MyLab Marketing: Improves Student Engagement Before, During, and After Class

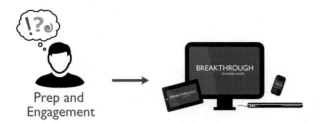

Prep and Engagement

- **NEW! VIDEO LIBRARY** – Robust video library with over 100 new book-specific videos that include easy-to-assign assessments, the ability for instructors to add YouTube or other sources, the ability for students to upload video submissions, and the ability for polling and teamwork.

- **Decision-making simulations – NEW and improved feedback for students.** Place your students in the role of a key decision-maker! Simulations branch based on the decisions students make, providing a variation of scenario paths. Upon completion students receive a grade, as well as a detailed report of the choices and the associated consequences of those decisions.

- **Video exercises – UPDATED with new exercises.** Engaging videos that bring business concepts to life and explore business topics related to the theory students are learning in class. Quizzes then assess students' comprehension of the concepts covered in each video.

- **Learning Catalytics –** A "bring your own device" student engagement, assessment, and classroom intelligence system helps instructors analyze students' critical-thinking skills during lecture.

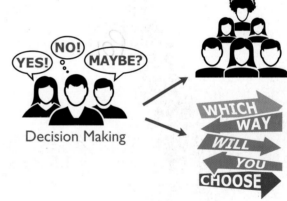

Decision Making

- **Dynamic Study Modules (DSMs) – UPDATED with additional questions.** Through adaptive learning, students get personalized guidance where and when they need it most, creating greater engagement, improving knowledge retention, and supporting subject-matter mastery. Also available on mobile devices.

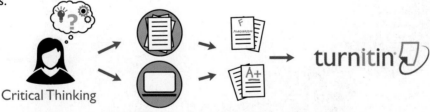

Critical Thinking

- **Writing Space – UPDATED with new commenting tabs, new prompts, and a new tool for students called Pearson Writer.** A single location to develop and assess concept mastery and critical thinking, the Writing Space offers automatic graded, assisted graded, and create your own writing assignments, allowing you to exchange personalized feedback with students quickly and easily.

  Writing Space can also check students' work for improper citation or plagiarism by comparing it against the world's most accurate text comparison database available from **Turnitin**.

- **Additional Features** – Included with the MyLab are a powerful homework and test manager, robust gradebook tracking, Reporting Dashboard, comprehensive online course content, and easily scalable and shareable content.

http://www.pearsonmylabandmastering.com

6212 7455

Consumer Behavior

Buying, Having, and Being

Twelfth Edition
Global Edition

Michael R. Solomon

Saint Joseph's University

Boston   Columbus   Indianapolis   New York   San Francisco   Amsterdam
Cape Town   Dubai   London   Madrid   Milan   Munich   Paris   Montréal   Toronto   Delhi
Mexico City   São Paulo   Sydney   Hong Kong   Seoul   Singapore   Taipei   Tokyo

Vice President, Business Publishing: Donna Battista
Editor-in-Chief: Stephanie Wall
Acquisitions Editor: Mark Gaffney
Editorial Assistant: Eric Santucci
Vice President, Product Marketing: Maggie Moylan
Director of Marketing, Digital Services and Products:
Jeanette Koskinas
Senior Product Marketing Manager: Alison Haskins
Executive Field Marketing Manager: Adam Goldstein
Field Marketing Manager: Lenny Ann Raper
Product Marketing Assistant: Jessica Quazza
Team Lead, Program Management: Ashley Santora
Program Manager: Jennifer M. Collins
Team Lead, Project Management: Jeff Holcomb
Project Manager: Becca Groves
Project Manager, Global Edition: Sudipto Roy
Associate Acquisitions Editor, Global Edition: Ishita Sinha
Senior Project Editor, Global Edition: Daniel Luiz

Manager, Media Production, Global Edition: M. Vikram Kumar
Senior Manufacturing Controller, Production, Global Edition:
Trudy Kimber
Operations Specialist: Carol Melville
Creative Director: Blair Brown
Art Director: Janet Slowik
Cover Image: © Lukasz Janyst/Shutterstock
Vice President, Director of Digital Strategy and Assessment:
Paul Gentile
Manager of Learning Applications: Paul DeLuca
Digital Editor: Brian Surette
Director, Digital Studio: Sacha Laustsen
Digital Studio Manager: Diane Lombardo
Digital Studio Project Manager: Monique Lawrence
Digital Studio Project Manager: Alana Coles
Digital Studio Project Manager: Robin Lazrus
Full-Service Project Management and Composition: Integra
Software Services Pvt. Ltd.

Pearson Education Limited
Edinburgh Gate
Harlow
Essex CM20 2JE
England

and Associated Companies throughout the world

Visit us on the World Wide Web at:
www.pearsonglobaleditions.com

ISBN 10:   1-292-15310-5
ISBN 13: 978-1-292-15310-0

British Library Cataloguing-in-Publication Data
A catalogue record for this book is available from the British Library.

10 9 8 7 6 5 4 3 2 1
19 18 17

Typeset in 9.5/12 Utopia by Integra Software Services Pvt. Ltd.
Printed in Malaysia (CTP-VVP)

BRIEF CONTENTS

CONTENTS

Chapter 4 ● Learning and Memory 130

Chapter 5 ● Motivation and Affect 172

Chapter 6 ● The Self: Mind, Gender, and Body 200

Chapter 7 ● Personality, Lifestyles, and Values 242

Section 3 • Choosing and Using Products 283

Chapter 8 • Attitudes and Persuasive Communications 284

Chapter 9 • Decision Making 334

Chapter 10 • Buying, Using, and Disposing 380

Michael R. Solomon, Ph.D., is Professor of Marketing in the Haub School of Business at Saint Joseph's University in Philadelphia. Before joining the Saint Joseph's faculty in the fall of 2006, he was the Human Sciences Professor of Consumer Behavior at Auburn University. Before moving to Auburn in 1995, he was chair of the Department of Marketing in the School of Business at Rutgers University, New Brunswick, New Jersey. Professor Solomon began his academic career in the Graduate School of Business Administration at New York University (NYU), where he also served as Associate Director of NYU's Institute of Retail Management. He earned his B.A. degrees in psychology and sociology *magna cum laude* at Brandeis University and a Ph.D. in social psychology at the University of North Carolina at Chapel Hill. In 1996 he was awarded the Fulbright/FLAD Chair in Market Globalization by the U.S. Fulbright Commission and the Government of Portugal, and he served as Distinguished Lecturer in Marketing at the Technical University of Lisbon. He held an appointment as Professor of Consumer Behaviour at the University of Manchester (United Kingdom) from 2007 to 2013.

Professor Solomon's primary research interests include consumer behavior and lifestyle issues; branding strategy; the symbolic aspects of products; the psychology of fashion, decoration, and image; services marketing; marketing in virtual worlds; and the development of visually oriented online research methodologies. He has published numerous articles on these and related topics in academic journals, and he has delivered invited lectures on these subjects in Europe, Australia, Asia, and Latin America. His research has been funded by the American Academy of Advertising, the American Marketing Association, the U.S. Department of Agriculture, the International Council of Shopping Centers, and the U.S. Department of Commerce. He currently sits on the editorial or advisory boards of *The Journal of Consumer Behaviour, Journal of Marketing Theory and Practice, Critical Studies in Fashion and Beauty,* and *Journal for Advancement of Marketing Education,* and he served an elected six-year term on the Board of Governors of the Academy of Marketing Science. Professor Solomon has been recognized as one of the 15 most widely cited scholars in the academic behavioral sciences/fashion literature, and as one of the 10 most productive scholars in the field of advertising and marketing communications.

Professor Solomon is a frequent contributor to mass media. His feature articles have appeared in such magazines as *Psychology Today, Gentleman's Quarterly,* and *Savvy.* He has been quoted in numerous national magazines and newspapers, including *Advertising Age, Adweek, Allure, Elle, Glamour, Mademoiselle, Mirabella, Newsweek,* the *New York Times, Self, Time, USA Today,* and the *Wall Street Journal.* He frequently appears on television and speaks on radio to comment on consumer behavior issues, including appearances on *The Today Show, Good Morning America, Inside Edition, Newsweek on the Air,* the *Entrepreneur Sales and Marketing Show,* CNBC, Channel One, the *Wall Street Journal* Radio Network, the WOR Radio Network, and National Public Radio. He acts as consultant to numerous companies on consumer behavior and marketing strategy issues and often speaks to business groups throughout the United States and overseas. In addition to this text, Professor Solomon is coauthor of the widely used textbook *Marketing: Real People, Real Choices.* He has three children, Amanda, Zachary, and Alexandra; a son-in-law, Orly; and three granddaughters, Rose, Evey, and Arya. He lives in Philadelphia with his wife Gail and their "other child," a pug named Kelbie Rae.

The twelfth edition of *Consumer Behavior* has been extensively revised and updated to reflect the major trends and changes in marketing that impact the study of consumer behavior. The most significant changes to the edition are:

- A totally reorganized Contents page that organizes material into four sections. The first section introduces the field of consumer behavior and then devotes an entire chapter to issues related to consumer well-being to reinforce to students the many commercial, environmental, ethical, and health issues our field touches. The second section dives deeper into micro influences such as perception and learning, and the third section examines how consumers make decisions and form attitudes toward products and services. The final section shows how macro variables such as group dynamics, culture, and communications platforms such as social media influence these decisions.
- New data feature *Data Powered by GfK*. New end of part cases using real consumer data from GfK.
- Six new end-of-chapter cases and six updated end-of-chapter cases.
- All new "CB As I See It" boxes in every chapter that feature prominent consumer behavior researchers who share their current work with students.
- A strong focus on social media and how digital technology influences consumer behavior.
- Significant coverage of major emerging topics including Big Data, the Digital Self, gamification, and contextual influences on decision making such as priming and nudging.
- New content added to every chapter, including the following key terms:

Ambicultural	Digital self
Automated attention analysis	Disclaimers
Bitcoin	Dispreferred marker effect
Brand arrogance	e-Sports
Brand immigrants	Embarrassment
Brand storytelling	Embodied cognition
Brand tourists	Empty self
CEO pay ratio	Enclothed cognition
Cognitive-affective model	Endcap displays
Cohabitate	Endowed progress effect
Collaborative consumption	Endowment effect
College wage premium	Envy
Conditioned superstition	Evaluations
Consumer culture theory (CCT)	Executive control center
Consumer fairy tales	Fatshionistas
Consumer hyperchoice	Feedback loop
Credit score	Female-to-male earnings ratio
Crytocurrency	Glamping
Dadvertising	Guilt

Gyges effect

Happiness

Happiness economy

Haul videos

Homeostatis

Hook

Hybrid products

Identity

IKEA effect

Imbibing idiot bias

Implementation intentions

Incidental brand exposure

Income inequality

Independence hypothesis

Internet trolls

Intersex children

Linkbaiting

Locavore

Loss aversion

Marketplace sentiments

Martyrdom effect

Material accumulation

Material parenting

Media snacker

Medical tourism

Medication adherence

Meerkating

Megaphone effect

Microfame

Mood congruency

Moods

Morning morality effect

Nanofame

Native advertising

Negative state relief

Net neutrality

Neuroendocrinological science

Near-field communication (NFC)

Normcore

P2P commerce

Paradox of fashion

Phablets

Power posing

Product authenticity

Product personalization

Reader-response theory

Red sneakers effect

Retail therapy

Sadvertising

Search engine optimization (SEO)

Search engines

Selfie

Shared endorsements

Sharing economy

Simple additive rule

Slacktivism

Social default

Spectacles

Status anxiety

Street art

Swatting

Swishing

Technology acceptance model (TAM)

The Personal Data Notification & Protection Act

The Student Digital Privacy Act

Third-gender movement

Unboxing videos

Vanity sizing

Virtual makeover

Virtual reality

Wearable computing

Weighted additive rule

I love to people-watch, don't you? People shopping, people flirting, people consuming. Consumer behavior is the study of people and the products that help to shape their identities. Because I'm a consumer myself, I have a selfish interest in learning more about how this process works—and so do you.

In many courses, students are merely passive observers; they learn about topics that affect them indirectly, if at all. Not everyone is a plasma physicist, a medieval French scholar, or a marketing professional. But we are all consumers. Many of the topics in this book have both professional and personal relevance to the reader, regardless of whether he or she is a student, professor, or businessperson. Nearly everyone can relate to the trials and tribulations of last-minute shopping; primping for a big night out; agonizing over an expensive purchase; fantasizing about a week in the Caribbean; celebrating a holiday or commemorating a landmark event, such as graduating or getting a driver's license; or (dreaming about) winning the lottery.

In this edition, I have tried to introduce you to the latest and best thinking by some bright scientists who develop models and studies of consumer behavior. But that's not enough. Consumer behavior is an applied science, so we must never lose sight of the role of "horse sense" when we apply our findings to life in the real world. That's why you'll find a lot of practical examples to back up these fancy theories.

What Makes This Book Different: Buying, Having, and Being

As this book's subtitle suggests, my vision of consumer behavior goes well beyond studying the act of *buying*—*having* and *being* are just as important, if not more so. Consumer behavior is more than buying things; it also embraces the study of how having (or not having) things affects our lives and how our possessions influence the way we feel about ourselves and about each other—our state of being. I developed the *wheel of consumer behavior* that appears at the beginning of text sections to underscore the complex—and often inseparable—interrelationships between the individual consumer and his or her social realities.

In addition to understanding why people buy things, we also try to appreciate how products, services, and consumption activities contribute to the broader social world we experience. Whether we shop, cook, clean, play basketball, hang out at the beach, or even look at ourselves in the mirror, the marketing system touches our lives. As if these experiences aren't complex enough, the task of understanding the consumer increases when we take a multicultural perspective.

We'll explore these ideas with intriguing and current examples as we show how the consumer behavior discipline relates to your daily life. Throughout the twelfth edition, you'll find up-to-the-minute discussions of topics such as dadvertising, meerkating, the imbibing idiot basis, swatting, and swishing. If you can't identify all of these terms, I can suggest a textbook that you should read immediately!

Going Global

The U.S. experience is important, but it's far from the whole story. This book also considers the many other consumers around the world whose diverse experiences with buying, having, and being we must understand. That's why you'll find numerous examples of marketing and consumer practices relating to consumers and companies outside the United States throughout the book. If we didn't know it before the tragic events of September 11, 2001, we certainly know it now: Americans also are global citizens, and it's vital that we all appreciate others' perspectives.

Digital Consumer Behavior: A Virtual Community

As more of us go online every day, there's no doubt the world is changing—and consumer behavior evolves faster than you can say "the Web." The twelfth edition continues to highlight and celebrate the brave new world of digital consumer behavior. Today, consumers and producers come together electronically in ways we have never known before. Rapid transmission of information alters the speed at which new trends develop and the direction in which they travel, especially because the virtual world lets consumers participate in the creation and dissemination of new products.

One of the most exciting aspects of the new digital world is that consumers can interact directly with other people who live around the block or around the world. As a result, we need to radically redefine the meaning of community. It's no longer enough to acknowledge that consumers like to talk to each other about products. Now we share opinions and get the buzz about new movies, CDs, cars, clothes—you name it—in electronic communities that may include a housewife in Alabama, a disabled senior citizen in Alaska, or a teen loaded with body piercings in Amsterdam. And many of us meet up in computer-mediated environments (CMEs) such as Facebook, Twitter, and Foursquare. I'm totally fascinated by what goes on in virtual worlds, and you'll see a lot of material in this edition that relates to these emerging consumer playgrounds.

We have just begun to explore the ramifications for consumer behavior when a Web surfer can project her own picture onto a Web site to get a virtual makeover or a corporate purchasing agent can solicit bids for a new piece of equipment from vendors around the world in minutes. These new ways of interacting in the marketplace create bountiful opportunities for businesspeople and consumers alike. You will find illustrations of the changing digital world sprinkled liberally throughout this edition. In addition, each chapter features boxes that I call *Net Profit,* which point to specific examples of the Internet's potential to improve the way we conduct business.

But is the digital world always a rosy place? Unfortunately, just as in the "real world," the answer is no. The potential to exploit consumers, whether by invading their privacy, preying on the curiosity of children, or simply providing false product information, is always there. That's why you'll also find boxes called *The Tangled Web* that point out some of the abuses of this fascinating new medium. Still, I can't imagine a world without the Web, and I hope you'll enjoy the ways it's changing our field. When it comes to the new virtual world of consumer behavior, you're either on the train or under it.

Consumer Research Is a Big Tent: The Importance of a Balanced Perspective

Like most of you who will read this book, the field of consumer behavior is young, dynamic, and in flux. It is constantly cross-fertilized by perspectives from many different disciplines: The field is a big tent that invites many diverse views to enter. I try to express the field's staggering diversity in these pages. Consumer researchers represent virtually every social science discipline, plus a few from the physical sciences and the arts for good measure. From this blending of disciplines comes a dynamic and complex research perspective, including viewpoints regarding appropriate research methods, and even deeply held beliefs about what are and what are not appropriate issues for consumer researchers to study in the first place.

The book also emphasizes how strategically vital it is to understand consumers. Many (if not most) of the fundamental concepts in marketing emanate from a manager's ability to know people. After all, if we don't understand why people behave as they do, how can we identify their needs? If we can't identify their needs, how can we satisfy their needs? If we can't satisfy people's needs, we don't have a marketing concept, so we might as well fold up our big tent and go home!

To illustrate the potential of consumer research to inform marketing strategy, the text contains numerous examples of specific applications of consumer behavior concepts by marketing practitioners, as well as examples of windows of opportunity where we could use these concepts (perhaps by alert strategists after they take this course!). The *Marketing Opportunity* boxes you'll find in each chapter highlight the fascinating ways in which marketing practitioners translate the wisdom they glean from consumer research into actual business activities.

The Good, the Bad, and the Ugly

A strategic focus is great, but this book doesn't assume that everything marketers do is in the best interests of consumers or of their environment. Likewise, as consumers we do many things that are not so positive, either. We suffer from addictions, status envy, ethnocentrism, racism, sexism, and many other -*isms*. Regrettably, there are times when marketing activities—deliberately or not—encourage or exploit these human flaws. This book deals with the totality of consumer behavior, warts and all. We'll highlight marketing mistakes or ethically suspect activities in boxes that I call *Marketing Pitfall*.

On a more cheerful note, marketers create wonderful (or at least unusual) things, such as holidays, comic books, Krispy Kreme donuts, nu-jazz music, Webkinz, and the many stylistic options that beckon to us in the domains of clothing, home design, the arts, and cuisine. I also take pains to acknowledge the sizable impact of marketing on popular culture. Indeed, the final section of this book captures recent work in the field that scrutinizes, criticizes, and sometimes celebrates consumers in their everyday worlds. I hope you will enjoy reading about such wonderful things as much as I enjoyed writing about them. Welcome to the fascinating world of consumer behavior!

The Tangled Web

From ihatestarbucks.com to boycottwalmart.meetup.com, irritated customers have launched hundreds of **gripe sites** to air their grievances against companies. The practice is so widespread that some firms proactively buy unflattering domain names to keep other ~~people from buying them~~. Xerox, for example, ~~...~~.com, xeroxcorporation ~~...~~rox.net. About 20,000 ~~...~~bucks.com." About one-~~...~~gistered to none other ~~...~~y slam; owners include ~~...~~ola, Toys "R" Us, Target, ~~...~~t.[32]

Marketing Opportunity

Successful companies understand that needs are a moving target. No organization—no matter how renowned for its marketing prowess—can afford to rest on its laurels. *Everyone* needs to keep innovating to stay ahead of changing customers and the marketplace. BMW is a great example. No one (not even rivals like Audi or Mercedes-Benz) would argue that the German automaker knows how to make a good car (though they may not agree with the company's claim to be "the ultimate driving machine"). Still, BMW's engineers and designers know they have to understand how drivers' needs will change in the future—even those loyal owners who love the cars they own today. The company is highly sensitive to such key trends as:

- A desire for environmentally friendly products
- Increasingly congested roadways and the movement by some cities such as London to impose fees on vehicles in central areas
- New business models that encourage consumers to rent products only while they need them rather than buying them outright

BMW's response: The company committed more than $1 billion to develop electric BMWi models such as its new i3 commuter car and i8 sports car. These futuristic-looking vehicles are largely made from lightweight carbon fiber to maximize the distance they can go between battery charges, and 25 percent of the interior ~~...~~ recycled or renewable ~~...~~dition, BMW started ~~...~~ (now in several Europe~~...~~ San Francisco) it calls ~~...~~ a computer chip in their ~~...~~ and leave it wherever t~~...~~ longer need it. That's fo~~...~~

Marketing Pitfall

When Hurricane Sandy devastated cities on the East Coast in 2012, some marketers rose to the occasion, whereas others stumbled in the wind. Gap, for example, tweeted, "We'll be doing lots of Gap.com shopping today. How about you?" American Apparel offered an incentive to shoppers: "In case you're bored during the storm, just Enter SANDYSALE at Checkout." Many of the storm victims were not amused. One tweeted, "Hey @americanapparel people have died and others are in need. Shut up about your #Sandy sale."

In contrast, Allstate ran radio commercials to let policyholders know how to file claims quickly. JetBlue Airways waived change and cancellation fees for people who had to rebook. How's this for a relationship builder? Duracell batteries sent a truck to New York City that offered free batteries and access to charging lockers for mobile devices and computers to desperate people who had been without power (or even worse, access to social media).[6]

Consumer Behavior in the Trenches

I'm a huge believer in the value of up-to-date information. Our field changes so rapidly that often yesterday's news is no news at all. True, there are "timeless" studies that demonstrate basic consumer behavior constructs as well today as they did 20 years ago or more (I may even have authored some of them!). Still, I feel a real obligation to present students and their professors with a current view of research, popular culture, and marketing activities whenever I can. For this reason, each time I start to contemplate my next edition, I write to colleagues to ask for copies of papers they have in press that they believe will be important in the future. Their cooperation with my request allows me to include a lot of fresh research examples; in some cases, these articles will not yet have been published when this book comes out.

I've also taken this initiative to the next level with a feature I call *CB As I See It*. In every chapter you'll find a "flesh-and-blood" consumer behavior professor who shares his or her perspective as a leading researcher in a particular area of specialization about an appropriate topic. I've let these esteemed colleagues largely speak for themselves, so now students can benefit from other voices who chime in on relevant research issues.

Data Powered by GfK

For this edition we've partnered with GfK, one of the largest market research organizations in the world, to provide students with actual consumer data to use in the end-of-part cases. This feature allows students to "get their hands dirty" with real issues and to develop their analytical skills. The data are real, and the problems are too. Each case presents the student with a scenario that he or she would face when working in industry and asks them to use that information to make decisions and marketing recommendations. Additional chapter level exercises that also incorporate actual GfK data can be found in the Marketing Metrics questions in MyLab Marketing.

Case Study

HONDA'S ASIMO

Meet ASIMO! He is 4 feet tall, with a pleasant childish voice, and the ability to recognize and interact with people; however, ASIMO is no child. He is the humanoid robot "brainchild" of scientists at Honda. ASIMO's technology includes two camera eyes to map its environment and recognize unique faces. Its body construction is so humanlike that it can run at 3.5 mph, toss a ball to play with a child, and use its opposable thumbs to open a bottle and serve you a cold drink. ASIMO is the perfect household companion.

Honda has not yet made ASIMO available to purchase for home use, but it is only a matter of time until families can have their own humanoid robot. But not everyone is interested.

describe wanting to create a social robot with a whimsical appearance, intentionally not human or animal. They believe that "robots will be their own kind of creature and should be accepted, measured, and valued on those terms."

If consumers are not ready for ASIMO, perhaps they are ready for some of its features. *Facial recognition technology (FRT),* the ability for a computer to "read" your face, is seeing strong development and application. According to some analysts, the FRT market is expected to grow from $1.92 billion to $6.5 billion within the next 5 years.

Advertisers and big brands are taking notice of FRT. Imagine a billboard in a mall that advertises Abercrombie to a teen girl and Target to a busy mom. Immersive Labs, recently acquired by Kairos, has developed digital billboards that mea-

Critical Thinking in Consumer Behavior: Case Study

Learning by doing is an integral part of the classroom experience. You'll find a *case study* at the end of each chapter, along with discussion questions to help you apply the case to the chapter's contents. Also included in the twelfth edition are the following items that will enhance the student learning experience:

- **Chapter Objectives** at the beginning of each chapter provide an overview of key issues to be covered in the chapter. Each *chapter summary* is then organized around the objectives to help you integrate the material you have read.
- **Review** at the end of each chapter helps you to study key issues.
- **The Consumer Behavior Challenge** at the end of each chapter is divided into two sections:
  - **Discuss** poses thoughtful issues that encourage you to consider pragmatic and ethical implications of the material you have read.

○ **Apply** allows you to "get your hands dirty" as you conduct mini-experiments and collect data in the real world to better grasp the application of consumer behavior principles.

Instructor Resources

At the Instructor Resource Center, www.pearsonglobaleditions.com/solomon, instructors can easily register to gain access to a variety of instructor resources available with this text in downloadable format.

The following supplements are available with this text:

- Instructor's Resource Manual
- Test Bank
- TestGen® Computerized Test Bank
- PowerPoint Presentations

Sarah Roche, a doctoral student at the University of Texas at San Antonio (and now a faculty member at Texas Wesleyan University), did yeoman service as she helped me to review recently published academic articles.

I'm also grateful for the many helpful comments on how to improve the twelfth edition that my peer reviewers provided. Special thanks go to the following individuals:

Karen L. Becker, The College of New Jersey
Carolyn Bonifield, University of Vermont
Dr. Jane Boyd Thomas, Winthrop University
Karthikeya Easwar, Georgetown University
Xiang Fang, Oklahoma State University
Andrew Forman, Hofstra University
Curtis P. Haugtvedt, Ohio State University
James Mason, Oklahoma State University
Carolyn F. Musgrove, Indiana University Southeast
Thomas A. Myers, Virginia Commonwealth University
Paul Jr., Indiana University
Glenna C. Pendleton, Northern Michigan University
Carol Salusso, Washington State University
Leah Schneider, University of Oregon
Gene Steidinger Jr., Loras College
Ebru Ulusoy, University of Maine
Mary G. Vermillion, DePaul University
Tommy E. Whittler, St. Vincent DePaul University
Yi-Chia Wu. University of Texas - Pan American
Weiling Zhuang, Eastern Kentucky University

These colleagues generously contributed their thoughts to my *CB As I See It* boxes:

Julie Baker, Texas A&M University
Stacey Menzel Baker, Creighton University
Jonah Berger, University of Pennsylvania
Malaika Brengman, Vrije Universiteit Brussel (Belgium)
Fredric Brunel, Boston University
Julien Cayla, Nanyang Business School (Singapore)
Pierre Chandon, INSEAD (France)
Jean-Charles Chebat, HEC-Montréal (Canada) and Technion (Israel)
Paul Connell, Stonybrook University
Giana Eckhardt, Royal Holloway, University of London (United Kingdom)
Amber Epp, University of Wisconsin–Madison
Jennifer Escalas, Vanderbilt University
Eileen Fischer, York University (Canada)
Ron Hill, Villanova
Paul Henry, University of Sydney (Australia)
Wendy Liu, University of California–San Diego
John Lynch, University of Colorado–Boulder
Nira Munichor, Hebrew University of Jerusalem (Israel)
Cele Otnes, University of Illinois at Urbana–Champaign
Michel Tuan Pham, Columbia University
Stefano Putoni, Erasmus University of Rotterdam (The Netherlands)

Derek Rucker, Northwestern University
Craig Thompson, University of Wisconsin–Madison
Debora Thompson, Georgetown University
Benjamin Voyer, ESCP Europe Business School (France) & London School of
     Economics (United Kingdom)
Michel Wedel, University of Maryland
Jerome Williams, Rutgers University

I thank David Nemi, Nassau Community College SUNY, for the creation of the Instructor's Manual and Test Item Files and Darci Wagner, Ohio University, for her work with the PowerPoints.

I would also like to thank the good people at Pearson who, as always, have done great work on this edition. A special thanks to Mark Gaffney, Stephanie Wall, Jen Collins, and Lenny Raper for their support; Becca Groves did a great job keeping me on course, and Melissa Pellerano was her usual conscientious self.

Without the tolerance of my friends and colleagues, I would never have been able to sustain the illusion that I was still an active researcher while I worked on this edition. I am grateful to my department chair, Dave Allan, and to Dean Joe DiAngelo for supporting their high-maintenance faculty member. Also, I am grateful to my students, who have been a prime source of inspiration, examples, and feedback. The satisfaction I garnered from teaching them about consumer behavior motivated me to write a book I felt they would like to read.

Last but not least, I would like to thank my family and friends for sticking by me during this revision. They know who they are; their names pop up in chapter vignettes throughout the book. My apologies for "distorting" their characters in the name of poetic license! My gratitude and love go out to my parents, Jackie and Henry, and my in-laws, Marilyn and Phil. Ditto to my super children, Amanda, Zachary, and Alexandra—and my high-tech son-in-law Orly—who always made the sun shine on gray days (not to mention my favorite pug, Kelbie Rae). My fabulous granddaughters Rose, Evey, and Arya added a special thrill. Finally, thanks above all to the love of my life: Gail, my wonderful wife, best friend, and the hottest grandmother on earth: I still do it all for you.

M.R.S.
Philadelphia, Pennsylvania
August 2015

Pearson would like to thank the following people for their contributions to the Global Edition:

Contributors:
Adele Berndt, Jönköping University (Sweden)
Nadia Rattoo, University of Central Lancashire (United Kingdom)
Muneeza Shoaib, Middlesex University Dubai (United Arab Emirates)
Diane Sutherland
Jon Sutherland

Reviewers:
Richard Glavee-Geo, Norges Teknisk-Naturvitenskapelige Universitet (Norway)
Jie Liu, Manchester Metropolitan University (United Kingdom)
Jimmy Wong Shiang Yang, SIM University (Singapore)
Frederick H.K. Yim, Hong Kong Baptist University (Hong Kong)

Consumer Behavior

CONSUMER BEHAVIOR

1: Foundations of Consumer Behavior

2: Internal Influences on Consumer Behavior

3: Choosing and Using Products

4: Consumers in Their Social and Cultural Settings

Section 1 • Foundations of Consumer Behavior

This introductory section provides an overview of the field of consumer behavior (CB). In Chapter 1, we look at how consumers influence the field of marketing and at how marketers influence us. We describe the discipline of consumer behavior and some of the different approaches to understanding what makes consumers tick. In Chapter 2 we'll look at the broad issue of well-being, at both the positive and negative ways the products we use affect us and we'll also focus on the central role of ethics in marketing decisions.

CHAPTERS AHEAD

Chapter 1 • Buying, Having, and Being: An Introduction to Consumer Behavior

Chapter Objectives

When you finish reading this chapter you will understand why:

1-1 Consumer behavior is a process.

1-2 Marketers have to understand the wants and needs of different consumer segments.

1-3 Our choices as consumers relate in powerful ways to the rest of our lives.

1-4 Our motivations to consume are complex and varied.

1-5 Technology and culture create a new "always-on" consumer.

1-6 Many different types of specialists study consumer behavior.

1-7 There are differing perspectives regarding how and what we should understand about consumer behavior.

Source: Supri Suharjoto/Shutterstock.com.

Gail has some time to kill before her Accounting class, so she pulls out her trusty iPhone to see what's going on in her social networks. Between studying for her Accounting and Marketing exams, she hasn't checked out anything interesting in days—even her Facebook friends around campus have been quiet. Enough of the serious stuff, she decides. It's time for some *really* educational surfing.

So, where to go first? Gail goes straight to Pinterest to see if anyone has pinned any new styles on her Shoe-aholic Board. Yes, definitely some new stuff to post for her sorority sisters. She flicks over to HerCampus ("a collegiette's guide to life^SM") to get the latest 411 on *The Bachelor* TV show. She's just about to jump to Gen Y Girl when she gets a text from Jewelmint.com to notify her that the site has a new jewelry option for her that's based on the profile she filled out when she registered. Sweet—it's a bracelet the actress Allison Williams from *Girls* recommends. With her PayPal account, it doesn't take Gail long to throw the bracelet in the digital cart and order it—and to share a photo of her haul on Facebook. Just on a whim, Gail opens the Tinder app on her phone; yes, as usual plenty of guys who want to meet up if she "swipes right." Not happening with these dweebs—a flurry of left swipes and she's done.[1] As Gail glances at the clock, she realizes she'd better come back to the real world or she'll miss her exam. OK, enough time for one quick post before she runs to catch the campus shuttle: Gail logs on to RateMyProfessors.com and writes a quick but glowing paragraph about how great her Consumer Behavior professor has been this semester ... not to mention that awesome textbook they're using.[2]

OBJECTIVE 1-1
Consumer behavior is
a process.

Consumer Behavior: People in the Marketplace

This book is about people like Gail—and *you*. It concerns the products and services we buy and use and the ways these fit into our lives. This introductory chapter describes some important aspects of the field of consumer behavior and some reasons why it's essential to understand how people interact with the marketing system. For now, though, let's return to one "typical" consumer: Gail, the business major. The preceding vignette allows us to highlight some aspects of consumer behavior that we will cover in the rest of the book.

Gail is a consumer; so let's compare her to other consumers. For some purposes, marketers find it useful to categorize her in terms of her age, gender, income, or occupation. These are descriptive characteristics of a population, or **demographics**. In other cases, marketers would rather know something about Gail's interests in clothing or music or the way she spends her leisure time. Knowledge of consumer characteristics plays an extremely important role in many marketing applications, such as when a manufacturer defines the market for a product or an advertising agency decides on the appropriate techniques to employ when it targets a certain group of consumers.

Gail's sorority sisters strongly influence her purchase decisions. The conversations we have with others transmit a lot of product information, as well as recommendations to use or avoid particular brands; this content often is more influential than what we see on television commercials, magazines, or billboards. The growth of the Web has created thousands of online **consumption communities**, where members share opinions and recommendations about anything from Barbie dolls to baseball fantasy league team line-ups to iPhone apps. Gail forms bonds with fellow group members because they use the same products. There is also pressure on each group member to buy things that will meet with the group's approval. A consumer may pay a steep price in the form of group rejection or embarrassment when he or she doesn't conform to others' conceptions of what is good or bad, "in" or "out."

As members of a large society, such as in the United States, people share certain cultural values, or strongly held beliefs about the way the world should function. Members of subcultures, or smaller groups within the culture, also share values; these groups include Hispanics, teens, Midwesterners, and even hipsters who listen to Arcade Fire, wear Band of Outsiders clothing, and eat vegan tacos.

Everyday Gail comes into contact with information about many competing *brands*. Some don't capture her attention at all, whereas others are just a turnoff because they don't relate to "looks," people, or ideas with which she identifies. The use of **market segmentation strategies** means an organization targets its product, service, or idea only to specific groups of consumers rather than to everybody—even if it means that other consumers who don't belong to this target market aren't attracted to it. That's why they make chocolate and vanilla ice cream (and even candied bacon flavor!).

Brands often have clearly defined images, or "personalities," that advertising, packaging, branding, and other marketing elements help to shape. Even the choice of a favorite Web site is very much a *lifestyle* statement: It says a lot about a person's interests, as well as something about the type of person he or she would like to be. People often purchase a product because they like its image or because they feel its "personality" somehow corresponds to their own. This is true even when they evaluate other people; after all, each of us is in a way a "brand" that others like or not—thus the popularity of dating apps such as Tinder that let people quickly choose among competing alternatives! Moreover, a consumer may believe that if he or she buys and uses the product or service, its desirable qualities will "magically" rub off on to him or her. When a product or service satisfies our specific needs or desires, we may reward it with many years of *brand loyalty*, which is a bond between product and consumer that is difficult for competitors to break.

Consumers form strong loyalties with their favorite brands or stores. If necessary, many are willing to camp out for a new product introduction, much like they would for scarce tickets at a big concert.
Source: Jeffrey Blackler/Alamy.

The appearance, taste, texture, or smell of the item influences our evaluations of products. A good Web site helps people to feel, taste, and smell with their eyes. We may be swayed by the shape and color of a package on the store shelf, as well as by more subtle factors, such as the symbolism in a brand name, in an advertisement, or even in the choice of a cover model for a magazine. These judgments are affected by—and often reflect—how a society feels people should define themselves at that point in time. Many product meanings lurk below the surface of packaging and advertising; we'll discuss some of the methods marketers and social scientists use to discover or apply these meanings.

Like Gail, we shape our opinions and desires based on a mix of voices from around the world, which is becoming a much smaller place as a result of rapid advancements in communications and transportation systems. In today's global culture, consumers often prize products and services that "transport" them to different places and allow them to experience the diversity of other cultures—even if only to watch others brush their teeth on YouTube.

What Is Consumer Behavior?

The field of **consumer behavior** covers a lot of ground: *It is the study of the processes involved when individuals or groups select, purchase, use, or dispose of products, services, ideas, or experiences to satisfy needs and desires.* Consumers take many forms, ranging from an 8-year-old child who begs her mother for a *Frozen* Elsa doll to an executive in a large corporation who helps to decide on a multimillion-dollar computer system. The items we consume include anything from canned peas to a massage, democracy, Juicy jeans, Reggaeton music, or a celebrity like Taylor Swift. The needs and desires we satisfy range from hunger and thirst to love, status, and even spiritual fulfillment. Also, as we'll see throughout this book, people get passionate about a broad range of products. Whether it's vintage Air Jordans, that perfect yoga mat, or the latest computer tablet, there's no shortage of brand fans who will do whatever it takes to find and buy what they crave.

Consumer Behavior Is a Process

In its early stages of development, researchers referred to the field as *buyer behavior*; this reflected the emphasis at that time (1960s and 1970s) on the interaction between consumers and producers at the time of purchase. Most marketers now recognize that consumer behavior is in fact an *ongoing process*, not merely what happens at the moment a consumer hands over money or a credit card and in turn receives some good or service.

The **exchange**, a transaction in which two or more organizations or people give and receive something of value, is an integral part of marketing.[3] Although *exchange theory* remains an important part of consumer behavior, the expanded view emphasizes the *entire* consumption process, which includes the issues that influence the consumer before, during, and after a purchase. Figure 1.1 illustrates some of the issues that we address during each stage of the consumption process.

A **consumer** is a person who identifies a need or desire, makes a purchase, and then disposes of the product during the three stages of the consumption process. In many cases, however, different people play a role in this sequence of events. The purchaser and user of a product might not be the same person, as when a parent picks out clothes for a teenager (and makes selections that can result in "fashion suicide" in the view of the teen). In other cases, another person may act as an *influencer* when he or she recommends certain products without actually buying or using them. A friend's grimace when you try on that new pair of pants may be more influential than anything your mother might say.

Finally, consumers may take the form of organizations or groups. One or several persons may select products that many will use, as when a purchasing agent orders a company's office supplies. In other organizational situations, a large group of people may make purchase decisions: for example, company accountants, designers, engineers, sales personnel, and others—all of whom will have a say in the various stages of the consumption process. As we'll see in Chapter 11, one important type of organization is the family, in which different family members weigh in about products and services that all will use.

Figure 1.1 STAGES IN THE CONSUMPTION PROCESS

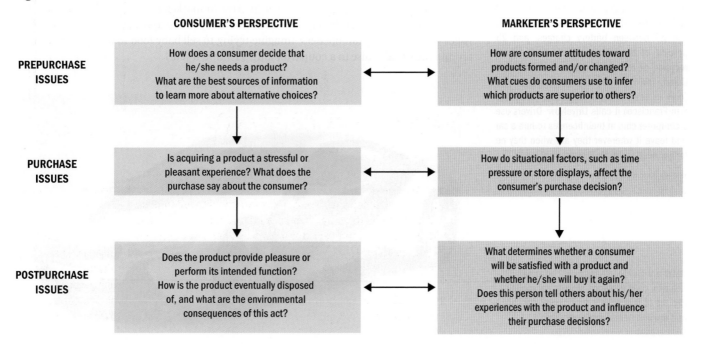

Successful companies understand that needs are a moving target. No organization—no matter how renowned for its marketing prowess—can afford to rest on its laurels. *Everyone* needs to keep innovating to stay ahead of changing customers and the marketplace. BMW is a great example. No one (not even rivals like Audi or Mercedes-Benz) would argue that the German automaker knows how to make a good car (though they may not agree with the company's claim to be "the ultimate driving machine"). Still, BMW's engineers and designers know they have to understand how drivers' needs will change in the future—even those loyal owners who love the cars they own today. The company is highly sensitive to such key trends as:

- A desire for environmentally friendly products
- Increasingly congested roadways and the movement by some cities such as London to impose fees on vehicles in central areas
- New business models that encourage consumers to rent products only while they need them rather than buying them outright

BMW's response: The company committed more than $1 billion to develop electric BMWi models such as its new i3 commuter car and i8 sports car. These futuristic-looking vehicles are largely made from lightweight carbon fiber to maximize the distance they can go between battery charges, and 25 percent of the interior plastic comes from recycled or renewable raw materials. In addition, BMW started a car-sharing service (now in several European cities as well as San Francisco) it calls DriveNow: Drivers use a computer chip in their licenses to hire a car and leave it wherever they are when they no longer need it. That's forward thinking.[4]

Consumers' Impact on Marketing Strategy

Why should managers, advertisers, and other marketing professionals bother to learn about consumer behavior? Simply, *it's good business*. The basic marketing concept that you (hopefully) remember from your basic Marketing class states that organizations exist to satisfy needs. Marketers can satisfy these needs only to the extent that they understand the people or organizations that will use the products and services they sell. *Voila!* That's why we study consumer behavior.

OBJECTIVE 1-2
Marketers have to understand the wants and needs of different consumer segments.

Consumers Are Different! How We Divide Them Up

Our society is evolving from a *mass culture* in which many consumers share the same preferences to a diverse one in which we each have almost an infinite number of choices—just think about how many shades of lipstick or necktie patterns compete for your attention. This change makes it more important than ever to identify distinct market segments and to develop specialized messages and products for those groups.

As we'll see later, building loyalty to a brand is a smart marketing strategy, so sometimes companies define market segments when they identify their most faithful customers or **heavy users**. As a rule of thumb, marketers use the **80/20 rule**: 20 percent of users account for 80 percent of sales. This guideline often holds up well, and in some cases even this lopsided split isn't big enough: A study of 54 million shoppers reported that only 2.5 percent of consumers account for 80 percent of sales for the average packaged-goods brand. The 1 percent of pet owners who buy 80 percent of Iams pet food spend $93 a year on the brand, and the 1.2 percent of beer drinkers who account for 80 percent of Budweiser sales spend $170 on Bud each year. Of the 1,364 brands the researchers studied, only 25 had a consumer base of more than 10 percent that accounted for 80 percent of volume.[5] So, just think of the 80/20 rule as a guideline rather than set in stone.

Aside from heavy usage of a product, we use many other dimensions to divide up a larger market. As we've already seen, *demographics* are statistics that measure observable aspects of a population, such as birth rate, age distribution, and income. The U.S. Census Bureau is a major source of demographic data on U.S. families, but many private firms gather additional data on specific population groups as well. The changes and trends that demographic studies reveal are of great interest to marketers because they can use the data to locate and predict the size of markets for many products, ranging from home mortgages to brooms and can openers. Imagine trying to sell baby food to a single male or an around the world cruise to a couple making $15,000 a year!

BMW anticipated changes in consumer behavior as it develops electric car models like the i8 that satisfy dual desires for style and environmental responsibility.
Source: BMW of North America, LLC.

In this book we explore many of the important demographic variables that make one consumer the same as or different from others. We also consider other important characteristics that are a bit subtler, such as differences in consumers' personalities and tastes that we can't objectively measure, yet may hugely impact our product choices. For now, let's summarize a few of the most important demographic dimensions, each of which we'll describe in more detail in later chapters.

Age

Consumers of different *age groups* obviously have different needs and wants. Although people who belong to the same age group differ in many other ways, they do tend to share a set of values and common cultural experiences that they carry throughout life.[7]

In some cases, marketers initially develop a product to attract one age group and then try to broaden its appeal later on. That's what the high-octane energy drink Red Bull does. The company aggressively introduced it in bars, nightclubs, and gyms to the product's core audience of young people. Over time, it became popular in other contexts, and the company began to sponsor the PGA European Tour to broaden its reach to older golfers (who probably aren't up partying all night). It also hands out free cans to commuters, cab drivers, and car rental agencies to promote the drink as a way to stay alert on the road.[8]

Gender

We start to make gender distinctions at an early age—even diapers come in pink versions for girls and blue for boys. Many products, from fragrances to footwear, target either men

Marketing Pitfall

When Hurricane Sandy devastated cities on the East Coast in 2012, some marketers rose to the occasion, whereas others stumbled in the wind. Gap, for example, tweeted, "We'll be doing lots of Gap.com shopping today. How about you?" American Apparel offered an incentive to shoppers: "In case you're bored during the storm, just Enter SANDYSALE at Checkout." Many of the storm victims were not amused. One tweeted, "Hey @americanapparel people have died and others are in need. Shut up about your #Sandy sale."

In contrast, Allstate ran radio commercials to let policyholders know how to file claims quickly. JetBlue Airways waived change and cancellation fees for people who had to rebook. How's this for a relationship builder? Duracell batteries sent a truck to New York City that offered free batteries and access to charging lockers for mobile devices and computers to desperate people who had been without power (or even worse, access to social media).[6]

Red Bull targets different age groups with its promotions.

Source: picturesbyrob/Alamy.

or women. The popular sunglass and athletic apparel brand Oakley now makes a concerted effort to boost the paltry 10 percent of its' revenue from women's products. The new "Made for More" campaign offers a revitalized line of workout gear; it actually asks women to sign an agreement that they will wear the clothing specifically for exercising rather than just running errands after Oakley learned that a majority of women agree that exercise and fitness are important to them. [9]

Family Structure

A person's family and marital status is yet another important demographic variable because this has a huge effect on consumers' spending priorities. Not surprisingly, young bachelors and newlyweds are the most likely to exercise; go to bars, concerts, and movies; and consume alcohol (enjoy it while you can!). Families with young children are big purchasers of health foods and fruit juices, whereas single-parent households and those with older children buy more junk food. Older couples and bachelors are most likely to use home maintenance services. [10]

Social Class and Income

People who belong to the same *social class* are approximately equal in terms of income and social standing in the community. They work in roughly similar occupations, and they tend to have similar tastes in music, clothing, leisure activities, and art. They also tend to

The Redneck Bank takes a unique approach to social class segmentation (yes, this is a real bank).

Source: Courtesy of www.redneckbank.com.

socialize with one another, and they share many ideas and values regarding the way they should live.[11] The distribution of wealth is of great interest to marketers because it determines which groups have the greatest buying power and market potential.

Race and Ethnicity

African Americans, Hispanic Americans, and Asian Americans are the three fastest-growing ethnic groups in the United States. As our society becomes increasingly multicultural, new opportunities develop to deliver specialized products to racial and ethnic groups and to introduce other groups to these offerings. McDonald's regards ethnic consumers as trendsetters. The restaurant chain often assesses their reactions to new menu items or advertisements before it rolls them out to the Caucasian market. For example, the fruit combinations in McDonald's smoothies are based on preferences the company's researchers discovered in ethnic communities.[12]

Geography

Many national marketers tailor their offerings to appeal to consumers who live in different parts of the country. Some southerners are fond of a "good ol' boy" image that leaves others scratching their heads. Although many northerners regard the name "Bubba" as a negative term, businesses in Dixie proudly flaunt the name. Bubba Co. is a Charleston-based firm that licenses products such as Bubba-Q-Sauce. In Florida, restaurants, sports bars, nightclubs, and a limousine firm all proudly bear the name Bubba.[13]

Lifestyles

Consumers also have different *lifestyles*, even if they share other demographic characteristics such as gender or age. The way we feel about ourselves, the things we value, the things we like to do in our spare time—all of these factors help to determine which products will push our buttons or even those that make us feel better. Procter & Gamble developed its heartburn medicine Prilosec OTC with an ideal customer in mind based on a lifestyle analysis. Her name is Joanne, and she's a mother older than age 35 who's more likely to get heartburn from a cup of coffee than from an overdose of pizza and beer. A P&G executive observed, "We know Joanne. We know what she feels. We know what she eats. We know what else she likes to buy in the store."[14]

Segmenting by Behavior: Relationships and "Big Data"

Marketers carefully define customer segments and listen to people in their markets as never before. Many of them now realize that a key to success is building relationships between brands and customers that will last a lifetime. Marketers who subscribe to this philosophy of **relationship marketing** interact with customers on a regular basis and give them solid reasons to maintain a bond with the company over time. A focus on relationships is even more vital, especially during the nasty economic conditions we've recently experienced; when times are tough, people tend to rely on their good friends for support!

Database marketing tracks specific consumers' buying habits closely and crafts products and messages tailored precisely to people's wants and needs based on this information. Walmart stores massive amounts of information on the 100 million people who visit its stores each week, and the company uses these data to fine-tune its offerings. For example, when the company analyzed how shoppers' buying patterns react when forecasters predict a major hurricane, it discovered that people do a lot more than simply stock up on flashlights. Sales of strawberry Pop-Tarts increase by about 700 percent, and the top-selling product of all is ... beer. Based on these insights, Walmart loads its trucks with toaster pastries and six-packs to stock local stores when a big storm approaches.[15]

At this very moment (and every moment thereafter until we croak), we all generate massive amounts of information that holds tremendous value for marketers. You may not see it, but we are practically buried by data that comes from many sources—sensors that collect climate information, the comments you and your friends make to your favorite social media sites, the credit card transactions we authorize, and even the GPS signals in

our smartphones that let organizations know where most of us are pretty much anytime day or night. This incredible amount of information has created a new field that causes tremendous excitement among marketing analysts (and other math geeks). The collection and analysis of extremely large datasets is called **Big Data**, and you'll be hearing a lot more about it in the next few years. Hint: If you have aptitude or interest in quantitative topics, this will be a desirable career path for you.

In a single day, consumers create 2.5 quintillion bytes of data (or 2.5 exabytes). New data pops up so quickly that this number doubles about every 40 months—and 90 percent of the data in the world today was created in the last 2 years alone. In addition to the huge *volume* of information marketers now have to play with, its *velocity* (speed) also enables companies to make decisions in real time that used to take months or years. For example, one group of researchers used the GPS phone signals that were coming from Macy's parking lots on Black Friday to estimate whether the department store was going to meet or exceed its sales projections for the biggest shopping day of the year—*before* the stores even reported their sales. This kind of intelligence allows financial analysts and marketing managers to move quickly as they buy and sell stocks or make merchandising decisions.

It's safe to say this data explosion will profoundly change the way we think about consumer behavior. Companies, nonprofits, political parties, and even governments now have the ability to sift through massive quantities of information that enables them to make precise predictions about what products we will buy, what charities we will donate to, what candidates we will vote for, and what levers they need to push to make this even more likely to happen. Walmart alone collects more than 2.5 petabytes of data every hour from its customer transactions (the equivalent of about 20 million filing cabinets' worth of text). Here are a few varied examples that illustrate how Big Data influences what we know and do:[16]

- When they monitor blips in Google queries for words like *flu* and *fever*, epidemiologists at the Centers for Disease Control can identify specific areas of the United States that have been hit by flu outbreaks even before the local authorities notice a rise in hospital admissions.
- Analysts for city police departments use massive amounts of crime data to identify "hot zones," where an abnormal amount of crimes occur. This intelligence enables them to assign and reassign law enforcement agents exactly where they need them.
- Although the Republicans outspent the Democrats during the 2012 presidential campaign, many attribute President Barack Obama's reelection to his campaign's masterful use of Big Data. The Democratic campaign systematically used huge datasets to help it decide exactly which voters needed an extra "nudge" to go to the polls and pull the lever for Obama. In subsequent elections the Republicans figured out how important it is to play catch-up and adopt their own Big Data strategies!

OBJECTIVE 1-3
Our choices as consumers relate in powerful ways to the rest of our lives.

Marketing's Impact on Consumers

Does marketing imitate life, or vice versa? After the movie *Wedding Crashers* became a big hit, hotels, wedding planners, and newlyweds reported an outbreak of uninvited guests who tried to gain access to parties across the United States.[17] For better or for worse, we all live in a world that the actions of marketers significantly influence.

Popular Culture Is Marketing Is Popular Culture ...

Marketing stimuli surround us as advertisements, stores, and products compete for our attention and our dollars. Marketers filter much of what we learn about the world, whether through the affluence they depict in glamorous magazines, the roles actors play in commercials, or maybe the energy drink a rock star just "happens" to hold during a photo shoot. Ads show us how we should act with regard to recycling, alcohol consumption, the types of houses and cars we might wish to own—and even how to evaluate others based on the products they buy or don't buy. In many ways we are also at the mercy of marketers, because we rely on them to sell us products that are safe and that perform as promised, to tell us the truth about what they sell, and to price and distribute these products fairly.

Popular culture—the music, movies, sports, books, celebrities, and other forms of entertainment that the mass market produces and consumes—is both a product of and an inspiration for marketers. It also affects our lives in more far-reaching ways, ranging from how we acknowledge cultural events such as marriage, death, or holidays to how we view

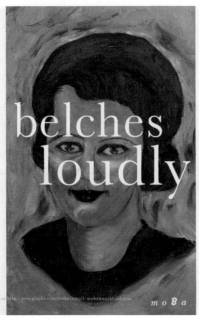

Some art speaks to you.
Some just belches loudly in your face.

Visit the permanent collection at 580 High Street, Dedham, Massachusetts – 617.325.8224 – Or on the Web at http://www.glyphs.com/moba-email: mobaworld.std.com   mo8a   museum   of   bad   art

We are surrounded by elements of popular culture—the good, the bad, and the ugly. This ad for the Museum of Bad Art reminds us of that.
Source: With permission of Museum of Bad Art.

social issues such as climate change, gambling, and addictions. Whether it's the Super Bowl, Christmas shopping, national health care, newspaper recycling, medical marijuana, body piercing, vaping, tweeting, or online video games, marketers play a significant role in our view of the world and how we live in it.

This cultural impact is hard to overlook, although many people do not seem to realize how much marketers influence their preferences for movie and musical heroes; the latest fashions in clothing, food, and decorating choices; and even the physical features that they find attractive or ugly in men and women. For example, consider the product icons that companies use to create an identity for their products. Many imaginary creatures and personalities, from the Pillsbury Doughboy to the Jolly Green Giant, at one time or another have been central figures in popular culture. In fact, it is likely that more consumers could recognize such characters than could identify past presidents, business leaders, or artists.

Marketers exert a huge impact on the way we live, for better and worse. Many companies and entrepreneurs are jumping on the new vaping bandwagon although the jury is still out as to whether this substitute for cigarette smoking is a good thing for smokers or simply a way to entice more young people to take up the smoking habit.
Source: Alex_Mac/Fotolia.

Although these figures never really existed, many of us feel as if we "know" them, and they certainly are effective *spokescharacters* for the products they represent.

All the World's a Stage

The sociological perspective of **role theory** takes the view that much of consumer behavior resembles actions in a play.[19] We as consumers seek the lines, props, and costumes necessary to put on a good performance. Because people act out many different roles, they sometimes alter their consumption decisions depending on the particular "play" they are in at the time. The criteria they use to evaluate products and services in one of their roles may be quite different from those they use in other roles. That's why it's important for marketers to provide each of us "actors" with the props we need to play all of our varied roles; these might include "up-and-coming executive," "geek," "hipster," or "big man on campus."

Marketing Opportunity

The interplay between marketing and/media and "real life" is obvious when you consider the history of the cultural observance American U.S. college students know as "Spring Break." Back in 1958 an English professor at Michigan State University heard some students talking about their Easter trip to Fort Lauderdale, Florida. He decided to go along to observe (they probably loved that), and upon his return he wrote a novel he called *Where the Boys Are*. That turned into a hit movie and the title song by Connie Francis rocked the charts. The year after the movie debuted in 1960, the number of students who visited Florida on their spring vacation ballooned from 20,000 to 50,000. MTV hosted a concert at Daytona Beach in 1986 that attracted major advertisers, and—thus began the commercialization of a rite that now attracts hundreds of thousands of devotees every year—maybe even you.[18]

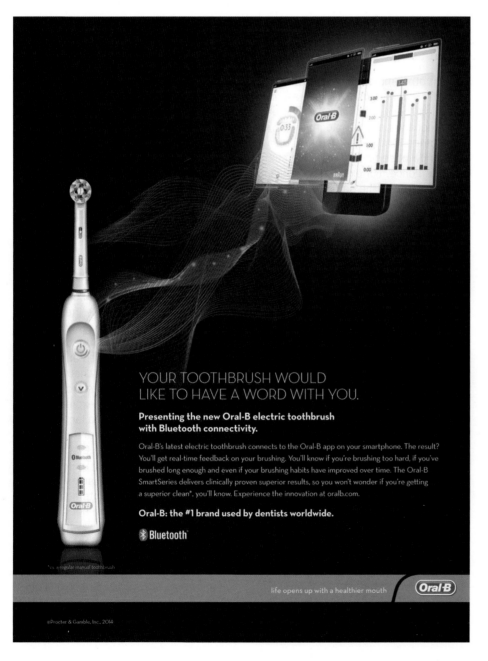

Technologies like Bluetooth connectivity allow consumers to interact with products more intimately, which in turn strengthens their relationships.

Source: Courtesy of The Procter & Gamble Company.

As we have seen, one trademark of marketing strategies today is that many organizations try very hard to build relationships with customers. The nature of these relationships can vary, but these bonds help us to understand some of the possible meanings products have for us. Furthermore, researchers find that, like friendships and love affairs with other people, our relationships with brands evolve over time. Some resemble deep friendships, whereas others are more like exciting but short-lived flings.[20]

Here are some of the types of relationships a person might have with a product:

- Self-concept attachment—The product helps to establish the user's identity.
- Nostalgic attachment—The product serves as a link with a past self.
- Interdependence—The product is a part of the user's daily routine.
- Love—The product elicits emotional bonds of warmth, passion, or other strong emotion.[21]

CB AS I SEE IT

Stefano Putoni-Erasmus, *University of Rotterdam*

Globalization is the defining social phenomenon of our times. Understanding its consequences for consumer behavior is crucial for marketers. A key way in which globalization influences consumer behavior is through the impact that globalization is having on the diversity of the societies in which we live. I think that many tensions associated with globalization stem from two opposing trends in how globalization influences diversity.

First, globalization leads to an *increase in diversity within countries*. Contemporary societies are vastly more diverse than they used to be, as can be easily noticed by taking a walk around Rotterdam—where I live—or

most other major cities. Second, globalization leads to a *decrease in diversity between countries*. Whereas few decades ago people in different countries lived very different lives, we can now observe a remarkable cultural convergence. For example, teenagers today listen to the same music, dress in the same way, and play the same games regardless of whether they live in Hong Kong or New York.

A paradox of globalization is thus that it both increases and decreases diversity. On the one hand, you can now eat sushi or Indian food in a sleepy Italian town. On the other hand, these restaurants look pretty much the same as those found in similarly sleepy towns in other countries or continents. These two trends raise important new questions for consumer researchers and I have tried to address some of them in my own work—focusing on both increasing diversity within countries and decreasing diversity between countries.

Here I would like to talk about one line of research, which I find especially interesting. It concerns the decrease in diversity between countries. One of the most visible aspects of globalization is the spread of English as the new *lingua franca*. The recent growth of English as the global language has been extraordinary and

the process is still gathering speed. With Bart de Langhe, Daniel Fenandes, and Stijn van Osselaer, I studied the impact of the rise of English as the global language for consumers' response to both marketing communications and marketing research. The basic contention of our articles is simple, as well as intuitive to any introspective bilingual: one's native language has special emotional qualities due to the connection of words with meaningful personal experiences. To make a concrete example, to a Dutch speaker, the word "oma" ("grandmother") is inescapably associated to his or her grandmother, whereas the English word lacks this link to personal memories and it is thus more emotionally neutral. Messages have therefore more emotional impact when expressed in one's native than second language.

Messages in English are common in many countries where English is not an official language. There are good reasons why companies decide to use English in their interactions with consumers who are not native speakers of English. However, our research highlights a potential drawback. For example, delivering emotional experiences is considered central in branding and it is harder to achieve this goal using a language that is not the consumer's native language.

Even a very inexpensive product like Peeps can play an important role in a culture.
Source: garytog/Fotolia.

OBJECTIVE 1-4
Our motivations to consume are complex and varied.

What Does It Mean to Consume?

What's the poop on Peeps? Every year, people buy about 1.5 billion of these mostly tasteless marshmallow chicks; about two-thirds of them sell around Easter. The newer version called Peeps Minis encourages people to eat them at other times as well, including quirky and obscure "holidays" such as "Bubble Wrap Appreciation Day" and "Lost Sock Memorial Day."[22]

Peeps have no nutritional value, but they do have a shelf life of two years. Maybe that's why not all Peeps get eaten. Devotees use them in decorations, dioramas, online slide shows, and sculptures. Some fans feel challenged to test their physical properties: On more than 200 Peeps Web sites, you can see fetishists skewering, microwaving, hammering, decapitating, and otherwise abusing the spongy confections.[23]

This fascination with a creepy little candy chick illustrates one of the fundamental premises of the modern field of consumer behavior: *People often buy products not for what*

Successful products satisfy needs and improve our lives in ways large and small. This South African ad subtly reminds us that our plans might go astray if we don't have a reliable form of transportation—and of course the quality auto parts that help to make that happen.
Source: Courtesy of Honda Motor Southern Africa.

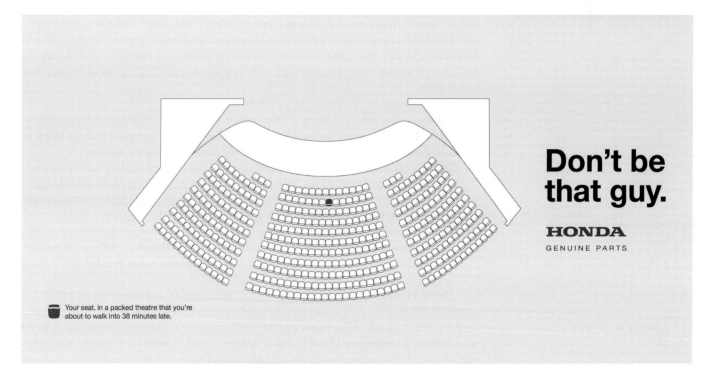

Your seat, in a packed theatre that you're about to walk into 38 minutes late.

Don't be that guy.

HONDA
GENUINE PARTS

they do, but for what they mean. This principle does not imply that a product's basic function is unimportant, but rather that the roles products play in our lives extend well beyond the tasks they perform. The deeper meanings of a product may help it to stand out from other similar goods and services. All things being equal, we choose the brand that has an image (or even a personality!) consistent with our underlying needs.

For example, although most people probably couldn't run faster or jump higher if they wear Nikes instead of Reeboks, many die-hard loyalists swear by their favorite brand. People choose between these archrivals (or other competitors) largely because of their *brand images*—meanings that have been carefully crafted with the help of legions of rock stars, athletes, slickly produced commercials, and many millions of dollars. So, when you buy a Nike "swoosh," you are doing more than choosing shoes to wear to the mall; you also make a lifestyle statement about the type of person you are or wish you were. For a relatively simple item made of leather and laces, that's quite a feat!

Our allegiances to sneakers, musicians, and even soft drinks help us define our place in modern society, and these choices also help each of us to form bonds with others who share similar preferences. This comment by a participant in a focus group captures the curious bonding that consumption choices can create: "I was at a Super Bowl party, and I picked up an obscure drink. Somebody else across the room went 'yo!' because he had the same thing. People feel a connection when you're drinking the same thing."[24]

As we'll see in Chapter 5, our motivations to consume range from the practical to the fanciful (see the Peeps discussion). In some cases, we decide to try a product because we want to learn more about the experience and in some way grow personally. For example, in one study undergraduates who were asked to try a new (fictitious) brand of beer were more likely to do so when they believed their level of expertise with the product was relatively low (imagine that!), and thus there was an opportunity to enhance their knowledge about different attributes of beer.[25] In other cases our choice of a product links more to our broader identity as a member of a larger entity such as an ethnic group or a country. In another study researchers found that emerging Chinese luxury brands such as Shanghai Tang and Shang Xia resonate with local consumers because they place a renewed value upon Chinese craftsmanship, values, and aesthetics.[26]

What Do We Need—*Really*?

A recent large survey explored some profound questions: How can we predict if someone will be happy? How does that feeling relate to living a meaningful life? The researchers concluded that happiness is linked to satisfying wants and needs, whereas meaningfulness relates to activities that express oneself and impact others in a positive way. Not surprisingly, people whose needs were satisfied were happier, but the findings went beyond that connection:

- Happiness was linked to being a taker rather than a giver, whereas meaningfulness went with being a giver rather than a taker. Happy people are more likely to think in the present rather than dwelling on the past or contemplating the future.
- Respondents who reported higher levels of worry, stress, and anxiety were less happy but had more meaningful lives. They spend a lot of time thinking about past struggles and imagining what will happen in the future. They are likely to agree that taking care of children and buying gifts for others are a reflection of who they are.
- The researchers concluded that "happiness without meaning characterizes a relatively shallow, self-absorbed or even selfish life, in which things go well, needs and desires are easily satisfied, and difficult or taxing entanglements are avoided."[27]

The distinction between a "happy" and a "meaningful" life brings up an important question: What is the difference between needing something and wanting it? The answer to this deceptively simple question actually explains a lot of consumer behavior! A **need** is something a person must have to live or achieve a goal. A **want** is a specific manifestation of a need that personal and cultural factors determine. For example, hunger is a basic

This ad from the United Arab Emirates appeals to our basic drive to reduce hunger.
Source: Designed and released by Publinet Advertising & Publicity LLC, Dubai, UAE.

need that all of us must satisfy; a lack of food creates a tension state that a person is motivated to reduce. But, the way he or she chooses to do that can take a lot of forms: One person's "dream meal" might include a cheeseburger, fries, and double-fudge Oreo cookies, whereas another might go for sushi followed by vegan and gluten-free chocolate cake balls.

The Global "Always-On" Consumer

OBJECTIVE 1-5
Technology and culture create a new "always-on" consumer.

Today many of us take for granted things that our grandparents only dreamed about. We instantly access people, places, and products with the click of a link. Many consumers travel to remote countries in a day rather than the weeks or months our ancestors needed, if they ever left their places of birth at all.

The majority of us now live in urban centers that bustle with people from many countries and that offer exotic foods from around the world. The United Nations defines a **megacity** as a metropolitan area with a total population of more than 10 million people. By 2011, there were already 20 such areas in the world. Researchers estimate that by 2030 three out of five people will live in cities, and more than 2 billion people will live in slums. Already, China boasts four shopping centers that are larger than the massive Mall of America in Minnesota, and soon it will be home to seven of the world's largest malls.[28]

This concentration in urban centers, combined with population growth in developing countries and increasing demands for modernization by billions of people in booming economies such as China, India, and Brazil, is both a blessing and a curse. Quality of life for many everyday citizens is better than even the elite who lived several centuries ago (even kings only bathed once a month). On the other hand, millions live in squalor, children around the world go to bed hungry, and we all feel the effects unbridled growth contributes to pollution of our air, soil, and water. As we'll see later in the book, all of these issues relate directly to our understanding of consumer behavior—and to the impact companies and customers have on our future and the world that we will leave to our children.

The Digital Native: Living a Social [Media] Life

It's fair to say that 24/7 access to smartphones and other social media devices has kindled a fascination among many of us with documenting *exactly* what we're doing and sharing the exciting news with others. A meal in a nice restaurant doesn't get touched until the

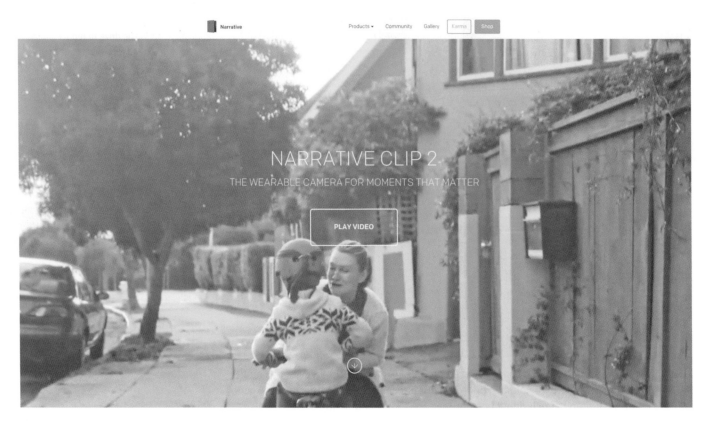

New products like the Narrative Clip allow people who feel the need to document their activities to do so easily.
Source: Courtesy of Narrative.

diner posts a photo of it on Instagram. We may not learn that the person we're dating has broken up with us until we see they have changed their relationship status on Facebook. Today you can even wear a tiny camera called the *Narrative Clip* that automatically snaps a photo every 30 seconds for those who feel the need to post an ongoing documentary of their everyday movements for posterity.[29]

There's little doubt that the digital revolution is one of the most significant influences on consumer behavior, and the impact of the Web will continue to expand as more and more people around the world log in. Many of us are avid Web surfers, and it's hard to imagine a time when texting, tweeting, Facebooking, or pinning favorite items on Pinterest weren't an accepted part of daily life—not to mention those who compulsively check in on Foursquare at their local Starbucks 10 times a day!

Electronic marketing makes our lives a lot easier. You can shop 24/7 without leaving home, you can read today's newspaper without getting drenched picking up a newsprint copy in a rainstorm, and you don't have to wait for the 6:00 pm news to find out what the weather will be like tomorrow—whether at home or around the globe. With the increasing use of handheld devices and wireless communications, you can get that same information—from stock quotes to the weather—even when you're away from your computer.

Also, it's not all about businesses selling to consumers (**B2C e-commerce**). The cyberspace explosion has created a revolution in consumer-to-consumer activity (**C2C e-commerce**): Welcome to the world of *virtual brand communities*. Just as e-consumers are not limited to local retail outlets in their shopping, they are not limited to their local communities when they look for friends or fellow fans of wine, hip-hop, or skateboarding.

Picture a small group of local collectors who meet once a month at a local diner to discuss their shared interests over coffee. Now multiply that group by thousands and include people from all over the world who are united by a shared passion for sports memorabilia, Barbie dolls, Harley-Davidson motorcycles, refrigerator magnets, or massive multiplayer online games (MMOGs) such as *World of Warcraft*. The Web also provides an easy way for consumers around the world to exchange information about their experiences with products, services, music, restaurants, and movies. The Hollywood Stock Exchange (hsx.com) offers a simulated entertainment stock market where traders predict the 4-week box office take for each film.[30] Amazon.com encourages shoppers to write reviews of books, and (just as Gail did) you can even rate your professors at RateMyProfessors.com (don't tell your prof about this one; it'll be our secret).[31] The popularity of chat rooms where consumers can go to discuss various topics with like-minded "Netizens" around the world grows every day, as do immersive **virtual worlds** such as *Second Life*, *Habbo Hotel*, and *Kaneva*. News reports tell us of the sometimes wonderful and sometimes horrific romances that have begun on the Internet as people check out potential mates on sites such as Match.com or OKCupid. In one month, the dating site Plenty of Fish alone had 122 million visits.[32] Or, chew on this: today in the United States, one-third of married couples met online![33]

If you're a typical student, you probably can't recall a time when the Internet was just a static, one-way platform that transmitted text and a few sketchy images. And believe it or not, in the last century even *that* crude technique didn't exist. You may have read about this in a history class: People actually *hand-wrote* letters to each other and waited for printed magazines to arrive in their mailboxes to learn about current events! The term **digital native** originated in a 2001 article to explain a new type of student who was starting to turn up on campus. These consumers grew up "wired" in a highly networked, always-on world where digital technology had always existed.[34]

Fast-forward a decade: Today the Internet is the backbone of our society. Widespread access to devices such as personal computers, digital video and audio recorders, web-cams, and smartphones ensures that consumers of practically any age who live in virtually any part of the world can create and share content. But information doesn't just flow from big companies or governments down to the people; today each of us can communicate with huge numbers of people by a click on a keypad, so information flows *across* people as well. Indeed, the recent decision by the Federal Communications Commission (FCC) to back the principle of **net neutrality** ensures that everyone—individual users and behemoth companies—is guaranteed equal access to the "pipes" we rely on to access cyberspace.

That's what we mean by a **horizontal revolution**. This horizontal revolution is characterized in part by the prevalence of social media. **Social media** are the online means of communication, conveyance, collaboration, and cultivation among interconnected and interdependent networks of people, communities, and organizations enhanced by technological capabilities and mobility.[36]

The Internet and its related technologies that gave birth to Web 2.0 make what we know today as social media possible and prevalent. Every day the influence of social media expands as more people join online communities. Facebook, a social utility that offers **synchronous interactions** (those that occur in real time, like when you text back-and-forth with a friend) and **asynchronous interactions** (those that don't require all participants to respond immediately, like when you text a friend and get an answer the next day), photo-sharing, games, applications, groups, e-retailing, and more, has more than one billion active users.[37]

People aren't just joining social communities. They are contributing too! Users upload 72 hours of video to YouTube every minute. In just 30 days on YouTube, more video is broadcast than in the past 60 years on the CBS, NBC, and ABC broadcasting networks combined.[38] Consider these mind-boggling social media stats:[39]

- If you were paid $1 for every time an article was posted on Wikipedia, you would earn $156.23 per hour.
- It took radio 38 years to reach 50 million listeners. TV took 13 years to reach 50 million users. The Internet took 4 years to reach 50 million people. In less than 9 months, Facebook added 100 million users.

Net Profit

Do you remember all those crazy Mentos/Diet Coke videos? At least 800 of them flooded YouTube after people discovered that when you drop the quarter-size candies into bottles of Diet Coke, you get a geyser that shoots 20 feet into the air. Needless to say, Mentos got a gusher of free publicity out of the deal, too.[35] Probably the biggest marketing phenomenon of this decade is **user-generated content**, whereby everyday people voice their opinions about products, brands, and companies on blogs, podcasts, and social networking sites such as Facebook and Twitter, and even film their own commercials that thousands view on sites such as YouTube. This important trend helps to define the era of **Web 2.0**: the rebirth of the Internet as a social, interactive medium from its original roots as a form of one-way transmission from producers to consumers.

- About 70 percent of Facebook users are outside the United States.
- Social networks have overtaken porn as the number-one online activity.
- Eighty percent of companies use LinkedIn as their primary recruiting tool.
- Twenty-five percent of search results for the world's top 10 brands are to user-generated content.
- People share more than 1.5 billion pieces of content on Facebook—*every* day.
- Eighty percent of Twitter usage is from mobile devices, and 17 percent of users have tweeted while on the toilet.

This is all exciting stuff, especially because social media platforms enable a **culture of participation**; a belief in democracy; the ability to freely interact with other people, companies, and organizations; open access to venues that allow users to share content from simple comments to reviews, ratings, photos, stories, and more; and the power to build on the content of others from your own unique point of view. Of course, just like democracy in the real world, we have to take the bitter with the sweet. There are plenty of unsavory things going on in cyberspace, and the hours people spend on Facebook, on online gambling sites, or in virtual worlds like *Second Life* have led to divorce, bankruptcy, or jail in the real world.

OBJECTIVE 1-6
Many different types of specialists study consumer behavior.

Consumer Behavior as a Field of Study

By now it should be clear that the field of consumer behavior encompasses many things, from the simple purchase of a carton of milk to the selection of a complex networked computer system; from the decision to donate money to a charity to devious plans to rip off a company.

There's an awful lot to understand, and many ways to go about it. Although people have certainly been consumers for a long time, it is only recently that consumption per se has been the object of formal study. In fact, although many business schools now require that marketing majors take a consumer behavior course, most colleges did not even offer such a course until the 1970s.

Where Do We Find Consumer Researchers?

Where do we find consumer researchers? Just about anywhere we find consumers. Consumer researchers work for manufacturers, retailers, marketing research firms, governments and nonprofit organizations, and of course colleges and universities. You'll find them in laboratories, running sophisticated experiments that involve advanced neural imaging machinery, or in malls interviewing shoppers. They may conduct focus groups or run large-scale polling operations. For example, when an advertising agency began to work on a new campaign for retailer JC Penney, it sent staffers to hang out with more than 50 women for several days. They wanted to really understand the respondents' lives, so they helped them to clean their houses, carpool, cook dinner, and shop. As one of the account executives observed, "If you want to understand how a lion hunts, you don't go to the zoo—you go to the jungle."[40]

Researchers work on many types of topics, from everyday household products and high-tech installations to professional services, museum exhibits, and public policy issues such as the effect of advertising on children. Indeed, no consumer issue is too sacred for researchers: Some intrepid investigators bravely explore "delicate" categories such as incontinence products and birth control devices. The marketing director for Trojan condoms noted that, "Unlike laundry, where you can actually sit and watch people do their laundry, we can't sit and watch them use our product." For this reason, Trojan relies on clinical psychologists, psychiatrists, and cultural anthropologists to understand how men relate to condoms.[41]

Interdisciplinary Influences on the Study of Consumer Behavior

Many different perspectives shape the young field of consumer behavior. Indeed, it is hard to think of a field that is more interdisciplinary. You can find people with training in a wide range of disciplines—from psychophysiology to literature—doing consumer research. Universities, manufacturers, museums, advertising agencies, and governments employ consumer researchers. Several professional groups, such as the Association for Consumer Research and the Society for Consumer Psychology, have been formed since the mid-1970s.

To gain an idea of the diversity of interests of people who do consumer research, consider the list of professional associations that sponsor the field's major journal, the *Journal of Consumer Research*: the American Association of Family and Consumer Sciences, the American Statistical Association, the Association for Consumer Research, the Society for Consumer Psychology, the International Communication Association, the American Sociological Association, the Institute of Management Sciences, the American Anthropological Association, the American Marketing Association, the Society for Personality and Social Psychology, the American Association for Public Opinion Research, and the American Economic Association. That's a pretty mixed bag.

Clearly there are a lot of researchers from diverse backgrounds who are into the study of consumer behavior. So, which is the "correct" discipline to look into these issues? You might remember a children's story about the blind men and the elephant. The gist of the story is that each man touched a different part of the animal and, as a result, the descriptions each gave of the elephant were quite different. This analogy applies to consumer research as well. Depending on the training and interests of the researchers studying it, they will approach the same consumer phenomenon in different ways and at different levels. Table 1.1 illustrates how we can approach a "simple" topic such as magazine usage from a range of perspectives.

TABLE 1.1   Interdisciplinary Research Issues in Consumer Behavior

Disciplinary Focus	Magazine Usage Sample Research Issues
Experimental Psychology: product role in perception, learning, and memory processes	How specific aspects of magazines, such as their design or layout, are recognized and interpreted; which parts of a magazine people are most likely to read.
Clinical Psychology: product role in psychological adjustment	How magazines affect readers' body images (e.g., do thin models make the average woman feel overweight?)
Microeconomics/Human Ecology: product role in allocation of individual or family resources	Factors influencing the amount of money a household spends on magazines.
Social Psychology: product role in the behavior of individuals as members of social groups	Ways that ads in a magazine affect readers' attitudes toward the products depicted; how peer pressure influences a person's readership decisions
Sociology: product role in social institutions and group relationships	Pattern by which magazine preferences spread through a social group (e.g., a sorority)
Macroeconomics: product role in consumers' relations with the marketplace	Effects of the price of fashion magazines and expense of items advertised during periods of high unemployment
Semiotics/Literary Criticism: product role in the verbal and visual communication of meaning	Ways in which underlying messages communicated by models and ads in a magazine are interpreted
Demography: product role in the measurable characteristics of a population	Effects of age, income, and marital status of a magazine's readers
History: product role in societal changes over time	Ways in which our culture's depictions of "femininity" in magazines have changed over time
Cultural Anthropology: product role in a society's beliefs and practices	Ways in which fashions and models in a magazine affect readers' definitions of masculine versus feminine behavior (e.g., the role of working women, sexual taboos)

Figure 1.2 THE PYRAMID OF
CONSUMER BEHAVIOR

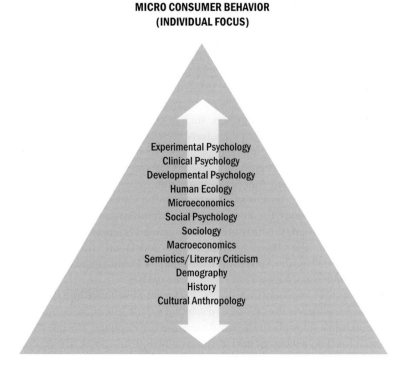

**MICRO CONSUMER BEHAVIOR
(INDIVIDUAL FOCUS)**

Experimental Psychology
Clinical Psychology
Developmental Psychology
Human Ecology
Microeconomics
Social Psychology
Sociology
Macroeconomics
Semiotics/Literary Criticism
Demography
History
Cultural Anthropology

**MACRO CONSUMER BEHAVIOR
(SOCIAL FOCUS)**

Figure 1.2 provides a glimpse of some of the disciplines that work in the field and the level at which each tackles research issues. We can roughly characterize them in terms of their focus on micro- versus macro-consumer behavior topics. The fields closer to the top of the pyramid concentrate on the individual consumer (micro issues), and those toward the base are more interested in the collective activities that occur among larger groups of people, such as consumption patterns members of a culture or subculture share (macro issues). As we make our way through this book, we'll focus on the issues at the top (micro) and then make our way to the bottom of the pyramid by the end of the course. Hang in there!

OBJECTIVE 1-7
There are differing perspectives regarding how and what we should understand about consumer behavior.

Two Perspectives on Consumer Research

One general way in which we classify consumer research is in terms of the fundamental assumptions the researchers make about what they study and how to study it. We call a set of beliefs that guide our understanding of the world a **paradigm**. As in other fields of study, a paradigm dominates the discipline of consumer behavior. However, some believe the discipline is in the middle of a *paradigm shift*, which occurs when a competing paradigm challenges the dominant set of assumptions.

The basic set of assumptions underlying the dominant paradigm at this point in time is **positivism** (sometimes called *modernism*). This perspective has significantly influenced Western art and science since the late 16th century. It emphasizes that human reason is supreme and that there is a single, objective truth that science can discover. Positivism encourages us to stress the function of objects, to celebrate technology, and to regard the world as a rational, ordered place with a clearly defined past, present, and future.

The newer paradigm of **interpretivism** (or *postmodernism*) questions these assumptions.[42] Proponents of this perspective argue that our society emphasizes science and

Don't let alcohol alter your reality.
Drink responsibly. Don't drink and drive.

MARCO
POLO
HOTEL
DUBAI

The expanded view of consumer behavior embraces much more than the study of what and why we buy; it also focuses on how marketers influence consumers and how consumers use the products and services marketers sell. In this case, a hotel in Dubai promotes responsible behavior.
Source: Courtesy of Marco Polo Hotel/Dubai; Brandcom Agency.

technology too much, and they feel that this ordered, rational view of behavior denies or ignores the complex social and cultural world in which we really live. Others feel that positivism puts too much emphasis on material well-being and that its logical outlook is directed by an ideology that stresses the homogenous views of a culture dominated by (dead) white males. And, as we'll see in the next chapter, some adherents to this view also believe researchers should not just study consumer issues, but act on them as well.

Interpretivists instead stress the importance of symbolic, subjective experience, and the idea that meaning is in the mind of the person—that is, we each construct our own meanings based on our unique and shared cultural experiences, so there are no right or wrong answers. In this view, the world in which we live is a **pastiche**, or mixture of images and ideas.[43] This perspective rejects the value we assign to products because they help us to create order; instead, it focuses on regarding consumption as offering a set of diverse experiences. Table 1.2 summarizes the major differences between these two perspectives on consumer research.

To appreciate how an interpretive framework helps us to understand marketing communications, let's refer to an analysis of one of the best-known and longest-running (1959–1978) advertising campaigns of all time: the work the advertising agency Doyle Dane Bernbach (DDB) did for the Volkswagen Beetle. This campaign, widely noted for its self-mocking wit, found many ways to turn the Beetle's homeliness, small size, and lack of power into positive attributes at a time when most car ads were emphasizing just the

TABLE 1.2	Positivist versus Interpretivist Approaches to Consumer Behavior	
Assumptions	**Positivist Approach**	**Interpretivist Approach**
Nature of reality Goal	Objective, tangible Single Prediction	Socially constructed Multiple understanding
Knowledge generated	Time-free, context independent	Time-bound, context dependent
View of causality	Existence of real causes	Multiple, simultaneous shaping events
Research relationship	Separation between researcher and subject	Interactive, cooperative with researcher being part of phenomenon under study

Source: Laurel Anderson Hudson, Julie L. Ozanne. Alternative Ways of Seeking Knowledge in Consumer Research. *Journal of Consumer Research*, Mar 1988, Vol. 14(4), 508–521 by permission of Oxford University Press/on behalf of the sponsoring society if the journal is a society journal.

opposite. In one famous advertising execution in this campaign, a black-and-white photo of a Beetle appeared above the tagline: "Lemon." The copy beneath the word went on to explain that a company inspector rejected this particular vehicle because he found a blemish on the glove box.

An interpretative analysis of these messages used concepts from literature, psychology, and anthropology to ground the appeal of this approach within a broader cultural context. Analysts linked the image DDB created for the humble car to other examples of what scholars of comedy call the "Little Man" pattern. This is a type of comedic character who is related to a clown or a trickster, a social outcast who is able to poke holes in the stuffiness and rigidity of bureaucracy and conformity. Other examples of the "Little Man" character include Hawkeye in the classic TV sitcom *M*A*S*H*, the comedian Woody Allen, and actor Charlie Chaplin. When one looks at the cultural meaning of marketing messages this way, it is perhaps no coincidence that IBM chose the Charlie Chaplin character some years later to help it "soften" its stuffy, intimidating image as it tried to convince consumers that its new personal computer products were user friendly.

In recent years the interpretivist focus has gained momentum and although it's still not the dominant focus of consumer researchers, it's quite commonplace to see research studies that adhere to this perspective, or its' current incarnation many refer to as **Consumer Culture Theory (CCT)**. This label refers generally to research that regards consumption from a social and cultural point of view rather than more narrowly as an economic exchange. CCT studies embrace a variety of topics that range from how the media shapes our conceptions of our bodies or how underprivileged people cope with poverty to how Harley-Davidson riders participate in an active community of bike lovers.[44]

Should Consumer Research Have an Academic or an Applied Focus?

Many researchers regard the field of consumer behavior as an applied social science. They argue that the value of the knowledge we generate should be judged in terms of its ability to improve the effectiveness of marketing practice. However, others argue that consumer behavior should not have a strategic focus at all; the field should not be a "handmaiden to business." It should instead focus on the understanding of consumption for its own sake rather than marketers applying this knowledge to making a profit.[45] Most consumer researchers do not hold this rather extreme view, but it has encouraged many to expand the scope of their work beyond the field's traditional focus on the purchase of consumer goods such as food, appliances, and cars to embrace social problems such as homelessness or preserving the environment. Certainly, it has led to some fiery debates among people working in the field!

CB AS I SEE IT
Craig Thompson, *University of Wisconsin-Madison*

Would you rather spend your time sipping a latte in a small, dimly light bohemian coffee shop or a bright, shiny Starbucks? Would you rather drive a fuel-efficient Prius or a powerful, four-wheel drive gas guzzling SUV? Would you rather buy your groceries at a Walmart superstore stocked to the ceiling with nationally advertised brands, or at a Whole Foods with a meticulously arranged produce display and an enticing selection of niche-oriented organic brands, or at a farmers market or CSA (Community Supported Agriculture) program where you can form a direct face-to-face relationship with the person producing your food?

From a conventional consumer behavior perspective, these different scenarios are no different from the myriad other choices that consumers make on a daily basis. Accordingly, they can be explained as the outcome of a given consumer's evaluation of the respective attributes offered by each alternative. Another prominent line of explanation would suggest that these choices are a form of identity signaling through which consumers

present a desired self-image to others (i.e., the socially conscious shopper, the sophisticated culinary omnivore; the frugal, down-to-earth consumer). Research that I have conducted with various colleagues over the last 15 years suggests that neither of these dominant explanations tell the full story about the motivations and meanings that underlie practices of *political consumerism*.

My conceptualization of political consumerism builds upon the works of the historian and social theorist Michel de Certeau, who analyzed the micro-politics of everyday actions. That is, practices through which individuals attempt to change the social conditions that organize and constrain their everyday actions. To illustrate the concept of structural constraints, consider the vast number of Americans who embark on a daily commute from their suburban homes to their place of work; a commute which consumes time, money (fuel costs, automobile depreciation) and often that generates frustration as one negotiates traffic delays and the like. And many Americans would love to forego this costly and stressful routine but they have few practical alternatives owing to a lack of convenient public transportation or housing costs which make living in the distant suburbs more affordable than center city neighborhoods which would be closer to their workplaces. While consumers can choose alternative modes of transportation (such as biking to work), a network of structural relations push consumers to accept, as a default choice, the standard practice of commuting and to bear its associated costs.

Political consumerism refers to situations where consumers seek to consciously resist these structural constraints through alternative consumption practices

and do so with a critical-reflexive knowledge of the specific conditions being challenged. My colleagues and I have consistently found that these resistant consumer choices and practices are collective rather individual in nature. In other words, consumers become socially linked to particular consumption communities that are mobilized by their opposition to some dominant structural influence and act upon a shared understanding (or ideology) of the ethical and cultural implications of their resistant consumer practices.

For example, Gokcen Coskuner-Balli and I conducted a study of community-supported agriculture; an alternative market system whereby consumers buy a share in a local farm (which typically costs between $300 to $600) and in return, they receive a weekly box of produce that they acquire at a centralized drop off site or in some cases, the farm itself. In this exchange relationship, the CSA farmer's planting decision and the success (or failure) of the crops determine what goes in the weekly basket as well as the volume of goods provided. Hence, consumers are foregoing their conventional ability to choose what they buy and CSA's "buy a share" pricing model makes it difficult to accurately determine just what they are paying for any particular item in their basket. Why do consumers enter into such an unconventional market relationship? In many cases, CSA consumers first become sensitized to the often-reported health risks associated with processed foods and the pesticides used in conventional agriculture. Thus, CSA offered these concerned consumers a means to incorporate fresh, organic produce into their diets. Importantly, many of these consumers were also responding to the evangelizing recommendations of friends and neighbors who were already members of a CSA. Once consumers commit to a CSA program, they gradually become socialized into the shared ideological values, beliefs, and ideas of the CSA community through their interactions with farmers, other CSA consumers, participation in farm events (e.g., tours, watermelon tasting events, apple picking) and last but not least, the newsletters that many CSA farms include in their weekly baskets. Over time, these consumers come to understand their participation in a CSA as a means to gain some degree of autonomy from the structural influences exerted by large agri-business firms and the array of consumer packaged goods they promote.

A very different ideological expression of the politics of consumption is offered by an analysis of avid Hummer owners that I conducted with Marius Luedicke and Markus Giesler. Prior to our study, Hummer owners had largely been stereotyped as ardent status-seekers who were oblivious to the socially irresponsible nature of their oversized version of conspicuous consumption. In contrast, we discovered that devout Hummer owners had constructed a collective identity in which they were proponents and defenders of liberty. Upon further investigation, we found that their understanding of freedom and its symbolic linkage to a mass-produced SUV was grounded in the ideology of American exceptionalism. This ideology portrays the United States as a proverbial City on the Hill that stands as beacon of freedom and liberty to the world. American exceptionalism further venerates the ideal of rugged individualism and promotes a belief that the United States, as a divinely blessed land, enjoys a boundless frontier of natural resources. For Hummer owners, their environmental critics were not only an affront to these hallowed values but were even akin to communists and socialists, in posing a threat to the sacrosanct American way of life. Paradoxically, the cultural backlash against the Hummer galvanized these owners' belief that driving a Hummer was a principled act of resistance against un-American "tree huggers" who sought to impose tyrannical constraints on their rugged individualist lifestyles and their capacity to experience the American frontier through their off-roading endeavors. Although the Hummer's cultural moment has passed, my colleagues and I believe that this underlying ideology of American exceptionalism can help to explain phenomena such as the high rate of climate change denial among political conservatives and even more extreme versions of politicized fossil fuel consumption, such as the automotive subculture known as "rolling coal." [http://en.wikipedia.org/wiki/Rolling_coal]

For example, Chipotle's award winning animated short film—*The Scarecrow* https://www.youtube.com/watch?v=lUtnas5ScSE—incorporates critiques of corporate farming that have been central to the ideology of community supported agriculture and other variations of the local food movement. Similarly, Dove's Campaign for Real Beauty reiterates feminist criticisms of the so-called beauty industry in the course of promoting its line of cosmetic and skin care products. One school of thought deems marketers' appropriation of resistant consumer ideologies and marketing strategies to be an inherently hypocritical and exploitative action that misleads consumers, as in so-called greenwashing campaigns. Others counter that such campaigns can contribute to positive social change by building broader social awareness of the problems and concerns being represented.

Taking It from Here: The Plan of the Book

This book covers many facets of consumer behavior, and in the chapters to come we will highlight many of the research perspectives that we only briefly described in this one. The plan of the book is simple: It goes from micro to macro. Think of it as a sort of photograph album of consumer behavior: Each chapter provides a "snapshot" of consumers, but the lens used to take each picture gets successively wider. First we'll focus on the crucially important topic of consumer well-being in the next chapter of Section 1 as we consider some of the consequences of our decisions for our environment and ourselves. In Section 2 we'll dive deeper into the facets of individual consumer behavior as we look at internal factors such as how we learn about products and services and then use this information to decide how we feel about them—and about ourselves as individuals. In Section 3 we zoom in on how exactly we choose products and services from a field of competitors and how we decide to purchase, use and even dispose of these products. Finally in Section 4 we expand the lens to consider external influences on these decisions such as the groups to which we belong and the opinions of others we access via both traditional and new media.

CHAPTER SUMMARY

Now that you have finished reading this chapter, you should understand why:

1. Consumer behavior is a process.

Consumer behavior is the study of the processes involved when individuals or groups select, purchase, use, or dispose of products, services, ideas, or experiences to satisfy needs and desires. A consumer may purchase, use, and dispose of a product, but different people may perform these functions. In addition, we can think of consumers as role players who need different products to help them play their various parts.

2. Marketers have to understand the wants and needs of different consumer segments.

Market segmentation is an important aspect of consumer behavior. Consumers can be segmented according to many dimensions, including product usage, demographics (the objective aspects of a population, such as age and sex), and psychographics (psychological and lifestyle characteristics). Emerging developments, such as the new emphasis on relationship marketing and the practice of database marketing, mean that marketers are much more attuned to the wants and needs of different consumer groups.

3. Our choices as consumers relate in powerful ways to the rest of our lives.

Marketing activities exert an enormous impact on individuals. Consumer behavior is relevant to our understanding of both public policy issues (e.g., ethical marketing practices) and the dynamics of popular culture.

4. Our motivations to consume are complex and varied.

Marketers try to satisfy consumer needs, but the reasons people purchase any product can vary widely. The identification of consumer motives is an important step to ensure that a product will satisfy appropriate needs. Traditional approaches to consumer behavior focus on the abilities of products to satisfy rational needs (utilitarian motives), but hedonic motives (e.g., the need for exploration or for fun) also play a key role in many purchase decisions.

5. Technology and culture create a new "always-on" consumer.

The Web and social media transform the way consumers interact with companies and with each other. Online commerce allows us to locate obscure products from around the world, and consumption communities provide forums for people to share opinions and product recommendations.

6. Many different types of specialists study consumer behavior.

The field of consumer behavior is interdisciplinary; it is composed of researchers from many different fields who share an interest in how people interact with the marketplace. We can categorize these disciplines by the degree to which their focus is micro (the individual consumer) or macro (the consumer as a member of groups or of the larger society).

7. There are differing perspectives regarding how and what we should understand about consumer behavior.

Researchers who study consumer behavior do so both for academic purposes and to inform marketing organizations about practical decisions. We can roughly divide research orientations into two approaches: The positivist perspective emphasizes the objectivity of science and the consumer as a rational decision maker. The interpretivist (or CCT) perspective, in contrast, stresses the subjective meaning of the consumer's individual experience and the idea that any behavior is subject to multiple interpretations rather than to one single explanation.

KEY TERMS

80/20 Rule, 30
Asynchronous interactions, 43
B2C e-commerce, 42
Big Data, 34

C2C e-commerce, 42
Consumer, 29
Consumer behavior, 28
Consumer Culture Theory (CCT), 48

Consumption communities, 27
Culture of participation, 44
Database marketing, 33
Demographics, 27

REVIEW

1-1 Provide a definition of consumer behavior.

1-2 What are demographics? Give three examples of demographic characteristics.

⭐ **1-3** What are consumption communities? Give three examples of consumption communities.

1-4 What is role theory, and how does it help us to understand consumer behavior?

1-5 How would you define a consumer?

1-6 Why do some marketers believe in the concept of relationship marketing?

1-7 How practical and useful is database marketing for most businesses?

1-8 Identify the three stages of the consumption process.

1-9 Have traditional patterns of consumption been radically changed by globalization?

⭐ **1-10** How could interdisciplinary research in consumer behavior explain the profile of a national newspaper or television news channel?

1-11 Name two different disciplines that study consumer behavior. How would their approaches to the same issue differ?

1-12 This chapter states "people often buy products not for what they do but for what they mean." Explain the meaning of this statement and provide an example.

⭐ **1-13** What are the major differences between the positivist and interpretivist paradigms in consumer research?

CONSUMER BEHAVIOR CHALLENGE

▪ DISCUSS

1-14 Each country or region will have a core of products and services that are consumed. Collectively, the consumption of these infers some kind of group bond. Identify examples of these specific products and services and comment on how they help to maintain group bonds.

1-15 What aspects of consumer behavior would interest a financial planner? A university administrator? A graphic arts designer? A social worker in a government agency? A nursing instructor?

1-16 Individuals can have different relationships with brands and products. It is suggested that an individual can have a self-concept attachment, a nostalgic attachment, interdependence, or love. Choose 8 to 10 brands or products that you use and comment on whether you feel any of these attachments towards them. What do your findings tell you about the power of each brand?

1-17 The chapter discussed a study that compared and contrasted people who lead "happy" lives versus those with "meaningful" lives. How does this distinction relate to the way you decide to spend your time and money? How does it relate to consumer behavior more generally? [46]

1-18 Businesses using social media to appear relevant and present in the lives of their consumers have seen some tremendous successes. Some, however, have exposed themselves to threats they could not have anticipated and have suffered huge losses in consumer perception. Yet, it seems that businesses cannot afford to ignore social media; they need to have a visible and vibrant presence on all platforms. The major problems are that the businesses become the subject of discussion. In these discussions, businesses have little control, and deleting comments is seen as exercising unreasonable censorship. Do you agree or disagree with this assertion?

1-19 PricewaterhouseCoopers (PwC) carried out an extensive survey of 6 continents, 19 territories, and 19,000 online shoppers for their Total Retail 2015 survey. [47] It revealed what many had predicted for some years, that the shift from high street retail to online retail was still gathering pace and showed few signs of slowing down.

PwC's model explains the continuing preference for online retail in terms of four retail disruptors. Their first disruptor considers the evolution of the conventional store. It is no longer the single point of sale for the business. In some respects, it is a window into the business and a form of catalog or showroom. PwC suggests that this is a natural evolution of the business model. The second and third disruptors (mobile technology and social networks) are the technological changes that have had a massive impact on retailing. Mobile technology means that purchases can be made anywhere, anytime, by anyone. Social networks are instant, real-time points of contact with consumers and are increasingly important places for reviews and feedback. At the same time, the buzz and excitement that can be generated by social media can create instant and massive demand for a product or service. The final disruptor is related to changes in the demographic make-up of society. The key 18–24 years' age group has a much greater affinity with brands than previous generations do; 43 percent follow brands online, they research brands more, and they are more inclined to watch videos about brands. The PwC survey revealed that 36 percent of consumers visit retail outlets at least once a week. It is still an important contact point.

A decade ago, only 25.3 percent of consumers had ever made an online purchase.[48] According to Dunn Humby, a global advertising company, multichannel purchasing is set to continue to change retail, with some brands seeing between 20 and 50 percent of sales through online shopping.[49]

To what extent is apparent that the merger of technology and culture driving this change from conventional retailing to online shopping? Will it mean the death of traditional retailing?

▋ APPLY

1-20 National marketers will often adapt the ways in which they market and promote products and services on a geographical basis. Is this the case in your country? Discuss with a company example.

1-21 The specific way we choose to satisfy a need depends on our unique history, learning experiences, and cultural environment. For example, two classmates may feel their stomachs rumble during a lunchtime lecture. If neither person has eaten since the night before, the strength of their respective needs (hunger) would be about the same. However, the ways each person goes about satisfying this need might be quite different. Conduct this exercise with classmates: "As you probably know, a prisoner who is sentenced to die traditionally gets to choose his or her 'last meal.' If you had to do this (let's hope not), describe your last meal in detail." Compare the responses you get, especially among people from different ethnic or cultural backgrounds. What similarities and differences emerge?

Case Study

HONDA'S ASIMO

Meet ASIMO! He is 4 feet tall, with a pleasant childish voice, and the ability to recognize and interact with people; however, ASIMO is no child. He is the humanoid robot "brainchild" of scientists at Honda. ASIMO's technology includes two camera eyes to map its environment and recognize unique faces. Its body construction is so humanlike that it can run at 3.5 mph, toss a ball to play with a child, and use its opposable thumbs to open a bottle and serve you a cold drink. ASIMO is the perfect household companion.

Honda has not yet made ASIMO available to purchase for home use, but it is only a matter of time until families can have their own humanoid robot. But not everyone is interested. Although some consumers have interacted with robotic kiosks that can process food orders and provide rudimentary in-store customer service, many are a bit nervous about an actual robot serving them meals or sitting down and telling them the news of the day. Why? Perhaps it is Hollywood's influence on our perception of robots. It might not be the sweet WALL-E that comes to mind when we think about robots, but the Terminator or another threatening machine.

Even robot developers have differing views on the roles robots could play or how they should look. Some see them as humanistic in appearance, serving as kind, compassionate companions for the aging or lonely. The movie *Her* explored the human-like connection that could exist with a computer-generated being. However, the developers of a robot called *Leonardo*

describe wanting to create a social robot with a whimsical appearance, intentionally not human or animal. They believe that "robots will be their own kind of creature and should be accepted, measured, and valued on those terms."

If consumers are not ready for ASIMO, perhaps they are ready for some of its features. *Facial recognition technology (FRT)*, the ability for a computer to "read" your face, is seeing strong development and application. According to some analysts, the FRT market is expected to grow from $1.92 billion to $6.5 billion within the next 5 years.

Advertisers and big brands are taking notice of FRT. Imagine a billboard in a mall that advertises Abercrombie to a teen girl and Target to a busy mom. Immersive Labs, recently acquired by Kairos, has developed digital billboards that measure the age range, gender, and even attention level of a passerby to deliver a tailored ad. With the addition of Immersive Labs, Kairos believes it has become the only facial biometrics company in the world that offers both facial recognition and emotion analysis tools.

According to researchers, FRT can do more than read your face and estimate general physical characteristics. It can map out a biometric profile that is as unique as your fingerprint. Red Pepper is a company that uses this advanced technology to develop Facedeals, a smartphone app that provides personalized offers to consumers. Here's how it works. You download the app, walk into a store with a Facedeals camera and are recognized. Facedeals interfaces with your Facebook information, analyzing your content for favorite brands, relationship status, places visited, and other information. Then Facedeals presents you with a personalized offer.

Google is considering letting individuals use a body motion, perhaps a "wink" or "eyebrow movement," as their FRT password. Forbes.com has unveiled an app where your webcam watches your facial responses when you view ads to learn what products and ads you like and dislike.

Although the marketing applications for FRT are numerous, companies should be aware that a recent study found that 75 percent of respondents were uncomfortable with in-store facial recognition technology that could identify them as a high value shopper and then alert a salesperson. That could change as technology continues to permeate our lives and as consumers become convinced of the value of real-time personalized offers made possible only by having their unique facial features recognized.

DISCUSSION QUESTIONS

CS 1-1 What are the most likely consumer market segments for robots? Which consumer characteristics would be important to determine these market segments? What types of roles do you envision robots playing for these consumers?

CS 1-2 Reflect on the value of FRT as a marketing tool. Give one example that illustrates how this technology can be most effectively used by marketers.

CS 1-3 Discuss the "creepiness" concerns that some consumers have about robots and FRT. How can marketers address or even overcome these issues?

Sources: http://Asimo.honda.com, accessed July 30, 2013; Sara Gates, "Google Facial Recognition Patent: Users May Be Able to Make a Face Instead of Entering a Password," http://www.huffingtonpost.com/2013/06/06/google-facial-recognition-patent-password_n_3398360.html, accessed July 30, 2013; Companies and Markets.com, "Facial Recognition Market to Be Worth $6.5 Billion by 2018," http://www.companiesandmarkets.com/News/Security/Facial-recognition-market-to-be-worth-6-5-billion-by-2018/NI7244, accessed July 30, 2013; Steve Parker, Jr., "Oh, It's Happening! Facial Recognition & Data-Driven Marketing," http://www.askingsmarterquestions.com/oh-it%E2%80%99s-happening-facial-recognition-data-driven-marketing/, accessed July 30, 2013; Michael Walsh, "Facedeals: Facial Recognition Marketing Stirs Privacy Discussion Along with Excitement," http://www.nydailynews.com/news/national/facedeals-facial-recognition-marketing-stirs-privacy-discussion-excitement-article-1.1137240#ixzz2aYzMgBZ2, accessed July 30, 2013; Gavin P. Sullivan, "Big Brother's Tracking Shines Light on Emerging Facial Recognition Technology," http://www.forbes.com/sites/mergermarket/2013/07/09/big-brothers-tracking-shines-light-on-emerging-facial-recognition-technology/, accessed July 30, 2013; Tarun Wadhwa, "What Do Jell-O, Kraft, and Adidas Have in Common? They All Want to Know Your Face," http://www.forbes.com/sites/singularity/2012/08/08/billboards-and-tvs-detect-your-face-and-juice-up-ads-tailored-just-for-you/, accessed July 30, 2013; "Three quarters of shoppers think facial recognition technology is "creepy," http://business-reporter.co.uk/2015/05/07/three-quarters-of-shoppers-think-facial-recognition-technology-is-creepy/, accessed May 10, 2015; Brian Brackeen, "Kairos Acquires IMRSV," https://www.kairos.com/blog/158-kairos-acquires-imrsv, accessed May 8, 2015; Michael Roppolo, "Coming in 2015: World's First Family Robot," http://www.cbsnews.com/news/jibo-wants-to-be-your-familys-first-robot-next-year/, accessed May 1, 2015; *Trends Magazine*, January 2015, Vol. 12, Issue 1, pp. 1–7.

MyLab Marketing

Go to the Assignments section of your MyLab to complete these writing exercises.

1.22 List the three stages in the consumption process. Describe the issues that you considered in each of these stages when you made a recent important purchase.

1.23 This chapter states that people play different roles and that their consumption behaviors may differ depending on the particular role they are playing. State whether you agree or disagree with this statement, giving examples from your personal life. Try to construct a "stage set" for a role you play, specifying the props, costumes, and script that you use to play a role (e.g., job interviewee, conscientious student, party animal).

NOTES

1. Molly Wood, "Led by Tinder, a Surge in Mobile Dating Apps," February 4, 2015, *New York Times*, http://www.NewYorkTimes.com/2015/02/05/technology/personaltech/led-by-tinder-the-mobile-dating-game-surges.html?ref=business, accessed February 28, 2015.

2. http://www.jewelmint.com, accessed July 18, 2013; http://www.oxygen.com, accessed July 18, 2013; http://www.ivillage.com, accessed July 18, 2013; http://www.hercampus.com, accessed July 18, 2013; http://www.RateMyProfessors.com, accessed July 18, 2013.

3. Michael R. Solomon, Greg W. Marshall, and Elnora W. Stuart, *Marketing: Real People, Real Choices*, 8th ed. (Upper Saddle River, NJ: Pearson Education, 2016).

4. http://www.bmw.com/com/en/insights/corporation/bmwi/vehicles.html, accessed February 27, 2015; https://us.drive-now.com/, accessed February 27, 2015; Joann Muller, "BMW's Car of the Future: Glued, Screwed & Rented," *Forbes* (November 3, 2011), http://www.forbes.com/sites/joannmuller/2011/11/03/bmws-vision-for-the-future-of-automobiles/, accessed December 21, 2012.

5. Jack Neff, "Study: Package-Goods Brands' Consumer Bases Very Small, Yet Diverse," *Advertising Age* (December 8, 2008), http://www.adage.com, accessed December 8, 2008.

6. Stuart Elliott, "Capitalizing on Disaster, Sometimes With Results That Match," *New York Times* (October 31, 2012), http://www.NewYorkTimes.com/2012/11/01/business/media/marketers-ride-the-coattails-of-a-storm-not-all-successfully.html, accessed December 21, 2012.

7. Natalie Perkins, "Zeroing in on Consumer Values," *Advertising Age* (March 22, 1993): 23.

8. Hannah Karp, "Red Bull Aims at an Older Crowd," *Wall Street Journal* (June 7, 2004): B3.

9. Mark J. Miller, "Oakley Looking to Get More In Tune with Female Customers," June 4, 2013, *Brandchannel*, http://www.brandchannel.com/home/post/2013/06/04/Oakley-Women-060413.aspx, accessed February 27, 2015.

10. Charles M. Schaninger and William D. Danko, "A Conceptual and Empirical Comparison of Alternative Household Life Cycle Models," *Journal of Consumer Research* 19 (March 1993): 580–594; Robert E. Wilkes, "Household Life-Cycle Stages, Transitions, and Product Expenditures," *Journal of Consumer Research* 22 (June 1995): 27–42.

11. Richard P. Coleman, "The Continuing Significance of Social Class to Marketing," *Journal of Consumer Research* 10 (December 1983): 265–280.

12. Burt Helm, "Ethnic Marketing: McDonald's Is Lovin' It," *Bloomberg Businessweek* (July 8, 2010), http://www.businessweek.com/magazine/-content/10_29/b4187022876832.htm, accessed December 21, 2012.

13. Motoko Rich, "Region's Marketers Hop on the Bubba Bandwagon," *Wall Street Journal Interactive Edition* (May 19, 1999).

14. Sarah Ellison, "Prilosec OTC Blitz by P&G Represents New Drug Foray," *Wall Street Journal* (September 12, 2003), http://www.wsj.com, accessed September 12, 2003.

15. Constance L. Hayes, "What Wal-Mart Knows About Customers' Habits," *New York Times* (November 14, 2004), http://www.NewYorkTimes.com, accessed November 14, 2004.

16. Lisa Arthur, *Big Data Marketing: Engage Your Customers More Effectively and Drive Value* (New York: Wiley, 2013); Andrew McAfee and Erik Brynjolfsson, *Big Data: The Management Revolution, Harvard Business Review* (October 2012), http://hbr.org/2012/10/big-data-the-management-revolution/ar/1, accessed December 21, 2012; "Bringing Big Data to the Enterprise," *IBM*, http://www-01.ibm.com/software/data/bigdata/, accessed December 21, 2012; Geoff Nunberg, "Forget YOLO: Why 'Big Data' Should Be the Word of the Year," *NPR* (December 20, 2012), http://www.npr.org/2012/12/20/167702665/geoff-nunbergs-word-of-the-year-big-data, accessed December 21, 2012.

17. Mylene Mangalindan, "Hollywood's 'Wedding Crashers' Inspires the Invitationless," *Wall Street Journal* (December 28, 2005): B1.

18. Pagan Kennedy, "Who Made That? (Spring Break)," *The New York Times Magazine* (March 24, 2013).

19. Erving Goffman, *The Presentation of Self in Everyday Life* (Garden City, NY: Doubleday, 1959); George H. Mead, *Mind, Self, and Society* (Chicago: University of Chicago Press, 1934); Michael R. Solomon, "The Role of Products as Social Stimuli: A Symbolic Interactionism Perspective," *Journal of Consumer Research* 10 (December 1983): 319–329.

20. Jennifer Aaker, Susan Fournier, and S. Adam Brasel, "When Good Brands Do Bad," *Journal of Consumer Research* 31 (2004): 1–16.

21. Susan Fournier, "Consumers and Their Brands: Developing Relationship Theory in Consumer Research," *Journal of Consumer Research* 24 (March 1998): 343–373.

22. Andrew Adam Newman, "Popular at Easter, Peeps Candy Extends to the Quirky Holidays," June 18, 2014, *New York Times*, http://www.NewYorkTimes.com/2014/06/19/business/media/popular-at-easter-peeps-candy-extends-to-the-quirky-holidays.html?ref=todayspaper&_r=0, accessed February 22, 2015.

23. http://www.marshmallowpeeps.com/products/valentines-day, accessed December 22, 2012; Thomas Vinciguerra, "Soft, Chewy and Taking Over the World," *New York Times* (July 5, 2006): Sec. 4, p. 2.

24. Quoted in "Bringing Meaning to Brands," *American Demographics* (June 1997): 34.

25. Joshua Clarkson, Chris Janiszewski, and Melissa D. Cinelli, "The Desire for Consumption Knowledge," *Journal of Consumer Research* 39, no. 6 (April 2013): 1313–1329.

26. Jonathan Schroeder, Janet Borgerson, and Zhiyan Wu, "A Brand Culture Approach to Brand Literacy: Consumer Co-creation and Emerging Chinese Luxury Brands," *Advances in Consumer Research* (2014): 42.

27. Roy F. Baumeister, Kathleen D. Vohs, Jennifer L. Aaker, and Emily N. Garbinsky, "Some Key Differences between a Happy Life and a Meaningful Life," *Journal of Positive Psychology* (2013), 8: 505-516

28. "Megacities," http://webs.schule.at/website/megacities/megacities_index_en.htm, accessed December 22, 2012; David Barbosa, "China, New Land of Shoppers, Builds Malls on Gigantic Scale," *New York Times* (May 25, 2005), http://www.NewYorkTimes.com, accessed May 25, 2005.

29. Bianca Bosker, "Nice To Meet You. I've Already Taken Your Picture," *Huffington Post*, February 10, 2014, http://www.huffingtonpost.com/2014/02/10/narrative-clip_n_4760580.html?&ncid=tweetlnkushpmg00000046, accessed February 22, 2015.

30. http://www.hsx.com, accessed December 22, 2012.

31. http://www.RateMyProfessors.com/, accessed February 28, 2015.

32. http://www.pof.com/inbox.aspx, accessed December 16, 2012; Irina Slutsky, "Get Hooked up with the Big Business of Online Dating," *Advertising Age* (February 14, 2011), http://adage.com/article/ad-age-graphics/online-dating-a-a-1-3-billion-market/148845/, accessed May 7, 2011.

33. "One-Third of Married Couples in U.S. Meet Online: Study," *New York Daily News*, June 4, 2013, http://www.nydailynews.com/life-style/one-third-u-s-marriages-start-online-dating-study-article-1.1362743, accessed February 28, 2015.

34. Marc Prensky, "Digital Natives, Digital Immigrants," *On the Horizon* 9, no. 5 (October 2001): 1–6.

35. Keith Schneider, "Recipe for Success: Take Mentos, Diet Coke. Mix," *New York Times* (February 20, 2007), http://www.NewYorkTimes.com/2007/02/20/business/smallbusiness/20eep.html, accessed December 22, 2012; Steve Spangler, "Mentos Diet Coke Geyser," SteveSpanglerScience.com, http://www.stevespanglerscience.com/experiment/original-mentos-diet-coke-geyser, accessed May 7, 2011; Suzanne Vranica and Chad Terhune, "Mixing Diet Coke and Mentos Makes a Gusher of Publicity," *Wall Street Journal* (June 12, 2006): B1.

36. Tracy Tuten and Michael R. Solomon, *Social Media Marketing* 2nd ed. (London: Sage, 2016).

37. http://newsroom.fb.com/Key-Facts, accessed December 22, 2012.

38. http://www.youtube.com/t/press_statistics, accessed December 22, 2012.

39. Parts of this section are adapted from Tracy Tuten and Michael R. Solomon, *Social Media Marketing* 2nd ed. (London: Sage, 2016).

40. Suzanne Vranica, "Ad Houses Will Need to Be More Nimble, Clients Are Demanding More and Better Use of Consumer Data, Web," *Wall Street Journal* (January 2, 2008): B3.

41. Jack Neff, "Mucus to Maxi Pads: Marketing's Dirtiest Jobs, Frank Talk about Diapers and Condoms Lifts Taboos and Helps Make a Difference in Consumers' Lives, Say Those in the Trenches," *Advertising Age* (February 17, 2009), http://www.adage.com, accessed February 17, 2009.

42. For an overview, see Eric J. Arnould and Craig J. Thompson, "Consumer Culture Theory (CCT): Twenty Years of Research," *Journal of Consumer Research* 31 (March 2005): 868–882.

43. Alladi Venkatesh, "Postmodernism, Poststructuralism and Marketing," paper presented at the American Marketing Association Winter Theory Conference, San Antonio, Texas, February 1992; see also Stella Proctor, Ioanna Papasolomou-Doukakis, and Tony Proctor, "What Are Television Advertisements Really Trying to Tell Us? A Postmodern Perspective," *Journal of Consumer Behavior* 1 (February 2002): 246–255; A. Fuat Firat, "The Consumer in Postmodernity," in NA: Advances in Consumer Research, eds. Rebecca H. Holman and Michael R. Solomon (1991), Vol. 18, Provo, UT: Association for Consumer Research: 70-76.

44. Eric J. Arnould and Craig J. Thompson, "Consumer Culture Theory (CCT): Twenty Years of Research," *Journal of Consumer Research* 31, no. 4 (2005): 868–882. doi:10.1086/426626; Russell W. Belk and John F. Sherry, eds., "Consumer Culture Theory," *Research in Consumer Behavior* 11 (2007) and subsequent volumes.

45. Morris B. Holbrook, "The Consumer Researcher Visits Radio City: Dancing in the Dark," in Elizabeth C. Hirschman and Morris B. Holbrook, eds., *Advances in Consumer Research* 12 (Provo, UT: Association for Consumer Research, 1985): 28–31.

46. Roy F. Baumeister, Kathleen D. Vohs, Jennifer L. Aaker, and Emily N. Garbinsky, "Some Key Differences between a Happy Life and a Meaningful Life," *Journal of Positive Psychology*, (2013), 8: 505-516

47. PwC, "Total Retail Survey 2015," http://www.pwc.com/gx/en/industries/retail-consumer/global-multi-channel-consumer-survey.html.

48. Enrique Bigne, Carla Ruiz, and Silvia Sanz, "The Impact of Internet User Shopping Patterns and Demographics on Consumer Mobile Buying Behaviour," *Journal of Electronic Commerce Research* (2005), 6, no. 3, http://web.csulb.edu/journals/jecr/issues/20053/paper3.pdf.

49. Julian Highley, "How Multichannel Grocery Shopping Is Changing the Way That Consumers Buy," dunnhumby, https://www.dunnhumby.com/how-multichannel-grocery-shopping-changing-way-consumers-buy.

Chapter 2 • Consumer and Social Well-Being

When you finish reading this chapter you will understand why:

2-1 Ethical business is good business.

2-2 Marketers have an obligation to provide safe and functional products as part of their business activities.

2-3 Consumer behavior impacts directly on major public policy issues that confront our society.

2-4 Consumer behavior can be harmful to individuals and to society.

Chapter Objectives

Source: DmitriMaruta/Shutterstock.

Tracy wheels her cart down the grocery aisles, absent-mindedly throwing in the usual fill-ins she always buys on her weekly trip. She reaches for a box of Tide laundry detergent and is about to toss it into the cart when she stops herself in midair: She just remembered her resolution to think a little more about the environmental impact of the cleaning products and other groceries she brings into the house. When her son Jon came home from school and asked her how she was helping to preserve the world for the next generation, she was embarrassed that she couldn't answer him. From the mouths of babes! Time for this 33-year-old to learn a lesson.

Might as well start with detergents—Tracy thinks about that news report she saw last week about the excessive use of chemicals and other additives that are bad for the water supply, not to mention the huge amount of fresh water U.S. consumers waste just to wash their clothes.

Tracy has always bought Tide; it's the same product her mother used for years. Now as she takes a closer look in the detergent section she notices a lot of other brands, including some "tree-hugger" ones she's never seen before like Dropps, Ecos, Method, and Seventh Generation. When she looks at each box, Tracy notices that some carry different "ecolabels" including one issued by the U.S. Environmental Protection Agency called DfE (Design for the Environment). Hmmm ... Tide doesn't have that on its box. On the other hand, the Tide package does recommend just using cold water instead of hot for the laundry, and Procter & Gamble (P&G) now sells a concentrated version that doesn't require as much soap to do the wash. Tracy also notices that the "green" brands seem to cost a bit more. Today every penny counts—how much of her precious grocery budget is worth sacrificing for a slightly less sudsy wash? All of these choices are really confusing. Maybe she should stick with what she knows and let others worry about the environment. Then again, what will she tell Jon the next time he asks about how "green" she is?

Business Ethics and Consumer Rights

Mainstream U.S. shoppers like Tracy increasingly choose "green" products that are better for the environment. On the other hand, there has been a lot of hype about "the green revolution"; since the recession, consumers are a lot more cost-conscious. To add to the confusion, even well-intentioned shoppers have trouble figuring out which brands really are better. It's practically a full-time job to sort out all the competing claims. One solution is for independent rating agencies to develop labeling systems that the shopper can use to decide among options—but even these systems can be overwhelming. There are more than 480 eco-label systems worldwide, and about a quarter of those are in North America.[1] The U.S. government is trying to encourage businesses and consumers to select green cleaning products; the Environmental Protection Agency (EPA) even signed a promotion agreement with NASCAR to raise awareness of the DfE label. In addition to DfE certification and other rating systems the cleaning industry sponsors, a few manufacturers and retailers even offer their own labels, such as SC Johnson's Greenlist and Eco-Scale by the Whole Foods grocery chain. Other major brands, like P&G's Tide, sell highly concentrated versions that are formulated to work with cold water. It's tough to make apples-to-apples comparisons, and these competing systems threaten to "throw the baby out with the bath water" if consumers like Tracy throw up their hands and just stick to what they know. Is it possible for marketers to "do good" and still "do well"; can they provide profits and still do what's right for customers and the environment?

The answer is simple: *Ethical business is good business.* A global survey by Nielsen reported that 50 percent of consumers are willing to pay more for goods and services from companies that have implemented programs to give back to society.[2] Consumers think better of the products a firm sells when the organization behaves ethically.[3]

Business ethics are rules of conduct that guide actions in the marketplace; these are the standards against which most people in a culture judge what is right and what is wrong, good or bad. These universal values include honesty, trustworthiness, fairness, respect, justice, integrity, concern for others, accountability, and loyalty.

Of course, notions of right and wrong differ among people, organizations, and cultures. Some businesses believe it is OK for salespeople to pull out all the stops to persuade customers to buy, even if this means they mislead them; other firms feel that anything less than total honesty with customers is terribly wrong. Because each culture has its own set of values, beliefs, and customs, companies around the world define ethical business behaviors quite differently. For example, one study found that because of differences in values (as we will discuss in Chapter 3), Mexican firms are less likely to have formal codes of ethics and they are more likely to bribe public officials than are U.S. or Canadian companies. However, because of different attitudes about work and interpersonal relationships, these companies also are more likely to treat lower-level employees better than do their northern neighbors.[4]

These cultural differences certainly influence whether business practices such as bribery are acceptable. Since 1977 the Foreign Corrupt Practices Act makes it illegal for U.S. executives to bribe foreigners to gain business. The Organization for Economic Cooperation and Development (OECD), to which most industrialized countries belong, also outlaws bribery. Still, these practices are common in many countries. In Japan, it's called *kuroi kiri* (black mist); in Germany, it's *schmiergeld* (grease money), whereas Mexicans refer to *la mordida* (the bite), the French say *pot-de-vin* (jug of wine), and Italians speak of the *bustarella* (little envelope). They're all talking about *baksheesh*, the Middle Eastern term for a "tip" to grease the wheels of a transaction. Giving "gifts" in exchange for getting business from suppliers or customers is acceptable and even expected in many countries.

Regardless of whether they do it intentionally, some marketers do violate their bonds of trust with consumers. In some cases, these actions are actually illegal, as when a manufacturer deliberately mislabels the contents of a package. Or a retailer may adopt a "bait-and-switch" selling strategy that lures consumers into the store when it offers inexpensive products with the sole intent to get them to switch to higher-priced goods.

In other cases, marketing practices have detrimental effects on society even though they are not explicitly illegal. Some companies erect billboards for alcohol and tobacco products in low-income neighborhoods; others sponsor commercials that objectify women as they pander to male viewers.

Needs and Wants: Do Marketers Manipulate Consumers?

One of the most common and stinging criticisms of marketing is that companies convince consumers they "need" many material things, and that they will be unhappy and inferior people if they do not have these "necessities." The issue is a complex one and is certainly worth considering: Do marketers give people what they want, or do they tell people what they *should* want?

Who controls the market, companies or consumers? This question is even more complicated as new ways of buying, having, and being are invented every day. It seems that the "good old days" of *marketerspace*—a time when companies called the shots and decided what they wanted their customers to know and do—are dead and gone. Many people now feel empowered to choose how, when, or if they will interact with corporations as they construct their own **consumerspace**. In this new environment, individuals dictate to companies the types of products they want and how, when, and where (or even if) they want to learn about those products. In turn, companies need to develop and leverage brand equity in bold new ways to attract the loyalty of these consumer "nomads." People still "need" companies—but in new ways and on their own terms. As we'll see throughout this book, profound changes in consumer behavior are influencing how people search for product information and evaluate alternative brands. In the brave new world of consumerspace, we have much greater potential to shape our own marketing destinies.[5]

Do Marketers Create Artificial Needs?

The marketing system has come under fire from both ends of the political spectrum. On the one hand, some members of the Religious Right believe that marketers contribute to the moral breakdown of society when they present images of hedonistic pleasure and encourage the pursuit of secular humanism at the expense of spirituality and the environment. A coalition of religious groups called the *National Religious Partnership for the Environment* claims that gas-guzzling cars and other factors that cause climate change are contrary to Christian moral teachings about protecting people and the Earth.[6]

On the other hand, some leftists argue that the same deceitful promises of material pleasure function to buy from people who would otherwise be revolutionaries working to change the system.[7] According to this argument, the marketing system creates demand—demand that only its products can satisfy.

A Response. As we saw in Chapter 1, *a need is a basic biological motive; a want represents one way that society has been taught to satisfy the need.* For example, thirst is a biologically based need. Marketers teach us to want Coca-Cola to satisfy that thirst rather than, say, goat's milk. Thus, the need is already there; marketers simply recommend ways to satisfy it. A basic objective of marketing is to create awareness that needs exist, not to create needs.

Is Marketing Necessary?

More than 50 years ago, the social critic Vance Packard wrote, "Large-scale efforts are being made, often with impressive success, to channel our unthinking habits, our

CB AS I SEE IT
Ronald Hill, *Villanova University*

The Judeo-Christian Bible, as well as most other religious and philosophical traditions, tell us that the "poor will always be with us." As a child who grew up in the 1950s and 1960s, I was often told to finish my meal, which inevitably included an unpleasant-tasting vegetable like Brussels sprouts, because "people are starving in India/Africa/Asia." Of course, I remarked to my mother that I was happy to donate them!

But what is it really like to be "poor" in a material landscape that is dominated by the abundance of goods and services in western and developed economies. Do the very poor in nations like the United States, France, and Australia have similar dreams, aspirations, and consumption behaviors to more affluent citizens, or do they respond differently because of unique circumstances? How about billions of people in sub-Saharan Africa, South Asia, and parts of Latin and South America who lack access to even the most modest portfolio of items that we take for granted in the developed West? Do they use the same material "lenses" as their affluent counterparts in other parts of the planet?

Let's look at three different studies that help inform this conversation. The first examined levels of materialism (or desire for goods and services) between impoverished versus affluent children in the United States. To have the starkest differences, poor youths came from neighborhoods where the average price of a home was $30,000; wealthier youths came from communities where the average home price was $1,000,000. Levels of material yearning were about the same at early ages (8–10) but increased significantly as they moved into middle and high school (11–17). What is most remarkable is that material longing declined for affluent children toward the end of this age range as their accomplishments inside and outside school supported self-esteem development. Unfortunately, such opportunities did not exist in the impoverished neighborhoods, leaving these youths with lower self-esteem and high materialism in a denuded living environment.

The second investigation considered thousands of consumers across 38 developed and developing nations. In both cases, persons who lived below the typical material abundance of their countries were less satisfied with their lives than individuals who lived above this level of material wealth. Thus, "haves" with positive social comparisons had greater life satisfaction than "have-nots" who suffered from negative comparisons. Interestingly, people living in the most impoverished nations reveal even greater differences, with their haves and have-nots experiencing even greater highs and lows.

The third study involved saving behaviors by citizens of impoverished versus affluent nations. Using the same 38 nations but more consumers, results demonstrate that poverty impacted relationships between saving behaviors and feelings of well-being in that persons living in poorer nations experienced an even greater boost in well-being from saving than their affluent nation complement. Although the reasons are somewhat complex, the simple answer is that failure to save in conditions of abject poverty can have catastrophic consequences including hunger, homelessness, and death.

purchasing decisions, and our thought processes by the use of insights gleaned from psychiatry and the social sciences."[8] The economist John Kenneth Galbraith charged that radio and television are important tools to accomplish this manipulation of the masses. Because consumers don't need to be literate to use these media, repetitive and compelling communications can reach almost everyone. This criticism may even be more relevant to online communications, where a simple click delivers a world of information to us.

Some people charge that marketers arbitrarily link products to desirable social attributes, so they foster a materialistic society where what we own defines our value as a person. One influential critic even argued that the problem is that we are not materialistic *enough*: We do not sufficiently value goods for the utilitarian functions they deliver but instead focus on the irrational value of goods for what they symbolize. According to this view, for example, "Beer would be enough for us, without the additional promise that in drinking it we show ourselves to be manly, young at heart, or neighborly. A washing machine would be a useful machine to wash clothes, rather than an indication that we are forward-looking or an object of envy to our neighbors."[9]

A Response. *Products meet existing needs, and marketing activities only help to communicate their availability.*[10] The *economics of information* perspective regards advertising as an important source of consumer information.[11] This view emphasizes the economic cost of the time we

This ad was created by the American Association of Advertising Agencies to counter charges that ads create artificial needs.

Source: Used with permission of American Association of Advertising Agencies.

spend to search for products. Accordingly, advertising is a service for which consumers are willing to pay because the information it provides reduces their search time.

Do Marketers Promise Miracles?

Westin Hotels launched its Westin Well-Being Movement to hotel guests as well as employees worldwide. Programs all relate to what the hospitality company calls "six pillars": "feel well," "work well," "move well," "eat well," "sleep well" and "play well."[12] Advertising leads us to believe that products have magical properties; the things we buy will transform our lives. We will be beautiful, successful, perhaps even live forever. In this respect, advertising functions as mythology does in primitive societies: It provides simple, anxiety-reducing answers to complex problems.

A poster for Westin Hotels' Well-Being Movement

Source: Courtesy of Starwood Hotels & Resorts Worldwide, Inc.

A Response. *Marketers simply do not know enough about people to manipulate them.* Consider that the failure rate for new products ranges from 40 percent to 80 percent. Although people think that advertisers have an endless source of magical tricks and scientific techniques to manipulate them, in reality the industry is successful when it tries to sell good products and unsuccessful when it sells poor ones.[13]

Materialism: Are You What You Own?

During World War II, members of "cargo cults" in the South Pacific literally worshiped cargo they salvaged from crashed aircraft or that washed ashore from ships. They believed that their ancestors piloted the ships and planes that passed near their islands, so they tried to attract them to their villages. They went so far as to construct fake planes from straw to lure the real ones overhead![14]

We may not worship products to that extent, but many of us certainly work hard to attain our vision of the good life, which abounds in material comforts. Most young people can't imagine a life without cell phones, MP3 players and other creature comforts. In fact, we can think of marketing as a system that provides certain standards of living to consumers. To some extent, then, the standards of living we expect and desire influence our lifestyles, either by personal experience or as a result of the affluent characters we see on TV in "reality shows" such as *Keeping Up With the Kardashians,* in movies, and in the pages of *Vogue* or *GQ.*[15] Exhibit A: The popular bumper sticker that reads "He Who Dies with the Most Toys Wins."

Our possessions play a central role in our lives, and our desire to accumulate them shapes our value systems. **Materialism** refers to the importance people attach to worldly possessions.[16] We sometimes take the bounty of products and services for granted, until we remember how recent this abundance is. For example, in 1950, two of five U.S. homes did not have a telephone, and in 1940 only half of all households had indoor plumbing.

Materialists are more likely to value possessions for their status and appearance-related meanings, whereas those who do not emphasize this value tend to prize products that connect them to other people or that provide them with pleasure when they use them.[17] As a result, high materialists prefer expensive products that they publicly consume. A study comparing specific items that low versus high materialists value found that people who were non-materialists cherished items with personal significance, such as a mother's wedding gown, picture albums, a rocking chair from childhood, or a garden. In contrast, high materialists preferred prestige goods such as jewelry, china, or a vacation home.[18]

Materialistic people also appear to link more of their self-identity to products. One study found that when people who score high on this value fear the prospect of dying, they form even stronger connections to brands.[19] Another study reported that consumers who are "love-smitten" with their possessions tend to use these relationships to compensate for loneliness and a lack of affiliation with social networks.[20] Yet another found that materialists tend to value a product before they buy it because they believe it will make them happy, but their satisfaction with it diminishes after the purchase when they realize this didn't happen.[21]

Nonetheless, consumers' appetites for material goods continue to grow—especially in developing markets where luxury goods reign supreme. Analysts predict modest growth in sales of luxury products in Europe and the United States, but huge growth in China as well as solid gains in new markets such as Azerbaijan, Brazil, Indonesia, Kazakhstan, Malaysia, Mexico, South Africa, Turkey, and Vietnam. Asian consumers now account for more than 50 percent of global luxury sales.[22]

Perhaps our expectations about accumulating material goods are evolving as U.S. consumers increasingly get access to more and more exotic products. Thus, materialists value (or perhaps even obsess about) the inherent qualities of what they buy, whether their purchases are diamonds or organic yogurt. One important dimension

The Whole Foods grocery chain targets shoppers who value health-oriented and locally-produced food products.
Source: Chris Howes/Wild Places Photography/Alamy.

today is **provenance**: Shoppers are willing to pay more for an item when they know exactly where it comes from, and they are assured that "real people" have thoughtfully selected the things from which they choose. This process of **curation**, which used to refer to an expert who carefully chooses pieces to include in a museum exhibit, now applies to a range of consumer products such as food, clothing, and travel. Whole Foods personalizes its inventory as it features the names of store employees on chalkboards throughout the store and often specifies the farms that grew the products.[23]

OBJECTIVE 2-2
Marketers have an obligation to provide safe and functional products as part of their business activities.

Consumers' Rights and Product Satisfaction

Fifty-four million dollars for a pair of missing pants? A judge in Washington, D.C., made headlines when he filed a $54 million lawsuit against his neighborhood dry cleaner because it lost a pair of his pinstriped suit pants. He claimed that a local consumer protection law entitled him to thousands of dollars for each day over nearly four years in which signs at the shop promised "same day service" and "satisfaction guaranteed." The suit dragged on for several months, but at the end of

The Tangled Web

From ihatestarbucks.com to boycottwalmart.meetup .com, irritated customers have launched hundreds of **gripe sites** to air their grievances against companies. The practice is so widespread that some firms proactively buy unflattering domain names to keep other people from buying them. Xerox, for example, registered xeroxstinks.com, xeroxcorporation-sucks.com, and ihatexerox.net. About 20,000 domain names end in "sucks.com." About one-third of these sites are registered to none other than the companies they slam; owners include Walmart Stores, Coca-Cola, Toys "R" Us, Target, and Whole Foods Market.[28]

the day the plaintiff went home with empty pockets.[24] And some people claim we have too many lawsuits in this country!

If you're not happy with a product or service, what can you do about it? You have three possible courses of action (though sometimes you can take more than one):[25]

1 **Voice response**—You can appeal directly to the retailer for redress (e.g., a refund).
2 **Private response**—You can express your dissatisfaction to friends and boycott the product or the store where you bought it.
3 **Third-party response**—Like the pantsless judge, you can take legal action against the merchant, register a complaint with the Better Business Bureau, or write a letter to the newspaper. These comments can be effective, especially when others join in. Cover Girl ran an advertising campaign targeted to female football fans that depicted a model wearing a Baltimore Ravens jersey with the tagline, "Get Your Game Face On." At about the same time, a prominent Ravens player made headlines in a series of allegations about NFL players who physically abused their wives and girlfriends. Protestors went online and altered the ad to make it look like the model had a black eye.[26] When enough people band together to express negative **marketplace sentiments** through activist organizations such as Greenpeace or in social media mass protests such as the one Cover Girl ran into, dramatic changes can result.[27]

In one study, business majors wrote complaint letters to companies. When the firm sent a free sample in response, this action significantly improved how the students felt

Mass protests can sometimes cause change.
Source: Frances Roberts/Alamy.

Consumers get creative when they want to vent their feelings about companies they don't like.
Source: Michael Matthews/Alamy.

about it. This didn't happen, however, when they *only* received a letter of apology—but no swag. Even worse, students who got no response reported an even more negative image than before. This shows that *any* kind of response is better than none.[29]

A number of factors influence which route we choose. People are more likely to take action if they're dissatisfied with expensive products such as household durables, cars, and clothing than for problems with inexpensive products.[30] Ironically, consumers who are satisfied with a store in general are <u>more</u> likely to complain if they experience something bad; they take the time to complain because they feel connected to the store. And, if a company resolves the problem, customers feel even better about it than if they hadn't complained in the first place![31] The moral: Although nobody likes criticism, organizations should encourage people to complain for these reasons:

1 They get the chance to correct the situation.
2 They will avoid an escalating problem that results when consumers take to social media to let others know they've been treated badly. People are more likely to spread the word about unresolved negative experiences to their friends than they are to boast about positive occurrences.
3 They collect valuable insights about customers' experiences that will (hopefully) help them to improve for future customers.
4 If consumers do not believe that the store will respond to their complaint, they will be more likely to simply switch than fight as they just take their business elsewhere.

Companies that score high in customer satisfaction often benefit from a big competitive advantage—especially when so many firms skimp on the attention they pay to customers. A five-year study of customer satisfaction in the Canadian banking industry provides typical results: Banks that provided better service commanded a larger "share of wallet" than did others (i.e., their customers entrusted them with a larger proportion of their money).[32]

Even so, more than half of the chief marketing officers (CMOs) who participated in a large survey reported that their companies *do not reward their employees* if customer satisfaction improves. More than one-third said they have no way to track word-of-mouth among customers, and less than 3 in 10 said their firms are good at resolving customers' complaints.[33] What is wrong with this picture?

When a product doesn't work as we expect or turns out to be unsafe (like the recent spate of hazardous products from China, ranging from toothpaste to dog food), it's the understatement of the year to say we're not satisfied. In these situations, marketers must immediately take steps to reassure us, or they risk losing a customer for life. If the company confronts the problem truthfully, we are often willing to forgive and forget. But if the firm seems to be dragging its heels or covering up, our resentment grows. This is what happened during the BP oil spill or when a disabled Carnival cruise ship sat at sea in 2013 while 4,200 passengers and crew suffered through five days with no plumbing or electricity, and little food, in the glare of an unrelenting media spotlight.[34]

Market Regulation

The subprime mortgage meltdown that led to the collapse of major investment banking and insurance companies such as Bear Stearns, Lehman Brothers, and AIG, as well as triggered the Great Recession of 2008 (and beyond), illustrates why many people look to governments and industry watchdogs to provide oversight and regulation rather than relying strictly on businesses to police themselves. Concern for the welfare of consumers has been an issue since at least the beginning of the 20th century, and activists continue to voice concerns about a range of issues such as child labor, exploitative advertising, and genetically engineered food.[35]

Partly as a result of consumers' efforts, the U.S. government established many federal agencies to oversee consumer-related activities. These include the Department of Agriculture, the Federal Trade Commission, the Food and Drug Administration, the Securities and Exchange Commission, and the EPA. After Upton Sinclair's 1906 book *The Jungle* exposed the awful conditions in the Chicago meatpacking industry, Congress was prompted to pass important pieces of legislation—the Pure Food and Drug Act in 1906 and the Federal Meat Inspection Act a year later—to protect consumers. A summary of some important consumer legislation enacted since that time appears in Table 2.1. You can find other information about consumer-related issues at consumerreports.org and cpsc.gov (the Consumer Product Safety Commission).

Table 2.2 lists major U.S. regulatory agencies and what they do. One of the most important ones for consumers is The Food and Drug Administration (FDA); it polices advertising claims as well as the contents of edible products and pharmaceuticals. For example, as part of an FDA crackdown on consumer drug advertising, Bayer HealthCare Pharmaceuticals launched a $20 million **corrective advertising** campaign for Yaz, the most popular birth control pill in the United States. This term means that the company must inform consumers that previous messages were wrong or misleading. The TV commercials, which ran during prime-time shows such as *Grey's Anatomy* and on cable networks, warn that nobody should take Yaz hoping that it will also cure pimples or premenstrual syndrome. Bayer was required to run these ads to correct previous messages after regulators decided the previous ads overstated the drug's ability to improve women's moods and clear up acne.[36]

Consumerism

"Absolut Impotence." So reads a parody of a vodka ad created by Adbusters, a nonprofit organization that advocates for "the new social activist movement of the information age." The editor of the group's magazine argues that America is no longer a country, but rather a multitrillion-dollar brand subverted by corporate agendas. He claims that "America™" is no different from McDonald's, Marlboro, or General Motors.[38]

Adbusters sponsors numerous initiatives, including *Buy Nothing Day* and *TV Turnoff Week*, that try to discourage rampant commercialism. These efforts, along with biting ads and commercials that lampoon advertising messages, are examples of **culture jamming**, which is a strategy to disrupt efforts by the corporate world to dominate

Marketing Pitfall

Advertisers, retailers, and manufacturers typically try to police themselves to ensure that their messages and products are not harmful or inaccurate. In addition to good intentions, they have a practical reason to do so: They don't want governments to do it for them. Indeed, sometimes these efforts even seem to go a bit over the top. Consider, for example, a ruling by the National Advertising Division (NAD) of the Council of Better Business Bureaus, which is one of these industry watchdogs. Acting on a complaint by rival Kimberly-Clark, P&G must add little flecks of cartoon toilet paper to the backsides of its Charmin cartoon bears in future ads for its toilet paper. Although P&G supported its claim that Charmin leaves "fewer pieces behind" than the Cottonelle brand (and showed the results of its test on the brand's Web site), the NAD decided that the test "did not accurately reflect the results consumers normally see and experience."[37]

TABLE 2.1	Sample of Federal Legislation Intended to Enhance Consumers' Welfare

Year	Act	Purpose
1953	Flammable Fabrics Act	Prohibits the transportation of flammable fabrics across state lines.
1958	National Traffic and Safety Act	Creates safety standards for cars and tires.
1958	Automobile Information Disclosure Act	Requires automobile manufacturers to post suggested retail prices on new cars.
1966	Fair Packaging and Labeling Act	Regulates packaging and labeling of consumer products. (Manufacturers must provide information about package contents and origin.)
1966	Child Protection Act	Prohibits sale of dangerous toys and other items.
1967	Federal Cigarette Labeling and Advertising Act	Requires cigarette packages to carry a warning label from the Surgeon General.
1968	Truth-in-Lending Act	Requires lenders to divulge the true costs of a credit transaction.
1969	National Environmental Policy Act	Established a national environmental policy and created the Council on Environmental Quality to monitor the effects of products on the environment.
1972	Consumer Products Safety Act	Established the Consumer Product Safety Commission to identify unsafe products, establish safety standards, recall defective products, and ban dangerous products.
1975	Consumer Goods Pricing Act	Bans the use of price maintenance agreements among manufacturers and resellers.
1975	Magnuson-Moss Warranty-Improvement Act	Creates disclosure standards for consumer product warranties and allows the Federal Trade Commission to set policy regarding unfair or deceptive practices.
1990	The Nutrition Labeling and Education Act	Reaffirms the legal basis for the Food and Drug Administration's new rules on food labeling and establishes a timetable for the implementation of those rules.
1998	Internet Tax Freedom Act	Established a moratorium on special taxation of the Internet, including taxation of access fees paid to America Online and other Internet Service Providers.
2010	Dodd-Frank Wall Street Reform and Consumer Protection Act	Prompted by the recession that began in 2008, intends to promote the financial stability of the United States by improving accountability and transparency in the financial system, to end "too big to fail," to protect the American taxpayer by ending bailouts, and to protect consumers from abusive financial services practices.

our cultural landscape. The movement believes that "culture jamming" will change the way information flows; the way institutions wield power; the way TV stations are run; and the way the food, fashion, automobile, sports, music, and culture industries set their agendas.[39]

Although some in corporate America may dismiss these extreme sentiments as the ravings of a lunatic fringe, their proponents deserve to be taken seriously. The recent scandals involving such corporate icons as BP, AIG, Enron, Martha Stewart, Arthur Andersen, Bear Stearns, and massive product recalls from companies such as General Motors and Blue Bell Creameries fueled a growing bonfire of mistrust and skepticism among the consuming public.

President John F. Kennedy ushered in the modern era of consumerism with his "Declaration of Consumer Rights" in 1962. These include the right to safety, the right to be informed, the right to redress, and the right to choice. The 1960s and 1970s were a time of consumer activism as consumers began to organize to demand better-quality products (and to boycott companies that did not provide them).

The publication of books such as Rachel Carson's *Silent Spring* in 1962, which attacked the irresponsible use of pesticides, and Ralph Nader's *Unsafe at Any Speed* in

| TABLE 2.2 | U.S. Regulatory Agencies and Responsibilities |

Regulatory agency	Responsibilities
Consumer Product Safety Commission (CPSC)	Protects the public from potentially hazardous products. Through regulation and testing programs, the CPSC helps firms make sure their products won't harm customers.
Environmental Protection Agency (EPA)	Develops and enforces regulations aimed at protecting the environment. Such regulations have a major impact on the materials and processes that manufacturers use in their products and thus on the ability of companies to develop products.
Federal Communications Commission (FCC)	Regulates telephone, radio, and television. FCC regulations directly affect the marketing activities of companies in the communications industries, and they have an indirect effect on all firms that use broadcast media for marketing communications.
Federal Trade Commission (FTC)	Enforces laws against deceptive advertising and product labeling regulations. Marketers must constantly keep abreast of changes in FTC regulations to avoid costly fines.
Food and Drug Administration (FDA)	Enforces laws and regulations on foods, drugs, cosmetics, and veterinary products. Marketers of pharmaceuticals, over-the-counter medicines, and a variety of other products must get FDA approval before they can introduce products to the market.
Interstate Commerce Commission (ICC)	Regulates interstate bus, truck, rail, and water operations. The ability of a firm to efficiently move products to its customers depends on ICC policies and regulation.

1965, which exposed safety defects in General Motors' Corvair automobile, prompted these movements. Many people have a vigorous interest in consumer-related issues, ranging from environmental concerns such as global warming and climate change, toxic waste, and so on, to excessive violence and sex on television or in the lyrics of popular rock and rap songs like Robin Thicke's controversial *Blurred Lines* music video that some people interpreted as encouraging rape. Indeed, after a public outcry Reebok had to drop the rapper Rick Ross from its endorsement roster after he released a song about spiking a woman's drink with the drug MDMA, also referred to as ecstasy or molly: "Put molly all in her champagne/ She ain't even know it/I took her home and I enjoyed that/she ain't even know it."[40]

Transformative Consumer Research

Indeed, some consumer researchers are themselves organizing, not only to study but also to rectify what they see as pressing social problems in the marketplace. This perspective is called *participatory action research (PAR)* or **transformative consumer research (TCR)**. It promotes research projects that include the goal of helping people or bringing about social change. Scientists who subscribe to this perspective view consumers as collaborators who work with them to realize this change rather than as a "phenomenon" on which to conduct research. Adherents of TCR work with at-risk populations, such as children, the disadvantaged, and the disabled, or on such topics as materialism, consumption of dangerous products, and compulsive consumption.[42]

Social Marketing and Corporate Social Responsibility (CSR)

The evidence is mounting that a brand's philanthropic activities can influence shopper behavior and ultimately purchase decisions. Consumers are especially interested in choosing brands that support causes they find personally relevant. These causes include medical cures and disease prevention, social change, faith-based initiatives, and animal and child welfare.[48]

Marketing Pitfall

When an organization wants to encourage people to contribute to its cause in some way, it seems like a good idea to provide an initial token display of support such as wearing a tshirt, signing a petition, or asking them to join a Facebook group. Makes sense, right? Not necessarily. Some critics are worried about the phenomenon they term **slacktivism**; small and relatively meaningless expressions of support for important causes such as liking a charity on Facebook that substitute for donations or volunteering. One study found that if the initial display is visible to others, this public behavior can actually *reduce* the likelihood that the person will contribute beyond that. Under some circumstances the need to make a positive impression on others is satisfied by the public display, so the person exhibits slacktivism and doesn't bother to do anything else to support the cause.[41]

CB AS I SEE IT

Stacey Menzel Baker, *Creighton University*

Consumer behavior researchers study the relationships among people possessions, places, brands, experiences, and other people. We know that consumers become attached to their cameras, cars, homes, coffee shops, communities, daily routines, favorite brands, commercial service providers, family, and friends. Such relationships are important in creating, maintaining, and, at times, reconstructing our identities. Thus, when one or more of these relationships is damaged, our identity may be altered.

Imagine a community devastated by a natural hazard event, such as a hurricane, tornado, or flood. Visual images of demolished homes, scattered personal possessions, uprooted trees, destroyed businesses, shell-shocked faces, and perhaps even caskets and flags may come to your mind. Such images make us acutely aware that essential relationships fundamentally important in the everyday lives of human beings have been damaged.

We become aware of our own humanity, and we become aware of collective suffering. [43] [44]

My research focuses on how people make sense of losses of material possessions and marketplace interactions, as well as how they rebuild their lives in the face of adversity. [45] One way people make sense of their losses is through storytelling, and material possessions and marketplace interactions figure prominently in their stories. For instance, a person living in a community where a tornado left 25 percent of the people homeless said:

> Their [mobile home] trailers were totally wiped out, and their possessions were everywhere.... Your entire life was on display, on public display ... like the pictures, these were private things.... People [were saying], "I had no idea how much a tornado exposed your entire life to the world." There's nobody that I know of that was able, unless they moved in after the tornado, there's nobody that didn't see something, there's nobody that didn't have pink insulation in their yard. Everyone had garbage that they had to clean up, and, you know, so we were all involved.

Notice that, though this person did not lose her home or many of her possessions, she felt the losses experienced by her neighbors. When we share in the vulnerability felt by others,[46] we are more likely to do something to help them relieve their pain. For instance, we may volunteer our time, make donations of money, food, or material goods, or organize community action groups.

People who experience disasters seek to reclaim their lives from the traumatic event. Material possessions and marketplace interactions play a prominent role in the reconstruction of their lives. For instance, 95 percent of Greensburg, Kansas, was destroyed by a tornado in 2007. The tornado wiped out businesses and most homes, and the community recovery became the focus of a documentary titled *Greensburg: A Story of Community Rebuilding* was produced by Leonardo DiCaprio and Craig Piligian and aired on Planet Green between 2008 and 2010.[47] Two people from the community featured in the documentary said:

> With the grand opening of this grocery store, it does feel like we are starting to get somewhere. Like our community is starting to come together. And the fact that we are doing such normal, everyday things now, that's really a blessing.

> It finally begins to set in. Today will be kind of moving day with everything coming in. It's good, but it's just a little overwhelming to see all of this coming in. It's all new. It's all different. But yet, it's gonna be our home.... All of a sudden you realize how much you lost.... And until I see it coming back, I didn't really realize the loss that we'd had. It was 40 years of memories that are gone— 40 years of some things we will never get back again. But yet, I still feel that we're blessed to be in this place.

Notice how important the grocery store is in making people feel like their community is still intact. Their collective identity is coming back. In a similar sense, notice how the new home is both a reminder of all that has been lost and all that has been gained. My research program revolves around consumer well-being and focuses on attachments that are disrupted, the vulnerability that we experience, and the resiliency we develop in the face of adversity. One clear take away is that the same types of relationships with stores, marketplace experiences that bring us pain when they are gone, also bring us a sense of normalcy and an eventual return to our everyday lives when they return, albeit in a different form.

As the emerging TCR perspective shows, the field of consumer behavior can help to improve our lives as consumers.[49] **Social marketing** strategies use the techniques that marketers normally employ to sell beer or detergent to encourage positive behaviors such as increased literacy and to discourage negative activities such as drunk driving.[50] Many researchers help to evaluate or create public policies to ensure that products are labeled accurately, to certify that people can comprehend important information in advertising messages, or to prevent children from being exploited by program-length toy commercials that masquerade as television shows.

Many firms today try to integrate **corporate social responsibility (CSR)** into their business models. CSR describes processes that encourage the organization to make a positive impact on the various stakeholders in its community including consumers, employees, and the environment. For example, the shoe company TOMS is well-known for its promise to give a needy child a pair of shoes for every pair it sells.

CSR is more than a nice idea; it's also good business. Consumer research convincingly shows that, all things equal, people are likely to choose a brand that gives back to the community. **Cause marketing** is a popular strategy that aligns a company or brand with a cause to generate business and societal benefits. Indeed, one survey reported that three out of five consumers bought a product or service in the previous year because of its association with a cause. An executive observed, "As a whole, Americans do have a heightened sensitivity to how they can help make a difference."[51]

Major Policy Issues Relevant to Consumer Behavior

It's hard to divorce consumer behavior from most of what goes on around us. The field intersects with many of the big issues we read about and debate every day. These range from human rights and humane working conditions to the safety of what we eat, the future of our environment, and our relationships with governments, corporations, and other organizations. In this section, we'll introduce three major issues—without pretending to cover *all* of the important ones.

Data Privacy and Identity Theft

A Carnegie Mellon professor demonstrated just how easy it is to find people online if you know what you're doing. In one study he showed that it was possible to deduce portions of a person's Social Security number from nothing but a photograph posted online.[52] Data breaches at major companies such as Target, Sony, and Home Depot continue to worry many people. The federal government is actively engaged with this problem and a variety of legislative proposals are being considered including **The Personal Data Notification & Protection Act of 2015** that would strengthen the obligations companies have to notify customers when their personal information has been exposed and **The Student Digital Privacy and Parental Rights Act of 2015** that would prevent companies from selling K-12 students' online data to third parties or otherwise sharing information unless it is for a school-related purpose.[53]

One of the biggest ethical issues many marketers face today relates to how much they can—or should—know about their customers. Virtually anyone who surfs the Web or who carries a cell phone (especially a smartphone with GPS capability) shares reams of personal information with all sorts of companies (whether they know it or not).

Clearly, we all benefit from technologies that allow companies to precisely tailor their messages to our needs based on the product information we look for. Indeed, industry researchers report that a lot of people actually don't mind the ads if they are personally relevant.[55] But some consumer advocates argue that we pay a high cost for this

The Tangled Web

Facebook recently introduced a "Tag Suggestions" feature that uses facial recognition to identify a user's friends in photos he or she uploads and automatically suggests nametags for them. Other programs like Picasa also incorporate facial recognition technology. This handy little tool removes the need to keep typing the same friends' names into photo albums. But is there a dark side to this capability? Because facial recognition analyzes and stores people's unique facial measurements, it may come with some serious privacy risks. For example in the near future it will be possible for marketers to identify people as they walk down the street – and link their faces to relevant information such as credit scores or medical records. Some firms already offer smart billboards that detect the gender and age of a passerby and show that person relevant ad messages. For now these boards don't analyze emotions or other personal characteristics, but what if they could detect a feeling like sadness and offer the person a message about antidepressants?[54]

convenience. As the director of one consumer group phrased it in a complaint to the Federal Trade Commission, "Online consumers are being bought and sold like chattel."[56]

Are we for sale? In some sense, yes. If you surf the Web (and who doesn't today?), it's likely that someone is carefully tracking your clicks—the search items you Google, the sites you visit, perhaps even the comments you post on Facebook. Your digital actions have actual financial value, because of the industry called **real-time bidding**; an electronic trading system that sells ad space on the Web pages people click on at the moment they visit them.

In the early days of the Internet, advertisers simply bought space on Web sites that generally matched the demographics of their target audience. Then they showed the same ad to everyone who came to the site—an inefficient approach people in the industry call "spray and pray." Today that picture has changed as companies develop complex algorithms that predict where consumers with specific profiles (e.g., "Asian Americans who make more than $100,000 a year, live in Los Angeles, and are in the market for a luxury car") will visit and serve up precisely tailored messages to these customers. By the way, these are not "live auctions" like you might see on eBay; they are conducted automatically on powerful computers that receive several million bids every second. Each auction typically takes less than 30 milliseconds. And because not all customers are as likely to buy or to spend as much as are others, these algorithms attach different values to them so higher value customers command higher auction prices. As the CEO of one of these trading companies explained, "The first impression seen by a high-value person on the opening page of a major newspaper first thing in the morning has a different value than a user from China who is 12 and has been on the Web all day long playing games." The real-time bidding business is growing rapidly: Analysts estimate that by 2017, the U.S. market alone will reach $8.3 billion.[57]

Identity theft occurs when someone steals your personal information and uses it without your permission. They may charge items on a credit card or perhaps access medical services via your health benefits. Identity theft is the most common consumer complaint, according to the Federal Trade Commission. It accounts for almost 20 percent of all problems consumers report.[58] Experts estimate that approximately 15 million Americans fall victim to identity theft each year, with financial losses exceeding $50 billion. And, as any victim knows, the financial aspects are not the only pain points because cancelling credit cards or otherwise correcting the situation can result in huge hassles.

Identity thieves get more sophisticated every day. They used to be content with stealing wallets and "dumpster diving" to obtain account numbers. Today, we increasingly fall prey to high-tech **phishing** scams in which people receive fraudulent emails that ask them to supply account information, as well as **botnets** (a set of computers that are penetrated by malicious software known as *malware* that allows an external agent to control their actions) that hijack millions of computers without any trace. Recently we've witnessed numerous hacks of corporate and government databases including Apple, Best Buy, *The New York Times*, Sony Pictures, and even NASA.

Locational privacy is a related issue. Every one of us who walks around with a phone transmits his or her approximate location, and those of us with GPS-enabled phones leave nothing to chance. In addition, many cars now have GPS devices that can share their location with a centralized service. We can purchase GPS trackers to keep tabs on our kids, aged relatives, or wayward pets. Some insurance companies offer steep discounts to drivers who use GPS tracking technology. The companies provide a small tracker in the car that reports driving habits and in some cases even whether the driver is cruising through unsafe neighborhoods. Other services allow anxious parents to track a teenager's driving and provide a "report card" on use of the family car.[59] A school district in Brazil goes a step farther: It requires 20,000 grade school students to wear uniforms embedded with GPS chips similar to those used in pet trackers. The chips automatically send parents a text message as soon as their children enter the school grounds, or if their children are more than 20 minutes late. A Texas school district implemented a similar plan though it later abandoned the idea and decided to install surveillance cameras on high school campuses instead.[60]

For all intents and purposes in today's wired world, consumers can run, but we can't hide: If someone wants to know where we are or where we've been, the data are there for the asking. As with Web tracking, there is value here: We can easily identify by looking at hundreds or even thousands of reviews the best sushi place within a block of our current location, or perhaps get a heads up on that policeman with the radar gun who is hiding behind that billboard up the highway. However, this is a mixed blessing if this information gets into the wrong hands. Consumers need to make tough tradeoffs between convenience and constant surveillance.

Market Access

Many of us take for granted that we are free to shop anywhere we want or that we can easily learn about our purchase options—everything we need is just a click of a mouse away, right? In reality, however, large numbers of people can't make this claim. For one reason or another their **market access** (i.e., their ability to find and purchase goods and services) is limited because of physical, mental, economic, or social barriers.

Disabilities

Disabled people are the largest minority market in the United States. One in 5 U.S. adults lives with a disability that interferes with daily life.[61] The Census Bureau reports that there are 54 million adults with disabilities who spend almost $200 billion annually, yet companies pay remarkably little attention to the unique needs of this vast group. Fully 11 million U.S. adults have a condition that makes it difficult for them to leave home to shop, so they rely almost exclusively on catalogs and the Internet to purchase products. Many people have limited mobility and are unable to gain easy access to stores, entertainment venues, educational institutions, and other locations. Bodily limitations or disfigurements may result in real or imagined stigmatization, so self-concept and interpersonal relationships may be problematic.[62] People who rely on wheelchairs for mobility often encounter barriers when they try to enter stores, move around the aisles, or enter dressing rooms that are too narrow to accommodate a chair. Others have mental illnesses, such as excessive anxiety in public places. These issues touch many of us; for example, 15 percent of Vietnam and 1991 Gulf War Veterans have been diagnosed with *post-traumatic stress disorder (PTSD)*, and 20 percent of veterans who served in Afghanistan and Iraq received care at a Veterans' Administration (VA) facility for the disorder since their return home. Large numbers of children also encounter difficulties with market access, whether offline or online.

The good news is that technology holds the potential to improve market access. Here are a few exciting new developments:

- The touch screen is a breakthrough for people who have problems with motor skills. They no longer need to manipulate a mouse, keyboard, or pen to use programs. A device like the iPad makes *touch-to-speak technology* affordable and easy to use. For example, a person who is unable to speak can communicate his or her preferences for meals, activities, and so on just by touching the screen. Other apps amplify sounds for the hard-of-hearing, or even encourage children with motor skills disabilities to engage in physical therapy.[63] The LookTel Money Reader app makes it possible for blind people to pay for products in cash; it can "read money" and tell the person the value of the bills he or she holds.[64]
- Dating websites for singles with health problems allow people with an array of disabilities, including paralysis and multiple sclerosis, to find partners. Dating 4 Disabled caters to people with physical diseases, while NoLongerLonely focuses on those with mental illness. Sites like these and others allow users to be blunt and honest about their own issues and what they seek in a partner. One site was created by a man whose brother suffered from Crohn's disease. He observed, "He was a good-looking boy, but when do you tell a girl that you have a colostomy bag? The first date? The third? There's no good time."[65]

Food Deserts

The Department of Agriculture defines a **food desert** as a Census tract where 33 percent of the population or 500 people, whichever is less, live more than a mile from a grocery store in an urban area or more than 10 miles away in a rural area. Healthy food options in these communities are hard to find or are unaffordable. Researchers estimate that in the United States about 23.5 million people live in food deserts.

Limited access to healthy choices can lead to poor diets and higher levels of obesity and other diet-related diseases. More broadly, this *food insecurity* increases the number of low- and moderate-income families who struggle to purchase the diet they need to sustain a healthy and active life.[66]

Literacy

Media literacy refers to a consumer's ability to access, analyze, evaluate, and communicate information in a variety of forms, including print and nonprint messages.[67]

Media literacy empowers people to be both critical thinkers and creative producers of an increasingly wide range of messages using image, language, and sound. This movement reminds us that we are bombarded with thousands of messages every day that espouse a particular point of view or try to persuade us to buy this or that. It's our job to critically evaluate this information and not everyone has the skills to do that. This task is even more difficult in the age of Google, where many of us assume that whatever comes up in a Google search or on Wikipedia is completely true and accurate (Hint: not by a long shot). As the tried-but-true phrase says, "*Caveat Emptor*"—let the buyer beware!

Unfortunately, some of us have an even bigger problem than evaluating the source of a message: We can't read it in the first place. The U.S. Department of Education estimates that about 1 in 7 U.S. adults are **functionally illiterate**.[68] This term describes a person whose reading skills are not adequate to carry out everyday tasks, such as reading the newspaper or the instructions on a pill bottle. Almost half of U.S. Americans read below a sixth-grade level.

This limitation impedes market access for a couple of reasons: First, the illiterate or "low-literate" consumer is at a disadvantage because he or she encounters difficulty in learning about the best purchase options. Second, this person may experience feelings of shame and embarrassment and avoid market situations where he or she will be forced to reveal the inability to read a label or other written material.[69] Some of these people (whom researchers term *social isolates*) cope with the stigma of illiteracy by avoiding situations in which they will have to reveal this problem. They may choose not to eat at a restaurant with an unfamiliar menu, for example.

Low-literate consumers rely heavily on visual cues, including brand logos and store layouts, to navigate in retail settings, but they often make mistakes when they select similarly packaged products (for example, brand line extensions). They also encounter problems with *innumeracy* (understanding numbers); many low-literate people have difficulty knowing, for example, whether they have enough money to purchase the items in their cart and unethical merchants may cheat them out of the correct amount of change. Not surprisingly, these challenges create an emotional burden for low-literate consumers, who experience stress, anxiety, fear, shame, and other negative emotions before, during, and after they shop.[70]

Sustainability and Environmental Stewardship

Almost everyone today is concerned about saving our planet. Worries about climate change, entire species going extinct, widespread exposure to carcinogens and harmful bacteria and many other issues are front and center. Some solutions are no-brainers: Unilever launched a campaign on Facebook and YouTube tied to its Axe brand to encourage reduced usage of hot water. The "Showerpooling" campaign asks fans to take a pledge to share a shower with a like-minded acquaintance or attractive stranger.[71]

Of course, that's a trivial approach to a big problem but real solutions are a huge priority for many individuals and organizations. A *sustainable business model* is not just about "do-gooder" efforts that reduce a company's carbon footprint or the amount of plastic that goes into landfills. Indeed, about 6 out of every 10 companies that convert to a sustainable

A recent study of more than 2000 hotel guests suggests that simply allowing consumers to pledge to practice sustainable behaviors increases the likelihood they will follow through. When guests made a specific commitment at check-in to hang their towels for reuse to reduce laundry waste (and received a lapel pin to symbolize their commitment), the number of towels actually hung increased by more than 40 percent. The researchers estimated the savings at this one hotel at over $50,000 and nearly 700,000 gallons of water.[75]

A Ford ad in Brazil promotes conservation.
Source: Courtesy of J. Walter Thompson Publicidade LTDA.

business model report that they have profited financially as well.[72] A **triple bottom-line orientation** refers to business strategies that strive to maximize return in three ways:

1. **The financial bottom line:** Provide profits to stakeholders.
2. **The social bottom line:** Return benefits to the communities where the organization operates.
3. **The environmental bottom line:** Minimize damage to the environment or even improve natural conditions.

The U.S. EPA defines the concept this way: "**Sustainability** is based on a simple principle: Everything that we need for our survival and well-being depends, either directly or indirectly, on our natural environment. Sustainability creates and maintains the conditions under which humans and nature can exist in productive harmony, that permit fulfilling the social, economic and other requirements of present and future generations."[73] Some people refer to this way of thinking as *cradle to cradle*; the target to aim for is a product made from natural materials that is fully reusable or recyclable so that the company actually uses zero resources to make it.

That is a tough goal, but many organizations work hard to get as close to it as they can—and consumers increasingly take notice. Many of us are much more mindful of these issues when we shop and when we make decisions about the foods we eat, the clothes we wear, the buildings in which we live and work, and the cars we drive. The consumer's focus on personal health is merging with a growing interest in global health. Some analysts call this new value **conscientious consumerism**.[74]

Green Marketing and Greenwashing

Because sustainability and related issues such as climate change, pollution, and toxic products are so pervasive, it is important to distinguish this term from another widely used buzzword: **Green marketing** describes a strategy that involves the development and promotion of environmentally friendly products and stressing this attribute when the manufacturer communicates with customers. Although some specialized companies such as Seventh Generation have successfully built a following around their green products, this strategy has not fared well in recent years. Nonetheless, there still is demand for environmentally friendly products: U.S. consumers spend more than $40 billion a year on them.

This ad from The Slovak Republic under-scores the growing priority consumers place upon organic foods.

Source: JANDL marketing a reklama, S.R.O.

This estimate includes $29.2 billion for organic food; more than $10 billion for hybrid, electric, and clean-diesel vehicles; more than $2 billion on energy-efficient light bulbs; and $640 million on green cleaning products.[76] However, sales are flat or lower than in prior years.

Why would this be? We know that consumers increasingly pay more attention to environmental issues, and many even say they will pay more for products that manu-facturers produce under ethical conditions (e.g., in humane workplaces and without harmful chemicals). In one typical study, the researchers gave subjects a description of a coffee company that either used or did not use Fair Trade principles to buy its beans. They found that participants were willing to pay an additional $1.40 for a pound of the coffee if it was ethically sourced and were negative about the company if it did not adhere to these principles. The study obtained similar results for shirts that were made with organic cotton.[77]

Still—as we'll see in more detail in Chapter 8—it is common to witness a disconnect between consumers' attitudes and their actual behavior. As the old saying goes, "the road to hell is paved with good intentions." Despite consumers' best intentions to "buy green," we can point to two major reasons for the gap between saying and doing:

First, green products are more expensive because the ingredients tend to cost more than their more conventional counterparts, and transportation costs are higher too because they are sold in smaller volumes than the big brands. Although many consumers profess a desire to buy environmentally friendly products, especially in tough economic times they have a tendency not to back these preferences with their cash. When the Great Recession hit in 2008, it took a lot of the steam out of the green movement. For example, in 2009, S.C. Johnson introduced a line of green products called Nature's Source and the company spent more than $25 million to advertise them. By 2010 the company slashed the line's advertising budget to zero.[78]

Unfortunately, the second reason for the lackluster showing of green products is largely self-inflicted. **Greenwashing** occurs when companies make false or exaggerated claims about how environmentally friendly their products are. Think about the old story of the "boy who cried wolf": Consumers simply don't believe most of the green claims companies make about their brands. Almost one-fourth of U.S. consumers say they have "no way of knowing" if a product is green or actually does what it claims. Their skepticism is probably justified: According to one report, more than 95 percent of consumer companies that market as "green" make misleading or inaccurate claims. Another survey found that the number of products that claim to be green has increased by 73 percent since 2009—but of the products investigated, almost one-third had fake labels, and 70 made green claims without offering any proof to back them up.[79] One survey reported that 71 percent of respondents say they will stop buying a product if they feel they've been misled about its environmental impact, and 37 percent are so angry about greenwashing that they believe this justifies a complete boycott of everything the company makes.[80]

As we saw in Chapter 1, it is typical to find that a relatively small number of consumers account for a large amount of the action with regard to a certain consumption activity or purchase. This certainly is true when we look at people who walk the walk, in addition to talking the talk, about modifying their behaviors to help the environment. Marketers point to a segment of consumers they call **LOHAS**—an acronym for "lifestyles of health and sustainability." This label refers to people who worry about the environment, want products to be produced in a sustainable way, and spend money to advance what they see as their personal development and potential. These so-called "Lohasians" (others refer to this segment as *cultural creatives*) represent a great market for products such as organic foods, energy-efficient appliances, and hybrid cars, as well as alternative medicine, yoga tapes, and ecotourism. One organization that tracks this group estimates that they make up between 13 percent to 19 percent of the adults in the United States; it values the market for socially conscious products at $290 billion.[81] Table 4.4 shows that the LOHAS market divides into six different sectors.

TABLE 2.4   LOHAS Market Sectors

Personal Health	Green Building
$117 billion	$100 billion
Natural, organic products	Home certification
Nutritional products	Energy Star appliances
Integrative health care	Sustainable flooring
Dietary supplements	Renewable energy systems
Mind body spirit products	Wood alternatives
Eco Tourism	**Natural Lifestyles**
$42 billion	$10 billion
Eco-tourism travel	Indoor & outdoor furnishings
Eco-adventure travel	Organic cleaning supplies
	Compact fluorescent lights
	Social change philanthropy
	Apparel
Alternative Transportation	**Alternative Energy**
$20 billion	$1 billion
Hybrid vehicles	Renewable energy credits
Biodiesel fuel	Green pricing
Car sharing programs	

Source: www.lohas.com/about.htm, accessed March 2, 2013.

OBJECTIVE 2-4

Consumer behavior can be harmful to individuals and to society.

The Dark Side of Consumer Behavior

A few years ago a crowd assembled for a big holiday sale at a Walmart store in New York. When the doors opened, the crowd trampled a temporary worker to death as people rushed to grab discounted merchandise off the store shelves. A lawsuit filed on behalf of the man's survivors claimed that in addition to providing inadequate security, the retailer "engaged in specific marketing and advertising techniques to specifically attract a large crowd and create an environment of frenzy and mayhem."[82] In subsequent years there have been additional incidents of trampling and even gunfire as people frantically jockey for position to scoop up the big sales. Just how far will people go to secure a bargain?

Despite the best efforts of researchers, government regulators, and concerned industry people, sometimes we are our own worst enemies. We think of individuals as rational decision makers, who calmly do their best to obtain products and services that will maximize the health and well-being of themselves, their families, and their society. In reality, however, consumers' desires, choices, and actions often result in negative consequences to individuals and the society in which they live.

Some of these actions are relatively benign, but others have more onerous consequences. Harmful consumer behaviors, such as excessive drinking or cigarette smoking, stem from social pressures. The cultural value many of us place on money encourages activities such as shoplifting and insurance fraud. Exposure to unattainable ideals of beauty and success creates dissatisfaction with our bodies or our achievements. We will touch on many of these issues later in this book, but for now, let's review some dimensions of the "dark side" of consumer behavior.

Consumer Terrorism

The terrorist attacks of 9/11 were a wake-up call to the free-enterprise system. They revealed the vulnerability of nonmilitary targets and reminded us that disruptions of our financial, electronic, and supply networks can potentially be more damaging to our way of life than the fallout from a conventional battlefield. Assessments by the Rand Corporation and other analysts point to the susceptibility of the nation's food supply as a potential target of **bioterrorism**.[83] More recently, many concerned policymakers, executives, and military commanders have added the prospect of **cyberterrorism** to the list of pressing concerns, especially in the light of high-profile attacks on the computer systems of large financial institutions such as American Express.[84]

Even before the anthrax scares of 2001, toxic substances placed in products threatened to hold the marketplace hostage. This tactic first drew public attention in the United States in 1982, when seven people died after taking Tylenol pills that had been laced with cyanide. A decade later, Pepsi weathered its own crisis when more than 50 reports of syringes found in Diet Pepsi cans surfaced in 23 states. In that case, Pepsi pulled off a public relations *coup de grace* by convincing the public that the syringes could not have been introduced during the manufacturing process. The company even showed an in-store surveillance video that caught a customer slipping a syringe into a Diet Pepsi can while the cashier's head was turned.[85] Pepsi's aggressive actions underscore the importance of responding to such a crisis head-on and quickly.

More recently, a publicity campaign for a late-night cartoon show backfired when it aroused fears of a terrorist attack and temporarily shut down the city of Boston. The effort consisted of 1-foot-tall blinking electronic signs with hanging wires and batteries that marketers used to promote the Cartoon Network TV show *Aqua Teen Hunger Force* (a surreal series about a talking milkshake, a box of fries, and a meatball). The signs were placed on bridges and in other high-profile spots in several U.S. cities. Most depicted a boxy, cartoon character giving passersby the finger. The bomb squads and other police personnel required to investigate the mysterious boxes cost the city of Boston more than $500,000—and a lot of frayed nerves.[86]

Addictive Consumption

A woman in New Zealand apparently died from drinking too much Coca-Cola. Her family said she drank about 2.2 gallons of the beverage every day for years. Prior to her death she had several rotten teeth removed, and she gave birth to a baby who was born without any tooth enamel. The 31-year-old mother of eight died following a cardiac arrhythmia after consuming more than two pounds of sugar and 970 mg of caffeine a day. Coca-Cola noted that the coroner's report, while singling out its product as a probable cause of death, stated that the company "cannot be held responsible for the health of consumers who drink unhealthy quantities of the product."[87]

Though we usually equate substance abuse with addiction to alcohol, drugs, or nicotine, it seems we can become dependent on almost anything—there is even a Chapstick Addicts support group with 250 active members![88] **Consumer addiction** is a physiological or psychological dependency on products or services. Many companies profit from selling addictive products or from selling solutions for kicking a bad habit.

A Chinese man got so upset about the amount of time his adult son spent playing videogames that he took a novel approach: He hired "digital hit men" in the form of other gamers to kill off all of his son's characters in the games.[89] How is that for "tough love?" Psychologists compare **social media addiction** to chemical dependency, to the point of inducing symptoms of withdrawal when users are deprived of their fix. As one noted, "Everyone is a potential addict—they're just waiting for their drug of choice to come along, whether heroin, running, junk food or social media."[90] Indeed, a survey reported 1 in 3 smartphone owners would rather give up sex than their phones![91] And, as many of us realize this fixation grows by the "enablers" around us as they exhibit the same behavior. Indeed one study documented that college students are much more likely to pull out their phones when someone with whom they were sitting had just done so.[92]

Internet addiction has been a big headache for several years already in South Korea, where 90 percent of homes connect to cheap, high-speed broadband. Many young Koreans' social lives revolve around the "PC *bang*," dimly lit Internet parlors that sit on practically every street corner. A government study estimates that up to 30 percent of South Koreans younger than 18 are at risk of Internet addiction. Many already exhibit signs of actual addiction, including an inability to stop themselves from using computers, rising levels of tolerance that drive them to seek ever-longer sessions online, and withdrawal symptoms such as anger and craving when they can't log on. Some users have literally dropped dead from exhaustion after playing online games for days on end.[93]

Other problems arise when people become overly involved in playing online games or posting on social network sites:

- In the United Kingdom, a 33-year-old widowed mother let her two dogs starve to death and neglected her three kids after becoming hooked on the online game *Small World*. A judge banned her from going on the Internet. The woman slept only two hours a night as she played the virtual reality game (in which dwarves and giants battle to conquer the world) almost nonstop for six months. Her children—aged 9, 10, and 13—had no hot food and "drank" cold baked beans from tins. When the family's two dogs died from neglect, she left their bodies rotting in the dining room for two months.[94]
- A U.S. woman pled guilty to a charge of second-degree murder in the death of her three-month-old son. The 22-year-old mother lost her temper when her child began crying while she was playing *FarmVille* on Facebook; she shook the baby until it died.
- **Cyberbullying** refers to the "willful and repeated harm inflicted through the use of computer, cell phones, and other electronic devices."[95] One study reported that 1 in 5 middle school students in the United States were subject to cyberbullying. As one seventh-grade girl observed, "It's easier to fight online, because you feel more brave and in control. On Facebook, you can be as mean as you want."[96] The problem has gotten so bad that the U.S. Department of Health and Human Services even has a website to combat it: Stopbullying.gov.[97]

The Tangled Web

Yik Yak is a hugely popular social app that has invaded numerous college campuses. The down side is that the site fosters cyberbullying because it does not require users to post a profile so they remain anonymous. It sorts messages only by geographic location and only posts within a 1.5-mile radius appear so it's ideal for a campus environment. Offensive "yaks" that derogate students by name or encourage violence and even gang rape appear more often than they should. It's like a graffiti-defaced bathroom wall at the student union—but on digital steroids. [98]

A government website focuses on the problem of cyberbullying.

Source: StopBullying.gov, U.S. Department of Health & Human Service.

- **Phantom Vibration Syndrome** describes the tendency to habitually reach for your cell phone because you feel it vibrating, even if it is off or you are not even wearing it at the time. One researcher reports that 70 percent of people who report heavy usage of mobile devices say they experience this phenomenon. The name derives from *phantom limb syndrome*, a condition in which someone who has lost a limb experiences sensory hallucinations that it is still attached to the body and functioning.[99]

Compulsive Consumption

Some consumers take the expression "born to shop" quite literally. They shop because they are compelled to do so rather than because shopping is a pleasurable or functional task. **Compulsive consumption** refers to repetitive and often excessive shopping performed as an antidote to tension, anxiety, depression, or boredom.[100] "Shopaholics" turn to shopping much the way addicted people turn to drugs or alcohol.[101] One man diagnosed with *compulsive shopping disorder (CSD)* bought more than 2,000 wrenches and never used any of them. Therapists report that women clinically diagnosed with CSD outnumber men by four to one. They speculate that women are attracted to items such as clothes and cosmetics to enhance their interpersonal relationships, whereas men tend to focus on gadgetry, tools, and guns to achieve a sense of power.

One out of 20 U.S. adults is unable to control the buying of goods that he or she does not really want or need. Some researchers say compulsive shopping may be related to low self-esteem. It affects an estimated 2 to 16 percent of the adult U.S. population.[102] In some cases, the consumer has little or no control over his or her consumption, much like a drug addict. Even the act of shopping itself is an addicting experience for some people. Three common elements characterize many negative or destructive consumer behaviors:[103]

1 The behavior is not done by choice.
2 The gratification derived from the behavior is short-lived.
3 The person experiences strong feelings of regret or guilt afterward.

Gambling is an example of a consumption addiction that touches every segment of consumer society. Whether it takes the form of casino gambling, playing the "slots," betting on sports events with friends or through a bookie, or even buying lottery tickets, excessive gambling can be quite destructive. Taken to extremes, gambling can result in lowered self-esteem, debt, divorce, and neglected children. According to one psychologist,

A French organization combats the sexual abuse of children by online predators.
Source: Courtesy of Innocence en Danger

gamblers exhibit a classic addictive cycle: They experience a "high" while in action and depression when they stop gambling, which leads them back to the thrill of the action. Unlike drug addicts, however, money is the substance that hard-core gamblers abuse. We can probably expect the problem to grow as the movement to legalize online gambling in some U.S. states picks up steam (it already is legal in Nevada, Delaware, and New Jersey).[104] There is a built-in market for this new format: Analysts estimate more than 170 million people play simulated casino games on social networks, more than triple the number of real money online gamblers.[105]

Consumed Consumers

Consumed consumers are people who are used or exploited, willingly or not, for commercial gain in the marketplace. Here are some examples:

- **Prostitutes**—Expenditures on prostitution in the United States alone are estimated at $20 billion annually. These revenues are equivalent to those in the domestic shoe industry.[106]
- **Organ, blood, and hair donors**—There is a lively global **red market** for body parts. By one estimate, you could make about $46 million if you donated every reusable part of your body (do not try this at home).[107] In the United States, millions of people sell their blood. A lively market also exists for organs (e.g., kidneys), and some women sell their hair to be made into wigs. Bidding for a human kidney on eBay went to more than $5.7 million before the company ended the auction (it's illegal to sell human organs online ... at least so far). The seller wrote, "You can choose either kidney.... Of course only one for sale, as I need the other one to live. Serious bids only."[108] Here is the retail price for some typical red market transactions in the United States (often much cheaper elsewhere):[109]
  - A pint of blood: $337
  - Hair (for extensions): $308
  - Cornea: $24,400
  - Heart: $997,700
- **Babies for sale**—Several thousand surrogate mothers have been paid to be medically impregnated and carry babies to term for infertile couples. A fertile woman between

the ages of 18 and 25 can "donate" one egg every 3 months and rake in $7,000 each time. Over 8 years, that's 32 eggs for a total of $224,000.[110] In one case in Germany, police arrested a couple when they tried to auction their 8-month-old son on eBay. The parents claimed that the offer, which read "Baby—collection only. Offer my nearly new baby for sale because it cries too much. Male, 70 cm long" was just a joke.[111]

Illegal Acquisition and Product Use

In addition to being self-destructive or socially damaging, many consumer behaviors are illegal as well. Analysts estimate the cost of crimes that consumers commit against business at more than $40 billion per year. A survey conducted by the McCann-Erickson advertising agency revealed the following tidbits:[112]

● Ninety-one percent of people say they lie regularly. One in 3 fibs about his or her weight, 1 in 4 about income, and 21 percent lie about their age. Nine percent even lie about their natural hair color.
● Four out of 10 Americans have tried to pad an insurance bill to cover the deductible.
● Nineteen percent say they've snuck into a theater to avoid paying admission.
● More than three out of five people say they've taken credit for making something from scratch when they have done no such thing. According to Pillsbury's CEO, this "behavior is so prevalent that we've named a category after it—speed scratch."

Consumer Theft and Fraud

Who among us has never received an email offering us fabulous riches if we help to recover a lost fortune from a Nigerian bank account? Of course, the only money changing hands will be yours if you fall for the pitch from a so-called *advance-fee fraud artist*. These con men have successfully scammed many victims out of hundreds of millions of dollars. However, a small but intrepid group of "counterscammers" sometimes give these crooks a taste of their own medicine by pretending to fall for a scam and humiliating the perpetrator. One common strategy is to trick the con artist into posing for pictures while holding a self-mocking sign and then posting these photos on Internet sites. Both online and offline, fraud is rampant.

Stealing from stores is the most common scam. Someone commits a retail theft every 5 seconds. **Shrinkage** is the industry term for inventory and cash losses from shoplifting and employee theft (it does not refer to the condition George experienced in a famous episode of the *Seinfeld* TV show). This is a massive problem for businesses that gets passed on to consumers in the form of higher prices (about 40 percent of the losses can be attributed to employees rather than shoppers). Shopping malls spend $6 million annually on security, and a family of four spends about $300 extra per year because of markups to cover shrinkage.[113]

Indeed, shoplifting is fastest-growing crime in the United States. A comprehensive retail study found that shoplifting is a year-round problem that costs U.S. retailers $9 billion annually. The most frequently stolen products are tobacco products, athletic shoes, logo and brand-name apparel, designer jeans, and undergarments. The average theft amount per incident is $58.43, up from $20.36 in a 1995 survey.[114] The problem is equally worrisome in Europe; retailers there catch well more than 1 million shoplifters every year. The United Kingdom has the highest rate of shrinkage (as a percent of annual sales), followed by Norway, Greece, and France. Switzerland and Austria have the lowest rates.[115]

The large majority of shoplifting is not done by professional thieves or by people who genuinely need the stolen items.[116] About two million Americans are charged with shoplifting each year, but analysts estimate that for every arrest, 18 unreported incidents occur.[117] About three-quarters of those shoplifters authorities catch are middle- or high-income people who shoplift for the thrill of it or as a substitute for affection. Shoplifting is also common among adolescents. Research evidence indicates that teen shoplifting is influenced by factors such as having friends who also shoplift. It is also more likely to occur if the adolescent does not believe that this behavior is morally wrong.[118]

And what about shoppers who commit fraud when they abuse stores' exchange and return policies? Some big companies, such as Guess, Staples, and Sports Authority, use new software that lets them track a shopper's track record of bringing items back.

They are trying to crack down on **serial wardrobers** who buy an outfit, wear it once, and return it; customers who change price tags on items, then return one item for the higher amount; and shoppers who use fake or old receipts when they return a product. The retail industry loses approximately $16 billion a year to these and other forms of fraudulent behavior. Retail analysts estimate that about 9 percent of all returns are fraudulent.[119]

Counterfeiting, where companies or individuals sell fake versions of real products to customers (who may or may not be aware of the switch), accounts for more than $600 billion in global losses annually. Many of us think of counterfeiters as guys who sell *faux* designer handbags or watches on the street, but in fact the problem is much more wide-spread—and often deadly. About 200,000 people in China die per year because they ingest fake pharmaceuticals.[120]

Anticonsumption

Some types of destructive consumer behavior are **anticonsumption**; events in which people deliberately deface or mutilate products and services. Anticonsumption ranges from relatively mild acts like spray-painting graffiti on buildings and subways to serious incidences of product tampering or even the release of computer viruses that can bring large corporations to their knees. It can also take the form of political protest in which activists alter or destroy billboards and other advertisements that promote what they feel to be unhealthy or unethical acts. For example, some members of the clergy in areas heavily populated by minorities have organized rallies to protest the proliferation of cigarette and alcohol advertising in their neighborhoods; these protests sometimes include the defacement of billboards promoting alcohol or cigarettes.

MyLab Marketing

To complete the problems with the ⭐, go to EOC Discussion Questions in the MyLab as well as additional Marketing Metrics questions only available in MyLab Marketing.

CHAPTER SUMMARY

Now that you have finished reading this chapter, you should understand why:

1. Ethical business is good business.

Business ethics are rules of conduct that guide actions in the marketplace; these are the standards against which most people in a culture judge what is right and what is wrong, good or bad. Marketers must confront many ethical issues, especially ones that relate to how much they make consumers "want" things they don't need or are not good for them. A related issue is materialism, which refers to the importance people attach to worldly possessions, and the role of business in encouraging this outlook.

2. Marketers have an obligation to provide safe and functional products as part of their business activities.

It is both ethically and financially smart to maximize customer satisfaction. In some cases, external bodies such as the government or industry associations regulate businesses to ensure that their products and advertising are safe, clear, and accurate. Consumer behavior

researchers may play a role in this process and those who do transformative consumer research (TCR) may even work to bring about social change. Companies also play a significant role in addressing social conditions through their corporate social responsibility (CSR) practices and social marketing campaigns that promote positive behaviors.

3. Consumer behavior impacts directly on major public policy issues that confront our society.

Our relationships with companies and other organizations are complex and many issues that impact quality of life relate directly to marketing practices. These include the trade-off between our privacy and the ability of companies to tailor their offerings to our individual needs. Other issues revolve around market access because many people are unable to navigate the marketplace as a result of disabilities, illiteracy, or other conditions. In addition, our fragile environment requires a commitment to sustainable business practices that attempt to maximize the triple bottom-line that emphasizes financial, social, and environmental benefits.

4. Consumer behavior can be harmful to individuals and to society.

Although textbooks often paint a picture of the consumer as a rational, informed decision maker, in reality many consumer activities are harmful to individuals or to society. The "dark side" of consumer behavior includes terrorism, addiction, the use of people as products (consumed consumers), and theft or vandalism (anticonsumption).

KEY TERMS

Anticonsumption, 83
Bioterrorism, 78
Botnets, 71
Business ethics, 57
Cause marketing, 70
Compulsive consumption, 80
Conscientious consumerism, 74
Consumed consumers, 81
Consumer addiction, 79
Consumerspace, 58
Corporate social responsibility (CSR), 70
Corrective advertising, 66
Counterfeiting, 83
Culture jamming, 67
Curation, 62
Cyberbullying, 79

Cyberterrorism, 78
Food desert, 73
Functionally illiterate, 73
Green marketing, 75
Greenwashing, 76
Gripe sites, 63
Identity theft, 71
Locational privacy, 71
LOHAS, 77
Market access, 72
Marketplace sentiments, 65
Materialism, 62
Media literacy, 73
Phantom vibration syndrome, 80
Phishing, 71
Provenance, 62

Real-time bidding, 71
Red market, 81
Serial wardrobers, 83
Shrinkage, 82
Slacktivism, 68
Social marketing, 70
Social media addiction, 79
Sustainability, 74
The Personal Data Notification & Protection Act, 70
The Student Digital Privacy and Parental Rights Act of 2015, 70
Transformative consumer research (TCR), 68
Transitional economies, 62
Triple bottom-line orientation, 74

REVIEW

2-1 What are *business ethics*, and why is this an important topic?

2-2 The economics of information perspective argues that advertising is important. Why?

⭐ **2-3** What are the main features of consumerspace? Does it actually work as a methodology?

2-4 Why should companies encourage consumers to complain? How can this benefit the business?

⭐ **2-5** What is greenwashing? Is it ethical? Are consumers likely to be convinced?

2-6 In what ways is corporate social responsibility different from social marketing?

⭐ **2-7** Why is market access an important aspect of consumer well-being? What are some important reasons why consumers can experience limited market access?

2-8 What is LOHAS, and how is it significant to marketers?

CONSUMER BEHAVIOR CHALLENGE

■ DISCUSS

2-9 According to Viktoria de Chevron Villette, Co-Founder of the Millennial 20/20 Summit, which bills itself as the world's first gathering of brands, businesses, and industry leaders who target the Millennial generation, cause marketing offers enormous opportunities to corporations.[121] How do you see cause marketing developing?

2-10 Should scientists who study consumer behavior remain impartial, or is it appropriate for them to become involved in the topics they research like those who adhere to the transformative consumer research perspective?

2-11 Because of higher competition and market saturation, marketers in industrialized countries try to develop third-world markets. Asian consumers alone spend $90 billion a year on cigarettes, and U.S. tobacco manufacturers push relentlessly into these markets. We find cigarette advertising, which often depicts glamorous Western models and settings, just about everywhere—on billboards, buses, storefronts, and clothing—and tobacco companies sponsor many major sports and cultural events. Some companies even hand out cigarettes and gifts in amusement areas, often to preteens. Should governments allow these practices, even if the products may be harmful to their citizens or divert money that poor people should spend on essentials? If you were a trade or health official in a third-world country, what guidelines, if any, might you suggest to regulate the import of luxury goods from advanced economies?

2-12 The chapter discusses the practice of serial wardrobing, where people return an outfit after they wear it for a special occasion such as a formal. What do you think of this practice? Is it OK to use an expensive product once and then get your money back?

2-13 "College students' concerns about the environment and vegetarianism are simply a passing fad; a way to look 'cool.'" Do you agree?

2-14 Across Europe, lawyers estimate that around 10 million consumers are entitled to U.S. $5 billion in compensation from airline companies. The compensation claim is for when their flights have either been delayed or cancelled, unless this was due to extraordinary circumstances out of the airline's control. The claims can date back as long as six years. In order to be eligible for a claim, the consumer had to have flown out of a European Union (EU) airport on an EU-registered airline. Despite the clear rulings on the compensation rights of consumers, thousands of claimants found their claims rejected by the airlines. The EU even clarified the ruling 2012 and streamlined the claim process. Does your justice system adequately meet the needs of both consumers and companies in terms of how it awards damages?

2-15 In the summer of 2013, Manchester United announced that it had agreed to an eight-year sponsorship contract with AON worth $245 million to have its name on the club's training ground at Carrington. The deal will see the facility renamed the AON Training Complex. This was a part of a complicated deal in which Manchester United would appear in the Far East for matches wearing AON-sponsored shirts. The deal was worth double the amount that AON had paid in 2009 for its four-year shirt sponsorship. However, the name Old Trafford, the club's home, was not for sale at any price. Naming rights, claimed the executive vice-chairman of the club, were not up for negotiation. Have sports clubs in your country or region sold their stadium names to sponsors? What was the reaction of fans to this move?

2-16 The Creative Bloq Web site (www.creativebloq.com/) featured a collection of the most controversial ad campaigns of 2013. All of them attracted a lot of criticism. The 10 chosen advertisements appeared across the world and were designed by a number of different agencies. What is your take on them? Are they offensive or controversial? Why did the brands approve them?

■ APPLY

2-17 According to a 2012 report by Enisa, the European Information Security Agency, 93 percent of consumers were concerned as to whether businesses protected the information they hold about them. According to the report, 47 percent of service providers actively use personal data as a commercial asset. Around the same percentage share that data with third parties. If they were given the choice, consumers would be inclined to choose a business that required more personal data over one that did not in exchange for lower prices. The consumers also thought that giving more information would provide them with a more personalized service.

The Special Euro Barometer study in 2011 stated that 90 percent of customers revealed their names and addresses online to businesses. At the same time, the Enisa study suggested that 60 percent of consumers would choose a more data-friendly business, but if they gained better deals, this figure rose to 83 percent.

Conduct a poll among 10 car owners of various ages, where you describe these programs, and ask respondents if they would like to participate in order to receive a discount on their purchases. What are the pros and cons? Share your findings with the class.

2-18 In 2015, the UK's Medicines and Healthcare products Regulatory Agency (MHRA) seized $22 billion worth of counterfeit medicines and devices. Amongst the drugs were slimming pills and anaemia tablets. The seizure came at the end of a month-long international campaign against the illegal internet trade involving 115 countries and $72 billion worth of seizures. Suggest how you might design a marketing campaign to combat this dangerous, life threatening fraud. Who would be your target audience?

Case Study

ONE FOR ONE: THE ART OF GIVING AT TOMS

The first thing that comes to mind when people think about TOMS is their corporate social responsibility and the One for One philosophy that is the guiding force of the company's philanthropic mission. The shoe company's origins go back to 2006, during founder's Blake Mycoskie's travels in Argentina. There he saw the poor health and living conditions of the people as well as the difficulties that children faced growing up without shoes. It was thus that he came up with the idea of matching every pair of shoes sold with a pair of new shoes for a child in need. Mycoskie set up TOMS shoes as a means of integrating responsible practice into business and gave a new meaning to corporate sustainability. His simple idea redefined twenty-first century social entrepreneurship and has developed into a meaningful business model that helps promote health, education, and economic opportunity for children and communities globally.

The main idea behind TOMS's One for One mission is to give the customers an opportunity to contribute positively to a child's life by giving them not only a pair of shoes, but also a safe means to walk to school and avoid diseases that a child could catch walking barefoot. For customers, this knowledge makes the act of buying shoes more than just a purchase. They are able to associate themselves with the company's social mission. So far, TOMS has given 35 million pairs of shoes to children in more than 70 countries; it does so by donating shoes to charitable organizations that include the provision of shoes in their community development programs. The shoes are provided according to the type of terrain and season for each community and region. Additionally, TOMS also creates local jobs by manufacturing shoes in countries where they are given.

Corporate social responsibility at TOMS also focuses on the environmental impact of its products and operations. The shoes are made of sustainable vegan materials and their manufacturing design includes natural hemp, organic cotton, or recycled polyester. Their shoes boxes are made from 80 percent recycled material and are printed with soy ink. Expanding its social mission beyond providing shoes to children in need, TOMS has started other missions, including eye care, clean water, and safer birth. TOMS says that giving is in its DNA, and this is apparent from the fact that it even has a position called Chief Giving Officer. This person is responsible for ensuring that the various charitable missions that TOMS undertakes are carried out properly.

In 2011, TOMS eyewear was launched, and it has helped restore sight to more than 275,00 people in need. Its eyewear mission operates in 13 countries and provides diagnostic services, medical treatment, vision correction procedures, and prescription glasses with each sale of eyewear. The mission supports sustainable community-based eye care programs and helps in the creation of local professional job opportunities by providing basic eye care training to local health volunteers and teachers.

The company works on its clean water mission through its coffee roasting division. In 2014, TOMS Roasting Co. was launched, and it has helped provide over 67,000 weeks of safe drinking water in six countries. With each sale of TOMS Roasting Co. Coffee, the company works with its "Giving Partners" to provide one week's supply of safe water to one person and also works to provide sustainable safe water systems for entire communities. In 2014, working on the same One for One philosophy, TOMS Bag Collection was launched in four countries. TOMS Bags works with its Giving Partners to provide training for skilled birth attendants, and with every bag sold, TOMS provides birth kits that help women deliver a baby safely. TOMS draws style and textile inspirations for its bag collection from the locations where it provides shoes, eye care, and water. The entire TOMS bag line communicates a global ethos that reinforces the company's pledge to make a difference in people's lives and works toward their well-being.

The manufacturing units for TOMS shoes are located in Argentina, Ethiopia, and China. The company is conscious of the challenges that come with a global supply network. Their global staff works closely with suppliers and vendors to ensure that TOMS ethical standards are maintained uniformly. Every year, the company ensures that its direct suppliers provide certification that the materials are sourced in conformity with the applicable local labor laws, including laws related to slavery and human trafficking. The company invests in its employees by providing training to them on various business and leadership issues, and it also provides training by third-party experts on labor laws to its supply chain employees.

Although widely recognized and appreciated, the TOMS One for One charity model has been questioned by some critics on broader and long-term social benefits. The critics argue that there are unintended negative consequences of the One for One charity model that come at the expense of the local businesses in the communities where TOMS carries out its charities. For example, they suggest, for example, that the local business of a small-scale cobbler who makes and sells shoes in a small town is greatly undermined when a truckload of free shoes arrives in their town. When a community gets free shoes, they will not buy shoes available at the local shop, and this will hurt the income of the local business. To make matters worse, if the free shoes are distributed at irregular time periods, the local shoe vendors are not able to plan the demand levels for their shoes.

Critics further argue that that giving free things fosters a poor self-image among the recipients. The critics do recognize that such a social mission has good intentions, but they contend that it only provides a small and temporary fix and does not actually alleviate poverty from the roots. As the proverb goes, it's better to teach a hungry person to fish than to just give them a fish to eat. Furthermore, they say that in addition to hindering local businesses, such a model creates dependency and makes the affluent buyers of One for One products complacent about devising other ways to improve poverty and other social issues.

Similarly, many organizations that support social enterprises and entrepreneurial ventures suggest that the free giving model of charity does not address deeper causes of poverty, and in fact be inhibits long-term solutions. Such models approach poverty with the notion that people are poor because they lack things, and they ignore the reasons behind poverty, like the lack of infrastructure to earn more and make a better living. Social causes should not focus only on giving but should also focus on finding ways through which families can earn and support themselves. Although the TOMS model still predominately revolves around the free-good charity approach, it is worth noting that in some ways TOMS has responded to such criticisms by expanding the scope of its social missions. It diversified its charitable missions by including eye care, safe birth and clean water missions as a way to engage in socially responsible causes that go beyond the free good charities.

Overall, looking at the popularity of the TOMS model from the consumer point of view, it can be said to be a marketing success. TOMS understands that more consumers want to buy from companies that incorporate sustainable and responsible business practices that are key elements of its ethos. To communicate its social message and raise awareness of global issues like poverty and blindness, the company holds events like One Day Without Shoes, Style Your Sole, and World Sight Day.

TOMS understands that consumers like tangibility in their charitable actions and good causes. They feel less passionate about a company that says it will spend 10 percent of its profits on research that will help the poor, but if a company says it will give shoes to or will put glasses on a poor child, the consumer will feel a direct connection. TOMS's One for One model has also inspired many other companies to adopted such practices as part of their corporate social responsibility. Once such example is the Canadian company The Mealshare, which also works on the "buy one, give one" principle: the non-profit company gives people the choice to feed someone in need every time they eat out. Another company that has meaningfully modified the TOMS charity model is TheNakedHippie, which works on the basis of "buy one, fund one." This T-shirt brand invests 100% of its profits in micro loans that help people in developing countries start small business to support themselves and their families.

DISCUSSION QUESTIONS

CS 2-1 Discuss TOMS's ethical foundation and its approach to social marketing and corporate social responsibility. Would TOMS have succeeded without its One for One business model?

CS 2-2 Given the increasing trend toward ethical consumerism or conscientious consumption, discuss how consumers evaluate TOMS's ethical supply chain and charitable causes as part of their decision making.

CS 2-3 Considering the viewpoints of the critics regarding TOMS's charity model, discuss its pros and cons. What type of sustainable charitable causes can TOMS pursue in the future that will attract more customers to its social marketing efforts?

Sources: Toms.com, "TOMS: One for One," 2015, http://www.toms.com/corporate-responsibility, accessed November 1, 2015; G. Cheeseman, "The Problem with the TOMS Shoes Charity Model," *Triple Pundit: People, Planet, Profit,* 2012, http://www.triplepundit.com/2012/04/problem-charity-model-toms-shoes/; Knowledge@Wharton, "The One-for-one Business Model: Avoiding Unintended Consequences," 2015, http://knowledge.wharton.upenn.edu/article/one-one-business-model-social-impact-avoiding-unintended-consequences/, accessed November 14, 2015; M. Ellen Biery, "Mixing Business Strategy, 'Social Responsibility,'" Forbes.com, 2011, accessed November 2, 2015; A. Edwards, "TheNakedHippie—about," Thenakedhippie.com, 2015, http://www.thenakedhippie.com/about.php, accessed November 20, 2015.

MyLab Marketing

Go to the Assignments section of your MyLab to complete these writing exercises.

2.19 A corporation that does something to ostensibly curb climate change is not only doing the right thing environmentally, but this is also a great marketing tool. In late 2015, many of the corporate sponsors of the Paris climate summit came under attack from a range of environmental groups for "greenwashing." The corporations were being accused of cynically using the high profile event as a way of making themselves look environmentally friendly. The environmental groups claimed that the main sponsors, including a bank and two utility companies, were hypocrites, as their operations suggest that they are anything but environmentally friendly.[123] Research seems to suggest that the majority of consumers agree and believe that many corporations exaggerate their green credentials. What are the likely consequences for a corporation that is exposed as having green-washed their activities?

2.20 According to a recent survey by the US National Retail Federation, shoplifting is the biggest and most rapidly growing cause of inventory shrinkage. Their survey suggested that 38 percent of loses can be attributed to shoplifting. This is closely followed by employee or internal theft at 34.5 per cent. Other causes included paperwork errors, vendor fraud and errors, and other unknown loses.[124] Inventory shrinkage does not just have implications for the retailer; it also means that retailers have to actively monitor their customers and be suspicious of their behavior. Shoplifting is a global problem, and few countries have answers to the problem. What are the implications of increased shoplifting? How does this affect retailers and customers?

NOTES

1. http://www.ecolabelindex.com/, accessed March 4, 2015.
2. "Nielsen 50% of Global Consumers Surveyed Willing to Pay More For Goods, Services from Socially Responsible Companies, Up From 2011," (August 6, 2013), http://www.nielsen.com/us/en/press-room/2013/nielsen-50-percent-of-global-consumers-surveyed-willing-to-pay-more-fo.html, accessed March 4, 2015.
3. Valerie S. Folkes and Michael A. Kamins, "Effects of Information about Firms' Ethical and Unethical Actions on Consumers' Attitudes," *Journal of Consumer Psychology* 8 (1999): 243–259.
4. Jacqueline N. Hood and Jeanne M. Logsdon, "Business Ethics in the NAFTA Countries: A Cross-Cultural Comparison," *Journal of Business Research* 55 (2002): 883–890.
5. Michael R. Solomon, *Conquering Consumerspace: Marketing Strategies for a Branded World* (New York: AMACOM, 2003).
6. Jeffrey Ball, "Religious Leaders to Discuss SUVs with GM, Ford Officials," *Wall Street Journal Interactive Edition* (November 19, 2002); Danny Hakim, "The S.U.V. Is a Beast, and It's Hairy, Too," *New York Times* (February 2, 2005), www.NewYorkTimes.com, accessed February 2, 2005; www.nrpe.org/issues, accessed May 11, 2009.
7. William Leiss, Stephen Kline, and Sut Jhally, *Social Communication in Advertising: Persons, Products, and Images of Well-Being* (Toronto: Methuen, 1986); Jerry Mander, *Four Arguments for the Elimination of Television* (New York: William Morrow, 1977).
8. Packard (1957), quoted in Leiss et al., *Social Communication,* 11.

9. Raymond Williams, *Problems in Materialism and Culture: Selected Essays* (London: Verso, 1980).

10. Leiss et al., *Social Communication.*

11. George Stigler, "The Economics of Information," *Journal of Political-Economy* (1961): 69.

12. Jane L. Levere, "Westin Creates Six Pillars of Well-Being in a Program for Guests and Employees," *New York Times* (March 19, 2014), http://www.NewYorkTimes.com/2014/03/20/business/media/westin-creates-six-pillars-of-well-being-in-a-program-for-guests-and-employees.html, accessed February 22, 2015.

13. Leiss et al., *Social Communication*, 11.

14. Russell W. Belk, "Possessions and the Extended Self," *Journal of Consumer Research* 15 (September 1988): 139–168; Melanie Wallendorf and Eric J. Arnould, "'My Favorite Things': A Cross-Cultural Inquiry into Object-Attachment, Possessiveness, and Social Linkage," *Journal of Consumer Research* 14 (March 1988): 531–547.

15. L. J. Shrum, Jaehoon Lee, James E. Burroughs, and Aric Rindfleisch, "Online Process Model of Second-Order Cultivation Effects: How Television Cultivates Materialism and Its Consequences of Life Satisfaction," *Human Communication Research* 37 (January 2011): 34–57; L. J. Shrum, James E. Burroughs, and Aric Rindfleisch, "Television's Cultivation of Material Values," *Journal of Consumer Research* 32, no. 3 (2005): 473–479.

16. Susan Schultz Kleine and Stacy Menzel Baker, "An Integrative Review of Material Possession Attachment," *Academy of Marketing Science Review*, no. 1 (2004).

17. Marsha L. Richins, "Special Possessions and the Expression of Material Values," *Journal of Consumer Research* 21 (December 1994): 522–533.

18. Richins, "Special Possessions."

19. Aric Rindfleisch, James E. Burroughs, and Nancy Wong, "The Safety of Objects: Materialism, Existential Insecurity, and Brand Connection," *Journal of Consumer Research* 36 (June 2009): 1–16.

20. John L. Lastovicka and Nancy J. Sirianni, "Truly, Madly, Deeply: Consumers in the Throes of Material Possession Love," *Journal of Consumer Research* Vol. 38, No. 2 (August 2011): 323-342.

21. Marsha L. Richins, "When Wanting Is Better than Having: Materialism, Transformation Expectations, and Product-Evoked Emotions in the Purchase Process," *Journal of Consumer Research* 40, no. 1 (June 2013): 1–18.

22. "Luxury Goods Market Predicted to Grow Six to Seven Percent in 2012, Defying Global Turmoil and Spreading to New Markets, According to Spring Update of Bain & Company's Luxury Goods Worldwide Market Study," Bain & Company, May 15, 2012, http://www.bain.com/about/press/press-releases/luxury-goods-market-predicted-to-grow-six-to-seven-percent-in-2012.aspx, accessed March 1, 2013.

23. Quoted in Michael Pavone, "How Whole Foods Became the Luxury Brand of Millennials," Fastcoexist.com, February 23, 2012, http://www.fastcoexist.com/1679351/how-whole-foods-became-the-luxury-brand-of-millennials, accessed March 1, 2013.

24. Ariel Sabar, "In Case of Missing Trousers, Aggrieved Party Loses Again," *New York Times* (June 26, 2007), www.NewYorkTimes.com, accessed June 26, 2007.

25. Mary C. Gilly and Betsy D. Gelb, "Post-Purchase Consumer Processes and the Complaining Consumer," *Journal of Consumer Research* 9 (December 1982): 323–328; Diane Halstead and Cornelia Droge, "Consumer Attitudes Toward Complaining and the Prediction of Multiple Complaint Responses," in Rebecca H. Holman and Michael R. Solomon, eds., *Advances in Consumer Research* 18 (Provo, UT: Association for Consumer Research, 1991): 210–216; Jagdip Singh, "Consumer Complaint Intentions and Behavior: Definitional and Taxonomical Issues," *Journal of Marketing* 52 (January 1988): 93–107.

26. Ryan Parker, "Covergirl Issues Statement After Protesters Alter NFL 'Game Face' Ads, *LA Times* (September 16, 2014), http://www.latimes.com/fashion/alltherage/la-ar-cover-girl-nfl-ads-protest-the-league-20140915-htmlstory.html, accessed March 4, 2015.

27. Ahir Gopaldas, "Marketplace Sentiments," *Journal of Consumer Research* 41, no. 4 (2014): 995–1014. doi: 10.1086/678034.

28. Emily Steel, "How to Handle 'IHateYourCompany.com': Some Firms Buy Up Negative Domain Names to Avert 'Gripe Sites,'" *Wall Street Journal* (September 5, 2008), http://online.wsj.com/news/articles/SB122057760688302147, accessed November 22, 2013. http://webreprints.djreprints.com/25744 30594663.html, accessed September 5, 2008.

29. Gary L. Clark, Peter F. Kaminski, and David R. Rink, "Consumer Complaints: Advice on How Companies Should Respond Based on an Empirical Study," *Journal of Services Marketing* 6 (Winter 1992): 41–50.

30. Alan Andreasen and Arthur Best, "Consumers Complain—Does Business Respond?" *Harvard Business Review* 55 (July–August 1977): 93–101.

31. Tibbett L. Speer, "They Complain Because They Care," *American Demographics* (May 1996): 13–14; cf. also Yany Grégoire, Thomas M. Tripp, and Renaud Legoux, "When Customer Love Turns into Lasting Hate: The Effects of Relationship Strength and Time on Customer Revenge and Avoidance," *Journal of Marketing* 73 (November 2009): 18–32; Ingrid Martin, "Expert-Novice Differences in Complaint Scripts," in Rebecca H. Holman and

Michael R. Solomon, eds., *Advances in Consumer Research* 18 (Provo, UT: Association for Consumer Research, 1991): 225–231; Marsha L. Richins, "A Multivariate Analysis of Responses to -Dissatisfaction," *Journal of the Academy of Marketing Science* 15 (Fall 1987): 24–31; John A. Schibrowsky and Richard S. Lapidus, "Gaining a Competitive Advantage by Analyzing Aggregate Complaints," *Journal of Consumer Marketing* 11 (1994): 15–26; Clay M. Voorhees, Michael K. Brady, and David M. Horowitz, "A Voice from the Silent Masses: An Exploratory and Comparative Analysis of Noncomplainers," *Journal of the Academy of Marketing Science* 34 (Fall 2006): 514–527.

32. Bruce Cooil, Timothy L. Keiningham, Lerzan Aksoy, and Michael Hsu, "A Longitudinal Analysis of Customer Satisfaction and Share of Wallet: Investigating the Moderating Effect of Customer Characteristics," *Journal of Marketing* 71 (January 2007): 67–83. For a study that looks at consumer variables moderating this relationship, cf. Kathleen Seiders, Glenn B. Voss, Dhruv Grewal, and Andrea L. Godfrey, "Do Satisfied Customers Buy More? Examining Moderating Influences in a Retailing Context," *Journal of Marketing* 69 (October 2005): 26–43.

33. "Voice of the Consumer Not Leveraged," Center for Media Research (February 3, 2009), www.mediapost.com, accessed February 3, 2009.

34. Robbie Brown, Kim Severson, and Barry Meier, "Cruise Line's Woes Are Far From Over as Ship Makes Port," *New York Times* (February 14, 2013), http://www.NewYorkTimes.com/2013/02/15/us/carnival-cruise-line-ship-triumph-towed-into-port.html?pagewanted=all&_r=0, accessed February 20, 2013.

35. Robert V. Kozinets and Jay M. Handelman, "Adversaries of Consumption: Consumer Movements, Activism, and Ideology," *Journal of Consumer Research* 31 (December 2004): 691–704; cf. also Paul C. Henry, "How Mainstream Consumers Think about Consumer Rights and Responsibilities," *Journal of Consumer Research* 37, no. 4 (2010), 670–687.

36. Natasha Singer, "A Birth Control Pill That Promised Too Much," *New York Times* (February 10, 2009), www.NewYorkTimes.com, accessed February 10, 2009.

37. Jack Neff, "NAD to Charmin: No Bare Bear Bottoms: P&G Must Show Some Pieces of TP on Bruin's Bums," *Advertising Age* (August 12, 2010), http://adage.com/article/adages/advertising-p-g-show-pieces-charmin-bears/145379/, accessed April 29, 2011.

38. "Adbusters," Adbusters Media Foundation, www.adbusters.org, accessed March 5, 2015.

39. "Adbusters.".

40. Victoria Uwumarogie, "Robin Thicke Concert Met With Protesters Who Still Say 'Blurred Lines' Promotes Rape," Madame Noire (March 5, 2014), http://madamenoire.com/406804/robin-thicke-concert/, accessed March 4, 2015; James C. McKinley, Jr., "Reebok Drops Rick Ross After Protest Over Lyrics," New York Times, (April 11, 2013), http://artsbeat.blogs.nytimes.com/2013/04/11/reebok-drops-rick-ross-after-protest-over-lyrics/?_r=0, accessed March 4, 2015.

41. K. Kristofferson, Katherine White, and J. Peloza, (2014). "The nature of slacktivism: How the social observability of an initial act of token support affects subsequent prosocial action," *Journal of Consumer Research* 40, no. 6: 1149–1166.

42. Julie L. Ozanne and Bige Saatcioglu, "Participatory Action Research," *Journal of Consumer Research* 35 (October 2008): 423–439.

43. Baker, Stacey Menzel and Courtney Nations Baker (2015), "Keeping the Bounce in Our Steps: Community Narratives of Vulnerability and Resiliency and their Relationship to Shared Material Resources," *Working Paper.*

44. Baker, Stacey Menzel and Ronald Paul Hill (2013), "A Community Psychology of Object Meanings: Identity Negotiation during Disaster Recovery," *Journal of Consumer Psychology*, 23 (3), 275c287.

45. Baker, Stacey Menzel (2009), "Vulnerability and Resilience in Natural Disasters: A Marketing and Public Policy Perspective," *Journal of Public Policy & Marketing*, 28 (Spring), 114–123. Baker, Stacey Menzel, Ronald Paul Hill, Courtney Nations Baker, and John D. Mittelstaedt, (2015), "Improvisational Provisioning in Disaster: The Mechanisms and Meanings of Ad Hoc Marketing Exchange Systems in Community," *Journal of Macromarketing*, in press.

46. Baker, Stacey Menzel, David M. Hunt, and Terri L. Rittenburg (2007), "Consumer Vulnerability as a Shared Experience: Tornado Recovery Process in Wright Wyoming," *Journal of Public Policy & Marketing*, 26 (Spring), 6–19.

47. DiCaprio, Leonardo and Craig Piligian (2008), *Greensburg: A Story of Community Rebuilding*, [documentary series], United States: Discovery Communications, LLC.

48. Shelia Shayon, Cause Marketing Does Affect Brand Purchase," *Broad Channel*, August 26, 2011, http://www.brandchannel.com/home/post/2011/08/26/Cause-Marketing-Does-Affect-Brand-Purchase.aspx, accessed February 3, 2015.

49. For consumer research and discussions related to public policy issues, see Paul N. Bloom and Stephen A. Greyser, "The Maturing of Consumerism," *Harvard Business Review* (November–December 1981): 130–139; George S. Day, "Assessing the Effect of Information Disclosure Requirements," *Journal of Marketing* (April 1976): 42–52; Dennis E. Garrett, "The Effectiveness

of Marketing Policy Boycotts: Environmental Opposition to Marketing," *Journal of Marketing* 51 (January 1987): 44–53; Michael Houston and Michael Rothschild, "Policy-Related Experiments on Information Provision: A Normative Model and Explication," *Journal of Marketing Research* 17 (November 1980): 432–449; Jacob Jacoby, Wayne D. Hoyer, and David A. Sheluga, *Misperception of Televised Communications* (New York: American Association of Advertising Agencies, 1980); Gene R. Laczniak and Patrick E. Murphy, *Marketing Ethics: Guidelines for Managers* (Lexington, MA: Lexington Books, 1985): 117–123; Lynn Phillips and Bobby Calder, "Evaluating Consumer Protection Laws: Promising Methods," *Journal of Consumer Affairs* 14 (Summer 1980): 9–36; Donald P. Robin and Eric Reidenbach, "Social Responsibility, Ethics, and Marketing Strategy: Closing the Gap Between Concept and Application," *Journal of Marketing* 51 (January 1987): 44–58; Howard Schutz and Marianne Casey, "Consumer Perceptions of Advertising as Misleading," *Journal of Consumer Affairs* 15 (Winter 1981): 340–357; Darlene Brannigan Smith and Paul N. Bloom, "Is Consumerism Dead or Alive? Some New Evidence," in Thomas C. Kinnear, ed., *Advances in Consumer Research* 11 (1984): 369–373.

50. Cf. Philip Kotler and Alan R. Andreasen, *Strategic Marketing for Nonprofit Organizations*, 4th ed. (Upper Saddle River, NJ: Prentice Hall, 1991); Jeff B. Murray and Julie L. Ozanne, "The Critical Imagination: Emancipatory Interests in Consumer Research," *Journal of Consumer Research* 18 (September 1991): 192–244; William D. Wells, "Discovery-Oriented Consumer Research," *Journal of Consumer Research* 19 (March 1993): 489–504.

51. Quoted in Chuck Raasch, "'Conscientious Consumption' Survives Recession," *USA Today* (November 29, 2012), http://www.usatoday.com/story/news/nation/2012/11/28/giving-back-post-great-recession/1634703/, accessed January 2, 2013; http://www.causemarketingforum.com/site/c.bkLUKcOTLkK4E/b.6443937/k.41E3/Background_and_Basics.htm, accessed February 16, 2013; Adam Kleinberg, "Brands from KFC to Gucci are Jumping on the Cause Marketing Bandwagon," *Advertising Age* (June 6, 2014), http://adage.com/article/agency-viewpoint/marketing-hot-pay-good/293537/, accessed March 4, 2015.

52. Chloe Albanesius, "Social Security Numbers Revealed ... With Facial-Recognition Software?" *PC* (August 1, 2011), http://www.pcmag.com/article2/0,2817,2389540,00.asp, accessed March 5, 2015.

53. FACT SHEET: Safeguarding American Consumers & Families, Office of the Press Secretary, The White House (January 12, 2015), http://www.whitehouse.gov/the-press-office/2015/01/12/fact-sheet-safeguarding-american-consumers-families, accessed March 5, 2015; Natasha Singer, "Legislators Introduce Student Digital Privacy Bill," *New York Times*, April 29, 2015, http://bits.blogs.nytimes.com/2015/04/29/legislators-introduce-student-digital-privacy-bill/?_r=0, accessed July 13, 2015; Somini Sengupta, "Letting Down Our Guard With Web Privacy," *New York Times*, March 30, 2013, http://www.New York Times.com/2013/03/31/technology/web-privacy-and-how-consumers-let-down-their-guard.html?pagewanted=1&ref=us, accessed February 23, 2015.

54. Natasha Singer, "Face Recognition Makes the Leap from Sci-Fi," *New York Times* (November 12, 2011), http://www.NewYorkTimes.com/2011/11/13/business/face-recognition-moves-from-sci-fi-to-social-media.html?_r=0, accessed February 20, 2015.

55. Karl Greenberg, "Fewer People Find Social Ads Annoying," *Marketing Daily* (December 10, 2012), http://www.mediapost.com/publications/article/188850/fewer-people-find-social-ads-annoying.html?edition=54351#axzz2EkcOH7Ua, accessed January 4, 2013.

56. Quoted in Natasha Singer, "YOU FOR SALE: Your Online Attention, Bought in an Instant," *New York Times* (November 17, 2012), http://www.NewYorkTimes.com/2012/11/18/technology/your-online-attention-bought-in-an-instant-by-advertisers.html?pagewanted=1, accessed January 4, 2013.

57. Singer, "YOU FOR SALE: Your Online Attention, Bought in an Instant," *New York Times* (November 17, 2012).

58. "Identity Theft Action Plan, Pennsylvania Commission on Crime and Delinquency," http://www.portal.state.pa.us/portal/server.pt/community/what_is_id_theft_/12993/identity_theft_statistics/587724, accessed February 16, 2013; "Identity Theft," Federal Trade Commission, http://www.consumer.ftc.gov/features/feature-0014-identity-theft, accessed February 16, 2013; "Identity Theft Victim Statistics," http://www.identitytheft.info/victims.aspx, accessed February 16, 2013; "Hacker 'Botnet' Hijacked Online Searches," Phys.org (February 7, 2013), http://phys.org/news/2013-02-hacker-botnet-hijacked-online.html, accessed February 16, 2013; Nicole Perlroth, "Hackers in China Attacked the *Times* for Last 4 Months," *New York Times* (January 30, 2013), http://www.NewYorkTimes.com/2013/01/31/technology/chinese-hackers-infiltrate-new-york-times-computers.html?pagewanted=all, accessed February 16, 2013.

59. "Save Money on Car Insurance Through GPS Tracking, LiveView GPS" (February 9, 2012), http://www.liveviewgps.com/blog/save-money-on-car-insurance-through-gps-tracking/, accessed February 16, 2013; http://www.motosafety.com/, accessed February 16, 2013.

60. Mariella Moon, "Uniforms with Microchip Notify Parents If Their Children Skip School," *Mashable* (March 26, 2012), http://mashable.com/2012/03/26/uniforms-with-microchip/?utm_medium=email&utm_source=newsletter, accessed January 4, 2013; Will Oremus, "Texas School District Drops RFID Chips, Will Track Kids With Surveillance Cameras Instead," *Future & Tense* (July 17, 2013), http://www.slate.com/blogs/future_tense/2013/07/17/texas_northside_school_district_drops_rfid_tracking_privacy_not_the_main.html, accessed March 5, 2015.

61. "Nearly 1 in 5 People Have a Disability in the U.S., Census Bureau Reports," U.S. Census Bureau (July 25, 2012), https://www.census.gov/newsroom/releases/archives/miscellaneous/cb12-134.html, accessed March 5, 2015; Susannah Fox, "Americans Living with Disability and Their Technology Profile," *PewInternet* (January 21, 2011), http://pewinternet.org/Reports/2011/Disability.aspx, accessed January 2, 2013; Terry L. Childers and Carol Kaufman-Scarborough, "Expanding Opportunities for Online Shoppers with Disabilities," *Journal of Business Research* 62 (2009), 572–578.

62. Michael R. Solomon, Kel Smith, Nadine Vogel, and Natalie T. Wood, "Virtual Freedom for People with Disabilities," *Society for Disability Studies, Philadelphia* (June 2010).

63. Zoe Fox, "4 Ways iPads Are Changing the Lives of People with Disabilities," *Mashable* (July 25, 2011), http://mashable.com/2011/07/25/ipads-disabilities/?utm_source=feedburner&utm_medium=email&utm_campaign=Feed%3A+Mashable+%28Mashable%29, accessed January 2, 2013.

64. http://www.looktel.com/moneyreader, accessed March 5, 2015; Nick Bilton," An iPhone App Helps the Blind Identify Currency," *New York Times* (March 9, 2011), http://bits.blogs.NewYorkTimes.com/2011/03/09/an-iphone-app-helps-the-blind-identify-currency/?scp=1&sq=app%20helps%20the%20blind&st=cse, accessed January 2, 2013.

65. Quoted in Karen Barrow, "Difference Is the Norm on These Dating Sites," *New York Times* (December 27, 2010), http://www.NewYorkTimes.com/2010/12/28/health/28dating.html?emc=eta1, accessed January 2, 2013.; http://www.dating4disabled.com/, accessed March 5, 2015; http://www.nolongerlonely.com/, accessed March 5, 2015.

66. "Healthy Food Financing Initiative," Office of Community Services, U.S. Department of Health and Human Services (January 18, 2011), http://www.acf.hhs.gov/programs/ocs/resource/healthy-food-financing–initiative-0, accessed January 4, 2013.

67. National Association for Media Literacy Education, http://namle.net/publications/media-literacy-definitions/, accessed March 1, 2013.

68. Robert Roy Britt, "14 Percent of U.S. Adults Can't Read," *Live Science* (January 10, 2009), http://www.livescience.com/3211-14-percent-adults-read.html, accessed March 1, 2013.

69. Natalie Ross Adkins and Julie L. Ozanne, "The Low Literate Consumer," *Journal of Consumer Research* 32, no. 1 (June 2005): 93–105.

70. Natalie Ross Adkins and Julie L. Ozanne, "The Low Literate Consumer," *Journal of Consumer Research* 32, no. 1 (2005): 93; Madhubalan Viswanathan, José Antonio Rosa, and James Edwin Harris, "Decision-Making and Coping of Functionally Illiterate Consumers and Some Implications for Marketing Management," *Journal of Marketing* 69, no. 1 (2005): 15.

71. Bruce Horovitz, "Axe Showerpool Promo Raises Eyebrows," *USA Today* (September 17, 2012), http://usatoday30.usatoday.com/money/business/story/2012/09/17/axe-showerpool-promo-raises–eyebrows/57797640/1, accessed March 1, 2013.

72. "5 Lessons from the Companies Making Sustainability More Profitable Than Ever," *Fast Company Co.Exist* (February 5, 2013), http://www.fastcoexist.com/1681339/5-lessons-from-the-companies-making-sustainability-more-profitable-than-ever, accessed March 1, 2013.

73. Quoted in "What Is Sustainability?" United States Environmental Protection Agency," http://www.epa.gov/sustainability/basicinfo.htm, accessed March 1, 2013.

74. Emily Burg, "Whole Foods Is Consumers' Favorite Green Brand," *Marketing Daily*, www.mediapost.com, accessed May 10, 2007.

75. K. Baca-Motes, A. Brown, A. Gneezy, E. A. Keenan, and L. D. Nelson, "Commitment and Behavior Change: Evidence from the Field," *Journal of Consumer Research* 39, no. 5: 1070–1084

76. Jack Neff, "As More Marketers Go Green, Fewer Consumers Willing to Pay for It," *Advertising Age* (September 24, 2012), http://adage.com/article/news/marketers-green-fewer-consumers-pay/237377/, accessed January 4, 2013.

77. Remi Trudel and June Cotte, "Does It Pay to Be Good?" *MIT Sloan Management Review* 61 (Winter 2009): 61–68.

78. Stephanie Clifford and Andrew Martin, "As Consumers Cut Spending, 'Green' Products Lose Allure," *New York Times* (April 21, 2011), http://www.NewYorkTimes.com/2011/04/22/business/energy-environment/22green.html?hp&_r=0, accessed March 1, 2013.

79. Wendy Koch, "'Green' Product Claims Are Often Misleading," *USA Today* (October 26, 2010), http://content.usatoday.com/communities/greenhouse/post/2010/10/green-product-claims/1?csp=34money&utm_source=feedburner&utm_medium=feed&utm_campaign=Feed%3A+Usatoday-comMoney-TopStories+%28Money+-+Top+Stories%29, accessed April 10, 2011.

80. Mark Dolliver, "Thumbs Down on Corporate Green Efforts," *Adweek* (August 31, 2010), http://www.adweek.com/aw/content_display/news/client/e3i842

60d4301c885f91b2cd8a712f323cf, accessed April 10, 2011; Sarah Mahoney, "Americans Hate Faux Green Marketers," *Marketing Daily* (March 25, 2011), http://www.mediapost.com/publications/?fa=Articles.showArticle&art_aid=147415&nid=125122, accessed April 10, 2011.

81. www.lohas.com/about.htm, accessed March 2, 2013.

82. Aditi Mathur, "Black Friday Turns Deadly; Hundreds Left Unconscious, Injured and Trampled," *International Business Times* (November 29 2011), http://www.ibtimes.com/black-friday-turns-deadly-hundreds-left–unconscious-injured-trampled-graphic-videos-375868, accessed March 2, 2013. http://www.ibtimes.com/black-friday-turns-deadly-hundreds-left–unconscious-injured-trampled-graphic-videos-375868, accessed November 3, 2013; Jack Neff, "Lawsuit: Marketing Blamed in Wal-Mart Trampling Death," *Advertising Age* (December 4, 2008), www.adage.com, accessed December 4, 2008; www.Freerepublic.Com/Focus/F-News/2142920/Posts, accessed December 4, 2008.

83. Kenneth E. Nusbaum, James C. Wright, and Michael R. Solomon, "Attitudes of Food Animal Veterinarians to Continuing Education in Agriterrorism," paper presented at the 53rd Annual Meeting of the Animal Disease Research Workers in Southern States, University of Florida (February 2001).

84. Christopher Harress. "Obama Says Cyberterrorism Is Country's Biggest Threat, U.S. Government Assembles 'Cyber Warriors,'" *International Business Times* (February 18, 2014), http://www.ibtimes.com/obama-says-cyberterrorism-countrys-biggest-threat-us-government-assembles-cyber-warriors-1556337, accessed March 5, 2015; Sean Gallagher, "Security Pros Predict "Major" Cyber Terror Attack This Year," *Ars Technica* (January 4, 2013), http://arstechnica.com/-security/2013/01/security-pros-predict-major-cyberterror-attack-this-year/, accessed April 3, 2013.

85. Betty Mohr, "The Pepsi Challenge: Managing a Crisis," *Prepared Foods* (March 1994): 13.

86. "Boston Officials Livid Over Ad Stunt," *New York Times* (February 1, 2007), www.NewYorkTimes.com, accessed February 1, 2007.

87. http://www.usatoday.com/story/news/nation/2013/02/12/coca-cola-soda-death/1912491/?morestories=obnetwork, accessed January 29, 2015.

88. http://www.experienceproject.com/groups/Am-Addicted-To-Chapstick/34083, accessed May 29, 2011.

89. Sam Laird, "Dad Hires Hit Men to Kill Son—in Video Games," *Mashable*, January 9, 2013, http://mashable.com/2013/01/09/dad-son-video-games/?WT.mc_id=en_my_stories&utm_campaign=My%2BStories&utm_medium=email&utm_source=newsletter?WT.mc_id=en_my_stories&utm_campaign=My%2BStories&utm_medium=email&utm_source=newsletter, accessed February 22, 2015.

90. Erik Sass, "Woman Kills Baby for Interrupting FarmVille," *Social Media & Marketing Daily* (October 28, 2010), http://www.mediapost.com/publications/?fa=Articles.showArticle&art_aid=138502&nid=120184, accessed April 30, 2011.

91. Bob Al-Greene, "Late-Night Gadget Use Damages Your Sleep Cycle," *Mashable* (November 19, 2012), http://mashable.com/2012/11/19/-gadgets-sleep/, accessed January 4, 2013.

92. Emily Price, "Cellphone Addiction May Be Contagious, Study Finds," *Mashable* (October 3, 2012), http://mashable.com/2012/12/03/cell-phone-addiction-contigous/? utm_source=feedburner&utm_medium=email&utm_campaign=Feed%3A+Mashable+%28Mashable%29, accessed February 18, 2015.

93. Martin Fackler, "In Korea, A Boot Camp Cure for Web Obsession," *New York Times* (November 18, 2007), www.NewYorkTimes.com/2007/11/18/Technology/18rehab.html, accessed November 19, 2007.

94. Chris Pollard, "A Cruel World," *The Sun (U.K.)* (September 13, 2010), http://www.diigo.com/cached?url=http%3A%2F%2Fwww.thesun.co.uk%2Fsol%2Fhomepage%2Fnews%2F3135278%2FMum-addicted-to-Small-World-neglected-kids-and-let-dogs-starve-to-death.html, accessed February 23, 2011.

95. Quoted in http://cyberbullying.us/, accessed March 2, 2013.

96. Quoted in Jan Hoffman, "Online Bullies Pull Schools Into the Fray," *New York Times* (June 27, 2010), http://www.NewYorkTimes.com/2010/06/28/style/28bully.html?pagewanted=1&_r=0&emc=eta1, accessed January 4, 2013.

97. http://www.stopbullying.gov/cyberbullying/what-is-it/, accessed March 5, 2015.

98. Jonathan Mahler, "Who Spewed That Abuse? Anonymous Yik Yak App Isn't Telling," *New York Times* (March 8, 2015), http://www.nytimes.com/2015/03/09/technology/popular-yik-yak-app-confers-anonymity-and-delivers-abuse.html?smid=nytcore-iphone-share&smprod=nytcore-iphone&_r=0, accessed March 10, 2015.

99. Matt Petronzio, "Do You Suffer from These 4 Tech Afflictions?" *Mashable* (June 1, 2012), http://mashable.com/2012/06/01/tech-addiction/?WT.mc_id=en_top_stories&utm_campaign=Top%2BStories&utm_medium=email&utm_source=newsletter, accessed January 4, 2013.

100. Derek N. Hassay and Malcolm C. Smith, "Compulsive Buying: An Examination of the Consumption Motive," *Psychology & Marketing* 13 (December 1996): 741–752.

101. Nancy M. Ridgway, Monika Kukar-Kinney, and Kent B. Monroe, "An Expanded Conceptualization and a New Measure of Compulsive Buying," *Journal of Consumer Research* 35, no. 4 (2008): 622–639; Thomas

C. O'Guinn and Ronald J. Faber, "Compulsive Buying: A Phenomenological Explanation," *Journal of Consumer Research* 16 (September 1989): 154.

102. Curtis L. Taylor, "Guys Who Buy, Buy, Buy," *Newsday* (October 6, 2006); Jim Thornton, "Buy Now, Pay Later," *Men's Health* (December, 2004): 109–112.

103. Georgia Witkin, "The Shopping Fix," *Health* (May 1988): 73; see also Arch G. Woodside and Randolph J. Trappey III, "Compulsive Consumption of a Consumer Service: An Exploratory Study of Chronic Horse Race Track Gambling Behavior," working paper #90-MKTG-04, A. B. Freeman School of Business, Tulane University (1990); Rajan Nataraajan and Brent G. Goff, "Manifestations of Compulsiveness in the Consumer-Marketplace Domain," *Psychology & Marketing* 9 (January 1992): 31–44; Joann Ellison Rodgers, "Addiction: A Whole New View," *Psychology Today* (September–October 1994): 32.

104. Deena Beasley and Nichola Groom, "States Race to Legalize Online Gambling," *The Huffington Post* (February 28, 2013), http://www.huffingtonpost.com/2013/03/01/online-gaming-legalized-in-new-jersey_n_2784866.html, accessed March 5, 2015.

105. Spencer E. Ante and Alexandra Berzon, "Gambling Industry Bets Virtual Money Turns Real," *Wall Street Journal* (December 20, 2012), http://-professional.wsj.com/article/SB10001424127887324731304578191741064162164.html, accessed January 4, 2013.

106. Helen Reynolds, *The Economics of Prostitution* (Springfield, IL: Thomas, 1986).

107. Patrick Di Justo, "How to Sell Your Body for $46 Million," *Wired* (August 2003): 47.

108. Amy Harmon, "Illegal Kidney Auction Pops Up on eBay's Site," *New York Times* (September 3, 1999), www.NewYorkTimes.com, accessed September 3, 1999.

109. Scott Carney, "Inside the Business of Selling Human Body Parts," *Wired* (January 31, 2011), http://www.wired.com/magazine/2011/01/ff_-red markets/2, accessed March 1, 2013.

110. Di Justo, "How to Sell Your Body for $46 Million."

111. Reuters, "German Parents Offer Baby on eBay," *New York Times* (May 25, 2008), www.NewYorkTimes.com/2008/05/25/world/europe/25ebayby.html?_r=1&scp=1&sq=baby ..., accessed May 25, 2008.

112. "Advertisers Face Up to the New Morality: Making the Pitch," *Bloomberg* (July 8, 1997).

113. "Shoplifting: Bess Myerson's Arrest Highlights a Multibillion-Dollar Problem That Many Stores Won't Talk About," *Life* (August 1988): 32.

114. "New Survey Shows Shoplifting Is a Year-Round Problem," *Business Wire* (April 12, 1998).

115. "Customer Not King, But Thief," *Marketing News* (December 9, 2002): 4.

116. Catherine A. Cole, "Deterrence and Consumer Fraud," *Journal of Retailing* 65 (Spring 1989): 107–120; Stephen J. Grove, Scott J. Vitell, and David Strutton, "Non-Normative Consumer Behavior and the Techniques of Neutralization," in Terry Childers et al., eds., *Marketing Theory and Practice*, 1989 AMA Winter Educators' Conference (Chicago: American Marketing Association, 1989): 131–135.

117. Mark Curnutte, "The Scope of the Shoplifting Problems," *Gannett News Service* (November 29, 1997).

118. Anthony D. Cox, Dena Cox, Ronald D. Anderson, and George P. Moschis, "Social Influences on Adolescent Shoplifting—Theory, Evidence, and Implications for the Retail Industry," *Journal of Retailing* 69 (Summer 1993): 234–246.

119. Stephanie Kang, "New Return Policy: Retailers Say 'No' to Serial Exchangers," *Wall Street Journal* (November 29, 2004): B1.

120. Leo Burnett, "Behind New System to Blunt Counterfeiting in China '1-Tag' Lets Consumers Authenticate Products and Avoid Potentially Hazardous Ripoffs," *AdAge Global* (January 31, 2011), http://adage.com/article/global-news/leo-burnett-creates-system-stop-counterfeiting-china/148571/, accessed January 2, 2013.

121. Viktoria de Chevron Villette, "Cause Marketing: Socially Relevant and Untapped," *Digital Marketing Magazine*, February 4, 2016, http://digitalmarketingmagazine.co.uk/digital-marketing-features/cause-marketing-socially-relevant-and-untapped/3141.

122. Medicines and Healthcare products Regulatory Agency, "UK leads the way with £15.8 million seizure in global operation targeting counterfeit and unlicensed medicines and devices," GOV.UK, https://www.gov.uk/government/news/uk-leads-the-way-with-158-million-seizure-in-global-operation-targeting-counterfeit-and-unlicensed-medicines-and-devices.

123. COP21: corporate sponsors accused of 'green-washing'(http://www.ft.com/cms/s/0/43986518-9426-11e5-b190-291e94b77c8f.html#axzz3uxPqpViJ); http://www.greenwashingindex.com/about-greenwashing; http://www.theguardian.com/environment/2014/sep/13/greenwashing-sticky-business-naomi-klein.

124. Kathy Grannis Allen, "Retailers Estimate Shoplifting, Incidents of Fraud Cost $44 Billion in 2014," *National Retail Federation*, June 23, 2015, https://nrf.com/media/press-releases/retailers-estimate-shoplifting-incidents-of-fraud-cost-44-billion-2014; Centre for Retail Research, "Retail Crime in the UK," http://www.retailresearch.org/ukretailcrime.php; Centre for Retail Research, "Retail Crime in the UK," http://www.designagainstcrime.com/projects/anti-shoplifting/

SECTION 1   ANALYZING THE ATHLETIC SHOE MARKET FOR SHOE FIEND

BACKGROUND

You are the marketing analyst for SHOE FIEND, an online ath-letic shoe store. To date, your company has done little formal marketing research about athletic shoe buyers in the United States. Using the 2014 Spring GfK MRI data, you recently ran a series of reports about the shoe-buying habits of several U.S. consumer segments. At this time, you have decided to focus on the five best-selling shoe brands on your Web site: Adidas, Asics, Nike, New Balance, and Reebok. After looking through the GfK MRI data report options, you decided that the most fitting question for your purposes was "Did you buy [SHOE BRAND] in the last 12 months?"

The report is designed to compare the shoe-buying habits of consumers across several different consumer characteristics: gender, age, and Internet use. In addition, you also created three subsegment schemes that combined two different segmentation variables: Gender and Age (men 18–34 and women 18–34) and Internet Use and Age (heavy Internet users 18–34 years old).

YOUR GOAL

First, review the data from the GfK MRI. You will use this information to make some inferences about the brand pref-erences of the different segments. You will combine the information in the GfK MRI with some financial assumptions provided by SHOE FIEND to make some recommendations for future marketing tactics.

THE DATA

The data in the report can be interpreted in the following manner:

- Market Segment Size (000s): The total number of U.S. adults that meet the criteria for the segment (regardless of whether they did or did not buy a particular shoe brand)
- Market Segment Size (%): The same as Market Segment Size (000s), but presented as a percentage of all U.S. Adults.
- Estimated Count (000s): The estimated number of U.S. adults within the segment who bought that particular pair of shoes at least once in the last 12 months.
- Percentage of Total: Among all U.S. adults who bought a particular brand of shoes in the last 12months, the percentage of them who belong to that particular segment.
- Percentage within market segment who bought in last year: The percentage of people within a particular segment who bought the shoe brand within the last 12 months
- Index: The likelihood of a member of the segment to have bought the particular shoe brand in the last 12 months, indexed to the likelihood of an average U.S. adult (the U.S. average equals an index value of 100). Thus, an index value of 120 can be interpreted as mem-bers of that segment being 20 percent more likely than the national average to have bought a particular brand of shoes in the last 12 months.

	Total	Men	Women	Adults 18–34	Men 18–34	Women 18–34	Internet 1 (Heavy Users)	Adults 18–34 and Heavy Internet
Market Segment Size (000s)	237,115	114,159	122,916	71,961	35,867	36,037	47,361	21,985
Market Segment Size (%)	100	48.1	51.8	30.3	15.1	15.2		9.3
ADIDAS								
Estimated Count (000s)	17,096	9,635	7,461	6,973	4,053	2,919	4,163	2,392
% of Total	100	56.36	43.64		23.71	17.08	24.35	13.99
% within Mkt. Seg. who bought last year	7.21	8.44	6.07	9.69	11.3	8.1	8.79	10.88
Index	100	117	84	134	157	112	122	
ASICS								
Estimated Count (000s)	11,186	4,851	6,335	2,948	1,321	1,627	2,453	899
% of Total	100	43.37	56.63	26.36	11.81	14.55	21.93	8.04
% within Mkt. Seg. who bought last year	4.72	4.25		4.1	3.68	4.51	5.18	4.09
Index	100	90	109	87	78	96	110	87

(Continued)

	Total	Men	Women	Adults 18–34	Men 18–34	Women 18–34	Internet 1 (Heavy Users)	Adults 18–34 and Heavy Internet
NIKE								
Estimated Count (000s)	49,453	24,685	24,768	20,808		9,966	12,233	6,818
% of Total	100	49.92	50.08	42.08	21.92	20.15	24.74	13.79
% within Mkt. Seg. who bought last year	20.87	21.63	20.16	28.93	30.23	27.64	25.82	31
Index	100	104	97	139	145	132	124	149
NEW BALANCE								
Estimated Count (000s)	25,338	12,488	12,850	4,931	2,681	2,250	4,816	1,638
% of Total	100	49.29	50.71	19.46	10.58	8.88	19.01	6.46
% within Mkt. Seg. who bought last year	10.69	10.94	10.46	6.86	7.47	6.24	10.17	7.45
Index	100	102	98	64	70	58	95	70
REEBOK								
Estimated Count (000s)	9,919	5,234	4,685	2,891	1,681	1,209	2,149	952
% of Total	100	52.77	47.23	29.14	16.95	12.19	21.66	9.6
% within Mkt. Seg. who bought last year	4.18	4.59	3.81	4.02	4.69	3.35	4.54	4.33
Index	100	110	91	96	112	80	108	103

Source: Spring 2014 GfK MRI

Task 1: Correct the Table:

Unfortunately, it appears that someone accidentally left some of the calculated values blank in the table. Luckily, you know you can use the other available information in the table to calculate the missing values.

● Q1: Calculate the market segment size (in percentage) for heavy Internet users

$$\text{CALCULATION} = \frac{\text{[Market Segment Size (000s) in the Internet 1 (Heavy Users) Column]}}{\text{[Market Segment Size (000s) in the Total Column]}}$$

● Q2: Calculate the percentage of total market for adults 18–34 who bought Adidas in the last 12 months.

$$\text{CALCULATION} = \frac{\text{[Estimated Count (000s in Adults 18–34]}}{\text{[Estimated Count (000s in Total)]}}$$

● Q3: Calculate the index for adults 18–34 who are heavy Internet users who bought Adidas in the last 12 months.

$$\text{CALCULATION} = 100 + \frac{\text{([percentage within market segment who bought last year in adults 18–34 heavy Internet]} - \text{[percentage within market segment who bought last year in total])}}{\text{[percentage within market segment who bought last year in total]}} \times 100$$

● Q4: For the Women column, calculate the percentage within market segment who bought Asics in the last 12 months.

$$\text{CALCULATION} = \frac{\text{[Estimated Count (000s)]}}{\text{[Market Segment Size (000s)]}}$$

● Q5: For Men 18–34, calculate the Estimated Count (000s) who bought Nike shoes in the last 12 months.

CALCULATION = [Market Segment Size (000s) for Men 18–34] × [Percentage within market segment who bought last year for Men 18–34]

Task 2: Making Inferences about Athletic Shoe Buyers

1 Generally speaking, does it appear that heavy Internet users are more or less likely than the average U.S. adult to have bought these shoe brands in the last 12 months?
2 If you were going to run a series of advertisements for SHOE FIEND targeting younger adult women, which brand would you recommend to feature on the advertisement? Which shoe brand would you be disinclined to feature? Why?
3 Lately, management for SHOE FIEND has worried that its positioning has completely overlooked serving the wants of "older" consumers (older than 45 years old). If SHOE FIEND decides to market toward older U.S. adults, which of the brands should SHOE FIEND be more conscientious about featuring?

Task 3: Estimating the Value of the Shoe Buying Segments

Using some assumptions provided by the CFO, you are tasked with estimating the annual sales (in dollars) for each shoe buying segment. To do so, you will need to make the following assumptions:

● Average number of pairs bought within 12 months
● Average price of shoe brand

These numbers are estimates that came from the internal efforts of your financial analyst team.

	If someone buys at least one pair of a shoe brand in the last 12 months, how many total pairs of that brand do they buy, on average?	Average price per shoe pair
Adidas	2.0	$70
Asics	2.0	$70
Nike	1.5	$75
New Balance	2.0	$70
Reebok	1.5	$65

1 What are the total estimated sales of these five shoe brands for heavy Internet users in the last 12 months?
2 For a random U.S. adult woman, how much would we estimate she spent on Asics shoes in the last 12 months?

DISCUSSION AND DEBATE

1. Based solely on the information that you analyzed, do you think it makes more sense for SHOE FIEND to: treat the whole market as homogeneous (no segmentation), use a single variable segmentation scheme (just gender, just age, just Internet usage), or a multivariate segmentation scheme? Regardless of your answer, identify the advantages and limitations associated with your argument.
2. You are about to ask a junior analyst at SHOE FIEND to run another GfK MRI report for you. Which additional variables do you think would be best to add into the report for segmentation purposes? Why?

 GfK US LLC, Mediamark Research & Intelligence division.

CONSUMER BEHAVIOR

In this section, we focus on the internal dynamics of consumers. Although "no man is an island," each of us are to some degree "self-contained" in terms of receiving information about the outside world. We are constantly confronted by advertising messages, products, and other people—not to mention our own thoughts about ourselves—that affect how we make sense of the world and of course what we choose to buy. Each chapter in this section looks at some aspect that may be "invisible" to others but is important to understand how consumers make choices.

Chapter 3 describes the process of perception; the way we absorb and interpret information about products and other people from the outside world. Chapter 4 focuses on how we store this information and how it adds to our existing knowledge about the world. Chapter 5 looks at motivation—why we do what we do—and how our emotional states influence us. Chapter 6 explores how our views about ourselves—particularly our sexuality and our physical appearance—affect what we do, want, and buy. Chapter 7 goes on to consider how our unique personalities, lifestyles and values also guide us as consumers.

CHAPTERS AHEAD

Chapter 3 • Perception

Source: LensKiss/Shutterstock.

The European vacation has been wonderful, and this stop in Lisbon is no exception. Still, after two weeks of eating his way through some of the continent's finest pastry shops and restaurants, Gary's getting a bit of a craving for his family's favorite snack—a good old American box of Oreos and an ice-cold carton of milk. Unbeknownst to his wife, Janeen, he had stashed away some cookies "just in case"; this was the time to break them out.

Now all he needs is the milk. On an impulse, Gary decides to surprise Janeen with a mid-afternoon treat. He sneaks out of the hotel room while she's napping and finds the nearest *grosa.* When he heads to the store's small refrigerated section, though, he's puzzled—no milk here. Undaunted, Gary asks the clerk, *"Leite, por favor?"* The clerk quickly smiles and points to a rack in the middle of the store piled with little white square boxes. No, that can't be right—Gary resolves to work on his Portuguese. He repeats the question, and again he gets the same answer.

Finally, he investigates, and sure enough, he sees that the labels say they contain something called ultra-heat-treated (UHT) milk. Nasty! Who in the world would drink milk out of a little box that's been sitting on a warm shelf for who knows how long? Gary dejectedly returns to the hotel, his snack-time fantasies crumbling like so many stale cookies.

Sensation

Although news to Gary, many people in the world do drink milk out of a box every day. UHT, pasteurized milk that has been heated until the bacteria that cause it to spoil are destroyed, can last for 5 to 6 months without refrigeration if unopened. The milk tastes slightly sweeter than fresh milk but otherwise it's basically the same.

Shelf-stable milk is particularly popular in Europe, where there is less refrigerator space in homes and stores tend to carry less inventory than in the United States. Seven out of 10 Europeans drink it routinely. Manufacturers keep trying to crack the U.S. market as well, though analysts doubt their prospects. To begin with, milk consumption in the United States is declining steadily as teenagers choose soft drinks instead, even though the Milk Industry Foundation pumped $44 million into an advertising campaign to promote milk drinking ("Got Milk?").

Beyond that, it's hard to convince Americans to drink milk out of a box. In focus groups, U.S. consumers say they have trouble believing the milk is not spoiled or unsafe. In addition, they consider the square, quart-sized boxes more suitable for dry food. Nonetheless, many schools and fast-food chains do buy UHT milk because of its long shelf life.[1] Although Americans may not think twice about drinking a McDonald's McFlurry made with shelf-stable milk, it's still going to be a long, uphill battle to change their minds about the proper partner for a bagful of Oreos.

Whether we experience the taste of Oreos, the sight of a Chloé perfume ad, or the sound of the band Imagine Dragons, we live in a world overflowing with sensations. Wherever we turn, a symphony of colors, sounds, and odors bombards us. Some of the "notes" in this symphony occur naturally, such as the loud barking of a dog, the shades of the evening sky, or the heady smell of a rose bush. Others come from people: The person who plops down next to you in class might wear swirling tattoos, bright pink pants, and enough nasty perfume to make your eyes water.

Marketers certainly contribute to this commotion. Consumers are never far from pop-up ads, product packages, radio and television commercials, and billboards—all clamoring for our attention. Even movie theaters are getting into the act; some are installing moving seats, scent machines, and compressed air blasts to simulate the feeling of bullets flying by.[2]

Sometimes we go out of our way to experience "unusual" sensations: feeling thrills from bungee jumping; playing virtual reality games; or going to theme parks such as Universal Studios, which offers "Fear Factor Live" attractions in which vacationers swallow gross things or perform stomach-churning stunts.[3]

However, only a select few try to cram down as many peanut butter and banana sandwiches, Moon Pies, or cheesesteaks as (in)humanly possible in events sponsored by Major League Eating/Federation of Competitive Eating (MLE/FCE). Other sensation-seekers happily blast teeth-rattling Lupe Fiasco cuts from their booming car speakers. Each of us copes with this sensory bombardment by paying attention to some stimuli and tuning out

Contestants at an eating contest.
Source: David Mark Erickson/Corbis.

others. And, the messages to which we *do* pay attention often wind up affecting us differently from what the sponsors intended; we each put our personal "spin" on things as we assign meanings consistent with our own unique experiences, biases, and desires. This chapter focuses on the process of how we absorb sensations and then use these to interpret the surrounding world.

Sensation refers to the immediate response of our sensory receptors (eyes, ears, nose, mouth, fingers, skin) to basic stimuli such as light, color, sound, odor, and texture. **Perception** is the process by which people select, organize, and interpret these sensations. The study of perception, then, focuses on what we *add* to these raw sensations to give them meaning.

Our brains receive external stimuli, or *sensory inputs*, on a number of channels. We may see a billboard, hear a jingle, feel the softness of a cashmere sweater, taste a new flavor of ice cream, or smell a leather jacket. These inputs are the raw data that begin the perceptual process. Sensory data from the external environment (e.g., hearing a tune on the radio) can generate internal sensory experiences; a song might trigger a young man's memory of his first dance and bring to mind the smell of his date's perfume or the feel of her hair on his cheek.

Marketers' messages are more effective when they appeal to several senses. For example, in a recent study one group read ad copy for potato chips that only mentioned the taste, whereas another group's ad copy emphasized the product's smell and texture, in addition to its taste. The participants in the second group came away thinking the chips would taste better than did those whose ad message only focused on taste.[4]

Each product's unique sensory qualities help it to stand out from the competition, especially if the brand creates a unique association with the sensation. The Owens-Corning Fiberglass Corporation was the first company to trademark a color when it used bright pink for its insulation material; it adopted the Pink Panther as its spokescharacter.[5] Harley-Davidson actually tried (unsuccessfully) to trademark the distinctive sound a "hog" makes when it revs up.

Hedonic Consumption

These responses are an important part of **hedonic consumption**: multisensory, fantasy, and emotional aspects of consumers' interactions with products.[6] Remember that in earlier chapters we talked about how physical cues "prime" us to react even when we're not aware of this impact. The sensations we experience are **context effects** that subtly influence how we think about products we encounter. Here are some examples from consumer research:

- Respondents evaluated products more harshly when they stood on a tile floor rather than a carpeted floor.[7]
- Fans of romance movies rate them higher when they watch them in a cold room (the researchers explain this is because they compensate for the low physical temperature with psychological warmth the movie provides).[8]
- When a product is scented, consumers are more likely to remember other attributes about it after they encounter it.[9]

OBJECTIVE 3-1

The design of a product often is a key driver of its success or failure.

The sensory experiences we receive from products and services play an increasingly key role when we choose among competing options. As manufacturing costs go down and the amount of "stuff" that people accumulate goes up, consumers want to buy things that will provide hedonic value in addition to simply doing what they're designed to do. A *Dilbert* comic strip poked fun at this trend when it featured a product designer who declared: "Quality is yesterday's news. Today we focus on the emotional impact of the product." Fun aside, the new focus on emotional experience is consistent with psychological research finding that people prefer additional *experiences* to additional *possessions* as their incomes rise.[10]

Method used aesthetic innovations to shake up the stale household cleaners market.
Source: Courtesy of Method Products.

Net Profit

Augmented reality (AR) refers to media that superimpose one or more digital layers of data, images, or video over a physical object. If you've ever watched a three-dimensional (3D) movie with those clunky glasses, you've experienced one form of AR. Or, if you've seen that yellow line in an NFL game that shows the first down marker, you've also encountered AR in a simple form.

More likely, though, in the next few years you'll live in AR through your smartphone or tablet. New apps like Google Goggles (for Android phones) and Layar (for Android and Apple devices) impose a layer of words and pictures on whatever you see in your phone's viewer. Microsoft's HoloLens technology blends holograms with what you see in your physical space so that you can actually manipulate digital images—for example, a user who wants to assemble a piece of furniture or fix a broken sink can actually "see" where each part connects to the next through the goggles.[13]

AR apps open new worlds of information (and marketing communications). Do you want to know the bio of the singer you see on a CD cover? Who painted that cool mural in your local bar? How much did that house you were looking at eventually sell for? Just point your smartphone at each and the information will be superimposed on your screen.[14] AR is about to be big business: Analysts project that revenue from AR apps will hit $5.2 billion by 2017.[15]

The imminent explosion of **virtual reality (VR)** technology in the consumer market also is driving the integration between physical sensations and digital information. Unlike AR that delivers a combination of both sensory experiences, VR provides a totally immersive experience that transports the user into an entirely separate 3D environment. Facebook purchased the Oculus VR company in 2014, and this was just the first step in what promises to be an avalanche of commercially available VR technology from major companies including Samsung, Sony and Google.[16]

In this environment, form *is* function. Two young entrepreneurs named Adam Lowry and Eric Ryan discovered that basic truth when they quit their day jobs to develop a line of house-cleaning products they called Method. Cleaning products—what a yawn, right?

Think again: For years, companies such as Procter & Gamble have plodded along, peddling boring boxes of soap powder to generations of housewives who suffered in silence, scrubbing and buffing, yearning for the daily respite of martini time. Lowry and Ryan gambled that they could offer an alternative: cleaners in exotic scents such as cucumber, lavender, and ylang-ylang that come in aesthetically pleasing bottles. The bet paid off. Within two years, the partners were cleaning up, taking in more than $2 million in revenue. Shortly thereafter, they hit it big when Target contracted to sell Method products in its stores.[11]

There's a method to Target's madness. Design is no longer the province of uppercrust sophisticates who never got close enough to a cleaning product to be revolted by it. The store chain helped to make designers such as Karim Rashid, Michael Graves, Philippe Starck, Todd Oldham, and Isaac Mizrahi household names. In fact, recent research evidence suggests that our brains are wired to appreciate good design: Respondents who were hooked up to a brain apparatus called a functional magnetic resonance imaging (fMRI) scanner showed faster reaction times when they saw aesthetically pleasing packages even compared to well-known brands such as Coca-Cola.[12] Mass-market consumers thirst for great design, and they reward those companies that give it to them with their enthusiastic patronage and loyalty. From razor blades such as the Gillette Sensor to the Apple Watch and even to the lowly trashcan, design *is* substance. Form *is* function.

Sensory Marketing

When guests at Omni luxury hotels visit the hotel chain's Web site to reserve a room, they hear the sound of soft chimes playing. The signature scent of lemongrass and green tea hits them as they enter the lobby. In their rooms, they find eucalyptus bath salts and Sensation Bars, minibars stocked with items such as mojito-flavored jellybeans, and miniature Zen gardens.

Welcome to the new era of **sensory marketing**, where companies think carefully about the impact of sensations on our product experiences. From hotels to carmakers to brewers, companies recognize that our senses help us decide which products appeal to

A virtual reality headset.
Source: Rommel Canlas/123RF.

us—and which ones stand out from a host of similar offerings in the marketplace. In this section, we'll take a closer look at how some smart marketers use our sensory systems to create a competitive advantage.

Vision

Sure, Apple's products usually work pretty well—but that's not why many people buy them. Sleek styling and simple, compact features telegraph an aura of modernity, sophistication, and just plain "cool." Marketers rely heavily on visual elements in advertising,

Paintlist, a smartphone app from the Dutch Boy paint brand, evaluates music provided by users to suggest colors that it says evoke similar moods.
Source: Courtesy of Marcus Thomas, LLC.

store design, and packaging. They communicate meanings on the *visual channel* through a product's color, size, and styling.

Colors may even influence our emotions more directly. Evidence suggests that some colors (particularly red) create feelings of arousal and stimulate appetite, and others (such as blue) create more relaxing feelings. American Express launched its Blue card after its research found that people describe the color as "providing a sense of limitlessness and peace."[17] Advertisements of products presented against a backdrop of blue are better liked than the same ads shown against a red background, and cross-cultural research indicates a consistent preference for blue whether people live in Canada or Hong Kong.[18] People even link moral judgments to colors; in a study, respondents evaluated undesirable consumer behaviors less negatively when described on a red (compared with green) background while they evaluated desirable consumer behaviors more positively when described on a green (compared with red) background.[19]

CB AS I SEE IT

Malaika Brengman *Vrije Universiteit Brussel, Belgium*

As you go shopping the lighting of the interior and the colors on the walls are probably the last thing you pay attention to. Still, while hardly noticed, these ambient cues in our surroundings influence our behavior as consumers in an important way.

I became intrigued about this subject when a study we conducted revealed that recycle stores with the color yellow in their store interior appeared to perform better. Reading more on the issue, I discovered an interesting experiment where television sets were presented either in a blue-colored store environment or a red-colored one. Could that possibly impact sales? The findings of this

study showed that apparently store color does matter! More television sets were sold in the blue-colored store than in the red-colored one. And even more impressing: more expensive television sets were chosen in the blue store condition.

Of course I wanted to find out how this was possible and more in particular which colors generate what effects. But what is color actually? Color is essentially our perception of the reflection of light. Without light, we cannot perceive any colors. The shapes and colors of the objects we perceive around us help us make sense of it all. But, as these perceptions are formed not only through our eyes, but also for a large part in our brain, color does not only provide objective information about our environment, it also affects our thoughts and feelings... and ultimately even our consumption behavior.

Triggered by the question what exact colors retail managers should apply to lure in shoppers and to persuade them to buy, I devoted my doctoral dissertation to this topic. In spite of the fact that some earlier studies did find that color influences the behavior of retail shoppers, it was still not entirely clear what specific colors would be most beneficial. In fact, researchers have often drawn inferences regarding color effects testing only two or four particular tones. I intended to conduct a more rigorous study,

examining the specific effects of the three dimensions of color (pigment, saturation and value), by testing a total of 32 store color variants. The findings of this investigation confirmed that the more the consumer appreciates the colors in a shop, the longer he will linger there and the more money he will be prepared to spend. A positive feeling of excitement, evoked by the interior color, also tends to lead to approach behavior, a willingness to stay longer and explore the store more. Arousal can however also revert into tension and stress, which is experienced as unpleasant and leads to avoidance. According to our findings, vivid or dark store interiors are not to be advised, but rather light interiors are recommended because they bring about a pleasant, relaxed feeling, which is conducive to purchase behavior. While blue, green, yellow or orange interiors are also recommended because they bring about positive feelings, certain hues such as yellow-green and red can best be avoided because they arouse feelings of stress.

This study proves that decisions about the color of a store interior should not be taken lightly, since they really influence the emotions of the shoppers, and their subsequent purchase behavior. Shoppers may also need to realize that a pleasant store environment can induce them to spend more than intended, which may not be so good if you are on a budget.

People who complete tasks when the words or images appear on red backgrounds perform better when they have to remember details; however, they excel at tasks requiring an imaginative response when the words or images are displayed on blue backgrounds. Olympic athletes who wear red uniforms are more likely to defeat competitors in blue uniforms, and men rate women who wear red as more attractive than those who wear blue. In one study, interior designers created bars decorated primarily in red, yellow, or blue and invited people to choose one to hang out in. More people chose the yellow and red rooms, and these guests were more social and active—and ate more. In contrast, partygoers in the blue room stayed longer.[20] Maybe the moral is: Get your prof to give you multiple-choice exams on red paper, essays on blue paper, and then celebrate afterward in a red room!

Some reactions to color come from learned associations (which we'll tackle in the next chapter). In Western countries, black is the color of mourning, whereas in some Eastern countries, notably Japan, white plays this role. In addition, we associate the color black with power. Teams in both the National Football League and the National Hockey League who wear black uniforms are among the most aggressive; they consistently rank near the top of their leagues in penalties during the season.[21] And, researchers have found evidence for racial differences in preferences for white- versus black-colored products. [22]

Not surprisingly, there are gender differences in color preferences. People associate darker colors with males and lighter colors with females.[23] Women are drawn toward brighter tones and they are more sensitive to subtle shadings and patterns. Some scientists attribute this to biology; females see color better than males do, and men are 16 times more likely to be color-blind.

Age also influences our responsiveness to color. As we get older, our eyes mature and our vision takes on a yellow cast. Colors look duller to older people, so they prefer white and other bright tones. This helps to explain why mature consumers are much more likely to choose a white car; Lexus, which sells heavily in this market, makes 60 percent of its vehicles in white. The trend toward brighter and more complex colors also reflects the increasingly multicultural makeup of the United States. For example, Hispanics tend to prefer brighter colors as a reflection of the intense lighting conditions in Latin America; strong colors retain their character in strong sunlight.[24] That's why Procter & Gamble uses brighter colors in makeup it sells in Latin countries.

Teams that wear black uniforms tend to play more aggressively.

Source: Nicholas Piccillo/Fotolia.

Scientists and philosophers have talked about the meanings of colors since the time of Socrates in the 5th century BC, but it took Sir Isaac Newton in the early 17th century to shine light through a prism and reveal the color spectrum. Even then, Newton's observations weren't totally scientific; he identified seven major colors to be consistent with the number of planets known at that time, as well as the seven notes of the diatonic scale.

We now know that perceptions of a color depend on both its physical wavelength and how the mind responds to that stimulus. Yellow is in the middle of wavelengths the human eye can detect, so it is the brightest and attracts attention. The *Yellow Pages* originally were colored yellow to heighten the attention level of bored telephone operators.[25] However, our culture and even our language affect the colors we see. For example, the Welsh language has no words that correspond to green, blue, gray, or brown in English, but it uses other colors that English speakers don't (including one that covers part of green, part of gray, and the whole of our blue). The Hungarian language has two words for what we call red; Navajo has a single word for blue and green, but two words for black.[26]

Because colors elicit such strong emotional reactions, the choice of a *color palette* is a key issue in package design. Companies used to arrive at these choices casually. For example, Campbell's Soup made its familiar can in red and white because a company executive liked the football uniforms at Cornell University! Today, however, color choices are a serious business. These decisions help to "color" our expectations of what's inside the package. When it launched a white cheese as a "sister product" to an existing blue "Castello" cheese, a Danish company introduced it in a red package under the name of Castello Bianco. They chose this color to provide maximum visibility on store shelves. Although taste tests were positive, sales were disappointing. A subsequent analysis of consumer interpretations showed that the red packaging and the name gave the consumers wrong associations with the product type and its degree of sweetness. Danish consumers had trouble associating the color red with the white cheese. Also, the name *Bianco* connoted a sweetness that was incompatible with the actual taste of the product. The company relaunched it in a white package and named it "White Castello." Almost immediately, sales more than doubled.[27]

Some color combinations come to be so strongly associated with a corporation that they become known as the company's **trade dress**, and courts may even grant exclusive use of specific color combinations: Eastman Kodak's trade dress protects its usage of its distinctive yellow, black, and red boxes. As a rule, however, judges grant trade dress protection only when consumers might be confused about what they buy because of similar coloration of a competitor's packages.[28]

Of course, fashion trends strongly influence our color preferences, so it's no surprise that we tend to encounter a "hot" color on clothing and in home designs in one season that something else replaces the next season (as when the *fashionistas* proclaim, "Brown is the new black!" or fans of the TV series counter with, "No, *Orange is the New Black*"). These styles do not happen by accident; most people don't know (but now *you* do) that a handful of firms produce **color forecasts** that manufacturers and retailers buy so they can be sure they stock up on the next hot hue. For example, Pantone, Inc. (one of these color arbiters) identified "Marsala"—a naturally robust and earthy wine red—as the color of the year for 2015.[29] Table 3.1 summarizes how experts link specific colors to marketing contexts.

Dollars and Scents

Odors stir emotions or create a calming feeling. They invoke memories or relieve stress. Die-hard New York Yankees fans can buy fragrances to bring back that stadium feeling: "New York Yankees" (for him) and "New York Yankees For Her."[30] As scientists continue to discover the powerful effects of smell on behavior, marketers come up with ingenious ways to exploit these connections. This form of sensory marketing takes interesting turns as manufacturers find new ways to put scents into products, including men's suits, lingerie, detergents, and aircraft cabins. And this just in: Burger King in Japan sells a "Flame Grilled" fragrance to customers who want to smell like a Whopper.[31]

One study found that consumers who viewed ads for either flowers or chocolate and who also were exposed to flowery or chocolaty odors spent more time processing the

TABLE 3. 1	Marketing Applications of Colors	
Color	**Associations**	**Marketing Applications**
Yellow	Optimistic and youthful	Used to grab window shoppers' attention
Red	Energy	Often seen in clearance sales
Blue	Trust and security	Banks
Green	Wealth	Used to create relaxation in stores
Orange	Aggressive	Call to action: subscribe, buy or sell
Black	Powerful and sleek	Luxury products
Purple	Soothing	Beauty or anti-aging products

Source: Adapted from Leo Widrich, "Why Is Facebook Blue? The Science Behind Colors in Marketing," *Fast Company* (May 6, 2013), http://www.fastcompany.com/3009317/why-is-facebook-blue-the-science-behind-colors-in-marketing?partner=newsletter, accessed February 23, 2015.

product information and were more likely to try different alternatives within each product category.[32] Another reported that subjects showed higher recall of a test brand's attributes if it was embedded with a scent—and this effect persisted as long as two weeks after the experiment.[33] Retailers like Hugo Boss often pump a "signature" scent into their stores; one study reported that "warm scents" such as vanilla or cinnamon as opposed to "cool scents" such as peppermint enhance shoppers' purchases of premium brands.[34]

Some of our responses to scents result from early associations that call up good or bad feelings, and that explains why businesses explore connections among smell, memory, and mood.[35] Researchers for Folgers found that for many people the smell of coffee summons up childhood memories of their mothers cooking breakfast, so the aroma reminds them of home. The company turned this insight into a commercial in which a young man in an army uniform arrives home early one morning. He goes to the kitchen, opens a Folgers' package, and the aroma wafts upstairs. His mother opens her eyes, smiles, and exclaims, "He's home!"[36]

We process fragrance cues in the *limbic system*, the most primitive part of the brain and the place where we experience immediate emotions. One study even found that the scent of fresh cinnamon buns induced sexual arousal in a sample of male students![37] In another study, women sniffed T-shirts that men had worn for two days (wonder how much they paid them to do that?) and reported which they preferred. The women were most attracted to the odor of men who were genetically similar to them, though not *too* similar. The researchers claimed the findings were evidence that we are "wired" to select compatible mates, but not those so similar as to cause inbreeding problems.[38]

OBJECTIVE 3-2

Products and commercial messages often appeal to our senses, but because of the profusion of these messages we don't notice most of them.

Sound

BMW recently began to use an **audio watermark** at the end of TV and radio ads around the world. "The company wants to establish what the brand sounds like," so all of its messages end with a melody "underscored by two distinctive bass tones that form the sound logo's melodic and rhythmic basis." BMW claims this sound signature represents "sheer driving pleasure."[39]

Music and other sounds affect people's feelings and behaviors. Some marketers who come up with brand names pay attention to **sound symbolism**; the process by which the way a word sounds influences our assumptions about what it describes and attributes, such as size. For example, consumers are more likely to recognize brand names that begin with a hard consonant like a K (Kellogg's) or P (Pepsi). We also tend to associate certain vowel and consonant sounds (or *phonemes*) with perceptions of large and small size. Mental rehearsal of prices containing numbers with small phonemes results in overestimation of price discounts, whereas mental rehearsal of prices containing numbers with large phonemes results in underestimation.[40] One study even found that the sound symbolism in a stock's ticker symbol helped to predict the company's performance during its first year of trading.[41]

Touch

Pretend for a moment that you are shopping for a sweater on the Internet. You navigate to http://www.landsend.com, scroll through the cardigans, and pause at one that appeals to you. You click on the sweater for more information. A larger photo appears, and the caption reads: "Imagine holding this sweater, feeling the soft, 100% cotton in your hands." What if you did as instructed? Would your perception of the sweater be any different than if you had not imagined feeling it?

One study demonstrated the potential power of touch: Britain's Asda grocery chain removed the wrapping from several brands of toilet tissue in its stores so that shoppers could feel and compare textures. The result, the retailer says, was soaring sales for its own in-store brand, resulting in a 50 percent increase in shelf space for the line.[42]

It seems that encouraging shoppers to touch a product encourages them to imagine they own it, and researchers know that people value things more highly if they own them: This is known as the **endowment effect**. One set of researchers reported that participants who simply touched an item (an inexpensive coffee mug) for 30 seconds or less created a greater level of attachment to the product; this connection in turn boosted what they were willing to pay for it.[43] Indeed, the power of touch even translates to online shopping where touchscreens create a stronger feeling of psychological ownership compared to products consumers explore using a touchpad or a mouse.[44]

Sensations that reach the skin, whether from a luxurious massage or the bite of a winter wind, stimulate or relax us. Researchers even have shown that touch can influence sales interactions. In one study, diners whom waitstaff touched gave bigger tips, and the same researchers reported that food demonstrators in a supermarket who lightly touched customers had better luck in getting shoppers to try a new snack product and to redeem coupons for the brand.[45] On the other hand, an accidental touch from a stranger (especially a male) leads to more negative evaluations of products a shopper encounters in a store.[46]

Some anthropologists view our experience of touch much like a primal language, one we learn well before writing and speech. Indeed, researchers are starting to identify the important role the **haptic** (touch) sense plays in consumer behavior. Haptic senses appear to moderate the relationship between product experience and judgment confidence. This confirms the commonsense notion that we're more sure about what we perceive when we can touch it (a major problem for those who sell products online). Individuals who score high on a "Need for Touch" (NFT) scale are especially sensitive to the haptic dimension. These people respond positively to such statements as:

- When walking through stores, I can't help touching all kinds of products.
- Touching products can be fun.
- I feel more comfortable purchasing a product after physically examining it.[47]

Some Japanese companies take this idea a step farther with their practice of **Kansei engineering**, a philosophy that translates customers' feelings into design elements. The designers of the Mazda Miata focused on young drivers who saw the car as an extension of their body, a sensation they call "horse and rider as one." After extensive research they discovered that making the stick shift exactly 9.5 centimeters long conveys the optimal feeling of sportiness and control.[48]

Taste

Our taste receptors obviously contribute to our experience of many products. So-called "flavor houses" develop new concoctions to please the changing palates of consumers.

The classic, contoured Coca-Cola bottle also attests to the power of touch. The bottle was designed approximately 90 years ago to satisfy the request of a U.S. bottler for a soft-drink container that people could identify even in the dark.
Source: © Rufus Stone/Alamy.

Scientists are right behind them as they build new devices to test these flavors. Alpha M.O.S. sells a sophisticated electronic tongue for tasting, and the company is working on what its executives call an *electronic mouth*, complete with artificial saliva, to chew food and to dissect its flavor. Coca-Cola and PepsiCo use the tongue to test the quality of corn

Product designers continue to experiment with natural user interfaces such as touchscreens.
Source: grafvision/shutterstock.com.

syrups, and Bristol-Myers Squibb and Roche use the device to formulate medicines that don't taste bitter.[50]

Cultural factors also determine the tastes we find desirable. A food item's image and the values we attach to it (such as how vegans regard beef menu items, which is not kindly) influence how we experience the actual taste.[51] For example, consumers' greater appreciation of different ethnic dishes contributes to increased desires for spicy foods, so the quest for the ultimate pepper sauce continues. More than 50 stores in the United States supply fiery concoctions with names such as Sting and Linger, Hell in a Jar, and Religious Experience (comes in Original, Hot, and Wrath).[52]

In India, salt combats the sensory assault of spicy food.

Source: Courtesy of Taproot India. Contributors: Santosh Padhi, Agnello Dias, Pranan Bhide, and Chintan Ruparel.

As the cost of raw materials skyrockets as a result of shortages caused by natural disasters such as the Tokyo earthquake and manmade ones like the conflict in the Middle East, some companies try to camouflage price increases as they shrink the size of packages instead of charging more. Sometimes marketers use code words to announce a change: they may label the smaller packages as "green" because there is less plastic or cardboard in a smaller box, more "portable" when they squeeze products into little carry bags, or "healthier" because smaller amounts translate into fewer calories. For example, Kraft brought out "Fresh Stacks" packages for its Nabisco Premium saltines and Honey Maid graham crackers. Each holds about 15 percent fewer crackers than the standard boxes for the same price. But, Kraft notes that because the new packages include more sleeves of crackers, they are more portable—and the company notes that as an added benefit the smaller boxes supply crackers that will be fresher when you get around to eating them. A packaging expert noted that typically, when the economy recovers, companies respond with a new "jumbo-size" product that is usually even more expensive per ounce. Then the process begins again: "It's a continuous cycle, where at some point the smallest package offered becomes so small that perhaps they're phased out and replaced by the medium-size package, which has been shrunk down."[53]

OBJECTIVE 3-3
Perception is a three-stage process that translates raw stimuli into meaning.

The Stages of Perception

Like computers, we undergo stages of *information processing* in which we input and store stimuli. Unlike computers, though, we do *not* passively process whatever information happens to be present. In the first place, we notice only a small number of the stimuli in our environment, simply because there are so many different ones out there vying for our attention. Of those we do notice, we attend to an even smaller number—and we might not process the stimuli that do enter consciousness objectively. Each individual interprets the meaning of a stimulus in a manner consistent with his or her own unique biases, needs, and experiences. As Figure 3.1 shows, these three stages of *exposure, attention*, and *interpretation* make up the process of perception.

Stage 1: Exposure

Exposure occurs when a stimulus comes within the range of someone's sensory receptors. Consumers concentrate on some stimuli, are unaware of others, and even go out of their way to ignore some messages. We notice stimuli that come within range for even a short time—*if* we so choose. However, getting a message noticed in such a short time (or even in a longer one) is no mean feat.

Sensory Thresholds

Before we consider what else people may choose not to perceive, let's consider what they are *capable* of perceiving. By this we mean that stimuli may be above or below a person's **sensory threshold** which is the point at which it is strong enough to make a conscious impact in his or her awareness.

If you have ever blown a dog whistle and watched your pooch respond to a sound you cannot hear, you won't be surprised to learn that there are some stimuli that people simply can't perceive. Some of us pick up sensory information that others, whose sensory channels have diminished because of disability or age, cannot. The science of **psychophysics** focuses on how people integrate the physical environment into their personal, subjective worlds.

It sounds like a great name for a rock band, but the **absolute threshold** refers to the minimum amount of stimulation a person can detect on a given sensory channel. The sound a dog whistle emits is at too high a frequency for human ears to pick up, so this stimulus is beyond our auditory absolute threshold. The absolute threshold is an important consideration when we design marketing stimuli. A highway billboard might have the most entertaining copy ever written, but this genius is wasted if the print is too small for passing motorists to see it. In contrast, the **differential threshold** refers to the ability of a sensory system to detect changes in or differences between two stimuli. The minimum difference we can detect between two stimuli is the **just noticeable difference (j.n.d.)**.

Figure 3.1 AN OVERVIEW OF THE PERCEPTUAL PROCESS

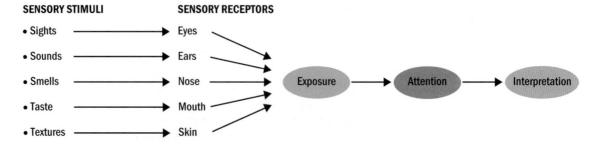

Figure 3.2 THE PEPSI LOGO OVER TIME
Source: Pepsi is a registered trademark of PepsiCo, Inc. Used with permission.

The dual issues of *if* and *when* consumers will notice a difference between two stimuli is relevant to many marketing situations. Sometimes a marketer may want to ensure that consumers notice a change, such as when a retailer offers merchandise at a discount. In other situations, the marketer may want to downplay the fact that it has made a change, such as when a store raises a price or a manufacturer reduces the size of a package. When a brand tries to modernize its logo, it has to walk a fine line because consumers tend to get tired of old-fashioned designs but they still want to be able to identify the familiar product. Figure 3.2 shows the evolution of the Pepsi label over time.

A consumer's ability to detect a difference between two stimuli is relative. A whispered conversation that might be unintelligible on a noisy street can suddenly become public and embarrassingly loud in a quiet library. It is the *relative difference* between the decibel level of the conversation and its surroundings, rather than the absolute loudness of the conversation itself, that determines whether the stimulus will register.

In the 19th century, a psychophysicist named Ernst Weber found that the amount of change required for the perceiver to notice a change systematically relates to the intensity of the original stimulus. The stronger the initial stimulus, the greater a change must be for us to notice it. This relationship is **Weber's Law**.

Consider how Weber's Law works for a product when it goes on sale. If a retailer believes that a markdown should be at least 20 percent for the reduction to make an impact on shoppers, it should cut the price on a pair of socks that retails for $10 to $8 (a $2 discount) for shoppers to realize a difference. However, a sports coat that sells for $100 would not benefit from a $2 discount; the retailer would have to mark it down $20 to achieve the same impact.

Weber's Law, ironically, is a challenge to green marketers who try to reduce the sizes of packages when they produce concentrated (and more earth-friendly) versions of

This Canadian beer ad pokes fun at subliminal advertising.
Source: © 2005. Molson USA, LLC.

YOU HAVE JUST BEEN EXPOSED TO MOLSON SUBLIMINAL ADVERTISING.

AT FIRST GLANCE, THIS IMAGE APPEARS MERELY CRISP AND REFRESHING. BUT WHAT HAPPENS WHEN WE MAGNIFY THE IMAGE BY POWER OF 10?

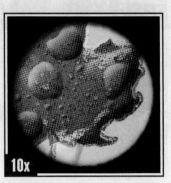

10x

NOTHING YET. JUST A COUPLE OF SWEAT BEADS ON A LABEL.

10,000x

BUT WE DIDN'T STOP THERE. WE EMBEDDED YET ANOTHER IMAGE DESIGNED TO MAKE YOU THIRST FOR JOHN MOLSON'S DELICIOUS BEER.

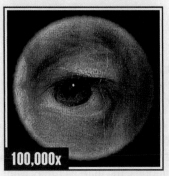

100,000x

DIFFICULT TO SEE AT THIS MAGNIFICATION, LET'S GO IN FURTHER.

their products. Makers of laundry detergent brands have to convince their customers to pay the same price for about half the detergent. Also, because of pressure from powerful retailers such as Walmart that want to fit more bottles on their shelves, the size of detergent bottles is shrinking significantly. Procter & Gamble, Unilever and Henkel all maintain that their new concentrated versions will allow people to wash the same number of loads with half the detergent. One perceptual trick they're using to try to convince consumers of this is the redesign of the bottle cap: Both P&G and Church & Dwight use a cap with a broader base and shorter sides to persuade consumers that they need a smaller amount.[54]

OBJECTIVE 3-4

Subliminal advertising is a controversial—but largely ineffective—way to talk to consumers.

Subliminal Perception

A German ad agency and the broadcaster Sky Deutschland are teaming up on a new advertising platform that targets weary commuters who rest their heads against the windows

YOU MAY NOT BE AWARE OF IT, BUT RIGHT NOW YOUR SUBCONSCIOUS IS JONESING FOR A COLD, CRISP MOLSON. WHY? BECAUSE WE SLIPPED THROUGH THE BACK DOOR OF YOUR BRAIN AND PLANTED A FEW VISUAL CUES DEEP IN YOUR MIND. ANY OF THE IMAGES BELOW SEEM STRANGELY FAMILIAR?

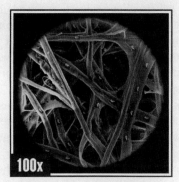

100x

MAGNIFIED AT 100X HOWEVER, WE BEGIN TO SEE SOMETHING.

1,000x

AN IMAGE OF JOHN MOLSON PRINTED ON THE PAPER FIBER OF THE BEER LABEL. THOUGH MINUTE, YOUR BRAIN PICKED UP ON THIS SUBLIMINAL CUE TO A 219-YEAR HERITAGE OF BREWING GREAT-TASTING BEER.

1,000,000x

AH, THERE IT IS: AN IMAGE OF PEOPLE SOCIALIZING WITH AN ICE-COLD MOLSON.

10,000,000x

A MICROSCOPIC REMINDER THAT MOLSON HAS BEEN BRINGING FRIENDS TOGETHER SINCE 1786. SHOULD YOU SUDDENLY AWAKEN IN A CROWDED BAR ORDERING A ROUND OF MOLSON FOR EVERYONE, WE DID THAT. AND YOU'RE WELCOME.

of train cars. They call it the "talking window"; it uses "bond conduction technology" that emits vibrations the brain reads as sounds. As the commuter starts to nod off, he or she will suddenly hear a voice inside their head that pitches a product.[55] That will get your attention!

Most marketers want to create messages *above* consumers' thresholds so people will notice them. Ironically, a good number of consumers instead believe that marketers design many advertising messages so they will be perceived unconsciously, or *below* the threshold of recognition. Another word for threshold is *limen*, and we term stimuli that fall below the limen *subliminal*. **Subliminal perception** refers to a stimulus below the level of the consumer's awareness.

This topic has captivated the public for more than 50 years, despite the fact that there is virtually no proof that this process has *any* effect on consumer behavior. A survey of U.S. consumers found that almost two-thirds believe in the existence of subliminal advertising, and more than one-half are convinced that this technique can get them to buy things they do not really want.[56] ABC rejected a Kentucky Fried Chicken (KFC) commercial that invited viewers to slowly replay the ad to find a secret message, citing the network's long-standing policy against subliminal advertising. KFC argued that the ad wasn't subliminal at all because the company told viewers about the message and how to find it. The network wasn't convinced.[57]

Like this KFC ad, most examples of subliminal advertising that people "discover" are not subliminal at all—on the contrary, the images are quite apparent. Remember, if you can see it or hear it, it's not subliminal; the stimulus is above the level of conscious awareness. Nonetheless, the continuing controversy about subliminal persuasion has been important in shaping the public's beliefs about advertisers' and market-ers' abilities to manipulate consumers against their will. A recent kerfuffle generated by a McDonald's Happy Meal toy illustrates that we tend to see or hear what we are looking for: When the company released a toy Minion (from the popular *Despicable Me* movie series), some outraged parents stated it was sending a "subliminal mes-sage" to their children. They claim that it speaks gibberish that sounds a lot like "what the" and a word that rhymes with duck. McDonald's response: "Minions speak 'Minionese' which is a random combination of many languages and nonsense words and sounds.... Any perceived similarities to words used within the English language is purely coincidental."[58]

Marketers supposedly send subliminal messages on both visual and aural channels. **Embeds** are tiny figures they insert into magazine advertising via high-speed photogra-phy or airbrushing. These hidden images, usually of a sexual nature, supposedly exert strong but unconscious influences on innocent readers. Some limited evidence hints at the possibility that embeds can alter the moods of men when they're exposed to sexually suggestive subliminal images, but the effect (if any) is subtle—and may even work in the opposite direction if this creates negative feelings among viewers.[59] To date, the only real impact of this interest in hidden messages is to sell more copies of "exposés" written by a few authors and to make some consumers (and students taking a consumer behavior class) look a bit more closely at print ads, perhaps seeing whatever their imaginations lead them to see.

Some research by clinical psychologists suggests that subliminal messages can influ-ence people under specific conditions, though it is doubtful that these techniques would be of much use in most marketing contexts. For this kind of message to have a prayer of working, an advertiser has to tailor it specifically to an individual rather than the mass messages suitable for the general public.[60] The stimulus should also be as close to the liminal threshold as possible. Here are other discouraging factors:

- There are wide individual differences in threshold levels. For a message to avoid con-scious detection by consumers who have low thresholds, it would have to be so weak that it would not reach those who have high thresholds.
- Advertisers lack control over consumers' distance and position from a screen. In a movie theater, for example, only a small portion of the audience would be in exactly the right seats to be exposed to a subliminal message.
- The viewer must pay absolute attention to the stimulus. People who watch a television program or a movie typically shift their attention periodically, and they might not even notice when the stimulus appears.
- Even if the advertiser induces the desired effect, it works only at a general level. For example, a message might increase a person's thirst—but not necessarily for a specific drink. Because the stimulus just affects a basic drive, a marketer could find that after all the bother and expense of creating a subliminal message, demand for competitors' products increases as well!

Clearly, there are better ways to get our attention—let's see how.

Stage 2: Attention

As you sit in a lecture, you might find your mind wandering (yes, even you!). One minute you are concentrating on the professor's words, and the next you catch yourself daydreaming about the upcoming weekend. Suddenly, you tune back in as you hear your name being spoken. Fortunately, it's a false alarm—the professor has called on another "victim" who has the same first name. But she's got your attention now.

Attention refers to the extent to which processing activity is devoted to a particular stimulus. As you know from sitting through both interesting and "less interesting" lectures, this allocation can vary depending on both the characteristics of the stimulus (i.e., the lecture itself) and the recipient (i.e., your mental state at the time).

Although we live in an "information society," we can have too much of a good thing. Consumers often live in a state of **sensory overload**; we are exposed to far more information than we can process. In our society, much of this bombardment comes from commercial sources, and the competition for our attention steadily increases. The average adult is exposed to about 3,500 pieces of advertising information every single day—up from about 560 per day 30 years ago.

Are you a **media snacker**? A recent study found that consumers in their 20s ("digital natives") switch media venues about 27 times per nonworking hour—the equivalent of more than 13 times during a standard half-hour TV show. As a Unilever marketing executive put it, "If you have consumers who are snacking on short amounts of time with different types of media channels, we have to think about how to communicate in short, 'snack-like' bits of messaging."[61] That means the fight for your attention—or what some marketers refer to as an **eyeball economy**—gets tougher every day.

Multitasking

Getting the attention of young people in particular is a challenge—as your professor probably knows! A large proportion of teens report that they engage in **multitasking**, where they process information from more than one medium at a time as they alternate among their cell phones, TVs, and laptops.[63] One study observed 400 people for a day and found that 96 percent of them were multitasking about a third of the time they used media.[64]

What impact does all this multitasking have on consumers' ability to absorb, retain, and understand information? One possible consequence: These bursts of stimulation provoke the body to secrete the dopamine hormone, which is addicting. When we go without these squirts, we feel bored. Some scientists warn that our cravings for more stimulation distract us from more prolonged thought processes and reduce our ability to concentrate (don't text and drive!). Researchers find that heavy multitaskers have more trouble focusing, and they experience more stress. One study found that people who are interrupted by email report significantly more stress than those who were allowed to focus on a task.[65]

Before you panic, there is some good news: Evidence suggests that the brains of Internet users become more efficient at finding information, whereas some videogame players develop better eyesight. One team of researchers found that players of fast-paced video games could track the movement of a third more objects on a screen than non-players. They say the games can improve reaction and the ability to pick out details amid clutter. For better or worse, technology seems to be rewiring our brains to try to pay attention to more stimuli. Today we consume three times as much information each day as people did in 1960. We constantly shift attention: Computer users at work change windows or check email or other programs nearly 37 times an hour. Computer users visit an average of 40 Web sites a day.[66]

Marketers constantly search for ways to break through the clutter and grab people's attention. Some tactics are straightforward, such as when manufacturers try to get their brands shelved at eye level in a store and toward the center of a display because they know that is where shoppers are most likely to look.[67] In the online world, advertisers keep innovating to get visitors to watch their messages. One of the most popular today

Marketing Pitfall

If you watch TV with a digital video recorder (DVR), you're 25 percent more likely to fast-forward past ads that don't interest you immediately. Another 25 percent of DVR users don't watch an entire commercial if it doesn't draw them in right away—no matter how entertaining it gets by the end. Ads that start out with a captivating story are more likely to hold an audience compared to those that get to the point more slowly. This finding may cast doubt on traditional ratings of advertisements where viewers in laboratory settings are forced to watch an entire commercial—in real life they may just zap through it.[62]

CB AS I SEE IT

Michel Wedel *University of Maryland*

Front-facing cameras are now integrated in almost all computers and mobile devices. Software that analyzes the images captured by these cameras enables consumers' eye movements and facial expressions to be recorded. This has made remote eye tracking studies on large panels of respondents for commercial and academic marketing research possible. But moreover, in a few years from now, this new technology will have become an integrated part of consumers' everyday lives. It will not only be implemented on laptop and desktop computers, but also on smartphones, tablets, digital billboards, kiosks, and smart TVs.

Users will interact with these devices through gaze- and voice-control. Much of this is already possible.

Software that records where consumers look can support visual cues and automatic alerts to direct consumer search during day-to-day tasks. This may help to make daily life safer, simpler, and more enjoyable. On digital devices, consumers will be able use their gaze to manipulate 3D images of objects, people, and virtual displays of public places and stores. For entertainment and education, they will be able to interact with avatars by looking at them. The avatar smiles when the viewer smiles and follows the viewer's gaze. Face and gaze recording can be used to improve focus and comprehension in real-time. Explanations may appear when comprehension is slow and gaze-cues may direct viewers' gaze to relevant materials and improve focus and comprehension. Recommendation engines will recommend news articles, blogs, books and reviews, based on what a user has looked at previously and what emotions were expressed. Face and gaze recording will also improve the targeting of marketing efforts. Gaze-based rendering and 3D vision will enhance online and virtual shopping experiences. Attentive and interactive TV sets, billboards, digital ads, and digital point of sale devices will adapt dynamically to the viewers' gaze, facial expression, and head- and body-movements to deliver commercial messages and services on electronic devices that are tailored to their moment-to-moment interests and emotions.

This new field of **automated attention analysis (AAA)**, the automated recording of how long people look at images, words, people, places and products, if their pupils dilate, how their heads and postures change, how fast they blink, and what emotions they show, will explode information about the visual behavior in consumers' day-to-day lives. The revolution in big gaze and face recording data will be similar to the revolution in Internet click-stream data that we have seen in the past decades. That wealth of data will be of great value to market research companies, manufacturers, service providers and retailers, and enable them to better tailor products, services and marketing effort to individual consumers' momentary interests and experiences. But, unleashing the promise of AAA will require academic developments in two interconnected areas: (1) computing procedures and statistical models to analyze gaze and face data based on (2) consumer behavior theory that explains visual attention and facial expressions in these new natural contexts. Then, unprecedented new insights into consumer information processing and decision making will become available that hold the promise of improving marketing effectiveness and consumer welfare.

is **rich media**; the use of animated.gif files or video clips to grab viewers' attention. LowerMyBills.com is notorious for its endless loops of silhouetted dancers and surprised office workers, whereas other ads spring into action when you move the cursor over them. Other rich media are online versions of familiar TV commercials that sit frozen on the Web site until you click them. *Teaser ads*, much like those you see on TV that give you a taste of the story but make you return later for the rest, also turn up on Web sites.[68]

Because the brain's capacity to process information is limited, consumers are selective about what they pay attention to. The process of **perceptual selection** means that people attend to only a small portion of the stimuli to which they are exposed. Consumers practice a form of "psychic economy" as they pick and choose among stimuli to avoid being overwhelmed. How do we choose? Both personal and stimulus factors help to decide.

Personal Selection Factors

How do marketers seem to "know" when you're hungry and choose those times to bombard you with food ads? The answer is they don't—at least not yet. **Perceptual vigilance** means we are more likely to be aware of stimuli that relate to our current needs.

The flip side of perceptual vigilance is **perceptual defense**. This means that we tend to see what we want to see—and we don't see what we don't want to see. If a stimulus threatens us in some way, we may not process it, or we may distort its meaning so that it's more acceptable. For example, a heavy smoker may block out images of cancer-scarred lungs because these vivid reminders hit a bit too close to home.

Still another factor is **adaptation**, which is the degree to which consumers continue to notice a stimulus over time. The process of adaptation occurs when we no longer pay attention to a stimulus because it is so familiar. A consumer can "habituate" and require increasingly stronger "doses" of a stimulus to notice it. A commuter who is en route to work might read a billboard message when the board is first installed, but after a few days it simply becomes part of the passing scenery. Several factors can lead to adaptation:

- **Intensity**—Less-intense stimuli (e.g., soft sounds or dim colors) habituate because they have less sensory impact.
- **Discrimination**—Simple stimuli habituate because they do not require attention to detail.
- **Exposure**—Frequently encountered stimuli habituate as the rate of exposure increases.
- **Relevance**—Stimuli that are irrelevant or unimportant habituate because they fail to attract attention.

Stimulus Selection Factors

In addition to the receiver's mind-set, characteristics of the stimulus itself play an important role to determine what we notice and what we ignore. Marketers need to understand these factors so they can create messages and packages that will have a better chance to cut through the clutter. For example, when researchers used infrared eye-tracking equipment to measure what ads consumers look at, they found that visually complex ads are more likely to capture attention.[69]

In general, we are more likely to notice stimuli that differ from others around them (remember Weber's Law). A message creates **contrast** in several ways:

- **Size**—The size of the stimulus itself in contrast to the competition helps to determine if it will command attention. Readership of a magazine ad increases in proportion to the size of the ad.[70]
- **Color**—As we've seen, color is a powerful way to draw attention to a product or to give it a distinct identity. Black & Decker developed a line of tools it called DeWalt to target the residential construction industry. The company colored the new line yellow instead of black; this made the equipment stand out against other "dull" tools.[71]
- **Position**—Not surprisingly, we stand a better chance of noticing stimuli that are in places we're more likely to look. That's why the competition is so heated among suppliers to have their products displayed in stores at eye level. In magazines, ads that are placed toward the front of the issue, preferably on the right-hand side, also win out in the race for readers' attention. (Hint: The next time you read a magazine, notice which pages you're more likely to spend time looking at.)[72] A study that tracked consumers' eye movements as they scanned telephone directories also illustrates the importance of message position. Consumers scanned listings in alphabetical order, and they noticed 93 percent of quarter-page display ads but only 26 percent of plain listings. Their eyes were drawn to color ads first, and these were viewed longer than black-and-white ones. In addition, subjects spent 54 percent more time viewing ads for businesses they ended up choosing, which illustrates the influence of attention on subsequent product choice.[73] Another study reported that advertisers can increase brand recall and choice if they change the location of brand logos and product depictions across ad exposures.[74] And products that are located in the center of a person's field of vision are more likely to receive attention.[75]

Position also is important in online advertising. Sophisticated eye-tracking studies clearly show that most search engine users view only a limited number of search results. When the typical shopper looks at a search page, his or her eye travels across the top of the search result, returns to the left of the screen, and then travels down to the last item shown on the screen without scrolling. Search engine marketers call this space on the screen where we are virtually guaranteed to view listings the **golden triangle** (see Figure 3.3).[76]

● **Novelty**—Stimuli that appear in unexpected ways or places tend to grab our attention. Packages that "stand out" visually on store shelves have an advantage, especially when the consumer doesn't have a strong preference for brands in the category and he or she needs to make rapid decisions.[77] One solution is to put ads in unconventional places, where there will be less competition for attention. These places include the backs of shopping carts, walls of tunnels, floors of sports stadiums, and yes, even public restrooms.[78] An outdoor advertising agency in London constructs huge ads in deserts and farm fields adjacent to airports so that passengers who look out the window can't help but pay attention. It prints the digital ads on pieces of PVC mesh that sit on frames a few inches above the ground.[79]

Figure 3.3 THE GOLDEN TRIANGLE

Eye-tracking studies reveal that people typically spend most of their time on a website looking at the "golden triangle" outlined by yellow, orange and red.

Source: Enquiro Search Solutions, Inc. (Now Mediative Performance LP).

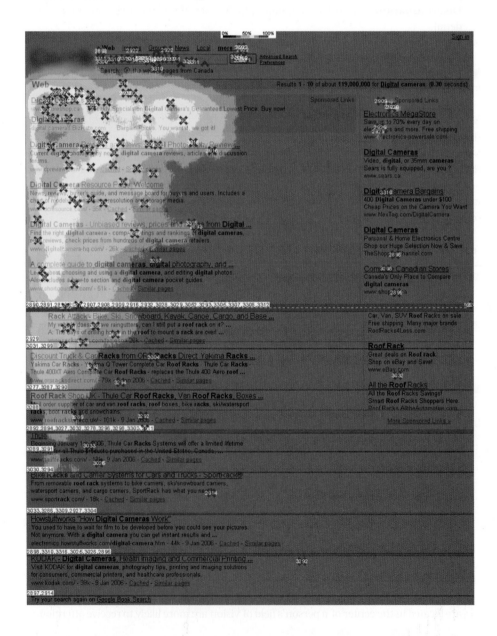

Indeed, one study indicates that novelty in the form of interruptions actually *intensifies* our experiences; distraction increases our enjoyment of pleasant stimuli because it amplifies our dislike of unpleasant stimuli. According to this research, people actually enjoy TV shows *more* when commercials interrupt them. A group of undergraduates watched an episode of an old sitcom (*Taxi*) with which they were unfamiliar. Half viewed the original broadcast, which included ads for a jeweler, a lawyer, and other businesses; the other half saw the show with all commercials deleted. Students who saw the original actually gave it higher evaluations. The researchers found a similar pattern when they interrupted people who were getting a massage. In contrast, subjects reported that the irritating sound of a vacuum cleaner was even worse when they got a break from listening to it and then had to hear it resume! The researchers interpret these results as the outcome of adaptation: We experience events more intensely at first but then get used to them. When we experience an interruption and then start over, we revert to the original intensity level.[80]

<table>
<tr><td>

OBJECTIVE 3-5

We interpret the stimuli to which we do pay attention according to learned patterns and expectations.

</td></tr>
</table>

Stage 3: Interpretation

Interpretation refers to the meanings we assign to sensory stimuli. Just as people differ in terms of the stimuli that they perceive, the meanings we assign to these stimuli vary as well. Many of these meanings depend on our socialization within a society: Even sensory perception is culturally specific. A team of anthropologists created a "kit" of stimuli to compare what people around the world perceive; this included color chips, scratch-and-sniff cards, sounds recorded at different frequencies, and so on. When they exposed the same stimuli to people in more than 20 different cultures, the results were dramatic: For example, prior research on mostly English-speaking people indicated that the typical person is not good at identifying the smell of everyday things like coffee, peanut butter, and chocolate; they usually identify about half of them correctly. However, people who live on the Malay Peninsula were more accurate.

Language differences drive some of these contrasts. The researchers found that English and Dutch speakers used different metaphors than Farsi and Turkish people to describe pitch; they think of sounds as thin or thick rather than high or low. When Dutch speakers heard a tone while they were shown a mismatched height bar (e.g., a high tone and a low bar) and were asked to sing the tone, they sang a lower tone – but this wasn't the case when they saw a thin or thick bar. In contrast, when Farsi speakers heard a tone and were shown a bar of mismatched thickness, they misremembered the tone but not when they were shown a bar mismatched for height.[81] As we'll see in Chapter 14, culture matters—a lot.

Two people can see or hear the same event, but their interpretation of it can be as different as night and day, depending on what they had expected the stimulus to be. In one study, kids ages 3 to 5 who ate McDonald's French fries served in a McDonald's bag overwhelmingly thought they tasted better than those who ate the same fries out of a plain white bag. Even carrots tasted better when they came out of a McDonald's bag—more than half the kids preferred them to the same carrots served in a plain package! Ronald would be proud.[82]

The meaning we assign to a stimulus depends on the **schema**, or set of beliefs, to which we assign it. This in turn leads us to compare the stimulus to other similar ones we encountered in the past. Identifying and evoking the correct schema is crucial to many marketing decisions because this determines what criteria consumers will use to evaluate the product, package, or message. Extra Strength Maalox Whip Antacid flopped even though a spray can is a pretty effective way to deliver the product. To consumers, aerosol whips mean dessert toppings, not medication.[83] When a college cafeteria gave menu items descriptive labels (e.g., Red Beans with Rice versus Traditional Cajun Red Beans with Rice, Chocolate Pudding versus Satin Chocolate Pudding) so that diners had more information about each option so they could more easily categorize it, sales increased by more than 25 percent.[84]

The location of a product's image on a package influences the way our brains make sense of it. For example, as a result of what we have learned about the law of gravity (heavy objects sink and light objects float), we assume that products that are lower down in a frame weigh more than products that appear higher in a frame. In addition, objects on the right of a frame appear heavier than products that appear on the left of a frame. This interpretation results from our intuition about levers: We know that the farther away an object is from a lever's fulcrum, the more difficult it is to raise the item. Because we read from left to right, the left naturally becomes the visual fulcrum and thus we perceive objects on the right as heavier. Manufacturers should bear these *package schematics* in mind because they may influence our feelings about the contents in a package for better or worse. Think, for example, about a diet food marketer who wants shoppers to regard the menu items as lighter.[85]

As we'll see in Chapter 7, products often assume a "brand personality" because we tend to assign them common human traits such as sophistication or sexiness. In other words, we *anthropomorphize* objects when we think of them in human terms, and this thought process may encourage us to evaluate products using schemas we apply to classify other people. A recent study illustrates how this works: Subjects saw an advertisement with a picture of a car that had been modified to make it appear as though it was either "smiling" or "frowning." In some cases, the text of the ad was written in the first person, to activate a human schema, whereas others saw the same ad written in the third person. When the human schema was active, those who saw the "smiling" car rated it more favorably than when they saw a "frowning" car.[86]

Stimulus Organization

One factor that determines how we will interpret a stimulus is the relationship we assume it has with other events, sensations, or images in memory. When RJR Nabisco introduced a version of Teddy Grahams (a children's product) for adults, it used understated packaging colors to reinforce the idea that the new product was for grown-ups. But sales were disappointing. Nabisco changed the box to bright yellow to convey the idea that this was a fun snack, and buyers' more positive association between a bright primary color and taste prompted adults to start buying the cookies.[87]

The stimuli we perceive are often ambiguous. It's up to us to determine the meaning based on our past experiences, expectations, and needs. A classic experiment demonstrated the process of "seeing what you want to see": Princeton and Dartmouth students separately viewed a movie of a particularly rough football game between the two rival schools. Although everyone was exposed to the same stimulus, the degree to which students saw infractions and the blame they assigned for those they did see depended on which college they attended.[88]

As this experiment demonstrates, we tend to project our own desires or assumptions onto products and advertisements. This interpretation process can backfire for marketers.

We recognize patterns of stimuli, such as familiar words. In this Austrian ad consumers will tend to see the word "kitchen" even though the letters are scrambled.
Source: Client: XXXLutz; Head of Marketing: Mag. Thomas Saliger; Agency: Demner, Merlicek & Bergmann; Account Supervisor: Andrea Kliment; Account Manager: Albin Lenzer; Creative Directors: Rosa Haider, Tolga Buyukdoganay; Art Directors: Tolga Buyukdoganay, Rene Pichler; Copywriter: Alistair Thompson.

Better ask for the free assembly service by **XXXLutz**

Planters LifeSavers Company found this out when it introduced Planters Fresh Roast, a vacuum-packed peanuts package. The idea was to capitalize on consumers' growing love affair with fresh-roast coffee by emphasizing the freshness of the nuts in the same way. A great idea—until irate supermarket managers began calling to ask who was going to pay to clean the peanut gook out of their stores' coffee-grinding machines.[89]

Interpretational Biases: The Eye of the Beholder

Our brains tend to relate incoming sensations to others already in memory, based on some fundamental organizational principles. These principles derive from *Gestalt psychology*, a school of thought based upon the notion that people interpret meaning from the *totality* of a set of stimuli rather than from any individual stimulus. The German word **Gestalt** roughly means *whole, pattern,* or *configuration,* and we summarize this term as "the whole is greater than the sum of its parts." A piecemeal perspective that analyzes each component of the stimulus separately can't capture the total effect. The Gestalt perspective provides several principles that relate to the way our brains organize stimuli:

- The **closure principle** states that people tend to perceive an incomplete picture as complete. That is, we tend to fill in the blanks based on our prior experience. This principle explains why most of us have no trouble reading a neon sign even if several of its letters are burned out. The principle of closure is also at work when we hear only part of a jingle or theme. Marketing strategies that use the closure principle encourage audience participation, which increases the chance that people will attend to the message.
- The **similarity principle** tells us that consumers tend to group together objects that share similar physical characteristics. Green Giant relied on this principle when the company redesigned the packaging for its line of frozen vegetables. It created a "sea of green" look to unify all of its different offerings.
- The **figure-ground principle** states that one part of a stimulus will dominate (the *figure*), and other parts recede into the background (the *ground*). This concept is easy to understand if one thinks literally of a photograph with a clear and sharply focused object (the figure) in the center. The figure is dominant, and the eye goes straight to it. The parts of the configuration a person will perceive as figure or ground can vary depending on the individual consumer, as well as other factors. Similarly, marketing messages that use the figure-ground principle can make a stimulus the focal point of the message or merely the context that surrounds the focus.

OBJECTIVE 3-6

The field of semiotics helps us to understand how marketers use symbols to create meaning.

Semiotics: The Meaning of Meaning

As we've seen, when we try to "make sense" of a marketing stimulus we interpret it in light of our prior associations. An experiment demonstrated how our assumptions influence our experiences; in this case, the study altered beer drinkers' taste preferences simply by telling them different stories about a specific brew's ingredients. The researcher offered bar patrons free beer if they would participate in a taste test (guess what: few refused the offer). Participants tasted two beers each, one a regular draft of Budweiser or Samuel Adams and the other the same beer with a few drops of balsamic vinegar added. Although most beer *aficionados* would guess that vinegar makes the drink taste bad, in fact 60 percent of the respondents who did not know which beer contained the vinegar actually preferred the doctored version to the regular one! But when tasters knew in advance which beer had vinegar in it before they took a swig, only one-third preferred that version.[90]

Much of the meaning we take away influences what we make of the symbolism we perceive. After all, on the surface many marketing images have virtually no literal connection to actual products. What does a cowboy have to do with a bit of tobacco rolled into a paper tube? How can a celebrity such as the basketball player LeBron James or the singer Rihanna enhance the image of a soft drink or a fast-food restaurant?

To help them understand how consumers interpret the meanings of symbols, some marketers turn to **semiotics**, a discipline that studies the correspondence between signs and

This Indian ad for paper products relies on the principle of similarity to create an image of a man.
Source: Courtesy of Taproot India. Contributors: Santosh Padhi, Agnello Dias, Ananth Nanavre, Amol Jadhav, and Amol Kamble.

symbols and their roles in how we assign meanings.[91] Semiotics is a key link to consumer behavior because consumers use products to express their social identities. Products carry learned meanings, and we rely on marketers to help us figure out what those meanings are. As one set of researchers put it, "Advertising serves as a kind of culture/consumption dictionary; its entries are products, and their definitions are cultural meanings."[92]

From a semiotic perspective, every marketing message has three basic components: an *object*, a *sign* (or symbol), and an *interpretant*. The **object** is the product that is the focus of the message (e.g., Marlboro cigarettes). The **sign** is the sensory image that represents the intended meanings of the object (e.g., the Marlboro cowboy). The **interpretant** is the meaning we derive from the sign (e.g., rugged, individualistic, American). Figure 3.4 diagrams this relationship.

According to semiotician Charles Sanders Peirce, signs relate to objects in one of three ways: They can resemble objects, connect to them, or tie to them conventionally. An **icon** is a sign that resembles the product in some way (e.g., the Ford Mustang has a galloping horse on the hood). An **index** is a sign that connects to a product because they share

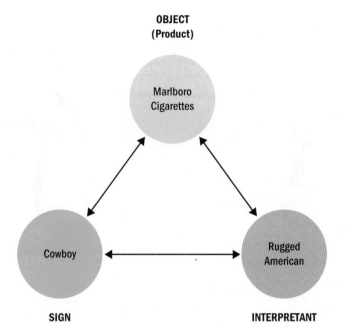

OBJECT
(Product)

Marlboro
Cigarettes

Cowboy

Rugged
American

SIGN
(Image)

INTERPRETANT
(Meaning)

Figure 3.4 Semiotic Relationships

some property (e.g., the pine tree on some of Procter & Gamble's Spic and Span cleanser products conveys the shared property of fresh scent). A **symbol** is a sign that relates to a product by either conventional or agreed-on associations (e.g., the lion in Dreyfus Fund ads provides the conventional association with fearlessness and strength that it carries [or hopes to carry] over to the company's approach to investments).[93]

A lot of time, thought, and money go into creating brand names and logos that clearly communicate a product's image (even when a name like Exxon is generated by a computer!). Starbucks removed the words *Starbucks Coffee* as it introduced a new logo that features only the famous siren character. The CEO explained this change means the company is thinking "beyond coffee."[94]

The choice of a logo is even more difficult when the brand has to travel across cultures. For example, as Chinese business becomes more global, companies refashion ancient Chinese pictograms into new corporate logos that resonate with both the East and the West. Chinese pictograms really are icons because the ancient symbols were once graphic depictions of the words they signify. China Telecom's logo features two interlocking letter Cs that together form the Chinese character for China but also represent the concept of "customer" and "competition." In addition, though, the symbol also resembles the horns of an ox, a hard-working animal. When the software company Oracle redesigned its logo for the Chinese market, it added three Chinese characters that signify the literal translation of the word *oracle:* "writing on a tortoise shell." The expression dates back to ancient China when mystics scrawled prophecies on bones. The California firm was enthusiastic about the translation because it conveyed Oracle's core competency—data storage.[95]

Hyperreality

Perhaps you recall a recent Budweiser Super Bowl commercial that was set in "Whatever, U.S.A." The action took place in a small town with blue streets, light poles and fencing—not to mention a hot tub, sand pit, and concert stage smack in the middle of the main street surrounded by hordes of young partiers. In reality, the company paid the ski town of Crested Butte, Colorado, a cool half-million dollars to let it redo the place for a weekend and fly in 1,000 revelers to film a Bud Light commercial. That amount was double the original offer—after many residents pushed back at Budweiser's plan to rent out their town.[96]

Not ringing a bell? How about the town of Mount Airy in North Carolina near the Virginia border? It was the inspiration for the mythical town of Mayberry in "The Andy Griffith Show." To attract tourists, the town has slowly transformed itself into the TV town:

Last Exit to Nowhere sells T-shirts that bear the logos of companies featured in works of fiction.

Source: Images from LastExittoNowhere.com.

If you visit the Mayberry Motor Inn, an Aunt Bee look-alike will show you around. You can tour around in a vintage police car like the one that Sheriff Andy Taylor drove (Andy Griffith was born in Mount Airy). If you're lucky you'll stumble on the actress who played Thelma Lou in the original show; she still signs autographs.[97]

One of the hallmarks of modern advertising is that it creates a condition of **hyperreality**. This refers to the process of making real what is initially simulation or "hype." Advertisers create new relationships between objects and interpretants when they invent connections between products and benefits, such as when an ad equates Marlboro cigarettes with the American frontier spirit. In a hyperreal environment, over time it's no longer possible to discern the true relationship between the symbol and reality. The "artificial" associations between product symbols and the real world take on lives of their own.

We see this a lot lately when fans create products that correspond to "realities" that never actually existed. These include Pinterest Boards for food mentioned in the steamy novel *Fifty Shades of Gray* and *The Unofficial Mad Men Cookbook, The Unofficial Harry Potter Cookbook, The Unofficial Narnia Cookbook, A Feast of Ice and Fire* (Game of Thrones), *and Abbey Cooks Entertain* (Downton Abbey)[98] Even the fictional GEICO gecko has published a book titled *You're Only Human: A Guide to Life*, that covers a range of topics from tattooing to flossing.[99]

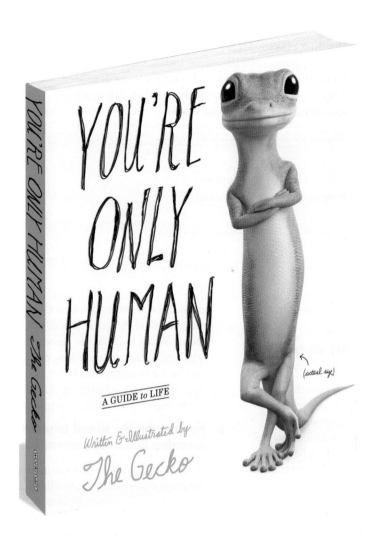

Perceptual Positioning

So, we know that we often interpret a product stimulus in light of what we've learned about a product category and the characteristics of existing brands. Our perception of a brand comprises both its functional attributes (e.g., its features, its price, and so on) and its symbolic attributes (its image and what we think it says about us when we use it). We'll look more closely at issues such as brand image in later chapters, but for now it's important to keep in mind that (as we stated in Chapter 1) our evaluation of a product typically is the result of what it means rather than what it does. This meaning—as consumers perceive it—constitutes the product's market position, and it may have more to do with our expectations of product performance as communicated by its color, packaging, or styling than with the product itself.

When a marketer understands how consumers think about a set of competing brands, it can use these insights to develop a **positioning strategy**, which is a fundamental component of a company's marketing efforts as it uses elements of the marketing mix (i.e., product design, price, distribution, and marketing communications) to influence the consumer's interpretation of its meaning in the marketplace relative to its competitors. For example, although consumers' preferences for the taste of one product over another are important, this functional attribute is only one component of product evaluation.

Marketers can use many dimensions to carve out a brand's position in the marketplace. These include:[100]

- **Lifestyle.** Grey Poupon mustard is a "higher-class" condiment.
- **Price leadership.** L'Oréal sells its Noisôme brand face cream in upscale beauty shops, whereas its Plenitude brand is available for one-sixth the price in discount stores—even though both are based on the same chemical formula.[101]

- **Attributes.** Bounty paper towels are "the quicker picker-upper."
- **Product class.** The Spyder Eclipse is a sporty convertible.
- **Competitors.** Northwestern Insurance is "the quiet company."
- **Occasions.** Wrigley's gum is an alternative at times when smoking is not permitted.
- **Users.** Levi's Dockers target men in their 20s to 40s.
- **Quality.** At Ford, "Quality is job 1."

MyLab Marketing

To complete the problems with the ⭐, go to EOC Discussion Questions in the MyLab as well as additional Marketing Metrics questions only available in MyLab Marketing.

CHAPTER SUMMARY

Now that you have finished reading this chapter, you should understand why:

1. The design of a product often is a key driver of its success or failure.

In recent years, the sensory experiences we receive from products and services have become a high priority when we choose among competing options. Consumers increasingly want to buy things that will give them hedonic value in addition to functional value. They often believe that most brands perform similarly, so they weigh a product's aesthetic qualities heavily when they select a brand.

2. Products and commercial messages often appeal to our senses, but because of the profusion of these messages we don't notice most of them.

Marketing stimuli have important sensory qualities. We rely on colors, odors, sounds, tastes, and even the "feel" of products when we evaluate them. Not all sensations successfully make their way through the perceptual process. Many stimuli compete for our attention, and we don't notice or accurately interpret the majority of them.

3. Perception is a three-stage process that translates raw stimuli into meaning.

Perception is the process by which physical sensations, such as sights, sounds, and smells, are selected, organized, and interpreted. The eventual interpretation of a stimulus allows it to be assigned meaning. A perceptual map is a widely used marketing tool that evaluates the relative standing of competing brands along relevant dimensions.

4. Subliminal advertising is a controversial—but largely ineffective—way to talk to consumers.

So-called subliminal persuasion and related techniques that expose people to visual and aural messages below the sensory threshold are controversial. Although evidence that subliminal persuasion is effective is virtually nonexistent, many

consumers continue to believe that advertisers use this technique. Some of the factors that determine which stimuli (above the threshold level) do get perceived include the amount of exposure to the stimulus, how much attention it generates, and how it is interpreted. In an increasingly crowded stimulus environment, advertising clutter occurs when too many marketing-related messages compete for attention.

5. We interpret the stimuli to which we do pay attention according to learned patterns and expectations.

We don't attend to a stimulus in isolation. We classify and organize it according to principles of perceptual organization. A *Gestalt*, or overall pattern, guides these principles. Specific grouping principles include closure, similarity, and figure-ground relationships. The final step in the process of perception is interpretation. Symbols help us make sense of the world by providing us with an interpretation of a stimulus that others often share. The degree to which the symbolism is consistent with our previous experience affects the meaning we assign to related objects.

6. The field of semiotics helps us to understand how marketers use symbols to create meaning.

Marketers try to communicate with consumers by creating relationships between their products or services and desired attributes. A semiotic analysis involves the correspondence between stimuli and the meaning of signs. The intended meaning may be literal (e.g., an icon such as a street sign with a picture of children playing). Or it may be indexical if it relies on shared characteristics (e.g., the red in a stop sign means danger). Meaning also can be conveyed by a symbol in which an image is given meaning by convention or by agreement of members of a society (e.g., stop signs are octagonal, whereas yield signs are triangular). Marketer-created associations often take on lives of their own as consumers begin to believe that hype is, in fact, real. We call this condition *hyperreality*.

KEY TERMS

REVIEW

3-1 Define hedonic consumption and provide an example.

3-2 How does the sense of touch influence consumers' reactions to products?

⭐ **3-3** Identify and describe the three stages of perception.

3-4 Why is Weber's Law a challenge for green marketers?

3-5 Does subliminal perception work? Why or why not?

3-6 Compare and contrast perceptual vigilance and perceptual defense.

3-7 "The whole is greater than the sum of its parts." Explain this statement.

⭐ **3-8** How do you identify a product's object, sign (or symbol), and interpretant?

3-9 What do we mean by the concept of augmented reality? Give an example that is not discussed in the chapter. How does this concept differ from virtual reality?

⭐ **3-10** How does semiotics help marketers understand consumer behavior?

CONSUMER BEHAVIOR CHALLENGE

■ DISCUSS

3-11 Subliminal advertising is not illegal in the United States, but it is in the United Kingdom and Australia. Should it be made illegal globally considering there is no proof it actually works?

3-12 The slogan for the movie *Godzilla* was "Size does matter." Should this be the slogan for the United States as well? Many marketers seem to believe so. The average serving size for a fountain drink has gone from 12 ounces to 20 ounces. An industry consultant explains that the 32-ounce Big Gulp is so popular because "people like something large in their hands. The larger the better." Some cities (most notably New York) have tried to ban sales of sugary drinks greater than 24 ounces but so far unsuccessfully.[102] Hardee's Monster Burger, complete with two beef patties and five pieces of bacon, weighs in at 63 grams of fat and more than 1,000 calories. The standard for TV sets used to be 19 inches; now it's 32 inches and growing. Hulking sport utility vehicles

(SUVs) have replaced tiny sports cars as the status vehicle of the new millennium. What's up with our fascination with bigness? Is this a uniquely U.S. preference? Do you believe that "bigger is better"? Is this a sound marketing strategy?

3-13 Augmented reality applications may reach the level of sophistication where we observe almost everything through the screen of our smartphones to receive an "enhanced" experience. Do you view this as a positive development or a problem?

3-14 Analysts believe that augmented reality (AR) apps will be worth $5.2 billion (approximately) by 2017. However, AR will not be available to everyone. Is your country's infrastructure ready for this next leap in technology?

3-15 Identify a locally produced brand that has retained its normal packaging size despite having less contents. Did the manufacturer make this change clear?

■ APPLY

3-16 Compile a list of ten or twelve products you enjoyed when you were a child. What are your recollections about their size and price? Find a stockist of the brands and compare your recollections with the current product offerings. Do the products appear to be the same size and have the same value? How would you apply Weber's Law to this comparison?

3-17 Interview three to five male and female friends each about their perceptions of mobile phones and their functionality. Construct a perceptual map for each model. Based on your map of mobile phones, do you see any areas that are not adequately served by current offerings? What (if any) gender differences did you notice regarding both the relevant dimensions raters use and how they place specific models along these dimensions?

3-18 Choose one of your favorite products that you have been buying for some years. How has it changed over the years? Is it better, bigger, smaller, easier to use, better tasting?

3-19 Colors and designs of products are chosen so that they appeal to particular target groups. Colors are used to attract male or female consumers. The design of logos and packaging are also created to be attractive and appealing. What is your view of the ideal color, design, and packaging that would attract male consumers compared to female ones?

3-20 Finding new locations for advertisements is a constant quest. Consider your own country or region. Where are advertisements appearing today where there were no advertisements in the past?

Case Study

A LUSH TREAT FOR THE SENSES

A visit to the Lush store is pure indulgence for the senses, and that's exactly what the store and its planners want its customers to expect, feel, and remember—a rich experience that leaves the senses and the mind invigorated. Lush manufactures a range of cosmetics including soaps, bathing foams, bath oils, creams, moisturizers, massage bars, cleansers, makeup, perfumes, and deodorants. The company was established in 1994 in Poole, in the United Kingdom, to provide cosmetics that are fresh, natural, and fun. Today, Lush has 130 shops in 50 countries around the world and firmly adheres to its original philosophy. Lush was ranked as the fourth-best company in the United Kingdom for Customer Experience Excellence in 2014, while its closest competitor Body Shop was in 38th place.

Lush is passionate about being fresh and organic, and this passion drives the company. Their products are made of the freshest organic fruits and vegetables, the finest essential oils, and safe synthesis. Their goal is clear and simple: they want to offer the freshest products ever. This commitment attracts the natural customer community and plays a vital role in how the company is perceived by its target customers. The company's appeal is further bolstered by a no-animal testing policy, environmentally friendly packaging and labelling, helpful and friendly staff, and a unique store design and ambiance.

The Lush experience starts even before one enters the shop. The exotic, natural fragrances of Lush products can be taken in from a distance, and shoppers are naturally drawn to the store. Once inside, all senses come alive within a few seconds. The colorful, unwrapped products are displayed like food on market stalls. The soaps are sold as chunky blocks that look like cheese,

the Bath bombs are piled up like fruit, the face masks are kept in cold pots in salad-bar type tables, and butter cream is arranged like cake. The unusual forms of the products and the creative stocking style grab the customer's attention, and their enchanting scents drives the consumer to look even further. The overall ambiance of the store is attractive and comfortable, with the walls and lighting creating a warm effect. The furniture is made of natural wood, and the flooring is done with natural stone that creates a very fitting environment for the fresh, natural products. The sounds in the store are a combination of background music and a market-type buzz created by the salespeople's active interaction and engagement with customers.

The location of Lush stores is mostly near high-end fashion stores, enabling them to target the latter's high-end customers and communicate a premium image. Lush hires and trains energetic and happy people who interact with the customers as if they are taking to their friends, showing them the things they love and encouraging them to touch the unwrapped products and smell them. The salespersons offer free skin and hair consultations and invite customers for a live demonstration or even a hand massage.

Lush carefully selects the words it uses on its labels, packages, store signage, Web sites, and advertising. The words "fresh," "natural," and "handmade" are used extensively. Labelling contains names of natural ingredients like chocolate, olives, sugar, cinnamon, coconut oil, and honey. The choice of words in different communications is creative, and this adds to its fun and green image; examples include the "Go Naked" campaign and the "Have a Sniff" point-of-purchase sign. The "Go Naked" campaign encouraged consumers to buy unpackaged products to help save resources that are wasted by over-packing products. More than 45 percent of lush products are sold naked; that is, without packaging. Similarly, the "Have a Sniff" sign next to the unwrapped products promotes the package-less style of Lush while also inviting customers to take in the scent of the products.

DISCUSSION QUESTIONS

CS 3-1 Based on your understanding of the perceptual process, discuss how Lush uses sensory marketing for its products and encourages its customers to process information.

CS 3-2 Are the decisions of Lush's consumers driven by a rational consumption appeal that uses the message of ethical, organic, fresh, and healthy products, or is it influenced by the hedonic consumption and the pleasurable multi-sensory experience they encounter in the stores?

Sources: KPMG Nunwood, "Lush vs. The Body Shop—Why Retail CEM Is Essential for CX," 2014, http://www.nunwood.com/lush-vs-body-shop-retail-customer-experience-management-essential-customer-experience-excellence/, accessed November 7, 2015; N. Bruins, "Why It's Lush to Focus on Consumer Experience," *k3reatil*, 2014, http://k3retail.com/blog/why-its-lush-to-focus-on-consumer-experience/, accessed November 3, 2015; Brandrepublic.com, "Case Study: Lush—The Scent of Success," 2015, http://www.brandrepublic.com/article/996257/case-study-lush—scent-success#HIJAoyEIpKzqjFob.99, accessed November 7, 2015; Lushusa.com, "A Lush Life," 2015, http://www.lushusa.com/A-Lush-Life/about-us, en_US, pg.html, accessed November 7, 2015.

MyLab Marketing

Go to the Assignments section of your MyLab to complete these writing exercises.

3.22 Many studies have shown that our sensory detection abilities decline as we grow older. Discuss the implications of the absolute threshold for marketers who want to appeal to the elderly.

3.23 The chapter discussed the "talking window," which a German ad agency is placing in subway cars. When the agency posted a YouTube video to promote the platform, one person commented, "At what point does it stop being advertising and start being harassment?" How would you answer this question?[103]

NOTES

1. Lisa Leake, "Why Some Milk is Not Refrigerated (and an Explanation of UHT)," (July 31st, 2013), http://www.100daysofrealfood.com/2013/07/31/uht-why-some-milk-is-not-refrigerated/, accessed March 5, 2015; http://www.milkunleashed.com/shelf-safe-milk/aseptic-packaging-uht-milk.html, accessed July 22, 2013; http://wiki.answers.com/Q/What_is_the_difference_between_fresh_milk_and_uht_treated_milk_and_any_advantages_and_disadvantages, accessed March 28, 2011; Craig Baumrucker, "Why Does Organic Milk Last So Much Longer Than Regular Milk?," *Scientific American* (June 6, 2008), www.scientificamerican.com/article.cfm?id=experts-organic-milk-lasts-longer, accessed June 30, 2009.

2. Brooks Barnes, "To Lure Young, Movie Theaters Shake, Smell and Spritz," *New York Times* (November 29, 2014), http://www.NewYorkTimes.com/2014/11/30/business/media/to-lure-young-movie-theaters-shake-smell-and-spritz.html?ref=technology, accessed February 23, 2015.

3. http://www.universalorlando.com/Theme_Parks/Universal_Studios_Orlando/Attractions/fear_factor_live.aspx, accessed March 28, 2011; Nat Ives, "Putting Some Terror in Family Outings," *New York Times* (January 17, 2005), www.NewYorkTimes.com, accessed January 17, 2005.

4. Ryan S. Elder and Aradhna Krishna, "The Effects of Advertising Copy on Sensory Thoughts and Perceived Taste," *Journal of Consumer Research* 36, no. 5 (2010): 748–756.

5. Glenn Collins, "Owens-Corning's Blurred Identity," *New York Times* (August 19, 1994): D4.

6. Elizabeth C. Hirschman and Morris B. Holbrook, "Hedonic Consumption: Emerging Concepts, Methods, and Propositions," *Journal of Marketing* 46 (Summer 1982): 92–101.

7. Joan Myers-Levy, Rui (Juliet) Zhu, and Lan Jiang, "Context Effects From Bodily Sensations: Examining Bodily Sensations Induced by Flooring and the Moderating Role of Product Viewing Distance," *Journal of Consumer Research* 37 (June 2010): 1–14.

8. Jiewen Hong and Yacheng Sun, "Warm It Up with Love: The Effect of Physical Coldness on Liking of Romance Movies," *Journal of Consumer Research* 39, no. 2 (August 2012): 293–306.

9. Aradhna Krishna, May O. Lwin, and Maureen Morrin, "Product Scent and Memory," *Journal of Consumer Research* 37 (June 2010): 57–67.

10. Virginia Postrel, "The New Trend in Spending," *New York Times* (September 9, 2004), www.NewYorkTimes.com, accessed September 9, 2004.

11. Emily Cadei, "Cleaning Up: S. F. Duo Putting a Shine on Its Product Line," *San Francisco Business Times Online Edition* 17, no. 16 (December 6, 2002).

12. Martin Reimann, Judith Zaichkowsky, Carolin Neuhaus, Thomas Bender, and Bernd Weber, "Aesthetic Package Design: A Behavioral, Neural, and Psychological Investigation," *Journal of Consumer Psychology* 20 (2010): 431–441.

13. http://www.microsoft.com/microsoft-hololens/en-us, accessed March 9, 2015.

14. Gabriel Kahn, "Chinese Characters Are Gaining New Meaning as Corporate Logos," *Wall Street Journal Interactive Edition* (July 18, 2002).

15. Natalie Zmuda, "Why Tommy Hilfiger Boosted Ad Budget by 60%, Aired First Branded TV Spot Since 2005," *Ad Age CMO Strategy*, http://adage.com/article/cmo-strategy/marketing-tommy-hilfiger-boosted-ad-budget-60/147258/, accessed April 28, 2011.

16. Andrew Rosenblum, "2015: The Year Virtual Reality Finally Reaches Living Rooms," *Popular Science* (January 12, 2015), http://www.popsci.com/virtual-reality-meets-its-public, accessed March 9, 2015.

17. Adam Bryant, "Plastic Surgery at AmEx," *Newsweek* (October 4, 1999): 55.

18. Amitava Chattopadhyay, Gerald J. Gorn, and Peter R. Darke, *Roses Are Red and Violets Are Blue—Everywhere? Cultural Universals and Differences in Color Preference among Consumers and Marketing Managers* (unpublished manuscript, University of British Columbia, Fall 1999); Joseph Bellizzi and Robert E. Hite, "Environmental Color, Consumer Feelings, and Purchase Likelihood," *Psychology & Marketing* 9 (1992): 347–363; Ayn E. Crowley, "The Two-Dimensional Impact of Color on Shopping," *Marketing Letters* 4 (January 1993); Gerald J. Gorn, Amitava Chattopadhyay, and Tracey Yi, *Effects of Color as an Executional Cue in an Ad: It's in the Shade* (unpublished manuscript, University of British Columbia, 1994).

19. Tine DeBock, Mario Pandelaere, and Patrick Van Kenhove, "When Colors Backfire: The Impact of Color Cues on Moral Judgment," *Journal of Consumer Psychology* 23, no. 3 (2013): 341–348.

20. Pam Belluck, "Reinvent Wheel? Blue Room. Defusing a Bomb? Red Room," *New York Times* (February 5, 2009), www.NewYorkTimes.com, accessed February 5, 2009.

21. Mark G. Frank and Thomas Gilovich, "The Dark Side of Self and Social Perception: Black Uniforms and Aggression in Professional Sports," *Journal of Personality & Social Psychology* 54 (1988): 74–85.

22. Ioannis Kareklas, Frédéric F. Brunel, and Robin A. Coulter, "Judgment Is Not Color Blind: The Impact of Automatic Color Preference on Product and Advertising Preferences," *Journal of Consumer Psychology* 24, no. 1 (2014): 87–95.

23. Gün R. Semin and Tomás A. Palma, "Why the Bride Wears White: Grounding Gender With Brightness," *Journal of Consumer Psychology* 24, no. 2 (2014): 217–225.

24. Pamela Paul, "Color by Numbers," *American Demographics* (February 2002): 31–36.

25. Marc Gobé, *Emotional Branding: The New Paradigm for Connecting Brands to People* (New York: Allworth Press, 2001).

26. Dirk Olin, "Color Cognition," *New York Times* (November 30, 2003), www .NewYorkTimes.com, accessed November 30, 2003.

27. "Ny Emballage og Ny Navn Fordoblede Salget," *Markedsforing* 12 (1992): 24. Adapted from Michael R. Solomon, Gary Bamossy, and Soren Askegaard, *Consumer Behavior: A European Perspective*, 2nd ed. (London: Pearson Education, 2001).

28. Meg Rosen and Frank Alpert, "Protecting Your Business Image: The Supreme Court Rules on Trade Dress," *Journal of Consumer Marketing* 11 (1994): 50–55.

29. http://www.pantone.com/pages/index.aspx?pg=21163&, accessed March 6, 2015.

30. Mark J. Miller, "Smell Ball! New York Yankees Scents a Branding Opportunity," *Brand Channel*, February 13, 2012, http://www .brandchannel.com/home/post/2012/02/13/New-York-Yankees-Fragrance-021312.aspx, accessed February 3, 2015.

31. The Associated Press, "Burger King to Offer Fragrance, Eau De Whopper," *New York Times* (March 20, 2015), http://www.nytimes.com/2015/03/21/business/burger-king-to-offer-fragrance-eau-de-whopper.html?_r=0, accessed March 21, 2015.

32. Deborah J. Mitchell, Barbara E. Kahn, and Susan C. Knasko, "There's Something in the Air: Effects of Congruent or Incongruent Ambient Odor on Consumer Decision-Making," *Journal of Consumer Research* 22 (September 1995): 229–238; for a review of olfactory cues in store environments, see also Eric R. Spangenberg, Ayn E. Crowley, and Pamela W. Henderson, "Improving the Store Environment: Do Olfactory Cues Affect Evaluations and Behaviors?" *Journal of Marketing* 60 (April 1996): 67–80.

33. Krishna Aradhna, May O. Lwin, and Maureen Morrin, "Product Scent and Memory," *Journal of Consumer Research* 37, no. 1 (2010): 57–67.

34. Adriana V. Madzharov, Lauren G. Block, and Maureen Morrin, "The Cool Scent of Power: Effects of Ambient Scent on Consumer Preferences and Choice Behavior," *Journal of Marketing* January 79, no. 1 (2015): 83–96, doi: http://dx.doi.org/10.1509/jm.13.0263.

35. Pam Scholder Ellen and Paula Fitzgerald Bone, "Does It Matter if It Smells? Olfactory Stimuli as Advertising Executional Cues," *Journal of Advertising* 27 (Winter 1998): 29–40.

36. Jack Hitt, "Does the Smell of Coffee Brewing Remind You of Your Mother?" *New York Times Magazine* (May 7, 2000): 73–77.

37. Maxine Wilkie, "Scent of a Market," *American Demographics* (August 1995): 40–49.

38. Nicholas Wade, "Scent of a Man Is Linked to a Woman's Selection," *New York Times* (January 22, 2002), www.NewYorkTimes.com, accessed January 22, 2002.

39. Dale Buss, "Audio Branding: BMW Uses New Sound Signature to Help Redefine the Brand," *Brand Channel*, March 20, 2013, http://www.brand channel.com/home/post/2013/03/20/BMW-Sound-Signature-032013 .aspx, accessed February 23, 2015; Sheila Shayon, "World Cup Winner: Coca-Cola for Sonic Branding," *BrandChannel* (July 12, 2010), http://www .brandchannel.com/home/post/2010/07/12/Coca-Cola-World-Cup-Wavin-Flag.aspx, accessed March 6, 2015.

40. Bruce G. Vanden Bergh, Janay Collins, Myrna Schultz, and Keith Adler, "Sound Advice on Brand Names," *Journalism Quarterly* 61, no. 4 (1984): 835–840; Eric Yorkston and Geeta Menon, "A Sound Idea: Phonetic Effects of Brand Names on Consumer Judgments," *Journal of Consumer Research* 31 (June 2004): 43–51; Keith S. Coulter and Robin A. Coulter, "Small Sounds, Big Deals: Phonetic Symbolism Effects in Pricing," *Journal of Consumer Research* 37, no. 2 (2010): 315–328.

41. L. J. Shrum, Sarah Roche, and Tina M. Lowrey, "What's in a Name: Sound Symbolism of Stock Ticker Symbols Predict Stock Performance," in June Cotte and Stacy Wood, eds., *NA—Advances in Consumer Research* 42 (Duluth, MN: Association for Consumer Research, 2014): 654–655.

42. Sarah Ellison and Erin White, "'Sensory' Marketers Say the Way to Reach Shoppers Is the Nose," *Advertising Age* (November 24, 2000): 1–3.

43. "You Can Look—But Don't Touch," *Science Daily* (January 20, 2009), www.sciencedaily.com, accessed January 30, 2009; Joann Peck and Suzanne B. Shu, "The Effect of Mere Touch on Perceived Ownership," *Journal of Consumer Research* 36, no. 3 (2009): 434–447.

44. Joann Peck, Victor A. Barger, and Andrea Webb, "In Search of a Surrogate for Touch: The Effect of Haptic Imagery on Perceived Ownership," *Journal of Consumer Psychology* 23, no. 2 (2013): 189–196; S. Adam Brasel and James Gips, "Tablets, Touchscreens, and Touchpads: How Varying Touch Interfaces Trigger Psychological Ownership and Endowment," *Journal of Consumer Psychology* 24, no. 2 (2014): 226–233.

45. Jacob Hornik, "Tactile Stimulation and Consumer Response," *Journal of Consumer Research* 19 (December 1992): 449–458.

46. Brett A. S. Martin, "A Stranger's Touch: Effects of Accidental Interpersonal Touch on Consumer Evaluations and Shopping Time," *Journal of Consumer Research* 39, no. 1 (June 2012): 174–184.

47. J. Peck and T. L. Childers, "Individual Differences in Haptic Information Processing: The 'Need for Touch' Scale," *Journal of Consumer Research* 30, no. 3 (2003): 430–442.

48. Material adapted from a presentation by Glenn H. Mazur, QFD Institute, 2002.

49. John Tagliabue, "Sniffing and Tasting with Metal and Wire," *New York Times* (February 17, 2002), www.NewYorkTimes.com, accessed February 17, 2002.

50. Claire Cain Miller, "To Win Over Users, Gadgets Have to be Touchable," *New York Times* (September 1, 2010), http://www.NewYorkTimes.com/2010/09/01/technology/01touch.html?_r=1&emc=tnt&tntemail0=y, accessed March 27, 2011.

51. Michael W. Allen, Richa Gupta, and Arnaud Monnier, "The Interactive Effect of Cultural Symbols and Human Values on Taste Evaluation," *Journal of Consumer Research* 35 (August 2008): 294–308.

52. Becky Gaylord, "Bland Food Isn't So Bad—It Hurts Just to Think about This Stuff," *Wall Street Journal* (April 21, 1995): B1.

53. Stephanie Clifford and Catherine Rampell, quoted in "Food Inflation Kept Hidden in Tinier Bags," *New York Times* (March 28, 2011), http://www.NewYorkTimes.com/2011/03/29/business/29shrink .html?pagewanted=all, accessed March 29, 2011.

54. Ellen Byron, "Selling Detergent Bottles' Big Shrink Suds Makers' Challenge: Convince Consumers Less Isn't Really Less," *Wall Street Journal* (May 21, 2007), www.wsj.com, accessed May 21, 2007.

55. David Knowles, "German Company Tests 'Talking Window' that Pumps Ads Into Brains of Train Passengers," *New York Daily News* (July 3, 2013), http://www.nydailynews.com/news/world/talking-window-advertising-technique-tested-germany-article-1.1391390, accessed February 23, 2015.

56. Michael Lev, "No Hidden Meaning Here: Survey Sees Subliminal Ads," *New York Times* (May 3, 1991): D7.

57. "ABC Rejects KFC Commercial, Citing Subliminal Advertising," *Wall Street Journal* (March 2, 2006), www.wsj.com, accessed March 2, 2006.

58. Quoted in Claire Groden, "Potty-Mouthed Minions Wreak Happy Meal Havoc," *Fortune* (July 9, 2015), http://fortune.com/2015/07/09/minions-mcdonalds-happy-meal/, accessed July 11, 2015.

59. Andrew B. Aylesworth, Ronald C. Goodstein, and Ajay Kalra, "Effect of Archetypal Embeds on Feelings: An Indirect Route to Affecting Attitudes?" *Journal of Advertising* 28, no. 3 (Fall 1999): 73–81.

60. Joel Saegert, "Why Marketing Should Quit Giving Subliminal Advertising the Benefit of the Doubt," *Psychology & Marketing* 4 (Summer 1987): 107–120; see also Dennis L. Rosen and Surendra N. Singh, "An Investigation of Subliminal Embed Effect on Multiple Measures of Advertising Effectiveness," *Psychology & Marketing* 9 (March–April 1992): 157–173; for a more recent review, see Kathryn T. Theus, "Subliminal Advertising and the Psychology of Processing Unconscious Stimuli: A Review of Research," *Psychology & Marketing* (May–June 1994): 271–290.

61. Quoted in Brian Steinberg, "Study: Young Consumers Switch Media 27 Times an Hour: Survey of 'Digital Natives' Indicates Brands Must Step Up Creative Game to Hold Their Attention," *Advertising Age* (April 9, 2012), http://adage.com/article/news/study-young-consumers-switch-media-27-times-hour/234008/?utm_source=digital_email&utm_medium =newsletter&utm_campaign=adage, accessed January 30, 2015.

62. Brian Steinberg, "How to Keep Ad Skippers from Fast-Forwarding Your Ad," *Advertising Age* (March 31, 2009), www.adage.com, accessed March 31, 2009.

63. Joseph Burris, "Plugged-in Generation Multi-Tasking Big Time," *Baltimore Sun* (February 17, 2010), http://articles.baltimoresun.com/2010-02-17/features/bal-md.pa.kids17feb17_1_cell-phones-multi-tasking-parental-controls, accessed May 5, 2011.

64. Sharon Waxman, "At an Industry Media Lab, Close Views of Multitasking," *New York Times* (May 15, 2006), http://www.NewYorkTimes.com/2006/05/15/technology/15research.html, accessed August 22, 2011.

65. Emma Innes, "Is Your Inbox Making You Ill? Reading Work Emails Causes Your Blood Pressure and Heart Rate to Soar," *Daily Mail* (June 4, 2013), http://www.dailymail.co.uk/health/article-2335699/Is-inbox-making-ill-Reading-work-emails-causes-blood-pressure-heart-rate-soar.html#ixzz3Tii7BFks, accessed March 7, 2015.

66. Stephanie Castillo, "Teens Told They Need to 'Focus on the Task at Hand' Make a Case for Multitasking," (October10, 2014), *Medical Daily*, http://www.medicaldaily.com/teens-told-they-need-focus-task-hand-make-case-multitasking-306721, accessed March 5, 2015; Matt Richtel, "Attached to Technology and Paying a Price," *New York Times* (June 6, 2010), http://www.NewYorkTimes.com/2010/06/07/technology/07brain.html?pagewanted=1, accessed April 17, 2011.

67. A. Selin Atalay, H. Onur Bodur, and Dina Rasolofoarison, "Shining in the Center: Central Gaze Cascade Effect on Product Choice," *Journal of Consumer Research* 39, no. 4 (December 2012): 848–866.

68. Lee Gomes, "As Web Ads Grow, Sites Get Trickier about Targeting You," *Wall Street Journal* (May 9, 2007): B1.

69. Rik Pieters, Michel Wedel, and Rajeev Batra, "The Stopping Power of Advertising: Measures and Effects of Visual Complexity," *Journal of Marketing* 74 (September 2010): 48–60.

70. Roger Barton, *Advertising Media* (New York: McGraw-Hill, 1964).

71. Suzanne Oliver, "New Personality," *Forbes* (August 15, 1994): 114.

72. Adam Finn, "Print Ad Recognition Readership Scores: An Information Processing Perspective," *Journal of Marketing Research* 25 (May 1988): 168–177.

73. Gerald L. Lohse, "Consumer Eye Movement Patterns on Yellow Pages Advertising," *Journal of Advertising* 26 (Spring 1997): 61–73.

74. Stewart A. Shapiro and Jesper H. Nielsen, "What the Blind Eye Sees: Incidental Change Detection as a Source of Perceptual Fluency," *Journal of Consumer Research* 39, no. 6 (2013):: 1202–1218

75. A. Selin Atalay, H. Onur Bodur, and Dina Rasolofoarison, "Shining in the Center: Central Gaze Cascade Effect on Product Choice," *Journal of Consumer Research* 39, no. 4 (2012): 848–866.

76. Linda Stern, "Bigger Than at Times Square," *Newsweek* (March 24, 2008), www.newsweek.com.

77. Milica Milosavljevic, Vidhya Navalpakkam, Christof Koch, and Antonio Rangel, "Relative Visual Saliency Differences Induce Sizable Bias in Consumer Choice," *Journal of Consumer Psychology* 22, no. 1 (2012): 67–74.

78. Chris Sherman, "A New F-Word for Google Search Results," *Search Engine Watch* (March 8, 2005), http://searchenginewatch.com/3488076, accessed June 29, 2010.

79. Michael R. Solomon and Basil G. Englis, "Reality Engineering: Blurring the Boundaries Between Marketing and Popular Culture," *Journal of Current Issues & Research in Advertising* 16, no. 2 (Fall 1994): 1–18; Michael McCarthy, "Ads Are Here, There, Everywhere: Agencies Seek Creative Ways to Expand Product Placement," *USA Today* (June 19, 2001): 1B.

80. Benedict Carey, "Liked the Show? Maybe It Was the Commercials," *New York Times* (March 2, 2009), http://topics.NewYorkTimes.com/topics/reference/timestopics/people/c/benedict_carey/index.html, accessed March 3, 2009.

81. T. M. Luhrmann, "Can't Place That Smell? You Must Be American: How Culture Shapes Our Senses," *New York Times*, September 5, 2014, http://www.NewYorkTimes.com/2014/09/07/opinion/sunday/how-culture-shapes-our-senses.html?ref=international, accessed February 23, 2015.

82. Nicholas Bakalar, "If It Says McDonald's, Then It Must Be Good," *New York Times* (August 14, 2007), www.NewYorkTimes.com, accessed August 14, 2007.

83. Robert M. McMath, "Image Counts," *American Demographics* (May 1998): 64.

84. Brian Wansink, James Painter, and Koert van Ittersum, "Descriptive Menu Labels' Effect on Sales," *Cornell Hotel & Restaurant Administration Quarterly* (December 2001): 68–72.

85. Xiaoyan Deng and Barbara E. Kahn, "Is Your Product on the Right Side? The 'Location Effect' on Perceived Product Heaviness and Package Evaluation," *Journal of Marketing Research* 46, no. 6 (December 2009): 725–738.

86. Pankaj Aggarwal and Ann L. McGill, "Is That Car Smiling at Me? Schema Congruity as a Basis for Evaluating Anthropomorphized Products," *Journal of Consumer Behavior* 34 (December 2007): 468–479.

87. Anthony Ramirez, "Lessons in the Cracker Market: Nabisco Saved New Graham Snack," *New York Times* (July 5, 1990): D1.

88. Albert H. Hastorf and Hadley Cantril, "They Saw a Game: A Case Study," *Journal of Abnormal & Social Psychology* 49 (1954): 129–134; see also Roberto Friedmann and Mary R. Zimmer, "The Role of Psychological Meaning in Advertising," *Journal of Advertising* (1988): 31–40.

89. Robert M. McMath, "Chock Full of (Pea)nuts," *American Demographics* (April 1997): 60.

90. Benedict Carey, "Knowing the Ingredients Can Change the Taste," *New York Times* (December 12, 2006), www.NewYorkTimes.com, accessed December 12, 2006.

91. David Glen Mick, "Consumer Research and Semiotics: Exploring the Morphology of Signs, Symbols, and Significance," *Journal of Consumer Research* 13 (September 1986): 196–213.

92. Teresa J. Domzal and Jerome B. Kernan, "Reading Advertising: The What and How of Product Meaning," *Journal of Consumer Marketing* 9 (Summer 1992): 48–64.

93. Arthur Asa Berger, *Signs in Contemporary Culture: An Introduction to Semiotics* (New York: Longman, 1984); David Glen Mick, "Consumer Research and Semiotics," 196–213; Charles Sanders Peirce, in Charles Hartshorne, Paul Weiss, and Arthur W. Burks, eds., *Collected Papers* (Cambridge, MA: Harvard University Press, 1931–1958); cf. also V. Larsen, D. Luna, and L. A. Peracchio, "Points of View and Pieces of Time: A Taxonomy of Image Attributes," *Journal of Consumer Research* 31, no. 1 (2004): 102–111.

94. Steven Heller, "A Makeover for the Starbucks Mermaid," *New York Times* (January 8, 2011), http://www.NewYorkTimes.com/2011/01/09/weekinreview/09heller.html?_r=1&scp=2&sq=starbucks&st=cse, accessed March 27, 2011.

95. Dexter Dining Room and Kitchen, *Metropolitan Home* (March 2009), www.metropolitanhome.com, accessed January 27, 2009.

96. Julie Turkewitz, "Town Becomes a Beer Ad, but Residents Don't Feel Like a Party," *New York Times* (September 4, 2014), http://www.NewYorkTimes.com/2014/09/05/us/colorado-town-prepares-to-become-beer-ad.html?ref=media, accessed February 23, 2015.

97. Kim Severson, "Inspiring Mayberry, and Then Becoming It," *New York Times* (June 21, 2013), http://www.New York Times.com/2013/06/22/us/in-north-carolina-inspiring-mayberry-and-then-becoming-it.html?_r=0, accessed February 23, 2015.

98. Hellen Lundell, "Fictional Food: Consumers Taking the Lead on Food Fabrication," *Heartbeat* (June 18, 2013), http://www.hartman-group.com/hartbeat/fictional-foodconsumers-taking-the-lead-on-food fabrication?utm_content=msolom01@sju.edu&tm_keyword=1fM92wXkAvpCt0zU6Ab&utm_source=tailoretmail&utm_term=Read+More%26nbsp%3b%C2%BB&utm_campaign=Fictional+food%2c+fad+or+fantasy%3f&tm_campaign=FICTIONAL+FOOD+CONSUMERS+TAKING+THE+LEAD+ON+FOOD+FABRICATION&, accessed February 23, 2015.

99. Dale Buss, "The GEICO Gecko Finds his Voice—and Puts it Into Book About Being 'Human'" *Brand Channel* (April 25, 2013), http://www.brandchannel.com/home/post/2013/04/25/Geico-Gecko-Book-042513.aspx, accessed February 23, 2015.

100. Adapted from Michael R. Solomon, Greg W. Marshall, and Elnora W. Stuart, *Marketing: Real People, Real Choices*, 8th ed. (Upper Saddle River, NJ: Pearson, 2016).

101. William Echikson, "Aiming at High and Low Markets," *Fortune* (March 22, 1993): 89.

102. Michael M. Grybaum, "Judge Blocks New York City's Limits on Big Sugary Drinks," *New York Times* (March 11, 2013), http://www.NewYorkTimes.com/2013/03/12/nyregion/judge-invalidates-bloombergs-soda-ban.html?pagewanted=all&_r=0, accessed April 3, 2013.

103. David Knowles, "German Company Tests 'Talking Window' that Pumps Ads into Brains of Train Passengers," *New York Daily News* (July 3, 2013), http://www.nydailynews.com/news/world/talking-window-advertising-technique-tested-germany-article-1.1391390, accessed February 23, 2015.

Chapter 4 • Learning and Memory

When you finish reading this chapter you will understand why:

4-1 It is important to understand how consumers learn about products and services.

4-2 Conditioning results in learning.

4-3 Learned associations with brands generalize to other products.

4-4 There is a difference between classical and instrumental conditioning, and both processes help consumers learn about products.

4-5 We learn about products by observing others' behavior.

4-6 Our brains process information about brands to retain them in memory.

4-7 The other products we associate with an individual product influence how we will remember it.

4-8 Products help us to retrieve memories from our past.

4-9 Marketers measure our memories about products and ads.

Source: Photos.com/Thinkstock.

Ah, Sunday morning! The sun is shining, the birds are singing, and Joe is feeling groovy! He puts on his vintage Levi's 501 jeans (circa 1968) and his Woodstock T-shirt (the "real" Woodstock, not that fake abomination they put on more recently, thank you) and saunters down to the kitchen. Joe smiles in anticipation of his morning plans. He's just returned from his college reunion and now it's time to "process" all the people he's seen and the stories he heard about their old antics. Joe cranks up the Lava Lamp, throws a Grateful Dead record on the turntable (ah, the sublime joys of vinyl), and sits back on his Barcalounger as he clutches a huge bowl filled to the brim with his all-time favorite cereal, Cap'n Crunch. Let the memories begin!

OBJECTIVE 4-1
It is important to understand how consumers learn about products and services.

How Do We Learn?

Joe journeys through time with the aid of many products that make him feel good because they remind him of earlier parts of his life. Products have capitalized on this nostalgia, too. PepsiCo launched its "Throwback" campaign; now it sells Pepsi Throwback, Mountain Dew Throwback, and Doritos Taco-Flavored chips in authentic packages from the past. Hostess brought back its 1970s characters Twinkie the Kid, Captain CupCake, King Ding Dong, and Happy Ho Ho to adorn its snack cake packages. Disney revived its *Tron* franchise. As a PepsiCo marketing executive explained, "Retro is very cool with 20-somethings, because it ties in with their desire for simpler, cleaner, more authentic lives. Many of them are engaged in identity self-creation through their Facebook pages, Instagram, Twitter and other social media, and they see nostalgia as a way to differentiate themselves."[1]

Learning is a relatively permanent change in behavior caused by experience. The learner need not have the experience directly, however; we can also learn when we observe events that affect others.[2] We learn even when we don't try: We recognize many brand names and hum many product jingles, for example, even for products we don't personally use. We call this casual, unintentional acquisition of knowledge **incidental learning**.

Learning is an ongoing process. Our knowledge about the world constantly updates as we are exposed to new stimuli and as we receive ongoing feedback that allows us to modify our behavior when we find ourselves in similar situations at a later time. The concept of learning covers a lot of ground, ranging from a consumer's simple association between a stimulus such as a product logo (e.g., Coca-Cola) and a response (e.g., "refreshing soft drink") to a complex series of cognitive activities (e.g., writing an essay on learning for a consumer behavior exam).

Psychologists who study learning advance several theories to explain the learning process. These theories range from those that focus on simple stimulus–response connections (*behavioral theories*) to perspectives that regard consumers as solvers of complex problems who learn abstract rules and concepts when they observe what others say and do (*cognitive theories*). It's important for marketers to understand these theories as well, because basic learning principles are at the heart of many consumer purchase decisions.

OBJECTIVE 4-2
Conditioning results in learning.

Behavioral Learning Theories

Behavioral learning theories assume that learning takes place as the result of responses to external events. Psychologists who subscribe to this viewpoint do not focus on internal thought processes. Instead, they approach the mind as a "black box" and emphasize the observable aspects of behavior. The observable aspects consist of things that go into the box (the stimuli or events perceived from the outside world) and things that come out of the box (the responses, or reactions to these stimuli).

Two major approaches to learning represent this view: *classical conditioning* and *instrumental conditioning*. According to the behavioral learning perspective, the feedback we receive as we go through life shapes our experiences. Similarly, we respond to brand names, scents, jingles, and other marketing stimuli because of the learned connections we form over time. People also learn that actions they take result in rewards and punishments; this feedback influences the way they will respond in similar situations in the future. Consumers who receive compliments on a product choice will be more likely to buy that brand again, whereas those who get food poisoning at a new restaurant are not likely to patronize that restaurant in the future.

Classical Conditioning

Classical conditioning occurs when a stimulus that elicits a response is paired with another stimulus that initially does not elicit a response on its own. Over time, this second stimulus causes a similar response because we associate it with the first stimulus. Ivan Pavlov, a Russian physiologist who conducted research on digestion in animals, first demonstrated this phenomenon in dogs. Pavlov induced classically conditioned learning when he paired a neutral stimulus (a bell) with a stimulus known to cause a salivation response in dogs (he squirted dried meat powder into their mouths). The powder was an **unconditioned stimulus (UCS)** because it was naturally capable of causing the response. Over time, the bell became a **conditioned stimulus (CS)**; it did not initially cause salivation, but the dogs learned to associate the bell with the meat powder and began to salivate at the sound of the bell only. The drooling of these canine consumers because of a sound, now linked to feeding time, was a **conditioned response (CR)**.

This basic form of classical conditioning that Pavlov demonstrated primarily applies to responses controlled by the *autonomic* (e.g., salivation) and *nervous* (e.g., eye blink) *systems*. That is, it focuses on visual and olfactory cues that induce hunger, thirst, sexual arousal, and other basic drives. When marketers consistently pair these cues with

Marketing Opportunity

Events we experience when we are young often exert a lasting influence on our preferences as we get older. Consider for example the lifelong impact on a fan when his team wins the World Series. A recent analysis used Facebook data on how many people "liked" and posted about a specific baseball team. It found that if a team wins the championship when a boy is 8 years old, this significantly increases the probability he will support the team as an adult regardless of how well the team did every other year of his life (the data doesn't hold up for females). The pattern persists until age 14 when it starts falling off; a World Series winner when a man is 20 years old is only one-eighth as likely to create an adult fan as when he was 8 years old. Thus, overall there are 1.65 Yankees fans for every Mets fan. However, the Mets' popularity spikes among those who were born in the years 1961 and 1978. It turns out that both sets of these fans happened to be 8 years old when the Mets won the World Series. Maybe winning *is* everything.[3]

Some advertising messages appeal to our motivation to avoid negative outcomes like bad breath. This Indian ad for a mint certainly does.
Source: McCann Erickson India.

conditioned stimuli, such as brand names, consumers may learn to feel hungry, thirsty, or aroused when they encounter these brand cues at a later point.

Classical conditioning can have similar effects for more complex reactions, too. Even a credit card becomes a conditioned cue that triggers greater spending, especially because as a stimulus it's present only in situations where we spend money. People learn they can make larger purchases with credit cards, and they also leave larger tips than when they pay by cash.[4] Small wonder that American Express reminds us, "Don't leave home without it."

Conditioning effects are more likely to occur after the conditioned (CS) and unconditioned (UCS) stimuli have been paired a number of times.[5] Repeated exposures—**repetition**—increase the strength of stimulus–response associations and prevent the decay of these associations in memory. Some research indicates that the intervals between exposures may influence the effectiveness of this strategy as well as the type of medium the marketer uses; the most effective repetition strategy is a combination of spaced exposures that alternate in terms of media that are more and less involving, such as television advertising complemented by print media.[6]

Many classic advertising campaigns consist of product slogans that companies repeat so often they are etched in consumers' minds. Conditioning will not occur or will take longer if the CS is only occasionally paired with the UCS. One result of this lack of association is **extinction**, which happens when the effects of prior conditioning diminish and finally disappear. This can occur, for example, when a product is overexposed in the marketplace so that its original allure is lost. The Izod Lacoste polo shirt, with its distinctive crocodile crest, is a good example of this effect. When the once-exclusive crocodile started to appear on baby clothes and many other items, it lost its cachet. Other contenders, such as the Ralph Lauren polo player, successfully challenged it as a symbol of casual elegance. Now that Izod is being more careful about where its logo appears, the brand is starting to regain its "cool" in some circles.

Stimulus Generalization

Stimulus generalization refers to the tendency of stimuli similar to a CS to evoke similar, conditioned responses. For example, Pavlov noticed in subsequent studies that his dogs would sometimes salivate when they heard noises that only vaguely resembled a bell, such as keys jangling.

People also react to other, similar stimuli in much the same way they responded to the original stimulus; we call this generalization a **halo effect**. A drugstore's bottle of private-brand mouthwash that is deliberately packaged to resemble Listerine mouthwash may evoke a similar response among consumers, who assume that this "me-too" product shares other characteristics of the original. Indeed, consumers in one study on shampoo brands tended to rate those with similar packages as similar in quality and performance as well.[7] This "piggybacking" strategy can cut both ways: When the quality of the me-too product turns out to be lower than that of the original brand, consumers may exhibit even more positive feelings toward the original. However, if they perceive the quality of the two competitors to be about equal, consumers may conclude that the price premium they pay for the original is not worth it.[8]

Stimulus Discrimination

Stimulus discrimination occurs when a UCS does not follow a stimulus similar to a CS. When this happens, reactions weaken and will soon disappear. Part of the learning process involves making a response to some stimuli but not to other, similar stimuli. Manufacturers of well-established brands commonly urge consumers not to buy "cheap imitations" because the results will not be what they expect.

Marketing Applications of Classical Conditioning Principles

Behavioral learning principles apply to many consumer phenomena, such as when a marketer creates a distinctive brand image or links a product to an underlying need. The transfer of meaning from an unconditioned stimulus to a conditioned stimulus explains why

Procter & Gamble opened a new line of Tide Dry Cleaners, named after its bestselling laundry detergent. P&G will rely on the more than 800,000 Facebook fans of Tide (what else do these people "like" on Facebook?) and other loyal detergent users to trust their clothes to the franchise stores. P&G plans to infuse the stores and its dry cleaning fluids with the familiar Tide scent just to underscore the connection.

Source: Courtesy of Boomburg via Getty Images.

The Tangled Web

People get attached to favorite logos, and social media platforms allow them to learn about any unsavory changes almost instantaneously. Gap misjudged consumers' attachment to its old logo when it introduced a new one without warning fans first. Within hours, consumers who were loyal to the old logo were burning up the blogosphere with indignant posts. Gap wrote on its Facebook page, "We know this logo created a lot of buzz and we're thrilled to see passionate debate unfolding!" As the criticism got more heated, the company did an about-face and finally surrendered on Facebook: "O.K. We've heard loud and clear that you don't like the new logo . . . we're bringing back the Blue Box tonight."[16]

Marketing Opportunity

Luxury carmakers are jumping into the licensing pool in droves. Bentley lends its name to colognes, furniture, skis, handbags and even a hotel suite at the St. Regis hotel in New York that costs $10,500 a night. The Ferrari prancing horse logo pops up on chess sets, Tod's loafers and Oakley sunglasses. Lamborghini, Maserati and Tesla now sell leather goods. Porsche (which like Lamborghini and Bentley now is owned by Volkswagen) has gone a step farther; it operates Porsche Design retail stores around the world. A spokeswoman observed, "Luggage, bikes, desk pieces, *couture* clothing—it all provides a continuation of the Porsche driving experience."[22]

"made-up" brand names, such as Marlboro, Coca-Cola, or Adidas, exert such powerful effects on consumers. The association between the Marlboro man and the cigarette is so strong that in some cases the company no longer even bothers to include the brand name in its ads that feature the cowboy riding off into the sunset. Indeed, recent research shows that these linkages cement early on; scans of children show how the pleasure and appetite centers of their brains light up when they view advertising images of fast-food companies such as the McDonald's logo.[9]

When researchers pair *nonsense syllables* (meaningless sets of letters) with such evaluative words as *beauty* or *success*, the meaning transfers to the fake words. This change in the symbolic significance of initially meaningless words shows that fairly simple associations can condition even complex meanings, and the learning that results can last a long time.[10] These associations are crucial to many marketing strategies that rely on the creation and perpetuation of **brand equity**, in which a brand has strong positive associations in a consumer's memory and commands a lot of loyalty as a result.[11]

OBJECTIVE 4-3

Learned associations with brands generalize to other products.

Marketing Applications of Repetition

One advertising researcher argued that any more than three exposures to a marketing communication are wasted. The first exposure creates awareness of the product, the second demonstrates its relevance to the consumer, and the third reminds him or her of the product's benefits.[12] However, even this bare-bones approach implies that we need repetition to ensure that the consumer is actually exposed to (and processes) the message at least three times. As we've seen, this exposure is by no means guaranteed, because people tend to tune out or distort many marketing communications. Marketers that attempt to condition an association must ensure that the consumers they target will be exposed to the stimulus a sufficient number of times to make it "stick."

However, it is possible to have too much of a good thing. Consumers can become so used to hearing or seeing a marketing stimulus that they no longer pay attention to it. One solution is to create variations of the same basic message to alleviate this problem of **advertising wear-out**. Toyota ran a commercial featuring a reworked version of The Fixx's song "Saved by Zero" to promote its no-interest payment options so many times that close to 10,000 fed-up viewers organized a *Facebook* group to petition the company for mercy. As one worn-out group member posted, "There have been worse commercials, and there have been commercials that were played this often; but never before has a commercial this bad been aired so much."[13]

How often should an advertiser repeat the ads it places on Web sites? Recent research indicates that the answer depends on whether the ad relates to the Web site's content, and whether or not competing ads are also present on the site. The study found support for the general idea that repetitive ad messages resulted in higher recall and interest in learning more about the advertised product (in this case, a laptop). However, repeating the same ad was primarily effective when competitors also showed ads on the site. Otherwise, it was better to vary the ad messages for the laptop (presumably because people tuned out the ad if it appeared repeatedly). These ads were also more effective when they appeared on a site where the content related to the advertised product.[14]

Marketing Applications of Conditioned Product Associations

Advertisements often pair a product with a positive stimulus to create a desirable association. Various aspects of a marketing message, such as music, humor, or imagery, can affect conditioning. In one study, for example, subjects who viewed a slide of pens paired with either pleasant or unpleasant music were more likely later to select the pen that appeared with the pleasant music.[15]

Marketing Applications of Stimulus Generalization

The iconic (and deceased) reggae singer Bob Marley's name and image appears on a vast range of products, including caps, lanyards, T-shirts, rolling papers, handbags and purses,

Universities create a revenue stream when they grant companies the rights to use their names and logos.
Source: RosalreneBetancourt/Alamy.

belts and buckles, beach towels, and knapsacks. His daughter Cedella launched High Tide swimwear to further extend the franchise, and his son Rohan created the Marley Coffee brand; each variety is named after a different Marley tune.[17]

The process of stimulus generalization often is central to branding and packaging decisions that try to capitalize on consumers' positive associations with an existing brand or company name. We clearly appreciate the value of this kind of linkage when we look at universities with winning sports teams: Loyal fans snap up merchandise, from clothing to bathroom accessories, emblazoned with the school's name. This business did

Bentley is among many luxury carmakers that is aggressively licensing its name in other product categories.
Source: Courtesy of Bentley Motors Limited.

not even exist 20 years ago when schools were reluctant to commercialize their images. Texas A&M was one of the first schools that even bothered to file for trademark protection, and that was only after someone put the Aggie logo on a line of handguns. Today it's a different story. Many college administrators crave the revenue they receive from sweatshirts, drink coasters, and even toilet seats emblazoned with school logos. Washington State University sells branded Wagyu beef raised by its staff and animal science students. It joins other college-branded delicacies, including Cornell Dairy Ice Cream and Texas A&M Jerky.[18]

Strategies that marketers base on stimulus generalization include:

- **Family branding**—Many products capitalize on the reputation of a company name. Companies such as Campbell's, Heinz, and General Electric rely on their positive corporate images to sell different product lines.
- **Product line extension**—Marketers add related products to an established brand. Dole, which we associate with fruit, introduced refrigerated juices and juice bars, whereas Sun Maid went from raisins to raisin bread. The gun manufacturer Smith & Wesson launched its own line of furniture and other home items. Starbucks Corp. and Jim Beam Brands teamed up to make Starbucks Coffee Liqueur. Condé Nast is opening bars and clubs linked to its *Vogue* and *GQ* magazines around the world.[19]
- **Licensing**—Companies often "rent" well-known names, hoping that the learned associations they have forged will "rub off" onto other kinds of products. Jamba Juice launched a clothing line.[20] Zippo Manufacturing Co., long known for its "windproof" cigarette lighters, markets a men's fragrance—and no, it doesn't smell like lighter fluid.[21]
- **Look-alike packaging**—Distinctive packaging designs create strong associations with a particular brand. Companies that make generic or private-label brands and want to communicate a quality image often exploit this linkage when they put their products in packages similar to those of popular brands.[23] How does this strategy affect consumers' perceptions of the original brand? One study found that a negative experience with an imitator brand actually *increased* consumers' evaluations of the original brand, whereas a positive experience with the imitator had the opposite effect of decreasing evaluations of the original brand.[24] Another study found that consumers tend to react positively to "copycat brands" as long as the imitator doesn't make grandiose claims that it can't fulfill.[25]

Of course, this strategy can make a lot of work for lawyers if the copycat brand gets *too* close to the original. Marketers of distinctive brands work hard to protect their designs and logos, and each year companies file numerous lawsuits in so-called *Lanham Act* cases that hinge on the issue of **consumer confusion**: How likely is it that one company's logo, product design, or package is so similar to another that the typical shopper would mistake one for the other? Levi Strauss has sued almost 100 other apparel manufacturers that it claims have borrowed its trademark pocket design of a pentagon surrounding a drawing of a seagull in flight or its distinctive tab that it sews into its garments' vertical seams.[26]

Companies with a well-established brand image try to encourage stimulus discrimination when they promote the unique attributes of their brand—hence the constant reminders for American Express Travelers Cheques: "Ask for them by name." However, a brand name that a firm uses so widely that it is no longer distinctive becomes part of the public domain and competitors are free to borrow it: think of well-worn names such as aspirin, cellophane, yo-yo, escalator, and even google (which started as a noun and is now also a verb). This high degree of acceptance can be a tough barrier to jump when you're a competitor: Microsoft hopes that over time we will choose to "bing" rather than "google" when we want information.

OBJECTIVE 4-4

There is a difference between classical and instrumental conditioning, and both processes help consumers learn about products.

Instrumental Conditioning

Instrumental conditioning (or *operant conditioning*) occurs when we learn to perform behaviors that produce positive outcomes and avoid those that yield negative outcomes. We most closely associate this learning process with the psychologist B. F. Skinner, who demonstrated the effects of instrumental conditioning by teaching pigeons and other animals to dance, play Ping-Pong, and perform other activities when he systematically rewarded them for desired behaviors.[27]

Whereas responses in classical conditioning are involuntary and fairly simple, we make those in instrumental conditioning deliberately to obtain a goal, and these may be more complex. We may learn the desired behavior over a period of time as a **shaping** process rewards our intermediate actions. For example, the owner of a new store may award prizes to shoppers who simply drop in; she hopes that over time they will continue to drop in and eventually even buy something.

Also, whereas classical conditioning involves the close pairing of two stimuli, instrumental learning occurs when a learner receives a reward *after* he or she performs the desired behavior. In these cases, learning takes place over time, while the learner attempts and abandons other behaviors that don't get reinforced. A good way to remember the difference is to keep in mind that in instrumental learning the person makes a response because it is *instrumental* to gain a reward or avoid a punishment. Over time, consumers come to associate with people who reward them and to choose products that make them feel good or satisfy some need.

Instrumental conditioning occurs in one of three ways:

1 When the environment provides **positive reinforcement** in the form of a reward, this strengthens the response and we learn the appropriate behavior. For example, a woman who gets compliments after wearing Obsession perfume learns that using this product has the desired effect, and she will be more likely to keep buying the product.

2 **Negative reinforcement** also strengthens responses so that we learn the appropriate behavior. A perfume company might run an ad showing a woman sitting home alone on a Saturday night because she did not wear its fragrance. The message this conveys is that she could have avoided this negative outcome if only she had used the perfume.

3 In contrast to situations where we learn to do certain things to avoid unpleasantness, **punishment** occurs when unpleasant events follow a response (such as when our friends ridicule us if we wear a nasty-smelling fragrance). We learn the hard way not to repeat these behaviors.

4 To help you understand the differences among these mechanisms, keep in mind that reactions from a person's environment to his or her behavior can be either positive or

Positive reinforcement occurs after consumers try a new product and like it.
Source: Provided courtesy of Frito-Lay North America, Inc.

negative, and that marketers can either apply or remove these outcomes (or anticipated outcomes). That is, under conditions of both positive reinforcement and punishment, the person receives a reaction when he or she does something. In contrast, negative reinforcement occurs when the person avoids a negative outcome—the removal of something negative is pleasurable and hence is rewarding.

Finally, when a person no longer receives a positive outcome, *extinction* is likely to occur, and the learned stimulus–response connection will not be maintained (as when a woman no longer receives compliments on her perfume). Thus, positive and negative reinforcement strengthen the future linkage between a response and an outcome because of the pleasant experience. This tie is weakened under conditions of both punishment and extinction because of the unpleasant experience. Figure 4.1 will help you to "reinforce" the relationships among these four conditions.

Figure 4.1 TYPES OF REINFORCEMENT

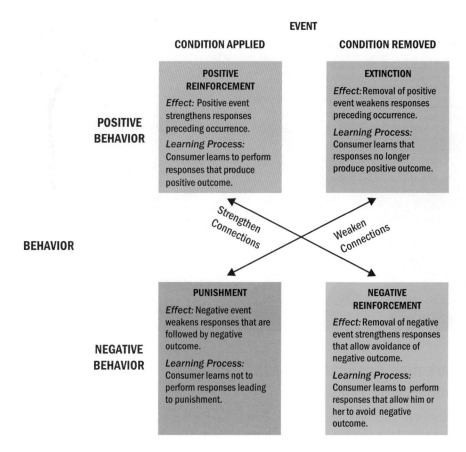

It's important for marketers to determine the most effective reinforcement schedule to use. This decision relates to the amount of effort and resources they must devote when they reward consumers who respond as they hope to their requests. Several schedules are possible:

- **Fixed-interval reinforcement**—After a specified time period has passed, the first response you make brings the reward. Under such conditions, people tend to respond slowly right after they get reinforced, but their responses get faster as the time for the next reinforcement approaches. For example, consumers may crowd into a store for the last day of its seasonal sale and not reappear until the next one.
- **Variable-interval reinforcement**—The time that must pass before you get reinforced varies based on some average. Because you don't know exactly when to expect the reinforcement, you have to respond at a consistent rate. This is the logic behind retailers' use of so-called *secret shoppers:* people who periodically test for service quality when they pose as customers at unannounced times. Because store employees never know exactly when to expect a visit, they must maintain high quality constantly "just in case."
- **Fixed-ratio reinforcement**—Reinforcement occurs only after a fixed number of responses. This schedule motivates you to continue performing the same behavior over and over. For example, you might keep buying groceries at the same store to earn a prize when you collect 50 register receipts.
- **Variable-ratio reinforcement**—You get reinforced after a certain number of responses, but you don't know how many responses are required. People in such situations tend to respond at high and steady rates, and this type of behavior is difficult to extinguish. This reinforcement schedule is responsible for consumers' attractions to slot machines. They learn that if they keep throwing money into the machine, they will eventually win something (if they don't go broke first).

Casino operators program slot machines to deliver rewards on a variable-ratio reinforcement schedule.

Source: Boggy/Fotolia.

Marketing Applications of Instrumental Conditioning Principles

Principles of instrumental conditioning are at work when a marketer rewards or punishes a consumer for a purchase decision. Businesspeople shape behavior when they gradually reinforce the appropriate actions consumers take. A car dealer might encourage a reluctant buyer to simply sit in a floor model, then suggest a test drive, and then try to close the deal.

Marketers have many ways to reinforce consumers' behaviors, ranging from a simple "thank you" after a purchase to substantial rebates and follow-up phone calls. For example, a life insurance company obtained a much higher rate of policy renewal among a group of new customers who received a thank-you letter after each payment, compared to a control group that did not receive any reinforcement.[28]

Frequency marketing is a popular technique that rewards regular purchasers with prizes that get better as they spend more. The airline industry pioneered this instrumental learning strategy when it introduced "frequent flyer" programs in the early 1980s to reward loyal customers. The practice has spread to many other businesses as well, ranging from grocery stores to casinos.

Gamification: The New Frontier for Learning Applications

Many of us grew up playing games, and some of us never stopped. In some sense, all of life is a game, insofar as there are winners and losers and challenges we must solve to reach various objectives. Many organizations are going to the next level; they're borrowing from basic principles of gaming to motivate consumers and employees across a broad spectrum of activity.

The fast-growing strategy of **gamification** turns routine actions into experiences as it adds gaming elements to tasks that might otherwise be boring or routine. Young people have grown up playing games; these activities structure their learning styles and influence the platforms to which they will gravitate.[29] Important elements of gaming include:

- A dynamic digital environment (whether in-store, on a laptop, or on a tablet or phone) that resembles a sophisticated videogame platform
- Multiple short- and long-term goals

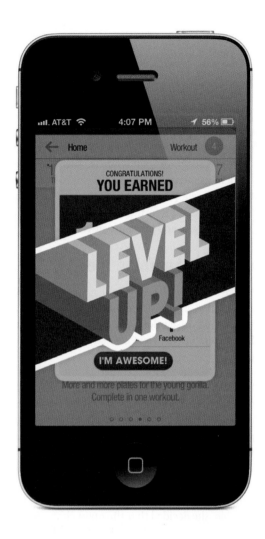

A phone app "gamfies" working out so that people will be more likely to break a sweat.
Source: Courtesy of Fitocracy, Inc.

- Rapid and frequent feedback
- A reward for most or all efforts in the form of a badge or a virtual product
- Friendly competition in a low-risk environment
- A manageable degree of uncertainty

At its most basic, gamification is simply about providing rewards to customers to encourage them to buy even more. These mechanisms used to take the form of buy-10-get-one-free punch cards, but today a host of sophisticated phone apps dispense rewards to eager shoppers—sometimes with a twist when marketers tinker with the reinforcement schedule. Indeed research shows that when a business "preloads" a frequent buyer card with a few punches this makes the reward look more attainable and motivates consumers to complete the rest. In a study on what the researchers term the **endowed progress effect**, a carwash gave one set of customers a buy-eight-get-one-free card, while a second set of customers got a 10-wash card that had been punched twice. Researchers reported that almost twice as many people in the second condition redeemed their cards even though in both cases customers had to pay for eight carwashes to get a free one. The connection to basic learning processes is clear. As one marketing professor explained, "All organisms, in different ways, are drawn to goals. The closer we are to achieving our goals, the more motivated we are to keep doing something. As mice on a runway get closer to a food pellet, they run faster…. as people get closer to having a completed card, the time between visits gets smaller." [30]

Many domains of human activity (and business) share the common need to motivate and reward people to achieve ascending levels of mastery. These include:

- **Store and brand loyalty.** Foursquare gives people virtual badges when they check in at a local cafe or restaurant. Some of them check in as often as they can to compete for the honor of being named "mayor" of the location.
- **Social marketing.** More than 75 utilities use a service from a company called Opower that awards badges to customers when they reduce their energy consumption. Customers can compare their progress with their neighbors' and broadcast their achievements on Facebook.
- **Employee performance.** Some restaurants enlist a service called Objective Logistics to rank the performances of waiters on a leaderboard, rewarding the good ones with plum shifts and more lucrative tables.[31]

Cognitive Learning Theory

Unlike behavioral theories of learning, **cognitive learning theory** approaches stress the importance of internal mental processes. This perspective views people as problem-solvers who actively use information from the world around them to master their environments. Supporters of this view also stress the role of creativity and insight during the learning process.

An Ocean Spray commercial for diet cranberry juice illustrates how marketers can harness their knowledge of cognitive theories to tweak marketing messages. The spot features two men, in the role of cranberry growers, who stand knee-deep in a bog. A group of women who are exercising joins them. Originally, the ad depicted the women having a party, but a cognitive scientist who worked on the campaign nixed that idea; she argued that the exercise class would send the diet message more quickly, whereas the party scene would confuse viewers who would spend too much time trying to figure out why the group was celebrating. This extra cognitive activity would distract from the ad's message. And, contrary to standard practice in advertising that the actors name the product as early as possible, she decided that the main characters should wait a few seconds before they mention the new diet product. She reasoned that viewers would need a second or so more time to process the images because of the additional action in the ad (the exercising). In a test of which ads got remembered best, this new version scored in the top 10 percent.[32]

Is Learning Conscious or Not?

A lot of controversy surrounds the issue of whether or when people are aware of their learning processes.[33] Whereas behavioral learning theorists emphasize the routine, automatic nature of conditioning, proponents of cognitive learning argue that even these simple effects are based on cognitive factors: They create expectations that a response will follow a stimulus (the formation of expectations requires mental activity). According to this school of thought, conditioning occurs because subjects develop conscious hypotheses and then act on them.

There is some evidence to support the existence of *nonconscious procedural knowledge.* People apparently do process at least some information in an automatic, passive way, a condition that researchers call "mindlessness" (we've all experienced that!).[34] When we meet someone new or encounter a new product, for example, we have a tendency to respond to the stimulus in terms of existing categories we have learned, rather than taking the trouble to formulate new ones. In these cases a *trigger feature*—some stimulus that cues us toward a particular pattern—activates a reaction. For example, men in one study rated a car in an ad as superior on a variety of characteristics if a seductive woman (the trigger feature) was present, despite the fact that the men did not believe the woman's presence actually had an influence on their evaluations.[35] We'll discuss these triggers in the context of *priming* in later chapters.

Nonetheless, many modern theorists regard some instances of automatic conditioning as cognitive processes, especially when people form expectations about the linkages between stimuli and responses. Indeed, studies using *masking effects*, which make it difficult for subjects to learn CS and UCS associations, show substantial reductions in conditioning.[36] An adolescent girl may observe that women on television and in real life seem to be rewarded with compliments and attention when they smell nice and wear alluring clothing. She figures out that the probability of these rewards occurring is greater when she wears perfume, so she deliberately wears a popular scent to obtain the reward of social acceptance. For now, the jury is out regarding the true impact of nonconscious processing and priming because this question currently is one of the hottest debates in the field of psychology.[37]

OBJECTIVE 4-5

We learn about products by observing others' behavior.

Observational Learning

Observational learning occurs when we watch the actions of others and note the reinforcements they receive for their behaviors. In these situations, learning occurs as a result of *vicarious* rather than direct experience. This type of learning is a complex process; people store these observations in memory as they accumulate knowledge and then they use this information at a later point to guide their own behavior. Particularly when we are preoccupied with other demands, we are likely to mimic others' behaviors as a **social default**.[38]

Modeling (not the runway kind) is the process of imitating the behavior of others. For example, a woman who shops for a new kind of perfume may remember the reactions her friend received when she wore a certain brand several months before, and she will mimic her friend's behavior in the hope that she will get the same feedback.

The modeling process is a powerful form of learning, and people's tendencies to imitate others' behaviors can have negative effects. Of particular concern is the potential of television shows and movies to teach violence to children. Children may be exposed to new methods of aggression by models (e.g., cartoon heroes) in the shows they watch. At some later point, when the child becomes angry, he or she may imitate these behaviors. A classic study demonstrates the effect of modeling on children's actions. Kids who watched an adult stomp on, knock down, and otherwise torture a large inflated "Bobo doll" repeated these behaviors when later left alone in a room with the doll; children who did not witness these acts did not.[39] Unfortunately, the relevance of this study to violent TV shows seems quite clear.

Figure 4.2 shows that for observational learning in the form of modeling to occur, the marketer must meet four conditions:[40]

1 The consumer's attention must be directed to the appropriate model, whom, for reasons of attractiveness, competence, status, or similarity, he or she must want to emulate.
2 The consumer must remember what the model says or does.
3 The consumer must convert this information into actions.
4 The consumer must be motivated to perform these actions.

Figure 4.2 THE OBSERVATIONAL LEARNING PROCESS

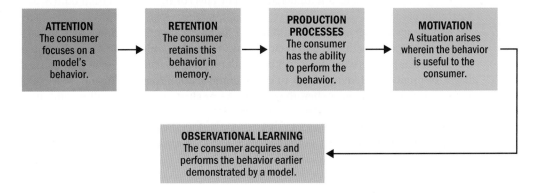

Marketing Applications of Cognitive Learning Principles

Our ability to learn vicariously when we observe the outcomes of what others do makes the lives of marketers much easier. They don't necessarily have to directly reward or punish consumers when they make a purchase (think how expensive or even ethically questionable that might be!). Instead, they can show what happens to desirable models who use or do not use their products; they know that consumers often will imitate these actions at a later time. For example, a perfume commercial might depict a throng of admirers who compliment a glamorous woman when she wears a certain fragrance. Needless to say, this learning process is more practical than providing the same attention to each woman who actually buys the perfume (unless your brand's market share is really, really small!).

Consumers' evaluations of the people they model go beyond simple stimulus–response connections. For example, a celebrity's image elicits more than a simple reflexive response of good or bad.[41] It is a complex combination of many attributes. In general, the degree to which a person emulates someone else depends on that model's level of *social attractiveness*. Attractiveness comes from several components, including physical appearance, expertise, or similarity to the evaluator (more on this in Chapter 8).

How Do We Learn to Be Consumers?

Ah, nothing like a luxurious spa day. But for a 4-year-old girl? Sensing big opportunities, many adult spas are adding separate services for young girls that go well beyond the old-fashioned mommy/daughter manicure. The International Spa Association reports that 25 percent of its members now offer services specifically for the younger-than-13 age group. Chains such as Sweet and Sassy pamper their "princesses" with custom-size robes and banana-scented facials.[42]

We don't spring from the womb with consumer skills in place. **Consumer socialization** is the process "by which young people acquire skills, knowledge, and attitudes relevant to their functioning in the marketplace."[43] Research supports the proposition that the brand preferences and product knowledge that occur in childhood persist into the later stages of consumers' lives.[44]

From where does this knowledge come? Friends and teachers certainly participate in this process. For instance, children talk to one another about consumer products, and this tendency increases as the kids age.[45] Especially for young children, though, the family and the media are two primary socialization sources.

Parents' Influence

Parents influence consumer socialization both directly and indirectly. They deliberately try to instill their own values about consumption in their children ("You're going to learn the value of a dollar!"). Parents also determine the degree to which their children come into contact with other information sources, such as television, salespeople, and peers.[46] Cultural expectations regarding children's involvement in purchase decisions influence when and how parents socialize their kids as consumers. For example, parents in traditional cultures such as Greece and India rely on later development timetables for consumer-related skills and understanding of advertising practices than do U.S. and Australian parents.[47]

Grown-ups also serve as significant models for observational learning. Children learn about consumption as they watch their parents' behaviors and imitate them. Marketers encourage this process when they package adult products in child versions. This "passing down" of product preferences helps to create brand loyalty; researchers find evidence of intergenerational influence when they study the product choices of mothers and their daughters.[48]

The process of consumer socialization begins with infants; within the first two years, children request products they want. By about age 5, most kids make purchases with the

Marketing Opportunity

The media play an especially large role in teaching us how to be girls and boys. TV programs, movies, and performers such as Miley Cyrus, Justin Bieber, and Iggy Azalea or "boy bands" like One Direction socialize us into gender roles. We'll dive more deeply into the importance of sexual identity for consumer behavior in Chapter 6, but for now it's worth noting how media role models help kids to learn about appropriate behaviors, or at least what society considers appropriate at any point in time:

Although Cinderella, Ariel and other princesses still offer a tried-and-true formula for girls that involves being "rescued" by a man, other heroines for girls teach a different lesson. Katniss from *The Hunger Games*, the Black Widow of *The Avengers*, Anna and Elsa of *Frozen*, and Tris from *Divergent* compete for girls' loyalty. The appeal of Katniss explains why Hasbro has done so well with the Nerf Rebelle Heartbreaker Exclusive Golden Edge Bow, a petunia-colored weapon with gold and white trim that shoots colorful foam darts. A similar product line, Zing's Air Huntress bows and sling shots, carries the slogan: "Ready. Aim. Girl Power." There's even a Barbie version of a Katniss doll complete with bow and arrow.[54]

The beauty industry is expanding to cater to the needs of young consumers.
Source: Alikssa/Fotolia.

help of parents and grandparents, and by age 8 most buy things on their own.[49] Figure 4.3 summarizes the sequence of stages as kids turn into consumers.

Parents exhibit different styles when they socialize their children:[50]

- *Authoritarian parents* are hostile, restrictive, and emotionally uninvolved. They do not have warm relationships with their children, they censor the types of media their children see, and they tend to have negative views about advertising.
- *Neglecting parents* also are detached from their children, and the parents don't exercise much control over what their children do.
- *Indulgent parents* communicate more with their children about consumption-related matters and are less restrictive. They believe that children should be allowed to learn about the marketplace without much interference.

Television and the Web: Electric Babysitters

Advertising starts to influence us at an early age. Today most kids divide their time among the TV set, the computer, and their cell phones. In the United States, about 80 percent of children age 5 and under use the Internet at least once a week. What's more, like their older brothers and sisters, little kids are avid multitaskers: A Nielsen

Figure 4.3 FIVE STAGES OF
CONSUMER DEVELOPMENT BY
EARLIEST AGE AT ONSET AND MEDIAN
AGE AT ONSET

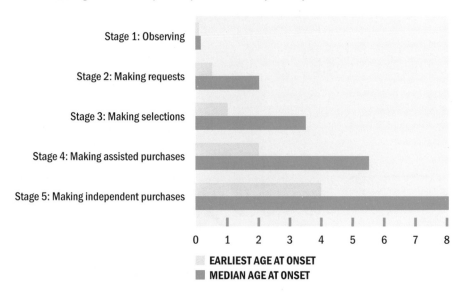

A CONSUMER IS BORN

Children start accompanying parents to the marketplace as early as one month old
and begin to make independent purchases as early as four years old.

study reported that 36 percent of kids ages 2 to 11 watch online content and TV at the same time.[51]

As we've seen, many marketers push their products on kids to encourage them to build a lifelong habit. The National Institutes of Health projects that a ban on fast-food advertising to children would cut the national obesity rate by as much as 18 percent.[52] In two studies, British researchers compared the effects of television advertising on the eating habits of 152 kids between the ages of 5 and 11. The kids watched 10 ads followed by a cartoon. In one session, the kids saw ads for toys before they watched a video. In another session, the researchers replaced the toy ads with food ads that commonly run during children's programs. After both viewings, held two weeks apart, the kids were allowed to snack as much as they wanted from a table of low-fat and high-fat snacks, including grapes, cheese-flavored rice cakes, chocolate buttons and potato chips. The 5- to 7-year-old kids who saw the food ads ate 14 to 17 percent more calories than those who saw the toy ads. The results were even more dramatic among 9- to 11-year-olds. Those in the food ad condition ate from 84 to 134 percent more calories than did those in the toy ad condition.[53]

Cognitive Development

A child's ability to make mature, "adult" consumer decisions obviously increases with age (not that grown-ups always make mature decisions). Marketers segment kids in terms of their **stage of cognitive development**, or their ability to comprehend concepts of increasing complexity. Some evidence indicates that young children learn consumption-related information surprisingly well.[55]

The Swiss psychologist Jean Piaget was the foremost proponent of the idea that children pass through distinct stages of cognitive development. He believed that a certain cognitive structure characterizes each stage as the child learns to process information.[56] In one classic demonstration of cognitive development, Piaget poured the contents of a short, squat glass of lemonade into a taller, thinner glass that actually held the same amount of liquid. Five-year-olds, who still believed that the shape of the glass determined its contents, thought this glass held more liquid than the first glass. They are in what Piaget termed a *preoperational stage of development*. In contrast, 6-year-olds tended to be unsure, but 7-year-olds knew the amount of lemonade had not changed.

Many developmental specialists no longer believe that children necessarily pass through these fixed stages at the same time. An alternative view proposes that they differ in information-processing capability or the ability to store and retrieve information from memory. Researchers who advocate this approach identify three developmental stages:[57]

1 **Limited**—Children who are younger than age 6 do not employ storage-and-retrieval strategies.
2 **Cued**—Children between the ages of 6 and 12 employ these strategies but only when prompted to do so.
3 **Strategic**—Children 12 and older spontaneously employ storage-and-retrieval strategies.

This sequence of development underscores the notion that children do not think in the same way adults do, and we can't expect them to use information the same way either. It also reminds us that they do not necessarily form the same conclusions as do adults when they encounter product information. Kids are not as likely to realize that something they see on TV is not "real," and as a result they are more vulnerable to persuasive messages. Younger kids aren't able to distinguish media depictions from reality, so the more a child watches *Phineas and Ferb* or *SpongeBob SquarePants*, the more he or she will accept the images it depicts as real.[58] Kids also see idealized images of what it is like to be an adult. Because children older than age 6 do about a quarter of their television viewing during prime time, adult programs and commercials have a big effect on them. For example, young girls who see adult lipstick commercials associate lipstick with beauty.[59]

CB AS I SEE IT

Paul Connell, *Stony Brook University*

When we are children, we must learn many things, including how to become a consumer. A large and growing literature has found that children gradually learn many of the skills necessary to be a consumer as they age. These skills include learning how to identify which price promotions are the best deal (such as buy one get one free or 60% off), understanding how advertising works, and what brands symbolize in the culture in which they live. A large and growing body of research conducted in the fields of marketing, psychology, communication, nutrition, and public health have contributed greatly to our understanding of how children progress from a

"blank slate" as infants to having an increasingly sophisticated understanding of marketing techniques as they approach adulthood. However, we still know surprisingly little about how our experiences with the marketplace when we are children might affect us years or even decades later in adulthood. Most of what we know is based on research conducted within the last decade, and much remains to be learned.

In the research I have worked on with Merrie Brucks and Jesper Nielsen at the University of Arizona, we investigate whether exposure to advertising in childhood has effects that persist into adulthood. Previous research strongly supports the idea that children first begin to understand that ads are distinct from the content they are embedded within, then begin to understand that the purpose of advertising is to persuade, and finally effectively use the knowledge they have gained about marketing techniques to evaluate marketing activities more critically. However, what happens when we are exposed to ads before we have learned that the purpose of advertising is to persuade (versus to entertain or inform) or before we have learned how to use our marketplace knowledge effectively?

We find that exposure to advertising in childhood indeed has effects that last well beyond the time of initial exposure. That is, when we are exposed to ads before we have begun to process ads similar to the way adults do (in our early teens), we have a greater tendency to develop strong emotional connections to elements featured in the advertising, such as brand characters. This emotional connection then causes us to evaluate the products associated with the advertising less critically. For example, we might think that a sugary or fattening snack is healthier than we would otherwise judge it to be. These biases are also quite resilient. Even after using well-known techniques for getting people to recognize and correct for judgment biases, people who harbored strongly positive feelings toward advertising elements such as brand characters resisted changing their judgments of these products. We even found the biases can translate to new products that do not even exist yet when they feature the same advertising elements. For example, a well-known brand character for a breakfast cereal could be used to promote a different food product and biased product evaluations can transfer to the new product.

Research underscores the idea that children's understanding of brand names evolves as they age. Kids learn to relate to brand names at an early age; they recognize brand names in stores, develop preferences for some brands over others, and request branded items by name. However, brand names function as simple perceptual cues for these children that let them identify a familiar object with particular features. *Conceptual brand meanings*, which specify the nonobservable abstract features of the product, enter into the picture in middle childhood (about age 8); children incorporate them into their thinking and judgments a few years later. By the time a child reaches 12 years of age, he or she thinks about brands on a conceptual or symbolic level and he or she is likely to incorporate these meanings into brand-related judgments.[60]

Several business ventures illustrate that using sound principles of consumer psychology can also make good financial sense. The trend started a long time ago with public television's *Sesame Street*, but today the for-profit networks are in the game as well. The first successful foray into the preschool market was *Blue's Clues* in 1996, which turned into a huge hit as viewers abandoned the smarmy *Barney & Friends*.

Now, when millions of preschoolers tune in to Nickelodeon's hit show *Dora the Explorer*, they don't realize that they view content based on **multiple-intelligence theory**. This influential perspective argues for other types of intelligence, such as athletic prowess or musical ability, beyond the traditional math and verbal skills psychologists use to measure IQ. Thus, when Dora consults her map, she promotes "spatial" skills. And when she asks her young viewers to help her count planks to build a bridge, Dora builds "interpersonal intelligence."[61]

Message Comprehension

Because children differ in their abilities to process product-related information, advertisers' direct appeals to them raise many serious ethical issues.[62] Children's advocacy groups argue that kids younger than age 7 do not understand the persuasive intent of commercials, and (as we've seen) younger children cannot readily distinguish between a commercial and programming. Kids' cognitive defenses are not yet sufficiently developed to filter out commercial appeals, so in a sense, altering their brand preferences may be likened to "shooting fish in a barrel," as one critic put it.[63] Figure 4.4 shows one attempt to assess whether kids can tell that a commercial is trying to persuade them.

Beginning in the 1970s, the Federal Trade Commission (FTC) took action to protect children. The agency limited commercials during "children's" programming (most often Saturday morning television) and required "separators" to help children discern when a program ended and a commercial began (e.g., "We'll be right back after these commercial messages"). The FTC reversed itself in the early 1980s during the deregulatory, pro-business climate of Ronald Reagan's administration. The 1990 Children's Television Act restored some of these restrictions. Still, critics argue that rather than sheltering children from marketplace influences, the dominant way that marketers view them is as what one calls "kid customers."[64]

On the bright side, however, it seems that food companies are finally taking action to combat the growing problem of childhood obesity that they helped to create. Numerous corporations, including Sara Lee, Burger King, Campbell Soup Company, Coca-Cola, Pepsi,

Figure 4.4 EXAMPLES OF SKETCHES RESEARCHERS USE TO MEASURE CHILDREN'S PERCEPTIONS OF COMMERCIAL INTENT

Dannon, General Mills, Hershey, Kellogg, Kraft Foods, Mars, McDonald's, and Nestlé, have joined the Council of Better Business Bureau's Children's Food and Beverage Initiative. They have pledged to market to kids 11 and younger only products that meet government or American Heart Association standards for "healthy" foods. In addition, this agreement restricts the use of third-party licensed characters in ads targeted to child audiences and sharply limits the usage of product images in places like elementary schools and video games.[65] In addition, the FTC recently strengthened privacy safeguards that cover mobile apps and Web sites targeted to children; now companies must obtain parental consent before they collect data from kids that could be used to identify, contact, or locate them.[66]

OBJECTIVE 4-6
Our brains process information about brands to retain them in memory.

Memory

Memory is a process of acquiring information and storing it over time so that it will be available when we need it. Contemporary approaches to the study of memory employ an *information-processing approach*. They assume that the mind is in some ways like a computer: Data are input, processed, and output for later use in revised form. Figure 4.5 summarizes the memory process:

1 In the **encoding** stage, information enters in a way the system will recognize.
2 In the **storage stage**, we integrate this knowledge with what is already in memory and "warehouse" it until it is needed.
3 During **retrieval**, we access the desired information.[67]

Many of our experiences are locked inside our heads, and they may surface years later if the right cues prompt them. Marketers rely on consumers to retain information they collect about products and services so they will apply it to future purchase decisions. We combine this *internal memory* with *external memory* when we decide what to buy. This includes all the product details on packages and other marketing stimuli that permit us to identify and evaluate brand alternatives in the marketplace.[68]

The grocery-shopping list is a good example of a powerful external memory aid. When consumers use shopping lists, they buy approximately 80 percent of the items on the list. The likelihood that a shopper will purchase a particular list item is higher if the person who wrote the list also participates in the shopping trip. This means that if marketers can induce consumers to plan to purchase an item before they go shopping, there is a high probability that they will buy it. One way to encourage this kind of advance planning

Figure 4.5 TYPES OF MEMORY

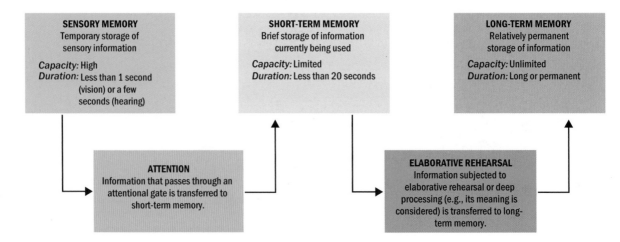

SENSORY MEMORY	SHORT-TERM MEMORY	LONG-TERM MEMORY
Temporary storage of sensory information	Brief storage of information currently being used	Relatively permanent storage of information
Capacity: High	*Capacity:* Limited	*Capacity:* Unlimited
Duration: Less than 1 second (vision) or a few seconds (hearing)	*Duration:* Less than 20 seconds	*Duration:* Long or permanent

ATTENTION
Information that passes through an attentional gate is transferred to short-term memory.

ELABORATIVE REHEARSAL
Information subjected to elaborative rehearsal or deep processing (e.g., its meaning is considered) is transferred to long-term memory.

is to provide peel-off stickers on packages so that, when consumers notice the supply is low, they can simply peel off the label and place it directly on a shopping list.[69] Or, a retailer can support a phone app that generates a shopping list for the user (you already can choose from an abundance of apps that do this).[70]

How Our Brains Encode Information

The way we *encode*, or mentally program, information helps to determine how our brains will store this information. In general, it's more likely that we'll retain incoming data when we associate it with other things already in memory. For example, we tend to remember brand names that we link to physical characteristics of a product category (e.g., Coffee-Mate creamer or Sani-Flush toilet bowl cleaner) or that we can easily visualize (e.g., Tide detergent or Ford Mustang cars) compared to more abstract brand names.[71] Similarly, our brains automatically react to images of familiar celebrities and use them to guide how we think about them to ascribe meaning to other images of people or products with which they appear.[72]

Sometimes we process a stimulus simply in terms of its *sensory meaning*, such as the literal color or shape of a package. We may experience a feeling of familiarity when, for example, we see an ad for a new snack food we have recently tasted. In many cases, though, we encode meanings at a more abstract level. *Semantic meaning* refers to symbolic associations, such as the idea that rich people drink champagne or that fashionable women have navel piercings. Let's take a closer look at how we encode these deeper meanings.

Episodic memories relate to events that are personally relevant.[73] As a result, a person's motivation to retain these memories will likely be strong. Couples often have "their song," which reminds them of their first date or wedding. We call some especially vivid associations *flashbulb memories* (where were you when you first heard that Osama bin Laden was dead?). In addition, recall of the past may affect future behavior. A college fund-raising campaign can raise more money when it evokes pleasant college memories than when it reminds alumni of unpleasant ones.

A **narrative**, or a description of a product that is written as a story, is often an effective way to convey product information. Our memories store a lot of the social information we acquire in story form; it's a good idea to construct ads in the form of a narrative

Certain events create flashbulb memories. Do you remember when you heard that Osama bin Laden was dead?

Source: Cal Vornberger/Alamy.

so they resonate with the audience. Narratives persuade people to construct mental representations of the information they see or hear. Pictures aid in this construction and allow us to develop more detailed mental representations.[74] Research supports the idea that we are more likely to positively evaluate and purchase brands when they connect with us like this.[75]

Memory Systems

Researchers describe three distinct memory systems: *sensory memory, short-term memory (STM)*, and *long-term memory (LTM)*. Each plays a role in processing brand-related information (see Figure 4.5).

Sensory Memory

Sensory memory stores the information we receive from our senses. This storage is temporary; it lasts a couple of seconds at most. For example, a man who walks past a donut shop gets a quick, enticing whiff of something baking inside. Although this sensation lasts only a few seconds, it is sufficient to allow him to consider whether he should investigate further. If he retains this information for further processing, it transfers to short-term memory.

Short-Term Memory

Short-term memory (STM) also stores information for a limited period of time, and it has limited capacity. Similar to a computer, this system is *working memory*; it holds the information we are currently processing. Our memories can store verbal input *acoustically* (in terms of how it sounds) or *semantically* (in terms of what it means).

We store this information as we combine small pieces into larger ones in a process we call **chunking**. A *chunk* is a configuration that is familiar to the person and that he or she can think about as a unit. For example, a brand name like 7 For All Mankind is a chunk that represents a great deal of detailed information about the product.

Initially, researchers believed that our STM was capable of processing between five and nine chunks of information at a time; they described this basic property as "the magical number 7+/−2." This is the reason our phone numbers today (at least in the United States) have seven digits.[76] It now appears that three to four chunks is the optimal size for efficient retrieval (we remember seven-digit phone numbers because we chunk the individual digits, so we may remember a three-digit exchange as one piece of information).[77] Phone calls aside, chunking is important to marketers because it helps determine how consumers keep prices in short-term memory when they comparison-shop.[78]

Long-Term Memory

Long-term memory (LTM) is the system that allows us to retain information for a long period of time. A cognitive process of **elaborative rehearsal** allows information to move from STM into LTM. This involves thinking about the meaning of a stimulus and relating it to other information already in memory. Marketers assist in the process when they devise catchy slogans or jingles that consumers repeat on their own.

How Our Memories Store Information

The relationship between STM and LTM is a source of some controversy. The traditional *multiple-store* perspective assumes that STM and LTM are separate systems. More recent research has moved away from the distinction between the two types of memory; it emphasizes the interdependence of the systems. According to **activation models of memory**, depending on the nature of the processing task different levels of processing occur that activate some aspects of memory rather than others.[81] The more effort it takes to process information (so-called *deep processing*), the more likely it is that information will transfer into LTM.

Marketing Opportunity

It's common for marketers to give a brand a vivid name that conjures up an image or story in our minds. Research suggests that this strategy results in higher consumer evaluations versus brand names composed of meaningless letters or numbers. One study reported that consumers rated cell phones from Samsung and LG more positively after they were the first in the industry to break the practice of naming the phones with combinations of letters and numbers—LG's phones instead sport names like Chocolate, Shine, Vu, Voyager, Dare, and Decoy, whereas Samsung started things off with the Black-Jack, UpStage, FlipShot, and Juke, and later added the Access, Instinct, and Glyde. During the same period these companies increased market share in this category. Compared to other phone brands, consumers rated these models as modern, creative, engaging, original, cool and easy to remember.[79]

CB AS I SEE IT
John Lynch, *University of Colorado-Boulder*

The most important idea in all of marketing is the consumer's *consideration set* – the set of alternatives actively considered for choice.

1. Most of the time you as a marketer *fail* to make a sale to a consumer, it is not because you were considered and found wanting: it is because you were never considered.
2. Most of the time if you as a marketer *do* make a sale, it is not because you were the best possible option for that consumer if he or she had searched exhaustively:

it is because the consumer failed to consider another alternative he or she would have liked better.

My colleagues and I believe that these principles explain how consumers respond to *resource scarcity* of money or time by retrieving from memory alternative ways to spend a resource. [80] In economics, a key idea is *opportunity cost* – any time you decide to spend a resource, you are supposed to ask whether that is the highest and best use of the resource. Should you spend $5 at Starbucks or save it for clothing? But newer work shows that only sometimes do consumers only think about opportunity costs, consistent with point 2 above.

Suppose you have plenty of cash in your wallet, and you are standing in line at McDonalds and thinking about what to order for breakfast. Experiments show that it may not even occur to you that you could spend that cash on something else later in the day. But when you have just a little cash in your wallet, later-in-the-day opportunity costs now pop into your head and enter your consideration set for how you are going to spend that money.

My colleagues and I find that the resource uses that enter your consideration sets are of two types, which we call *priority plans* and *efficiency plans*. In priority planning, consumers realize opportunity costs because they don't feel like they have enough of the resource to have everything in their consideration sets; they decide to sacrifice less important uses. In efficiency planning, consumers try to cope with a shortage without giving up anything by using the resource more efficiently—e.g., clipping coupons to save money, or combining shopping trips to save time.

We find that when consumers perceive little constraint, neither efficiency plans nor priority plans enter their consideration sets. When consumers feel moderate constraint, plans of both types start popping into their heads. But the efficiency plans feel good and the priority plans feel bad, so only when consumers are seriously constrained do priority plans start to pop into their heads faster and more frequently. When we consumers prioritize too little and too late, that can get us in a lot of trouble. It's all about how memory affects our consideration sets!

OBJECTIVE 4-7
The other products we associate with an individual product influence how we will remember it.

Associative Networks

According to activation models of memory, an incoming piece of information gets stored in an **associative network** that contains many bits of related information. We each have organized systems of concepts that relate to brands, manufacturers, and stores stored in our memories; the contents, of course, depend on our own unique experiences.

Think of these storage units, or *knowledge structures*, as complex spider webs filled with pieces of data. Incoming information gets put into nodes that connect to one another (if you haven't guessed, this is also why we call cyberspace the World Wide Web). When we view separate pieces of information as similar for some reason, we chunk them together under some more abstract category. Then, we interpret new, incoming information to be consistent with the structure we have created.[82] This

Figure 4.6 AN ASSOCIATIVE
NETWORK FOR PERFUMES

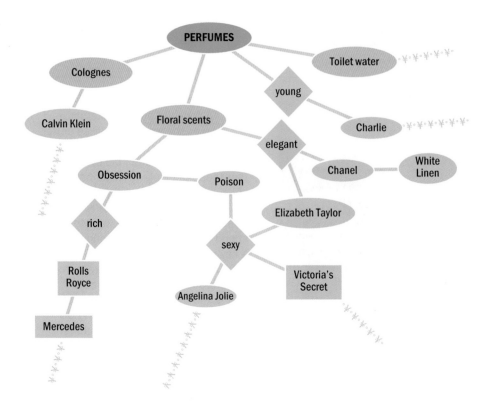

The Tangled Web

Social networks such as Facebook have revolutionized how people store and share memories. However, at least some users are starting to feel that maybe these platforms do this a bit too well: They don't necessarily want others (especially employers, parents, and other authority figures) to know about all of their "awesome" experiences. As a result a number of newer platforms including Wickr, Vidburn, and even Facebook's own Poke allow photos or messages to be viewed for a few seconds before they vanish into cyberspace. The biggest hit is Snapchat, which posts and then destroys more than 60 million photos or messages every day—already a tenth of the activity that occurs on the much bigger Facebook platform. One of Snapchat's founders explained the thinking behind the app: "It became clear how awful social media is. "There is real value in sharing moments that don't live forever."[84]

helps explain why we are better able to remember brands or stores that we believe "go together"; for example, when Titleist golf balls rather than Chanel fragrances sponsors a golf tournament.[83]

In the associative network, links form between nodes. For example, a consumer might have a network for "perfumes." Each node represents a concept related to the category. This node can be an attribute, a specific brand, a celebrity the consumer identifies with a specific perfume brand, or even a related product. A network for perfumes might include concepts such as the brand names Viva La Juicy by Juicy Couture, Calvin Klein Eternity, and Elizabeth Arden Red Door, as well as attributes such as sexy and elegant.

When we ask the consumer to list perfumes, this consumer recalls only those brands that show up in the appropriate category. The task of a new entrant that wants to position itself as a category member (e.g., a new luxury perfume) is to provide cues that facilitate its placement in the appropriate category. Figure 4.6 shows a sample network for perfumes.

Spreading Activation

A marketing message may activate our memory of a brand directly (for example, when it shows us a picture of the package), or it may do so indirectly when it links to something else that's related to the brand in our knowledge structure. If it activates a node, it will also activate other linked nodes, much as tapping a spider's web in one spot sends movement reverberating across the web. Meaning thus spreads across the network, and we recall concepts, such as competing brands and relevant attributes, that we use to form attitudes toward the brand.

This process of **spreading activation** allows us to shift back and forth among levels of meaning. The way we store a piece of information in memory depends on the type of meaning we initially assign to it. This meaning type, in turn, will determine how and when something activates the meaning. Thus, we could store the memory trace for an Axe men's fragrance ad in one or more of the following ways:

- **Brand-specific**—Memory is stored in terms of claims the brand makes ("it's macho").
- **Ad-specific**—Memory is stored in terms of the medium or content of the ad itself (a macho-looking guy uses the product).

- **Brand identification**—Memory is stored in terms of the brand name (e.g., "Axe").
- **Product category**—Memory is stored in terms of how the product works or where it should be used (a bottle of Axe sits in a guy's medicine cabinet).
- **Evaluative reactions**—Memory is stored as positive or negative emotions ("that looks cool").[85]

Levels of Knowledge

Within a knowledge structure, we code elements at different levels of abstraction and complexity. *Meaning* concepts (such as "macho") get stored as individual nodes. We may combine these concepts into a larger unit we call a *proposition* (or a *belief*). A proposition links two nodes together to form a more complex meaning, which can serve as a single chunk of information. For example, "Axe is cologne for macho men" is a proposition (though not necessarily a correct one!).

In turn, we integrate propositions to produce an even more complex unit called a **schema**. As we saw in Chapter 3, a schema is a cognitive framework we develop through experience. We encode information more readily when that information is consistent with an existing schema.[86] The ability to move up and down among levels of abstraction greatly increases processing flexibility and efficiency. For this reason, young children who do not yet have well-developed schemas are not able to make as efficient use of purchase information as are older children.[87]

One type of schema especially relevant to consumer behavior is a **script**; a sequence of events an individual expects to occur. As consumers we learn **service scripts** that guide our behavior in commercial settings. We expect a certain sequence of events, and we may become uncomfortable if the service departs from our script. A service script for a visit to the dentist might include such events as (1) drive to the dentist, (2) read old magazines in the waiting room, (3) hear name called and sit in dentist's chair, (4) dentist injects something into gums, (5) dentist turns on high-pitched drill, and so on. This desire to follow a script helps to explain why such service innovations as automatic bank machines, self-service gas stations, or "scan-your-own" grocery checkouts have met with resistance by some consumers who have trouble adapting to new sequences of events.[88]

Marketing Opportunity

Individual cognitive or physiological factors are responsible for some of the differences in retrieval ability among people.[89] Older adults consistently display inferior recall ability for current items, such as prescription drug instructions, although they may recall events that happened to them when they were younger with great clarity.[90] The recent popularity of puzzles, such as Sudoku and Brain Box, and centers that offer "mental gymnastics" attests to emerging evidence that we can keep our retrieval abilities sharp by exercising our minds, just as we keep our other muscles toned when we work out on a regular basis.

There is a growing market for products that enable consumers to practice "mental gymnastics."
Source: Boominbox Limited.

How We Retrieve Memories When We Decide What to Buy

It hasn't been smooth sailing for the cruise industry lately, following several highly-publicized incidents where things were not exactly ship-shape on board. One of the most embarrassing and high-profile accidents stranded several thousand guests on a Carnival ship in the Gulf of Mexico with no electricity or working toilets, but plenty of smartphones to record the dismal conditions. Carnival's potential cruisers are skittish, so the cruise line launched a $25 million public relations offensive to lure people back on board. The campaign asks previous customers to use social media to post images and videos of happy experiences that will contribute to Carnival's "Moments that Matter" commercial. The ad's voiceover says, "We never forget the moments that matter. We hang them on our walls. We share them with everyone. And hold onto them forever. Since the day we first set sail, millions of lasting moments have been made with us. What will yours be?" Sure enough, the campaign received more than 30,000 submissions, presumably from passengers who enjoyed both the midnight chocolate buffet and working plumbing.[91]

We've seen that *retrieval* is the process whereby we recover information from long-term memory. As evidenced by the popularity of the board game *Trivial Pursuit* or the TV show *Are You Smarter Than a Fifth Grader?*, we have a vast quantity of information stored in our heads—a lot of which is not useful unless you play the game! Although most of the information that enters LTM does not go away, it may be difficult or impossible to retrieve unless the appropriate cues are present. What factors influence the likelihood that we will remember the marketing messages that organizations work so hard to create?

Situational factors also influence retrieval; these relate to the environment in which we encounter the message. Not surprisingly, recall is enhanced when we pay more attention to the message in the first place. Some evidence indicates that we can more easily retrieve information about a **pioneering brand** (the first brand to enter a market) from memory than we can for **follower brands** that ride their coattails because the first product's introduction is likely to be distinctive, and for the time being, no competitors divert our attention.[92] In addition, we are more likely to recall descriptive brand names than those that do not provide adequate cues as to what the product is.[93]

Not surprisingly, the way a marketer presents the message influences the likelihood that we'll be able to recall it later. The **spacing effect** describes the tendency for us to recall printed material more effectively when the advertiser repeats the target item periodically, rather than presenting it repeatedly in a short time period.[94] The viewing environment of a marketing message also affects recall. For example, commercials we see during baseball games yield the lowest recall scores among sports programs because the activity is stop-and-go rather than continuous. Unlike football or basketball, the pacing of baseball gives many opportunities for attention to wander even during play. General Electric discovered that its commercials fared better in television shows with continuous activity, such as stories or dramas, compared to variety shows or talk shows that are punctuated by a series of acts.[95] A large-scale analysis of TV commercials found that viewers recall commercials shown first in a series of ads better than those they see last.[96]

Finally, it goes without saying that the nature of the ad itself plays a big role in determining whether it's memorable. One study on print advertising reported that we are far more likely to remember spectacular magazine ads, including multipage spreads, three-dimensional pop-ups, scented ads, and ads with audio components. For example, a Pepsi Jazz two-page spread, which incorporated a three-dimensional pop-up of the opened bottle, a small audio chip that played jazz music from the bottle's opening, and a scratch-and-sniff tab that let readers smell its black cherry vanilla flavor, scored an amazing 100 percent in reader recall.[97] Unfortunately, that kind of multimedia treatment is expensive; not every ad can mimic a Broadway production!

What Makes Us Forget?

Marketers obviously hope that consumers will not forget about their products. However, in a poll of more than 13,000 adults, more than half were unable to remember any specific ad they had seen, heard, or read in the past 30 days. How many can you remember right now? Clearly, forgetting by consumers is a big headache for marketers (not to mention a problem for students when they study for exams!). In one major study, only 23 percent of the respondents could recall a new product introduced in the past year.[98]

Early memory theorists assumed that memories simply fade with the passage of time. In a process of **decay**, the structural changes that learning produces in the brain simply go away. Forgetting also occurs as a result of **interference**; as we learn additional information, it displaces the previous information. Consumers may forget stimulus–response associations if they subsequently learn new responses to the same or similar stimuli; we call this process *retroactive interference*. Or prior learning can interfere with new learning, a process we term *proactive interference*. Because we store pieces of information in memory as nodes that link to one another, we are more likely to retrieve a meaning concept that is connected by a larger number of links. But as we learn new responses, a stimulus loses its effectiveness in retrieving the old response.[99]

These interference effects help to explain problems in remembering brand information. Consumers tend to organize attribute information by brand.[100] Additional attribute information regarding a brand or similar brands may limit the person's ability to recall old brand information. Recall may also be inhibited if the brand name is composed of frequently used words. These words cue competing associations; as a result, we retain less brand information.[101] In one study, brand evaluations deteriorated more rapidly when ads for the brand appeared with messages for 12 other brands in the same category than when researchers showed the ad along with ads for 12 dissimilar products.[102] Thus, when we increase the uniqueness of one brand, it impairs the recall of other brands.[103] However, when we call a competitor by name, this can result in poorer recall for our own brand.[104]

State-Dependent Retrieval

Is it true that you'll do better on an exam if you study for it in the classroom in which you'll take the test? Perhaps. The phenomenon of **state-dependent retrieval** illustrates that we are better able to access information if our internal state is the same at the time of recall as when we learned the information. So, we are more likely to recall an ad if our mood or level of arousal at the time of exposure is similar to that in the purchase environment. When marketers re-create the cues that were present when they first presented the information, they can enhance recall. For example, on its box Life cereal uses a picture of "Mikey" from its long-running TV commercials, which facilitates recall of brand claims and favorable brand evaluations.[105]

Familiarity and Recall

As a general rule, when we are already familiar with an item we're more likely to recall messages about it. Indeed, this is one of the basic goals of marketers who try to create and maintain awareness of their products. The more experience a consumer has with a product, the better use he or she makes of product information.[106]

However, there is a possible fly in the ointment: As we noted previously in this chapter, some evidence indicates that extreme familiarity can result in inferior learning and recall. When consumers are highly familiar with a brand or an advertisement, they may not pay much attention to a message for it because they do not believe that any additional effort will increase their knowledge.[107] We call this process *automaticity*.[108] For example, when researchers expose consumers to a radio ad that repeats the audio track from a television ad they've already seen, they do little critical, evaluative processing; they just mentally replay the video portion of the ad.[109]

We may also encounter a **highlighting effect**, which occurs when the order in which consumers learn about brands determines the strength of association between these brands and their attributes. Consumers more strongly associate common attributes with early-learned brands and unique attributes with late-learned brands. More generally, we are more likely to recognize words, objects, and faces we learn early in life than similar items we learn later. This applies to brands as well; managers who introduce new entries into a market with well-established brand names need to work harder to create learning and memory linkages by exposing consumers to information about them more frequently.[110]

Salience and Recall

The **salience** of a brand refers to its prominence or level of activation in memory. Stimuli that stand out in contrast to their environments are more likely to command attention, which, in turn, increases the likelihood that we will recall them. The **von Restorff Effect** is well-known to memory researchers; it shows that almost any technique that increases the novelty of a stimulus also improves recall. This explains why unusual advertising or distinctive packaging tends to facilitate brand recall.[111]

The tactic of introducing a surprise element in an ad can boost recall, even if the new information is not relevant to the remaining material.[112] In addition, *mystery ads*, in which the ad doesn't identify the brand until the end, are more effective if we want to build associations in memory between the product category and that brand—especially in the case of relatively unknown brands.[113]

Furthermore, the *intensity* and type of emotions we experience at the time also affect the way we recall the event later. We recall **mixed emotions** (e.g., those with positive and negative components) differently than **unipolar emotions** that are either wholly positive or wholly negative. The latter become even more polarized over time, so that we recall good things as even better than they really were and bad things as even worse (maybe the "good old days" weren't really so good after all!).[114]

The Viewing Context

Regardless of how awesome a commercial is, the show in which it appears influences its impact. Nielsen (one company that measures who watches which media) reports that viewers who enjoy a program are more likely to respond positively to a commercial and to say they want to buy the advertised product. Nielsen studied the responses of 10,000 people across 50 shows and 200 brands. Viewers are almost one-third more likely to remember brands whose products were placed in shows they enjoy. The impact of this factor varies across show format; it's weaker in sitcoms but much stronger in "lifestyle programs" such as *Extreme Makeover: Home Edition*.[115]

It also helps when the marketer's message is consistent with the theme or events in the program, and it's even better when the advertised product actually makes a reference to the show. The Discovery Channel documented this effect during a broadcast of its program *Mythbusters*, which uses science to test the validity of urban legends. The network ran a brief ad for Guinness beer in which a character asked another whether it was a "myth that Guinness only has 125 calories." Viewers who saw this ad remembered the name of the Guinness brand 41 percent more often than they did when they saw a traditional ad for the beer. Other similar **hybrid ads** that include a program tie-in deliver similar results.[116]

Pictorial Versus Verbal Cues

Is a picture worth a thousand words? There is some evidence for the superiority of visual memory over verbal memory, but this advantage is unclear because it is more difficult to measure recall of pictures.[117] However, the available data indicate that we are more likely to recognize information we see in picture form at a later time.[118] Certainly, visual aspects of an ad are more likely to grab a consumer's attention. In fact, eye-movement studies indicate that about 90 percent of viewers look at the dominant picture in an ad before they bother to view the copy.[119]

Although pictorial ads may enhance recall, they do not necessarily improve comprehension. One study found that television news items presented with illustrations (still pictures) as a backdrop result in improved recall for details of the news story, even though understanding of the story's content does not improve.[120] Another study confirmed that consumers typically recall ads with visual figures more often and they like them better.[121]

OBJECTIVE 4-9
Marketers measure our memories about products and ads.

How We Measure Consumers' Recall of Marketing Messages

Because marketers pay so much money to place their messages in front of consumers, they hope that people will actually remember these ads later on. It seems that they have good reason to be concerned. In one study, fewer than 40 percent of television viewers made positive links between commercial messages and the corresponding products; only 65 percent noticed the brand name in a commercial, and only 38 percent recognized a connection to an important point.[122]

Even more sadly, only 7 percent of television viewers can recall the product or company featured in the most recent television commercial they watched. This figure represents less than half the recall rate recorded in 1965. We can explain this drop-off in terms of such factors as the increase of 30- and 15-second commercials and the practice of airing television commercials in clusters rather than in single-sponsor programs.[123]

The news is a bit brighter for online marketing messages, especially when they repeat commercials that first appeared on television. Research by Google shows that recall improves when spots reappear before YouTube videos.[124] Apple reports similar results for "iAds," mobile ads that pop up on iPhones and iPods.[125]

Recognition versus Recall

One indicator of good advertising is, of course, the impression it makes on us. But how can we define and measure this impact? Two basic measures of impact are **recognition** and **recall**. In the typical *recognition test*, researchers show ads to subjects one at a time and ask if they have seen them before. In contrast, *free recall tests* ask consumers to

Visual aspects of an ad grab a consumer's attention, especially when they are novel. That is certainly the case for this "pile of trash" that is actually an outdoor ad on a Dutch street for the MINI Cooper.
Source: Courtesy of UbachsWisbrun/JWT.

Facebook's Timeline feature helps consumers to recall the brands they have "liked" over time.
Source: Justin Sullivan/Getty Images.

independently think of what they have seen without being prompted for this information first; obviously, this task requires greater effort on their part.

Under some conditions, these two memory measures tend to yield the same results, especially when the researchers try to keep the viewers' interest in the ads constant (though that may be an overly artificial way to study true memory for ads).[126] Generally, though, recognition scores tend to be more reliable and do not decay over time the way recall scores do.[127] Recognition scores are almost always better than recall scores because recognition is a simpler process and the consumer has more retrieval cues available.

Both types of retrieval play important roles in purchase decisions, however. Recall tends to be more important in situations in which consumers do not have product data at their disposal, so they must rely on memory to generate this information.[128] However, recognition is more likely to be an important factor in a store, where retailers confront consumers with thousands of product options (i.e., external memory is abundantly available) and the task simply may be to recognize a familiar package. Unfortunately, package recognition and familiarity can have negative consequences; for example, consumers may ignore warning labels because they take those messages for granted and don't really notice them.[129]

Problems with Memory Measures

Although measuring an ad's memorability is important, analysts have questioned whether existing measures accurately assess these dimensions, for several reasons. First, the results we obtain from a measuring instrument are not necessarily based on what we measure, but rather on something else about the instrument or the respondent. This form of contamination is a **response bias**. For example, people tend to give "yes" responses to questions, regardless of what the item asks. In addition, experimental subjects often are eager to be "good subjects": They try to figure out what the experimenter is looking for and give the response they think they are supposed to give. This tendency is so strong that in some studies the rate at which subjects claim they recognize *bogus ads* (ads they have not seen before) is almost as high as their recognition rate for those they really have seen![130]

Memory Lapses

People are also prone to forget information or retain inaccurate memories (yes, even younger people). Typical problems include *omitting* (leaving facts out), *averaging* (the tendency to "normalize" memories by not reporting extreme cases), and *telescoping* (inaccurate recall of time).[131] These distortions are not just a problem in court cases that rely on eyewitness testimony; they also call into question the accuracy of product usage databases that rely on consumers to recall their purchase and consumption of food and household items. For example, one study asked people to describe what portion of various foods—small, medium, or large—they ate in a typical meal. However, the researchers used different definitions of "medium." Regardless of the definition they gave, about the same number of people claimed they typically ate "medium" portions.[132] In other situations, we may "fool ourselves" by distorting past memories. For example, some people who work toward a goal like losing weight or saving money may exaggerate (to themselves) how much progress they've made to justify current indulgences. That tendency points to the importance of documenting your progress (your Fitbit monitoring device doesn't lie) to keep yourself on track.[133]

OBJECTIVE 4-9
Products help us to retrieve memories from our past.

Bittersweet Memories: The Marketing Power of Nostalgia

The Disney theme parks ran a marketing campaign called "Let the Memories Begin." It focused on vacation memories; TV commercials, online ads, and brochures featured photos and videos shot by park guests. Disney projected images of visitors on building facades each night.[134] The company understands just how powerful memories can be.

The pictures we take of ourselves using products and services (like when we pose for selfies with Mickey at Disney World) can themselves serve as powerful retrieval cues. Indeed, the three types of possessions consumers most value are furniture, visual art, and photos. These objects are likely to jog memories of the past.[135] Researchers find that valued possessions can evoke thoughts about prior events on several dimensions, including sensory experiences, friends and loved ones, and breaking away from parents or former partners.[136] That helps to explain the popularity of photo-sharing sites like Flickr and Instagram; Flickr alone hosts more than 5 billion pictures and offers "Share This" tools for use on Facebook and Twitter.[137]

Nostalgia describes the bittersweet emotion that arises when we view the past with both sadness and longing.[138] References to "the good old days" are increasingly common, as advertisers call up memories of youth and hope that these feelings will translate to what they're selling today. A **retro brand** is an updated version of a brand from a prior historical period. These products trigger nostalgia, and researchers find that they often inspire consumers to think back to an era when (at least in our memories) life was more stable, simple, or even utopian. Simply, they let us "look backward through rose-colored glasses. One study reported that people who were asked to think about the past were willing to pay more for products than those who were asked to think about new or future memories.[139]

Our prior experiences also help to determine what we like today. Consumer researchers created a *nostalgia index* that measures the critical ages during which our preferences are likely to form and endure over time. It turns out that a good predictor of whether people will like a specific song is how old they were when that song was popular. On average, we are most likely to favor songs that were popular when we were 23.5 years old (so pay attention to the hot songs if you haven't turned 23 yet). Our preferences for fashion models peak at age 33, and we tend to like movie stars who were popular when we were 26 or 27 years old.[140]

Products are particularly important as memory markers when our sense of the past is threatened, as, for example, when an event such as divorce, relocation, or graduation challenges a consumer's current identity.[141] Our cherished possessions often have *mnemonic* qualities that serve as a form of external memory when they prompt us to retrieve episodic memories. For example, family photography allows consumers to create their own retrieval cues; the 11 billion amateur photos we take annually form a kind of external memory bank for our culture. A stimulus is, at times, able to evoke a weakened response even years after we first perceived it. We call this effect **spontaneous recovery**, and this reestablished connection may explain consumers' powerful emotional reactions to songs or pictures they have not been exposed to in quite a long time. Some recent nostalgia campaigns include:

Fossil's product designs evoke memories of earlier, classic styles.
Source: Used with permission of Fossil Inc. Photography by Thom Jackson and Jon Kirk.

- Freezy Freakies gloves that sprouted designs when exposed to cold temperatures were all the rage 20 years ago, when the manufacturer sold about 300,000 pairs per year. The gloves were made with thermochromic ink that turns to bright colors when the temperature plunges. This technology resurfaced more recently on Coors Light cans that shine blue when the beer is cold and fade to white when it becomes warm. Now two brothers have licensed the Freezy Freakies brand to make adult versions of the gloves that are sure to light up fond memories for many people.[142]

- Coca-Cola is reviving Surge, a citrus-flavor soda that it discontinued more than a decade ago. The brand is coming back after a Millennial fan base called "The Surge Movement" spent years lobbying for it to return. The Surge Movement's Facebook page has more than 150,000 likes.

- Calvin Klein collaborated with luxury fashion store MyTheresa.com to reissue 1990's–era clothing styles from the collection that launched Kate Moss's modeling career.

- Microsoft promotes its Internet Explorer browser with a video it calls "Child of the '90s." It begins, "You might not remember us, but we met in the '90s," and goes on to remind its Millennial target audience of childhood favorites like virtual pets ("the only thing buzzing in your pocket") and the tabletop game Hungry Hungry Hippos.[143]

Marketers often resurrect popular characters and stories from days gone by; they hope that consumers' fond memories will motivate them to revisit the past. We had a 1950s' revival in the 1970s, and consumers in the 1980s got a heavy dose of memories from the 1960s. Today, it seems that popular characters only need to be gone for a few years before someone tries to bring them back. Many companies have responded as they dig deep into their vaults to bring back old favorites. New commercials position Chevrolet as a classic U.S. brand. Planters Peanuts recruited the actor Robert Downey, Jr., as the new voice of Mr. Peanut. "Retired" brand names, including Meister Brau beer, the brokerage firm Shearson, Handi-Wrap plastic wrap, and Wonder Bread were sold at auction to companies that want to bring them back to life.[144] The biggest retro success story in recent years: the Old Spice Guy campaign that went viral and revived a men's deodorant brand that is more than 70 years old.

MyLab Marketing

To complete the problems with the ✪, go to EOC Discussion Questions in the MyLab as well as additional Marketing Metrics questions only available in MyLab Marketing.

CHAPTER SUMMARY

Now that you have finished reading this chapter, you should understand why:

1. It is important to understand how consumers learn about products and services.

Learning is a change in behavior caused by experience. Learning can occur through simple associations between a stimulus and a response or via a complex series of cognitive activities.

2. Conditioning results in learning.

Behavioral learning theories assume that learning occurs as a result of responses to external events. Classical conditioning occurs when a stimulus that naturally elicits a response (an unconditioned stimulus) is paired with another stimulus that does not initially elicit this response. Over time, the second stimulus (the conditioned stimulus) elicits the response even in the absence of the first.

3. Learned associations with brands generalize to other products.

This response can also extend to other, similar stimuli in a process we call *stimulus generalization*. This process is the basis for such marketing strategies as licensing and family branding, where a consumer's positive associations with a product transfer to other contexts.

4. There is a difference between classical and instrumental conditioning, and both processes help consumers learn about products.

Operant, or instrumental, conditioning occurs as the person learns to perform behaviors that produce positive outcomes and avoid those that result in negative outcomes. Whereas classical conditioning involves the pairing of two stimuli, instrumental learning occurs when a response to a stimulus leads to reinforcement. Reinforcement is positive if a reward follows a response. It is negative if the person avoids a negative outcome by not performing a response. Punishment occurs when an unpleasant event follows a response. Extinction of the behavior will occur if reinforcement no longer occurs.

5. We learn about products by observing others' behavior.

Cognitive learning occurs as the result of mental processes. For example, observational learning occurs when the consumer performs a behavior as a result of seeing someone else performing it and being rewarded for it.

6. Our brains process information about brands to retain them in memory.

Memory is the storage of learned information. The way we encode information when we perceive it determines how we will store it in memory. The memory systems we call *sensory memory*, *short-term memory*, and *long-term memory* each play a role in retaining and processing information from the outside world.

7. The other products we associate with an individual product influence how we will remember it.

We don't store information in isolation; we incorporate it into a knowledge structure where our brains associate it with other related data. The location of product information in associative networks, and the level of abstraction at which it is coded, help to determine when and how we will activate this information at a later time. Some factors that influence the likelihood of retrieval include the level of familiarity with an item, its salience (or prominence) in memory, and whether the information was presented in pictorial or written form.

8. Marketers measure our memories about products and ads.

We can use either recognition or recall techniques to measure memory for product information. Consumers are more likely to recognize an advertisement if it is presented to them than they are to recall one without being given any cues. However, neither recognition nor recall automatically or reliably translates into product preferences or purchases.

9. Products help us to retrieve memories from our past.

Products also play a role as memory markers; consumers use them to retrieve memories about past experiences (autobiographical memories), and we often value them because they are able to do this. This function also encourages the use of nostalgia in marketing strategies.

KEY TERMS

Activation models of memory, 152
Advertising wear-out, 134
Associative network, 153
Behavioral learning theories, 131
Brand equity, 134
Chunking, 152
Classical conditioning, 131
Cognitive learning theory, 142
Conditioned response (CR), 131
Conditioned stimulus (CS), 131
Consumer confusion, 137
Consumer socialization, 144
Decay, 157
Elaborative rehearsal, 152
Encoding, 150
Endowed progress effect, 141
Episodic memories, 151
Extinction, 132
Family branding, 136
Fixed-interval reinforcement, 139
Fixed-ratio reinforcement, 139
Follower brands, 156
Frequency marketing, 140
Gamification, 140
Halo effect, 133

Highlighting effect, 157
Hybrid ads, 158
Incidental learning, 131
Instrumental conditioning, 137
Interference, 157
Learning, 130
Licensing, 136
Long-term memory (LTM), 152
Look-alike packaging, 136
Memory, 150
Mixed emotions, 158
Modeling, 143
Multiple-intelligence theory, 149
Narrative, 151
Negative reinforcement, 137
Nostalgia, 161
Observational learning, 143
Pioneering brand, 156
Positive reinforcement, 137
Product line extension, 136
Punishment, 137
Recall, 159
Recognition, 159
Repetition, 132
Response bias, 160

Retrieval, 150
Retro brand, 161
Salience, 158
schema, 155
Script, 155
Sensory memory, 152
Service scripts, 155
Shaping, 137
Short-term memory (STM), 152
Social default, 143
Spacing effect, 156
Spontaneous recovery, 161
Spreading activation, 154
Stage of cognitive development, 146
State-dependent retrieval, 157
Stimulus discrimination, 133
Stimulus generalization, 133
Storage stage, 150
Unconditioned stimulus (UCS), 131
Unipolar emotions, 158
Variable-interval reinforcement, 139
Variable-ratio reinforcement, 139
von Restorff effect, 158

REVIEW

4-1 What is the difference between an unconditioned stimulus and a conditioned stimulus?

4-2 People react to other, similar stimuli in much the same way as they responded to an original stimulus. What is this phenomenon, and how does it work?

4-3 What are the dangers of advertising wear-out, and how might a marketer avoid it?

4-4 Advertisers like to use celebrities and well-known faces to help promote their products and services. Is this a good idea?

4-5 Why are brand marketers concerned with stimulus discrimination?

⭐ **4-6** What is the major difference between behavioral and cognitive theories of learning?

4-7 Name the three stages of information processing as we commit information about products to memory.

4-8 What is *external memory*, and why is it important to marketers?

4-9 How can marketers use sensory memory?

4-10 What advantages does narrative bring to advertising?

4-11 List the three types of memory, and explain how they work together.

⭐ **4-12** How is associative memory like a spider web?

4-13 How does the likelihood that a person wants to use an ATM machine relate to a schema?

4-14 Why does a pioneering brand have a memory advantage over follower brands?

4-15 If a consumer is familiar with a product, advertising for it can work by either enhancing or diminishing recall. Why?

4-16 Why are retro brands so popular? What is the key ingredient that makes them successful?

4-17 What is a schema? Give an example.

4-18 How would you explain the terms *salience* and *recall*?

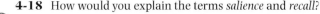 **4-19** How do different types of reinforcement enhance learning? How does the strategy of frequency marketing relate to conditioning?

4-20 How does learning new information make it more likely that we'll forget things we've already learned?

CONSUMER BEHAVIOR CHALLENGE

■ DISCUSS

4-21 To hasten kids' introduction to social media, a team of Finnish designers invented a block-sorting toy that also works like Twitter. It allows preverbal kids to grab colorful blocks with icons for sleeping, eating, or brushing their teeth; the kids then fit them into slots to indicate what they're up to. The device then transmits the "status update" to light up the corresponding block-shape on the same toy in another household.[145] Should very young children be introduced to social media this way?

4-22 According to Gianfranco Zaccai of Continuum, focus groups kill innovation. He claims that in the 40 years he has been involved in the marketing industry, working with some of the most brilliant minds, he has never seen an innovation developed as a result of a focus group. He maintains that this is because of what focus groups can and cannot do. Do you agree?

4-23 Sales of retro trainer brands, food brands, board games, and even vehicles (such as the relaunch of Vespa in India) are all examples of the growth of nostalgia marketing. Nostalgia marketing taps into the memories of the consumer and sells them an idealized version of their past. According to Jannine LaSaleta at the Grenoble Ecole de Management in France, nostalgia marketing aims to provide consumers with a feeling of social connectedness.[146] It makes them value money less and leads them to spend more freely. Nostalgia marketing can be applied to any stage in the consumers' life. It does not just mean that the marketing has to refer to products or services that the consumer associates with their childhood or adolescence. How do you think nostalgia marketing works? How might nostalgia marketing work for several markets at the same time?

4-24 Using commercial music for advertising is nothing new, but advertisers need to be very careful with their choices, as sometimes things can go wrong unexpectedly. In 2013, General Motors was forced to pull an advertisement for one of its Chevrolet models in China amid accusations of racism. The company had chosen the 2012 song "Booty Swing" by Parov Stelar, which sampled heavily from "Oriental Swing" by Lil Hardin Armstrong and Her Swing Orchestra. In the lyrics, there were lines that suggested that the Chinese were "ching-chong, chop-suey" and that the Japanese could not pronounce the letter "r."

Although many musicians embrace the opportunity to earn royalties from the use of their music in advertising, some are adamant that their music should never be used. One such example is Adam Yauch, aka MCA, an original member of the Beastie Boys who died in 2012. His will left his entire estate to his widow with the caveat that in no event could his music or any of his creations be used in advertising. It was clear he did not approve.

Some musicians are only too happy to accept an additional revenue stream from the use of their music in advertisements. Not only do they receive royalties for its use, but this might also stimulate sales. What is your view on the use of popular music in advertisements?

■ APPLY

4-25 Just how well do you recall jingles and tunes used by brands in commercials? As a group, compile a list and see how many of these all of you can remember. Is there something specific that triggers recall? Are they original jingles or tunes or are they "borrowed"?

4-26 In 2012, 14 of Singapore's biggest food-and-beverage businesses committed themselves to a radical rethinking of the way in which they advertise to children. The pledge, called the "Responsible Advertising to Children Pledge" was part of a commitment made by the companies to assist Singaporeans to attain a healthy and active lifestyle. The signatories were all renowned brands – Coca-Cola, Ferraro, General Mills, Kellogg's, Kerry, Mars, McCain, McDonald's, Mondelēz, Nestlé, Pepsico, FrieslandCampina, Suntory, and Unilever. They all agreed to advertise their products incorporating nutrient details that were based on independently verifiable scientific tests. Further, they undertook to apply these guidelines to any advertising aimed at under 12-year-olds or not advertise at all.

4-27 Choose a well-established product sold in your country. Identify its key attributes. How could the brand be leveraged? Can you suggest any brand extensions that could be developed? What about licensing? Just how far could you go with the development?

4-28 As a group, identify at least 10 long-established local brands that are specific to your country or region. What

is it about them that has ensured their longevity? Identify the features and attributes of each brand, from the packaging and design to the product itself.

Case Study

DO AVATARS DREAM ABOUT VIRTUAL SHEEP?

When he ventures online, he's a muscular, bronzed, 23-year-old surfer. But, after a few hours chilling in the virtual world of *The Sims 4*, it's time for this shy, 110-pound student to get back to work. Sound weird? It's not. He is one of the more than one billion people worldwide who inhabit a virtual world in digital form. Welcome to the world of avatars! In the years since virtual worlds came into being, marketers have been working to understand how the time people spend in virtual worlds influences the way they learn about brands and whether it impacts their relationship with the brand in the real world.

In *The Sims 4* and other sites, users create an avatar to represent themselves online. Some people create avatars that look a lot like them in the real world, but many residents choose avatars that represent the person they would like to be, fantasy creatures, or even individuals of the opposite gender. With these alternate personalities they go out and explore virtual worlds. So what does this mean to marketers? A lot more than some pixels on a computer screen. Avatars interact with real brands in these virtual worlds. They can purchase products such as jeans for their avatars, and they can attend events such as concerts or lectures. Marketers can gain insights about how consumers learn about brands by analyzing the behavior of their avatars in virtual settings.

But it's not just virtual worlds that want to understand how to make money from the legions of avatars out there. Web site designers and developers also realize the importance of avatars that interact with visitors on corporate Web sites. Several companies such as Sitepal offer software applications that design avatars to greet and guide visitors. Some of these avatars take the form of famous people, including rock stars, actors, and historical figures. Sitepal can even help a company to set up

an avatar-powered testimonial page where satisfied customers can "talk" to potential customers visiting the company's site. Research suggests that avatars might increase users' satisfaction with the Web sites and affect purchases.

Apparel brands continue to experiment with the use of avatars to help customers have a better online experience in determining the right fit for clothing. Start-up company Fitle has developed a three-dimensional system that will enable a consumer to create an avatar with a virtual representation of their body that is close to 99 percent accurate. Their system is being designed to interface with the catalogs of 250 partner brands that would allow users to "try on" clothing and create virtual wardrobes. The impact on how consumers would learn about different brands of clothing and their fit seems like a potential game-changer for the apparel industry.

Organizations and educators are continuing to explore the impact of avatars and virtual worlds. Companies can host their business meetings online and encourage employees to develop their own avatars when they attend the meetings. Several university presidents have even held online forums with students and create avatars to discuss current issues of concern with their students. The world of avatars and virtual worlds will continue to challenge marketers in the years to come.

DISCUSSION QUESTIONS

CS 4-1 How might classical conditioning operate for a consumer who visits a new tutoring Web site and is greeted by the Web site's avatar who resembles Albert Einstein?

CS 4-2 How might instrumental conditioning influence a consumer who purchases a new outfit for his avatar in a virtual world?

CS 4-3 Do consumers build associative networks from their avatar's experience? If so, would the associations from their avatar experience be any different from other shopping experiences? How would these networks impact the consumer's ability to organize and retrieve information that they have learned?

_____

Sources: Audrey Waters, "Number of Virtual World Users Breaks 1 Billion, Roughly Half Under Age 15," readwrite.com (October 1, 2010), http://readwrite.com/2010/10/01/number_of_virtual_world_users_breaks_the_1_ billion#awesm=~omeiEn2UL1brEV, accessed November 4, 2013; www.sitepal.com, accessed November 4, 2013 and May 26, 2015; Natalie T. Wood and Michael R. Solomon, (2011), "Adonis or Atrocious: Spokesavatars and Source Effects in Immersive Digital Environments," in Matthew S. Eastin, Terry Daugherty, and Neal M. Burns, eds., *Handbook of Research on Digital Media and Advertising: User Generated Content Consumption* (IGI Global), 521–534; Stu Robarts, "Fitle Gives Users a 3-D Avatar of Themselves for Trying on Clothes," (July 29, 2014), http://www.gizmag.com/fitle-3d-clothing-avatar/33167/, accessed May 30, 2015.

MyLab Marketing

Go to the Assignments section of your MyLab to complete these writing exercises.

4.29 New passive monitoring systems allow us to pay tolls automatically or simply show our phones equipped with systems like Apple Pay. Convenient, for sure. But these systems also eliminate the transparency of the connection between the stimulus and the response. As a result we don't think as much about the costs when we use them. Is this a problem for consumers?

4.30 The Snapchat app provides a way for social media users to share content with their friends that disappears after a brief time. In Europe, Google is fighting an intense legal battle over what some call the "right to be forgotten"; users want the option to dictate to Google whether it will be allowed to display results when people search about them. On the other hand, some people who believe that "information wants to be free" say that if a person posts online it should be with the expectation that the content will be permanent and that you forfeit control over others' right to access it. Which argument is correct?

NOTES

1. Jenna Goudreau, "These Old Brands Are Poised for a 2011 Comeback: Nostalgia Will Help Sell to Consumers Who Aren't Happy with the Present," *Forbes* (December 31, 2010), http://today.msnbc.msn.com/id/40856091/ns/today-entertainment, accessed July 22, 2013.
2. Robert A. Baron, *Psychology: The Essential Science* (Boston: Allyn & Bacon, 1989).
3. Seth Stephens-Davidowitz, "They Hook You When You're Young," *New York Times* (April 19, 2014), http://www.NewYorkTimes.com/2014/04/20/opinion/sunday/they-hook-you-when-youre-young.html?_r=0, accessed February 22, 2015.
4. Richard A. Feinberg, "Credit Cards as Spending Facilitating Stimuli: A Conditioning Interpretation," *Journal of Consumer Research* 13 (December 1986): 348–356; Goudreau, "These Old Brands Are Poised for a 2011 Comeback."
5. R. A. Rescorla, "Pavlovian Conditioning: It's Not What You Think It Is," *American Psychologist* 43 (1988): 151–160; Elnora W. Stuart, Terence A. Shimp, and Randall W. Engle, "Classical Conditioning of Consumer Attitudes: Four Experiments in an Advertising Context," *Journal of Consumer Research* 14 (December 1987): 334–339.
6. C. Janiszewski, H. Noel, and A. G. Sawyer, "A Meta-analysis of the Spacing Effect in Verbal Learning: Implications for Research on Advertising Repetition and Consumer Memory," *Journal of Consumer Research* 30, no. 1 (2003): 138–149.
7. James Ward, Barbara Loken, Ivan Ross, and Tedi Hasapopoulous, "The Influence of Physical Similarity of Affect and Attribute Perceptions from National Brands to Private Label Brands," in Terence A. Shimp et al., eds., *American Marketing Educators' Conference* (Chicago: American Marketing Association, 1986): 51–56.
8. Judith Lynne Zaichkowsky and Richard Neil Simpson, "The Effect of Experience with a Brand Imitator on the Original Brand," *Marketing Letters* 7, no. 1 (1996): 31–39.
9. Roger Dobson, "Logos 'Brand' Youthful Minds: Children's Brains Are Found to Light Up at the Sight of Fast-Food Logos," *The Independent* (September 23, 2012), http://www.independent.co.uk/news/science/logos-brand-youthful-minds-8165962.html, accessed January 21, 2013.
10. Randi Priluck Grossman and Brian D. Till, "The Persistence of Classically Conditioned Brand Attitudes," *Journal of Advertising* 21, no. 1 (1998): 23–31; Chris T. Allen and Thomas J. Madden, "A Closer Look at Classical Conditioning," *Journal of Consumer Research* 12 (December 1985): 301–315; Chester A. Insko and William F. Oakes, "Awareness and the Conditioning of Attitudes," *Journal of Personality & Social Psychology* 4 (November 1966): 487–496; Carolyn K. Staats and Arthur W. Staats, "Meaning Established by Classical Conditioning," *Journal of Experimental Psychology* 54 (July 1957): 74–80.
11. Kevin Lane Keller, "Conceptualizing, Measuring, and Managing Customer-Based Brand Equity," *Journal of Marketing* 57 (January 1993): 1–22.
12. Herbert Krugman, "Low Recall and High Recognition of Advertising," *Journal of Advertising Research* (February–March 1986): 79–80.
13. Brian Steinberg, "Ad Nauseam: Repetition of TV Spots Risks Driving Consumers Away, Fragmenting Media, Smaller Budgets Make for More of the Same Ads," *Crain's Detroit Business* (December 1, 2008), www.Crainsdetroit.Com/Article/20081201/Email01/812010278/1092, accessed December 1, 2008.
14. Yaveroglu Donthu and Naveen Donthu, "Advertising Repetition and Placement Issues in On-Line Environments," *Journal of Advertising* 37 (Summer 2008): 31–43.
15. Gerald J. Gorn, "The Effects of Music in Advertising on Choice Behavior: A Classical Conditioning Approach," *Journal of Marketing* 46 (Winter 1982): 94–101.
16. Stuart Elliot, "Gap Inc. Puts 'GAP' Back in Logo," *New York Times* (October 12, 2010), http://mediadecoder.blogs.NewYorkTimes.com/2010/10/12/gap-inc-puts-gap-back-in-logo/?scp_1&sq_gap%20logo&st_cse, accessed March 27, 2011.

17. Mark J. Miller, "Bob Marley Brand Expands from Music to Coffee to Swimwear," Brandchannel (February 21, 2012), http://www.brand channel.com/home/post/2012/02/21/Bob-Marley-Brand-Exten sions-022112.aspx, accessed January 7, 2013.

18. Kirk Johnson, "A University Steak to Go with That Sweatshirt?" *New York Times* (March 2, 2013), http://www.NewYorkTimes.com/2013/03/03/us/how-about-a-university-steak-with-your-sweatshirt.html?ref=todayspaper, accessed March 4, 2013.

19. Dale Buss, "Condé Nast Extends Magazine Brands into Bar and Restaurant Scene," *Broad Channel* (April 12, 2013), http://www.brandchannel.com/home/post/2013/04/12/Conde-Nast-Brand-Extensions-041213.aspx, accessed February 3, 2015.

20. Dan Macsai, "Jamba Juice Launches Clothing Line," *Fast Company* (July 1, 2010), http://www.fastcompany.com/magazine/147/unwanted-wear-your-smoothie.html?partner=homepage_newsletter, accessed April 6, 2011.

21. http://www.zippofragrances.com/VediMacro.phtml?goTo=1&IDMacro=1 321&sLang=EN, accessed March 4, 2013; James R. Hagerty, "Zippo Preps for a Post-Smoker World," *Wall Street Journal* (March 8, 2011), http://online.wsj.com/article/SB1000142405274870407680457618041117 3921454.html?mod=dist_smartbrief&mod=WALLSTREETJOURNAL_hp_ MIDDLENexttoWhatsNewsThird, accessed April 6, 2011.

22. Quoted in Rebecca R. Ruiz, "Luxury Cars Imprint Their Brands on Goods From Cologne to Clothing," *New York Times*, February 2015, http://www .NewYorkTimes.com/2015/02/21/automobiles/luxury-cars-imprint-their-brands-on-goods-from-cologne-to-clothing.html?smid=NewYork Timescore-iphone-share&smprod=newyorktimesscore-iphone&_r=0, accessed February 22, 2015.

23. "Look-Alikes Mimic Familiar Packages," *New York Times* (August 9, 1986): D1.

24. Zaichkowsky and Simpson, "The Effect of Experience with a Brand Imitator on the Original Brand."

25. Luk Warlop and Joseph W. Alba, "Sincere Flattery: Trade-Dress Imitation and Consumer Choice," *Journal of Consumer Psychology* 14, nos. 1 & 2 (2004): 21–27.

26. Michael Barbaro and Julie Creswell, "Levi's Turns to Suing Its Rivals," *New York Times* (January 29, 2007), www.NewYorkTimes.com/2007/01/29/ business/29jeans.html, accessed June 30, 2009.

27. For a comprehensive approach to consumer behavior-based operant conditioning principles, see Gordon R. Foxall, "Behavior Analysis and Consumer Psychology," *Journal of Economic Psychology* 15 (March 1994): 5–91.

28. J. Blaise Bergiel and Christine Trosclair, "Instrumental Learning: Its Application to Customer Satisfaction," *Journal of Consumer Marketing* 2 (Fall 1985): 23–28.

29. Several books have recently been published on this topic; for example, Gabe Zichermann and Christopher Cunningham (2011), *Gamification by Design: Implementing Game Mechanics in Web and Mobile Apps*, New York: O'Reilly Media; Jane McGonigal (2011), *Reality Is Broken: Why Games Make Us Better and How They Can Change the World*, New York: Penguin Press; and Byron Reeves and J. Leighton, Read (2009), *Total Engagement: Using Games and Virtual Worlds to Change the Way People Work and Businesses Compete*, Boston, Harvard Business Review Press.

30. Quoted in John Grossmann, "Using Smartphones and Apps to Enhance Loyalty Programs," *New York Times*, January 28, 2015, http://www.newy orktimes.com/2015/01/29/business/smallbusiness/using-smartphones-and-apps-to-enhance-small-business-loyalty-programs.html?smid=New York Timescore-iphone-share&smprod=New York Timescore-iphone, accessed February 22, 2015; Joseph C. Nunes and Xavier Drèze, "The Endowed Progress Effect: How Artificial Advancement Increases Effort," *Journal of Consumer Research* (March 2006) 32: 504–512.

31. Nick Wingfield, "All the World's a Game, and Business Is a Player," *New York Times* (December 23, 2012), http://www.New York Times .com/2012/12/24/technology/all-the-worlds-a-game-and-business-is-a-player.html?emc=eta1, accessed January 7, 2013.

32. Suzanne Vranica, "Agencies Don Lab Coats to Reach Consumers, Firms Deploy Scientists Within Creative Groups to Make Messages Stick," *Wall Street Journal* (June 4, 2007): B8.

33. Cf., for example, E. M. Eisenstein and J. W. Hutchinson, "Action-Based Learning: Goals and Attention in the Acquisition of Market Knowledge," *Journal of Marketing Research* 43, no. 2 (2006): 244–258.

34. Ellen J. Langer, *The Psychology of Control* (Beverly Hills, CA: Sage, 1983).

35. Robert B. Cialdini, *Influence: Science and Practice*, 2nd ed. (New York: William Morrow, 1984); Y. Rottenstreich, S. Sood, and L. Brenner, "Feeling and Thinking in Memory-Based versus Stimulus-Based Choices," *Journal of Consumer Research* 33, no. 4 (2007): 461–469.

36. Chris T. Allen and Thomas J. Madden, "A Closer Look at Classical Conditioning," *Journal of Consumer Research* 12 (December 1985): 301–315; see also Terence A. Shimp, Elnora W. Stuart, and Randall W. Engle, "A Program of Classical Conditioning Experiments Testing Variations in the Conditioned Stimulus and Context," *Journal of Consumer Research* 18 (June 1991): 1–12.

37. Sally L. Satel, "Primed for Controversy," *New York Times* (February 23, 2013), http://www.NewYorkTimes.com/2013/02/24/opinion/sunday/ psychology-research-control.html, accessed March 4, 2013.

38. Young Eun Huh, Joachim Vosgerau, and Carey K. Morewedge, "Social Defaults: Observed Choices Become Choice Defaults," *Journal of Consumer Research* 41, no. 3: 746–760

39. Terence A. Shimp, "Neo-Pavlovian Conditioning and Its Implications for Consumer Theory and Research," in Thomas S. Robertson and Harold H. Kassarjian, eds., *Handbook of Consumer Behavior* (Upper Saddle River, NJ: Prentice Hall, 1991): 162-187.

40. Albert Bandura, *Social Foundations of Thought and Action: A Social Cognitive View* (Upper Saddle River, NJ: Prentice Hall, 1986).

41. Bandura, *Social Foundations.*

42. Julie Turkewitz, "After a Spa Day, Looking Years Younger (O.K., They're Only 7)," *New York Times*, January 2, 2015, http://www.NewYorkTimes .com/2015/01/03/us/after-a-spa-day-looking-years-younger-ok-theyre-only-7.html, accessed February 3, 2015.

43. Scott Ward, "Consumer Socialization," in Harold H. Kassarjian and Thomas S. Robertson, eds., *Perspectives in Consumer Behavior* (Glenview, IL: Scott, Foresman, 1980), 380; cf. also Patricia Robinson and Steven Maxwell Kates, "Children and Their Brand Relationships," *Advances in Consumer Research* 32, no. 1 (2005); Terry O'Sullivan, "Advertising and Children: What Do the Kids Think?" *Qualitative Market Research* 8, no. 4 (2005): 371.

44. Paul M. Connell, Merrie Brucks, and Jesper H. Nielsen, "How Childhood Advertising Exposure Can Create Biased Product Evaluations That Persist into Adulthood," *Journal of Consumer Research* 41, no. 1 (June 2014): 119–134.

45. Thomas Lipscomb, "Indicators of Materialism in Children's Free Speech: Age and Gender Comparisons," *Journal of Consumer Marketing* (Fall 1988): 41–46.

46. George P. Moschis, "The Role of Family Communication in Consumer Socialization of Children and Adolescents," *Journal of Consumer Research* 11 (March 1985): 898–913.

47. Gregory M. Rose, Vassilis Dalakas, and Fredric Kropp, "A Five-Nation Study of Developmental Timetables, Reciprocal Communication and Consumer Socialization," *Journal of Business Research* 55 (2002): 943–949.

48. Elizabeth S. Moore, William L. Wilkie, and Richard J. Lutz, "Passing the Torch: Intergenerational Influences as a Source of Brand Equity," *Journal of Marketing* 66 (April 2002): 17–37.

49. James U. McNeal and Chyon-Hwa Yeh, "Born to Shop," *American Demographics* (June 1993): 34–39.

50. Karl Greenberg, "Study: Kids Influence Family's Use of Media," *Marketing Daily* (June 10, 2010), http://www.mediapost.com/publications/article/ 129877/study-kids-influence-familys-use-of-media.html, accessed April 19, 2011; Les Carlson, Sanford Grossbart, and J. Kathleen Stuenkel, "The Role of Parental Socialization Types on Differential Family Communication Patterns Regarding Consumption," *Journal of Consumer Psychology* 1, no. 1 (1992): 31–52; cf. also Sonya A. Grier, Janell Mensinger, Shirley H. Huang, Shiriki K. Kumanyika, and Nicolas Stettler, "Fast-Food Marketing and Children's Fast-Food Consumption: Exploring Parents' Influences in an Ethnically Diverse Sample," *Journal of Public Policy & Marketing* 26 (Fall 2007): 221–235.

51. Erik Sass, "Four Out of Five Kids Ages Five and Under Are on the Web," *Marketing Daily* (March 17, 2011), http://www.mediapost.com/ publications/?fa=Articles.showArticle&art_aid=146941&nid=124844, accessed April 19, 2011.

52. Emily Bryson York, "NIH: Banning Fast Food Ads Will Make Kids Less Fat," *Advertising Age* (November 19, 2008), http://adage.com/results .php?endeca=1&return=endeca&search_offset=0&search_order_ by=score&search_advanced=1&searchprop=AdAgeAll&search_phrase= banning+fast+food+ads+will+make+kids+less+fat&searchmode=match all&sortby=date&range=adage&variable=90&date_range=specific&date_ begin=11%2F19%2F08&date_end=&x=42&y=20, accessed November 24, 2008.

53. Andrew Martin, "Kellogg to Curb Marketing of Foods to Children," *New York Times* (June 14, 2007), www.NewYorkTimes.com, accessed June 14, 2007; Tara Parker-Pope, "Watching Food Ads on TV May Program Kids to Overeat," *Wall Street Journal* (July 10, 2007): D1.

54. Hilary Stout and Elizabeth A. Harris, "Today's Girls Love Pink Bows as Playthings, But These Shoot," *New York Times*, March 22, 2014, http://www .newyorktimes.com/2014/03/23/business/todays-girls-love-pink-bows-as-playthings-but-these-shoot.html?hp&_r=0, accessed February 21, 2015.

55. Laura A. Peracchio, "How Do Young Children Learn to Be Consumers? A Script-Processing Approach," *Journal of Consumer Research* 18 (March

1992): 425–440; Laura A. Peracchio, "Young Children's Processing of a Televised Narrative: Is a Picture Really Worth a Thousand Words?" *Journal of Consumer Research* 20 (September 1993): 281–293; see also M. Carole Macklin, "The Effects of an Advertising Retrieval Cue on Young Children's Memory and Brand Evaluations," *Psychology & Marketing* 11 (May–June 1994): 291–311.

56. Jean Piaget, "The Child and Modern Physics," *Scientific American* 196, no. 3 (1957): 46–51; see also Kenneth D. Bahn, "How and When Do Brand Perceptions and Preferences First Form? A Cognitive Developmental Investigation," *Journal of Consumer Research* 13 (December 1986): 382–393.

57. Deborah L. Roedder, "Age Differences in Children's Responses to Television Advertising: An Information-Processing Approach," *Journal of Consumer Research* 8 (September 1981): 144–153; see also Deborah Roedder John and Ramnath Lakshmi-Ratan, "Age Differences in Children's Choice Behavior: The Impact of Available Alternatives," *Journal of Marketing Research* 29 (May 1992): 216–226; Jennifer Gregan-Paxton and Deborah Roedder John, "Are Young Children Adaptive Decision Makers? A Study of Age Differences in Information Search Behavior," *Journal of Consumer Research* 21, no. 4 (1995): 567–580.

58. For a study on the effects of commercial programming on creative play, cf. Patricia M. Greenfield, Emily Yut, Mabel Chung, Deborah Land, Holly Kreider, Maurice Pantoja, and Kris Horsley, "The Program-Length Commercial: A Study of the Effects of Television/Toy Tie-Ins on Imaginative Play," *Psychology & Marketing* 7 (Winter 1990): 237–256.

59. Gerald J. Gorn and Renee Florsheim, "The Effects of Commercials for Adult Products on Children," *Journal of Consumer Research* 11 (March 1985): 962–967. For a study that assessed the impact of violent commercials on children, see V. Kanti Prasad and Lois J. Smith, "Television Commercials in Violent Programming: An Experimental Evaluation of Their Effects on Children," *Journal of the Academy of Marketing Science* 22, no. 4 (1994): 340–351.

60. Gwen Bachmann Achenreiner and Deborah Roedder John, "The Meaning of Brand Names to Children: A Developmental Investigation," *Journal of Consumer Psychology* 13, no. 3 (2003): 205–219.

61. Paula Lyon Andruss, "'Dora' Translates Well," *Marketing News* (October 13, 2003): 8.

62. Gary Armstrong and Merrie Brucks, "Dealing with Children's Advertising: Public Policy Issues and Alternatives," *Journal of Public Policy & Marketing* 7 (1988): 98–113.

63. Bonnie Reece, "Children and Shopping: Some Public Policy Questions," *Journal of Public Policy & Marketing* (1986): 185–194.

64. Daniel Cook, University of Illinois, personal communication, December 2002; Daniel Cook, "Contradictions and Conundrums of the Child Consumer: The Emergent Centrality of an Enigma in the 1990s," paper presented at the Association for Consumer Research, October 2002.

65. http://www.bbb.org/us/children-food-beverage-advertising-initiative/, accessed June 14, 2011; John Eggerton, "Sara Lee Agrees to Limit Food Marketing to Kids," *Broadcasting & Cable* (September 23, 2010), http://www.broadcastingcable.com/article/457541-Sara_Lee_Agrees_to_Limit_Food_Marketing_to_Kids.php, accessed April 19, 2011.

66. Natasha Singer, "New Online Privacy Rules for Children," *New York Times* (December 19, 2012), http://www.NewYorkTimes.com/2012/12/20/technology/ftc-broadens-rules-for-online-privacy-of-children.html, accessed January 4, 2013.

67. R. C. Atkinson and I. M. Shiffrin, "Human Memory: A Proposed System and Its Control Processes," in K. W. Spence and J. T. Spence, eds., *The Psychology of Learning and Motivation: Advances in Research and Theory*, vol. 2 (New York: Academic Press, 1968): 89–195.

68. James R. Bettman, "Memory Factors in Consumer Choice: A Review," *Journal of Marketing* (Spring 1979): 37–53. For a study that explores the relative impact of internal versus external memory on brand choice, see Joseph W. Alba, Howard Marmorstein, and Amitava Chattopadhyay, "Transitions in Preference over Time: The Effects of Memory on Message Persuasiveness," *Journal of Marketing Research* 29 (1992): 406–416.

69. Lauren G. Block and Vicki G. Morwitz, "Shopping Lists as an External Memory Aid for Grocery Shopping: Influences on List Writing and List Fulfillment," *Journal of Consumer Psychology* 8, no. 4 (1999): 343–375.

70. Tanya Menoni, "7 Time-Saving Grocery List Apps for the iPhone," *About Tech*, http://ipod.about.com/od/bestiphoneapps/tp/6-Time-Saving-Iphone-Grocery-List-Apps.htm, accessed March 16, 2015.

71. Kim Robertson, "Recall and Recognition Effects of Brand Name Imagery," *Psychology & Marketing* 4 (Spring 1987): 3–15.

72. Robin J. Tanner and Ahreum Maeng, "A Tiger and a President: Imperceptible Celebrity Facial Cues Influence Trust and Preference," (December 2012), *Journal of Consumer Research* 39, no. 4: 769–783.

73. Endel Tulving, "Remembering and Knowing the Past," *American Scientist* 77 (July–August 1989): 361.

74. Rashmi Adaval and Robert S. Wyer, Jr., "The Role of Narratives in Consumer Information Processing," *Journal of Consumer Psychology* 7, no. 3

(1998): 207–246; cf. also R. F. Baumeister and L. S. Newman, "How Stories Make Sense of Personal Experiences: Motives that Shape Autobiographical Narratives," *Personality & Social Psychology Bulletin* 20, no. 6 (1994): 676–690; J. Bruner, *Actual Minds, Possible Worlds* (Cambridge, MA: Harvard University Press, 1986).

75. Jennifer Edson Escalas, "Narrative Processing: Building Consumer Connections to Brands," *Journal of Consumer Psychology* 14, nos. 1 & 2 (2004): 168–180.

76. George A. Miller, "The Magical Number Seven, Plus or Minus Two: Some Limits on Our Capacity for Processing Information," *Psychological Review* 63 (1956): 81–97.

77. James N. MacGregor, "Short-Term Memory Capacity: Limitation or Optimization?" *Psychological Review* 94 (1987): 107–108.

78. M. Vanhuele, G. Laurent, and X. Drèze, "Consumers' Immediate Memory for Prices," *Journal of Consumer Research* 33, no. 2 (2006): 163–172.

79. Beth Snyder Bulik, "What's in a (Good) Product Name? Sales Cellphone Study Finds 'Cognitive' Monikers Work; Numerics Flop," February 2, 2009, www.namedevelopment.com/Articles/Good-Cellphone-Names.html, accessed February 27, 2009.

80. Stephen A. Spiller (2011) "Opportunity Cost Consideration." *Journal of Consumer Research* 38, no. 4 (2011): 595-610. Philip M. Fernbach, Christina Kan, and John G. Lynch (2015), "Squeezed: Coping with Constraint through Efficiency and Prioritization," *Journal of Consumer Research*, 41 (5), 1204-1227.

81. See Catherine A. Cole and Michael J. Houston, "Encoding and Media Effects on Consumer Learning Deficiencies in the Elderly," *Journal of Marketing Research* 24 (February 1987): 55–64; A. M. Collins and E. F. Loftus, "A Spreading Activation Theory of Semantic Processing," *Psychological Review* 82 (1975): 407–428; Fergus I. M. Craik and Robert S. Lockhart, "Levels of Processing: A Framework for Memory Research," *Journal of Verbal Learning & Verbal Behavior* 11 (1972): 671–684.

82. Walter A. Henry, "The Effect of Information-Processing Ability on Processing Accuracy," *Journal of Consumer Research* 7 (June 1980): 42–48.

83. T. B. Cornwell, M. S. Humphreys, A. M. Maguire, C. S. Weeks, and C. L. Tellegen, "Sponsorship-Linked Marketing: The Role of Articulation in Memory," *Journal of Consumer Research* 33, no. 3 (2006): 312–321.

84. Quoted in Jenna Wortham, "A Growing App Lets You See It, Then You Don't," *New York Times*, February 8, 2013, http://www.NewYorkTimes.com/2013/02/09/technology/snapchat-a-growing-app-lets-you-see-it-then-you-dont.html?_r=0, accessed February 22, 2015.

85. Kevin Lane Keller, "Memory Factors in Advertising: The Effect of Advertising Retrieval Cues on Brand Evaluations," *Journal of Consumer Research* 14 (December 1987): 316–333. For a discussion of processing operations that occur during brand choice, see Gabriel Biehal and Dipankar Chakravarti, "Consumers' Use of Memory and External Information in Choice: Macro and Micro Perspectives," *Journal of Consumer Research* 12 (March 1986): 382–405.

86. Susan T. Fiske and Shelley E. Taylor, *Social Cognition* (Reading, MA: Addison-Wesley, 1984).

87. Deborah Roedder John and John C. Whitney Jr., "The Development of Consumer Knowledge in Children: A Cognitive Structure Approach," *Journal of Consumer Research* 12 (March 1986): 406–417.

88. Michael R. Solomon, Carol Surprenant, John A. Czepiel, and Evelyn G. Gutman, "A Role Theory Perspective on Dyadic Interactions: The Service Encounter," *Journal of Marketing* 49 (Winter 1985): 99–111.

89. S. Danziger, S. Moran, and V. Rafaely, "The Influence of Ease of Retrieval on Judgment as a Function of Attention to Subjective Experience," *Journal of Consumer Psychology* 16, no. 2 (2006): 191–195.

90. Roger W. Morrell, Denise C. Park, and Leonard W. Poon, "Quality of Instructions on Prescription Drug Labels: Effects on Memory and Comprehension in Young and Old Adults," *The Gerontologist* 29 (1989): 345–354.

91. Mark J. Miller, "Carnival Hopes to Jog Passengers' Positive Memories in New Cruise Campaign," *Brand Channel* (September 19, 2013), http://www.brandchannel.com/home/post/2013/09/19/Carnival-Comeback-Campaign-091913.aspx, accessed February 22, 2015.

92. Frank R. Kardes, Gurumurthy Kalyanaram, Murali Chandrashekaran, and Ronald J. Dornoff, "Brand Retrieval, Consideration Set Composition, Consumer Choice, and the Pioneering Advantage" (unpublished manuscript, The University of Cincinnati, Ohio, 1992).

93. Judith Lynne Zaichkowsky and Padma Vipat, "Inferences from Brand Names," paper presented at the European meeting of the Association for Consumer Research, Amsterdam (June 1992).

94. H. Noel, "The Spacing Effect: Enhancing Memory for Repeated Marketing Stimuli," *Journal of Consumer Psychology* 16, no. 3 (2006): 306–320; for an alternative explanation, see S. L. Appleton-Knapp, R. A. Bjork, and T. D. Wickens, "Examining the Spacing Effect in Advertising: Encoding Variability, Retrieval Processes, and Their Interaction," *Journal of Consumer Research* 32, no. 2 (2005): 266–276.

95. Herbert E. Krugman, "Low Recall and High Recognition of Advertising," *Journal of Advertising Research* (February–March 1986): 79–86.

96. Rik G. M. Pieters and Tammo H. A. Bijmolt, "Consumer Memory for Television Advertising: A Field Study of Duration, Serial Position, and Competition Effects," *Journal of Consumer Research* 23 (March 1997): 362–372.

97. Erik Sass, "Study Finds Spectacular Print Ads Get Spectacular Recall," *Marketing Daily* (February 23, 2007), www.mediapost.com, accessed February 23, 2007.

98. Aaron Baar, "New Product Messages Aren't Making Intended Impressions," *Marketing Daily* (March 6, 2008), http://publications.mediapost.com/Index.Cfm?Fuseaction=Articles.Showarticle&Art_Aid=779, accessed March 6, 2008.

99. Raymond R. Burke and Thomas K. Srull, "Competitive Interference and Consumer Memory for Advertising," *Journal of Consumer Research* 15 (June 1988): 55–68.

100. Eric J. Johnson and J. Edward Russo, "Product Familiarity and Learning New Information," *Journal of Consumer Research* 11 (June 1984): 542–550.

101. Joan Meyers-Levy, "The Influence of Brand Name's Association Set Size and Word Frequency on Brand Memory," *Journal of Consumer Research* 16 (September 1989): 197–208.

102. Michael H. Baumgardner, Michael R. Leippe, David L. Ronis, and Anthony G. Greenwald, "In Search of Reliable Persuasion Effects: II. Associative Interference and Persistence of Persuasion in a Message-Dense Environment," *Journal of Personality & Social Psychology* 45 (September 1983): 524–537.

103. Joseph W. Alba and Amitava Chattopadhyay, "Salience Effects in Brand Recall," *Journal of Marketing Research* 23 (November 1986): 363–370.

104. Margaret Henderson Blair, Allan R. Kuse, David H. Furse, and David W. Stewart, "Advertising in a New and Competitive Environment: Persuading Consumers to Buy," *Business Horizons* 30 (November–December 1987): 20.

105. Kevin Lane Keller, "Memory Factors in Advertising: The Effect of Advertising Retrieval Cues on Brand Evaluations," *Journal of Consumer Research* 14 (December 1987): 316–333.

106. Eric J. Johnson and J. Edward Russo, "Product Familiarity and Learning New Information," *Journal of Consumer Research* 11 (June 1984): 542–550.

107. Eric J. Johnson and J. Edward Russo, "Product Familiarity and Learning New Information"; John G. Lynch and Thomas K. Srull, "Memory and Attentional Factors in Consumer Choice: Concepts and Research Methods," *Journal of Consumer Research* 9 (June 1982): 18–37.

108. Joseph W. Alba and J. Wesley Hutchinson, "Dimensions of Consumer Expertise," *Journal of Consumer Research* 13 (March 1988): 411–454; Julie A. Edell and Kevin Lane Keller, "The Information Processing of Coordinated Media Campaigns," *Journal of Marketing Research* 26 (May 1989): 149–164; cf. also Jeff Galak, Joseph P. Redden, and Justin Kruger, "Variety Amnesia: Recalling Past Variety Can Accelerate Recovery from Satiation," *Journal of Consumer Research* 36, no. 4 (2009): 575–584.

109. Marcus Cunha, Jr., and Juliano Laran, "Asymmetries in the Sequential Learning of Brand Associations: Implications for the Early Entrant Advantage," *Journal of Consumer Research* 35, no. 5 (2009): 788–799; Julie A. Edell and Kevin Lane Keller, "The Information Processing of Coordinated Media Campaigns," *Journal of Marketing Research* 26 (May 1989): 149–164; cf. also Galak, Redden, and Kruger, "Variety Amnesia: Recalling Past Variety Can Accelerate Recovery from Satiation."

110. Cunha, Jr., and Laran, "Asymmetries in the Sequential Learning of Brand Associations: Implications for the Early Entrant Advantage"; Andrew W. Ellis, Selina J. Holmes, and Richard L. Wright, "Age of Acquisition and the Recognition of Brand Names: On the Importance of Being Early," *Journal of Consumer Psychology* 20, no. 1 (2010): 43–52.

111. John G. Lynch and Thomas K. Srull, "Memory and Attentional Factors in Consumer Choice: Concepts and Research Methods," *Journal of Consumer Research* 9 (June 1982): 18–37; Joseph W. Alba and Amitava Chattopadhyay, "Salience Effects in Brand Recall," *Journal of Marketing Research* 23 (November 1986): 363–370; Elizabeth C. Hirschman and Michael R. Solomon, "Utilitarian, Aesthetic, and Familiarity Responses to Verbal versus Visual Advertisements," in Thomas C. Kinnear, ed., *Advances in Consumer Research* 11 (Provo, UT: Association for Consumer Research, 1984): 426–431.

112. Susan E. Heckler and Terry L. Childers, "The Role of Expectancy and Relevancy in Memory for Verbal and Visual Information: What Is Incongruency?" *Journal of Consumer Research* 18 (March 1992): 475–492.

113. Russell H. Fazio, Paul M. Herr, and Martha C. Powell, "On the Development and Strength of Category-Brand Associations in Memory: The Case of Mystery Ads," *Journal of Consumer Psychology* 1, no. 1 (1992): 1–13.

114. Jennifer Aaker, Aimee Drolet, and Dale Griffin, "Recalling Mixed Emotions," *Journal of Consumer Research* 35 (August 2008): 268–278.

115. Alex Mindlin, "Commercials Bask in a Show's Glow," *New York Times Online* (December 17, 2007), www.NewYorkTimes.com, accessed December 17, 2008.

116. Suzanne Vranica, "New Ads Take on Tivo, Tie-Ins to TV Shows Aim to Prevent Fast-Forwarding," *Wall Street Journal* (October 5, 2007): B4.

117. Hirschman and Solomon, "Utilitarian, Aesthetic, and Familiarity Responses to Verbal versus Visual Advertisements."

118. Terry Childers and Michael Houston, "Conditions for a Picture-Superiority Effect on Consumer Memory," *Journal of Consumer Research* 11 (September 1984): 643–654; Terry Childers, Susan Heckler, and Michael Houston, "Memory for the Visual and Verbal Components of Print Advertisements," *Psychology & Marketing* 3 (Fall 1986): 147–150.

119. Werner Krober-Riel, "Effects of Emotional Pictorial Elements in Ads Analyzed by Means of Eye Movement Monitoring," in Thomas C. Kinnear, ed., *Advances in Consumer Research* 11 (Provo, UT: Association for Consumer Research, 1984): 591–596.

120. Hans-Bernd Brosius, "Influence of Presentation Features and News Context on Learning from Television News," *Journal of Broadcasting & Electronic Media* 33 (Winter 1989): 1–14.

121. Edward F. McQuarrie and David Glen Mick, "Visual and Verbal Rhetorical Figures Under Directed Processing versus Incidental Exposure to Advertising," *Journal of Consumer Research* 29 (March 2003): 579–587; cf. also Ann E. Schlosser, "Learning Through Virtual Product Experience: The Role of Imagery on True Versus False Memories," *Journal of Consumer Research* 33, no. 3 (2006): 377–383.

122. "Only 38% of T.V. Audience Links Brands with Ads," *Marketing News* (January 6, 1984): 10.

123. "Terminal Television," *American Demographics* (January 1987): 15.

124. Susan Kuchinskas, "Home > Media > Video Brands Increase Recall with TV/Digital Mix, Google Says," *ClizkZ* (December 6, 2011), http://www.clickz.com/clickz/news/2130484/brands-increase-recall-tv-digital-mix-google, accessed January 7, 2013.

125. Kunur Patel, "Apple, Campbell's Say iAds Twice as Effective as TV A Nielsen Study Shows iPhone Users Are Paying Attention, While TV Viewers Not So Much," *Ad Age/Digital* (February 3, 2011), http://adage.com/article/digital/apple-campbell-s-iads-effective-tv/148630/, accessed January 7, 2013.

126. Richard P. Bagozzi and Alvin J. Silk, "Recall, Recognition, and the Measurement of Memory for Print Advertisements," *Marketing Science* 2 (1983): 95–134.

127. Adam Finn, "Print Ad Recognition Readership Scores: An Information Processing Perspective," *Journal of Marketing Research* 25 (May 1988): 168–177.

128. James R. Bettman, "Memory Factors in Consumer Choice: A Review," *Journal of Marketing* (Spring 1979): 37–53.

129. Mark A. Deturck and Gerald M. Goldhaber, "Effectiveness of Product Warning Labels: Effects of Consumers' Information Processing Objectives," *Journal of Consumer Affairs* 23, no. 1 (1989): 111–125.

130. Surendra N. Singh and Gilbert A. Churchill, Jr., "Response-Bias-Free Recognition Tests to Measure Advertising Effects," *Journal of Advertising Research* (June–July 1987): 23–36.

131. William A. Cook, "Telescoping and Memory's Other Tricks," *Journal of Advertising Research* 27 (February–March 1987): 5–8.

132. "On a Diet? Don't Trust Your Memory," *Psychology Today* (October 1989): 12.

133. F. May, and C. Irmak, C. "Licensing Indulgence in the Present by Distorting Memories of Past Behavior," *Journal of Consumer Research* 41, no. 3 (2014): 624–641.

134. Hugo Martin, "Disney's 2011 Marketing Campaign Centers on Family Memories," *Los Angeles Times* (September 23, 2010), http://latimesblogs.latimes.com/money_co/201009/disney-to-market-on-memories.html, accessed April 4, 2011.

135. Russell W. Belk, "Possessions and the Extended Self," *Journal of Consumer Research* 15 (September 1988): 139–168.

136. Morris B. Holbrook and Robert M. Schindler, "Nostalgic Bonding: Exploring the Role of Nostalgia in the Consumption Experience," *Journal of Consumer Behavior* 3, no. 2 (December 2003): 107–127.

137. Alexia Tsotsis, "Flickr Dips Its Toes into Social with Twitter and Facebook 'Share This' Features," *TechCrunch* (March 30, 2011), http://techcrunch.com/2011/03/30/flickr-dips-its-toes-into-social-with-twitter-and-face book-share-this-features/, accessed April 6, 2011.

138. Susan L. Holak and William J. Havlena, "Feelings, Fantasies, and Memories: An Examination of the Emotional Components of Nostalgia," *Journal of Business Research* 42 (1998): 217–226.

139. Jannine D. Lasaleta, Constantine Sedikides, and Kathleen D. Vohs, "Nostalgia Weakens the Desire for Money," *Journal of Consumer Research* (October 2014): 713–729.

140. Robert M. Schindler and Morris B. Holbrook, "Nostalgia for Early Experience as a Determinant of Consumer Preferences," *Psychology &*

Marketing 20, no. 4 (April 2003): 275–302; Morris B. Holbrook and Robert M. Schindler, "Some Exploratory Findings on the Development of Musical Tastes," *Journal of Consumer Research* 16 (June 1989): 119–124; Morris B. Holbrook and Robert M. Schindler, "Market Segmentation Based on Age and Attitude Toward the Past: Concepts, Methods, and Findings Concerning Nostalgic Influences on Consumer Tastes," *Journal of Business Research* 37, no. 1 (September 1996): 27–40.

141. Russell W. Belk, "The Role of Possessions in Constructing and Maintaining a Sense of Past," in Marvin E. Goldberg, Gerald Gorn, and Richard W. Pollay, eds., *Advances in Consumer Research* 16 (Provo, UT: Association for Consumer Research, 1989): 669–678.

142. Claire Martin, "Freezy Freakies, a Colorful Blast From Winters Past," *New York Times*, February 14, 2015, http://www.NewYorkTimes.com/2015/02/15/business/freezy-freakies-a-colorful-blast-from-winters-past.html?smid=*NewYorkTimes*core-iphone-share&smprod=*NewYork Times*core-iphone, accessed February 23, 2015.

143. Katherine Duncan, "Blast from the Past: Nostalgia Becomes a Marketing Strategy," *Entrepreneur* (December 16, 2014), http://www.entrepreneur.com/article/239684, accessed February 23, 2015.

144. Martinne Geller, "Exclusive: Flowers Foods to Win Hostess' Wonder Bread," *Chicago Tribune* (February 27, 2013), http://articles.chicagotribune.com/2013-02-27/business/sns-rt-us-hostess-flowersbre91q0tf-20130227_1_bread-brands-beefsteak-brand-hostess-brands, accessed March 4, 2013; Stuart Elliot, "From Retired Brands, Dollars and Memories," *New York Times* (December 8, 2010), http://www.NewYorkTimes.com/2010/12/09/business/media/09adco.html?_r=1&adxnnl=1&ref=media&adxnnlx=1301951891-EMjJs87oEc62npAZxAn7Gw, accessed April 4, 2011; Goudreau, "These Old Brands Are Poised for a 2011 Comeback."

145. http://passiripatti.com/2010/11/social-media-for-toddlers/,accessed June 14, 2011; "Sign of the Times: Toy Blocks That Teach Toddlers Social Networking," *Fast Company* (November 30, 2010), http://www.fastcodesign.com/1662781/toy-blocks-become-twitter-for-toddlers?partner=homepage_newsletter, accessed April 19, 2011.

146. Kate Taylor, "3 Ways Brands Are Marketing Nostalgia in the Age of Throwback Thursday," January 13, 2015, *Entrepreneur*, http://www.entrepreneur.com/article/241716.

147. Thomas F. Jones, "Our Musical Heritage Is Being Raided," *San Francisco Examiner* (May 23, 1997).

148. Kevin Goldman, "A Few Rockers Refuse to Turn Tunes into Ads," *New York Times* (August 25, 1995): B1.

149. Charles Duhigg, "Warning: Habits May Be Good for You," *New York Times Magazine* (July 17, 2008), www.ntyimes.com/2008/07/13/Business/13habit.html, accessed July 17, 2008.

Chapter 5 • Motivation and Affect

When you finish reading this chapter you will understand why:

5-1 Products can satisfy a range of consumer needs.

5-2 Consumers experience different kinds of motivational conflicts that can impact their purchase decisions.

5-3 Consumers experience a range of affective responses to products and marketing messages.

5-4 The way we evaluate and choose a product depends on our degree of involvement with the product, the marketing message, or the purchase situation.

Source: Phil Date/Shutterstock.

A s Basil scans the menu at the trendy health-food restaurant Paula has dragged him to, he reflects on what a man will give up for love. Now that Paula has become a die-hard vegan, she's slowly but surely working on him to forsake those juicy steaks and burgers for healthier fare. He can't even hide from tofu and other delights at school; the dining facility in his dorm just started to offer "veggie" alternatives to its usual assortment of greasy "mystery meats" and other delicacies he loves.

Paula is totally into it; she claims that eating this way not only cuts out unwanted fat but also is good for the environment. Just his luck to fall head-over-heels for a "tree-hugger." As Basil gamely tries to decide between the stuffed artichokes with red pepper vinaigrette and the grilled marinated zucchini, fantasies of a sizzling 14-ounce T-bone dance before his eyes.

OBJECTIVE 5-1
Products can satisfy a range of consumer needs.

The Motivation Process: Why Ask Why?

Paula certainly is not alone in her belief that eating green is good for the body, the soul, and the planet. According to a 2014 Harris Interactive study, approximately 5 percent of U.S. Americans are vegetarian (close to 16 million people) and about half of these vegetarians are vegan. Indeed the number of vegans in the United States has doubled since 2009.

Vegetarianism refers only to a diet that excludes meat (some animal products that do not involve the death of an animal, such as milk, cheese, and butter, may be included). *Veganism*, in contrast, links to a set of ethical beliefs about use of and cruelty to animals. In addition to objecting to hunting or fishing, adherents protest cruel animal training; object to the degrading use of animals in circuses, zoos, rodeos, and races; and also oppose the testing of drugs and cosmetics on animals.[1]

The forces that drive people to buy and use products are generally straightforward—for example, when a person chooses what to have for lunch. As hard-core vegans demonstrate, however, even the basic food products we consume also relate to wide-ranging beliefs regarding what we think is appropriate or desirable. In some cases, these emotional responses create a deep commitment to the product. Sometimes people are not even fully aware of the forces that drive them toward some products and away from others.

To understand motivation is to understand *why* consumers do what they do. Why do some people choose to bungee-jump off a bridge or compete on reality shows, whereas others spend their leisure time playing chess or gardening? Whether it is to quench a thirst, kill boredom, or attain some deep spiritual experience, we do everything for a reason, even if we can't articulate what that reason is. We teach marketing students from Day 1 that the goal of marketing is to satisfy consumers' needs. However, this insight is useless unless we can discover what those needs are and why they exist. A beer commercial once asked, "Why ask why?" In this chapter, we'll find out.

Motivation refers to the processes that lead people to behave as they do. It occurs when a need is aroused that the consumer wishes to satisfy. The need creates a state of tension that drives the consumer to attempt to reduce or eliminate it. This need may be *utilitarian* (i.e., a desire to achieve some functional or practical benefit, as when a person loads up on green vegetables for nutritional reasons) or it may be *hedonic* (i.e., an experiential need, involving emotional responses or fantasies as when a person feels "righteous" by eating kale). The desired end state is the consumer's **goal**. Marketers try to create products and services to provide the desired benefits and help the consumer to reduce this tension.

One question that keeps some consumer researchers up at night is whether a person even needs to be aware of a motivation to achieve a goal. The evidence suggests that motives can lurk beneath the surface, and cues in the environment can activate a goal even when we don't know it: Marketers are just beginning to explore the effects of **incidental brand exposure**:

- People who were exposed to a sign in a room of the brand name "Apple" provided responses on an unrelated task that were more unique compared to those who saw a sign with the IBM brand name.[2]
- College students who used a "cute" ice cream scoop to help themselves to ice cream took a larger amount than those who used a plain scoop; the researchers explained that the whimsical object drove them to be more self-indulgent even though they weren't aware of this effect.[3]
- Some students scored higher on difficult Graduate Records Examination questions when they took the test using a Massachusetts Institute of Technology pen and delivered a better athletic performance when they drank water from a Gatorade cup during strenuous exercise.[4]

Motivational Strength

Whether the need is utilitarian or hedonic, the magnitude of the tension it creates determines the urgency the consumer feels to reduce it. We call this degree of arousal a **drive**.

Drive Theory

Drive theory focuses on biological needs that produce unpleasant states of arousal (e.g., your stomach grumbles during a morning class). The arousal this tension causes motivates us to reduce it and return to a balanced state called **homeostasis**. Some researchers believe that this need to reduce arousal is a basic mechanism that governs much of our behavior. Indeed there is research evidence for the effectiveness of so-called **retail therapy**; apparently the act of shopping restores a sense of personal control over one's environment and as a result can alleviate feelings of sadness.[5] Go for it!

If a behavior reduces the drive, we naturally tend to repeat it. Your motivation to leave class early to grab a snack would be greater if you hadn't eaten in 24 hours than if you had eaten only two hours earlier. If you did sneak out and got indigestion afterward, say, from wolfing down a package of Twinkies, you would be less likely to repeat this behavior the next time you want a snack. One's degree of motivation, then, depends on the distance between one's present state and the goal.

Drive theory runs into difficulties when it tries to explain some facets of human behavior that run counter to its predictions. People often do things that increase a drive state rather than decrease it. For example, we may *delay gratification*. If you know you are going out for a lavish dinner, you might decide to forego a snack earlier in the day even though you are hungry at that time.

Expectancy Theory

Most current explanations of motivation focus on cognitive factors rather than biological ones to understand what motivates behavior. **Expectancy theory** suggests that expectations of achieving desirable outcomes—positive incentives—rather than being pushed from within motivate our behavior. We choose one product over another because we expect this choice to have more positive consequences for us. Thus, we use the term *drive* here loosely to refer to both physical and cognitive processes.

Motivational Direction

Motives have direction as well as strength. They are goal-oriented in that they drive us to satisfy a specific need. We can reach most goals by a number of routes, and the objective of a company is to convince consumers that the alternative it offers provides the best chance to attain the goal. For example, a consumer who decides that she needs a pair of jeans to help her reach her goal of being admired by others can choose among Levi's, Wranglers, True Religion, Diesel, 7 for All Mankind, and many other alternatives, each of which promises to deliver certain benefits.

Needs versus Wants

As we saw in Chapter 1, a *need* reflects a basic goal such as keeping yourself nourished or protected from the elements. In contrast a *want* is a specific pathway to achieving this objective that depends a lot on our unique personalities, cultural upbringing, and our observations about how others we know satisfy the same need. One person's cool

A want (like fast food) is a specific way to satisfy a need (like hunger).
Source: Dennis Tarnay, Jr./Alamy.

For some, jumping out of an airplane is a valuable hedonic experience.
Source: Kovalenko Inna.

downtown loft is another's suburban McMansion. In some cases, we don't even know we have a "want" until we can no longer have it: A lot of people didn't know they wanted *foie gras* ice cream sandwiches until California made them illegal. California banned *foie gras* in 2012, arguing that it was cruel to force-feed a duck to fatten its liver. Demand for delicacies made with the expensive and unobtainable dish spiked. A federal court overturned the ban in 2015, much to the relief of fatty liver connoisseurs.[6]

When we focus on a *utilitarian need*, we emphasize the objective, tangible attributes of products, such as miles per gallon in a car; the amount of fat, calories, and protein in a cheeseburger; or the durability of a pair of blue jeans. *Hedonic needs* are subjective and experiential; here we might look to a product to meet our needs for excitement, self-confidence, or fantasy—perhaps to escape the mundane or routine aspects of life.[7] Many items satisfy our hedonic needs (there's even a popular resort called Hedonism). Luxury brands in particular thrive when they offer the promise of pleasure to the user—how badly do you "need" that Armani suit or Coach bag?[8]

Of course, we can also be motivated to purchase a product because it provides *both* types of benefits. For example, a woman (perhaps a politically incorrect one) might buy a mink coat because of the luxurious image it portrays and because it also happens to keep her warm through the long, cold winter. Indeed, recent research on novel consumption experiences indicates that even when we choose to do unusual things (like eating bacon ice cream or staying in a freezing ice hotel), we may do so because we have what the authors term a **productivity orientation**. This refers to a continual striving to use time constructively: Trying new things is a way to check them off our "bucket list" of experiences we want to achieve before we move on to others.[9]

OBJECTIVE 5-2 Consumers experience different kinds of motivational conflicts that can impact their purchase decisions.	**Motivational Conflicts** A goal has *valence*, which means that it can be positive or negative. We direct our behavior toward goals we value positively; we are motivated to *approach* the goal and to seek out products that will help us to reach it. However, as we saw in Chapter 4's discussion of negative reinforcement, sometimes we're also motivated to *avoid* a negative outcome rather than achieve a positive outcome.

We structure purchases or consumption activities to reduce the chances that we will experience a nasty result. For example, many consumers work hard to avoid rejection by their peers (an avoidance goal). They stay away from products that

Figure 5.1 TYPES OF MOTIVATIONAL CONFLICT

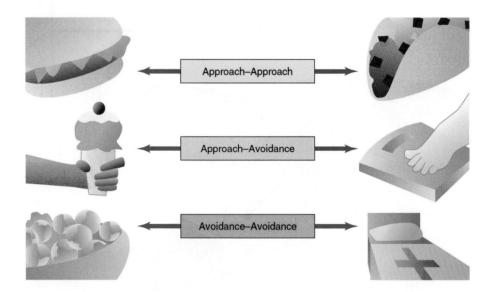

they associate with social disapproval. Products such as deodorants and mouthwash frequently rely on consumers' negative motivation when ads depict the onerous social consequences of underarm odor or bad breath.

Because a purchase decision can involve more than one source of motivation, consumers often find themselves in situations in which different motives, both positive and negative, conflict with one another.[10] Marketers attempt to satisfy consumers' needs by providing possible solutions to these dilemmas. As Figure 5.1 shows, there are three general types of conflicts we should understand.

Approach–Approach Conflict

A person has an **approach–approach conflict** when he or she must choose between two desirable alternatives. A student might be torn between going home for the holidays and going on a skiing trip with friends. Or, he or she might have to choose between two CDs to download (assuming that he or she is going to pay for one of them!). The **theory of cognitive dissonance** is based on the premise that people have a need for order and consistency in their lives and that a state of *dissonance* (tension) exists when beliefs or behaviors conflict with one another. We resolve the conflict that arises when we choose between two alternatives through a process of *cognitive dissonance reduction*, where we look for a way to reduce this inconsistency (or dissonance) and thus eliminate unpleasant tension.

Postdecision dissonance occurs when a consumer must choose between two products, both of which possess good and bad qualities. When he or she chooses one product and not the other, the person gets the bad qualities of the product he or she buys and loses out on the good qualities of the one he or she didn't buy. This loss creates an unpleasant, dissonant state that he wants to reduce. We tend to convince ourselves, after the fact, that the choice we made was the smart one as we find additional reasons to support the alternative we did choose—perhaps when we discover flaws with the option we did not choose (sometimes we call this *rationalization*). A marketer can bundle several benefits together to resolve an approach–approach conflict. For example, Miller Lite's claim that it is "less filling" *and* "tastes great" allows the drinker to "have his beer and drink it too."

Approach-Avoidance Conflict

Many of the products and services we desire have negative consequences attached to them as well as positive ones. We may feel guilty or ostentatious when we buy a luxury product such as a fur coat or we might feel like gluttons when we crave a tempting package of Twinkies. An **approach–avoidance conflict** occurs when we desire a goal but wish to avoid it at the same time.

Some solutions to these conflicts include the proliferation of fake furs, which eliminate guilt about harming animals to make a fashion statement, and the success of diet programs like Weight Watchers that promise good food without the calories.[11] Many marketers try to help consumers overcome guilt by convincing them that they deserve these luxuries. As the model for L'Oréal cosmetics exclaims, "Because I'm worth it!"

Avoidance-Avoidance Conflict

Sometimes we find ourselves caught "between a rock and a hard place." We may face a choice with two undesirable alternatives: for instance, the option of either spending more money on an old car or buying a new one. Don't you hate when that happens? Marketers frequently address an **avoidance–avoidance conflict** with messages that stress the unforeseen benefits of choosing one option (e.g., when they emphasize special credit plans to ease the pain of car payments).

How We Classify Consumer Needs

Numerous psychologists have tried to define a universal inventory of needs they could trace systematically to explain virtually all behavior.

Murray's Psychogenic Needs

One such inventory that the psychologist Henry Murray developed delineates a set of 20 *psychogenic needs* that (sometimes in combination) result in specific behaviors. These needs include such dimensions as *autonomy* (being independent), *defendance* (defending the self against criticism), and even *play* (engaging in pleasurable activities).[12]

Murray's framework is the basis for a number of personality tests that modern-day psychologists use, such as the Thematic Apperception Test (TAT). In the TAT, the analyst shows test subjects four to six ambiguous pictures and asks them to write answers to four direct questions about the pictures:

1 What is happening?
2 What led up to this situation?
3 What is being thought?
4 What will happen?

The theory behind the test is that people will freely project their own subconscious needs onto the neutral stimulus. By getting responses to the pictures, the analyst really gets at the person's true needs for achievement or affiliation or whatever other need may be dominant. Murray believed that everyone has the same basic set of needs but that individuals differ in their priority rankings of these needs.[13]

Specific Needs and Buying Behavior

Other motivational approaches have focused on specific needs and their ramifications for behavior. For example, individuals with a high *need for achievement* strongly value personal accomplishment.[14] They place a premium on products and services that signify success because these consumption items provide feedback about the realization of their goals. These consumers are good prospects for products that provide evidence of their achievement. One study of working women found that those who were high in achievement motivation were more likely to choose clothing they considered businesslike and less likely to be interested in apparel that accentuated their femininity.[15] Some other important needs that are relevant to consumer behavior include:

- *Need for affiliation* (to be in the company of other people):[16] The need for affiliation is relevant to products and services for people in groups, such as participating in team sports, frequenting bars, and hanging out at shopping malls.
- *Need for power* (to control one's environment):[17] Many products and services allow us to feel that we have mastery over our surroundings. These products range from "hopped-up" muscle cars and loud boom boxes (oversized portable radios that impose one's musical tastes on others) to luxury resorts that promise to respond to every whim of their pampered guests.

● *Need for uniqueness* (to assert one's individual identity):[18] Products satisfy the need for uniqueness when they pledge to bring out our distinctive qualities. For example, Cachet perfume claims to be "as individual as you are."

Maslow's Hierarchy of Needs

The psychologist Abraham Maslow originally developed his influential **Hierarchy of Needs** to understand personal growth and how people attain spiritual "peak experiences."[19] Marketers later adapted his work to understand consumer motivations.[19] Maslow's *hierarchical* structure implies that the order of development is fixed—that is, we must attain a certain level before we activate a need for the next, higher one. Marketers embraced this perspective because it (indirectly) specifies certain types of product benefits people might look for, depending on their stage of mental or spiritual development or on their economic situation.[20]

Figure 5.2 presents this model. At each level, the person seeks different kinds of product benefits. Ideally, an individual progresses up the hierarchy until his or her dominant motivation is a focus on "ultimate" goals, such as justice and beauty. Unfortunately, this state is difficult to achieve (at least on a regular basis); most of us have to be satisfied with occasional glimpses, or *peak experiences*. One study of men aged 49 to 60 found that these respondents engaged in three types of activities to attain self-fulfillment: (1) *sport and physical activity*, (2) *community and charity*, and (3) *building and renovating*. Regardless of whether these activities were related to their professional work, these so-called *magnetic points* gradually took the place of those that were not as fulfilling.[21]

Marketers' applications of this hierarchy have been somewhat simplistic, especially because the same product or activity can gratify different needs. For example, one study found that gardening could satisfy needs at every level of the hierarchy:[22]

● **Physiological**—"I like to work in the soil."
● **Safety**—"I feel safe in the garden."
● **Social**—"I can share my produce with others."
● **Esteem**—"I can create something of beauty."
● **Self-actualization**—"My garden gives me a sense of peace."

Another problem with taking Maslow's Hierarchy of Needs too literally is that it is culture-bound; its assumptions may apply only to Western culture. People in other

Safety is a lower-level need in Maslow's Hierarchy of Needs
Source: Courtesy of Volvo do Brasil.

SAFETY FIRST.

Volvo Trucks. Driving Progress

Figure 5.2 MASLOW'S HIERARCHY OF NEEDS

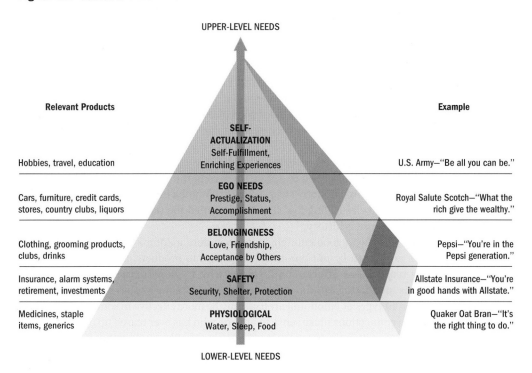

UPPER-LEVEL NEEDS

Relevant Products

Example

SELF-ACTUALIZATION
Self-Fulfillment,
Enriching Experiences

Hobbies, travel, education

U.S. Army—"Be all you can be."

EGO NEEDS
Prestige, Status,
Accomplishment

Cars, furniture, credit cards,
stores, country clubs, liquors

Royal Salute Scotch—"What the
rich give the wealthy."

BELONGINGNESS
Love, Friendship,
Acceptance by Others

Clothing, grooming products,
clubs, drinks

Pepsi—"You're in the
Pepsi generation."

SAFETY
Security, Shelter, Protection

Insurance, alarm systems,
retirement, investments

Allstate Insurance—"You're
in good hands with Allstate."

PHYSIOLOGICAL
Water, Sleep, Food

Medicines, staple
items, generics

Quaker Oat Bran—"It's
the right thing to do."

LOWER-LEVEL NEEDS

cultures (or, for that matter, even some in Western cultures) may question the order of the levels it specifies. A religious person who has taken a vow of celibacy would not necessarily agree that physiological needs must be satisfied before self-fulfillment can occur.

Similarly, many Asian cultures value the welfare of the group (belongingness needs) more highly than needs of the individual (esteem needs). The point is that this hierarchy, although marketers widely apply it, is helpful primarily because it reminds us that consumers may have different need priorities in different consumption situations and at different stages in their lives—not because it *exactly* specifies a consumer's progression up the ladder of needs.

A basic activity like gardening can satisfy people at different levels depending upon their motivation to engage in it.
Source: Todd Arena/123RF.

OBJECTIVE 5-3

Consumers experience a range of affective responses to products and marketing messages.

Affect

Zumba began in the 1990s as a Colombian dance fitness program, but today it's an international sensation. Every week about 14 million people in more than 150 countries take classes that combine elements of dance moves adapted from various sources such as hip-hop, salsa, merengue, mambo, belly dancing and Bollywood, with some squats and lunges thrown in for good measure. The Zumba company started as an infomercial producer, but the regimen was popularized when the CEO's brother, an out-of-work advertising executive, had a revelation and convinced him to change focus. The brother recalls that he saw a movie billboard with some exuberant dancers: "Immediately, I called my brother and said, 'You're selling the wrong thing. You're selling fitness when you should be selling this emotion.' I wanted to turn Zumba into a brand where people felt that kind of free and electrifying joy." The two invented the tagline, "Ditch the workout; join the party!" The rest is history.[23]

We may not all be in good enough shape to endure a Zumba workout, but many of our decisions are driven by our emotional responses to products. Social scientists refer to these raw reactions as **affect**. That explains why so many marketing activities and messages focus on altering our moods or linking their products to an affective response, although different types of emotional arousal may be more effective in some contexts than others.[24] These connections make sense to anyone who has ever teared up during a sappy TV commercial or written an angry letter after getting shabby treatment at a hotel.

Types of Affective Responses

Affect describes the experience of emotionally laden states, but the nature of these experiences ranges from evaluations, to moods, to full-blown emotions. **Evaluations** are valenced (i.e., positive or negative) reactions to events and objects that are not accompanied by high levels of physiological arousal. For example, when a consumers evaluates a movie as being positive or negative, this usually involves some degree of affect accompanied by low levels of arousal (possible exceptions such as *Fifty Shades of Gray* notwithstanding!). **Moods** involve temporary positive or negative affective states accompanied by moderate levels of arousal. Moods tends to be diffuse and not necessarily linked to a particular event (e.g. you might have just "woken up on the wrong side of the bed this morning"). **Emotions** such as happiness, anger, and fear tend to be more intense and often relate to a specific triggering event such as receiving an awesome gift.[25]

Marketers find many uses for affective states. They often try to link a product or service with a positive mood or emotion (just think of a sappy Hallmark greeting card). Of

Zumba exercise routines focus on providing an emotional experience.
Source: Photo by Danny Martindale/WireImage/ Getty Images.

course a variety of products from alcohol to chocolate are consumed at least partly for their ability to enhance mood. Numerous companies evaluate the emotional impact of their ads; some such as Unilever and Coca-Cola use sophisticated technology that interprets how viewers react to ads by their facial expressions.[26]

On other occasions marketing communications may deliberately evoke negative affect, such as regret if you forget to play the lottery. Perhaps a more productive way to harness the power of negative affect is to expose the consumer to a distressing image and then provide a way to improve it. For example, a nonprofit organization might run an ad showing a starving child when it solicits donations. Helping others as a way to resolve one's own negative moods is known as **negative state relief**. Recently we've seen a trend in advertising toward inspirational stories that manipulate our emotions like a roller-coaster: Think about the commercials Budweiser likes to run about a puppy who befriends a horse, gets lost, finds his way home, etc. This practice even has a name: **sadvertising**.[27]

A study shows that this emotional element is especially potent for decisions that involve outcomes the person will experience shortly as opposed to those that involve a longer time frame.[28] Another study attests to the interplay between our emotions and how we access information in our minds that allows us to make smarter decisions. These researchers reported evidence for what they call an **emotional oracle effect**: People who trusted their feelings were able to predict future events better than those who did not; this occurred for a range of situations including the presidential election, the winner of *American Idol*, movie box office success, and the stock market. The likely reason is that those with more confidence were better able to access information they had learned that could help them make an informed forecast.[29]

Mood Congruency

We've already seen that cognitive dissonance occurs when our various feelings, beliefs, or behaviors don't line up, and we may be motivated to alter one or more of these to restore consistency. We'll talk more about that in our discussion of attitudes in Chapter 8.

Mood congruency refers to the idea that our judgments tend to be shaped by our moods. For example, consumers judge the same products more positively when they are in a positive as opposed to a negative mood. This is why advertisers attempt to place their ads after humorous TV programming or create uplifting ad messages that put viewers in a good mood. Similarly, retailers work hard to make shoppers happy by playing "up" background music and encouraging staff to be friendly. Then of course there's the traditional "three-martini" business lunch...

Positive Affect

As part of its global "Open Happiness" campaign, Coca-Cola set up a vending machine at the National University of Singapore that trades free coke beverages for hugs. The machine, which is outfitted in Coca-Cola's signature colors and fonts, reads, "hug me" in large letters on the front.[30]

Our feelings also can serve as a source of information when we weigh the pros and cons of a decision. Put simply, the fact that the prospect of owning a specific brand will make a person feel good can give it a competitive advantage—even if the brand is similar on a functional level to other competing brands. That helps to explain why many of us will willingly pay a premium for a product that on the surface seems to do the same thing as a less expensive alternative—whether in the case of the hottest new Apple iPhone, a Justice shirt, or even a pricey university. A passionate commitment to one brand has famously been termed a **lovemark** by the head of the Saatchi & Saatchi advertising agency.

Happiness

Happiness is a mental state of well-being characterized by positive emotions. What makes us happy? Although many of us believe owning more shiny material goods is the key to happiness, research says otherwise. Several studies have reported that a greater emphasis on acquiring *things* actually links to lower levels of happiness! Indeed some

CB AS I SEE IT

Michel Tuan Pham, *Columbia University*

Theories of how consumers make choices and decisions have historically emphasized processes that are cognitive and seemingly "rational." Consumers, we are told, function a bit like computers: They search and receive product-related information from the environment (e.g., the electrical consumption of a dishwasher), combine this information with other information stored in their memory (e.g., the reputation of a particular brand), and integrate the whole into an overall decision using rules that reflect what consumers care about (e.g.,

their willingness to trade-off brand reputation for lower prices). The metaphor typically advanced is that of a consumer using *Consumer Reports*® to make decisions.

Anyone who has observed consumers operate in the real world knows that the above-described model offers a poor description of many consumption decisions. In particular, this computer-like model doesn't capture the important role that feelings and emotions play in consumers' decisions and behavior. Think of the pride and contentment of a mother buying new shoes for her growing toddler, the joy of a young child learning that she is going to Disneyland, the excitement of a teenager planning his next birthday party, or the anger of a customer who feels cheated by a company. How does one capture that?

For the past 25 years, I have studied how feelings and emotions influence consumers' decisions and behavior. My findings show that feelings and emotions indeed do matter. Part of the reason why they matter is that contrary to the assumed incompatibility between emotion and rationality, consumers typically consider their feelings and emotions to be informative. On this point, I think that they are generally right. If a product doesn't "feel right," one should probably stay away from it,

even if it seems like a good deal; and if a product "feels right," one is likely to be happy with it in the long run—something that I have called *emotional rationality.*

Another reason why feelings and emotions matter is that a lot of the seemingly logical arguments that consumers use to explain their decisions are in fact *post hoc* rationalizations of their immediate feelings toward the products that they evaluate. Consumers may reason that they like a new BMW because it has good mileage or because their current car is getting old, whereas in fact these rationales only came to their minds because they were immediately attracted by the car's pleasing aesthetic. First emotional impressions thus matter a lot in business.

My research further shows that feelings and emotions are not just good or bad, pleasant or unpleasant. Their specific content makes a big difference. Pride isn't the same as excitement; anxiety isn't the same as sadness; and joy isn't the same as relaxation. Each of these distinct emotions moves consumers in different directions. A big challenge for marketers will be to understand how to induce the "right" emotions among consumers, which is something that I am currently working on in my latest research.

recent evidence suggests we are "wired" to engage in **material accumulation**, which is what researchers term the instinct to earn more than we can possibly consume, even when this imbalance makes us unhappy. In the first phase of a study to explore this idea, respondents were asked to listen to obnoxious white noise on a headset. They were told they could earn pieces of Dove chocolate when they listened to the white noise a certain number of times. They also were asked to estimate how may pieces of chocolate they could eat in a 5-minute period after this phase. Respondents on average endured enough white noise to earn far more chocolates then even they predicted they could eat. In other words, they endured negative experiences to earn more than they knew they could possibly consume.[31]

Happiness is an extreme state of well-being accompanied by positive emotions.
Source: Phil Date/Shutterstock.

Other work suggests that experiences beat out material acquisitions. In one study respondents were asked to think of either a material purchase (defined as a purchase made with the primary intention of acquiring a material possession) or an experiential purchase (defined as a purchase made with the primary intention of acquiring a life experience). Even though the two scenarios were matched for the price paid, respondents were happier when they thought of experiential purchases.[32] In addition, the drivers of happiness also seem to vary throughout the life span. Younger people are more likely to associate happiness with excitement, whereas older people are more likely to associate this state with feelings of calm and peacefulness.[33]

Negative Affect

Although we may assume that marketers want to make us happy all the time, that's hardly the case. Marketing messages can make us sad, angry or even depressed—and sometimes that's done on purpose!

Disgust

Many researchers believe that the primitive emotion of disgust evolved to protect us from contamination; we learned over the years to avoid putrid meat and other foul substances linked to pathogens. As a result, even the slight odor of something nasty elicits a universal reaction—the wrinkling of the nose, curling of the upper lips, and protrusion of the tongue. Wrinkling the nose has been shown to prevent pathogens from entering through the nasal cavity, and sticking out the tongue aids in the expulsion of tainted food and is a common precursor to vomiting.

OK, now that you're sufficiently grossed out, what (you may ask in disgust) does this have to do with marketing and persuasion? Well, disgust also exerts a powerful effect on our judgments. People who experience this emotion become harsher in their judgments of moral offenses and offenders. In one experiment, people who sat in a foul-smelling room or at a desk cluttered with dirty food containers judged acts such as lying on a résumé or keeping a wallet found on the street as more immoral than individuals who were asked to make the same judgments in a clean environment. In another study, survey respondents who were randomly asked to complete the items while they stood in front of a hand sanitizer gave more conservative responses than those who stood in another part of the hallway.[35]

The Tangled Web

The next time you're feeling down and you think about cheering yourself by checking your Facebook page, think again: Researchers report that the longer people stay on Facebook, the worse they feel. Apparently this activity makes you feel like you're wasting your life; people say that compared to browsing the Internet (or perhaps, studying) Facebook checking is less meaningful or useful. This judgment in turns leads to bad feelings.[34]

Talk about a rude awakening—and the need to make a quick decision! This unforgiving clock brings new meaning to the phrase, "you snooze, you lose." If you don't get up to turn off the alarm when it sounds, it's going to cost you.
Source: wireframe.ru.

Advertisers used to avoid using negative imagery so they wouldn't turn people off, but many now realize that it actually can be productive to elicit extreme feelings such as disgust to get their message across:

● To discourage people from consuming sugary drinks, The New York Department of Health showed a man imbibing a soft drink—as he does the beverage turns into gobs of fat.
● Febreze ran a TV commercial where blindfolded people in a foul room believe it's actually a nice location because the air freshener covers up the stench.
● Lamisil is a medication for toenail fungus, so it's not too hard to generate feelings of disgust. The company created a creature it called "Digger" that excavates its way under people nails—a safe bet it accomplished its objective.

Envy

Envy is a negative emotion associated with the desire to reduce the gap between oneself and someone who is superior on some dimension. Researchers distinguish between two types of envy: *Benign envy* occurs when we believe the other person actually deserves a coveted brand (like an iPhone). Under these circumstances the person may be willing to pay more to obtain the same item. *Malicious envy* occurs when the consumer believes the other person does not deserve his or her superior position. In this case the consumer may not desire the product the other person owns, but he or she may be willing to pay more for a different brand in the same category (like a Samsung Galaxy) to set them apart from the other person.[36]

Guilt

Guilt is "an individual's unpleasant emotional state associated with possible objections to his or her actions, inaction, circumstances, or intentions."[37] Marketers may try to invoke a feeling of guilt when they want consumers to engage in prosocial behaviors like giving to charities. These "guilt appeals" can be particularly effective when others are present because this approach activates a sense of social responsibility. However, extreme guilt appeals can backfire so often a more subtle approach is preferable.[38]

Embarrassment

Embarrassment is an emotion driven by a concern for what others think about us. To be embarrassed, we must be aware of, and care about, the audience that evaluates us.[39] This reaction also pops up in the consumer environment when we purchase socially sensitive products such as condoms, adult diapers, tampons, or hair-lice shampoo.[40] In these situations consumers get creative as they try to reduce embarrassment; they might try to hide a sensitive product among others in a shopping basket or choose a cashier who looks "more friendly" when they check out.

How Social Media Tap into Our Emotions

Since 1972, the tiny country of Bhutan has measured the Gross National Happiness of its citizens.[41] Now the city of Somerville, MA, is testing an app called H(app)athon, which combines survey questions about well-being with data collected automatically by phone to monitor how happy residents are. New devices like Fitbits and services like the Nike + Training Club allow many of us to continuously monitor our well-being; at least in terms of steps walked or how well we slept.[42] Proponents of a **happiness economy** claim that well-being is the new wealth, and social media technology is what allows us to accumulate it.

A lot of our social media activity involves expressing affect, both positive and negative. We may share particularly good or bad feelings on Facebook or Twitter, or even resort to corny emoticons like :) in texts or emails, to convey how we feel. To push sales of its Jell-O brand, Kraft unveiled a "Mood Monitor" on Twitter, in which it will randomly send coupons to users it finds who type in a :(emoticon. Kraft will monitor the Twittersphere and the company will launch coupons whenever the national average of smiley faces dips below 51 percent.[43] LOL!

In fact, it's so common for people to express their moods and also their emotional reactions to products that these posts can be a treasure trove for marketers who want to learn more about how their offerings make people feel. A technique called **sentiment analysis** refers to a process (sometimes also called *opinion mining*) that scours the social media universe to collect and analyze the words people use when they describe a specific product or company. When people feel a particular way, they are likely to choose certain words that tend to relate to the emotion. From these words, the researcher creates a **word-phrase dictionary** (sometimes called a *library*) to code the data. The program scans the text to identify whether the words in the dictionary appear.

Consider this example based on Canon's PowerShot A540. A review on *Epinions*, a product review site, included this statement: "The Canon PowerShot A540 had good aperture and excellent resolution." A sentiment analysis would extract the entities of interest from the sentence, identifying the product as the Canon PowerShot A540 and the relevant dimensions as aperture and resolution. The sentiment would then be extracted for each dimension: the sentiment for aperture is *good*, whereas that for resolution is *excellent*. Text-mining software would collect these reactions and combine them with others to paint a picture of how people are talking about the product. There are several sentiment analysis programs that do similar things; a new one called ToneCheck even reports on the emotions it detects in people's emails.[45]

The Tangled Web

Facebook routinely adjusts its users' news feeds, without their knowledge, to see what happens when they see different ad formats or numbers of ads. The company got into hot water recently when it admitted that it had manipulated the news feeds of more than 600,000 randomly selected users to change the number of positive and negative posts they saw. The goal was to determine if these posts then influenced what users posted. Sure enough, moods are contagious: people who saw more positive posts responded by writing more positive posts. Similarly, seeing more negative content prompted the viewers to be more negative in their own posts. Although Facebook argued that users give blanket consent to the company's research as a condition of using the service, many critics suggested the company had crossed an ethical boundary.[44]

OBJECTIVE 5-4
The way we evaluate and choose a product depends on our degree of involvement with the product, the marketing message, or the purchase situation.

Consumer Involvement

Imagine this conversation between two shoppers at a car dealership:

Consumer #1: I want the one I read about in the latest issue of *Car and Driver* magazine: It has a six-cylinder turbo engine, a double-clutch transmission, a 90 strokebore, and 10:1 compression ratio.
Consumer #2: I want a red one.

Involvement is "a person's perceived relevance of the object based on their inherent needs, values, and interests."[46] Figure 5.3 shows that different factors may create involvement. These factors can be something about the person, something about the object, or something about the situation.

Figure 5.3 CONCEPTUALIZING INVOLVEMENT

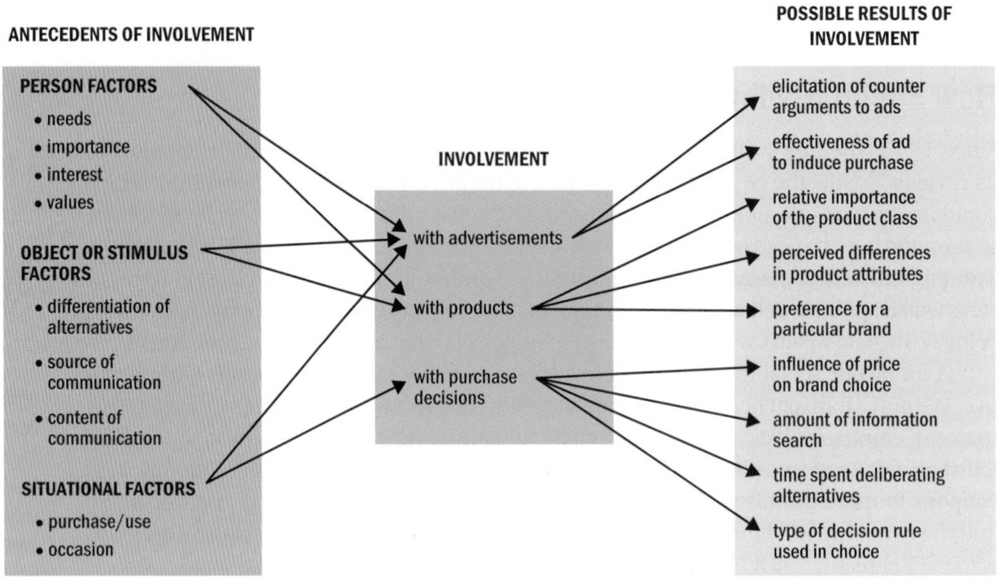

ANTECEDENTS OF INVOLVEMENT

POSSIBLE RESULTS OF INVOLVEMENT

PERSON FACTORS
- needs
- importance
- interest
- values

OBJECT OR STIMULUS FACTORS
- differentiation of alternatives
- source of communication
- content of communication

SITUATIONAL FACTORS
- purchase/use
- occasion

INVOLVEMENT

with advertisements

with products

with purchase decisions

elicitation of counter arguments to ads

effectiveness of ad to induce purchase

relative importance of the product class

perceived differences in product attributes

preference for a particular brand

influence of price on brand choice

amount of information search

time spent deliberating alternatives

type of decision rule used in choice

INVOLVEMENT = f (Person, Situation, Object)

The level of involvement may be influenced by one or more of these three factors. Interactions among persons, situation, and object factors are likely to occur.

Marketing Opportunity

As we saw in Chapter 4, *gamification* is a red-hot marketing strategy today; it refers to the application of gaming principles to non-gaming contexts. This approach offers a way to dramatically increase involvement, especially for activities that can benefit from a bit of motivation. When the Federal Deposit Insurance Corporation (FDIC) wanted to promote financial literacy, the government agency created its Money Smart program. It's designed to look like a board game similar to *Monopoly* and it challenges players to learn financial skills such as setting up a bank account, paying bills on time and avoiding identity theft. The game attracted more than 40,000 users in a year.[53] Closer to home, when the business school at Syracuse University wanted to ramp up undergraduates' interest in corporate finance, it did so by placing students into one of four "houses" for the year à la *Harry Potter*, each with its own name and shield. Students can earn points for attending optional lectures and other finance-related activities. The winning team at the end of the year gets a party with the Dean, but also a "house cup" just like in the movie.[54]

Our motivation to attain a goal increases our desire to acquire the products or services that we believe will satisfy it. However, as we see in the case of Consumer #2 at the car dealership, not everyone is motivated to the same extent. Involvement reflects our level of motivation to process information about a product or service we believe will help us to solve a problem or reach a goal.[47] Think of a person's degree of involvement as a continuum that ranges from absolute lack of interest in a marketing stimulus at one end to obsession at the other. **Inertia** describes consumption at the low end of involvement, where we make decisions out of habit because we lack the motivation to consider alternatives. Table 5.1 shows one of the most widely used scales to assess level of involvement.

Depending on whether the need we want to satisfy is utilitarian or hedonic (see Chapter 1), as our involvement increases we think more about the product ("I've spent the last three days researching mortgage interest rates") or we experience a strong emotional response ("I get goose bumps when I imagine what my daughter will look like in that bridal gown").[48] Not surprisingly, we tend to find higher levels of involvement in product categories that demand a big investment of money (like houses) or self-esteem (like clothing) and lower levels for mundane categories like household cleaners or hardware.[49] Still, bear in mind that virtually anything can qualify as highly involving to some people—just ask a "tool guy" to talk about his passion for hammers or plumbing supplies.

When Apple put its first iPhone on sale, thousands of adoring iCultists around the country (including the mayor of Philadelphia) waited in front of Apple stores for days to be one of the first to buy the device—even though they could order the phone online and have it delivered in 3 days. Somehow that was too long to wait for a cell phone with a touchscreen. As one loyal consumer admitted, "If Apple made sliced bread, yeah, I'd buy it."[50]

Cult products such as Apple—or Hydrox, Harley-Davidson, Jones Soda, Chick-Fil-A, Manolo Blahnik designer shoes (think Carrie on *Sex and the City*), and the Boston Red Sox—command fierce consumer loyalty, devotion, and maybe even worship by consumers.[51] A large majority of consumers agree that they are willing to pay more for a brand when they feel a personal connection to the company.[52]

TABLE 5.1 A Scale to Measure Involvement

To Me [Object to Be Judged] Is

1. important	_:_:_:_:_:_:_	unimportant*
2. boring	_:_:_:_:_:_:_	interesting
3. relevant	_:_:_:_:_:_:_	irrelevant*
4. exciting	_:_:_:_:_:_:_	unexciting*
5. means nothing	_:_:_:_:_:_:_	means a lot to me
6. appealing	_:_:_:_:_:_:_	unappealing*
7. fascinating	_:_:_:_:_:_:_	mundane*
8. worthless	_:_:_:_:_:_:_	valuable
9. involving	_:_:_:_:_:_:_	uninvolving*
10. not needed	_:_:_:_:_:_:_	needed

Types of Involvement

A freelance software programmer named Winter is on a mission to visit every Starbucks in the world. To date he's been to more than 12,000 outlets in numerous countries. When he learned that a Starbucks store in British Columbia was scheduled to close the next day, he spent $1,400 to fly there immediately just to order a cup of coffee in the nick of time. He chronicles his odyssey on his Web site, starbuckseverywhere.net.[55]

OK, maybe Winter needs to get a life. Still, his passion demonstrates that involvement takes many forms. It can be cognitive, as when a "gearhead" is motivated to learn all he or she can about the latest specs of a new tablet, or emotional, as when the thought of a new Armani suit gives a clotheshorse the chills.[56] What's more, the act of *buying* the Armani may be highly involving for people who are passionately devoted to shopping.

To further complicate matters, advertisements such as those Nike or Adidas produce may themselves be involving for some reason (e.g., because they make us laugh or cry or inspire us to exercise harder). So, it seems that involvement is a fuzzy concept because it overlaps with other things and means different things to different people. Indeed, the

The FDIC "gamified" the need to build financial literacy.
Source: FDIC.

This Brazilian ad for hair-loss product appeals to men who take their impending baldness seriously.
Source: Art Director: Pedro Vargens, Creative Directors: Bruno Richter and Victor Vicente.

Marketing Opportunity

When we have the opportunity to personalize a product, our involvement increases because the item reflects our unique preferences. But how about when we build the product ourselves? Researchers term this the **IKEA Effect**; self-made (or at least assembled) products including furniture, Legos, and even origami enhance the value we attach to them because our own labor is involved.[61] Of course, there may also be that unsettling feeling when you finish assembling a bookcase and there's still one part left over....

consensus is that there are actually several broad types of involvement we can relate to the product, the message, or the perceiver.[57]

Product Involvement

Product involvement is a consumer's level of interest in a particular product. The more closely marketers can tie a brand to an individual, the higher the involvement they will create.

As a rule, product decisions are likely to be highly involving if the consumer believes there is a lot of **perceived risk**. This means the person believes there may be negative consequences if he or she chooses the wrong option. Risk is greater when a product is expensive or complicated. In some cases perceived risk also is a factor when others can see what we choose, and we may be embarrassed if we make the wrong choice.[58] Remember that a product does not necessarily have to cost a fortune or be hard to use to be risky—for example, a college senior who is going to a job interview may obsess about sweating too much and give a lot of thought to the brand of deodorant he or she uses that morning.

We value things more when our own labor contributes to making or assembling them.
Source: Maridav/Fotolia.

CB AS I SEE IT
Debora Thompson, *Georgetown University*

Companies increasingly involve consumers in the process of developing advertising and other marketing actions. Such **co-creation** of marketing with consumers is expected to significantly increase their engagement with the brand. However, not much is known about the response of consumers who have not been directly involved in the co-creation process, but are simply informed that the company undertook co-creation activity with some unspecified fellow consumers. My research has explored when and why informing the audience that an ad was created by another consumer will increase message

persuasiveness. Through several lab experiments in which consumers watched TV ads for several brands, my colleagues and I have found that informing consumers that an ad is consumer-generated triggers two conflicting responses: skepticism about the competence of the ad creator and identification with the ad creator. Skepticism emerges when the audience challenges the ability of regular consumers to design effective advertising, perhaps recognizing that effective advertising requires particular skill and expertise. Identification emerges when the audience perceives similarities between themselves and the consumer creating the ad. The effectiveness of disclosing advertising co-creation, therefore, depends on factors that hinder skepticism and heighten identification with the ad creator. Interestingly, we found that attributing the ad to a consumer backfires when the ad creator is simply portrayed as an unspecified fellow consumer or when the audience consists of non-loyal consumers who do not share with the ad creator a commitment towards the brand. However, this negative effect can be mitigated and even reversed under high distraction viewing conditions, when consumers' ability to activate their critical thoughts is limited, and when the audience identifies with the

consumer creating the ad, such as when the ad creator is depicted as sharing a background trait with the viewers or when the consumer is loyal to the brand.

Overall, my research shows that although marketers should continue to engage consumers and benefit from their creativity, they should be careful about how they publicize this fact to the population at large. To reap greater benefits from consumer-generated campaigns, it is important to develop a narrative not only about the initiative itself, but also about the consumer creating the ad. Marketers can prevent the heightened skepticism about the skills of ordinary consumers as content creators by increasing identification between the ad creator and the ad recipient. This can be done by disseminating information about the co-creation process via public relations efforts, TV ads, and online videos, or through social networking sites (e.g., developing "the making of the ad" videos). Finally, my research suggests that the disclosure of consumer-generated ads should be driven by a careful assessment of the brand's growth objectives. Consumer-generated advertising campaigns are likely to be a more effective tactic to engage and retain a brand's loyal customers, rather than to attract and grow the share of customers who are not presently loyal to the brand.

Figure 5.4 lists five kinds of risk—including objective (e.g., physical danger) and subjective (e.g., social embarrassment) factors—as well as the products each type tends to affect. Perceived risk is less of a problem for consumers who have greater "risk capital," because they have less to lose from a poor choice. For example, a highly self-confident person might worry less than a vulnerable, insecure person who chooses a brand that peers think isn't cool.

Mass customization describes the personalization of products and services for individual customers at a mass-production price.[59] This product involvement strategy applies to a wide range of products and services, from newspaper Web sites that allow readers to choose which sections of the paper they want to see, to Dell computers that you can configure, to Levi's blue jeans that have a right leg one inch shorter than a left leg to fit an asymmetrical body (this is more common than you think).[60] Mars Snackfood USA

Figure 5.4 FIVE TYPES OF PERCEIVED RISK

	BUYERS MOST SENSITIVE TO RISK	**PURCHASES MOST SUBJECT TO RISK**
MONETARY RISK	Risk capital consists of money and property. Those with relatively little income and wealth are most vulnerable.	High-ticket items that require substantial expenditures are most subject to this form of risk.
FUNCTIONAL RISK	Risk capital consists of alternative means of performing the function or meeting the need. Practical consumers are most sensitive.	Products or services whose purchase and use requires the buyer's exclusive commitment are most sensitive.
PHYSICAL RISK	Risk capital consists of physical vigor, health, and vitality. Those who are elderly, frail, or in ill health are most vulnerable.	Mechanical or electrical goods (such as vehicles or flammables), drugs and medical treatment, and food and beverages are most sensitive.
SOCIAL RISK	Risk capital consists of self-esteem and self-confidence. Those who are insecure and uncertain are most sensitive.	Socially visible or symbolic goods, such as clothes, jewelry, cars, homes, or sports equipment are most subject to social risk.
PSYCHO-LOGICAL RISK	Risk capital consists of affiliations and status. Those lacking self-respect or attractiveness to peers are most sensitive.	Expensive personal luxuries that may engender guilt, durables, and services whose use demands self-discipline or sacrifice are most sensitive.

introduced M&M's Faces to encourage consumers to bond with its chocolates: At mymms.com, you can upload a photo and order a batch of M&Ms with a face and personal message printed on the candy shell.

When a consumer is highly involved with a specific product, this is the Holy Grail for marketers because it means he or she exhibits **brand loyalty**: Repeat purchasing behavior that reflects a conscious decision to continue buying the same brand.[62] Note that this definition states that the consumer not only buys the brand on a regular basis, but that he or she also has a strong positive attitude toward it rather than simply buying it out of habit. In fact, we often find that a brand-loyal consumer has more than simply a positive attitude; frequently he or she is passionate about the product. "True-blue" users react more vehemently when a company alters, redesigns, or (God forbid) eliminates a favorite brand. One simple test to find out if you're brand loyal: If the store is temporarily out of your favorite brand, will you buy a different product or hold off until you can get your first choice?

Although everyone wants to cultivate brand-loyal customers, there is a wrinkle that sometimes confounds even the most effective marketers. We often engage in *brand switching*, even if our current brand satisfies our needs. When researchers for British brewer Bass Export studied the U.S. beer market, they discovered that many drinkers have a repertoire of two to six favorite brands rather than one clear favorite.[63]

Sometimes, it seems we simply like to try new things; we crave variety as a form of stimulation or to reduce boredom. **Variety-seeking**, the desire to choose new alternatives over more familiar ones, even influences us to switch from our favorite products to ones we like less! This can occur even before we become *satiated*, or tired, of our favorite. Research supports the idea that we are willing to trade enjoyment for variety because the unpredictability *itself* is rewarding.[64]

We're especially likely to look for variety when we are in a good mood, or when there isn't a lot of other stuff going on.[65] So, even though we have favorites, we still like to sample other possibilities. However, when the decision situation is ambiguous, or when there is little information about competing brands, we tend to opt for the safe choice.

Message Involvement

It started with Jay Z's celebrated campaign to promote his autobiographical *Decoded* book. The agency Droga5 created a national scavenger hunt when it hid all 320 pages of the book (mostly blown-up versions) in outdoor spots in 13 cities that somehow related to the text on each page (e.g. on cheeseburger wrappers in New York). Coldplay borrowed a page from this book more recently to promote its album *Ghost Stories*. The band hid lyric sheets inside ghost stories in libraries around the world and gave out clues on Twitter.[66] This represents an emerging way to engage consumers: In **alternate reality games (ARGs)**, thousands of people participate in a fictional story or competition to solve a mystery.

As these novel scavenger hunts illustrate, media vehicles possess different qualities that influence our motivation to pay attention to what they tell us, known as **message involvement**. Print is a *high-involvement medium* (whether it appears on a "dead tree" or in an e-book). The reader actively processes the information and (if desired) he or she is able to pause and reflect on it before turning the page.[67] In contrast, television is a *low-involvement medium* because it requires a passive viewer who exerts relatively little control (remote-control "zipping" notwithstanding) over content.

TV's passive nature explains why advertisers try to place their ads in shows such as *American Idol* that engage viewers; they want to increase the likelihood their audience will pay attention when their messages come on the screen. Research evidence indicates that a viewer who is more involved with a television show will respond more positively to commercials he or she sees during that show, and that these spots will have a greater chance to influence purchase intentions.[69] In fact, some messages (including really well-made advertisements) are so involving that they trigger a stage of **narrative transportation**, where people become immersed in the storyline. One recent study showed that people who are feeling lucky engage in this process when they look at an advertisement for a lottery; once immersed, it is hard to distract them from the message.[70] Not a great thing for compulsive gamblers, but a powerful effect nonetheless.

Although consumers' involvement levels with a product message vary, marketers do not have to simply sit back and hope for the best. If they are aware of some basic factors that increase or decrease attention, they can take steps to increase the likelihood that product information will get through. A marketer can boost a person's motivation to process relevant information via one or more of the following techniques:[71]

● **Use novel stimuli, such as unusual cinematography, sudden silences, or unexpected movements, in commercials.** When a British firm called Egg Banking introduced a credit card to the French market, its ad agency created unusual commercials to make people question their assumptions. One ad stated, "Cats always land on their paws," and then two researchers in white lab coats dropped a kitten off a rooftop—never to see it again (animal rights activists were not amused).[72]

● **Use prominent stimuli, such as loud music and fast action, to capture attention.** In print formats, larger ads increase attention. Also, viewers look longer at colored pictures than at black-and-white ones.

● **Include celebrity endorsers.** As we'll see in Chapter 8, people process more information when it comes from someone they admire or at least know about, whether Michael Jordan, Bill Gates, or maybe even Kim Kardashian.

Net Profit

The Nielsen research company wanted to see if the social media activity people participated in while they watched a TV show related to how involved they were with the action in the program. Sure enough, when they hooked up 300 people to brain monitors as they watched prime-time TV shows in a 2015 study, they found a strong relationship with the number of messages on *Twitter* during the same segments on these shows when they aired on live TV. Nielsen concludes that *Twitter* chatter is an accurate indicator of the overall audience's interest in a show, right down to the specific scene. In a separate study Nielsen also found that the volume of tweets about new shows before they launch can predict which premieres will attract the largest audiences.[68]

A novel or unexpected image can heighten involvement, especially for a less-than-thrilling business like an optician.
Source: luerzersarchive.net.

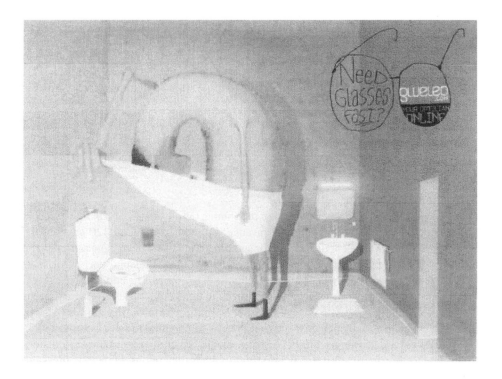

● **Provide value that customers appreciate.** Charmin bathroom tissue set up public toilets in Times Square that hordes of grateful visitors used. Thousands more people (evidently with time on their hands) visited the brand's Web site to view the display.[73]

● **Invent new media platforms to grab attention.** Procter & Gamble printed trivia questions and answers on its Pringles snack chips with ink made of blue or red food coloring, and a company called Speaking Roses International patented a technology to laser-print words, images, or logos on flower petals.[74] An Australian firm creates hand stamps that nightclubs use to identify paying customers; the stamps include logos or ad messages so partiers' hands become an advertising platform.[75]

Product involvement often depends on the situation we're in. The Charmin toilet tissue brand sponsors a Web site, appropriately named SitOrSquat.com. The site helps travelers find the cleanest public restrooms wherever they happen to be. The brand manager explains, "Our goal is to connect Charmin with innovative conversations and solutions as a brand that understands the importance of bringing the best bathroom experience to consumers, even when they're away from home." According to Charmin, SitOrSquat lists over 52,000 toilets in 10 countries.
Source: Courtesy of P&G/Charmin.

- **Encourage viewers to think about actually using the product.** If a person can imagine this, he or she is more likely to want to obtain the real thing. Research shows that even subtle cues in an advertisement can encourage this mental rehearsal. One simple example is orienting an image of a cup with its handle to the right so that (for a right-handed person) it matches the dominant hand and facilitates mental stimulation.[76]

- **Create spectacles where the message is itself a form of entertainment.** In the early days of radio and television, ads literally were performances; show hosts integrated marketing messages into the episodes. Today live advertising that features attention-grabbing events called **spectacles** is making a comeback as marketers try harder and harder to captivate jaded consumers:[77] Axe body products sponsored a posh Hamptons (New York) nightclub for the whole season; it became The Axe Lounge, sporting branding on the DJ booth and menu and Axe products in the restrooms.

Situational Involvement

Situational involvement describes engagement with a store, Web site, or a location where people consume a product or service. One way to increase this kind of involvement is to personalize the messages shoppers receive at the time of purchase. For example, a few marketers tailor the recommendations they give shoppers in a store based on what they picked up from a shelf. At some Dunkin' Donuts locations, a person who orders a morning coffee sees an ad at the cash register that pushes hash browns or breakfast sandwiches. Many retailers and event planners today focus on enhancing customers' experiences in stores, dealerships, and stadiums. Industry insiders refer to this as a "butts-in-seats" strategy. That's why some fans who attend Atlanta Falcons football games get visited by a cheerleader in the stands for a photo op, and also why Chrysler is ramping up its efforts to get people to test drive cars at dealerships and auto shows. As the head of the car company's "experiential marketing unit" explained, "We know a physical experience with a vehicle is a great way to allow people to try it out and move up on their consideration list.[78]

Net Profit

Would you pay hard-earned money to watch *other* people play videogames? If you answer yes, you're part of the booming **e-sports** phenomenon. These sports boast stars, uniforms, and rivalries, but the players are clicking their mouses rather than swinging their bats. In a world championship game in Seoul, 40,000 fans packed a stadium built for the soccer World Cup to cheer on their favorite League of Legends team.[79]

E-Sports is a rapidly growing phenomenon around the world.
Source: Jean Chung/The New York Times/Redux.

MyLab Marketing

To complete the problems with the ⭐, go to EOC Discussion Questions in the MyLab as well as additional Marketing Metrics questions only available in MyLab Marketing.

CHAPTER SUMMARY

1. Products can satisfy a range of consumer needs.

Marketers try to satisfy consumers' needs, but the reason any product is purchased can vary widely. The identification of consumer motives is an important step to ensure that a product will meet the appropriate need(s). Traditional approaches to consumer behavior have focused on the abilities of products to satisfy rational needs (utilitarian motives), but hedonic motives (such as the need for exploration or fun) also guide many purchase decisions. Maslow's Hierarchy of Needs demonstrates that the same product can satisfy different needs.

2. Consumers experience different kinds of motivational conflicts that can impact their purchase decisions.

Motivation refers to the processes that lead people to behave as they do. It occurs when a need is aroused that the consumer wishes to satisfy. A goal has *valence*, which means that it can be positive or negative. We direct our behavior toward goals we value positively; we are motivated to *approach* the goal and to seek out products that will help us to reach it. However, we may also be motivated to *avoid* a negative outcome rather than achieve a positive outcome.

3. Consumers experience a range of affective responses to products and marketing messages.

Affective responses can be mild (evaluations), moderate (moods), or strong (emotions). Marketers often try to elicit a positive emotional response via advertising or other communication channels so that consumers form a bond (or lovemark) with their offering. A lot of the content on social media reflects affective responses that people post, so these platforms are a rich source of information for marketers to gauge how consumers feel about their brands.

4. The way we evaluate and choose a product depends on our degree of involvement with the product, the marketing message, or the purchase situation.

Product involvement can range from low where consumers make purchase decisions based on inertia, to high where they form strong bonds with favorite brands (cult products). Marketing strategies also need to consider consumers' extent of engagement with the messages about their products and the environments in which consumption of these products occur.

KEY TERMS

Affect, 180
Alternate reality games (ARGs), 191
Approach–approach conflict, 176
Approach–avoidance conflict, 176
Avoidance–avoidance conflict, 177
Brand loyalty, 190
Co-creation, 189
Cult products, 186
Drive, 173
Drive theory, 173
Embarrassment, 184
Emotional oracle effect, 181
Emotions, 180
Envy, 184
Evaluations, 180
E-sports, 193

Expectancy theory, 174
Goal, 173
Guilt, 184
Happiness, 181
Happiness economy, 185
Hierarchy of Needs, 178
Homeostasis, 173
IKEA Effect, 188
Incidental brand exposure, 173
Inertia, 186
Involvement, 185
Lovemark, 181
Mass customization, 189
Material accumulation, 182
Message involvement, 191
Mood congruency, 181

Moods, 180
Motivation, 173
Narrative transportation, 191
Negative state relief, 181
Perceived risk, 188
Product involvement, 188
Productivity orientation, 175
Retail therapy, 173
Sadvertising, 181
Sentiment analysis, 185
Situational involvement, 193
Spectacles, 193
Theory of cognitive dissonance, 176
Variety-seeking, 191
Word-phrase dictionary, 185

REVIEW

5-1 What is *motivation* and why is this idea so important to marketers?

⭐ **5-2** Describe three types of motivational conflicts. Cite an example of each from a current marketing campaign.

5-3 Explain the difference between a need and a want.

5-4 What is *cognitive dissonance?*

⭐ **5-5** What are some of the key problems with Maslow's hierarchy of needs?

⭐ **5-6** List three types of perceived risk, and give an example of each.

5-7 What is the difference between a *mood* and an *emotion?*

5-8 What is *mood congruency* and how do advertisers use it?

5-9 What is it about a cult product that allows a higher price point?

5-10 What are some strategies marketers can use to increase consumers' involvement with their products?

CONSUMER BEHAVIOR CHALLENGE

■ DISCUSS

5-11 Does money buy happiness? Why or why not?

5-12 Many consumers today seem to be obsessed with monitoring their emotions. They post about their feelings, track their sleep patterns, and fret about how often they're "liked" on social media. Should happiness be quantified?

5-13 Crisis, fear, and guilt are very common themes in marketing and advertising. Humanitarian disasters are the backdrops favored by charities to elicit donations. Fear of burglary or weather damage fuels home and contents insurance marketing. Gyms rely on our guilt about putting on a few pounds over the winter months. These are all dominant emotions—should marketers use these emotions as integral parts of their marketing campaigns?

5-14 A group of psychologists argued that we need to revise Maslow's Hierarchy of Needs. They propose we should delete "self-actualization" from the pinnacle and replace it with "parenting." Right below this peak, they added "mate retention" and "mate acquisition." They claim that too many people see Maslow's triangle as "aspirational"—a description of what fulfilled individuals "should" do—rather than as an explanation of how human motivation actually works. Their perspective is evolutionary; if the only purpose of art, music, and literature is self-fulfillment, how does that contribute to the survival of the species? One of the proponents of this view observes, "If you are a good poet or a good musician, there is a reproductive payoff: women are attracted to men with these abilities. What a man is saying when he is playing his guitar up there is 'look at my good genes.'" What do you think—do our motivations to buy, have, and be ultimately come down to survival of our gene pool?[80]

5-15 The chapter discusses a study that says our moods actually get worse when we spend a lot of time on Facebook because we feel like we're wasting our time. Do you agree?

■ APPLY

5-16 Our online behaviors also can satisfy needs at different levels of Maslow's Hierarchy of Needs, especially when we participate in social networks such as Facebook. Web-based companies can build loyalty if they keep these needs in mind when they design their offerings:

- We satisfy physiological needs when we use the Web to research topics such as nutrition or medical questions.
- The Web enables users to pool information and satisfy safety needs when they call attention to bad practices, flawed products, or even dangerous predators.
- Profile pages on Facebook let users define themselves as individuals.
- Online communities, blogs, and social networks provide recognition and achievement to those who cultivate a reputation for being especially helpful or expert in some subject.
- Users can seek help from others and connect with people who have similar tastes and interests.
- Access to invitation-only communities provides status.
- Spiritually based online communities can provide guidance to troubled people.[81]

Interview people you know about their motivations to participate in social media. Ask them to provide a list of the platforms they access most, then for each probe about their reasons to visit these. What needs do these sites appear to satisfy? How might these insights help you to devise ideas for new social media products?

5-17 Interview members of a celebrity fan club. Describe their level of involvement with the "product," and devise some marketing strategies to reach this group.

5-18 Crowdfunding is a relatively new frontier for marketing and consumer behavior. The main feature of this type of business arrangement and its related marketing revolves around attracting a sufficient number of interested backers to fund the project. The reward for involvement is the eventual delivery of the product and any rewards or additional features that are either included as a reward tier for larger contributions or "unlocked" once the basic funding figure has been exceeded. However, the relationship between the developers of the product and the backers is no longer a simple case of gathering pre-sales funding to validate the demand for the product. Increasingly, backers are involved in the actual development and direction that the product takes. The project developer responds to the requirements of the backers; after all, it is their funds that underpin the financial viability of the whole project. Crowdfunding certainly shortens the development cycle for new products, but it is developing far beyond the original idea of peer-to-peer lending or involvement.[82]

Research the development of crowdfunding across two or more crowdfunding platforms. How has the development and launch of products been influenced by the involvement of the customers or backers? How has the product been marketed? Has the product, once launched, featured the involvement of backers in the marketing messages? In your view, is this backer involvement and influence a feature that is likely to continue to develop? What challenges will marketers face in the future both during the project crowdfunding phase and the eventual launch of the product on the market?

Case Study

HAS THE DEATH OF THE WATCH BEEN GREATLY EXAGGERATED? APPLE GETS INTO THE GAME

It used to be that putting on a watch was just a standard part of getting dressed in the morning. How could you hope to move successfully throughout your day, making it to appointments on time, if you weren't wearing a watch on your wrist to let you know what time it is?

Today however, we're surrounded by technology devices at work, home, and even away from home that readily display the time of day. The outcome? Many have come to view the personal watch as an unnecessary device. As a result, the watch industry has been struggling to find ways to remain relevant, searching for the key to how they can motivate consumers to purchase a time-keeping device that many consider redundant with the desktops, laptops, tablets, and cellphones to which they are so connected.

As industry analysts have pointed out, watches may actually be "superfluous" and there are claims that "telling time is secondary today." And even for those more diehard consumers who still wear a watch, according to Marshall Cohen, chief industry analyst in New York at the NPD Group, "there's no practical need for any watch-wearing holdouts to pay a lot for a timepiece."

Apple says, not true! It believes that the death of the watch has been greatly exaggerated and in response, the company recently introduced the Apple Watch. These devices range in price from $350 to more than $10,000. The new watches, far from simply telling the time, are actually mini-computers that allow the wearer to check and send messages, surf the Internet, monitor heart rate, and pay in a store.

The watches' introduction has been both praised and criticized. Some point to Apple's ability to interest consumers in any number of technology devices and believe that the Apple Watch will be yet another success story for the company. An early reviewer, *Wall Street Journal's* Geoffrey Fowler, believes that his dependence on other devices has decreased since putting on the Apple Watch and that it's helped him to be more focused. But others cite consumers' waning interest in watches in general, the difficulties in functioning with such a small screen, and they wonder who would really be motivated to make the investment in the entry level model, let alone the top of the line, Apple Watch Edition, with an attention-getting price tag of $17,000!

So what does Apple think will motivate consumers to buy one of these new gadgets? They talk about consumers' need to quickly and subtly get access to information, which is not always possible with a clunkier tablet or cell phone. Tim Bajarin,

Creative Strategies analyst says, "the flexibility of "glanceable information" is more valuable than people realize today." He also mentions that the new watches will offer options for non-verbal communication, tapping a button to send a message, for instance. Apple CEO Tim Cook calls it "the most personal device we've ever created—it's not just with you, it's on you" and claims that it's the most advanced timepiece ever created, period.

Analysts forecast that Apple will ship 7.5 million watches in the months following its introduction. But critics still wonder if consumers can be convinced that there's a real need for the devices. On top of that, there's a potentially saturated market to consider, with 10 million competing smartwatches shipped in the year before Apple's entry into the product category. Another form of competition comes from the established luxury brand watches that may have already cornered the higher end of the market. Proponents of luxury watches believe that Apple can't match their unique qualities—prestige, resale value, their ability to be passed down as an heirloom, exclusivity, and a less obtrusive look which may be safer for the wearer.

While blogger John Gruber commented on a recent podcast: "I still have no idea why I would want to wear it," early adopters of the Apple Watches and others who believe in the power of Apple to succeed were not surprised by recent announcements from the company about an upgraded operating system and improvements that will make the watches' apps work even better.

So, who knows how this story will turn out—will Apple be the game-changer that played a significant role in how we think about the evolution of the personal watch or will it be seen as having momentarily misstepped into an industry whose death was already a foregone conclusion?

DISCUSSION QUESTIONS

CS 5.1 Discuss the possible reasons to buy a watch today. Connect each motivation you identify with an appropriate motivational theory from the chapter.

CS 5.2 What does Apple really believe will motivate consumers to purchase the Apple Watch? Are there different motivations at the low versus high (luxury version) price point?

CS 5.3 How do marketers of watches use marketing and advertising to motivate consumers to buy them? Give specific examples.

Sources: Kathleen Beckett, "Who Wears What, Why?" http://www.nytimes .com/2014/03/28/fashion/who-wears-what-why.html?emc=edit_tnt_20

140327&nlid=33295816&tntemail0=y&_r=1, accessed May 15, 2015; Jessica Guynn, "Apple Prices Apple Watch," http://www.usatoday.com/story/tech/2015/03/09/apple-watch-event/24536117/, accessed May 28, 2015; Micah Singleton, "Who Will Buy a $10,000 Apple Watch Edition?" http://www.theverge.com/2015/3/10/8164135/apple-watch-price-target-market-who-will-buy, accessed June 2, 2015; Farhad Manjoo and Vanessa Friedman, "Affairs of the Wrist: The Apple Watch Comes Between Them," June 11, 2015, http://www.nytimes.com/2015/06/11/

fashion/affairs-of-the-wrist-the-apple-watch-comes-between-them.html, accessed June 12, 2015; John Paul Titlow, "The Apple Watch Just Got A Lot More Useful," http://www.fastcompany.com/3047207/fast-feed/the-apple-watch-just-got-a-lot-more-useful, accessed June 9, 2015; Geoffrey Fowler, "Apple Watch Review: The Smartwatch Finally Makes Sense," http://www.wsj.com/articles/apple-watch-review-the-smartwatch-finally-makes-sense-1428494495, accessed June 10, 2015.

MyLab Marketing

Go to the Assignments section of your MyLab to complete these writing exercises.

5.19 The basic lesson of Maslow's Hierarchy of Needs is that we must first satisfy basic needs before we progress up the ladder (a starving man is not interested in status symbols, friendship, or self-fulfillment). This implies that consumers value different product attributes depending on what is currently available to them. In today's economic environment, the hierarchy helps to explain why many consumers take a closer look at the price and reliability of a product rather than whether it will impress their friends. How do you believe the recession changed the way consumers evaluate products? Do you agree that the priorities many now place on "value-priced" brands is the "new normal," or will our attitudes change as the economy improves?

5.20 Our emotional reactions to marketing cues are so powerful that some high-tech companies study mood in small doses (in 1/30 of a second increments) as they analyze people's facial reactions when they see ads or new products. They measure happiness as they look for differences between, for example, a *true smile* (which includes a relaxation of the upper eyelid) and a *social smile* (which occurs only around the mouth). Whirlpool used this technique to test consumers' emotional reactions to a yet-to-be-launched generation of its Duet washers and dryers. The company's goal: To design an appliance that will actually make people happy. Researchers discovered that even though test subjects said they weren't thrilled with some out-of-the-box design options, such as unusual color combinations, their facial expressions said otherwise.[83] Does the ability to study our emotional reactions at such a specific level give marketers an unfair advantage?

NOTES

1. "Is 2014 the Year of the Vegan,?" *One Green Planet*, http://www.one-greenplanet.org/news/is-2014-the-year-of-the-vegan/, accessed March 3, 2015; "Vegetarianism in America," Vegetarian Times, http://www.vegetariantimes.com/features/archive_of_editorial/667, accessed May 9, 2011.

2. Gráinne M. Fitzsimmons, Tanya L. Chartrand and Gavan J. Fitzsimons, "Automatic Effects of Brand Exposure on Motivated Behavior: How Apple Makes You 'Think Different,'" *Journal of Consumer Research* 35 (2008): 21–35.

3. Gergana Y. Nenkov and Maura L. Scott, "So Cute I Could Eat It Up": Priming Effects of Cute Products on Indulgent Consumption," *Journal of Consumer Research* August 2014, vol. 41, 2: 326-341; http://www.jcr-admin.org/files/pressPDFs/041814131740_676581.pdf.

4. Ji Kyung Park, and Deborah Roedder John, "I Think I Can, I Think I Can: Brand Use, Self-Efficacy, and Performance. *Journal of Marketing Research* 51, no. 2 (2014): 233–247.

5. Scott I. Rick, Beatriz Pereira, and Katherine A. Burson, "The Benefits of Retail Therapy: Making Purchase Decisions Reduces Residual Sadness," *Journal of Consumer Psychology* 24, no. 3 (2014): 373–380.

6. Josh Barro, "How Forbidding Foie Gras Increased the Appetite for It," *New York Times*, (Janury 20, 2015), http://www.nytimes.com/2015/01/

20/upshot/how-forbidding-foie-gras-increased-the-appetite-for-it.html?smid=nytcore-iphone-share&smprod=nytcore-iphone&_r=1&abt=0002&abg=0, accessed January 30, 2015.

7. Russell W. Belk, Guliz Ger, and Soren Askegaard, "The Fire of Desire: A Multisited Inquiry into Consumer Passion," *Journal of Consumer Research* 30 (2003): 326–351; cf. also Yu Chen, "Possession and Access: Consumer Desires and Value Perceptions Regarding Contemporary Art Collection and Exhibit Visits," *Journal of Consumer Research* 35 (April 2009): 925–940.

8. Henrik Hagtvedt and Vanessa M. Patrick, "The Broad Embrace of Luxury: Hedonic Potential as a Driver of Brand Extendibility," *Journal of Consumer Psychology* 19, no. 4 (2009): 608–618.

9. Anat Keinan and Ran Kivetz, "Productivity Orientation and the Consumption of Collectable Experiences," *Journal of Consumer Research* 37, no. 6 (April 2011):935–935. DOI: 10.1086/657163.

10. Thomas Kramer and Song-Oh Yoon, "Approach-Avoidance Motivation and the Use of Affect as Information," *Journal of Consumer Psychology* 17, no. 2 (2007): 128–138.

11. www.weightwatchers.com/index.aspx, accessed June 30, 2009.

12. See Paul T. Costa and Robert R. McCrae, "From Catalog to Classification: Murray's Needs and the Five-Factor Model," *Journal of Personality & Social Psychology* 55 (1988): 258–265; Calvin S. Hall and Gardner Lindzey,

Theories of Personality, 2nd ed. (New York: Wiley, 1970); James U. McNeal and Stephen W. McDaniel, "An Analysis of Need-Appeals in Television Advertising," *Journal of the Academy of Marketing Science* 12 (Spring 1984): 176–190.

13. Michael R. Solomon, Judith L. Zaichkowsky, and Rosemary Polegato, *Consumer Behaviour: Buying, Having, and Being—Canadian Edition* (Scarborough, Ontario: Prentice Hall Canada, 1999).

14. See David C. McClelland, *Studies in Motivation* (New York: Appleton-Century-Crofts, 1955).

15. Mary Kay Ericksen and M. Joseph Sirgy, "Achievement Motivation and Clothing Preferences of White-Collar Working Women," in Michael R. Solomon, ed., *The Psychology of Fashion* (Lexington, MA: Lexington Books, 1985): 357–369.

16. See Stanley Schachter, *The Psychology of Affiliation* (Stanford, CA: Stanford University Press, 1959).

17. Eugene M. Fodor and Terry Smith, "The Power Motive as an Influence on Group Decision Making," *Journal of Personality & Social Psychology* 42 (1982): 178–185.

18. C. R. Snyder and Howard L. Fromkin, *Uniqueness: The Human Pursuit of Difference* (New York: Plenum, 1980).

19. Abraham H. Maslow, *Motivation and Personality*, 2nd ed. (New York: Harper & Row, 1970).

20. An integrative view of consumer goal structures and goal-determination processes proposes six discrete levels of goals wherein higher-level (versus lower-level) goals are more abstract, more inclusive, and less mutable. In descending order of abstraction, these goal levels are life themes and values, life projects, current concerns, consumption intentions, benefits sought, and feature preferences. See Cynthia Huffman, S. Ratneshwar, and David Glen Mick, "Consumer Goal Structures and Goal-Determination Processes: An Integrative Framework," in S. Ratneshwar, David Glen Mick, and Cynthia Huffman, eds., *The Why of Consumption* (London: Routledge, 2000): 9–35.

21. Paul Henry, "Magnetic Points for Lifestyle Shaping: The Contribution of Self-Fulfillment, Aspirations and Capabilities," *Qualitative Market Research* 9, no. 2 (2006): 170.

22. Study conducted in the Horticulture Department at Kansas State University, cited in "Survey Tells Why Gardening's Good," *Vancouver Sun* (April 12, 1997): B12; see also Paul Hewer and Douglas Brownlie, "Constructing 'Hortiporn': On the Aesthetics of Stylized Exteriors," *Advances in Consumer Research* 33, no. 1 (2006): 36-42.

23. http://www.zumba.com/en-US, accessed March 3, 2015; Quoted in Alexandra Bruell, "How Zumba Built a Brand with a Cult Following in Just a Few Years," *Ad Age/CMO Strategy* (August 20, 2012), http://adage.com/article/cmo-interviews/zumba-built-a-cult-a-years/236737/, accessed January 11, 2013.

24. Fabrizio Di Muro and Kyle B. Murray, "An Arousal Regulation Explanation of Mood Effects on Consumer Choice," *Journal of Consumer Research* 39, no. 3 (October 2012): 574–584, http://www.jstor.org/-stable/10.1086/664040; Cassie Mogilner, Jennifer Aaker, and Sepandar D. Kamvar, "How Happiness Affects Choice," *Journal of Consumer Research* 39, no. 2 (August 2012): 429–443, http://www.jstor.org/stable/10.1086/663774; For a study that looks at cross-cultural differences in expression of emotion, cf. Ana Valenzuela, Barbara Mellers, and Judi Strebel, "Pleasurable Surprises: A Cross-Cultural Study of Consumer Responses to Unexpected Incentives," *Journal of Consumer Research* 36, no. 5 (2010): 792–805; cf. also Samuel K. Bonsu, Aron Darmody, and Marie-Agnès Parmentier, "Arrested Emotions in Reality Television," *Consumption Markets & Culture* 13, no. 1 (2010): 91–107. Parts of this section were adapted from Michael R. Solomon, Rebekah Russell-Bennett, and Josephine Previte, *Consumer Behaviour: Buying, Having, Being*, 3rd ed. (Frenchs Forest, NSW: Pearson Australia, 2012).

25. Portions of this section are adapted from Michael R. Solomon, Katherine White and Darren W. Dahl, *Consumer Behaviour: Buying, Having, Being*, 6th Canadian Edition, (Toronto: Pearson, 2014).

26. Steve McClellan, "Unilever, Coca-Cola Utilize Facial Analysis To Enhance Ad Tests *Mediapost* (January 18, 2013), http://www.mediapost.com/publications/article/191418/unilever-coca-cola-utilize-facial-analysis-to-enh.html?edition=55665#axzz2IcmSJS00, accessed February 22, 2015.

27. Rae Ann Fera, "The Rise Of Sadvertising: Why Brands Are Determined To Make You Cry," *Fast Company*, http://www.fastcocreate.com/3029767/the-rise-of-sadvertising-why-brands-are-determined-to-make-you-cry?partner=newsletter#!, accessed January 29, 2015.

28. Hannah H. Chang and Michel Tuan Pham, "Affect as a Decision-Making System of the Present," *Journal of Consumer Research* 40, no. 1 (2013): 42–63.

29. Michel Tuan Pham, Leonard Lee, and Andrew T. Stephen, "Feeling the Future: The Emotional Oracle Effect," *Journal of Consumer Research* 39, no. 3 (October 2012): 461–477.

30. Lauren Indvik, "Hug a Vending Machine, Get a Free Coke," April 9, 2012, http://mashable.com/2012/04/09/coca-cola-hug-machine/?WT.mc_id=en_business&utm_campaign=Business&utm_medium=email&utm_source=newsletter, accessed January 11, 2013.

31. Matt Richtel, "You Can't Take It With You, But You Still Want More," *New York Times* (January 4, 2014) http://www.nytimes.com/2014/01/05/business/you-cant-take-it-with-you-but-you-still-want-more.html?ref=business, accessed February 22, 2015.

32. Leaf Van Boven and Thomas Gilovich, "To Do or to Have? That Is the Question," *Journal of Personality and Social Psychology* 85, no. 6: 1193–1202. 2003,

33. Elizabeth Dunn, Lara B. Aknin and Michael I Norton, "Spending Money on Others Promotes Happiness," *Science* 319 (2008): 1687–1688; Cassie Mogilner, "The Pursuit of Happiness: Time, Money, and Social Connection," *Psychological Science* 21, no. 9 (2011): 1348–1354; Cassie Mogilner, Sepandar D. Kamvar and Jennifer Aaker, "The Shifting Meaning of Happiness," *Social Psychological and Personality Science* (July 2, 2011): 395–402.

34. Rebecca Hiscott, "Why You Feel Terrible After Spending Too Much Time On Facebook," *The Huffington Post*, July 17, 2014, http://www.huffingtonpost.com/2014/07/17/facebook-study_n_5595890.html, accessed January 29, 2015.

35. Peter Lieberman and David Pizarro, "All Politics Is Olfactory," *New York Times* (October 23, 2010), http://www.nytimes.com/2010/10/24/opinion/24pizarro.html?_r=1&ref=todayspaper, accessed April 29, 2011.

36. Niels Van de Ven, Marcel Zeeienberg, and Rik Pieters, "The Envy Premium in Product Evaluation," *Journal of Consumer Research* 37, no. 6 (2011): 984–998.

37. Roy F. Baumeister, Arlene M. Stillwell, and Todd F. Heatherton, "Guilt: An Interpersonal Approach," *Psychological Bulletin* 115 (1994): 243–267.

38. Debra Z. Basil, Nancy M. Ridgway, and Michael D. Basil, "Guilt Appeals: The Mediating Effective of Responsibility," *Psychology & Marketing* 23, no. 12 (2006): 1035–1054.

39. Loraine Lau-Gesk and Aimee Drolet, "The Publicly Self-Conscious Consumer: Prepare to Be Embarrassed," *Journal of Consumer Psychology* 18, no. 2 (2008):127–136.

40. Aubrey Wilson and Christopher West, "The Marketing of Unmentionables," *Harvard Business Review* (January–February 1981): 91–102.

41. Gross National Happiness Commission, Government of Bhutan, http://www.gnhc.gov.bt/, accessed March 2, 2015.

42. Anya Kamenetz, "A City-Wide Quest For Happiness, Powered By Sensors and Data," *Fast Company* (June 3, 2013), http://www.fastcompany.com/3011057/tech-forecast/a-city-wide-quest-for-happiness-powered-by-sensors-and-data?partner=newsletter, accessed January 29, 2015; http://happathon.com/, accessed March 3, 2015.

43. E. J. Schultz, "Turning the Frown Upside Down: Kraft's Jell-O Plans Twitter Mood Monitor," *Advertising Age* (May 8, 2011), http://adage.com/article/news/kraft-s-jell-o-plans-twitter-mood-monitor/227439/, accessed May 10, 2011.

44. Vindu Goel, "Facebook Tinkers with Users' Emotions in News Feed Experiment, Stirring Outcry, *New York Times* (June 29, 2014), http://www.nytimes.com/2014/06/30/technology/facebook-tinkers-with-users-emotions-in-news-feed-experiment-stirring-outcry.html, accessed January 29, 2015.

45. http://tonecheck.com, accessed March 3, 2015; Tracy Tuten and Michael R. Solomon, *Social Media Marketing*, 2nd ed. (London: SAGE, 2016); Jennifer Van Grove, "How a Sentiment Analysis Startup Profits by Checking Emotion in E-mail," *Mashable* (January 20, 2011), http://mashable.com/2011/01/20/lymbix/?utm_source=feedburner&utm_medium=email&utm_campaign=Feed%3A+Mashable+%28Mashable%29, accessed April 29, 2011.

46. Judith Lynne Zaichkowsky, "Measuring the Involvement Construct in Marketing," *Journal of Consumer Research* 12 (December 1985): 341–352.

47. Andrew Mitchell, "Involvement: A Potentially Important Mediator of Consumer Behavior," in William L. Wilkie, ed., *Advances in Consumer Research* 6 (Provo, UT: Association for Consumer Research, 1979): 191–196.

48. Richard L. Celsi and Jerry C. Olson, "The Role of Involvement in Attention and Comprehension Processes," *Journal of Consumer Research* 15 (September 1988): 210–224.

49. Barbara J. Phillips and Edward F. McQuarrie, (2010). "Narrative and Persuasion in Fashion Advertising," *Journal of Consumer Research* 37 (October 2010): 368–392; Ronald E. Goldsmith, Leisa R. Flynn, and Ronald A. Clark, "Materialistic, Brand Engaged, and Status Consuming Consumers and Clothing Behaviors," *Journal of Fashion Marketing and Management* 16, no. 1 (2012): 102–120.

50. Jeremy W. Peters, "Gave Up Sleep and Maybe a First-Born, But at Least I Have an iPhone," *New York Times Online* (June 30, 2007), http://www.nytimes.com/2007/06/30/technology/30phone.html?scp=1&sq=Gave%20up%20Sleep%20and%20Maybe%20a%20First-Born,%20but%20at%20Least%20I%20Have%20an%20iPhone&st=Search, accessed August 24, 2011.

51. Ronald W. Pimentel and Kristy E. Reynolds, "A Model for Consumer Devotion: Affective Commitment with Proactive Sustaining Behaviors," *Academy of Marketing Science Review* no. 5 (2004), www.amsreview.org/articles/pimentel05-2004.pdf, accessed March 17, 2015.

52. Tanya Irwin, "'Breakout Brands' Connect With Customers," *Marketing Daily* (November 4, 2012), http://www.mediapost.com/publications/-article/186468/breakout-brands-connect-with-customers.html?edition=53137 #ixzz2HcbTBfx7, accessed January 10, 2013.

53. Ronald Smit, "Advance to Go: Winning with Gamification, *Wired* (June 19, 2013), http://www.wired.com/2013/06/advance-to-go-winning-with-gamification/, accessed February 21, 2015.

54. Natalie Kitroeff, "Syracuse University Turns to Harry Potter to Motivate Business Students," *Bloomburg Business* (September 12, 2014) http://www.bloomberg.com/bw/articles/2014-09-12/syracuse-university-uses-a-harry-potter-game-to-motivate-b-schoolers, accessed February 21, 2015.

55. www.starbuckseverywhere.net, accessed March 3, 2015; Julie Jargon, "A Fan Hits a Roadblock on Drive to See Every Starbucks," *Wall Street Journal* (May 23, 2009), http://online.wsj.com/article/SB124301100481847767.html, accessed May 25, 2009.

56. Judith Lynne Zaichkowsky, "The Emotional Side of Product Involvement," in Paul Anderson and Melanie Wallendorf, eds., *Advances in Consumer Research* 14 (Provo, UT: Association for Consumer Research): 32–35.

57. For a discussion of interrelationships between situational and enduring involvement, see Marsha L. Richins, Peter H. Bloch, and Edward F. McQuarrie, "How Enduring and Situational Involvement Combine to Create Involvement Responses," *Journal of Consumer Psychology* 1, no. 2 (1992): 143–153. For more information on the involvement construct, see "Special Issue on Involvement," *Psychology & Marketing* 10, no. 4 (July–August 1993).

58. Alba and Hutchinson, "Dimensions of Consumer Expertise"; Bettman and Park, "Effects of Prior Knowledge and Experience and Phase of the Choice Process on Consumer Decision Processes"; Merrie Brucks, "The Effects of Product Class Knowledge on Information Search Behavior," *Journal of Consumer Research* 12 (June 1985): 1–16; Joel E. Urbany, Peter R. Dickson, and William L. Wilkie, "Buyer Uncertainty and Information Search," *Journal of Consumer Research* 16 (September 1989): 208–215.

59. Joseph B. Pine, II, and James H. Gilmore, *Markets of One: Creating Customer-Unique Value through Mass Customization* (Boston: Harvard Business School Press, 2000), www.managingchange.com/masscust/overview.htm, accessed May 30, 2005.

60. Neeraj Arora, Xavier Drèze, Anindya Ghose, James D. Hess, Raghuram Iyengar, Bing Jing, Yogesh Joshi, V. Kumar, Nicholas Lurie, Scott Neslin, S. Sajeesh, Meng Su, Niladri Syam, Jacquelyn Thomas, and Z. John Zhang, "Putting One-to-One Marketing to Work: Personalization, Customization, and Choice," *Marketing Letters* (2008): 305–321; Mike Beirne, "Mars Gives M&M's a Face," *Brandweek* (May 22, 2008), www.brandweek.com/bw/news/recent_display.jsp?vnu_content_Id=1003807134, accessed May 22, 2008.

61. Michael I. Norton, Daniel Mochon, and Dan Ariely, "The IKEA Effect: When Labor Leads to Love," *Journal of Consumer Psychology* 22, no. 3 (2012): 453–460.

62. Jacob Jacoby and Robert Chestnut, *Brand Loyalty: Measurement and Management* (New York: Wiley, 1978).

63. David F. Midgley, "Patterns of Interpersonal Information Seeking for the Purchase of a Symbolic Product," *Journal of Marketing Research* 20 (February 1983): 74–83.

64. Cyndee Miller, "Scotland to U.S.: 'This Tennent's for You,'" *Marketing News* (August 29, 1994): 26.

65. Rebecca K. Ratner, Barbara E. Kahn, and Daniel Kahneman, "Choosing Less-Preferred Experiences for the Sake of Variety," *Journal of Consumer Research* 26 (June 1999): 1–15.

66. Tim Nudd, "Coldplay Hides Lyrics From New Album Inside Libraries in 9 Countries: Look for the Ghost Stories," *Adweek* (May 1, 2014), http://www.adweek.com/adfreak/coldplay-hides-lyrics-new-album-inside-libraries-9-countries-157410, accessed February 22, 2015.

67. Herbert E. Krugman, "The Impact of Television Advertising: Learning Without Involvement," *Public Opinion Quarterly* 29 (Fall 1965): 349–356.

68. Vindu Goel, "Study of TV Viewers Backs Twitter's Claims to Be Barometer of Public Mood," *New York Times* (March 8, 2015), http://bits.blogs.nytimes.com/2015/03/08/twitter-chatter-reveals-what-we-like-to-watch/?smid=nytcore-iphone-share&smprod=nytcore-iphone, accessed March 10, 2015.

69. Kevin J. Clancy, "CPMs Must Bow to 'Involvement' Measurement," *Advertising Age* (January 20, 1992): 26.

70. Brent McFerran, Darren W. Dahl, Gerald J. Gorn, and Heather Honea, "Motivational Determinants of Transportation into Marketing Narratives," *Journal of Consumer Psychology* 20, no. 3 (2010): 306–316.

71. David W. Stewart and David H. Furse, "Analysis of the Impact of Executional Factors in Advertising Performance," *Journal of Advertising Research* 24 (1984): 23–26; Deborah J. MacInnis, Christine Moorman, and Bernard J. Jaworski, "Enhancing and Measuring Consumers' Motivation, Opportunity, and Ability to Process Brand Information from Ads," *Journal of Marketing* 55 (October 1991): 332–353.

72. Elaine Sciolino, "Disproving Notions, Raising a Fury," *New York Times* (January 21, 2003), www.nytimes.com, accessed January 21, 2003.

73. Louise Story, "Times Sq. Ads Spread via Tourists' Cameras," *New York Times* (December 11, 2006), www.nytimes.com, accessed December 11, 2006.

74. "Read My Chips? Pringles Has Plans to Print Jokes, Trivia on Its Potatoes," *Wall Street Journal* (May 20, 2004): C13; David Serchuk, "A Rose with Another Name," *Forbes* (December 27, 2004): 52.

75. "Ads That Stay with You," *Newsweek* (November 19, 2007), www.newsweek.com/Id/68904, accessed November 19, 2007.

76. R. S. Elder and A. Krishna, "The 'Visual Depiction Effect' in Advertising: Facilitating Embodied Mental Simulation Through Product Orientation," *Journal of Consumer Research* 38, no. 6 (April 2012): 988–1003.

77. Stephanie Clifford, "Axe Body Products Puts Its Brand on the Hamptons Club Scene," *New York Times* (May 22, 2009): B6; Alana Semuels, "Honda Finds a Groovy New Way to Pitch Products: The Musical Road," *Los Angeles Times* (October 13, 2008), www.latimes.com/Business/La-Fi-Roads13-2008 oct13,0,4147014.Story, accessed October 13, 2008; Eric Pfanner, "A Live Promotion, At 14,000 Feet," *New York Times* (June 6, 2008), www.nytimes.com, accessed June 6, 2008; Les Luchter, "Jameson Whiskey Texts Targets on N.Y. Streets," *Marketing Daily* (August 8, 2008), www.mediapost.com, accessed August 8, 2008; Doreen Carvajal, "Dancers in the Crowd Bring Back 'Thriller,'" *New York Times* (March 10, 2008), www.nytimes.com, accessed March 10, 2008; Eric Pfanner, "When Consumers Help, Ads Are Free," *New York Times* (June 21, 2009), www.nytimes.com, accessed June 22, 2009.

78. "This Is How the NFL Is Getting Butts Back in the Bleachers," *Adweek* (August 26, 2014), http://www.adweek.com/news/advertising-branding/how-nfl-getting-butts-back-bleachers-159687, accessed March 3, 2015; Quoted in Larry P. Vellequette, "Chrysler's Butts-In-Seats Marketing Gets a Boost, *Automotive News* (December 2, 2013), http://www.autonews.com/article/20131202/RETAIL03/312029970/chryslers-butts-in-seats-marketing-gets-a-boost, accessed March 18, 2015.

79. David Segal, "Behind League of Legends, E-Sports's Main Attraction," *New York Times* (October 10, 2014), http://www.nytimes.com/2014/10/12/technology/riot-games-league-of-legends-main-attraction-esports.html?smid=nytcore-ipad-share&smprod=nytcore-ipad&_r=0, accessed February 19, 2015.

80. Lisa Belkin, "Living to Be a Parent," *New York Times* (September 10, 2010), http://www.NewYorkTimes.com/2010/09/12/magazine/12fob-wwln-t.html?_r=1&ref=magazine, accessed April 10, 2011.

81. Adapted in part from Jack Loechner, "Emotional Business Bonding on Social Networks," *Research Brief*, Center for Media Research (December 27, 2007), http://blogs.mediapost.com/research_brief/?p=1603, accessed December 27, 2007.

82. Nadine Scholz, "The Relevance of Crowdfunding: The Impact on the Innovation Process of Small Entrepreneurial Firms," *Springer*, 2015.

83. Jeffrey Zaslow, "Happiness Inc.," *Wall Street Journal* (March 18, 2006): P1.

Chapter 6 • The Self: Mind, Gender, and Body

Chapter Objectives

When you finish reading this chapter you will understand why:

6-1 The self-concept strongly influences consumer behavior.

6-2 Products often define a person's self-concept.

6-3 Gender identity is an important component of a consumer's self-concept.

6-4 The way we think about our bodies (and the way our culture tells us we should think) is a key component of self-esteem.

6-5 Every culture dictates certain types of body decoration or mutilation.

Source: gpointstudio/Shutterstock.

Lisa is trying to concentrate on the report her client expects by five o'clock. She has worked hard to maintain this important account for the firm, but today she is distracted thinking about her date with Eric last night. Although things seemed to go OK, she couldn't shake the feeling that Eric regards her more as a friend than as a potential romantic partner. As she leafs through *Glamour* and *Cosmopolitan* during her lunch hour, Lisa is struck by all the articles that offer tips on how to become more attractive by dieting, exercising, and wearing sexy clothes. She begins to feel depressed as she looks at the svelte models in the many advertisements for perfumes, apparel, and makeup. Each woman is more glamorous and beautiful than the last. Surely they've had "adjustments"; women simply don't look that way in real life. Then again, it's unlikely that Eric could ever be mistaken for Brad Pitt on the street. Still, in her down mood, Lisa actually thinks that maybe she should look into cosmetic surgery. Even though she's never considered herself unattractive, maybe if she got a new nose or removed that mole on her cheek she'd feel better about herself. Who knows, she might look so good she'll get up the nerve to submit a photo to that Web site Tinder that everyone's talking about. But on second thought, is Eric even worth it?

OBJECTIVE 6-1
The self-concept strongly influences consumer behavior.

The Self

Are you what you buy? Lisa isn't the only person who feels that her physical appearance and possessions affect her "value" as a person. We choose many products, from cars to cologne, because we want to highlight or hide some aspect of the self. In this chapter, we'll focus on how consumers' feelings about themselves shape their consumption practices, particularly as they strive to fulfill their society's expectations about how a male or female should look and act.

Does the Self Exist?

Most of us can't boast of coming close to Katy Perry's 66 million followers on Twitter, but many of us do have hundreds of followers, in addition to legions of Facebook friends.[1] The explosion of these and other social networking services enables everyone to focus on himself or herself and share mundane or scintillating details about life with anyone who's interested (*why* they are interested is another story!).

An emphasis on the unique nature of the self is much greater in Western societies.[3] Many Eastern cultures stress the importance of a **collective self**, where a person derives his or her identity in large measure from a social group. Both Eastern and Western cultures believe that the self divides into an inner, private self and an outer, public self. Where cultures differ is in terms of which part they see as the "real you"; the West tends to subscribe to an independent understanding of the self, which emphasizes the inherent separateness of each individual.

Non-Western cultures, in contrast, tend to focus on an interdependent self where we define our identities largely by our relationships with others.[4] For example, a Confucian perspective stresses the importance of "face": others' perceptions of the self and maintaining one's desired status in their eyes. One dimension of face is *mien-tzu*, the reputation one achieves through success and ostentation. Some Asian cultures developed explicit rules about the specific garments and even colors that certain social classes and occupations were allowed to display. These traditions live on today in Japanese style manuals that set out detailed instructions for dressing and how to address people of differing status.[5] That orientation is a bit at odds with such Western conventions as "casual Friday," which encourages employees to express their unique selves through dress (at least short of muscle shirts and flip-flops).

Self-Concept

The **self-concept** summarizes the beliefs a person holds about his or her own attributes and how he or she evaluates the self on these qualities. Although your overall self-concept may be positive, there certainly are parts of it you evaluate more positively than others. For example, Lisa feels better about her professional identity than she does about her feminine identity.

The self-concept is a complex structure. We describe attributes of self-concept along such dimensions as *content* (e.g., facial attractiveness versus mental aptitude), *positivity* (i.e., self-esteem), *intensity and stability* over time, and *accuracy* (i.e., the degree to which one's self-assessment corresponds to reality).[6] As we'll see later in this chapter, consumers' self-assessments can be quite distorted, especially with regard to their physical appearance. In addition, our own estimates of how much we change over time vary as well: A recent study that included both young and old people asked more than 19,000 respondents about their preferences in the past (foods, vacations, hobbies, and bands) and also to predict how their tastes will change in the future. Regardless of age, people acknowledged that their prior choices had changed quite a bit over time, but they still tended to predict that they would not change as they got older.[7]

A person's self-concept is a work in progress. Some parts are fairly stable, but each of us modifies some elements of it as we make our way through life—and particularly as we discover new ideas, social groups we admire, and yes, images we receive from the culture around us that endorse certain types of people over others. Each element that contributes to our self-concept is an **identity**. One way to define identity is "any category label with which a consumer self-associates that is amenable to a clear picture of what a person in that category looks like, thinks, feels and does." Some of these identities are pretty stable

Net Profit

Today it seems natural to think of ourselves as potential celebs waiting for our 15 minutes of fame (as the pop icon Andy Warhol once predicted). The Internet supplies **microfame** for many people like the blogger Perez Hilton and the buxom singer Tila Tequila. Indeed some analysts propose that microfame has morphed into **nanofame** as the glare of the internet spotlight shines brighter and increasingly faster—you may (or may not!) remember the temporarily famous "Alex from Target" (a cashier turned overnight heartthrob on Twitter) or "Left Shark" who was an awkward backup dancer during Katy Perry's 2015 Super Bowl performance. One easy avenue to nanofame: The Vine platform that lets users share 6-second videos. It boasts more than 200 people who have more than a million followers each.[2]

Marketing Pitfall

A word to the wise: Corporate recruiters often complain about students who show up for job interviews in sloppy or revealing clothing; these applicants failed to "read the memo" about which role they're expected to play in professional settings! Opportunities for impression management abound, and this includes how you act at business dinners or networking events. Indeed researchers found evidence of an **imbibing idiot bias**: Even when they are not actually impaired, people who simply *hold* an alcoholic beverage are perceived to be less intelligent than those who do not. Job candidates who ordered wine during an interview held over dinner were viewed as less intelligent and less hireable than candidates who ordered soda. Ironically, the job candidates themselves believed that ordering wine rather than soda helped them to appear more intelligent![18]

(e.g., mother, African American), whereas other identities are more temporary and likely to change (e.g., Libertarian, college student, Prius driver).[8]

As we'll see in Chapter 7, marketers try hard to understand which consumers adopt certain identities and then develop products and messages that meet the needs of people who link themselves to a given identity. So for example a person who sees herself as environmentally responsible is more likely than someone who doesn't think much about that to drive a Prius hybrid vehicle. "Green" products are more likely to get that person's attention.

Self-Esteem

Self-esteem refers to the positivity of a person's self-concept. People with low self-esteem expect that they will not perform very well, and they will try to avoid embarrassment, failure, or rejection. When Sara Lee developed a new line of snack cakes, for example, researchers found that consumers low in self-esteem preferred portion-controlled snack items because they felt they lacked self-control.[9] In contrast, a more recent study found that individuals who are made to feel powerful spend more money on themselves ("because I'm worth it!"), whereas those who experience a feeling of powerlessness spend more on others than on themselves.[10]

How do marketers influence self-esteem? Exposure to ads such as the ones Lisa checked out can trigger a process of **social comparison**, in which the person tries to evaluate her appearance by comparing it to the people depicted in these artificial images.[11] This is a basic human tendency, and many marketers tap into our need for benchmarks when they supply idealized images of happy, attractive people who just happen to use their products. An ad campaign for Clearasil is a good example. In one typical ad, two teenage boys enter a kitchen where a 40-ish mother is mixing something in a bowl. When her son leaves the room, his friend hits on Mom. The ad's tagline: "Clearasil may cause confidence."

In a study that illustrates the social comparison process, female college students who were exposed to beautiful women in advertisements afterward expressed lowered satisfaction with their own appearance, as compared to other participants who did not view ads with attractive models.[12] Another study reported that young women alter their perceptions of their own body shapes and sizes after they watch as little as 30 minutes of TV programming.[13] Researchers report similar findings for men.[14] This process even operates when we decide how much to eat: A study found that people who were served food by a server who was either fat or thin chose different portion sizes.[15]

Real and Ideal Selves

When a consumer compares some aspect of himself or herself to an ideal, this judgment influences self-esteem. He or she might ask, "Am I as good-looking as I would like to be?" or "Do I make as much money as I should?" The **ideal self** is a person's conception of how he or she would like to be, whereas the **actual self** refers to our more realistic appraisal of the qualities we do and don't have. We choose some products because we think they are consistent with our actual self, whereas we buy others to help us reach an ideal standard. We also often engage in a process of **impression management** in which we work hard to "manage" what others think of us; we strategically choose clothing and other products that will show us off to others in a good light.[16]

Impression management applies to all sorts of behaviors, from professional contexts and dating to markers of religious observance. For example, an increasing number of Islamic men in Egypt have a *zebibah* (Arabic for "raisin")—a dark circle of callused skin or a bump—between the hairline and the eyebrows. It marks the spot where the worshipper repeatedly presses his forehead into the ground during his daily prayers (observant Muslims pray five times a day). Some add prayers so that the bump will become even more pronounced; the owner of the mark thus broadcasts his degree of piousness on his head. As an Egyptian newspaper editor explains, "there is a kind of statement in it. Sometimes as a personal statement to announce that he is a conservative Muslim and sometimes as a way of outbidding others by showing them that he is more religious or to say that they should be like him."[17]

Fantasy: Bridging the Gap Between the Selves

Most people experience a discrepancy between their real and ideal selves, but for some consumers this gap is especially large. These people are especially good targets for marketing communications that employ *fantasy appeals*.[19] A **fantasy** or daydream is a self-induced shift in consciousness, which is sometimes a way to compensate for a lack of external stimulation or to escape from problems in the real world.[20] Many products and services succeed because they appeal to our fantasies. An ad may transport us to an unfamiliar, exciting situation; things we purchase may permit us to "try on" interesting or provocative roles. And, with today's technology, such as the *virtual makeovers* that several Web sites offer, consumers can experiment with different looks before they actually take the plunge in the real world. *Vogue*'s "Makeup Simulation" application (now available in Japan) allows women to see how brands such as Clinique would look on their (simulated) faces. Johnson & Johnson's ROC Skincare offers its "Skin Correxion Tool" to simulate the effects of anti-aging products.[21]

Multiple Selves

In a way, each of us really is a number of different people—for example, your mother probably would not recognize the "you" that emerges at a party at 2:00 am! We have as many selves as we do different social roles. Depending on the situation, we act differently, use different products and services, and even vary in terms of how much we *like* the aspect of ourselves we put on display. A person may require a different set of products to play each of her roles: She may choose a sedate, understated perfume when she plays her professional self, but splash on something more provocative on Saturday night as she transitions to her *femme fatale* self.

The **dramaturgical perspective** on consumer behavior views people as actors who play different roles. We each play many roles, and each has its own script, props, and costumes.[22] The self has different components, or *role identities*, and only some of these are active at any given time. Some identities (e.g., husband, boss, student) are more central to the self than others, but other identities (e.g., dancer, gearhead, or advocate for the homeless) may dominate in specific situations.[23] Indeed, some roles may conflict with one another. For example, one study of Iranian young people who live in the United Kingdom described what the authors termed the **torn self**, where respondents struggle with retaining an authentic culture while still enjoying Western freedom (and dealing with assumptions of others who believe they might be terrorists).[24]

A message about multiple selves from Chile.
Source: Courtesy of Prolam Young & Rubicam.

Marketing Pitfall

The automaker Renault avoided a big problem when a French judge ruled that the company could go forward with its plan to release a new electric car named Zoe—even though the two plaintiffs in the case already had the name Zoe Renault. The lawyer who brought the unsuccessful suit argued that the girls would endure a lifetime of grief, as would the other 35,000 people in France who are also named Zoe. He claimed, "Can you imagine what little Zoes would have to endure on the playground, and even worse, when they get a little bit older and someone comes up to them in a bar and says, 'Can I see your air bags?' or 'Can I shine your bumper?'"[25]

Strategically, this means a marketer may want to ensure that the appropriate role identity is active before pitching products that customers need to play a particular role. One obvious way to do this is to place advertising messages in contexts in which people are likely to be well aware of that role identity; for example, when fortified drink and energy bar product companies hand out free product samples to runners at a marathon.

If each person potentially has many social selves, how does each develop? How do we decide which self to "activate" at any point in time? The sociological tradition of **symbolic interactionism** stresses that relationships with other people play a large part to form the self.[26] According to this perspective, we exist in a symbolic environment. We assign meaning to any situation or object when we interpret the symbols in this environment. As members of society, individuals learn to agree on shared meanings. Thus, we "know" that a red light means stop, the "golden arches" mean fast food, and "blondes have more fun." That knowledge is important to understand consumer behavior because it implies that our possessions play a key role as we evaluate ourselves and decide "who we are."[27]

The Looking-Glass Self

Bloomingdales and some other clothing stores are testing interactive dressing rooms: When you choose a garment, the mirror superimposes it on your reflection so that you can see how it would look on your body without having to go to the trouble of trying it on.[28] Exciting stuff, but in a way this fancy technology simply simulates the "primping" process many shoppers undergo when they prance in front of a mirror and try to imagine how a garment will look on them—and whether others will approve or not.

Sociologists call the process of imagining others' reactions "taking the role of the other," or the **looking-glass self**.[29] According to this view, our desire to define ourselves operates as a sort of psychological sonar: We take readings of our own identity when we "bounce" signals off others and try to project their impression of us. Like the distorted mirrors in a funhouse, our appraisal of who we are varies depending on whose perspective we consider and how accurately we predict their evaluations of us. In symbolic interactionist terms, we *negotiate* these meanings over time. Essentially we continually ask ourselves the question: "*Who am I* in this situation?" Those around us greatly influence how we answer this query because we also ask, "Who do *other people* think I am?" We tend to pattern our behavior on the perceived expectations of others, as a form of **self-fulfilling prophecy**. When we act the way we assume others *expect* us to act, we often confirm these perceptions.

A confident career woman may sit morosely at a nightclub, imagining that others see her as a dowdy, unattractive woman with little sex appeal (regardless of whether these perceptions are true). A self-fulfilling prophecy like the one we described comes into play here because these "signals" influence the woman's actual behavior. If she doesn't believe she's attractive, she may choose frumpy, unflattering clothing that actually does make her less attractive. The next morning at work, however, her self-confidence at the office may cause her to assume that others hold her "executive self" in even higher regard than they actually do (we all know people like that)!

Self-Consciousness

Have you ever walked into a class in the middle of a lecture? If you were convinced that all eyes were on you as you awkwardly searched for a seat, you can understand the feeling of *self-consciousness*. In contrast, sometimes we behave with shockingly little self-consciousness. For example, we may do things in a stadium, at a riot, or at a fraternity party that we would never do if we were highly conscious of our behavior (and add insult to injury when we post these escapades to our Facebook page!).[30] Of course, certain cues in the environment, such as walking in front of a mirror, are likely to promote self-consciousness. That feeling in turn may influence behavior. For example, one pair of researchers is looking at whether grocery shoppers who push a cart with an attached mirror will buy more produce and healthy foods because their heightened self-consciousness makes them more weight conscious.[31]

Some people seem to be more sensitive in general to the image they communicate to others. However, we all know people who act as if they're oblivious to the impression they make. A heightened concern about the nature of one's public "image" also results in more concern about the social appropriateness of products and consumption activities.

Consumers who score high on a scale of **public self-consciousness** express more interest in clothing and use more cosmetics than others who score lower.[32] In one study, highly self-conscious subjects expressed greater willingness to buy personal products, such as a douche or a gas-prevention remedy, that are somewhat embarrassing to buy but may avoid awkward public incidents later.[33]

Similarly, high **self-monitors** are more attuned to how they present themselves in their social environments, and their estimates of how others will perceive their product choices influence what they choose to buy.[34] A scale to measure self-monitoring asks consumers how much they agree with statements such as "I guess I put on a show to impress or entertain others" or "I would probably make a good actor." Perhaps not surprisingly, publicly visible types such as college football players and fashion models tend to score higher on these dimensions.[35]

Self-consciousness on steroids—perhaps that's what we're experiencing in what historians looking back might call "The Era of the Selfie." A **selfie**, or a picture a smartphone user takes of himself or herself on a smartphone (whether or not it's attached to a "selfie stick") is a common form of communication, especially for Millennials. There are more than 35 million of them posted on Instagram alone. Then add in the growing practice of posting streaming video of yourself on platforms including Periscope, Camio, and Meerkat, and you've got a major cultural phenomenon. Indeed the term **meerkating**, which describes the act of someone shooting a live video stream, has become a verb as thousands of people create their own running self-documentaries.

What explains the infatuation many of us seem to have with photographing ourselves? One simple reason: Because we can. Obviously the widespread adoption of smartphones makes it easy to do. But there may be other reasons as well. One explanation hinges on the concept of the **empty self**. This perspective points to the decline of shared points of reference over the last 50 years as we witnessed a decline in family, community, and traditions. As a result, people have shifted inward and a focus on the self is an unconscious way to compensate for what we have lost. Indeed when we look at young people (more on this in Chapter 13), we do observe a decline in marriage rates and a low amount of trust people place in government, corporations, and organized religion. The increasing focus on self-reliance in turn creates a culture of narcissism, where we are obsessed with what we do and feel the need to constantly record it (updating our relationship status on Facebook, posting selfies and photos of our meals on Instagram, etc.).[36]

Perhaps that's an overly bleak assessment, but it does help to explain why the average Millennial checks his or her smartphone 43 times per day, and why 83 percent of Millennials report that they sleep with their smartphones every night.[37] Here's the irony: Research shows that although people believe taking pictures during an event enhances their enjoyment, the opposite is true. There is a tendency to become preoccupied with documenting the moment—the more pictures people take, the less they say they enjoy the actual experience.[38]

Are We What We Buy?

Way back in 1890, the famous psychologist William James wrote, "A man's self is the sum total of all that he can call his." And that was before iPhones, Diesel jeans, and Igloo dormsize refrigerators! **Self-image congruence models** suggest that we choose products when their attributes match some aspect of the self.[42] And, when we choose a product that we think is aesthetically pleasing this choice makes us feel better about ourselves.[43] Indeed recent research that included brain wave measures such as functional magnetic resonance imaging (fMRI) showed that when a person has a close relationship with a brand this activates the insula, a brain area responsible for urging, addiction, loss aversion, and interpersonal love.[44]

These emotional connections even make people defensive of their favorite brands if they see negative information about them. A comment by a respondent (a 32-year-old male) in one study nicely illustrates this bond: "My BMW is my wingman, my twin. I

The Tangled Web

Job applicants who post outrageous selfies (that must have been a pretty wild party ...) may come to regret their actions as potential employers start to check out their pages before they look at the would-be candidates' résumés. Some even turn to services such as Reputation.com that scour the Internet to remove embarrassing postings before the boss (or Mom) sees them.[39] Cell phones have spawned yet another way for teens to share intimate details about themselves online. The phenomenon of **sexting**, in which kids post nude or seminude photos of themselves online, is growing. In one recent survey of a sample of college students, more than half of respondents admitted to sexting as minors, and most were unaware that these acts have potential legal consequences.[40] Your online photos may be a lot more public than you think, and marketers find ways to use them, too. Digital marketing companies scan photo-sharing sites such as Instagram, Flickr, and Pinterest when they work for major advertisers. They use scanning software that identifies whether a person is holding a brand with a logo (like a Coke can) and what the person is doing in the picture. This information is useful to send targeted messages to consumers and to provide feedback to clients about how people use their brands. For example, Kraft Foods pays a company to find out what people drink when they eat macaroni and cheese.[41]

Marketing Opportunity

Identity marketing is a promotional strategy whereby consumers alter some aspects of their selves to advertise for a branded product. Air New Zealand created "cranial billboards" in exchange for a round-trip ticket to New Zealand—30 Los Angeles participants shaved their heads and walked around with an ad for the airline on their skulls.[56] Temporary tattoos of brand logos are common these days. Indeed this idea is hardly new; bubble gum companies in the 19th century distributed crudely made versions of the tattoos, and then in 1890, Cracker Jack used them as one of their "prize in every box" promotions.[57] More recently, Reebok set up a pop-up tattoo shop at an event in Sweden and gave away thousands of dollars in prizes to the fan who got the biggest version of the brands' new triangle logo (not a temporary one). The lucky winner's right thigh is, shall we say, Reebok's for life.[58]

would never diss it for another car because that would be like dissing my twin brother or worse, dissing myself."[45] This guy's fondness for his vehicle is hardly unique; more than a third of Americans have nicknames for their cars. That bond explains the wording of a recent TV commercial for SafeAuto insurance as a Mom drives her kids around in a well-used minivan: "For years you and this supercharged piece of eye candy have done much more than make car payments, buy gas and change the oil. You've lived, really lived, and you're most certainly not done ..."[46]

Congruence models assume a process of *cognitive matching* between product attributes and the consumer's self-image.[47] Over time we tend to form relationships with products that resemble the bonds we create with other people: These include love, unrequited love (we yearn for it but can't have it), respect, and perhaps even fear or hate ("why is my computer out to get me?").[48] Researchers even report that after a "breakup" with a brand, people tend to develop strong negative feelings and will go to great lengths to discredit it, including bad-mouthing and even vandalism.[49]

Research largely supports the idea of congruence between product usage and self-image. One of the earliest studies to examine this process found that car owners' ratings of themselves tended to match their perceptions of their cars: Pontiac drivers saw themselves as more active and flashy than did Volkswagen drivers.[50] Indeed, a German study found that observers were able to match photos of male and female drivers to pictures of the cars they drove almost 70 percent of the time.[51] Researchers also report congruity between consumers and their most preferred brands of beer, soap, toothpaste, and cigarettes relative to their least preferred brands, as well as between consumers' self-images and their favorite stores.[52] Some specific attributes useful to describe matches between consumers and products include rugged/delicate, excitable/calm, rational/emotional, and formal/informal.[53]

Although these findings make some intuitive sense, we cannot blithely assume that consumers will always buy products whose characteristics match their own. It is not clear that consumers really see aspects of themselves in down-to-earth, functional products that don't have complex or humanlike images. It is one thing to consider a brand personality for an expressive, image-oriented product, such as perfume, and quite another to impute human characteristics to a toaster.

Another problem is the old "chicken-and-egg" question: Do people buy products because they see these as similar to themselves, or do people assume that these products must be similar to themselves because they bought them? The similarity between a person's self-image and the images of products purchased does tend to increase over the time the product is owned, so we can't rule out this explanation.

Remember that the reflected self helps shape self-concept, which implies that people see themselves as they imagine others see them. Because what others see includes a person's clothing, jewelry, furniture, car, and so on, it stands to reason that these products also help to create the perceived self. A consumer's possessions place him or her into a social role, which helps to answer the question, "Who am I now?"

People use an individual's consumption behaviors to identify that person's social identity. In addition to checking out a person's clothes and grooming habits, we make inferences about personality based on his or her choice of leisure activities (e.g., squash versus bowling), food preferences (e.g., tofu and beans versus steak and potatoes), cars, and home decorating choices. When researchers show people pictures of someone's living room, for example, study participants make surprisingly accurate guesses about the occupant's personality.[54] In the same way that a consumer's use of products influences others' perceptions, the same products can help to determine his or her own self-concept and social identity.[55]

We are *attached* to an object to the extent we rely on it to maintain our self-concept.[59] Objects act as a security blanket when they reinforce our identities, especially in unfamiliar situations. For example, students who decorate their dorm rooms with personal items are less likely to drop out of college. This coping process may protect the self from being diluted in a strange environment.[60] When a pair of researchers asked children of various ages to create "who am I?" collages, for which they chose pictures that represented their selves, older kids between middle childhood and early adolescence inserted more photos of branded merchandise. Also, as they aged, their feelings about these objects evolved from

CB AS I SEE IT
Derek D. Rucker, *Northwestern University*

What meaning do you attach to products and brands? If you are like many consumers, products and brands have psychological utility in addition, and perhaps in some cases exceeding, their functional value. A Louis Vuitton handbag is not just a container for holding personal objects; a Ferrari is not simply a vehicle to get a consumer from point A to point B; and a sweatshirt of one's undergraduate alma mater is not merely a piece of clothing to stay warm. Rather, each of these objects has the potential to signal one's identity to both the self and others. Of particular interest to me is how

psychological threat—when one feels unsuccessful in an important domain of the self-concept— shapes the type of products one desires. Specifically, the notion that people might cope with threat through consumption is termed, **compensatory consumption**.

In my first foray into compensatory consumption, I demonstrated that psychological threats in the form of feeling powerless could affect consumption. Feeling powerless represents a psychological threat in that people often desire power (i.e., control over precious resources in relation to others). My colleague Adam Galinsky and I proposed that, as power is intimately associated with status, when consumers feel powerless they might exhibit a shift in preferences towards objects associated with status. To test this idea, we instructed undergraduate students to write about a time they felt powerless or powerful. Subsequently, participants indicated their reservation price for a framed portrait of their university that was either described as scarce (high-status) or as common (low-status). Participants who had written about a past experience of feeling powerless were willing to pay more for the framed portrait of their university, but only when that framed portrait was represented as scarce (i.e., high status). Essentially, consumers, seemingly unbeknownst to themselves, sought consumption

to offset the psychological state of feeling powerless.

However, the fact consumers engage in compensatory consumption does not mean consumption is always an antidote for a psychological threat. In work with Monika Lisjak, Andrea Bonezzi, and Soo Kim, we demonstrated that compensatory consumption can worsen psychological threat. For example, in one experiment we first threatened participants' perceptions of their intelligence and then we gave them the opportunity to either select a product that signaled intelligence or a product that signaled sociability. Finally, we measured participants' tendency to ruminate on (i.e., repeatedly think about) the threatening experience. We found that participants who chose a product that signaled success in the domain of threat, which in theory can offset the threat, heightened rumination about the threat. Furthermore, additional experiments suggest that, as a consequence of rumination, participants perform poorer on tasks that involved subsequent attention, such as completing math problems.

My current work continues to try to understand how consumers protect their sense of self in the face of psychological threat. I hope to answer the question of when consumption is a sound salve for threat versus a hollow substitute as a means to understand the powerful and transformative effects of brands and products.

concrete relationships (e.g., "I own it") to more sophisticated, abstract relationships (e.g., "It is like me").[61]

Our use of consumption information to define the self is especially important when we have yet to completely form a social identity, such as when we have to play a new role in life. Think, for example, of the insecurity many of us felt when we first started college or reentered the dating market after leaving a long-term relationship. **Symbolic self-completion theory** suggests that people who have an incomplete self-definition tend to complete this identity when they acquire and display symbols they associate with that role.[62]

Adolescent boys, for example, may use "macho" products such as cars and cigarettes to bolster developing masculinity; these items act as a "social crutch" during a period of uncertainty about their new identity as adult males. As we mature into a role, we actually rely less on the products people associate with it: When kids start to skateboard, they often invest in pro skateboard "decks" with graphics and branding that cost between $40 and $70 even without the "trucks" (wheels and axles). But—to the chagrin of the skateboard industry—as they get more serious about boarding, many think it's just fine to buy *blank decks*, the plain wood boards that cost only $15 to $30.[63]

The contribution of possessions to self-identity is perhaps most apparent when we lose these treasured objects. One of the first acts of institutions that want to repress individuality and encourage group identity, such as prisons or the military, is to confiscate personal possessions.[64] Victims of burglaries and natural disasters commonly report feelings of alienation, depression, or of being "violated." One consumer's comment after she was robbed is typical: "It's the next worse thing to being bereaved; it's like being raped."[65] Burglary victims exhibit a diminished sense of community, lowered feelings of privacy, and less pride in their houses' appearance than do their neighbors.[66]

A study of postdisaster conditions, where consumers may have lost literally everything but the clothes on their backs following a fire, hurricane, flood, or earthquake, highlights the dramatic impact of product loss. Some people are reluctant to undergo the process of re-creating their identities by acquiring new possessions. Interviews with disaster victims reveal that some hesitate to invest the self in new possessions and so become more detached about what they buy. This comment from a woman in her 50s is representative of this attitude: "I had so much love tied up in my things. I can't go through that kind of loss again. What I'm buying now won't be as important to me."[67]

OBJECTIVE 6-2
Products often define a person's self-concept.

The Extended Self

As we noted previously, many of the props and settings consumers use to define their social roles become parts of their selves. Those external objects that we consider a part of us constitute the **extended self**. In some cultures, people literally incorporate objects into the self: they lick new possessions, take the names of conquered enemies (or in some cases eat them), or bury the dead with their possessions.[68]

Consumers continue to discover new ways to integrate man-made products into our physical bodies. The use of foreign materials to replace or supplement human body

A spouse often becomes part of a person's extended self—for better or worse.
Source: Courtesy of Clemenger BBDO.

SPENDING TOO MUCH TIME WITH THE WIFE?

STAY A LITTLE LONGER

parts is not necessarily new (remember George Washington's infamous wooden teeth), but recent advances in technology continue to erode the barrier between self and not self. Here are some examples:[69]

- According to the American Society for Aesthetic Plastic Surgery, Americans get more than 9 million cosmetic surgical and nonsurgical procedures in a year. The most frequently performed surgical procedure is breast augmentation, which typically involves the integration of man-made silicon implants with the patient's organic material.
- More than 4 million Americans have an artificial knee.
- At least prior to his recent arrest for murder that made global headlines, the South African track star Oscar Pistorious competed against world-class runners with two artificial legs made of carbon. Nike teamed with orthopedics company Össur to introduce its first sprinting prosthesis, called the Nike Sole, perhaps the first commercially scalable transformation of disabled athletes into "superabled" athletes.
- More than 200,000 people now have cochlear implants that deliver sound from a microphone directly to the auditory nerve. Other neural implants recognize when epileptic seizures are about to occur and stimulate the brain to stop them. A woman paralyzed from the waist down who wore a motorized exoskeleton walked the route of the London Marathon over a period of 17 days.

We don't usually go that far, but some people do cherish possessions as if they were a part of them. In fact, some of us willingly (and perhaps eagerly) label ourselves as *fanatics* about a cherished product.[71] Consider shoes, for example: You don't have to be Carrie of *Sex and the City* fame to acknowledge that many people feel a strong bond to their footwear. The singer Mariah Carey recently posted a photo of her huge shoe closet on Instagram and labeled it, "Always my favorite room in the house... #shoes #shoes #moreshoes."[72]

One study found that people commonly view their shoes as magical emblems of self, Cinderella-like vehicles for self-transformation. Based on data collected from consumers, the researcher concluded that (like their sister Carrie) women tend to be more attuned to the symbolic implications of shoes than men. A common theme that emerged was that a pair of shoes obtained when younger—whether a first pair of leather shoes, a first pair of high heels, or a first pair of cowboy boots—had a big impact even later in life. These experiences were similar to those that occur in such well-known fairy tales and stories as Dorothy's red shoes in *The Wizard of Oz*, Karen's magical red shoes in Hans Christian Anderson's *The Red Shoes*, and Cinderella's glass slippers.[73]

In addition to shoes, of course, many material objects—ranging from personal possessions and pets to national monuments or landmarks—help to form a consumer's identity. Just about everyone can name a valued possession that has a lot of the self "wrapped up" in it, whether it is a beloved photograph, a trophy, an old shirt, a car, or a cat. Indeed, usually we can construct a pretty accurate "biography" of someone when we simply catalog the items he displays in his bedroom or office. A study illustrates that the product/self doesn't even have to be that strong to influence a consumer's self-concept. In one experiment, researchers approached women in a shopping mall and gave them one of two shopping bags to walk around with for an hour. Women who received a bag from Victoria's Secret later reported to the researchers that they felt more sensual and glamorous. In another experiment, MBA students were asked to take notes for 6 weeks using a pen embossed with the MIT logo; they reported feeling smarter at the end of the term.[74]

As Figure 6.1 shows, we describe four levels of the extended self, ranging from personal objects to places and things that allow people to feel as though they are rooted in their larger social environments:[75]

1 **Individual level**—Consumers include many of their personal possessions in self-definition. These products can include jewelry, cars, clothing, and so on. The saying "You are what you wear" reflects the belief that one's things are a part of one's identity.

Net Profit

Many consumers try to bolster their self-esteem as they accumulate evidence of their achievements. In a results-oriented and competitive society, we continue to find ways to trumpet our successes. In Chapter 4 we discussed the growing trend of *gamification*, which involves rewarding people for accomplishing tasks. We display evidence of these rewards, or **badges**, by way of car bumper stickers ("My son is an honor student") or even grownup equivalents of the merit badges that the Boy Scouts award. Adults can buy their own Nerd Merit Badges recognizing geeky achievements, including "Open Source" (contribution to an open-source project), "Family Tech Support," or "I Have an Actual Human Skeleton in My Office." When they go online to **geospatial platforms** that use their smartphones to identify their physical locations, consumers earn pins on Gowalla to certify that they've eaten in certain restaurants, or badges on Foursquare that testify to personal qualities such as "Photogenic," "Gossip Girl," or even "Crunked" (for hitting more than four bars in a single night).[70]

Figure 6.1 LEVELS OF THE EXTENDED
SELF

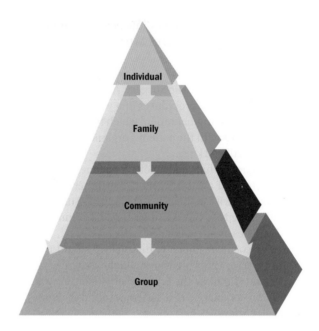

2 **Family level**—This part of the extended self includes a consumer's residence and the furnishings in it. We can think of the house as a symbolic body for the family, and the place where we live often is a central aspect of who we are.

3 **Community level**—It is common for consumers to describe themselves in terms of the neighborhood or town from which they come. For farm families or other residents with close ties to a community, this sense of belonging is particularly important.

4 **Group level**—We regard our attachments to certain social groups as a part of the self; we'll consider some of these consumer *subcultures* in later chapters. A consumer also may feel that landmarks, monuments, or sports teams are a part of the extended self.

Embodied Cognition

To what extent do the products we buy influence how we define ourselves? Social scientists who study relationships between thoughts and behaviors increasingly talk about the theory of **embodied cognition**. A simple way to explain this perspective is that "states of the body modify states of the mind."[76] In other words, our behaviors and observations of what we do and buy shape our thoughts rather than vice versa. One of the most powerful examples is the idea that our body language actually changes how we see ourselves; in the most widely viewed TED talk ever, a social psychologist discusses how **power posing** (standing in a confident way even if you don't feel confident) affects brain activity. Again, the self-fulfilling prophecy at work.[77]

The embodied cognition approach is consistent with consumer behavior research that demonstrates how changes in self-concept can arise from usage of brands that convey different meanings. Indeed one pair of researchers used the term **enclothed cognition** in their work that showed how the symbolic meaning of clothing changes how people behave. In one study they asked respondents to wear a lab coat, which people associate with attentiveness and precise work. Indeed they found that subjects who wore the lab coat displayed enhanced performance on tasks that required them to pay close attention. But they also introduced a twist: When respondents were told the garment was in fact a painter's coat rather than a doctor's lab coat, the effects went away. In other words, the respondents interpreted the symbolic meaning of the clothing and then altered their behavior accordingly.[78]

Residents of the Blue Mars virtual world use their iPhones to vote on the most attractive avatars.

Source: Image courtesy of Avatar Reality.

It's tempting to point out that a study your humble author conducted more than 30 years ago on the "dress for success" phenomenon found similar results for students in job interview settings. In perhaps the best Ph.D. dissertation ever written (at least in your author's opinion), male candidates who wore professional attire acted more assertively and confidently during the interviews, and on average even asked for higher starting salaries![79]

The Digital Self

We've already talked about impression management, but our wired world takes this process to a new level.[80] Today we have access to "post-production" tools to engineer our identities. These free or inexpensive applications allow virtually anyone to dramatically modify his or her **digital self** at will as we strategically "modify" the profile photos

The Tangled Web

"I can leave Facebook whenever I want!" Actually, for many people it's not so easy. Researchers looked at Facebook posts, blogs, discussion groups, and online magazines to find "breakup stories" that would help them to understand what people go through when they decide to end their relationship with this social network. Many people talked about the things they're missing: friends' birthdays, the ability to play online games, and the ability to use various online services. Their descriptions were laced with strong emotions that ranged from sadness to the kind of relief an addict might feel if he or she succeeds in breaking out of a bad habit.

we post on Facebook or the descriptions we share on online dating sites. In addition, many of us create additional identities in the form of avatars in virtual worlds like *Second Life* and massive multiplayer online games (MMOGs) such as *World of Warcraft*. U.S. Americans alone spend about $1.6 billion per year to buy virtual goods just for their avatars. Our physical bodies continue to merge with our digital environments; we're moving from "you are what you wear" to "you are what you post." We also take pieces of these digital identities back with us to the physical world. Respondents in one study placed more value on digital items that reflect their physical identities, such as digital photos and written communications.[81]

Wearable Computing

Get ready for the invasion of **wearable computing**. Whether devices we wear on our wrist like the Apple Watch, on our face like Google Glass, or woven into our clothing, increasingly our digital interactions will become attached to our bodies—and perhaps even inserted *into* our bodies as companies offer ways to implant computer chips into our wrists. There are obvious privacy concerns as these products pick up steam, but advocates argue they offer numerous benefits as well. These attachable computers will be cheaper, provide greater accuracy because sensors are closer to our bodies, and be more convenient because we won't have to carry around additional hardware.[82] Already numerous wearables with big health implications are available or under development:[83]

- Sensing for sleep disorders by tracking breath, heart rate, and motion
- Detecting possible onset of Alzheimer's by monitoring a person's gait via a GPS embedded in his or her shoes
- Tracking ingestion of medication via sensors that are activated by stomach fluid
- Measuring blood sugar via a contact lens with a chip that can track activity in a patient's tears
- Assessing the impact of blows to a football player's head via sensors inserted in his helmet.

Virtual Makeovers

New **virtual makeover** technologies make it even easier for each of us to involve the digital self as we choose products to adorn our physical selves. These platforms allow the shopper to superimpose images on their faces or bodies so that they can quickly and easily see how products would alter appearance, without taking the risk of actually buying the item first. L'Oréal offers a Makeup Genius app that turns the front-facing iPhone and iPad camera into a makeup mirror so that the customer can virtually try on hundreds of cosmetics products. The shopper can change facial expressions and lighting conditions; the virtual makeup stays on her face. The online glasses merchant Warby Parker allows consumers to upload a picture of themselves and try on frames virtually. Other apps such as Perfect 365 and Face Tune let you touch up your photo so you can remove a pimple, a wrinkle, or even a few pounds before you post it on Instagram or Facebook for others to admire.[84]

OBJECTIVE 6-3

Gender identity is an important component of a consumer's self-concept.

Gender Identity

The Indian government banned a TV spot for Axe men's deodorant: The spot shows a man who turns into a walking chocolate figurine after he sprays himself with the brand's Dark Temptation deodorant. As he walks through the city, women throw themselves at him as they lick him and bite off various parts of his body. Although the same ad played in Argentina and Europe without any problem, traditional Indian culture doesn't approve of such blatant imagery. The government yanked another ad for Amul Macho underwear, in which a young woman comes to a river to do

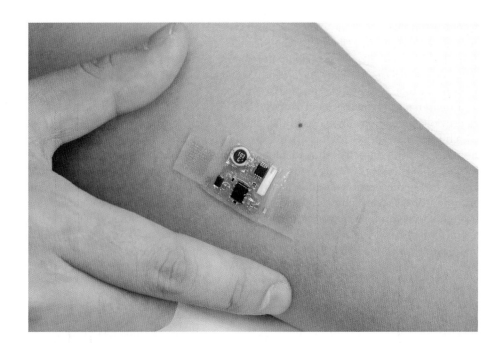

her husband's laundry, pulls out a pair of boxer shorts, and begins to wash them by hand as she gives sultry looks to the camera and throws her head back in a suggestive manner, as a voiceover says, "Amul Macho. Crafted for fantasies." Members of a Hindu organization called The Army of Ram (a Hindu god) attacked a group of female college students in a bar because they were drinking and dancing with men.[85] Clearly, expectations for the appropriate behavior of men and women are not set in stone around the world.

Gender identity is an important component of a consumer's self-concept. People often conform to their culture's expectations about how those of their gender should act, dress, or speak; we refer to these sets of expectations as **sex roles**. Of course, these guidelines change over time, and they differ radically across societies. In India and elsewhere, for example, a society communicates its assumptions about the proper roles of men and women as it defines ideal behaviors for each gender.

It's not clear to what extent gender differences are innate rather than culturally shaped, but they're certainly evident in many consumption situations. Consider the gender differences market researchers observe when they compare the food preferences of men to those of women. Women eat more fruit; men are more likely to eat meat. As one food writer put it, "Boy food doesn't grow. It is hunted or killed."[86] Indeed, consumers do tend to view meat as a masculine product. In one case a company that sells soy patties found that men viewed the food as feminine, so its solution was to add artificial grill marks on the patties to make them look like cuts of meat.[87]

The sexes also differ sharply in the quantities of food they eat: When researchers at Hershey discovered that women eat smaller amounts of candy, they created a white chocolate confection called Hugs, one of the most successful food introductions of all time. In contrast, a man in a Burger King Whopper ad ditches his date at a fancy restaurant, complaining that he is "too hungry to settle for chick food." Pumped up on Whoppers, a swelling mob of men shake their fists, punch one another, toss a van off a bridge, and sing, "I will eat this meat until my innie turns into an outie," and "I am hungry. I am incorrigible. I am man."[88]

Sex Role Socialization

When students write reviews of faculty members on the popular website *Rate My Professors*, they use different words depending on whether the professor is male or female. Women professors usually come out on the losing end of these reviews. In a study that examined 14 million reviews on the site, positive words such as *smart* and *genius* are more much more likely to describe males than females across 25 different disciplines. Other terms that fit female stereotypes pop up in reviews of female professors, including *bossy*, *strict*, and *demanding* (as well as *nurturing*). Women are also much more likely to be called out by the fashion police with terms such as *frumpy*.[89]

Children pick up on the concept of gender identity at an earlier age than researchers previously believed—by as young as age 1 in some cases. By the age of 3, most U.S. children categorize driving a truck as masculine and cooking and cleaning as feminine.[90] Even characters that cartoons portray as helpless are more likely to wear frilly or ruffled dresses.[91] Many commercial sources, in addition to parents and friends, provide lessons in **gender socialization** for both girls and boys. An advertisement for Sony's Bravia televisions is typical: The spot shows a man and a woman gazing through a storefront window at a Bravia LCD. Unaware of each other, the two simultaneously whisper: "Nice picture." Suddenly, two buttons appear on the screen that read: "Ending for Men" and "Ending for Women." The male ending is either a funny clip from a sports show or a cartoon spoof of a martial-arts movie. Women see either a 1950s-era musical centered on shoes or a tearjerker about a female doctor who saves the life of an orphan.[92]

Marketers tend to reinforce cultural expectations regarding the "correct" way for boys and girls, men and women, to look and act. Many societies expect males to pursue **agentic goals**, which stress self-assertion and mastery. However, they teach females to value **communal goals**, such as affiliation and building harmonious relations.[93] A recent comprehensive review of the research literature reported five basic conclusions about gender differences:[94]

1 Males are more self-oriented, whereas females are more other-oriented
2 Females are more cautious responders
3 Females are more responsive to negative data
4 Males process data more selectively and females more comprehensively; and
5 Females are more sensitive to differentiating conditions and factors.

Gender Identity Versus Sexual Identity

Gender-role identity is a state of mind as well as body. A person's biological gender (i.e., male or female) does not totally determine whether he or she will exhibit **sex-typed traits**—characteristics we stereotypically associate with one gender or the other. A consumer's subjective feelings about his or her sexuality are crucial as well.[95]

At the same time, new evidence is emerging about the effects of biology on consumer behavior. **Neuroendocrinological science** focuses on the potential role of hormonal influences on preferences for different kinds of products or people.[96] Much of this work is based on evolutionary logic that underscores how people are "wired" from birth to seek out mates who can produce optimal offspring that will be more likely to survive in a competitive environment. For example, evidence suggests that women who are at peak fertility (near ovulation in their monthly menstrual cycle) are attracted to men who display evidence of higher levels of testosterone (male hormone), and these women are also more interested in attending social gatherings (presumably to increase their chances of locating a suitable mate). One set of experiments showed that at peak fertility women (nonconsciously) chose products that enhanced their appearance by wearing sexy rather than conservative clothing. The researchers claim this is because of a desire to attract men's attention away from attractive rivals. Another set of studies found that ovulating women are more likely to prefer variety in product choice; the authors report that this variety seeking relates to a desire to be exposed to new men during this time.[97]

Unlike maleness and femaleness, masculinity and femininity are *not* biological characteristics. A behavior that one culture considers to be masculine might get a different response in another. For example, the norm in the United States is that male friends avoid touching each other (except in "safe" situations such as on the football field). In some

Latin and European cultures, however, it is common for men to hug and kiss one another as a form of greeting. Note that even this norm continues to evolve, as U.S. teenagers of both sexes adopt the new fad of hugging as a standard form of greeting (sometimes accompanied by the high-five or the fist-bump) and male friends (encouraged by the MTV show of the same name) feel free to talk about having a **bromance** (affection between straight male friends).[98]

Sex-Typed Products

Obviously many products are intimately associated with one gender or the other, especially if they link to a culture's definition of what is sexually appealing. Thus, the results of a recent French study shouldn't be too surprising: In a series of field experiments, men were more likely to complete a survey or pick up a dropped glove if a female confederate wore high heels rather than flats. The higher the heel, the greater the likelihood of cooperation. As you might guess, the relationship did not hold for females.[99] Note: Gender-specific linkages like this may indeed have a biological basis. Some (though hardly all) social scientists speculate that high heels change a woman's posture in a way that men are "wired" to notice. As one account puts it, "The waist looks slimmer, the backside protrudes, the chest thrusts out, and a pedestrian gait becomes what anthropologists call 'the courtship strut.'"[100]

A popular book once proclaimed, *Real Men Don't Eat Quiche*. In addition to quiche, marketers promote many **sex-typed products**. They reflect stereotypical masculine or feminine attributes, and consumers associate them with one gender or another.[102] For example, ePad Femme is the "world's first tablet made exclusively for women." It comes preloaded with a pink background and a number of apps related to yoga, grocery shopping, weight loss, and cooking.[103]

Female Sex Roles

In the 1949 movie *Adam's Rib*, Katharine Hepburn played a stylish and competent lawyer. This film was one of the first to show that a woman can have a successful career and still be happily married. Today, the evolution of a new managerial class of women has forced marketers to change their traditional assumptions about women as they target this growing market. For example, Suzuki appeals to the growing number of women in India who achieve financial independence and buy their own cars. Its Zen Estilo (*estilo* means "style" in Spanish) model comes in eight colors, including "purple fusion," "virgin blue," and "sparkling olive."[104]

Still, it's premature to proclaim the death of traditional sex-role stereotypes. This is certainly true in Islamic countries that require women to be completely covered in public

Many products acquire a gender identity.
Source: Courtesy of Greatest Common Factory and SafeAuto Bill Sallans.

This ad for Bijan illustrates how sex role identities are culturally bound by contrasting the expectations of how women should appear in two different countries.
Source: Courtesy of Bijan Fragrances c/o Fashion World.

and that prohibit them from working as salespeople in stores open to the public (even if the store sells female intimate apparel).[105]

To further complicate matters, sex roles constantly evolve. In a complex society like ours, we often encounter contradictory messages about "appropriate" behavior, and we may find ourselves putting on a different face as we jump from situation to situation. An exploration of what the authors labeled **contemporary young mainstream female achievers (CYMFA)** identified different roles these women play in different contexts. For example, as a mother or partner they enact a highly feminine role; as a tough, pitiless businessperson, they play a masculine role; and with a friend they might evoke both roles at once.[106]

Male Sex Roles

A European ad for designer Dolce & Gabbana depicts a group of sweaty men in tight jeans who surround a woman wearing spike heels who is pinned to the ground. Other ads featuring long-time household products spokescharacter Mr. Clean claim that only a strong man is powerful enough to tackle dirt.[107] To promote the Dr. Pepper Ten drink, the company sent a mobile "Man Cave" to U.S. cities. The trailer parked in "testosterone zones" such as ball fields or car shows, where it gave men a place to watch TV and play video games. The accompanying advertising campaign featured a muscled commando type who totes a space-age weapon. "Hey ladies, enjoying the film?" he asks. "'Course not. Because this is our movie, and Dr. Pepper Ten is our soda."[108]

Our culture's stereotype of the ideal male is a tough, aggressive, muscular man who enjoys "manly" sports. When global entrepreneur and CEO of Virgin Airlines

Gun Goddess sells feminine accessories to women who own or use firearms.
Source: GunGoddess.com.

Richard Branson lost a racing bet to the owner of Air Asia, his "sentence" was to dress as a female flight attendant for the winner's airline. The winner gloated, "I'm looking forward to him sucking up to me as a stewardess!"[109] A study that tracked advertising in eight male magazines with primarily male readerships (ranging from *Maxim* to *Golf Digest*) reported that most contain many ads that can contribute to "hyper-masculinity" because of heavy emphasis on violence, dangerousness, and callous attitudes toward women and sex.[110]

Just as for women, however, the true story is more complicated than being "a man's man." Indeed, scholars of **masculinism** study the male image and the complex cultural meanings of masculinity.[111] Like women, men receive mixed messages about how they are supposed to behave and feel. Chevrolet's "Guy's Night Out" commercial depicts a new dad's night out with friends where they wind up watching his toddler's sing-a-long CD.

One study examined how U.S. men pursue masculine identities through their everyday consumption. The researchers suggest that men try to make sense out of three different models of masculinity that they call *breadwinner, rebel,* and *man-of-action hero.* On the one hand, the breadwinner model draws from the U.S. myth of success and celebrates respectability, civic virtues, pursuit of material success, and organized achievement. The rebel model, on the other hand, emphasizes rebellion, independence, adventure, and potency. The man-of-action hero is a synthesis that draws from the best of the other two models.[112]

Androgyny

The British department store chain Selfridges is known for unusual promotions and events (this is the store where actress Lindsay Lohan ripped off her clothes and ran through the aisles, much to the delight of the London tabloids).[113] The store even went brand-free for 2 years to give customers a break. Now the merchant is going gender-free in its 2-month

A male sex-typed product.
Source: IWC Schaffhausen.

IWC.
Engineered for men.

IWC
SCHAFFHAUSEN
SINCE 1868

Don't fly too high!

Pilot's Watch Double Chronograph. Ref. 3778: A watch? Or a machine? A 46-mm stainless-steel case, mechanical double chronograph movement with a split-seconds hand for intermediate time and a soft-iron inner case to protect the movement against magnetic fields make this timepiece an indestructible, and at the same time high-precision masterpiece from the Schaffhausen-based watch manufacturers. All it needs to make it fly is a pilot. **IWC. Engineered for men.**

Mechanical chronograph movement I Self-winding I 44-hour power reserve when fully wound I Date and day display I Small hacking seconds I Stopwatch function with hours, minutes and seconds I Split-seconds hand for intermediate timing (figure) I Soft-iron inner case for protection against magnetic fields I Screw-in crown I Sapphire glass, convex, antireflective coating on both sides I Water-resistant 6 bar I Stainless steel

Agender Project. It will feature unisex fashion lines and put mannequins in storage to "show the collections in a non-gender-specific way." One possible motivation for the experiment: The store finds that more female shoppers are buying menswear for themselves and now it wants to encourage men to be adventurous about crossing to the other side of the aisle as well.[114] Come on, guys, rock those skirts....

Androgyny refers to the possession of both masculine and feminine traits.[115] Researchers make a distinction between *sex-typed people*, who are stereotypically masculine or feminine, and *androgynous* people, whose orientation isn't as clearly defined. Clearly, the "normality" of sex-typed behaviors varies across cultures. For example, although acceptance of homosexuality varies in Asian cultures, it doesn't occur to most Asians to assume that a man with some feminine qualities is gay. A survey of Korean consumers found that more than 66 percent of men and 57 percent of women younger than age 40 live self-described "androgynous" lifestyles—with men having more traditionally female traits and women having more traditionally male ones than they might have years ago. But the respondents didn't link that with sexual orientation. Although Koreans nickname males with feminine interests "flower men," they don't consider this to be a derogatory term.[116] In Japan, men that people call *gyaru-o* ("male gals") are common on city streets. Tanned and meticulously dressed (and usually heterosexual), these fops cruise Tokyo's stylish boutiques.[117]

Some research indicates that sex-typed people are more sensitive to the sex role depictions of characters in advertising. In one study, subjects read two versions of a beer advertisement couched in either masculine or feminine terms. The masculine version contained phrases such as "X beer has the strong aggressive flavor that really asserts itself with good

Androgyny refers to the possession of both masculine and feminine traits.
Source: kitty/Shutterstock.

food and good company," and the feminine version made claims such as "Brewed with tender care, X beer is a full-bodied beer that goes down smooth and gentle." People who rated themselves as highly masculine or highly feminine preferred the version that was described in (respectively) very masculine or very feminine terms.[118]

Researchers developed a scale to identify "nontraditional males" (NTMs) who exhibit stereotypically female tendencies. The scale included statements such as these:

● I enjoy looking through fashion magazines.
● In our family, I take care of the checkbook and pay the bills.
● I am concerned about getting enough calcium in my diet.
● I am good at fixing mechanical things.
● I would do better than average in a fistfight.

Not too surprisingly, strong differences emerged between men who rated the statements along traditional sex-role lines and those who had nontraditional orientations When asked how they would like others to see them, NTMs were more likely than traditional males (TMs) to say that they would like to be considered stylish, sophisticated, up to date, and trendsetting. They were also more likely to say that they would like to be seen as sensitive, spiritual, affectionate, organized, and thrifty, but less likely to say they would like to be seen as "outdoorsy."

Androgyny can open new markets if marketers can expand the reach of their target audience. Some companies that sell exclusively to one gender may therefore decide to test the waters with the other sex when they promote **gender-bending products**, which are traditionally sex-typed items adapted to the opposite gender, such as the recent profusion of merchants that sell pink guns for women. Here are some other gender benders:[119]

- Rubbermaid introduced a line of grooming tools specifically for men, including tweezers and clippers. As a manager explained, "Most men don't want to go to what we call the 'pink aisle' of the store to get tweezers and clippers that are made for women. They want products that look masculine and are made for their specific grooming needs."
- Old Spice has long been known as the brand Dad keeps in his medicine cabinet, but young women who like the scent and the relatively low price are tuning into the deodorant as well. This resurgence is a bit ironic because the first product the company introduced in 1937 was a women's fragrance.
- Febreze is an odor-neutralizing line of products that Procter & Gamble (P&G) markets to women for housecleaning. However, P&G finds that a lot of men spray it on their clothes to delay doing laundry. And in Vietnam, where the product is called Ambi Pur, men who ride motor scooters use it as a deodorizing spray for their helmets.[120]

Gay, Lesbian, Bisexual, and Transgender (GLBT) Consumers

The proportion of the population that is gay or lesbian is difficult to determine, and efforts to measure this group have been controversial.[121] A 2015 Gallup report based on responses from more than 300,000 adult Americans found that on average 3.6 percent of respondents who live in the 50 largest metropolitan areas (that researchers refer to as *Metropolitan Statistical Areas* or *MSAs*) self-identified as GLBT.[122]

To put things in perspective, the GLBT market is about as large as the Asian American population (currently at about 12 million people). These consumers spend in the range of $250 billion to $350 billion a year. A Simmons study of readers of gay publications found that these readers are almost 12 times more likely to hold professional jobs, twice as likely

Axe's Anarchy brand is a gender-bender.
Source: Courtesy of Unilever.

to own a vacation home, and eight times more likely to own a notebook computer compared to heterosexuals.[123]

Gay relationships are increasingly mainstream in most parts of the United States. A Gallup survey in 2014 found that 55 percent of Americans favor same-sex marriage, whereas nearly 8 of 10 young adults support it.[124] Therefore, it's not surprising to see more and more marketing communications that routinely include gay couples. A recent Banana Republic campaign features pairs of models who also are couples in real life. One of these is two men, both interior designers. The chief creative officer of the agency that created the campaign observed, the goal is "to reflect our world and how we live in a true, genuine way."[125] Even the Oreo cookie brand took a public stand when in support of Gay Pride Month the company posted a photo on its Facebook page of an Oreo with six different colors of cream—one for each color of the rainbow, a symbol gay rights supporters use to show diversity. The post drew many thousands of comments. Some called for a product boycott, but most like this one were more supportive: "Thank you Oreo and Nabisco for your Pride. Not only did you make an awesome statement about love and acceptance, but that cookie looked freaking delicious!!"[126]

Of late the cultural spotlight has turned on transgender people, helped along by the media attention paid to a character in the popular TV show *Orange is the New Black* and the debut of former athlete and current reality TV star Bruce Jenner in her new identity as Caitlin Jenner on the cover of *Vogue*. Our definitions of gender continue to evolve as a global **third gender movement** picks up steam: Australia's High Court recently ruled that a person there was allowed to register gender as "nonspecific" on official documents. Nepal issues citizenship papers with a "third gender" category and Germany allows parents of **intersex children**—those born with both genitals, or ambiguous sex characteristics—to mark their birth certificates with an X.[127] United Colors of Benetton caused a stir when its product campaign included Lea T, a trans-sexual Brazilian model.[128]

Marketing Opportunity

Now that the U.S. Supreme Court has ruled in favor of same-sex marriage, businesses are searching for ways to meet the needs of this lucrative market. Americans already spend more than $50 billion per year on weddings and the explosion of gay weddings is projected to add at least another $2 billion to this figure. The online magazine *EquallyWed* offers tips on wedding planning and OutVite.com sells "custom printed gay and lesbian stationery." After it received pressure from gay rights groups, the *Today* show on NBC invited same-sex couples to compete in its annual wedding contest. *Brides'* magazine ran its first feature about a wedding between one of the magazine's photo editors and her longtime girlfriend. A year previously, *Martha Stewart Weddings* published a pictorial of two gay grooms stomping on a glass and sharing a kiss.[129]

OBJECTIVE 6-4
The way we think about our bodies (and the way our culture tells us we should think) is a key component of self-esteem.

The Body

For many women, trying on jeans is a painful exercise. Levi Strauss launched an online fitting service called the Curve ID System to make the process a little more comfortable. The digital offering is available in 20 languages and 50 countries; it is based on 60,000 women's figures worldwide and its goal is to provide a more customized experience to ease the frustration many women feel as they search for the perfect pair of jeans.[130] Still, you may want to consider some Spanx shapewear for some "tummy-taming," "butt boosting," or "thigh trimming" before you wear your new pants in public.[131]

A person's physical appearance is a large part of his or her self-concept. **Body image** refers to a consumer's subjective evaluation of his or her physical self. Our evaluations don't necessarily correspond to what those around us see. A man may

In a series of Dove ads in China, pregnant bellies are painted with questions from unborn girls. "If you knew I would grow to be a flat-nosed girl, will you still welcome me?" asks one. "If you knew I'd grow up to weigh 140 jin [154 lbs], would I still be your baby?" asks another. The third: "I'll soon come to the world, but if I grow to only have an A bra cup, will you tease me?" Many Chinese women worry about being labelled a "leftover woman" or a "spinster," terms for women who reach the age of 26 and are still single.[133]

Source: Phil Date/Shutterstock.

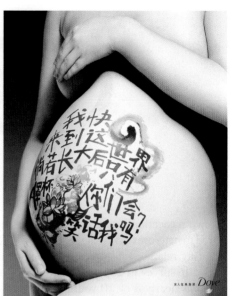

think of himself as being more muscular than he really is, or a woman may feel she appears fatter than is actually the case. Whether these perceptions are accurate is almost a moot point because our body insecurities weigh us down whether they're justified or not.[132]

Some marketers exploit consumers' tendencies to distort their body images when they prey on our insecurities about appearance. They try to create a gap between the real and the ideal physical selves and consequently motivate a person to purchase products and services he or she thinks will narrow that gap. Even social media apparently impacts how we feel about our bodies. A recent study of Facebook users reported that one-half of them felt more self-conscious about their body images after they looked at photos of themselves and others on the site.[134]

Ideals of Beauty

BeautifulPeople.com is an online dating site that allows only attractive people to join (you have to have your photo approved by members). Now it's expanding its service to employers who want to hire "good-looking staff." One of the site's managers explains, "Attractive people tend to make a better first impression on clients, win more business and earn more."[135] He might be right: One study reported that on average a U.S. worker who was among the bottom one-seventh in looks, as assessed by randomly chosen observers, earned 10 to 15 percent less per year than a similar worker whose looks were assessed in the top one-third—a lifetime difference, in a typical case, of about $230,000.[136] Who says "beauty is only skin deep?"

Our satisfaction with the physical image we present to others depends on how closely we think the image corresponds to the ideal our culture values. An **ideal of beauty** is a particular model, or *exemplar*, of appearance. Ideals of beauty for both men and women may include physical features (e.g., a well-rounded derriere for women or a well-defined six-pack for men) as well as clothing styles, cosmetics, hairstyles, skin tone (pale versus tan), and body type (petite, athletic, voluptuous, etc.). Our desires to match up to these ideals—for better or worse—drive a lot of our purchase decisions. What's more, the pressure to exhibit these traits starts earlier and earlier: The retailer Abercrombie & Fitch first came under fire a few years ago for selling thongs to preteens.

More recently, critics blasted the chain because it offers padded bikini tops to the same age group.[137]

Is Beauty Universal?

As we noted, the evidence continues to mount that at least some of our tastes for physical features are "wired in" genetically. What cues lead us to view some faces as beautiful or handsome as opposed to others? Specifically, people appear to favor features we associate with good health and youth because these signal reproductive ability and strength. These characteristics include large eyes, high cheekbones, and a narrow jaw. Believe it or not, another cue that people across ethnic and racial groups use to signal sexual desirability is whether the person's facial features are balanced (i.e., if the two sides of the face are in proportion to one another). This is a signal of good health. Sure enough, people with symmetrical features on average start having sex 3 to 4 years earlier than those with unbalanced features.[138]

Men also use a woman's body shape as a sexual cue; an evolutionary explanation is that feminine curves provide evidence of reproductive potential. During puberty, a typical female gains almost 35 pounds of "reproductive fat" around the hips and thighs that supply the approximately 80,000 extra calories she will need to support a pregnancy. Most fertile women have waist-to-hip ratios of 0.6 to 0.8, an hourglass shape that also happens to be the one men rank highest. Even though preferences for overall weight change over time, waist-to-hip ratios tend to stay in this range. Even the super thin model Twiggy (who pioneered the "waif look" decades before Kate Moss) had a ratio of 0.73.[139]

How do women infer that a potential male mate has desirable characteristics of strength and health? They tend to favor men with heavy lower faces (an indication of a high concentration of androgens that impart strength), those who are slightly above average in height, and those with prominent brows. In one study, women viewed a series of male headshots that had been digitally altered to exaggerate or minimize masculine traits. They saw men with square jaws and well-defined brow ridges as good short-term partners, whereas they preferred those with feminine traits, such as rounder faces and fuller lips, for long-term mates. Overwhelmingly, participants said those with more masculine features were likely to be risky and competitive and also more apt to fight, challenge bosses, cheat on spouses, and put less effort into parenting. They assumed that men with more feminine faces would be good parents and husbands, hard workers, and emotionally supportive mates.[140]

These findings also relate to the emerging—and controversial—work in neuroendocrinological science we discussed earlier in the chapter. In another study, researchers showed women in Japan and Scotland a series of computer-generated photos of male faces that were systematically altered in terms of such dimensions as the size of the jaw and the prominence of the eyebrow ridge.[141] Women in the study preferred the heavier masculine features when they were ovulating, but these choices shifted during other parts of their monthly cycles.

Jaw size aside, the way we "package" our bodies still varies enormously, and that's where marketers come in: Advertising and other forms of mass media play a significant role in determining which forms of beauty we consider desirable at any point in time. An ideal of beauty functions as a sort of cultural yardstick. Consumers compare themselves to some standard (often one the fashion media advocate at that time), and they are dissatisfied with their appearance to the extent that they don't match up to it. This may lower their own self-esteem or, in some cases, possibly diminish the effectiveness of an ad because of negative feelings a highly attractive model arouses.[142]

Our language provides phrases to sum up these cultural ideals. We may talk about a "bimbo," a "girl-next-door," or an "ice queen," or we may refer to specific women who have come to embody an ideal, such as J-Lo, Gwyneth Paltrow, the late Princess Diana,

While Americans spend billions of dollars per year to fix less-than-perfect teeth, a new craze among Japanese women is to pay to have straight teeth made crooked. People in the U.S. refer negatively to this look as "snaggleteeth," or "fangs," but many Japanese men find what they call *yaeba* (double tooth) attractive. Blogs celebrate the yaeba look and woman pay dentists to attach pieces of plastic to their real teeth to achieve it.[143]

Source: © Philip Bigg/Alamy.

and before her the late Princess Grace.[144] Similar descriptions for men include "jock," "pretty boy," and "bookworm," or a "Brad Pitt type," a "Wesley Snipes type," and so on.

Ideals of Female Beauty Evolve Over Time

Although beauty may "only be skin deep," throughout history women have worked hard to attain it. They starved themselves; painfully bound their feet; inserted plates into their lips; spent countless hours under hair dryers, in front of mirrors, and beneath tanning lights; and opted for breast reduction or enlargement operations.

We characterize periods of history by a specific "look," or ideal of beauty. Often these relate to broader cultural happenings, such as today's emphasis on fitness and toned bodies. A look at U.S. history reveals a succession of dominant ideals. For example, in sharp contrast to today's emphasis on health and vigor, in the early 1800s it was fashionable to appear delicate to the point of looking ill. The poet John Keats described the ideal woman of that time as "a milk white lamb that bleats for man's protection." Other past looks include the voluptuous, lusty woman that Lillian Russell made popular; the athletic Gibson Girl of the 1890s; and the small, boyish flapper of the 1920s exemplified by the silent movie actress Clara Bow.[145] Marilyn Monroe died in 1962, but she represents a cultural ideal of beauty that persists to this day. M.A.C. introduced a line of cosmetics named after her and Macy's launched a Marilyn clothing line.[146]

In much of the 19th century, the desirable waistline for U.S. women was 18 inches, a circumference that required the use of corsets pulled so tight that they routinely caused headaches, fainting spells, and possibly even the uterine and spinal disorders common among women of the time. Although modern women are not quite as "straight-laced," many still endure such indignities as high heels, body waxing, eyelifts, and liposuction. In addition to the millions women spend on cosmetics, clothing, health clubs, and fashion magazines, these practices remind us that—rightly or wrongly—the desire to conform to current standards of beauty is alive and well.

Our culture communicates these standards—subtly and not so subtly—virtually everywhere we turn: on magazine covers, in department store windows, on TV shows. Feminists argue that fashion dolls, such as the ubiquitous Barbie, reinforce an unnatural ideal of thinness. When we extrapolate the dimensions of these dolls to average female body sizes, indeed they are unnaturally long and thin.[147] If the traditional Barbie doll were a real woman, her dimensions would be 38–18–34! Mattel conducted "plastic surgery" on Barbie to give her a less pronounced bust and slimmer hips, but she is still not exactly dumpy.[148] The company now sells an even more realistic Barbie featuring wider hips and a smaller bust.[149]

As we've seen, the ideal body type of Western women changes over time—check out portraits of models from several hundred years ago by Botticelli and others to appreciate by just how much. These changes periodically cause us to redefine *sexual dimorphic markers*, which are those aspects of the body that distinguish between the sexes. The first part of the 1990s saw the emergence of the controversial "waif" look in which successful models (most notably Kate Moss) had bodies that resembled those of young boys. Using heights and weights from winners of the Miss America pageant, nutrition experts concluded that many beauty queens were in the undernourished range. In the 1920s, contestants had a body mass index in the range now considered normal (20 to 25). Since then, an increasing number of winners have had indexes under 18.5, which is the World Health Organization's standard for undernutrition.[150]

Similarly, a study of almost 50 years of *Playboy* centerfolds shows that the women have become less shapely since Marilyn Monroe graced the first edition with a voluptuous hourglass figure of 37–23–36. However, a magazine spokesman comments, "As time has gone on and women have become more athletic, more in the business world and more inclined to put themselves through fitness regimes, their bodies have changed, and we reflect that as well...."[151] Fair enough. Indeed, a recent reexamination of centerfold data shows that the trend toward increasing thinness seems to have stabilized and may actually have begun to reverse. Still, although the women shown in the magazine became somewhat heavier over the 21-year period the researchers reviewed, the Playmates remain markedly below weights medical experts consider normal for their age group.[152] Ironically, when researchers ask women to predict how men will rate women of different body shapes, women choose thinner figures than do men. In other words, they think men prefer skinny fashion model types, when in fact the shapes men choose come closer to the "real" women.[153]

The Western Ideal of Female Beauty

The French Parliament is talking about legislation that would regulate the minimum weight for fashion models. It wants to combat widespread problems among women who starve themselves to stay thin enough to succeed in this competitive business. If this law passes, a 5'7" model would need to weigh at least 120 pounds for a modeling agency to avoid criminal penalties. The "you can never be too thin or too rich" debate goes on in other countries as well, especially after the well-publicized deaths of several malnourished models—including a French woman who at one point before she died weighed only 55 pounds.

Some people exaggerate the connection between self-esteem and appearance to such an extent that they sacrifice their health to attain what they consider to be a desirable body image. Women in particular tend to pick up messages from the media that the quality of their bodies reflects their self-worth, so it is not surprising that most (though certainly not all) major **body image distortions** occur among females. These psychological disorders cause the patient to believe that his or her body literally is bigger or smaller than others see it.

Researchers link a distorted body image to eating disorders, which are particularly prevalent among young women. People with *anorexia* perceive themselves as too fat, and they virtually starve themselves in the quest for thinness. This condition often results in *bulimia*, which involves two stages. First, binge eating occurs (usually in private), in which a person may consume more than 5,000 calories at one time. The binge is followed by induced vomiting, abuse of laxatives, fasting, or overly strenuous exercise—a "purging" process that reasserts the woman's sense of control.

Most eating disorders occur among white, upper-middle-class teens and college-age women. Victims often have brothers or fathers who are hypercritical of their weight; these disorders are also associated with a history of sexual abuse.[154] In addition, one's peers can encourage binge eating; groups such as athletic teams, cheerleading squads, and sororities may reinforce this practice. In one study of a college sorority, members' popularity within the group increased the more they binged.[155]

What Is Today's Ideal of Female Beauty?

Of course the pendulum is always moving because cultural changes modify the ideals of beauty that are dominant at one point in time. In late 2014 Kim Kardashian supposedly "broke the Internet" when many thousands of people clicked on a link to see a revealing photo of her large (and allegedly PhotoShop enhanced) backside on the cover of *Paper* magazine.[156] A hit music video by Jennifer Lopez and Iggy Azalea called "Booty" helped to drive the trend toward, shall we say, a more pronounced female silhouette.

It's not surprising that standards are changing because the typical woman's body is no longer as "petite" as it used to be. The most commonly purchased dress today is a size 14; it was a size 8 in 1985! The size and shape of the "average" U.S. consumer is dramatically different from what it was 60 years ago; essentially the fashion industry is selling clothing to super thin women who don't exist (at least not many of them do). The U.S. government estimates that two-thirds of U.S. adults are overweight or obese. Nevertheless, apparel companies still develop clothing lines based on a 1941 military study that set sizing standards based on a small sample of mostly white, young (and presumably physically fit) female soldiers. Indeed, even the sizes we wear send messages about body ideals. Clothing manufacturers often offer **vanity sizing**, where they deliberately assign smaller sizes to garments. Women prefer to buy the smaller size, even if the label is inaccurate. Those who have low self-esteem related to appearance think of themselves more positively and believe they are thinner when they wear vanity sizes.[157]

In addition, standards based on this outdated snapshot of U.S. women need to recognize the diversity of today's ethnic population: According to current criteria, 78 percent of African American women and 72 percent of Hispanic women are overweight, compared with 58 percent of white women. Non-Caucasian body shapes differ as well; for example, Hispanic Americans and Asian Americans tend to be shorter than their Caucasian counterparts.

For several years Dove's Campaign for Real Beauty has drawn attention to unrealistic beauty ideals as it features women with imperfect bodies in advertising. One ad read, "Let's face it, firming the thighs of a size 8 supermodel wouldn't have been much of a challenge." Unilever initiated the campaign after its research showed that many women didn't believe its products worked because the women who used them in its ads didn't look realistic.[158] When the company asked 3,200 women around the world to describe their looks, most summed themselves up as "average" or "natural." Only 2 percent called themselves "beautiful."

The growing popularity of "full-figured" women, such as Oprah, Queen Latifah, and Rosie O'Donnell, and plus-size spokesmodels, such as Emme, also has helped to improve the self-esteem of larger women. In reality, plus-size clothes have been available for almost a century, ever since a Lithuanian immigrant, Lena Bryant (her name was later misspelled as "Lane" on a business form), transformed a maternity-wear business into a line for stout women in the 1920s. Today, mass-market stores like Forever 21 and Target and upscale designers like Elie Tahari have turned their attention to the larger woman.

Nonetheless, **fattism** is deeply ingrained in our culture: As early as nursery school age, children prefer drawings of peers in wheelchairs, on crutches, or with facial disfigurements to those of fat children. One survey of girls aged 12 to 19 reported that 55 percent said they see ads "all the time" that make them want to go on a diet.[159] A recent advertising controversy testifies to our thinness mania: It was bad enough when Pepsi unveiled its new "skinny" diet soda can. When the company paired the launch with Fashion Week—the huge promotion for an industry that celebrates skinny models (some of whom have died from anorexia)—the National Eating Disorders Association protested and Pepsi had to apologize. The organization also persuaded Apple to shut down an ad campaign because it was built around the message, "You can never be too thin or too powerful."[160]

However larger consumers are fighting back against these stereotypes. As the name of a Dutch magazine proclaims, *Big is Beautiful*.[161] A recent study focused on **fatshionistas**, plus-sized consumers who want more options from mainstream fashion marketers. A blog post the researchers found sums up the alienation many of these women feel:

> For many of us who were fat as children and teens, clothes shopping was nothing short of tortuous. Even if our parents were supportive, the selection of "husky" or "half-sizes" for kids was the absolute pits. When that sort of experience is reinforced as a child, we often take it into adulthood.... We simply have been socialized not to expect better than to be treated as fashion afterthoughts.

The researchers investigated the triggers that mobilize these women to try to change the market to make it friendlier to shoppers who don't conform to a pencil-thin ideal of beauty. They found that indeed these consumers can agitate for change, especially when they create a common community of like-minded people (the "Fat Acceptance Movement") who can rally behind others who have successfully challenged the status quo.

One "heroine" of this movement is the indie-rock singer Beth Ditto, who at slightly more than 5 feet tall weighs more than 200 pounds. She has successfully defied the "fat" stereotype and even launched her own fashion line. Ditto also was the opening model at a Jean Paul Gaultier runway show during Paris Fashion Week.[162] And recently Target launched a plus-size product line after a popular blogger with almost 70,000 Instagram followers started a boycott against the stores because of its lack of plus-size inventory. In an open letter to the company, she wrote: "All I want is the clothing you offer all your other regular sized customers, but you always leave me out.... You have once again made me feel like a second-class customer and because of that I'm going to have to discontinue my relationship with you altogether." Guess what? Target made her a brand ambassador for its new line, AVA & VIV.[163] There really is something to this social media stuff.

Ideals of Male Beauty

It's hard not to notice that many business leaders and celebrities recently have sprouted a lot of facial hair. Beards were a no-no for over a century; in the early to mid-1800s people commonly associated them with socialists and others on the margins of society. Friedrich Engels (who co-authored *The Communist Manifesto* with Karl Marx) once sponsored a "moustache evening" to taunt the clean-shaven members of the bourgeois class.

Then in the latter part of the century the "beard movement" came into fashion as the Gold Rush and the Civil War made shaving optional; and some rebelled against a world of "woman-faced men." As Robber Barons like full-bearded Jay Gould and Andrew Carnegie flouted their millions, beards now became linked to capitalists. The pendulum swung yet again, however, as workers' rebellions evoked images of bearded men committing violent acts against their bosses. King C. Gillette invented the safety razor in 1901, and the clean-shaven look was back. Now, the pendulum has moved again: Google's co-founder Sergey Brin, Goldman Sachs's chief executive, Lloyd C. Blankfein, and Marc Benioff, the billionaire founder and chief executive of Salesforce, all sport prominent facial hair.[164]

As this brief history of facial hair illustrates, a society's ideals of beauty for men change as well. Who could confuse Justin Bieber with Johnny Depp? Male ideals involve length of hair, the presence and type of facial hair (or not), musculature, and of course clothing styles and accessories (anyone for a "murse" aka "man bag?"). We also distinguish among ideals of beauty for men in terms of facial features, musculature, and facial hair. In fact, one national survey that asked both men and women to comment on male aspects of appearance found that the dominant standard of beauty for men is a strongly masculine, muscled body, though women tend to prefer men with less muscle mass than men themselves strive to attain.[165]

The Tangled Web

At least 400 Web sites attract young people with "ana" and "mia," nicknames for anorexia and bulimia. These "communities" offer tips on crash dieting, bingeing, vomiting, and hiding weight loss from concerned parents. **Group dieting** is a growing problem as consumers patronize blog rings devoted to excessive weight loss—especially when they challenge female college students to lose as much weight as possible before events such as spring break. In one typical post, a woman confessed to eating "one cracker, one strawberry and a little bit of soup" in a 24-hour period, whereas another recounted a lunch of a slice of mango and a stick of gum. These sites, often adorned with photos of ultrathin celebrities and slogans such as "Diet Coke Is Life," appeal to followers of an underground movement called *pro-ana* (pro-anorexia) who sometimes identify themselves in public when they wear red bracelets.

Advertisers appear to have the males' ideal in mind; a study of men who appear in advertisements found that most sport the strong and muscular physique of the male stereotype.[166] More than 40 percent of boys in middle school and high school say they exercise regularly to increase muscle mass. Perhaps more troubling, 38 percent say they use protein supplements, and nearly 6 percent admit they have experimented with steroids.[167]

OBJECTIVE 6-5

Every culture dictates certain types of body decoration or mutilation.

Body Decoration and Mutilation

People in every culture adorn or alter their bodies in some way. Decorating the physical self serves a number of purposes:[168]

- **To separate group members from nonmembers**—One Native American tribe, the Chinook, pressed the head of a newborn between two boards for a year, which permanently altered its shape. In our society, teens go out of their way to adopt distinctive hair and clothing styles that will separate them from adults.
- **To place the individual in the social organization**—Many cultures engage in puberty rites during which a boy symbolically becomes a man. Some young men in part of Ghana paint their bodies with white stripes to resemble skeletons to symbolize the death of their child status. In Western cultures, this rite may involve some form of mild self-mutilation or engaging in dangerous activities.
- **To place the person in a gender category**—The Tchikrin, American Indians of South America, insert a string of beads in a boy's lip to enlarge it. Western women wear lipstick to enhance femininity. At the turn of the 20th century, small lips were fashionable because they represented women's submissive role at that time.[169] Today, big, red lips are provocative and indicate an aggressive sexuality.
- **To enhance sex-role identification**—We can compare the modern use of high heels, which podiatrists agree are a prime cause of knee and hip problems, backaches, and fatigue, with the traditional Asian practice of foot binding to enhance femininity. As one doctor observed, "When [women] get home, they can't get their high-heeled shoes off fast enough. But every doctor in the world could yell from now until Doomsday, and women would still wear them."[170]
- **To indicate desired social conduct**—The Suya of South America wear ear ornaments to emphasize the importance placed on listening and obedience in their culture. In Western society, some gay men may wear an earring in the left or right ear to signal what role (submissive or dominant) they prefer in a relationship.

The e-commerce site Rent the Runway replaces models with regular women and allows visitors to search for women of a certain age, height, weight, and even bust size to see how that dress looks on someone similar. Shoppers can review dresses they have rented and have the option to list their height, weight, and chest size alongside their reviews. That feature allows other women to search for customers who have similar dimensions and ask them questions. The strategy seems to be working: The company found that the conversion rate for shoppers who clicked on real photos was double that of shoppers who clicked on models' photos.[171]

Source: Rent the Runway.

RENT THE RUNWAY

A Russian artist takes body decoration to a new extreme: He describes himself as a platypus – and indeed his lips extend more than two inches from his face.
Source: News Dog Media.

Marketing Pitfall

In a previous era, wealthy women avoided the sun at all costs lest people get the impression that they had to work for a living outdoors. The bias toward pale skin extends to other cultures as well. An ad on Malaysian television showed an attractive college student who can't get a second glance from a boy at the next desk. "She's pretty," he says to himself, "but ...." Then she applies Pond's Skin Lightening Moisturizer by Unilever PLC, and she reappears looking several shades paler. Now the boy wonders, "Why didn't I notice her before?" In many Asian cultures, people also historically equate light skin with wealth and status, and they associate dark skin with the laboring class that toils in the fields. This stereotype persists today: In a survey, 74 percent of men in Malaysia, 68 percent in Hong Kong, and 55 percent in Taiwan said they are more attracted to women with fair complexions. About a third of the female respondents in each country said they use skin-whitening products. Olay has a product it calls White Radiance, and L'Oréal sells a White Perfect line.[176]

In contrast, Caucasians in the U.S. today equate a tanned complexion with health, physical activity and an abundance of leisure time... Indoor tanning at salons with names such as Eternal Summer and Tan City is popular among many U.S. young people, despite evidence that links this practice to skin cancer. A recent analysis found that tanning beds account for as many as 400,000 cases of skin cancer in the United States each year, including 6,000 cases of melanoma, which is the deadliest form of the disease. The rate of melanoma among women younger than 40 has risen significantly in recent years. Public health officials report that one-third of Caucasian teenage girls say they have engaged in indoor tanning. And, about half of the top-rated colleges in the United States offer tanning beds either on campus or in off-campus housing.[177] Is skin cancer too high a price to pay to attain an ideal of beauty?

- **To indicate high status or rank**—The Hidates, American Indians of North America, wear feather ornaments that indicate how many people they have killed. In our society, some people wear glasses with clear lenses, even though they do not have eye problems, to enhance their perceived status.
- **To provide a sense of security**—Consumers often wear lucky charms, amulets, and rabbits' feet to protect them from the "evil eye." Some modern women wear a "mugger whistle" around their necks for a similar reason.

Body Anxiety

A billboard that shows a woman wearing a tank top and raising her arm to show off her underarm proclaims, "Dear New Jersey: When people call you 'the Armpit of America,' take it as a compliment. Sincerely, Dove." It's part of a campaign for Dove Advanced Care, a new deodorant product with moisturizers for underarms."[172] It looks like women have another body part to worry about.

Because many consumers experience a gap between their real and ideal physical selves, they often go to great lengths to change aspects of their appearance. From girdles to bras, cosmetics to plastic surgery, tanning salons to diet drinks, a multitude of products and services promise to alter aspects of the physical self. It is difficult to overstate the importance of the physical self-concept (and consumers' desires to improve their appearances) to many marketing activities. To rub salt into the wound, there is evidence that exposure to these messages increases the desire to conform to a cultural ideal (such as thinness for women) but also decreases a person's belief that they can attain this ideal. One recent study reported that when women in a weight loss program were repeatedly exposed to images of a thin model, they saw their dieting goals as less attainable and actually consumed more unhealthy snacks.[173]

Cosmetic Surgery

Consumers increasingly choose to have cosmetic surgery to change a poor body image or simply to enhance appearance.[174] In Venezuela, billboards advertise bank loans to obtain breast augmentations; a political candidate even tried to finance his campaign by raffling off a breast lift.[175] Cosmetic procedures are so fashionable that a woman with implants is often casually referred to as "an operated woman." South Korea, which boasts the highest rate of cosmetic surgery of any country, is attracting hordes of Chinese consumers who flock there for double eyelid surgery or more radical facial restructuring that often involves painful procedures to alter their faces into a V-shape that results in delicate features their culture values.. The Korean government even provides funding to promote the country's

In Venezuela, women are confronted with a culture of increasingly enhanced physiques fueled by beauty pageants and plastic surgery.

Source: Meridith Kohut/The New York Times.

medical tourism business. This term describes a rapidly growing sector of the global economy that encourages consumers to travel to other countries for surgical procedures that might be unavailable, more dangerous, or more expensive where they live.[178]

According to the American Academy of Cosmetic Surgery, doctors in the United States perform nearly 860,000 cosmetic-surgery procedures each year—and men make up more than 150,000 of the patients. As cosmetic surgery becomes increasingly acceptable (even expected in some circles), consumers and the medical profession expand the scope of body parts they want to alter. Perhaps spurred by fashions such as low-rise jeans and spandex workout gear that call attention to the derrière, for example, buttock augmentation surgery is gaining in popularity. The operation typically costs about $20,000, so clearly it's not intended for the bottom of the market.[179]

The craze for "modifications" even extends to younger consumers who (one would think) don't need it—at least not yet. The American Society of Plastic Surgeons reports that doctors give about 12,000 Botox injections to U.S. teens aged 13 to 19 annually. Although there are some sound medical reasons for this, such as abnormal twitching of the eyelid or involuntary contractions of neck muscles, apparently most young patients elect to have the treatment to address perceived imperfections such as a too-gummy smile and a too-square jaw. Some teenagers mistakenly think that Botox can prevent wrinkles.[180]

Tattoos

Tattoos—both temporary and permanent—today are a popular form of body adornment.[181] Mattel Inc. even released Totally Stylin' Tattoos Barbie, which comes with tiny tattoos her young owners can put on her body. The doll also comes with wash-off tats kids can use to ink themselves.[182]

Although consumers young and old (okay, mostly young) sport body art to make statements about the self, these skin designs actually serve some of the same functions that other kinds of body painting do in primitive cultures. Tattoos (from the Tahitian *ta-tu*) have deep roots in folk art. Until recently, the images were crude and were primarily death symbols (e.g., a skull), animals (especially panthers, eagles, and snakes), pinup women, or military designs. More current influences include science fiction themes, Japanese symbolism, and tribal designs.

Historically, people associated tattoos with social outcasts. For example, authorities in 6th-century Japan tattooed the faces and arms of criminals to identify them, and these markings served the same purpose in 19th-century prisons and 20th-century

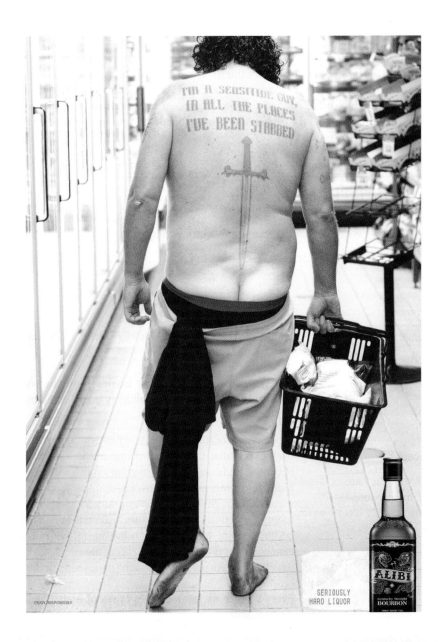

concentration camps. Marginal groups, such as bikers or Japanese *yakuza* (gang members), often use these emblems to express group identity and solidarity.

Today, a tattoo is a fairly risk-free way to express an adventurous side of the self. About 1 in 5 Americans have at least one, and women are twice as likely to sport a tattoo compared to men. The most popular ink site for women: the ankle.[183]

As more people jump on the tattoo bandwagon it's inevitable that some of them will regret this decision later (perhaps when they wake up in the morning?). Tattoo removal centers with names such as Dr. Tattoff, Tat2BeGone, and Tattoo MD meet the need to deal with so-called "tattoo regret." Industry data indicate that at least 45,000 Americans undergo tattoo removal each year. Unfortunately—at least for now—it's a lot more complicated to remove a tattoo than to put one on. A design that cost several hundred dollars could require several thousand dollars and many laser sessions to remove.[184] The moral: Before you get a significant other's name etched onto your body, be pretty sure you plan to stay together.

Body Piercing

Like tattoos, body piercing evolved from a practice associated with fringe groups to a popular fashion statement. Historians credit the initial impetus for the mainstreaming of what had been an underground West Coast fad to Aerosmith's 1993 video for the song "Cryin'," in which actress Alicia Silverstone gets both a navel ring and a tattoo.[185] Piercings can range from a hoop protruding from a navel to scalp implants, where metal posts are inserted in the skull (do not try this at home!). Publications such as *Piercing Fans International Quarterly* see their circulations soar, and Web sites attract numerous followers. According to one recent estimate, about 14 percent of Americans have at least one body piercing other than in an earlobe. About three-fourths of these people are female; the most popular site is the navel.[186]

MyLab Marketing

To complete the problems with the ✪, go to EOC Discussion Questions in the MyLab as well as additional Marketing Metrics questions only available in MyLab Marketing.

CHAPTER SUMMARY

1. The self-concept strongly influences consumer behavior.

Consumers' self-concepts are reflections of their attitudes toward themselves. Whether these attitudes are positive or negative, they will help to guide many purchase decisions; we can use products to bolster self-esteem or to "reward" the self.

2. Products often define a person's self-concept.

We choose many products because we think that they are similar to our personalities. The symbolic interactionist perspective of the self implies that each of us actually has many selves, and we require a different set of products as props to play each role. We view many things other than the body as part of who we are. People use valued objects, cars, homes, and even attachments to sports teams or national monuments to define the self, when they incorporate these into the extended self.

3. Gender identity is an important component of a consumer's self-concept.

Sex roles, or a society's conceptions about masculinity and femininity, exert a powerful influence on our expectations about the brands we should consume. Advertising plays an important role because it portrays idealized expectations about gender identity.

4. The way we think about our bodies (and the way our culture tells us we should think) is a key component of self-esteem.

A person's conception of his or her body also provides feedback to self-image. A culture communicates specific ideals of beauty, and consumers go to great lengths to attain these. Many consumer activities involve manipulating the body, whether through dieting, cosmetic surgery, piercing, or tattooing. Sometimes these activities are carried to an extreme because people try too hard to live up to cultural ideals. One common manifestation is eating disorders, diseases in which women in particular become obsessed with thinness.

5. Every culture dictates certain types of body decoration or mutilation.

Body decoration or mutilation may serve such functions as separating group members from nonmembers, marking the individual's status or rank within a social organization or within a gender category (e.g., homosexual), or even providing a sense of security or good luck.

KEY TERMS

Actual self, 202
Agentic goals, 214
Androgyny, 218
Badges, 209
Body image, 221
Body image distortions, 225
Bromance, 215
Collective self, 201
Communal goals, 214

Compensatory consumption, 207
Contemporary young mainstream
    female achievers (CYMFA), 216
Digital self, 211
Dramaturgical perspective, 203
Embodied cognition, 210
Empty self, 205
Enclothed cognition, 210
Extended self, 208

Fantasy, 203
Fatshionistas, 227
Fattism, 226
Gender identity, 213
Gender socialization, 214
Gender-bending products, 220
Geospatial platforms, 209
Group dieting, 227
Ideal of beauty, 222

REVIEW

6-1 What is the Big Five?

 6-2 Compare and contrast the real versus the ideal self. List three products for which a person is likely to use each type of self as a reference point when he or she considers a purchase.

6-3 How might the "digital self" differ from a consumer's self-concept in the real world, and why is this difference potentially important to marketers?

 6-4 Have ideals of beauty in the United States changed during the past 50 years? If so, how?

6-5 What is vanity sizing?

6-6 What does "the looking-glass self" mean? How do feelings about the self influence what we buy?

6-7 How do Eastern and Western cultures differ in terms of how people think about the self?

6-8 How are subjective views of body image exploited by marketers?

CONSUMER BEHAVIOR CHALLENGE

■ DISCUSS

6-9 To what extent do your purchasing habits reflect your own personality?

6-10 Are you what you *post online*?

6-11 According to the Web site Voucher Codes, "pester power" costs U.K. parents $750 per year. The children were clearly influenced by advertising, and parents often used diversionary tactics to put them off the scent. One parent in 10, according to the study, gave in and made the purchase whether the child needed the item or not. What is pester power, and is it a problem in your country?

6-12 How might a marketer frame a marketing campaign aimed at contemporary young mainstream female achievers (CYMFA)? Are there any key differences or similarities to the broader female market that can be used?

6-13 One consequence of the continual evolution of sex roles is that men are concerned as never before with their appearance. Men spend $7.7 billion on grooming products globally each year. A wave of male cleansers, moisturizers, sunscreens, depilatories, and body sprays washes up on U.S. shores, largely from European marketers. L'Oréal Paris reports that men's skincare products are now its fastest-growing sector. In Europe, 24 percent of men younger than age 30 use skincare products—and 80 percent of young Korean men do. Even some cosmetics products, like foundation and eyeliner, are catching on in some segments, though men aren't comfortable owning up to using them. In fact, a British makeup product looks like a ballpoint pen so men can apply it secretly at the office.[187] Over the past decade, the media paid a lot of attention to so-called "metrosexuals": straight males who are interested in fashion, home design, gourmet cooking, and personal care products. How widespread is this phenomenon? Do you see men in your age group focusing on these interests? Should marketers change how they think of male sex roles today?

6-14 Some activists object to Axe's male-focused marketing because they claim it demeans women. In contrast, Dove's "Natural Beauty" campaign gets kudos because it promotes more realistic expectations for girls. Guess what? The same company—Unilever—owns both Axe and Dove. Is it hypocritical for a big company to sponsor positive messages about women in one of its divisions while it sends a different message in another?

6-15 Jenny Darroch of the Drucker School of Management focuses much of her research on how to market to women. She believes that around 85 percent of all family household purchases occur as a result of a decision made by a woman. The other major consideration is the growth of demographic data and how it is being used to target women as decision makers. Darroch is firmly of the opinion that marketers need to consider whether gender plays a role in a purchasing decision.[188] The motivation behind a potential purchase may be entirely gender-driven. A potential automobile purchase might mean that a man is more interested in style and performance while a woman is more concerned with practicalities such as space, affordability, and fuel consumption. What marketing advice would you suggest when targeting female customers?

6-16   The clothing chain H&M features computer-generated models on its Web site. The company drew criticism for presenting only picture-perfect people; for example, the Norwegian Broadcasting Corporation accused the chain of "creating unrealistic physical ideals." A

company spokesman defended the move by explaining that these unreal bodies would ensure that the garments remain the focus of online shoppers' attention. In contrast, the teen-oriented magazine *Seventeen* pledged to always feature "real girls" in its pages. This change was in response to an online petition that gathered nearly 85,000 signatures in just 4 days. The 14-year-old reader who posted the petition stated, "For the sake of all the struggling girls all over America, who read *Seventeen* and think these fake images are what they should be, I'm stepping up. I know how hurtful these photoshopped images can be."[189] What do you think of this argument—does the use of only "perfect" bodies create a problem for real shoppers?

■ APPLY

6-17   If our possessions do indeed come to be a part of us, how do we bring ourselves to part with these precious items? Researchers find that people often take steps to distance themselves from a favored object before they get rid of it. Strategies they identified include taking pictures and videos of the objects; moving them into an out-of-the way location such as a garage or an attic; or washing, ironing, and wrapping the item. Interview people you know who have disposed of a product that was important to them—for example, a well-used car or a favorite sweatshirt that finally had too many holes to keep. What steps did they take to "divest" themselves of this attachment (such as removing personal items from a car before selling it, etc.).[190]

6-18   Construct a "consumption biography" of a friend or family member. Make a list of or photograph his or her favorite possessions, and see if you or others can describe this person's personality just from the information provided by this catalog.

6-19   Interview victims of burglaries, or people who have lost personal property in floods, hurricanes, or other natural disasters. How do they go about reconstructing their possessions, and what effect did the loss appear to have on them? Similarly, poll your class: If their house or apartment was on fire and they could only take one possession with them as they evacuate, what would it be?

6-20   Some people sacrifice their health to attain what they consider to be a desirable body image. Is this a problem in your country?

6-21   Clearly some products and services are necessarily gender orientated, but many products are needlessly

gender-specific. Many women would also point out that female versions of a product are often more expensive too. Identify some products that are needlessly gender-specific.

6-22   How do people you know feel about their cars? Interview some of them about the "relationships" they have. Do they decorate their cars? Do they have nicknames for them? And, check out a video on YouTube called "I Love My Car" to really see how deep these relationships can go.

6-23   Many advertisers routinely purchase stock photography when they need an image of a certain kind of person to insert in an ad. Many photos of women reflect common stereotypes, ranging from the crisp businesswoman who wears a suit and glasses and holds a briefcase to the smiling mother who pours milk into cereal bowls for her kids at breakfast. Sheryl Sandberg, the Facebook executive who is an advocate for women in business, started an organization called Lean In to promote leadership. Lean In has now partnered with Getty Images, one of the biggest stock photography companies, to offer an image collection that represents women differently. The new collection depicts women as surgeons, painters, bakers, soldiers and hunters. There are girls riding skateboards and women lifting weights.[191] Look through a sample of current magazines and collect images of women. To what extent do they represent a range of roles? Categorize these images according to the type of product advertised and the situation the photo depicts (e.g., multitasking woman holding a tablet and a baby, happy homemaker, etc.). Based on what you find, what messages do our media give us about gender roles today?

Case Study

L'ORÉAL AGE PERFECT—BECAUSE THEY'RE WORTH IT

L'Oréal Paris's signature slogan "Because I'm worth it" is one of the most recognizable of all time. It was first introduced in 1973 by L'Oreal Paris when it was launching its hair color products in the United States; since then, the company has grown into a cosmetics giant that markets a range of beauty and makeup products in more than 130 countries, and the slogan still resonates with women's conceptions of beauty and self-esteem around the world.

L'Oréal Paris adopted a very modern approach to its communication strategy when it ran the "Because I'm worth it" advertising campaign. Before the campaign, advertising mostly involved male voiceovers talking about women's products. L'Oréal initiated the trend of women speaking for themselves, highlighting their self-confidence, independence, and self-fulfillment. A 23-year-old female copy writer from McKann Erickson created the slogan at the height of the feminist movement in the 1970s. The slogan struck the right chord, communicating independence, respect, and recognition for women. This led to the development of a long line of successful celebrity endorsements by more than 35 diverse international female ambassadors, including Jane Fonda, Eva Longoria, Jennifer Lopez, Beyoncé, and Aishwarya Rai. The slogan has changed little over the years, the only variations being "Because you're worth it" and "Because we're worth it" to adapt to the changing times and circumstances.

Over the years, L'Oréal has continued to partner with female brand ambassadors belonging to different age groups from across the globe. Many of L'Oréal's brand ambassadors have been relatively younger female celebrities, a global trend in the cosmetic industry. But L'Oréal has shown a higher degree of inclusivity by offering specific beauty products for older women like the L'Oréal Age Perfect Range. L'Oréal recognized that women's concepts of beauty are evolving, and older women increasingly prefer age-appropriate beauty products that address their specific needs. L'Oréal's Age Perfect range offers many products that cater to such needs, including Excellence Hair Color, Cell Renewal Day Cream, Glow Renewal Day/Night Cream, and Eye Renewal Eye Cream.

For its Age Perfect Range, L'Oréal partnered with the acclaimed actress Dame Helen Mirren in 2015. L'Oréal's decision to have Dame Mirren as a spokesperson for the Age Perfect brand has been welcomed in the beauty world for its celebration of older women. The ads for the Age Perfect Range present Dame Mirren as very candid, un-retouched; she promotes the idea of aging with a confident attitude, saying "Grow another year bolder." In one of the ads for Age Perfect, Helen makes a bold statement by wearing a black leather jacket, a sleek fitting skirt, and bright red lipstick. She gives a twist to the brand's famous tagline by asking, "So are we worth it?" and answers with a mischievous grin, "More than ever."

By endorsing its Age Perfect line through bold celebrity ambassadors, L'Oréal reinforces its brand personality, promoting itself as a brand that is still relevant to women's self-concept and self-importance in the twenty-first century. With the Age Perfect range, L'Oréal overtly endorses that the idea that beauty and the use of cosmetics are not limited to younger women, and it encourages older women to indulge themselves and enjoy and take pride in growing older. It reinforces this message in several slogans: "The older we get, the more fabulous we become," "Now is our time. Now is our Perfect Age," "It's taken over 60 years to look this good. We are so worth it!"

Through many online tips and tutorials, L'Oréal also shows how many Age Perfect products can be used. These tips include advice for haircuts, hair color, hair volume, foundation, lip color, eyeshades and mascara, eyebrows, makeup remover, cleansers, and moisturizers. The focus is on helping women understand how products from the Age Perfect line can be used according to their age and image.

L'Oréal's Age Perfect has been well received for its inclusivity, but the Age Perfect line has also allowed the company to effectively segment the female cosmetics market. In practice, the approach combines experimentation and redefining one's looks with the help of age-appropriate products that will address the specific beauty needs of older women—all while encouraging women to develop a bold attitude as an expression of their beauty.

DISCUSSION QUESTIONS

CS 6-1 Discuss the success of L'Oréal's slogan "Because I am worth it" over time, and how it has managed to connect with women. What is role of cosmetics in the way women of different ages look at themselves and define their self-concept and self-esteem?

CS 6-2 Comment on the role of female celebrities in delivering L'Oréal's brand message. How do you think the message of self-worth would be received by women if L'Oréal did not use celebrities in its marketing?

CS 6-3 Discuss the appeal of the Age Perfect advertising campaign for the older women. Actress Helen Mirren insisted that her facial features, including wrinkles and age spots, were not to be air brushed or retouched. Do you think this strategy will work better than glossy and airbrushed campaigns?

Sources: L'Oréal Paris, "Age Perfect for Helen Mirren's Golden Age," 2015, http://www.loreal-paris.co.uk/perfectage, accessed November 26, 2015; E. McLonan, "My Beauty Secrets—by Dame Helen: At 69, She Still Looks Stunning," *Mail Online,* 2015, http://www.dailymail.co.uk/femail/article-2926043/My-beauty-secrets-Dame-Helen-69-looks-stunning-reveals-new-ad-campaign-Helen-Mirren-tells-exclusively-does-it.html, accessed November 26, 2015; YouTube, "The History of 'Because You're Worth It,'" 2015, https://www.youtube.com/watch?v=j6DHRFuCEwA, accessed November, 26 2015; YouTube, "Helen Mirren Stars in the NEW Age Perfect TV Advert from L'Oréal Paris," 2015, https://www.youtube.com/watch?v=2ZPIqfpM3-s, accessed November 26, 2015.

MyLab Marketing

Go to the Assignments section of your MyLab to complete these writing exercises.

6-24 The chapter discusses the "empty self" explanation for the popularity of selfies among young people. Do you agree?

6-25 Societies and cultures view body decoration and mutilation in different ways. But people in nearly every society adorn or alter their bodies in some way. What are the main reasons for decorating the physical self in this way? How do these decorations inform us about these individuals?

NOTES

1. http://www.statista.com/statistics/273172/twitter-accounts-with-the-most-followers-worldwide/accessed March 18, 2015.
2. Alex Williams, "15 Minutes of Fame? More Like 15 Seconds of Nanofame," *New York Times* (February 6, 2015), http://www.nytimes.com/2015/02/08/style/15-minutes-of-fame-more-like-15-seconds-of-nanofame.html?smid=nytcore-ipad-share&smprod=nytcore-ipad&_r=0, accessed February 16, 2015.
3. Harry C. Triandis, "The Self and Social Behavior in Differing Cultural Contexts," *Psychological Review* 96, no. 3 (1989): 506–520; H. Markus and S. Kitayama, "Culture and the Self: Implications for Cognition, Emotion, and Motivation," *Psychological Review* 98 (1991): 224–253.
4. Markus and Kitayama, "Culture and the Self."
5. Nancy Wong and Aaron Ahuvia, "A Cross-Cultural Approach to Materialism and the Self," in Dominique Bouchet, ed., *Cultural Dimensions of International Marketing* (Denmark: Odense University, 1995): 68–89.
6. Morris Rosenberg, *Conceiving the Self* (New York: Basic Books, 1979); M. Joseph Sirgy, "Self-Concept in Consumer Behavior: A Critical Review," *Journal of Consumer Research* 9 (December 1982): 287–300; www.mediapost.com, accessed February 15, 2007; Roy F. Baumeister, Dianne M. Tice, and Debra G. Hutton, "Self-Presentational Motivations and Personality Differences in Self-Esteem," *Journal of Personality* 57 (September 1989): 547–575; Ronald J. Faber, "Are Self-Esteem Appeals Appealing?" in Leonard N. Reid, ed., *Proceedings of the 1992 Conference of the American Academy of Advertising* (1992): 230–235.
7. John Tierney, "Why You Won't Be the Person You Expect to Be?" *New York Times* (January 3, 2013), http://www.nytimes.com/2013/01/04/ scence/study-in-science-shows-end-of-history-illusion.html?_r=0, accessed January 23, 2013.
8. Americus Reed, Mark R. Forehand, Stefano Puntoni, and Luk Warlop, "Identity-based Consumer Behavior," *International Journal of Research in Marketing* 29, no. 4 (2012): 310–321.
9. Emily Yoffe, "You Are What You Buy," *Newsweek* (June 4, 1990): 59.
10. Derek D. Rucker, David Dubois, and Adam D. Galinsky, "Generous Paupers and Stingy Princes: Power Drives Consumer Spending on Self Versus Others," *Journal of Consumer Research* 37, no. 6 (April 2011): 1015–1029.
11. Michael Häfner, "How Dissimilar Others May Still Resemble the Self: Assimilation and Contrast After Social Comparison," *Journal of Consumer Psychology* 14, nos. 1 & 2 (2004): 187–196.
12. Marsha L. Richins, "Social Comparison and the Idealized Images of Advertising," *Journal of Consumer Research* 18 (June 1991): 71–83; Mary C. Martin and Patricia F. Kennedy, "Advertising and Social Comparison: Consequences for Female Preadolescents and Adolescents," *Psychology & Marketing* 10 (November–December 1993): 513–530; cf. also Claudia Townsend and Sanjay Sood, "Self-Affirmation Through the Choice of Highly Aesthetic Products," *Journal of Consumer Research* 39, no. 2 (2012): 415–428.
13. Philip N. Myers, Jr., and Frank A. Biocca, "The Elastic Body Image: The Effect of Television Advertising and Programming on Body Image Distortions in Young Women," *Journal of Communication* 42 (Summer 1992): 108–133.
14. Charles S. Gulas and Kim McKeage, "Extending Social Comparison: An Examination of the Unintended Consequences of Idealized Advertising Imagery," *Journal of Advertising* 29 (Summer 2000): 17–28.
15. Brent McFerran, Darren W. Dahl, Gavan J. Fitzsimons, and Andrea C. Morales, "Might an Overweight Waitress Make You Eat More? How the Body Type of Others Is Sufficient to Alter Our Food Consumption," *Journal of Consumer Psychology* 20, no. 2 (2010): 146–151; cf. also Michael

Häfner and Debra Trampe, "When Thinking Is Beneficial and When It Is Not: The Effects of Thin and Round Advertising Models," *Journal of Consumer Psychology* 19, no. 4 (2009): 619–628; Brent McFerran, Darren W. Dahl, Gavan J. Fitzsimons, and Andrea C. Morales, "I'll Have What She's Having: Effects of Social Influence and Body Type on the Food Choices of Others," *Journal of Consumer Research* 36, no. 6 (April 2010): 173–180.
16. For the seminal treatment of this process, cf. Erving Goffman, *The Presentation of Self in Everyday Life* (New York: Doubleday, 1959).
17. Quoted in Michael Slackman, "Fashion and Faith Meet, on Foreheads of the Pious," *New York Times* (December 18, 2007), www.nytimes.com, accessed March 25, 2015.
18. Scott I. Rick and Maurice E. Schweitzer, "The Imbibing Idiot Bias: Consuming Alcohol Can be Hazardous to Your (Perceived) Intelligence," *Journal of Consumer Psychology* 23, no. 2 (2013): 212–219.
19. Harrison G. Gough, Mario Fioravanti, and Renato Lazzari, "Some Implications of Self Versus Ideal-Self Congruence on the Revised Adjective Check List," *Journal of Personality & Social Psychology* 44, no. 6 (1983): 1214–1220.
20. Steven Jay Lynn and Judith W. Rhue, "Daydream Believers," *Psychology Today* (September 1985): 14.
21. Parham Aarabi, "How Brands are Using Facial Recognition to Transform Marketing," *VB News* (April 13, 2013), http://venturebeat.com/2013/04/13/marketing-facial-recognition/, accessed February 20, 2015.
22. Erving Goffman, *The Presentation of Self in Everyday Life* (Garden City, NY: Doubleday, 1959); Michael R. Solomon, "The Role of Products as Social Stimuli: A Symbolic Interactionism Perspective," *Journal of Consumer Research* 10 (December 1983): 319–329.
23. Americus Reed II, "Activating the Self-Importance of Consumer Selves: Exploring Identity Salience Effects on Judgments," *Journal of Consumer Research* 31, no. 2 (2004): 286–295.
24. Aliakbar Jafari and Christina Goulding, "'We Are Not Terrorists!' UK-Based Iranians, Consumption Practices and the 'Torn Self,'" *Consumption Markets & Culture* 11 (June 2008): 73–91.
25. Quoted in Fred Meier, "Girls Named Zoe Lose Suit Against Renault for Naming Electric Car Zoe," *DriveOn* (November 10, 2010), http://content.usatoday.com/communities/driveon/post/2010/11/girls-lose-renault-zoe-electric-car-lawsuit-over-name/1, accessed April 10, 2011.
26. George H. Mead, *Mind, Self and Society* (Chicago: University of Chicago Press, 1934).
27. Debra A. Laverie, Robert E. Kleine, and Susan Schultz Kleine, "Reexamination and Extension of Kleine, Kleine, and Kernan's Social Identity Model of Mundane Consumption: The Mediating Role of the Appraisal Process," *Journal of Consumer Research* 28 (March 2002): 659–669.
28. Jennifer Elias, "Can This Company Finally Get The Retail Fashion World Online?" *Fast Company* (June 24, 2014), http://www.fastcolabs.com/3026831/can-this-company-finally-get-the-retail-fashion-world-online, accessed March 19, 2015.
29. Charles H. Cooley, *Human Nature and the Social Order* (New York: Scribner's, 1902).
30. Jay G. Hull and Alan S. Levy, "The Organizational Functions of the Self: An Alternative to the Duval and Wicklund Model of Self-Awareness," *Journal of Personality & Social Psychology* 37 (1979): 756–768; Jay G. Hull, Ronald R. Van Treuren, Susan J. Ashford, Pamela Propsom, and Bruce W. Andrus, "Self-Consciousness and the Processing of Self-Relevant Information," *Journal of Personality & Social Psychology* 54, no. 3 (1988): 452–465.

31. Michael Moss, "Nudged to the Produce Aisle by a Look in the Mirror," *New York Times* (August 27, 2013), http://www.nytimes.com/2013/08/28/dining/wooing-us-down-the-produce-aisle.html?_r=0, accessed February 23, 2015.

32. Arnold W. Buss, *Self-Consciousness and Social Anxiety* (San Francisco: Freeman, 1980); Lynn Carol Miller and Cathryn Leigh Cox, "Public Self-Consciousness and Makeup Use," *Personality & Social Psychology Bulletin* 8, no. 4 (1982): 748–751; Michael R. Solomon and John Schopler, "Self-Consciousness and Clothing," *Personality & Social Psychology Bulletin* 8, no. 3 (1982): 508–514.

33. Loraine Lau-Gesk and Aimee Drolet, "The Publicly Self-Conscious Consumer: Prepare to Be Embarrassed," *Journal of Consumer Psychology* 18 (April 2008): 127–136.

34. Morris B. Holbrook, Michael R. Solomon, and Stephen Bell, "A Re-Examination of Self-Monitoring and Judgments of Furniture Designs," *Home Economics Research Journal* 19 (September 1990): 6–16; Mark Snyder, "Self-Monitoring Processes," in Leonard Berkowitz, ed., *Advances in Experimental Social Psychology* (New York: Academic Press, 1979): 85–128.

35. Mark Snyder and Steve Gangestad, "On the Nature of Self-Monitoring: Matters of Assessment, Matters of Validity," *Journal of Personality & Social Psychology* 51 (1986): 125–139; Timothy R. Graeff, "Image Congruence Effects on Product Evaluations: The Role of Self-Monitoring and Public/Private Consumption," *Psychology & Marketing* 13 (August 1996): 481–499; Richard G. Netemeyer, Scot Burton, and Donald R. Lichtenstein, "Trait Aspects of Vanity: Measurement and Relevance to Consumer Behavior," *Journal of Consumer Research* 21 (March 1995): 612–626.

36. Philip Cushman, "Why the Self Is Empty: Toward a Historically Situated Psychology," *American Psychologist* 45 (1990): 599–611.

37. Peter Noel-Murray, "Are Selfies and Smartphones the New Comfort Food? How Millennials Satisfy the 'Empty Self,'" *Psychology Today* (October 2, 2014), https://www.psychologytoday.com/blog/inside-the-consumer-mind/201410/are-selfies-and-smartphones-the-new-comfort-food, accessed March 19, 2015.

38. Gia Nardini, Robyn A. LeBoeuf, and Richard J. Lutz, (2013). "When a Picture Is Worth Less Than a Thousand Words" *Association for Consumer Research 2013 North American Conference*, Chicago (USA), (October 4, 2013.)

39. http://www.reputation.com/, accessed March 25, 2015.

40. Heidi Strohmaier, Megan Murphy, and David DeMatteo, "Youth Sexting: Prevalence Rates, Driving Motivations, and the Deterrent Effect of Legal Consequences," *Sexuality Research and Social Policy* 11, no. 3 (September 2014): 245–255, http://link.springer.com/article/10.1007/s13178-014-0162-9, accessed March 19, 2015.

41. Douglas Macmillan and Elizabeth Dwoskin, "Smile! Marketing Firms Are Mining Your Selfies," *Wall Street Journal* (October 9, 2014), http://www.wsj.com/articles/smile-marketing-firms-are-mining-your-selfies-1412882222?KEYWORDS=selfies, accessed February 22, 2015.

42. Jennifer L. Aaker, "The Malleable Self: The Role of Self-Expression in Persuasion," *Journal of Marketing Research* 36 (February 1999): 45–57; Sak Onkvisit and John Shaw, "Self-Concept and Image Congruence: Some Research and Managerial Implications," *Journal of Consumer Marketing* 4 (Winter 1987): 13–24.

43. Claudia Townsend and Sanjay Sood, "Self-Affirmation Through the Choice of Highly Aesthetic Products," *Journal of Consumer Research* 40, no. 1 (2013): 256–269.

44. Martin Reimann, Raquel Castaño, Judith Zaichkowsky, and Antoine Bechara, "How We Relate to Brands: Psychological and Neurophysiological Insights Into Consumer–Brand Relationships," *Journal of Consumer Psychology* 22, no 1 (2012): 128–142.

45. Quoted in Shirley Y. Y. Cheng, Tiffany Barnett White, and Lan Nguyen Chaplin, "The Effects of Self-brand Connections on Responses to Brand Failure: A New Look at the Consumer–Brand Relationship," *Journal of Consumer Psychology* 22, no. 2 (2012): 280–288.

46. Andrew Adam Newman, "Playing on America's Love for Its 2-Ton Darlings," *New York Times* (December 26, 2013), http://www.nytimes.com/2013/12/27/business/media/playing-on-americas-love-for-its-2-ton-darlings.html, accessed February 24, 2015.

47. C. B. Claiborne and M. Joseph Sirgy, "Self-Image Congruence as a Model of Consumer Attitude Formation and Behavior: A Conceptual Review and Guide for Further Research," paper presented at the Academy of Marketing Science Conference, New Orleans, 1990.

48. Susan Fournier and Julie L. Yao, "Reviving Brand Loyalty: A Reconceptualization within the Framework of Consumer-Brand Relationships," *International Journal of Research in Marketing* 14, no. 5 (December 1997): 451–472; Caryl E. Rusbult, "A Longitudinal Test of the Investment Model: The Development (and Deterioration) of Satisfaction and Commitment in Heterosexual Involvements," *Journal of Personality & Social Psychology* 45, no. 1 (1983): 101–117.

49. Allison R. Johnson, Maggie Matear, and Matthew Thomson, "A Coal in the Heart: Self-Relevance as a Post-Exit Predictor of Consumer Anti-Brand Actions," *Journal of Consumer Research* 38, no. 1 (June 2011): 108–125.

50. A. L. E. Birdwell, "A Study of Influence of Image Congruence on Consumer Choice," *Journal of Business* 41 (January 1964): 76–88; Edward L. Grubb and Gregg Hupp, "Perception of Self, Generalized Stereotypes, and Brand Selection," *Journal of Marketing Research* 5 (February 1986): 58–63.

51. Benedict Carey, "With That Saucy Swagger, She Must Drive a Porsche," *New York Times* (June 13, 2006), www.nytimes.com, accessed March 25, 2015.

52. Ira J. Dolich, "Congruence Relationship Between Self-Image and Product Brands," *Journal of Marketing Research* 6 (February 1969): 80–84; Danny N. Bellenger, Earle Steinberg, and Wilbur W. Stanton, "The Congruence of Store Image and Self Image as It Relates to Store Loyalty," *Journal of Retailing* 52, no. 1 (1976): 17–32; Ronald J. Dornoff and Ronald L. Tatham, "Congruence Between Personal Image and Store Image," *Journal of the Market Research Society* 14, no. 1 (1972): 45–52.

53. Naresh K. Malhotra, "A Scale to Measure Self-Concepts, Person Concepts, and Product Concepts," *Journal of Marketing Research* 18 (November 1981): 456–464.

54. Jack L. Nasar, "Symbolic Meanings of House Styles," *Environment & Behavior* 21 (May 1989): 235–257; E. K. Sadalla, B. Verschure, and J. Burroughs, "Identity Symbolism in Housing," *Environment & Behavior* 19 (1987): 579–587.

55. Solomon, "The Role of Products as Social Stimuli"; Robert E. Kleine III, Susan Schultz-Kleine, and Jerome B. Kernan, "Mundane Consumption and the Self: A Social-Identity Perspective," *Journal of Consumer Psychology* 2, no. 3 (1993): 209–235; Newell D. Wright, C. B. Claiborne, and M. Joseph Sirgy, "The Effects of Product Symbolism on Consumer Self-Concept," in John F. Sherry Jr. and Brian Sternthal, eds., *Advances in Consumer Research* 19 (Provo, UT: Association for Consumer Research, 1992): 311–318; Susan Fournier, "A Person-Based Relationship Framework for Strategic Brand Management" (doctoral dissertation, University of Florida, 1994); Liad Weiss and Gita V. Johar, "Egocentric Categorization and Product Judgment: Seeing Your Traits in What You Own (And Their Opposite in What You Don't)," *Journal of Consumer Research* 40, no. 1 (2013): 185–201.

56. www.airnewzealand.com/aboutus/mediacentre/cranial-billboards-campaign.htm, accessed March 5, 2013.

57. "The History of Temporary Tattoos," *TemporaryTattoos.com* (May 25, 2013), http://temporarytattoos.com/the-history-of-temporary-tattoos/, accessed March 20, 2013.

58. Gabriel Beltrone, "Woman Gets a Giant Reebok Tattoo, and Her Very Own Ad to Go with It," *Adweek* (September 17, 2014), http://www.adweek.com/adfreak/woman-gets-giant-reebok-tattoo-and-her-very-own-ad-well-160192, accessed March 20, 2015.

59. A. Dwayne Ball and Lori H. Tasaki, "The Role and Measurement of Attachment in Consumer Behavior," *Journal of Consumer Psychology* 1, no. 2 (1992): 155–172.

60. William B. Hansen and Irwin Altman, "Decorating Personal Places: A Descriptive Analysis," *Environment & Behavior* 8 (December 1976): 491–504.

61. Lan Nguyen Chaplin and Deborah Roedder John, "The Development of Self-Brand Connections in Children and Adolescents," *Journal of Consumer Research* 32 (June 2005): 119–129.

62. Robert A. Wicklund and Peter M. Gollwitzer, *Symbolic Self-Completion* (Hillsdale, NJ: Erlbaum, 1982).

63. Paul Glader, "Avid Boarders Bypass Branded Gear," *Wall Street Journal* (July 27, 2007), http://www.wsj.com/articles/SB118549628157679731, accessed March 24, 2015.

64. Erving Goffman, *Asylums* (New York: Doubleday, 1961).

65. Floyd Rudmin, "Property Crime Victimization Impact on Self, on Attachment, and on Territorial Dominance," *CPA Highlights, Victims of Crime Supplement* 9, no. 2 (1987): 4–7.

66. Barbara B. Brown, "House and Block as Territory," paper presented at the Conference of the Association for Consumer Research, San Francisco, 1982.

67. Shay Sayre and David Horne, "I Shop, Therefore I Am: The Role of Possessions for Self-Definition," in Shay Sayre and David Horne, eds., *Earth, Wind, and Fire and Water: Perspectives on Natural Disaster* (Pasadena, CA: Open Door Publishers, 1996): 353–370; cf. also Jill G. Klein and Laura Huang, "After All Is Lost: Meeting the Material Needs of Adolescent Disaster Survivors," *Journal of Public Policy & Marketing* 26, no. 1 (Spring 2007): 1–12.

68. Ernest Beaglehole, *Property: A Study in Social Psychology* (New York: Macmillan, 1932).

69. Adapted from Jagdish N. Sheth and Michael R. Solomon, "Extending the Extended Self in a Digital World," *Journal of Marketing Theory and Practice* 22, no. 2 (2014): 123–132.

70. https://foursquare.com/user/2509238/badges/foursquare, accessed March 25, 2015; Rob Walker, "Lifelong Earning," *New York Times* (June 11, 2010), http://www.nytimes.com/2010/06/13/magazine/13fob-consumed-t.html?emc=eta1, accessed April 10, 2011.

71. Scott Smith, Dan Fisher, and S. Jason Cole, "The Lived Meanings of Fanaticism: Understanding the Complex Role of Labels and Categories in Defining the Self in Consumer Culture," *Consumption, Markets & Culture* 10 (June 2007): 77–94.

72. Quoted in Cavan Sieczkowski, "Mariah Carey's Shoe Closet Is Probably Bigger Than Your Apartment," *Huffington Post* (July 20, 2015), http://www.huffingtonpost.com/entry/mariah-careys-shoe-closet-is-probably-bigger-than-your-apartment_55acf41de4b0caf721b322ca, accessed July 21, 2015.

73. Russell W. Belk, "Shoes and Self," *Advances in Consumer Research* (2003): 27–33.

74. Park Ji Kyung and Deborah Roedder John, "Got to Get You into My Life: Do Brand Personalities Rub Off on Consumers?" *Journal of Consumer Research* 37, no. 4 (2010): 655–669.

75. Russell W. Belk, "Possessions and the Extended Self," *Journal of Consumer Research* 15 (September 1988): 139–168.

76. Andrew D. Wilson and Sabrina Golonka, "Embodied Cognition Is Not What You Think it Is," *Frontiers in Psychology* (February 12, 2013), http://journal.frontiersin.org/article/10.3389/fpsyg.2013.00058/full, accessed March 19, 2015, doi: 10.3389/fpsyg.2013.00058

77. Amy Cuddy, "Your Body Language Shapes Who You Are," TED talk filmed June 2012, http://www.ted.com/talks/amy_cuddy_your_body_language_shapes_who_you_are?language=en, accessed March 21, 2015.

78. Adam Hajo and Adam D. Galinsky, "Enclothed Cognition," *Journal of Experimental Social Psychology* 48, no. 4 (July 2012): 918–925.

79. Michael R. Solomon (1981), "Dress for Success: Clothing Appropriateness and the Efficacy of Role Behavior," *Dissertation Abstracts International*, 42 (6), Ph.D. Dissertation, Department of Psychology, University of North Carolina at Chapel Hill.

80. Adapted from Jagdish N. Sheth, and Michael R. Solomon, "Extending the Extended Self in a Digital World," *Journal of Marketing Theory and Practice* 22, no. 2 (2014): 123–132; cf. also Russell W. Belk, "Extended Self in a Digital World," *Journal of Consumer Research* 40, no. 3 (2013): 477–500.

81. Nick Yee, Jeremy N. Bailenson, Mark Urbanek, Francis Chang, and Dan Merget, "The Unbearable Likeness of Being Digital: The Persistence of Nonverbal Social Norms in Online Virtual Environments," *Cyberpsychology & Behavior* 10, no. 1 (2007): 116–121.

82. Nick Bilton, "Wearable Technology That Feels Like Skin," *New York Times* (October 8, 2014), http://www.nytimes.com/2014/10/09/fashion/wearable-technology-that-feels-like-skin.html?smid=nytcore-iphone-share&smprod=nytcore-iphone&_r=0, accessed February 26, 2015.

83. Adapted from a presentation by Prof. Thanigavelan Jambulingam, Saint Joseph's University, January 22, 2015; mc10.com, http://www.mc10inc.com/consumer-products/sports/checklight/, accessed March 25, 2015.

84. Hilary Stout, "Mirror, Mirror in the App: What's the Fairest Shade and Shadow of Them All?" *New York Times* (May 14, 2014), http://www.nytimes.com/2014/05/15/business/mirror-mirror-in-the-app-whats-the-fairest-shade-of-all.html?_r=0, accessed March 25, 2015.

85. Somini Sengupta, "Attack on Women at an Indian Bar Intensifies a Clash of Cultures," *New York Times* (February 8, 2009), www.nytimes.com, accessed February 8, 2009; Niraj Sheth and Tariq Engineer, "As the Selling Gets Hot, India Tries to Keep Cool, New-Age Dilemma: Too Sexy? Just Fun? The Chocolate Man," *Wall Street Journal* (September 9, 2008), www.wsj.com, accessed September 9, 2008.

86. Diane Goldner, "What Men and Women Really Want ... to Eat," *New York Times* (March 2, 1994): C1(2).

87. Paul Rozin, Julia M. Hormes, Myles S. Faith, and Brian Wansink, "Is Meat Male?: A Quantitative Multimethod Framework to Establish Metaphoric Relationships," *Journal of Consumer Research* 39, no. 3 (2012): 629–643.

88. Nina M. Lentini, "McDonald's Tests 'Angus Third Pounder' in California," *Marketing Daily* (March 27, 2007), www.mediapost.com, accessed March 27, 2007.

89. Scott Jaschik, "Rate My Word Choice," *Inside Higher Ed* (February 9, 2015), https://www.insidehighered.com/news/2015/02/09/new-analysis-rate-my-professors-finds-patterns-words-used-describe-men-and-women, accessed February 25, 2015.

90. Glenn Collins, "New Studies on 'Girl Toys' and 'Boy Toys,'" *New York Times* (February 13, 1984): D1.

91. Susan B. Kaiser, "Clothing and the Social Organization of Gender Perception: A Developmental Approach," *Clothing & Textiles Research Journal* 7 (Winter 1989): 46–56.

92. Suzanne Vranica, "Sony Tries to Lure DVR Ad-Skippers," *Wall Street Journal* (September 20, 2006): A20.

93. Joan Meyers-Levy, "The Influence of Sex Roles on Judgment," *Journal of Consumer Research* 14 (March 1988): 522–530.

94. Joan Meyers-Levy and Barbara Loken, "Revisiting Gender Differences: What We Know and What Lies Ahead," *Journal of Consumer Psychology* 25, no. 1 (2015): 129–149.

95. Meyers-Levy and Loken, "Revisiting Gender Differences."; Eileen Fischer and Stephen J. Arnold, "Sex, Gender Identity, Gender Role Attitudes, and Consumer Behavior," *Psychology & Marketing* 11 (March–April 1994): 163–182.

96. Julie King, "What Biology Can Tell Us About Consumers," *Canada One* (March 1, 2011), http://www.canadaone.com/ezine/mar11/biology_consumers.html, accessed March 25, 2015.

97. Kristina M. Durante, Vladas Griskevicius, Sarah E. Hill, Carin Perilloux, and Norman P. Li, "Ovulation, Female Competition, and Product Choice: Hormonal Influences on Consumer Behavior," *Journal of Consumer Research* 37, no. 6 (April 2011): 921–934.; Kristina M. Durante and Ashley Rae Arsena, "Playing the Field: The Effect of Fertility on Women's Desire for Variety," *Journal of Consumer Research* 41 no. 6 (2015): 1372–1391.

98. Sarah Kershaw, "For Teenagers, Hello Means 'How About a Hug?'" *New York Times* (May 27, 2009), www.nytimes.com, accessed May 28, 2009.

99. Nicolas Guéguen, "High Heels Increase Women's Attractiveness," *Archives of Sexual Behavior* (2014), http://link.springer.com/article/10.1007%2Fs10508-014-0422-z#page-1, DOI 10.1007/s10508-014-0422-z, accessed March 25, 2015.

100. Quoted in Kathleen Kelleher, "For Many Women, High Heels Are a Way to Elevate the Spirit," *LA Times* (March 27, 2000), http://articles.latimes.com/2000/mar/27/news/cl-13018, accessed March 23, 2015.

101. Mark J. Miller, "It's Official: 'Breastaurant Trademarked by Texas Sports Bar," *Brandchannel* (April 12, 2013), http://www.brandchannel.com/home/post/2013/04/12/Breastaurant-Trademark-041213.aspx, accessed February 25, 2015.

102. Clifford Nass, Youngme Moon, and Nancy Green, "Are Machines Gender Neutral? Gender-Stereotypic Responses to Computers with Voices," *Journal of Applied Social Psychology* 27, no. 10 (1997): 864–876; Kathleen Debevec and Easwar Iyer, "Sex Roles and Consumer Perceptions of Promotions, Products, and Self: What Do We Know and Where Should We Be Headed," in Richard J. Lutz, ed., *Advances in Consumer Research* 13 (Provo, UT: Association for Consumer Research, 1986): 210–214; Joseph A. Bellizzi and Laura Milner, "Gender Positioning of a Traditionally Male-Dominant Product," *Journal of Advertising Research* (June–July 1991): 72–79.

103. Michelle Jaworski, "The 'First Tablet for Women' Is as Awful as It Sounds," *The Daily Dot* (March 13, 2013), http://www.dailydot.com/society/epad-femme-tablet-for-women/, accessed March 23, 2015.

104. Eric Bellman, "Suzuki's Stylish Compacts Captivate India's Women," *Wall Street Journal* (May 11, 2007): B1.

105. Craig S. Smith, "Underneath, Saudi Women Keep Their Secrets," *New York Times* (December 3, 2002), www.nytimes.com, accessed December 3, 2002.

106. Marylouise Caldwell, Ingeborg Astrid Kelppe, and Paul Henry, "Prosuming Multiple Gender Role Identities: A Multi-Country Written and Audio-Visual Exploration of Contemporary Young Mainstream Female Achievers," *Consumption, Markets & Culture* 10 (June 2007): 95–115.

107. Doreen Carvajal, "Europe Takes Aim at Sexual Stereotyping in Ads," *New York Times* (September 9, 2008), http://www.nytimes.com/2008/09/10/business/media/10adco.html?_r=0 accessed September 10, 2008.

108. Quoted in Natalie Zmuda, "Can Dr Pepper's Mid-Cal Soda Score a 10 with Men?" *Advertising Age* (February 21, 2011), http://adage.com/article/news/dr-pepper-10-avoid-marketing-missteps-pepsi-coke/148983/, accessed April 10, 2011.

109. Quoted in Barry Silverstein, "Ever the Publicity Hound, Branson Readies to Be an Airline Hostess," *BrandChannel* (November 18, 2010), http://www.brandchannel.com/home/post/2010/11/18/Richard-Branson-Loses-Bet.aspx, accessed April 10, 2011.

110. Sarah Mahoney, "Study: Men's Mags May Be Bad For Men," *Marketing Daily* (March 2, 2013), http://www.mediapost.com/publications/article/194617/study-mens-mags-may-be-bad-for-men.html?edition=57304#axzz2MuwUQkdG, accessed February 25, 2015.

111. Barbara B. Stern, "Masculinism(s) and the Male Image: What Does It Mean to Be a Man?" in Tom Reichert and Jacqueline Lambiase, eds., *Sex in Advertising: Multi-Disciplinary Perspectives on the Erotic Appeal* (Mahwah, NJ: Erlbaum, 2003): 215–228.

112. Douglas B. Holt and Craig J. Thompson, "Man-of-Action Heroes: The Pursuit of Heroic Masculinity in Everyday Consumption," *Journal of Consumer Research* 31 (September): 425–440.

113. Lucy Vine, "Lindsay Lohan Gets Naked and Streaks in London's Selfridges Laughing Hysterically," *Mirror* (June 23, 2014), http://www.mirror.co.uk/3am/celebrity-news/lindsay-lohan-gets-naked-streaks-3746464, accessed March 22, 2015.

114. Quoted in Mark J. Miller, "Selfridges Will Go Gender-Free in Latest Retail Experiment," *Brandchannel* (January 29, 2015), http://www.brandchannel.com/home/post/2015/01/29/150129-Selfridges-Gender-Free.aspx?utm_campaign=150129-Selfridges-Agender&utm_source=newsletter&utm_medium=email, accessed February 25, 2015.

115. Sandra L. Bem, "The Measurement of Psychological Androgyny," *Journal of Consulting & Clinical Psychology* 42 (1974): 155–162; Deborah E. S. Frable, "Sex Typing and Gender Ideology: Two Facets of the Individual's Gender Psychology That Go Together," *Journal of Personality & Social Psychology* 56, no. 1 (1989): 95–108.

116. Geoffrey A. Fowler, "Asia's Lipstick Lads," Wall Street Journal (May 27, 2005), www.wsj.com, accessed May 27, 2005.

117. Matt Alt and Hiroko Yoda, "Big Primpin' in Tokyo," *Wired* (May 2007): 46.

118. Leila T. Worth, Jeanne Smith, and Diane M. Mackie, "Gender Schematicity and Preference for Gender-Typed Products," *Psychology & Marketing* 9 (January 1992): 17–30.

119. Rupal Parekh, "Gender-Bending Brands an Easy Way to Increase Product Reach," *Advertising Age* (March 2, 2009), www.adage.com, accessed March 24, 2015; Sarah Mahoney, "Best Buy Opens Store Designed for Women," *Retail Customer Experience* (October 6, 2008), http://www.retailcustomerexperience.com/news/best-buy-opens-store-designed-for-women/, accessed March 24, 2015; Kevin Helliker, "The Solution to Hunting's Woes? Setting Sights on Women," *Wall Street Journal* (October 1, 2008), http://online.wsj.com/Article/Sb122281550760292225, accessed October 2, 2008; Stephanie Clifford, "Frito Lay Tries to Enter the Minds (and Lunch Bags) of Women," *New York Times* (February 24, 2009), http://www.nytimes.com/2009/02/25/business/media/25adco.html?, accessed March 24, 2015; Karl Greenberg, "Harley Says Guys Ride Back Seat in May," *Marketing Daily* (February 3, 2009), www.mediapost.com, accessed February 3, 2009.

120. Lauren Coleman-Lochner, "Old Spice Attracting Women in Gender-Bending Hit for P&G," *Bloomburg Business* (March 12, 2015), http://www.bloomberg.com/news/articles/2014-03-12/old-spice-attracting-women-in-gender-bending-hit-for-p-g, accessed March 20, 2015.

121. Projections of the incidence of homosexuality in the general population often are influenced by assumptions of the researchers, as well as the methodology they employ (e.g., self-report, behavioral measures, fantasy measures). For a discussion of these factors, see Edward O. Laumann, John H. Gagnon, Robert T. Michael, and Stuart Michaels, The *Social Organization of Homosexuality* (Chicago: University of Chicago Press, 1994).

122. Frank Newport and Gary J. Gates, "San Francisco Metro Area Ranks Highest in LGBT Percentage," *Gallup* (March 20, 2015), http://www.gallup.com/poll/182051/san-francisco-metro-area-ranks-highest-lgbt-percentage.aspx?utm_source=Social%20Issues&utm_medium=newsfeed&utm_campaign=tiles, accessed March 20, 2015.

123. For an academic study of this subculture, cf. Steven M. Kates, "The Dynamics of Brand Legitimacy: An Interpretive Study in the Gay Men's Community," *Journal of Consumer Research* 31 (September 2004): 455–464.

124. Justin McCarthy, "Same-Sex Marriage Support Reaches New High at 55%," *Gallup*, http://www.gallup.com/poll/169640/sex-marriage-support-reaches-new-high.aspx, accessed March 22, 2015.

125. Stuart Elliott, "Banana Republic Ads With Real-Life Unions Include a Gay Couple," *New York Times* (February 20, 2014), http://www.nytimes.com/2014/02/21/business/media/banana-republic-ads-with-real-life-unions-includes-a-gay-couple.html?_r=1, accessed February 21, 2015.

126. Quoted in Meghan Neal, "Oreo Sees Support, But Also Backlash and Boycott, for Gay Pride Rainbow Cookie," *New York Daily News*, July 27, 2012, http://www.nydailynews.com/news/national/oreo-sees-support-backlash-boycott-gay-pride-rainbow-cookie-article-1.1103369, accessed February 21, 2015.

127. Julia Baird, "Neither Female Nor Male," *New York Times* (April 6, 2014), http://www.nytimes.com/2014/04/07/opinion/neither-female-nor-male.html?ref=opinion, accessed February 21, 2015.

128. Matthew Chapman, "Benetton to Feature Trans-Sexual Brazilian Model in Spring/Summer Campaign," *marketingmagazine.co.uk* (January 23, 2013), http://www.brandrepublic.com/news/1168021/Benetton-feature-trans-sexual-Brazilian-model-Spring-Summer-campaign/, accessed February 21, 2015.

129. Sreekar Jasthi, "The Economic Impact of Gay Marriage: A $2.5 Billion Question," *Nerd Wallet* (November 12, 2014), http://www.nerdwallet.com/blog/cities/economics/economic-impact-gay-marriage-2-5-billion-question/, accessed March 22, 2015; Kevin Sack, "When the Bride Takes a Bride, Businesses Respond," *New York Times* (July 15, 2010), http://www.nytimes.com/2010/07/16/us/16marriage.html?emc=eta1, accessed March 22, 2015; http://equallywed.com/, accessed March 22, 2015; http://www.outvite.com/?Cobrand=OutVite&Site=OutVite&vk=1777211146, accessed March 22, 2015.

130. Sheila Shayon, "Levi's for Women: Shape, Not Size, Matters," *BrandChannel* (September 17, 2010), http://www.brandchannel.com/home/post/2010/09/17/Levis-Women-Curve-ID-Digital.aspx, accessed April 10, 2011; http://us.levi.com/shop/index.jsp?categoryId=3146849&AB=CMS_Home_CurveID_081010, accessed May 28, 2011.

131. http://www.spanx.com/category/index.jsp?categoryId=2992553&clickid=topnav_shapers_txt, accessed March 24, 2015.

132. Abe Sauer, "How Unilever is Translating the Dove Real Beauty Campaign for China," *Brandchannel* (July 15, 2013), http://www.brandchannel.com/home/post/2013/07/15/Dove-Real-Beauty-China-Campaign-071513.aspx, accessed January 30, 2015.

133. Ibid.

134. Samantha Murphy, "No, You're Not Fat—Facebook Just Makes You Think You Are," *Mashable* (March 30, 2012), http://mashable.com/2012/03/30/facebook-makes-you-feel-fat/?WT.mc_id=en_social-media&utm_campaign=Social%2BMedia&utm_medium=email&utm_source=newsletter, accessed January 11, 2013.

135. Samantha Murphy Kelly, "Job Site Wants Only Beautiful Candidates," *Mashable* (June 2, 2013), http://mashable.com/2013/06/02/beautiful-people-job-site/?WT.mc_id=en_my_stories&utm_campaign=My%2BStories&utm_medium=email&utm_source=newsletter, accessed January 30, 2015.

136. Daniel S. Hamermesh, "Ugly? You May Have a Case," *New York Times Magazine* (August 27, 2011), http://www.nytimes.com/2011/08/28/opinion/sunday/ugly-you-may-have-a-case.html?ref=opinion, accessed March 22, 2015.

137. Nina Mandell, "Padded Swimsuits for All? Abercrombie and Fitch Marketing Padded Tops to Young Girls," *New York Daily News* (March 27, 2011), http://www.nydailynews.com/lifestyle/fashion/2011/03/27/2011-03-27_padded_swimsuits_for_all_abercrombie_and_fitch_marketing_padded_tops_to_young_gi.html, accessed April 10, 2011.

138. Emily Flynn, "Beauty: Babes Spot Babes," *Newsweek* (September 20, 2004): 10.

139. For some results that provide exceptions to this overall phenomenon, cf. Elizabeth Cashdan, "Waist-to-Hip Ratio Across Cultures: Trade-Offs Between Androgen- and Estrogen-Dependent Traits," *Current Anthropology* 49, no. 6 (2008): 1099–1107.

140. Abigail W. Leonard, "How Women Pick Mates vs. Flings," *LiveScience* (January 2, 2007), www.livescience.com/health/070102_facial_features.html, accessed January 3, 2007.

141. Corky Siemaszko, "Depends on the Day: Women's Sex Drive a Very Cyclical Thing," *New York Daily News* (June 24, 1999): 3.

142. Amanda B. Bower, "Highly Attractive Models in Advertising and the Women Who Loathe Them: The Implications of Negative Affect for Spokesperson Effectiveness," *Journal of Advertising* 30 (Fall 2001): 51–63.

143. Austin Considine, "A Little Imperfection for That Smile?" New York Times (October 21, 2011), http://www.nytimes.com/2011/10/23/fashion/in-japan-a-trend-to-make-straight-teeth-crooked-noticed.html, accessed December 2, 2013.

144. Basil G. Englis, Michael R. Solomon, and Richard D. Ashmore, "Beauty Before the Eyes of Beholders: The Cultural Encoding of Beauty Types in Magazine Advertising and Music Television," *Journal of Advertising* 23 (June 1994): 49–64; Michael R. Solomon, Richard Ashmore, and Laura Longo, "The Beauty Match-Up Hypothesis: Congruence Between Types of Beauty and Product Images in Advertising," *Journal of Advertising* 21 (December 1992): 23–34.

145. Lois W. Banner, *American Beauty* (Chicago: University of Chicago Press, 1980); for a philosophical perspective, see Barry Vacker and Wayne R. Key, "Beauty and the Beholder: The Pursuit of Beauty Through Commodities," *Psychology & Marketing* 10 (November–December 1993): 471–494.

146. Mark J. Miller, "Macy's Introduces Marilyn Monroe Collection to a Racier Generation," *Brandchannel* (March 6, 2013), http://www.brandchannel.com/home/post/2013/03/06/Macys-Marilyn-Monroe-030613.aspx, accessed March 23, 2015.

147. Elaine L. Pedersen and Nancy L. Markee, "Fashion Dolls: Communicators of Ideals of Beauty and Fashion," paper presented at the International Conference on Marketing Meaning, Indianapolis, IN, 1989; Dalma Heyn, "Body Hate," *Ms.* (August 1989): 34; Mary C. Martin and James W. Gentry, "Assessing the Internalization of Physical Attractiveness Norms," *Proceedings of the American Marketing Association Summer Educators' Conference* (Summer 1994): 59–65.

148. Lisa Bannon, "Barbie Is Getting Body Work, and Mattel Says She'll Be 'Rad,'" *Wall Street Journal Interactive Edition* (November 17, 1997).

149. Lisa Bannon, "Will New Clothes, Bellybutton Create 'Turn Around' Barbie," *Wall Street Journal Interactive Edition* (February 17, 2000).

150. "Report Delivers Skinny on Miss America," *Montgomery Advertiser* (March 22, 2000): 5A.

151. "Study: Playboy Models Losing Hourglass Figures," CNN.com (December 20, 2002), www.CNN.com.

152. Anthony H. Ahrensa, Sarah F. Etua, James J. Graya, James E. Mosimanna, Mia Foley Sypecka, and Claire V. Wiseman, "Cultural Representations of Thinness in Women, Redux: *Playboy* Magazine's Depiction of Beauty from 1979 to 1999," *Body Image* (September 2006): 229–235.

153. Quoted in Will Lassek, Steve Gaulin, and Hara Estroff Marano, "Eternal Curves," *Psychology Today* (July 03, 2012), http://www.psychologytoday.com/articles/201206/eternal-curves, accessed January 11, 2013.

154. Jane E. Brody, "Personal Health," *New York Times* (February 22, 1990): B9.

155. Christian S. Crandall, "Social Contagion of Binge Eating," *Journal of Personality & Social Psychology* 55 (1988): 588–598.

156. Charlotte Alter, "What Does It Mean to 'Break the Internet'?" *Time* (November 12, 2014), http://time.com/3580977/kim-kardashian-break-the-internet-butt/, accessed March 23, 2015.

157. Nilüfer Z. Aydinoğlu and Aradhna Krishna, "Imagining Thin: Why Vanity Sizing Works," *Journal of Consumer Psychology* 22, no. 4 (2012): 565–572.

158. Erin White, "Dove 'Firms' with Zaftig Models: Unilever Brand Launches European Ads Employing Non-Supermodel Bodies," *Wall Street Journal* (April 21, 2004): B3.

159. David Goetzl, "Teen Girls Pan Ad Images of Women," *Advertising Age* (September 13, 1999): 32; Carey Goldberg, "Citing Intolerance, Obese People Take Steps to Press Cause," *New York Times* (November 5, 2000), http://www.nytimes.com/2000/11/05/us/fat-people-say-an-intolerant-world-condemns-them-on-first-sight.html, accessed September 1, 2011.

160. Shirley S. Wang, "Diet Pepsi's 'Skinny Can' Campaign Riles Eating Disorders Group," *Wall Street Journal* (February 15, 2011), http://blogs.WallStreetJournal.com/health/2011/02/15/diet-pepsis-skinny-can-campaign-riles-eating-disorders-group/, accessed April 10, 2011.

161. http://www.bigisbeautiful.nl/, accessed March 22, 2015.

162. Quoted in Daiane Scaraboto and Eileen Fischer, "Frustrated Fatshionistas: An Institutional Theory Perspective on Consumer Quests for Greater Choice in Mainstream Markets," *Journal of Consumer Research* 39, no. 6 (2013): 1234–1257.

163. Sheila Shayon, "Target Launches First Plus-Size Collection Following Blogger Boycott," *Brandchannel* (January 21, 2015), http://www.brandchannel.com/home/post/2015/01/21/150121-Target-Plus-Size.aspx?utm_campaign=150121-Target-Plus-Size&utm_source=newsletter&utm_medium=email, accessed February 3, 2015.

164. Stephanie Clifford, "High Fashion, No Airbrushing," *New York Times* (October 19, 2012), http://www.nytimes.com/2012/10/20/business/rent-the-runway-uses-real-women-to-market-high-fashion.html?ref=todayspaper&_r=0, accessed January 11, 2013.

165. Stephen Mihm, "Why C.E.O.s Are Growing Beards," *New York Times* (November 28, 2014), http://www.nytimes.com/2014/11/30/opinion/sunday/why-ceos-are-growing-beards.html?module=Search&mabReward=relbias%3Ar%2C%7B%221%22%3A%22RI%3A9%22%7D&_r=0, accessed January 30, 2015.

166. Jill Neimark, "The Beefcaking of America," *Psychology Today* (November–December 1994): 32.

167. Richard H. Kolbe and Paul J. Albanese, "Man to Man: A Content Analysis of Sole-Male Images in Male-Audience Magazines," *Journal of Advertising* 25 (Winter 1996): 1–20.

168. Douglas Quenqua, "Muscular Body Image Lures Boys into Gym, and Obsession," *New York Times* (November 19, 2012), http://www.nytimes.com/2012/11/19/health/teenage-boys-worried-about-body-image-take-risks.html?hp, accessed January 11, 2013.

169. Ruth P. Rubinstein, "Color, Circumcision, Tattoos, and Scars," in Michael R. Solomon, ed., *The Psychology of Fashion* (Lexington, MA: Lexington Books, 1985): 243–254; Peter H. Bloch and Marsha L. Richins, "You Look 'Mahvelous': The Pursuit of Beauty and Marketing Concept," *Psychology & Marketing* 9 (January 1992): 3–16.

170. Sondra Farganis, "Lip Service: The Evolution of Pouting, Pursing, and Painting Lips Red," *Health* (November 1988): 48–51.

171. Michelle Hancock, "High Heels: The Agony and the Ecstacy," *The Telegraph* (April 1, 1986), http://news.google.com/newspapers?nid=2209&dat=19860401&id=xp4rAAAAIBAJ&sjid=NfwFAAAAIBAJ&pg=6255,163038, accessed September 19, 2013.

172. Andrew Adam Newman, "Dove Tells Women to Love Their Armpits," *New York Times* (February 27, 2014), http://www.nytimes.com/2014/02/28/business/media/dove-tells-women-to-love-their-armpits.html, accessed February 24, 2015.

173. Anne-Kathrin Klesse, Caroline Goukens, Kelly Geyskens, and Ko de Ruyter, "Repeated Exposure to the Thin Ideal and Implications for the Self: Two Weight Loss Program Studies," *International Journal of Research in Marketing* 29, no. 4 (2013): 355–362.

174. Andrew Adam Newman, "Celebrating Black Beauty and Advocating Diversity," *New York Times* (April 18, 2013), http://www.nytimes.com/2013/04/19/business/media/celebrating-black-beauty-and-advocating-diversity.html, accessed February 2, 2015; Thomas Fuller, "A Vision of Pale Beauty Carries Risks for Asia's Women," *International Herald Tribune Online* (May 14, 2006), accessed May 16, 2006.

175. Sherry L. Pagoto, Stephenie C. Lemon, Jessica L. Oleski, Jonathan M. Scully, Gin-Fei Olendzki, Martinus M. Evans, Wenjun Li, L. Carter Florence, Brittany Kirkland, and Joel J. Hillhouse, "Availability of Tanning Beds on US College Campuses," *JAMA Dermatology* 151, no. 1 (2015): 59–63, http://archderm.jamanetwork.com/article.aspx?articleid=1919438, accessed March 24, 2015, doi:10.1001/jamadermatol.2014.3590; Sabrina Tavernise, "Warning: That Tan Could Be Hazardous: Indoor Tanning Poses Cancer Risks, Teenagers Learn," *New York Times* (January 10, 2015), http://www.nytimes.com/2015/01/11/health/indoor-tanning-poses-cancer-risks-teenagers-learn.html?_r=1, accessed February 3, 2015.

176. John W. Schouten, "Selves in Transition: Symbolic Consumption in Personal Rites of Passage and Identity Reconstruction," *Journal of Consumer Research* 17 (March 1991): 412–425; Janet Whitman, "Extreme Makeovers Blur Line Between Medicine and Cosmetics," *Wall Street Journal* (January 7, 2004), www.wsj.com, accessed January 7, 2004.

177. William Neuman, "Mannequins Give Shape to a Venezuelan Fantasy," *New York Times* (November 6, 2013), http://www.nytimes.com/2013/11/07/world/americas/mannequins-give-shape-to-venezuelan-fantasy.html?hp, accessed February 3, 2015; Simon Romero, "Chávez Tries to Rally Venezuela against a New Enemy: Breast Lifts," *New York Times* (March 14, 2011), http://www.nytimes.com/2011/03/15/world/americas/15venezuela.html?scp=1&sq=breast&st=cse, accessed April 10, 2011.

178. Alexandra Stevenson, "Plastic Surgery Tourism Brings Chinese to South Korea," *New York Times* (December 23, 2014), http://www.nytimes.com/2014/12/24/business/international/plastic-surgery-tourism-brings-chinese-to-south-korea.html?ref=international&_r=0, accessed January 30, 2015.

179. Natasha Singer, "How to Stuff a Wild Bikini Bottom," *New York Times* (March 2, 2006), www.nytimes.com, accessed March 2, 2006.

180. Catherine Saint Louis, "This Teenage Girl Uses Botox. No, She's Not Alone," *New York Times* (August 11, 2010), http://www.nytimes.com/2010/08/12/fashion/12SKIN.html?_r=1&scp=2&sq=botox&st=cse, accessed April 10, 2011.

181. Dannie Kjeldgaard and Anders Bengtsson, "Consuming the Fashion Tattoo," in Geeta Menon and Akshay R. Rao, eds., *Advances in Consumer Research* 32 (Duluth, MN: Association for Consumer Research, 2005): 172–177.

182. Tiffany Hsu and Don Lee, "At 50 Years Old, Barbie Gets Tattoos—And a Megastore in China," *Los Angeles Times* (March 6, 2009), http://articles.latimes.com/2009/mar/06/business/fi-tattoobarbie6, accessed March 6, 2009.

183. Dana Blanton, "Fox News Poll: Tattoos aren't just for rebels anymore," *Fox News* (March 14, 2014), http://www.foxnews.com/us/2014/03/14/fox-news-poll-tattoos-arent-just-for-rebels-anymore/, accessed March 24, 2015.

184. Mona Chalabi, "Dear Mona, How Many People Regret Their Tattoos?" *FiveThirtyEight* (November 6, 2014), http://fivethirtyeight.com/datalab/how-many-people-regret-their-tattoos/, accessed March 24, 2015; Natasha Singer, "Erasing Tattoos, Out of Regret or for a New Canvas," *New York Times* (June 17, 2007), www.nytimes.com, accessed June 17, 2007.

185. www.pathfinder.com:80/altculture/aentries/p/piercing.html, accessed August 22, 1997.

186. "Body Piercing Statistics," *Statistic Brain* (March 17, 2015), http://www.statisticbrain.com/body-piercing-statistics/, accessed March 24, 2015.

187. Vivian Manning-Schaffel, "Metrosexuals: A Well-Groomed Market?" *Brand Channel* (May 22, 2006), www.brandchannel.com, accessed May 22, 2006; Jack Neff, "A Lipstick Index for Men? Philips' Norelco Posits That Guys Are Growing Beards to Protest Recession," *Advertising Age* (April 2, 2009), www.adage.com, accessed April 2, 2009; Aaron Baar, "Move Over, Ladies: Men Are Walking Down Beauty Aisles," *Marketing Daily* (December 22, 2008), www.mediapost.com, accessed December 22, 2008.

188. Jenny Darroch, "Marketing to Women: What to Do/What Not to Do…Without Appearing Too Contradictory," *The Huffington Post*, October 27, 2014, http://www.huffingtonpost.com/jenny-darroch/marketing-to-women-what-t_b_6050500.html.

189. Quoted in Lauren Indvik, *Mashable* (July 3, 2012), http://mashable.com/2012/07/03/seventeen-real-girls-petition/?utm_source=feedburner&utm_medium=email&utm_campaign=Feed%3A+Mashable+%28Mashable%29, accessed January 11, 2013.

190. Jesse Chandler and Norbert Schwarz, "Use Does Not Wear Ragged the Fabric of Friendship: Thinking of Objects as Alive Makes People Less Willing to Replace Them," *Journal of Consumer Psychology* 20, no. 2 (2010): 138–145.

191. Claire Cain Miller, "LeanIn.org and Getty Aim to Change Women's Portrayal in Stock Photos," *New York Times* (February 9, 2014), http://www.nytimes.com/2014/02/10/business/leaninorg-and-getty-aim-to-change-womens-portrayal-in-stock-photos.html?_r=1, accessed February 25, 2015.

Chapter 7 • Personality, Lifestyles, and Values

Chapter Objectives

When you have finished reading this chapter you will understand why:

7-1 A consumer's personality influences the way he or she responds to marketing stimuli, but efforts to use this information in marketing contexts meet with mixed results.

7-2 Brands have personalities.

7-3 A lifestyle defines a pattern of consumption that reflects a person's choices of how to spend his or her time and money, and these choices are essential to define consumer identity.

7-4 It can be more useful to identify patterns of consumption than knowing about individual purchases when organizations craft a lifestyle marketing strategy.

7-5 Psychographics go beyond simple demographics to help marketers understand and reach different consumer segments.

7-6 Underlying values often drive consumer motivations.

Source: Alfgar/Shutterstock

Jackie and Hank, executives in a high-powered Los Angeles advertising agency, are exchanging ideas about how they are going to spend the big bonus everyone in the firm is getting for landing a new account. They can't help but snicker at their friend Rose in accounting, who avidly surfs the Internet for information about a state-of-the-art home theater system she plans to install in her condo. What a couch potato! Hank, who fancies himself a bit of a daredevil, plans to blow his bonus on a thrill-seeking trip to Colorado, where a week of outrageous bungee jumping awaits him (assuming he lives to tell about it, but that uncertainty is half the fun). Jackie replies, "Been there, done that.... Believe it or not, I'm staying put right here—heading over to Santa Monica to catch some waves." Seems that the surfing bug has bitten her since she stumbled onto Jetty Girl, an online resource for women who surf.[1]

Jackie and Hank marvel at how different they are from Rose, who's content to spend her downtime watching sappy old movies or actually reading books. All three make about the same salary, and Jackie and Rose were sorority sisters at USC. How can their tastes be so different? Oh well, they figure, that's why they make chocolate and vanilla.

OBJECTIVE 7-1
A consumer's personality influences the way he or she responds to marketing stimuli, but efforts to use this information in marketing contexts meet with mixed results.

Personality

Jackie and Hank are typical of many people who search for new (and even risky) ways to spend their leisure time. This desire translates into big business for the "adventure travel" industry, which provides white-knuckle experiences.[2] In the old days, the California beach culture relegated women to the status of land-locked "Gidgets" who sat on shore while their boyfriends rode the surf. Now (inspired by the female surfers in the movie *Blue Crush* and then by Bethany Hamilton, the woman documented in the movie *Soul Surfer* who lost her left arm to a shark and returned to the sport), women fuel the sport's resurgence in popularity. Roxy rides the wave with its collections of women's surf apparel; it even includes a feature on its Web site that lets users design their own bikinis.[3]

Just what does make Jackie and Hank so different from their more sedate friend Rose? One answer may lie in the concept of **personality**, which refers to a person's unique psychological makeup and how it consistently influences the way a person responds to his or her environment. Do all people *have* personalities? Certainly we can wonder about some we meet! Actually, even though the answer seems like a no-brainer, some psychologists argue that the concept of personality may not be valid. Many studies find that people do not seem to exhibit stable personalities. Because people don't necessarily behave the same way in all situations, they argue that this is merely a convenient way to categorize people.

Intuitively, this argument is a bit hard to accept, because we tend to see others in a limited range of situations, and so they *do* appear to act consistently. However, we each know that we ourselves are not all *that* consistent; we may be wild and crazy at times and serious and responsible at others. Although certainly not all psychologists have abandoned the idea of personality, many now recognize that a person's underlying characteristics are but one part of the puzzle, and situational factors often play a large role in determining behavior.[4] Although we may undergo dramatic changes as we grow up, in adulthood measures of personality stay relatively stable. Studies of thousands of people's scores on the widely used measurement instrument the **Minnesota Multiphasic Personality Inventory (MMPI)** confirm that our personalities tend to stabilize by the age of 30. For example, most of us become less interested in thrill seeking as we focus more on self-discipline. Enjoy it while you can![5]

Consumer Behavior on the Couch: Freudian Theory

The famous psychologist Sigmund Freud proposed that much of one's adult personality stems from a fundamental conflict between a person's desire to gratify his or her physical needs and the necessity to function as a responsible member of society. This struggle plays out in the mind among three systems. (Note: These systems do *not* refer to physical parts of the brain.) Let's quickly review each.

Freudian Systems

The **id** is about immediate gratification; it is the "party animal" of the mind. It operates according to the **pleasure principle**; that is, our basic desire to maximize pleasure and avoid pain guides our behavior. The id is selfish and illogical. It directs a person's psychic energy toward pleasurable acts without any regard for consequences.

The **superego** is the counterweight to the id. This system is essentially the person's conscience. It internalizes society's rules (especially as parents teach them to us) and tries to prevent the id from seeking selfish gratification. Finally, the **ego** is the system that mediates between the id and the superego. It's basically a referee in the fight between temptation and virtue. The ego tries to balance these opposing forces according to the **reality principle**, which means it finds ways to gratify the id that the outside world will find acceptable. (Hint: This is where Freudian theory applies to marketing.) These conflicts occur on an unconscious level, so the person is not necessarily aware of the underlying reasons for his or her behavior.

How is Freud's work relevant to consumer behavior? In particular, it highlights the potential importance of unconscious motives that guide our purchases. The implication is that consumers cannot necessarily tell us their true motivation when they choose products, even if we can devise a sensitive way to ask them directly. The Freudian perspective also raises the possibility that the ego relies on the symbolism in products to compromise between the demands of the id and the prohibitions of the superego. People channel their unacceptable desire into acceptable outlets when they use products that signify these underlying desires. This is the connection between product symbolism and motivation: The product stands for, or represents, a consumer's true goal, which is socially unacceptable or unattainable. By acquiring the product, the person vicariously experiences the forbidden fruit.

"Sometimes a Cigar Is Just a Cigar": Products as Sexual Symbols

Most Freudian applications in marketing relate to a product's supposed sexual symbolism. For example, some analysts speculate that owning a sports car is a substitute for sexual gratification (especially for men going through a "midlife crisis"). Indeed, some people do seem inordinately attached to their cars, and they may spend many hours lovingly washing and polishing them. An Infiniti ad reinforces the belief that cars symbolically satisfy consumers' sexual needs in addition to their functional ones when it describes one model as "what happens when you cross sheet metal and desire." Other approaches focus on male-oriented symbolism—so-called *phallic symbols*—that appeals to women. Although Freud joked that, "sometimes a cigar is just a cigar," many popular applications of Freud's ideas revolve around the use of objects that resemble sex organs (e.g., cigars, trees, or swords for male sex organs; tunnels for female sex organs). This focus stems from Freud's analysis of dreams, which he believed communicate repressed desires in the form of symbolically rich stories.

Motivational Research

In the 1950s, **motivational research** borrowed Freudian ideas to understand the deeper meanings of products and advertisements. This approach adapted psychoanalytical (Freudian) interpretations with a heavy emphasis on unconscious motives. It basically assumed that we channel socially unacceptable needs into acceptable outlets—including product substitutes.

This perspective relies on *depth interviews* with individual consumers. Instead of asking many consumers a few general questions about product usage and combining these responses with those of many other consumers in a representative statistical sample, a motivational researcher talks to only a few people but probes deeply into each respondent's purchase motivations. A depth interview might take several hours, and it's based on the assumption that the respondent cannot immediately articulate his or her *latent* or underlying motives. A carefully trained interviewer can derive these only after extensive questioning and interpretation.

Ernest Dichter, a psychoanalyst who trained with Freud's disciples in Vienna in the early part of the 20th century, pioneered this work. Dichter conducted in-depth interview studies on more than 230 different products, and actual marketing campaigns incorporated many of his findings.[6] For example, Esso (now Exxon in the United States) for many years reminded consumers to "Put a Tiger in Your Tank" after Dichter found that people responded well to this powerful animal symbolism containing vaguely sexual undertones. Table 7.1 provides a summary of major consumption motivations he identified.

Some critics reacted to the motivational studies that ad agencies conducted in much the same way they did to subliminal perception studies (see Chapter 3). They charged that this approach gave advertisers the power to manipulate consumers.[7] However, many consumer researchers felt the research lacked sufficient rigor and validity because the interpretations are so subjective.[8] Because the analyst based his conclusions on his own judgment after he interviewed a small number of people, critics were dubious about whether the findings would generalize to a larger market. In addition, because the original motivational

| TABLE 7.1 | A Motivational Researcher Identifies Consumption Motives |

Motive	Associated Products
Power-masculinity-virility	Power: Sugary products and large breakfasts (to charge oneself up), bowling, electric trains, hot rods, power tools Masculinity-virility: Coffee, red meat, heavy shoes, toy guns, buying fur coats for women, shaving with a razor
Security	Ice cream (to feel like a loved child again), full drawer of neatly ironed shirts, real plaster walls (to feel sheltered), home baking, hospital care
Eroticism	Sweets (to lick), gloves (to be removed by woman as a form of undressing), a man lighting a woman's cigarette (to create a tension-filled moment culminating in pressure, then relaxation)
Moral purity-cleanliness	White bread, cotton fabrics (to connote chastity), harsh household cleaning chemicals (to make housewives feel moral after using), bathing (to be equated with Pontius Pilate, who washed blood from his hands), oatmeal (sacrifice, virtue)
Social acceptance	Companionship: Ice cream (to share fun), coffee, Love and affection: Toys (to express love for children), sugar and honey (to express terms of affection) Acceptance: Soap, beauty products
Individuality	Gourmet foods, foreign cars, cigarette holders, vodka, perfume, fountain pens
Status	Scotch: ulcers, heart attacks, indigestion (to show one has a high-stress, important job!), carpets (to show one does not live on bare earth like peasants)
Femininity	Cakes and cookies, dolls, silk, tea, household curios
Reward	Cigarettes, candy, alcohol, ice cream, cookies
Mastery over environment	Kitchen appliances, boats, sporting goods, cigarette lighters
Disalienation (a desire to feel connectedness to things)	Home decorating, skiing, morning radio broadcasts (to feel "in touch" with the world)
Magic-mystery	Soups (having healing powers), paints (change the mood of a room), carbonated drinks (magical effervescent property), vodka (romantic history), unwrapping of gifts

Source: Adapted from Jeffrey F. Durgee, "Interpreting Dichter's Interpretations: An Analysis of Consumption Symbolism," in *The Handbook of Consumer Motivation, Marketing and Semiotics: Selected Papers from the Copenhagen Symposium*, eds. Hanne Hartvig-Larsen, David Glen Mick, and Christian Alstead (Copenhagen, 1991).

researchers were heavily influenced by orthodox Freudian theory, their interpretations usually involved sexual themes. This emphasis tends to overlook other plausible causes for behavior. Still, motivational research had great appeal to at least some marketers for several reasons:

- Motivational research is less expensive to conduct than large-scale, quantitative survey data collection because interviewing and data-processing costs are relatively minimal.
- The knowledge a company derives from motivational research may help it develop marketing communications that appeal to deep-seated needs and thus provide a more powerful hook to reel in consumers. Even if they are not necessarily valid for all consumers in a target market, these insights can still be valuable to an advertiser who wants to create copy that will resonate with customers.
- Some of the findings seem intuitively plausible after the fact. For example, motivational studies concluded that we associate coffee with companionship, that we avoid prunes because they remind us of old age, and that men fondly equate the first car they owned as an adolescent with the onset of their sexual freedom.

Other interpretations were hard for some researchers to swallow, such as the observation that women equate the act of baking a cake with birth, or that men are reluctant to give blood because they feel it drains their vital fluids. However, we do sometimes say a pregnant woman has "a bun in the oven," and Pillsbury claims that "nothing says lovin' like something from the oven." When the Red Cross hired motivational researcher Dichter to boost blood donation rates, he reported that men (but not women) tended to drastically overestimate the amount of blood they gave. As a result, the Red Cross counteracted men's fear of losing their virility when the organization symbolically equated the act of giving blood with fertilizing a female egg: "Give the gift of life." Despite its drawbacks, some ad agencies today still use some forms of motivational research. The approach is most useful, however, when we use it as an exploratory technique to provide insights that inform more rigorous research approaches.

Neo-Freudian Theories

Freud's work had a huge influence on subsequent theories of personality. Although he opened the door to the realization that explanations for behavior may lurk beneath the surface, many of his colleagues and students felt that an individual's personality is more influenced by how he or she handles relationships with others than by how he or she resolves sexual conflicts. We call these theorists *Neo-Freudian* (meaning following from or being influenced by Freud).

Karen Horney

One of the most prominent neo-Freudians was Karen Horney. This pioneering psychotherapist described people as moving toward others (*compliant*), away from others (*detached*), or against others (*aggressive*).[9] Indeed, one early study found that compliant people are more likely to gravitate toward name-brand products, detached types are more likely to be tea drinkers, and males the researchers classified as aggressive preferred brands with a strong masculine orientation (e.g., Old Spice deodorant).[10] Other well-known neo-Freudians include Alfred Adler, who proposed that a prime motivation is to overcome feelings of inferiority relative to others; and Harry Stack Sullivan, who focused on how personality evolves to reduce anxiety in social relationships.[11]

Carl Jung

Carl Jung was also one of Freud's disciples. However, Jung didn't accept Freud's emphasis on sexual aspects of personality. He went on to develop his own method of psychotherapy that he called *analytical psychology.* Jung believed that the cumulative experiences of past generations shape who we are today. He proposed that we each share a *collective unconscious*, a storehouse of memories we inherit from our ancestors. For example, Jung would argue that many people are afraid of the dark because their distant ancestors had good reason to fear it. These shared memories create **archetypes**, or universally recognized ideas and behavior patterns. Archetypes involve themes, such as birth, death, or the devil, that appear frequently in myths, stories, and dreams.

Jung's ideas may seem a bit far-fetched, but advertising messages do in fact often include archetypes. For example, some of the archetypes Jung and his followers identified include the "old wise man" and the "earth mother."[12] These images appear frequently in marketing messages that feature characters such as wizards, revered teachers, or even Mother Nature. Our culture's current infatuation with stories such as *Harry Potter* and *The Lord of the Rings* speaks to the power of these images—to say nothing of the "wizard" who helps you repair your laptop.

Young & Rubicam (Y&R), a major advertising agency, uses the archetype approach in its BrandAsset® Archetypes model, as depicted in Figure 7.1. The model proposes healthy relationships among archetypes as well as unhealthy ones. A healthy personality is one in which the *Archetypes* overwhelm their corresponding *Shadows*; a sick personality results when one or more Shadows prevail. When a brand's Shadows dominate, this cues the agency to take action to guide the brand to a healthier personality, much as one would try to counsel a psychologically ill person.[13]

A second, similar approach popularized by authors Mark and Pearson uses a typology of 12 brand archetypes. These include categories such as "Hero," "Magician," "Lover," and "Jester." This perspective draws on theories of human motivation to create two sets of contrasts: belonging/people versus independence/self-actualization, and risk/mastery versus stability/control.[14] Table 7.2 (on page 248) summarizes some of these archetype/brand relationships.

Figure 7.1 BRANDASSET VALUATOR® ARCHETYPES

Characteristics

Magician - thought
logical, analytical, insightful

Sage - peace
wise, visionary, mentoring

Patriarch - belief
dignified, authoritative, inspirational

Matriarch - order
organized, systematic, controlled

Angel - dreams
optimistic, innocent, pure

Mother Earth - body
stable, genuine, nurturing

Enchantress - soul
mysterious, sensual, tempting

Queen - being
relaxed, comforting, sociable

Actress - feelings
glamorous, dramatic, involved

Warrior - ego
confident, powerful, heroic

Troubadour - joy
joyous, free-spirited, agile

Jester - spirit
witty, resilient, daring

THOUGHT · SUBSTANCE · EMOTIONS · ENERGY

Shadow Characteristics

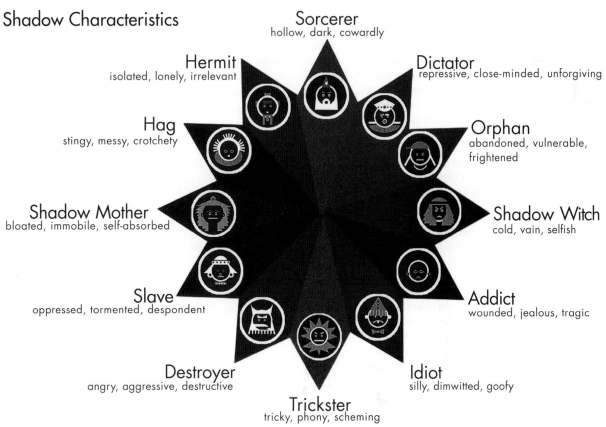

Sorcerer
hollow, dark, cowardly

Hermit
isolated, lonely, irrelevant

Dictator
repressive, close-minded, unforgiving

Hag
stingy, messy, crotchety

Orphan
abandoned, vulnerable, frightened

Shadow Mother
bloated, immobile, self-absorbed

Shadow Witch
cold, vain, selfish

Slave
oppressed, tormented, despondent

Addict
wounded, jealous, tragic

Destroyer
angry, aggressive, destructive

Idiot
silly, dimwitted, goofy

Trickster
tricky, phony, scheming

Source: BrandAsset® Consulting: A Young & Rubican Brands Company.

TABLE 7.2   Selected Mark and Pearson Brand Archetypes

Archetype	Description	Example brands	As consumers
Leaving a Thumbprint on the World			
"Hero" **Core desire:** To prove worth through courageous action **Goal:** Exert mastery in a way that improves the world **Fear:** Weakness, vulnerability, and wimping out **Strategy:** Become strong and competent	Everything seems lost … but then the Hero rides over the hill and saves the day. The Hero triumphs over evil, adversity, and challenges; in doing so, the Hero inspires others. Heroes are ambitious and seek out challenges. The Hero generally wants to make the world a better place. Their motto is: "Where there is a will, there's a way."	Hero brands include: the Marines, the Olympics, the NASA space program, Nike, Red Cross, and Under Armour. Hero movies include: *Star Wars* and *Saving Private Ryan.* Famous Heroes include: Martin Luther King, Jr., Nelson Mandela, John F. Kennedy, and Superman.	Hero consumers expect companies, and indeed brands, to articulate their values, mission, and vision in a clear way. Increasingly, Hero consumers expect those corporate visions to reflect some sense of social responsibility. Heroes evaluate brands and companies not just on the quality of the product or service but also the strengths and ethics of the firm's convictions.
"Magician" **Core desire:** Knowledge of fundamental laws and how the world works **Goal:** Make dreams come true **Fear:** Unanticipated negative consequences **Strategy:** Develop vision and live it	Most basic to the Magician is the desire to search out the fundamental laws of how things work and to apply these principles to getting things done. The most typical applications of magical lore are to heal the mind, heart, and body; to find the fountain of youth and the secret of longevity. Or to invent products to make things happen. The Magician's motto is: "It can happen."	Magician brands include all those that foster "magical moments": Sony, Google, Moët and Chandon, Verve Clicquot, MasterCard, and Disney. Television shows characterized by the Magician include: *City of Angels, Touched by an Angel,* and *Seventh Heaven.*	As customers, Magicians believe that who you are is as important as the quality of your products or services. You are always, therefore, selling yourself, your values, and your own consciousness when marketing to Magicians. Magicians are motivated by personal transformation; therefore, firms offering transformative experiences will appeal most to Magicians.
No Man Is an Island			
"Lover" **Core desire:** Attain intimacy and experience sensual pleasure **Goal:** Being in a relationship with people **Fear:** Being alone, a wall-flower unwanted and unloved **Strategy:** Become more and more attractive physically, emotionally, and in every other way	The Lover archetype governs all sorts of love, from parental love, to friendship, to spiritual love, but most important is romantic love. The Lover is always active in intense and personal friendships. Lovers think of themselves as being wonderfully appreciative of others. They also typically dislike competition. This can often lead to jealousy and mean-spirited behavior. The Lover's motto is: "I only have eyes for you."	Lover brands include: Coco Chanel, Christian Dior, The Body Shop, Revlon, Godiva, Victoria's Secret, Hallmark, and Häagen Dazs. Lover archetypes in movies include: *Titanic, Pretty Woman,* and *Casablanca.* Famous Lover people include: Sofia Vergara, Sophia Loren, Elizabeth Taylor, and George Clooney.	The Lover wants a deeper kind of connection—one that is intimate, genuine, and personal (sometimes also sensual). Lovers often identify products with certain relationships. Lovers develop deep relationships with products and companies, especially those that help them feel special and loved. These types of consumers also like being singled out for attention; for example: "mailing to special customers only."
"Jester" **Core desire:** To live in the moment with full enjoyment **Goal:** To have a great time and lighten up the world **Fear:** Boredom and being boring **Strategy:** Play, make jokes, and be funny	The Jester archetype includes: the clown, the trickster, and anyone at all who loves to play or act up. While it is possible to have fun on our own, the Jester calls us out to come and play with one another. Jester figures enjoy life and interaction for their own sake. They also love being the life of the party! The Jester's motto is: "If I can't dance, I don't want to be a part of your revolution."	Jester brands include: M&Ms, Snickers, Skittles, Pringles, Coke, Pepsi, and Bud Light. Famous Jester people include: Robin Williams, Johnny Carson, Chris Rock, and Will Smith.	The Jester in every one of us loves humor. Jesters like funny commercials because they entertain them and make them feel good, creating a halo effect around the product. Jester ads and packaging highlight bright colors and lots of action—the more outrageous, the better. Overall, the Jester loves the fun of marketing. They are not frightened by knowing we are in a new time.

Source: Adapted from Michael R. Solomon, Rebekah Russell-Bennett, and Josephine Previte, *Consumer Behaviour: Buying, Having, Being,* 3rd ed., Frenchs Forest, NSW: Pearson Australia, 2012.

Trait Theory

Popular online matchmaking services such as match.com and eharmony.com offer to create your "personality profile" and then hook you up with other members whose profiles are similar. This approach to personality focuses on the quantitative measurement of **personality traits**, which we define as the identifiable characteristics that define a person.

What are some crucial personality traits? Consumer researchers have looked at many to establish linkages to product choice, such as "need for uniqueness," "introversion/extroversion" (whether people are shy or outgoing), and "attention to social comparison information." Some research evidence suggests that ad messages that match how a person thinks about himself or herself are more persuasive.[16]

Another trait relevant to consumer behavior is **frugality**. Frugal people deny short-term purchasing whims; they choose instead to resourcefully use what they already own. For example, this personality type tends to favor cost-saving measures such as timing showers and bringing leftovers from home to have for lunch at work.[18] Obviously, during tough economic times many people reveal their "inner frugalista" as they search for ways to save money. Indeed, as the Great Recession invaded, Google searches for the term *frugality* increased by roughly 2,500 percent. Whereas many of us splurged on expensive cars or Jimmy Choo shoes (or both) in the past, many analysts predict that more of us will

Net Profit

Certainly messages and products that promote uniqueness so that a consumer can make a statement via individualized choices are bound to appeal to some more than others. Technological developments encourage **product personalization** strategies that enable each buyer to customize an item and in some cases to design it online. Continuum, a new clothing company, allows women to create their own bikini design. After she uploads her measurements, the company uses three-dimensional printing to generate the product in nylon.[17]

Products like these from a German company appeal to people who like to be well-organized.
Source: Photo courtesy of The Container Store.

After elfa
The same space — with the same contents — is transformed into a well-functioning and beautiful closet!

Your design is customized to suit your unique storage needs.

Real wood accents add warmth to your space.

All of the vertical space is used to create additional storage.

Shoes are organized, easy to access and take up little space.

You have visibility to what you've stored, which saves time.

The Container Store   containerstore.com | 800.733.3532

be frugal down the road, even when the economy improves. They expect to see us buy smaller houses and (gasp!) live within our means as we forsake heavy credit card debt. How accurate is this prediction? Maybe the answer depends on how many of us truly have frugal personality traits versus those who are merely "taking a break" until the economy improves. Recent surveys of U.S. college students indicate that frugal consumers are less materialistic and not as involved as brands compared to others; they're also less likely to be concerned about others' opinions regarding what they buy.[19]

According to the research firm Mindset Media, personality traits are better predictors of the type of media consumers choose than are demographic variables such as age, gender, and income. The company also claims that the TV shows you watch offer marketers insights into your personality and the types of brands you're likely to prefer, based on your dominant personality traits and the (perceived) matchup with a brand's image. To find out which personalities are attracted to which TV shows it recently analyzed self-reported data from about 25,000 TV viewers across more than 70 TV shows. These are some of the media/trait/brand linkages the company generated in its analysis:[20]

- Viewers of *Mad Men* are emotionally sensitive and intellectually curious types who often tend to be dreamers rather than realists. Good brand matches are Apple and the Audi A6.
- Viewers of *Family Guy* are rebels who don't like authority, rules, or structure they deem unfair, and usually won't hesitate to make their feelings known with anger or sarcasm. Good brand matches are DiGiorno and the Ford F150.
- Viewers of *Dancing with the Stars* are traditionalists who prefer stability and the tried-and-true. They respect authority and generally have their feet firmly grounded. Good brand matches are Kraft and the Chrysler Town and Country car.
- Viewers of *The Office* consider themselves superior to others and like to brag about their accomplishments. They also like to be in charge. Good brand matches are Starbucks and the BMW Series 3.

The Big Five Personality Traits

The most widely recognized approach to measuring personality traits is the so-called **Big Five** (also known as the Neo-Personality Inventory). This is a set of five dimensions that form the basis of personality: openness to experience, conscientiousness, extroversion, agreeableness, and neuroticism. Table 7.3 describes these dimensions.

TABLE 7.3   Description of Big Five Personality Dimensions

	Description	Example of Measurement Items (agree/disagree)
Openness to experience	The degree to which a person is open to new ways of doing things	Love to think up new ways of doing things
Conscientiousness	The level of organization and structure a person needs	Am always prepared
Extroversion	How well a person tolerates stimulation from people	Talk to a lot of different people at parties
Agreeableness	The degree to which we defer to other people	Take time out for others
Neuroticism (emotional instability)	How well a person copes with stress	Get upset easily

Source: Michael R. Solomon, Rebekah Russell-Bennett, and Josephine Previte, *Consumer Behaviour: Buying, Having, Being,* 3rd ed., Frenchs Forest, NSW: Pearson Australia, 2012.

TABLE 7.4	The Four Dimensions of the Myers-Briggs Type Indicator®	
Focus of attention	Extroversion (E) External world	Introversion (I) Internal world
Take in information	Sensing (S) Sequential, step-by-step	Intuition (N) Big picture
Make decisions	Thinking (T) Step back from the situation, take an objective view	Feeling (F) Step into the situation, take a subjective view
Deal with the outer world	Judging (J) A planned approach to meeting the deadline in a scheduled way	Perceiving (P) A spontaneous approach to meeting the deadline with a rush of activity

Source: Adapted from Meyers-Briggs Type Indicator® (MBTI®),https://www.cpp.com (products page/mbti/index.aspx), accessed March 29, 2015.

The **Myers-Briggs Type Indicator**®, which is based on Jung's work, is another widely used personality test. When you apply for a job it is quite possible your potential employer will ask you to take this test. Depending on a respondent's preferences within each of four dimensions as Table 7.4 shows, he or she is assigned to one of 16 four-letter types.[21] Jung believed each of us has "inborn predispositions" along these dimensions that then interact with the environment to shape personality.

The publishers of the Myers-Briggs test also relate these dimensions to social media usage. For example, they report that people who use platforms such as Facebook, Twitter, and LinkedIn are more likely to be Extroverts, use Intuition, and arrive at decisions by Thinking.[22]

Problems with Trait Theory in Consumer Research

Because consumer researchers categorize large numbers of consumers according to whether they exhibit various traits, we can apply this approach to segment markets. If a car manufacturer, for example, determines that drivers who fit a given trait profile prefer a car with certain features, it can use this information to great advantage. The notion that consumers buy products that are extensions of their personalities makes intuitive sense. As we'll see shortly, many marketing managers endorse this idea as they try to create *brand personalities* to appeal to different types of consumers.

Unfortunately, the use of standard personality trait measurements to predict product choices has met with mixed success at best. In general, marketing researchers simply have not been able to predict consumers' behaviors on the basis of measured personality traits. These are some logical explanations for these less-than-stellar results:[23]

- Many of the scales are not sufficiently valid or reliable; they do not adequately measure what they are supposed to measure, and their results may not be stable over time.
- Psychologists typically develop personality tests for specific populations (e.g., people who are mentally ill); marketers then "borrow" them to apply to a more general population where they have questionable relevance.
- Often marketers don't administer the tests under the appropriate conditions; people who are not properly trained may give them in a classroom or at a kitchen table.
- The researchers often make changes in the instruments to adapt them to their own situations and needs; in the process, they may add or delete items and rename variables. These *ad hoc* changes dilute the validity of the measures and also reduce researchers' ability to compare results across consumer samples.
- Many trait scales measure gross, overall tendencies (e.g., emotional stability or introversion); marketers then use these results to make predictions about purchases of specific brands.

● In many cases, marketers ask consumers to respond to a large number of scales with no advance thought about how they will relate these measures to consumer behavior. The researchers then use a "shotgun approach" because they follow up on anything that happens to look interesting. As any statistician will tell you, this approach capitalizes on chance and can produce distorted results that may not be reproducible (or surface at all) in other studies.

Although marketing researchers largely abandoned the use of personality measures after many studies failed to yield meaningful results, some researchers have not given up on the early promise of this line of work. More recent efforts (mainly in Europe) try to learn from past mistakes. Researchers use more specific measures of personality traits that they have reason to believe are relevant to economic behavior. They try to increase the validity of these measures, primarily by including multiple measures of behavior rather than just a single personality scale. In addition, these researchers tone down their expectations of what personality traits can tell them about consumers. They now recognize that traits are only part of the solution; they have to incorporate personality data with information about people's social and economic conditions for it to be useful.[24] As a result, some more recent research has had better success at relating personality traits to such consumer behaviors as alcohol consumption among young men or shoppers' willingness to try new, healthier food products.[25] Table 7.5 provides some examples of consumer research studies that tie personality traits to product purchase and use.

TABLE 7.5   The Influence of Personality Traits on Consumer Behavior

Personality Trait	Influence on Consumer Behavior
Superstition	Sports fan behavior such as "lucky socks," the direction of one's cap on the head, purchase of good luck charms, refusal to purchase particular items because of bad luck (i.e., opals, peacock feathers, apricots)
Pro-environment	Individual recycling efforts, decreased car usage, increased use of public transport
Romanticism	Movie genre choice, more likely to take risks, prefer warm countries to visit, prefer luxury travel
Willingness to spend money	Spendthrifts save less money and carry more debt than tightwads, so they are higher users of credit cards; more likely to buy hedonic items than tightwads
Enjoyment of shopping	People who enjoy shopping are more likely to spend time searching for products, resulting in increased product knowledge
Need for cognition (enjoyment of thinking)	People who enjoy thinking respond better to words than pictures and are more motivated to spend time processing the words and reading the "fine print."
Need for affect (enjoyment of processing feelings)	People who enjoy feelings respond better to pictures than words; more likely to engage in compulsive behavior; pictures may encourage impulse buying
Impulsiveness	More likely to experience pleasure than guilt when overeating
Need for uniqueness	People who want to "stand out from the crowd" tend to be opinion leaders; they are more likely to be sources of information about brands and products for other people
Susceptibility to interpersonal influence (how influenced a person is by another)	A person who is easily influenced by others is more likely to prefer wines that offer social benefits such as prestige
Self-consciousness	People who are concerned with the way they appear to others are less likely to complain directly to a business or in front of others
Extroversion	Extroverts experience more positive emotions when consuming
Neuroticism	Neurotic people are less likely to repurchase or complain (they just leave), regardless of their level of satisfaction

Source: Michael R. Solomon, Rebekah Russell-Bennett, and Josephine Previte, *Consumer Behaviour: Buying, Having, Being*, 3rd ed., Frenchs Forest, NSW: Pearson Australia, 2012.[26]

OBJECTIVE 7-2
Brands have
personalities.

Brand Personality

Are Apple users better than the rest of us? Many of us know an "Apple-holic" who likes to turn up his or her nose at the uneducated masses that have to get by with their primitive PCs or Android phones. In fact, a survey of 20,000 people claims that iPad users are unkind and have little empathy; it labels them a "selfish elite." It also described them as "six times more likely to be wealthy, well-educated, power-hungry, over-achieving, sophisticated, unkind and non-altruistic 30- to 50-year-olds. They are self-centered workaholics with an overwhelming interest in business and finance who cherish 'power and achievement' and will not cross the street to help others."[27] Ouch! That's a pretty harsh way to describe people who happen to gravitate toward a successful brand. Do products as well as their owners actually have personalities? Let's step back to explore this intriguing question.

In 1886, a momentous event occurred in marketing history: The Quaker Oats man first appeared on boxes of hot cereal. Quakers had a reputation in 19th-century America for being shrewd but fair, and peddlers sometimes dressed as members of this religious group to cash in on their credibility. When the cereal company decided to "borrow" this imagery for its packages, it hoped customers might make the same association.[28]

Today, thousands of brands also borrow personality traits of individuals or groups to convey an image they want customers to form of them. A **brand personality** is the set of traits people attribute to a product as if it were a person.[29] An advertising agency wrote the following memo to help it figure out how to portray one of its clients. Based on this description of the "client," can you guess who he is? "He is creative ... unpredictable ... an imp.... He not only walks and talks, but has the ability to sing, blush, wink, and work with little devices like pointers.... He can also play musical instruments.... His walking motion is characterized as a 'swagger.' ... He is made of dough and has mass."[30] Of course, we all know today that packaging and other physical cues create a "personality" for a product (in this case, the Pillsbury Doughboy).

It's increasingly common for marketers to think carefully about brand personality as they embrace the communications approach known as **brand storytelling**. This perspective emphasizes the importance of giving a product a rich background to involve customers in its history or experience. Brand storytelling is based on the tradition of **reader-response theory**, which is a widely accepted perspective in literature that focuses on the role of the reader in interpreting a story rather than just relying upon the author's version. This approach recognizes that the consumer does not just want to listen to a manufactured set of details, but he or she wants to participate in the story by "filling in the blanks."[31]

One popular genre of brand storytelling is what a set of researchers described as an **underdog brand biography**. This includes details about a brand's humble origins and how it defied the odds to succeed. Such a story resonates with consumers because they can identify with these struggles. Thus, Google, HP, and Apple like to talk about the garages in which they started. The label on a Nantucket Nectars bottle describes how the company started "with only a blender and a dream."[32]

Anthropomorphism refers to the tendency to attribute human characteristics to objects or animals. We may think about a cartoon character or mythical creation as if it were a person and even assume that it has human feelings. Again, consider familiar spokescharacters such as Chester Cheetah from Pringles, the Keebler Elves, or the Michelin Man—or the frustration some people feel when they come to believe their computer is smarter than they are or even that it's "conspiring" to make them crazy! As we saw in our discussion of *sex-typed products* in Chapter 6, there is a common tendency in particular to ascribe a gender to a product. We tend to gravitate toward products that are the same as our own gender. In one study, a promotional message that depicted a fragrance, digital camera, and car as either male or female resulted in more positive evaluations when the item's (presumed) gender was the same as the respondent's.[34]

In a sense, a brand personality is a statement about the brand's market position. Understanding this is crucial to marketing strategy, especially if consumers don't see the brand the way its makers intend them to and they must attempt to *reposition* the product

Marketing Pitfall

Even colleges have brand personalities—though, as with other products, these images aren't always an accurate (or desirable) reflection of the place. ESPN had to pull the plug on an advertising campaign for its collegiate basketball coverage after managers learned that Anomaly, the advertising agency ESPN had retained for the campaign, intended to recruit actors who would play the stereotypical students at numerous schools. The idea was to have the students stationed at a call center; they would phone consumers to convince them to watch their school play on TV. Here are just a few of the "brand personalities" a leaked memo described:

- Tennessee: "a slutty girl who would hang out at the cowgirl hall of fame."
- Duke: "a smart, with it, young white male. He's handsome. He's from money. He is, in short, the kind of guy everyone can't stand. He is the kind of guy everyone wants to be."
- Oklahoma: "is awesome and he thinks everything is awesome. He's very enthusiastic about all things call center and all things life and he wants to share this contagious enthusiasm with everyone he meets. Wide-eyed, as naive as they come."
- Purdue: "child prodigy. 14-year-old. Or open to an 18-year-old who looks 14. Aeronautical engineering. Wiz kid. Think McLovin from *Superbad*."
- Kansas: "straight off the farm. However, he takes great pains to point out that Kansas is very cosmopolitan, as witnessed by their record, their burgeoning tech industry, and their hybrid corns (bonus: modified by fish genes!)."
- Villanova: "the poor man's Duke—he's not quite as handsome, he's not quite as rich, he's not quite as dapper. After 2 or 3 beers though, who cares? ... he's friendly enough."
- Pittsburgh: "a tomboy. She obviously grew up in the neighborhood and isn't going to take any guff from anyone and she'll wallop you in the eye with a crowbar if you suggest different. So don't. Think Tina Fey type."
- Georgetown: "a 4.36 GPA who's lived in 9 world-class cities, but all the time in her sister's shadow (her GPA is 4.37). She's sort of the female Duke, except most people like her. Think Reese Witherspoon."[33]

Quaker Oats was one of the first companies
to create a distinct personality for its brand.
Source: FoodPhotography/Alamy.

(i.e., give it a personality makeover). That's the problem Volvo now faces: Its cars are
renowned for safety, but drivers don't exactly see them as exciting or sexy. A safe and solid
brand personality makes it hard to sell a racy convertible like the C70 model, so a British
ad tried to change that perception with the tagline, "Lust, envy, jealousy. The dangers
of a Volvo." Just as with people, however, you can only go so far to convince others that
your personality has changed. Volvo has been trying to jazz up its image for years, but for
the most part consumers don't buy it. In a previous attempt in the United Kingdom, the
company paired action images like a Volvo pulling a helicopter off a cliff with the headline
"Safe Sex"—but market research showed that people didn't believe the new image. As one

CB AS I SEE IT
Nira Munichor, Hebrew University of Jerusalem

Think of an arrogant person you know. What is your evaluation of this person? How successful do you think he or she is? How does this person make you feel? How uncomfortable are you in his or her presence? Now, picture an arrogant brand, a brand that conveys superiority in addition to a certain level of disrespect for others. For example, a brand that states that it is "Hated by many. Loved by few,"

and that informs you that "You're not worthy." Which attributes do you think such a brand has? Do you think the brand is high-quality? And would you buy a product of such a brand?

My colleague, Professor Yael Steinhart, and I have been investigating **brand arrogance** and the effects it has on consumers' decisions, behaviors, and even well-being. Arrogance is an interesting trait in that it comprises both positive and negative aspects. On one hand, consumers think of arrogant brands (like arrogant people) as being high in status and quality, which suggests that consumers should find these brands appealing. On the other hand, arrogance makes consumers feel uncomfortable and inferior, and they might therefore be put off by arrogant brands (just as they might be put off by arrogant people).

How does the complex array of positive and negative associations that arrogant brands evoke influence consumers' purchase decisions? All told, does arrogance make a brand more or less attractive for consumers? We have discovered that the answers to these questions depend on who the consumer is, and, in particular, how positive or negative the consumer's

self-evaluation is. When people feel good about themselves, namely, when they have high self-esteem and high self-confidence, they tend to be less sensitive to criticism. Similarly, consumers with positive self-perceptions are less sensitive to the sense of inferiority that arrogant brands induce. Consequently, these consumers focus on the positive connotations inherent in brand arrogance, and are inclined to prefer an arrogant brand over a comparable non-arrogant alternative. In contrast, consumers with negative self-perceptions, those who feel unconfident and have low self-esteem, find it difficult to tolerate any additional harm to their self-view. These consumers are therefore motivated to resist arrogant brands that might cause them to feel inferior, and to prefer alternatives.

Interestingly, arrogant brand resistance, which at first glance might seem to be a defensive act of withdrawal, appears to be beneficial for consumers, and may help them improve their self-perceptions. We have found that consumers with negative self-evaluations feel better about themselves after they resist an arrogant brand.

brand consultant observed, "You get the sort of feeling you get when you see your grandparents trying to dance the latest dance. Slightly amused and embarrassed."[35]

Many of the most recognizable figures in popular culture are spokescharacters for long-standing brands, such as the Jolly Green Giant, the Keebler Elves, Mr. Peanut, or Charlie the Tuna.[36] These personalities periodically get a makeover to keep their meanings current. For example, Bayer recast Speedy Alka-Seltzer: In the 1950s and later, he was an all-around good guy who was ready to help with any sort of indigestion. Today, he appears as a "wingman" for men in their 20s and 30s who tend to "overindulge" on food and drink. (Do you know anyone who fits this description?) The creative director on the campaign explained that the goal is to introduce Speedy as "the good-times enabler who shows up whenever guys are being guys."[37]

Forging a successful brand personality often is key to building brand loyalty, but it's not as easy to accomplish as it might appear. One reason is that many consumers (particularly younger ones) have a sensitive "BS detector" that alerts them when a brand doesn't live up to its claims or is somehow inauthentic. When this happens, the strategy may backfire as consumers rebel. They may create Web sites to attack the brand or post

A study found that consumers infer strong differences in a wine's "personality" based on the bottle's label design.

Source: Reprinted with permission from *Journal of Marketing*, published by the American Marketing Association, Ulrich R. Orth & Keven Malkewitz, May 2008, Vol. 72, p. 73.

Personality Traits		Low	High
Sincerity	Down-to-earth Honest Wholesome Cheerful		
Excitement	Daring Spirited Imaginative Up-to-date		
Competence	Reliable Intelligent Successful		
Sophistication	Upper class Charming		
Ruggedness	Outdoorsy Tough		

parodies that make fun of it on YouTube. One set of researchers terms this phenomenon a **Doppelgänger brand image** (one that looks like the original but is in fact a critique of it). For example, many consumers were immensely loyal to the Snapple brand until Quaker purchased it. These loyalists felt that Quaker had stripped the brand of its offbeat, grassroots sensibility; one shock jock renamed it "Crapple" on his radio show.[38]

Many of the most recognizable figures in popular culture are spokescharacters for long-standing brands.
Source: Franck Fotos/Alamy.

So, how do people think about brands? We use some personality dimensions to compare and contrast the perceived characteristics of brands in various product categories, including these:[39]

- Old-fashioned, wholesome, traditional
- Surprising, lively, "with it"
- Serious, intelligent, efficient
- Glamorous, romantic, sexy
- Rugged, outdoorsy, tough, athletic

Indeed, consumers appear to have little trouble assigning personality qualities to all sorts of inanimate products, from personal care products to more mundane, functional ones—even kitchen appliances. Whirlpool's research showed that people saw its products as more feminine than they saw competing brands. When respondents were asked to imagine the appliance as a person, many of them pictured a modern, family-oriented woman living in the suburbs—attractive but not flashy. In contrast, they envisioned the company's Kitchen Aid brand as a modern professional woman who was glamorous, wealthy, and enjoyed classical music and the theater.[40]

A product that creates and communicates a distinctive brand personality stands out from its competition and inspires years of loyalty. However, personality analysis helps marketers identify a brand's weaknesses that have little to do with its functional qualities: Adidas asked kids in focus groups to imagine that the brand came to life and was at a party and to tell what they would expect the brand to be doing there. The kids responded that Adidas would be hanging around the keg with its pals, talking about girls. Unfortunately, they also said Nike would *be with* the girls![41] The results reminded Adidas' brand managers that they had some work to do.[42]

Just as we rely on all sorts of cues to infer a human being's personality including facial features, body type, clothing, home decoration, and so on the same is true when we try to figure out brand personality. A product's design is an obvious cue (Apple is "sleek," IKEA is "practical"). Packaging is another, as we saw in Chapter 3, that shapes and colors link to meanings.

Another important cue is a brand name: Although Shakespeare wrote "a rose by any other name would smell as sweet," in reality a name does make a difference. That's why you order mahi-mahi instead of dolphin, Chilean sea bass instead of Patagonian toothfish, and you buy dried plums rather than prunes. Companies typically pay professional "namers" up to $75,000 to come up with a good one that makes a memorable statement about brand personality, and of course millions more to put the marketing muscle behind it that makes the name a household word.

Although Steve Jobs came up with Apple (and stuck with it despite a lawsuit from The Beatles) and Sir Richard Branson thought of Virgin, in many cases the naming decision is carefully made by a team of branding experts and sometimes carefully scrutinized as well. This is especially true for pharmaceutical products because the Food and Drug Administration (FDA) makes sure that the name doesn't make claims it can't support: Rogaine, the hair-restoring medication, was originally named Regain but the FDA didn't approve. In addition, it's important that a drug name can't be mistaken for another medication. A heartburn treatment named Losec became Prilosec so that people wouldn't confuse it with the diuretic Lasix (that would not be a happy day for the patient). The FDA goes so far as to conduct handwriting tests on proposed names to be sure pharmacists won't fill a prescription with a similar drug.[43]

In other categories, the goal is more straightforward: Break through the clutter and get noticed. Today that sometimes means a name that borders on the vulgar, but it gets our attention. Hapi Food cereal (that offers laxative properties) switched its name to Holy Crap cereal after a customer used that term to describe the product's benefits. You can buy a Kickass Cupcake, and wash it down with wines called Sassy Bitch or Fat Bastard. The HVLS Fan Company (short for high volume, low speed) was moving sluggishly until the owner changed the name to Big Ass Fans.[44]

Marketing Pitfall

When a regional carrier called USAir was purchased in the late 1990s, the buyer decided that the name sounded too regional. He hired a branding firm to find a new one. The rebranding process took 9 months and was reported to cost almost $40 million. The new name: US Airways.

OBJECTIVE 7-3

A lifestyle defines a pattern of consumption that reflects a person's choices of how to spend his or her time and money, and these choices are essential to define consumer identity.

Lifestyles and Consumer Identity

Are you an **e-sports** fan, or is the idea of getting your kicks by watching *other* people play video games a bit strange? Maybe Amazon knows something you don't; the company paid almost $1 billion to acquire the Twitch Web site where many of these contests occur.[45] Although still under the radar for many of us, competitive video gaming has become a major "athletic" activity. Millions of people watch e-sports on television. Today some video game players are celebrities with their own fan base and merchandise. The

E-sports attracts millions of fans around the world.
Source: Imaginechina/Corbis.

sport is especially hot in South Korea, where a couple is as likely to go on a date to a game club as to the movies. One live tournament there drew 100,000 spectators. [46] Take that, Super Bowl.

Consumers who choose to spend hours watching their heroes play videogames make choices: how to spend their time and how to spend their money. Each of us makes similar choices everyday and often two quite similar people in terms of basic categories such as gender, age, income, and place of residence still prefer to spend their time and money in markedly different ways. We often see this strong variation among students at the same university, even though many of them come from similar backgrounds. A "typical" college student (if there is such a thing) may dress much like his or her friends, hang out in the same places, and like the same foods, yet still indulge a passion for marathon running, stamp collecting, or acid jazz. According to *The Urban Dictionary*, some of the undergraduates at your school may fall into one of these categories:[48]

- **Metro:** You just can't walk past a Banana Republic store without making a purchase. You own 20 pairs of shoes, half a dozen pairs of sunglasses, just as many watches, and you carry a man-purse. You see a stylist instead of a barber because barbers don't do highlights. You can make lamb shanks and risotto for dinner and Eggs Benedict for breakfast ... all from scratch. You shave more than just your face. You also exfoliate and moisturize.
- **Hesher:** A Reebok-wearing, mulleted person in acid-washed jeans and a Judas Priest T-shirt who still lives in his or her parents' basement, swears that he or she can really rock out on his or her Ibanez Stratocaster copy guitar, and probably owns a Nova that hasn't run in five years.
- **Emo:** Someone into soft-core punk music that integrates high-pitched, overwrought lyrics and inaudible guitar riffs. He or she wears tight wool sweaters, tighter jeans, itchy scarves (even in the summer), ripped chucks with their favorite band's signature, black square-rimmed glasses, and ebony greasy unwashed hair that is required to cover at least three-fifths of the face at an angle.

In traditional societies, class, caste, village, or family largely dictate a person's consumption options. In a modern consumer society, however, each of us is free (at least within our budgets) to select the set of products, services, and activities that define our self and, in turn, create a social identity we communicate to others. **Lifestyle** defines a

The Tangled Web

The explosive popularity of e-sports has created a downside for some celebrity gamers. In the last few years, a popular—and costly—prank that initially targeted movie and music stars has made its way into the e-sports world. It's called **swatting**, and it involves phone calls and texts to police departments that falsely report wrongdoing at a celebrity's home (such as the rapper Lil Wayne). These alarms prompt a visit from a SWAT team that descends on the house. The competitive nature of e-sports creates rivalries and grudges and some players decide this is a fun and public way to get back at another player.[47]

Thousands of people who are into cosplay strut their stuff at Comic Con conventions.
Source: Jamie Pham Photography/Alamy.

Marketing Opportunity

Trend trackers find some of the most interesting—and rapidly changing—microcultures in Japan, where young women start many trends that eventually make their way around the world. One is *Onna Otaku* (she-nerds): girls who get their geek on as they stock up on femme-friendly comics, gadgets, and action figures instead of makeup and clothes. Another is the growing **cosplay** movement, a form of performance art in which participants wear elaborate costumes that represent a virtual world avatar or other fictional character. These outfits often depict figures from *manga, anime*, or other forms of graphic novels, but they can also take the form of costumes from movies such as *The Matrix, Star Wars, Harry Potter*, or even *Ace Ventura: Pet Detective* (cosplay cafés in Tokyo feature waitresses who dress as maids). This role-playing subculture appears in various forms in Western culture as well, as anyone who attended one of the many Comic Con conventions held in U.S. cities can attest.[50]

pattern of consumption that reflects a person's choices of how to spend his or her time and money. These choices play a key role in defining consumer identity.[49] Whether Tuners, Dead Heads, or skinheads, each lifestyle subculture exhibits its own unique set of norms, vocabulary, and product insignias. These subcultures often form around fictional characters and events, and they help to define the extended self (see Chapter 6). Numerous lifestyles thrive on their collective worship of mythical and not-so-mythical worlds and characters that range from the music group Phish to Hello Kitty.

Marketers also think about lifestyle in terms of how much time we have available to do what we'd like and what we choose to do with that leisure time. In 2014, Americans between the ages of 25 and 54 who are employed on average spent 8.7 hours working, 2.5 hours on leisure activities, and 1 hour eating and drinking in a typical day.[51] In contrast, although full-time college students on average also devote an hour per day to eating and drinking, they spent 3.3 hours on educational activities, 2.2 hours working, 1.4 hours traveling, 4 hours on leisure—and 0.8 hour on grooming.[52] Figure 7.2 shows how U.S. consumers more generally allocate their time.

A **lifestyle marketing perspective** recognizes that people sort themselves into groups on the basis of the things they like to do, how they like to spend their leisure time, and how they choose to spend their disposable income.[53] The growing number of niche magazines and Web sites that cater to specialized interests reflects the spectrum of choices available to us in today's society. The downside of this is obvious to the newspaper industry; several major papers have already had to shut down their print editions because people consume most of their information online.

A lifestyle is much more than how we allocate our discretionary income. It is a statement about who one is in society and who one is not. Group identities, whether of hobbyists, athletes, or drug users, gel around distinctive consumption choices. Social scientists use a number of terms to describe such self-definitions in addition to lifestyle, including *taste public, consumer group, symbolic community*, and *status culture*.[54]

A goal of lifestyle marketing is to allow consumers to pursue their chosen ways to enjoy their lives and express their social identities. For this reason, a key aspect of this strategy is to focus on people who use products in desirable social settings. The desire to associate a product with a social situation is a long-standing one for advertisers, whether they include the product in a round of golf, a family barbecue, or a night at a glamorous club surrounded by the hip-hop elite.[55] Thus, people, products, and settings combine to express a *consumption style*, as Figure 7.3 diagrams.

Figure 7.2 HOW U.S. CONSUMERS ALLOCATE THEIR TIME

Courtesy of The Hartman Group, Inc.

OBJECTIVE 7-4

It can be more useful to identify patterns of consumption than knowing about individual purchases when organizations craft a lifestyle marketing strategy.

Product Complementarity and Co-Branding Strategies

The designer Ralph Lauren has crafted a classic lifestyle brand that people around the world associate with U.S. taste. He built his Polo empire on an image that evokes country homes and sheepdogs. At the company's elegant flagship store in Manhattan that is a refurbished mansion, one business journalist wrote, "While men who look like lawyers search for your size shirt and ladies who belong at deb parties suggest complementary bags and shoes, you experience the ultimate in lifestyle advertising." Not bad for a guy born in the Bronx to a Jewish housepainter; his original name was Ralph Lifshitz. Now the Lauren empire is expanding beyond clothing, fragrances, and home accessories to restaurants in Paris, Chicago, and New York. You can eat the American Dream while you wear it.[56]

Figure 7.3 CONSUMPTION STYLE

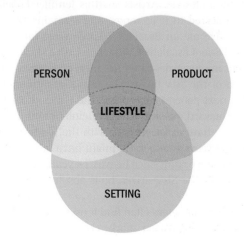

We get a clearer picture of how people use products to define lifestyles when we see how they make choices in a variety of product categories. A lifestyle marketing perspective implies that we must look at *patterns of behavior* to understand consumers. As one study noted, "All goods carry meaning, but none by itself.... The meaning is in the relations between all the goods, just as music is in the relations marked out by the sounds and not in any one note."[57]

Indeed, many products and services do seem to "go together," usually because the same types of people tend to select them. In many cases, products do not seem to "make sense" if companion products don't accompany them (e.g., fast food and paper plates, or a suit and tie) or are incongruous in the presence of other products that have a different personality (e.g., a Chippendale chair in a high-tech office or discount cigarettes paired with a solid gold lighter).

Therefore, an important part of lifestyle marketing is to identify the set of products and services that consumers associate with a specific lifestyle. In fact, research evidence suggests that even a relatively unattractive product becomes more appealing when consumers link it with other products that they do like.[58] Furthermore, when people consume multiple products that are labeled with the same brand they actually like them more: They believe that these items were deliberately developed to go together.[59]

The meshing of objects from many different categories to express a single lifestyle idea is at the heart of many consumption decisions, including coordinating an outfit for a big date (shoes, garments, fragrance, etc.), decorating a room (tables, carpet, wallpaper, etc.), and designing a restaurant (menu, ambience, waitperson uniforms, etc.). Many people today evaluate products not just in terms of function but also in terms of how well their design coordinates with other objects and furnishings. Marketers who understand these cross-category relationships may pursue **co-branding strategies** where they team up with other companies to promote two or more items. Some marketers even match up their spokescharacters in ads; the Pillsbury Doughboy appeared in a commercial with the Sprint Guy to pitch cell phones, the lonely Maytag repairman was in an ad for the Chevrolet Impala, and the Taco Bell Chihuahua (now retired) showed up in a commercial for GEICO insurance.[60]

Product complementarity occurs when the symbolic meanings of different products relate to one another.[61] Consumers use these sets of products we call a **consumption constellation** to define, communicate, and perform social roles.[62] For example, we identified the U.S. "yuppie" of the 1980s by such products as a Rolex watch, a BMW automobile, a Gucci briefcase, a squash racket, fresh pesto, white wine, and brie cheese. Researchers find that even children are adept at creating consumption constellations, and as they get older they tend to include more brands in these cognitive structures.[63]

OBJECTIVE 7-5

Psychographics go beyond simple demographics to help marketers understand and reach different consumer segments.

Psychographics

When Cadillac introduced its Escalade SUV, critics scoffed at the bizarre pairing of this old-line luxury brand with a truck. However, consumers quickly associated the vehicle with the hip-hop lifestyle. Artists such as Jennifer Lopez, Outkast, and Jay Z referred to it in songs, and Jermaine Dupri proclaimed, "Gotta have me an Escalade." Three years later, Cadillac rolled out its 18-foot Escalade EXT pickup with a sticker price of $50,000.

The Escalade brand manager describes the target customer for luxury pickups as a slightly earthier version of the SUV buyer. She says that although the two drivers may own $2 million homes next door to each other, the typical luxury SUV driver is about 50, has an MBA from Harvard, belongs to a golf club, maintains connections with his college friends, and works hard at keeping up with the Joneses. In contrast, the luxury pickup driver is roughly 5 years younger. He might have inherited his father's construction business, and he's been working since he was 18 years old. He may or may not have attended college, and unlike the SUV driver, he is absolutely still connected to his high school friends.[64]

As this example shows, marketers often find it useful to develop products that appeal to different lifestyle subcultures. When marketers combine personality variables with

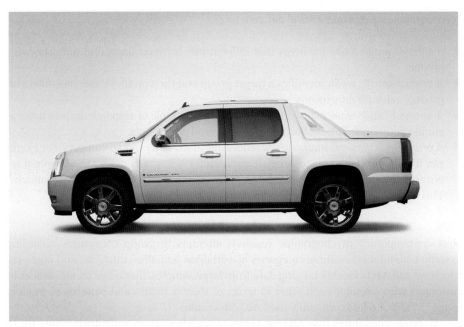

Cadillac developed a luxury SUV and then a luxury pickup to appeal to two distinct psychographic segments.
Source: Evox Productions/Drive Images/Alamy.

knowledge of lifestyle preferences, they have a powerful lens they can focus on consumer segments. It's common to create a fictional profile of a "core customer" who inspires product design and communications decisions. For example, Chip Wilson, who founded the popular clothing company Lululemon, relied on a "muse" he made up: A 32-year-old professional single woman named Ocean who makes $100,000 a year. He described Ocean as "engaged, has her own condo, is traveling, fashionable, has an hour and a half to work out a day." This ideal user, according to Wilson, appeals to all women: "If you're 20 years old or you're graduating from university, you can't wait to be that woman. If you're 42 years old with a couple children, you wish you had that time back." Lululemon added a male "muse" when the company moved into menswear: Duke is 35 and an "athletic opportunist" who surfs in the summer and snowboards in the winter. When he got involved in a new company, Kit and Ace, sure enough Wilson helped to come up with two new muses: "Kit, a 29-year-old single woman who 'is looking to buy her first apartment, but is still renting. She works in the creative area, like in graphic design or fashion, and loves to bike on weekends,' and Ace, a 32-year-old similarly groovy guy, who drinks strong coffee, 'likes to go to breweries and hangs out with his friends. He does CrossFit once a week and spins three times a week, loves brunch on the weekends.'"[65] Sound like anyone you know (hint: definitely not your humble author!)?

Psychographics involves the "use of psychological, sociological, and anthropological factors ... to determine how the market is segmented by the propensity of groups within the market—and their reasons—to make a particular decision about a product, person, ideology, or otherwise hold an attitude or use a medium."[66] Marketers use many psychographic variables to segment consumers, but all of these dimensions go beyond surface characteristics to investigate consumers' motivations for purchasing and using products. Demographics allow us to describe *who* buys, but psychographics tells us *why* they do. A classic example involves a popular Canadian advertising campaign for Molson Export beer that included insights from psychographic findings. The company's research showed that Molson's target customers tend to be like boys who never grew up, who were uncertain about the future, and who were intimidated by women's newfound freedoms. Accordingly, the ads featured a group of men, "Fred and the boys," whose get-togethers emphasized male companionship, protection against change, and the reassuring message that the beer "keeps on tasting great."[67]

How Do We Perform a Psychographic Analysis?
Psychographic studies take several different forms:

- A *lifestyle profile* looks for items that differentiate between users and nonusers of a product.
- A *product-specific profile* identifies a target group and then profiles these consumers on product-relevant dimensions.
- A *general lifestyle segmentation study* places a large sample of respondents into homogenous groups based on similarities of their overall preferences.
- A *product-specific segmentation study* tailors questions to a product category. For example, if a researcher wants to conduct research for a stomach medicine, she might rephrase the item, "I worry too much" as, "I get stomach problems if I worry too much." This allows her to more finely discriminate among users of competing brands.[68]

AIOs
Most contemporary psychographic research attempts to group consumers according to some combination of three categories of variables: activities, interests, and opinions, which we call **AIOs** for short. Using data from large samples, marketers create profiles of customers who resemble each other in terms of their activities and patterns of product usage.[69] Table 7.6 lists commonly used AIO dimensions.

To group consumers into AIO categories, researchers give respondents a long list of statements and ask them to indicate how much they agree with each one. Thus, we can "boil down" a person's lifestyle by discovering how he or she spends time, what he or she finds interesting and important, and how he or she views himself or herself and the world around him or her.

Typically, the first step in conducting a psychographic analysis is to determine which lifestyle segments yield the bulk of customers for a particular product. This strategy reflects *the 80/20 rule* we first discussed in Chapter 1. This rule reminds us that, in many cases, only one or a few lifestyle segments account for the majority of sales.[70]

Psychographic techniques help marketers to identify their heavy users. Then they can better understand how they relate to the brand and the benefits they derive from it. For instance, marketers at the beginning of the walking-shoe craze assumed that all purchasers were basically burned-out joggers. Subsequent psychographic research showed that there were actually several different groups of "walkers," ranging from those who walk to get to work to those who walk for fun. This realization resulted in shoes that manufacturers aimed at different segments, from Footjoy Joy-Walkers to Nike Healthwalkers.

The makers of the popular Sigg water bottle, which is available in many different designs, actually choose from about 3,000 different concepts each year with specific customers in mind. These include the Whole Foods Woman, who lives in a city, practices yoga, and buys organic produce; and the Geek Chic Guy, who listens to Radiohead and wears vintage Converse sneakers.
Source: Winston Wong/Alamy.

Marketers use the results of these studies to:

- **Define the target market** This information allows the marketer to go beyond simple demographic or product usage descriptions (e.g., middle-aged men or frequent users).
- **Create a new view of the market** Sometimes marketers create their strategies with a "typical" customer in mind. This stereotype may not be correct because the actual customer may not match these assumptions. For example, marketers of a face cream for women were surprised to find that older, widowed women were their heavy users rather than the younger, sociable women to whom they were pitching their appeals.

TABLE 7.6   AIO Dimensions

Activities	Interests	Opinions	Demographics
Work	Family	Themselves	Age
Hobbies	Home	Social issues	Education
Social events	Job	Politics	Income
Vacation	Community	Business	Occupation
Entertainment	Recreation	Economics	Family size
Club membership	Fashion	Education	Dwelling
Community	Food	Products	Geography
Shopping	Media	Future	City size
Sports	Achievements	Culture	Stage in life cycle

Source: William D. Wells and Douglas J. Tigert, "Activities, Interests, and Opinions," *Journal of Advertising Research* 11 (August 1971): 27–35. © 1971 by The Advertising Research Foundation. Used with permission.

- **Position the product** Psychographic information can allow the marketer to emphasize features of the product that fit in with a person's lifestyle.
- **Better communicate product attributes** The artist or copywriter obtains a much richer mental image of the target consumer than he or she can simply by looking at dry statistics. For example, research that the Schlitz beer brand conducted found that heavy beer drinkers tended to feel that life's pleasures were few and far between. In response, the brewer developed commercials with the tagline, "You only go around once, so reach for all the gusto you can."[71]
- **Develop product strategy** Understanding how a product fits, or does not fit, into consumers' lifestyles allows the marketer to identify new product opportunities, chart media strategies, and create environments most consistent and harmonious with these consumption patterns.
- **Market social and political issues** A psychographic study of men aged 18 to 24 who drink and drive highlights the potential for this perspective to help in the eradication of harmful behaviors. Researchers divided this segment into four groups: "good timers," "well adjusted," "nerds," and "problem kids." They found that one group in particular—"good timers"—was more likely to believe that it is fun to be drunk, that the chances of having an accident while driving drunk are low, and that drinking increases one's appeal to the opposite sex. Because the study showed that this group is also the most likely to drink at rock concerts and parties, is most likely to watch MTV, and tends to listen to album-oriented rock radio stations, reaching "good timers" with a prevention campaign became easier.[72]

Marketers constantly search for new insights so they can identify and reach groups of consumers united by common lifestyles. To meet this need, many research companies and advertising agencies develop their own **lifestyle segmentation typologies**. Respondents answer a battery of questions that allow the researchers to cluster them into a set of distinct lifestyle groups. The questions usually include a mixture of AIOs plus other items relating to feelings about specific brands, favorite celebrities, and media preferences. Companies that want to learn more about their customers and potential customers then buy one or more of these systems for their own use.

International VALS is a segmentation methodology that can be used to gain deeper consumer insights in different countries and can be useful for country-specific strategic marketing planning and communication strategies. International VALS presents country-specific frameworks based on cultural differences between attitudes and behaviors as they exist in different countries, including VALS for China, the Dominican Republic, Japan, Nigeria, the United Kingdom, and Venezuela.

Japan VALS and UK VALS will be discussed in this section to highlight how consumers from different countries can be segmented based on their society's attitudes and behaviors.

Japan-VALS™ divides Japanese society into different segments based on two key consumer attributes: primary motivation (*tradition, achievement,* and *self-expression*) and attitudes about social change (*innovation* and *self-expression*). Primary motivation describes what a person is most interested in: life, occupational duties, and recreational interests.

- **Integrators** rank the highest on the Japan-VALS measure of innovation. They are active, trend-setting, informed, affluent, well-traveled, and use a variety of media.
- **Self-Innovators and Self-Adapters** score high on self-expression. They are fashionable, socially active, and seek adventure.
- **Ryoshiki Innovators and Ryoshiki Adapters** are driven by occupations with a personal focus on education, career achievement, and professional knowledge. Home, family, and social status are their guiding concerns.
- **Traditional Innovators and Traditional Adapters** are primarily focused on matters of tradition, like religions and customs, and are conservative in their opinions. They have a preference for traditional home styling and fashion.

Achievers focus on hard work, professional pursuits, family, knowledge, influence, and qualifications.

- **High Pragmatics and Low Pragmatics** are less active, less informed, and have no obvious interests and lifestyle choices. They do not score high on any life-orientation dimension.
- **Sustainers** score lowest on the innovation and self-expression dimensions and prefer to sustain the past. They lack money, youth, and high education.

United Kingdom VALS (UK VALS™) categorizes consumers into one of six core groups. Segments are defined based on primary motivation (*tradition, achievement,* and *self-expression*), resources (*high* or *low*), and innovation.

- **Activators** are most open to change, new ideas, and products. They are forerunners of innovation and have a wide range of interests. This group is further divided by motivation: *tradition activators, achievement activators,* and *self-expression activators.*
- **Traditionalists** are primarily conservative and prefer to manage social change by reassessing new ideas based on tried and tested ones with established standards and ethical codes.
- **Achievers** base their accomplishments on hard work and professional pursuits. They are success-oriented and tend to focus on family, knowledge, influence, and qualifications.
- **Seekers** prefer individuality, self-discovery, and action. They actively seek self-gratification, excitement, and sociability.
- **Pragmatics** prefer to play safe and do not want to steer away from their peer group. They have a relatively low attachment to any particular lifestyle. Pragmatics can be differentiated on the basis on motivation: *Pragmatic Involvers* are motivated by tradition, *Pragmatic Rationals* are motivated by achievement, and *Pragmatic Aspirationals* are motivated by self-expression.
- **Constraineds** tend to stick to familiar things and the past. They are family-focused and have a few friends who share their opinions and ideas.

OBJECTIVE 7-6
Underlying values
often drive consumer
motivations.

Values

A religious official in Saudi Arabia decreed that children there should not be allowed to watch Mickey Mouse because the cartoon character is a "soldier of Satan."[73] This observation may surprise most of us, but then again we don't live in this deeply conservative Islamic culture. A **value** is a belief that some condition is preferable to its opposite. For example, it's safe to assume that most people prefer freedom to slavery. Others avidly pursue products and services that will make them look younger rather than older. A person's set of values plays an important role in consumption activities. Consumers purchase many products and services because they believe these products will help to attain a value-related goal.

Everyone wants to be clean, but some societies are more fastidious than others and won't accept products and services that they think cut corners. Italian women on average spend 21 hours a week on household chores other than cooking—compared with only 4 hours for Americans, at least according to Procter & Gamble's (P&G) research. The Italian women wash kitchen and bathroom floors at least four times a week, Americans only once. Italian women typically iron nearly all their wash, even socks and sheets, and they buy more cleaning supplies than women elsewhere do.

Because of these traits, they should be ideal customers for cleaning products, right? That's what Unilever thought when it launched its all-purpose Cif spray cleaner there, but it flopped. Similarly, P&G's best-selling Swiffer wet mop bombed big time. Both companies underestimated this market's desire for products that are tough cleaners, not timesavers. Only about 30 percent of Italian households have dishwashers because many women don't trust machines to get dishes as clean as they can get them by hand, manufacturers say. Many of those who do use machines tend to thoroughly rinse the dishes before they load them into the dishwasher. The explanation for this value: After World War II, Italy remained a poor country until well into the 1960s, so labor-saving devices, such as washing machines, which had become popular in wealthy countries, arrived late. Italian women joined the workforce later than many other European women and in smaller numbers. Young Italian women increasingly work outside the home, but they still spend nearly as much time as their mothers did on housework.

When Unilever did research to determine why Italians didn't take to Cif, they found that these women weren't convinced that a mere spray would do the job on tough kitchen grease or that one product would adequately clean different surfaces (it turns out that 72 percent of Italians own more than eight different cleaning products). The company reformulated the product and then reintroduced it with different varieties instead of as an all-in-one. It also made the bottles 50 percent bigger because Italians clean so frequently, and changed its advertising to emphasize the products' cleaning strength rather than convenience. P&G also reintroduced its Swiffer, this time adding beeswax and a Swiffer duster that is now a bestseller. It sold 5 million boxes in the first 8 months, twice the company's forecasts.[83]

Two people can believe in and exhibit the same behaviors (e.g., vegetarianism), but their underlying **belief system** may be quite different (e.g., animal activism versus health concerns). The extent to which people share a belief system is a function of individual, social, and cultural forces. Advocates of a belief system often seek out others with similar beliefs so that social networks overlap; as a result, believers tend to be exposed to information that supports their beliefs (e.g., tree-huggers rarely hang out with loggers).[74]

Core Values

The actress Kim Kardashian wasn't pleased when her picture ran on the cover of *Cosmopolitan Turkey*, especially when it was released on the same date that some countries commemorate the alleged Armenian genocide in the last days of the Ottoman Empire. Because *Cosmopolitan* publishes in 64 different countries, it is difficult to be sure readers everywhere experience the content the same way. In addition to political differences, marketers have to be sensitive to cultural values: In some countries, because of local norms about modesty, some female readers have to hide the magazine from their husbands! Different cultures emphasize varying belief systems that define what it means to be female, feminine, or appealing—and what people consider appropriate to see in print on these matters. Publishers of the Chinese version aren't even permitted to mention sex at all, so they replace articles about uplifting cleavage with uplifting stories about youthful dedication. Ironically, there isn't much down-and-dirty material in the Swedish edition either—but for the opposite reason: The culture is so open about this topic that it doesn't grab readers' attention the way it would in the United States.[75]

In many cases, of course, values are universal. Who does not desire health, wisdom, or world peace? What sets cultures apart is the *relative importance*, or ranking, of these universal values. This set of rankings constitutes a culture's **value system**.[76] For example, one study found that North Americans have more favorable attitudes toward advertising messages that focus on self-reliance, self-improvement, and the achievement of personal goals as opposed to themes stressing family integrity, collective goals, and the feeling of harmony with others. Korean consumers exhibited the reverse pattern.[77]

We characterize every culture in terms of its members' endorsement of a value system. Not every individual will endorse these values equally; in some cases, values may even seem to contradict one another (e.g., U.S. Americans appear to value both conformity and individuality and try to find some accommodation between the two). Nonetheless, it is usually possible to identify a general set of **core values** that uniquely define a culture. For example, core values such as freedom, youthfulness, achievement, materialism, and activity characterize U.S. culture.

Of course, these values certainly evolve over time. Some analysts argue that our focus on acquiring physical objects is shifting a bit toward the consumption of experiences instead. This movement is consistent with research that shows experiential purchases provide greater happiness and satisfaction because they allow us to connect with others and form a bigger part of our social identities. Indeed, one study demonstrated that highly materialistic consumers actually experience pleasure before a purchase because they believe it will transform their lives, but they then experience negative emotions after they buy the item when they realize this is not the case.[78] And, as we saw in Chapter 2 increasingly in the United States we find that many consumers value sustainability and reward companies that are environmentally friendly. That helps to explain why among young consumers the Chipotle restaurant chain is so popular. The company promotes sustainable agriculture practices and the humane treatment of animals it uses for meat.[79]

How do we determine what a culture values? We term the process of learning the beliefs and behaviors endorsed by one's own culture **enculturation**. In contrast, we call the process of learning the value system and behaviors of another culture (often a priority for those who wish to understand consumers and markets in foreign countries)

The Chipotle chain is popular among young consumers, partly because of its sustainable business practices.
Source: Helen Sessions/Alamy.

acculturation. *Socialization agents*, including parents, friends, and teachers, impart these beliefs to us. In one study, for example, the researchers explored the domain of hunting. They described the process by which family members and friends mentor young men as they learn how to hunt. These socialization agents used stories and traditions to guide the men as they moved through the stages of pre-hunter, neophyte, and apprentice, until they finally become competent hunters.[80]

The media are another important socialization agent; we learn a lot about a culture's priorities when we look at the values that advertising communicates. For example, sales strategies differ significantly between the United States and China. U.S. commercials are more likely to present facts about products and suggestions from credible authorities, whereas Chinese advertisers tend to focus more on emotional appeals without bothering too much about substantiating their claims. U.S. ads tend to be youth-oriented, whereas Chinese ads are more likely to stress the wisdom of older people.[81]

As we've seen, *values* are general ideas about good and bad goals. From these flow *norms*, or rules that dictate what is right or wrong, acceptable, or unacceptable. We explicitly decide on *enacted norms*, such as the rule that a green traffic light means "go" and a red one means "stop." Many norms, however, are much more subtle. We discover these **crescive norms** as we interact with others. The following are all types of crescive norms:[82]

- A **custom** is a norm that controls basic behaviors, such as division of labor in a household or how we practice particular ceremonies.
- A **more** ("mor-ay") is a custom with a strong moral overtone. It often involves a *taboo*, or forbidden behavior, such as incest or cannibalism. Violation of a more often meets with strong sanctions. In Islamic countries such as Saudi Arabia, people consider it sacrilege to display underwear on store mannequins or to feature a woman's body in advertising, so retailers have to tread lightly; one lingerie store designed special headless and legless mannequins with only the slightest hint of curves to display its products.[84]
- A **convention** is a norm that regulates how we conduct our everyday lives. These rules often deal with the subtleties of consumer behavior, including the "correct" way to furnish one's house, wear one's clothes, or host a dinner party. The Chinese government tried to change citizens' conventions when the country geared up for the Olympics in Beijing: Local habits were at odds with what planners knew foreign visitors expected to encounter. For one, it's common to spit on the sidewalk; the sinus-clearing, phlegmy

CB AS I SEE IT
Giana Eckhardt, Royal Holloway University of London

Did you use Airbnb rather than a hotel the last time you traveled? Or use Uber to get home rather than take a taxi? Or decided to rely on Zipcar instead of bringing your car to campus? If yes, you are a part of the Sharing Economy, heralded by sources ranging from *Fortune* magazine to President Obama as a major growth sector. The sharing economy represents a major shift in lifestyle for consumers: consumers no longer want to own, but prefer to access goods and services. That way,

they do not have the obligations and burdens of ownership, such as finding a space to park their car or having to deal with the upkeep of their bicycle, when a bike sharing service is more convenient. But what is sharing? Sharing is a form of social exchange that takes place among people known to each other, without any profit. Sharing is an established practice, and dominates particular aspects of our life, such as within the family. By sharing and collectively consuming the household space of the home, family members establish a communal identity, for example.

My colleague Fleura Bardhi and I are interested in whether the form of exchange happening in the "sharing economy" is really sharing. We have found that when sharing is market-mediated—when a company is an intermediary between consumers who don't know each other—it is no longer sharing at all. Rather, consumers are paying to access someone else's goods or services for a particular period of time. It is an economic exchange, and we have labeled this *access-based consumption*.

Our research on Zipcar, the world's leading car-sharing company, illustrates some of the characteristics of access-based consumption. Consumers

don't feel any psychological sense of ownership over the cars, nor do they feel a sense of reciprocal obligations that arise when sharing with one another. They experience Zipcar in the anonymous way one experiences a hotel; they know others have used the cars, but have no desire to interact with them. They don't view other Zipsters as co-sharers of the cars, but rather are mistrustful of them, and rely on the company to police the sharing system so it's equitable for everyone. Finally, consumers do not want to be a part of a community, with either other Zipsters or with the company itself. Thus, our research challenges the romanticized view of the sharing economy as being collaborative and altruistically motivated.

It is important to highlight the benefits that access provides in contrast to the disadvantages of ownership and sharing. These consist of convenient and cost-effective access to valued resources, flexibility, and freedom from the financial, social, and emotional obligations embedded in ownership and sharing. There is still a lot to learn about sharing, access, and ownership, though, and we are currently researching how these concepts may vary across generations, across cultures, and across social classes.

---

prespit hawking sound is so common that one foreigner dubbed it "the national anthem of China." In addition to the extensive cleanup the government conducted (it even restricted city traffic to reduce smog levels), it imposed a hefty fine for public spitting to get people accustomed to holding in their saliva before hordes of fans descended on the city.[85]

All three types of crescive norms may jointly define a culturally appropriate behavior. For example, a more may tell us what kind of food it's okay to eat. These norms vary across cultures, so a meal of dog is taboo in the United States, Hindus shun steak, and Muslims avoid pork products. A custom dictates the appropriate hour at which we should serve the meal. Conventions tell us how to eat the meal, including such details as the utensils we use, table etiquette, and even the appropriate apparel to wear at dinnertime. We often take these conventions for granted. We just assume that they are the "right" things to do (again, until we travel to a foreign country!). Much of what we know about these norms we learn

An etiquette class is one form of socialization agent that teaches people about their culture's values and how to act "appropriately" in different settings.
Source: John Robertson/Alamy.

vicariously as we observe the behaviors of actors in television commercials, sitcoms, print ads, and other media. That reminds us why the marketing system is such an important element of culture.

How Do Values Link to Consumer Behavior?

Despite their importance, values haven't helped us to understand consumer behavior as much as we might expect. One reason is that broad-based concepts such as freedom, security, or inner harmony are more likely to affect general purchasing patterns than to differentiate between brands within a product category. This is why some researchers distinguish among broad-based *cultural values* such as security or happiness, *consumption-specific values* such as convenient shopping or prompt service, and *product-specific values* such as ease of use or durability, which affect the relative importance people in different cultures place on possessions.[86]

A study of product-specific values looked in depth at Australians who engage in extreme sports such as surfing, snowboarding, and skateboarding. The researchers identified four dominant values that drove brand choice: freedom, belongingness, excellence, and connection. For example, one female surfer they studied embraced the value of belongingness. She expressed this value when she wore popular brands of surfing apparel even when these major brands had lost their local roots by going mainstream. In contrast, another surfer in the study valued connection: he expressed this as he selected only locally made brands and supported local surfing events.[87]

Some aspects of brand image, such as sophistication, tend to be common across cultures, but others are more likely to be relevant in specific places. The Japanese tend to value peacefulness, whereas Spaniards emphasize passion, and the value of ruggedness appeals to Americans.[88] Because values drive much of consumer behavior (at least in a general sense), we might say that virtually *all* consumer research ultimately relates to identifying and measuring values. Let's briefly describe some specific attempts by researchers to measure cultural values and apply this knowledge to marketing strategy.

The Rokeach Value Survey

The psychologist Milton Rokeach identified a set of **terminal values**, or desired end states, that apply to many different cultures. The *Rokeach Value Survey* also includes a set of **instrumental values**; actions we need to take to achieve these terminal values.[89] Table 7.7 lists these two sets of values.

Some evidence indicates that differences in these global values do translate into product-specific preferences and differences in media usage. Nonetheless, marketing researchers have not widely used the Rokeach Value Survey.[90] One reason is that our society is evolving into smaller and smaller sets of *consumption microcultures* within a larger culture, each with its own set of core values (more on this in Chapter 13). For example, in the United States, a sizable number of people are strong believers in natural health practices and alternative medicine. This focus on wellness instead of mainstream medical approaches to sickness influences many of their behaviors, from food choices to the use of alternative medical practitioners, as well as their opinions on political and social issues.[91]

The List of Values (LOV)

The **List of Values (LOV) scale** isolates values with more direct marketing applications. This instrument identifies nine consumer segments based on the values members endorse and relates each value to differences in consumption behaviors. These segments include consumers who place priorities on such values as a sense of belonging, excitement, warm relationships with others, and security. For example, people who endorse the sense-of-belonging value are older, are more likely to read *Reader's Digest* and *TV Guide*, drink and entertain more, and prefer group activities more than people who do not endorse this value as highly. In contrast, those who endorse the value of excitement are younger and prefer *Rolling Stone* magazine.[92]

The Means–End Chain Model

The **means–end chain model** assumes that people link specific product attributes (indirectly) to terminal values: We choose among alternative means to attain some end state that we value (such as freedom or safety). Thus, we value products to the extent that they provide the means to some end we desire. A technique researchers call **laddering** uncovers consumers' associations between specific attributes and these general consequences. Using this approach, they help consumers climb up the "ladder" of abstraction that connects functional product attributes with desired end states.[93] Based on consumer feedback, they then create *hierarchical value maps* that show how specific product attributes get linked to end states.

Syndicated Surveys

A number of companies track changes in values through large-scale surveys. They sell the results of these studies to marketers, who receive regular updates on changes and trends. This approach originated in the mid-1960s, when Playtex was concerned about sagging girdle sales (pun intended). The company commissioned the market research firm of Yankelovich, Skelly & White to see why sales had dropped. Their research linked the decline to a shift in values regarding appearance and naturalness. Playtex went on to design lighter, less restrictive garments, while Yankelovich went on to track the impact of

TABLE 7.7   Terminal and Instrumental Values

Instrumental Values	Terminal Values
Ambitious	A comfortable life
Broad-minded	An exciting life
Capable	A sense of accomplishment
Cheerful	A world of peace
Clean	A world of beauty
Courageous	Equality
Forgiving	Family security
Helpful	Freedom
Honest	Happiness
Imaginative	Inner harmony
Independent	Mature love
Intellectual	National security
Logical	Pleasure
Loving	Salvation
Obedient	Self-respect
Polite	Social recognition
Responsible	True friendship
Self-controlled	Wisdom

Source: Copyright 1983 From Measuring the Cultural Values Manifest in Advertising," *Current Issues and Research in Advertising* (1983): 71–92 by Richard Pollay. Reproduced by permission of the American Academy of Advertising (http://www.aaoa.wildapricot.org)

these types of changes in a range of industries. Gradually, the firm developed the idea of one big study to track U.S. attitudes. In 1970, it introduced the Yankelovich *Monitor*™, which is based on 2-hour interviews with 4,000 respondents.[94]

Today, many other syndicated surveys also track changes in values. Advertising agencies perform some of these so that they can stay on top of important cultural trends and help shape the messages they craft for clients. These services include the International VALS™ survey we discussed, GlobalScan (operated by the advertising agency Backer Spielvogel Bates), New Wave (the Ogilvy & Mather advertising agency), and the Lifestyles Study conducted by the DDB World Communications Group.

MyLab Marketing

To complete the problems with the ⭐, go to EOC Discussion Questions in the MyLab as well as additional Marketing Metrics questions only available in MyLab Marketing.

CHAPTER SUMMARY

Now that you have finished reading this chapter, you should understand why:

1. **A consumer's personality influences the way he or she responds to marketing stimuli, but efforts to use this information in marketing contexts meet with mixed results.**

   The concept of *personality* refers to a person's unique psychological makeup and how it consistently influences the way a person responds to his or her environment. Marketing strategies based on personality differences have met with mixed success, partly because of the way researchers have measured and applied these differences in *personality traits* to consumption contexts. Some analysts try to understand underlying differences in small samples of consumers by employing techniques based on Freudian psychology and variations of this perspective, whereas others have tried to assess these dimensions more objectively in large samples using sophisticated, quantitative techniques

2. **Brands have personalities.**

   A brand personality is the set of traits people attribute to a product as if it were a person. Consumers assign personality qualities to all sorts of inanimate products. Like our relationships with other people, these designations can change over time; therefore, marketers need to be vigilant about maintaining the brand personality they want consumers to perceive. Forging a desirable brand personality often is key to building brand loyalty.

3. **A lifestyle defines a pattern of consumption that reflects a person's choices of how to spend his or her time and money, and these choices are essential to define consumer identity.**

   A consumer's *lifestyle* refers to the ways he or she chooses to spend time and money and how his or her consumption choices reflect these values and tastes. Lifestyle research is useful for tracking societal consumption preferences and also for positioning specific products and services to different segments. Marketers segment based on lifestyle differences; they often group consumers in terms of their AIOs (activities, interests, and opinions).

4. **It can be more useful to identify patterns of consumption than knowing about individual purchases when organizations craft a lifestyle marketing strategy.**

   We associate interrelated sets of products and activities with social roles to form *consumption constellations*. People often purchase a product or service because they associate it with a constellation that, in turn, they link to a lifestyle they find desirable. *Geodemography* involves a set of techniques that use geographical and demographic data to identify clusters of consumers with similar psychographic characteristics.

5. **Psychographics go beyond simple demographics to help marketers understand and reach different consumer segments.**

   Psychographic techniques classify consumers in terms of psychological, subjective variables in addition to observable characteristics (demographics). Marketers have developed systems to identify consumer "types" and to differentiate them in terms of their brand or product preferences, media usage, leisure time activities, and attitudes toward broad issues such as politics and religion.

6. **Underlying values often drive consumer motivations.**

   Products take on meaning because a person thinks the products will help him or her to achieve some goal that is linked to a value, such as individuality or freedom. A set of core values characterizes each culture, to which most of its members adhere.

KEY TERMS

Acculturation, 268
AIOs, 264
Anthropomorphism, 253
Archetypes, 246
Belief system, 268
Big Five, 250
Brand arrogance,255

Brand personality, 253
Brand storytelling, 253
Co-branding strategies, 262
Consumption constellation, 262
Convention, 269
Core values, 268
Cosplay, 260

Crescive norms, 269
Custom, 269
Doppelgänger brand image, 256
Ego, 243
Enculturation, 268
E-sports, 258
Frugality, 249

REVIEW

7-1 How does Freud's work on the unconscious mind relate to marketing practice?

 7-2 Enculturation helps us learn the beliefs and behaviors of our own society. Could an external marketer learn the same things through acculturation?

 7-3 What is the basic philosophy behind a lifestyle marketing strategy?

7-4 How can marketers stay on top of changes in lifestyle trends?

CONSUMER BEHAVIOR CHALLENGE

■ DISCUSS

7-5 The state church in Iceland is the Evangelical Lutheran Church. Just over 92 percent of the population class themselves as being Lutherans, but not all are practicing members of the church.[95] Another 3 percent belong to other Lutheran groups. Less than 1 percent of the population are Catholic. Some still follow the ancient gods from the Norse sagas. What coercive norms would you expect in Iceland as a marketer?

7-6 Is there such a thing as personality? If so, how might you integrate knowledge about consumers' personality traits into a marketing strategy?

7-7 The Great Recession is over, so things are looking up for many consumers. Still, is frugality the "new normal" or will many of us revert to the free-spending days before the bubble burst in 2008?

7-8 Taking your own country as an example, how would you link values to consumer behavior?

■ APPLY

7-9 Products and services exist in a carefully created ecosystem of complementary products and services. Each one influences the demand, sales, and price of the others. What are a gym's complementary products and services?

7-10 Starbucks is solidly established as a go-to location for coffee, tea, and pastries but to grow the company needs to expand its offerings so that customers spend more of their time (and money) there. The chain is experimenting with a new concept, Starbuck Evenings, where after 4:00 each afternoon the store flips to a different menu that includes wine, beer, small plates like truffle mac and cheese, sandwiches, and salads.[96] Is Starbucks too entrenched in our "coffeehouse lifestyle" or does the chain have room to expand? What recommendations would you make to Starbucks to help the company expand its lifestyle marketing strategy?

7-11 Using media that target college students, construct a consumption constellation for this social role. What set of products, activities, and interests tend to appear in advertisements depicting "typical" college students? How realistic is this constellation?

7-12 Extreme sports. YouTube. Pinterest. Veganism. Can you predict what will be "hot" in the near future? Identify a lifestyle trend that is just surfacing in your universe. Describe this trend in detail, and justify your prediction. What specific styles or products relate to this trend?

Case Study

RED BULL: GIVING WINGS TO A WAY OF LIFE

When Red Bull was launched in 1987 by the Austrian entrepreneur Dietrich Mateschitz, it created a new beverage category: energy drinks. Since then, the energy drink segment has grown substantially, with Red Bull establishing itself as the undisputed market leader worldwide—it is available in 167 countries and has sold around 50 billion cans to date. Red Bull has not only created a new product category but has also cultivated a way of life that is widely admired by athletes, musicians, artists, and students around the world.

The brand's logo of two red muscular bulls and its iconic slogan promising to give the consumer "wings" are a statement for the thrill-seeking consumer. Red Bull fans are attracted to the brand's proposition of fun, adventure, creativity, and challenge. It resonates well with the 18–35 age group by embracing the culture of extreme sports, music, and art.

Over time, the Red Bull brand has become bigger than the product itself. Red Bull does not intend to bring the product to the people, but to bring people to the product. Red Bull's strategy is to associate itself with experiences and events that are popular with its target customers and thereby create a unique brand identity. The company delivers such experiences by heavily sponsoring extreme sports events like motor racing, snowboarding, kite surfing, soapbox races, and Formula One races. Red Bull also creates its own events, like Red Bull X Fighters, Red Bull Air Race, and Red Bull Paper Wings, all of which attract huge audiences.

The Red Bull Flugtag is one of their popular annual events, and the participants live the brand's slogan: they construct their own homemade flying machines and jump into water. Another event that showcased the brand's spirit of adventure was Red Bull Stratos, which was the company's breakthrough space-diving mission. The event was streamed live on October 14, 2012, showing Austrian sky diver Felix Baumgatner in a Red Bull labelled costume take a free fall from the edge of space, breaking the speed of sound and landing on the ground in a Red Bull parachute. The company had heavily publicized the event and it was followed by avid Red Bull fans right from the planning stages. The live streaming of the event had 8 million views on YouTube, a new record in itself.

Red Bull activities involve a mix of sports, games, athlete and team sponsorships, music events, and other sports culture events like Red Bull BC One (breakdancing), and Red Bull Art of Motion (free-running). The Red Bull Web site features more than 134 events and activities to engage its users. No matter what activity its users choose, one thing is shared among all—the Red Bull state of mind.

Red Bull started its own Media House in 2007 to offer its followers more options to know and experience the Red Bull lifestyle. It produces content across multiple media: print, television,

online, and feature films. Some of the productions of Red Bull Media House include the film *The Art of Flight*, the brand's magazine *Red Bulletin*, and the TV show *Red Bull Signature Series*, in partnership with NBC. With the establishment of the media house, the Red Bull brand has actually transcended the original product and become a full-fledged creator of its own brand experience. Red Bull continues to hold autographed events across the globe and produce its own content, incorporating storytelling material that attracts readers, viewers, and listeners to the brand.

Red Bull is not merely satisfying a functional need; it is offering its consumers a vision and promising values through which they can define themselves. Through this approach, the drink that vitalizes the body and mind becomes a consumer lifestyle choice of extreme experience. In addition, through the Red Bull Media House, the company is set to take content marketing to the extreme as well. Many in the marketing and advertising world are ready to hail Red Bull as a publishing empire that also just happens to sell a drink.

DISCUSSION QUESTIONS

CS7-1 Based on your understanding of the personality attributes influencing consumer behavior, describe how consumers identify themselves with the brand personality of Red Bull. What goal and values are the consumers of Red Bull trying to achieve?

CS7-2 Discuss how Red Bull can be considered a lifestyle brand. Looking at the diverse activities that Red Bull associates itself with, is there a single way to define the Red Bull lifestyle?

CS7-3 Discuss the product complementarity of Red Bull's energy drink and media house. Do you think that Red Bull as a lifestyle brand is strong enough to venture into publishing extreme content? What does this mean for its original product and the rising competition it is facing in different global markets?

Sources: Red Bull company Website, http://energydrink.redbull.com/company, accessed October 20, 2015; Kim Bhasin, "Red Bull Is Absolutely Obsessed with Its 'Gives You Wings' Slogan," *Business Insider* (October 15, 2012); Kim Bhasin, "Felix Baumgartner's Jump Was the Biggest Risk Red Bull Has Ever Taken," *Business Insider* (October 15, 2012); Catherine Smith, "Red Bull Stratos YouTube Live Stream Attracts Record Number of Viewers (UPDATE)," *The Huffington Post*, October 14, 2012; Rob Howard, "Cult Brand Secrets: Red Bull," *Cult*, March 14, 2014, http://www.cult.ca/blog/cult-brand-secrets-red-bull#sthash.dAHOWxeK.dpuf, accessed October 20 2015; Henry Faustine, "Red Bull: The Brand That Gives Content Wings," *Digital for Life*, November 6, 2012, http://www.digitalforreallife.com/2012/11/red-bull-the-brand-that-gives-content-wings/, accessed October 18, 2015; James O' Brien, "How Red Bull Takes Content Marketing to the Extreme," *Mashable*, December 19, 2012, http://mashable.com/2012/12/19/red-bull-content-marketing/#J_9pBDtlN5qy, accessed October 18, 2015.

MyLab Marketing

Go to the Assignments section of your MyLab to complete these writing exercises.

7-13 Collect a sample of ads that appeal to consumers' values. What value is being communicated in each ad, and how is this done? Is this an effective approach to designing a marketing communication?

7-14 Identify three distinct "taste cultures" within your school. Can you generate a "consumption constellation" for each (clothing, music, leisure activities, etc.)?

NOTES

1. http://www.jettygirl.com/blog/, accessed March 29, 2015.
2. For an interesting ethnographic account of skydiving as a voluntary high-risk consumption activity, see Richard L. Celsi, Randall L. Rose, and Thomas W. Leigh, "An Exploration of High-Risk Leisure Consumption Through Skydiving," *Journal of Consumer Research* 20 (June 1993): 1–23.
3. http://www.imdb.com/title/tt1596346/, accessed March 29, 2015; http://www.roxy.com/surf/, accessed March 29, 2015.
4. See J. Aronoff and J. P. Wilson, *Personality in the Social Process* (Hillsdale, NJ: Erlbaum, 1985); Walter Mischel, *Personality and Assessment* (New York: Wiley, 1968).
5. Robert R McCraie and Paul T. Costa, "The Stability of Personality: Observations and Evaluations," *Current Directions in Psychological Science* (1994): 173–175.
6. Ernest Dichter, *A Strategy of Desire* (Garden City, NY: Doubleday, 1960); Ernest Dichter, *The Handbook of Consumer Motivations* (New York: McGraw-Hill, 1964); Jeffrey F. Durgee, "Interpreting Dichter's Interpretations: An Analysis of Consumption Symbolism," in *The Handbook of Consumer Motivations* (unpublished manuscript, Rensselaer Polytechnic Institute, Troy, New York, 1989); Pierre Martineau, *Motivation in Advertising* (New York: McGraw-Hill, 1957).
7. Vance Packard, *The Hidden Persuaders* (New York: D. McKay, 1957).
8. Harold Kassarjian, "Personality and Consumer Behavior: A Review," *Journal of Marketing Research* 8 (November 1971): 409–418.
9. Karen Horney, *Neurosis and Human Growth* (New York: Norton, 1950).
10. Joel B. Cohen, "An Interpersonal Orientation to the Study of Consumer Behavior," *Journal of Marketing Research* 6 (August 1967): 270–278; Pradeep K. Tyagi, "Validation of the CAD Instrument: A Replication," in Richard P. Bagozzi and Alice M. Tybout, eds., *Advances in Consumer Research* 10 (Ann Arbor, MI: Association for Consumer Research, 1983): 112–114.
11. For a comprehensive review of classic perspectives on personality theory, see Calvin S. Hall and Gardner Lindzey, *Theories of Personality*, 2nd ed. (New York: Wiley, 1970).
12. See Carl G. Jung, "The Archetypes and the Collective Unconscious," in H. Read, M. Fordham, and G. Adler, eds., *Collected Works*, vol. 9, part 1 (Princeton, NJ: Princeton University Press, 1959).
13. This material was contributed by Rebecca H. Holman, senior vice president and director, Consumer Knowledge Structures, The Knowledge Group, Young & Rubicam Brands, July 2005.
14. Margaret Mark and Carol S. Pearson, *The Hero and the Outlaw: Building Extraordinary Brands Through the Power of Archetypes* (New York: McGraw-Hill, 2001). This section borrows from a discussion in Michael R. Solomon, Rebekah Russell-Bennett, and Josephine Previte, *Consumer Behaviour: Buying, Having, Being*, 3rd ed. (Frenchs Forest, NSW: Pearson Australia, 2012).
15. E. B. Boyd, "How a Personality Test Designed to Pick Astronauts Is Taking the Pain Out of Customer Support," *Fast Company* (December 1, 2010), http://www.fastcompany.com/1706766/how-a-system-designed-to-weed-out-nasa-astronauts-is-taking-the-pain-out-of-customer-support-call?partner=homepage_newsletter, accessed April 13, 2011.
16. Caglar Irmak, Beth Vallen, and Sankar Sen, "You Like What I Like, but I Don't Like What You Like: Uniqueness Motivations in Product Preferences," *Journal of Consumer Research* 37, no. 3 (October 2010): 443–455; E. A. Kim, S. Ratneshwar, E. Roesler, and T. G. Chowdhury, "Attention to Social Comparison Information and Brand Avoidance Behaviors," *Marketing Letters* (2014): 1–13; Adam Duhachek and Dawn Iacobucci, "Consumer Personality and Coping: Testing Rival Theories of Process," *Journal of Consumer Psychology* 15, no. 1 (2005): 52–63; S. Christian Wheeler, Richard E. Petty, and George Y. Bizer, "Self-Schema Matching and Attitude Change:

Situational and Dispositional Determinants of Message Elaboration," *Journal of Consumer Research* 31 (March, 2005): 787–797.
17. http://continuumfashion.com/N12.php, accessed March 29, 2015; "3D Printing Hits The Fashion World," *Forbes* (August 7, 2013), http://www.forbes.com/sites/rachelhennessey/2013/08/07/3-d-printed-clothes-could-be-the-next-big-thing-to-hit-fashion/, accessed February 16, 2015.
18. John L. Lastovicka, Lance A. Bettencourt, Renee Shaw Hughner, and Ronald J. Kuntze, "Lifestyle of the Tight and Frugal: Theory and Measurement," *Journal of Consumer Research* 26 (June 1999): 85–98; The Hartman Group, "The Continuing Economic Maelstrom & the US Consumer: Implications for CPG, *Restaurant and Retail* January 2009," http://www.hartman-group.com/publications/white-papers/the-continuing-economic-maelstrom-the-us-consumer, accessed September 3, 2011; Joseph Lazzaro, "US Savings Rate Soars to 14-Year High," *Daily Finance* (June 1, 2009), www.dailyfinance.com/2009/06/01/us-savings-rate-soars-to-14-year-high, accessed June 1, 2009; Andrea K. Walker, "Economy Breeds a Frugal Consumer," *Baltimore Sun* (April 20, 2009), www.baltimoresun.com/business/bal-te.bz.shoppinghabits19apr20,0,1577826.story, accessed June 1, 2009.
19. Ronald E. Goldsmith, Leisa Reinecke Flynn, and Ronald A. Clark, "The Etiology of the Frugal Consumer," *Journal of Retailing and Consumer Services* 21, no. 2 (2014): 175–184. doi: 10.1016/j.jretconser.2013.11.005.
20. Adapted from information presented in Beth Snyder Bulik, "You Are What You Watch: Market Data Suggest Research Links Personality Traits to Consumers' Viewing Habits, Helps Marketers Match Brands with Audiences," *Advertising Age* (November 1, 2010), http://adage.com/article/news/research-links-personality-traits-tv-viewing-habits/146779/, accessed April 13, 2011.
21. Adapted from https://www.cpp.com/products/mbti/index.aspx, accessed March 6, 2013.
22. Stephanie Buck, "What Type of Social Media Personality Are You?" Mashable.com (August 13, 2012), http://mashable.com/2012/08/13/what-type-of-social-media-personality-are-you-infographic/?utm_medium=email&utm_source=newsletter, accessed March 6, 2013.
23. Jacob Jacoby, "Personality and Consumer Behavior: How Not to Find Relationships," in *Purdue Papers in Consumer Psychology*, no. 102 (Lafayette, IN: Purdue University, 1969); Harold H. Kassarjian and Mary Jane Sheffet, "Personality and Consumer Behavior: An Update," in Harold H. Kassarjian and Thomas S. Robertson, eds., *Perspectives in Consumer Behavior*, 4th ed. (Glenview, IL: Scott Foresman, 1991): 291–353; John Lastovicka and Erich Joachimsthaler, "Improving the Detection of Personality Behavior Relationships in Consumer Research," *Journal of Consumer Research* 14 (March 1988): 583–587. For an approach that ties the notion of personality more directly to marketing issues, see Jennifer L. Aaker, "Dimensions of Brand Personality," *Journal of Marketing Research* 34 (August 1997): 347–357.
24. Girish N. Punj and David W. Stewart, "An Interaction Framework of Consumer Decision-Making," *Journal of Consumer Research* 10 (September 1983): 181–196.
25. J. F. Allsopp, "The Distribution of On-Licence Beer and Cider Consumption and Its Personality Determinants Among Young Men," *European Journal of Marketing* 20, no. 3 (1986): 44–62; Gordon R. Foxall and Ronald E. Goldsmith, "Personality and Consumer Research: Another Look," *Journal of the Market Research Society* 30, no. 2 (April 1988): 111–125; J. Z. Sojka and J. L. Giese, "Using Individual Differences to Detect Consumer Shopping Behavior," *International Review of Retail, Distribution and Consumer Research* 13, no. 4 (2003): 337–353; P. Albanese, "Personality and Consumer Behaviour: An Operational Approach," *European Journal of Marketing* 27, no. 8 (1993): 28–37; M. B. Holbrook and T. J. Olney, "Romanticism

and Wanderlust: An Effect of Personality on Consumer Preferences," *Psychology and Marketing* 12, no. 3 (1995): 207–222; Hans Baumgartner, "Towards a Personology of the Consumer," *Journal of Consumer Research* 29 (September 2002): 286–292.

26. J. C. Mowen and B. Carlson, "Exploring the Antecedents and Consumer Behavior Consequences of the Trait of Superstition," *Psychology and Marketing* 20, no. 12 (2003): 1045–65; M. Cleveland, M. Kalamas, and M. Laroche, "Shades of Green, Linking Environmental Locus of Control and Pro-environmental Behaviors," *Journal of Consumer Marketing* 22, no. 4/5 (2005): 198–212; J. C. Mowen, The 3M Model of Motivation and Personality: Theory and Empirical Applications to Consumer Behavior (Massachusetts: Kluwer Academic Publishers, 2000); M. B. Holbrook and T. J. Olney, "Romanticism and Wanderlust: An Effect of Personality on Consumer Preferences," *Psychology and Marketing* 12, no. 3 (1995): 207–22; S. I. Rick, C. E. Cryder, and G. Loewenstein, "Tightwads and Spendthrifts," *Journal of Consumer Research* 34 (April 2008): 767–81; J. Z. Sojka and J. L. Giese, "The Influence of Personality Traits on the Processing of Visual and Verbal Information," Marketing Letters 12, no. 1 (2001): 91–106; R. A. Clark and R. E. Goldsmith, "Market Mavens: Psychological Influences," *Psychology and Marketing* 22 (April 2005): 289–312; U. R. Orth, "Consumer Personality and Other Factors in Situational Brand Choice Variation," *Journal of Brand Management* 13, no. 2 (2005): 115–33; M. Marquis and P. Filiatrault, "Understanding Complaining Responses Through Consumers' Self-Consciousness Disposition," *Psychology and Marketing* 19, no. 3 (2002): 267–91; T. A. Mooradian and J. M. Olver, "'I Can't Get No Satisfaction': The Impact of Personality and Emotion on Postpurchase Processes," *Psychology and Marketing* 14, no. 4 (1997): 379–92.

27. Quoted in Stuart O'Brien, "iPad Owners Are 'Self-Centered Workaholics,'" *Mobile Entertainment* (July 30, 2010), http://www.mobile-ent.biz/news/read/ipad-owners-are-self-centered-workaholics, accessed April 13, 2011.

28. Thomas Hine, "Why We Buy: The Silent Persuasion of Boxes, Bottles, Cans, and Tubes," *Worth* (May 1995): 78–83.

29. Jennifer Aaker, Kathleen D. Vohs, and Cassie Mogilner, "Nonprofits Are Seen as Warm and For-Profits as Competent: Firm Stereotypes Matter," *Journal of Consumer Research* 37, no. 2 (August 2010): 224–237.

30. Bradley Johnson, "They All Have Half-Baked Ideas," *Advertising Age* (May 12, 1997): 8.

31. Jon Hamm, "Why Agencies and Brands Need to Embrace True Story telling," *Adweek* (September 23, 2013), http://www.adweek.com/news/advertising-branding/why-agencies-and-brands-need-embrace-true-sto rytelling-152534, accessed March 29, 2015.

32. Neeru Paharia, Anat Keinan, Jill Avery, and Juliet B. Schor, "The Underdog Effect: The Marketing of Disadvantage and Determination through Brand Biography," *Journal of Consumer Research* 37, no. 5 (February 2011): 775–790.

33. Michael Hiestand, "ESPN Drops Ad Campaign That Was to Portray College Stereotypes," *USA Today* (November 14, 2008), www.usatoday.com/money/advertising/2008-11-13-espn-ad-campaign-killed_N.html, accessed November 14, 2008.

34. Ellis A. Hende and Ruth Mugge, "Investigating Gender-Schema Congruity Effects on Consumers' Evaluation of Anthropomorphized Products," *Psychology & Marketing* 31, no.2 (2014): 264–277.

35. Quoted in Erin White, "Volvo Sheds Safe Image for New, Dangerous Ads," *Wall Street Journal* (June 14, 2002), www.wsj.com, accessed June 14, 2002; Viknesh Vijayenthiran, "Volvo's Upmarket Plans Hindered by Brand Image, Poor CO2 Emissions," *Motor Authority* (November 24, 2008), www.motorauthority.com/volvo-continuing-with-plans-to-move-upmarket.html, accessed June 1, 2009.

36. Yongjun Sung and Spencer F. Tinkham, "Brand Personality Structures in the United States and Korea: Common and Culture-Specific Factors," *Journal of Consumer Psychology* 15, no. 4 (2005): 334–350; Beverly T. Venable, Gregory M. Rose, Victoria D. Bush, and Faye W. Gilbert, "The Role of Brand Personality in Charitable Giving: An Assessment and Validation," *Journal of the Academy of Marketing Science* 33 (July 2005): 295–312.

37. Quoted in Stuart Elliott, "A 1950s Brand Mascot Fights 21st-Century Indigestion," *New York Times* (March 5, 2008), www.nytimes.com, accessed March 5, 2008.

38. Craig J. Thompson, Aric Rindfleisch, and Zeynep Arsel, "Emotional Branding and the Strategic Value of the Doppelganger Brand Image," *Journal of Marketing* 70, no. 1 (2006): 50.

39. Jennifer L. Aaker, "Dimensions of Brand Personality," *Journal of Marketing Research* 34 (August 1997): 347–357.

40. Tim Triplett, "Brand Personality Must Be Managed or It Will Assume a Life of Its Own," *Marketing News* (May 9, 1994): 9.

41. Seth Stevenson, "How to Beat Nike," *New York Times* (January 5, 2003), www.nytimes.com, accessed January 5, 2003.

42. Susan Fournier, "Consumers and Their Brands: Developing Relationship Theory in Consumer Research," *Journal of Consumer Research* 24, no. 4 (March 1998): 343–373.

43. Neal Gabler, "The Weird Science of Naming New Products," *New York Times Magazine*(January 15, 2015),http://www.nytimes.com/2015/01/18/magazine/the-weird-science-of-naming-new-products.html?smid=nytcore-iphone-share&smprod=nytcore-iphone, accessed February 3, 2015.

44. John Grossman, "Risqué Names Reap Rewards for Some Companies," *New York Times* (April 23, 2014), http://www.nytimes.com/2014/04/24/business/smallbusiness/risque-names-reap-rewards-for-some-companies.html, accessed February 3, 2015.

45. Karyne Levy, "Here's Why Amazon Just Paid Nearly $1 Billion for a Site Where You Watch People Play Video Games," *Business Insider* (August 25, 2014), http://www.businessinsider.com/heres-why-amazon-paid-almost-1-billion-for-twitch-2014-8#ixzz3VnhCim1P, accessed March 29, 2015.

46. Paul Mozur, "For South Korea, E-Sports is National Pastime," *New York Times* (October 19, 2014), http://www.nytimes.com/2014/10/20/technology/league-of-legends-south-korea-epicenter-esports.html, accessed February 16, 2015.

47. Chris Pereira, "Three Swatting Incidents Attributed to Teenage Minecraft Player," *Gamespot*, (March 28, 2015), http://www.gamespot.com/articles/three-swatting-incidents-attributed-to-teenage-min/1100-6426236/, accessed March 29, 2015; Richard Lewis, "On Twitch, SWAT Teams are Becoming Dangerous Props for Trolls," *The Daily Dot* (August 22, 2014), http://www.dailydot.com/esports/swatting-twitch-trend-prank/, accessed March 29, 2015.

48. These definitions are adapted from entries in *The Urban Dictionary*, www.urbandictionary.com, accessed March 16, 2013.

49. Benjamin D. Zablocki and Rosabeth Moss Kanter, "The Differentiation of Life-Styles," *Annual Review of Sociology* (1976): 269–297; Mary Twe Douglas and Baron C. Isherwood, *The World of Goods* (New York: Basic Books, 1979).

50. http://www.comic-con.org/about, accessed March 29, 2015; "Cosplay," www.cosplay.com, accessed March 29, 2015; Lisa Katayama, "Anatomy of a Nerd; Japanese Schoolgirl Watch," *Wired* (March 2006), www.wired.com/wired/archive/14.03/play.html?pg=3, accessed March 29, 2015.

51. "American Time Use Survey," Bureau of Labor Statistics, http://www.bls.gov/tus/charts/, accessed March 29, 2015.

52. "American Time Use Survey," Bureau of Labor Statistics, http://www.bls.gov/tus/charts/students.htm, accessed March 29, 2015.

53. Zablocki and Kanter, "The Differentiation of Life-Styles."

54. Richard A. Peterson, "Revitalizing the Culture Concept," *Annual Review of Sociology* 5 (1979): 137–166.

55. William Leiss, Stephen Kline, and Sut Jhally, *Social Communication in Advertising* (Toronto: Methuen, 1986).

56. Quoted in "Polo/Ralph Lauren Corporation History," *Funding Universe*, http://www.fundinguniverse.com/company-histories/polo-ralph-lauren-corporation-history/, accessed March 29, 2015; Mark J. Miller, "Ralph Lauren Ready to Open First Restaurant in New York City," *Brandchannel* (December 12, 2014), http://www.brandchannel.com/home/post/2014/12/12/141212-Ralph-Lauren-New-York-Restaurant-Polo-Bar.aspx?utm_campaign=141212-Ralph-Lauren-New-York-Restaurant-Polo-Bar&utm_source=newsletter&utm_medium=email, accessed February 22, 2015.

57. Douglas and Isherwood, *The World of Goods*, quoted on pp. 72–73.

58. Christopher K. Hsee and France Leclerc, "Will Products Look More Attractive When Presented Separately or Together?" *Journal of Consumer Research* 25 (September 1998): 175–186.

59. R. Rahinel and J. P. Redden, "Brands as Product Coordinators: Matching Brands Make Joint Consumption Experiences More Enjoyable," *Journal of Consumer Research* 39, no. 6 (2013): 1290–1299.

60. Brian Steinberg, "Whose Ad Is This Anyway? Agencies Use Brand Icons to Promote Other Products; Cheaper Than Zeta-Jones," *Wall Street Journal* (December 4, 2003), www.wsj.com, accessed December 4, 2003.

61. Michael R. Solomon, "The Role of Products as Social Stimuli: A Symbolic Interactionism Perspective," *Journal of Consumer Research* 10 (December 1983): 319–329.

62. Michael R. Solomon and Henry Assael, "The Forest or the Trees? A *Gestalt* Approach to Symbolic Consumption," in Jean Umiker-Sebeok, ed., *Marketing and Semiotics: New Directions in the Study of Signs for Sale* (Berlin: Mouton de Gruyter, 1988), 189–218; Michael R. Solomon, "Mapping Product Constellations: A Social Categorization Approach to Symbolic Consumption," *Psychology & Marketing* 5, no. 3 (1988): 233–258; see also Stephen C. Cosmas, "Life Styles and Consumption Patterns," *Journal of Consumer Research* 8, no. 4 (March 1982): 453–455; Russell W. Belk, "Yuppies as Arbiters of the Emerging Consumption Style," in Richard J. Lutz, ed., *Advances in Consumer Research* 13 (Provo, UT: Association for Consumer Research, 1986): 514–519.

63. Lan Nguyen Chaplin and Tina M. Lowrey, "The Development of Consumer-Based Consumption Constellations in Children," *Journal of Consumer Research,* 36, no. 5 (2010): 757–777.

64. Danny Hakim, "Cadillac, Too, Shifting Focus to Trucks," *New York Times* (December 21, 2001), http://www.nytimes.com/2001/12/21/business/cadillac-too-shifting-focus-to-trucks.html, accessed September 3, 2011.

65. Quoted in Amy Wallace, "Chip Wilson, Lululemon Guru, Is Moving On," *New York Times Magazine* (February 2, 2015), http://www.ny times.com/2015/02/08/magazine/lululemons-guru-is-moving-on .html?smid=nytcore-iphone-share&smprod=nytcore-iphone&_r=0, accessed February 3, 2015.

66. See Lewis Alpert and Ronald Gatty, "Product Positioning by Behavioral Life Styles," *Journal of Marketing* 33 (April 1969): 65–69; Emanuel H. Demby, "Psychographics Revisited: The Birth of a Technique," *Marketing News* (January 2, 1989): 21; William D. Wells, "Backward Segmentation," in Johan Arndt, ed., *Insights into Consumer Behavior* (Boston: Allyn & Bacon, 1968): 85–100.

67. Ian Pearson, "Social Studies: Psychographics in Advertising," *Canadian Business* (December 1985): 67.

68. Rebecca Piirto Heath, "Psychographics: Qu'est-Ce Que C'est?," *Marketing Tools* (November–December 1995).

69. Alfred S. Boote, "Psychographics: Mind Over Matter," *American Demographics* (April 1980): 26–29; William D. Wells, "Psychographics: A Critical Review," *Journal of Marketing Research* 12 (May 1975): 196–213.

70. Joseph T. Plummer, "The Concept and Application of Life Style Segmentation," *Journal of Marketing* 38 (January 1974): 33–37.

71. Berkeley Rice, "The Selling of Lifestyles," *Psychology Today* (March 1988): 46.

72. John L. Lastovicka, John P. Murry, Erich A. Joachimsthaler, Gurav Bhalla, and Jim Scheurich, "A Lifestyle Typology to Model Young Male Drinking and Driving," *Journal of Consumer Research* 14 (September 1987): 257–263.

73. Robert F. Worth, "Arab TV Tests Societies' Limits with Depictions of Sex and Equality," *New York Times* (September 26, 2008), www.nytimes .com/2008/09/27/World/Middleeast/27beirut.Html?_R=1&Scp=1&Sq=N..., accessed September 26, 2008.

74. Ajay K. Sirsi, James C. Ward, and Peter H. Reingen, "Microcultural Analysis of Variation in Sharing of Causal Reasoning about Behavior," *Journal of Consumer Research* 22 (March 1996): 345–372.

75. Vercihan Ziflioğlu, "TV Celebrity Kardashian Lashes Out at Turkish Cosmo Cover," *Hürriyet Daily News* (April 12, 2011), http://www.hurriyetdailynews .com/n.php?n=american-tv-personality-angry-for-her-photos-on-turkish-magazine-2011-04-12, accessed May 10, 2011; David Carr, "Romance in *Cosmo's* World Is Translated in Many Ways," *New York Times* (May 26, 2002), www.nytimes.com, accessed May 26, 2002.

76. Milton Rokeach, *The Nature of Human Values* (New York: Free Press, 1973).

77. Sang-Pil Han and Sharon Shavitt, "Persuasion and Culture: Advertising Appeals in Individualistic and Collectivistic Societies," *Journal of Experimental Social Psychology* 30 (1994): 326–350.

78. Thomas Gilovich, Amit Kumar, and Lily Jampol, "A Wonderful Life: Experiential Consumption and the Pursuit of Happiness," *Journal of Consumer Psychology* 25, no. 1 (2015): 152–165; Marsha L. Richins, "When Wanting Is Better than Having: Materialism, Transformation Expectations, and Product-Evoked Emotions in the Purchase Process," *Journal of Consumer Research* 40, no. 1 (2013): 1–18.

79. Noam Cohen, "Chipotle Blurs Lines With a Satirical Series About Industrial Farming," *New York Times* (January 27, 2014), http://www.nytimes .com/2014/01/27/business/media/chipotle-blurs-lines-with-a-satirical-series-about-industrial-farming.html?_r=1, accessed February 23, 2015.

80. Jon Littlefield and Julie L. Ozanne, "Socialization into Consumer Culture: Hunters Learning to Be Men," *Consumption Markets & Culture* 14, no. 4 (2011): 333–360.

81. Carolyn A. Lin, "Cultural Values Reflected in Chinese and American Television Advertising," *Journal of Advertising* 30 (Winter 2001): 83–94.

82. George J. McCall and J. L. Simmons, *Social Psychology: A Sociological Approach* (New York: Free Press, 1982).

83. Deborah Ball, "Women in Italy Like to Clean but Shun the Quick and Easy: Convenience Doesn't Sell When Bathrooms Average Four Scrubbings a Week," *Wall Street Journal* (April 25, 2006): A1.

84. Arundhati Parmar, "Out from Under," *Marketing News* (July 21, 2003): 9–10.

85. Jim Yardley, "No Spitting on the Road to Olympic Glory, Beijing Says," *New York Times* (April 17, 2007), www.nytimes.com, accessed April 17, 2007.

86. Donald E. Vinson, Jerome E. Scott, and Lawrence R. Lamont, "The Role of Personal Values in Marketing and Consumer Behavior," *Journal of Marketing* 41 (April 1977): 44–50; John Watson, Steven Lysonski, Tamara Gillan, and Leslie Raymore, "Cultural Values and Important Possessions: A Cross-Cultural Analysis," *Journal of Business Research* 55 (2002): 923–931.

87. Pascale Quester, Michael Beverland, and Francis Farrelly, "Brand–Personal Values Fit and Brand Meanings: Exploring the Role Individual Values Play in Ongoing Brand Loyalty in Extreme Sports Subcultures," *Advances in Consumer Research* 33, no. 1 (2006): 21–28.

88. Jennifer Aaker, Veronica Benet-Martinez, and Jordi Garolera, "Consumption Symbols as Carriers of Culture: A Study of Japanese and Spanish Brand Personality Constructs," *Journal of Personality & Social Psychology* 81, no. 3 (2001): 492–508.

89. Milton Rokeach, *Understanding Human Values* (New York: Free Press, 1979); see also J. Michael Munson and Edward McQuarrie, "Shortening the Rokeach Value Survey for Use in Consumer Research," in Michael J. Houston, ed., *Advances in Consumer Research* 15 (Provo, UT: Association for Consumer Research, 1988), 381–386.

90. B. W. Becker and P. E. Conner, "Personal Values of the Heavy User of Mass Media," *Journal of Advertising Research* 21 (1981): 37–43; Vinson, Scott, and Lamont, "The Role of Personal Values in Marketing and Consumer Behavior."

91. Craig J. Thompson and Maura Troester, "Consumer Value Systems in the Age of Postmodern Fragmentation: The Case of the Natural Health Microculture," *Journal of Consumer Research* 28 (March 2002): 550–571.

92. Sharon E. Beatty, Lynn R. Kahle, Pamela Homer, and Shekhar Misra, "Alternative Measurement Approaches to Consumer Values: The List of Values and the Rokeach Value Survey," *Psychology & Marketing* 2 (1985): 181–200; Lynn R. Kahle and Patricia Kennedy, "Using the List of Values (LOV) to Understand Consumers," *Journal of Consumer Marketing* 2 (Fall 1988): 49–56; Lynn Kahle, Basil Poulos, and Ajay Sukhdial, "Changes in Social Values in the United States During the Past Decade," *Journal of Advertising Research* 28 (February–March 1988): 35–41; see also Wagner A. Kamakura and Jose Alfonso Mazzon, "Value Segmentation: A Model for the Measurement of Values and Value Systems," *Journal of Consumer Research* 18 (September 1991): 28; Jagdish N. Sheth, Bruce I. Newman, and Barbara L. Gross, *Consumption Values and Market Choices: Theory and Applications* (Cincinnati, OH: South-Western, 1991).

93. Thomas J. Reynolds and Jonathan Gutman, "Laddering Theory, Method, Analysis, and Interpretation," *Journal of Advertising Research* (February–March 1988): 11–34; Beth Walker, Richard Celsi, and Jerry Olson, "Exploring the Structural Characteristics of Consumers' Knowledge," in Melanie Wallendorf and Paul Anderson, eds., *Advances in Consumer Research* 14 (Provo, UT: Association for Consumer Research, 1986), 17–21; Tania Modesto Veludo-de-Oliveira, Ana Akemi Ikeda, and Marcos Cortez Campomar, "Laddering in the Practice of Marketing Research: Barriers and Solutions," *Qualitative Market Research: An International Journal* 9, no. 3 (2006): 297–306. For a critique of this technique, cf. Elin Brandi Sørenson and Søren Askegaard, "Laddering: How (Not) to Do Things with Words," *Qualitative Market Research: An International Journal* 10, no. 1 (2007): 63–77.

94. "25 Years of Attitude," *Marketing Tools* (November–December 1995): 38–39.

95. World Council of Churches, "Evangelical Lutheran Church of Iceland," https://www.oikoumene.org/en/member-churches/evangelical-lutheran-church-of-iceland.

96. Dale Buss, "Night and Day, Starbucks Grows Up as a Global Lifestyle Brand," *Brandchannel* (December 20, 2012), http://www.brandchannel.com/home/post/2012/12/20/Starbucks-Night-and-Day-122012.aspx, accessed February 22, 2015.

SECTION 2   EVOLVING TRENDS IN FITNESS AND FRENCH FRIES

BACKGROUND AND GOAL

Your close friend has finally saved up enough money to open up his dream business—a fitness gym! He hopes to one day turn his gym into a national chain, but for now he plans on opening just two locations in the large U.S. city where he lives. He recently read a news article about how fitness trends in his city are consistent with overall trends in the United States, so he asked you to do a little research about fitness membership trends in the nation. In addition, he asked you to look up membership trends for three likely competitors: Planet Fitness, LA Fitness, and 24 Hour Fitness. In addition, your friend has noted that some recent trends for gyms have included some rather curious practices, like giving away free pizza and candy to its members! He is wondering if you may be able to provide some insight, even if indirect, about such trends and how they may apply to his new gym.

You used GfK MRI's data to find information about U.S. adult gym membership trends in 2012 and 2014. Your plan is to use the two different time points to make some inferences about where the future of fitness gym marketing may be heading. In addition, you also found historical trends about U.S. adult spending at fast-food restaurants. Although not exactly the same as free pizza at gyms, you decided to look at the data to consider whether you can glean any insights. You also found some information about the types of cable channels, Websites, and apps different fitness consumers use; you plan on using this information to give some advice to your friend about how to advertise for his new gym.

THE DATA

The data in the report are all reported in the millions (000,000s) and interpreted in a similar way:

- "Bought Fast Food" and "Spent More than $100 on FF": Both questions deal with someone's fast-food consumption in the past 6 months from either Spring 2014 or Spring 2012. The first question is a simple count of whether someone spent any money on fast food, whereas the second question estimates the number of people who spent more than $100 on fast food in the past 6 months.
- "Member of Gym": This question is an estimate of U.S. adults who have had a membership in any sort of fitness gym in the last 12 months from either Spring 2014 or Spring 2012. This number includes any gym, not just 24 Hour Fitness, Planet Fitness, and LA Fitness.
- "LA Fitness", "24 Hour Fitness", and "Planet Fitness": These questions are the estimated count of U.S. adults who had a membership to the gym within the last 12 months from either Spring 2014 or Spring 2012.

Year	Bought Fast Food		Spent More Than $100 on FF		Member of Gym		LA Fitness		24 Hour Fitness		Planet Fitness	
	2012	2014	2012	2014	2012	2014	2012	2014	2012	2014	2012	2014
Total	169.0	168.5	55.3	56.5	43.2	52.1	2.9	4.2	4.5	3.6	2.6	4.9
HH < $40,000	49.9	50.3	12.3	12.5	7.5	10.9	0.5	1.0	0.8	0.6	0.6	1.3
HH $40,000–$74,999	48.5	45.8	15.5	15.2	10.5	12.2	0.7	1.2	0.8	0.9	0.6	1.3
HH $75,000+	70.6	72.4	27.5	28.8	25.2	28.9	1.7	2.0	2.9	2.0	1.3	2.3
Men	81.4	80.8	29.4	30.0	20.4	24.3	1.3	1.9	2.5	1.9	1.3	2.3
Women	87.7	87.8	25.9	26.5	22.8	27.7	1.6	2.3	2.0	1.6	1.2	2.5

All numbers reported in millions (000,000s)
Source: Spring 2012 and Spring 2014 GfK MRI

- Which of the three income groups had the largest increase in gym membership from 2012 to 2014? If this was expressed in terms of percentage increase, which income group experienced the largest increase from 2012 to 2014?
- Which of the three gyms had the largest market share in 2012? In 2014?
- From 2012 to 2014, does it appear that LA Fitness, 24 Hour Fitness, and Planet Fitness comprise a greater or lesser share of the total gym membership market? Why?

DISCUSSION

1. Compare the membership trends between LA Fitness, 24 Hour Fitness, and Planet Fitness. Are membership trends similar or different across genders and income groups? Consider the different marketing mixes of the three gyms; what do you think may account for the differences in membership trends? (Tip: You can use a tool like *Google News* to search for news articles about each gym in 2012 or 2014.)

2. Your friend told you that he envisions his gym being a place where people who are "intimidated" about going to the gym will feel safe and empowered to work out. Assuming this aspect of your friend's gym is going to be part of his positioning, which of the three competing gyms would you consider to be his most serious competitor? Why?

3. Which income group has experienced the greatest increase in fast food spending from 2012 to 2014? Do you think this information is relevant for your friend when thinking about the marketing mix of his gym? Why or why not?

 GfK US LLC, Mediamark Research & Intelligence division.

WHO'S DRIVING YOU HOME TONIGHT?
NEVER DRINK AND DRIVE

DRIVE DRY
A brandhouse INITIATIVE
DRIVEDRY

CONSUMER BEHAVIOR

1: Foundations of Consumer Behavior

2: Internal Influences on Consumer Behavior

4: Social and Cultural Settings

Consumers in Their

3: Choosing and Using Products

Section 3 • Choosing and Using Products

In Section 3 we look at how consumers think about products, the steps they use to choose one, and what happens after we buy something. Chapter 8 focuses on how we form feelings and thoughts about products and how marketers influence us. In Chapter 9 we look at the steps we use to identify the best solution to a consumption problem. Chapter 10 highlights how factors at the time of purchase influence our choices and then what happens after we buy.

CHAPTERS AHEAD

Chapter 8 • Attitudes and Persuasive Communications

Chapter Objectives

Source: Blend Images/Corbis

Saundra is hanging out at the mall, idly texting some friends about some stuff she saw in a few stores. When she checks her Facebook page, she sees several of them are chatting about their college application plans. She groans to herself; it's starting already! She's just starting her senior year of high school, and already everybody's thinking about what happens next year. Saundra realizes it's time to bite the bullet and really start to look into this; her Mom will certainly be happy. But it's all so confusing. She's been getting bombarded with enticing ads and brochures from so many different schools. They're hard to escape; some arrive by snail mail and others keep hitting her with emails and texts. A few have invited her to take virtual campus tours on their Web sites, and one even wants her to enter a virtual world version of the campus as an avatar to walk around and "talk" to current students. It's amazing to see how different their pitches are, too. Sure, some universities tout their academic excellence, but others play up their international programs, job placement programs, and even amenities (rock climbing walls!). Of course, she's familiar with some of the schools that are starting to court her, and she already has a pretty good idea in her mind of what they're about. But others feel like a blank slate; so far at least, she has absolutely no idea about what it would be like to be a student at these schools. As Saundra starts to post some Facebook queries about where people are looking, she realizes it's going to be an intense year.

OBJECTIVE 8-1
It is important for consumer researchers to understand the nature and power of attitudes.

The Power of Attitudes

People use the term *attitude* in many contexts. A friend might ask you, "What is your attitude toward abortion?" A parent might scold, "Young man, I don't like your attitude." Some bars even euphemistically refer to happy hour as "an attitude adjustment period." For our purposes, though, an **attitude** is a lasting, general evaluation of people (including oneself), objects, advertisements, or issues.[1] We call anything toward which one has an attitude an **attitude object (A$_o$)**. As Saundra will learn (and no doubt you did too) during her college search process, we assimilate information from a variety of sources and often put a lot of effort into forming an attitude toward many things, including a complex attitude object like a university.

An attitude is lasting because it tends to endure over time. It is general because it applies to more than a momentary event, such as hearing a loud noise, though you might, over time, develop a negative attitude toward all loud noises. Consumers have attitudes toward a wide range of attitude objects, from product-specific behaviors (e.g., you use Crest toothpaste rather than Colgate) to more general, consumption-related behaviors (e.g., how often you should brush your teeth). Attitudes help to determine whom you choose to date, what music you listen to, whether you will recycle aluminum cans, or whether you choose to become a consumer researcher for a living. In this chapter we'll consider the contents of an attitude, how we form attitudes, and how we measure them. We will also review some of the surprisingly complex relationships between attitudes and behavior and then take a closer look at how marketers can change these attitudes.

Psychologist Daniel Katz developed the **functional theory of attitudes** to explain how attitudes facilitate social behavior.[2] According to this pragmatic approach, attitudes exist *because* they serve some function for the person. Consumers who expect that they will need to deal with similar situations at a future time will be more likely to start to form an attitude in anticipation.[3] Two people can each have an attitude toward some object for different reasons. As a result, it's helpful for a marketer to know *why* an attitude is held before he or she tries to change it. These are different attitude functions:

- **Utilitarian function**—The **utilitarian function** relates to the basic principles of reward and punishment we learned about in Chapter 4. We develop some attitudes toward products simply because they provide pleasure or pain. If a person likes the taste of a cheeseburger, that person will develop a positive attitude toward cheeseburgers. Ads that stress straightforward product benefits (e.g., you should drink Diet Coke "just for the taste of it") appeal to the utilitarian function.
- **Value-expressive function**—Attitudes that perform a **value-expressive function** relate to the consumer's self-concept (Chapter 6) or central values (Chapter 7). A person forms a product attitude in this case because of what the product says about him or her as a person. Value-expressive attitudes also are highly relevant to the psychographic analyses we discussed in Chapter 7, which consider how consumers cultivate a cluster of activities, interests, and opinions to express a particular social identity.
- **Ego-defensive function**—Attitudes we form to protect ourselves either from external threats or internal feelings perform an **ego-defensive function**. An early marketing study showed that housewives resisted the use of instant coffee because it threatened their conception of themselves as capable homemakers (this doesn't seem to be a big issue for most anymore!).[4] Products that promise to help a man project a "macho" image (e.g., Marlboro cigarettes) appeal to his insecurities about his masculinity. Another

example is deodorant ads that stress the dire, embarrassing consequences when you're caught with underarm odor in public.

● **Knowledge function**—We form some attitudes because we need order, structure, or meaning. A **knowledge function** applies when a person is in an ambiguous situation ("it's OK to wear casual pants to work, but only on Friday") or when he or she confronts a new product (e.g., "Bayer wants you to know about pain relievers").

OBJECTIVE 8-2
Attitudes are more
complex than they first
appear.

The ABC Model of Attitudes

When Subaru of America began work on a new marketing strategy, the automaker discovered that even though most auto buyers had heard of the brand, few had strong emotional connections to it. However, current Subaru owners expressed strong passion and even love for the brand. To ramp up this emotional connection for non-owners as well, the new campaign targets people who are in three different stages of buying a car—what Subaru calls the *heart*, the *head*, and the *wallet*. The *heart* stage focuses on the love that owners show for their cars; commercials share personal stories of their attachment. The *head* stage ads, in contrast, present the rational side of specific models as they emphasize how the cars benefit their owners in terms of reliability, economy, and so on. Then, the *wallet* ads deal with the financial details of actually buying a Subaru; these include special offers from local dealers.[5]

Like the Subaru campaign, an attitude has three components: affect, behavior, and cognition. As we saw in Chapter 5, **affect** describes how a consumer *feels* about an attitude object. **Behavior** refers to the *actions* he or she takes toward the object or in some cases at least his or her intentions to take action about it (but, as we will discuss at a later point, an intention does not always result in an actual behavior). **Cognition** is what he or she *believes* to be true about the attitude object. You can remember these three components of an attitude as the **ABC model of attitudes**.

The ABC model emphasizes the interrelationships among knowing, feeling, and doing. We can't determine consumers' attitudes toward a product if we just identify their cognitions (beliefs) about it. For example, a researcher may find that shoppers "know" a particular camcorder has a power zoom lens, auto focus, and a flying erase head, but simply knowing this doesn't indicate whether they feel these attributes are good, bad, or irrelevant, or whether they would actually buy the camcorder.

Hierarchies of Effects

Which comes first: knowing, feeling, or doing? It turns out that each element may lead things off, depending on the situation. Attitude researchers developed the concept of a **hierarchy of effects** to explain the relative impact of the three components. Each hierarchy specifies that a fixed sequence of steps occur *en route* to an attitude. Figure 8.1 summarizes these three different hierarchies.

The High-Involvement Hierarchy: Think → Feel → Do

The **high-involvement hierarchy** assumes that a person approaches a product decision as a problem-solving process. First, he or she forms beliefs about a product as she accumulates knowledge (*beliefs*) regarding relevant attributes. Next, he or she evaluates these beliefs and forms a feeling about the product (*affect*).[6] Then he or she engages in a relevant behavior, such as when he or she buys a product that offers the attributes he or she feels good about. This hierarchy assumes that a consumer is highly involved when he or she makes a purchase decision (see Chapter 5).[7] He or she is motivated to seek out a lot of information, carefully weigh alternatives, and come to a thoughtful decision.

The Low-Involvement Hierarchy: Think → Do → Feel

The **low-involvement hierarchy of effects** assumes that the consumer initially doesn't have a strong preference for one brand over another; instead, he or she acts on the basis of

Figure 8.1 THREE HIERARCHIES OF EFFECTS

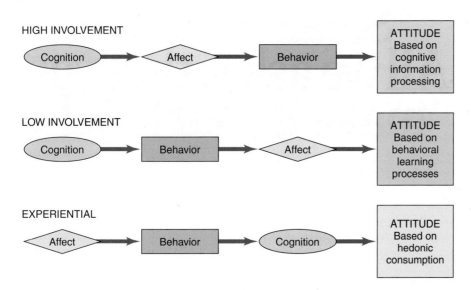

limited knowledge and forms an evaluation only *after* he or she has bought the product.[8] The attitude is likely to come about through behavioral learning, as good or bad experiences reinforce his or her initial choice.

The possibility that consumers simply don't care enough about many decisions to carefully assemble a set of product beliefs and then evaluate them is important. This implies that all of our well-intentioned efforts to influence beliefs and carefully communicate information about product attributes may fall on deaf ears. Consumers aren't necessarily going to pay attention anyway; they are more likely to respond to simple stimulus–response connections when they make purchase decisions. For example, a consumer who chooses among paper towels might remember that "Bounty is the quicker picker-upper" rather than systematically comparing all the brands on the shelf. Get a life!

The notion of consumers' low involvement is a bitter pill for some marketers to swallow. Who wants to admit that what they market is not important to the people who buy it? A brand manager for, say, a brand of bubble gum or cat food may find it hard to believe that consumers don't put that much thought into purchasing the product because he or she spends many waking (and perhaps sleeping) hours thinking about it.

For marketers, the ironic silver lining to this low-involvement cloud is that under these conditions, consumers are not motivated to process a lot of complex, brand-related information. Instead, they will be swayed by principles of behavioral learning, such as the simple responses that conditioned brand names or point-of-purchase displays elicit (as we discussed in Chapter 4).

The Experiential Hierarchy: Feel → Do → Think

According to the **experiential hierarchy of effects**, we act on the basis of our emotional reactions. The experiential perspective highlights the idea that intangible product attributes, such as package design, advertising, brand names, and the nature of the setting in which the experience occurs, can help shape our attitudes toward a brand. We may base these reactions on *hedonic* motivations, such as whether using the product is exciting like the Nintendo Wii or aesthetically pleasing like the Apple iPhone.

Even the emotions the communicator expresses have an impact. A smile is infectious; in a process we term *emotional contagion*, messages that happy people deliver enhance our attitude toward the product.[9] Numerous studies demonstrate that the mood a person is in when he or she sees or hears a marketing message influences how he or she will process the ad, the likelihood that he or she will remember the information he

This ad for New York's famous Smith & Wollensky restaurant emphasizes that marketers and others associated with a product or service are often more involved with it than are their customers.
Source: Courtesy of Smith & Wollensky Steak House.

Steak is our life. All we ask is that you make it your lunch.

Smith & Wollensky.
The quintessential New York City steakhouse.
49th St. & 3rd Ave. (212) 753-1530.

Winner of The *Wine Spectator's* 1987 Grand Award.

Product design and other aesthetic attributes helps to influence attitudes when consumers choose on the basis of their emotional reactions.
Source: Rob Cousins/Alamy.

or she sees, and how he or she will feel about the advertised item and related products in the future.

Researchers continue to debate whether cognition and affect are independent or linked when we form attitudes based on hedonic consumption. The **cognitive-affective model** proposes that an emotional reaction is just the last step in a series of cognitive processes that follows sensory recognition of a stimulus and retrieval of information from memory that helps to categorize it. In contrast the **independence hypothesis** argues that affect and cognition are separate systems so that it's not always necessary to have a cognition to elicit an emotional response. This perspective focuses more on the impact of aesthetic experiences as opposed to the consumption of products that provide primarily functional benefits. [10]

<table>
<tr><td>OBJECTIVE 8-3
We form attitudes in several ways.</td><td></td></tr>
</table>

How Do We Form Attitudes?

We all have lots of attitudes, and we don't usually question how we got them. Certainly, you're not born with the heartfelt conviction that, say, Pepsi is better than Coke, or that emo music liberates the soul. From where do these attitudes come?

We form an attitude in several different ways, depending on the particular hierarchy of effects that operates. As we saw in Chapter 4, we simply may form an attitude toward a brand as a result of classical conditioning: A marketer repeatedly pairs an attitude object such as the Pepsi name with a catchy jingle ("You're in the Pepsi Generation"). Or we can form an attitude because of instrumental conditioning: The marketer reinforces us when we consume the attitude object (e.g., you take a swig of Pepsi and it quenches your thirst). Finally, this learning can result from a complex cognitive process. For example, teenagers may model the behavior of friends and media endorsers, such as Beyoncé, who drink Pepsi because they believe that this will allow them to fit in with the desirable lifestyle that Pepsi commercials portray.

All Attitudes Are Not Created Equal

It's important to distinguish among types of attitudes because not all form in the same way.[11] One consumer may be highly brand-loyal; she has an enduring, deeply held positive attitude toward an attitude object, and it would be difficult to weaken this involvement. However, another woman may be a more fickle consumer: She may have a mildly positive attitude toward a product but be quite willing to abandon it when something better comes along. In this section, we'll consider the differences between strongly and weakly held attitudes and briefly review some of the major theoretical perspectives researchers use to explain how attitudes form and relate to our other attitudes.

Consumers vary in their *commitment* to an attitude; the degree of commitment relates to their level of involvement with the attitude object (see Chapter 5).[12] Let's look at three (increasing) levels of commitment:

1 **Compliance**—At the lowest level of involvement, **compliance**, we form an attitude because it helps us to gain rewards or avoid punishment. This attitude is superficial; it is likely to change when others no longer monitor our behavior or when another option becomes available. You may drink Pepsi because the cafeteria sells it, and it is too much trouble to go elsewhere for a Coca-Cola.

2 **Identification**—**Identification** occurs when we form an attitude to conform to another person's or group's expectations. Advertising that depicts the dire social consequences when we choose some products over others relies on the tendency of consumers to imitate the behavior of desirable models (more on this in Chapter 11).

3 **Internalization**—At a high level of involvement we call **internalization**, deep-seated attitudes become part of our value system. These attitudes are difficult to change because they are so important to us. The infamous Coke debacle of the 1980s (still a

standard in marketing textbooks today) illustrates what can happen when a marketer messes with strongly held attitudes. In this case, Coca-Cola decided to change its flavor formula to meet the needs of younger consumers who often preferred a sweeter taste (more characteristic of Pepsi). The company conducted rigorous blind *taste tests* that showed people who didn't know what brands they were drinking preferred the flavor of the new formula. Much to its surprise, when New Coke hit the shelves, the company faced a consumer revolt as die-hard Coke fans protested. This allegiance to Coke was obviously more than a minor taste preference for these people; the brand was intertwined with their social identities and took on intense patriotic and nostalgic properties.

OBJECTIVE 8-4

A need to maintain consistency among all of our attitudinal components often motivates us to alter one or more of them.

The Consistency Principle

Have you ever heard someone say, "Pepsi is my favorite soft drink. It tastes terrible," or "I love my boyfriend. He's the biggest idiot I've ever met"? Probably not (at least until the couple gets married!), because these beliefs or evaluations don't go together. According to the **principle of cognitive consistency**, we value harmony among our thoughts, feelings, and behaviors, and a need to maintain uniformity among these elements motivates us. This desire means that, if necessary, we change our thoughts, feelings, or behaviors to make them consistent with other experiences. That boyfriend may slip up and act like a moron occasionally, but his girlfriend (eventually) will find a way to forgive him—or dump him. The consistency principle is an important reminder that we don't form our attitudes in a vacuum: A big factor is how well they fit with other, related attitudes we already hold.

We've already reviewed this phenomenon in Chapter 5, when we learned about the *theory of cognitive dissonance*. We saw there that when a person is confronted with inconsistencies among attitudes or behaviors, he or she will take some action to resolve this "dissonance"; perhaps he will change his or her attitude or modify his or her behavior to restore consistency. The theory has important ramifications for consumer behavior. We often confront situations in which there is some conflict between our attitudes toward a product or service and what we actually do or buy.[13]

According to the theory, our motivation to reduce the negative feelings of dissonance makes us find a way for our beliefs and feelings to fit together. The theory focuses on situations in which two cognitive elements clash. A *cognitive element* is something a person believes about himself or herself, a behavior he or she performs, or an observation about his or her surroundings. For example, the two cognitive elements "I know smoking cigarettes causes cancer" and "I smoke cigarettes" are *dissonant* with one another. This psychological inconsistency creates a feeling of discomfort that the smoker tries to reduce. The magnitude of dissonance depends on both the importance and number of dissonant elements.[14] In other words, we're more likely to observe dissonance in high-involvement situations where there is more pressure to reduce inconsistencies.

We reduce dissonance when we eliminate, add, or change elements. A person can stop smoking (*eliminating*), or remember Great-Aunt Sophie who smoked until the day she died at age 95 (*adding*). Alternatively, he or she might question the research that links cancer and smoking (*changing*), perhaps by believing industry-sponsored studies that try to refute this connection.

Dissonance theory can help to explain why evaluations of a product tend to increase *after* we buy the product. The cognitive element, "I made a stupid decision," is dissonant with the element, "I am not a stupid person," so we tend to find even more reasons to like something after it becomes ours. A classic study at a horse race demonstrated this *postpurchase dissonance*. Bettors evaluated their chosen horse more highly and were more confident of its success *after* they placed a bet than before. Because the bettor financially commits to the choice, he or she reduces dissonance by elevating the attractiveness of the chosen alternative relative to the nonchosen ones.[15] One implication of this phenomenon is that consumers actively seek support for their decisions so they can justify them; therefore, marketers should supply their customers with additional reinforcement after they purchase to bolster these decisions.

As it gets increasingly difficult for cigarette smokers to indulge their habit in public places like offices, they have to work harder to reduce cognitive dissonance in order to justify the effort to continue this practice.
Source: Scott Griessel/Fotolia.

Self-Perception Theory

Do we always change our attitudes to be in line with our behavior because we're motivated to reduce cognitive dissonance? **Self-perception theory** provides an alternative explanation of dissonance effects.[16] It assumes that we observe our own behavior to determine just what our attitudes are, much as we assume that we know what another person's attitude is when we watch what he does. The theory states that we maintain consistency as we infer that we must have a positive attitude toward an object if we have bought or consumed it (assuming that we freely made this choice). Thus, you might say to yourself, "I guess I must be into Facebook pretty big time. I seem to spend half my life on it."

Self-perception theory helps to explain the effectiveness of a strategy salespeople call the **foot-in-the-door technique**: They know that consumers are more likely to comply with a big request if they agree to a smaller one first.[17] The name for this technique comes from the old practice of door-to-door selling; salespeople learn to plant their foot in a door so the prospect doesn't slam it on them. A good salesperson knows that he or she is more likely to get an order if he or she can persuade the customer to open the door and talk. By agreeing to do so, the customer signals that he or she is willing to listen to the salesperson's pitch. Placing an order is consistent with the self-perception that "I'm the kind of person who is willing to buy something from a salesperson who knocks on my door."[18] Recent research also points to the possibility that when salespeople ask consumers to make a series of choices, these decisions are cognitively demanding and deplete the resources the person has available to monitor his or her behavior. As a result, the target will opt for easier decisions down the road; in some cases, it may be easier just to comply with the request than to search for reasons why you shouldn't.[19]

Social Judgment Theory

Social judgment theory also assumes that people assimilate new information about attitude objects in light of what they already know or feel.[20] The initial attitude acts as a frame of reference, and we categorize new information in terms of this existing standard. Just as our decision that a box is heavy depends in part on the weight of other boxes we lift, we develop a subjective standard when we judge attitude objects.

One important aspect of the theory is that people differ in terms of the information they will find acceptable or unacceptable. They form **latitudes of acceptance and rejection** around an attitude standard. They will consider and evaluate ideas falling within the latitude favorably, but they are more likely to reject out of hand those that fall outside of this zone. People tend to perceive messages within their latitude of acceptance as more consistent with their position than those messages actually are. We call this exaggeration an *assimilation effect*.

However, we tend to see messages that fall in our latitude of rejection as even more unacceptable than they actually are; this results in an exaggeration we call a *contrast effect*.[21] As a person becomes more involved with an attitude object, his or her latitude of acceptance gets smaller. In other words, consumers accept fewer ideas farther from their own position and they tend to oppose even mildly divergent positions. Discriminating buyers have smaller latitude of acceptance (e.g., "choosy mothers choose Jif peanut butter"). However, relatively uninvolved consumers consider a wider range of alternatives. They are less likely to be brand loyal and are more likely to switch brands.

Balance Theory

Have you ever heard the expression, "Any friend of Joe's is a friend of mine?" How about "My enemy's enemy is my friend?" **Balance theory** considers how people perceive relations among different attitude objects, and how they alter their attitudes so that these remain consistent (or "balanced").[22] One study even found that when a person observes two other individuals who are eating similar food, they assume they must be friends![23]

A balance theory perspective involves relations (always from the perceiver's subjective point of view) among three elements, so we call the resulting attitude structures *triads*. Each triad contains (1) a person and his or her perceptions of (2) an attitude object and (3) some other person or object. The theory specifies that we want relations among elements in a triad to be harmonious. If they are unbalanced, this creates tension that we are motivated to reduce by changing our perceptions to restore balance.

We link elements together in one of two ways: They can have either a *unit relation*, where we think that a person is somehow connected to an attitude object (something like a belief), or they can have a *sentiment relation*, where a person expresses liking or disliking for an attitude object. You might perceive that a dating couple has a positive sentiment

A woman who dislikes men in earrings has to resolve a state of imbalance if she wants to date a guy who wears one.
Source: youngnova/123RF.

relation. On getting married, they will have a positive unit relation. If they get divorced, they sever the unit relation.

To see how balance theory might work, consider the following scenario:

● Kristin would like to date Dan, who is in her consumer behavior class. In balance theory terms, Kristin has a positive sentiment relation with Dan.

● One day, Dan shows up in class wearing an earring. Dan has a positive unit relation with the earring.

● Men who wear earrings are a turnoff to Kristin. She has a negative sentiment relation with men's earrings.

Figure 8.2 BALANCE THEORY

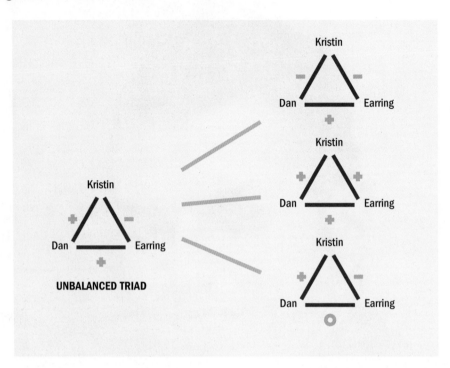

UNBALANCED TRIAD

Marketing Opportunity

Consumers often like to publicize their connections with successful people or organizations (no matter how shaky the connection) to enhance their own standing. Researchers call this tactic **basking in reflected glory**. A series of studies at Arizona State University (ASU) showed how students' desires to identify with a winning image—in this case, ASU's football team—influenced their consumption behaviors. After the team played a game each weekend, observers recorded the incidence of school-related items, such as ASU T-shirts and caps that students walking around campus wore. The researchers correlated the frequency of these behaviors to the team's performance. If the team won on Saturday, students were more likely to show off their school affiliation (basking in reflected glory) the following Monday than if the team lost. And the bigger the point spread, the more likely they were to observe students who wore clothes with the ASU logo.[24]

According to balance theory, Kristin faces an unbalanced triad. As Figure 8.2 shows, she will experience pressure to restore balance by altering some aspect of the triad. How can she do this? She could decide that she does not like Dan after all. Or her liking for Dan could prompt her to decide that earrings on men are really pretty cool. She might even try to negate the unit relation between Dan and the earring by deciding that he must wear it as part of a fraternity initiation (this reduces the free-choice element). Finally, she could choose to "leave the field" by accepting a date with Dan's roommate Doug who doesn't wear an earring (but who has an awesome tattoo). Note that although the theory does not specify which of these routes Kristin will choose, it does predict that she will change one or more of her perceptions to achieve balance. Although this example is an oversimplified representation of most attitude processes, it helps to explain a number of consumer behavior phenomena.

Balance theory reminds us that when we have balanced perceptions, our attitudes also are likely to be stable. However, when we experience inconsistencies, we also are more likely to change our attitudes. Balance theory helps explain why consumers like to be linked to positively valued objects. When you form a unit relation with a popular product (e.g., you wear a popular designer's clothing, drive a hot car, or follow a popular singer), this may improve the chances that other people will include you as a positive sentiment relation in their triads.

At the college level, many schools in addition to ASU reap huge revenues when they license their school's name and logo. Universities with strong athletic programs, such as Michigan State, Miami, and Auburn, clean up when they sell millions of dollars worth of merchandise (everything from T-shirts to toilet seats). Yale was a relative latecomer to this game, but the director of licensing explained the decision to profit from the use of the school's name and the likeness of bulldog mascot Handsome Dan: "We recognize that our name means a lot—even to people who didn't go here. Plus, this way we can crack down on the Naked Coed Lacrosse shirts out there with Yale on them."[25]

When a school's team wins a game, students (and fans) are more likely to wear merchandise that link them to the institution as they "bask in reflected glory."
Source: Rose-Marie Murray/Alamy.

CB AS I SEE IT

Jennifer Escalas, *Vanderbilt University*

Do you have a favorite celebrity? One whom you follow on Twitter or Instagram? If that celebrity uses a particular brand, would you buy it? Kim Kardashian receives ten thousand dollars to tweet about a product. Abercrombie and Fitch paid *Jersey Shore* stars *not* to wear their products on the reality television show. Companies like Adly.com offer thousands of celebrities endorsement deals on social media; they utilize stars like Katy Perry, Justin Bieber, and Taylor Swift, who combined have nearly 200 million Twitter followers.

My research with Jim Bettman explores how celebrity endorsement works, focusing on the symbolic meanings associated with celebrities, and how that meaning can be linked to brands. We believe that people engage in consumption (at least in part) to create themselves and communicate aspects about themselves to others. For example, consumers may communicate who they are by the car they drive. You probably think that someone who drives a Prius is different from a person who drives a Mercedes. Why is that? It's because there are different symbolic meanings associated with the two brands. Prius is a hybrid, so the driver is likely concerned about the environment. Mercedes are expensive, so the driver is likely to be wealthy.

Marketers spend a lot of time (and money!) developing unique images for their brands. Celebrity endorsement is one way for marketers to connect symbolic meanings to the image of their brand. Celebrities often personify various characteristics that may be useful to consumers when they construct and communicate their self-concepts, such as being stylish, rugged, smart, sexy, successful, or even rebellious.

Consumers do not look to all celebrities for meaning indiscriminately. They are more likely to accept meanings from brands associated with a celebrity who represents either who they are or who they would like to be, and to reject meanings associated with a celebrity who represents either who they are not or who they would not like to become. Furthermore, for a celebrity endorsement to work well, there should be a match between the celebrity image and the brand image. It doesn't make sense for former President George W. Bush to endorse Urban Outfitters.

Our studies show that when self-concept construction is especially important, celebrity endorsements have a stronger effect. We look at settings where consumers' identities are compromised by such factors as low self-esteem, loneliness, or stress, which create a liminal state where self-identity needs to be reconstructed. We find that consumers with low self-esteem respond favorably to advertisements that feature aspirational celebrities that the consumer wishes to be more like. We believe these consumers use the celebrity's image, which is associated with the brand, to build their own self-esteem. We also find that lonely consumers and consumers experiencing high levels of stress respond more favorably to brands advertised with a celebrity endorser who they like. Thus, we find that celebrity endorsement can serve a therapeutic function for consumers with compromised identities by providing useful symbolic meanings for self-identity construction.

This "balancing act" is at the heart of **celebrity endorsements**, in which marketers hope that the star's popularity will transfer to the product or when a nonprofit organization recruits a celebrity to discourage harmful behaviors.[26] We will consider this strategy at length later in this chapter. For now, it pays to remember that creating a unit relation between a product and a star can backfire if the public's opinion of the celebrity endorser shifts from positive to negative. For example, Pepsi pulled an ad that featured Madonna after she released a controversial music video involving religion and sex; it also happened when celebrity bad girl Paris Hilton got busted. The strategy can also cause trouble if people question the star–product unit relation: This occurred when the late singer Michael Jackson, who also did promotions for Pepsi, subsequently confessed that he didn't even drink soda.

OBJECTIVE 8-5

Attitude models identify specific components and combine them to predict a consumer's overall attitude toward a product or brand.

Attitude Models

When market researchers want to assess consumers' attitudes toward beer brands, they might simply go to a bar and ask a bunch of guys, "How do you feel about Budweiser?" However, as we saw previously, attitudes can be a lot more complex than that. One problem is that many attributes or qualities may link to a product or service; depending on the individual, some of these will be more or less important ("Less filling!" "Tastes great!"). Another problem is that when a person decides to take action toward an attitude object, other factors influence his or her behavior, such as whether he or she feels that his family or friends would approve. **Attitude models** specify the different elements that might work together to influence people's evaluations of attitude objects.

Multiattribute Attitude Models

A simple response does not always tell us everything we need to know, either about *why* the consumer feels a certain way toward a product or about what marketers can do to change her attitude. Our beliefs (accurate or not) about a product often are key to how we evaluate it. Warner-Lambert discovered this when it conducted research for its Fresh Burst Listerine mouthwash. A research firm paid families so it could set up cameras in their bathrooms and watch their daily routines (maybe they should have just checked out YouTube). Participants who bought both Fresh Burst and rival Scope said they used mouthwash to make their breath smell good. But Scope users swished around the liquid and then spit it out, whereas Listerine users kept the product in their mouths for a long time (one respondent held the stuff in until he got in the car and finally spit it out in a sewer a block away!). These findings told Listerine that the brand still hadn't shaken its medicine-like image.[27]

Because attitudes are so complex, marketing researchers may use **multiattribute attitude models** to understand them. This type of model assumes that consumers' attitude toward an attitude object (A_o) depends on the beliefs they have about several of its attributes. When we use a multiattribute model, we assume that we can identify these specific beliefs and combine them to derive a measure of the consumer's overall attitude. We'll describe how these models work with the example of a consumer who evaluates a complex attitude object that should be familiar to you: a college.

Basic multiattribute models contain three specific elements:[28]

- *Attributes* are characteristics of the A_o. A researcher tries to identify the attributes that most consumers use when they evaluate the A_o. For example, one of a college's attributes is its scholarly reputation.
- *Beliefs* are cognitions about the specific A_o (usually relative to others like it). A belief measure assesses the extent to which the consumer perceives that a brand possesses a particular attribute. For example, a student might believe that the University of North Carolina is strong academically (or maybe this is consistency theory at work because your humble author went to graduate school there!).

● *Importance weights* reflect the relative priority of an attribute to the consumer. Although people might consider an A_o on a number of attributes, some attributes are likely to be more important than others (i.e., consumers will give them greater weight). Furthermore, these weights are likely to differ across consumers. In the case of colleges and universities, for example, one student might stress research opportunities, whereas another might assign greater weight to athletic programs.

The most influential multiattribute model is called the **Fishbein Model**, named after its primary developer.[29] The model measures three components of attitude:

● *Salient beliefs* people have about an A_o (i.e., those beliefs about the object a person considers during evaluation).
● *Object-attribute linkages*, or the probability that a particular object has an important attribute.
● *Evaluation* of each of the important attributes.

When we combine these three elements, we compute a consumer's overall attitude toward an object (we'll see later how researchers modify this equation to increase its accuracy). The basic formula is:

$$A_{jk} = \Sigma \beta_{ijk} I_{ik}$$

where
  i = attribute
  j = brand
  k = consumer
  I = the importance weight given attribute i by consumer k
  β = consumer k's belief regarding the extent to which brand j possesses attribute i
  A = a particular consumer's (k's) attitude score for brand j

We obtain the overall attitude score (A) when we multiply consumers' rating of each attribute for all the brands they considered by the importance rating for that attribute.

To see how this basic multiattribute model works, let's suppose we want to predict which college our friend Saundra from the beginning of the chapter is likely to attend. After months of waiting anxiously, Saundra gets accepted to four schools. Because she must now decide among these, we would first like to know which attributes Saundra will consider when she forms an attitude toward each school. We can then ask Saundra to assign a rating regarding how well each school performs on each attribute and also determine the relative importance of the attributes to her.

By summing scores on each attribute (after we weight each by its relative importance), we compute an overall attitude score for each school. Table 8.1 shows these hypothetical ratings. Based on this analysis, it seems that Saundra has the most favorable attitude toward Smith. She is clearly someone who would like to attend a college for women with a solid academic reputation rather than a school that offers a strong athletic program or a party atmosphere.

Marketing Applications of the Multiattribute Model

Suppose you were the director of marketing for Northland College, another school Saundra considered. How might you use the data from this analysis to improve your image?

Capitalize on Relative Advantage. If prospective students view one brand as superior on a particular attribute, a marketer needs to convince consumers like Saundra that this particular attribute is important. For example, although Saundra rates Northland's social atmosphere highly, she does not believe this attribute is a valued aspect for a college. As Northland's marketing director, you might emphasize the importance of an active social

		Beliefs (B)			
Attribute (i)	importance (I)	Smith	Princeton	Rutgers	Northland
Academic reputation	6	8	9	6	3
All women	7	9	3	3	3
Cost	4	2	2	6	9
Proximity to home	3	2	2	6	9
Athletics	1	1	2	5	1
Party atmosphere	2	1	3	7	9
Library facilities	5	7	9	7	2
Attitude score		163	142	153	131

TABLE 8.1   The Basic Multiattribute Model: Saundra's College Decision

life, varied experiences, or even the development of future business contacts that a student forges when he or she makes strong college friendships.

Strengthen Perceived Product/Attribute Linkages. A marketer may discover that consumers do not equate his brand with a certain attribute. Advertising campaigns often address this problem when they stress a specific quality to consumers (e.g., "new and improved"). Saundra apparently does not think much of Northland's academic quality, athletic programs, or library facilities. You might develop an informational campaign to improve these perceptions (e.g., "little-known facts about Northland").

Add a New Attribute. Product marketers frequently try to distinguish themselves from their competitors when they add a product feature. Northland College might try to emphasize some unique aspect, such as a hands-on internship program for business majors that takes advantage of ties to the local community.

Influence Competitors' Ratings. Finally, you can decrease your competitors' higher ratings with a *comparative advertising* strategy. In this case, you might publish an ad that lists the tuition rates of a number of area schools with which Northland compares favorably and emphasize the value for the money its students get.

Do Attitudes Predict Behavior?

Consumer researchers have used multiattribute models for many years, but a major problem plagues them: In many cases, a person's attitude doesn't predict behavior. In a classic demonstration of "do as I say, not as I do," many studies report a low correlation between a person's reported attitude toward something and actual behavior toward it. Some researchers are so discouraged that they question whether attitudes are of any use at all when we try to understand behavior. Hence the popular expression, "the road to hell is paved with good intentions."

In response, researchers tinkered with the Fishbein Model to improve its predictive ability. They call the newer version the **theory of reasoned action**.[32] This model contains several important additions to the original, and although the model is still not perfect, it does a better job of prediction.[33] Let's look at some of the modifications to this model.

Intentions Versus Behavior

Attitudes possess both direction and strength. A person may like or dislike an attitude object with varying degrees of confidence or conviction. It is helpful to distinguish between

❙ Marketing Pitfall

The (in)consistency between attitudes and behavior links to a major public health problem: **medication adherence**. This term describes the extent to which people fill and actually take prescribed medicines. Although some patients unfortunately don't adhere to prescriptions because they can't afford them, many simply forget to swallow their pills. This breakdown between attitudes and behavior threatens many people's health and it also adds huge costs to the healthcare system. An industry study estimates it costs U.S. taxpayers $290 billion annually.[30] The CVS chain found that even for chronic diseases, one-third of their customers stopped taking their prescribed medicine after a month, and half stopped after a year. CVS aggressively reminds people to fill their prescriptions with texts, e-mails, and phone calls.[31] Still, even these methods are only part of the solution: People still need to actually take the pills once they get them home.

Marketers focus on how a product's attributes are "new and improved" when they want to strengthen the linkage to a quality they think consumers desire.
Source: Balint Radu/Fotolia.

attitudes we hold firmly and those that are more superficial, especially because a person who holds an attitude with greater conviction is more likely to act on it. One study on environmental issues and marketing activities found, for example, that people who express greater conviction in their feelings regarding environmentally responsible behaviors such as recycling show greater consistency between attitudes and behavioral intentions.[34]

Social pressure also can help motivate consumers to engage in socially responsible behaviors. One study assessed this possibility when it compared the effectiveness of different ways a hotel might encourage guests to reuse their towels. When researchers used a social appeal ("the majority of guests reuse their towels"), this worked better than a functional appeal ("help save the environment"). They also found that compliance was boosted when they phrased the requests in terms of directly relevant others ("the majority of guests in this room reuse their towels") compared to more general group appeals ("the majority of men and women reuse their towels").[35] As this example illustrates, the theory acknowledges the power of other people to influence what we do. Much as we may hate to admit it, what we think others would *like* us to do may override our own preferences. Thus, **normative influence** can result in a contradiction between what we say we will do and what we actually do when the moment of truth arrives.

Let's take a closer look at Saundra's college choice. You saw in Table 8.1 that she was eager to attend a predominantly female school. However, if she felt that this choice would be unpopular (perhaps her friends would think she was too nerdy), she might ignore or downgrade this preference when she made her decision. Researchers added a new element, the **subjective norm (SN)**, to account for the effects of what we believe other people think we should do. They use two factors to measure SN: (1) the intensity of a *normative belief (NB)* that others believe we should take or not take some action and (2) the *motivation to comply (MC)* with that belief (i.e., the degree to which the consumer takes others' anticipated reactions into account when she evaluates a purchase).

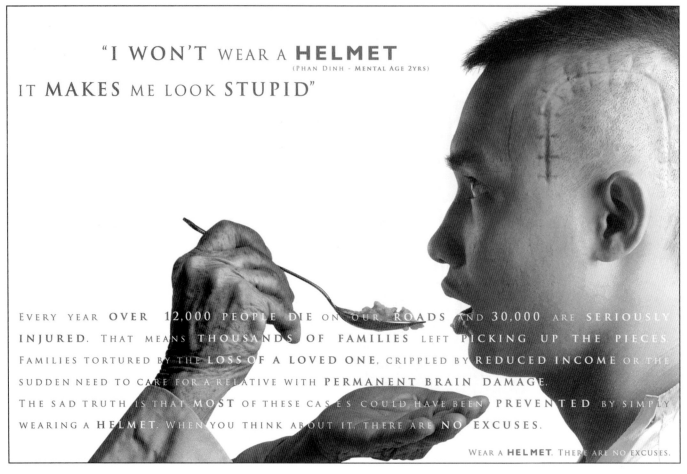

This Vietnamese ad employs social pressure (the subjective norm) to address people's attitudes toward wearing helmets.
Source: Asia Injury Prevention Foundation.

The newer model also measures **attitude toward the act of buying (A_{act})**, rather than only the attitude toward the product itself. In other words, it focuses on the perceived consequences of a purchase. Knowing how someone feels about buying or using an object turns out to be more valid than merely knowing the consumer's evaluation of the object itself.[36]

To understand this distinction, consider a marketing researcher who wants to measure college students' attitudes toward safe sex and wearing condoms. Although many college students interviewed would probably report a positive attitude toward condom use, can the researcher conclude from the responses that these respondents will actually buy and use them? The researcher might get more accurate results if the same students were asked how likely they are to *buy* condoms. A person might have a positive A_0 toward condoms, but A_{act} (attitude toward the act of obtaining the attitude object) might be negative because of the embarrassment or the hassle involved.

Obstacles to Predicting Behavior in the Theory of Reasoned Action

Despite improvements to the Fishbein Model, problems arise when researchers misapply it. As our discussion about measuring personality traits in Chapter 7 showed, sometimes researchers use a model in ways it was not intended or where certain assumptions about human behavior may not be warranted.[37] Here are some other obstacles to prediction researchers encounter:

- The model tries to predict actual behavior (e.g., taking a diet pill), not the *outcomes* of behavior that some studies assess (e.g., losing weight).
- Some outcomes are beyond our control, such as when the purchase requires the cooperation of other people. For instance, a woman might *want* to get a mortgage, but this intention will be worthless if she cannot find a banker to give her one.

- The basic assumption that behavior is intentional may be invalid in a variety of cases, including impulsive acts, sudden changes in situation, novelty seeking, or even simple repeat buying. One study found that such unexpected events as having guests, changes in the weather, or reading articles about the healthfulness of certain foods significantly affected actual behaviors.[38]
- Measures of attitude often do not really correspond to the behavior they are supposed to predict, either in terms of the A_o or when the act will occur. One common problem is a difference in the level of abstraction researchers employ. For example, knowing a person's attitude toward sports cars may not predict whether he or she will purchase a BMW Z3. It is important to match the level of specificity between the attitude and the behavioral intention.
- A similar problem relates to the *time frame* of the attitude measure. In general, the longer the time between the attitude measurement and the behavior it is supposed to assess, the weaker the relationship will be. For example, predictability improves greatly if we ask a consumer the likelihood that he or she will buy a house in the next week as opposed to within the next 5 years.
- We form stronger and more predictive attitudes through direct, personal experience with an A_o than those we form indirectly through advertising.[39] According to the **attitude accessibility perspective**, behavior is a function of the person's immediate perceptions of the A_o, in the context of the situation in which he or she encounters it. An attitude will guide the evaluation of the object but *only* if a person's memory activates it when he or she encounters the object. These findings underscore the importance of strategies that induce trials (e.g., by widespread product sampling to encourage the consumer to try the product at home, taste tests in grocery stores, test drives at car dealers, etc.) as well as those that maximize exposure to marketing communications.

In addition, most researchers apply the theory of reasoned action in Western settings. Certain assumptions inherent in the model may not necessarily apply to consumers from other cultures. Several cultural roadblocks diminish the universality of the theory of reasoned action:[40]

- The model predicts the performance of a voluntary act. Across cultures, however, many activities, ranging from taking exams and entering military service to receiving an inoculation or even choosing a marriage partner, are not necessarily voluntary.
- The relative impact of subjective norms may vary across cultures. For example, Asian cultures tend to value conformity and "face saving," so it is possible that subjective norms involving the anticipated reactions of others to the choice will have an even greater impact on behavior for many Asian consumers. Indeed, a study conducted during an election in Singapore successfully predicted how people would vote as it assessed their voting intentions beforehand. These intentions were in turn influenced by such factors as voters' attitudes toward the candidate, attitudes toward the political party, and subjective norms, which in Singapore includes an emphasis on harmonious and close ties among members of the society.
- The model measures behavioral intentions and thus presupposes that consumers are actively thinking ahead and planning future behaviors. The intention concept assumes that consumers have a linear time sense; they think in terms of past, present, and future. As we'll discuss in Chapter 10, not all cultures subscribe to this perspective on time.
- A consumer who forms an intention implicitly claims that he or she is in control of his or her actions. Some cultures (e.g., Muslim peoples) tend to be fatalistic and do not necessarily believe in the concept of free will. Indeed, one study that compared students from the United States, Jordan, and Thailand found evidence for cultural differences in assumptions about fatalism and control over the future.

Figure 8.3 THEORY OF TRYING

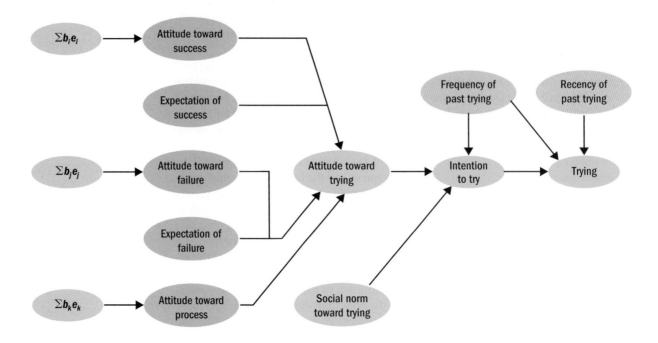

Trying to Consume

Other theorists propose different perspectives on the attitude–behavior connection. For example, the **multiple pathway anchoring and adjustment (MPAA) model** emphasizes multiple pathways to attitude formation, including outside-in (object-centered) and inside-out (person-centered) pathways.[41]

Another perspective tries to address some of these problems because it focuses instead on consumers' goals and what they believe they have to do to attain them. The **theory of trying** states that we should replace the criterion of behavior in the reasoned action model with *trying* to reach a goal. As Figure 8.3 shows, this perspective recognizes that additional factors might intervene between intent and performance—both personal and environmental barriers might prevent the individual from attaining the goal. For example, a person who intends to lose weight may have to deal with numerous issues: He may not believe he is capable of slimming down, he may have a roommate who loves to cook and who leaves tempting goodies lying around the apartment, his friends may be jealous of his attempts to diet and encourage him to pig out, or he may be genetically predisposed to obesity and cutting down on calories simply will not produce the desired results.[42]

Persuasion: How Do Marketers Change Attitudes?

BUY NOW! Advertisers constantly bombard us with messages imploring us to change our attitudes—and of course buy their products. These persuasion attempts can range from logical arguments to graphic pictures, from peers who try to intimidate us to celebrities who try to charm us. Now we'll review some of the factors that help gauge the effectiveness of marketing communications. Our focus will be on some basic aspects of communication that specifically help to determine how and if consumers will form new attitudes or modify existing ones.

Persuasion involves an active attempt to change attitudes. This is of course job number 1 for many marketing communications. Later we'll learn more about how marketers try to accomplish this, but for now we'll set the stage by listing some basic psychological principles that influence people to change their minds or comply with a request:[43]

Scarcity makes products more desirable.
Source: carmenbobo/Fotolia.

- **Reciprocity**—We are more likely to give if first we receive. That's why including money in a mail survey questionnaire (in some cases, as little as a nickel or dime) increases the response rate compared to surveys that come without financial incentives in the envelope.
- **Scarcity**—Like people, items are more attractive when they aren't available. In one study, researchers asked people to rate the quality of chocolate chip cookies. Participants who only got one cookie liked them better than did those who evaluated more of the same kind of cookie. That helps explain why we tend to value "limited-edition" items.
- **Authority**—We believe an authoritative source much more readily than one that is less authoritative. That explains why the U.S. public's opinion on an issue can shift by as much as 2 percent when the *New York Times* (but not the *National Enquirer*) runs an article about it.
- **Consistency**—As we saw previously in this chapter, people try not to contradict themselves in terms of what they say and do about an issue. In one study, students at an Israeli university who solicited donations to help disabled people doubled the amount they normally collected in a neighborhood if they first asked the residents to sign a petition supporting this cause 2 weeks before they actually asked for the donations.
- **Liking**—We agree with those we like or admire. A study found that good-looking fund-raisers raised almost twice as much as other volunteers who were not as attractive.
- **Consensus**—We consider what others do before we decide what to do. People are more likely to donate to a charity if they first see a list of the names of their neighbors who have already done so.

Decisions, Decisions: Tactical Communications Options

Suppose Audi wants to create an advertising campaign for a new ragtop it targets to young drivers. As it plans this campaign, the automaker must develop a message that will arouse desire for the car. To craft persuasive messages that might persuade someone to buy this car instead of the many others available, we must answer several questions:

- Who will drive the car in the ad? A NASCAR driver? A career woman? A reality show star? The source of a message helps determine whether consumers will accept it.
- How should we construct the message? Should it emphasize the negative consequences of being left out when others drive cool cars and you still tool around in your old clunker? Should it directly compare the car with others already on the market, or maybe present a fantasy in which a tough-minded female executive meets a dashing stranger while she cruises down the highway in her Audi?

- What media should we use? Should the ad run in a magazine? Should we air it on TV? Sell the product door-to-door? Post the material on a Web site or create a Facebook group? Convince bloggers to write about it? Reward shoppers who check in on Foursquare at an Audi dealership? If we do produce a print ad, should we run it in the pages of *Vogue? Good Housekeeping? Car and Driver?* Sometimes *where* you say something is as important as *what* you say. Ideally, we should match the attributes of the medium with those of what we sell. For example, advertising in magazines with high prestige is more effective when we want to communicate messages about overall product image and quality, whereas specialized expert magazines do a better job when we want to convey factual information.[44]

- What characteristics of the target market might lead its members to accept the ad? If targeted users are frustrated in their daily lives, they might be more receptive to a fantasy appeal. If they're status-oriented, maybe a commercial should show bystanders who swoon with admiration as the car cruises by.

OBJECTIVE 8-6

The communications model identifies several important components for marketers when they try to change consumers' attitudes toward products and services.

The Elements of Communication

Marketers traditionally rely on the **communications model** in Figure 8.4. This model specifies the elements they need to control to communicate with their customers. One of these is a *source*, where the communication originates. Another is the *message* itself. There are many ways to say something, and the structure of the message has a significant effect on how we perceive it. We must transmit the message via a *medium*, which could be TV, radio, magazines, billboards, personal contact, or even a matchbook cover. One or more *receivers* interpret the message in light of their own experiences. Finally, the source receives *feedback* so that the marketer can use receivers' reactions to modify aspects of the message as necessary.

An Updated View: Interactive Communications

The traditional communications model is not entirely wrong, but it also doesn't tell the whole story—especially in today's dynamic world of interactivity, where consumers have many more choices available to them and greater control over which messages they *choose* to process.[45]

In fact, the popular strategy we call **permission marketing** acknowledges that a marketer will be more successful when he or she communicates with consumers who have already agreed to listen to him or her; consumers who "opt out" of listening to the message probably weren't good prospects in the first place.[46] In contrast, those who say they want to learn more are likely to be receptive to marketing communications they have chosen to see or hear. As the permission marketing concept reminds us, we don't have to simply sit

Figure 8.4 THE TRADITIONAL COMMUNICATIONS MODEL

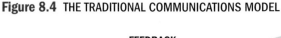
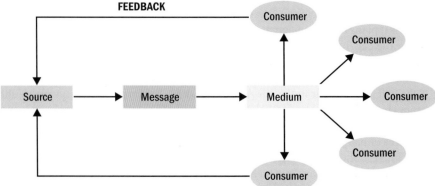

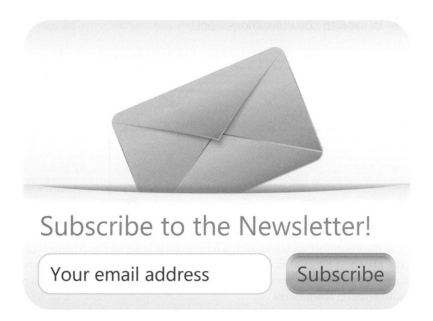

there and take it. We have a voice in deciding what messages we choose to see and when, and we exercise that option more and more.

Social scientists developed the traditional model to understand mass communications in which a source transmits information to many receivers at one time—typically via a *broadcast* medium such as television. This perspective essentially views advertising as the process of transferring information to the buyer before a sale. It regards a message as *perishable*—the marketer repeats the same message to a large audience and then the message "vanishes" when a new campaign takes its place. As we'll see, that model doesn't work as well now that we can *narrowcast*, or finely tune our messages to suit small groups of receivers (sometimes even one person at a time).

OBJECTIVE 8-7
The consumer who processes a message is not the passive receiver of information marketers once believed him or her to be.

How long has it been since you posted to your Facebook page? Exciting technological and social developments make us rethink the picture of passive consumers as people increasingly play more proactive roles in communications. In other words, we are to a greater extent *partners*—rather than couch potatoes—in the communications process. Our input helps to shape the messages we and others like us receive; furthermore, we may seek out these messages rather than sit home and wait to see them on TV or in the paper. For example, the popular social media platform *Pinterest* allows users to create digital scrapbooks, but in the process it serves as a voyage of discovery as people pull images from many sources (often other users' Boards). This kind of new medium allows consumers to "dream out loud" and also guide one another toward many new styles and brands.[47] Figure 8.5 illustrates this updated approach to interactive communications.

One of the early instigators of this communications revolution was the humble handheld remote control device. As VCRs (remember them?) began to be commonplace in homes, suddenly consumers had more input into what they wanted to watch—and when. No longer did the TV networks decide when we could watch our favorite shows, and we didn't have to miss the new episode of *Hawaii Five-O* because it was on at the same time as the Bears game.

Since that time, of course, our ability to control our media environment has mushroomed. Just ask some of the millions of us who use digital video recorders (DVRs) such as TiVo to watch TV shows whenever we wish—and who blithely skip over the commercials.[48] Many others have access to video-on-demand or pay-per-view TV. Home-shopping networks encourage us to call in and discuss our passion for cubic zirconium jewelry live

Figure 8.5 AN UPDATED COMMUNICATIONS MODEL

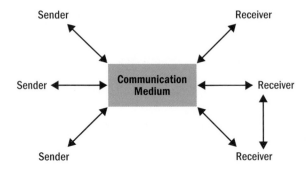

on the air. Caller ID devices and answering machines allow us to decide if we will accept a phone call during dinner and to know if a telemarketer lurks on the other end before we pick up the phone. A bit of Web surfing allows us to identify kindred spirits around the globe, to request information about products, and even to provide suggestions to product designers and market researchers.

<table>
<tr><td>

OBJECTIVE 8-8

Several factors influence the effectiveness of a message source.

</td><td>

The Source

Regardless of whether we receive a message by "snail mail" (net-heads' slang for the postal service), email, or SMS text, common sense tells us that if different people say or write the same words, the message can still affect us differently. Researchers have dis-

</td></tr>
</table>

cussed the power of *source effects* for more than 60 years. When we attribute the same message to different sources and measure the degree of attitude change that occurs after listeners hear it, we can isolate which characteristics of a communicator cause attitude change.[49]

Under most conditions, the source of a message can have a big impact on the likelihood that receivers will accept it. Marketers can choose a spokesperson because she is an expert, attractive, famous, or even a "typical" consumer who is both likable and trustworthy. *Credibility* and *attractiveness* are two particularly important source characteristics (i.e., how much we either believe or like the communicator).[50]

How do marketing specialists decide whether to stress credibility or attractiveness when they select a message source? There should be a match between the needs of the recipient and the potential rewards the source offers. When this match occurs, the recipient is more motivated to process the message. An attractive source, for example, is more effective for receivers who tend to be sensitive about social acceptance and others' opinions, whereas a credible, expert source is more powerful when she speaks to internally oriented people.[51] However, even a credible source's trustworthiness evaporates if she endorses too many products.[52]

The choice may also depend on the type of product. A positive source can reduce risk and increase message acceptance overall, but particular types of sources are more effective to reduce different kinds of risk. Experts excel when we want to change attitudes toward utilitarian products that have high performance risk, such as vacuums, because they are complex and may not work as we expect. Celebrities work better when they focus on products such as jewelry and furniture that have high social risk, where the users are more concerned about the impression others have of them. Finally, "typical" consumers, who are appealing sources because of their similarity to the recipient, tend to be most effective when they provide real-life endorsements for everyday products that are low risk, such as cookies.[53]

Source Credibility

Source credibility refers to a communicator's expertise, objectivity, or trustworthiness. This dimension relates to consumers' beliefs that this person is competent and that he or she will provide the necessary information we need when we evaluate competing products.

A credible source is particularly persuasive when the consumer has yet to learn much about a product or form an opinion of it.[54] Indeed, a study demonstrated that simply letting consumers know a firm is profitable leads them to put more stock in what the company says in its advertising.[55] On the other hand, some subtle cues can diminish credibility: Consider for example those super fast **disclaimers** you often hear at the end of a commercial message that supply additional information the advertiser is required to provide ("possible side effects may include nausea, diarrhea, or death"). Although people tend to assume that people who speak faster are more intelligent, they may trust them less. When consumers don't already have a positive attitude toward a product, a fast-paced disclaimer leads them to think the advertiser has ulterior motives and they trust the company less.[56]

Sincerity is particularly important when a company tries to publicize its *corporate social responsibility (CSR)* activities that benefit the community. As we saw in Chapter 2, a company's image can skyrocket when consumers believe it's genuinely doing good things. But this effort can backfire if people question the organization's motivations (e.g., if they think the firm spends more to talk about its good deeds than to actually do them).[57] Not too surprisingly, people who see deceptive advertising experience a feeling of distrust that carries over to other messages from that source and even to other sources because they are more likely to assume that advertising in general is not credible—a true case of poisoning the well for other marketers![58]

One widely used technique to generate credibility is to pay an expert or a celebrity to tout a product, but this kind of endorsement doesn't come cheap. However, typically the investment is worth it simply because market analysts use the announcement of an endorsement contract to evaluate a firm's potential profitability, which affects its expected return. On average, then, the impact of endorsements on stock returns appears to be so positive that it offsets the cost of hiring the spokesperson.[59] Indeed, a study on the use of celebrities in marketing reported that ads containing a celebrity endorser produced 9.4 percent higher consumer readership than ads without a celebrity endorser. In its analysis of almost 80,000 print ads, Starch Advertising Research concluded, "in terms of helping with the first task in ... getting consumers to read your ad, these data show that a celebrity endorsement moves the readership needle."[60]

The drawing power of famous people may even be "wired in": One study found that compared to "ordinary" faces, our brains pay more attention to famous faces and more efficiently process information about these images.[61] Celebrities increase awareness of a firm's advertising and enhance both company image and brand attitudes.[62] A celebrity endorsement strategy can be an effective way to differentiate among similar products. This is especially important when consumers do not perceive many actual differences among competitors, as often occurs when brands are in the mature stage of the product life cycle.

Although in general more positive sources tend to increase attitude change, there are exceptions to this rule. Sometimes we can think a source is obnoxious, yet it is still effective. A case in point is the irritating redhead in Wendy's commercials who says "Now That's Better." In some instances the differences in attitude change between positive sources and less-positive sources become erased over time. After a while, people appear to "forget" about the negative source and change their attitudes anyway. We call this process the **sleeper effect**.[63]

The source effects issue has gained even more attention recently as a result of a hot trend in marketing known as **native advertising**. This term refers to digital messages designed to blend into the editorial content of the publications in which they appear. The idea is to capture the attention of people who might resist ad messages that pop up in the middle of an article or program. These messages may look a lot like a regular article, but they often link to a sponsor's content. For example, native ads on *Vanity Fair* magazine's Web site resemble editorial contributions complete with a byline, but the author is listed as "Vanity Fair Agenda." An advertising executive commented, native ads "should not come across as anything that doesn't belong. That is what we mean by native; it belongs."[64]

A message's credibility increases if receivers think the source's qualifications are relevant to the product he or she endorses. This linkage can overcome other objections people may have to the endorser or the product. Ronald Biggs, whose claim to fame was

The Tangled Web

In recent years we've witnessed a new attempt to manipulate attitudes that some call **sock puppeting**. This term describes a company executive or other biased source that poses as someone else as he or she touts the organization in social media. For example, it came to light that the CEO of Whole Foods had posted derogatory comments about rival Wild Oats without revealing his true identity. More recently, a nonprofit research organization called GiveWell that rates the effectiveness of charities had to discipline two of its founders who pretended to be other people on blogs and then referred people to the group's Web site.[65]

Similar problems may dilute the credibility of *Wikipedia*, the open-source online encyclopedia that is beloved by many students. Anyone can edit entries, so their reliability is not assured. Although other alert contributors may eventually correct false or self-serving entries, there is still room for organizations to color content in a way that serves their goals. For example, a visitor edited the *Wikipedia* entry for the SeaWorld theme parks to change all mentions of "orcas" to "killer whales"; he or she also deleted a paragraph that criticized SeaWorld's "lack of respect toward its orcas." It turns out the changes originated at a computer located in Anheuser-Busch—the company that happens to own SeaWorld. An employee of PepsiCo deleted several paragraphs of the Pepsi entry that focused on its detrimental health effects, and a person at Walmart altered an entry about how the retailer pays its employees.

Another form of sock puppeting is so-called *paid influencer programs* that attempt to start online conversations about brands when they encourage bloggers to write about them. These "sponsored conversations" can be effective, but again marketers need to be careful about the potential to distort source recommendations. Kmart awarded a shopping spree to a group of bloggers who agreed to post about their experiences. Panasonic flew bloggers to the Consumer Electronics Show in Las Vegas, where they posted about the show and Panasonic products unveiled there. Mercedes gave a blogger use of an SUV for a week in exchange for posts about it.

Marketing messages that consumers perceive as **buzz** (those that are authentic and consumer generated) tend to be more effective than those they categorize as **hype** (those that are inauthentic, biased, and company generated). However, the digital environment makes it easier for a hype message to masquerade as buzz if the source does not disclose that it is in fact sponsored. The Federal Trade Commission (FTC) toughened its stance on this problem in 2013, when the regulatory agency issued guidelines for organizations that advertise in digital media. For example, the FTC says, "Required disclosures must be clear and conspicuous. In evaluating whether a disclosure is likely to be clear and conspicuous, advertisers should consider its placement in the ad and its proximity to the relevant claim. The closer the disclosure is to the claim to which it relates, the better."[66] The agency is trying to address abuses like the situation in which a the PR firm for a video game developer had its own employees pose as consumers and post positive game reviews at the iTunes store.[67]

his role in the *Great Train Robbery* in the United Kingdom, successfully served as a spokesman in Brazil for a company that makes door locks—a topic about which he is presumably knowledgeable![68]

It's important to note that what is credible to one consumer segment may be a turnoff to another. Indeed, rebellious or even deviant celebrities may be attractive to some simply for that reason. Tommy Hilfiger cultivated a rebellious, street-smart image when he used rappers Snoop Doggy Dogg—aka Snoop Dog, aka Snoop Lion, aka Snoopzilla—to help launch his clothing line and Coolio, a former crack addict and thief and Diddy (aka Puffy) as a runway model.[69] Parents may not be thrilled by these message sources—but isn't that the point? Charlie Sheen, please report to the studio ....

A consumer's beliefs about a product's attributes will weaken if he or she perceives that the source is biased.[70] **Knowledge bias** implies that a source's knowledge about a topic is not accurate. **Reporting bias** occurs when a source has the required knowledge but we question his or her willingness to convey it accurately—as when a racket manufacturer pays a star tennis player to use its products exclusively. The source's credentials might be appropriate, but the fact that consumers see the expert as a "hired gun" compromises believability.

Source Attractiveness: "What Is Beautiful Is Good"

A British dairy company enlisted Johnny Rotten, the lead singer of the Sex Pistols, to appear in a commercial (or *advert*, as they say in the United Kingdom) to promote its butter. Sales went up substantially when the punk legend plugged the product (rotten butter?).[71] **Source attractiveness** refers to the social *value* recipients attribute to a communicator. This value relates to the person's physical appearance, personality, social status, or similarity to the receiver (we like to listen to people who are like us). Our desire to know what our peers think helps to explain why both Facebook and Google now allow **shared endorsements**; users who follow or rate a product or service may find that their endorsements show up on the advertiser's page.[72]

Some sources like Johnny Rotten appeal to us because they are cool, brainy, or just plain famous. However, many simply are nice to look at. Almost everywhere we turn, beautiful people try to persuade us to buy or do something. As Chapter 6 showed us, our society places a high premium on physical attractiveness. We assume that good-looking people are smarter, hipper, and happier than the rest of us. This is an example of a **halo effect**, which occurs when we assume that persons who rank high on one dimension excel on others as well. We can explain this effect in terms of the consistency principle we discussed previously in this chapter; we are more comfortable when all of our judgments about a person correspond.

As a result, physically attractive people often get a boost in life because people assume they excel on other dimensions as well. Occasionally this halo effect can backfire if observers infer that someone has exploited their attractiveness (e.g. women who get labeled as "gold diggers"). One study found that good-looking children are less likely to get assistance from adults (at least for fairly mild problems) because people assume they are more competent and thus better able to help themselves. One implication of this work is that ironically charitable organizations may want to consider using less attractive kids as models to solicit donations![73] Note: Psychologists also refer to the opposite, *forked-tail effect* that describes our assumptions that an unattractive person also isn't good at other things. There are a lot of angels and devils out there.

Star Power: Celebrities as Communications Sources

Celebrities hawk everything from grills (George Foreman) to perfumes (Jennifer Lopez). As our discussion about the consistency principle illustrates, these messages are more effective when there's a logical connection between the star and the product. When Bob Dylan pitches Victoria's Secret lingerie (yes, he really did), marketers may need to reread their consumer behavior textbook.[74] Then again, teen idol Justin Bieber puts his name on almost everything ... including nail polish![75]

Celebrities, major and minor, frequently serve as communications sources in advertisements, promotions and infomercials.

Source: Blend Images/Corbis.

Star power works because celebrities embody *cultural meanings*—they symbolize important categories like status and social class: A "working-class hero" (Mike of *Mike & Molly*), gender (the effeminate Cam on *Modern Family*), age (the youthful President Grant on *Scandal*), and even personality types (the nerdy Sheldon on *The Big Bang Theory*, cool Adam Levine on *The Voice*). Ideally, the advertiser decides what meanings the product should convey (that is, how it should position the item in the marketplace) and then chooses a celebrity who embodies a similar meaning. The product's meaning thus moves from the manufacturer to the consumer, using the star as a vehicle.[76]

Nonhuman Endorsers

A celebrity endorsement strategy has its drawbacks. As we previously noted, stars' motives may be suspect if they plug products that don't fit their images or if consumers begin to believe the celebrities never met a product they didn't like (for a fee). They may be involved in a scandal or deviate from a brand's desired image—for example, the Milk Processor Education Program suspended "Got Milk?" ads featuring Mary-Kate and Ashley Olsen after Mary-Kate entered a treatment facility for an undisclosed health issue.

For these reasons, some marketers seek alternative sources, including cartoon characters and mascots. As the marketing director for a company that manufactures costumed

Marketing Pitfall

Celebrities (and their managers) don't necessarily jump at the chance to endorse just any product. After all, they have a brand image to protect as well. For years one popular strategy has been to film commercials overseas and stipulate that they are not to air at home. The practice is so widespread in Japan that it's even got its own portmanteau word: *Japander*, a combination of Japanese and pandering, which describes a western star acting in Japan advertisements and endorsing products they are unlikely to use in order to make a large amount of money quickly. It also implies embarrassing oneself in Japanese media. Check out japander.com to see actors such as Arnold Schwarzenegger, George Clooney, and Jennifer Aniston in commercials they'd prefer their U.S. fans didn't see.[77]

Spokescharacters boost the effectiveness of advertising claims.

Source: Pat Canova/Alamy.

characters for sports teams and businesses points out, "You don't have to worry about your mascot checking into rehab."[78] Researchers report that **spokescharacters**, such as the Pillsbury Doughboy, Chester Cheetah, and the GEICO Gecko, do, in fact, boost viewers' recall of claims that ads make and also yield higher brand attitudes.[79] Some of the most popular spokescharacters in recent years include Old Spice's The Man Your Man Could Smell Like (played by former NFL athlete Isaiah Mustafa), Snoopy (who appears in commercials for MetLife), the talking M&Ms, Flo for Progressive insurance, and Allstate's Mayhem Man.[80]

As we saw in Chapter 7, an *avatar* is one increasingly popular alternative to a flesh-and-blood endorser. *Avatar* is a Hindu term for a deity that appears in superhuman or animal form. In the computing world, it means a character you can move around inside a visual, graphical world. Consumers who inhabit virtual worlds such as *Second Life*, *Habbo Hotel*, and *The Sims* design their avatars to reflect their own unique personalities, desires, and fantasies.

The advantages of using virtual avatars compared to flesh-and-blood models include the ability to change the avatar in real time to suit the needs of the target audience. From an advertising perspective, they are likely to be more cost effective than hiring a real person. From personal-selling and customer-service perspectives, they handle multiple customers at one time, they are not geographically limited, and they are operational 24/7; therefore, they free up company employees and sales personnel to perform other activities.[81]

OBJECTIVE 8-9

The way a marketer structures his or her message determines how persuasive it will be.

The Message

Subtle aspects of the way a source delivers a message can influence our interpretation of what he or she says. For example, if a source refers to the brand as "you," "we," or more abstractly "the brand" this changes how people feel about the product. A more intimate reference can bolster feelings about brands with whom the consumer has a positive relationship, but it can also be off-putting if it's inconsistent with how the person feels about the product.[82]

Even the layout in a print ad sends a message about how the consumer should relate to the advertised item. A brand that wants customers to see it as a "friend" by depicting a model using it is more effective when the product image appears horizontally and near the model. On the other hand, if a brand wants customers to see it as a "leader" the advertiser will have better luck if it physically places the brand above the user and farther away "(it's lonely at the top).[83]

A major study of more than 1,000 commercials identified factors that determine whether a commercial message will be persuasive. The single most important feature: Does the communication stress a unique attribute or benefit of the product?[84] Table 8.2 lists some other good and bad elements of commercial messages.

Consumers may find commercials confusing, but what's even worse is when we find them annoying. In a landmark study of irritating advertising, researchers examined more than 500 prime-time network commercials that had registered negative reactions by consumers. The most irritating commercials were for feminine hygiene products, hemorrhoid medication or laxatives, and women's underwear. The researchers identify these as prime offenders:

- The commercial shows a sensitive product (e.g., hemorrhoid medicine) and emphasizes its usage.
- The situation is contrived or overdramatized.
- A person is put down in terms of appearance, knowledge, or sophistication.

TABLE 8.2   Characteristics of Good and Bad Messages

Positive effects	Negative effects
Showing convenience of use	Extensive information on components, ingredients, or nutrition
Showing new product or improved features	Outdoor setting (message gets lost)
Casting background (i.e., people are incidental to message)	Large number of on-screen characters
Indirect comparison to other products	Graphic displays
Demonstration of the product in use	
Demonstration of tangible results (e.g., bouncy hair)	
An actor playing the role of an ordinary person	
No principal character (i.e., more time is devoted to the product)	

Source: Adapted from David W. Stewart and David H. Furse, "The Effects of Television Advertising Execution on Recall, Comprehension, and Persuasion," *Psychology & Marketing* 2 (Fall 1985): 135–60. Copyright © 1985 by John Wiley & Sons, Inc. Reprinted by permission.

- An important relationship, such as a marriage, is threatened.
- There is a graphic demonstration of physical discomfort.
- The commercial created uncomfortable tension because of an argument or an antagonistic character.
- It portrays an unattractive or unsympathetic character.
- It includes a sexually suggestive scene.
- The commercial suffers from poor casting or execution.

Characteristics of the message itself help determine its impact on attitudes. These variables include *how* we say the message as well as *what* we say. Depending on the marketer's objectives and the nature of the product, different kinds of messages produce different results. A marketer faces some crucial issues when she creates a message:

- Should the message be conveyed in words or pictures?
- How often should the message be repeated?
- Should the message draw a conclusion, or should this be left up to the listener?
- Should the message present both sides of an argument?
- Should the message explicitly compare the product to competitors?
- Should the message include a blatant sexual appeal?
- Should the message arouse negative emotions such as fear?
- How concrete or vivid should the arguments and imagery be?
- Should the message be funny?

Should We Use Pictures or Words?

The saying "One picture is worth a thousand words" captures the idea that visuals are effective, especially when the communicator wants to influence receivers' emotional responses. For this reason, advertisers often rely on vivid illustrations or photography.[85]

However, a picture is not always as effective when it communicates factual information. Ads that contain the same information elicit different reactions when the marketer presents them in visual versus verbal form. The verbal version affects ratings on the utilitarian aspects of a product, whereas the visual version affects aesthetic evaluations. Verbal elements are more effective when an accompanying picture reinforces them, especially if they *frame* the illustration (the message in the picture strongly relates to the copy).[86]

Because it requires more effort to process, a verbal message is most appropriate for high-involvement situations, such as print contexts where the reader really pays attention to the advertising. Verbal material decays more rapidly in memory, so these messages require more frequent exposures to obtain the desired effect. Visual images, in contrast, allow the receiver to *chunk* information at the time of encoding (see Chapter 4). Chunking results in a stronger memory trace that aids retrieval over time.[87]

The concrete discussion of a product attribute in ad copy also influences the importance of that attribute because it draws more attention. For example, in a study where participants read two versions of ad copy for a watch, the version that claimed "According to industry sources, three out of every four watch breakdowns are due to water getting into the case," was more effective than the version that simply said, "According to industry sources, many watch breakdowns are due to water getting into the case."[88]

Should We Repeat the Message?

Repetition can be a double-edged sword for marketers. As we noted in Chapter 4, we usually need multiple exposures to a stimulus before learning occurs. Contrary to the saying "familiarity breeds contempt," people tend to like things that are more familiar to them, even if they were not that keen on them initially.[89] Psychologists call this the **mere exposure phenomenon**.

Advertisers find positive effects for repetition even in mature product categories: Repeating product information boosts consumers' awareness of the brand, even though the marketer says nothing new.[90] However, as we saw in Chapter 6, too much repetition creates *habituation*, whereby the consumer no longer pays attention to the stimulus

Figure 8.6 TWO-FACTOR THEORY OF MESSAGE REPETITION

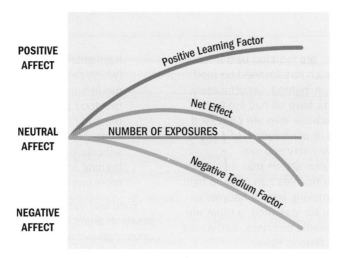

because of fatigue or boredom. Excessive exposure can cause advertising wear-out, which can result in negative reactions to an ad after we see it too much.[91] Research evidence indicates that "three's the charm" when it comes to exposing an audience to a product claim. Additional messages tend to trigger skepticism and actually reverse any positive impact.[92]

The **two-factor theory** explains the fine line between familiarity and boredom; it proposes that two separate psychological processes operate when we repeatedly show an ad to a viewer. The positive side of repetition is that it increases familiarity and thus reduces uncertainty about the product. The negative side is that over time boredom increases with each exposure. At some point the amount of boredom exceeds the amount of uncertainty the message reduces, and this results in wear-out. Figure 8.6 depicts this pattern. Its effect is especially pronounced when each exposure is of a fairly long duration (such as a 30-second commercial).[93]

The two-factor perspective implies that advertisers can overcome this problem if they limit the amount of exposure per repetition (e.g., use 15-second spots instead of longer commercials). They can also maintain familiarity but alleviate boredom if they slightly vary the content of ads over time—although each spot differs, the campaign still revolves around a common theme. Recipients who see varied ads about the product absorb more information about product attributes and experience more positive thoughts about the brand than do those who see the same information repeatedly. This additional information also allows the person to resist attempts to change his or her attitude in the face of a counterattack by a competing brand.[94]

How Do We Structure the Argument?

Many marketing messages are like debates or trials: A source presents an argument and tries to convince the receiver to shift his or her opinion. As you've no doubt guessed, the *way* we present the argument may be as important as *what* we say. It's often a good idea to relate the product to a person's identity to ramp up involvement as we discussed in Chapter 5. On the other hand, there's the temptation to push too hard. A recent study shows how that can happen: Respondents were asked to focus on their attitudes toward environmental issues to activate that aspect of their identities. Then they were divided into three groups, each of which was shown a separate slogan for Charlie's Soap, a real biodegradable cleanser. One message just said the soap was "a good choice for consumers." A second version related to the issue by calling the soap "a good choice for green consumers." The third message pushed the envelope farther: "the only choice for green consumers!" Although many real managers predicted that the last choice would be most effective, in fact the second one was most effective because the last choice just pushed too hard.[96]

Net Profit

The Pandora music site attracts about 70 million listeners, who tune in to playlists Pandora creates based on their initial preferences for certain artists. The site uses a music intelligence algorithm to dissect the characteristics of favorite songs and serve up others that are similar. Pandora's engineers constantly tweak the playlists as they experiment with variations of the experience. For example, do listeners want to hear mostly familiar songs, or do they want to discover new music? One of the biggest issues they wrestle with: How frequently should Pandora repeat the same song or artist in a playlist? The site constantly tries new variations to arrive at the optimal number of repetitions, but it turns out a lot depends on other factors such as the time of day and where listeners are when they tune in. For example, Pandora's data show that users welcome new music instead of the same old same old, but when they're at work not so much. The company continues to tweak its algorithm as it tries to answer the elusive question, "Can you have too much of a good thing?"[95]

CB AS I SEE IT
Pierre Chandon INSEAD, *France*

I am interested in food marketing, how it makes people fat, and how consumer research can help find solutions that improve health without killing the pleasure of eating or the food industry.

The obesity epidemic is largely driven by ever-increasing food portion sizes. Yet, our efforts to fight obesity have focused on trying to influence *what* people eat instead of *how much* they eat. Traditional public policy solutions (warnings, labels,

taxes, bans) are resisted by the food industry, which has focused on food reformulation instead. Unfortunately, these efforts have all had limited success because they are perceived as a threat to our freedom to eat the food that we know and like.

My research shows that regulators and food companies can unite to fight obesity by making people happier to spend more for less food, a triple win for public health, business, and eating enjoyment. Here is how:

- *Improve perception of food portion and package sizes.* Visual biases make us strongly underestimate today's supersized portions and resist downsizing. Drawing on our knowledge of these biases, we can increase acceptance of portion downsizing, by bringing original small sizes back to lunchroom menus (to reframe perceptions of and preferences for a "normal" size), or by using "stealth" downsizing that elongates, instead of shortening, packages in supermarkets.
- *Focus on the sensory pleasure of eating, rather than on food quantity, or even health.* We show that

highlighting sensory pleasure (which peaks with the first mouthful) leads school kids and fast-food patrons to choose, prefer, and pay more for smaller portions. This can be done easily in schools through sensory imagery training and in restaurants with more vivid menu descriptions.

Food and eating are fascinating research areas because they touch upon cognitive as well as social psychology, but also economics, sociology, and even the branch of philosophy related to taste (aesthetics). Because we all eat, it is rare to find someone who is not interested in the factors that, unbeknownst to us, influence what, when, and how much we eat. For example, in another study, I showed that people eat more, and less healthy, after their favorite football team was defeated, especially if it was a narrow defeat against a rival of the same strength, and eat less and more healthy after a victory. We also show that this happens because fans see the defeat of their team as their own failure (we say "we lost," not "they lost"), which makes it harder to self-regulate.[97]

Most messages merely present one or more positive attributes about the product or reasons to buy it. These are *supportive arguments*. An alternative is to use a *two-sided message*, in which the message presents both positive and negative information. Research indicates that two-sided ads can be quite effective, yet marketers rarely use them.[98]

Why would a marketer want to devote advertising space to publicize a product's negative attributes? Under the right circumstances, **refutational arguments** that first raise a negative issue and then dismiss it can be quite effective. This approach increases source credibility because it reduces *reporting bias*; this means that the receiver assumes the source has carefully considered both sides of the argument. Also, people who are skeptical about the product may be more receptive to a balanced argument instead of a "whitewash."[99] For example, after General Motors declared bankruptcy, an ad declared: "Let's be completely honest: No company wants to go through this."[100] Research evidence indicates that when experts have strong arguments on their side, they are actually more effective if they express some uncertainty rather than stating unequivocally that they are correct.[101]

This doesn't mean the marketer should go overboard and confess to major problems with the product (though hopefully there aren't any major ones to admit to). The typical refutational strategy discusses relatively minor attributes that may present a problem or fall short when the customer compares a product to competitors. Positive, important attributes then refute these drawbacks. For example, Avis got a lot of mileage when it claimed to be only the "No. 2" car rental company, whereas an ad for Volkswagen woefully described one of its cars as a "lemon" because there was a scratch on the glove compartment chrome strip.[102] A two-sided strategy appears to be the most effective when the audience is well educated (and presumably more impressed by a balanced argument).[103] It is also best to use when receivers are not already loyal to the product—"preaching to the choir" about possible drawbacks may raise doubts unnecessarily.

One important structural question: Should the argument draw conclusions, or should the marketer merely present the facts and let the consumer arrive at his or her own decision? On the one hand, consumers who make their own inferences instead of having ideas spoon-fed to them will form stronger, more accessible attitudes. On the other hand, leaving the conclusion ambiguous increases the chance that the consumer will not form the desired attitude.

The response to this issue depends on the consumer's motivation to process the ad and the complexity of the arguments. If the message is personally relevant, people will pay attention to it and spontaneously form inferences. However, if the arguments are hard to follow or consumers lack the motivation to follow them, it's safer for the ad to draw conclusions.[104]

Should We Compare Our Product to Our Competitors?

In 1971 the FTC issued guidelines that encouraged advertisers to name competing brands in their ads. The government did this to improve the information available to consumers in ads, and indeed recent evidence indicates that, at least under some conditions, this type of presentation does result in more informed decision making.[105] However, advertisers need to tread lightly, especially when they risk ruffling the feathers of other companies. Fox rejected a commercial that Sodastream submitted for the 2015 Super Bowl because the actress Scarlett Johansson sensually sips her homemade soda and says, "Sorry, Coke and Pepsi."[106]

Comparative advertising refers to a message that compares two or more recognizable brands and weighs them in terms of one or more specific attributes.[107] An Arby's campaign to promote its chicken sandwiches used this approach: One commercial, set in a fictitious McDonald's boardroom, featured a young man who tries to convince McDonald's executives to serve a healthier type of chicken. He proposes that McDonald's offers 100 percent all-natural chicken instead of 70 percent chicken—the other 30 percent allegedly consisting of phosphates, salt, and water added to the chicken. The room erupts in laughter. At the end of the spot, a voice-over says that, unlike McDonald's, Arby's chicken sandwiches contain 100 percent natural chicken.

This strategy can cut both ways, especially if the sponsor depicts the competition in a nasty or negative way. Although some comparative ads result in desired attitude changes, they may also be lower in believability and stir up **source derogation** (i.e., the consumer may doubt the credibility of a biased presentation).[108] Indeed, in some cultures (such as Asia), comparative advertising is rare because people find such a confrontational approach offensive.

New Message Formats: The Social Media Revolution

The novel "ice-bucket challenge" that swept the Internet in fall 2014 was a novel way to harness social media for a good cause; the movement that asked people to take a selfie of themselves dousing their heads in a bucket of ice water went viral and raised more than $115 million for A.L.S. research. Researchers explain this success by pointing to several elements of the message including: the 24-hour deadline to either take the cold shower or pay the money (a specific goal as opposed to a more abstract one); the public nature of the challenge that allowed participants to share their selfies online; and the slight amount of self-sacrifice that was involved. Yes, people tend to donate more money when they have to suffer a bit for the cause; researchers label this the **martyrdom effect**. As one put it, "We're supposed to prefer pleasure to pain but, when it comes to charity, you don't hear about massage-a-thons or dessert-a-thons." [109]

The "ice-bucket challenge" that swept the Internet was a novel way to harness social media for a good cause.
Source: Jurgen Falchle/Fotolia

An array of new ways to transmit information in both text and picture form offers marketers exciting alternatives to traditional advertising on TV, billboards, magazines, and so on.[110] **M-commerce** (mobile commerce), where marketers promote their goods and services via wireless devices, including cell phones, PDAs, and iPods, is red-hot. European and Asian consumers already rely on their cell phones to connect them to the world in ways we are only starting to see in the United States. In Asia, tiny cell phone screens have become electronic wallets that buy Cokes from vending machines and devices that dole out McDonald's coupons on the phone screen. Among the Chinese, cell phones have become such important status symbols that relatives at funeral rites burn paper cell phone effigies so the dead will have their mobiles in the afterlife.

If you're on Facebook, Twitter, or LinkedIn (and the odds are good that you are), you're one of the billions of people who use **social media** applications globally. This term refers to the set of technologies that enable users to create content and share it with thousands or even millions of others. We'll dive into social media in more detail in Chapter 14. In addition to "the obvious suspects" (i.e. popular social media platforms including Facebook,

Pinterest, Foursquare, Tumblr, and so on), there are many other alternatives for marketers that want to harness these new technologies to communicate with customers. Some of these may even use multiple platforms, unfold over a period of time, and integrate social media with real world experiences. A **transmedia storytelling** strategy typically includes communications media that range from Web sites, blogs, and email to recorded phone calls and even graffiti messages scrawled in public spaces.

Reality Engineering

OBJECTIVE 8-10
Many modern marketers are reality engineers.

The Pennsylvania city of Altoona temporarily renamed itself "POM Wonderful Presents: The Greatest Movie Ever Sold" to promote a popular movie that parodies product-placement advertising; the movie's producers sold the title to the maker of POM Wonderful pomegranate juice for $1 million.[113] **Reality engineering** occurs when marketers appropriate elements of popular culture and use them as promotional vehicles.[114] It's hard to know what's real anymore; specialists even create "used jeans" when they apply chemical washes, sandpaper, and other techniques to make a new pair of jeans look like they're ready for retirement. The industry has a term for this practice that sums up the contradiction: *new vintage*![115]

The grassroots efforts we often witness today to capture our attention epitomize **guerrilla marketing**: Promotional strategies that use unconventional means and venues to encourage word of mouth about products. This has nothing to do with monkey business; the term implies that the marketer "ambushes" the unsuspecting recipient because the message pops up in a place where he or she wasn't expecting to see an advertisement. These campaigns often recruit legions of real consumers who agree to engage in some kind of street theater or perhaps place messages in unconventional locations like public restrooms or on city sidewalks to get in the face of media-saturated consumers.

Reality engineers have many tools at their disposal; they plant products in movies, pump scents into offices and stores, attach video monitors in the backs of taxicabs, buy ad space on police patrol cars, or film faked "documentaries" such as *The Blair Witch Project*.[116] This process is accelerating: Historical analyses of Broadway plays, best-selling novels, and the lyrics of hit songs, for example, clearly show large increases in the use of real brand names over time.[117]

Here are some examples of reality engineering:

- Mattel announced that it was putting a "for sale" sign on the Barbie Malibu Dreamhouse, where the doll character supposedly has lived in comfort since the introduction of Malibu Barbie in 1971. The campaign mixed actual and imaginary elements. A section of the real estate Web site Trulia carried the for-sale listing that described the property as "the dreamiest of dream houses."[118]
- The Quill.com division of the office supply retail chain Staples carries a line of products from the Dunder Mifflin Paper Company of Scranton, PA. As any fan knows, that is the fictional setting of the TV show *The Office*, which recently went off the air after nine seasons.[119]
- The Coachella music festival made headlines with a "virtual performance" (via hologram) of the deceased performer Tupac Shakur. YouTube reported more than 15 million views of the spectacle within 48 hours, and Tupac's greatest hits album made the *Billboard 200* for the first time in 12 years. Plans are underway to debut holograms of other dead stars including Elvis Presley and Michael Jackson.[120]
- A New York couple funded their $80,000 wedding by selling corporate plugs; they inserted coupons in their programs and tossed 25 bouquets from 1-800-FLOWERS.

Product Placement

When the new James Bond movie, *Spectre*, came out in 2015 the heroes and villains chased one another in flashy cars including an Aston Martin, Range Rover, and Jaguar C-X75.[121] A music video for the Jennifer Lopez song "Live It Up" (featuring Pitbull) hyped

Swarovski, Nokia, Ice Watches, and Beluga vodka. Apple took top honors in 2014 movie product placements; its products appeared in about one-fourth of all number-one box-office hits during the year that ran the gamut from *Birdman* to *Sex Tape*. Target stores played a role in episodes of the CW's *Jane the Virgin* TV show and a Toyota car was written into the plot of an episode of ABC's *Modern Family*.[122]

That's quite a change; In the not-so-distant past, TV networks demanded that producers "geek" (alter) brand names before they appeared in a show, as when *Melrose Place* changed a Nokia cell phone to a "Nokio."[123] Today, real products pop up everywhere. Well-established brands lend an aura of realism to the action, while upstarts benefit tremendously from the exposure. In the movie version of *Sex and the City*, Carrie's assistant admits that she "borrows" her pricey handbags from a rental Web site called Bag Borrow or Steal. The company's head of marketing commented about the mention, "It's like the *Good Housekeeping* Seal of Approval. It gives us instant credibility and recognition."[124]

Bag Borrow or Steal got a free plug (oops, they got another one here!). In many cases, however, these "plugs" are no accident. **Product placement** is the insertion of real products in fictional movies, TV shows, books, and plays. Many types of products play starring (or at least supporting) roles in our culture; the most visible brands range from Coca-Cola and Nike apparel to the Chicago Bears football team and the Pussycat Dolls band.[125]

Product placement is by no means a casual process: Marketers pay about $25 billion per year to plug their brands in TV and movies. Several firms specialize in arranging these appearances; if they're lucky, they manage to do it on the cheap when they get a client's product noticed by prop masters who work on the shows. For example, in a cafeteria scene during an episode of *Grey's Anatomy*, it was no coincidence that the character Izzie Stevens happened to drink a bottle of Izze Sparkling Pomegranate fruit beverage. The placement company that represents PepsiCo paid nothing to insert the prop in that case, but it probably didn't get off so easily when the new brand also showed up in HBO's *Entourage* and CBS's *The Big Bang Theory* and *The New Adventures of Old Christine*.[126]

Today, most major releases brim with real products, even though a majority of consumers believe the line between advertising and programming is becoming too fuzzy and distracting (though as we might expect, concerns about this blurring of boundaries are more pronounced among older people than younger).[127] A study reported that consumers respond well to placements when the show's plot makes the product's benefit clear. Similarly, audiences had a favorable impression when a retailer provided furniture, clothes, appliances, and other staples for the struggling families who get help on ABC's *Extreme Makeover: Home Edition*.[128]

Some researchers claim that product placement aids consumer decision making because the familiarity of these props creates a sense of cultural belonging while they generate feelings of emotional security. Another study found that placements consistent with a show's plot do enhance brand attitudes, but incongruent placements that aren't consistent with the plot affect brand attitudes *negatively* because they seem out of place.[129]

Advergaming

If you roar down the streets in the *Need for Speed Underground 2* video racing game, you'll pass a Best Buy store as well as billboards that hawk Old Spice and Burger King.[130] *America's Army*, produced by the U.S. government as a recruitment tool, is one of the most successful advergames. Twenty-eight percent of those who visit the *America's Army* Web page click through to the recruitment page.

About three-quarters of U.S. consumers now play video games, yet to many marketers the idea of integrating their brands with the stories that games tell is still a well-kept secret. Others, including Axe, Mini Cooper, and Burger King, have figured this out: They create game narratives that immerse players in the action. Orbitz offers playable banner-games that result in the highest click-through rate of any kind of advertising the online travel site does. However, these linkages sometimes draw criticism if they seem to encourage violent behavior. Recently, as the game maker Electronic Arts (EA) took steps to launch its *Medal of Honor Warfighter* game, the company put up a Web site that included links to the catalogs of the manufacturers of the real kinds of guns, knives, and combat-style gear the game includes, such as a powerful sniper's rifle and accessories for assault weapons. After gamers protested, EA disabled the links.[131]

Even so, the future is bright for **advergaming**, where online games merge with interactive advertisements that let companies target specific types of consumers. These placements can be short exposures such as a billboard that appears around a racetrack, or they can take the form of branded entertainment and integrate the brand directly into the action. The mushrooming popularity of user-generated videos on YouTube and other sites creates a growing market to link ads to these sources as well. This strategy is growing so rapidly that there's even a new (trademarked) term for it. **Plinking™** is the act of embedding a product or service link in a video.

Why is this new medium so hot?[132]

- Compared to a 30-second TV spot, advertisers can get viewers' attention for a much longer time. Players spend an average of 5 to 7 minutes on an advergaming site.
- Physiological measures confirm that players are highly focused and stimulated when they play a game.
- Marketers can tailor the nature of the game and the products in it to the profiles of different users. They can direct strategy games to upscale, educated users, while they gear action games to younger users.
- The format gives advertisers great flexibility because game makers now ship PC video games with blank spaces in them to insert virtual ads. This allows advertisers to change messages on the fly and pay only for the number of game players that actually see them. Sony Corporation now allows clients to directly insert online ads into PlayStation 3 videogames; the in-game ads change over time through a user's Internet connection.
- There's great potential to track usage and conduct marketing research. For example, an inaudible audio signal coded into Activision's *Tony Hawk's Underground 2* skating game on PCs alerts a Nielsen monitoring system each time the test game players view Jeep product placements within the game.

Types of Message Appeals

A persuasive message can tug at the heartstrings or scare you, make you laugh, make you cry, or leave you yearning to learn more. In this section, we'll review the major alternatives available to communicators.

Emotional Versus Rational Appeals

Colgate-Palmolive's Total brand was the first toothpaste to claim that it fights gingivitis, a benefit that let Colgate inch ahead of Procter & Gamble's Crest for the first time in decades. Colgate initially made a scientific pitch for its new entry because it emphasized Total's germ-fighting abilities. In newer ads, however, former model Brooke Shields cavorted with two children (not hers) as soft music played in the background. She stated, "Having a healthy smile is important to me. Not just as an actress but as a mom."[133]

So, which is better: to appeal to the head or to the heart? The answer often depends on the nature of the product and the type of relationship consumers have with it. It's hard to gauge the precise effects of rational versus emotional appeals. Although recall of ad content tends to be better for "thinking" ads than for "feeling" ads, conventional measures of advertising effectiveness (e.g., day-after recall) may not be adequate to assess cumulative effects of emotional ads. These open-ended measures assess cognitive responses, and they may penalize feeling ads because the reactions are not as easy to articulate.[134]

Sex Appeals

A risqué ad campaign for Kraft's Zesty Italian salad dressing attracted the attention of a conservative activist group called One Million Moms. Members took to the Web to protest a print ad featuring a hunky male model having a naked picnic. They described the ad, which appeared in an issue of *People* magazine, as the most disgusting ad they had ever seen produced by Kraft. They implied that the food giant was selling itself through blatant eroticism. Kraft defended its campaign as a light-hearted and coy way of engaging with their consumers. They said that the response they received has been overwhelmingly positive.

Echoing the widely held belief that "sex sells," many marketing communications for products from perfumes to autos feature heavy doses of erotic suggestions that range from subtle hints to blatant displays of skin. Of course, the prevalence of **sex appeals** varies from country to country. Even U.S. firms run ads elsewhere that would not go over at home. For example, a "cheeky" ad campaign designed to boost the appeal of U.S.-made Lee jeans among Europeans features a series of bare buttocks. The messages are based on the concept that if bottoms could choose jeans, they would opt for Lee: "Bottoms feel better in Lee Jeans."[135]

Perhaps not surprisingly, female nudity in print ads generates negative feelings and tension among female consumers, whereas men's reactions are more positive—although women with more liberal attitudes toward sex are more likely to be receptive.[136] In a case of turnabout being fair play, another study found that males dislike nude males in ads, whereas females responded well to undressed males—but not totally nude ones like the guy in the Kraft ad.[137] Women also respond more positively to sexual themes when they occur in the context of a committed relationship rather than just gratuitous lust.[138]

So, does sex work? Although erotic content does appear to draw attention to an ad, its use may actually be counterproductive. In one survey, an overwhelming 61 percent of the respondents said that sexual imagery in a product's ad makes them *less* likely to buy it.[139] Ironically, a provocative picture can be *too* effective; it can attract so much attention as to hinder processing and recall of the ad's contents. Sexual appeals appear to be ineffective when marketers use them merely as a "trick" to grab attention. They do, however, appear to work when the product is *itself* related to sex (e.g., lingerie or Viagra).[140]

A research firm explored how men and women look at sexually themed ads and what effect, if any, what they choose to look at might have on the ads' effectiveness. One part of the study used special software to follow the visual behavior of respondents as they looked at print ads. The ad sample consisted of two U.S. print ads, one sexual and one nonsexual, from each of five product categories. When the participants looked at a sexual ad, men tended to ignore the text as they focused instead on the woman in it, whereas the women participants tended first to explore the ad's text elements. Men said they liked the sexual ads more, they liked the products advertised in them more, and they would be more likely to buy those products. In contrast, women scored the sexual ads lower than the nonsexual ones on all three of those criteria.[141]

Humor Appeals

A TV commercial for Metamucil showed a National Park Service ranger who pours a glass of the laxative down Old Faithful and announces that the product keeps the famous geyser "regular." Yellowstone National Park started getting letters from offended viewers. Park officials also had their own concerns: They didn't want people to think that the geyser needed "help" or that it's OK to throw things down into it![142]

Do **humor appeals** work? Overall, funny advertisements do get attention. One study found that recognition scores for *humorous* liquor ads were better than average. However, the verdict is mixed as to whether humor affects recall or product attitudes in a significant way.[143] One reason silly ads may shift opinions is that they provide a source of *distraction*. A funny ad inhibits **counterarguing** (in which a consumer thinks of reasons why he or she doesn't agree with the message); this increases the likelihood of message acceptance because the consumer doesn't come up with arguments against the product.[144]

Fear Appeals

Volkswagen's advertising campaign for its Jetta model's safety features got a lot of people to sit up and take notice. The spots show passengers in deep conversation as they drive down the street, completely unprepared for the vehicles that suddenly appear and collide

Marketing Pitfall

A series of funny ads created by a German agency didn't make everyone laugh. Grey Germany did three condom ads for a pharmacy chain. They implied that if more people used condoms the world would have been spared such figures as Mao Tse-Tung, Adolf Hitler, and Osama bin Laden. Each execution depicted a swimming sperm with a likeness of one of the despised characters. Critics complained that the ads were racist, offensive, and inappropriate; the campaign apparently didn't exactly enhance the retailer's image.[145]

violently with their cars. One spot also showed a passenger's head striking an airbag. The spots ended with a focus on the stunned passengers and the damaged Jetta. The ads seemed so real that the company received several calls asking whether the people in the ad were hurt.

Fear appeals emphasize the negative consequences that can occur unless the consumer changes a behavior or an attitude. These types of messages are fairly common in advertising, although they are more common in social marketing contexts in which organizations encourage people to convert to healthier lifestyles by quitting smoking, using contraception, or relying on a designated driver. Several countries including the United States are looking at tough new guidelines for cigarette advertising and packaging. These options include requiring a range of horrific images to appear directly on the cigarette packaging (and in cigarette ads) to show people who have suffered from the ravages of cigarettes, such as a man with cigarette smoke coming out of a tracheotomy hole in his throat and a cadaver on an autopsy table. In 2013 a U.S. Court of Appeals ruled that these images, along with the phone number 1-800-QUIT-NOW, are "unabashed attempts to evoke emotion" and "browbeat consumers" to stop buying the companies' products. However, the FDA still plans to continue the fight.[146]

This tactic, if and when it's implemented, may well scare away would-be smokers, but do fear appeals work more generally? Most research on this topic indicates that these negative messages are most effective when the advertiser uses only a moderate threat and when the ad presents a solution to the problem. Otherwise, consumers will tune out the ad because they can do nothing to solve or avoid the threat.[147]

When a weak threat is ineffective, there may be insufficient elaboration of the harmful consequences of the behavior. When a strong threat doesn't work, there may be too much elaboration that interferes with the processing of the recommended change in behavior; the receiver is too busy thinking of reasons the message doesn't apply to him or her to pay attention to the offered solution.[148] A study that manipulated subjects' degree of anxiety about AIDS, for example, found that they evaluated condom ads most positively when the ads used a moderate threat. Copy that promoted use of the condom because "Sex is a risky business" (moderate threat) resulted in more attitude change than either a weaker threat that emphasized the product's sensitivity or a strong threat that discussed the certainty of death from AIDS.[149]

Similarly, scare tactics have not generally been an effective way to convince teenagers to curb their use of alcohol or drugs. Teens simply tune out the message or deny its relevance to them.[150] However, a study of adolescent responses to social versus physical threat appeals in drug prevention messages found that social threat (such as being ostracized by one's peers) is a more effective strategy.[151]

The Message as Art Form: Metaphors Be with You

Just like novelists, poets, and artists, marketers are storytellers. Their communications take the form of stories because they describe intangible product benefits. The storyteller, therefore, must express these in some concrete form so that consumers will get the message.

Advertising creatives rely (consciously or not) on well-known literary devices to communicate these meanings. For example, characters such as Mr. Goodwrench, the Jolly Green Giant, and Charlie the Tuna may personify a product or service. Many ads take the form of an **allegory**, which is a story about an abstract trait or concept that advertisers tell in the context of a person, animal, vegetable, or object.

A **metaphor** places two dissimilar objects into a close relationship such that "A is B," whereas a **simile** compares two objects, "A is like B." A and B, however dissimilar, share some quality that the metaphor highlights. Metaphors allow the marketer to apply meaningful images to everyday events. In the stock market, "white knights" battle "hostile raiders" with the help of "poison pills"; Tony the Tiger equates cereal with strength and "you're in good hands with Allstate" insurance.[152]

Resonance is another type of literary device advertisers frequently use. It is a form of presentation that combines a play on words with a relevant picture. Whereas

WHO'S DRIVING YOU HOME TONIGHT?
NEVER DRINK AND DRIVE   DRIVE DRY
A brandhouse INITIATIVE

metaphor substitutes one meaning for another by connecting two things that are in some way similar, resonance employs an element that has a double meaning—such as a *pun,* in which two words sound similar but have different meanings. For example, an ad for a diet strawberry shortcake dessert might bear the copy "berried treasure" so that the brand conveys qualities we associate with buried treasure such as valuable and hidden. An ad for ASICS athletic shoes proclaimed, "We believe women should be running the country" as it depicted a woman jogging, whereas a Bounce fabric softener ad asked "Is there something creeping up behind you?" as it showed a woman's dress bunched up on her back as a result of static. Because the text departs from expectations, it creates a state of tension or uncertainty on the part of the viewer until he or she figures out the wordplay. Once the consumer "gets it," he or she may prefer the ad to a more straightforward message.[153]

Just as a novelist or artist can tell a story in words or pictures, we can choose several ways to address our consumer audiences. Advertisers structure commercials like other art forms; as we've seen, they borrow conventions from literature and art to communicate.[154] One important distinction is between a *drama* and a *lecture.*[155] A lecture is like a speech: The source speaks directly to the audience to inform them about a product or to persuade them to buy it. Because a lecture clearly implies an attempt at persuasion, the audience will regard it as such. Assuming it motivates listeners, they weigh the merits of the message along with the source's credibility. Cognitive responses occur (e.g., "How much did Coke pay him to say that?"). Consumers accept the appeal if it overcomes objections and is consistent with their beliefs.

The Source Versus the Message: Do We Sell the Steak or the Sizzle?

OBJECTIVE 8-11
Audience characteristics help to determine whether the nature of the source or the message itself will be relatively more effective.

We've discussed two major components of the communications model: the source and the message. At the end of the day, which component persuades consumers to change their attitudes? Should we worry more about *what* we say or *how* we say it and *who* says it?

Surprise! The answer is it depends. As we saw in Chapter 5, consumers' level of involvement determines which cognitive

Figure 8.7 THE ELABORATION LIKELIHOOD MODEL (ELM) OF PERSUASION

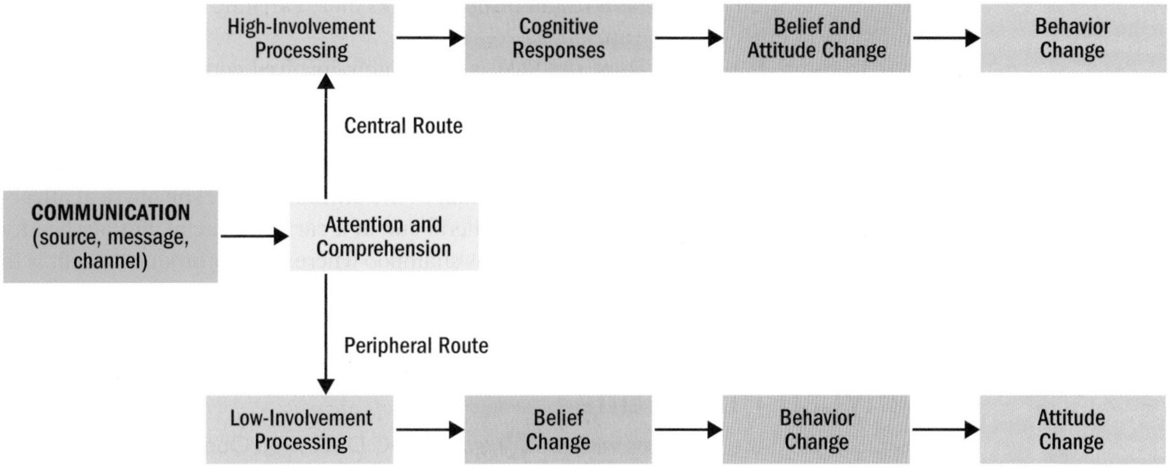

processes will activate when they receive a message. This in turn influences which aspects of a communication they process. Like travelers who come to a fork in the road, they choose one path or the other. The direction they take determines which aspects of the marketing communication will work and which will fall on deaf ears.

The **Elaboration Likelihood Model (ELM)** assumes that, under conditions of high involvement, we take the *central route* to persuasion. Under conditions of low involvement, we take a *peripheral route* instead. Figure 8.7 diagrams this model.[156]

The Central Route to Persuasion

According to the ELM, when we find the information in a persuasive message relevant or interesting, we pay careful attention to it. In this event, we focus on the arguments the marketer presents and generate *cognitive responses* to this content. An expectant mother who hears a radio message that warns about drinking while pregnant might say to herself, "She's right. I really should stop drinking alcohol now that I'm pregnant." Or she might offer counterarguments, such as, "That's a bunch of baloney. My mother had a cocktail every night when she was pregnant with me, and I turned out fine." If people generate counterarguments in response to a message, it's less likely that they will yield to the message, whereas if they generate further supporting arguments, it's more likely they'll comply.[157]

The central route to persuasion involves the standard hierarchy of effects we discussed earlier in this chapter. Recall this assumes that we carefully form and evaluate beliefs; the strong attitudes that result in turn guide our behavior. The implication is that message factors, such as the quality of arguments an ad presents, will determine attitude change. Prior knowledge about a topic results in more thoughts about the message and also increases the number of counterarguments.[158]

The Peripheral Route to Persuasion

In contrast, we take the peripheral route when we're not really motivated to think about the marketer's arguments. Instead, we're likely to use other cues to decide how to react to the message. These cues include the product's package, the attractiveness of the source, or the context in which the message appears. We call sources of information extraneous to the actual message *peripheral cues* because they surround the actual message.

The peripheral route to persuasion highlights the **paradox of low involvement**: When we *don't* care as much about a product, the way it's presented (e.g., who endorses it or the visuals that go with it) increases in importance. The implication here is that we may buy low-involvement products chiefly because the marketer designs a "sexy" package, chooses a popular spokesperson, or creates a stimulating shopping environment. In other words, especially when a consumer engages in emotional or behavioral decision making, these environmental cues become more important than when he or she performs cognitive decision making; as a result, he or she looks more carefully at the product's performance or other objective attributes.

To recap, the basic idea of the ELM is that highly involved consumers look for the "steak" (e.g., strong, rational arguments). Those who are less involved go for the "sizzle" (e.g., the colors and images in packaging or famous people's endorsements). It is important to remember, however, that the *same* communications variable can be both a central and a peripheral cue, depending on its relation to the attitude object. The physical attractiveness of a model might serve as a peripheral cue in a car commercial, but her beauty might be a central cue for a product such as shampoo where a major product benefit is to enhance attractiveness.[159]

MyLab Marketing

To complete the problems with the ⭐, go to EOC Discussion Questions in the MyLab as well as additional Marketing Metrics questions only available in MyLab Marketing.

CHAPTER SUMMARY

Now that you have finished reading this chapter, you should understand why:

1. It is important for consumer researchers to understand the nature and power of attitudes.

An *attitude* is a predisposition to evaluate an object or product positively or negatively. We form attitudes toward products and services, and these attitudes often determine whether we will purchase or not.

2. Attitudes are more complex than they first appear.

Three components make up an attitude: beliefs, affect, and behavioral intentions.

3. We form attitudes in several ways.

Attitude researchers traditionally assumed that we learn attitudes in a fixed sequence: First we form beliefs (*cognitions*) about an attitude object, then we evaluate that object (*affect*), and then we take some action (*behavior*). Depending on the consumer's level of involvement and the circumstances, though, his attitudes can result from other hierarchies of effects as well. A key to attitude formation is the function the attitude holds for the consumer (e.g., is it utilitarian or ego defensive?).

4. A need to maintain consistency among all of our attitudinal components often motivates us to alter one or more of them.

One organizing principle of attitude formation is the importance of consistency among attitudinal components—that

is, we alter some parts of an attitude to be in line with others. Such theoretical approaches to attitudes as cognitive dissonance theory, self-perception theory, and balance theory stress the vital role of our need for consistency.

5. Attitude models identify specific components and combine them to predict a consumer's overall attitude toward a product or brand.

Multiattribute attitude models underscore the complexity of attitudes: They specify that we identify and combine a set of beliefs and evaluations to predict an overall attitude. Researchers integrate factors such as subjective norms and the specificity of attitude scales into attitude measures to improve predictability.

6. The communications model identifies several important components for marketers when they try to change consumers' attitudes toward products and services.

Persuasion refers to an attempt to change consumers' attitudes. The communications model specifies the elements marketers need to transmit meaning. These include a source, a message, a medium, a receiver, and feedback.

7. The consumer who processes a message is not the passive receiver of information marketers once believed him or her to be.

The traditional view of communications regards the perceiver as a passive element in the process. New developments in interactive communications highlight the need to consider the active roles a consumer plays when he or she obtains product information and builds a relationship with a company. Advocates of permission marketing argue that it's more effective to send messages to consumers who have already indicated an interest in learning about a product than trying to hit people "cold" with these solicitations.

8. Several factors influence the effectiveness of a message source.

Two important characteristics that determine the effectiveness of a source are its attractiveness and credibility. Although celebrities often serve this purpose, their credibility is not always as strong as marketers hope. Marketing messages that consumers perceive as buzz (those that are authentic and consumer generated) tend to be more effective than those they categorize as hype (those that are inauthentic, biased, and company generated).

9. The way a marketer structures his or her message determines how persuasive it will be.

Some elements of a message that help to determine its effectiveness include the following: conveyance of the message in words or pictures; employment of an emotional or a rational appeal; frequency of repetition; conclusion drawing; presentation of both sides of the argument; and inclusion of fear, humor, or sexual references. Advertising messages often incorporate elements from art or literature, such as dramas, lectures, metaphors, allegories, and resonance.

10. Many modern marketers are reality engineers.

Reality engineering occurs when marketers appropriate elements of popular culture to use in their promotional strategies. These elements include sensory and spatial aspects of everyday existence, whether in the form of products that appear in movies, scents pumped into offices and stores, billboards, theme parks, or video monitors attached to shopping carts.

11. Audience characteristics help to determine whether the nature of the source or the message itself will be relatively more effective.

The relative influence of the source versus the message depends on the receiver's level of involvement with the communication. The Elaboration Likelihood Model (ELM) specifies that source effects are more likely to sway a less-involved consumer, whereas a more-involved consumer will be more likely to attend to and process components of the actual message.

KEY TERMS

ABC model of attitudes, 286
Advergaming, 318
Affect, 286
Allegory, 321
Attitude object (A_o), 285
Attitude, 285
Attitude accessibility perspective, 301
Attitude models, 296
Attitude toward the act of buying (A_{act}), 300
Balance theory, 292
Basking in reflected glory, 294
Behavior, 286
Buzz, 308
Celebrity endorsements, 296
Cognition, 286
Cognitive-affective model, 289
Communications model, 304
Comparative advertising, 315
Compliance, 289
Counterarguing, 320
Disclaimers, 307
Ego-defensive function, 285
Elaboration Likelihood Model (ELM), 323
Experiential hierarchy of effects, 287
Fear appeals, 321
Fishbein Model, 297

Foot-in-the-door technique, 292
Functional theory of attitudes, 285
Guerrilla marketing, 317
Halo effect, 308
Hierarchy of effects, 286
High-involvement hierarchy, 286
Humor appeals, 320
Hype, 308
Identification, 289
Independence hypothesis, 289
Internalization, 289
Knowledge bias, 308
Knowledge function, 286
Latitudes of acceptance and rejection, 292
Low-involvement hierarchy of effects, 286
Martyrdom effect, 315
M-commerce, 316
Medication adherence, 298
Mere exposure phenomenon, 312
Metaphor, 321
Multiattribute attitude models, 296
Multiple pathway anchoring and adjustment (MPAA) model, 302
Native advertising, 307
Normative influence, 299
Paradox of low involvement, 323
Permission marketing, 304

Persuasion, 302
Plinking™, 319
Principle of cognitive consistency, 290
Product placement, 318
Reality engineering, 317
Refutational arguments, 314
Reporting bias, 308
Resonance, 321
Self-perception theory, 291
Sex appeals, 320
Shared endorsements, 308
Simile, 321
Sleeper effect, 307
Social judgment theory, 292
Social media, 316
Sock puppeting, 307
Source attractiveness, 308
Source credibility, 306
Source derogation, 315
Spokescharacters, 310
Subjective norm (SN), 299
Theory of Reasoned Action, 298
Theory of Trying, 302
Transmedia storytelling, 317
Two-Factor Theory, 313
Utilitarian function, 285
Value-expressive function, 285

REVIEW

8-1 How can an attitude play an ego-defensive function?

⭐ **8-2** Describe the ABC model of attitudes.

8-3 List the three hierarchies of attitudes, and describe the major differences among them.

8-4 How do levels of commitment to an attitude influence the likelihood that it will become part of the way we think about a product in the long term?

8-5 We sometimes enhance our attitude toward a product after we buy it. How does the theory of cognitive dissonance explain this change?

8-6 What is the foot-in-the-door technique? How does self-perception theory relate to this effect?

8-7 What are latitudes of acceptance and rejection? How does a consumer's level of involvement with a product affect his latitude of acceptance?

8-8 According to balance theory, how can we tell if a triad is balanced or unbalanced? How can consumers restore balance to an unbalanced triad?

8-9 Describe a multiattribute attitude model and list its key components.

⭐ **8-10** "Do as I say, not as I do." How does this statement relate to attitude models?

8-11 What is a subjective norm, and how does it influence our attitudes?

8-12 What are three obstacles to predicting behavior even if we know a person's attitudes?

8-13 Describe the Theory of Reasoned Action. Why might it not be equally valuable when we apply it to non-Western cultures?

8-14 List three psychological principles related to persuasion.

⭐ **8-15** Describe the elements of the traditional communications model, and tell how the updated model differs.

8-16 What is source credibility, and what are two factors that influence our decision as to whether a source is credible?

8-17 What is the difference between buzz and hype?

8-18 What is a halo effect, and why does it happen?

8-19 What is an avatar, and why might an advertiser choose to use one instead of hiring a celebrity endorser?

8-20 Marketers must decide whether to incorporate rational or emotional appeals in a communications strategy. Describe conditions that are more favorable to one or the other.

8-21 When should a marketer present a message visually versus verbally?

8-22 How does the Two-Factor Theory explain the effects of message repetition on attitude change?
   (a) When is it best to present a two-sided message versus a one-sided message?

8-23 Do humorous ads work? If so, under what conditions?
   (a) Should marketers ever try to arouse fear to persuade consumers?

8-24 Why do marketers use metaphors to craft persuasive messages? Give two examples of this technique.

8-25 What is the difference between a lecture and a drama?

8-26 Describe the Elaboration Likelihood Model, and summarize how it relates to the relative importance of *what* is said versus *how* it's said.

CONSUMER BEHAVIOR CHALLENGE

■ DISCUSS

8-27 The Federal Trade Commission recently sponsored a conference on "Blurred Lines: Advertising or Content?" that reflects the agency's concerns about the resemblance between native ads and "real" articles. [160] The chapter discusses the problem of *sock puppeting* where executives masquerade as everyday consumers and post negative reviews about their competitors. Numerous cases have come to light of hotels, restaurants, and other businesses that pay customers to write positive evaluations on review sites. *Wikipedia* can be edited by anyone. Do we care about source credibility anymore? What does the future look like for source effects in an age when anyone can post content, and pretend it came from a credible source?

8-28 Corporate sponsorship of universities in the United States and the United Kingdom is commonplace; the sponsored universities have attracted millions of dollars. Chinese universities are following suit. However, this process was strongly criticized following the sponsorship of a building at Tsinghua University in 2011.

The No. 4 Teaching Building was adorned with big gold letters proclaiming it to be the Jeanswest Building. Within days of the sign going up, it was defaced with spray paint. Students at the university believed the institution had "sold out" and that it was a laughing stock across China. The sign was eventually taken down. The university was trying to raise $114 million in sponsorship and had offered the naming rights for 14 of its buildings. Had Tsinghua University crossed the line and brought the institution into disrepute?

8-29 Across the globe there is a growing demand for free mobile phone content, mainly in the form of apps. In turn, this is having a marked influence on mobile advertising. The biggest increase in mobile advertising is taking place in the Asia Pacific region. According to the analyst firm Gartner, the region is the largest market for mobile advertising. Gartner predicts that mobile advertising will grow at a rate of 400 percent until 2016. At that point, the market will be worth an estimated $24.5

billion. How do you think the marketplace will react to this new advertising medium as it becomes more common?[161]

8-30 Against the backdrop of Chinese consumers' fear of buying contaminated food, a new industry emerged in 2013. Online suppliers promised products directly from the farm. This followed a food scare surrounding contaminated rice and cooking oil. Two of the new businesses, COFO Ltd. And Shunfeng Express, are aiming to capture a market share of the 1.3 billion Chinese consumers in a position to pay for the premium and guaranteed range of organic products. Online sales of fresh produce reached $6.5 billion in 2013, which represented a growth in excess of 400 percent. Is it ethical to base a business model on fear?

8-31 Google updated its terms of service to allow shared endorsements though it's likely most users don't read these terms too carefully. Not everyone is thrilled about finding out his or her comments appear in an ad without giving explicit permission. Users who claimed the company had not adequately notified them about how it was using endorsements sued Facebook.[162] What should be the platform's obligation to ask permission? Are we as consumers responsible for whatever it does so long as we agree to the site's terms of service (and read the fine print)?

8-32 Jeff Chown and Mick Carter of Davie Brown Entertainment work with brands such as AT&T, Gillette, Nokia, and Pizza Hut. They try to match these major brands with the world's most popular celebrities and sports stars. They use a celebrity database index to look at consumer perceptions of celebrities and score them across a range of different attributes such as appeal, trust, awareness, aspiration, endorsement, influence, and whether they are seen as trendsetters. Perhaps one of the most important considerations is consumer awareness. If no one knows who the celebrity is, then it is irrelevant that they might have all of the other key attributes. Chown and Carter also look at an attribute they call "breakthrough," which is the ability of the celebrity to capture the attention of the consumer.[163] If you were a marketer and looking for a celebrity for clients, what kind of attributes would you be looking for? Consider a celebrity for a bank and for an energy drink.

8-33 What do you understand by *sock puppeting*? Is it ethical?

8-34 Should corporations use their activities in the field of CSR as marketing tools? Is the point of CSR to be a better corporate neighbor rather than a tool to market products and services?

8-35 Discuss some conditions that would cause you to advise a marketer to use a comparative advertising strategy.

8-36 The American Medical Association encountered a firestorm of controversy when it agreed to sponsor a line of healthcare products that Sunbeam manufactured (a decision it later reversed). Should trade or professional organizations, journalists, professors, and others endorse specific products at the expense of other offerings?

8-37 Many, many companies rely on celebrity endorsers as communications sources to persuade. Especially when they target younger people, these spokespeople often are "cool" musicians, athletes, or movie stars. In your opinion, who would be the most effective celebrity endorser today, and why? Who would be the least effective? Why?

8-38 Swiss Legend, a watch brand, gets famous people to wear its colorful timepieces. One way it does this is to give away its products at awards shows. Publicists call this common practice "gifting the talent": Companies provide stars with "goody bags" full of complimentary products.[164] What do you think about the practice of "gifting the talent" to accumulate endorsements? Is this a sound strategy? Is it ethical for celebrities to accept these gifts?

8-39 Watchdog groups have long decried product placements because they blur the line between content and advertising without adequately informing viewers. The networks themselves appear to be divided on how far they want to open the gate. According to one study, the effectiveness of product placement varies by product category and type of placement. Consumers indicate that product placements have the most influence on their grocery, electronics, and apparel purchases. The most common platform for a placement is to get a brand shown on a T-shirt or other piece of an actor's wardrobe.[165] What do you think about this practice? Under what conditions is product placement likely to influence you and your friends? When (if ever) is it counterproductive?

8-40 Research featured in the *Journal of Consumer Psychology* would seem to suggest that chewing gum or eating makes a consumer completely immune to the effects of advertising. Most advertising relies on fairly simple features, such as a powerful and memorable message or, in many cases, by repeating the advertisement so that the full effects of the mere exposure phenomenon work on the audience. Eating, it would seem, interrupts both of these effects. The advertisement reaches our minds by pre-vocalising the message. We then silently articulate the message to ourselves. The mechanics of chewing something means that the individual creates oral-motor interference.

There are important messages for advertisers to learn if this is truly the case—they should avoid advertising when they know that people might be eating. They should also avoid advertising in social situations; the audience might not be paying attention and they might be eating too.[166] The other important message is to avoid advertising around digital content. The audience is pre-vocalising the content they are interested in and will ignore banner advertisements. The only way advertising will work in these cases is to interrupt the digital content. In your view, does this mean that the concept of mere exposure is no longer applicable as a concept and practice? What does this mean for advertising?

■ APPLY

8-41 Think of a behavior someone does that is inconsistent with his or her attitudes (e.g., attitudes toward cholesterol, drug use, or even buying things to make him or her stand out or attain status). Ask the person to elaborate on why he or she does the behavior, and try to identify the way the person resolves dissonant elements.

8-42 Devise an attitude survey for a set of competing automobiles. Identify areas of competitive advantage or disadvantage for each model you include.

8-43 Construct a multiattribute model for a set of local restaurants. Based on your findings, suggest how restaurant managers could improve their establishment's image via the strategies described in this chapter.

8-44 Locate foreign ads at sites like japander.com in which celebrities endorse products that they don't pitch on their home turf. Ask friends or classmates to rate the attractiveness of each celebrity, then show them these ads and ask them to rate the celebrities again. Does the star's "brand image" change after it's paired with cheesy ads? Based on these results, what advice would you give to a manager who has to choose among endorsement offers for a famous client?

8-45 Why would a marketer consider saying negative things about her product? When is this strategy feasible? Can you find examples of it?

8-46 Collect ads that rely on sex appeal to sell products. How often do they communicate benefits of the actual product?

8-47 UK-based Reverse Graffiti specializes in guerrilla marketing. They sell DIY Snow Graffiti packages for under $300. The package includes a stencil, a biodegradable spray maker, and a pair of latex gloves, and a full set of instructions. Is guerrilla marketing just vandalism under an assumed title?

8-48 The chapter discusses the important problem of medication adherence. How can healthcare marketers strengthen the link between intentions and behavior to boost the rate at which people actually take their prescribed medications? Devise a communications strategy to increase the adherence rate.

8-49 In Europe, comparative advertising is a dangerous area to get involved in. There are many legal pitfalls, and many consumers do not respond well to advertisements that depict competitors in a poor light. Some consumers get the impression that if a brand needs to mention another brand in their advertising, then they are worried about them. Find some examples of comparative advertising in your country. Are they effective and persuasive?

8-50 Collect examples of ads that rely on the use of metaphors or resonance. Do you feel these ads are effective? If you were marketing the products, would you feel more comfortable with ads that use a more straightforward, "hard-sell" approach? Why or why not?

8-51 The elaboration likelihood model (ELM) assumes that under conditions of high-involvement, we take the central route to persuasion. What does this mean, and how does it work?

8-52 According to this chapter, "Just like novelists, poets, and artists, marketers are storytellers." To what extent can this be taken seriously? There is certainly a case for it when you consider the fact that communications can often take the form of stories, as they need to illustrate an intangible aspect of product or service. The story is a concrete form of getting the message across. Do you agree?

Case Study

SHAMPOO BUYING: A "BAD HAIR" DAY?

When was the last time you purchased shampoo or other hair care products? How long did it take you to choose? How did you decide?

The hair care aisle of a typical drugstore has more than 200 choices for shampoo. The packages promote a myriad of benefits including repair, protection, hydration, control, and nourishment. How does a consumer make the match between his or her needs and the brand benefits? It's not easy to choose, and therefore not a surprise that many shoppers spend about 20 minutes in this aisle when they select a shampoo brand.

The confusion builds when you consider that it is not just shampoo that we buy. There are gels, mousses, hairsprays, shine enhancers, and conditioners. A recent Mintel survey shows that three-quarters of consumers use conditioner in addition to shampoo, and these numbers are even higher for women.

One way that consumers try to simplify the purchase process is by referring to compelling advertising, so ad agencies work hard to create effective messages that can reinforce current brand loyalty or persuade consumers to try a new brand. Hair care product advertising relies heavily on television, print, the Internet, and outdoor advertising, most commonly in the form of billboards. In addition, many ad campaigns feature appealing celebrity endorsers such as Katie Holmes, Nicole Scherzinger, and Sofia Vergara.

And it's not only women in the United States who scratch their heads over these choices. To the women of Singapore and the Philippines, the choice of hair conditioner poses the same challenges. To connect with women in these countries, Unilever tried a nontraditional campaign to show the benefit of Cream Silk Hair Fall Defense, a conditioner brand the company sells in those countries. Cream Silk's core benefit is the "strength" it gives hair. With the help of advertising agency JWT, Unilever was able to break through the advertising clutter and deliver its message in an entirely new format.

JWT began by contacting Paul Goh, the leading violin bow-maker in Singapore. For this promotion, Mr. Goh was asked to switch out the horsehair violin bows he traditionally used and exchange them with human hair on four of his violin bows. This hair had been washed and conditioned with Cream Silk. To demonstrate the strength of the hair, a string quartet used the bows as it played during a 4-hour concert in a busy shopping mall in Manila. Good news for Unilever: The entire concert concluded without even one broken hair on the violin bows! You can view the video yourself on YouTube; just search "The Human Hair Quartet."

According to JWT, the event was fully successful in engaging Cream Silk's target market. The people who flocked to the concert rose to as high as 600 at one point. Over 450 samples of the shampoo were distributed. A survey conducted at the event showed that most of the consumers left with a positive impression about Cream Silk. What do you think? If you were looking for stronger hair, would this advertising convince you? How is this approach superior or inferior to others that conditioner brands typically use?

DISCUSSION QUESTIONS

CS 8-1 Describe Cream Silk's promotion within the context of the multiattribute model: Which attribute(s) were central to the promotion and how does the model explain what the company was trying to accomplish with the "Human Hair Quartet?" What limitations might this model have for predicting consumer's attitudes and purchase behavior towards Cream Silk? (Hint: Take a look at the Theory of Reasoned Action.)

CS 8-2 In contrast to the Cream Silk promotion, Old Spice used its characteristically quirky approach to persuade men to try its hair care products. The integrated campaign, "That's the Power of Hair," incorporated a popular Huey Lewis tune, an interactive Web site, and funny ads featuring animated hair. Discuss the type of message appeal and the Elaboration Likelihood Model route each campaign used.

Sources: "Shampoo, Conditioners and Styling Products—US—April 2013," Mintel Oxygen, accessed August 4, 2013; "JWT and Unilever Demonstrate the Power of Cream Silk with First Ever Human Hair Quartet," J. Walter Thompson, http://www.jwt.com/en/news/singapore/singapore/jwtandunile-verdemonstratethepowerofcreamsilkwithfirsteverhumanhairquartet/, accessed August 5, 2013; Andrew Adam Newman, "In Shampoo Ads for Men, It's Not Just the Hair, It's What It Does For You," (February 18, 2014), http://www.nytimes.com/2014/02/18/business/media/in-shampoo-ads-for-men-its-not-just-the-hair-its-what-it-does-for-you.html?_r=0, accessed May 25, 2015.

MyLab Marketing

Go to the Assignments section of your MyLab to complete these writing exercises.

8-53 A government agency wants to encourage people who have been drinking to use designated drivers. What advice could you give the organization about constructing persuasive communications? Discuss some factors that might be important, including the structure of the communications, where they should appear, and who should deliver them. Should it use fear appeals? If so, how?

8-54 Contrast the hierarchies of effects the chapter outlines. How should marketers take these different situations into account when they choose their marketing mix?

NOTES

1. Robert A. Baron and Donn Byrne, *Social Psychology: Understanding Human Interaction*, 5th ed. (Boston: Allyn & Bacon, 1987).
2. Daniel Katz, "The Functional Approach to the Study of Attitudes," *Public Opinion Quarterly* 24 (Summer 1960): 163–204, Richard J. Lutz, "Changing Brand Attitudes Through Modification of Cognitive Structure," *Journal of Consumer Research* 1 (March 1975): 49–59.
3. Russell H. Fazio, T. N. Lenn, and E. A. Effrein, "Spontaneous Attitude Formation," *Social Cognition* 2 (1984): 214–234.
4. Sharon Shavitt, "The Role of Attitude Objects in Attitude Functions," *Journal of Experimental Social Psychology* 26 (1990): 124–148; see also J. S. Johar and M. Joseph Sirgy, "Value Expressive Versus Utilitarian Advertising Appeals: When and Why to Use Which Appeal," *Journal of Advertising* 20 (September 1991): 23–34.
5. Aaron Baar, "New Subaru Campaign Takes Aim with Cupid's Arrow," *Marketing Daily* (April 28, 2008), http://publications.mediapost.com/Index.Cfm?Fuseaction=Articles.San&S=81435&Nid=420..., accessed April 28, 2008.
6. Michael Ray, "Marketing Communications and the Hierarchy-of-Effects," in Peter Clark, ed., *New Models for Mass Communication Research* (Beverly Hills, CA: Sage, 1973), 147–176.
7. Herbert Krugman, "The Impact of Television Advertising: Learning Without Involvement," *Public Opinion Quarterly* 29 (Fall 1965): 349–356;

Robert Lavidge and Gary Steiner, "A Model for Predictive Measurements of Advertising Effectiveness," *Journal of Marketing* 25 (October 1961): 59–62.
8. Stephanie Thompson, "Bad Breakup? There, There, B&J Know Just How You Feel," *Advertising Age* (January 24, 2005): 8.
9. Daniel J. Howard and Charles Gengler, "Emotional Contagion Effects on Product Attitudes," *Journal of Consumer Research* 28 (September 2001): 189–201; Andrew B. Aylesworth and Scott B. MacKenzie, "Context Is Key: The Effect of Program-Induced Mood on Thoughts About the Ad," *Journal of Advertising* 27 (Summer 1998): 17; Angela Y. Lee and Brian Sternthal, "The Effects of Positive Mood on Memory," *Journal of Consumer Research* 26 (September 1999): 115–128; Michael J. Barone, Paul W. Miniard, and Jean B. Romeo, "The Influence of Positive Mood on Brand Extension Evaluations," *Journal of Consumer Research* 26 (March 2000): 386–401. For a study that compared the effectiveness of emotional appeals across cultures, see Jennifer L. Aaker and Patti Williams, "Empathy Versus Pride: The Influence of Emotional Appeals Across Cultures," *Journal of Consumer Research* 25 (December 1998): 241–261. For research that relates mood (depression) to acceptance of health-related messages, see Punam Anand Keller, Isaac M. Lipkus, and Barbara K. Rimer, "Depressive Realism and Health Risk Accuracy: The Negative Consequences of Positive Mood," *Journal of Consumer Research* 29 (June 2002): 57–69.

10. Punam Anand, Morris B. Holbrook, and Debra Stephens, "The Formation of Affective Judgments: The Cognitive–Affective Model Versus the Independence Hypothesis," *Journal of Consumer Research* 15 (December 1988): 386–391; Richard S. Lazarus, "Thoughts on the Relations Between Emotion and Cognition," *American Psychologist* 37, no. 9 (1982): 1019–1024; Robert B. Zajonc, "Feeling and Thinking: Preferences Need No Inferences," *American Psychologist* 35, no. 2 (1980): 151–175.

11. See Sharon E. Beatty and Lynn R. Kahle, "Alternative Hierarchies of the Attitude–Behavior Relationship: The Impact of Brand Commitment and Habit," *Journal of the Academy of Marketing Science* 16 (Summer 1988): 1–10.

12. J. R. Priester, D. Nayakankuppan, M. A. Fleming, and J. Godek, "The A(2)SC(2) Model: The Influence of Attitudes and Attitude Strength on Consideration Set Choice," *Journal of Consumer Research* 30, no. 4 (2004): 574–587.

13. Chester A. Insko and John Schopler, *Experimental Social Psychology* (New York: Academic Press, 1972).

14. Insko and Schopler, *Experimental Social Psychology*.

15. Robert E. Knox and James A. Inkster, "Postdecision Dissonance at Post Time," *Journal of Personality & Social Psychology* 8, no. 4 (1968): 319–323.

16. Daryl J. Bem, "Self-Perception Theory," in Leonard Berkowitz, ed., *Advances in Experimental Social Psychology* (New York: Academic Press, 1972): 1–62; cf. more recently Keisha M. Cutright, Eugenia C. Wu, Jillian C. Banfield, Aaron C. Kay, and Gavan J. Fitzsimons, "When Your World Must Be Defended: Choosing Products to Justify the System," *Journal of Consumer Research* 38, no. 1 (June 2011): 62–77.

17. Jonathan L. Freedman and Scott C. Fraser, "Compliance Without Pressure: The Foot-in-the-Door Technique," *Journal of Personality & Social Psychology* 4 (August 1966): 195–202. For further consideration of possible explanations for this effect, see William DeJong, "An Examination of Self-Perception Mediation of the Foot-in-the-Door Effect," *Journal of Personality & Social Psychology* 37 (December 1979): 221–231; Alice M. Tybout, Brian Sternthal, and Bobby J. Calder, "Information Availability as a Determinant of Multiple-Request Effectiveness," *Journal of Marketing Research* 20 (August 1988): 280–290.

18. David H. Furse, David W. Stewart, and David L. Rados, "Effects of Foot-in-the-Door, Cash Incentives and Follow-ups on Survey Response," *Journal of Marketing Research* 18 (November 1981): 473–478; Carol A. Scott, "The Effects of Trial and Incentives on Repeat Purchase Behavior," *Journal of Marketing Research* 13 (August 1976): 263–269.

19. Bob Fennis, Loes Janssen, and Kathleen D. Vohs, "Acts of Benevolence: A Limited-Resource Account of Compliance with Charitable Requests," *Journal of Consumer Research* (2009): 906–925.

20. See Joan Meyers-Levy and Brian Sternthal, "A Two-Factor Explanation of Assimilation and Contrast Effects," *Journal of Marketing Research* 30 (August 1993): 359–368.

21. Mark B. Traylor, "Product Involvement and Brand Commitment," *Journal of Advertising Research* (December 1981): 51–56.

22. Fritz Heider, *The Psychology of Interpersonal Relations* (New York: Wiley, 1958).

23. K. Woolley and A. Fishbach, "A Recipe for Friendship: Similarity in Food Consumption Promotes Affiliation and Trust," talk presented at the October 2014 Association for Consumer Research, Baltimore, MD.

24. Robert B. Cialdini, Richard J. Borden, Avril Thorne, Marcus Randall Walker, Stephen Freeman, and Lloyd Reynolds Sloan, "Basking in Reflected Glory: Three (Football) Field Studies," *Journal of Personality & Social Psychology* 34: 366–375.

25. Quoted in Jon Weinbach, "Ad Score! Major League Soccer Teams Will Sell Ad Space on Players' Jerseys," *Wall Street Journal* (September 28, 2006): B1.

26. Debra Z. Basil and Paul M. Herr, "Attitudinal Balance and Cause-Related Marketing: An Empirical Application of Balance Theory," *Journal of Consumer Psychology* 16, no. 4 (2006): 391–403.

27. Leslie Kaufman, "Enough Talk," *Newsweek* (August 18, 1997): 48–49.

28. Allan Wicker, "Attitudes Versus Actions: The Relationship of Verbal and Overt Behavioral Responses to Attitude Objects," *Journal of Social Issues* 25 (Autumn 1969): 65.

29. Martin Fishbein, "An Investigation of the Relationships Between Beliefs About an Object and the Attitude Toward that Object," *Human Relations* 16 (1983): 233–240.

30. Medication Adherence in America 2013, National Community Pharmacists Association, https://www.ncpanet.org/pdf/reportcard/AdherenceReportCard_Abridged.pdf, accessed March 30, 2015.

31. Stephanie Clifford, "Using Data to Stage-Manage Paths to the Prescription Counter," *New York Times* (June 19, 2013), http://bits.blogs.nyt.com/2013/06/19/using-data-to-stage-manage-paths-to-the-prescription-counter/, accessed February 3, 2015.

32. Icek Ajzen and Martin Fishbein, "Attitude–Behavior Relations: A Theoretical Analysis and Review of Empirical Research," *Psychological Bulletin* 84 (September 1977): 888–918.

33. Morris B. Holbrook and William J. Havlena, "Assessing the Real-to-Artificial Generalizability of Multi-Attribute Attitude Models in Tests of New Product Designs," *Journal of Marketing Research* 25 (February 1988): 25–35; Terence A. Shimp and Alican Kavas, "The Theory of Reasoned Action Applied to Coupon Usage," *Journal of Consumer Research* 11 (December 1984): 795–809.

34. R. P. Abelson, "Conviction," *American Psychologist* 43 (1988): 267–75; Richard E. Petty and Jon A. Krosnick, *Attitude Strength: Antecedents and Consequences* (Mahwah, NJ: Erlbaum, 1995); Ida E. Berger and Linda F. Alwitt, "Attitude Conviction: A Self-Reflective Measure of Attitude Strength," *Journal of Social Behavior & Personality* 11, no. 3 (1996): 557–572.

35. Noah J. Goldstein, Robert B. Cialdini, and Vladas Griskevicius, "A Room with a Viewpoint: Using Social Norms to Motivate Environmental Conservation in Hotels," *Journal of Consumer Research* 35 (October 2008): 472–482.

36. Blair H. Sheppard, Jon Hartwick, and Paul R. Warshaw, "The Theory of Reasoned Action: A Meta-Analysis of Past Research with Recommendations for Modifications and Future Research," *Journal of Consumer Research* 15 (December 1988): 325–343.

37. Joseph A. Cote, James McCullough, and Michael Reilly, "Effects of Unexpected Situations on Behavior–Intention Differences: A Garbology Analysis," *Journal of Consumer Research* 12 (September 1985): 188–194.

38. Robert E. Smith and William R. Swinyard, "Attitude–Behavior Consistency: The Impact of Product Trial Versus Advertising," *Journal of Marketing Research* 20 (August 1983): 257–267.

39. For a recent similar application, cf. Nader T. Tavassoli and Gavan J. Fitzsimons, "Spoken and Typed Expressions of Repeated Attitudes: Matching Response Modes Leads to Attitude Retrieval Versus Construction," *Journal of Consumer Research* 33, no. 2 (2006): 179–187.

40. Kulwant Singh, Siew Meng Leong, Chin Tiong Tan, and Kwei Cheong Wong, "A Theory of Reasoned Action Perspective of Voting Behavior: Model and Empirical Test," *Psychology & Marketing* 12, no. 1 (January 1995): 37–51; Joseph A. Cote and Patriya S. Tansuhaj, "Culture Bound Assumptions in Behavior Intention Models," in Thomas K. Srull, ed., *Advances in Consumer Research* 16 (Provo, UT: Association for Consumer Research, 1989), 105–109.

41. Joel B. Cohen and Americus Reed II, "A Multiple Pathway Anchoring and Adjustment (MPAA) Model of Attitude Generation and Recruitment," *Journal of Consumer Research* 33 (June 2006): 1–15.

42. Richard P. Bagozzi and Paul R. Warshaw, "Trying to Consume," *Journal of Consumer Research* 17 (September 1990): 127–140.

43. Robert B. Cialdini and Kelton V. L. Rhoads, "Human Behavior and the Marketplace," *Marketing Research* (Fall 2001): 13.

44. Gert Assmus, "An Empirical Investigation into the Perception of Vehicle Source Effects," *Journal of Advertising* 7 (Winter 1978): 4–10. For a more thorough discussion of the pros and cons of different media, see Stephen Baker, *Systematic Approach to Advertising Creativity* (New York: McGraw-Hill, 1979).

45. Alladi Venkatesh, Ruby Roy Dholakia, and Nikhilesh Dholakia, "New Visions of Information Technology and Postmodernism: Implications for Advertising and Marketing Communications," in Walter Brenner and Lutz Kolbe, eds., *The Information Superhighway and Private Households: Case Studies of Business Impacts* (Heidelberg: Physica-Verlag, 1996), 319–337; Donna L. Hoffman and Thomas P. Novak, "Marketing in Hypermedia Computer-Mediated Environments: Conceptual Foundations," *Journal of Marketing* 60, no. 3 (July 1996): 50–68. For an early theoretical discussion of interactivity in communications paradigms, see B. Aubrey Fisher, *Perspectives on Human Communication* (New York: Macmillan, 1978).

46. Seth Godin, *Permission Marketing: Turning Strangers into Friends, and Friends into Customers* (New York: Simon & Schuster, 1999).

47. Barbara J. Phillips, Jessica Miller, and Edward F. McQuarrie, "Dreaming Out Loud on Pinterest: New Forms of Indirect Persuasion," *International Journal of Advertising*, 33, no. 4 (2014): 633.

48. Brad Stone, "The War for Your TV," *Newsweek* (July 29, 2002): 46–47.

49. Carl I. Hovland and W. Weiss, "The Influence of Source Credibility on Communication Effectiveness," *Public Opinion Quarterly* 15 (1952): 635–650; for a recent treatment, cf. Yong-Soon Kang and Paul M. Herr, "Beauty and the Beholder: Toward an Integrative Model of Communication Source Effects," *Journal of Consumer Research* 33 (June 2006): 123–130.

50. Herbert Kelman, "Processes of Opinion Change," *Public Opinion Quarterly* 25 (Spring 1961): 57–78; Susan M. Petroshius and Kenneth E. Crocker, "An Empirical Analysis of Spokesperson Characteristics on Advertisement and Product Evaluations," *Journal of the Academy of Marketing Science* 17 (Summer 1989): 217–226.

51. Kenneth G. DeBono and Richard J. Harnish, "Source Expertise, Source Attractiveness, and the Processing of Persuasive Information: A Functional Approach," *Journal of Personality & Social Psychology* 55, no. 4 (1988): 541–546.

52. Joseph R. Priester and Richard E. Petty, "The Influence of Spokesperson Trustworthiness on Message Elaboration, Attitude Strength, and Advertising Effectiveness," *Journal of Consumer Psychology* 13, no. 4 (2003): 408–421.

53. Hershey H. Friedman and Linda Friedman, "Endorser Effectiveness by Product Type," *Journal of Advertising Research* 19, no. 5 (1979): 63–71. For a study that looked at nontarget market effects—the effects of advertising intended for other market segments—see Jennifer L. Aaker, Anne M. Brumbaugh, and Sonya A. Grier, "Non-Target Markets and Viewer

Distinctiveness: The Impact of Target Marketing on Advertising Attitudes," *Journal of Consumer Psychology* 9, no. 3 (2000): 127–140.

54. S. Ratneshwar and Shelly Chaiken, "Comprehension's Role in Persuasion: The Case of Its Moderating Effect on the Persuasive Impact of Source Cues," *Journal of Consumer Research* 18 (June 1991): 52–62.

55. Steven S. Posavac, Michal Herzenstein, Frank R. Kardes, and Suresh Sundaram, "Profits and Halos: The Role of Firm Profitability Information in Consumer Inference," *Journal of Consumer Psychology* 20, no. 3 (2010): 327–337.

56. Kenneth C. Herbst, Eli J. Finkel, David Allan, and Gráinne M. Fitzsimons, "On the Dangers of Pulling a Fast One: Advertisement Disclaimer Speed, Brand Trust, and Purchase Intention," *Journal of Consumer Research* 38, no. 5 (2012): 909–919.

57. Yeosun Yoon, Zeynep Gurhan-Canli, and Norbert Schwarz, "The Effect of Corporate Social Responsibility (CSR) Activities on Companies with Bad Reputations," *Journal of Consumer Psychology* 16, no. 4 (2006): 377–390.

58. Peter R. Darke and Robin J. B. Ritchie, "The Defensive Consumer: Advertising Deception, Defensive Processing, and Distrust," *Journal of Marketing Research* 44 (February 2007): 114–127.

59. Jagdish Agrawal and Wagner A. Kamakura, "The Economic Worth of Celebrity Endorsers: An Event Study Analysis," *Journal of Marketing* 59 (July 1995): 56–62.

60. "Report: Charlie Sheen May Not Shine, But Stars Are Aligned as Print Ad Activists," *NYSportsJournalism.com* (February 25, 2011), http://nysports journalism.squarespace.com/study-stars-shine-in-print-ads/?SSScroll Position=0&VK=94964620, accessed April 30, 2011.

61. Heather Buttle, Jane E. Raymond, and Shai Danziger, "Do Famous Faces Capture Attention?," paper presented at Association for Consumer Research Conference, Columbus, OH (October 1999).

62. Michael A. Kamins, "Celebrity and Noncelebrity Advertising in a Two-Sided Context," *Journal of Advertising Research* 29 (June–July 1989): 34; Joseph M. Kamen, A. C. Azhari, and J. R. Kragh, "What a Spokesman Does for a Sponsor," *Journal of Advertising Research* 15, no. 2 (1975): 17–24; Lynn Langmeyer and Mary Walker, "A First Step to Identify the Meaning in Celebrity Endorsers," in Rebecca H. Holman and Michael R. Solomon, eds., *Advances in Consumer Research* 18 (Provo, UT: Association for Consumer Research, 1991): 364–371.

63. Anthony R. Pratkanis, Anthony G. Greenwald, Michael R. Leippe, and Michael H. Baumgardner, "In Search of Reliable Persuasion Effects: III. The Sleeper Effect Is Dead, Long Live the Sleeper Effect," *Journal of Personality & Social Psychology* 54 (1988): 203–218.

64. Stuart Elliott, "A Message that Tries to Blend In," *New York Times* (December 12, 2013), http://www.nyt.com/2013/12/13/business/media/a-message-that-tries-to-blend-in.html?_r=0, accessed February 23, 2015.

65. Stephanie Strom, "Nonprofit Punishes a 2nd Founder for Ruse," *New York Times* (January 15, 2008), www.nyt.com/2008/01/15/us/15givewell .html?ex=1201064400&en=97effb249, accessed January 15, 2008; Ross D. Petty and J. Craig Andrews, "Covert Marketing Unmasked: A Legal and Regulatory Guide for Practices That Mask Marketing Messages," *Journal of Public Policy & Marketing* (Spring 2008): 7–18; James B. Stewart, "Whole Foods CEO Threatens Merger, Fuels Arbitrage," *Smart Money* (July 18, 2007), www.smartmoney.com/investing/stocks/whole-foods-ceo-threatens-merger-fuels-arbitrage-21550/?hpadref=1, accessed June 4, 2009; Brian Morrissey, "'Influencer Programs' Likely to Spread," *Adweek* (March 2, 2009), http:// www.adweek.com/news/advertising-branding/influencer-programs-likely-spread-98542, accessed March 2, 2009; Katie Hafner, "Seeing Corporate Fingerprints in Wikipedia Edits," *New York Times* (August 19, 2007), www.nyt .com/2007/08/19/technology/19wikipedia.html?_r=1&oref=slogin, accessed August 19, 2007; Brian Bergstein, "New Tool Mines: Wikipedia Trustworthiness Software Analyzes Reputations of the Contributors Responsible for Entries," *MSNBC* (September 5, 2007), www.msnbc.msn.com/id/20604175, accessed September 5, 2007; http://wikiscanner.virgil.gr, accessed June 4, 2009.

66. Quoted in ".com Disclosures: How to Make Effective Disclosures in Digital Advertising," Federal Trade Commission (March 2013), https://www.ftc .gov/sites/default/files/attachments/press-releases/ftc-staff-revises-online-advertising-disclosure-guidelines/130312dotcomdisclosures.pdf, accessed March 31, 2015.

67. Ameet Sachdev, "FTC Cracks Down on Fake Online Endorsements: Agency Attempts to Punish Fake Reviews, Force Disclosure," *Chicago Tribune* (October 11, 2010), http://articles.chicagotribune.com/2010-10-11/business/ct-biz-1011-web-reviews-20101011_1_ftc-cracks–endorsements-mary-engle, accessed April 15, 2011.

68. "Robber Makes It Biggs in Ad," *Advertising Age* (May 29, 1989): 26.

69. Gaby Wilson, "A$AP Rocky Wears Throwback Tommy Hilfiger on Under the Influence of Music Tour," MTV.com (August 7, 2013), http://style.mtv .com/2013/08/07/asap-rocky-tommy-hilfiger/, accessed March 31, 2015; "Snoop Doggy Dogg aka Snoop Lion has Changed His Name to Snoopzilla," news.com.au (October 17, 2013), http://www.news.com.au/entertainment/music/snoop-doggy-dogg-aka-snoop-lion-has-changed-his-name-to-snoopzilla/story-e6frfn09-1226741490306, accessed March 31, 2015.

70. Alice H. Eagly, Andy Wood, and Shelly Chaiken, "Causal Inferences About Communicators and Their Effect in Opinion Change," *Journal of Personality & Social Psychology* 36, no. 4 (1978): 424–435.

71. Patrick Loughran, "Sex Pistol Sends Dairy Crest Butter Sales Soaring," *Times of London* (February 3, 2009), www.timesonline.co.uk, accessed February 4, 2009.

72. Claire Cain Miller and Vindu Goel, "Google to Sell Users' Endorsements," *New York Times* (October 11, 2013), http://www.nyt.com/2013/10/12/tech nology/google-sets-plan-to-sell-users-endorsements.html?pagewanted=1& ref=todayspaper, accessed February 19, 2015.

73. R. J. Fisher and Y. Ma, "The Price of Being Beautiful: Negative Effects of Attractiveness on Empathy for Children in Need," *Journal of Consumer Research* 41, no. 2 (2014): 436–450.

74. Brian Steinberg, "Bob Dylan Gets Tangled Up in Pink: Victoria's Secret Campaign Drafts Counterculture Hero; Just Like the Rolling Stones," *Wall Street Journal* (April 2, 2004): B3.

75. Robert Klara, "Brands by Bieber," *Brandweek* (January 1, 2011), http:// www.adweek.com/news/advertising-branding/brands-bieber-126241, accessed February 23, 2011.

76. Grant McCracken, "Who Is the Celebrity Endorser? Cultural Foundations of the Endorsement Process," *Journal of Consumer Research* 16, no. 3 (December 1989): 310–321.

77. Quoted in www.japander.com, accessed March 7, 2013.

78. Nat Ives, "Marketers Run to Pull the Plug When Celebrity Endorsers Say the Darnedest Things," *New York Times* (July 16, 2004), www.nyt.com, accessed July 16, 2004.

79. Judith A. Garretson and Scot Burton, "The Role of Spokescharacters as Advertisement and Package Cues in Integrated Marketing Communications," *Journal of Marketing* 69 (October, 2005): 118–132.

80. Jeff Bercovici, "America's Most Loved Spokescharacters," *Forbes* (March 14, 2011), http://www.forbes.com/2011/03/11/old-spice-snoopy-m-and-m-most-loved-spokescharacters.html, accessed April 30, 2011.

81. Natalie T. Wood and Michael R. Solomon, eds., *Virtual Social Identity* (Newport, CA: Sage, 2010).

82. Aner Sela, S. Christian Wheeler, and Gülen Sarial-Abi, "We Are Not The Same as You and I: Causal Effects of Minor Language Variations on Consumers' Attitudes Toward Brands," *Journal of Consumer Research* 3, no. 3 (2012): 644–661.

83. Xun Huang, Xiuping Li, and Meng Zhang, "'Seeing' the Social Roles of Brands: How Physical Positioning Influences Brand Evaluation," *Journal of Consumer Psychology* 23, no. 4 (2013): 509–514.

84. Kathy Crosett, "Consumers Confused by TV Commercials," *Adology* (October 4, 2010), http://www.marketingforecast.com/archives/7538, accessed May 30, 2011; David W. Stewart and David H. Furse, "The Effects of Television Advertising Execution on Recall, Comprehension, and Persuasion," *Psychology & Marketing* 2 (Fall 1985): 135–160.

85. Robert C. Grass and Wallace H. Wallace, "Advertising Communication: Print vs. TV," *Journal of Advertising Research* 14 (1974): 19–23.

86. Elizabeth C. Hirschman and Michael R. Solomon, "Utilitarian, Aesthetic, and Familiarity Responses to Verbal Versus Visual Advertisements," in Thomas C. Kinnear, ed., *Advances in Consumer Research* 11 (Provo, UT: Association for Consumer Research, 1984): 426–431.

87. Terry L. Childers and Michael J. Houston, "Conditions for a Picture-Superiority Effect on Consumer Memory," *Journal of Consumer Research* 11 (September 1984): 643–654.

88. Scott B. MacKenzie, "The Role of Attention in Mediating the Effect of Advertising on Attribute Importance," *Journal of Consumer Research* 13 (September 1986): 174–195.

89. Robert B. Zajonc, "Attitudinal Effects of Mere Exposure," *Journal of Personality & Social Psychology* 8 (1968): 1–29.

90. Giles D'Souza and Ram C. Rao, "Can Repeating an Advertisement More Frequently Than the Competition Affect Brand Preference in a Mature Market?" *Journal of Marketing* 59 (April 1995): 32–42.

91. George E. Belch, "The Effects of Television Commercial Repetition on Cognitive Response and Message Acceptance," *Journal of Consumer Research* 9 (June 1982): 56–65; Marian Burke and Julie Edell, "Ad Reactions Over Time: Capturing Changes in the Real World," *Journal of Consumer Research* 13 (June 1986): 114–118; Herbert Krugman, "Why Three Exposures May Be Enough," *Journal of Advertising Research* 12 (December 1972): 11–14.

92. Susannah Jacob, "The Power of Three: Three Is the Right Number for Persuasion, a Study Says," *New York Times* (January 3, 2014), http://www .nyt.com/2014/01/05/fashion/Three-Persuasion-The-Power-of-Three .html?ref=style, accessed January 30, 2015.

93. Robert F. Bornstein, "Exposure and Affect: Overview and Meta-Analysis of Research, 1968–1987," *Psychological Bulletin* 106, no. 2 (1989): 265–289; Arno Rethans, John Swasy, and Lawrence Marks, "Effects of Television Commercial Repetition, Receiver Knowledge, and Commercial Length: A Test of the Two-Factor Model," *Journal of Marketing Research* 23 (February 1986): 50–61.

94. Curtis P. Haugtvedt, David W. Schumann, Wendy L. Schneier, and Wendy L. Warren, "Advertising Repetition and Variation Strategies: Implications

for Understanding Attitude Strength," *Journal of Consumer Research* 21 (June 1994): 176–189.

95. John Paul Titlow, "At Pandora, Every Listener is a Test Subject," *Fast Company* (August 14, 2013), http://www.fastcolabs.com/3015729/in-pandoras-big-data-experiments-youre-just-another-lab-rat, accessed February 18, 2015.

96. Amit Bhattacharjee, Jonah Berger and Geeta Menon, "When Identity Marketing Backfires: Consumer Agency in Identity Expression," *Journal of Consumer Research* 41, no. 2 (2014): 294–309.

97. Pierre Chandon and Brian Wansink, "Is Obesity Caused by Calorie Underestimation? A Psychological Model of Meal Size Estimation," *Journal of Marketing Research* 44, no. 1 (2007):84–99; Nailya Ordabayeva and Pierre Chandon, "Predicting and Managing Consumers' Package Size Impressions," *Journal of Marketing* 77, no. 5 (2013): 123–137; Yann Cornil and Pierre Chandon, "Pleasure as a Substitute for Size: Using Multisensory Imagery to Increase Preferences for Smaller Food Portions," 2014; Yann Cornil and Pierrre Chandon, "From Fan to Fat? Vicarious Losing Increases Unhealthy Eating But Self-Affirmation Is an Effective Remedy," *Psychological Science* 24, no. 10 (2013): 1936–1946; Brian Wansink and Pierre Chandon, "Slim by Design: Redirecting the Accidental Drivers of Mindless Overeating," *Journal of Consulting and Clincial Psychology* 24, no. 3 (2014): 413–431.

98. Linda L. Golden and Mark I. Alpert, "Comparative Analysis of the Relative Effectiveness of One- and Two-Sided Communication for Contrasting Products," *Journal of Advertising* 16 (1987): 18–25; Michael A. Kamins, "Celebrity and Noncelebrity Advertising in a Two-Sided Context," *Journal of Advertising Research* 29 (June–July 1989): 34; Robert B. Settle and Linda L. Golden, "Attribution Theory and Advertiser Credibility," *Journal of Marketing Research* 11 (May 1974): 181–185.

99. Cf. Alan G. Sawyer, "The Effects of Repetition of Refutational and Supportive Advertising Appeals," *Journal of Marketing Research* 10 (February 1973): 23–33; George J. Szybillo and Richard Heslin, "Resistance to Persuasion: Inoculation Theory in a Marketing Context," *Journal of Marketing Research* 10 (November 1973): 396–403.

100. Rupal Parekh and Jean Halliday, "New Ad Introduces Consumers to 'New GM,'" *Advertising Age* (June 1, 2009), http://adage.com/article?article_id=137010, accessed June 6, 2009.

101. Uma R. Karmarkar and Zakary L. Tormala, "Believe Me, I Have No Idea What I'm Talking About: The Effects of Source Certainty on Consumer Involvement and Persuasion," *Journal of Consumer Research* 36 (April 2009): 1033–1049.

102. Golden and Alpert, "Comparative Analysis of the Relative Effectiveness of One- and Two-Sided Communication for Contrasting Products"; Gita Venkataramani Johar and Anne L. Roggeveen, "Changing False Beliefs from Repeated Advertising: The Role of Claim-Refutation Alignment," *Journal of Consumer Psychology* 17, no. 2 (2007): 118–127.

103. George E. Belch, Michael A. Belch, and Angelina Villareal, "Effects of Advertising Communications: Review of Research," in *Research in Marketing* 9 (Greenwich, CT: JAI Press, 1987): 59–117.

104. Frank R. Kardes, "Spontaneous Inference Processes in Advertising: The Effects of Conclusion Omission and Involvement on Persuasion," *Journal of Consumer Research* 15 (September 1988): 225–233.

105. Belch, Belch, and Villareal, "Effects of Advertising Communications: Review of Research"; Cornelia Pechmann and Gabriel Esteban, "Persuasion Processes Associated with Direct Comparative and Noncomparative Advertising and Implications for Advertising Effectiveness," *Journal of Consumer Psychology* 2, no. 4 (1994): 403–432.

106. Bruce Horovitz, "Sodastream's Super Bowl Spot Gets Rejected—Again," *USA Today* (January 25, 2014), http://www.usatoday.com/story/money/business/2014/01/25/5-biggest-advertisers-going-for-it-in-super-bowl/4835695//business/2014/01/24/sodastream-banned-super-bowl-ad-coke-pepsi-scarlett-johannson/4838575/, accessed February 16, 2015.

107. Cornelia Dröge and Rene Y. Darmon, "Associative Positioning Strategies Through Comparative Advertising: Attribute vs. Overall Similarity Approaches," *Journal of Marketing Research* 24 (1987): 377–389; Darrell Muehling and Norman Kangun, "The Multidimensionality of Comparative Advertising: Implications for the FTC," *Journal of Public Policy & Marketing* (1985): 112–128; Beth A. Walker and Helen H. Anderson, "Reconceptualizing Comparative Advertising: A Framework and Theory of Effects," in Rebecca H. Holman and Michael R. Solomon, eds., *Advances in Consumer Research* 18 (Provo, UT: Association for Consumer Research, 1991), 342–347; William L. Wilkie and Paul W. Farris, "Comparison Advertising: Problems and Potential," *Journal of Marketing* 39 (October 1975): 7–15; R. G. Wyckham, "Implied Superiority Claims," *Journal of Advertising Research* (February–March 1987): 54–63.

108. Stephen A. Goodwin and Michael Etgar, "An Experimental Investigation of Comparative Advertising: Impact of Message Appeal, Information Load, and Utility of Product Class," *Journal of Marketing Research* 17 (May 1980): 187–202; Gerald J. Gorn and Charles B. Weinberg, "The Impact of Comparative Advertising on Perception and Attitude: Some Positive Findings," *Journal of Consumer Research* 11 (September 1984): 719–727; Terence A. Shimp and David C. Dyer, "The Effects of Comparative Advertising Mediated by Market Position of Sponsoring Brand," *Journal of Advertising* 3 (Summer 1978): 13–19; R. Dale Wilson, "An Empirical

Evaluation of Comparative Advertising Messages: Subjects' Responses to Perceptual Dimensions," in B. B. Anderson, ed., *Advances in Consumer Research* 3 (Ann Arbor, MI: Association for Consumer Research, 1976), 53–57.

109. Quoted in Ian McGugan, "The Ice-Bucket Racket," *New York Times Magazine* (November 14, 2014), http://www.nyt.com/2014/11/16/magazine/the-ice-bucket-racket.html?module=Search&mabReward=relbias%3Ar%2C%7B%221%22%3A%22RI%3A10%22%7D&_r=0, accessed January 30, 2015.

110. Geoffrey A. Fowler, "Asia's Mobile Ads," *Wall Street Journal* (April 25, 2005), www.wsj.com, accessed April 25, 2005; Brooks Barnes, "Coming to Your Cell: Paris Hilton," *Wall Street Journal* (March 17, 2005), www.wsj.com, accessed March 17, 2005; Alice Z. Cuneo, "Marketers Dial in to Messaging," *Advertising Age* (November 1, 2004): 18; Stephen Baker and Heather Green, "Blogs Will Change Your Business," *BusinessWeek* (May 2, 2005): 56.

111. http://www.iamtryingtobelieve.com/, accessed March 31, 2015; Matt Linderman, "Year Zero' project = "the way a viral campaign should be run," signalvnoise (May 1, 2007), https://signalvnoise.com/posts/403-year-zero-project-the-way-a-viral-campaign-should-be-run, accessed March 31, 2015.

112. Jon Zahlaway, "Nine Inch Nails' *Year Zero* Plot Hits the Web," *SoundSpike*, February 22, 2007, http://www.livedaily.com/news/11570.html?t=102, May 30, 2011.

113. Erica Orden, "This Book Brought to You by …," *Wall Street Journal* (April 26, 2011), http://professional.wsj.com/article/SB10001424052748704132204576285372092660548.html?mg=reno-WallStreetJournal, accessed April 28, 2011.

114. Michael R. Solomon and Basil G. Englis, "Reality Engineering: Blurring the Boundaries Between Marketing and Popular Culture," *Journal of Current Issues & Research in Advertising* 16, no. 2 (Fall 1994): 1–17.

115. Austin Bunn, "Not Fade Away," *New York Times* (December 2, 2002), www.nyt.com, accessed December 2, 2002.

116. Marc Santora, "Circle the Block, Cabby, My Show's On," *New York Times* (January 16, 2003), www.nyt.com, accessed January 16, 2003; Wayne Parry, "Police May Sell Ad Space," *Montgomery Advertiser* (November 20, 2002): A4.

117. This process is described more fully in Michael R. Solomon, *Conquering Consumerspace: Marketing Strategies for a Branded World* (New York: AMACOM, 2003); cf. also T. Bettina Cornwell and Bruce Keillor, "Contemporary Literature and the Embedded Consumer Culture: The Case of Updike's Rabbit," in Roger J. Kruez and Mary Sue MacNealy, eds., *Empirical Approaches to Literature and Aesthetics: Advances in Discourse Processes* 52 (Norwood, NJ: Ablex, 1996), 559–572; Monroe Friedman, "The Changing Language of a Consumer Society: Brand Name Usage in Popular American Novels in the Postwar Era," *Journal of Consumer Research* 11 (March 1985): 927–937; Monroe Friedman, "Commercial Influences in the Lyrics of Popular American Music of the Postwar Era," *Journal of Consumer Affairs* 20 (Winter 1986): 193.

118. Stuart Elliott, "Leaving Behind Malibu in Search of a New Dream Home," *New York Times* (February 6, 2013), http://www.nyt.com/2013/02/07/business/media/barbie-to-sell-her-malibu-dreamhouse.html?_r=0, accessed February 17, 2013.

119. http://www.quill.com/content/index/authentic-dunder-mifflin-office-supplies/default.cshtml, accessed April 1, 2015; Stuart Elliott, "Expanding Line of Dunder Mifflin Products Shows Success in Reverse Product Placement," *New York Times* (November 23, 2012), http://mediadecoder.blogs.nyt.com/2012/11/23/expanding-line-of-dunder-mifflin-products-shows-success-in-reverse-product–placement/, accessed February 17, 2013.

120. Mark J. Miller, "Hologram Virtual Performances Put Dead Celebs on the Comeback Trail," *Brandchannel* (June 19, 2012), http://www.brandchannel.com/home/post/2012/06/19/Hologram-Virtual–Performances-061912.aspx, accessed February 17, 2013.

121. Mark J. Miller, "007 Branding: Jaguar Land Rover Joins SPECTRE Product Placement Roster," *Brandchannel* (February 10, 2015), http://www.brandchannel.com/home/post/2015/02/10/150210-James-Bond-SPECTRE-Product-Placement.aspx, accessed February 23, 2015.

122. Abe Sauer, "Announcing the 2015 Brandcameo Product Placement Awards," (February 20, 2015), *Brandchannel*, http://www.brandchannel.com/home/post/150220-2015-Brandcameo-Product-Placement-Awards.aspx, accessed March 31, 2015.

123. Fara Warner, "Why It's Getting Harder to Tell the Shows from the Ads," *Wall Street Journal* (June 15, 1995): B1.

124. Quoted in Simona Covel, "Bag Borrow or Steal Lands the Role of a Lifetime, Online Retailer Hopes to Profit from Mention in 'Sex and the City,'" *Wall Street Journal* (May 28, 2008), http://online.wsj.com/article/SB121184149016921095.html?mod=rss_media_and_marketing, accessed May 28, 2008; www.bagborroworsteal.com, accessed April 1, 2015.

125. "Top 10 Product Placements in First Half of '07," *Marketing Daily* (September 26, 2007), www.mediapost.com, accessed September 26, 2007.

126. Brian Steinberg, "Getting Izze to Izzie on 'Grey's Anatomy': How PepsiCo Placed Beverage Brand in ABC Show without Paying a Thing," *Advertising Age* (April 1, 2009), www.adage.com, accessed April 1, 2009.

127. Claire Atkinson, "Ad Intrusion Up, Say Consumers," *Advertising Age* (January 6, 2003): 1.

128. Motoko Rich, "Product Placement Deals Make Leap from Film to Books," *New York Times* (June 12, 2006), www.nyt.com, accessed June 12, 2006.

129. Cristel Antonia Russell, "Investigating the Effectiveness of Product Placements in Television Shows: The Role of Modality and Plot Connection Congruence on Brand Memory and Attitude," *Journal of Consumer Research* 29 (December 2002): 306–318; Denise E. DeLorme and Leonard N. Reid, "Moviegoers' Experiences and Interpretations of Brands in Films Revisited," *Journal of Advertising* 28, no. 2 (1999): 71–90; Barbara B. Stern and Cristel A. Russell, "Consumer Responses to Product Placement in Television Sitcoms: Genre, Sex and Consumption," *Consumption, Markets & Culture* 7 (December 2004): 371–394.

130. Louise Story, "More Marketers Are Grabbing the Attention of Players During Online Games," *New York Times* (January 24, 2007), www.nyt.com, accessed January 24, 2007; Shankar Gupta, "King of the Advergames," www.mediapost.com, accessed December 22, 2006; "Plinking," *Fast Company* (April 2007): 31; Sarah Sennott, "Gaming the Ad," *Newsweek* (January 31, 2005): E2; "Advertisements Insinuated into Video Games," *New York Times* (October 18, 2004), www.nyt.com, accessed October 18, 2004; Jack Loechner, "Advergaming," *Research Brief* (October 24, 2007), http://www.mediapost.com/publications/?fa=Articles.showArticle&art_aid=69570&passFuseAction=PublicationsSearch.showSearchReslts&art_searched=&page_number=0, accessed September 13, 2011; Tim Zuckert, "Become One with the Game, Games Offer Brands a Unique Way to Be the Entertainment—Not Just Sponsor It," *Advertising Age* (June 16, 2008), www.adage.com, accessed June 16, 2008.

131. Barry Meier and Andrew Martin, "Real and Virtual Firearms Nurture a Marketing Link," *New York Times* (December 24, 2012), http://www.nyt.com/2012/12/25/business/real-and-virtual-firearms-nurture-marketing-link.html, accessed February 17, 2013.

132. Nick Wingfield, "Sony's PS3 to Get In-Game Ads," *Wall Street Journal* (June 4, 2008): B7; Jeffrey Bardzell, Shaowen Bardzell, and Tyler Pace, *Player Engagement and In-Game Advertising* (November 23, 2008), http://class.classmatandread.net/pp/oto.pdf, accessed September 13, 2011.

133. Louise Kramer, "In a Battle of Toothpastes, It's Information vs. Emotion," *New York Times* (January 17, 2007): C6.

134. Hubert A. Zielske, "Does Day-After Recall Penalize 'Feeling' Ads?" *Journal of Advertising Research* 22 (1982): 19–22.

135. Allessandra Galloni, "Lee's Cheeky Ads Are Central to New European Campaign," *Wall Street Journal* (March 15, 2002), www.wsj.com, accessed March 15, 2002.

136. Belch, Belch, and Villareal, "Effects of Advertising Communications: Review of Research"; Alice E. Courtney and Thomas W. Whipple, "Sex Stereotyping in Advertising," *Signs* 10 (Spring 1985): 583–585; Michael S. LaTour, "Female Nudity in Print Advertising: An Analysis of Gender Differences in Arousal and Ad Response," *Psychology & Marketing* 7, no. 1 (1990): 65–81; B. G. Yovovich, "Sex in Advertising—The Power and the Perils," *Advertising Age* (May 2, 1983): M4–M5. For an interesting interpretive analysis, see Richard Elliott and Mark Ritson, "Practicing Existential Consumption: The Lived Meaning of Sexuality in Advertising," in Frank R. Kardes and Mita Sujan, eds., *Advances in Consumer Behavior* 22 (1995): 740–745; Jaideep Sengupta and Darren W. Dahl, "Gender-Related Reactions to Gratuitous Sex Appeals," *Journal of Consumer Psychology* 18 (2008): 62–78.

137. Penny M. Simpson, Steve Horton, and Gene Brown, "Male Nudity in Advertisements: A Modified Replication and Extension of Gender and Product Effects," *Journal of the Academy of Marketing Science* 24, no. 3 (1996): 257–262.

138. Jaideep Sengupta and Darren W. Dahl, "Gender-Related Reactions to Gratuitous Sex Appeals," *Journal of Consumer Psychology* 18 (2008): 62–78; Darren W. Dahl, Jaideep Sengupta, and Kathleen Vohs, "Sex in Advertising: Gender Differences and the Role of Relationship Commitment," *Journal of Consumer Research* 36 (August 2009): 215–231.

139. Mark Dolliver, "Seeing Too Much Sex in Ads, or Too Little?" *Adweek* (December 6, 2010), http://teens.adweek.com/aw/content_display/datacenter/research/e3i5b647315f27310efc8f6df37dcb48e9b, accessed April 15, 2011.

140. Michael S. LaTour and Tony L. Henthorne, "Ethical Judgments of Sexual Appeals in Print Advertising," *Journal of Advertising* 23, no. 3 (September 1994): 81–90.

141. "Does Sex Really Sell?" *Adweek* (October 17, 2005): 17.

142. Katharine Q. Seelye, "Metamucil Ad Featuring Old Faithful Causes a Stir," *New York Times* (January 19, 2003), www.nyt.com, accessed January 19, 2003.

143. Thomas J. Madden, "Humor in Advertising: An Experimental Analysis," working paper, no. 83-27, University of Massachusetts, 1984; Thomas J. Madden and Marc G. Weinberger, "The Effects of Humor on Attention in Magazine Advertising," *Journal of Advertising* 11, no. 3 (1982): 8–14; Marc G. Weinberger and Harlan E. Spotts, "Humor in U.S. Versus U.K. TV Commercials: A Comparison," *Journal of Advertising* 18 (1989): 39–44; see

also Ashesh Mukherjee and Laurette Dubé, "The Use of Humor in Threat-Related Advertising" (unpublished manuscript, McGill University, June 2002).

144. David Gardner, "The Distraction Hypothesis in Marketing," *Journal of Advertising Research* 10 (1970): 25–30.

145. Chris Abraham, "Global Web Means Your 'Fart Jokes' Can Be Heard Out of Context," *Advertising Age* (June 15, 2009), http://adage.com/digitalnext/article?article_id=137273, accessed June 16, 2009.

146. U.S. Gives Up on Graphic Cigarette Package Warnings – for Now, *Advertising Age* (March 20, 2013), http://adage.com/article/news/u-s-graphic-cigarette-package-warnings/240436/, accessed April 1, 2015.

147. Michael L. Ray and William L. Wilkie, "Fear: The Potential of an Appeal Neglected by Marketing," *Journal of Marketing* 34, no. 1 (1970): 54–62.

148. Punam Anand Keller and Lauren Goldberg Block, "Increasing the Effectiveness of Fear Appeals: The Effect of Arousal and Elaboration," *Journal of Consumer Research* 22 (March 1996): 448–459.

149. Ronald Paul Hill, "An Exploration of the Relationship Between AIDS-Related Anxiety and the Evaluation of Condom Advertisements," *Journal of Advertising* 17, no. 4 (1988): 35–42.

150. Randall Rothenberg, "Talking Too Tough on Life's Risks?" *New York Times* (February 16, 1990): D1.

151. Denise D. Schoenbachler and Tommy E. Whittler, "Adolescent Processing of Social and Physical Threat Communications," *Journal of Advertising* 25, no. 4 (Winter 1996): 37–54.

152. Barbara B. Stern, "Medieval Allegory: Roots of Advertising Strategy for the Mass Market," *Journal of Marketing* 52 (July 1988): 84–94.

153. Edward F. McQuarrie and David Glen Mick, "On Resonance: A Critical Pluralistic Inquiry into Advertising Rhetoric," *Journal of Consumer Research* 19 (September 1992): 180–197.

154. Cf. Linda M. Scott, "The Troupe: Celebrities as Dramatis Personae in Advertisements," in Rebecca H. Holman and Michael R. Solomon, eds., *Advances in Consumer Research* 18 (Provo, UT: Association for Consumer Research, 1991): 355–363; Barbara Stern, "Literary Criticism and Consumer Research: Overview and Illustrative Analysis," *Journal of Consumer Research* 16 (1989): 322–334; Judith Williamson, *Decoding Advertisements* (Boston: Marion Boyars, 1978).

155. John Deighton, Daniel Romer, and Josh McQueen, "Using Drama to Persuade," *Journal of Consumer Research* 16 (December 1989): 335–343.

156. Richard E. Petty, John T. Cacioppo, and David Schumann, "Central and Peripheral Routes to Advertising Effectiveness: The Moderating Role of Involvement," *Journal of Consumer Research* 10, no. 2 (1983): 135–146.

157. Jerry C. Olson, Daniel R. Toy, and Philip A. Dover, "Do Cognitive Responses Mediate the Effects of Advertising Content on Cognitive Structure?" *Journal of Consumer Research* 9, no. 3 (1982): 245–262.

158. Julie A. Edell and Andrew A. Mitchell, "An Information Processing Approach to Cognitive Responses," in S. C. Jain, ed., *Research Frontiers in Marketing: Dialogues and Directions* (Chicago, IL: American Marketing Association, 1978): 178-183.

159. Richard E. Petty, John T. Cacioppo, Constantine Sedikides, and Alan J. Strathman, "Affect and Persuasion: A Contemporary Perspective," *American Behavioral Scientist* 31, no. 3 (1988): 355–371.

160. Stuart Elliott, "A Message That Tries to Blend In," *New York Times* (December 12, 2013), http://www.nyt.com/2013/12/13/business/media/a-message-that-tries-to-blend-in.html?_r=0, accessed February 23, 2015.

161. Kunur Patel, "Apple, Campbell's Say iAds Twice as Effective as TV," *Ad Age Digital* (February 3, 2011), http://adage.com/article/digital/apple-campbell-s-iads-effective-tv/148630/, accessed April 15, 2011.

162. Claire Cain Miller and Vindu Goel, "Google to Sell Users' Endorsements," *New York Times* (October 11, 2013), http://www.nyt.com/2013/10/12/technology/google-sets-plan-to-sell-users-endorsements.html?pagewanted=1&ref=todayspaper, accessed February 19, 2015.

163. Warc, "Celebrity Endorsement: The Trigonometry of Talent," http://www.warc.com/Topics/AdmapSeptember2012.topic.

164. Rob Walker, "The Gifted Ones," *New York Times Magazine* (November 14, 2004), www.nyt.com, accessed September 29, 2007.

165. Center for Media Research, "Product Placement, Sampling, and Word-of-Mouth Collectively Influence Consumer Purchases" (October 22, 2008), www.mediapost.com, accessed October 22, 2008; Brian Steinberg and Suzanne Vranica, "Prime-Time TV's New Guest Stars: Products," *Wall Street Journal* (January 12, 2004), www.wsj.com, accessed January 12, 2004; Karlene Lukovitz, "'Storyline' Product Placements Gaining on Cable," *Marketing Daily* (October 5, 2007), www.mediapost.com, accessed October 5, 2007.

166. Sascha Topolinski, Sandy Lindner, and Anna Freudenberg, "Popcorn in the Cinema: Oral Interference Sabotages Advertising Effects," *Journal of Consumer Psychology* 24, no. 2 (April 2014): 169–176.

Chapter 9 • Decision Making

Source: stefanocapra/Fotolia

Richard has had it! There's only so much longer he can go on watching TV on his tiny, antiquated set. It was bad enough trying to squint at *The Walking Dead*. The final straw was when he couldn't tell the Titans from the Jaguars during an NFL football game. When he went next door to watch the second half on Mark's home theater setup, he finally realized what he was missing. Budget or not, it was time to act: A man has to have his priorities.

Where to start looking? The Web, naturally. Richard checks out a few comparison-shopping Web sites, including pricegrabber.com and bizrate.com. After he narrows down his options, he ventures out to check on a few sets in person. He figures he'll probably get a decent selection (and an affordable price) at one of those huge "big box" stores. Arriving at Zany Zack's Appliance Emporium, Richard heads straight for the Video Zone in the back; he barely notices the rows of toasters, microwave ovens, and stereos on his way. Within minutes, a smiling salesperson in a cheap suit accosts him. Even though he could use some help, Richard tells the salesperson he's only browsing. He figures these guys don't know what they're talking about, and they're simply out to make a sale no matter what.

Richard examines some of the features on the 60-inch flatscreens. He knew his friend Evey had a set by Prime Wave that she really liked, and his sister Alex warned him to stay away from the Kamashita. Although Richard finds a Prime Wave model loaded to the max with features such as a sleep timer, on-screen programming menu, cable-compatible tuner, and picture-in-picture, he chooses the less expensive Precision 2000X because it has one feature that really catches his fancy: stereo broadcast reception.

Later that day, Richard is a happy man as he sits in his easy chair and watches Sheldon match wits with Leonard, Howard, and the others on *The Big Bang Theory*. If he's going to be a couch potato, he's going in style.

What's Your Problem?

OBJECTIVE 9-1
The three categories of consumer decision making are cognitive, habitual, and affective.

Richard's decision represented his response to a problem. In fact *every* consumer decision we make is a response to a problem. Of course, the type and scope of these problems varies enormously; our needs range from simple physiological priorities such as quenching thirst to whether we will spend our hard-earned money on a television to abstract intellectual or aesthetic quandaries such as choosing a college major—or perhaps what to wear to that upcoming Rihanna concert.

Because some purchase decisions are more important than others, the amount of effort we put into each differs. Sometimes the decision-making process is almost automatic; we seem to make snap judgments based on little information. At other times it resembles a full-time job. A person may literally spend days or weeks agonizing over an important purchase such as a new home, a car, or even an iPhone versus a Samsung Galaxy.

We make some decisions thoughtfully and rationally as we carefully weigh the pros and cons of different choices. In other cases we let our emotions guide us to one choice over another as we react to a problem with enthusiasm, joy, or even disgust. Still other actions actually *contradict* what those rational models predict. For example, **purchase momentum** occurs when our initial impulse purchases actually increase the likelihood that we will buy even more (instead of less as we satisfy our needs); it's like we get "revved up" and plunge into a spending spree (we've all been there!).[1]

Hyperchoice

Given the range of problems we all confront in our lives, clearly it is difficult to apply a one-size-fits-all explanation to the complexities of consumer behavior. Things get even more complicated when we realize just how many choices we have to make in today's information-rich environment. Ironically, for many of us one of our biggest problems is not having too few choices, but rather too many.

This condition of **consumer hyperchoice** forces us to make repeated decisions that may drain psychological energy while decreasing our abilities to make smart choices.[2] A study conducted in a grocery store illustrates how having too much can handicap our thought processes. Shoppers tried samples of flavored fruit jams in two different conditions: in the "limited choice" condition they picked from six flavors, whereas those in the "extensive choice" group saw 24 flavors. Thirty percent of consumers in the limited group actually bought a jar of jam as a result, and a paltry 3 percent of those in the extensive group did.

Part of what we're going to discuss in this chapter already is familiar ground to you. In Chapter 4 we reviewed approaches to learning that link options to outcomes, where over time we come to link certain choices to good or bad results. In Chapter 5 we talked about affective decision making; how our emotional responses drive many of our choices. And, in Chapter 8 we reviewed three hierarchies of effects, or the sequence of steps involving thinking, feeling, and eventually doing. These ideas really relate to types of decision making because they remind us that depending on the situation and the importance of what we're dealing with, our choices can be dominated by "hot" emotions, "cold" information processing, or even "lukewarm" snap decisions. Figure 9.1 summarizes the three "buckets" of consumer decision making.

Figure 9.1 THE THREE "BUCKETS" OF CONSUMER DECISION MAKING

Cognitive — deliberate, rational, sequential

Habitual — behavioral, unconscious, automatic

Affective — emotional, instantaneous

Researchers now realize that decision makers actually possess a *repertoire* of strategies. The perspective of **constructive processing** argues that we evaluate the effort we'll need to make a particular choice and then tailor the amount of cognitive "effort" we expend to get the job done.[3] When the task requires a well-thought-out, rational approach, we'll invest the brainpower to do it. Otherwise, we look for shortcuts such as "just do what I usually do," or perhaps we make "gut" decisions based on our emotional reactions. In some cases, we actually create a **mental budget** that helps us to estimate what we will consume over time so that we can regulate what we do in the present. If the dieter knows he will be chowing down at a big BBQ tomorrow, he may decide to skip that tempting candy bar today.[4]

Self-Regulation

The buckets of decision making don't necessarily work independently of one another. Think for example about Orlando, a 28-year-old marketing manager who has decided to embark on a weight-loss program. The pressure is on to drop the pounds before he marries Amanda this summer. Orlando knows he needs a plan if he has any chance to succeed.

A person's efforts to change or maintain his or her actions over time, whether these involve dieting, living on a budget, or training to run a marathon, involve careful planning that is a form of **self-regulation**. If we have a self-regulatory strategy, this means that we specify in advance how we want to respond in certain situations. These "if-then" plans or **implementation intentions** may dictate how much weight we give to different kinds of information (emotional or cognitive), a timetable to carry out a decision, or even how we will deal with disruptive influences that might interfere with our plans (like a bossy salesperson who tries to steer us to a different choice).[5]

Orlando may engage in cognitive decision making as he carefully selects a diet and perhaps compiles a list of foods he will "ban" from his kitchen. In addition, he may have to recognize that he has a behavioral pattern of snacking on junk food in the mid-afternoon whether he's really hungry or not. Simple, but powerful, behavioral cues in the environment like that Snickers bar sitting on his coworker Arya's desk can lead us to quick and sometimes rash actions (how will Orlando explain the "disappearance" of that candy bar to Arya?) He may also have to recognize that some emotional "triggers" set him off so when his boss yells at him his first response is to reach for the sweets to cheer himself up.

Orlando may have to "argue" with himself as he weighs the long-term benefits of a successful diet against short-term temptations. In some cases, this involves some creative tinkering with the facts—for example, consumers engage in **counteractive construal** when they exaggerate the negative aspects of behaviors that will interfere with the ultimate goal.[6] Orlando may inflate the number of calories in the snack to help him to resist its lure. He may even go public with his weight loss plan by posting his weekly weigh-in on a phone app like DietBet so that others can watch his progress—and even bet on his success or failure.[7]

Dynamic speed displays provide a feedback loop to help drivers regulate their speed.
Source: cre250/Fotolia.

In recent years, researchers and marketers have become more aware of the role they can play in changing consumer behavior by helping people to regulate their own actions. This help may take the form of simple feedback like a phone app for dieters or perhaps a wearable computing device like the Fitbit that tells you how many steps you take in a day (and how many more you should take). These applications provide a **feedback loop** to help with self-regulation. The basic premise is amazingly simple: Provide people with information about their actions in real time, and then give them a chance to change those actions so that you push them to improve. A common feedback loop we increasingly see on highways comes from those "dynamic speed displays" that use a radar sensor to flash "Your Speed" when you pass one. This isn't new information; all you have to do is look at

CB AS I SEE IT

Wendy Liu, University of California, San Diego

One of the toughest tasks for a consumer is to exert self-control in order to achieve some long-term results. For example, one may wish to save money for a down payment on a house, or to keep a healthy diet and exercise routine for long-term fitness. The conventional wisdom says that planning can help people achieve these long-term goals. For example, one can plan out exactly how much to spend in a given month, and such a budget will help keep one's spending in check. One can also plan out one's food consumption the next day, in the hopes that one will stick to the plan and stay on track towards one's fitness goal. But if only self-control was this easy! Alas, the world is filled with temptations that conspire to lead us astray, and as we all have personally experienced, it's much easier to make a great plan of self-control than to carry out the plan.

Recent research has added deeper understanding to the art and science of goal setting and planning, as it finds that all plans are not created equal. Whereas some planning activities facilitate self-control, others might actually hinder self-control efforts. Further, people in different circumstances may need different kinds of planning.

For example, my colleague and I asked one group of study participants to make a detailed plan for their food intake for the day, whereas another group were not asked to make such a plan. Looking at their plans, we saw that everyone made fairly healthy plans. Thus everyone had great intentions. The key is, would they stick to their plans when faced with a temptation?

Later we offered all participants an unhealthy snack. Was the group who planned better able to resist the snack, compared to those who didn't plan? What we found is that the effectiveness of planning depended upon the current fitness status of the participants; in particular, how far the person is from his or her goal weight. For those participants who are pretty close to their goal weight (i.e., only a couple of pounds to lose), planning indeed facilitated self-control as those who planned were less likely to take the snack than those who did not plan. However, among those who are far away from their goal weight, the concrete planning actually backfired; those who planned were even more likely than those who didn't plan to take the snack.

Why is this happening? We found that for those who are far from their goal weight, making a concrete, detailed plan further highlighted for them how difficult it would be for them to lose weight, and they became demotivated to stick to their plan. In general, researchers have found that nearness to the goal is a significant differentiator for self-control strategies. Strategies that work for those with only one mile to walk differ from that for those with a mountain to climb.

---

your speedometer to know the same thing. Yet on average these displays result in a 10 percent reduction in driving speed among motorists for several miles following exposure to the feedback loop.[8]

Now, the bad news: As any frustrated dieter knows, self-regulation doesn't necessarily work. Just because we devise a well-meaning strategy doesn't mean we'll follow it. Sometimes our best-laid intentions go awry literally because we're too tired to fight temptation. Research shows that our ability to self-regulate declines as the day goes on. The **Morning Morality Effect** shows that people are more likely to cheat, lie, or even commit fraud in the afternoon than in the morning. Scientists know that the part of the brain they call the **executive control center** that we use for important decision making, including moral judgments, can be worn down or distracted even by simple tasks like memorizing numbers.[9] As one researcher nicely put it, "To the extent that you're cognitively tired, you're more likely to give in to the devil on your shoulder."[10]

Other studies show that, ironically the act of planning itself can undermine our ability to attain goals. When a person is not happy with his or her progress toward a goal like weight loss, the act of thinking about what he or she needs to do to improve performance can cause emotional distress. This angst in turn results in less self-control.[11] As we saw in the last chapter's discussion of attitudes and behavior, "the road to hell is paved with good intentions!"

OBJECTIVE 9-2

A cognitive purchase decision is the outcome of a series of stages that results in the selection of one product over competing options

Cognitive Decision Making

Traditionally, consumer researchers approached decision making from a **rational perspective**. According to this view, people calmly and carefully integrate as much information as possible with what they already know about a product, painstakingly weigh the pluses and minuses of each alternative, and arrive at a satisfactory decision. This kind of careful, deliberate thinking is especially relevant to activities such as financial planning that call for a lot of attention to detail and many choices that impact a consumer's quality of life.[13] When marketing managers believe that their customers in fact do undergo this kind of planning, they should carefully study steps in decision making to understand just how consumers weigh information, form beliefs about options, and choose criteria they use to select one option over others. With these insights in hand, they can develop products and promotional strategies that supply the specific information people look for in the most effective formats.[14]

Steps in the Cognitive Decision-Making Process

Let's think about Richard's process of buying a new TV that we described at the beginning of the chapter. He didn't suddenly wake up and crave a new flatscreen. Richard went through several steps between the time he felt the need to replace his TV and when he actually brought one home. We describe these steps as (1) problem recognition, (2) information search, (3) evaluation of alternatives, and (4) product choice. Of course, as we saw in Chapter 4, after we make a decision, its outcome affects the final step in the process, in which learning occurs based on how well the choice worked out. This learning process in turn influences the likelihood that we'll make the same choice the next time the need for a similar decision occurs. And so on and so on. Figure 9.2 provides an overview of this decision-making process. Let's briefly look at each step.

Step 1: Problem Recognition

Ford's plan to promote its Fusion hybrid model focused on people who aren't thinking about buying a new car—at least not right now. Its TV commercials target what the auto industry terms the "upper funnel," or potential buyers down the road. Ford's research found that a large number of U.S. drivers still are unaware of the Fusion. The company is confident that it can close sales if and when customers decide to buy a new car. But, its weak spot is to get people into the frame of mind where they want to do that. To create desire where none yet exists, visitors to a special Web site entered to win a trip and a new Fusion. Ford publicized the sweepstakes on Twitter and Facebook; during the first two weeks of the promotion, almost 70,000 people requested more information about the car.[15]

Problem recognition occurs at what Ford terms the upper funnel, when we experience a significant difference between our current state of affairs and some state we desire. As we noted at the beginning of the chapter, this *problem* requires a *solution*. A person who unexpectedly runs out of gas on the highway has a problem, as does the person who becomes dissatisfied with the image of his car, even though there is nothing mechanically wrong with it. Although the quality of Richard's TV had not changed, he altered his *standard of comparison*, and as a result he had a new problem to solve: how to improve his viewing experience.

Figure 9.2 STAGES IN CONSUMER DECISION MAKING

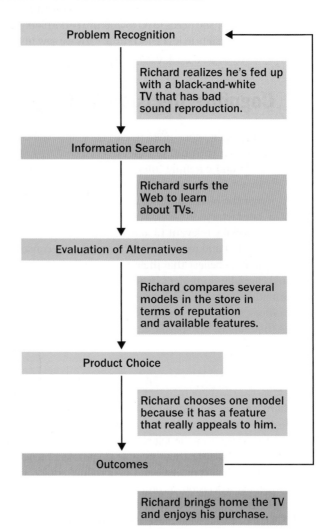

Marketing Pitfall

Product labels assist us with problem solving, but some are more useful than others. Here are some examples of the not-so-helpful variety:[20]

- Instructions for folding up a portable baby carriage: "Step 1: Remove baby."
- On a Conair Pro Style 1600 hair dryer: "WARNING: Do not use in shower. Never use while sleeping."
- At a rest stop on a Wisconsin highway: "Do not eat urinal cakes."
- On a bag of Fritos: "You could be a winner! No purchase necessary. Details inside."
- On some Swanson frozen dinners: "Serving suggestion: Defrost."
- On Tesco's Tiramisu dessert (printed on bottom of box): "Do not turn upside down."
- On Marks & Spencer bread pudding: "Product will be hot after heating."
- On packaging for a Rowenta iron: "Do not iron clothes on body."
- On Nytol sleeping aid: "Warning: May cause drowsiness."

Figure 9.3 shows that a problem arises in one of two ways. The person who runs out of gas experiences a decline in the quality of his *actual state* (*need recognition*). In contrast, the person who craves a newer, flashier car moves his *ideal state* (*opportunity recognition*) upward. Either way, there is a gulf between the actual state and the ideal state.[16] Richard perceived a problem because of opportunity recognition: He moved his ideal state upward in terms of the quality of TV reception he craved.

Step 2: Information Search

Once a consumer recognizes a problem, he or she needs the 411 to solve it. **Information search** is the process by which we survey the environment for appropriate data to make a reasonable decision. You might recognize a need and then search the marketplace for specific information (a process we call *prepurchase search*). However, many of us, especially veteran shoppers, enjoy browsing just for the fun of it or because we like to stay up to date on what's happening in the marketplace. Those shopaholics engage in *ongoing search*.[17]

As a general rule, we search more when the purchase is important, when we have more of a need to learn more about the purchase, or when it's easy to obtain the relevant information.[18] Consumers differ in the amount of search they tend to undertake, regardless of the product category in question. All things equal, younger, better-educated people who enjoy the shopping/fact-finding process tend to conduct more information searches. Women are more inclined to search than are men, as are those who place greater value on style and the image they present.[19]

Figure 9.3 PROBLEM RECOGNITION: SHIFTS IN ACTUAL OR IDEAL STATES

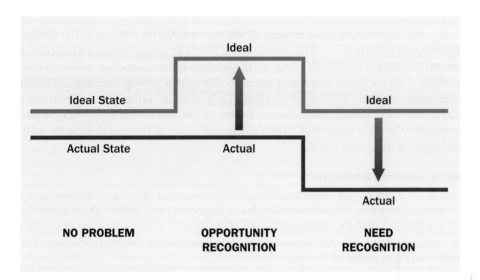

Does knowing something about the product make it more or less likely that we will engage in search? The answer to this question isn't as obvious as it first appears: Product experts and novices use different strategies when they make decisions. "Newbies" who know little about a product should be the most motivated to find out more about it. However, experts are more familiar with the product category, and thus they should be better able to understand the meaning of any new product information they might acquire.

So, who searches more? The answer is neither: Search tends to be greatest among those consumers who are *moderately knowledgeable* about the product. Typically we find an inverted-U relationship between knowledge and search effort, as Figure 9.4 shows. People with limited expertise may not feel they are competent to search extensively. In fact, they may not even know where to start. Richard, who did not spend a lot of time

Figure 9.4 THE RELATIONSHIP BETWEEN AMOUNT OF INFORMATION SEARCH AND PRODUCT KNOWLEDGE

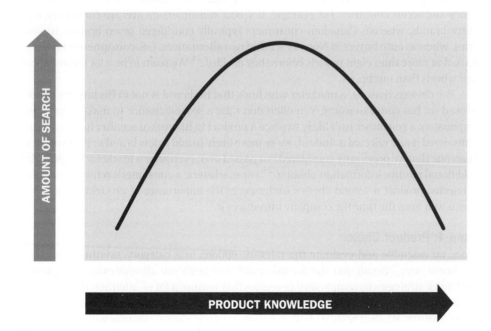

researching his purchase, is typical. He visited one store, and he looked only at brands with which he was already familiar. In addition, he focused on only a small number of product features.[21]

Because experts have a better sense of what information is relevant to the decision, they engage in *selective search*, which means their efforts are more focused and efficient. In contrast, novices are more likely to rely on the opinions of others and on "nonfunctional" attributes, such as brand name and price, to distinguish among alternatives. Finally, novice consumers may process information in a "top-down" rather than a "bottom-up" manner; they focus less on details than on the big picture. For instance, they may be more impressed by the sheer amount of technical information an ad presents than by the actual significance of the claims it makes.[22]

Step 3: Evaluate Alternatives

Much of the effort we put into a purchase decision occurs at the stage where we have to put the pedal to the metal and actually choose a product from several alternatives. This may not be easy; modern consumer society abounds with choices. In some cases, there may be literally hundreds of different brands (as in cigarettes) or different variations of the same brand (as in shades of lipstick).

Ask a friend to name all the brands of perfume she can think of. The odds are she will reel off three to five names rather quickly, then stop and think awhile before she comes up with a few more. She's probably familiar with the first set of brands, and in fact she probably wears one or more of these. Her list may also contain one or two brands that she doesn't like; to the contrary, they come to mind because she thinks they smell nasty or are unsophisticated. Note also that there are many, many more brands on the market that she did not name at all.

If your friend goes to the store to buy perfume, it is likely that she will consider buying some or most of the brands she listed initially. She might also entertain a few more possibilities if these come to her attention while she's at the fragrance counter (for example, if an employee "ambushes" her with a scent sample as she walks down the aisle).

We call the alternatives a consumer knows about the **evoked set** and the ones he or she seriously considers the **consideration set**.[23] Recall that Richard did not know much about the technical aspects of television sets, and he had only a few major brands in memory. Of these, two were acceptable possibilities and one was not.

Consumers often consider a surprisingly small number of alternatives, especially with all the choices available to us. A cross-national study found that people generally include just a few products in their consideration set, although this amount varies by product category and across countries. For example, U.S. beer consumers on average considered only three brands, whereas Canadian consumers typically considered seven brands. In contrast, whereas auto buyers in Norway studied two alternatives, U.S. consumers on average looked at more than eight models before they decided.[24] We seem to be a lot pickier about our wheels than our brews.

For obvious reasons, a marketer who finds that his brand is not in his target market's evoked set has cause to worry. You often don't get a second chance to make a good first impression; a consumer isn't likely to place a product in his evoked set after he has already considered it and rejected it. Indeed, we're more likely to add a new brand to the evoked set than one that we previously considered but passed over, even after a marketer has provided additional positive information about it.[25] For marketers, a consumer's reluctance to give a rejected product a second chance underscores the importance of ensuring that it performs well from the time the company introduces it.

Step 4: Product Choice

Once we assemble and evaluate the relevant options in a category, eventually we have to choose one.[26] Recall that the decision rules that guide our choices range from simple and quick strategies to complicated processes that require a lot of attention and cognitive processing.[27] Our job isn't getting any easier as companies overwhelm us with more and more features. We deal with 50-button remote controls, digital cameras with hundreds of

As feature creep becomes more of a problem, just providing clear instructions to users is a major "pain point" for many manufacturers.
Source: supercavie/Shutterstock.

mysterious features and book-length manuals, and cars with dashboard systems worthy of the space shuttle. Experts call this spiral of complexity **feature creep**. As evidence that the proliferation of gizmos is counterproductive, Philips Electronics found that at least half of the products buyers return have nothing wrong with them; consumers simply couldn't understand how to use them! What's worse, on average the buyer spent only 20 minutes trying to figure out how to use the product and then gave up.

Why don't companies avoid this problem? One reason is that we often assume the more features the better. It's only when we get the product home that we realize the virtue of simplicity. In one study, consumers chose among three models of a digital device that varied in terms of how complex each was. More than 60 percent chose the one with the most features. Then, when the participants got the chance to choose from up to 25 features to customize their product, the average person chose 20 of these add-ons. But when they actually used the devices, it turns out that the large number of options only frustrated them; they ended up being much happier with the simpler product. As the saying goes, "Be careful what you wish for."[28]

Step 5: Postpurchase Evaluation
Another old saying goes, "the proof of the pudding is in the eating." In other words, the true test of our decision-making process is whether we are happy with the choice we made after we undergo all these stages. **Postpurchase evaluation** closes the loop; it occurs when we experience the product or service we selected and decide whether it meets (or maybe even exceeds) our expectations. We'll take a closer look at that in the next chapter.

Neuromarketing

Is there a "buy button" in your brain? Some corporations, including Google, CBS, Disney, and Frito-Lay, have teamed up with neuroscientists to find out.[29] **Neuromarketing** uses functional magnetic resonance imaging (or fMRI), a brain-scanning device that tracks blood flow as we perform mental tasks to take an up-close look at how our brains respond to marketing messages and product design features. In recent years, researchers have discovered that regions in the brain, such as the amygdala, the hippocampus, and the

CB AS I SEE IT

Frédéric Brunel, *Boston University*

Today, more than ever, competitors are often able to match each other on product features, quality and price. As a result, many have argued that the key to differentiating offers, creating value and winning and keeping customers is via superior product design. Whether we think of electronics goods, food packages, household or industrial goods, these design investments and increased attention to product visual appearance is evident everywhere around us. However, my colleagues Rishtee Kumar-Batra and Suchi Chandran and I have been wondering if selling a more attractive product is always a winning strategy. In particular, we have been trying to understand if *some products might end up looking too good?*

A product's visual design is often the first piece of product information that is perceived by consumers and it is key in creating initial impressions, sustaining interest and signaling an owner's identity to others. The accepted common wisdom is that *"more beautiful should the better"*; in other words, superior-looking products will be more liked by consumers and more successful in the market. The role of physical attractiveness is not only true for products, but it is also true for how we perceive others. For example, in psychology, *implicit personality theory* research has shown that, in the absence of additional information, more attractive individuals are perceived to be more intelligent and more socially competent. Yet, psychologists have also shown that when someone is considered *highly* attractive, there is a backfiring effect and perceptions of intelligence and social competence go down.

In our research, we extend these social psychological principles to the study of visual product design. For example, in a study involving the design of kitchen toasters, we show that although design A is perceived as visually less attractive than design B, and design B is perceived as visually less attractive than design C, perceptions of product quality and product performances are highest for design B (the reasonably attractive design), not design C

(the highly attractive design). We found this robust pattern of results across multiple product categories (e.g., vacuum cleaners, USB drives, or computer mice). Our results therefore support the proposition that consumers' perceptions are based on two general sets of beliefs: Belief 1 *"a beautiful product is a good product,"* but also Belief 2, *"when a product is too beautiful, it can't be as good."*

Further, our research into this phenomenon has shown also that Belief 1 is perceptually based and automatic and does not require cognitive efforts, whereas Belief 2 is only at play when consumers have sufficient cognitive resources to engage in this type of more elaborate thinking. We also showed that Belief 2 is invoked when the product brand is not disclosed or when the disclosed brand does not have strong brand equity. For strong brands, we did not find the inverted U-shaped relationship; in these cases the results suggest that *"more beautiful is always better."*

In conclusion, our research confirms that investments in superior visual product designs generally are good strategies. However, weaker or newer brands should be careful not to overreach. They need to proceed with caution in order to take advantage of their design investments, otherwise they risk a backfiring effect on perceptions of quality and performance.

hypothalamus, are dynamic switchboards that blend memory, emotions, and biochemical triggers. These interconnected neurons shape the ways in which fear, panic, exhilaration, and social pressure influence our choices.

Scientists know that specific regions of the brain light up in these scans to show increased blood flow when a person recognizes a face, hears a song, makes a decision, or senses deception. Now they hope to harness this technology to measure consumers' reactions to movie trailers, automobiles, the appeal of a pretty face, and even their loyalty to specific brands. DaimlerChrysler took brain scans of men as they looked at photos of cars and confirmed that sports cars activated their reward centers. The company's scientists

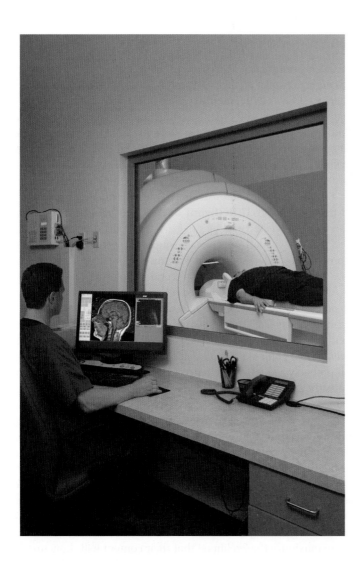

Neuromarketing techniques rely on sophisticated devices like the fMRI to understand how our brains respond to marketing messages.
Source: James Steidl/123RF.

found that the most popular vehicles—the Porsche- and Ferrari-style sports cars—-triggered activity in a section of the brain they call the *fusiform face area*, which governs facial recognition. A psychiatrist who ran the study commented, "They were reminded of faces when they looked at the cars. The lights of the cars look a little like eyes."

A study that took brain scans of people as they drank competing soft-drink brands illustrates how loyalty to a brand affects our reactions, even at a basic, physiological level. When researchers monitored brain scans of 67 people who took a blind taste test of Coca-Cola and Pepsi, each soft drink lit up the brain's reward system. The participants were evenly split as to which drink they preferred—even though three out of four participants *said* they preferred Coke. When told they were drinking Coke, the regions of the brain that control memory lit up, and this activation drowned out the area that simply reacts to taste cues. In this case, Coke's strong brand identity trumped the sensations coming from respondents' taste receptors.

In another application, Frito-Lay gave electroencephalograms (EEGs), which measure fluctuations in the electrical activity directly below the scalp, to test subjects to learn how they respond to Cheetos cheese puffs. Researchers reported that people had a powerful reaction to the orange residue of cheese dust the snack leaves on their hands; one account described this as "a sense of giddy subversion that consumers enjoy over the messiness of the product." Frito-Lay went on to develop an advertising campaign it called "The Orange Underground"; the edgy Cheetos mascot Chester Cheetah encouraged people to commit subversive acts with the product. In one spot, a guy sitting on a plane sticks Cheetos up the nostrils of his snoring seatmate. Do not try this.

Online Decision Making

With the tremendous number of Web sites and apps available and the huge number of people who spend big chunks of their day online, how can people organize information and decide where to click? A **cybermediary** often is the answer. This term describes a Web site or app that helps to filter and organize online market information so that customers can identify and evaluate alternatives more efficiently. Many consumers regularly link to comparison-shopping sites, such as Bizrate.com or Pricegrabber.com, for example, that list online retailers that sell a given item along with the price each charges.[30] *Directories* and *portals*, such as Yahoo! or The Knot, are general services that tie together a large variety of different sites. *Forums, fan clubs,* and *user groups* offer product-related discussions to help customers sift through options. **Intelligent agents** are sophisticated software programs that use *collaborative filtering* technologies to learn from past user behavior to recommend new purchases.[31] When you let Amazon.com suggest a new book, the site uses an intelligent agent to propose novels based on what you and others like you have bought in the past.

What's the most common way for us to conduct information search today? Google it, of course! Although there are other **search engines** out there such as Microsoft's Bing, Yahoo! or even You Tube, Google's version of the software that examines the Web for matches to terms like "home theater system" or "tattoo removal services" is so dominant—with 96 percent of the world's mobile search market—the name has become a verb. However, even a giant like Google can't rest on its laurels because changes in how we search will probably reduce our reliance on search engines. Increasingly consumers bypass Google as they go directly on their smartphones or tablets to apps like Yelp to read and write product reviews.[32]

However, as anyone who's ever Googled knows, the Web delivers enormous amounts of product and retailer information in seconds. The biggest problem Web surfers face these days is to narrow down their choices, not to beef them up. In cyberspace, simplification is key. Still, the sad reality is that in many cases we simply don't search as much as we might. If we Google a term, most of us are only likely to look at the first few results at the top of the list.

Indeed, that's one reason why **search engine optimization (SEO)** is so important today; this term refers to the procedures companies use to design the content of Web sites and posts to maximize the likelihood that their content will show up when someone searches for a relevant term. Our goal is to persuade people to access our content. Just like an expert fisherman chooses his spot and carefully selects the right lure to catch a fish, SEO experts create online content that will attract the attention of the *search algorithms,* or mathematical formulas, that companies like Google use to determine which entries will turn up in a search. The algorithm will hunt for certain keywords, and it also will consider who uses them. For example, if a lot of influential people share an entry, the formula will weight it more. Site creators try to ensure that they use the right keywords and that these show up in one or more elements of the post including:

- **Meta tag:** Code embedded in a Web page. Meta tags are visible to site visitors but only by viewing the source code for the page.
- **Title tag:** An HTML tag that defines the page's title. The title is displayed in the browser's title bar, in search engine results, and in RSS feeds.
- **Heading tag:** An HTML tag that is used to section and describe content.
- **Title:** The headline or the main indicator of a page's content. Although a traditional headline in a magazine article may be indirect, an optimized title needs to be more literal. Search algorithms are smart, but they don't get puns or jokes. For example, a print ad for an expensive Louis Vuitton handbag may read "High Fashion Replicas Indistinguishable from the Real Thing." An optimized title might read "Shop Wise: 5 Tips for Ensuring that a Vuitton Bag Is Real, Not Fake, Fashion" to ensure that the search would index on keywords such as *Vuitton, shop,* and *bag.* Titles also should use a **hook** that increases the likelihood people will click on it. Social media pros refer to the careful crafting of a title that markets the content as **linkbaiting**.[33]

Can you imagine choosing a restaurant before you check it out online? Increasingly many of us rely on online reviews to steer us toward and away from specific restaurants, hotels, movies, garments, music, and just about everything else. A survey of 28,000 respondents in 56 countries reported that online user ratings are the second-most trusted source of brand information (after recommendations from family and friends). We usually put a lot of stock in what members of our social networks recommend. Unfortunately, user ratings don't link strongly to actual product quality that objective evaluation services like *Consumer Reports* provide. And, there's evidence that mobile reviews may be less helpful than desktop reviews, even when the same reviewer writes both. Comments posted via mobile devices are more emotional and more negative.[34]

Regardless of their accuracy, customer product reviews are a key driver of satisfaction and loyalty. Another advantage these reviews provide is that consumers learn about other, less popular options they may like as well, and at the same time products such as movies, books, and CDs that aren't "blockbusters" are more likely to sell. At the online DVD rental company Netflix, for example, fellow subscribers recommend about two-thirds of the films that people order. In fact, between 70 and 80 percent of Netflix rentals come from the company's back catalog of 38,000 films rather than recent releases.[35]

This aspect of online customer review is one important factor that's fueling an important business model called the **long tail**.[36] The basic idea is that we no longer need to rely solely on big hits (such as blockbuster movies or best-selling books) to find profits. Companies can also make money if they sell small amounts of items that only a few people want—*if* they sell enough different items. For example, Amazon.com maintains an inventory of 3.7 million books, compared to the 100,000 or so you'll find in a large retail store like Barnes & Noble. Most of these stores will sell only a few thousand copies (if that), but the 3.6 million books that Barnes & Noble *doesn't* carry make up a quarter of Amazon's revenues! Other examples of the long tail include successful microbreweries and TV networks that make money on reruns of old shows on channels like the *Game Show Network*.

How Do We Put Products into Categories?

Consumers are in the middle of a love affair with yogurt, and new varieties like Greek yogurt do well among people who crave healthy, filling snacks. Now we see other offerings that allow people to drink their yogurt in the form of smoothies, kefir and other blends that blur the lines among beverages, desserts, snacks and even supplements like probiotics.[37] How can consumers make sense of these new products?

Remember that when consumers process product information, they don't do it in a vacuum. They evaluate its attributes in terms of what they already know about the item or other similar products. A person who thinks about a particular 35-mm camera will most likely compare it to *other* 35-mm cameras rather than to a disposable camera. Because the *category* in which a consumer places a product determines the other products he or she will compare it to, the way we classify a brand in our minds plays a big role in how we evaluate it.[38]

And, as is the case with drinkable yogurts, sometimes companies like to play with these categories; they create new ones when they introduce **hybrid products** that feature characteristics from two distinct domains. Thus, we have the crossover utility vehicle (CUV) that mixes a passenger car and a sport utility vehicle (SUV) and the recent "cronut" craze (a combination croissant and donut) that started with a New York bakery and made its leap to national stardom courtesy of Dunkin' Donuts.[39]

A recent study that examined how consumers use calorie information demonstrates why the categories we use to define products are important. When people saw menus that listed the calorie count of individual items, they chose more dietetic items. However, when the lower calorie items were grouped into a single "low-calorie" category on the menu, diners actually selected them less frequently. The researchers explain that consumers have negative associations with low-calorie labels, so they're more likely to dismiss these options in the early stages of the decision process. As a result individual items are less likely to make the cut into diners' consideration sets so ironically this menu information results in less healthier choices overall.[40]

Consumers cognitively represent product information in a **knowledge structure**. This term refers to a set of beliefs and the way we organize these beliefs in our minds. These structures matter to marketers like Stonyfield, Green Valley and Trader Joe's that sell yogurt-related items because they want to ensure that customers correctly group their products. Typically, we represent a product in a knowledge structure at one of three levels. To understand this idea, consider how someone might respond to these questions about an ice cream cone: What other products share similar characteristics, and which would you consider as alternatives to eating a cone? These questions may be more complex than they first appear. At one level, a cone is similar to an apple because you could eat both as a dessert. At another level, a cone is similar to a piece of pie because you could eat either for dessert and both are fattening. At still another level, a cone is similar to an ice cream sundae—you could eat either for dessert, both are made of ice cream, and both are fattening. Figure 9.5 depicts these three levels.

It's easy to see that the foods a person associates with the category "fattening dessert" influence his or her decision about what to eat after dinner. The middle level, or *basic level category*, is typically the most useful for classifying products. At this level, the items we group together tend to have a lot in common with each other, but still permit us to consider a broad enough range of alternatives. The broader *superordinate category* is more abstract, whereas the more specific *subordinate category* often includes individual brands.[41] Of course, not all items fit equally well into a category. Apple pie is a better example of the subordinate category "pie" than is rhubarb pie, even though both are types of pies. This is because it's more *prototypical*, and most people would think of apple as a pie flavor before they thought of rhubarb. In contrast, true pie experts probably know a lot about both typical and atypical category examples.[42]

Strategic Implications of Product Categorization

The way we categorize products has a lot of strategic implications for marketers. That's because this process affects which products consumers will compare to our product and also the criteria they'll use to decide if they like us or the other guys.

Position a Product. The success of a *positioning strategy* hinges on the marketer's ability to convince the consumer to consider its product within a given category. For example, the orange juice industry tried to reposition orange juice as a drink people can enjoy all day long ("It's not just for breakfast anymore"). However, soft-drink companies attempt the opposite when they portray sodas as suitable for breakfast consumption. They are trying to make their way into consumers' "breakfast drink" category, along with orange juice, grapefruit juice, and coffee. Of course, this strategy can backfire, as Pepsi-Cola discovered when it introduced Pepsi a.m. and positioned it as a coffee substitute. The company did such a good job of categorizing the drink as a morning beverage that customers wouldn't drink it at any other time, and the product failed.[43]

Figure 9.5 LEVELS OF CATEGORIZATION

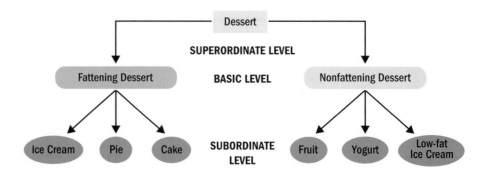

This ad for Sunkist lemon juice attempts to establish a new category for the product by repositioning it as a salt substitute.
Source: Courtesy of Sunkist Growers

Identify Competitors. At the abstract, superordinate level, many different product forms compete for membership. The category "entertainment" might comprise both bowling and the ballet, but not many people would substitute one of these activities for the other. Products and services that on the surface are quite different, however, actually compete with each other at a broad level for consumers' discretionary dollars. Although bowling or ballet may not be a likely tradeoff for many people, a symphony might try to lure away season ticket holders to the ballet by positioning itself as an equivalent member of the superordinate category "cultural event." We're often faced with choices between noncomparable categories, where we can't directly relate the attributes in one to those in another (the old problem of comparing apples and oranges). When we can create an overlapping category that encompasses both items (e.g., entertainment, value, usefulness) and then rate each alternative in terms of that superordinate category comparison, the process is easier.[44]

Create an Exemplar Product. As we saw with the case of apple pie versus rhubarb pie, if a product is a really good example of a category, then it is more familiar to consumers and they more easily recognize and recall it.[45] The characteristics of **category exemplars** tend to exert a disproportionate influence on how people think of the category in general.[46] In a sense, brands we strongly associate with a category get to "call the shots": They define the criteria we use to evaluate all category members.

Locate Products in a Store. Product categorization also can affect consumers' expectations regarding the places where they can locate a desired product. If products do not clearly fit into categories (e.g., is a rug furniture?), this may diminish our ability to find them or figure out what they're supposed to be once we do. For instance, a frozen dog food that pet owners had to thaw and cook before they served it to Fido failed in the market, partly because people could not adapt to the idea of buying dog food in the "frozen foods for people" section of their grocery stores.

Evaluative Criteria

When Richard looked at different television sets, he focused on one or two product features and completely ignored several others. He narrowed down his choices as he only

TABLE 9.1	Hypothetical Alternatives for a TV Set			
		Brand Ratings		
Attribute	**Importance Ranking**	**Prime Wave**	**Precision**	**Kamashita**
Size of screen	1	Excellent	Excellent	Excellent
Stereo broadcast capability	2	Poor	Excellent	Good
Brand reputation	3	Excellent	Excellent	Poor
Onscreen programming	4	Excellent	Poor	Poor
Cable-ready capability	5	Good	Good	Good
Sleep timer	6	Excellent	Poor	Good

considered two specific brand names, and from the Prime Wave and Precision models, he chose one that featured stereo capability. Table 9.1 summarizes the attributes of the TV sets that Richard considered. Now, let's see how a comparison of these attributes can alter Richard's choice of a specific brand depending on the rules he uses to consider them.

Evaluative criteria are the dimensions we use to judge the merits of competing options. When he compared alternative products, Richard could have chosen from among many criteria that ranged from functional attributes ("Does this TV come with remote control?") to experiential ones ("Does this TV's sound reproduction make me imagine I'm in a concert hall?").

Another important point is that criteria on which products *differ* from one another carry more weight in the decision process than do those where the alternatives are *similar*. If all brands a person considers rate equally well on one attribute (e.g., if all TVs come with remote control), Richard needs to find other reasons to choose one over another. **Determinant attributes** are the features we actually use to differentiate among our choices.

This French ad provides a vivid way to suggest an evaluative criterion.
Source: SOORUZ/PUBLICIS Conseil Paris/ Photographers: Cesar Ancelle-Hancelle/Jacques Demarcillac–Producer: Charles Denis.

Marketers often educate consumers about which criteria they should use as determinant attributes. For example, consumer research from Church & Dwight indicated that many consumers view the use of natural ingredients as a determinant attribute. As a result, the company promoted its toothpaste made from baking soda, which the company already manufactured for Church & Dwight's Arm & Hammer brand.[47]

To effectively recommend a new decision criterion, a marketer should convey three pieces of information:[48]

1 It should point out that there are significant differences among brands on the attribute.
2 It should supply the consumer with a decision-making rule, such as *if* ... (deciding among competing brands), *then* ... (use the attribute as a criterion).
3 It should convey a rule that is consistent with how the person made the decision on prior occasions. Otherwise, she is likely to ignore the recommendation because it requires too much mental work.

Under conditions of high cognitive involvement, people tend to think carefully about the pros and cons of different options, almost like a computer that would follow a somewhat complicated formula to make a decision. This is a **compensatory rule**; it allows a product to make up for its shortcomings on one dimension by excelling on another. There are two basic types of compensatory rules:

1 The **simple additive rule** leads to the option that has the largest number of positive attributes. A person may use this process when it's difficult to get more information. It's not the best solution because some of the attributes may not be meaningful to the customer. Thus, we may be impressed by a brand that boasts a laundry list of features even though most of them are not determinant attributes.
2 A **weighted additive rule** allows the consumer to take into account the relative importance of the attributes by weighting each one. If this sounds familiar, it should: The calculation process strongly resembled the multiattribute attitude model we discussed in Chapter 8.

Compensatory rules require the decision maker to carefully consider the attributes of competing options, but we all know that we don't necessarily do that. When we make habitual or emotional decisions we typically use a **noncompensatory rule**.[51] This means that if an option doesn't suit us on one dimension, we just reject it out of hand and

Marketing Opportunity

Consumers today often want to know just where the things they buy came from. The J. Peterman Company clothing catalogs tell stories about the apparel they sell, and upscale grocery stores such as Whole Foods provide great detail about the specific farms where produce and meat were raised. **Product authenticity** is becoming a determinant attribute. Researchers claim that although authenticity can be a hard concept to pin down, it seems to be composed of three attributes: heritage, sincerity, and commitment to quality.[49] That explains why many companies like to tout their "authentic" story; for example New Balance describes its Maine factory like this: "Built in 1945, the Depot Street building is the workplace of almost 400 associates. Each pair of shoes they produce is a proud work of craftsmanship that carries a little bit of the long history that is the town and its people."[50]

move on to something else rather than think about how it might meet our needs in other ways: "I've never heard of that brand," or maybe "That color is gross."

- The **lexicographic rule** says, "select the brand that is the best on the most important attribute." If a decision maker feels that two or more brands are equally good on that attribute, he or she then compares them on the second-most important attribute. This selection process goes on until the tie is broken. In Richard's case, because both the Prime Wave and Precision models were tied on his most important attribute (a 60-inch screen), he chose the Precision because of its rating on his second-most important attribute: its stereo capability.
- The **elimination-by-aspects rule** is similar to the lexicographic rule because the buyer also evaluates brands on the most important attribute. In this case, though, he or she imposes specific cut-offs. For example, if Richard had been more interested in having a sleep timer on his TV (i.e., if it had a higher importance ranking), he might have stipulated that his choice "must have a sleep timer." Because the Prime Wave model had one and the Precision did not, he would have chosen the Prime Wave.
- Whereas the two former rules involve processing by attribute, the **conjunctive rule** entails processing by brand. As with the elimination-by-aspects procedure, the decision maker establishes cut-offs for each attribute. He chooses a brand if it meets all the cutoffs, but rejects a brand that fails to meet any one cut-off. If none of the brands meet all the cutoffs, he may delay the choice, change the decision rule, or modify the cutoffs he chooses to apply.

If Richard stipulated that all attributes had to be rated "good" or better, he would not have been able to choose any of the available options. He might then have modified his decision rule, conceding that it was not possible to attain these high standards in his price range. In this case, perhaps Richard could decide that he could live without on-screen programming, so he would reconsider the Precision model.

If we're willing to allow good and bad product qualities to cancel each other out, we arrive at a different choice. For example, if Richard were not concerned about having stereo reception, he might have chosen the Prime Wave model. But because this brand doesn't feature this highly ranked attribute, it doesn't stand a chance when he uses a non-compensatory rule.

OBJECTIVE 9-4
We often rely on rules-of-thumb to make routine decisions.

Habitual Decision Making

Richard's meditations about the exact TV to buy probably don't resemble most of the choices he makes. If he's anything like most of us, he deals with dozens of decisions everyday and he makes most of them almost automatically. "Cream and sugar?" "Fries with that?"

The decision-making steps we've reviewed are well and good, but common sense tells us we don't undergo this elaborate sequence every time we buy something.[52] If we did, we'd spend our entire lives making these decisions. This would leave us little time to enjoy the things we eventually decide to buy. Some of our buying behaviors simply don't seem "rational" because they don't serve a logical purpose (you don't use that navel ring to hold a beach towel). **Habitual decision making** describes the choices we make with little or no conscious effort. Many purchase decisions are so routine we may not realize we've made them until we look in our shopping carts! Although decisions we make on the basis of little conscious thought may seem dangerous or at best stupid, this process actually is quite efficient in many cases. The journalist Malcolm Gladwell hit the bestseller list with his book *Blink*, which demonstrated how snap judgments that occur in the blink of an eye can be surprisingly accurate. [53, 54]

When a person buys the same brand over and over, does this mean it's just a habit or is he or she truly loyal to that product? The answer is, it depends: In some cases, the explanation really is just **inertia**, which means that it involves less effort to throw a familiar package into the cart. **Brand loyalty** is a totally different story. This describes a pattern of repeat purchasing behavior that involves a *conscious decision* to continue buying the same brand.

As you might imagine, though both inertia and brand loyalty yield the same result the latter is harder to achieve, but also much more valuable because it represents a true commitment by the consumer. One simple test that may help to tell the difference: If the consumer discovers that a store is out of his or her normal brand, will he or she just choose another one or defer the purchase to find this brand somewhere else? If the answer is "my way or the highway," that marketer has a loyal customer.

Priming and Nudging

OBJECTIVE 9-3
The way information about a product choice is framed can prime a decision even when the consumer is unaware of this influence

A study of the influence of company logos found that, when respondents were exposed to a brief flash of either an Apple or an IBM logo on a screen, their behavior changed *even though they weren't even aware they had seen the logo*. Creativity, nonconformity, and innovation are traits many consumers associate with the Apple brand, whereas they link tradition, intelligence, and responsibility with IBM.[55] Sure enough, those who saw the Apple logo subsequently provided more creative and innovative responses on a task than those who saw the IBM logo.

Researchers continue to identify factors that bias our decisions, and many of these are factors that operate beneath the level of conscious awareness.[56] In one study, respondents' attitudes toward an undesirable product—curried grasshoppers! —improved when they were asked to approach it. This physical movement typically links to liking; even our own body movements or other physiological reactions can influence what goes on in our minds.[57] To help understand this process, try to force yourself to smile or frown and then carefully gauge your feelings; you may find that the old prescription to "put on a happy face" to cheer yourself up may actually have some validity.[58]

Often it's just a matter of **framing**, or how we pose the question to people or what exactly we ask them to do. For example, people hate losing things more than they like getting things; economists call this tendency **loss aversion**. In one study, teachers who had the opportunity to improve student performance didn't make the grade in terms of improved test scores. However, those who got extra money at the beginning of the year and were told they would lose it if their students did not show sufficient progress managed to bring up their scores.

To see how framing works, consider the following scenario: You've scored a free ticket to a sold-out football game. At the last minute, though, a sudden snowstorm makes it somewhat dangerous to get to the stadium. Would you still go? Now, assume the same game and snowstorm—except this time you paid a small fortune for the ticket. Would you head out in the storm in this case?

Researchers who work on **prospect theory** analyze how the value of a decision depends on gains or losses; they identify principles of **mental accounting** that relate to the way we frame the question as well as external issues that shouldn't influence our choices, but do anyway. In this case, researchers find that people are more likely to risk their personal safety in the storm if they *paid* for the football ticket than if it's a freebie. Only the most die-hard fan would fail to recognize that this is an irrational choice because the risk is the same regardless of whether you got a great deal on the ticket. Researchers call this decision-making bias the **sunk-cost fallacy**: If we've paid for something, we're more reluctant to waste it.

The notion that even subtle changes in a person's environment can strongly influence the choices he or she makes has emerged on center stage in the study of consumer behavior in recent years. Unlike standard economic theory that regards people as rational decision makers, the rapidly growing field of **behavioral economics** focuses on the effects of psychological and social factors on the economic decisions we make, and many of these choices are anything but "rational." Indeed it turns out that it's quite possible to modify the choices of individuals and groups merely by tinkering with the way we present information to them. This research holds enormous implications, especially for public policy issues because it turns out the way organizations frame their messages can exert a big influence on the numbers of consumers who will stop smoking, eat healthy foods, or save more money for retirement. There are important ethical issues as well, especially as studies continue to identify ways that organizations including governments and companies can subtly but powerfully influence what we "freely" choose to do.[59]

Much of the emerging work in behavioral economics focuses on the role of **priming**: Cues in the environment that make us more likely to react in a certain way even though we're unaware of these influences. A *prime* is a stimulus that encourages people to focus on some specific aspect of their lives such as their financial well-being or the environment:

- A group of undergraduates was primed to think about money; they saw phrases like "she spends money liberally," or pictures that would make them think of money. Then this group and a control group that wasn't focused on money answered questions about moral choices they would make. Those students who had been primed to think of money consistently exhibited weaker ethics. They were more likely to say they would steal a ream of paper from the university's copying room and more likely to say they would lie for financial gain.[60]
- When people see pictures of "cute" products, they are more likely to engage in indulgent behavior such as eating larger portions of ice cream. [61]
- In a field study in a wine store, researchers played either stereotypically French or German music on alternate days. On the days when French music was in the background, people bought more French versus German wine and the reverse happened on German music days. Follow-up questionnaires indicated customers were not aware of the impact of the music on their choices.[62]

Much of the current work in behavioral economics demonstrates how a **nudge**—a deliberate change by an organization that intends to modify behavior—can result in dramatic effects. [63] A simple "nudge" that changes how people act is to switch from asking consumers to "opt in" to a program to asking them to "opt out" of a program if they don't want to participate. In Europe, countries that ask drivers to indicate if they want to be an organ donor convince less than 20 percent of drivers to do so. In contrast, those that require drivers to opt out if they *don't* want to be donors get more than 95 percent participation.

This **default bias**—where we are more likely to comply with a requirement than to make the effort not to comply— can be applied to numerous choice situations. For example, people are more likely to save for retirement if their employers automatically deduct a set amount from their paychecks than if they have to set up this process themselves. It is also how many software companies and social media platforms encourage users to adopt their products and privacy policies (e.g., when you must opt out of Facebook's right to share your data with others).[64]

Heuristics: Mental Shortcuts

The default bias we previously described illustrates that we often take the easy way out when we make decisions. Unlike the cognitive decision strategies we've already described we use when we want to arrive at the best result possible—a **maximizing solution**—in fact we often are quite content to exert less mental effort and simply receive an adequate outcome—a **satisficing solution**. This "good enough" perspective on decision making is called **bounded rationality**.

We've seen that many habitual decisions we make are subject to mental accounting biases. In addition, we often fall back on other shortcuts to simplify our choices. For example, Richard made certain assumptions instead of conducting an extensive information search. In particular, he assumed that the selection at Zany Zack's was more than sufficient, so he did not bother to shop at any other stores.[65]

We refer to these shortcuts as **heuristics**. These "mental rules-of-thumb" range from the general ("higher-priced products are higher-quality products" or "buy the same brand I bought last time") to the specific ("buy Domino, the brand of sugar my mother always bought").[66] Sometimes these shortcuts may not be in our best interests. A car shopper

TABLE 9.2	Market Beliefs
Brand	All brands are basically the same.
	Generic products are just name brands sold under a different label at a lower price.
	The best brands are the ones that are purchased the most.
	When in doubt, a national brand is always a safe bet.
Store	Specialty stores are great places to familiarize yourself with the best brands; but once you figure out what you want, it's cheaper to buy it at a discount outlet.
	A store's character is reflected in its window displays.
	Salespeople in specialty stores are more knowledgeable than other sales personnel.
	Larger stores offer better prices than small stores.
	Locally owned stores give the best service.
	A store that offers a good value on one of its products probably offers good values on all of its items.
	Credit and return policies are most lenient at large department stores.
	Stores that have just opened usually charge attractive prices.
Prices/Discounts/Sales	Sales are typically run to get rid of slow-moving merchandise.
	Stores that are constantly having sales don't really save you money.
	Within a given store, higher prices generally indicate higher quality.
Advertising and Sales Promotion	"Hard-sell" advertising is associated with low-quality products.
	Items tied to "giveaways" are not a good value (even with the freebie).
	Coupons represent real savings for customers because they are not offered by the store.
	When you buy heavily advertised products, you are paying for the label, not for higher quality.
Product/Packaging	Largest-sized containers are almost always cheaper per unit than smaller sizes.
	New products are more expensive when they're first introduced; prices tend to settle down as time goes by.
	When you are not sure what you need in a product, it's a good idea to invest in the extra features, because you'll probably wish you had them later.
	In general, synthetic goods are lower in quality than goods made of naturals materials.
	It's advisable to stay away from products when they are new to the market; it usually takes the manufacturer a little time to work the bugs out.

Source: Adapted from Calvin P. Duncan, "Consumer Market Beliefs: A Review of the Literature and an Agenda for Future Research," in Marvin E. Goldberg. Gerald Gorn, and Richard W. Pollay eds., *Advances in Consumer Research* 17 (Provo, UT: Association for Consumer Research, 1990):729–35.

who personally knows one or two people who have had problems with a particular vehicle, for example, might assume that he would have similar trouble with it rather than taking the time to find out that it actually has an excellent repair record.[67] Table 9.2 lists a set of **market beliefs** that many of us share. Let's summarize a few of the most prevalent heuristics we commonly use.

Covariation

A person who sells a used car probably makes sure the car's exterior is clean and shiny. Potential buyers often judge the vehicle's mechanical condition by its appearance, even though this means they may drive away in a clean, shiny clunker.[68] When we only have incomplete product information, we often base our judgments on our beliefs about **covariation**—our associations among events that may or may not actually influence one another.[69]

Country of origin

A product's "address" matters. We Americans like to buy Italian shoes, Japanese cars, and microwave ovens built in South Korea. Consumers strongly associate certain items with specific countries, and products from those countries often attempt to benefit from these linkages. That's why **country of origin (COO)** often is an important heuristic. Indeed, marketers often go out of their way to link a brand with a country to capitalize on associations people have with a specific COO: French wines, Italian sports cars, even Häagen-Dazs ice cream with that authentic Danish taste (but actually owned by Nestlé and made in Scandinavian strongholds like New Jersey).

A Dutch shoe ad reminds us that a product's address matters.

Source: Courtesy of Grey/Copenhagen.

Familiar brand names

In a study the Boston Consulting Group conducted of the market leaders in 30 product categories, 27 of the brands that were number one in 1930 (such as Ivory Soap and Campbell's Soup) still were at the top more than 50 years later.[70]

Higher prices

Many people assume that a higher-priced alternative is better quality than a lower-priced option.[71] This assumption is often correct; you do tend to get what you pay for. However, let the buyer beware: The price–quality relationship is not always justified.[72]

Collective Decision Making

OBJECTIVE 9-5

Marketers often need to understand *consumers'* behavior rather than a consumer's behavior.

As if the decision-making process we've reviewed in this chapter wasn't complicated enough, the full story is even more "interesting." That's because many of the decisions we make are *collaborative.* In these cases, other people participate in the problem-solving sequence—from initial problem recognition and information search to evaluation of alternatives and product choice. To further muddy the waters, these decisions often include two or more people who may not have the same level of investment in the outcome, the same tastes and preferences, or the same consumption priorities. If you've ever debated where to go out to eat with your friends, or perhaps bickered about whose turn it is to do the dishes, you get the picture. You can read 50 restaurant reviews on Yelp!, and still it's like pulling teeth to reach a consensus.

In this section we examine **collective decision-making** situations in which more than one person chooses the products or services that multiple consumers use. First, we'll look at organizational decision making, in which multiple employees select goods or services on behalf of a larger group. We then focus more specifically on one of the most important organizations to which we belong: the family unit. We'll consider how members of a family negotiate among themselves and how important changes in modern family structure affect this process.

Why do we lump together big corporations and small families? One important similarity is that in both cases individuals or groups play a number of specific roles when they choose products or services for their organizational unit.[73] Depending on the decision, the choice may include some or all of the group members, and different group members play important roles in what can be a complicated process. These roles include the following:

- **Initiator**—The person who brings up the idea or identifies a need.
- **Gatekeeper**—The person who conducts the information search and controls the flow of information available to the group. In organizational contexts, the gatekeeper identifies possible vendors and products for the rest of the group to consider.
- **Influencer**—The person who tries to sway the outcome of the decision. Some people may be more motivated than others to get involved, and participants also possess different amounts of power to get their point across.
- **Buyer**—The person who actually makes the purchase. The buyer may or may not actually use the product.
- **User**—The person who actually consumes the product or service.

OBJECTIVE 9-6
The decision-making process differs when people choose what to buy on behalf of an organization rather than for personal use.

B2B Decision Making

Many employees of corporations or other organizations make purchase decisions on a daily basis. **Organizational buyers** are people who purchase goods and services on behalf of companies for the companies' use in manufacturing, distribution, or resale. These individuals buy from **business-to-business (B2B) marketers** that must satisfy the needs of organizations such as corporations, government agencies, hospitals, and retailers. In terms of sheer volume, B2B is where the action is: Roughly $2 trillion worth of products and services change hands among organizations, which is actually *more* than end consumers purchase.

Organizational buyers have a lot of responsibility. They decide on the vendors with whom they want to do business and what specific items they require from these suppliers. The items they consider range in price and significance from paper clips (by the case, not the box) to multimillion-dollar computer systems. A number of factors influence the organizational buyer's perception of the purchase situation. These include his or her *expectations* of the supplier (e.g., product quality, the competence and behavior of the firm's employees, and prior experiences in dealing with that supplier), the *organizational climate* of the company (i.e., how it rewards performance and what it values), and the buyer's *assessment* of his or her own performance (e.g., whether he or she believes in taking risks).[74]

Like other consumers, organizational buyers engage in a learning process in which employees share information with one another and develop an "organizational memory" that consists of shared beliefs and assumptions about the best choices to make.[75] Just as the "market beliefs" we discussed previously influence a consumer while shopping with the family on the weekend, the same thing happens at the office. He or she (perhaps with fellow employees) solves problems as they search for information, evaluate alternatives, and decide.[76] There are, of course, some important differences between the two situations.

How Does B2B Decision Making Compare to Consumer Decision Making?

Let's summarize the major differences between organizational and industrial purchase decisions versus individual consumer decisions:[77]

- The purchase decisions that companies make frequently involve many people, including those who do the actual buying, those who directly or indirectly influence this decision, and the employees who will actually use the product or service.
- Organizations and companies often use precise technical specifications that require a lot of knowledge about the product category.
- Impulse buying is rare (industrial buyers do not suddenly get an "urge to splurge" on lead pipe or silicon chips). Because buyers are professionals, they base their decisions on past experience and they carefully weigh alternatives.
- Decisions often are risky, especially in the sense that a buyer's career may ride on his judgment.
- The dollar volume of purchases is often substantial; it dwarfs most individual consumers' grocery bills or mortgage payments. One hundred to 250 organizational customers typically account for more than half of a supplier's sales volume, which gives the buyers a lot of influence over the supplier.
- B2B marketing often emphasizes personal selling more than advertising or other forms of promotion. Dealing with organizational buyers typically requires more face-to-face contact than when marketers sell to end consumers.

We must consider these important features when we try to understand the purchasing decisions organizations make. Having said that, however, there are actually more similarities between organizational buyers and ordinary consumers than many people realize. True, organizational purchase decisions do tend to have a higher economic or functional component compared to individual consumer choices, but emotional aspects do play a role. Organizational buyers may appear to the outsider to be models of rationality, but at times they base their decisions on brand loyalty, on long-term relationships with particular suppliers or salespeople, or even on aesthetic preferences. Even investors, who are supposed to make cold, calculated judgments about the worth of companies based on financial indicators, sometimes are influenced instead by other concerns; for instance, they may be biased toward companies that provide better working conditions for employees or that are unusual in some other way.[78]

As you'd expect, the organizational decision-making process depends on the purchase. As when individuals choose, the more complex, novel, or risky the decision, the more effort the group devotes to information search and to evaluating alternatives. However, if these buyers rely on a fixed set of suppliers for routine purchases, this greatly reduces their information search and effort.[79] Typically, a group of people (members of a **buying center**) plays different roles in more complex organizational decisions. As we will see later on, this joint involvement is somewhat similar to family decision making, in which family members are likely to participate in more important purchases. Note: Unlike a shopping center, a buying center does not refer to a physical place, but rather the group of people who make the decision.

The classic **buyclass theory of purchasing** divides organizational buying decisions into three types that range from the least to the most complex. Three decision-making dimensions describe the purchasing strategies of an organizational buyer:[80]

1 The level of information he or she must gather prior to the decision.
2 The seriousness with which he or she must consider all possible alternatives.
3 The degree to which he or she is familiar with the purchase.

In practice, these three dimensions relate to how much cognitive effort the buyer expends when he decides. Three types of "buyclasses," or strategies determined by these

Organizations often assemble teams to make purchasing decisions.
Source: Courtesy of Capstone Turbine Corporation.

dimensions, encompass most organizational decision situations.[81] Table 9.3 summarizes these strategies.

- A **straight rebuy** is a habitual decision. It's an automatic choice, as when an inventory level reaches a preestablished reorder point. Most organizations maintain an approved vendor list, and as long as experience with a supplier is satisfactory, there is little or no ongoing information search or evaluation.
- A **modified rebuy** situation involves limited decision making. It occurs when an organization wants to repurchase a product or service but also wants to make some minor modifications. This decision might involve a limited search for information among a few vendors. One or a few people will probably make the final decision.
- A **new task** involves extensive problem solving. Because the company hasn't made a similar decision already, there is often a serious risk that the product won't perform as

| TABLE 9.3 | Types of Organizational Buying Decisions |

Buying Situation	Extent of Effort	Risk	Buyer's Involvement
Straight rebuy	Habitual decision-making	Low	Automatic reorder
Modified rebuy	Limited problem solving	Low to moderate	One or a few
New task	Extensive problem solving	High	Many

Source: Adapted from Patrick J. Robinson, Charles W. Faris, and Yoram Wind, *Industrial Buying and Creative Marketing* (Boston: Allyn & Bacon, 1967).

it should or that it will be too costly. This is when the organization designates a buying center with assorted specialists to evaluate the purchase, and they typically gather a lot of information before they come to a decision.

B2B E-Commerce

Business-to-business (B2B) e-commerce refers to Internet interactions between two or more businesses or organizations. This includes exchanges of information, products, services, or payments. The Web revolutionized the way companies communicate with other firms and even the way they share information with their own people. Today the majority of B2B companies, even those that until recently relied heavily on "old-school" techniques such as cold calls and mailed newsletters, use social media to connect with customers and business partners.[82]

In the simplest form of B2B e-commerce, the Internet provides an online catalog of products and services that businesses need. Companies like Dell Computer use their Internet site to deliver online technical support, product information, order status information, and customer service to corporate customers. Early on, Dell discovered that it could serve the needs of its customers more effectively if it tailored its Internet presence to different customer segments. Today Dell's Internet site allows shoppers to get recommendations based on their customer segment (home, home office, government, small business, and education). The company saves millions of dollars a year as it replaces hard-copy manuals with electronic downloads. For its larger customers, Dell provides customer-specific, password-protected pages that allow business customers to obtain technical support or to place an order.[83]

Prediction Markets

Are all of us smarter than each of us? A **prediction market** is one of the hottest trends in organizational decision-making techniques. This approach asserts that groups of people with knowledge about an industry are, collectively, better predictors of the future than are any of them as individuals. In a prediction market framework, companies from Microsoft to Eli Lilly and Hewlett-Packard empower their employees as "traders." Like a stock market, traders place bets on what they think will happen regarding future sales, the success of new products, or how other firms in a distribution channel will behave, —and they often receive a cash reward if their "stock picks" pan out. For example, the pharmaceutical giant Eli Lilly routinely places multimillion-dollar bets on drug candidates that face overwhelming odds of failure. The relatively few new compounds that do succeed have to make enough money to cover the losses the others incur. Obviously, the company will benefit if it can separate the winners from the losers earlier in the process. Lilly ran an experiment in which about 50 of its employees involved in drug development, including chemists, biologists, and project managers, traded six mock drug candidates through an internal market. The group correctly predicted the three most successful drugs.[84] Or, surf over to the Hollywood Stock Exchange (hsx.com) to check out

There's no 'u' in Threadless, but there should be. You pick the great ideas, you pick what we sell, you pick the next big thingy!

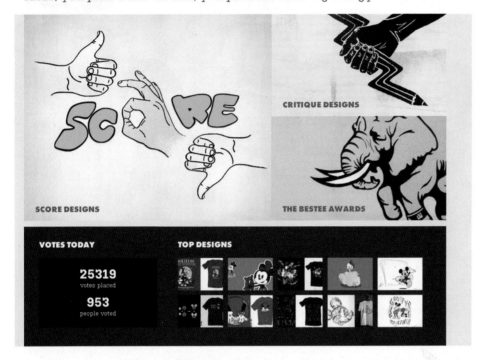

which celebrities and new movie releases traders think will succeed or bomb; you can bet Hollywood executives do![85]

Prediction markets are one element of **crowdsourcing**, which describes the growing practice of soliciting ideas for new products and even advertising campaigns from a user community. Under this model, companies no longer market to customers, they market *with* them.[86] The **wisdom of crowds** perspective (from a book by that name) argues that, under the right circumstances, groups are smarter than the smartest people in them. If this is true, it implies that large numbers of consumers can predict successful products.[87]

OBJECTIVE 9-7
Members of a family unit play different roles and have different amounts of influence when the family makes purchase decisions.

The Intimate Corporation: Family Decision Making

The decision process within a household unit resembles a business conference. Certain matters go on the table for discussion, different members advocate different actions based on their differing priorities and agendas, and there may be power struggles to rival any tale of corporate intrigue. In just about every living situation, whether it's a conventional family or students who share a sorority house or apartment, group members assume different roles just as purchasing agents, engineers, account executives, and others do within a company.

Marketing Opportunity

Companies as diverse as Budweiser (which crowdsourced its new Black Crown beer) to handbag designer Alexander Wang today offer products that originated from ideas employees or customers submitted.[88] At Threadless, customers rank T-shirt designs ahead of time, and the company prints the winning ideas. Every week, contestants upload T-shirt designs to the site, where about 700 compete to be among the six that it prints during that time. Threadless visitors score designs on a scale of 0 to 5, and the staff members select winners from the most popular entrants. *Threadless sells out of every shirt it offers.*[89]

ModCloth, an online retailer of affordable women's clothing and accessories, launched an entire private label collection made up mostly of designs submitted and voted on by its Facebook community. At Kickstarter.com, a crowdsourced funding site, participants have pledged more than $320 million to fund greater than 18,000 projects that range from movies to a Bluetooth-enabled watch.[90]

American Girl produces historical-period characters complete with books, dolls, and accessories, as well as modern-period dolls. The company also operates The American Girl Place, where young girls who own the dolls drag their parents and grandparents to attractions including dioramas and a doll hair salon. Consumer researchers who studied the American Girl phenomenon concluded that part of the brand's huge popularity is due to its multigenerational appeal. After they interviewed numerous girls, mothers, and grandmothers, they found that consumers of all ages valued the opportunities for family connection and also learning about their heritage and those of other cultures.[91]

Source: Reprinted with permission of American Girl, Inc.

How Families Decide

Families make two basic types of decisions:[92]

1 In a **consensual purchase decision** members agree on the desired purchase; they disagree only in terms of how they will make it happen. In these circumstances, the family will most likely engage in problem solving and consider alternatives until they find a way to satisfy everyone in the group. For example, in a family that decides to get a dog, some of the members (you can guess who) voice concerns about who will take care of it. The solution is to draw up a chart that assigns family members to specific duties.

2 In an **accommodative purchase decision** however, group members have different preferences or priorities and can't agree on a purchase that satisfies everyone's needs. It is here that they use bargaining, coercion, and compromise to achieve agreement on what to buy or who gets to use it. Conflict occurs when there is incomplete correspondence in family members' needs and preferences. Although household spending and budgeting is the most common source of conflict in these disputes, TV viewing choices come in a close second![93]

Decisions create conflict among family members to the extent that the issue is somehow important or novel; conflict also occurs if individuals have strong opinions about good and bad alternatives. The degree to which these factors generate conflict determines the type of decision the family will make.[94] Some specific factors that determine how much family decision conflict there will be include:[95]

- **Interpersonal need**—(a person's level of investment in the group): A teenager may care more about what her family buys for the house than will a college student who lives in a dorm.
- **Product involvement and utility**—(the degree to which a person will use the product to satisfy a need): A mother who is an avid coffee drinker will obviously be more interested in the purchase of a new coffeemaker than will her teenage son who swigs Coke by the gallon.
- **Responsibility**—(for procurement, maintenance, payment, and so on): People are more likely to have disagreements about a decision if it entails long-term consequences and commitments. For example, a family decision about getting a dog may involve conflict over who will be responsible for walking and feeding it.
- **Power**—(or the degree to which one family member exerts influence over the others): In traditional families, the husband tends to have more power than the wife, who in turn has more than the oldest child, and so on. Conflict can arise when one person continually uses the power he has within the group to satisfy his own priorities. For example, if a child believed that his life would end if he did not receive a Kinect for his birthday, he might be more willing to "cash in some chips" and throw a tantrum.

Marketers need to figure out who makes the buying decisions in a family because this information tells them who to target and whether they need to reach both spouses to influence a choice. Researchers pay special attention to which spouse plays the role of the **family financial officer (FFO)**—the individual who keeps track of the family's bills and decides how to spend any surplus funds. In traditional families (and especially those with low educational levels), women are primarily responsible for family financial management: The man makes it and the woman spends it. Each spouse "specializes" in certain activities.[96] The pattern is different among families where more modern sex-role norms operate. These couples believe that both people should participate in family maintenance activities. In these cases, husbands assume more responsibility for laundering, housecleaning, grocery shopping, and so on, in addition to such traditionally "male" tasks as home maintenance and garbage removal.[97]

The **synoptic ideal** calls for the husband and wife to act as joint decision makers. Together they thoughtfully weigh alternatives, assign one another well-defined roles, and calmly make mutually beneficial consumer decisions. This model is widely accepted among U.S. couples, especially younger ones: They agree the ideal marriage is one in

Roommates have to make collaborative decisions just as spouses do.
Source: Gadelshina Dina/Shutterstock.

which husband and wife both work and share child care and household duties. That's a big change from just 20 years ago, when less than half of the population approved of the dual-income family, and less than half of 1 percent of husbands knew how to operate a sponge mop.[98]

Still, the synoptic ideal is just that—an ideal. In real life, couples often don't have the luxury to make calm and rational joint decisions. Instead spousal decision making may be more about choosing whatever option will result in less conflict. A couple "reaches" rather than "makes" a decision. Researchers simply describe this process as "muddling through."[99] One common technique to simplify the decision-making process uses *heuristics*, like the ones we discussed previously in the chapter. The following decision-making patterns, which realtors frequently observe when a couple decides on a new house, illustrate how couples use heuristics:

- The couple defines their areas of common preference on obvious, objective dimensions rather than subtler, hard-to-define cues. For example, they may easily agree on the number of bedrooms they need in the new home, but they have a harder time when they need to agree on how the home should look.
- The couple negotiates a system of *task specialization* in which each is responsible for certain duties or decision areas and does not intrude on the other's "turf." For many couples, sex roles often dictate just what these territories are. For example, the wife may do advance scouting for houses that meet their requirements, and the husband determines whether the couple can obtain a mortgage.
- The likelihood of one partner conceding to the wishes of the other depends on how passionately each person desires a specific outcome. One spouse yields to the influence of the other in many cases simply because his or her preference for a certain attribute is not particularly intense. In other situations, he is more willing to fight for what he wants (in other words, "choose your battles").[100] In cases where intense preferences for different attributes exist, rather than attempting to influence each other, spouses will "trade off" a less-intense preference for a more strongly felt desire. For example, a husband who is somewhat indifferent about kitchen design may give in to his wife in exchange for permission to design his own "Man Cave."

So, who "wears the pants" in the family? Sometimes it's not obvious which spouse makes the decisions. Indeed, although many men literally wear the pants, it's women who buy them. Haggar's research showed that nearly half of married women bought pants for their husbands without the husbands being present, so the firm started to advertise its menswear products in women's magazines. When one family member chooses a product, this is an **autonomic decision**. In traditional households, for example, men often have sole responsibility to select a car, whereas decorating choices fall to women. **Syncretic decisions**, such as a vacation destination, involve both partners. These choices are common for vacations, homes, appliances, furniture, home electronics, and long-distance phone services. As the couple's educational level increases, they are more likely to make decisions together.[101]

One analysis of family decision making took a closer look at the idea that family members mutually construct a **family identity** that defines the household both to members and to outsiders.[103] According to this perspective (which is similar to the role theory approach to consumer behavior we discussed in Chapter 1), family rituals, narratives (stories the members tell about the family), and everyday interactions help families maintain their structure, maintain their family character (day-to-day characteristics of family life), and clarify members' relationships to one another. The value of this approach to marketers is that it reminds us of how often products and services help to define the family identity. For example, a father might take his young children out for ice cream every Saturday afternoon, so this becomes a predictable ceremony that defines their relationship. Or, a mom might seek the comfort of her Beats headphones to shield her from the noise when her kids play after school, while a TiVo "saves marriages" because it allows family members to compromise when they decide who gets access to the TV.

CB AS I SEE IT

Amber Epp *University of Wisconsin–Madison*

Family influence is inescapable because, even as consumers make decisions, they are always immersed in family relationships. As a dominant cultural institution, family is a main organizing force that shapes consumers' choices and experiences in the marketplace. More so than other types of decisions, families' choices often are scrutinized in the public eye and lead to feelings of guilt and stress about whether they are making the "right" decisions. Parents might ask, are we eating healthy meals? What rules should we have about technology use?

Do we spend enough family time together? Constant sharing on social media makes parenting (or certain images of parenting) more visible and transparent, increasing expectations and raising the pressure on parents to make good choices. Nowhere is this reality more evident than in current debates surrounding child care.

Increasingly, parents are outsourcing an expanding array of caregiving activities. Services now exist for everything a parent could imagine including nannies, potty training, planning birthday parties, etiquette classes, teaching children how to ride a bike, helping with school projects, and accompanying kids on college tours. These services blur the boundaries between family and the market, and prompt new questions about what is acceptable to outsource and how parents make sense of these sometimes contentious decisions.

In a recent study, my co-author and I conducted in-depth interviews with 23 sets of parents across five major cities to address three research questions: (1) how do parents make choices about which care activities to outsource? (2) what tensions emerge when parents outsource, and how are these tensions managed? and (3) how do parents justify and revise the mix of resources they use in care provision?

We found that when parents outsource care they experience tensions of control, intimacy, and substitutability. For instance, when contemplating whether or not to enlist others for help in planning a child's birthday party, parents might ask, isn't it my job as a parent to do this (substitutability)? What if the party planner doesn't do things the way I want them to be done (control)? Shouldn't I be the person who created the excitement and joy on my child's face (intimacy)? Despite struggling with these questions and resulting tensions, parents still outsourced. However, parents generated specific strategies to manage tensions such as customizing services, using them infrequently, or deconstructing care (e.g., baking the birthday cake themselves, but hiring someone else to plan and coordinate).

Our data also suggest that *who* parents outsource to (e.g., family, village, public, or market) matters immensely, as each has the potential to spark or relieve different tensions. For example, although family and village resources frequently heighten control tensions, the market often resolves control tensions more effectively because of its for-hire, contractual nature. Modern-day parental support comes in many forms, but the optimal mix of resources varies across families and depends on the tensions parents face.[104]

The Wife

As women continue to work outside the home in great number, their influence on household purchase decisions grows accordingly. The share of mothers employed full- or part-time has quadrupled since the 1950s and today accounts for nearly three-quarters of women with children at home. The number of women who are their families' sole or primary breadwinner also has soared, to 40 percent today from 11 percent in 1960.

When the husband is the primary or sole breadwinner, household spending decisions divide roughly equally. He makes about a third of them, she makes a third, and they make a third jointly. However, it's increasingly common for the wife to command a higher salary than the husband; almost 40 percent of married working women bring in more than their partner. When the wife earns more she is likely to make a much higher proportion of decisions about how the family unit spends its money. This is true even in areas where men traditionally make decisions: Women make up almost half of the $200 billion consumer-electronics business, and $105 billion of the $256 billion home-improvement market.[107]

Of course women pay a price for this enhanced role. Working mothers often struggle with what one researcher calls the **juggling lifestyle**: a frenzied, guilt-ridden compromise between conflicting cultural ideals of motherhood and professionalism.[108] This frantic way of life isn't surprising in light of a survey by the U.S. Department of Labor showing that the average working woman spends about twice as much time as the average working man on household chores and the care of children. She also gets about an hour less sleep each night than the average stay-at-home mom.[109]

And, despite this shift in decision-making responsibilities, women are still primarily responsible for the continuation of the family's **kin-network system**. They maintain ties among family members, both immediate and extended. Women are more likely to coordinate visits among relatives, stay in touch with family members, send greeting cards, and arrange social engagements.[110] This organizing role means that women often make important decisions about the family's leisure activities, and they are more likely to decide with whom the family will socialize.

The Husband

It's increasingly common to tune into TV commercials that depict a domestic version of fathers who tenderly and wisely look after the kids. Indeed this updated picture even has its own name: **Dadvertising**. A Cheerios commercial, for example, shows a confident dad taking charge of a hectic weekday morning. The campaign also features a dedicated Tumblr page and Twitter hashtag, #HowToDad.[111]

As we've seen, women's roles within the family decision-making unit are changing, but so are those of men. For one thing, single men remain a powerful and often ignored force in the marketplace. Right now, 3 out of 10 men are single, and more than 80 percent of them make the sole or key big-ticket decisions in their households.

Another driver of this change is that as we've just seen, more women are working outside the home and at better-paying jobs. This means that a growing number of husbands today stay home with the kids: The Census Bureau reports that one-fifth of fathers with preschool-age children and working wives are the primary caretaker. As one marketing executive observed, "Kids are going to grow up with dads that give them baths and drive them to soccer and are cutting up oranges for team snacks." Already, by some estimates men do more than half of the grocery shopping in the United States.

This shift causes marketers to reexamine how they sell a range of products as they try to appeal to Dads: Both Lego and Mattel now offer construction toys. Procter & Gamble is developing special sections at big retailers as the company finds that women aren't as likely as before to choose personal care products for their husbands. The so-called "man aisle" organizes men's products in one place with shelf displays and even small TV monitors to help them pick out the appropriate items.[112]

Group Shopping

We shop differently when we're doing it with a group. For example, people who shop with at least one other person tend to make more unplanned purchases, buy more, and cover more areas of a store than do those who browse solo.[113] The famous Tupperware party is a successful example of a **home shopping party** that capitalizes on group pressures to boost sales.[114]

The Mega Bloks Barbie Build 'n Style line construction sets are marketed to girls but also are intended to appeal to their Dads.
Source: BARBIE and associated trademarks and trade dress are owned by, and used under permission from, Mattel. © 2015 Mattel. All Rights Reserved.

Social shopping is an emerging form of e-commerce that allows an online shopper to simulate the experience of shopping with others in a brick-and-mortar store. New technologies allow a consumer to "try on" a garment via an avatar and also to access[115] feedback from others in his or her social network either prior to or after deciding on a purchase. As the technology continues to mature, social shopping may offer an even more compelling purchase experience than the in-store interactions it replaces. The social shopping mechanisms now being introduced at a rapid rate take the form of product ratings, reviews, product montages, design competitions, style advice, live outfit reviews, visual scrapbooking, and crowdsourced advice. Table 9.4 summarizes some of the current approaches to social shopping.

Home shopping parties capitalize on group pressure to generate sales.
Source: Madhourses/Shutterstock.

TABLE 9.4	Social Shopping Applications						
Social Shopping Web Site Categories							
Virtual Wish Lists/ Scrapbooking	**Try It On Sites and Apps**	**Pre-purchase Feedback**	**Competitions**	**Social Shopping Advocacy**	**Group Purchasing Sites**	**Linking and Networking 'Sign On'**
Supply	Gotryiton	ASOS	ASOS	Klout	Living Social	Facebook Connect
Polyvore	Fashionism	Facebook		The Fancy	Groupon	Modcloth
Pinterest	Justboughtit	Twitter		Sneakpeeq	BuyWithMe	Wanelo
vi.sualize.us		Motilo		Fab		
Mydeco		Daily Grommet				

Source: Adapted from Rachel Ashman, Michael R. Solomon and Julia Wolny, "An Old Model for a New Age: Applying the EKB in Today's Participatory Culture," *Journal of Customer Behaviour*, 2015, 14(2): 127–146.

MyLab Marketing

To complete the problems with the ✪, go to EOC Discussion Questions in the MyLab as well as additional Marketing Metrics questions only available in MyLab Marketing.

CHAPTER SUMMARY

Now that you have finished reading this chapter, you should understand why:

1. **The three categories of consumer decision making are cognitive, habitual, and affective.**

   Consumer decision making is a central part of consumer behavior, but the way we evaluate and choose products (and the amount of thought we put into these choices) varies widely, depending on such dimensions as the degree of novelty or risk related to the decision. We almost constantly need to make decisions about products. Some of these decisions are important and entail great effort, whereas we make others on a virtually automatic basis. Perspectives on decision making range from a focus on habits that people develop over time to novel situations involving a great deal of risk in which consumers must carefully collect and analyze information before making a choice. Many of our decisions are highly automated; we make them largely by habit. The way we evaluate and choose a product depends on our degree of involvement with the product, the marketing message, or the purchase situation. Product involvement can range from low, where purchase decisions are made via inertia, to high, where consumers form strong bonds with what they buy.

2. **A cognitive purchase decision is the outcome of a series of stages that results in the selection of one product over competing options.**

   A typical decision involves several steps. The first is problem recognition, when we realize we must take some action. This recognition may occur because a current possession malfunctions or perhaps because we have a desire for something new. Once the consumer recognizes a problem and sees it as sufficiently important to warrant some action, he or she begins the process of information search. This search may range from performing a simple memory scan to determine what he or she has done before to resolve the same problem to extensive fieldwork during which he or she consults a variety of sources to amass as much information as possible. The World Wide Web has changed the way many of us search for information. Today, our problem is more likely to weed out excess detail than to search for more information. Comparative search sites and intelligent agents help to filter and guide the search process. We may rely on cybermediaries, such as Web portals, to sort through massive amounts of information as a way to simplify the decision-making process. In the evaluation of alternatives stage, the options a person considers constitute his or her evoked set. Members of the evoked set usually share some characteristics; we categorize them similarly. The way the person mentally groups products influences which alternatives she will consider, and usually we associate some brands more strongly with these categories (i.e., they are more prototypical). When the consumer eventually must make a product choice from among alternatives, he uses one of several decision rules. Noncompensatory rules eliminate alternatives that are deficient on any of the criteria we've chosen. Compensatory rules, which we are more likely to apply in high-involvement situations, allow us to consider each alternative's good and bad points more carefully to arrive at the overall best choice. Once the consumer makes a choice, he or she engages in postpurchase evaluation to determine whether it was a good one; this assessment in turn influences the process the next time the problem occurs.

3. The way information about a product choice is framed can prime a decision even when the consumer is unaware of this influence.

Principles of mental accounting demonstrate that the way a problem is framed and whether it is put in terms of gains or losses influences what we decide. In addition, other cues in the environment—including subtle ones of which we may not even be aware—may prime us to choose one option over another. A prime is a stimulus that encourages people to focus on some specific aspect of their lives. Much of the current work in behavioral economics demonstrates how a nudge—a deliberate change by an organization that intends to modify behavior—can result in dramatic effects.

4. We often rely on rules-of-thumb to make routine decisions.

In many cases, people engage in surprisingly little search. Instead, they rely on various mental shortcuts, such as brand names or price, or they may simply imitate others' choices. We may use heuristics, or mental rules-of-thumb, to simplify decision making. In particular, we develop many market beliefs over time. One of the most common beliefs is that we can determine quality by looking at the price. Other heuristics rely on well-known brand names or a product's country of origin as signals of product quality. When we consistently purchase a brand over time, this pattern may be the result of true brand loyalty or simply inertia because it's the easiest thing to do.

5. Marketers often need to understand consumers' behavior rather than a consumer's behavior.

More than one person actually makes many purchasing decisions. Collective decision making occurs whenever two or more people evaluate, select, or use a product or service. In organizations and in families, members play several different roles during the decision-making process. These roles include gatekeeper, influencer, buyer, and user.

6. The decision-making process differs when people choose what to buy on behalf of an organization rather than for personal use.

Organizational buyers are people who make purchasing decisions on behalf of a company or other group. Although many of the same factors that affect how they make decisions in their personal lives influence these buyers, their organizational choices tend to be more rational. Their decisions are also likely to involve more financial risk, and as the choices become more complex, it is probable that a greater number of people will be involved in making the decision. The amount of cognitive effort that goes into organizational decisions relates to internal factors, such as the individuals' psychological characteristics, and external factors, such as the company's willingness to tolerate risk. One of the most important determinants is the type of purchase the company wants to make: The extent of problem-solving required depends on whether the product or service it procures is simply a reorder (a straight rebuy), a reorder with minor modifications (modified rebuy), or something it has never bought before or something complex and risky (new task). Online purchasing sites revolutionize the way organizational decision makers collect and evaluate product information in business-to-business (B2B) e-commerce.

7. Members of a family unit play different roles and have different amounts of influence when the family makes purchase decisions.

Marketers have to understand how families make decisions. Spouses in particular have different priorities and exert varying amounts of influence in terms of effort and power. Working women tend to command more power in purchasing decisions, but on the other hand the significant growth in the number of stay-at-home fathers also influences this dynamic.

KEY TERMS

REVIEW

9-1 Why can "mindless" decision making actually be *more* efficient than devoting a lot of thought to what we buy?

9-2 List the steps in the model of cognitive decision making.

9-3 What is purchase momentum, and how does it relate (or not relate) to the model of rational decision making?

⭐ **9-4** Explain how a consumer can display signs of purchase momentum.

9-5 Name two ways in which a consumer problem arises.

9-6 Give an example of the sunk-cost fallacy.

9-7 What is prospect theory? Does it support the argument that we are rational decision makers?

9-8 "Marketers need to be extra sure their product works as promised when they first introduce it." How does this statement relate to what we know about consumers' evoked sets?

9-9 Describe the difference between a superordinate category, a basic level category, and a subordinate category.

9-10 What is an example of an exemplar product?

⭐ **9-11** List three product attributes that consumers use as product quality signals and provide an example of each.

9-12 How does a brand name work as a heuristic?

9-13 Describe the difference between inertia and brand loyalty.

⭐ **9-14** What is the difference between a noncompensatory and a compensatory decision rule? Give one example of each.

9-15 What is a prime? How does it differ from a nudge?

9-16 What are some factors that influence how an organizational buyer evaluates a purchase decision?

9-17 What is a prediction market?

9-18 Distinguish between straight rebuy and modified rebuy.

9-19 How can a marketer manipulate the social and physical surroundings in a retail store to influence purchasing decisions? How does it work?

9-20 In terms of temporal factors, what does slow or fast mean?

9-21 *Helicopter moms* may be an American phenomenon, but is there anything similar to this in your own country?

9-22 Describe the role of *family financial officer*. How does this role change over time?

9-23 What is meant by the concept of the synoptic deal? Is it relevant in most cases?

9-24 How would you distinguish between a consensual purchase decision and an accommodative one? Provide an example of each of them.

CONSUMER BEHAVIOR CHALLENGE

■ DISCUSS

9-25 Excessive food consumption may link to emotional issues such as feelings of inferiority or low self-esteem. In some situations people consume products (especially food) as a reaction to prior life experiences such as loss of a loved one or perhaps abuse as a child. A British man whom the U.K. news media once dubbed "the world's fattest man" when he weighed in at 980 pounds is a case in point. He explained that as an adult his insatiable desire to constantly eat stemmed from an abusive father and sexual abuse by a relative: "I still had all these things going around in my head from my childhood. Food replaced the love I didn't get from my parents." (The good news: after a gastric bypass operation this man has lost almost two-thirds of his body weight).[116] Obviously this is an extreme case, and it certainly doesn't mean that everyone who struggles with his or her weight is a victim of abuse! Nonetheless, emotion often plays a role—a dieter may feel elated when he weighs in at three pounds less than last week; however, if he fails to make progress he may become discouraged and actually sabotage himself with a Krispy Kreme binge.[117] Is it ethical for food companies to exploit these issues by linking their products to enhanced moods?

9-26   The chapter discusses ways that organizations can use "nudges" to change consumer behavior. Critics refer to them as *benevolent paternalism* because they argue they force people to "eat their vegetables" by restricting the freedom to choose. For example, several cities including New York and Philadelphia have tried (unsuccessfully thus far) to ban the sales of extra large portions of sugary drinks. What's your take on these efforts – should local, state or federal governments be in the business of nudging citizens to be healthier?

9-27   Why is it difficult to place a product in a consumer's evoked set after the person has already rejected that product? What strategies might a marketer use to accomplish this goal?

9-28   Technology has the potential to make our lives easier as it reduces the amount of clutter we need to work through to access the information on the Internet that really interests us. However, perhaps intelligent agents that make recommendations based only on what we and others like us have chosen in the past limit us, in that they reduce the chance that we will stumble on something (e.g., a book on a topic we've never heard of or a music group that's different from the style we usually listen to) through serendipity. Will the proliferation of "shopping bots" make our lives too predictable by only giving us more of the same? If so, is this a problem?

9-29   It's increasingly clear that many postings on blogs and product reviews on Web sites are fake or are posted there to manipulate consumers' opinions. How big a problem is this if consumers increasingly look to consumer-generated product reviews during the stage of information search? What steps, if any, can marketers take to nip this problem in the bud?

9-30   Commercial Alert, a consumer group, is highly critical of neuromarketing. The group's executive director wrote, "What would happen in this country if corporate marketers and political consultants could literally peer inside our brains and chart the neural activity that leads to our selections in the supermarket and voting booth? What if they then could trigger this neural activity by

various means, so as to modify our behavior to serve their own ends?"[118] What do you think? Is neuromarketing dangerous?

9-31   Research supports the argument that the way we pay for a product changes the way we perceive it. More specifically, credit cards prime people to focus less on the costs of the item and more on the benefits. Using plastic decouples the expense of the purchase so we tend to buy more when we can charge it.[119] Newer innovations like digital wallets take this a step further so payment—at least at the time of purchase—is even less painful. Are these formats going to create problems if they prime us to think more about short-term gratification and less about the long-term hit to our budgets? Do marketers have an obligation to try to prevent these problems?

9-32   As more people enter virtual worlds like Second Life and Kaneva, family decision-making research may have to include our virtual partners (and children?) as well.[120] Do you agree? How do you think consumer researchers could use a virtual world to help them understand decision making in the real world?

9-33   Industrial purchase decisions are totally rational. Aesthetic or subjective factors don't—and shouldn't—play a role in this process. Do you agree?

9-34   We can think of college students who live away from home as having a substitute "family." Whether you live with your parents, with a spouse, or with other students, how are decisions made in your college residence "family"? Do some people take on the role of mother, father, or child? Give a specific example of a decision that had to be made and the roles members played.

9-35   There is an increasing trend toward using crowdsourcing as a research and development tool. According to Gartner, by 2017 around 75 percent of all product development capabilities carried out by consumer goods manufacturers will be derived from crowdsourcing.[121] Their predictions went on to suggest that consumer goods companies that use crowdsourcing would see a distinct 1 percent increase in their revenue compared to competitors that did not use crowdsourcing. According to Gartner, consumer goods companies are actively seeking consumer engagement. It is technological development that is making this approach more popular and workable; companies use online communities to help them solve problems and develop new consumer-created products and ideas.

This type of crowdsourcing is a great way to interact with customers. It enables a business to turn customers into loyal brand advocates and to reward them for the ideas that they contribute. These initiatives aim to encourage the most qualified and creative individuals to offer their ideas and to improve projects and products. Crowdsourcing is not a cheap alternative; it takes investment to be able to scan and evaluate the ideas that are being generated. Some companies, such as Kimberly-Clark, actually invite parents to submit ideas.

They also offer help develop the ideas and provide funds to create prototypes. If, in the end, the company does not want the product, they will help the parents find a manufacturing partner. Another example comes from Madison Electric Products, which manufactures products for the professional electrician. They rebranded in 2010 and used crowdsourcing as an integral part of the process—the company developed new products based on the ideas and opinions of electricians who responded to the crowdsourcing. The inventors of the new products could choose to sell their idea to the company, earn royalties on sales, or licence their idea to the company. Since 2010, every one of the company's new product launches has derived from crowdsourced ideas. The company can thus be assured that they are developing and marketing products that their professional market needs and will buy. Madison Electric Products discovered that it was vital to quickly evaluate ideas and respond to contributors.

Is it right to use ideas from customers with little or no reward? How would you go about ensuring that a crowdfunded project attracted a high and consistent level of participation?

APPLY

9-36 Find examples of electronic recommendation agents on the Web. Evaluate these. Are they helpful? What characteristics of the sites you locate are likely to make you buy products you wouldn't have bought on your own?

9-37 Neuromarketing is a growing area of marketing, but few really understand the science behind it. Some suggest that it is a means by which the decision-making processes and behaviors of the consumer can be truly understood; they believe that consumers do not actually know their own mind, and that neuromarketing reveals the truth.[122] On the one hand, it is claimed that neuromarketing effectively casts the consumer as an unknowing, passive, and unreliable entity; on the other, neuromarketing claims to speak for the consumer using technology rather than opinion—consumer opinions have become secondary and neuromarketers can speak for them. Is neuromarketing correct in positing that consumers are really driven by emotion rather than rational choice?

9-38 Define the three levels of product categorization the chapter describes. Diagram these levels for a health club.

9-39 Choose a friend or parent who grocery shops on a regular basis and keep a log of his or her purchases of common consumer products during the term. Can you detect any evidence of brand loyalty in any categories based on consistency of purchases? If so, talk to the person about these purchases. Try to determine if his or her choices are based on true brand loyalty or on inertia. What techniques might you use to differentiate between the two?

9-40 Hershey's stresses the determinant attribute of product authenticity when the chocolate company states: "Hershey, PA is where it all started more than 100 years ago, and it's still where the famous Hershey's Kisses are made."[123] Find examples of other companies that appeal to their heritage. How effective are these messages?

9-41 Form a group of three. Pick a product and develop a marketing plan based on either cognitive or habitual decision making. What are the major differences in emphasis between the two perspectives? Which is the most likely type of decision-making process for the product you selected?

9-42 Identify a person who is about to make a major purchase. Ask that person to make a chronological list of all the information sources he or she consults before deciding what to buy. How would you characterize the types of sources he or she uses (i.e., internal versus external, media versus personal, etc.)? Which sources appeared to have the most impact on the person's decision?

9-43 Perform a survey of country of origin stereotypes. Compile a list of five countries and ask people what products they associate with each. What are their evaluations of the products and likely attributes of these different products? The power of a country stereotype can also be demonstrated in another way. Prepare a brief description of a product, including a list of features, and ask people to rate it in terms of quality, likelihood of purchase, and so on. Make several versions of the description, varying only the country from which it comes. Do ratings change as a function of the country of origin?

9-44 Ask a friend to "talk through" the process he or she used to choose one brand rather than others during a recent purchase. Based on this description, can you identify the decision rule that he or she most likely employed?

9-45 Think of a product you recently shopped for online. Describe your search process. How did you become aware that you wanted or needed the product? How did you evaluate alternatives? Did you wind up buying online? Why or why not? What factors would make it more or less likely that you would buy something online versus in a traditional store?

9-46 Can you replicate Richard's decision-making process as he chose a TV brand for other consumers or other products? Create a grid for a different product category that lists available brands and the features each offers. (Hint: Product Web sites for computers, cars, and other complex products often generate these grids when they allow you to choose the "compare products" option.) Present this grid to several respondents and ask each to talk aloud as they evaluate their options. Based on their description, can you identify which decision rule they seem to use?

9-47 Extraneous characteristics of the choice situation can influence our selections, even though they wouldn't *if* we were totally rational decision makers. Create two versions of this scenario (alternate the text you see in parentheses as directed) and ask a separate group of people to respond to each:

> You are lying on the beach on a hot day. All you have to drink is ice water. For the past hour you have been thinking about how much you would enjoy a nice cold bottle of your favorite brand of beer. A companion gets up to go make a phone call and offers to bring back a beer from the only nearby place where beer is sold (either a fancy resort hotel or a small, run-down grocery store, depending on the version you're given). He says that the beer might be expensive and so asks how much you are willing to pay for it. What price do you tell him?

When researchers gave both versions of this question to respondents, they found that the median price participants who read the fancy-resort version gave was $2.65, but those who got the grocery-store version were only willing to pay $1.50. In both versions, the consumption act is the same, the beer is the same, and they don't consume any "atmosphere" because they drink the beer on the beach.[124] How do these results compare to yours?

9-48 Arrange to interview two married couples, one younger and one older. Prepare a response form that lists five product categories—groceries, furniture, appliances, vacations, and automobiles—and ask each spouse to indicate, without consulting the other, whether purchases in each category are made by joint or unilateral decisions, and to indicate whether the unilateral decisions are made by the husband or the wife. Compare each couple's responses for agreement between husbands and wives relative to who makes the decisions, and compare both couples' overall responses for differences relative to the number of joint versus unilateral decisions. Report your findings and conclusions.

9-49 Collect ads for three different product categories that target families. Find another set of ads for different brands of the same items that don't feature families. Prepare a report comparing the probable effectiveness of the two approaches. Which specific categories would most likely benefit from a family emphasis?

9-50 Pick three married couples and ask each husband and wife to list the names of all cousins, second cousins, and so on for both sides of the family. Based on the results, what can you conclude about the relative role of men and women in maintaining the kin-network system?

Case Study

TESLA MOTORS: DRIVING FORWARD WITH A NEW CONSUMER DECISION JOURNEY

The consumer decision-making process is undergoing major change and will never be the same. Consumers are more informed than ever, with access to virtually endless information. But that wealth of information is leading to many distractions and frustrations along the path to purchase. What experts used to illustrate as a linear or funnel-like decision making path now looks more like a circular, looping journey where distractions often lead consumers to revisit information search and alternative evaluation, just when it seemed like a purchase decision should have been reached.

Dr. Carl Marci at Innerscope Research says "the linear path to the register has been replaced with a roller-coaster ride that spans platforms and screens, through social media and traditional word of mouth." In his blog, Nigel Hollis describes moving away from a consumer loop into a view of a "cloud of turbulent and sometimes conflicting influences" and points to Sue Elms' suggestion that marketers need to plan for "meaningful coincidences" rather than targeting consumers at specific points on the path to purchase.

Marketers must replace outdated strategies that are based on misinterpretations of the decision journey. Today's reality is the prevalence of consumers moving seamlessly back and forth between physical and virtual shopping worlds, while using a variety of devices across multiple channels. "The Path to Purchase: Tracking the Consumer Journey," tells us that 67 percent of shopper journeys now start online; 65 percent of those journeys are purely mobile. Despite that, many consumers still feel a compelling connection to physical shopping for firsthand involvement with the product and the actual purchase. In this kind of an environment, marketers must find new ways to offer "frictionless" customer experiences, remembering that "every touchpoint is a brand experience and an opportunity to engage the consumer."

One company that has responded to this changing consumer decision journey is Tesla Motors, a manufacturer of high-end all-electric cars. Tesla Motors came on the scene in 2006, introducing its first vehicle, the sporty all-electric Roadster with a 200-mile range and a price tag of $100,000. The car won *Time*'s Best Inventions award in the transportation category. Following its unique purchase process, the company took orders ahead of time for the cars and went into production in 2008.

In 2012 it introduced the new Model S electric luxury sedan and by the end of 2013 had sold 18,000 through a non-traditional channel structure, becoming the best-selling full-size luxury sedan overall in the market. The Model S won *Motor Trend*'s Car of the Year and was awarded a five-star safety rating by the National Highway Safety Administration.

Next up, Tesla will be delivering the Model X, a crossover SUV. It has also announced the introduction of the latest version of the Model S, the Model S 70D, an all-wheel drive version with a 250-mile range and has plans to roll out a Model 3, which will sell at a price point of $35,000, appealing to a much broader target market. In 2015, Tesla expected to sell 55,000 vehicles overall, up 74 percent from 2014.

So how has Tesla reinvented the consumer's car buying journey? They believe they have overcome the notoriously frustrating process and created a new model of buying and owning a car through a customized, socially engaging buying experience. Their approach attempts to create that frictionless, engaging set of consumer touch points and experiences that's so important. As pointed out by Paul J. D'Arcy, "Since people start (their decision journey) online, Tesla designed its process around online information, commerce and community." This strategy emphasizes an engaging, content-rich online experience, using a corporate Web site and social media. The Web site is clean and clear, but information-intensive and features a blog by Elon Musk, a majority owner and "lead product architect," who has become the visible face of the company.

Tesla also wants consumers to feel a personal, emotional connection to the brand—to be passionate about owning a Tesla and to want to share that passion with other consumers. It has made user forums and a user community important parts of the online experience. The company does virtually no traditional advertising; it relies more on creating fans of the brand who are willing to generate word of mouth excitement about the vehicles.

However, keeping in mind the role that physical interaction with products can play, the company has introduced "tiny, brand-centric storefronts in upscale shopping malls." These kiosk stores typically feature one vehicle and have a brand expert on hand. The stores are aimed at making the brand more accessible to the general public through high visibility, low maintenance outlets. The car design is so unique and compelling that consumers are drawn in while they're doing other shopping and can ask questions without the high-pressure, commission-driven sales tactics typically associated with car dealerships. When consumers are ready to buy they place a refundable deposit online or they can arrange for a test drive by making a deposit.

The stores have become a big part of the company's advertising. As one observer said about consumers snapping pictures of the Tesla car as they drove by the store window, "That's how cool this car is. You feel like you're part of something bigger, a new age of motor vehicles." In addition, the media have picked up on the buzz created by the brand, a lot of it through social media, and played their own public relations role in increasing awareness of the company and its vehicles.

Tesla is working hard to rewrite the traditional attitudes that consumers have about vehicles and the things they consider in the purchase process. The company's consistent message is that it is building the best car ever, not just the best electric car. It wants to disassociate the company from the typical perceptions that consumers have of gas vehicles and their attributes—dirty, complex, unreliable, hard to maintain. In fact, Tesla service centers have white floors to emphasize the clean nature of the vehicles and the lack of mess involved in servicing them.

Despite the unusual purchase process Tesla Motors has created (or maybe because of it!), the demand for its vehicles continues to outpace production, with buyers placing orders for customized cars well in advance of their production and receipt of the vehicle. It also continues to push forward with game-changing innovation—adding to its network of 2,000 car superchargers worldwide, working to perfect autonomous-driving technology, achieving better mileage range and safety features, and bringing the price of the vehicles within reach of more consumers.

CS9-1 How does Tesla Motors' marketing strategy connect with the changes going on in the consumer decision journey today? Do you believe that they can be successful over the long-term with this kind of an approach?

CS9-2 The chapter identifies three different categories of consumer decision making: cognitive, habitual, and affective. How does Tesla seem to view the type of decision making that consumers go through when they purchase their vehicles?

Sources: Carl Marci, "The Path to Purchase is Paved With Emotion," http://www.cmo.com/articles/2015/3/19/the-path-to-purchase-is-paved-with-pure-emotion.html, accessed June 5, 2015; Nigel Hollis, "Goodbye Purchase Funnel, Hello Loyalty Loop?" http://www.millwardbrown.com/global-navigation/blogs/post/mb-blog/2012/01/19/Goodbye-purchase-funnel-hello-loyalty-loop.aspx, accessed June 10, 2015; Edwin van Bommel, David Edelman, and Kelly Ungerman, "Digitizing the Consumer Decision Journey," http://www.mckinsey.com/insights/marketing_sales/digitizing_the_consumer_decision_journey?cid=other-eml-ttn-mip-mck-oth-1412, accessed June 5, 2015; Chris Newberry, "The Path to Purchase: Tracking the Consumer Journey," http://www.marketingtechnews.net/news/2015/jan/09/path-purchase-tracking-consumer-journey/, accessed June 13, 2015; Paul J. D'Arcy, January 2013, http://scienceofrevenue.com/tag/tesla-marketing-strategy/, accessed June 16, 2015; Casey Neal, "Tesla Motors: Inspiration in Design, Innovation in Marketing," February, 19, 2015, http://www.brittonmdg.com/the-britton-blog/tesla-motors-inspiration-in-design-innovation-in-marketing, accessed June 16, 2015; Simon Reynolds, "Why You Should Copy Tesla's Way of Marketing," http://www.forbes.com/sites/siimonreynolds/2013/09/01/why-you-should-copy-teslas-way-of-marketing/, accessed June 17, 2015; "Cheaper Tesla Model Expected to Debut at 2015 Detroit Show," http://www.autotrader.com/research/article/car-news/218158/cheaper-tesla-model-e-expected-to-debut-at-2015-detroit-show.jsp, accessed June 5, 2015; Steve Fowler, "Tesla Model 3 to Challenge BMW 3 Series," March 5, 2015, http://www.autoexpress.co.uk/tesla/87867/tesla-model-3-to-challenge-bmw-3-series-world-exclusive.

MyLab Marketing

Go to the Assignments section of your MyLab to complete these writing exercises.

9-51 If people are not always rational decision makers, is it worth the effort to study how they make purchasing decisions?

9-52 According to retail analysts Mintel, 84 percent of women state that they influence important household financial decisions, compared to just 49 percent of men.[125] In a stereotypical nuclear family, the members are parts of a decision-making unit. Within the household there are power struggles and intrigue, just like on the board of a corporation. Each individual may have a clear set of requirements and strategies that they deploy to influence decision-making situations. How do the household member roles inform us about the decision-making unit? Do the recognized roles have any relevance to non-stereotypical households? Does the framework have any value in other cultures and societies?

NOTES

1. Ravi Dhar, Joel Huber, and Uzma Khan, "The Shopping Momentum Effect," paper presented at the Association for Consumer Research, Atlanta, GA, October 2002.
2. David Glen Mick, Susan M. Broniarczyk, and Jonathan Haidt, "Choose, Choose, Choose, Choose, Choose, Choose, Choose: Emerging and Prospective Research on the Deleterious Effects of Living in Consumer Hyperchoice," *Journal of Business Ethics* (2004), 52: 207–211; Barry Schwartz, *The Paradox of Choice: Why More is Less*, New York: HarperCollins Publishers, 2005.
3. James R. Bettman, "The Decision Maker Who Came in from the Cold" (presidential address), in Leigh McAllister and Michael Rothschild, eds., *Advances in Consumer Research* 20 (Provo, UT: Association for Consumer Research, 1993): 7–11; John W. Payne, James R. Bettman, and Eric J. Johnson, "Behavioral Decision Research: A Constructive Processing Perspective," *Annual Review of Psychology* 4 (1992): 87–131.
4. Parthasarathy Krishnamurthy and Sonja Prokopec, "Resisting That Triple-Chocolate Cake: Mental Budgets and Self-Control," *Journal of Consumer Research* 37 (June 2010): 68–79.
5. Peter M. Gollwitzer and Paschal Sheeran, "Self-Regulation of Consumer Decision Making and Behavior: The Role of Implementation Intentions," *Journal of Consumer Psychology*, 19 (2009): 593–607.
6. Ying Zhang, Szu-chi Huang, and Susan M. Broniarczyk, "Counteractive Construal in Consumer Goal Pursuit," *Journal of Consumer Research* 37 (June 2010): 129–142.
7. DietBet.com, accessed April 4, 2015;
8. Thomas Goetz, "Harnessing the Power of Feedback Loops," *Wired* (June 19, 2011), http://www.wired.com/2011/06/ff_feedbackloop/all/1, accessed February 3, 2015.
9. Maryan Kouchadki and Isaac H. Smith, "The Morning Morality Effect: The Influence of Time of Day on Unethical Behavior," *Psychological Science* (January 2014), 25 no. 1: 95–102.
10. Quoted in Matt Richtel, "That Devil on Your Shoulder Likes to Sleep In," *New York Times* (November 1, 2014), http://www.nytimes.com/2014/11/02/business/that-devil-on-your-shoulder-likes-to-sleep-in.html?module=Search&mabReward=relbias%3As%2C%7B%221%22%3A%22RI%3A6%22%7D, accessed February 16, 2015.
11. Claudia Townsend and Wendy Liu, "Is Planning Good for You? The Differential Impact of Planning on Self-Regulation," *Journal of Consumer Research* 39, No. 4 (December 2012): 688–703.
12. "Can Facebook Make You Fat and Poor?," *Mashable* (December 13, 2012), http://mashable.com/2012/12/13/facebook-fat-poor/?WT.mc_id=en_my_stories&utm_campaign=My%2BStories&utm_medium=email&utm_source=newsletter?WT.mc_id=en_my_stories&utm_campaign=My%2BStories&utm_medium=email&utm_source=newsletter, accessed February 25, 2015; Keith Wilcox and Andrew T. Stephen, "Are Close Friends the Enemy? Online Social Networks, Self-Esteem, and Self-Control," *Journal of Consumer Research* 40, no. 1 (2013): 90–103.
13. John G. Lynch, Richard G. Netemeyer, Stephen A. Spiller, and Alessandra Zammit, "A Generalizable Scale of Propensity to Plan: The Long and the Short of Planning for Time and for Money," *Journal of Consumer Research* 37 (June 2010): 108–128; Anick Bosmans, Rik Pieters, and Hans Baumgartner, "The Get Ready Mind-Set: How Gearing Up for Later Impacts Effort Allocation Now," *Journal of Consumer Research* 37 (June 2010): 98–107.
14. John C. Mowen, "Beyond Consumer Decision-Making," *Journal of Consumer Marketing* 5, no. 1 (1988): 15–25.
15. Jean Halliday, "With Fusion Campaign, Ford Targets 'Upper Funnel' Car Buyers: $60M to $80M Ad Blitz Aimed at Consumers Not Yet Ready to Buy New Vehicle," *Advertising Age* (March 2, 2009), www.advertisingage.com, accessed March 2, 2009.
16. Gordon C. Bruner, II, and Richard J. Pomazal, "Problem Recognition: The Crucial First Stage of the Consumer Decision Process," *Journal of Consumer Marketing* 5, no. 1 (1988): 53–63.
17. Peter H. Bloch, Daniel L. Sherrell, and Nancy M. Ridgway, "Consumer Search: An Extended Framework," *Journal of Consumer Research* 13 (June 1986): 119–126.
18. "Mental Accounting and Consumer Choice," *Marketing Science* 4 (1985): 199–214.
19. Girish N. Punj and Richard Staelin, "A Model of Consumer Search Behavior for New Automobiles," *Journal of Consumer Research* 9 (March 1983): 366–380. For recent work on online search that decomposes search strategies in terms of type of good, cf. Peng Huang, Nicholas H. Lurie, and Sabyasachi Mitra, "Searching for Experience on the Web: An Empirical Examination of Consumer Behavior for Search and Experience Goods," *Journal of Marketing* 73 (March 2009): 55–69.
20. Examples provided by Dr. William Cohen, personal communication, October 1999.
21. Cobb and Hoyer, "Direct Observation of Search Behavior"; Moore and Lehmann, "Individual Differences in Search Behavior for a Nondurable"; Punj and Staelin, "A Model of Consumer Search Behavior for New Automobiles"; Brian T. Ratchford, M. S. Lee, and D. Toluca, "The Impact of the Internet on Information Search for Automobiles," *Journal of Marketing Research* 40, no. 2 (2003): 193–209.
22. James R. Bettman and C. Whan Park, "Effects of Prior Knowledge and Experience and Phase of the Choice Process on Consumer Decision Processes: A Protocol Analysis," *Journal of Consumer Research* 7 (December 1980): 234–248.
23. Mary Frances Luce, James R. Bettman, and John W. Payne, "Choice Processing in Emotionally Difficult Decisions," *Journal of Experimental Psychology: Learning, Memory, & Cognition* 23 (March 1997): 384–405; example provided by Professor James Bettman, personal communication (December 17, 1997).
24. Some research suggests that structural elements of the information available, such as the number and distribution of attribute levels, will influence how items in a consideration set are processed; cf. Nicholas H. Lurie, "Decision-Making in Information-Rich Environments: The Role of Information Structure," *Journal of Consumer Research* 30 (March 2004): 473–486.
25. John R. Hauser and Birger Wernerfelt, "An Evaluation Cost Model of Consideration Sets," *Journal of Consumer Research* 16 (March 1990): 393–408.
26. Mita Sujan and James R. Bettman, "The Effects of Brand Positioning Strategies on Consumers' Brand and Category Perceptions: Some Insights from Schema Research," *Journal of Marketing Research* 26 (November 1989): 454–467.

27. See William P. Putsis, Jr., and Narasimhan Srinivasan, "Buying or Just Browsing? The Duration of Purchase Deliberation," *Journal of Marketing Research* 31 (August 1994): 393–402.

28. Robert E. Smith, "Integrating Information from Advertising and Trial: Processes and Effects on Consumer Response to Product Information," *Journal of Marketing Research* 30 (May 1993): 204–219.

29. Carmen Nobel, "Neuromarketing: Tapping Into the 'Pleasure Center' of Consumers," *Forbes* (February 1, 2013), http://www.forbes.com/sites/hbsworkingknowledge/2013/02/01/neuromarketing-tapping-into-the-pleasure-center-of-consumers/, accessed April 2, 2015; www.neuroscience marketing.com/blog, accessed April 2, 2015; Martin Reimann, Oliver Schilke, Bernd Weber, Carolin Neuhaus, and Judith L. Zaichkowsky, "Functional Magnetic Resonance Imaging in Consumer Research: A Review and Application," *Psychology & Marketing* 28, no. 6 (2011): 608–637; Sandra Blakeslee, "If You Have a 'Buy Button' in Your Brain, What Pushes It?" *New York Times* (October 19, 2004), www.nytimes.com, accessed October 19, 2004; Clive Thompson, "There's a Sucker Born in Every Medial Prefrontal Cortex," *New York Times* (October 26, 2003), www.nytimes.com, accessed September 29, 2007.

30. Michael Porter, *Competitive Advantage* (New York: Free Press, 1985).

31. Jeffrey M. O'Brien, "You're Soooooooo Predictable," *Fortune* (November 27, 2006): 230.

32. Claire Cain Miller, "Mobile Apps Drive Rapid Change in Searches *New York Times* (January 7, 2013), http://www.nytimes.com/2013/01/08/business/mobile-apps-drive-rapid-changes-in-search-technology.html?ref=business, accessed February 22, 2015.

33. Tracy W. Tuten and Michael R. Solomon, *Social Media Marketing* 2nd ed. London: SAGE, 2016.

34. Nicholas Lurie, Sam Ransbotham, and Hongju Liu, "The Content and Impact of Mobile vs. Desktop Reviews." Paper presented at the 2013 annual meeting of the Association for Consumer Research, Chicago, IL; Bart de Langhe, Philip Fernback, and Donald Lichtenstein, "Navigating by the Stars: What Do Online User Ratings Reveal About Product Quality?" Paper presented at the 2014 annual meeting of the Association for Consumer Research, Baltimore, MD.

35. "Customer Product Reviews Drive Online Satisfaction and Conversion," *Marketing Daily* (January 24, 2007), www.mediapost.com, accessed January 24, 2007.

36. Chris Anderson, *The Long Tail: Why the Future of Business Is Selling Less of More* (New York: Hyperion, 2006).

37. "Drinking Yogurt Taste Test: The Best And The Worst (PHOTOS)," *HuffPost Taste* (April 3, 2013), http://www.huffingtonpost.com/2013/04/03/best-drinking-yogurt_n_2993975.html, accessed July 29, 2015.

38. Cait Poyner and Stacy Wood, "Smart Subcategories: How Assortment Formats Influence Consumer Learning and Satisfaction," *Journal of Consumer Research* 37 (June 2010): 159–175; Kenneth C. Manning and David E. Sprott, "Price Endings, Left-Digit Effects, and Choice," *Journal of Consumer Research* 36, no. 2 (2009): 328–335; Sandra J. Milberg, Francisca Sinn, and Ronald C. Goodstein, "Consumer Reactions to Brand Extensions in a Competitive Context: Does Fit Still Matter?" *Journal of Consumer Research* 37, no. 3 (2010): 543–553; David Sleeth-Keppler and S. Christian Wheeler, "A Multidimensional Association Approach to Sequential Consumer Judgments," *Journal of Consumer Psychology* 21, no. 1 (2011): 14–23; Aner Sela, Jonah Berger, and Wendy Liu, "Variety, Vice, and Virtue: How Assortment Size Influences Option Choice," *Journal of Consumer Research* 35, no. 6 (2009): 941–951.

39. Noah Rayman, "Dunkin' Donuts Now Has Its Own Version of the Cronut," *Time* (October 27, 2014), http://time.com/3542225/dunkin-donuts-croissant-donut-cronut/, accessed April 3, 2015.

40. Jeffrey R. Parker and Donald R. Lehmann, "How and When Grouping Low-Calorie Options Reduces the Benefits of Providing Dish-Specific Calorie Information," *Journal of Consumer Research* 41, no. 1 (2014): 213–235; cf. also Avni M. Shah, James R. Bettman, Peter A. Ubel, Punam Anand Keller, and Julie A. Edell, "Surcharges Plus Unhealthy Labels Reduce Demand for Unhealthy Menu Items," *Journal of Marketing Research* 51, no. 6 (2014): 773–789.

41. Robert M. McMath, "The Perils of Typecasting," *American Demographics* (February 1997): 60.

42. Eleanor Rosch, "Principles of Categorization," in E. Rosch and B. B. Lloyd, eds., *Recognition and Categorization* (Hillsdale, NJ: Erlbaum, 1978); cf. also Joseph Lajos, Zsolt Katona, Amitava Chattopadhyay, and Miklos Savary, "Category Activation Model: A Spreading Activation Network Model of Subcategory Positioning When Categorization Uncertainty Is High," *Journal of Consumer Research* 36, no. 1 (June 2009): 122–136; cf also M.

S. Isaac and R. M. Schindler, "The Top-Ten Effect: Consumers' Subjective Categorization of Ranked Lists," *Journal of Consumer Research* 40, no. 6 (2014): 1181–1202.

43. Michael R. Solomon, "Mapping Product Constellations: A Social Categorization Approach to Symbolic Consumption," *Psychology & Marketing* 5, no. 3 (1988): 233–258.

44. Elizabeth C. Hirschman and Michael R. Solomon, "Competition and Cooperation among Culture Production Systems," in Ronald F. Bush and Shelby D. Hunt, eds., *Marketing Theory: Philosophy of Science Perspectives* (Chicago: American Marketing Association, 1982): 269–272.

45. Michael D. Johnson, "The Differential Processing of Product Category and Noncomparable Choice Alternatives," *Journal of Consumer Research* 16 (December 1989): 300–339.

46. Mita Sujan, "Consumer Knowledge: Effects on Evaluation Strategies Mediating Consumer Judgments," *Journal of Consumer Research* 12 (June 1985): 31–46.

47. Ronald Alsop, "How Boss's Deeds Buff a Firm's Reputation," *Wall Street Journal* (January 31, 2007): B1.

48. Stuart Elliott, "Pepsi-Cola to Stamp Dates for Freshness on Soda Cans," *New York Times* (March 31, 1994): D1; Emily DeNitto, "Pepsi's Gamble Hits Freshness Dating Jackpot," *Advertising Age* (September 19, 1994): 50.

49. Julie Napoli, Sonia J. Dickinson, Michael B. Beverland and Francis Farrelly, "Measuring Consumer-Based Brand Authenticity," *Journal of Business Research* 67, no. 6 (2014): 1090–1098.

50. George E. Newman and Ravi Dhar, "Authenticity Is Contagious: Brand Essence and the Original Source of Production," *Journal of Marketing Research* 51, no. 3 (June 2014): 371–386; Quoted in Matthew Hutson, "Quenching Consumers' Thirst for 'Authentic' Brands," *New York Times*, (December 27, 2014), http://www.nytimes.com/2014/12/28/business/quenching-consumers-thirst-for-authentic-brands.html?module=Search&mabReward=relbias%3Ar%2C%7B%221%22%3A%22RI%3A11%22%7D&_r=0, accessed February 18, 2015.

51. C. Whan Park, "The Effect of Individual and Situation-Related Factors on Consumer Selection of Judgmental Models," *Journal of Marketing Research* 13 (May 1976): 144–151.

52. Richard W. Olshavsky and Donald H. Granbois, "Consumer Decision-Making—Fact or Fiction," *Journal of Consumer Research* 6 (September 1989): 93–100; Geoffrey C. Kiel and Roger A. Layton, "Dimensions of Consumer Information Seeking Behavior," *Journal of Marketing Research* 28 (May 1981): 233–239; see also Narasimhan Srinivasan and Brian T. Ratchford, "An Empirical Test of a Model of External Search for Automobiles," *Journal of Consumer Research* 18 (September 1991): 233–242; Alex Mindlin, "Buyers Search Online, But Not by Brand," *New York Times* (March 13, 2006), www.nytimes.com, accessed March 13, 2006; Cathy J. Cobb and Wayne D. Hoyer, "Direct Observation of Search Behavior," *Psychology & Marketing* 2 (Fall 1985): 161–179; Sharon E. Beatty and Scott M. Smith, "External Search Effort: An Investigation across Several Product Categories," *Journal of Consumer Research* 14 (June 1987): 83–95; William L. Moore and Donald R. Lehmann, "Individual Differences in Search Behavior for a Nondurable," *Journal of Consumer Research* 7 (December 1980): 296–307. Tanya L. Chartrand, Joel Huber, Baba Shiv, and Robin J Tanner, "Nonconscious Goals and Consumer Choice," *Journal of Consumer Research* 35, 2 (August 2008): 189–201. Beth Snyder Bulik, "Behavioral Economics Helping Marketers Better Understand Consumers Practice Gives Advertisers Insight into Shoppers' Brand Selection," *Ad Age CMO Strategy* (July 26, 2010), http://adage.com/article/cmo-strategy/behavioral-economics-helping-marketers–under stand-consumers/145091/, accessed April 17, 2011; cf. also Robin L. Soster, Ashwani Monga, and William O. Bearden, "Tracking Costs of Time and Money: How Accounting Periods Affect Mental Accounting," *Journal of Consumer Research* 37, no. 4 (2010): 712–721.

53. Malcolm Gladwell, *Blink: The Power of Thinking without Thinking* (New York: Little Brown & Company, 2005).

54. Geoffrey C. Kiel and Roger A. Layton, "Dimensions of Consumer Information Seeking Behavior," *Journal of Marketing Research* 28 (May 1981): 233–239; see also Narasimhan Srinivasan and Brian T. Ratchford, "An Empirical Test of a Model of External Search for Automobiles," *Journal of Consumer Research* 18 (September 1991): 233–242; Alex Mindlin, "Buyers Search Online, But Not by Brand," *New York Times* (March 13, 2006), www.nytimes.com, accessed March 13, 2006; Cathy J. Cobb and Wayne D. Hoyer, "Direct Observation of Search Behavior," *Psychology & Marketing* 2 (Fall 1985): 161–179; Sharon E. Beatty and Scott M. Smith, "External Search Effort: An Investigation across Several Product Categories," *Journal of Consumer Research* 14 (June 1987): 83–95; William L. Moore and Donald R. Lehmann, "Individual Differences

in Search Behavior for a Nondurable," *Journal of Consumer Research* 7 (December 1980): 296–307.

55. Tanya L. Chartrand, Joel Huber, Baba Shiv, and Robin J Tanner, "Nonconscious Goals and Consumer Choice," *Journal of Consumer Research* 35, no. 2 (August 2008): 189–201.

56. Beth Snyder Bulik, "Behavioral Economics Helping Marketers Better Understand Consumers Practice Gives Advertisers Insight into Shoppers' Brand Selection," *Ad Age CMO Strategy* (July 26, 2010), http://adage.com/article/cmo-strategy/behavioral-economics-helping-marketers–understand-consumers/145091/, accessed April 17, 2011; cf. also Robin L. Soster, Ashwani Monga, and William O. Bearden, "Tracking Costs of Time and Money: How Accounting Periods Affect Mental Accounting," *Journal of Consumer Research* 37, no. 4 (2010): 712–721.

57. Aparna A. Labroo and Jesper H. Nielsen, "Half the Thrill Is in the Chase: Twisted Inferences from Embodied Cognitions and Brand Evaluations," *Journal of Consumer Research* 37 (June 2010): 143–158.

58. Leslie Z. McArthur, Michael R. Solomon, and Rebecca H. Jaffe, "Weight Differences in Emotional Responsiveness to Proprioceptive and Pictorial Stimuli," *Journal of Personality and Social Psychology* 39, no. 2 (1980): 308–319.

59. Steven J. Levitt and Stephen G. Dubner, *Freakonomics: A Rogue Economist Explores the Hidden Side of Everything* (New York, NY: Harper Perennial, 2009); Dan Ariely, *Predictably Irrational: The Hidden Forces That Shape Our Decisions* (New York: HarperCollins, 2008).

60. Eduardo Porter, "How Money Affects Morality," *New York Times* (January 3, 2013), http://economix.blogs.nytimes.com/2013/06/13/how-money-affects-morality/, accessed February 23, 2015.

61. Gergana Y. Nenkov and Maura L. Scott, "So Cute I Could Eat It Up": Priming Effects of Cute Products on Indulgent Consumption," *Journal of Consumer Research* 41, no. 2 (August 2014): 326–341.

62. Adrian C. North, David J. Hargreaves, and Jennifer McKendrick, "The Influence of In-Store Music on Wine Selections," *Journal of Applied Psychology* 84, no. 2 (1999): 271–276.

63. Rob Girling, "Design's Next Frontier: Nudging Consumers into Making Better Life Choices," *Fast Company* (February 15, 2012), http://www.fastcodesign.com/1669055/designs-next-frontier-nudging-consumers-into-making-better-life-choices?partner=homepage_newsletter, accessed February 18, 2015; for examples in the health and wellness area, cf. Zoe Chance, Margarita Gorlin, and Ravi Dhar, "Why Choosing Healthy Foods Is Hard, and How to Help: Presenting the 4Ps Framework for Behavior Change," *Customer Needs and Solutions* 1, no. 4 (2014): 253–262.

64. Richard H. Thaler and Cass R. Sunstein, *Nudge: Improving Decisions About Health, Wealth, and Happiness* (New York: Penguin Books, 2009); Rob Girling, *Design's Next Frontier: Nudging Consumers Into Making Better Life Choices, Co. Design* (February 29, 2012), http://www.fastcodesign.com/1669055/designs-next-frontier-nudging-consumers-into-making-better-life-choices?partner=homepage_newsletter, accessed February 16, 2013; John A. Bargh and Tanya L. Chartrand, "The Unbearable Automaticity of Being," *American Psychologist* 54, no. 7 (1999): 462–479; J. A. Bargh and M. J. Ferguson, "Beyond Behaviourism: On the Automaticity of Higher Mental Processes," *Psychological Bulletin* 126, no. 6 (2000): 925–945.

65. Laurie J. Flynn, "Like This? You'll Hate That (Not All Web Recommendations Are Welcome)," *New York Times* (January 23, 2006), www.nytimes.com, accessed January 23, 2006.

66. Robert A. Baron, *Psychology: The Essential Science* (Boston: Allyn &-Bacon, 1989); Valerie S. Folkes, "The Availability Heuristic and Perceived Risk," *Journal of Consumer Research* 15 (June 1989): 13–23; Daniel Kahneman and Amos Tversky, "Prospect Theory: An Analysis of Decision under Risk," *Econometrica* 47, no. 2 (1979): 263–291.

67. Wayne D. Hoyer, "An Examination of Consumer Decision-Making for a Common Repeat Purchase Product," *Journal of Consumer Research* 11 (December 1984): 822–829; Calvin P. Duncan, "Consumer Market Beliefs: A Review of the Literature and an Agenda for Future Research," in Marvin E. Goldberg, Gerald Gorn, and Richard W. Pollay, eds., *Advances in Consumer Research* 17 (Provo, UT: Association for Consumer Research, 1990): 729–735; Frank Alpert, "Consumer Market Beliefs and Their Managerial Implications: An Empirical Examination," *Journal of Consumer Marketing* 10, no. 2 (1993): 56–70.

68. Michael R. Solomon, Sarah Drenan, and Chester A. Insko, "Popular Induction: When Is Consensus Information Informative?" *Journal of Personality* 49, no. 2 (1981): 212–224.

69. Howard Beales, Michael B. Mazis, Steven C. Salop and Richard Staelin, "Consumer Search and Public Policy," *Journal of Consumer Research* 8, no. 1 (June 1981): 11–22.

70. Adam Bryant, "Message in a Beer Bottle," *Newsweek* (May 29, 2000): 43.

71. Calvin P. Duncan, "Consumer Market Beliefs: a Review of the Literature and an Agenda For Future Research", in *NA - Advances in Consumer Research* 17, eds. Marvin E. Goldberg, Gerald Gorn, and Richard W. Pollay (Provo, UT: Association for Consumer Research, 1990): 729–736.

72. Chr. Hjorth-Andersen, "Price as a Risk Indicator," *Journal of Consumer Policy* 10 (1987): 267–281; David M. Gardner, "Is There a Generalized Price–Quality Relationship?" *Journal of Marketing Research* 8 (May 1971): 241–243; Kent B. Monroe, "Buyers' Subjective Perceptions of Price," *Journal of Marketing Research* 10 (1973): 70–80.

73. Fred E. Webster and Yoram Wind, *Organizational Buying Behavior* (Upper Saddle River, NJ: Prentice Hall, 1972).

74. See J. Joseph Cronin, Jr., and Michael H. Morris, "Satisfying Customer Expectations: The Effect on Conflict and Repurchase Intentions in Industrial Marketing Channels," *Journal of the Academy of Marketing Science* 17 (Winter 1989): 41–49; Thomas W. Leigh and Patrick F. McGraw, "Mapping the Procedural Knowledge of Industrial Sales Personnel: A Script-Theoretic Investigation," *Journal of Marketing* 53 (January 1989): 16–34; William J. Qualls and Christopher P. Puto, "Organizational Climate and Decision Framing: An Integrated Approach to Analyzing Industrial Buying," *Journal of Marketing Research* 26 (May 1989): 179–192.

75. James M. Sinkula, "Market Information Processing and Organizational Learning," *Journal of Marketing* 58 (January 1994): 35–45.

76. Allen M. Weiss and Jan B. Heide, "The Nature of Organizational Search in High Technology Markets," *Journal of Marketing Research* 30 (May 1993): 220–233; Jennifer K. Glazing and Paul N. Bloom, "Buying Group Information Source Reliance," *Proceedings of the American Marketing Association Educators' Conference* (Summer 1994): 454.

77. B. Charles Ames and James D. Hlaracek, *Managerial Marketing for Industrial Firms* (New York: Random House Business Division, 1984); Edward F. Fern and James R. Brown, "The Industrial/Consumer Marketing Dichotomy: A Case of Insufficient Justification," *Journal of Marketing* 48 (Spring 1984): 68–77.

78. Jaakko Aspara, "Aesthetics of Stock Investments," *Consumption Markets & Culture* 12 (June 2009): 99–131.

79. Daniel H. McQuiston, "Novelty, Complexity, and Importance as Causal Determinants of Industrial Buyer Behavior," *Journal of Marketing* 53 (April 1989): 66–79.

80. Patrick J. Robinson, Charles W. Faris, and Yoram Wind, *Industrial Buying and Creative Marketing* (Boston: Allyn & Bacon, 1967).

81. Erin Anderson, Wujin Chu, and Barton Weitz, "Industrial Purchasing: An Empirical Examination of the Buyclass Framework," *Journal of Marketing* 51 (July 1987): 71–86.

82. Julie Moreland, "Does 'Liking' a Bulldozer Help Sell More of Them?" *Fast Company*, (November 29, 2012), http://www.fastcompany.com/3003479/does-liking-bulldozer-help-sell-more-them?partner=newsletter, accessed January 30, 2015.

83. http://www.dell.com/us/business/p/, accessed June 14, 2011.

84. Barbara Kiviat, "The End of Management," *Time Inside Business* (July 12, 2004), www.time.com/time/magazine/article/0,9171,994658,00.html, accessed October 5, 2007.

85. ww.hsx.com, accessed April 13, 2015.

86. Cf. C. Page Moreau and Kelly B. Herd, "To Each His Own? How Comparisons with Others Influence Consumers' Evaluations of Their Self–Designed Products," *Journal of Consumer Research* 36, no. 5 (February 2010): 806–819; Wendy Liu and David Gal, "Bringing Us Together Or Driving Us Apart: The Effect of Soliciting Consumer Input on Consumers' Propensity to Transact with an Organization," *Journal of Consumer Research* 38, no. 2 (August 2011): 242–259.

87. James Surowiecki, *The Wisdom of Crowds* (New York: Anchor, 2005); Jeff Howe, "The Rise of Crowdsourcing," *Wired* (June 2006), www.wired.com/wired/archive/14.06/crowds.html, accessed April 12, 2015.

88. Emma Hutchings, "Budweiser Will Crowdsource Its Next Beer," *Mashable* (November 7, 2012), http://mashable.com/2012/11/07/budweiser-crowdsourced-beer/, accessed March 19, 2013; Stephanie Buck, "Alexander Wang Teams Up with Samsung for Crowdsourced Handbag," *Mashable* (February 11, 2013), http://mashable.com/2013/02/11/alexander-wang-samsung/, accessed March 19, 2013.

89. www.threadless.com, accessed April 12, 2015; Mark Weingarten, "Designed to Grow," *Business 2.0* (June 2007): 35–37. For a contrarian view, cf. Joseph P. Simmons, Leif D. Nelson, Jeff Galak, and Shane Frederick, "Intuitive Biases in Choice Versus Estimation: Implications for the Wisdom of Crowds," *Journal of Consumer Research* 38, no. 1 (June 2011): 1–15.

90. Lauren Indvik, "ModCloth Launches Clothing Collection of User-Generated Designs," *Mashable* (May 23, 2012), http://mashable.com/2012/05/23/

modcloth-user-generated-fashion-label/?WT.mc_id=en_business&utm_campaign=Business&utm_medium=email&utm_source=newsletter, accessed January 10, 2013; kickstarter.com, accessed April 12, 2015.

91. Nina Diamond, John F. Sherry Jr., Albert M. Muñiz Jr., Mary Ann McGrath, Robert V. Kozinets, and Stefania Borghini, "American Girl and the Brand Gestalt: Closing the Loop on Sociocultural Branding Research," *Journal of Marketing* 73 (May 2009): 118–134.

92. Harry L. Davis, "Decision-Making Within the Household," *Journal of Consumer Research* 2 (March 1972): 241–260; Michael B. Menasco and David J. Curry, "Utility and Choice: An Empirical Study of Wife/Husband Decision-Making," *Journal of Consumer Research* 16 (June 1989): 87–97; Conway Lackman and John M. Lanasa. "Family Decision-Making Theory: An Overview and Assessment," *Psychology & Marketing* 10 (March–April 1993): 81–94.

93. Shannon Dortch, "Money and Marital Discord," *American Demographics* (October 1994): 11.

94. For research on factors affecting how much influence adolescents exert in family decision-making, see Ellen Foxman, Patriya Tansuhaj, and Karin M. Ekstrom, "Family Members' Perceptions of Adolescents' Influence in Family Decision-Making," *Journal of Consumer Research* 15 (March 1989): 482–491; Sharon E. Beatty and Salil Talpade, "Adolescent Influence in Family Decision-Making: A Replication with Extension," *Journal of Consumer Research* 21 (September 1994): 332–341; for a study that compared the influence of parents versus siblings, cf. June Cotte and Stacy L. Wood, "Families and Innovative Consumer Behavior: A Triadic Analysis of Sibling and Parental Influence," *Journal of Consumer Research* 31, no. 1 (2004): 78–86.

95. Daniel Seymour and Greg Lessne, "Spousal Conflict Arousal: Scale Development," *Journal of Consumer Research* 11 (December 1984): 810–821.

96. Karlene Lukovitz, "Women in Wealthy Homes Make 2 of 3 Buying Decisions," *Marketing Daily* (May 15, 2008), www.mediapost.com, accessed May 15, 2008; Dennis L. Rosen and Donald H. Granbois, "Determinants of Role Structure in Family Financial Management," *Journal of Consumer Research* 10 (September 1983): 253–258; Robert F. Bales, Interaction Process Analysis: A Method for the Study of Small Groups (Reading, MA: Addison-Wesley, 1950). For a cross-gender comparison of food shopping strategies, see Rosemary Polegato and Judith L. Zaichkowsky, "Family Food Shopping: Strategies Used by Husbands and Wives," *Journal of Consumer Affairs* 28, no. 2 (1994): 278–299.

97. Alma S. Baron, "Working Parents: Shifting Traditional Roles," *Business* 37 (January–March 1987): 36; William J. Qualls, "Household Decision Behavior: The Impact of Husbands' and Wives' Sex Role Orientation," *Journal of Consumer Research* 14 (September 1987): 264–279; Charles M. Schaninger and W. Christian Buss, "The Relationship of Sex-Role Norms to Household Task Allocation," *Psychology & Marketing* 2 (Summer 1985): 93–104.

98. Natalie Angier, "The Changing American Family," *New York Times* (November 25, 2013), http://www.nytimes.com/2013/11/26/health/families.html?_r=0, accessed February 20, 2015.

99. C. Whan Park, "Joint Decisions in Home Purchasing: A Muddling-Through Process," *Journal of Consumer Research* 9 (September 1982): 151–162; see also William J. Qualls and Francoise Jaffe, "Measuring Conflict in Household Decision Behavior: Read My Lips and Read My Mind," in John F. Sherry Jr. and Brian Sternthal, eds., *Advances in Consumer Research* 19 (Provo, UT: Association for Consumer Research, 1992): 522–531.

100. Kim P. Corfman and Donald R. Lehmann, "Models of Cooperative Group Decision-Making and Relative Influence: An Experimental Investigation of Family Purchase Decisions," *Journal of Consumer Research* 14 (June 1987): 1–13.

101. Diane Crispell, "Dual-Earner Diversity," *American Demographics* (July 1995): 32–37.

102. Elisha Hartwig, "Half of Parents Join Facebook to Creep on Their Kids," *Mashable* (February 16, 2013), http://mashable.com/2013/02/16/facebook-parents-kids/?utm_source=feedburner&utm_medium=email&utm_campaign=Feed%3A+Mashable+%28Mashable%29, accessed February 23, 2015.

103. Amber M. Epp and Linda L. Price, "Family Identity: A Framework of Identity Interplay in Consumption Practices," *Journal of Consumer Research* 35 (June 2008): 50–70; Robert Lohrer, "Haggar Targets Women with $8M Media Campaign," *Daily News Record* (January 8, 1997): 1.

104. Amber M. Epp and Sunaina Velagaleti, "Outsourcing Parenthood: How Families Manage Care Assemblages Using Paid Commercial Services," *Journal of Consumer Research*, 41 (December 2014): 911–935.

105. Erik Sass, "Facebook Is Now Leading Source of Evidence in Divorce Cases," *Social Media & Marketing Daily* (March 10, 2011), http://www.mediapost.com/publications/?fa=Articles.showArticle&art_aid=146421&nid=124595, accessed April 19, 2011.

106. Richard Alleyne, "Facebook Increasingly Implicated in Divorce," *The Telegraph* (UK) (January 21, 2011), http://www.telegraph.co.uk/technology/facebook/8274601/Facebook-increasingly-implicated-in-divorce.html, accessed January 2, 2013.

107. Natalie Angier, "The Changing American Family," *New York Times* (November 25, 2013), http://www.nytimes.com/2013/11/26/health/families.html?_r=0, accessed February 20, 2015; Belinda Luscombe, "Woman Power: The Rise of the Sheconomy," *Time Magazine* (November 22, 2010), http://www.time.com/time/magazine/article/0,9171,2030913-3,00.html, accessed April 19, 2011; Sarah Mahoney, "New Rules of Mama Marketing: Older, Greener," *Marketing Daily* (July 12, 2010), http://www.mediapost.com/publications/?fa=Articles.showArticle&art_aid=131754, accessed April 19, 2011.

108. Craig J. Thompson, "Caring Consumers: Gendered Consumption Meanings and the Juggling Lifestyle," *Journal of Consumer Research* 22 (March 1996): 388–407.

109. Edmund L. Andrews, "Survey Confirms It: Women Outjuggle Men," *New York Times* (September 15, 2004), http://www.nytimes.com/2004/09/15/politics/15labor.html, accessed April 10, 2015.

110. Micaela DiLeonardo, "The Female World of Cards and Holidays: Women, Families, and the Work of Kinship," *Signs* 12 (Spring 1942): 440–453.

111. Tanya Irwin, "Study: Men Defy Marketing Stereotypes," *Marketing Daily* (April 25, 2011), http://www.mediapost.com/publications/article/149272/study-men-defy-marketing-stereotypes.html, accessed April 10, 2015; Stephanie Clifford, "More Dads Buy the Toys, So Barbie, and Stores, Get Makeovers," *New York Times* (December 3, 2012), http://www.nytimes.com/2012/12/04/business/more-dads-buy-the-toys-so-barbie-and-stores-get-makeovers.html?_r=0, accessed April 10, 2015. Emily Bryson York, "Retailers Adjust Marketing As More Men Take Over Grocery Shopping," *Los Angeles Times* (December 29, 2011), http://articles.latimes.com/2011/dec/29/business/la-fi-male-shoppers-20111229, accessed April 10, 2015; Gokcen Coskuner-Balli and Craig J. Thompson, "The Status Costs of Subordinate Cultural Capital: At-Home Fathers' Collective Pursuit of Cultural Legitimacy through Capitalizing Consumption Practices," *Journal of Consumer Research* 40, no. 1 (June 2013): 19–41.

112. Quoted in Molly Soat, "Cheerios Leverages the Power of 'Dadvertising'," *Marketing News Weekly* (February 25, 2015), https://www.ama.org/publications/eNewsletters/Marketing-News-Weekly/Pages/cheerios-how-to-dad.aspx, accessed April 10, 2015.

113. Donald H. Granbois, "Improving the Study of Customer In-Store Behavior," *Journal of Marketing* 32 (October 1968): 28–32; Tamara F. Mangleburg, Patricia M. Doney, and Terry Bristol, "Shopping with Friends and Teens' Susceptibility to Peer Influence," *Journal of Retailing* 80 (2004): 101–116.

114. Len Strazewski, "Tupperware Locks in New Strategy," *Advertising Age* (February 8, 1988): 30.

115. Rachel Ashman, Michael R. Solomon and Julia Wolny, "An Old Model for a New Age: Applying the EKB in Today's Participatory Culture," *Journal of Customer Behaviour*, 2015, 14(2): 127–146.

116. Quoted in Sarah Lyall, "One-Third the Man He Used to Be, and Proud of It," *New York Times* (February 6, 2013), http://www.nytimes.com/2013/02/06/world/europe/paul-mason-is-one-third-the-man-he-used-to-be.html?_r=0, accessed February 6, 2013.

117. Claudia Townsend and Wendy Liu, "Is Planning Good for You? The Differential Impact of Planning on Self-Regulation," *Journal of Consumer Research* 38 (December 2012): 688–703.

118. Sandra Blakeslee, "If You Have a 'Buy Button' in Your Brain, What Pushes it?" *New York Times* (October 9, 2004), http://www.nytimes.com/2004/10/19/science/19neuro.html?_r=0, accessed April 2, 2013.

119. Promothesh Chatterjee and Randall L. Rose, "Do Payment Mechanisms Change the Way Consumers Perceive Products?," *Journal of Consumer Research*, (2012), 38, 6: 38–43.

120. Emily Friedman, "Does Virtual Cheating Still Count?," *ABC News* (August 13, 2007), http://abcnews.go.com/Technology/story?id=3473291&page=1, accessed August 13, 2007; Regina Lynn, "Virtual Rape Is Traumatic, but Is It a Crime?" *Wired* (May 4, 2007); www.wired.com/culture/lifestyle/commentary/sexdrive/2007/05/sexdrive_0504, accessed June 16, 2009; "Representative Kirk Wants to Ban Second Life's 'Rape Rooms' from Schools," *Virtual Worlds News* (May 7, 2008), www.virtualworldsnews.com/2008/05/representative.html?cid=113790134, accessed June 16, 2009.

121. "Gartner Reveals Top Predictions for IT Organizations and Users for 2014 and Beyond," Gartner Newsroom, October 8, 2013, http://www.gartner.com/newsroom/id/2603215

122. Tanja Schneider and Steve Woolgar, "Technologies of Ironic Revelation: Enacting Consumers in Neuromarkets," Institute for Science, Innovation and Society (InSIS) and Saïd Business School, University of Oxford, *Consumption Markets & Culture* 15, no. 2 (June 2012): 169–189.

123. Quoted in George E. Newman and Ravi Dhar, "Authenticity Is Contagious: Brand Essence and the Original Source of Production," *Journal of Marketing Research* 51, no. 3 (2014): 371–386.

124. Daniel Kahneman and Amos Tversky, "Prospect Theory: An Analysis of Decision under Risk," *Econometrica* 47 (March 1979): 263–291; Timothy B. Heath, Subimal Chatterjee, and Karen Russo France, "Mental Accounting and Changes in Price: The Frame Dependence of Reference Dependence," *Journal of Consumer Research* 22, no. 1 (June 1995): 90–97.

125. Sean Poulter, "Mothers Make the Important Financial Decisions in Most Families…and Choose Where to Go on Holiday, Research Finds," *The Daily Mail*, http://www.dailymail.co.uk/news/article-3228614/Mothers-make-important-financial-decisions-families-choose-holiday-research-finds.html#ixzz48kOAQ8Oq; "Spousal Roles in Family Purchase Decision Making Process," http://shodhganga.inflibnet.ac.in/bitstream/10603/10360/9/09_chapter%201.pdf; Lars Perner, "Families and Family Decision Making," http://www.consumerpsychologist.com/cb_Family_Decision_Making.html.

Chapter 10 • Buying, Using, and Disposing

Chapter Objectives

When you finish reading this chapter you will understand why:

10-1 Many factors at the time of purchase dramatically influence the consumer's decision-making process.

10-2 The information a store's layout, Web site, or salespeople provides strongly influences a purchase decision.

10-3 The growth of a "sharing economy" changes how many consumers think about buying rather than renting products.

10-4 Our decisions about how to dispose of a product are as important as how we decide to obtain it in the first place.

Source: Mandy Godbehear/Shutterstock.

Kyle is really psyched. The big day has actually arrived: He's going to buy a car! He's had his eye on that silver 2009 Honda Accord parked in the lot of Jon's Auto-Rama for weeks now. Although the sticker says $2,999, Kyle figures he can probably get this baby for a cool $2,000. Besides, Jon's dilapidated showroom and seedy lot make it look like just the kind of place that's hungry to move some cars. Kyle did his homework on the Web. First he found out the wholesale value of similar used Accords from the Kelley Blue Book (kbb.com), and then he scouted out some cars for sale in his area at cars.com. So, Kyle figures he's coming in loaded for bear—he's going to show these guys they're not dealing with some newbie. Unlike some of the newer, flashy car showrooms he's been in lately, this place is a real nuts-and-bolts operation; it's so dingy and depressing he can't wait to get out of there and take a shower. Kyle dreads the prospect of haggling over the price, but he hopes to convince the salesperson to take his offer because he knows the real market value of the car he wants. At the Auto-Rama lot, big signs on all the cars proclaim that today is Jon's Auto-Rama Rip Us Off Day! Things look better than Kyle expected—maybe he can get the car for even less than he hoped. He's a bit surprised when a salesperson comes over to him and introduces herself as Kristen. He expected to deal with a middle-aged man in a loud sport coat (a stereotype he has about used-car salespeople), but this is better luck: He reasons that he won't have to be so tough if he negotiates with a woman his age. Kristen laughs when he offers her $1,800 for the Honda; she points out that she can't take such a low bid for such a sweet car to her boss or she'll lose her job. Kristen's enthusiasm for the car convinces Kyle all the more that he has to have it. When he finally writes a check for $2,700, he's exhausted from all the haggling. What an ordeal! In any case, Kyle reminds himself that he at least convinced Kristen to sell him the car for less than the sticker price, and maybe he can fix it up and sell it for even more in a year or two. That Web surfing really paid off: He's a tougher negotiator than he thought.

OBJECTIVE 10-1

Many factors at the time of purchase dramatically influence the consumer's decision-making process.

Situational Effects on Consumer Behavior

Many consumers dread the act of buying a car. But change is in the wind, as dealers transform the car showroom. Car shoppers like Kyle log on to Internet buying services, call auto brokers who negotiate for them, buy cars at warehouse clubs, and visit giant auto malls where they can easily comparison shop. Indeed, the average car buyer today visits only 1.6 auto dealerships, as compared to five just a decade ago.[1] Kyle's experience when he bought a car illustrates some of the concepts we'll discuss in this chapter. He did a lot of legwork beforehand, and elements of the physical environment where he bought his Honda influenced his decision. Making a purchase is often not a simple, routine matter where you just pop into a store and make a quick choice.

As Figure 10.1 illustrates, many contextual factors affect our choice, such as our mood, whether we feel time pressure to make the purchase, and the particular reason we need the product. In some situations, such as when we buy a car or a home, the salesperson or realtor plays a pivotal role in our final selection. Also, today people like Kyle often use the Web to arm themselves with product and price information before they even enter a dealership or a store; this puts more pressure on retailers to deliver the value their customers expect.

The Consumption Situation

A **consumption situation** includes a buyer, a seller, and a product or service—but also many other factors, such as the reason we want to make a purchase and how the physical environment makes us feel.[2] Common sense tells us that we tailor our purchases to specific occasions and that the way we feel at a specific point in time affects what we want to do—or buy. Smart marketers understand these patterns and plan their efforts to coincide with situations in which we are most prone to purchase. For example, book clubs invest heavily in promotional campaigns in June because many people want to stock up on "beach books" to read during the summer; for the same reason, we get tons of featured fun fiction books for our Kindles and Nooks in April and May. Our moods even change radically during the day, so at different times we might be more or less interested in what a marketer offers. Social media platforms also are looking at ways to adapt quickly to situational changes. Facebook is testing ads targeted in real time based on users' status updates ("What's on your mind?") and wall posts. Theoretically, a user who posts near the end of his workday that "It's Miller time" could immediately be served a promotion from Miller Coors or another beer company.[3]

A study used a technique called the *day reconstruction method* to track these changes. More than 900 working women kept diaries of everything they did during the day, from reading the paper in the morning to falling asleep in front of the TV at night. The next day

Figure 10.1 ISSUES RELATED TO PURCHASE AND POSTPURCHASE ACTIVITIES

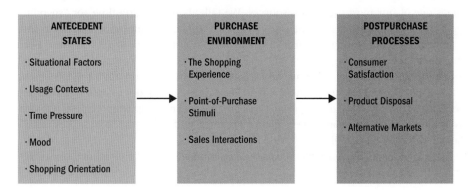

ANTECEDENT STATES	PURCHASE ENVIRONMENT	POSTPURCHASE PROCESSES
· Situational Factors	· The Shopping Experience	· Consumer Satisfaction
· Usage Contexts	· Point-of-Purchase Stimuli	· Product Disposal
· Time Pressure	· Sales Interactions	· Alternative Markets
· Mood		
· Shopping Orientation		

they relived each diary entry and rated how they felt at the time (annoyed, happy, etc.). Overall, researchers found that the study participants woke up a little grumpy but soon entered a state of mild pleasure. This mood increased by degrees through the day, though it was punctuated by occasional bouts of anxiety, frustration, and anger. Not surprisingly, the subjects were least happy when they engaged in mundane activities like commuting to work and doing housework, whereas they rated sex, socializing with friends, and relaxing as most enjoyable. Contrary to prior findings, however, the women were happier when they watched television than when they shopped or talked on the phone. They ranked taking care of children low, below cooking and not far above housework. The good news: Overall, people seem to be pretty happy, and these ratings aren't influenced much by factors such as household income or job security. By far, the two factors that most upset daily moods were a poor night's sleep and tight work deadlines.[4]

In addition to the functional relationships between products and usage situation, another reason to take environmental circumstances seriously is that a person's **situational self-image**—the role he or she plays at any one time—helps to determine what he or she wants to buy or consume.[5] A guy who tries to impress his date as he plays the role of "man-about-town" may spend more lavishly, order champagne instead of beer, and buy flowers; purchases he would never consider when he hangs out with his friends, slurps brew, and plays the role of "one of the boys." Let's see how these dynamics affect the way people think about what they buy.

If we systematically identify important usage situations, we can tailor market segmentation strategies to ensure that our offerings meet the specific needs these situations create. For example, we often tailor our furniture choices to specific settings. We prefer different styles for a city apartment, a beach house, or an executive suite. Similarly, we distinguish motorcycles in terms of how riders use them, including commuting, riding them as dirt bikes, or on a farm versus highway travel.[6]

Table 10.1 gives one example of how a marketer fine-tunes its segmentation strategy to the usage situation. When we list the major contexts in which people use a product (e.g., snow skiing and sunbathing for a suntan lotion) and the different types of people who use the product, we can construct a matrix that identifies specific product features we should emphasize for each situation. During the summer, a lotion manufacturer might promote the fact that the bottle floats and is hard to lose, but during the winter season it could tout its nonfreezing formula.

A consumer's physical and social environment affects his or her motives to use a product, as well as how he or she will evaluate the item. Important cues include his or her immediate environment as well as the amount and type of other consumers who are there as well. Dimensions of the physical environment, such as decor, odors, and even temperature, can significantly influence consumption. One study even found that if a Las Vegas casino pumped certain odors into the room, patrons fed more money into the slot machines![7] We'll take a closer look at some of these factors a bit later in this chapter when we consider how important store design is to consumer behavior.

Temporal Factors

Time is one of our most precious resources. We talk about "making time" or "spending time," and we frequently remind others that "time is money." Common sense tells us that we think more about what we want to buy when we have the luxury to take our time. Even a normally meticulous shopper who never buys before he or she compares prices might sprint through the mall at 9:00 pm on Christmas Eve to scoop up anything left on the shelves if he or she needs a last-minute gift. The same logic applies to online marketing; **open rates** (the percentage of people who open an email message from a marketer) vary throughout the day. The peak time for high open rates: mid-day on weekdays (presumably when all those at work take a lunch break).[8]

Time is an economic variable; it is a resource that we must divide among our activities.[9] We try to maximize satisfaction when we allocate our time to different tasks. Of

TABLE 10.1 A Person-Situation Segmentation Matrix for Suntan Lotion: Our Social and Physical Surroundings

Situation	Young Children Fair Skin	Young Children Dark Skin	Teenagers Fair Skin	Teenagers Dark Skin	Adult Women Fair Skin	Adult Women Dark Skin	Adult Men Fair Skin	Adult Men Dark Skin	Benefits/Features
Beach/boat sunbathing	Combined insect repellent				Summer perfume				a. Product serves as windburn protection b. Formula and container can stand heat c. Container floats and is distinctive (not easily lost)
Home-poolside sunbathing					Combined moisturizer				a. Product has large pump dispenser b. Product won't stain wood, concrete, furnishings
Sunlamp bathing					Combined moisturizer and massage oil				a. Product is designed specifically for type of lamp b. Product has an artificial tanning ingredient
Snow skiing					Winter perfume				a. Product provides special protection from special light rays and weather b. Product has antifreeze formula
Person benefit/ features	Special protection a. Protection is critical b. Formula is non-poisonous		Special protection a. Product fits in jean pocket b. Product used by opinion leaders		Special protection Female perfume		Special protection Male perfume		

Source: Adapted from Peter R. Dickson, "Person-Situation: Segmentation's Missing Link," *Journal of Marketing* 46 (Fall 1982): 62. By permission of American Marketing Association.

course, people's allocation decisions differ; we all know people who seem to play all of the time, and others who are workaholics. An individual's priorities determine his or her **timestyle**.[10] People in different countries also "spend" this resource at different rates. A social scientist compared the pace of life in 31 cities around the world as part of a study on timestyles.[11] He and his assistants timed how long it takes pedestrians to walk 60 feet and the time postal clerks take to sell a stamp. Based on these responses, he claims that the fastest and slowest countries are:

Fastest countries—(1) Switzerland, (2) Ireland, (3) Germany, (4) Japan, (5) Italy
Slowest countries—(31) Mexico, (30) Indonesia, (29) Brazil, (28) El Salvador, (27) Syria

Many consumers believe they are more pressed for time than ever before; marketers label this feeling **time poverty**. The problem appears to be more perception than fact. The reality is that we simply have more options for spending our time, so we feel pressured by the weight of all of these choices. In 1965, the average U.S. woman spent about 32 hours per week on housework; the time today is about half of that. Of course, there are plenty of husbands who share these burdens more: The average U.S. man spent just more than 4 hours per week on household tasks and that number has more than doubled. Women report feeling more rushed than men, though even they have more leisure time now than they did in the 1960s (about 30 hours of free time in a typical week).[12]

In addition to physical cues, other people who are in the situation affect purchase decisions. In some cases, the sheer presence or absence of **co-consumers**, the other patrons in a setting, actually is a product attribute; think about an exclusive resort or boutique that promises to provide privacy to privileged customers. At other times, the presence of others can have positive value. A sparsely attended ball game or an empty bar can be a depressing sight. The *type* of consumers who patronize a store or service or who use a product affects our evaluations. We often infer something about a store when we examine its customers. For this reason, some restaurants require men to wear jackets for dinner (and supply rather tacky ones if they don't), and bouncers at some "hot" night-spots handpick people who wait in line based on whether they have the right "look" for the club. To paraphrase the comedian Groucho Marx, "I would never join a club that would have me as a member!"

"Time flies when you're having fun," but other situations (like some classes—but certainly not consumer behavior) seem to last forever. Our experience of time is subjective; our immediate priorities and needs determine how quickly time flies. It's important for marketers to understand **psychological time** because we're more likely to be in a consuming mood at certain times than we are at others.

A study examined how the timestyles of a group of U.S. women influenced their consumption choices.[13] The researchers identified four dimensions of time: (1) the *social dimension* refers to individuals' categorization of time as either "time for me" or "time with/for others"; (2) the *temporal orientation dimension* depicts the relative significance individuals attach to past, present, or future; (3) the *planning orientation dimension* alludes to different time management styles varying on a continuum from analytic to spontaneous; and (4) the *polychronic orientation dimension* distinguishes between people who prefer to do one thing at a time from those who have multitasking timestyles. After they interviewed and observed these women, the researchers identified a set of five metaphors that they say capture the participants' perspectives on time:

- **Time is a pressure cooker**—These women are usually analytical in their planning, other-oriented, and monochronic in their timestyles. They treat shopping in a methodical manner and they often feel under pressure and in conflict.
- **Time is a map**—These women are usually analytical planners; they exhibit a future temporal orientation and a polychronic timestyle. They often engage in extensive-information search and comparison shop.
- **Time is a mirror**—Women in this group are also analytical planners and have a polychronic orientation. However, they have a past temporal orientation. Because of their risk averseness in time use, these women are usually loyal to products and services they know and trust. They prefer convenience-oriented products.
- **Time is a river**—These women are usually spontaneous in their planning orientation and have a present focus. They go on unplanned, short, and frequent shopping trips.
- **Time is a feast**—These women are analytical planners with a present temporal orientation. They view time as something they consume to pursue sensory pleasure and gratification, and for this reason they value hedonic consumption and variety-seeking.

McDonald's is testing a "Create Your Taste" platform that allows customers to skip the line and order from a kiosk, where they can customize their burger with a selection of buns, cheese, and toppings. The chain is hoping to boost satisfaction by giving diners greater control and less waiting time.[14] The psychological dimension of time—how we actually experience it—is an important factor in **queuing theory**, the mathematical study of waiting lines. As we all know, our experience when we wait has a big effect on our evaluations of what we get at the end of the wait. Although we assume that something must be pretty good if we have to wait for it, the negative feelings that long waits arouse can quickly turn people off.[15]

OBJECTIVE 10-2

The information a store's layout, Web site, or salespeople provides strongly influences a purchase decision.

The Shopping Experience

Many analysts who study consumer satisfaction, or those who design new products or services to increase it, recognize that it is crucial to understand how people actually interact with their environment to identify potential problems. To do so, they typically conduct **focus groups**, in which a small set of consumers comes into a facility to try a new item while company personnel observe them from behind a mirror. However, some researchers advocate a more up-close-and-personal approach that allows them to watch people in the actual environment where they consume the product. This perspective originated in the Japanese approach to **total quality management (TQM)**, which is a complex set of management and engineering procedures that aims to reduce errors and increase quality.

To help companies achieve more insight, researchers go to the **gemba**, which to the Japanese means "the one true source of information." According to this philosophy, it's essential to send marketers and designers to the precise place where consumers use the product or service rather than to ask laboratory subjects to use it in a simulated environment.

Figure 10.2 illustrates this idea in practice. Host Foods, which operates food concessions in major airports, sent a team to the *gemba*—in this case, an airport cafeteria—to identify problem areas. Employees watched as customers entered the facility, and then followed them as they inspected the menu, procured silverware, paid, and found a table. The findings were crucial to Host's redesign of the facility. For example, the team identified a common problem that many people traveling solo experience: the need to put down one's luggage to enter the food line and the feeling of panic you get because you're not able to keep an eye on your valuables when you get your meal. This simple insight allowed Host to modify the design of its facilities to improve a patron's line-of-sight between the food area and the tables.[16]

Mood

In Chapter 5 we discussed the importance of affect on the buying experience. Our mood at the time of purchase can really affect what we feel like buying.[17] If you don't believe it, try grocery shopping on an empty stomach! Or make a decision when you're stressed, and you'll understand how a physiological state impairs information-processing and problem-solving abilities.[18]

Two basic dimensions, *pleasure* and *arousal*, determine whether we will react positively or negatively to a consumption environment.[19] What it boils down to is that you can either enjoy or not enjoy a situation, and you can feel stimulated or not. As Figure 10.3 indicates, different combinations of pleasure and arousal levels result in a variety of emotional states. An arousing situation can be either distressing or exciting, depending on whether the context is positive or negative (e.g., a street riot versus a street festival). So, a specific mood is some combination of pleasure and arousal. The state of happiness is high in pleasantness

Figure 10.2 GOING TO THE GEMBA

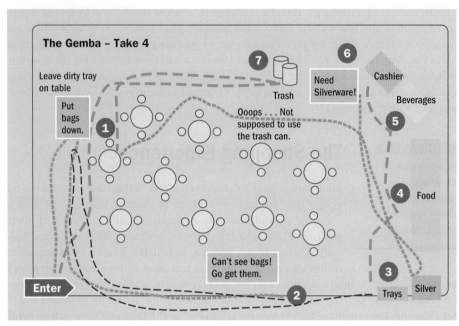

Source: © Quality Function Deployment Institute. Used with permission.

and moderate in arousal, whereas elation is high on both dimensions.[20] A mood state (either positive or negative) biases our judgments of products and services in that direction.[21] Put simply, we give more positive evaluations when we're in a good mood (this explains the popularity of the business lunch!).

Many factors, including store design, the weather, and whether you just had a fight with your significant other, affect your mood. Music and television programming do as well.[22] When we hear happy music or watch happy programs, we experience more positive reactions to commercials and products.[23] And when we're in a good mood, we process

Figure 10.3 DIMENSIONS OF EMOTIONAL STATES

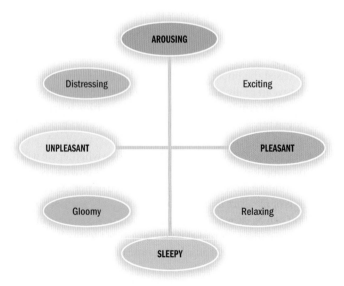

The business lunch is a tried-and-true way to get clients in a good mood.
Source: bikeriderlondon/Shutterstock.

ads with less elaboration. We pay less attention to the specifics of the message and we rely more on heuristics (see Chapter 9).[24]

When the Going Gets Tough, the Tough Go Shopping

We all know some people who shop simply for the sport of it, and others whom we have to drag to a mall. Shopping is how we acquire needed products and services, but social motives for shopping also are important. Thus, shopping is an activity that we can perform for either utilitarian (functional or tangible) or hedonic (pleasurable or intangible) reasons.[25]

So, do people hate to shop or love it? We segment consumers in terms of their **shopping orientation**, or general attitudes about shopping. These orientations vary depending on the particular product categories and store types we consider. One consumer might hate to shop for a car, but love to browse in music stores. A shopper's motivation influences the type of shopping environment that will be attractive or annoying; for example, a person who wants to locate and buy something quickly may find loud music, bright colors, or complex layouts distracting, whereas someone who is there to browse may enjoy the sensory stimulation.[26]

Some scale items that researchers use to assess our shopping motivations illustrate the diverse reasons we may shop. One item that measures hedonic value is "During the trip, I felt the excitement of the hunt." When we compare that type of sentiment to a functional statement, "I accomplished just what I wanted to on this shopping trip," there's a clear contrast between these two dimensions.[27] Hedonic shopping motives include the following:[28]

- **Social experiences**—The shopping center or department store replaces the traditional town square or county fair as a community gathering place. Many people (especially in suburban or rural areas) have almost no other places to spend their leisure time. That probably explains the popularity of late-night games college students in some rural areas play at their local Walmart. In addition to sports such as scavenger hunts, aisle football, and a relay race limbo under the shopping-cart stand, "10 in

10" is a big attraction. To play this game, students form into teams; each team has 10 minutes to put 10 items from anywhere in the store in a shopping cart. Then they turn their cart over to the opposing team, which has to figure out where the items came from and return them to the shelves where they belong (not so easy in a store stocked with more than 100,000 different items). The first team back to the checkout counters with an empty cart wins.[29] Note: If you get busted for playing this game, you did *not* learn about it here.

- **Sharing of common interests**—Stores frequently offer specialized goods that allow people with shared interests to communicate.
- **Affiliation**—Shopping centers are a natural place to congregate. The shopping mall is a favorite "hangout" for teenagers. It also represents a controlled, secure environment for the elderly, and many malls now feature "mall walkers' clubs" for early morning workouts.
- **Status**—As every salesperson knows, some people savor the experience of being waited on, even though they may not necessarily buy anything. One men's clothing salesman offered this advice: "Remember their size, remember what you sold them last time. Make them feel important! If you can make people feel important, they are going to come back. Everybody likes to feel important!"[30] When a team of researchers conducted in-depth interviews with women to understand what makes shopping a pleasurable experience, they found one motivation was role-playing. For example, one respondent dressed up for shopping excursions to upscale boutiques because she liked to pretend she was wealthy and have salespeople fall all over her.[31]
- **The thrill of the hunt**—Some people pride themselves on their knowledge of the marketplace. They may love to haggle and bargain, and even view this process as a sport.

E-Commerce: Clicks Versus Bricks

Pssst ... want to hear a secret? People are buying a lot of stuff online these days. Oh, you knew that already. Consumers worldwide spend about $1.5 trillion per year on e-commerce sites.[32] Analysts predict that soon about one-fourth of these transactions will occur on a mobile device. Already, about three-fourths of the world's population has access to a mobile phone and users download about 30 billion apps in a year.[33] Then add in the explosive growth of tablets: We're even more likely to use these devices when we're in the mood to shop. Their bigger screens make it easier to browse items, and often even more efficient than computers because shoppers can zoom in or drag items to their carts with their fingers.[34] That helps to explain why in recent years people have purchased even more merchandise from tablets than they have from phones (or from the newer so-called **phablets**, which are a hybrid of a phone and a tablet).

The experience of acquiring a product or service may be quite different offline versus online. This aspect of the transaction provides value over and above what you actually buy. We clearly see this difference between the two worlds when we compare how people gamble in casinos versus online. When researchers interviewed 30 gamblers to explore these experiences, they found sharp contrasts. Those who enjoy casino gambling have a strong sense of connection to fellow gamblers, so it's very much a social experience. Online gamblers enjoy the anonymity of the Internet. Casino gamblers get turned on by the sensual experiences and excitement of the casino, whereas online gamblers gravitate more to the feeling of safety and control they get because they stay at home. Casino gamblers talked about the friendly atmosphere, whereas those who stayed online reported behaviors that a real casino wouldn't tolerate, such as taunts and bullying.[35] Although both groups aim to have fun and hope to make money, it's a safe bet that their experiences are quite different.

As more and more Web sites pop up to sell everything from refrigerator magnets to Mack trucks, marketers continue to debate how the online world affects their business. In particular, many lose sleep as they wonder whether e-commerce will replace traditional retailing, work in concert with it, or perhaps even fade away to become another fad your kids will laugh about someday (OK, that's not real likely). Still, the rising availability of

Net Profit

Is cash obsolete? In the past few years we've seen a firestorm of activity to promote various kinds of virtual currency and encourage consumers to switch from cash and credit cards to **digital wallets**, which are electronic devices that allow an individual to make e-commerce transactions. A lot of this activity is propelled by the spread of **near field communications (NFC)** technology that allows devices near to one another (like a smartphone and a NFC terminal in a store) to establish radio communication. Apple Pay is a mobile payment service that lets users use their iPhones and Apple Watches to pay in stores and online. Google's joined an initiative called SoftCard backed by AT&T, T-Mobile, and Verizon; Samsung bought Loop Pay to enable customers to pay digitally. Twitter bought CardSpring, a mobile payments infrastructure company that allows merchants to offer deals to consumers that can be loaded onto to their credit cards so when you pay the discount is automatically applied to the purchase. Facebook is testing a new "Buy" feature that allows users to make purchases from businesses directly from within a social network.[36] The controversial **Bitcoin** system uses peer-to-peer technology to operate with no central authority or banks; it's the most prominent form of **cryptocurrency** that relies upon encryption techniques rather than banks to regulate the generation of units of currency and verify the transfer of funds. Some big companies including Dell, Expedia, PayPal, and Microsoft already work with partners to process bitcoin payments.[37] Don't unload those benjamins in your wallet just yet, but get ready for the currency revolution.

comparison shopping phone apps does threaten the existence of many retailers as consumers engage in what they call **showrooming**. This means that a shopper visits a store like Best Buy to explore options for big-ticket items like TVs or appliances and then he or she finds a cheaper price for the specific model online.

For marketers, the growth of online commerce is a sword that cuts both ways. On the one hand, they reach customers around the world even if they're physically located 100 miles from nowhere. On the other hand, they now compete not only with the store across the street but also with thousands of Web sites that span the globe. Also, when consumers obtain products directly from the manufacturer or wholesaler, this eliminates the intermediary—the loyal, store-based retailers that carry the firm's products and sell them at a marked-up price.[38] In addition, as we discussed in Chapter 2, there are huge issues relating to data security and privacy yet to be resolved.

So what makes e-commerce sites successful? Some e-tailers take advantage of technology to provide extra value to their customers that their land-locked rivals can't. eBay offers a feature within its Fashion app called "See It On" that allows the user to virtually try on sunglasses in real time. He or she can adjust the fit; choose different styles, frames, lenses, and colors to find the perfect look; and then browse through eBay to find the perfect price.[39] Other new fashion sites, such as Net-a-Porter and Gilt Groupe, directly connect buyers and sellers so that designers can be more nimble and react quickly to changing consumer tastes. Indeed, the high-fashion site ModaOperandi bills itself as a **pretailer**; it provides exclusive styles by prodding manufacturers to produce runway pieces they wouldn't otherwise make because store buyers weren't sure anyone would pay the money for them.[40]

More generally, online shoppers value these aspects of a Web site:

- The ability to click on an item to create a pop-up window with more details about the product, including price, size, colors, and inventory availability.
- The ability to click on an item and add it to your cart without leaving the page you're on.
- The ability to "feel" merchandise through better imagery, more product descriptions, and details.
- The ability to enter all data related to your purchase on one page, rather than going through several checkout pages.
- The ability to mix and match product images on one page to determine whether they look good together.[41]

Retailing as Theater

The competition for customers becomes even more intense as nonstore alternatives, from Web sites and print catalogs to TV shopping networks and home shopping parties, continue to multiply. With all of these shopping alternatives available, how can a traditional store compete? Many malls are giant entertainment centers, almost to the point that their traditional retail occupants seem like an afterthought. Today, it's commonplace to find carousels, miniature golf, skating rinks or batting cages in a suburban mall. Hershey opened a make-believe factory smack in the middle of Times Square. It features four steam machines and 380 feet of neon lighting, plus a moving message board that lets visiting chocoholics program messages to surprise their loved ones.[42]

The quest to entertain means that many stores go all out to create imaginative environments that transport shoppers to fantasy worlds or provide other kinds of stimulation. We call this strategy **retail theming**. Innovative merchants today use four basic kinds of theming techniques:

1 Landscape themes rely on associations with images of nature, Earth, animals, and the physical body. Bass Pro Shops, for example, creates a simulated outdoor environment, including pools stocked with fish.

2 Marketscape themes build on associations with man-made places. An example is The Venetian hotel in Las Vegas, which lavishly recreates parts of the real Italian city.

Marketing Opportunity

One popular theming strategy is to convert a store into a **being space**. This kind of environment resembles a sort of commercial living room, where we can go to relax, be entertained, hang out with friends, escape the everyday, or even learn. When you think of *being spaces*, Starbucks probably comes to mind. The coffee chain's stated goal is to become our "third place" where we spend the bulk of our time, in addition to home and work. Starbucks led the way when it outfitted its stores with comfy chairs and Wi-Fi. But there are many other marketers who meet our needs for exciting commercial spaces—no matter what those needs are. In Asia, venues such as Manboo and Fujiyama Land provide havens where gamers can do their thing 24/7—and even take a shower on-site during a break. Other spaces cater to the needs of **minipreneurs** (one-person businesses) as they offer work-centered being spaces. At New York's Paragraph, writers who need a quiet place to ruminate can hang out in a loft that's divided into a writing room and a lounge area. TwoRooms ("You Work, They Play") provides office space and child care for home-based workers.[44]

Reflecting the ever-quickening pace of our culture, many of these *being spaces* come and go rapidly—on purpose. **Pop-up stores** appear in many forms around the world. Typically, these are temporary installations that do business only for a few days or weeks and then disappear before they get old. For example, the Swatch Instant Store sells limited-edition watches in a major city until the masses discover it; then it closes and moves on to another "cool" locale. The Dutch beer brand Dommelsch organized pop-up concerts: Fans entered barcodes they found on cans, beer bottles, and coasters on the brewer's Web site to discover dates and locations. You may even run into a pop-up store on your campus; several brands, including the Brazilian flip-flop maker Havaianas, Victoria's Secret's Pink, and sustainable-clothing brand RVL7, run pop-up projects around the United States.[45]

3 Cyberspace themes build on images of information and communications technology. eBay's retail interface instills a sense of community among its vendors and traders.

4 Mindscape themes draw on abstract ideas and concepts, introspection and fantasy, and often possess spiritual overtones. The Kiva day spa in downtown Chicago offers health treatments based on a theme of American Indian healing ceremonies and religious practices.[43]

Store Image

As so many stores compete for customers, how do we ever pick one over others? Just like products (see Chapter 7), stores have "personalities." Some shops have clearly defined images (either good or bad). Others tend to blend into the crowd. What factors shape this personality, or **store image**? Some of the important dimensions of a store's image are location, merchandise, suitability, and the knowledge and congeniality of the sales staff.

These design features typically work together to create an overall impression. When we think about stores, we don't usually say, "Well, that place is fairly good in terms of convenience, the salespeople are acceptable, and services are good." We're more likely to proclaim, "That place gives me the creeps," or "It's so much fun to shop there." We quickly get an overall impression of a store, and the feeling we get may have more to do with intangibles, such as interior design and the types of people we find in the aisles, than with the store's return policies or credit availability. As a result, some stores routinely pop up in our consideration sets (see Chapter 9), whereas we never consider others ("Only geeks shop there!").[46]

Atmospherics

Retailers want you to come in—and stay. Careful store design increases the amount of space the shopper covers, and stimulating displays keep them in the aisles longer. This "curb appeal" translates directly to the bottom line: Researchers tracked grocery shopper's movements by plotting the position of their cell phones as they moved about a store. They found that when people lingered just 1 percent longer, sales rose by 1.3 percent.

Of course, grocers know a lot of tricks after years of observing shoppers. For example, they call the area just inside a supermarket's entrance the "decompression zone": People tend to slow down and take stock of their surroundings when they enter the store, so store designers use this space to promote bargains rather than to sell. Similarly, Walmart's

Bass Pro Shops use a landscape theme to connect shoppers with Nature.
Source: Stuart Abraham/Alamy.

CB AS I SEE IT

Julie Baker, *Texas Christian University*

How does the architecture of a retail storefront influence you as a shopper? What visual features of the design either encourage you to enter, or cause you to avoid a retailer? These are questions that my co-author Nancy Sirianni and I are researching in our study on consumer responses to retail storefronts.

We know that consumers depend heavily on visual cues found in the physical environment when making decisions, especially when they have no past experience with an entity, like a retail store. Storefront features such as windows, doorways, lighting,

awnings, building materials used, and architectural style are visual cues that shape consumers' perceptions of and feelings about a store, which in turn influence their preference and choice.

In addition, individuals have two basic needs regarding the environments with which they interact: to understand and to explore. Understanding focuses on how a space is laid out, and includes *coherence* (whether an environment appears organized) and *legibility* (whether it appears that an individual can navigate within the environment). Exploration focuses on whether one wants to discover more within the environment, and includes *mystery* (the promise that one could see more upon entering a setting) and *complexity* (how much is going on in a particular view). Storefront design can reflect differing degrees of coherence, legibility, mystery and complexity. For example, we have found that darkened windows and awnings are design features that shoppers correlate with mystery, while architectural symmetry and windows that shoppers can see through increase coherence and legibility. Ornamentation and multiple colors are associated with complexity.

Whether shoppers are attracted to a storefront design that leads to understanding or exploration depends on store characteristics

and consumer characteristics. To illustrate, one store characteristic that we propose influences preference is the type of store. If a store is utilitarian in nature, where the products/services sold fulfill basic needs (i.e., a drugstore or dry cleaner), consumers should prefer storefronts that promote understanding. On the other hand, if the store is more hedonic in nature, where the products/services sold are more pleasurable (i.e., boutiques or spa settings), consumers should prefer storefronts that encourage exploration. An example of a shopper characteristic that would influence preference is the personality of that shopper. One of our study respondents told us," I am very clean and organized, so I would avoid any store that appears messy." Similarly, a shopper's gender could influence storefront preference. Females have been found to perceive the same architectural design to be more complex than did males.

Retail managers and retail architects can use this knowledge to collaborate in designing retail storefronts that encourage shoppers to enter their stores. Storefront architecture is a visible and effective brand-building strategy for retailers and provides a way for designers and managers to control shoppers' perceptions of stores.

"greeters" help customers to settle in to their shopping experience. Once they get a serious start, the first thing shoppers encounter is the produce section. Fruits and vegetables can easily be damaged, so it would be more logical to buy these items at the end of a shopping trip. But fresh, wholesome food makes people feel good (and righteous) so they're less guilty when they throw the chips and cookies in the cart later.[47]

Because marketers recognize that a store's image is an important part of the retailing mix, store designers pay a lot of attention to **atmospherics**, the "conscious designing of space and its various dimensions to evoke certain effects in buyers."[48] These dimensions include colors, scents, and sounds. For example, stores with red interiors tend to make people tense, whereas a blue decor imparts a calmer feeling.[49]

A store's atmosphere in turn affects what we buy. In one study, researchers asked shoppers how much pleasure they felt five minutes after they entered a store. Those who

Patrons tend to drink more when they listen to country-and-western music than to other types.

Source: Radharc Images/Alamy.

Net Profit

Mobile shopping apps on smartphones provide imaginative new ways for retailers to guide shoppers through the experience, as they do everything for you: locate merchandise, identify the nearest restroom in a mall, or scout out sales. Some help you remember where you parked your car; others actually provide reward points when you visit certain stores. The apps also promise to provide a solution to the major hassles that drive consumers away from brick-and-mortar stores, especially long checkout times and incompetent sales associates. One survey reported that nearly 3 in 10 store visits ended with an average of $132 unspent because shoppers gave up in frustration and abandoned their carts. The study also found that more than 40 percent of shoppers who received guidance from a retail associate armed with a handheld mobile computer reported an improved shopping experience. To rub salt into the wound, more than half of store employees agreed that because use of online shopping tools is escalating, their customers were more knowledgeable about their products than the salespeople are! More than one-third of U.S. shoppers have downloaded at least one food or beverage app.[59] Note: Some recent research indicates that when shoppers use in-store mobile technology their behavior changes. Shoppers buy more unplanned items and also concentrate

enjoyed their experience spent more time and money.[50] To boost the entertainment value of shopping (and to lure online shoppers back to brick-and-mortar stores), some retailers create **activity stores** that let consumers participate in the production of the products or services they buy there. One familiar example is the Build-A-Bear Workshop chain, where customers dress bear bodies in costumes.[51]

In addition to visual stimuli, all sorts of sensory cues influence us in retail settings.[52] For example, patrons of country-and-western bars drink more when the jukebox music is slower. According to a researcher, "Hard drinkers prefer listening to slower-paced, wailing, lonesome, self-pitying music."[53] Music also can affect eating habits. Another study found that diners who listened to loud, fast music ate more food. In contrast, those who listened to Mozart or Brahms ate less and more slowly. The researchers concluded that diners who choose soothing music at mealtimes can increase weight loss by at least 5 pounds a month![54]

In-Store Decision Making

Despite all their efforts to "pre-sell" consumers through advertising, marketers increasingly recognize that the store environment exerts a strong influence on many purchases. Women tell researchers, for example, that store displays are one of the major information sources they use to decide what clothing to buy.[55]

This influence is even stronger when we shop for food: Analysts estimate that shoppers decide on about two out of every three supermarket purchases while they walk through the aisles.[56] Research evidence indicates that consumers use **mental budgets** for grocery trips that are typically composed of both an itemized portion and *in-store slack*. This means they typically decide beforehand on an amount they plan to spend, but then they have an additional amount in mind (slack) they are willing to spend on unplanned purchases—if they come across any they really want to have.[57] Here are some "tricks of the trade":

- Sell sweets at eye level, midway along aisles, where shoppers' attention lingers longest.
- Use the ends of aisles to generate big revenues—endcap displays account for 45 percent of soft drink sales.

- Use free-standing displays toward the rear of the supermarket and on the left side of aisles. Shoppers tend to move through a store in a counterclockwise direction and they are more likely to choose items from shelves to their left.
- Sprinkle the same product throughout the store, rather than grouping it in one spot to boost sales through repetitive exposure.
- Group ingredients for a meal in one spot.
- Post health-related information on kiosks and shelf tags to link groceries to good health in shoppers' minds, even though only 23 percent of them say they always look for nutritional information on labels.[58]

Spontaneous Shopping

When a shopper suddenly decides to buy something in the store, one of two different processes explains why:

1 He or she engages in **unplanned buying** when he or she is unfamiliar with a store's layout or perhaps he or she is under some time pressure. Or, if he or she sees an item on a store shelf, this might remind her he or she needs it. About one-third of all unplanned buying occurs because a shopper recognizes a new need while he or she is in the store.[62]
2 He or she engages in **impulse buying** when he or she experiences a sudden urge she simply can't resist, like the sketch of a "typical" impulse purchaser an actual consumer drew in Figure 10.4.[63]

Retailers typically place so-called *impulse items*, such as candy and gum, near the checkout to cater to these urges. Similarly, many supermarkets install wider aisles to

Figure 10.4 ONE CONSUMER'S IMAGE OF AN IMPULSE BUYER

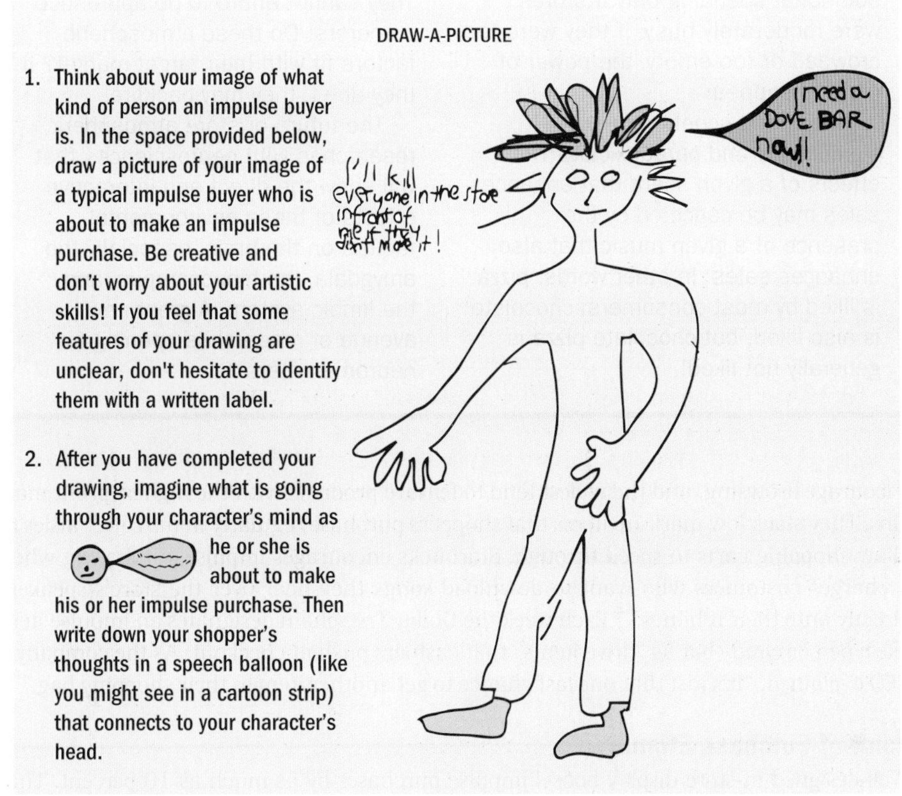

DRAW-A-PICTURE

1. Think about your image of what kind of person an impulse buyer is. In the space provided below, draw a picture of your image of a typical impulse buyer who is about to make an impulse purchase. Be creative and don't worry about your artistic skills! If you feel that some features of your drawing are unclear, don't hesitate to identify them with a written label.

2. After you have completed your drawing, imagine what is going through your character's mind as he or she is about to make his or her impulse purchase. Then write down your shopper's thoughts in a speech balloon (like you might see in a cartoon strip) that connects to your character's head.

Source: Dennis Rock, "Is Impulse Buying (Yet) a Useful Marketing Concept?" (unpublished manuscript, University of Southern California, Los Angeles, 1990): Fig. 7-A.

less on the information they find in the store. Ironically, if they talk on their phones while they shop they are less likely to buy items they planned to purchase and actually spend less because they are distracted.[60]

Even more futuristic tech is on the horizon:[61]

- Major retailers like Macy's and Target are deploying **beacons** in their stores. These devices communicate with smartphone apps indoors through a Bluetooth signal. They can share a coupon with a shopper's phone as he or she browses in the aisles, or reward consumers with points even for just entering the store.
- **Augmented reality (AR)** superimposes a layer of digital information over a physical environment. AR apps like Blippar allow the shopper to access additional information from product packages. For example, a woman who buys a Maybelline cosmetic product could hold her phone over the box to bring up a model who shares tips about how to apply makeup.
- **Virtual reality (VR)** is a computer-simulated interface that creates the impression the user is physically present. In contrast to AR, VR substitutes a completely different sensory for the user. Headsets like the Oculus Rift can provide a totally immersive experience as shoppers can browse a three-dimensional "store" just by putting one on. The U.K.-based Tesco grocery chain launched a virtual supermarket in Germany that allows shoppers to navigate a store in a 360-degree virtual environment, and the Marriott hotel chains offers a "4D Teleporter" that transports guests to exotic locales (at least virtually). The experience includes sensory inputs such as the sun on your face, wind in your hair, ground rumbling, and sea spray hitting your skin.

CB AS I SEE IT

Jean-Charles Chebat, *HEC-Montréal, Canada and Technion, Israel.*

What shoppers do and avoid in stores and malls significantly depends on intangible environmental factors, such as ambient scents, background music and colors. Store atmosphere affects emotions, basically arousal and pleasure, that affect shoppers' cognitive activity and behavior, mostly how much time and money shoppers spend in stores. Many retailers compete on such atmospheric strategies. These atmospheric factors enhance the perception of the mall, perception of the store within the mall and, in turn its products and services within the store. That's what I call *Meta-Packaging*.

Background music volume and tempo affect arousal and pleasure and, in turn, shoppers' cognitive activity, which helps them make purchase decisions. They also affect the relation between shoppers and service personnel. Soothing music makes products look more attractive. It also changes the perceived duration of the time spent walking through shopping malls. Crowding moderates the effects of music: fast ambient music improves shoppers experience under low crowding but has the opposite effects under high crowding (and conversely for slow ambient music).

Did you ever try the effects of your fragrance or after shave on other persons? They make candidates for a job perceived as more competent. Same with products and stores! If ambient scents are appropriate, they stimulate positive thoughts about the store and its products/services. The effects of arousing scents in malls are moderated by crowding: ambient citrus scents provoke additional spending only if stores were moderately busy. If they were too crowded or too empty, the power of citrus disappear.

Music and scents interact significantly and paradoxically. The effects of a given scent that enhances sales may be canceled by the presence of a given music that also enhances sales. In other words: pizza is liked by most consumers, chocolate is also liked; but chocolate pizza is generally not liked!

Retailers should be aware of its powerful commercial effects of colors. Cold colors are appeasing, increase the cognitive activity and help shoppers make buying decisions. The appropriateness of colors depends on culture: French Canadians prefer shopping environments in warm colors, English Canadians prefer colder colors.

Shoppers' behavior significantly depend on whom they shop with. The mall seems more attractive, stimulating and interesting when shopping with friends than when shopping alone or with family members. Other shoppers affect shoppers' behavior significantly. Shoppers interact with other shoppers and affect their behavior even if they don't know each other.

These sensory factors tell shoppers instantly if the store is meant for shoppers like themselves, in terms of social class, gender and generation. It is of utmost importance for retailers to test their effects before using them. They cannot afford to be apprentice sorcerers! Do these atmospheric factors fit with their target market? If they don't, they may backfire!

The future of store atmospheric research is with neurosciences that will show the direct and interactive effects of these environmental factors on the brain, especially the amygdala, the hippocampus, and the limbic system. A great new avenue of research is opening for neuromarketers.

---

encourage browsing, and the widest tend to feature products with the highest profit margins. They stack low mark-up items that shoppers purchase regularly in narrower aisles to allow shopping carts to speed through. Starbucks encourages impulse purchasing when it charges customers who want to download songs they hear over the store's speakers directly onto their iPhones.[64] Each week the Dollar Tree chain designates an impulse item like a pen or candy bar as "drive items" that cashiers push at checkout. As the company's CEO explained, "It's just that one last chance to get another item in their shopping bag."[65]

Point-of-Purchase Stimuli

Well-designed in-store display boosts impulse purchases by as much as 10 percent. That explains why U.S. companies spend about \$19 billion each year on **point-of-purchase (POP) stimuli**.[66] A POP can be an elaborate product display or demonstration, a coupon-dispensing machine, or an employee who gives out free samples of a new cookie in the grocery aisle.

The importance of POP in shopper decision making explains why product packages increasingly play a key role in the marketing mix as they evolve from the functional to the fantastic:

- In the past 100 years, Pepsi changed the look of its can, and before that its bottles, only 10 times. Now the company switches designs every few weeks. It's also testing cans that spray an aroma when you open one to match the flavor of the drink, such as a wild cherry scent misting from a Wild Cherry Pepsi can.
- Coors Light bottles sport labels that turn blue when the beer is chilled to the right temperature.
- Huggies' Henry the Hippo hand soap bottles have a light that flashes for 20 seconds to show children how long they should wash their hands.
- Evian's "palace bottle" turns up in restaurants and luxury hotels. The water bottle has an elegant swanlike neck and sits on a small silver tray.
- Unilever North America sells Axe shower gel bottles shaped like video game joysticks.
- Some companies are considering the insertion of a computer chip and tiny speaker inside a package. This gimmick might be useful for cross-promotion. For example, a package of cheese could say "I go well with Triscuit crackers" when a shopper takes it off the shelf. Of course, this attention-getting trick could backfire if everyone starts to do it. As one ad executive commented, "If you're walking down a row in a supermarket and every package is screaming at you, it sounds like a terrifying, disgusting experience."[67]

The Salesperson: A Lead Role in the Play

The salesperson is one of the most important players in the retailing drama.[68] As we saw way back in Chapter 1, exchange theory stresses that every interaction involves a trade of value. Each participant gives something to the other and hopes to receive something in return.[69] A (competent) salesperson offers a lot of value because his or her expert advice makes the shopper's choice easier.

A buyer–seller situation is like many other **dyadic encounters** (two-person groups); it's a relationship in which both parties must reach some agreement about the roles of each participant during a process of **identity negotiation**.[70] Some of the factors that help to define a salesperson's role (and effectiveness) are his or her age, appearance, educational level, and motivation to sell.[71]

In addition, more effective salespersons usually know their customers' traits and preferences better than do ineffective salespersons, and they adapt their approach to meet the needs of each specific customer.[73] The ability to be adaptable is especially vital when customers and salespeople have different *interaction styles*.[74] We each vary in the degree of assertiveness we bring to interactions. At one extreme, *nonassertive* people believe it's not socially acceptable to complain, and sales situations may intimidate them. *Assertive* people are more likely to stand up for themselves in a firm but nonthreatening way. *Aggressives* may resort to rudeness and threats if they don't get their way (we've all run into these folks).[75]

OBJECTIVE 10-3
The growth of a "sharing economy" changes how many consumers think about buying rather than renting products.

Ownership and the Sharing Economy

A funny thing is happening when people buy products: They no longer want to buy them. Instead we're witnessing the rise of the **sharing economy**, or what is sometimes called **collaborative consumption**. In this business model people rent what they need rather than buying it. Collaborative consumption communities typically offer a Web site that allows individuals to

list their services and a ratings system that allows both buyers and sellers to rate their experiences.

Need to use a car? Go to Zipcar and rent one by the hour. How about a camera, a power drill, or a blender? Go to SnapGoods and rent one of those too. Park your pet with a dogsitter rather than an impersonal kennel at Dog Vacay. You can even get a low interest loan from other individuals at Lending Club. The sharing economy is revolutionizing industries including taxis (Uber and Lyft), hospitality (Airbnb), used books (Bookmooch), and even errand running (TaskRabbit).

What is fueling this revolution? Primarily technology that dramatically lowers transaction costs, so that it's much easier to share assets and track them across large numbers of people. Online payment systems make it easy to exchange money. Social networks create communities and build trust among strangers who can access each other's histories. Sellers can make money from assets they don't use much; think about how many hours a typical owner actually uses an electric drill compared to how much it costs to buy one. Many of us only use our cars a few hours per week, but we still pay a monthly loan, maintenance, parking fees and so on; car owners who use RelayRides to rent their vehicles on average make $250 a month and some make more than $1,000.

As a major player in the sharing economy, Zipcar is changing how many urban dwellers think about transportation.
Source: Islemount Images/Alamy.

However, it's not just ease of use that explains the rise of the sharing economy. We also can point to a change in attitudes toward ownership, especially among younger consumers. A global survey that talked to more than 10,000 respondents reported that one-third of Millennials already belong to a sharing service or expect to join one soon. Many people believe overconsumption is putting our planet at risk, and half say they could happily live without most of the items they own. This is consistent with discussions we've had in prior chapters about the weak relationship researchers find between owning more "stuff" and happiness.[76] In addition, many people appreciate the intimacy of exchanging items with "real people" rather than getting them from big companies. Many seem more than willing to do things with total strangers our mothers used to warn us against: They stay in their homes, get in their cars, and even wear their clothes.[77] That's one reason the notion of doing business with other consumers rather than with companies goes by the name **P2P commerce** (peer-to-peer).

OBJECTIVE 10-4
Our decisions about how to dispose of a product are as important as how we decide to obtain it in the first place.

Postpurchase Satisfaction and Disposal

Our overall reactions to a product after we've bought it—what researchers call **consumer satisfaction/dissatisfaction (CS/D)**—obviously play a big role in our future behavior. It's a lot easier to sell something once than to sell it again if it bombed the first time. We evaluate the things we buy as we use them and integrate them into our daily consumption activities.[78]

Postpurchase Satisfaction

What exactly do consumers look for in products? That's easy: They want quality and value.[79] However, these terms have slippery meanings that are hard for us to pin down. We infer quality when we rely on cues as diverse as brand name, price, product warranties, and even our estimate of how much money a company invests in its advertising.[80]

Satisfaction or dissatisfaction is more than a reaction to how well a product or service performs. According to the **expectancy disconfirmation model**, we form beliefs about product performance based on our prior experience with the product or communications about the product that imply a certain level of quality.[81] When something performs the way we thought it would, we may not think much about it. If it fails to live

These watches are made from recycled
Nespresso coffeemaker cartridges.
Source: Courtesy of Blancier Handmade Watches.

up to expectations, this may create negative feelings. However, if performance happens to exceed our expectations, we're happy campers.

This perspective underscores how important it is to manage expectations. We often trace a customer's dissatisfaction to his or her erroneous expectations of the company's ability to deliver a product or service. *No* company is perfect. It's just not realistic to think that everything will always turn out perfectly (although some firms don't even come close!). For a while the hotel chain Holiday Inn adopted the slogan "No surprises" to assure guests of flawless service. Inevitably, there *were* surprises (no operator to answer the phone, an unmade bed) and the company had to drop its promise of perfection.

Product Disposal

Green issues don't end at the cash register. There is also the matter of what we do with our things when we're done with them. **Product disposal** is also an important element of consumer behavior.

Food waste winds up in landfills where it decomposes and emits methane, a potent greenhouse gas.
Source: Zavalnyuk Sergey/123RF.

Because we do form strong attachments to some products, it can be painful to get rid of them. Our possessions anchor our identities; our past lives on in our things.[82] Some Japanese people ritually "retire" worn-out sewing needles, chopsticks, and even computer chips when they burn them in a ceremony to thank them for years of good service.[83]

Still, we all have to get rid of our "stuff" at some point, either because it has served its purpose or perhaps because it no longer fits with our view of ourselves (as when newly-weds "upgrade" to a real place). Concern about the environment, coupled with a need for convenience, makes ease of product disposal a key attribute in categories from razors to diapers.

In many cases we acquire a new product even though the old one still functions—that's one of the hallmarks of our materialistic society. Some reasons to replace an item include a desire for new features, a change in the individual's environment (e.g., a refrigerator is the wrong color for a freshly painted kitchen), or a change in the person's role or self-image.[84]

Recycling

The issue of product disposition is vital because of its enormous public policy implications. We live in a throwaway society, which creates problems for the environment and also results in a great deal of unfortunate waste. In the United States alone, we waste about 60 million metric tons of food a year with an estimated value of $162 billion. Indeed, analysts say that one-third of the food produced globally is never consumed! To make matters worse, most food waste winds up in landfills where it decomposes and emits methane, a potent greenhouse gas.[85]

How do people decide whether to discard products or recycle them? Because we discard two billions tons of trash per year (and more in the United States than any other country), this is a pretty important question. One study reported that the perceived effort involved in recycling was the best predictor of whether people would go to the trouble. This pragmatic dimension outweighed general attitudes toward recycling and the environment in predicting one's intention to recycle.[86] Of course, one way to ease the pain is to reward consumers for recycling. The H&M store chain sponsors a Garment Recycling Program; customers can bring any garment from any brand in any condition into an H&M store. For every bag of clothes donated, H&M gives customers a 15 percent discount on the next item they buy.[87]

Lateral Cycling

During **lateral cycling**, one consumer exchanges something he or she owns for something the other person owns. Reusing other people's things is especially important in our throwaway society because, as one researcher put it, "there is no longer an 'away' to throw things to."[88] Although traditional marketers don't pay much attention to used-product sellers, factors such as concern about the environment, demands for quality, and cost and fashion consciousness make these "secondary" markets more important.[89]

In fact, economic estimates of this **underground economy** range from 3 to 30 percent of the gross national product of the United States and up to 70 percent of the gross domestic product of other countries. In the United States alone, there are more than 3,500 flea markets—including at least a dozen huge operations such as the 60-acre Orange County Marketplace in California—that operate nationwide to produce upward of $10 billion in gross sales.[90]

The new trend of **recommerce** (a play on the term *e-commerce*) shows that many consumers want to squeeze more value out of their possessions by selling or trading them.[91] This focus has given birth to the **swishing** movement, where people organize parties to exchange clothing or other personal possessions with others.[92]

The underground economy in the form of flea markets and other used-product sales formats is a significant element in the U.S. market.

Source: Stephanie Keith/Polaris/Newscom.

MyLab Marketing

To complete the problems with the ⭐, go to EOC Discussion Questions in the MyLab as well as additional Marketing Metrics questions only available in MyLab Marketing.

CHAPTER SUMMARY

1. Many factors at the time of purchase dramatically influence the consumer's decision-making process.

Many factors affect a purchase. These include the consumer's antecedent state (e.g., his or her mood, time pressure, or disposition toward shopping). Time is an important resource that often determines how much effort and search will go into a decision. Our moods are influenced by the degree of pleasure and arousal a store environment creates.

The usage context of a product is a segmentation variable; consumers look for different product attributes depending on the use to which they intend to put their purchase. The presence or absence of other people (co-consumers)—and the types of people they are—can also affect a consumer's decisions. The shopping experience also is a pivotal part of the purchase decision. In many cases, retailing is like theater: The consumer's evaluation of stores and products may depend on the type of "performance" he witnesses. The actors (e.g., salespeople), the setting (the store environment), and the props (e.g., store displays) influence this evaluation. Like a brand personality, a number of factors, such as perceived convenience, sophistication, and expertise of salespeople, determine store image. With increasing competition from nonstore alternatives, creating a positive shopping experience has never been more important. Online shopping is growing in importance, and this new way to acquire products has both good (e.g., convenience) and bad (e.g., security) aspects.

2. **The information a store's layout, Web site, or salespeople provides strongly influences a purchase decision.**

Because we don't make many purchase decisions until we're actually in the store, **Point-of-purchase (POP)** stimuli are important sales tools. These include product samples, elaborate package displays, place-based media, and in-store promotional materials such as "shelf talkers." POP stimuli are particularly useful in promoting impulse buying, which happens when a consumer yields to a sudden urge for a product. Increasingly, mobile shopping apps are also playing a key role. The consumer's encounter with a salesperson is a complex and important process. The outcome can be affected by such factors as the salesperson's similarity to the customer and his or her perceived credibility.

3. **The growth of a "sharing economy" changes how many consumers think about buying rather than renting products.**

In the rapidly growing sharing economy people rent what they need rather than buy it. New technologies make this process much easier and online networks allow us to form bonds of trust with strangers. In addition, many consumers no longer place a premium on owning products and prefer to "borrow" them only for the specific times when they actually need them.

4. **Our decisions about how to dispose of a product are as important as how we decide to obtain it in the first place.**

Concern about the environment and waste make the issue of product disposal key in many categories. In addition to understanding if and how consumers recycle, newer recommerce models such as swishing are emerging that enable people to share more of their used goods with one another rather than disposing of them.

KEY TERMS

Activity stores, 392
Atmospherics, 391
Augmented reality (AR), 393
Beacons, 393
Being space, 389
Bitcoin, 388
Co-consumers, 384
Collaborative consumption, 395
Consumer satisfaction/dissatisfaction (CS/D), 397
Consumption situation, 381
Cryptocurrency, 388
Digital wallet, 388
Dyadic encounters, 395
Expectancy disconfirmation model, 397
Focus groups, 385

Gemba, 385
Impulse buying, 393
Identity negotiation, 395
Lateral cycling, 400
Mental budgets, 392
Minipreneurs, 389
Mobile shopping apps, 392
NFC (Near Field Communications), 388
Open rates, 382
P2P commerce, 397
Phablets, 388
Point-of-purchase (POP) stimuli, 394
Pop-up stores, 389
Pretailer, 389
Product disposal, 398
Psychological time, 384

Queuing theory, 385
Recommerce, 400
Retail theming, 389
Sharing economy, 395
Shopping orientation, 387
Showrooming, 389
Situational self-image, 382
Store image, 390
Swishing, 400
Time poverty, 384
Timestyle, 383
Total quality management (TQM), 385
Underground economy, 400
Unplanned buying, 393
Virtual reality (VR), 393

REVIEW

10-1 What is time poverty, and how can it influence our purchase decisions?

⭐ **10-2** A consumption situation has a buyer, seller, and a product. What else would you add?

⭐ **10-3** List three separate motivations for shopping, and give an example of each.

10-4 What are some important pros and cons of e-commerce?

10-5 List three factors that help to determine store image.

10-6 What is the difference between unplanned buying and impulse buying?

10-7 How do business models in the sharing economy differ from traditional purchase processes?

10-8 What is the difference between recycling and lateral cycling?

CONSUMER BEHAVIOR CHALLENGE

■ DISCUSS

10-9 Are pop-up stores simply a fad, or a retailing concept that's here to stay?

10-10 Think about exceptionally good and bad salespeople you have encountered as a shopper. What qualities seem to differentiate them from others?

10-11 Discuss the concept of *timestyle*. Based on your own experiences, how might we segment consumers in terms of their timestyles?

10-12 Consumers who participate in the sharing economy seem willing to interact with total strangers. Despite safety and privacy concerns, what is the long-term outlook for this change in the way we think about interacting with people whom we don't know? How can businesses help to diminish worries some people may have about these practices?

10-13 A tourism study based in Penang focused on why tourists buy products and services.[93] What is the probable link between this and self-image?

10-14 Spontaneous purchases of desirable products is something all retailers want. The problem is that spontaneous purchasing also means spontaneous thefts. However, security can be expensive and, above all, it deters consumer interaction and impulse buys.[94] By creating a theft-free environment, retailers find themselves creating a negative selling environment. How big a problem is shoplifting, and is store design partly to blame?

10-15 According to the global property advisor CBRE, some 88 percent of all European shoppers look for a good range of retailers and an inclusive shopping experience when they choose the location for their shopping trips. The consumers also cite price, cleanliness, and convenience as being important. These factors particularly apply to the 18–24 age groups. From CBRE's research it is clear that a retail environment's success or failure depends on the shopping experience it offers. Consumers demand a better experience, while retailers are only concerned with footfalls and sales. Retail centers need to offer better quality dining, entertainment, and special events to enhance the shopping experience. What advice would you offer a retail center about food and entertainment?

10-16 Courts often prohibit special-interest groups from distributing literature in shopping malls. Mall managements claim that these centers are private property. However, these groups argue that the mall is the modern-day version of the town square and as such is a public forum. Find some recent court cases involving this free-speech issue, and examine the arguments pro and con. What is the current status of the mall as a public forum? Do you agree with this concept?

10-17 Marketers use "tricks" to minimize psychological waiting time. These techniques range from altering customers' perceptions of a line's length to providing distractions that divert attention from waiting:[95]

One hotel chain received excessive complaints about the wait for elevators, so it installed mirrors near the elevator banks. People's natural tendency to check their appearance reduced complaints, even though the actual waiting time was unchanged.

Airline passengers often complain about the wait to claim their baggage. In one airport, they would walk 1 minute from the plane to the baggage carousel and then wait 7 minutes for their luggage. When the airport changed the layout so that the walk to the carousel took 6 minutes and bags arrived 2 minutes after that, complaints disappeared.[96]

Restaurant chains are scrambling to put the "fast" back into fast food, especially for drive-through lanes, which now account for 65 percent of revenues. In a study that ranked the speed of 25 fast-food chains, cars spent an average of 203.6 seconds from the menu board to departure. Wendy's was clocked the fastest at 150.3 seconds. To speed things up and eliminate spills, McDonald's created a salad that comes in a container to fit into car cup holders. Arby's is working on a "high viscosity" version of its special sauce that's less likely to spill. Burger King is testing see-through bags so customers can quickly check their orders before speeding off.[97]

What are your waiting line "pain points?" How can companies change their processes to make these situations easier or more enjoyable for you?

■ **APPLY**

10-18   Conduct naturalistic observation at a local mall. Sit in a central location and observe the activities of mall employees and patrons. Keep a log of the nonretailing activity you observe (e.g., special performances, exhibits, socializing, etc.). Does this activity enhance or detract from business the mall conducts? As malls become more like high-tech game rooms, how valid is the criticism that shopping areas only encourage more loitering by teenage boys, who don't spend a lot in stores and simply scare away other customers?

10-19   Select three competing clothing stores in your area and conduct a store image study for them. Ask a group of consumers to rate each store on a set of attributes and plot these ratings on the same graph. Based on your findings, are there any areas of competitive advantage or disadvantage you could bring to the attention of store management?

10-20   Using Table 10.1 as a model, construct a person–situation segmentation matrix for a brand of perfume.

10-21   IKEA, the Swedish furniture and home design company, has 283 stores in 26 countries and generated profits of $3.2 billion in 2015. Their stores have a unique layout that cuts across image and atmosphere and creates an environment designed to confuse their customers. Their stores are maze-like; customers follow a distinct trail through them. The idea is to show the furniture in different settings to illustrate its versatility. Customers get disorientated with left and right turns and make impulse buys just in case they cannot find their way back to the product. By the time the customer gets to the warehouse area near the cash registers (the only place to get larger items and load them onto a cart), the customer is amazed at the low price and does not question the purchase. Smaller items such as candles or cushions are bought on impulse as the customer traverses the store. IKEA themselves deny that the store layout is designed to confuse customers; they claim that the showrooms are designed to get ideas across and provide customers with a context in which to see the products. In 2015, IKEA announced that they were changing the layout of their stores. Research this change and decide whether they are right or wrong to change the layout.

10-22   A Nielsen survey in 2015 showed that 60 percent of consumers browsed online before they made a purchase in-store. However, 51 percent of consumers browsed in-store and then went home to make their purchase online. Carry out a survey with friends and family. Are their practices similar? Why do they choose this method?

10-23   Interview three consumers who have used a sharing economy service, such as Zipcar, Airbnb, Snapgoods, etc. How would you characterize their experiences compared to more traditional models?

Case Study

RECYCLING PLASTICS BOTTLES, SAVING THE PLANET

Plastic—what would we do without it? It's an important part of our everyday life and serves as the packaging to many of the products we use on a daily basis. It's easy it is to use, versatile as a packaging material, and very convenient. But it's also one of the biggest contributors to waste. In the open ocean between Hawaii and San Francisco and between Africa and Australia are areas where plastic accumulates and is carried by ocean currents, resulting in the Great Pacific Garbage Patch and the Indian Ocean Garbage Patch, respectively. Needless to say, this represents a major hazard to wildlife in the area, but they also pose dangers to shipping traffic.

Current statistics suggest that about 27 percent of plastic bottles are recycled, which means that there is potential to change behavior and increase levels of recycling. Recycled plastic bottles can be turned into a number of other products, including clothing and sleeping bags. Both Coca-Cola and Pepsi have identified recycling as a major issue in this industry, but the majority of the sales of their beverages are in plastic bottles—more than 60 percent of it, in fact. This makes it important to develop alternatives to petroleum-based plastic (PET or polyethylene) bottles for packaging. One such innovation is the creation of a plastic bottle made from recyclable plant material.

Plastic bottles are generally made from petroleum, so using other ingredients means a lower carbon footprint. Both international brands have developed alternatives that attempt to not only reduce the carbon footprint associated with the traditional plastic bottle, but also to enable the bottle to be recycled and reused. Coca-Cola has introduced the plantbottle, which is made of 30 percent sugarcane and the waste from sugarcane products. This bottle functions and feels exactly like a traditional plastic bottle, but it is not biodegradable, so consumers have to be encouraged to recycle them. The first prototype of this bottle was introduced in 2009, and more than 35 million of them have now been sold in 40 countries. At the moment, only 30 percent of the bottle is from a plant-based source, though research is currently underway to increase this to 100 percent. Pepsi's bottle is also made of plant waste, and this material allows for these bottles to be turned into new Pepsi bottles.

To encouraging consumers to recycle their plastic bottles, various strategies have been developed by Coca-Cola and Pepsi that reward consumers for their recycling activities. In Singapore, the Happiness Recycled campaign included a recycling machine in public places that rewarded consumers every time they recycled a plastic Coke bottle. The empty Coke bottle was placed in a specially-developed bottle recycling machine, and in return the consumer was rewarded with a number of different items. Some of the items that the machine dispensed were flowers, t-shirts, and caps, all made from recycled plastic bottles. Each also contained a note encouraging consumers to continue recycling. A total of 51,827 bottles were recycled in this campaign, and a video of the campaign that was uploaded on YouTube got 45,000 views.

Pepsi has partnered with international non-government agencies and local citizens in various countries in Waste to Wealth initiatives. This initiative encourages recycling by providing an income for those who collect recyclable items. Other organizations that also have products that retail in plastic bottles, such as Nestlé and Johnson & Johnson, have also introduced education and reward programs to increase the recycling rates of these items.

In the United Kingdom, rewards have been given to consumers based on the pledges made to recycle in a campaign launched by Tesco and Coca-Cola. The purpose of the pledges is to educate families about the importance of recycling while also highlighting the importance of nature and the environment. Rewards have been given to those pledging their support, such as a discount voucher or loyalty points for the store rewards program. A family holiday to France was also one of the rewards. The campaign sought to enhance education about recycling as well as the level of involvement (and fun)—all geared towards increasing the levels of recycling in the United Kingdom.

Rewards from various organizations are not the only way to encourage recycling. In other European countries, consumers pay a deposit on the plastic bottle when buying their beverages. When these bottle is returned, it is placed in a recycling machine that returns the deposit to the consumer in the form of a voucher. This voucher is then presented to the retailer to get the deposit back.

DISCUSSION QUESTIONS

CS 10-1 How do Coca-Cola, Pepsi, Unilever, and Johnson & Johnson benefit from their various strategies with regard to plastic disposal? How do you feel about what they are doing?

CS 10-2 Why do you think Coca-Cola decided to include rewards and other experiences in their recycling campaign in Singapore? Do you think they were appropriate rewards?

CS 10-3 Suggest other ways to increase recycling in your community (besides those indicated here).

Sources: Care to Recycle Web site, http://caretorecycle.com/; The Coca-Cola Company, "Happiness Recycled: Coca-Cola Singapore Increases Recycle Rates with 'Recycle Happiness Machine,'" http://www.coca-colacompany.com/stories/happiness-recycled-coca-cola-singapore-increases-recycle-rates-with-recycle-happiness-machine/; Jessica Shankleman, "Coca-Cola, Nestle, Tesco Launch Campaigns to up Recycling Rates," GreenBiz, http://www.greenbiz.com/blog/2014/09/16/coca-cola-nestle-tesco-campaign-up-recycling-rates; Heritage Pioneer Corporate Group, "What Is the Coca-Cola PlantBottle?", http://www.hpcorporategroup.com/what-is-the-coca-cola-plantbottle.html; MRC Polymers, "Recycling Facts," http://www.mrcpolymers.com/PlasticRecyclingFacts.php; Laura Parker, "Plane Search Shows World's Oceans Are Full of Trash," *National Geographic*, April 4, 2014, http://news.nationalgeographic.com/news/2014/04/140404-garbage-patch-indian-ocean-debris-malaysian-plane/; Pepsico, "Packaging," Pepsico.com, http://www.pepsico.com/Purpose/Environmental-Sustainability/Packaging-and-Waste; Marc Gunther, "Why Are Major Beverage Companies Refusing to Use a 90% Recycled Can?", *The Guardian*, October 30, 2014, http://www.theguardian.com/sustainable-business/2014/oct/30/recycled-aluminum-novelis-ford-cocacola-pepsi-miller-budweiser-beer.

MyLab Marketing

Go to the Assignments section of your MyLab to complete these writing exercises.

10-26 People have more leisure time than ever. Why do they feel so rushed, and how can marketers address this problem?

10-27 Is the customer always right? Why or why not?

NOTES

1. Phil LeBeau, "Americans Rethinking How They Buy Cars," *CNBC* (February 26, 2014), http://www.cnbc.com/id/101445202, accessed April 7, 2015.
2. Pradeep Kakkar and Richard J. Lutz, "Situational Influence on Consumer Behavior: A Review," in Harold H. Kassarjian and Thomas S. Robertson, eds., *Perspectives in Consumer Behavior*, 3rd ed. (Glenview, IL: Scott, Foresman, 1981): 204–214.
3. Christopher Heine, "Will Facebook Ads Soon Reflect 'What's On Your Mind?'" *ClickZ* (March 23, 2011), http://www.clickz.com/clickz/news/2036901/facebook-ads-soon-reflect-whats-mind, accessed April 17, 2011.
4. Benedict Carey, "TV Time, Unlike Child Care, Ranks High in Mood Study," *New York Times* (December 3, 2004), www.nytimes.com, accessed December 3, 2004.
5. Carolyn Turner Schenk and Rebecca H. Holman, "A Sociological Approach to Brand Choice: The Concept of Situational Self-Image," in Jerry C. Olson, ed., *Advances in Consumer Research* 7 (Ann Arbor, MI: Association for Consumer Research, 1980): 610–614.
6. Peter R. Dickson, "Person–Situation: Segmentation's Missing Link," *Journal of Marketing* 46 (Fall 1982): 56–64.
7. Alan R. Hirsch, "Effects of Ambient Odors on Slot-Machine Usage in a Las Vegas Casino," *Psychology & Marketing* 12 (October 1995): 585–594.
8. Tanya Irwin, "ReachMail: Email Marketers Should Focus on Mid-Day," *Marketing Daily* (March 17, 2011), http://www.mediapost.com/publications/?fa5Articles.showArticle&art_aid5146883&nid5124807, accessed April 18, 2011.

9. Carol Felker Kaufman, Paul M. Lane, and Jay D. Lindquist, "Exploring More Than 24 Hours a Day: A Preliminary Investigation of Polychronic Time Use," *Journal of Consumer Research* 18 (December 1991): 392–401.

10. Laurence P. Feldman and Jacob Hornik, "The Use of Time: An Integrated Conceptual Model," *Journal of Consumer Research* 7 (March 1981): 407–419; see also Michelle M. Bergadaa, "The Role of Time in the Action of the Consumer," *Journal of Consumer Research* 17 (December 1990): 289–302; cf. also Niklas Woermann and Joonas Rokka, "Timeflow: How Consumption Practices Shape Consumers' Temporal Experiences," *Journal of Consumer Research* 41, no. 6 (2015): 1486–1508.

11. Alan Zarembo, "What If There Weren't Any Clocks to Watch?" *Newsweek* (June 30, 1997): 14; based on research reported in Robert Levine, *A Geography of Time: The Temporal Misadventures of a Social Psychologist, or How Every Culture Keeps Time Just a Little Bit Differently* (New York: Basic Books, 1997).

12. Sharon Jayson, "Men Vs. Women: How Much Time Spent on Kids, Job, Chores?" *USA TODAY* (March 14, 2013), http://www.usatoday.com/story/news/nation/2013/03/14/men-women-work-time/1983271/, accessed April 6, 2015; Vivian Giang, "How Everything We Tell Ourselves About How Busy We Are is a Lie," *Fast Company* (September 5, 2014), http://www.fastcompany.com/3035253/the-future-of-work/how-everything-we-tell-ourselves-about-how-busy-we-are-is-a-lie, accessed April 6, 2015.

13. June S. Cotte, S. Ratneshwar, and David Glen Mick, "The Times of Their Lives: Phenomenological and Metaphorical Characteristics of Consumer Timestyles," *Journal of Consumer Research* 31 (September 2004): 333–345.

14. Dale Buss, "Everything's Possible: McDonald's Pins Turnaround on 'Experience of the Future'," *Brandchannel* (December 8, 2014), http://www.brandchannel.com/home/post/2014/12/08/141208-McDonalds-Experience-of-the-Future.aspx?utm_campaign=141208-McDonalds&utm_source=newsletter&utm_medium=email, accessed February 25, 2015.

15. Dhruv Grewal, Julie Baker, Michael Levy, and Glenn B. Voss, "The Effects of Wait Expectations and Store Atmosphere Evaluations on Patronage Intentions in Service-Intensive Retail Store," *Journal of Retailing* 79 (2003): 259–268; cf. also Shirley Taylor, "Waiting for Service: The Relationship Between Delays and Evaluations of Service," *Journal of Marketing* 58 (April 1994): 56–69.

16. Material adapted from a presentation by Glenn H. Mazur, QFD Institute, 2002.

17. Laurette Dubé and Bernd H. Schmitt, "The Processing of Emotional and Cognitive Aspects of Product Usage in Satisfaction Judgments," in Rebecca H. Holman and Michael R. Solomon, eds., *Advances in Consumer Research* 18 (Provo, UT: Association for Consumer Research, 1991): 52–56; Lalita A. Manrai and Meryl P. Gardner, "The Influence of Affect on Attributions for Product Failure," in Rebecca H. Holman and Michael R. Solomon, eds., *Advances in Consumer Research* 18 (Provo, UT: Association for Consumer Research, 1991): 249–254.

18. Kevin G. Celuch and Linda S. Showers, "It's Time to Stress Stress: The Stress–Purchase/Consumption Relationship," in Rebecca H. Holman and Michael R. Solomon, eds., *Advances in Consumer Research* 18 (Provo, UT: Association for Consumer Research, 1991): 284–289; Lawrence R. Lepisto, J. Kathleen Stuenkel, and Linda K. Anglin, "Stress: An Ignored Situational Influence," in Rebecca H. Holman and Michael R. Solomon, eds., *Advances in Consumer Research* 18 (Provo, UT: Association for Consumer Research, 1991): 296–302.

19. Velitchka D. Kaltcheva and Barton A. Weitz, "When Should a Retailer Create an Exciting Store Environment?" *Journal of Marketing* 70 (January 2006): 107–118.

20. John D. Mayer and Yvonne N. Gaschke, "The Experience and Meta-Experience of Mood," *Journal of Personality & Social Psychology* 55 (July 1988): 102–111.

21. Meryl Paula Gardner, "Mood States and Consumer Behavior: A Critical Review," *Journal of Consumer Research* 12 (December 1985): 281–300; Scott Dawson, Peter H. Bloch, and Nancy M. Ridgway, "Shopping Motives, Emotional States, and Retail Outcomes," *Journal of Retailing* 66 (Winter 1990): 408–427; Patricia A. Knowles, Stephen J. Grove, and W. Jeffrey Burroughs, "An Experimental Examination of Mood States on Retrieval and Evaluation of Advertisement and Brand Information," *Journal of the Academy of Marketing Science* 21 (April 1993): 135–143; Paul W. Miniard, Sunil Bhatla, and Deepak Sirdeskmuhk, "Mood as a Determinant of Postconsumption Product Evaluations: Mood Effects and Their Dependency on the Affective Intensity of the Consumption Experience," *Journal of Consumer Psychology* 1, no. 2 (1992): 173–195; Mary T. Curren and Katrin R. Harich, "Consumers' Mood States: The Mitigating Influence of Personal Relevance on Product Evaluations," *Psychology & Marketing* 11 (March–April 1994): 91–107; Gerald J. Gorn, Marvin E. Goldberg, and Kunal Basu, "Mood, Awareness, and Product Evaluation," *Journal of Consumer Psychology* 2, no. 3 (1993): 237–256.

22. Gordon C. Bruner, "Music, Mood, and Marketing," *Journal of Marketing* 54 (October 1990): 94–104; Basil G. Englis, "Music Television and Its Influences on Consumers, Consumer Culture, and the Transmission of Consumption Messages," in Rebecca H. Holman and Michael R. Solomon, eds., *Advances in Consumer Research* 18 (Provo, UT: Association for Consumer Research, 1991): 111–114.

23. Marvin E. Goldberg and Gerald J. Gorn, "Happy and Sad TV Programs: How They Affect Reactions to Commercials," *Journal of Consumer Research* 14 (December 1987): 387–403; Gorn, Goldberg, and Basu, "Mood, Awareness, and Product Evaluation"; Curren and Harich, "Consumers' Mood States."

24. Rajeev Batra and Douglas M. Stayman, "The Role of Mood in Advertising Effectiveness," *Journal of Consumer Research* 17 (September 1990): 203; John P. Murry, Jr., and Peter A. Dacin, "Cognitive Moderators of Negative-Emotion Effects: Implications for Understanding Media Context," *Journal of Consumer Research* (March 1996), 22: 439–447.

25. For a scale to assess these dimensions of the shopping experience, see Barry J. Babin, William R. Darden, and Mitch Griffin, "Work and/or Fun: Measuring Hedonic and Utilitarian Shopping Value," *Journal of Consumer Research* 20 (March 1994): 644–656.

26. Kaltcheva and Weitz, "When Should a Retailer Create an Exciting Store Environment?"

27. Babin, Darden, and Griffin, "Work and/or Fun."

28. Edward M. Tauber, "Why Do People Shop?" *Journal of Marketing* 36 (October 1972): 47–48.

29. Ann Zimmerman and Laura Stevens, "Attention, Shoppers: Bored College Kids Competing in Aisle 6," *Wall Street Journal* (February 23, 2005), http://professional.wsj.com/article/SB110911598024661430-H9jfYNklaF4oJ2sZ32IaqiAm5.html?mg5reno-wsj, accessed September 11, 2011.

30. Robert C. Prus, *Making Sales: Influence as Interpersonal Accomplishment* (Newbury Park, CA: Sage Publications, 1989): 225.

31. Michael-Lee Johnstone and Denise M. Conroy, "Dressing for the Thrill: An Exploration of Why Women Dress Up to Go Shopping," *Journal of Consumer Behaviour* 4, no. 4 (2005): 234.

32. "Global B2C Ecommerce Sales to Hit $1.5 Trillion This Year," emarketer.com (February 3, 2014), http://www.emarketer.com/Article/Global-B2C-Ecommerce-Sales-Hit-15-Trillion-This-Year-Driven-by-Growth-Emerging-Markets/1010575#sthash.LyNbIrRR.dpuf, accessed April 6, 2015.

33. Alex Fitzpatrick, "75% of World Has Access to Mobile Phones," *Mashable* (July 17, 2012), http://mashable.com/2012/07/18/mobile-phones-worldwide/ ?utm_source=feedburner&utm_medium=email&utm_campaign=Feed%3A+Mashable+%28Mashable%29, accessed February 22, 2015.

34. Claire Cain Miller, "Do People Actually Shop on Phones? The Answer Is Decidedly Yes," *New York Times* (January 9, 2013), http://bits.blogs.nytimes.com/2013/01/09/do-people-actually-shop-on-phones-the-answer-is-decidedly-yes/, accessed February 22, 2015.

35. June Cotte and Kathryn A. LaTour, "Blackjack in the Kitchen: Understanding Online Versus Casino Gambling," *Journal of Consumer Research* 35 (February 2009): 742–758.

36. Vindu Goel, "Coming Soon to Social Media: Click to Buy Now," *New York Times* (July 17, 2014), http://bits.blogs.nytimes.com/2014/07/17/coming-soon-to-social-media-click-to-buy-now/?_php=true&_type=blogs&_r=0, accessed February 19, 2015.

37. Alex Washburn, "Digital Wallets: End of the Beginning or Beginning of the End?," *Wired* (February 2015), http://www.wired.com/2015/02/digital-wallets-end-of-the-beginning-or-beginning-of-the-end/, accessed April 6, 2015; Jacob Davidson, "No, Big Companies Aren't Really Accepting Bitcoin," *Money* (January 9, 2015), http://time.com/money/3658361/dell-microsoft-expedia-bitcoin/, accessed April 6, 2015.

38. Rebecca K. Ratner, Barbara E. Kahn, and Daniel Kahneman, "Choosing Less-Preferred Experiences for the Sake of Variety," *Journal of Consumer Research* 26 (June 1999): 1–15.

39. http://announcements.ebay.com/tag/see-it-on-sunglasses/, accessed April 6, 2015.

40. http://modaoperandi.com/, accessed April 6, 2015; http://www.net-a-porter.com, accessed April 6, 2015; http://www.threadless.com/, accessed April 6, 2015; www.modcloth.com, accessed April 6, 2015.

41. www.allurent.com/newsDetail.php?newsid520, accessed January 29, 2007.

42. Vanessa O'Connell, "Fictional Hershey Factory Will Send Kisses to Broadway," *Wall Street Journal* (August 5, 2002), www.wsj.com, accessed August 5, 2002.

43. Millie Creighton, "The Seed of Creative Lifestyle Shopping: Wrapping Consumerism in Japanese Store Layouts," in John F. Sherry Jr., ed., *Servicescapes: The Concept of Place in Contemporary Markets* (Lincolnwood, IL: NTC Business Books, 1998): 199–228; also cf. Robert V. Kozinets, John F. Sherry, Diana Storm, Adam Duhachek, Krittinee Nuttavuthisit, and Benet DeBerry-Spence, "Ludic Agency and Retail Spectacle," *Journal of Consumer Research* 31 (December 2004): 658–672.

44. http://www.paragraphny.com/, accessed March 12, 2013.

45. Jennifer Saranow, "Retailers Give It the Old College Try," *Wall Street Journal* (August 28, 2008): B8; *March 2007 Trend Briefing*, www.trendwatching.com/briefing, accessed March 30, 2007.

46. Susan Spiggle and Murphy A. Sewall, "A Choice Sets Model of Retail Selection," *Journal of Marketing* 51 (April 1987): 97–111.

47. "The Science of Shopping: The Way the Brain Buys," *The Economist* (December 18, 2008), www.economist.com, accessed April 6, 2015.

48. Philip Kotler, "Atmospherics as a Marketing Tool," *Journal of Retailing* (Winter 1973–1974): 10; Anna Mattila and Jochen Wirtz, "Congruency of Scent and Music as a Driver of In-Store Evaluations and Behavior," *Journal of Retailing* 77, no. 2 (2001): 273–289; J. Duncan Herrington, "An Integrative Path Model of the Effects of Retail Environments on Shopper Behavior," in Robert L. King, ed., *Marketing: Toward the Twenty-First Century* (Richmond, VA: Southern Marketing Association, 1991): 58–62; see also Ann E. Schlosser, "Applying the Functional Theory of Attitudes to Understanding the Influence of Store Atmosphere on Store Inferences," *Journal of Consumer Psychology* 7, no. 4 (1998): 345–369.

49. Joseph A. Bellizzi and Robert E. Hite, "Environmental Color, Consumer Feelings, and Purchase Likelihood," *Psychology & Marketing* 9 (September–October 1992): 347–363.

50. Robert J. Donovan, John R. Rossiter, Gilian Marcoolyn, and Andrew Nesdale, "Store Atmosphere and Purchasing Behavior," *Journal of Retailing* 70, no. 3 (1994): 283–294; cf. also L. W. Turley and Jean-Charles Chebat, "Linking Retail Strategy, Atmospheric Design and Shopping Behaviour," *Journal of Marketing Management* 18, no. 1–2 (2002): 125–144.

51. http://www.buildabear.com/shopping/, accessed March 12, 2013.

52. Charles S. Areni and David Kim, "The Influence of In-Store Lighting on Consumers' Examination of Merchandise in a Wine Store," *International Journal of Research in Marketing* 11, no. 2 (March 1994): 117–125.

53. "Slow Music Makes Fast Drinkers," *Psychology Today* (March 1989): 18.

54. Brad Edmondson, "Pass the Meat Loaf," *American Demographics* (January 1989): 19.

55. "Through the Looking Glass," *Lifestyle Monitor* 16 (Fall–Winter 2002).

56. Jennifer Lach, "Meet You in Aisle Three," *American Demographics* (April 1999): 41.

57. Karen M. Stilley, J. Jeffrey Inman, and Kirk L. Wakefield, "Planning to Make Unplanned Purchases? The Role of In-Store Slack in Budget Deviation," *Journal of Consumer Research* 37, no. 2 (2010): 264–278.

58. Michael Moss, "Nudged to the Produce Aisle by a Look in the Mirror," *New York Times* (August 27, 2013), http://www.nytimes.com/2013/08/28/dining/wooing-us-down-the-produce-aisle.html?_r=0, accessed February 23, 2015.

59. "Mobile Draws in Deal-Seeking Grocery Shoppers," *eMarketer.com* (April 22, 2014), http://www.emarketer.com/Article/Mobile-Draws-Deal-Seeking-Grocery-Shoppers/1010778#sthash.Z9ofCJ1Z.dpuf, accessed April 6, 2015; Yohana Desta, "7 Fresh Apps to Upgrade Grocery Shopping," *Mashable* (April 8, 2014), http://mashable.com/2014/04/08/apps-grocery-shopping/, accessed April 6, 2015; "Motorola Survey: Shoppers Better Connected to Information than Store Associates," *Chain Store Age* (January 17, 2011), http://www.chainstoreage.com/article/motorola-survey-shoppers-better-connected-information- store-associates, accessed April 30, 2011; Kris Hudson, "Malls Test Apps to Aid Shoppers," *Wall Street Journal* (April 26, 2011), http://online.wsj.com/article/SB10001424052748704336504576258740640080926.html?mod5dist_smart brief, accessed April 29, 2011.

60. Michael Sciandra and Jeff Inman, "Smart Phones, Bad Decisions? The Impact of In-store Mobile Technology Use on Consumer Decisions," in eds. Simona Botti and Aparna Labroo—*Advances in Consumer Research* 41 (Duluth, MN: Association for Consumer Research, 2013).

61. Cooper Smith, "How Beacons—Small, Low-Cost Gadgets—Will Influence Billions in US Retail Sales," *Tech Insider* (February 9, 2015), http://www.businessinsider.com/beacons-impact-billions-in-reail-sales-2015-2, accessed April 6, 2015; Zach Sokol, "A Virtual Reality Tesco Is Opening Shop In Berlin," *The Creators Project* (March 18, 2014), http://thecreatorsproject.vice.com/blog/tescos-using-virtual-reality-goggles-to-possibly-allow-people-to-buy-groceries-from-bed, accessed April 6, 2015; Jordan Crook, "With $45 Million In Funding, Augmented Reality Platform Blippar is Rethinking Search," *Techcrunch*, (March 6, 2015), http://techcrunch.com/2015/03/06/with-45-million-in-funding-augmented-reality-platform-blippar-is-rethinking-search/#.h5cyu1:Ehw2, accessed April 6, 2015; https://travel-brilliantly.marriott.com/our-innovations/oculus-get-teleported, accessed April 6, 2015.

62. Easwar S. Iyer, "Unplanned Purchasing: Knowledge of Shopping Environment and Time Pressure," *Journal of Retailing* 65 (Spring 1989): 40–57; C. Whan Park, Easwar S. Iyer, and Daniel C. Smith, "The Effects of Situational Factors on In-Store Grocery Shopping," *Journal of Consumer Research* 15 (March 1989): 422–433.

63. Iyer, "Unplanned Purchasing"; Park, Iyer, and Smith, "The Effects of Situational Factors on In-Store Grocery Shopping."

64. Matt Richtel, "At Starbucks, Songs of Instant Gratification," *New York Times* (October 1, 2007), www.nytimes.com, accessed October 1, 2007.

65. Quoted in Shelly Banjo and Sara Germano, "The End of the Impulse Shopper," *The Wall Street Journal* (November 25, 2014), http://www.wsj.com/articles/the-end-of-the-impulse-shopper-1416872108, accessed February 23, 2015.

66. Emily Steel, "Luring Shoppers to Stores," *Wall Street Journal* (August 26, 2010), http://online.wsj.com/article/SB10001424052748704545409045 7545184198006313 2.html, accessed April 18, 2011.

67. Quoted in Louise Story, "Product Packages Now Shout to Get Your Attention," *New York Times* (August 10, 2007), www.nytimes.com, accessed August 10, 2007.

68. Cf. Robert B. Cialdini, *Influence: Science and Practice*, 2nd ed. (Glenview, IL: Scott, Foresman, 1988).

69. Richard P. Bagozzi, "Marketing as Exchange," *Journal of Marketing* 39 (October 1975): 32–39; Peter M. Blau, *Exchange and Power in Social Life* (New York: Wiley, 1964); Marjorie Caballero and Alan J. Resnik, "The Attraction Paradigm in Dyadic Exchange," *Psychology & Marketing* 3, no. 1 (1986): 17–34; George C. Homans, "Social Behavior as Exchange," *American Journal of Sociology* 63 (1958): 597–606; Paul H. Schurr and Julie L. Ozanne, "Influences on Exchange Processes: Buyers' Preconceptions of a Seller's Trustworthiness and Bargaining Toughness," *Journal of Consumer Research* 11 (March 1985): 939–953; Arch G. Woodside and J. W. Davenport, "The Effect of Salesman Similarity and Expertise on Consumer Purchasing Behavior," *Journal of Marketing Research* 8 (1974): 433–436.

70. Mary Jo Bitner, Bernard H. Booms, and Mary Stansfield Tetreault, "The Service Encounter: Diagnosing Favorable and Unfavorable Incidents," *Journal of Marketing* 54 (January 1990): 7–84; Robert C. Prus, *Making Sales* (Newbury Park, CA: Sage Publications, 1989); Arch G. Woodside and James L. Taylor, "Identity Negotiations in Buyer–Seller Interactions," in Elizabeth C. Hirschman and Morris B. Holbrook, eds., *Advances in Consumer Research* 12 (Provo, UT: Association for Consumer Research, 1985): 443–449.

71. Barry J. Babin, James S. Boles, and William R. Darden, "Salesperson Stereotypes, Consumer Emotions, and Their Impact on Information Processing," *Journal of the Academy of Marketing Science* 23, no. 2 (1995): 94–105; Gilbert A. Churchill, Jr., Neil M. Ford, Steven W. Hartley, and Orville C. Walker, Jr., "The Determinants of Salesperson Performance: A Meta-Analysis," *Journal of Marketing Research* 22 (May 1985): 103–118.

72. www.customerssuck.com, accessed April 6, 2015.

73. Siew Meng Leong, Paul S. Busch, and Deborah Roedder John, "Knowledge Bases and Salesperson Effectiveness: A Script-Theoretic Analysis," *Journal of Marketing Research* 26 (May 1989): 164; Harish Sujan, Mita Sujan, and James R. Bettman, "Knowledge Structure Differences Between More Effective and Less Effective Salespeople," *Journal of Marketing Research* 25 (February 1988): 81–86; Robert Saxe and Barton Weitz, "The SOCCO Scale: A Measure of the Customer Orientation of Salespeople," *Journal of Marketing Research* 19 (August 1982): 343–351; David M. Szymanski, "Determinants of Selling Effectiveness: The Importance of Declarative Knowledge to the Personal Selling Concept," *Journal of Marketing* 52 (January 1988): 64–77; Barton A. Weitz, "Effectiveness in Sales Interactions: A Contingency Framework," *Journal of Marketing* 45 (Winter 1981): 85–103.

74. Jagdish N. Sheth, "Buyer-Seller Interaction: A Conceptual Framework," in *Advances in Consumer Research* 3 (Cincinnati, OH: Association for Consumer Research, 1976): 382–386; Kaylene C. Williams and Rosann L. Spiro, "Communication Style in the Salesperson-Customer Dyad," *Journal of Marketing Research* 22 (November 1985): 434–442.

75. Marsha L. Richins, "An Analysis of Consumer Interaction Styles in the Marketplace," *Journal of Consumer Research* 10 (June 1983): 73–82.

76. Cf. also Marsha L. Richins, "When Wanting is Better Than Having: Materialism, Transformation Expectations, and Product-Evoked Emotions in the Purchase Process," *Journal of Consumer Research* 40, no. 1 (2013): 1–18.

77. "Airbnb, Snapgoods and 12 More Pioneers of the 'Share Economy'," *Forbes*, http://www.forbes.com/pictures/eeji45emgkh/airbnb-snapgoods-and-12-more-pioneers-of-the-share-economy/, accessed April 7, 2015; "The New Consumer and the Sharing Economy," *Havas*, http://www.havas.com/insights/studies/actualites/the-new-consumer-and-the-sharing-economy, accessed April 7, 2015; Joel Stein, "Strangers Crashed My Car, Ate My Food and Wore My Pants," *Time* (January 29, 2015), http://time.com/3686877/uber-lyft-sharing-economy/, accessed April 7, 2015.

78. Rama Jayanti and Anita Jackson, "Service Satisfaction: Investigation of Three Models," in Rebecca H. Holman and Michael R. Solomon, eds., *Advances in Consumer Research* 18 (Provo, UT: Association for Consumer Research, 1991): 603–610; David K. Tse, Franco M. Nicosia, and Peter C. Wilton, "Consumer Satisfaction as a Process," *Psychology & Marketing* 7 (Fall 1990): 177–193. For a recent treatment of satisfaction issues from a more interpretive perspective, see Susan Fournier and David Glen Mick, "Rediscovering Satisfaction," *Journal of Marketing* 63 (October 1999): 5–23.

79. Robert Jacobson and David A. Aaker, "The Strategic Role of Product Quality," *Journal of Marketing* 51 (October 1987): 31–44. For a review of issues regarding the measurement of service quality, see J. Joseph Cronin, Jr., and Steven A. Taylor, "Measuring Service Quality: A Reexamination and Extension," *Journal of Marketing* 56 (July 1992): 55–68.

80. Amna Kirmani and Peter Wright, "Money Talks: Perceived Advertising Expense and Expected Product Quality," *Journal of Consumer Research* 16 (December 1989): 344–353; Donald R. Lichtenstein and Scot Burton, "The Relationship Between Perceived and Objective Price-Quality," *Journal of Marketing Research* 26 (November 1989): 429–443; Akshay R. Rao and Kent B. Monroe, "The Effect of Price, Brand Name, and Store Name on Buyers' Perceptions of Product Quality: An Integrative Review," *Journal of Marketing Research* 26 (August 1989): 351–357; Shelby Hunt, "Post-Transactional Communication and Dissonance Reduction," *Journal of Marketing* 34 (January 1970): 46–51; Daniel E. Innis and H. Rao Unnava, "The Usefulness of Product Warranties for Reputable and New Brands," in Rebecca H. Holman and Michael R. Solomon, eds., *Advances in Consumer Research* 18 (Provo, UT: Association for Consumer Research, 1991): 317–322; Terence A. Shimp and William O. Bearden, "Warranty and Other Extrinsic Cue Effects on Consumers' Risk Perceptions," *Journal of Consumer Research* 9 (June 1982): 38–46.

81. Gilbert A. Churchill, Jr., and Carol F. Surprenant, "An Investigation into the Determinants of Customer Satisfaction," *Journal of Marketing Research* 19 (November 1983): 491–504; John E. Swan and I. Frederick Trawick, "Disconfirmation of Expectations and Satisfaction with a Retail Service," *Journal of Retailing* 57 (Fall 1981): 49–67; Peter C. Wilton and David K. Tse, "Models of Consumer Satisfaction Formation: An Extension," *Journal of Marketing Research* 25 (May 1988): 204–212. For a discussion of what may occur when customers evaluate a new service for which comparison standards do not yet exist, see Ann L. McGill and Dawn Iacobucci, "The Role of Post-Experience Comparison Standards in the Evaluation of Unfamiliar Services," in John F. Sherry, Jr., and Brian Sternthal, eds., *Advances in Consumer Research* 19 (Provo, UT: Association for Consumer Research, 1992): 570–578; William Boulding, Ajay Kalra, Richard Staelin, and Valarie A. Zeithaml, "A Dynamic Process Model of Service Quality: From Expectations to Behavioral Intentions," *Journal of Marketing Research* 30 (February 1993): 7–27.

82. Russell W. Belk, "The Role of Possessions in Constructing and Maintaining a Sense of Past," in Marvin E. Goldberg, Gerald Gorn, and Richard W. Pollay, eds., *Advances in Consumer Research* 17 (Provo, UT: Association for Consumer Research, 1989): 669–676.

83. David E. Sanger, "For a Job Well Done, Japanese Enshrine the Chip," *New York Times* (December 11, 1990): A4.

84. Jacob Jacoby, Carol K. Berning, and Thomas F. Dietvorst, "What About Disposition?" *Journal of Marketing* 41 (April 1977): 22–28.

85. Ron Nixon, "Food Waste is Becoming Serious Economic and Environmental Issue, Report Says," *New York Times* (February 25, 2015), http://www .nytimes.com/2015/02/26/us/food-waste-is-becoming-serious-economic-and-environmental-issue-report-says.html?_r=1, accessed February 26, 2015.

86. Debra J. Dahab, James W. Gentry, and Wanru Su, "New Ways to Reach Non-Recyclers: An Extension of the Model of Reasoned Action to Recycling Behaviors," in Frank R. Kardes and Mita Sujan, eds., *Advances in Consumer Research* 22 (Provo, UT: Association for Consumer Research): 251–256. For other research, cf. Jesse R. Catlin and Yitong Wang, Recycling Gone Bad: When the Option to Recycle Increases Resource Consumption. *Journal of Consumer Psychology* 23, no. 1 (2013): 122–127; R. Trudel and J. J. Argo, "The Effect of Product Size and Form Distortion on Consumer Recycling Behavior," *Journal of Consumer Research* 40, no. 4 (2013), 632–643.

87. Alicia Ciccone, "H&M Launches Garment Recycling Program Across All Markets," *Brandchannel*, (February 21, 2013), http://www.brandchannel .com/home/post/2013/02/21/HM-Garment-Recycling-Program-022113.aspx, accessed February 23, 2015.

88. John F. Sherry, Jr., "A Sociocultural Analysis of a Midwestern American Flea Market," *Journal of Consumer Research* 17 (June 1990): 13–30.

89. Allan J. Magrath, "If Used Product Sellers Ever Get Organized, Watch Out," *Marketing News* (June 25, 1990): 9; Kevin McCrohan and James D. Smith, "Consumer Participation in the Informal Economy," *Journal of the Academy of Marketing Science* 15 (Winter 1990): 62.

90. John F. Sherry, Jr., "Dealers and Dealing in a Periodic Market: Informal Retailing in Ethnographic Perspective," *Journal of Retailing* 66 (Summer 1990): 174.

91. "Recommerce," Trendwatching.com, October 2011, http://www.trend watching.com/trends/recommerce/, accessed April 8, 2015.

92. http://www.swishing.com/, accessed April 7, 2015.

93. Muhannad M A Abdallat, "Actual Self-Image, Ideal Self-Image and the Relation between Satisfaction and Destination Loyalty," *Tourism & Hospitality* 1, no. 4 (2012), http://www.omicsgroup.org/journals/actual-self-image-ideal-self-image-and-the-relation-between-satisfaction-and-destination-loyalty-2167-0269.1000102.pdf.

94. Shelly Branch, "Maybe Sex Doesn't Sell, A&F Is Discovering," *Wall Street Journal* (December 12, 2003), www.wsj.com, accessed December 12, 2003.

95. David H. Maister, "The Psychology of Waiting Lines," in John A. Czepiel, Michael R. Solomon, and Carol F. Surprenant, eds., *The Service Encounter: Managing Employee/Customer Interaction in Service Businesses* (Lexington, MA: Lexington Books, 1985): 113–124.

96. David Leonhardt, "Airlines Using Technology in a Push for Shorter Lines," *New York Times* (May 8, 2000), www.nytimes.com, accessed May 8, 2000.

97. Jennifer Ordonez, "An Efficiency Drive: Fast-Food Lanes, Equipped with Timers, Get Even Faster," *Wall Street Journal* (May 18, 2000), www.wsj .com, accessed May 18, 2000.

SECTION 3   CATS, KIBBLE, AND CABLE TV

BACKGROUND AND GOAL

You were hired by PROSPEROUS PETS, a small regional chain of boutique pet care stores. PROSPEROUS PETS focuses on serving dog and cat owners for all of their pet needs, including pet sitting, pet training, grooming, toys, and food. PROSPEROUS PETS tends to serve customers who consider their dogs and cats "surrogate children," and who, are willing to spend top dollar on quality services and products.

PROSPEROUS PETS is preparing to launch its first television advertising campaign. The top management team has whittled the list of cable channels to potentially advertise on down to 11. Your task is to analyze additional information about the viewers of these 11 stations and come up with a short list of cable channels that you believe will be best for PROSPEROUS PETS. To aid you in your task, management handed you three reports generated from GfK MRI. The first report deals with the quantity of pets owned by viewers of each channel, the second report deals with the types of pet services used by channel viewers, and the final report is about where people buy their pet food.

THE DATA

The data in each of the three reports can be interpreted in a similar manner.

- The (mils) column is the estimated number (in millions) of people or U.S. households who exhibited the target behavior in the row and column. For example, 15.1 million U.S. adults report watching the cable channel AMC as well as who own one dog.
- The vertical percentage (%) column is the estimated percentage of all people in a column who watch the channel reported in the table's row. For example, of all people who own one dog, 23.8 percent of them also report watching AMC.
- The horizontal percentage (%) column is the estimated percentage of all people in a row who also exhibit the behavior reported in the table's column. For example, of all people who watch AMC, 29.7 percentage of them own one dog.

These three pieces of information can be informative on their own. However, they can also be used to calculate other useful metrics.

Task 1: Understanding the Data
Use the information provided in Table 1 to answer the following questions:

1 If someone owns a dog, what is the percentage chance they watch Fox News? What if they own a cat?

2 Which channel is much more likely to be watched by someone with four or more dogs than an average American? What is the Index value for this channel? An Index value of 100 is the benchmark for an average U.S. adult to have four or more dogs.

3 Which channel is much *less* likely to be watched by someone with four or more cats than compared to an average American? What is the Index value?

4 If we wanted to reach the most two to three dog-owning households by advertising on only a single cable channel, which channel would we pick?

5 Based on these results, is it fair to say that Animal Planet watchers are more likely to own either a cat or dog compared to the national average?

6 Regardless of the number of dogs or cats someone owns (including zero!), about how many U.S. adults in total said they watch the Cooking Channel?

TABLE 1 Pet Ownership and Cable Channel Viewing

Target	1 dog (mils)	Vert %	Horz %	2-3 dogs (mils)	Vert %	Horz %	4+ dogs (mils)	Vert %	Horz %	1 cat (mils)	Vert %	Horz %	2-3 cats (mils)	Vert %	Horz %	4+ cats (mils)	Vert %	Horz %
Total	63.8	100.0	26.9	39.5	100.0	16.7	5.8	100.0	2.4	29.0	100.0	12.2	21.4	100.0	9.0	5.6	100.0	2.4
HH subscribes to Cable	31.4	49.3	26.9	16.8	42.4	14.3	1.9	32.9	1.6	14.4	49.5	12.3	9.7	45.4	8.3	2.1	37.0	1.8
AMC	15.1	23.8	29.7	9.2	23.3	18.1	1.3	21.8	2.5	6.9	23.9	13.6	5.0	23.2	9.7	1.4	25.3	2.8
Animal Planet	15.5	24.2	29.8	11.4	28.9	22.0	1.6	27.5	3.1	7.5	25.8	14.4	6.0	28.0	11.6	1.6	27.9	3.0
Comedy Central	9.8	15.4	28.9	7.1	17.9	20.8	0.9	15.0	2.6	4.5	15.4	13.1	3.9	18.3	11.6	0.9	15.3	2.5
Cooking Channel	8.4	13.2	26.8	4.9	12.5	15.8	0.9	15.7	2.9	3.4	11.7	10.8	3.1	14.4	9.9	0.7	12.0	2.2
Discovery Channel	19.3	30.3	28.3	13.4	33.9	19.6	1.8	32.0	2.7	9.0	31.2	13.2	7.0	32.5	10.2	1.7	30.1	2.5
Food Network	16.2	25.4	28.6	9.7	24.5	17.1	1.5	26.4	2.7	7.0	24.2	12.4	5.6	26.0	9.8	1.3	22.5	2.2
Fox News Channel	19.1	30.0	28.0	11.3	28.7	16.6	1.6	28.6	2.4	8.3	28.5	12.1	5.9	27.8	8.7	1.4	25.7	2.1
History Channel	21.4	33.6	27.9	15.2	38.5	19.8	2.2	37.7	2.8	9.9	34.2	12.9	8.2	38.5	10.7	2.2	39.2	2.9
HGTV	14.8	23.2	30.8	8.6	21.9	18.0	1.2	20.5	2.5	5.8	20.1	12.1	4.9	22.9	10.2	1.2	21.0	2.5
Syfy	10.0	15.6	25.6	7.9	20.0	20.3	1.6	27.0	4.0	5.2	17.9	13.3	4.4	20.5	11.3	1.3	23.3	3.4
Weather Channel	19.6	30.7	26.4	12.5	31.7	16.9	2.0	34.7	2.7	9.5	32.7	12.8	6.8	31.6	9.1	2.0	36.0	2.7

Source: Spring 2014 GfK MRI

Use the information provided in Table 2 to answer the following question:

1 Your friend assumed that Animal Planet is the best channel to find pet owners who use pet services frequently. Do your data support or contradict her belief? Why?

TABLE 2 Pet Service Usage and Cable Channel Viewing

Target	Has Pet Insurance (mils)	Vert %	Horz %	Used Pet Daycare (mils)	Vert %	Horz %	Used Pet Grooming (mils)	Vert %	Horz %	1 Vet Visit (mils)	Vert %	Horz %	2-3 Vet Visits (mils)	Vert %	Horz %	4+ Vet Visits (mils)	Vert %	Horz %
Total	7.1	100.0	3.0	3.5	100.0	1.5	31.9	100.0	13.5	34.8	100.0	14.7	42.1	100.0	17.8	24.1	100.0	10.2
HH subscribes to Cable	3.3	46.5	2.8	1.6	46.7	1.4	16.1	50.4	13.7	16.8	48.3	14.4	19.9	47.3	17.1	11.0	45.8	9.4
AMC	1.5	21.8	3.0	0.9	26.0	1.8	7.9	24.7	15.5	7.8	22.4	15.3	10.2	24.2	20.1	5.3	22.1	10.4
Animal Planet	1.6	23.1	3.2	0.7	19.0	1.3	8.0	25.1	15.5	8.3	23.7	15.9	11.1	26.4	21.5	6.6	27.5	12.8
Comedy Central	1.1	15.6	3.3	0.7	19.5	2.0	5.4	16.9	15.9	5.5	15.9	16.3	7.1	16.8	20.9	4.4	18.1	12.9
Cooking Channel	0.8	11.7	2.7	0.4	11.8	1.3	4.2	13.1	13.4	4.6	13.2	14.6	5.7	13.4	18.1	2.9	12.1	9.3
Discovery Channel	2.0	28.3	2.9	1.1	31.2	1.6	10.4	32.5	15.2	10.5	30.1	15.3	13.9	33.1	20.4	7.8	32.4	11.4
Food Network	1.8	25.2	3.2	1.1	31.5	1.9	8.7	27.4	15.5	8.6	24.8	15.2	10.8	25.7	19.1	6.2	25.8	11.0
Fox News Channel	1.8	25.8	2.7	0.9	24.7	1.3	10.2	31.8	14.9	10.4	29.8	15.2	12.4	29.5	18.2	6.9	28.8	10.2
History Channel	2.4	33.7	3.1	1.2	34.5	1.6	11.9	37.4	15.6	11.9	34.1	15.5	15.3	36.3	19.9	8.8	36.5	11.5
HGTV	1.6	22.3	3.3	0.8	22.4	1.6	8.3	26.0	17.3	7.5	21.6	15.7	9.6	22.7	19.9	6.2	25.7	12.9
Syfy	1.4	20.1	3.7	0.4	11.8	1.0	5.3	16.6	13.6	6.0	17.1	15.3	8.0	19.1	20.7	4.2	17.2	10.7
Weather Channel	1.9	26.4	2.5	1.0	27.9	1.3	10.6	33.2	14.3	10.7	30.9	14.5	13.4	31.9	18.1	8.4	34.7	11.3

Source: Spring 2014 GfK MRI

Use the information provided in Table 3 to answer the following questions:

1 Assuming people only buy from one of the three options, how many people in total bought their pet food from a discount store, a pet specialty store, or directly from their veterinarian? What percentage of this total bought from their veterinarian?

2 Which cable channel had the largest percentage of viewers who buy their pet food from a veterinarian ?

TABLE 3   Pet Food Buying and Cable Channel Viewing

Target	Discount Store			Pet specialty shop			Veterinarian		
	(mils)	Vert %	Horz %	(mils)	Vert %	Horz %	(mils)	Vert %	Horz %
Total	22.8	100.0	9.6	53.2	100.0	22.5	10.2	100.0	4.3
HH subscribes to Cable	10.6	46.3	9.0	25.9	48.6	22.1	5.2	50.8	4.4
AMC	5.9	25.8	11.5	12.2	22.9	23.9	2.4	23.1	4.6
Animal Planet	5.9	25.7	11.3	13.6	25.5	26.2	2.8	27.1	5.3
Comedy Central	3.6	15.9	10.7	9.0	16.9	26.6	1.7	16.8	5.0
Cooking Channel	2.9	12.6	9.2	6.9	13.1	22.2	1.3	13.1	4.3
Discovery Channel	7.5	33.0	11.0	17.0	32.0	24.9	3.4	33.0	4.9
Food Network	5.3	23.3	9.4	13.7	25.8	24.2	2.4	23.4	4.2
Fox News Channel	6.7	29.2	9.8	15.3	28.8	22.4	3.3	31.9	4.8
History Channel	8.6	37.8	11.2	18.2	34.2	23.8	3.7	36.2	4.8
HGTV	5.2	22.8	10.8	12.5	23.4	26.0	2.5	24.3	5.2
Syfy	4.1	18.0	10.6	9.0	17.0	23.2	2.0	19.4	5.1
Weather Channel	7.7	33.8	10.4	16.1	30.3	21.7	3.5	34.0	4.7

Source: Spring 2014 GfK MRI

DISCUSSION AND DEBATE

1. Based only on the information provided, which three cable channels would you recommend as the best choices for promoting the business? Which three cable channels do you think are the poorest fit?

2. What other additional information would you like to have so that you could make a more informed recommendation? Why is it important? How could you find out this information?

3. If PROSPEROUS PETS told you that its services were much more profitable than its product (toys, food, etc.) sales, would that change your recommendation? Why or why not?

GfK US LLC, Mediamark Research & Intelligence division.

SMELLS LIKE YOU'RE BEING AN IDIOT.

What do you hope to smell there, sir? Gooseberry You don't even know what gooseberries smell like Perhaps next time instead of playing pretend, you should ask for an Export Dry. Crisp and refreshing but still full of flavour, Export Dry is a sophisticated lager that tastes incredible and smells like beer. So what are you waiting for? Oh, ok, well how long do you think that will take?

> LET NOTHING COME BETWEEN A MAN AND A GREAT BEER

CONSUMER BEHAVIOR

1: Foundations of Consumer Behavior

2: Internal Influences on Consumer Behavior

3: Choosing and Using Products

This fourth and final section focuses on the external factors that influence our identities as consumers and the decisions we make. Chapter 11 provides an overview of group processes and the role that social media plays in consumer decision making. In Chapter 12 we focus on the ways our income and social status relative to others helps to define who we are. Chapter 13 discusses the subcultures that help to determine how we buy and consume. Finally, in Chapter 14, we dive into broad yet powerful cultural influences on consumer behavior.

CHAPTERS AHEAD

Chapter 11 • Groups and Social Media

When you finish reading this chapter, you will understand why:

11-1 Other people and groups, especially those that possess social power, influence our decisions.

11-2 Word-of-mouth communication is the most important driver of product choice.

11-3 Opinion leaders' recommendations are more influential than others when we decide what to buy.

11-4 Social media changes the way we learn about and select products.

Source: Ljupco Smokovski/Shutterstock.

Zach leads a secret life. During the week, he is a straitlaced stock analyst for a major investment firm. However, his day job only pays the bills to finance his real passion: cruising on his Harley-Davidson Road Glide Custom. His Facebook posts are filled with lunchtime laments about how much he'd rather be out on the road (hopefully his boss won't try to friend him). Actually, Zach feels it's worth the risk: He's participating in Harley's social media promotion that encourages riders to post their stories ("freedom statements") on Facebook and Twitter to see if they'll include one of his posts on a Harley banner ad.[1] His girlfriend Karen worries a bit about his getting totaled in an accident, but Zach knows if he stays alert the only way that will probably happen is if he can't kick his habit of texting her while he's driving the bike.

Come Friday evening, it's off with the Brooks Brothers suit and on with the black leather, as he trades in his Lexus for his treasured Harley. A dedicated member of Harley Owners Group (HOG), Zach belongs to the rich urban bikers (RUBs) faction of Harley riders. Everyone in his group wears expensive leather vests with Harley insignias and owns customized "low riders." Just this week, Zach finally got his new Harley perforated black leather jacket at the company's Motorclothes Merchandise Web page.[2] As one of the Harley Web pages observed, "It's one thing to have people buy your products. It's another thing to have them tattoo your name on their bodies." Zach had to restrain himself from buying more Harley stuff; there were vests, eyewear, belts, buckles, scarves, watches, jewelry, and even housewares ("home is the road") for sale. He settled for a set of Harley salt-and-pepper shakers that would be perfect for his buddy Doug's new crib.

Zach's experiences on social media platforms make him realize the lengths to which some of his fellow enthusiasts go to make sure others know they are Hog riders. Two of his riding buddies are in a lively competition to be "mayor" of the local Harley dealership on Foursquare, whereas many others tweet to inform people about a group ride that will occur later in the day—kind of a flash mob on wheels.

Zach spends a lot of money to outfit himself to be like the rest of the group, but it's worth it. He feels a real sense of brotherhood with his fellow RUBs. The group rides together in two-column formation to bike rallies that sometimes attract up to 300,000 cycle enthusiasts. What a sense of power he feels when they all cruise together—it's them against the world!

Of course, an added benefit is the business networking he's accomplished during his jaunts with his fellow professionals who also wait for the weekend to "ride on the wild side; these days it would be professional suicide to let your contacts get cold, and you can't just count on LinkedIn to stay in the loop."[3]

Groups

OBJECTIVE 11-1
Other people and groups, especially those that possess social power, influence our decisions.

Humans are social animals. We belong to groups, try to please others, and look to others' behavior for clues about what we should do in public settings. In fact, our desire to "fit in" or to identify with desirable individuals or groups is the primary motivation for many of our consumption behaviors. We may go to great lengths to please the members of a group whose acceptance we covet.[4]

Social identity theory argues that each of us has several "selves" that relate to groups. These linkages are so important that we think of ourselves not just as "I," but also as "we." In addition, we favor others that we feel share the same identity—even if that identity is superficial and virtually meaningless. In numerous experiments that employ the **minimal group paradigm**, researchers show that even when they arbitrarily assign subjects to one group or another, people favor those who wind up in the same group.[5]

Zach's biker group is an important part of his identity, and this membership influences many of his buying decisions. He has spent many thousands of dollars on parts and accessories since he became a RUB. His fellow riders bond via their consumption choices, so total strangers feel an immediate connection with one another when they meet. The publisher of *American Iron*, an industry magazine, observed, "You don't buy a Harley because it's a superior bike, you buy a Harley to be a part of a family."[6]

Zach doesn't model himself after just *any* biker—only the RUB members with whom he really identifies can exert that kind of influence on him. For example, Zach's group doesn't have much to do with outlaw clubs whose blue-collar riders sport big Harley tattoos. The members of his group also have only polite contact with "Ma and Pa" bikers, whose rides are the epitome of comfort and feature such niceties as radios, heated handgrips, and floorboards.

Social Power

Why are groups so persuasive? The answer lies in the potential power they wield over us. **Social power** describes "the capacity to alter the actions of others."[8] To the degree to which you are able to make someone else do something, regardless of whether that person does it willingly, you have power over that person. The following classification of power bases helps us to distinguish among the reasons a person exerts power over another, the

Marketing Opportunity

We tend to think of running as something you do on your own, but today you're much more likely to run with a group. People train with friends and participate in charity runs together. Many of us are moving away from running alone at home; sales of home cardio equipment like treadmills are way down. Instead people gravitate to competitions like the Tough Mudder obstacle course or fitness classes. New Balance is picking up on this trend as the shoe manufacturer promotes its "Runnovation" campaign that focuses on running as a social activity. One print ad carries the headline, "Redefine girls' night out" as it shows a group of women running together. "Some go out. Others go out and make excellent happen. The night is yours. This is Runnovation."[7]

degree to which the influence is voluntary, and whether this influence will continue to have an effect even when the source of the power isn't around.[9]

- **Referent power**—If a person admires the qualities of a person or a group, he tries to copy the referent's behaviors (e.g., choice of clothing, cars, leisure activities). Prominent people in all walks of life affect our consumption behaviors by virtue of product endorsements (e.g., Lady Gaga for Polaroid), distinctive fashion statements (e.g., Kim Kardashian's displays of high-end designer clothing), or championing causes (e.g., Brad Pitt for UNICEF). **Referent power** is important to many marketing strategies because consumers voluntarily modify what they do and buy to identify with a referent.

- **Information power**—A person possesses **information power** simply because he or she knows something others would like to know. Editors of trade publications such as *Women's Wear Daily* often possess tremendous power because of their ability to compile and disseminate information that can make or break individual designers or companies. People with information power are able to influence consumer opinion by virtue of their access to the knowledge that provides some kind of competitive advantage.

- **Legitimate power**—Sometimes we grant power by virtue of social agreements, such as the authority we give to police officers, soldiers, and yes, even professors. The **legitimate power** a uniform confers wields authority in consumer contexts, including teaching hospitals where medical students don white coats to enhance their standing with patients.[10] Marketers "borrow" this form of power to influence consumers. For example, an ad that shows a model who wears a white doctor's coat adds an aura of legitimacy or authority to the presentation of the product ("I'm not a doctor, but I play one on TV").

- **Expert power**—U.S. Robotics signed up British physicist Stephen Hawking to endorse its modems. A company executive commented, "We wanted to generate trust. So we found visionaries who use U.S. Robotics technology, and we let them tell the consumer how it makes their lives more productive." Hawking, who has Lou Gehrig's disease and speaks via a synthesizer, said in one TV spot, "My body may be stuck in this chair, but with the Internet my mind can go to the end of the universe."[11] Hawking's **expert power** derives from the knowledge he possesses about a content area. This helps to explain the weight many of us assign to professional critics' reviews of restaurants, books, movies, and cars—even though, with the advent of blogs and open source references such as *Wikipedia*, it's getting a lot harder to tell just who is really an expert![12]

- **Reward power**—A person or group with the means to provide positive reinforcement (see Chapter 4) has **reward power**. The reward may be the tangible kind, such as the contestants on *Survivor* experience when their comrades vote them off the island. Or it can be more intangible, such as the gushing feedback the judges on *The Voice* deliver to contestants.

- **Coercive power**—We exert **coercive power** when we influence someone because of social or physical intimidation. A threat is often effective in the short term, but it doesn't tend to stick because we revert to our original behavior as soon as the bully leaves the scene. Fortunately, marketers rarely try to use this type of power (unless you count those annoying calls from telemarketers!). However, we can see elements of this power base in the fear appeals we talked about in Chapter 8, as well as in intimidating salespeople who try to succeed with a "hard sell."

Reference Groups

Just because we find ourselves in the company of others doesn't necessarily mean they impact what we say or do. A **reference group** is an actual or imaginary individual or group that significantly *influences* an individual's evaluations, aspirations, or behavior.[13] For our friend Zach, the RUBs with whom he hangs out are a reference group.

Members of a reference group can motivate us (or maybe our pets?) to lose weight, stop smoking or make other lifestyle changes.
Source: Courtesy of Jardiland and ROSAPARK agency Picture by www.lippoth.com, Photoshop artists: Graziella Vermeil & Pierrick Le Gros.

Research on smoking cessation programs powerfully illustrates the impact of reference groups. The study found that smokers tend to quit in sets: When one person quits, this creates a ripple effect that motivates others in his social network to give up the death sticks also. The researchers followed thousands of smokers and nonsmokers for more than 30 years, and they also tracked their networks of relatives, coworkers, and friends. They discovered that over the years, the smokers tended to cluster together (on average in groups of three). As the overall U.S. smoking rate declined dramatically during this period, the number of clusters in the sample decreased, but the remaining clusters stayed the same size; this indicated that people quit in groups rather than as individuals. Not surprisingly, some social connections were more powerful than others. A spouse who quit had a bigger impact than did a friend, whereas friends had more influence than siblings. Coworkers had an influence only in small firms where everyone knew one another.[14]

Reference group influences don't work the same way for all types of products and consumption activities. For example, we're not as likely to take others' preferences into account when we choose products that are not complex, that are low in perceived risk, or that we can try before we buy.[15] Although two or more people normally form a group, we often use the term *reference group* a bit more loosely to describe *any* external influence that provides social cues.[16] The referent may be a cultural figure that has an impact on many people (e.g., the Pope) or a person or group whose influence operates only in the consumer's immediate environment (e.g., the "popular" kids in high school). Reference groups that affect consumption can include parents, fellow motorcycle enthusiasts, the Tea Party, or even the Chicago Bears, the Dave Matthews Band, or Spike Lee.

A **membership reference group** consists of people we actually know. In contrast although we don't know those in an **aspirational reference group**, we admire them anyway. These people are likely to be successful businesspeople, athletes, performers, or anyone else who rocks our world. Not surprisingly, many marketing communications that specifically adopt a reference group appeal concentrate on highly visible celebrities; they link these people to brands so that the products they use or endorse also take on this aspirational quality. For example, an amateur basketball player who idolizes Miami Heat

The Tangled Web

The Web has spawned the rise of a new kind of avoidance group: **antibrand communities**. These groups also coalesce around a celebrity, store, or brand, but in this case they're united by their disdain for it. The site starbucked.com asks, "Starbucked enough by corporate crap product and service?" and provides the locations of independent coffee houses.[23] The U.K.-based anti-McDonald's site McSpotlight claims, "McDonald's spends over $2 billion a year broadcasting their glossy image to the world. This is a small space for alternatives to be heard." At Hel*Mart.com you can find links to numerous groups that oppose the practices of Walmart.

One team of researchers that studies these communities observes that they tend to attract social idealists who advocate non-materialistic lifestyles. After they interviewed members of online communities who oppose these three companies, they concluded that these antibrand communities provide a meeting place for those who share a moral stance; a support network to achieve common goals; a way to cope with workplace frustrations (many members actually work for the companies they bash!); and a hub for information, activities, and related resources.[24]

star Dwyane Wade might drool over a pair of Air Jordan 12 Dwyane Wade PE shoes.[17] One study of business students who aspired to the "executive" role found a strong relationship between products they associated with their *ideal selves* (see Chapter 6) and those they assumed that real executives own.[18]

Reference groups impact our buying decisions both positively and negatively. In most cases, we model our behavior to be in line with what we think the group expects us to do. Sometimes, however, we also deliberately do the *opposite* if we want to distance ourselves from **avoidance groups**. You may carefully study the dress or mannerisms of a group you dislike (e.g., "nerds," "druggies," or "preppies") and scrupulously avoid buying anything that might identify you with that group. Rebellious adolescents do the opposite of what their parents desire to make a statement about their independence. In one study, college freshmen reported consuming less alcohol when they associated it with their avoidance groups.[20]

Your motivation to distance yourself from a negative reference group can be as powerful or more powerful than your desire to please a positive group.[21] That's why advertisements occasionally show an undesirable person who uses a competitor's product. This kind of execution subtly makes the point that you can avoid winding up like *that* kind of person if you just stay away from the products he buys. As a once-popular book reminded us, "Real men *don't* eat quiche!"[22]

Conformity

The early Bohemians who lived in Paris around 1830 made a point of behaving, well, differently from others. One flamboyant figure of the time earned notoriety because he walked a lobster on a leash through the gardens of the Royal Palace. His friends drank wine from human skulls, cut their beards in strange shapes, and slept in tents on the floors of their garrets.[25] Sounds a bit like some frat houses we've visited.

Although in every age there certainly are those who "march to their own drummers," most people tend to follow society's expectations regarding how they should act and look (with a little improvisation here and there, of course). **Conformity** is a change in beliefs or actions as a reaction to real or imagined group pressure. For a society to function, its members develop **norms** or informal rules that govern behavior. Without these rules, we would have chaos. Imagine the confusion if a simple norm such as "always stop for a red traffic light" did not exist.

We conform in many small ways every day, even though we don't always realize it. Unspoken rules govern many aspects of consumption. In addition to norms regarding appropriate use of clothing and other personal items, we conform to rules that include gift-giving (we expect birthday presents from loved ones and get upset if they don't

Fantasy camps connect fans with their aspirational reference groups.
Source: Courtesy of Rock 'n' Roll Fantasy Camp.

materialize), sex roles (men often pick up the check on a first date), and personal hygiene (our friends expect us to shower regularly).

The pressure to conform conflicts with another motivation we've already discussed: The need to be unique. How can we reconcile these two goals? One study suggests that we try to have it both ways: We line up with a group on one dimension such as choosing a popular brand, but we differentiate ourselves on another by choosing a unique attribute such as color.[27]

Within limits, people approve of others who exhibit nonconforming behavior. This may be because we assume someone who makes unconventional choices is more powerful or competent, so he or she can afford to go out on a limb. Researchers term this the **Red Sneakers Effect** (to describe a brave person who sports a pair of red kicks in a professional setting). Indeed, they find that nonconforming behaviors under some conditions do lead to more positive impressions, but these disappear when the observer is unsure why the brave soul is violating a norm or if they decide the violator is not doing it intentionally (i.e. he or she is just clueless).[28]

Although we observe conformity in many settings (just remember high school!), we don't mimic others' behaviors all the time. What makes it more likely that we'll conform? These are some common culprits:[29]

- **Cultural pressures**—Different cultures encourage conformity to a greater or lesser degree. Americans like to say, "the squeaky wheel gets the grease," whereas in Japan a popular expression is "the nail that stands up gets hammered down." In a study, groups of passengers who arrived at an airport were asked to complete a survey: They were offered a handful of pens to use, for example four orange and one green. People of European descent more often chose the one pen that stood out, and Asians chose the color that was like the majority of the others.[30]

- **Fear of deviance**—The individual may have reason to believe that the group will apply *sanctions* to punish nonconforming behaviors. It's not unusual to observe adolescents who shun a peer who is "different" or a corporation or university that passes over a person for promotion because he or she is not a "team player."

- **Commitment**—The more people are dedicated to a group and value their membership in it, the greater their motivation to conform to the group's wishes. Rock groupies and followers of TV evangelists may do anything their idols ask of them, and terrorists become martyrs for their cause. According to the **Principle of Least Interest** the person who is *least* committed to staying in a relationship has the most power because that party doesn't care as much if the other person rejects him.[31] Remember that on your next date.

- **Group unanimity, size, and expertise**—As groups gain in power, compliance increases. It is often harder to resist the demands of a large number of people than only a few, especially when a "mob mentality" rules.

- **Susceptibility to interpersonal influence**—This trait refers to an individual's need to have others think highly of him or her. Consumers who don't possess this trait are *role-relaxed*; they tend to be older, affluent, and have high self-confidence. Subaru created a communications strategy to reach role-relaxed consumers. In one of its commercials, a man proclaims, "I want a car.... Don't tell me about wood paneling, about winning the respect of my neighbors. They're my neighbors. They're not my heroes."[32]

- **Environmental cues**—One study reported that people are more likely to conform when they make decisions in a warm room. Apparently the warmth caused participants to feel closer to other decision makers and this feeling led them to assume the others' opinions were more valid. In one part of the study the researchers analyzed betting behavior at a racetrack over a 3-year period. Sure enough, people were more likely to bet on the "favorite" horse on warmer days.[33]

The Tangled Web

When we make decisions as part of a group, we tend to have fewer restraints on our behavior. For example, we sometimes behave more wildly at costume parties or on Halloween than we do when others can easily identify us. This is the phenomenon of **deindividuation** a process whereby individual identities become submerged within a group. Deindividuation happens online as well. Researchers call this the **Gyges Effect**. The term comes from a myth called The Ring of Gyges: A shepherd discovers a ring that makes him invisible at will. He uses the anonymity of the ring to seduce the queen, assassinate the king, and take over the kingdom. In the present day, this myth reminds us that the anonymity of the Internet can cause otherwise moral people to experience a loss of inhibition and post things they would never say to a person in the real world. People who do this are known in the industry as **Internet trolls**. They post threats about rape and other violence, or bullying comments.[26] Trolls pose a big problem for social networks. As the head of Twitter wrote in a leaked memo, "I'm frankly ashamed of how poorly we've dealt with this issue during my tenure as CEO."

Source: Corepics VOF/Shutterstock.

Marketing Pitfall

Social loafing happens when we don't devote as much time and effort to a task as we could because our contribution is part of a larger group effort.[34] You may have experienced this if you've worked on a group project for a class! Waitpersons are painfully aware of social loafing: People who eat in groups tend to tip less per person than when they eat alone.[35] For this reason, many restaurants automatically tack on a fixed gratuity for groups of six or more.

Brand Communities

Before it released the popular Xbox game *Halo 2*, Bungie Studios put up a Web site to explain the story line. However, there was a catch: The story was written from the point of view of the Covenant (the aliens who are preparing to attack Earth in the game)—and in *their* language. Within 48 hours, avid gamers around the world shared information in gaming chat rooms to crack the code and translate the text. More than 1.5 million people preordered the game before its release.[36]

A **brand community** is a group of consumers—like those zealous Halo players—who share a set of social relationships based on usage of or interest in a product. In virtually any category, you'll find passionate brand communities (in some cases devoted to brands that don't even exist anymore); examples include the 3Com Ergo Audrey (discontinued Internet appliance), Apple Newton (discontinued personal digital assistant), BMW MINI (car), Garmin (GPS device), Jones Soda (carbonated beverage), Lomo and Holga (cameras), Tom Petty and the Heartbreakers (musical group), StriVectin (cosmeceutical), and *Xena: Warrior Princess* (TV program).

Unlike other kinds of communities, these members typically don't live near each other—except when they may meet for brief periods at organized events or **brandfests** that community-oriented companies such as Jeep or Harley-Davidson sponsor. These events help owners to "bond" with fellow enthusiasts and strengthen their identification with the product as well as with others they meet who share their passion.

Researchers find that people who participate in these events feel more positive about the sponsor's products as a result, and this enhances brand loyalty. They tend to forgive product failures or lapses in service quality, and they're less likely to switch brands even if they learn that competing products are as good or better. Furthermore, these community members become emotionally involved in the company's welfare, and they often serve as brand missionaries because they carry its marketing message to others.[38]

Researchers find that brand community members do more than help the product build buzz; their inputs actually create added value for themselves and other members as they develop better ways to use and customize products. It's common for experienced

Source: Andrew Rich/Getty Images.

users to coach "newbies" in ways to maximize their enjoyment of the product, so that more and more people benefit from a network of satisfied participants.[39] Figure 11.1 demonstrates this process of **collective value creation**.

OBJECTIVE 11-2
Word-of-mouth communication is the most important driver of product choice.

Word-of-Mouth Communication

Altoids breath mints have been around for 200 years, but the brand caught fire among a larger market only near the end of the 20th century. How did this happen? The revival began when the mint attracted a devoted following among smokers and coffee drinkers who hung out in the blossoming Seattle club scene during the 1980s. Until 1993, when Kraft bought manufacturer Callard & Bowser, only those "in the know" sucked the mints. The brand's marketing manager persuaded Kraft to hire advertising agency Leo Burnett to develop a modest promotional

Figure 11.1 THE PROCESS OF COLLECTIVE VALUE CREATION IN BRAND COMMUNITIES

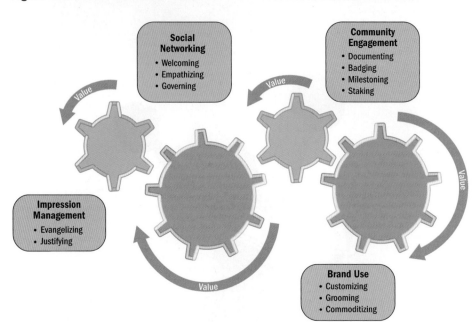

Source: Reprinted with permission from *Journal of Marketing*, "How Brand Community Practices Create Value," published by the American Marketing Association, Hope Jensen, Albert M. Muniz, and Eric J. Arnould, September 2009, 73, 30–51.

campaign. The agency decided to publicize the candy with subway posters sporting retro imagery and other "low tech" media to avoid making the product seem mainstream—that would turn off the original audience.[41] Young people started to tune into this "retro" treat, and its popularity skyrocketed.

As the Altoids success story illustrates, today grassroots efforts that motivate consumers to spread a brand's message are what makes a hit product. **Word-of-mouth (WOM)** is product information that individuals transmit to other individuals. Because we get the word from people we know, WOM tends to be more reliable and trustworthy than messages from more formal marketing channels. And, unlike advertising, WOM often comes with social pressure to conform to these recommendations.[42]

Despite the huge sums of money marketers pump into lavish ads, WOM is far more powerful: It influences up to 50 percent of all consumer goods sales.[43] If you think carefully about the content of your own conversations in the course of a normal day, you will probably agree that much of what you discuss with friends, family members, or coworkers is product-related: When you compliment someone on her dress and ask her where she bought it, recommend a new restaurant to a friend, or complain to your neighbor about the shoddy treatment you got at the bank, you engage in WOM.

As far back as the Stone Age (well, the 1950s, anyway), communications theorists challenged the assumption that advertising primarily determines what we buy. As a rule, *advertising is more effective to reinforce our existing product preferences than to create new ones.*[44] Studies in both industrial and consumer purchase settings underscore the idea that although information from impersonal sources creates brand awareness, consumers rely on WOM in the later stages of evaluation and adoption.[45] Quite simply, the more positive information consumers get about a product from peers, the more likely they will be to adopt the product.[46]

WOM is especially powerful when the consumer is relatively unfamiliar with the product category. We often encounter these situations in the case of new products (e.g., medications to prevent hair loss) or those that are technologically complex (e.g., smartphones). One way to reduce uncertainty about the wisdom of a purchase is to talk

CB AS I SEE IT

Eileen Fischer, *York University*

You know that being involved in a brand community can create value for customers. But do you think that means the actions that consumers who are members of those communities are invariably beneficial for brands? Do you expect that marketers in a product category will routinely benefit when consumers come together to share their knowledge and opinions about those products? Research is beginning to show that there can be many unanticipated consequences when consumers who care passionately about brands or products start interacting with one another online.

My colleague Marie-Agnès Parmentier and I recently examined the interactions of avid fans of the reality television series, *America's Next Top Model*. We followed their posts to multiple online forums, such as *Television Without Pity* and *Fans of Reality Television,* over a 10-year period, starting from the show's launch in 2003, through its popularity peak in 2008–2009, through to 2012 by which time its audience had fallen so low that rumors of its cancellation were circulating.[40]

We wanted to know if avid fans had played a role in the dissipation of the show's audience, and we found three fan-fuelled processes that played a role. First, avid fans "reframed" new elements introduced to the show as being inconsistent with its founding narratives. For example, the show initially positioned itself as embodying a high fashion narrative and taught its audience that high fashion models are supposed to have unconventional looks, be extremely tall, and very thin; only women with such characteristics are eligible to do the kinds of prestigious modeling work reserved for "top models." When the show featured an entire competition restricted to petite contestants, fans were quick to point out that the high fashion narrative was contradicted by the show's inclusion of contestants who could never work as top models. Second, avid fans "remixed" elements introduced to the show by its creators. For example, when

fans were displeased because they thought a contestant who was not the most qualified won a competition owing to favoritism exhibited by the show's creator, Tyra Banks, they created and circulated widely both texts and images that drew from materials produced by the show, but that parodied the ANTM brand. The parodies were clever, and some drew the attention of mainstream media, which publicized them widely. Third, avid fans "rejected" new elements of the show as being inferior to those they replaced. For example, fans loudly complained that the people who replaced long-time cast members Nigel Barker, J. Alexander, and Jay Manuel when each was fired in 2012 knew less about the fashion industry and lacked professional credibility. Their complaints were widely disseminated by mainstream media. Our study shows that avid brand fans—especially those who remain active participants in its community—can play a role in undermining the very brand they love.

Marketers can't control what happens once consumers start interacting with one another, and unforeseen consequences are likely. Discouraging consumers from sharing their passions with others seems unrealistic. Paying close attention may afford marketers a chance to see what's unfolding and to take appropriate action.

---

about it. Talking gives the consumer an opportunity to generate supporting arguments for the purchase and to garner support for this decision from others. For example, the strongest predictor of a person's intention to buy a residential solar water heating system is the number of solar heat users the person knows.[47]

Numerous professionals, such as doctors, accountants, and lawyers, as well as services marketers like lawn-care companies and cleaning services, depend primarily on WOM to generate business. In many cases, consumers recommend a service provider to a friend or coworker, and in other cases businesspeople make recommendations to their customers. For example, only 0.2 percent of respondents in one study reported that they choose a physician based on advertising. Instead, they rely primarily on advice from family and friends.[48]

Buzz Building

In the "old days," here's how a toy company would launch a new product: Unveil a hot holiday toy during a spring trade fair, run a November–December saturation television ad campaign during cartoon prime time to plug the toy during Christmas season, sit back and watch as desperate parents scrambled through the aisles at Toys "R" Us, and then wait for the resulting media coverage to drive still more sales.

Fast forward to a more recent toy story: A Hong Kong company called Silverlit Toys makes the $30 Picoo Z helicopter. At one point a Google search for the term *Picoo* produced more than 109,000 URLs, with many of those links pointed to major online global gift retailers like Hammacher Schlemmer and Toys "R" Us. Do you think this huge exposure was the result of a meticulously planned promotional strategy? Think again. By most accounts, a 28-year-old tech worker in Chicago started the Picoo Z buzz; he bought his helicopter after he read about it on a hobbyist message board. A few months later, he uploaded his homemade video of the toy on YouTube. Within 2 weeks, 15 of his friends had also bought the toy, and they in turn posted their own videos and pointed viewers to the original video. Internet retailers who troll online conversations

This Israeli ad illustrates how "facts" often mutate when people repeat them.
Source: Gitam BBDO, Tel Aviv; Karmel Abuzlaf, Guy Bar, Shani Gershi; Eitan Cohen; Arnon Rotem; Miriam Moshinksy.

for fresh and exciting buzz identified the toy and started to add their own links to the clips. Within a few short months, there were hundreds of Picoo Z videos and more than a million people viewed them.[49] The moral of the story: Stimulate WOM to build **buzz** around a product or service, then sit back and let your customers do the heavy lifting.

Negative WOM

We know that WOM is a powerful weapon; unfortunately it's a two-edged sword that cuts both ways for marketers. Informal discussions among consumers can make or break a product or store. Furthermore, consumers weigh **negative word-of-mouth** more heavily than they do positive comments. Especially when we consider a new product or service, we're likely to pay more attention to negative information than to positive information and to tell others about our nasty experience.[50] Research shows that negative WOM reduces the credibility of a firm's advertising and influences consumers' attitudes toward a product as well as their intention to buy it.[51] Dell found this out the hard way when bloggers denounced the computer maker's quality and service levels; then the popular media picked up this discontent and magnified it.[52]

As we transmit information to one another, it tends to change. The resulting message usually does not resemble the original at all. The British psychologist Frederic Bartlett used the method of **serial reproduction** to examine how content mutates. Like the game of "Telephone" many of us played as kids, he asked a subject to reproduce a stimulus, such as a drawing or a story. He then gave another subject this reproduction and asked him to copy it, and repeated this process several times. Figure 11.2 illustrates how a message

Figure 11.2 THE TRANSMISSION OF MISINFORMATION

changes as people reproduce it. Bartlett found that distortions almost inevitably follow a pattern: They tend to change from ambiguous forms to more conventional ones as subjects try to make them consistent with their preexisting schemas (see Chapter 3). He called this process *assimilation* and he noted that it often occurs as people engage in *leveling*, when they omit details to simplify the structure; or *sharpening*, when they exaggerate prominent details.

OBJECTIVE 11-3

Opinion leaders' recommendations are more influential than others' when we decide what to buy.

Opinion Leadership

As Cold Stone Creamery expands to Japan, the ice cream store projects a somewhat different image than it has in the United States. The chain wants to be ultracool as it generates a buzz among fashion-conscious "office ladies"—as the Japanese call young, single, female professionals. These women are influential in Japan; their reactions to a new product can make or break it. To woo this group, Cold Stone sponsored a fashion show for young women (assuming the models can fit into the dresses after sampling a few of the chain's caloric creations), and fashion magazines staged photo shoots at the stores.[53]

Although consumers get information from personal sources, they do not usually ask just *anyone* for advice about purchases. If you decide to buy a new stereo, you will most likely seek advice from a friend who knows a lot about sound systems. This friend may own a sophisticated system, or she may subscribe to specialized magazines such as *Stereo Review* and spend her free time browsing through electronics stores. However, you may have another friend who has a reputation for being stylish and who spends his free time reading *Gentleman's Quarterly* and shopping at trendy boutiques. You might not bring up your stereo problem with him, but you may take him with you to shop for a new fall wardrobe.

Everyone knows people who are knowledgeable about products and whose advice others take seriously. These individuals, or **opinion leaders**, are frequently able to influence others' attitudes or behaviors.[54] Clearly, some people's recommendations carry more weight than others. Opinion leaders are extremely valuable information sources because they possess the social power we discussed earlier in the chapter:

- They are technically competent, so they possess expert power.[55]
- They prescreen, evaluate, and synthesize product information in an unbiased way, so they possess knowledge power.[56]
- They are socially active and highly interconnected in their communities.[57]
- They are likely to hold offices in community groups and clubs and to be active outside of the home. As a result, opinion leaders often wield legitimate power by virtue of their social standing.
- They tend to be similar to the consumer in terms of their values and beliefs, so they possess referent power. Note that although opinion leaders are set apart by their interest or expertise in a product category, they are more convincing to the extent that they are *homophilous* rather than *heterophilous*. **Homophily** refers to the degree to which a pair of individuals is similar in terms of education, social status, and beliefs.[58] Effective opinion leaders tend to be slightly higher in terms of status and educational attainment than those they influence, but not so high as to be in a different social class.
- Opinion leaders are often among the first to buy new products, so they absorb much of the risk. This experience reduces uncertainty for the rest of us who are not as courageous. Furthermore, whereas company-sponsored communications tend to focus exclusively on the positive aspects of a product, the hands-on experience of opinion leaders makes them more likely to impart *both* positive and negative information about product performance. Thus, they are more credible because they have no "axe to grind."

How Influential Is an Opinion Leader?

Ford's prelaunch campaign for its crossover SUV Flex model aimed to get buzz going as it gave opinion leaders an exclusive look at the new car. In five cities, the company invited radio deejays, musicians, and other creative people to take a tour of the Flex. These influentials went on an urban odyssey as fleets of the vehicles took them to art galleries, nightclubs, and other hot spots. In a separate campaign to plug its Fiesta model, the carmaker selected 100 young people who got free use of a car for 6 months in return for blogging about it.[59]

When social scientists initially developed the concept of the opinion leader, they assumed that certain influential people in a community would exert an overall impact on group members' attitudes. Later work, however, questioned the assumption that there is such a thing as a *generalized opinion leader* whose recommendations we seek for all types of purchases. Few people are capable of being expert in a number of fields (even though they may believe otherwise). Sociologists distinguish between those who are *monomorphic*, or expert in a limited field, and those who are *polymorphic*, or expert in several fields.[60] Even opinion leaders who are polymorphic, however, tend to concentrate on one broad domain, such as electronics or fashion. For example, Mediamark Research & Intelligence estimates that 10.5 percent of the U.S. adult population, whom it labels "Big Circle Influentials," are the key influencers for personal finance decisions.[61]

A reexamination of the traditional perspective on opinion leadership reveals that the process isn't as clear-cut as some researchers thought.[62] The original framework is called the **two-step flow model of influence** It proposes that a small group of *influencers* disseminates information because they can modify the opinions of a large number of other people.

When the authors ran extensive computer simulations of this process, they found that the influence is driven less by influentials and more by the interaction among those who are easily influenced; they communicate the information vigorously to one another and they also participate in a two-way dialogue with the opinion leader as part of an **influence network** These conversations create **information cascades** that occur when a piece of information triggers a sequence of interactions (much like an avalanche). One study tracked, on an hourly basis, the rate at which 50 million Facebook users installed 2,700 apps. The researchers found clear evidence of an information cascade: Once an app was installed about 55 times in one day, its popularity took off. As Facebook friends got notified when someone installed the app, this feedback in turn prompted them to do it as well.[63]

Types of Opinion Leaders

We've seen that early conceptions of the opinion leader role assumed a static, one-way process: The opinion leader absorbs information from the mass media and in turn transmits data to opinion receivers. This view also confuses the functions of several different types of consumers.

Opinion leaders may or may not be purchasers of the products they recommend. Early purchasers also tend to be *innovators*; they like to take risks and try new things. Researchers call opinion leaders who also are early purchasers *innovative communicators*. One study identified characteristics of college men who were innovative communicators for fashion products. These men were among the first to buy new fashions, and other students were likely to follow their lead when they made their own purchases. Other characteristics of the men included the following:[65]

- They were socially active.
- They were appearance conscious and narcissistic (i.e., they were quite fond of themselves and self-centered).
- They were involved in rock culture.
- They were heavy readers of magazines like *Playboy* and *Sports Illustrated*.
- They were likely to own more clothing, and a broader range of styles, than other students.

The Tangled Web

It's not unusual for us to observe *herding behavior* among consumers as they blindly mimic what others in their group do. *Information cascades* can bias what people choose as they take their cues from what others select rather than choosing what they genuinely like. In a study that looked at how an individual's music preferences depend on knowing what other people choose, test subjects listened to 72 songs by new bands. A control group made their own individual judgments about which songs to select, but in other groups the participants could see how many people downloaded particular songs. This feedback made a huge difference in what people chose. For example if a song spiked early in the study and respondents could see a lot of people chose it, many more people jumped on the bandwagon and downloaded it as well. And it turns out these cascades occurred regardless of whether or not people genuinely liked the songs: The same thing happened when the subjects were given false information about which songs a lot of other people were downloading.[64] Round up the herd!

Opinion leaders also are likely to be *opinion seekers*. They are generally more involved in a product category and so they actively search for information. As a result, they are more likely to talk about products with others and to solicit others' opinions as well.[66] Contrary to the older, static view of opinion leadership, most product-related conversation does not take place in a "lecture" format where one person does all the talking. A lot of product-related conversation occurs in the context of a casual interaction rather than as formal instruction.[67]

The Market Maven

To publicize Clinical Therapy, a lotion brand from Vaseline, the company's advertising campaign mapped the social network of Kodiak, a small town in Alaska. Company reps took over a storefront and gave away free bottles of the product. In return, the recipients had to identify the person in town who recommended Clinical Therapy to them. Through this process they found a woman whom many of the townspeople named as their source.[68]

The Alaskan woman Vaseline found (no, she isn't former Governor Sarah Palin) is a **market maven**; she is a person who likes to transmit marketplace information of all types. These shopaholics are not necessarily interested in the products they recommend; they simply enjoy staying on top of what's happening in the marketplace. They come closer to the function of a generalized opinion leader because they tend to have a solid overall knowledge of how and where to procure products. They're also more confident in their own ability to make smart purchase decisions.

The Surrogate Consumer

In addition to everyday consumers who influence others' purchase decisions, a class of marketing intermediary we call the **surrogate consumer** often guides what we buy. This term refers to a third party we retain to provide input into our purchase decisions. Unlike the opinion leader or market maven, we usually compensate the surrogate for his or her advice. Interior decorators, stockbrokers, professional shoppers, and college admissions consultants are surrogate consumers.

Regardless of whether they actually make the purchase on behalf of the consumer, surrogate consumers can be enormously influential. The client essentially relinquishes control over several or all decision-making functions, such as information search, the evaluation of alternatives, or the actual purchase. For example, a client may commission an interior decorator to redo her house, and we may entrust a broker to make crucial buy/sell decisions on our behalf. Marketers tend to overlook surrogates when they try to convince consumers to buy their goods or services. This can be a big mistake, because they may mistarget their communications to end consumers when they should focus on the surrogates who actually sift through product information and recommend a purchase to their clients.[69]

How Do We Find Opinion Leaders?

When PepsiCo launched its Sierra Mist Ruby Splash flavor, the company hired a firm to identify local people in different cities who could help it recruit a select group of "influencers." The requirements were specific: Influencers had to love lemon-lime beverages, be ages 18 to 34, and be musicians, skateboard shop owners, people who love to throw backyard barbeques, or others who had laid-back lifestyles and who were well-known in their communities. One influencer, for example, was a musician who hosted a backyard jam session for 20 friends; before the event, a crew dropped off ice-cold cans of the soft drink as well as branded sunglasses, misters, and car fresheners with a Ruby Splash scent. Another opinion leader owned a skateboard store; he hosted an outdoor movie night to debut a new surf film. In all, the company sponsored more than 300 of these mini-events in a 2-month period. Nice job if you can get it.[70]

Unfortunately, because most opinion leaders are everyday consumers rather than celebrities, they are harder to find. A celebrity or an influential industry executive is by definition easy to locate. That person has national or at least regional visibility or has a listing in published directories or on social media. In contrast, opinion leaders tend to operate

PepsiCo recruited "influencers" to spread the word when it launched a new Sierra Mist flavor.
Source: Paul Sakuma/AP Images.

at the local level and they may influence only a small group of consumers rather than an entire market segment.

Self-Designation

The most commonly used technique to identify opinion leaders is simply to ask individual consumers whether they consider themselves to *be* opinion leaders. Figure 11.3 shows one of the measurement scales researchers use for this kind of self-designation.

Figure 11.3 OPINION LEADER SCALE

Please rate yourself on the following scales relating to your interactions with friends and neighbors regarding _____.

1. In general, do you talk to your friends and neighbors about _____:

very often				never
5	4	3	2	1

2. When you talk to your friends and neighbors about _____ do you:

give a great deal of information				give very little information
5	4	3	2	1

3. During the past six months, how many people have you told about a new _____?

told a number of people				told no one
5	4	3	2	1

4. Compared with your circle of friends, how likely are you to be asked about new _____?

very likely to be asked				not at all likely to be asked
5	4	3	2	1

5. In discussion of new _____, which of the following happens most?

you tell your friends about _____				your friends tell you about _____
5	4	3	2	1

6. Overall in all of your discussions with friends and neighbors are you:

often used as a source of advice				not used as a source of advice
5	4	3	2	1

Although respondents who report a greater degree of interest in a product category indeed are more likely to be opinion leaders, we must view the results of surveys that discover self-designated opinion leaders with some skepticism. Some people have a tendency to inflate their own importance and influence, whereas others who really are influential might not admit to this quality or be conscious of it if they are.[71] The fact that we transmit advice about products does not mean other people *take* that advice.

Sociometry: The Kevin Bacon Phenomenon

The play *Six Degrees of Separation* is based on the premise that everyone on the planet indirectly knows everyone else—or at least knows people who in turn know them. Indeed, social scientists estimate that the average person has 1,500 acquaintances and that five to six intermediaries can connect any two people in the United States.[72] A popular game called **Six Degrees of Kevin Bacon** challenges players to link the actor Kevin Bacon with other actors in much the same way.[73]

Sociometric methods trace communication patterns among members of a group. These techniques allow researchers to systematically map out the interactions among group members. Like the Vaseline campaign in Alaska we described previously, this means we interview consumers and find out who they ask for product information. In many cases, one or a few people emerge as the "nodes" in a map—and *voilà*, we've found our opinion leaders. This method is the most precise, but it is difficult and expensive to implement because it involves close study of interaction patterns in small groups. For this reason, it's best to apply a sociometric technique in a closed, self-contained social setting, such as in hospitals, in prisons, and on military bases, where members are largely isolated from other social networks.

Sociometric techniques don't just look at who talks (or texts) to whom; they also consider the type of relationships among members of a social network. **Tie strength** refers to the nature of the bond between people. It can range from *strong primary* (e.g., one's spouse) to *weak secondary* (e.g., an acquaintance whom one rarely sees). Although strong ties are important, weak ties are as well because they perform a *bridging function*. This type of connection allows a consumer access between subgroups. For example, you might have a regular group of friends that is a primary reference group (strong ties). If you have an interest in tennis, one of these friends might introduce you to a group of people in her dorm who play on the tennis team. As a result, you gain access to their valuable expertise through this bridging function. This referral process demonstrates the **strength of weak ties**.

We use sociometric analyses to better understand *referral behavior* and to locate strengths and weaknesses in terms of how one's reputation flows through a community.[74] To understand how a network guides what we buy, consider a study researchers conducted among women who lived together in a sorority house. They found evidence that subgroups, or *cliques*, within the sorority were likely to share preferences for various products. In some cases, the sisters even shared their choices of "private" (i.e., socially inconspicuous) products (probably because of shared bathrooms in the sorority house).[75]

OBJECTIVE 11-4
Social media changes the way we learn about and select products.

The Social Media Revolution

The odds are good that you've already accessed social media today. If you checked into your Facebook page (of course not during class!), fired off a tweet, read a restaurant review on Yelp, or maybe even killed off some nasty orcs on *World of Warcraft*, you're part of the social media revolution that is changing how consumers interact with the marketplace and with one another. Many of us love to share details about our lives that our parents probably would never discuss in public. Somehow events don't seem "official" until we post them: A change in relationship status on Facebook, a photo of a luscious restaurant appetizer on Instagram, a funky necklace pinned onto a Pinterest Board.

Sometimes people define social media in terms of hardware (like Samsung smartphones) or software (like Snapchat), but really it's first and foremost about **online community**: The

collective participation of members who together build and maintain a site.[76] Indeed, many of us become so enmeshed in our social networks that we feel the need to check them constantly to be sure we stay on top of what our (online) friends are up to 24/7 (oops, better stop reading this chapter and scan your Facebook, Twitter, or Foursquare posts!). Do you know anyone like that? Some refer to this compulsion as **fear of missing out (FOMO)**. Certainly there are advantages to always feeling connected, but perhaps the downside is a vague feeling of regret or inadequacy that lurks in the background in case we chose not to be somewhere—or even worse, that we weren't invited in the first place![77]

Whether we feel left out or not, it seems clear that our passion for social media exerts a big impact on our emotions and experiences during the course of a typical day. Indeed, one study even found that people on Twitter tend to follow others who share their mood: People who are happy tend to retweet or reply to others who are happy, whereas those who are sad or lonely tend to do the same with others who also post negative sentiments.[78]

Online Social Networks and Brand Communities

Let's take a closer look at the underlying fabric of social media. Each online platform, such as Facebook, Pinterest, or Twitter, consists of a **social network** a set of socially relevant nodes connected by one or more relations.[79] **Nodes** are members of the network (e.g., the more than 1 billion Facebook users) who are connected to one another. Ties stem from affiliations, such as kinship, friendship and affective bonds, shared experiences, and common hobbies and interests. When we think of community, we tend to think of people, but in principle, members of a network can be organizations, articles, countries, departments in a company, or any other definable unit. A good example is your university alumni association. The association is a community of networked individuals and organizations. Social networks are sometimes called **social graphs** though this term may also refer to a diagram of the interconnections of units in a network.

Flows occur between nodes. Flows are exchanges of resources, information, or influence among members of the network. On Facebook you share news, updates about your life, opinions on your favorite books and movies, photos, videos, and notes. As you share content, you create flows from among those in your network. In social media, these flows of communication go in many directions at any point in time and often on multiple platforms—a condition we term **media multiplexity**. Flows are not simply two-way or three-way; they may go through an entire community, a list or group within a network, or several individuals independently. For marketers, flows are especially important because they are the actionable components of any social network system in terms of the sharing of information, delivery of promotional materials, and sources of social influence.

Successful online communities possess several important characteristics:

- **Standards of behavior:** Rules that specify what members can and can't do on the site. Some of these rules are spelled out explicitly (e.g., if you buy an item on eBay, you agree that you have entered into a legal contract to pay for it), but many of them are unspoken. A simple example is discouragement of the practice of **flaming** when a POST CONTAINS ALL CAPITAL LETTERS TO EXPRESS ANGER.
- **Member contributions:** A healthy proportion of users need to contribute content. If not, the site will fail to offer fresh material and ultimately traffic will slow. Participation can be a challenge, though. Remember the *80/20 rule* we discussed way back in Chapter 1? It applies to online consumption as well. The fact is that most members of an online community are **lurkers**. That's kind of a creepy term, but it just means they absorb content that others post rather than contributing their own. Researchers estimate that only 1 percent of a typical community's users regularly participate, and another nine percent do so only intermittently. The remaining 90 percent just observe what's on the site. Although they don't contribute content, they do offer value to advertisers that simply want to reach large numbers of people.

    But what happens when we want to engage consumers more actively? How can a site convert lurkers into active users? The easier it is to participate, the more likely it is that the community can generate activity among a larger proportion of visitors. In part, this means ensuring that there are several ways to participate that vary in ease of use. Facebook is an example of an online community that has figured out how to offer several forms of participation. Members can post status updates (easy), make comments, upload pictures, share notes and links, play social games, answer quizzes, decorate their profiles, upload videos, and create events (a bit harder), among other forms of participation.
- **Degree of connectedness:** Powerful groups are cohesive; this means the members identify strongly with them and are highly motivated to stay connected. Online groups may be even more cohesive than physical groups, even though many of the members will never meet one another in person. For example, compared to the "six degrees of separation" norm we discussed, researchers estimate that Facebook's members on average have only four degrees of separation from each other. Although some users have designated only one friend and others have thousands, the median is about 100 friends. The researchers found that most pairs of Facebook users could be connected

All Friends   Maintained Relationships

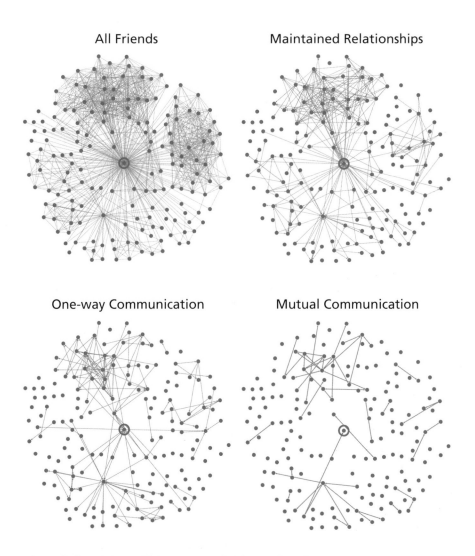

One-way Communication   Mutual Communication

A graphical representation of one person's network neighborhood on Facebook.
Source: Courtesy of Dr. Cameron Marlow, Stanford University.

through four intermediate users, and this number shrank to three within a single country.[80] Because many of us devote so much time and energy to our online group relationships, connectedness also reflects our real world relationships (it's common for people to learn that their partner has broken up with them only after they see a change in "relationship status" on Facebook!). One study that analyzed 1.3 million Facebook users and about 8.6 billion links among them reported that couples who are in a relationship are more likely to stay together if they share a lot of mutual Facebook friends, and they're more likely to break up within a few months if this indicator dips sharply because it implies their social lives aren't overlapping much.[81]

● **Network effects** The quality of the site improves as the number of users increases. For example, Amazon's ability to recommend books to you based on what other people with similar interests buy gets better as it tracks more and more people who enter search queries.

Social Games

A **social game** is a multiplayer, competitive, goal-oriented activity with defined rules of engagement and online connectivity among a community of players. Successful mobile games such as *Candy Crush* and *Angry Birds* boast millions of avid followers.[82] These applications usually incorporate one or more elements of game design, such as **leaderboards** that indicate how each player is doing relative to others in the game and **badges** that show the community the challenges the player has mastered so far.

Social games are built on several layers, including platform, mode, milieu, and genre.[83] Let's briefly review the basic dimensions of social games:

- A **game platform** refers to the hardware systems on which the game is played. Platforms include *game consoles* (consoles are interactive, electronic devices used to display video games, such as Sony's PlayStation3, Microsoft's Xbox 360, and Nintendo's Wii), computers (including both online games and those that require software installation on the player's computer hard drive), and portable devices that may include smartphones or devices specifically for game play such as the Sony PSP or Nintendo DS.[84]
- **Mode** refers to the way players experience the game world. It includes aspects such as whether a player's activities are highly structured, whether the game is single-player or multiplayer, whether the game is played in close physical proximity to other players (or by virtual proximity), and whether the game is real-time or turn-based.
- **Milieu** describes the visual nature of the game, such as science fiction, fantasy, horror, and retro.
- The **genre** of a game refers to the method of play. Popular genres include simulation, action, and role-playing. *Simulation games* depict real-world situations as accurately as possible. There are several subgenres, including racing simulators, flight simulators, and "Sim" games that enable players to simulate the development of an environment. Among social games, simulations include the highly popular *FarmVille*, *Pet Resort*, and *FishVille*. Action games consist of two major subgenres: *first-person shooters (FPS)*, where you "see" the game as your avatar sees it, and third-person games. In *role-playing games* (RPGs), the players play a character role with the goal of completing some mission. Perhaps the best-known RPG started its life as a tabletop game: *Dungeons and Dragons*. Players adopt the identity of a character in the game story and go about completing tasks and collecting points and items as they strive to accomplish the intended goal.

Digital Word-of-Mouth

Viral marketing occurs when an organization motivates visitors to forward online content to their friends; the message quickly spreads much like a cold virus moves among residents of a dorm. It usually takes off when the online content is entertaining or just plain weird. This strategy stirred up a huge amount of interest in "lap giraffes," for example.

Net Profit

MMORPGs—*massive multiplayer online role-playing games*—truly encompass the social aspects of gaming. *World of Warcraft* is one of the largest MMORPGs with millions of players from around the world; other popular ones include *Haven* and *The Sims*.[85] The money people spend in virtual worlds like these grows rapidly. Indeed, **digital virtual consumption (DVC)** may well be the next frontier of marketing. Today in the United States alone, consumers spend well more than $2 billion per year (yes, billion) to buy **virtual goods** for their online characters.[86] Thousands of in-world residents design, create, and purchase clothing, furniture, houses, vehicles, and other products their avatars need, and many do it in style as they acquire the kind of "bling" they can only dream about in real life. Some forward-thinking marketers understand that these platforms are the next stage they can use to introduce their products into people's lives, whether real or virtual. Today, for example, people who play *The Sims* can import actual pieces of furniture from IKEA into their virtual homes.

Source: Bloomberg/Getty Images.

Thousands of people started to look for these cuddly pets after an online message circulated about them. One hitch: There is no such thing as a lap giraffe. The scam was part of a marketing campaign for the cable provider DirecTV. More than half a million people put their names on a waiting list to receive one of the tiny animals. Presumably they're still waiting to get their new pets delivered.[87]

There's no doubt many of us love to share the news with others; news about new styles, new music, and especially new stuff that we've bought. Of course we do this in the form of online reviews in forums like Yelp or TripAdvisor. However the urge to share even creates new genres of communication such as **haul videos** that feature a proud *fashionista* describing clothing items she just bought, and **unboxing videos** that illustrate in painstaking detail exactly how to remove electronics products from their boxes and assemble them for use (if you don't believe it, Google these terms!).

Twitter has emerged as a powerful social network, as this Australian ad reminds us.
Source: Courtesy of STIHL Pty Ltd.

The viral marketing explosion highlights the power of the **Megaphone Effect**. Web 2.0 makes a huge audience available to everyday consumers. Some fashion bloggers build an impressive following as they share their views about what's hot and what's not. For example, more than 30,000 people read this post:

> Found the perfect gray socks while shopping at Uniqlo in Tokyo with my mom/favorite shopping partner (she's always down to stop randomly to eat and shares my love for finding wearable things in unlikely places). Vaguely sheer and just the right length. This sounds extremely trivial, and sort of is, but I've been looking for something like them forever now.[88]

Researchers report that written communication about brands is more likely to include mentions of interesting or unusual brands, and the motivation to post about these items is driven to a greater extent by the desire for self-enhancement. When people share their opinions about products with their social networks, they may do so to satisfy one of several goals: To manage the impression they make on others, to regulate emotions by expressing affective reactions, to share and acquire information, to bond with others, and to persuade others to change their opinions.[89]

Unlike a spontaneous conversation in the physical world, when consumers write about products they have more time to think strategically about what they're saying—and

CB AS I SEE IT

Jonah Berger, *The Wharton School, University of Pennsylvania*

Why do some things go viral? And why do some products and brands get more WOM than others?

It's clear that WOM is both frequent and important. People share all sorts of opinions, news, and information with their friends and colleagues. There are more than 500 million tweets and greater than 100 billion emails sent every day. In fact, you probably received an email, text, or social media update from someone while you were reading this sentence.

Further, interpersonal communication has a big impact on consumer behavior. Think about the last book you read or movie you watched. Chances are you heard about it from someone else. Indeed, WOM generates more than twice the sales of paid advertising.

As a result, companies and organizations are making WOM a big part of their marketing strategy. They're trying to create viral videos and starting accounts on every new social media property they can find.

But in all this hype around the newest technology, people have forgotten about something much more important: the psychology. Why does some content go viral while other stuff collects only a couple views? Why do some products get lots of WOM, whereas others are barely discussed? And how by understanding this science, can people get their product, ideas, and behaviors to become popular?

It turns out that six key factors drive much of what people talk about and share. In *Contagious: Why Things Catch On,* I put them in an acronym called S.T.E.P.P.S. That stands for Social

Currency, Triggers, Emotion, Public, Practical Value, and Stories. Each of these is a psychological principle that drives people to share all sorts of news, stories, and information.

Take Emotion. We analyzed 3 months of *New York Times* articles, almost 7,000 piece of content, to look at what made the most emailed list. Examining everything from world news and politics to sports and style we looked at which articles were highly shared and why. In general, we found that articles that evoked more emotion were more likely to be shared. The more people care, the more they share.

Further, more positive content was more likely to make the most emailed list. Sharing positive things puts others in a better mood, and reflects better on the sender. Most people want to be seen as Positive Pollys rather than Negative Nellys.

Even beyond valence though, the specific type of emotion articles evoked also mattered. Articles that evoked more high arousal emotions, like anger, anxiety, and inspiration were 21 to 34 percent more likely to go viral. Emotions that activate us can drive us to pass things on.

about how these judgments reflect on them.[90] Indeed, much of what we post is actually about ourselves; one study reported that 80 percent of tweets people send focus on themselves rather than other topics.[91]

A study that analyzed *Twitter* data illustrates the care people take to portray themselves in a positive light, but to avoid acting like they're bragging when they tweet about products they've bought or experienced. When the researchers looked at posts regarding two luxury brands—Louis Vuitton and Mercedes—they found that people commonly mention these items "in passing" as they comment on what they're doing or feeling at the moment, or even try to downplay the brand's positive characteristics to avoid looking too snobbish.[92]

Other researchers identified a somewhat similar phenomenon they call the **Dispreferred Marker Effect**. Online posts that are really negative may make the writer look harsh and judgmental, so people sometimes soften them by couching them in *dispreferred markers*, including phrases such as, "I'll be honest," "God bless it," or "I don't want to be mean, but ..." Sure enough, readers of these kinds of posts evaluated the writer more positively than they did posters who just laid out the bad news, warts and all.[93]

Digital Opinion Leaders

Quick, what's your Klout Score? Klout claims to precisely measure just how influential each of us is in cyberspace. The site assesses more than 12 billion pieces of data every day to compute a score from 0 to 100 for anyone who is online. Several indicators go into this number, including the ratio of comments or retweets a person generates compared to the amount of content he or she posts as well as the relative influence of the people who share this content. Not surprisingly celebrities including Justin Bieber and Zooey Deschanel boast high Klout scores, but plenty of influential people in other walks of life do too. Now Klout for Business allows brands to identify consumers with high scores so they can try to enlist them in spreading digital WOM about their brands. The matchmaking service Tawkify uses Klout scores as well, to pair people up for dates. One of the company's executives observed, "We've found that Klout scores are an authentic measurement of sophistication,

Klout scores measure how influential people are in online social networks.
Source: Courtesy of Klout, Inc.

wit, cultural savvy and appeal—a much truer and more trustworthy measurement than the typical online dating site bull-hockey-factors of height, weight and income."[94]

Previously we saw that opinion leaders are people who are more influential than most when they recommend purchases to others. In online groups, opinion leaders sometimes are called **power users**. They have a strong communications network that gives them the ability to affect purchase decisions for a number of other consumers, directly and indirectly.[95]

Much like their offline counterparts, power users are active participants at work and in their communities. Their social networks are large and well developed. Others trust them and find them to be credible sources of information about one or more specific topics. They tend to have a natural sense of intellectual curiosity, which may lead them to new sources of information. And they post an awful lot of brand-related content: Forrester Research has dubbed these brand-specific mentions **influence impressions**. In advertising lingo, an *impression* refers to a view or an exposure to an advertising message. Forrester estimates that, each year, U.S. consumers generate 256 billion influence impressions as people talk about their lives with each other, telling stories and experiences that invariably include brands.[96] These influence impressions are primarily delivered by—you guessed it—power users: Only 6.2 percent of social media users are responsible for about 80 percent of these brand mentions. Forrester calls these influencers **mass connectors**.

MyLab Marketing

To complete the problems with the ✪, go to EOC Discussion Questions in the MyLab as well as additional Marketing Metrics questions only available in MyLab Marketing.

CHAPTER SUMMARY

1. Other people and groups, especially those that possess social power, influence our decisions.

We belong to or admire many different groups, and a desire for them to accept us often drives our purchase decisions. Individuals or groups whose opinions or behavior are particularly important to consumers are reference groups. Both formal and informal groups influence the individual's purchase decisions, although such factors as the conspicuousness of the product and the relevance of the reference group for a particular purchase determine how influential the reference group is.

Individuals have influence in a group to the extent that they possess social power. Types of social power include information power, referent power, legitimate power, expert power, reward power, and coercive power.

Brand communities unite consumers who share a common passion for a product. Brandfests, which companies organize to encourage this kind of community, can build brand loyalty and reinforce group membership.

We conform to the desires of others for two basic reasons: (1) People who model their behavior after others because they take others' behavior as evidence of the correct way to act are conforming because of informational social influence; and (2) those who conform to satisfy the expectations of others or to be accepted by the group are affected by normative social influence. Group members often do things they would not do as individuals because their identities become merged with the group; they become deindividuated.

2. Word-of-mouth communication is the most important driver of product choice.

Much of what we know about products we learn through word-of-mouth (WOM) communication rather than formal advertising. We tend to exchange product-related information in casual conversations. Although WOM often is helpful to make consumers aware of products, it can also hurt companies when damaging product rumors or negative WOM occur.

3. Opinion leaders' recommendations are more influential than others when we decide what to buy.

Opinion leaders who are knowledgeable about a product and whose opinions are highly regarded tend to influence others' choices. Specific opinion leaders are somewhat hard to identify, but marketers who know their general characteristics can try to target them in their media and promotional strategies. Other influencers include market mavens, who have a general interest in marketplace activities; and surrogate consumers, who are compensated for their advice about purchases.

4. **Social media changes the way we learn about and select products.**

Social media platforms significantly increase our access to others' opinions about products and services. Virtual consumption communities unite those who share a common passion for products that include apparel, cars, music, beer, political candidates, etc. Many social media users post content online that satisfies motive for self-enhancement as well as the desire to share opinions and experiences about products and services. Consumers may engage with these brands via social games. Viral marketing techniques enlist individuals to spread online WOM about brands. Online opinion leaders play a pivotal role in disseminating influential recommendations and product information.

KEY TERMS

Antibrand communities, 417
Aspirational reference group, 417
Avoidance groups, 418
Badges, 433
Brand community, 420
Brandfests, 420
Buzz, 425
Coercive power, 416
Collective value creation, 421
Conformity, 418
Deindividuation, 419
Digital virtual consumption (DVC), 434
Dispreferred Marker Effect, 437
Expert power, 416
Flaming, 432
Flows, 432
Fear of Missing Out (FOMO), 431
Game platform, 434
Genre, 434
Gyges Effect, 419
Haul videos, 435
Homophily, 426
Influence impressions, 438

Influence network, 427
Information cascades, 427
Information power, 416
Internet trolls, 419
Leaderboards, 433
Legitimate power, 416
Lurkers, 432
Market maven, 428
Mass connectors, 438
Media multiplexity, 432
Megaphone Effect, 436
Membership reference group, 417
Milieu, 434
Minimal group paradigm, 395
MMORPGs, 434
Mode, 434
Negative word-of-mouth, 425
Network effects, 433
Nodes, 432
Norms, 418
Online community, 430
Opinion leaders, 426
Power users, 438

Principle of Least Interest, 419
Red Sneakers Effect, 419
Reference group, 416
Referent power, 416
Reward power, 416
Serial reproduction, 425
Six Degrees of Kevin Bacon, 430
Social game, 433
Social graphs, 432
Social loafing, 420
Social identity theory, 415
Social network, 432
Social power, 415
Sociometric methods, 430
Strength of weak ties, 430
Surrogate consumer, 428
Tie strength, 430
Two-Step Flow Model of Influence, 427
Unboxing videos, 435
Viral marketing, 434
Virtual goods, 434
Word-of-mouth (WOM), 422

REVIEW

11-1 What is *buzz building*, and how does it work?

11-2 What is meant by *homophily*?

⭐ **11-3** Describe some ways in which marketers use the Internet to encourage positive word-of-mouth.

11-4 Could a marketer create a generalized opinion leader?

11-5 What is an opinion leader? Give three reasons why they are powerful influences on consumers' opinions.

11-6 Is there such a thing as a generalized opinion leader? Why or why not?

11-7 What is *klout*, and how is it measured?

11-8 How do you find a suitable opinion leader?

11-9 What is *FOMO*, and why might it be important?

⭐ **11.10** List three types of social power, and give an example of each.

⭐ **11-11** What is a brand community, and why is it of interest to marketers?

11-12 Define conformity and give an example of it. Name three reasons why people conform.

11-13 How does the Principle of Least Interest relate to your success in a romantic relationship?

CONSUMER BEHAVIOR CHALLENGE

■ DISCUSS

11-14 A recent sociometric study on obesity (similar to the one we read about regarding clusters of smokers) provides a striking example of how our social networks influence what we do. The researchers analyzed a sample of more than 12,000 people who participated in the Framingham Heart Study, which closely documented their health from 1971 to 2003. They discovered that obesity can spread from person to person, much like a virus. The investigators knew who was friends with whom, as well as who was a spouse or sibling or neighbor, and they knew how much each person weighed at various times over three decades so they could reconstruct what happened over the years if study participants became obese. Guess what? When one person gains weight, close friends tend to gain weight, too. A person's chances of becoming obese if a close friend put on the pounds increased by 57 percent! The friend's influence remained even if he or she lived hundreds of miles away. The researchers speculated that the reason for this *social contagion* effect is that when our best buds get fat, this alters our perception of normal body weight so we aren't as concerned when we put on a few pounds as well.[97]

How does social contagion work in your life?

11-15 The Rio Olympics 2016 once again proved that major sporting events would struggle to attract the necessary finance and backing if it were not for the brands that sponsor them.[98] Brand owners know that the Olympic Games constitute arguably the most effective international marketing opportunity in the world. Olympic partners know that their logos and names will reach billions of viewers in over 200 countries. The revenues that are generated the commercial partnerships account for over 40 percent of Olympic revenues. Commercial partners also provide much-needed technical and products support before, during, and after the games. There are various levels of sponsorship that entitle sponsors to make use of Olympic images and trademarks. To what extent do you agree with the view that the Olympics have become a brandfest?

11-16 McCann Worldgroup manages over 50 brand community pages with over 4 million fans. None of the communication strategies are exactly the same. The focus of the efforts is common across the pages: to make sure that a fully integrated campaign creates and maintains engagement between the brands and their consumers. In Malaysia, Facebook has over 12.5 million users and has become a vital channel to create deep and meaningful relationships with consumers.[99] McCann believes that brands are beginning to realize that they need to invest in social media contacts with their customers. Customers are becoming increasingly savvy and empowered, and every close brand friend they create can become a brand advocate. There is clearly a great deal of persuasion still required; a study by *Deloitte Digital* and *MIT Sloan Management Review* suggests that 80 percent of brand owners recognize the importance of social media in creating brand communities, but the majority have no idea how to measure the effectiveness. What would you advise brand owners to do about social media and brand communities? How would you assess the effectiveness of campaigns?

11-17 SureBzz claims it is the first and leading word-of-mouth marketing service in India. The business works by creating a community of "SureBzzers." This community is then used to spread the word about a brand, product, or service to other consumers. SureBzz uses demographic and behavioral data points to help identify the right kind of person to spread the "buzz" about the brand. Each SureBzzer has the opportunity to experience the product or service first-hand; this is in order to ensure that the "buzz" is genuine. Typically, they are given samples, trials, and coupons. SureBzzers are encouraged to share their opinions on Facebook, Twitter, blogs, and other social media. The SureBzzers submit reports to the company that are then checked. How is the data used from this point?

11-18 In 2013 in the United Kingdom, Channel 4's program *Dispatches* featured an investigation into brands buying social media interactions. The documentary discovered that low-paid workers in Bangladeshi were being used as "click farms." They were employed to create Facebook likes, Twitter followers, and multiple YouTube views.[100] The episode resulted in calls for immediate action to stop the practice. What action should be taken to prevent this?

11-19 The strategy of viral marketing gets customers to sell a product to other customers on behalf of the company. That often means convincing your friends to climb on the bandwagon, and sometimes you get a cut if they buy something.[101] Some might argue that that means you're selling out your friends (or at least selling to your friends) in exchange for a piece of the action. Others might say you're simply sharing the wealth with your buddies. Have you ever passed along names of your friends to a company or Web site? If so, what happened? How do you feel about this practice?

■ APPLY

11-20 Who are the fashion opinion leaders in your country? How do they match up with the desired profile for such leaders?

11-21 A study on antibranding documented hostility among consumers who object to the gas-guzzling Hummer vehicle. One driver posted this message: "The H2 is a death machine. You'd better hope that you don't collide with an H2 in your economy car. You can kiss your ass goodbye thanks to the H2's massive weight and raised bumpers. Too bad you couldn't afford an urban assault vehicle of your own."[102]

Identify an antibranding site for another product. What functions do the site seem to serve? How can people who participate there be considered part of a community?

11-22 Choose 10 people and ask them about their latest major purchase of a product or service. How did they decide that they needed that product or service? What made them choose the brand? Were they influenced by the views of an opinion leader in their decision-making process?

11-23 List at least 10 of your friends. They can be close friends or acquaintances. Try to rank them in terms of their influence on your purchasing behavior. To what extent are you more likely to trust and follow the opinions of your closer friends compared to your acquaintances? What types of product and service purchases have they influenced?

11-24 The power of unspoken social norms often becomes obvious only when we violate them. To witness this result firsthand, try one of the following: Stand facing the back wall in an elevator, serve dessert before the main course, offer to pay cash for dinner at a friend's home, wear pajamas to class, or tell someone *not* to have a nice day.

11-25 Identify a set of avoidance groups for your peers. Can you identify any consumption decisions that you and your friends make with these groups in mind?

11-26 Several colleges have sponsored "social media detox" events. Students at Saint Mary's College of California were challenged to "Disconnect, Power Off and Unplug" in order to rediscover "The Lost Art of Solitude;" no Internet for a month! The library at Wake Forest University created a "ZieSta Room" where technology is banned.[103]

Do a "detox" of your own for 48 hours. No cellphones. No Facebook. No social media of any kind. Keep a diary of your experiences.

Case Study

SOCIAL MEDIA AND HUMOR

Stokers has come a long way since its beginnings in a market town in West Lancashire, England, back in 1895, when Alfred Stoker started a business selling fabric and millinery. The furniture retail firm grew to a total of 10 stores, and in 2001, it initiated its online presence with a Web site. Stokers began promoting itself, like many other companies, through Google ads in 2008; in 2010, it launched its Facebook page, followed by Twitter in 2011.

And yet—again, like many other companies—Stokers failed to recognize the impact of social media; posts on Facebook would remain outdated and negative reviews on Facebook were left unaddressed, all of which often lead to a negative impression of a brand online. Although the idea of having a Facebook page had been around for years, what to do with the site had brought many companies both confusion and frustration.

Stokers realized that firm changes needed to be made to turn the companies' online consumer experience around. It chose to focus on Facebook over Twitter as a first step to promote its products. Once a firm understanding of using social media was established, the company intended to explore other relevant social media—Twitter, Pinterest, and Instagram.

To begin, Stokers emulated other companies in using Facebook as a means to gather consumer information and increase product exposure. For example, it created competitions that required users to leave their details in order to enter a competition, thus creating a new populated database of interested consumers. This was an encouraging beginning, but Stokers wanted to take it to another level of engagement. Keeping consumers interested in products and encouraging them to return to the site was seen as a key objective. After various attempts to do just that, Stokers realized that it was the use of humor that resulted in a significantly high level of engagement with customers.

Research indicates if humor is associated with a product, then consumers tend to have a higher consumer preference toward it. Humor can also facilitate positive associations between a product and a consumer. A vital element of social media marketing is getting consumers to actively engage, and the addition of humor has been consistently found to increase likes on social media posts.

So it should come as no surprise that Stokers soon identified (through engagement figures) that the humor posts on its Facebook page received approximately 500 percent more engagement than posts that related to particular products only. The number of visitors to the Facebook page also increased by 75 percent. The increased interaction on the social media sites led to an increased activity of approximately 113 percent on the Web site. Other measures, like Web optimization, were also taken to ensure the Web site uploaded quickly, and this saw a 27 percent reduction in the bounce rate.

With figures like the above to reflect upon, the company made significant changes. The staff at Stokers were given clear directions for their daily social media activities. Any negative comments are picked up and dealt with straight away.

It is difficult to quantify a direct sales relation to a particular element of digital marketing, as it involves a combination of many things: email marketing, site optimization, Google Ads, and traditional marketing. Yet the numbers are telling—digital marketing as a whole led to a significant increase in sales in the target segment of garden furniture. In the first year, there was a 75 percent increase in sales, and in the second year it rose to 200 percent.

Looking back, the lessons are clear. Social media will not work for a company that just has a Facebook page, even if it posts regularly. This alone will not necessarily ensure active engagement from consumers. Social media posts also require constant monitoring and updating from the company to avoid becoming stagnant and outdated. Customers need a higher level of engagement. However, companies need to be mindful of choosing appropriate social media and ensure that any humor employed is appropriate for their products and services.

Humor in general works well with social media, with global brands like Oreo, Skittles, Taco Bell, and Old Spice taking full advantage of it to connect with consumers. Old Spice, for instance, is known to start mock battles with companies like Taco Bell, who then respond in the same spirit. Popchips' Facebook page provides consumers with entertaining images and funny puns. Nandos also uses humor in its social media and has received a positive response from its customers. Entertaining content is one of the top five reasons people follow particular brands or individuals online, and as more companies embrace this, it can only lead to better and more engaging customer experiences.

DISCUSSION QUESTIONS

CS 11-1 Select and analyze a few online campaigns where the humor is used with the product and without the product. Are there any differences in the number of posts or responses to these? Which method do you think works best, using humor alongside the product or without the product? Give examples.

CS 11-2 Are there any products where humor is not appropriate? How does this translate in the online world? Give examples.

Sources: Stokers, "Our Heritage," www.stokers.co.uk; Jelena Ilic, *Humour on Facebook.* (2012) 2nd International Conference on Foreign Language Teaching and Applied Linguistics (FLTAL'12), 4–6 May 2012, Sarajevo; A. Malhotra and C.K. Malhotra, "How to Create Brand Engagement on Facebook," *MIT Sloan Management Review* 54, No. 2, December 18, 2012; M. Strick, R. Van Baaren, R. Holland, and A. Van Knippenberg, "Humour in Advertisements Enhances Product Liking by Mere Association," *Psychology of Popular Media Culture*, 1(S), (2011): 16–31; Casey Fleischmann, "How Nando's Uses Social Media [CASE STUDY]," *Link Humans*, http://linkhumans.com/case-study/nandos, accessed November 27, 2015; Amy Elderkin, "How Big Brands Are Using Humour on Social Media (and Why You Should Too)," *Hootsuite*, July 13, 2015, http://blog.hootsuite.com/how-big-brands-are-using-humour-on-social-media/, accessed November 27, 2015.

MyLab Marketing

Go to the Assignments section of your MyLab to complete these writing exercises.

11-27 Although social networking is red hot, could its days be numbered? Many people have concerns about privacy issues. Others feel that platforms such as Facebook are too overwhelming. As one media executive comments, "Nobody has 5,000 real friends. At the end of the day it just becomes one big cauldron of noise." What's your stand on this: Can we have too much of a good thing? Will people start to tune out all of these networks?[104]

11-28 The adoption of a certain brand of shoe or apparel by athletes can be a powerful influence on students and other fans. Should high school and college coaches be paid to determine what brand of athletic equipment their players wear?

NOTES

1. http://freecountry.harley-davidson.com/landing.php, accessed April 11, 2015.

2. http://www.harley-davidson.com/shop/mens-motorcycle-clothes, accessed April 11, 2015.

3. Details adapted from John W. Schouten and James H. McAlexander, "Market Impact of a Consumption Subculture: The Harley-Davidson Mystique," in Fred van Raaij and Gary Bamossy, eds., *Proceedings of the 1992 European Conference of the Association for Consumer Research* (Amsterdam, 1992); John

W. Schouten and James H. McAlexander, "Subcultures of Consumption: An Ethnography of the New Bikers," *Journal of Consumer Research* 22 (June 1995): 43–61. See also Kelly Barron, "Hog Wild," *Forbes* (May 15, 2000), http://www.forbes.com/forbes/2000/0515/6511068a.html, accessed September 20, 2013.

4. Joel B. Cohen and Ellen Golden, "Informational Social Influence and Product Evaluation," *Journal of Applied Psychology* 56 (February 1972): 54–59; Robert E. Burnkrant and Alain Cousineau, "Informational and

Normative Social Influence in Buyer Behavior," *Journal of Consumer Research* 2 (December 1975): 206–215; Peter H. Reingen, "Test of a List Procedure for Inducing Compliance with a Request to Donate Money," *Journal of Applied Psychology* 67 (1982): 110–118.

5. Henri Tajfel and John C. Turner, "The Social Identity Theory of Intergroup Behaviour," in S. Worchel and W. G. Austin (Eds.), *Psychology of Intergroup Relations* (Chicago, IL: Nelson-Hall, 1986): 7–24.

6. Dyan Machan, "Is the Hog Going Soft?," *Forbes* (March 10, 1997): 114–119.

7. Andrew Adam Newman, "Campaign Redefines Running as a Social Activity," *New York Times* (July 8, 2013), http://www.nytimes.com/2013/07/09/business/media/campaign-redefines-running-as-a-social-activity.html?_r=3&adxnnl=1&adxnnlx=1375297677-/ALie05m6JiubQ4oXE4qig, accessed April 11, 2015.

8. Kenneth J. Gergen and Mary Gergen, *Social Psychology* (New York: Harcourt Brace Jovanovich, 1981): 312.

9. J. R. P. French, Jr., and B. Raven, "The Bases of Social Power," in D. Cartwright, ed., *Studies in Social Power* (Ann Arbor, MI: Institute for Social Research, 1959): 150–167.

10. Michael R. Solomon, "Packaging the Service Provider," *The Service Industries Journal* 5 (March 1985): 64–72.

11. Tamar Charry, "Unconventional Spokesmen Talk Up U.S. Robotics' Fast Modems in a New TV Campaign," *New York Times* (February 6, 1997), http://www.nytimes.com/1997/02/06/business/unconventional-spokes men-talk-up-us-robotics-fast-modems-in-a-new-tv-campaign.html?scp=44&sq=Tamar+Charry&st=nyt, accessed September 13, 2011.

12. Patricia M. West and Susan M. Broniarczyk, "Integrating Multiple Opinions: The Role of Aspiration Level on Consumer Response to Critic Consensus," *Journal of Consumer Research* 25 (June 1998): 38–51.

13. C. Whan Park and V. Parker Lessig, "Students and Housewives: Differences in Susceptibility to Reference Group Influence," *Journal of Consumer Research* 4 (September 1977): 102–110.

14. Gina Kolata, "Study Finds Big Social Factor in Quitting Smoking," *New York Times* (May 22, 2008), www.nytimes.com/2008/05/22/science/22smoke .html?ex=1369195200&en=0a10910fcde1a1ac&ei=5124&partner=per malink&exprod=permalink, accessed May 22, 2008.

15. Jeffrey D. Ford and Elwood A. Ellis, "A Re-examination of Group Influence on Member Brand Preference," *Journal of Marketing Research* 17 (February 1980): 125–132; Thomas S. Robertson, *Innovative Behavior and Communication* (New York: Holt, Rinehart & Winston, 1980), Ch. 8.

16. Gergen and Gergen, *Social Psychology*.

17. http://www.sneakerfiles.com/2011/06/15/air-jordan-xii-12-dwyane-wade-player-exclusive/, accessed June 15, 2011; Jennifer Edson Escalas and James R. Bettman, "You Are What You Eat: The Influence of Reference Groups on Consumers' Connections to Brands," *Journal of Consumer Psychology* 13, no. 3 (2003): 339–348.

18. A. Benton Cocanougher and Grady D. Bruce, "Socially Distant Reference Groups and Consumer Aspirations," *Journal of Marketing Research* 8 (August 1971): 79–81.

19. Susan B. Barnes, "Fantasy Camps: Get a Taste of a Different Life," *USA Today* (September 16, 2014), http://experience.usatoday.com/weekend/story/my-weekend-experience/2014/09/16/fantasy-camps-around-the-usa/15682941/, accessed April 11, 2015; quoted in Barry Rehfeld, "At These Camps, Everybody Is a Star (If Only for a Day)," *New York Times* (June 12, 2005), http://www.nytimes.com/2005/06/12/business/yourmoney/12fantasy.html?n=Top%2FReference%2FTimes%20Topics%2FSubjects%2FM%2FMusic&_r=0, accessed April 11, 2015.

20. Jonah Berger and Lindsay Rand, "Shifting Signals to Help Health: Using Identity Signaling to Reduce Risky Health Behaviors," *Journal of Consumer Research* 35, no. 3 (2008): 509–518.

21. Basil G. Englis and Michael R. Solomon, "To Be and Not to Be: Reference Group Stereotyping and the Clustering of America," *Journal of Advertising* 24 (Spring 1995): 13–28; Michael R. Solomon and Basil G. Englis, "I Am Not, Therefore I Am: The Role of Anti-Consumption in the Process of Self-Definition" (special session at the Association for Consumer Research meetings, October 1996, Tucson, Arizona); cf. also Brendan Richardson and Darach Turley, "Support Your Local Team: Resistance, Subculture and the Desire for Distinction," *Advances in Consumer Research* 33, no. 1 (2006): 175–180.

22. Bruce Feirstein, *Real Men Don't Eat Quiche* (New York: Pocket Books, 1982); www.auntiefashions.com, accessed December 31, 2002; Katherine White and Darren W. Dahl, "Are All Out-Groups Created Equal? Consumer Identity and Dissociative Influence," *Journal of Consumer Research* 34 (December 2007): 525–536.

23. www.starbucked.com, accessed April 26, 2015; http://www.mcspotlight .org/index.shtml, accessed April 26, 2015; http://www.hel-mart.com/links.php, accessed April 26, 2015.

24. Candice R. Hollenbeck and George M. Zinkhan, "Consumer Activism on the Internet: The Role of Anti-Brand Communities," *Advances in Consumer Research* 33, no. 1 (2006): 479–485.

25. Luc Sante, "Be Different! (Like Everyone Else!)," *New York Times Magazine* (October 17, 1999), www.nytimes.com, accessed October 3, 2007.

26. Quoted in Stephen Marce, "The Epidemic of Facelessness," *New York Times* (February 14, 2015), http://www.nytimes.com/2015/02/15/opinion/sunday/the-epidemic-of-facelessness.html?ref=opinion&_r=0, accessed February 24, 2015; "Internet Trolls And The Gyges Effect," *Milinism* (August 24, 2013), https://milinism.wordpress.com/2013/08/24/internet-trolls-and-the-gyges-effect/, accessed February 24, 2015.

27. Cindy Chan, Jonah Berger and Leaf Van Boven, "Identifiable but Not Identical: Combining Social Identity and Uniqueness Motives in Choice," *Journal of Consumer Research* 39, no. 3 (October 2012): 561–573.

28. Silvia Bellezza, Francesca Gino and Anat Keinan, "The Red Sneakers Effect: Inferring Status and Competence from Signals of Nonconformity," *Journal of Consumer Research* 41, no. 1 (2014): 35–54.

29. For a study that attempted to measure individual differences in proclivity to conformity, see William O. Bearden, Richard G. Netemeyer, and Jesse E. Teel, "Measurement of Consumer Susceptibility to Interpersonal Influence," *Journal of Consumer Research* 15 (March 1989): 473–481.

30. T. M. Luhrmann, "Wheat People vs. Rice People: Why Are Some Cultures More Individualistic Than Others?," *New York Times* (December 3, 2014), http://www.nytimes.com/2014/12/04/opinion/why-are-some-cultures-more-individualistic-than-others.html?ref=international, accessed February 16, 2015.

31. John W. Thibaut and Harold H. Kelley, *The Social Psychology of Groups* (New York: Wiley, 1959); W. W. Waller and Reuben Hill, *The Family, a Dynamic Interpretation* (New York: Dryden, 1951).

32. Bearden, Netemeyer, and Teel, "Measurement of Consumer Susceptibility to Interpersonal Influence"; Lynn R. Kahle, "Observations: Role-Relaxed Consumers: A Trend of the Nineties," *Journal of Advertising Research* (March–April 1995): 66–71; Lynn R. Kahle and Aviv Shoham, "Observations: Role-Relaxed Consumers: Empirical Evidence," *Journal of Advertising Research* (May–June 1995): 59–62.

33. Xun Huang, Meng Zhang, Michael K. Hui, and Robert S. Wyer, Jr., "Warmth and Conformity: The Effects of Ambient Temperature on Product Preferences and Financial Decisions," *Journal of Consumer Psychology* 24, no. 2 (2014): 241–250.

34. B. Latané, K. Williams, and S. Harkins, "Many Hands Make Light the Work: The Causes and Consequences of Social Loafing," *Journal of Personality & Social Psychology* 37 (1979): 822–832.

35. S. Freeman, M. Walker, R. Borden, and B. Latane, "Diffusion of Responsibility and Restaurant Tipping: Cheaper by the Bunch," *Personality & Social Psychology Bulletin* 1 (1978): 584–587.

36. http://halo.xbox.com/en-us/intel/titles/halo2, accessed June 15, 2011; Kris Oser, "Microsoft's Halo 2 Soars on Viral Push," *Advertising Age* (October 25, 2004): 46.

37. Quoted in Sheila Shayon, "Teen Girls: Shopping and Texting, Texting and Shopping," *Brandchannel* (November 26, 2010), http://www.brandchannel .com/home/post/2010/11/26/Teen-Girls-Snapshot-Shopping-and-Social-Media.aspx, accessed February 23, 2011.

38. Hope Jensen Schau, Albert M. Muñiz, Jr., and Eric J. Arnould, "How Brand Community Practices Create Value," *Journal of Marketing* 73 (September 2009), 30–51; John W. Schouten, James H. McAlexander, and Harold F. Koenig, "Transcendent Customer Experience and Brand Community," *Journal of the Academy of Marketing Science* 35 (2007): 357–368; James H. McAlexander, John W. Schouten, and Harold F. Koenig, "Building Brand Community," *Journal of Marketing* 66 (January 2002): 38–54; Albert Muñiz and Thomas O'Guinn, "Brand Community," *Journal of Consumer Research* (March 2001): 412–432; Scott A. Thompson and Rajiv K. Sinha, "Brand Communities and New Product Adoption: The Influence and Limits of Oppositional Loyalty," *Journal of Marketing* 72 (November 2008): 65–80.

39. Rama K. Jayanti and Jagdip Singh, "Framework for Distributed Consumer Learning in Online Communities," *Journal of Consumer Research* 36, no. 6 (2010): 1058–1081.

40. Marie-Agnès Parmentier and Eileen Fischer, "Things Fall Apart: The Dynamics of Brand Audience Dissipation," *Journal of Consumer Research* 41 (February 2015): 1228–1251.

41. Pat Wechsler, "A Curiously Strong Campaign," *BusinessWeek* (April 21, 1997): 134.

42. Johan Arndt, "Role of Product-Related Conversations in the Diffusion of a New Product," *Journal of Marketing Research* 4 (August 1967): 291–295.

43. Jacques Bughin, Jonathan Doogan and Ole Jørgen Vetvik, "A New Way to Measure Word-Of-Mouth Marketing," *McKinsey Quarterly* (April 2010), http://www.mckinsey.com/insights/marketing_sales/a_new_way_to_measure_word-of-mouth_marketing, accessed April 26, 2015.

44. Elihu Katz and Paul F. Lazarsfeld, *Personal Influence* (Glencoe, IL: Free Press, 1955).

45. John A. Martilla, "Word-of-Mouth Communication in the Industrial Adoption Process," *Journal of Marketing Research* 8 (March 1971):

173–178; see also Marsha L. Richins, "Negative Word-of-Mouth by Dissatisfied Consumers: A Pilot Study," *Journal of Marketing* 47 (Winter 1983): 68–78.

46. Arndt, "Role of Product-Related Conversations in the Diffusion of a New Product."

47. Leonard-Barton, "Experts as Negative Opinion Leaders in the Diffusion of a Technological Innovation."

48. Nancy Wagner, "Referral Programs as a Marketing Strategy," *AzCentral*, http://yourbusiness.azcentral.com/referral-programs-marketing-strategy-6364.html, accessed April 11, 2015.

49. http://www.silverlit-flyingclub.com/, accessed April 11, 2015.

50. Richard J. Lutz, "Changing Brand Attitudes Through Modification of Cognitive Structure," *Journal of Consumer Research* 1 (March 1975): 49–59. For some suggested remedies to bad publicity, see Mitch Griffin, Barry J. Babin, and Jill S. Attaway, "An Empirical Investigation of the Impact of Negative Public Publicity on Consumer Attitudes and Intentions," in Rebecca H. Holman and Michael R. Solomon, eds., *Advances in Consumer Research* 18 (Provo, UT: Association for Consumer Research, 1991): 334–341; Alice M. Tybout, Bobby J. Calder, and Brian Sternthal, "Using Information Processing Theory to Design Marketing Strategies," *Journal of Marketing Research* 18 (1981): 73–79; see also Russell N. Laczniak, Thomas E. DeCarlo, and Sridhar N. Ramaswami, "Consumers' Responses to Negative Word-of-Mouth Communication: An Attribution Theory Perspective," *Journal of Consumer Psychology* 11, no. 1 (2001): 57–73.

51. Robert E. Smith and Christine A. Vogt, "The Effects of Integrating Advertising and Negative Word-of-Mouth Communications on Message Processing and Response," *Journal of Consumer Psychology* 4, no. 2 (1995): 133–151; Paula Fitzgerald Bone, "Word-of-Mouth Effects on Short-Term and Long-Term Product Judgments," *Journal of Business Research* 32 (1995): 213–223.

52. Keith Schneider, "Brands for the Chattering Masses," *New York Times* (December 17, 2006), www.nytimes.com, accessed October 3, 2007.

53. Amy Chozick, "Cold Stone Aims to Be Hip in Japan Ice-Cream Chain, Uses Word-of-Mouth as Part of Bid for an Urban Image," *Wall Street Journal* (December 14, 2006): B10.

54. Everett M. Rogers, *Diffusion of Innovations*, 3rd ed. (New York: Free Press, 1983); cf. also Duncan J. Watts and Peter Sheridan Dodds, "Influentials, Networks, and Public Opinion Formation," *Journal of Consumer Research* 34 (December 2007): 441–458; Morris B. Holbrook and Michela Addis, "Taste Versus the Market: An Extension of Research on the Consumption of Popular Culture," *Journal of Consumer Research* 34 (October 2007): 415–424.

55. Dorothy Leonard-Barton, "Experts as Negative Opinion Leaders in the Diffusion of a Technological Innovation," *Journal of Consumer Research* 11 (March 1985): 914–926; Rogers, *Diffusion of Innovations*; cf. also Jan Kratzer and Christopher Lettl, "Distinctive Roles of Lead Users and Opinion Leaders in the Social Networks of Schoolchildren," *Journal of Consumer Research* 36, no. 4 (December 2009): 646–659.

56. Herbert Menzel, "Interpersonal and Unplanned Communications: Indispensable or Obsolete?," in Edward B. Roberts, ed., *Biomedical Innovation* (Cambridge, MA: MIT Press, 1981), 155–163.

57. Meera P. Venkatraman, "Opinion Leaders, Adopters, and Communicative Adopters: A Role Analysis," *Psychology & Marketing* 6 (Spring 1989): 51–68.

58. Rogers, *Diffusion of Innovations*.

59. Karl Greenberg, "Ford Puts Trendsetters Behind Wheel in VIP Events," *Marketing Daily* (November 11, 2008), www.mediapost.com/publications/?fa=Articles.san&s=94582&Nid=49281&p=407, accessed November 11, 2008.

60. Robert Merton, *Social Theory and Social Structure* (Glencoe, IL: Free Press, 1957).

61. Center for Media Research, "Inconspicuous, But Influential" (December 26, 2008), www.mediapost.com, accessed December 26, 2008; Charles W. King and John O. Summers, "Overlap of Opinion Leadership Across Consumer Product Categories," *Journal of Marketing Research* 7 (February 1970): 43–50; see also Ronald E. Goldsmith, Jeanne R. Heitmeyer, and Jon B. Freiden, "Social Values and Fashion Leadership," *Clothing & Textiles Research Journal* 10 (Fall 1991): 37–45; John O. Summers, "Identity of Women's Clothing Fashion Opinion Leaders," *Journal of Marketing Research* 7 (1970): 178–185.

62. Duncan J. Watts and Peter Sheridan Dodds, "Influentials, Networks, and Public Opinion Formation," *Journal of Consumer Research* 34 (December 2007): 441–458.

63. Tanya Irwin, "Study: Facebook Users Show 'Herding Instinct,'" *Marketing Daily* (October 12, 2010), http://www.mediapost.com/publications/?fa=Articles.showArticle&art_aid=137340&nid=119587, accessed April 29, 2011.

64. Cass R. Sunstein and Reid Hastie, "Making Dumb Groups Smarter," *Harvard Business Review* (December 2014), https://hbr.org/2014/12/making-dumb-groups-smarter, accessed April 11, 2015; Matthew J. Salganik, Peter Sheridan Dodds and Duncan J. Watts, "Experimental Study of Inequality and Unpredictability in an Artificial Cultural Market," *Science* 311 (February 10, 2006): 854–856, http://www.princeton.edu/~mjs3/salganik_dodds_watts06_full.pdf, accessed April 11, 2015; Matthew J. Salganik and Duncan J. Watts, "Leading the Herd Astray: An Experimental Study of Self-fulfilling Prophecies in an Artificial Cultural Market," *Social Psychology Quarterly* 71, no. 4 (2008): 338–355, http://www.princeton.edu/~mjs3/salganik_watts08.pdf, accessed April 11, 2015.

65. Steven A. Baumgarten, "The Innovative Communicator in the Diffusion Process," *Journal of Marketing Research* 12 (February 1975): 12–18.

66. Laura J. Yale and Mary C. Gilly, "Dyadic Perceptions in Personal Source Information Search," *Journal of Business Research* 32 (1995): 225–237.

67. Russell W. Belk, "Occurrence of Word-of-Mouth Buyer Behavior as a Function of Situation and Advertising Stimuli," in Fred C. Allvine, ed., *Combined Proceedings of the American Marketing Association*, series no. 33 (Chicago: American Marketing Association, 1971): 419–422.

68. Stephanie Clifford, "Spreading the Word (and the Lotion) in Small-Town Alaska," *New York Times* (October 8, 2008), www.nytimes.com/2008/10/08/business/media/09adco.html, accessed October 9, 2008.

69. Michael R. Solomon, "The Missing Link: Surrogate Consumers in the Marketing Chain," *Journal of Marketing* 50 (October 1986): 208–218.

70. Patricia Odell, "Pepsi Uses 'Influencers' to Launch a New Product," *PROMO* (June 18, 2009), www.promomagazine.com, accessed June 18, 2009.

71. William R. Darden and Fred D. Reynolds, "Predicting Opinion Leadership for Men's Apparel Fashions," *Journal of Marketing Research* 1 (August 1972): 324–328. A modified version of the opinion leadership scale with improved reliability and validity appears in Terry L. Childers, "Assessment of the Psychometric Properties of an Opinion Leadership Scale," *Journal of Marketing Research* 23 (May 1986): 184–188.

72. Dan Seligman, "Me and Monica," *Forbes* (March 23, 1998): 76.

73. http://www.thekevinbacongame.com/, accessed April 11, 2015.

74. Peter H. Reingen and Jerome B. Kernan, "Analysis of Referral Networks in Marketing: Methods and Illustration," *Journal of Marketing Research* 23 (November 1986): 370–378.

75. Peter H. Reingen, Brian L. Foster, Jacqueline Johnson Brown, and Stephen B. Seidman, "Brand Congruence in Interpersonal Relations: A Social Network Analysis," *Journal of Consumer Research* 11 (December 1984): 771–783; see also James C. Ward and Peter H. Reingen, "Sociocognitive Analysis of Group Decision-Making Among Consumers," *Journal of Consumer Research* 17 (December 1990): 245–262.

76. Some material in this section is adapted from Tracy Tuten and Michael R. Solomon, *Social Media Marketing* 2nd ed. (London: SAGE, 2015).

77. Jenna Wortham, "Feel Like a Wallflower? Maybe It's Your Facebook Wall," *New York Times* (April 9, 2011), http://www.nytimes.com/2011/04/10/business/10ping.html?_r=0, accessed March 19, 2013; Lizzie Crocker, "Are Twentysomethings Too Afraid of Missing Out?" *The Daily Beast* (November 9, 2012), http://www.thedailybeast.com/articles/2012/11/09/are-twenty-somethings-too-afraid-of-missing-out.html, accessed March 19, 2013.

78. Nick Bilton, "Twitter Users Congregate Based on Mood, Study Says," *New York Times* (March 16, 2011), http://bits.blogs.nytimes.com/2011/03/16/twitter-users-congregate-based-on-mood-study-says/, accessed April 29, 2011.

79. Alexandra Marin and Barry Wellman, "Social Network Analysis: An Introduction," in *Handbook of Social Network Analysis* (London: Sage, 2010). Chapter 2, 11-25.

80. "Facebook Users Have Four Degrees of Separation from Each Other!" *IBN Live*, November 23, 2011, http://ibnlive.in.com/news/facebook-its-now-4-degrees-of-separation/205084-11.html, accessed February 23, 2015.

81. Steve Lohr, "Researchers Draw Romantic Insights from Maps of Facebook Networks," *New York Times* (October 28, 2013), http://bits.blogs.nytimes.com/2013/10/28/spotting-romantic-relationships-on-facebook/, accessed April 11, 2015.

82. Drew Elliott, "Opportunities for Brands in Social Games," *Ogilvy PR Blog* (May 2010), http://blog.ogilvypr.com/2010/05/opportunities-for-brands-in-social-games/, accessed July 12, 2010.

83. Thomas Apperley, "Genre and Game Studies: Toward a Critical Approach to Video Game Genres," *Simulation & Gaming* 37, no. 1 (2006): 6–23.

84. Interactive Advertising Bureau, *IAB Game Advertising Platform Status Report*, http://www.iab.net/media/file/games-reportv4.pdf, accessed May 31, 2011.

85. Apperley, "Genre and Game Studies: Toward a Critical Approach to Video Game Genres."

86. Mike Snider, "Virtual Goods Spending Topped $2 Billion in U.S. in 2011," *Game Hunters* (February 29, 2012), http://content.usatoday.com/communities/gamehunters/post/2012/02/virtual-goods-spending-topped-2-billion-in-us-in-2011/1, accessed March 19, 2013; Janice Denegri-Knot and Mike Molesworth, "Concepts and Practices of Digital Virtual Consumption," *Consumption Markets & Culture* 13, no. 2 (2010): 109–132; Natalie T. Wood and Michael R. Solomon, "Adonis or Atrocious: Spokesavatars and Source Effects in Immersive Digital Environments," in Matthew S. Eastin, Terry Daugherty, and Neal M. Burns, eds., *Handbook of Research on Digital Media and Advertising: User Generated Content Consumption* (Hershey, PA: IGI Global, 2011): 521–534.

87. Michael Waltzer, "Petite Lap Giraffe: A Tiny Viral Marketing Success," *Brandchannel* (April 5, 2011), http://www.brandchannel.com/home/post/2011/04/05/Petite-Lap-Giraffe.aspx, accessed June 15, 2011.

88. Quoted in Edward F. McQuarrie, Jessica Miller and Barbara J. Phillips, "The Megaphone Effect: Taste and Audience in Fashion Blogging," *Journal of Consumer Research* 40, no. 1 (2013): 136–158.

89. Jonah Berger, "Word of Mouth and Interpersonal Communication: A Review and Directions for Future Research," *Journal of Consumer Psychology* 24, no. 4 (2014): 586–607; Eva Buechel, Jonah Berger "Facebook Therapy: Why People Share Self-Relevant Content Online," presented at the 2012 Association for Consumer Research conference, Vancouver: BC.

90. Jonah Berger and Raghuram Iyengar, "Communication Channels and Word Of Mouth: How the Medium Shapes the Message," *Journal of Consumer Research* 40, no. 3 (2013): 567–579; cf. also Andreas B. Eisingerich, HaeEun Helen Chun, Yeyi Liu, He Jia, and Simon J. Bell, "Why Recommend a Brand Face-to-face but not on Facebook? How Word-of-mouth on Online Social Sites Differs From Traditional Word-of-mouth," *Journal of Consumer Psychology* 25, no. 1 (2015): 120–128.

91. John Tierney, "Good News Beats Bad on Social Networks," *New York Times* (March 18, 2013), http://www.nytimes.com/2013/03/19/science/good-news-spreads-faster-on-twitter-and-facebook.html, accessed March 19, 2013.

92. Tejvir Sekhon, Barbara Bickart, Remi Trudel, and Susan Fournier, "Being a Likable Braggart: How Consumers Use Brand Mentions for Self-presentation on Social Media," in *Consumer Psychology in a Social Media World* (London, Routledge 2016); cf. also Yinlong Zhang, Lawrence Feick and Vikas Mittal, "How Males and Females Differ in Their Likelihood of Transmitting Negative Word of Mouth," *Journal of Consumer Research* 40, no. 6 (2014): 1097–1108.

93. Ryan Hamilton, Kathleen D. Vohs, and Ann L. McGill, "We'll Be Honest, This Won't Be the Best Article You'll Ever Read: The Use of Dispreferred Markers in Word-of-Mouth Communication," *Journal of Consumer Research* 41, no. 1 (June 2014): 197–212.

94. Quoted in Brian Anthony Hernandez, "Dating Site Finds You a Mate Based on Your Klout Score," *Mashable* (April 6, 2012), http://mashable.com/2012/04/16/tawkify-klout-scores-dating/?utm_medium=email&utm_source=newsletter, accessed April 15, 2015. http://klout.com/home, accessed April 11, 2015; Samantha Murphy Kelly, "Klout for Business Aims to Help Brands Reach Social Influencers," *Mashable* (March 30, 2013), http://mashable.com/2013/03/20/klout-for-business/?utm_medium=email&utm_source=feedburner&utm_campaign=Feed%3A+Mashable+%28Mashable%29, accessed February 22, 2015; Brian Anthony Hernandez, "Dating Site Finds You a Mate Based on Your Klout Score," *Mashable* (April 16, 2012), http://mashable.com/people/brian-anthony-hernandez/, accessed February 22, 2015.

95. Ed Keller and Jon Berry. *The Influentials* (New York: Simon & Schuster, 2003).

96. "Introducing Peer Influence Analysis: 500 Billion Peer Impressions Each Year," *Empowered*, (April 20, 2010), http://forrester.typepad.com/groundswell/2010/04/introducing-peer-influence-analysis.html, accessed December 31, 2010.

97. Gina Kolata, "Find Yourself Packing It On? Blame Friends," *New York Times* (July 26, 2007), www.nytimes.com, accessed July 26, 2007.

98. Rio 2016, "Sponsors," http://www.rio2016.com/en/more-information/partners.

99. "McCann Worldgroup Goes into Social Central Mode," *Marketing*, August 16, 2012, http://www.marketingmagazine.com.my/breaking-news-2012/mccann-worldgroup-goes-into-social-central-mode.

100. Matthew Chapman, "Dispatches Investigation into Social Media Malpractice Requires 'Immediate Action'," *Marketing*, August 06, 2013, http://www.marketingmagazine.co.uk/article/1194216/dispatches-investigation-social-media-malpractice-requires-immediate-action.

101. Thomas E. Weber, "Viral Marketing: Web's Newest Ploy May Make You an Unpopular Friend," *Wall Street Journal* (September 13, 1999), www.wsj.com, accessed September 13, 1999.

102. Marius K. Luedicke, "Brand Community Under Fire: The Role of Social Environments for the Hummer Brand Community," *Advances in Consumer Research* 33, no. 1 (2006): 486–493.

103. Carl Straumsheim, "Intersession Solitude," *Inside Higher Ed* (January 15, 2015), https://www.insidehighered.com/news/2015/01/15/saint-marys-college-calif-students-disconnect-power-and-unplug-interim-term-course, accessed February 26, 2015.

104. Quoted in Suzanne Vranica, "Ad Houses Will Need to Be More Nimble, Clients Are Demanding More and Better Use of Consumer Data, Web," *Wall Street Journal* (January 2, 2008): B3.

Chapter 12 • Income and Social Class

Chapter Objectives

When you finish reading this chapter you will understand why:

12-1 Our confidence in our future, as well as in the overall economy, determines how freely we spend and the types of products we buy.

12-2 We group consumers into social classes that say a lot about where they stand in society.

12-3 Individuals' desires to make a statement about their social class, or the class to which they hope to belong, influence the products they like and dislike.

Source: Sakala/Shutterstock.

Finally, the big day has come! Phil is going home with Marilyn to meet her parents. He was doing some contracting work at the securities firm where Marilyn works, and it was love at first sight. Even though Phil attended the "School of Hard Knocks" on the streets of Brooklyn and Marilyn was fresh out of Princeton, somehow they knew they could work things out despite their vastly different backgrounds. Marilyn hinted that her family has money, but Phil doesn't feel intimidated. After all, he knows plenty of guys from his old neighborhood who wheeled-and-dealed their way into six figures. He certainly can handle one more big shot in a silk suit who flashes a roll of bills and who shows off his expensive modern furniture with mirrors and gadgets everywhere you look.

When they arrive at the family estate in Connecticut, Phil looks for a blinged-out Escalade parked in the circular driveway, but he only sees a beat-up Jeep Cherokee, which must belong to one of the servants. Once inside, Phil is surprised by how simply the house is decorated and by how shabby everything seems. A faded Oriental rug covers the hall entryway and all of the furniture looks really old.

Phil is even more surprised when he meets Marilyn's father. He had half-expected Mr. Caldwell to be wearing a tuxedo and holding a large brandy snifter like the rich people he's seen in the movies. In fact, Phil has put on his best shiny Italian suit in anticipation, and he wore his large cubic zirconium pinky ring so this guy would know that he has some money, too. When Marilyn's father emerges from his study wearing an old rumpled cardigan sweater and tennis sneakers, Phil realizes he's definitely not one of those guys from the old neighborhood.

OBJECTIVE 12-1
Our confidence in our future, as well as in the overall economy, determines how freely we spend and the types of products we buy.

Income and Consumer Identity

As Phil's eye-opening experience at the Caldwells' house suggests, there are many ways to spend money, and there's also a wide gulf between those who have it and those who don't. Perhaps an equally wide gap exists between those who have had it for a long time and those who "made it the hard way—by earning it!" As this chapter begins, we briefly consider how general economic conditions affect the way we allocate our money. Then, to reflect the adage that says, "The rich are different," we'll explore how people who occupy different positions in society consume in very different ways.

To Spend or Not to Spend, That Is the Question

Consumer demand for goods and services depends on both our ability and our willingness to buy. Although demand for necessities tends to be stable over time, we postpone or eliminate other expenditures if we don't feel that now is a good time to spend money.[1] For example, you may decide to "make do" with your current clunker for another year rather than buy a new car right away. Even businesses like warehouse clubs that sell staples by the case feel the pain when shoppers postpone their purchases; stores such as Costco and Sam's Club post big losses when people no longer buy their discounted jewelry and clothing, even though sales of paper towels and pickles hold steady.[2]

Discretionary income is the money available to a household over and above what it requires to have a comfortable standard of living. How much money do people need to be "comfortable?" One study that analyzed survey data from more than 450,000 respondents concluded that the magic number is an annual income of $75,000. Emotional well-being steadily rises as people get to this level, but it does not significantly increase after that.[3]

Economists estimate that U.S. consumers wield about $400 billion a year in discretionary spending power. People aged 35 to 55, whose incomes are at a peak, account for about half of this amount. As the population ages and income levels rise, the way a typical U.S. household spends its money changes. The most noticeable shift is to allocate a much larger share of a budget to shelter and transportation and less to food and apparel. (Note: This doesn't mean that higher-income households buy less food and clothing; it's just that the *proportion* of dollars they spend on these categories decreases.)

Especially in the wake of the Great Recession of 2009, many consumers experience doubts about their individual and collective futures, and they are anxious to hold on to what they have. Of course, not everyone has the same attitudes about money and its importance. We all know *tightwads* who hate to part with even a penny (and who actually experience emotional pain when they hand over their cash) and *spendthrifts* who enjoy nothing more than buying everything in sight. Research on this issue finds that (stereotypes aside) U.S. tightwads outnumber spendthrifts. Men are more likely than women to be tightwads, as are older people and those with more education. How do we tell a tightwad from someone who's just being frugal? One of the researchers puts it this way: "The evidence suggests that frugality is driven by a pleasure of saving, as compared with tightwaddism, which is driven by a pain of paying."[4]

Money has complex psychological meanings; we equate it with success or failure, social acceptability, security, love, freedom, and yes, even sex appeal.[5] There are therapists who specialize in treating money-related disorders, and they report that some people even feel guilty about their success and deliberately make bad investments to reduce this feeling! Some other clinical conditions include *atephobia* (fear of being ruined), *harpaxophobia* (fear of becoming a victim of robbers), *peniaphobia* (fear of poverty), and *aurophobia* (fear of gold).[6]

A study explored some interesting links between our need for acceptance and feelings about cash. In one case, participants were either led to believe that a group had rejected them or that it had accepted them. They then completed measures that reflected their desire for money. Those whom the group rejected scored higher on these measures. At another stage, subjects counted either real money or pieces of paper and then experienced physical pain. Those who counted money reported they felt less pain than did those who just counted paper![7]

Consumer Confidence

Our expectations about the future affect our current spending, and these individual decisions add up to affect a society's economic well-being.[8] Consumers' beliefs about what the future holds are an indicator of **consumer confidence**. This measure reflects how optimistic or pessimistic people are about the future health of the economy and how they predict they'll fare down the road. These beliefs are important because they influence how much money people pump into the economy when they make discretionary purchases.

Many businesses take forecasts about anticipated spending seriously, and periodic surveys "take the pulse" of the U.S. consumer. The Conference Board conducts a survey of consumer confidence, as does the Survey Research Center at the University of Michigan. The following are the types of questions they pose to consumers:[9]

- Would you say that you and your family are better off or worse off financially than a year ago?
- Will you be better off or worse off a year from now?
- Is now a good time or a bad time for people to buy major household items, such as furniture or a refrigerator?
- Do you plan to buy a car in the next year?

When people are somewhat pessimistic about their prospects and about the state of the economy, as they are now, they tend to cut back on what they spend and take on less debt. When consumers feel optimistic about the future, they reduce the amount they save, they take on more debt, and they splurge on discretionary items. A range of factors influence the overall **savings rate** including individual consumers' pessimism or optimism about their personal circumstances, such as a sudden increase in personal wealth as the result of an inheritance and global events such as the Great Recession.

Income Inequality and Social Mobility

Take a moment to think about this: The 80 richest people in the world are worth $1.9 trillion. This is about the same amount shared by the 3.5 billion people who are in the bottom half of the world's income. And, the most affluent one percent of people worldwide control more than half the globe's total wealth.[10] In the last few years the label **One Percenter** entered our nation's vocabulary. Beginning with the Occupy Wall Street movement where we saw protestors camping out in cities across the United States, the spotlight has been on the people who earn the top 1 percent of income in our country. The wealthiest 160,000 U.S. families have as much wealth as the poorest 145 million families.[11]

Today one of the biggest issues we hear about is **income inequality**, that is, the extent to which resources are distributed unevenly within a population. One consequence of rising inequality is that more consumers worry about "falling behind" if a breadwinner loses his or her job or if the family can no longer afford the cost of housing, transportation, and other necessities. For example, a researcher who conducted an in-depth study of residents of a rural trailer park identified one segment of consumers she called the *Reluctant Emigrants*. These people once lived in fixed-site homes but various economic problems forced them to move to the more affordable trailer park. Because their lives are on a downward trajectory, their primary concerns focus on security and protection.[12]

Citigroup strategists coined the term **plutonomy** to describe an economy that's driven by a fairly small number of rich people.[13] This term seems increasingly appropriate to describe the United States because the share of households that are in the middle-income bracket (earning $35,000 to $100,000 per year) steadily shrinks.[14] One indicator of income inequality is the **CEO pay ratio**, which compares the salary of a company's

Income inequality is emerging as one of the most important issues for many people in the U.S.A.
Source: Kevork Djansezian/Getty Images.

chief executive to the earnings of a typical employee. That number grew from 20 in 1965 to 295.9 in 2013.[15] This gap is larger than most other countries. Recent reports indicate that the United States has the largest income inequality among developed countries. The only countries with a bigger disparity are Chile, Mexico, and Turkey.[16]

Social mobility refers to the "passage of individuals from one social class to another."[17] *Horizontal mobility* occurs when a person moves from one position to another that's roughly equivalent in social status; for instance, a nurse becomes an elementary school teacher. *Downward mobility* is, of course, movement none of us wants, but unfortunately we observe this pattern fairly often, as farmers and other displaced workers go on welfare rolls or join the ranks of the homeless. By one estimate, between 2.3 million and 3.5 million Americans experience homelessness in a year's time.[18]

Despite that discouraging trend, demographics decree that overall there must be *upward mobility* in our society. The middle and upper classes reproduce less (i.e., have fewer children per family) than the lower classes (an effect demographers call *differential fertility*), and they tend to restrict family size to below replacement level (i.e., they often have only one child). Therefore, so the reasoning goes, over time those of lower status must fill positions of higher status.[19]

Despite the well-deserved reputation of the United States as the "land of opportunity," social mobility today is a harder climb in the United States than in many other developed economies such as Canada, Denmark, Australia, Norway, Finland, Sweden, Germany, and Spain. One widely cited report, for example, found that the economic advantage of having an affluent father is much more likely to influence the fortune of his son in the United States than in most other Western countries.[20] Another analysis found that the likelihood of staying in the *same* social class as your parents is 0.47 in the United States, compared to only 0.15 in Denmark.[21]

Within the United States, we see the most social mobility in the Northeast, Great Plains, and West, whereas the odds of moving up are much lower in the Southeast and Midwest. One apparent factor for this difference is that, all things equal, there is more upward mobility in metropolitan areas where poor families live alongside relatively more well-off people rather than being segregated into low-income neighborhoods. Mobility also is more robust in areas with a greater number of two-parent households, better schools, and more civic engagement such as memberships in religious and community groups.[22]

Marketing Pitfall

A person's **credit score**, that is based on his or her outstanding debt and payment histories, used to be an obscure figure that credit card and mortgage companies consulted to decide if he or she qualified for a loan. Today that score has become a badge that many use to "keep score" of a person's worth. Some companies consider this magic score when they make hiring decisions, and increasingly individuals even use it to identify suitable dating partners. As one financial advisor put it, "Credit scores are like the dating equivalent of a sexually transmitted disease test. It's a shorthand way to get a sense of someone's financial past the same way an S.T.D. test gives some information about a person's sexual past." Another executive stated, "It's the only grade that matters after you graduate." Several dating sites including Creditscoredating.com and Datemycreditscore.com use this measure to screen potential suitors for members.[23]

In our society, wealth is still more likely to be earned than inherited although this pattern seems to be shifting.

Source: From 2000 advertising campaign. Courtesy of The Phoenix Companies, Inc.

The Great Recession and Materialism

The Great Recession officially lasted from December 2007 to June 2009. During this period we witnessed the largest drop in employment since the Great Depression. Even today, we feel the aftershocks of this economic upheaval.[24] The loss of wealth prompted drastic changes in consumer spending that almost overnight altered the landscape of consumer behavior. The "go-go" years seem like a distant memory as many people suddenly put the brakes on their BUY NOW mentality. The new mantra: Make do with what you have. Save. Question every expense: Do you really need that Starbucks latte, that $80 haircut, that fashion magazine? Thriftiness is in, eye-popping bling is out.

Some online dating sites use credit scores to screen potential suitors.

Source: Creditscoredating.com.

Even many *fashionistas* turned into **frugalistas**—they refuse to sacrifice style, but they achieve it on a budget. Now it's cool to visit Web sites and blogs that celebrate frugality, such as Dollar Stretcher (stretcher.com), All Things Frugal (allthingsfrugal.com), and Frugal Mom (frugalmom.net).[25] Today our economy is steadily recovering as income continues to rise each year. However, as of 2014 median income still is about 3 percent lower than it was before the troubles began.[26] Only time will tell if frugality becomes "the new normal."

In Chapter 2 we talked about *materialism*; the value people place on their possessions. As a by-product of the Great Recession, many consumers have been forced to reconsider the value of their possessions. One woman observed, "The idea that you need to go bigger to be happy is false. I really believe that the acquisition of material goods doesn't bring about happiness." This doesn't necessarily mean that people will stop buying—but perhaps, at least for a while, they will do so more carefully.

Another factor is just how much of a "buzz" we get from the stuff we buy. The research evidence points to the idea that consumers get more "bang for their buck" when they buy a bunch of smaller things over time, rather than blowing it all on one big purchase. This is as a result of what psychologists call **hedonic adaptation**; it basically means that to maintain a fairly stable level of happiness, we tend to become used to changes, big or small, wonderful or terrible. That means that over time the rush from a major purchase will dissipate and we're back to where we started (emotionally speaking). So, the next time you get a bonus or find an envelope stuffed with cash on the street, take a series of long weekends instead of splurging on that 3-week trip to Maui.[28]

Income-Based Marketing

A popular saying goes, "You can never be too thin or too rich." As we recover from the Great Recession, the average American's standard of living continues to improve—though many consumers still don't get a full ticket to the American Dream. About 45 million people live in poverty, including roughly 20 percent of children younger than age 18. Two factors contribute to an (overall) upward income trajectory: a shift in women's roles and increases in educational attainment:[29]

1 Mothers with preschool children are the fastest-growing segment of working people. Furthermore, many of them work in high-paying occupations, such as medicine and architecture, which men used to dominate. Although women are still a minority

Micro-sized apartments are popping up in big cities as an affordable option for people who want to live on their own.
Source: Courtesy of Panoramic Interests.

in most professional occupations, their ranks continue to swell. Unfortunately, the **female-to-male earnings ratio** is 0.78, which means that on average a woman earns 78 cents for every dollar a man brings home. The good news is that working wives account for almost half of household earnings today.

2 Although picking up the tab for college often entails great sacrifice, it still pays off in the long run. The **college wage premium**, which describes the gap between what workers with a college degree earn compared with those without one, has grown dramatically. Compared to a premium of about 40 percent in the late 1970s, today degree holders earn 80 percent more. The Federal Reserve Board estimates that during a lifetime on average a person with a degree will earn $830,000 more than someone with just a high school diploma.[30] So, hang in there!

Targeting the Top of the Pyramid: High-Income Consumers

Many marketers try to target affluent, upscale markets. This often makes sense, because these consumers obviously have the resources to spend on costly products that command higher profit margins. However, it is a mistake to assume that we should place everyone with a high income into the same market segment. As we noted previously, social class involves more than absolute income. It is also a way of life, and several factors—including where they got their money, how they got it, and how long they have had it—significantly affect wealthy people's interests and spending priorities.[31]

Despite our stereotype of rich people who just party all day long, one study found that the typical millionaire is a 57-year-old man who is self-employed, earns a median household income of $131,000, has been married to the same wife for most of his adult life, has children, has never spent more than $399 on a suit or more than $140 for a pair of shoes, and drives a Ford Explorer (the humble billionaire investor Warren Buffett comes to mind). Interestingly, many affluent people don't consider themselves to be rich. One tendency researchers notice is that these people indulge in luxury goods while they pinch pennies on everyday items; they buy shoes at Neiman Marcus and deodorant at Walmart, for example.[32]

SRI Consulting Business Intelligence divides consumers into three groups based on their attitudes toward luxury:

1 **Luxury is functional**—These consumers use their money to buy things that will last and have enduring value. They conduct extensive prepurchase research and make logical decisions rather than emotional or impulsive choices.

2 **Luxury is a reward**—These consumers tend to be younger than the first group but older than the third group. They use luxury goods to say, "I've made it." The desire to be successful and to demonstrate their success to others motivates these consumers to purchase conspicuous luxury items, such as high-end automobiles and homes in exclusive communities.

3 **Luxury is indulgence**—This group is the smallest of the three and tends to include younger consumers and slightly more males than the other two groups. To these consumers, the purpose of owning luxury is to be extremely lavish and self-indulgent. This group is willing to pay a premium for goods that express their individuality and make others take notice. They have a more emotional approach to luxury spending and are more likely than the other two groups to make impulse purchases.[33]

People who have had money for a long time tend to use their fortunes a lot differently. *Old money* families (e.g., the Rockefellers, DuPonts, Fords, etc.) live primarily on inherited funds. One commentator called this group "the class in hiding."[34] Following the Great Depression of the 1930s, moneyed families became more discreet about exhibiting their wealth. Many fled from mansions such as those we still find in Manhattan (the renovated Vanderbilt mansion now is Ralph Lauren's flagship store) to hideaways in Virginia, Connecticut, and New Jersey.

Mere wealth is not sufficient to achieve social prominence in these circles. You also need to demonstrate a family history of public service and philanthropy, and tangible markers of these contributions often enable donors to achieve a kind of immortality (e.g., Rockefeller University, Carnegie Hall, or the Whitney Museum).[35] "Old money" consumers distinguish among themselves in terms of ancestry and lineage rather than wealth.[36] Furthermore, they're secure in their status. In a sense, they have trained their whole lives to be rich.

In contrast to people with old money, today there are many people—including high-profile billionaires such as Bill Gates, Mark Zuckerberg, and Sir Richard Branson—who are "the working wealthy."[37] The Horatio Alger myth, where a person goes from "rags to riches" through hard work and a bit of luck, is still a powerful force in our society. That's why a commercial that showed the actual garage where the two cofounders of Hewlett-Packard first worked struck a chord in so many.

Although many people do in fact become "self-made millionaires," they often encounter a problem (although not the worst problem one could think of!) after they have become wealthy and change their social status. The label ***nouveau riche*** describes consumers who recently achieved their wealth and who don't have the benefit of years of training to learn how to spend it.

Pity the poor nouveau riches many suffer from *status anxiety*. They monitor the cultural environment to ensure that they do the "right" thing, wear the "right" clothes, get seen at the "right" places, use the "right" caterer, and so on.[38] Their flamboyant consumption is an example of *symbolic self-completion* (we discussed this in Chapter 6) because they try to display symbols they believe have "class" to make up for an internal lack of assurance about the "correct" way to behave.[39] In major Chinese cities such as Shanghai, some people wear pajamas in public as a way to flaunt their newfound wealth. As one consumer explained, "Only people in cities can afford clothes like this. In farming villages, they still have to wear old work clothes to bed."[40]

Targeting the Bottom of the Pyramid: Low-Income Consumers

Although poor people obviously have less to spend than do rich ones, they have the same basic needs as everyone else. Low-income families purchase staples, such as milk, orange juice, and tea, at the same rates as average-income families. Minimum wage–level households spend more than average on out-of-pocket healthcare costs, rent, and the food they eat at home.[41]

And, of course, the market size is huge: Although there are 6.6 billion consumers in the world, only 1.5 billion of them possess enough purchasing power to buy $10,000 worth of products for themselves and their families. The other 5.1 billion people— 78 percent of the global population—are low-income consumers.[42] Analysts refer to this vast number of consumers as the **bottom of the pyramid**. Figure 12.1 provides one framework to help marketers make needed changes to provide for the needs of low-income consumers around the world.

The 4 A's of addressing low-income consumers

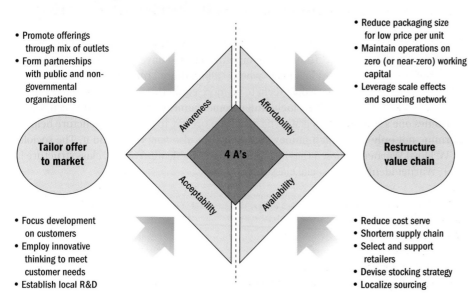

- Promote offerings through mix of outlets
- Form partnerships with public and non-governmental organizations

Tailor offer to market

- Focus development on customers
- Employ innovative thinking to meet customer needs
- Establish local R&D

Awareness
Affordability
4 A's
Acceptability
Availability

- Reduce packaging size for low price per unit
- Maintain operations on zero (or near-zero) working capital
- Leverage scale effects and sourcing network

Restructure value chain

- Reduce cost serve
- Shorten supply chain
- Select and support retailers
- Devise stocking strategy
- Localize sourcing

Figure 12.1 THE 4 A's
Source: Anderson and Niels Billou, "Serving the World's Poor: Innovation at the Base of the Economic Pyramid," *Journal of Business Strategy*, 28, 2: 14–21, reprinted in A. T. Kearney, *Serving the Low-Income Consumer: How to Tackle This Mostly Ignored Market*, 2011, http://www.atkearney .com/index.php/Publications/serving-the-low-income-consumer.html

The Digital Divide between the rich and the poor is still a reality.
Source: Deshakalyan Chowdhury/AFP/ Getty Images.

The Tangled Web

Because so much of what happens in the world today happens online, people who don't have access to the Internet can be at a real disadvantage. The so-called **Digital Divide** between the rich and the poor is still a reality. According to a study by the Pew Research Center, 87 percent of U.S. households making more than $75,000 have broadband access at home. In contrast, only 40 percent of U.S. households making less than $30,000 have access. Whereas 95 percent of high-income households use the Internet at home in some fashion, just 57 percent of the poorest do. Not surprisingly, affluent people are also much more likely to own cell phones, computers, e-readers, and other entertainment devices.[44]

To compound the problem, it seems that when poorer children do use technology, they don't use it as constructively. Data show that these kids spend much more time than do children from affluent families to use their gadgets to watch videos, play games, and connect on social networking sites, rather than for educational purposes. One reason for this gap is that low-income parents are more likely to use these media as an "electronic babysitter" when they go off to work. According to one study, children of parents who do not have a college degree spent 90 minutes more per day with media compared to more affluent families.[45]

Some multinational companies have woken up to the potential of this huge market. They focus on engineering innovations that allow them to produce inexpensive products that still function as people need them to:[43]

- The Nokia 105 is a tiny mobile phone that costs about $20.00. It includes a dust-proof keyboard, flashlight, alarm clock, and FM radio. The phone's battery charge lasts 35 days on standby.
- General Electric (GE) designed the Lullaby baby warmer with feedback from Indian doctors and nurses who advised on practical changes to turn a high-end product into one that many parents can access. The company replaced an expensive hand crank that lifts the baby's head with a simple plastic triangle that fits under the mattress. The mattress is covered in a tough plastic that resists tears, and GE developed an inexpensive LED device to replace the fluorescent bulbs other warmers use to create heat.
- A startup company called d.light sells portable solar lighting units in 62 countries to people who don't have steady access to electricity.

OBJECTIVE 12-2
We group consumers into social classes that say a lot about where they stand in society.

Social Class and Consumer Identity

Members of every society divide into the "haves" and the "have-nots" (though the amount people "have" is relative). The United States is a place where "all men are created equal," but even so some people seem to be more equal than others. A complex set of variables, including income, family background, and occupation, determines one's standing in society. The place you occupy in the social structure helps to determine not only how much money you spend but also *how* you spend it. The sociologist W. Lloyd Warner proposed the most influential classification of U.S. class structure in 1941. Warner identified six social classes:[46]

1 Upper Upper
2 Lower Upper
3 Upper Middle
4 Lower Middle
5 Upper Lower
6 Lower Lower

Other social scientists have proposed variations on this system over the years, but Warner's six levels summarize fairly well the way we still think about class, even though the proportion of consumers who fall into each category fluctuates over time.

Pick a Pecking Order

In many animal species, a social organization develops whereby the most assertive or aggressive animals exert control over the others and have the first pick of food, living space, and even mating partners. Chickens, for example, exhibit a clearly defined **dominance–submission hierarchy**. Within this hierarchy, each hen has a position in which she is submissive to all the hens above her and she dominates all the ones below her (hence the origin of the term *pecking order*).[47]

People are not much different. We also develop a pecking order that ranks us in terms of our relative standing in society. This rank determines our access to such resources as education, housing, and consumer goods. People try to move up in the social order to improve their ranking. This desire to improve one's lot in life, and often to let others know that one has done so, is at the core of many marketing strategies.

Just as marketers carve society into groups for segmentation purposes, sociologists describe divisions of society in terms of people's relative social and economic resources. Some of these divisions involve political power, whereas others revolve around purely economic distinctions. Karl Marx, the 19th-century economic theorist, argued that a person's relationship to the *means of production* determined his position in a society. The haves control resources, and they use the labor of others to preserve their privileged positions. The have-nots depend on their own labor for survival, so these people have the most to gain if they change the system. The German sociologist Max Weber showed that the rankings people develop are not one-dimensional. Some involve prestige or "social honor" (he called these *status groups*), some rankings focus on power (or *party*), and some revolve around wealth and property (*class*).[48]

We use the term **social class** more generally to describe the overall rank of people in a society. People who belong to the same social class have approximately equal social standing in the community. They work in roughly similar occupations, and they tend to have similar lifestyles by virtue of their income levels and common tastes. These people tend to socialize with one another and share many ideas and values regarding the way life should be lived.[49]

Indeed, "birds of a feather do flock together." We tend to marry people in a social class similar to our own, a tendency sociologists call **homogamy** or *assortative mating*. Well more than 90 percent of married high school dropouts marry someone who also dropped out or who has only a high school diploma. On the other side of the spectrum, less than 1 percent of the most highly educated Americans have a spouse who did not complete high school.[50]

Social class is as much a state of being as it is of having: It's also a matter of what you do with your money and how you define your role in society. Although we may not like the idea that some members of society are better off or "different" from others, most consumers do acknowledge the existence of different classes and the effect of class membership on consumption. As one wealthy woman observed when researchers asked her to define social class:

> I would suppose social class means where you went to school and how far. Your intelligence. Where you live . . . [w]here you send your children to school. The hobbies you have. Skiing, for example, is higher than the snowmobile . . . . It can't be [just] money, because nobody ever knows that about you for sure.[51]

In school, some kids seem to get all the breaks. They have access to many resources, such as special privileges, fancy cars, large allowances, or dates with other popular classmates. At work, some coworkers get promoted to high-prestige jobs with higher salaries and perks such as a parking space, a large office, or the keys to the executive washroom.

Social Stratification

Indeed, in virtually every context some people rank higher than others—even if they just have a larger number of Twitter followers. Patterns of social arrangements evolve whereby some members get more resources than others by virtue of their relative standing, power, or control in the group.[52] The process of **social stratification** refers to this creation of artificial divisions, "those processes in a social system by which scarce and valuable resources are distributed unequally to status positions that become more or less permanently ranked in terms of the share of valuable resources each receives."[53]

Whether rewards go to the "best and the brightest" or to someone who happens to be related to the boss, allocations are rarely equal within a social group. Most groups exhibit a structure, or **status hierarchy** in which some members are better off than others. They may have more authority or power, or other members simply like or respect them.

In a system in which (like it or not) we define people to a great extent by what they do for a living, **occupational prestige** is one way we evaluate their "worth." Hierarchies of occupational prestige tend to be quite stable over time and across cultures. Researchers find similarities in occupational prestige in countries as diverse as Brazil, Ghana, Guam, Japan, and Turkey.[54]

A typical ranking includes a variety of professional and business occupations at the top (e.g., CEO of a large corporation, physician, and college professor); whereas jobs that hover near the bottom include shoe shiner, ditch digger, and garbage collector. Because a person's occupation links strongly to his or her use of leisure time, allocation of family resources, aesthetic preferences, and political orientation, many social scientists consider it the single best indicator of social class.

A **worldview** is another way to differentiate among social classes. To generalize, the world of the working class (i.e., the lower-middle class) is more intimate and constricted. For example, working-class men are likely to name local sports figures as heroes and are less likely to take long vacation trips to out-of-the-way places.[55] Immediate needs, such as a new refrigerator or TV, tend to dictate buying behavior, whereas the higher classes focus on more long-term goals, such as saving for college tuition or retirement.[56] Working-class consumers depend heavily on relatives for emotional support and tend to orient themselves in terms of the local community rather than the world at large. They are more likely to be conservative and family oriented. Maintaining the appearance of one's home and property is a priority, regardless of the size of the house.

One study that looked at social class and how it relates to consumers' feelings of *empowerment* reported that lower-class men aren't as likely to feel they have the power to affect their outcomes. Respondents varied from those who were what the researcher

Occupational prestige plays an important role in defining a status hierarchy.
Source: wavebreakmedia/Shutterstock.

calls *potent actors* (those who believe they have the ability to take actions that affect their world) to *impotent reactors* (those who feel they are at the mercy of their economic situations). This orientation influenced consumption behaviors; for example, the professionals in the study who were likely to be potent actors set themselves up for financial opportunity and growth. They took broad perspectives on investing and planned their budgets strategically.[57]

Although they would like to have more in the way of material goods, working-class people do not necessarily envy those who rank above them in social standing.[58] They may not view the maintenance of a high-status lifestyle as worth the effort. As one blue-collar consumer commented, "Life is very hectic for those people. There are more breakdowns and alcoholism. It must be very hard to sustain the status, the clothes, and the parties that are expected. I don't think I'd want to take their place."[59]

This person may be right. Although good things appear to go hand-in-hand with higher status and wealth, the picture is not that clear. The social scientist Émile Durkheim observed that suicide rates are much higher among the wealthy; he wrote in 1897, "The possessors of most comfort suffer most."[60] Durkheim's wisdom may still be accurate today. Many well-off consumers seem to be stressed or unhappy despite or even because of their wealth, a condition some call **affluenza**.[61]

Cosmopolitanism is an aspect of worldview that is starting to receive more attention by consumer behavior researchers, who define a cosmopolitan as someone who tries to be open to the world and who strives for diverse experiences (not to be confused with the popular cocktail). This is a quality that used to be linked to the wealthy, but now—with improved access to media and of course the Internet—it's no longer necessary to be rich to express an interest in a range of culturally diverse products. Cosmopolitans respond well to brands that have a "worldly" (i.e., international or global) image. They think it's important to own consumer electronics products and are more likely to engage in social media activities.[62] A scale to identify these consumers includes statements like these:

- I enjoy exchanging ideas with people from other cultures or countries.
- I am interested in learning more about people who live in other countries.
- I find people from other cultures stimulating.

Income versus Social Class

Although we equate money with social class, they are by no means synonymous.[63] Additional income does not necessarily propel someone to a higher class. One problem is that even if a family adds one or more wage earners and increases its household income, each additional job is likely to be lower in status than the primary wage earner's job. In addition, these members don't necessarily pool their earnings toward the common good of the family.[64]

So, is social class or income a better predictor of consumer behavior? The answer partly depends on the type of product: Do people buy it largely for its functional value (what it does), or for its symbolic value (the impression it conveys to others)?

- Social class is a better predictor of purchases that have symbolic aspects but low to moderate prices (e.g., cosmetics, liquor).
- Income is a better predictor of major expenditures that do not have status or symbolic aspects (e.g., major appliances).
- We need both social class and income data to predict purchases of expensive, symbolic products (e.g., cars, homes).

How Do We Measure Social Class?

Because social class is a complex concept that depends on a number of factors, it is not surprising that social scientists disagree on the best way to measure it. Early measures included the *Index of Status Characteristics* from the 1940s and the *Index of Social Position*

CB AS I SEE IT

Paul Henry, *University of Sydney, Australia*

How often do you think about class?

Social class is usually something we don't think much about. Have you ever heard of the phrase "birds of a feather flock together?" We tend to hang round with people like ourselves because we feel comfortable with similar people. We live in areas where people are from the same class. We work and socialize with people like us. The people around us share our values and priorities. They share our cultural and social preferences to fashion, food, rules of etiquette, mannerisms, and ways of speaking. All these commonalities become taken-for-granted and normalized ways of being and doing.

Class only comes to the fore when we walk into another neighborhood and are confronted with people who are not like us. The signals are usually subtle; slightly different mannerisms, aesthetic tastes, appearance, and dress sense. Yet our gut reaction is that we are in a place where we don't quite fit in. You can easily test this out by recalling your own reactions to different suburbs you have visited. Imagine the different kind of clientele in the shops, bars, and restaurants. Think about how the people are different to you. What is it that makes you think that this is not a place where you fit in so well?

Class is of course intimately related to income and wealth, but class is more than about money. Think about some these other kinds of social markers that serve to distinguish people as upper or lower class. Take, for example the case of a working-class family that suddenly wins the lottery. Will their tastes and mannerisms change in line with the extra money; or would they still stand out when moving to an upmarket neighbourhood?

The research I've conducted finds subtle differences between classes in how people plan their finances and manage their money. It's partly about money managing skills and partly about outlook. Money planning skills can be partially taught but distinctive outlook is harder to change. Outlook includes things like degree of personal confidence, ambitiousness, belief in future possibilities for growth and comfort with challenge and change. People who are stronger in these forms of outlook set more ambitious financial goals, develop more elaborate plans to achieve them and persist more doggedly their attainment.

On the other hand if you lack personal confidence, set smaller goals and more easily give up, then a self-fulfilment prophesy sets in—more limited financial potential. Another part of the problem for people with poorer financial resources lies in the fact that they are more focused on meeting week-by-week costs. This is obviously stressful, emotionally wearing, and reinforces a short-term focus, where long-term goal setting recedes. Constant financial stress and frustration at lack of progress can leave many people at the bottom of the social scale feeling hopeless, fatalistic, and prone to spending any spare money on things that provide instant gratification: cigarettes, alcohol, fast food, and gambling. This sets up a downward health spiral that adds yet another layer of disadvantage.

from the 1950s.[65] These indices combined individual characteristics (e.g., income, type of housing) to arrive at a label of class standing. The accuracy of these composites is still a subject of debate among researchers; a study claimed that for segmentation purposes, raw education and income measures work as well as composite status measures.[66]

U.S. consumers generally have little difficulty placing themselves in either the working class (lower-middle class) or middle class.[67] Blue-collar workers with relatively high-prestige jobs still tend to view themselves as working class, even though their income levels are equivalent to those of many white-collar workers.[68] This fact reinforces the idea that the labels of "working class" or "middle class" are subjective. Their meanings say at least as much about self-identity as they do about economic well-being.

Marketing researchers were among the first to propose that we can distinguish people of different social classes from one another. However, many of the methods they originally used to place consumers into classes are badly dated and have little validity today.[69] One reason is that social scientists designed most measures of social class with the traditional nuclear family in mind; this unit included a male wage earner in the middle of his career and a female full-time homemaker. These measures have trouble accounting for two-income families, young singles living alone, or households headed by women, which are so prevalent today.

Another problem with measuring social class is the increasing anonymity of our society. Earlier studies relied on the *reputational method*, where researchers conducted extensive interviews within an area to determine the reputations and backgrounds of individuals. When they used information and also traced people's interaction patterns, they could generate a comprehensive view of social standing within a community. However, this approach is virtually impossible to implement in most communities today. One compromise is to interview individuals to obtain demographic data and to combine these data with the interviewer's subjective impressions of each person's possessions and standard of living.

One problem when we assign any group of people to a social class is that they may not exhibit equal standing on all of the relevant dimensions. A person might come from a low-status ethnic group but have a high-status job, whereas another who did not finish high school may live in a fancy part of town. Social scientists use the concept of **status crystallization** to assess the impact of social class inconsistency.[70] The logic is that when these indicators are not consistent, stress occurs, because the rewards from each part of such an "unbalanced" person's life are variable and unpredictable. People who exhibit such inconsistencies tend to be more receptive to social change than are those whose identities are more firmly rooted.

A related problem occurs when a person's social-class standing creates expectations that he or she can't meet. Some people find themselves in the not-unhappy position of making more money than we expect of those in their social class. This means they are *overprivileged*, a condition we define as an income that is at least 25 to 30 percent greater than the median for one's class.[71] In contrast, *underprivileged* consumers, who earn at least 15 percent less than the median, must often allocate a big chunk of their income to maintaining the impression that they occupy a certain status. For example, some people talk about being "house-poor"; they pay so much for a lavish home that they can't afford to furnish it. Today, many homeowners unfortunately find themselves in this position. Although the number of foreclosures on U.S. houses is less than half of what we saw in 2009 and 2010 after the housing bubble burst during the Great Recession, there still were 1.12 million filings in 2014.[72]

We traditionally assume that husbands define a family's social class, whereas wives must live it. Women achieve their social status through their husbands.[73] Indeed, the evidence indicates that physically attractive women do tend to "marry up in social class to a greater extent than attractive men do. Women trade the resource of sexual appeal, which historically has been one of the few assets they were allowed to possess, for the economic resources of men.[74]

We must strongly question the accuracy of this assumption in today's world. Many women now contribute equally to the family's well-being, and they work in positions of comparable or even greater status than their spouses. Employed women tend to average both their own and their husband's positions when they estimate their own subjective status.[75] Nevertheless, a prospective spouse's social class is often an important "product attribute" when someone in the "marriage market" evaluates his or her options.

Social Class Around the World

Every society has some type of hierarchical class structure that determines people's access to products and services. Let's take a quick look at a few important ones.

China

An economic boom is creating a middle class of more than 130 million people that analysts project will grow to more than 400 million in 10 years. During the Cultural Revolution, Mao's Red Guards seized on even the smallest possessions—a pocket watch or silk scarf—as evidence of "bourgeois consciousness." Change came rapidly in the early 1990s, after Mao's successor Deng Xiaoping uttered the phrase that quickly became the credo of the new China: "To get rich is glorious."

Because costs in China are low, a family with an annual income below the U.S. poverty threshold of about $14,000 can enjoy middle-class comforts, including stylish clothes, Chinese-made color televisions, DVD players, and cell phones. Wealthier Chinese entrepreneurs indulge in Cuban Cohiba cigars that sell for $25 each, a quarter of the average Chinese laborer's monthly wage. In bustling Shanghai, newly minted "yuppies" drop their kids off for golf lessons; visit Maserati and Ferrari showrooms; buy some luxury items from Louis Vuitton, Hugo Boss, or Prada; then pick up some Häagen-Dazs ice cream before they head to an Evian spa to unwind.

Nike, which consumers in a survey named China's coolest brand, profits mightily from the rise of the Chinese middle class. Nike shoes are a symbol of success, and the company opens an average of 1.5 new stores a day there. The company worked for a long time to attain this status, starting when it outfitted top Chinese athletes and sponsored all the teams in China's pro basketball league. Still, becoming a fashion icon (and persuading consumers to spend twice the average monthly salary for a pair of shoes) is no mean feat in a country that's not exactly sports crazy. So Nike affiliated with the NBA (which began to televise games in China) and brought over players such as Michael Jordan for visits. Slowly but surely, in-the-know Chinese came to call sneakers "Nai-ke."[76]

Japan

Japan is a highly brand-conscious society where upscale, designer labels are incredibly popular. Although the devastation from the 2011 tsunami reduced demand for luxury goods among many Japanese, their love affair with top brands started in the 1970s when the local economy was booming and many Japanese could buy Western luxury accessories for the first time. Some analysts say Japan's long slump since that time may have fostered a psychological need to splurge on small luxuries to give people the illusion of wealth and to forget their anxieties about the future. Single, working women are largely responsible for fueling Japan's luxury-goods spending; about three-quarters of Japanese women aged 25 to 29 work outside the home. These "office ladies" typically save money because they live with their parents, so this leaves them with cash on hand to spend on clothes, accessories, and vacations.[78]

The Middle East

In contrast to the Japanese, few Arabic women work. This makes a search for the latest in Western luxury brands a major leisure activity for those with money. A major expansion of Western luxury brands is under way across the Middle East, home to some of the fashion industry's best customers. High-end retailers such as Saks Fifth Avenue and Giorgio Armani operate opulent stores that cater to this attractive market. Like China, there also is a growing middle class of more than 150 million people. If the 22 countries in the Arab League were a single country, it would be the world's eighth-largest economy—bigger than India or Russia. It's also a young economy; more than half of the people are younger than 25 years of age.[79]

The United Kingdom

England is an extremely class-conscious country, and at least until recently inherited position and family background largely predetermined consumption patterns. Traditionally people defined three classes: upper, middle, and working. Members of the upper class were educated at schools such as Eton and Oxford, and they spoke like Henry Higgins in *My Fair Lady*. We can still find remnants of this rigid class structure. "Hooray Henrys" (wealthy young men) play polo at Windsor and hereditary peers still dominate the House of Lords.

Marketing Pitfall

The quality of life has improved dramatically for many Chinese in the last few decades, but this sudden prosperity comes with a price tag. Before the country's financial transformation, most people were fairly equal (although poor), and the ratio of males to females was about even as well. Thus, it was not a big deal for matchmakers to arrange suitable matches between men and women; the Chinese called this process *men-dang hudui*, meaning roughly "family doors of equal size." Most people never dated anyone other than their future spouse before they got married.

The economic boom upended this stable structure, so that now there are sharp inequalities of wealth. Roughly 300 million people have moved from rural areas to cities in the last 30 years. As a result the traditional matchmaker solution that paired members from an intimate community no longer is viable. To compound the problem, more Chinese women postpone marriage to pursue careers, and the gender gap is huge largely a result of the government's one-child policy that for years encouraged parents to have boys rather than girls. Researchers estimate that soon China will have a surplus of 24 million unmarried men. Many of them now search for a mate online as Chinese dating services bring in more than $300 million each year. Wealthy men buy their way out of the problem; in one case a company sent 200 women who enrolled in their service to a powerful executive so that he could select a bride. However, men of more modest means struggle to get the attention of potential mates, particularly if they are unable to afford an apartment in expensive cities like Beijing. And although women have a huge numerical advantage, they face strong pressure to find a suitable mate before they turn 28; to be single after this age stigmatizes them with the label "leftover woman."[77]

However, the dominance of inherited wealth appears to have faded in Britain's traditionally aristocratic society, as British entrepreneurs like Sir Richard Branson (of the Virgin empire) redefine the economy. The United Kingdom was particularly hard hit by the Great Recession, and a new emphasis on frugality altered people's priorities. In addition, populist outrage grew after it came to light that legislators had billed the government for excessive expenses—among other abuses, British taxpayers footed a £2,000 bill for one M.P. to clean the moat surrounding his castle.[80]

The *Great British Class Survey* conducted by the BBC asked more than 161,000 people for their input about social class. The study concluded the number of distinct classes in the United Kingdom today has grown from three to seven. These range from the "elite" at the top who possess money, social connections, and upper-crust cultural preferences, to the *precariat* (precarious proletariat) at the bottom who live from day to day with severely constrained resources. The new middle categories include the "technical middle class," a group that has a lot of money but few social connections or cultural activity, and "emergent service workers," a young, urban group that has little money but a lot of social connections and cultural interests. Not all Britons agreed with the new classifications. As one wrote to a newspaper, "There are only two classes: those with tattoos, and those without."[81]

India

India's economy is booming despite the global recession, and affluent consumers prize higher-end global brands—even though nearly half of India's population lives on less than $1.25 a day. Brands like Gucci, Jimmy Choo, and Hermès scramble to open stores in high-end hotels or new superluxury malls, where the management often stations guards at the doors to keep the destitute outside.[83]

A recent flap illustrates the rapid changes in Indian society. *Vogue India* ran a 16-page spread of poor people surrounded by luxury goods: a toothless old woman holds a child who wears a Fendi bib, a woman and two other people ride on a motorbike as she sports a Hermès bag that sells for more than $10,000, a street beggar grips a Burberry umbrella. A columnist denounced the spread as "not just tacky but downright distasteful." The

Marketing Pitfall

British consumers are well aware of a type of person they call **chavs**. This label refers to young, lower-class men and women who mix flashy brands and accessories from big names such as Burberry with track suits. Their style icons include soccer star David Beckham and his wife, Victoria (aka Posh Spice). Despite their (alleged) tackiness, some marketers like chavs because they spend a lot of their disposable income on fashion, food, and gadgets. France's Danone, which makes HP Sauce, a condiment the British have poured over bacon sandwiches and fries for a century, launched a series of ads to play up to the chav culture. One features a brawl over the sauce at a wedding buffet; another includes glammy soccer players' wives mingling cattily at a party. On the other hand the upscale Burberry brand was long a favorite of chavs, and its image is only starting to recover. As one author wrote, "a lot of people thought that Burberry would be worn by the person who mugged them." The association between chavs and Burberry hats and scarves got so bad that for awhile some restaurants and clubs barred entry to anyone who wore the distinctive plaid design.[82]

Chavs are a common social class stereotype in England.

Source: JJ Augustin Inc., Publishers.

magazine's editor commented that the shoot's message is simply that "fashion is no longer a rich man's privilege. Anyone can carry it off and make it look beautiful."[84]

One of Bollywood's biggest stars, Shahrukh Khan, is "brand ambassador" for Tag Heuer watches, which cost thousands of dollars. He gives them away on the Indian version of *Who Wants to Be a Millionaire?*, which is the show that also formed the basis for the hit movie *Slumdog Millionaire*. India's ascendancy is fairly recent; for decades after the country became independent from Britain, its economy was socialistic and traditional with a rigid class hierarchy: Dalits, formerly known as the Untouchables, are at the bottom and forced into menial jobs, whereas Brahmins historically occupied the highest rung of the social ladder.[85]

Analysts project that soon there will be about 267 million middle-class Indian consumers, a growth of about 67 percent over just a 5-year period. Although the middle class currently represents less than 15 percent of India's population, it still accounts for about one-half of the cars, computers, and air conditioners in the country.[86] Today, young Indian consumers watch MTV and read international fashion magazines. They exert a strong influence on the country's rapid growth, especially because India's population is relatively young; 54 percent of the people are younger than 25 years of age.[87]

OBJECTIVE 12-3

Individuals' desires to make a statement about their social class, or the class to which they hope to belong, influence the products they like and dislike.

Status Symbols and Social Capital

It's getting more difficult to clearly link certain brands or stores with a specific class. That's because a lot of "affordable luxuries" now are within reach of many consumers who could not have acquired them in the past. Think of college women you may know who buy pricey bags from Louis Vuitton or Coach, and then eat ramen noodles for dinner. To make matters even more confusing, a wealthy family may well buy its wine at Costco and its bath towels at Target—and proudly gloat about the steals they snagged.[88]

Rising incomes in many economically developing countries, such as South Korea and China, coupled with decreasing prices for quality consumer goods and services, create explosive demand for luxury products or at least "affordable" versions of these goods. The biggest emerging markets go by the acronym **BRIC nations**: Brazil, Russia, India, and China. China and India alone account for more than 20 percent of the world's gross domestic product (GDP); 30 years ago this percentage was less than 5. In recent years the rapid growth has slowed as a result of a number of factors including the United States' newfound dominance in the oil industry and, ironically, the maturation of these economies (especially in China) from lower-priced, production oriented systems to greater levels of consumption as incomes rise. Still analysts expect overall growth to continue even if at a slower rate. In 2014, China overtook the United States as the largest economy in the world.[89]

This change fuels demand for mass-consumed products that still offer some degree of *panache*. Companies such as H&M, Zara, EasyJet, and L'Oréal provide creature comforts to a consumer segment that analysts label **mass class**. This term describes the hundreds of millions of global consumers who now enjoy a level of purchasing power that's sufficient to let them afford high-quality products—except for big-ticket items such as college educations, housing, or luxury cars. The mass-class market, for example, spawned several versions of affordable cars: Latin Americans have their Volkswagen Beetle (they affectionately call it *el huevito*, "the little egg"); Indian consumers have their Maruti 800 (it sells for as little as US $4,860); and the Fiat Palio, the company's "world car," targets people in emerging countries such as Brazil, Argentina, India, China, and Turkey.[90]

"What Do You Use That Fork For?" Taste Cultures, Codes, and Cultural Capital

A **taste culture** describes consumers in terms of their aesthetic and intellectual preferences. This concept helps to illuminate the important, yet sometimes subtle, distinctions in consumption choices among the social classes.[93] For example, a comprehensive

Marketing Pitfall

Research evidence shows that people who identify with a relatively low-status category desire objectives they associate with high status as a way to enhance social standing.[91] This desire to compensate can ironically work against these individuals in the long run. For example, nutritionists point to supersized food portions and megasized cups of sugary drinks as prime culprits in the obesity epidemic we see in the United States. A research project demonstrated an obstacle to battling this problem: Underprivileged consumers view larger-sized portions as status symbols. When study respondents were made to feel they had less power, they chose bigger food portions to compensate. They were even more likely to do so when their choices were public. The researchers note the irony of this situation: The short-term status display may ultimately lead to even lower status because of the stigma of obesity in our society.[92]

analysis of social-class differences using data from 675,000 households supports the *mass class* phenomenon we discussed previously: Differences in consumption patterns between the upper and upper-middle classes and between the middle and working classes are disappearing. However, strong differences still emerge in terms of how consumers spend their discretionary income and leisure time. Upper- and upper-middle-class people are more likely to visit museums and attend live theater, and middle-class consumers are more likely to camp and fish. The upper classes are more likely to listen to all-news programs, whereas the middle classes are more likely to tune in to country music.[94]

In one of the classic studies of social differences in taste, researchers catalogued homeowners' possessions as they sat in their living rooms and asked them about their income and occupation. As Figure 12.2 shows, they identified clusters of furnishings and decorative items that seemed to appear together with some regularity, and they found different clusters depending on the consumer's social status. For example, they tended to find a cluster that consisted of religious objects, artificial flowers, and still-life portraits in relatively lower-status living rooms, whereas they were likely to catalogue a cluster of abstract paintings, sculptures, and modern furniture in a higher-status home.[95]

Another approach to social class focuses on the **codes** (the ways consumers express and interpret meanings) people within different social strata use. It's valuable for marketers to map these codes because they can use concepts and terms that their target customers will relate to. Marketing appeals we construct with class differences in mind result in quite different messages. For example, a life insurance ad that a company targets to a lower-class person might depict, in simple, straightforward terms, a hard-working family man who feels good immediately after he buys a policy. An upscale appeal might depict a more affluent older couple surrounded by photos of their children and grandchildren. It might include extensive copy that plugs the satisfaction of planning for the future.

This ad from New Zealand pokes fun at the tendency of some consumers to show off their cultural capital excessively.
Source: Courtesy of DB Breweries.

Figure 12.2 LIVING ROOM CLUSTERS AND SOCIAL CLASS

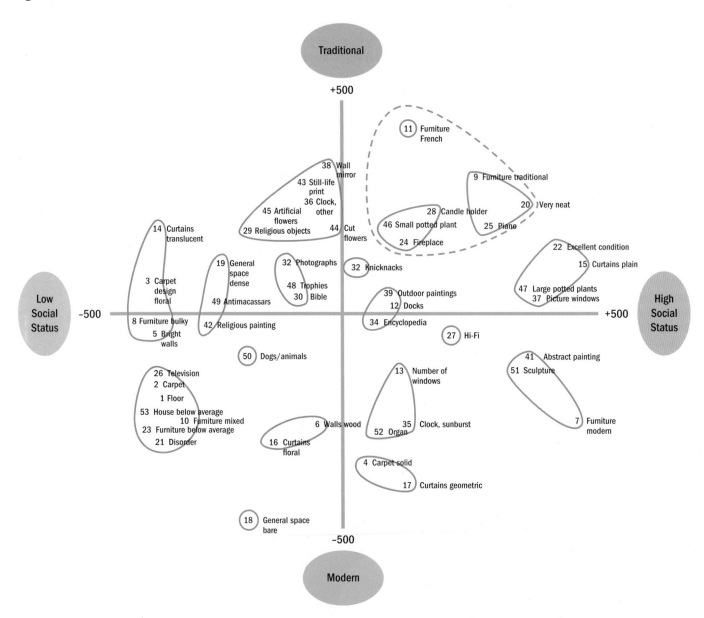

These two ways to communicate product benefits incorporate different types of codes. **Restricted codes** focus on the content of objects, not on relationships among objects. **Elaborated codes**, in contrast, are more complex and depend on a more sophisticated worldview. These code differences extend to the way consumers approach basic concepts such as time, social relationships, and objects. Table 12.1 summarizes some differences between these two code types.

Clearly, not all taste cultures are created equal. The upper classes have access to resources that enable them to perpetuate their privileged position in society. Pierre Bourdieu was a French theorist who wrote at length about how people compete for resources, or *capital*. Bourdieu did large-scale surveys to track people's wealth, and he related this "economic capital" to patterns of taste in entertainment and the arts. He concluded that "taste" is a status-marking force, or **habitus**, that causes consumption preferences to cluster together.

TABLE 12. 1   Effects of Restricted versus Elaborated Codes

	Restricted Codes	Elaborated Codes
General characteristics	Emphasize description and contents of objects Have implicit meanings (context dependent)	Emphasize analysis and interrelationship between objects; i.e., hierarchical organization and instrumental connections Have explicit meanings
Language	Use few qualifiers, i.e., few adjectives or adverbs Use concrete, descriptive, tangible symbolism	Have language rich in personal, individual qualifiers Use large vocabulary, complex conceptual hierarchy
Social relationships	Stress attributes of individuals over formal roles	Stress formal role structure, instrumental relationships
Time	Focus on present; have only general notion of future	Focus an instrumental relationship between present activities and future rewards
Physical space	Locate rooms, spaces in context of other rooms and places: e.g., "front room," "corner store"	Identify rooms, spaces in terms of usage; formal ordering of spaces; e.g., "dining room," "financial district"
Implications for marketers	Stress inherent product quality, contents (or trust-worthiness, goodness of "real-type"), spokesperson Stress implicit of fit of product with total lifestyle Use simple adjectives, descriptions	Stress differences, advantages vis-à-vis other products in terms of some autonomous evaluation criteria Stress product's instrumental ties to distant benefits Use complex adjectives, descriptors

Source: Adapted from Jeffrey F. Durgee, "How Consumer Sub-Cultures Code Reality: A Look at Some Code Types," in Richard J. Lutz, ed., *Advances in Consumer Research* 13 (Provo, UT: Association of Consumer Research, 1986): 332.

Later analyses of U.S. consumers largely confirm these relationships; for example, higher-income people are more likely than the average consumer to attend the theater, whereas lower-income people are more likely to attend a wrestling match.[96]

Social and Cultural Capital

The Burning Man Festival began in 1986 as a Summer Solstice celebration on a San Francisco beach that attracted a small group of people. Some of them built an eight-foot tall wooden man and set it on fire. Over the years the event attracted more and more people who celebrated "alternative lifestyles" with bizarre costumes, primitive camps and ample mind-altering substances. As the event grew, organizers moved it to the desert to accommodate more attendees. Since that time, however, this countercultural festival has evolved into something quite different: A huge annual retreat in the Black Rock Desert north of Reno, Nevada, that attracts wealthy technology moguls who engage in one-upmanship to show one another just how much money they can flaunt in the name of weirdness. Luminaries from Facebook, Amazon, Google, Twitter, Uber, and other hot Silicon Valley outfits go **glamping** in splendor with their entourages, and fees purportedly reach $25,000 per person. They arrive in tricked-out RVs like the ones celebrities stay in on movie sets; these connect together to create private enclaves that other attendees can't penetrate. Guests arrive on private jets and spend the week dining on sushi and lobster as they "get back to nature" in style.[97]

The transformation of Burning Man from what used to be known as a countercultural celebration to a showcase for wealth illustrates Bourdieu's concept of **social capital**. Exclusivity functions like a big, beefy nightclub bouncer who decides who he will admit past the velvet rope. An important form of "currency" is access to exclusive networks where business and political deals happen. In the process, paradoxically it's not unusual to find that the people who originated the activity can no longer afford to participate, like the original Burning Man "hippies" or long-time residents who get priced out of gentrifying urban neighborhoods.

Bourdieu also reminds us of the importance of **cultural capital**. This term refers to a set of distinctive and socially rare tastes and practices—knowledge of "refined" behavior that admits a person into the realm of the upper class.[98] The elites in a society collect a set of skills that enable them to hold positions of power and authority, and they pass these on to their children (think etiquette lessons and debutante balls). These resources gain in value because class members restrict access to them. That's part of the reason why people compete so fiercely for admission to elite colleges. Much as we hate to admit it, the rich *are* different.

Online Social Capital

Because we spend so much time in digital environments, it's natural that the same social class dynamics operate in these spaces. Let's use the social media platform Foursquare to understand how online social capital works. People visit Foursquare because they can check in at locations and announce their arrivals to their community of friends. Some check-ins earn badges and coupons from participating retailers. The more people who become involved, the more valuable the community, and involvement grows based on activities that participants value. For instance, people who are into Foursquare crave the status of being designated as "mayor" of a location like their local Starbucks. As long as people value this title, the Foursquare community will attract enthusiastic participants. If and when people move on to something else, the social capital that flows from being a mayor will slow to a trickle. At that point, we're on to the next hot site. As it declines, the community experiences a big drop off in participation, adherence to norms, perceived reputation, and trust among members.[99] Think about formerly popular online communities like MySpace or Friendster to understand how platforms can lose their cool almost overnight.

In the online world, many people hold others in high regard for their opinions as much as, or maybe even more than, for their money. The "psychic income" we get when we post reviews that others validate creates a **reputation economy**, in which the "currency" people earn is approval rather than cold hard cash.[100] Retailers may "sort" clientele in terms of their ability to afford the retailers' products or services (e.g., some investment firms only accept clients with a certain net worth). Volunteers who edit *Wikipedia* entries may devote 20 to 40 hours per week. Exclusive dating sites like hotenough.org weed out unattractive people. The site's home page claims, "Through our screening process, we have filtered the masses leaving only your area's most attractive, fit, trendy singles and have now included an exclusive section for our 40+ singles, the 'BABY BOOMER SECTION.' Hot Enough offers three tiers of hotties, so if you're fit and trendy, then rest assured there is a place for you."[101]

In general, we know that a community is healthier and more desirable when it is able to offer a lot of social capital as an inducement for people to join; that's one reason why the competition is fierce to get admitted to Ivy League universities. This is true in the online world as well. In the online world, bloggers acquire social capital when a lot of other people start to rate their posts highly and perhaps retweet them.[102] And, like exclusive country clubs, **online gated communities** that selectively allow access to some people may offer a high degree of social capital to the lucky few who pass the test.

The social network This.com is an invitation-only platform that allows a user to post only one link a day to focus those in the know on a particular topic. Journalists and industry insiders jockey ferociously to receive a coveted invite.[103] Or, consider ASmallWorld.com, a social networking site that gives the wealthy access to one another in cyberspace—while keeping the rest of us out. It's an invitation-only site that's grown to about 150,000 registered users. The site's founders promote it as a Facebook for the social elite. A few postings help to understand why. One person wrote, "I need to rent 20 very luxury sports cars for an event in Switzerland .... The cars should be: Maserati—Ferrari—Lamborghini—Aston Martin ONLY!" Another announced: "If anyone is looking for a private island, I now have one available for purchase in Fiji."[104]

Status Symbols

We tend to evaluate ourselves, our professional accomplishments, our appearance, and our material well-being relative to others. The popular phrase "keeping up with the Joneses" (in Japan, it's "keeping up with the Satos") refers to a desire to compare your standard of living with your neighbors'—and exceed it if you can.

Often it's not enough just to have wealth or fame; what matters is that you have more of it than others. One study demonstrated that we assign value to *loyalty programs* (e.g., when airlines award you special status based on the number of miles you fly) at least in part based on our level in the hierarchy relative to other members. Subjects were assigned to "gold status" in a program where they were in the only tier, or a program where there

CB AS I SEE IT

Benjamin G. Voyer, *ESCP Europe Business School & London School of Economics, United Kingdom*

What do you typically associate with luxury and luxury goods? High quality, well-crafted products, or perhaps simply a waste of money? The display of refined tastes or a mere attempt to show off? Luxury goods constitute a unique product and service category in marketing and are interesting for a simple reason: they often challenge everything we know about traditional products and services! The buying behavior of luxury consumers, and the meaning of luxury possessions, has been the focus of much research in the field. Luxury consumption has been linked to wealth, social class, and economic power. Research suggests that consumers use luxury

goods to enhance their status, especially when buying brands with prominent designer logos.

Recently, researchers have started to examine conspicuous consumption from a different angle, looking at whether status-enhancing consumption was compatible with the notion of sustainability. Throughout history, luxury goods have been associated with unsustainability or unhealthiness. Plato, for instance, suggested that societies in which people were consuming luxury goods were "unhealthy" or "healthy" societies, on the other hand, were those in which people would limit themselves to necessities. Overall, luxury consumption has often been perceived as a social and moral transgression, denoting values of hedonism, expense, and affluence.

In this context, could it be that consumers actually find sustainable luxury goods less desirable than nonsustainable ones? We answered this question in a series of studies conducted with colleague Daisy Beckham and looked at whether luxury was seen as compatible with sustainability. In a first study, we found that consumers were more likely to associate luxury brands with words related to unsustainability (e.g., pollution, smoke, greed, fumes) versus words related to sustainability (e.g., conservation, green, trees, ecology).

In another study, we looked at the effect of a "sustainability label" on consumers' perceptions of luxury goods. We asked participants to rate a series of six luxury handbags, three of them being randomly described as sustainable. We found that luxury bags receiving the label "sustainable edition" were rated, on average, as being less luxurious than bags without such a label. We also found that the more expensive consumers rated a luxury handbag, the less sustainable they thought it was. The only consumers who responded favorably to a sustainability label were those who valued sustainability as an important decision criterion when buying a handbag. A follow-up focus group revealed that participants perceived luxury as being conceptually opposed to the idea of sustainability, and that for some, sustainable luxury products would not carry the same status-enhancing effects than regular luxury products.

What is the bottom line of all this? Given that many consumers use luxury goods to communicate about social status, which is typically associated with breaking norms and rules, it seems that a sustainability label is paradoxically detrimental to the marketing of luxury goods. This is something that can be counterintuitive for luxury brands, which often communicate on product features, which are thought to enhance the perception of quality and prestige of their products (e.g., Made in France labels).

Counterfeit luxury goods are a major headache for companies that cater to high-end customers.
Source: © Neil Setchfield/Alamy.

Marketing Pitfall

Luxury goods often serve as status symbols, but the proliferation of inexpensive counterfeit products threatens to diminish their value ("Hey buddy, wanna buy a 'genuine' Rolex for $20?"). Fakes are a major headache for many manufacturers, especially in Asia; Officials in China estimate that 15 to 20 percent of the products made there are counterfeit.[107]

How do people who bought the real thing react when they see imitations of their prized handbags or watches parading by them on the street? Researchers who interviewed consumers who purchased luxury fashion brands in India and Thailand identified three coping strategies:

1. **Flight**—They stop using the brand because they don't want to be mislabeled as a lesser-status person who buys fake brands.
2. **Reclamation**—They go out of their way to emphasize their long relationship with the brand, but express concern that its image will be tarnished.
3. **Abranding**—They disguise their luxury items in the belief that truly high-status people do not need to display expensive logos, whereas those who do betray lower status.[108]

was also a silver tier. Although both groups were "gold," those in the program that also offered a lower level felt better about it.[105]

A major motivation to buy is not to enjoy these items but rather to let others know that we can afford them. These products are **status symbols**. The popular bumper-sticker slogan, "He who dies with the most toys, wins," summarizes the desire to accumulate these badges of achievement. Status-seeking is a significant source of motivation to procure appropriate products and services that we hope will let others know we've "made it." A study demonstrated how people turn to status symbols to prop up their self-concepts, especially when they feel badly or uncertain about other aspects of their lives. When subjects in auctions were made to feel that they had little power, they spent more to purchase items to compensate for this deficit.[106]

As we discussed previously, the rise of a mass class market means that many luxury products have gone down-market. Does this mean that Americans no longer yearn for status symbols? Hardly. The market continues to roll out ever-pricier goods and services, from $12,000 mother–baby diamond tennis bracelet sets to $600 jeans, $800 haircuts, and $400 bottles of wine. Although it seems that almost everyone can flaunt a designer handbag (or at least a counterfeit version with a convincing logo), our country's wealthiest consumers employ 9,000 personal chefs, visit plastic surgeons, and send their children to $400-an-hour math tutors. A sociologist explained, "Whether or not someone has a flat-screen TV is going to tell you less than if you look at the services they use, where they live and the control they have over other people's labor, those who are serving them."[109]

Of course, the particular products that count as status symbols vary across cultures and locales:

● Although to most Americans the now-defunct Hummer vehicle is a symbol of excess, Iraqis still regard the huge gas-guzzlers as an alluring symbol of power. An Iraqi Hummer dealer observed, "In Iraq, people judge you by your car, and you're not a man without one." People there use an Arabic phrase to explain the need to have the biggest car: *hasad thukuri*, which roughly translates as "penis envy."[110]

- In China, children are status symbols (partly because the government strongly discourages couples from having more than one baby). Parents want to show off their pampered child and are eager to surround their "little emperors" with luxury goods. Chinese families spend one-third to one-half of their disposable income on their children.[111]

- The Russian economy has fallen on hard times lately because of economic sanctions and falling oil prices. Still there are many *nouveau riches* who made a fortune over the past decide and crave luxury goods to show off their newfound wealth. Some buy the GoldVish cell phone that glitters with 120 carats of diamonds encrusting a case of white gold. The desire to spend as much as possible on indulgences fuels a popular joke in Moscow: A wealthy businessman tells a friend he bought a tie for $100. The friend responds, "You fool! You can get the same tie for $200 just across the street."[112]

- In Indonesia, as in many countries, a cell phone is a status symbol—but instead of a sleek iPhone, a decade-old Nokia model users call "the Brick" is the one to have. This "smart phone" never took off in the West; its bulky design makes it look dated. But in Jakarta, its heft is what people like about it. At a whopping half-pound, it doesn't fit into a pocket, so it's visible when models, politicians, and other celebrities cart it around with them. Nokia even sells a gold-plated version for $2,500. In the world of status symbols, anything goes as long as others don't have it.[113]

The social analyst Thorstein Veblen first discussed the motivation to consume for the sake of consuming at the turn of the 20th century. For Veblen, we buy things to create **invidious distinction**; this means that we use them to inspire envy in others through our display of wealth or power. Veblen coined the term **conspicuous consumption** to refer to people's desires to provide prominent visible evidence of their ability to afford luxury goods. The material excesses of his time motivated Veblen's outlook. Veblen wrote in the era of the "Robber Barons," where the likes of J. P. Morgan, Henry Clay Frick, and William Vanderbilt built massive financial empires and flaunted their wealth as they competed to throw the most lavish party. Some of these events were legendary, as this account describes:

> There were tales, repeated in the newspapers, of dinners on horseback; of banquets for pet dogs; of hundred-dollar bills folded into guests' dinner napkins; of a hostess who attracted attention by seating a chimpanzee at her table; of centerpieces in which lightly clad living maidens swam in glass tanks, or emerged from huge pies; of parties at which cigars were ceremoniously lighted with flaming banknotes of large denominations.[114]

Sounds like they really lived it up back in the old days, right? Well, maybe the more things change, the more they stay the same: The wave of corporate scandals involving companies such as AIG, Enron, WorldCom, and Tyco infuriated many consumers when they discovered that some top executives lived it up even as other employees were laid off. One account of a $1 million birthday party the chief executive of Tyco threw for his wife is eerily similar to a Robber Baron shindig: The party reportedly had a gladiator theme and featured an ice sculpture of Michelangelo's *David* with vodka streaming from his penis into crystal glasses. The company also furnished the executive's New York apartment with such "essentials" as a $6,000 shower curtain, a $2,200 gilt wastebasket, and a $17,100 "traveling toilette box."[115]

This phenomenon of conspicuous consumption was, for Veblen, most evident among what he termed the **leisure class** people for whom productive work is taboo. In Marxist terms, such an attitude reflects a desire to link oneself to ownership or control of the means of production, rather than to the production itself. Those who control these resources, therefore, avoid any evidence that they actually have to work for a living, as the term *idle rich* suggests.

To Veblen, wives are an economic resource. He criticized the "decorative" role of women, as rich men showered them with expensive clothes, pretentious homes, and a life of leisure as a way to advertise their own wealth (note that today he might have argued the same for a smaller number of husbands). Today we refer to these women as **trophy wives**. Fashions such as high-heeled shoes, tight corsets, billowing trains on dresses, and elaborate

This French ad suggests that even dogs marry "trophy wives."
Source: Courtesy of CLM-BBDO and Mars Petfood, Clive Stewart Photography.

hairstyles all conspired to ensure that wealthy women could barely move without assistance, much less perform manual labor. Similarly, the Chinese practice of foot-binding prevented female members of the aristocracy from walking; servants carried them from place to place. In recent years the tables have turned as older women—who increasingly boast the same incomes and social capital as their male peers—seek out younger men as arm candy. These so-called **cougars** (a term popularized by the TV show *Cougar Town*) are everywhere; surveys estimate that about one-third of women older than age 40 date younger men.[116]

Consumers engage in conspicuous consumption as a way to display status markers, yet the prominence of these markers varies from products with large recognizable emblems to those with no logo at all. Those "in the know" often can recognize a subtle status marker when another member of their elite group displays it, such as the distinctive design of a bag or watch—these are "quiet signals." In contrast, some people may feel the need to almost hit others over the head with their bling; they use "loud signals."

One set of researchers labels these differences **brand prominence**. They assign consumers to one of four consumption groups (patricians, parvenus, poseurs, and proletarians) based on their wealth and need for status. When they looked at data on luxury goods, the authors found different classes gravitated toward different types of brand prominence. Brands like Louis Vuitton, Gucci, and Mercedes vary in terms of how blatant their status appeals (e.g., prominent logos) are in advertisements and on the products themselves—or in other words, in the type of **status signaling** they employ.

Thinking back to our discussion about "old money" compared with "new money," for example, it's not surprising that those who are wealthier and don't have a high need for status (patricians) rely on "quiet signals" and likely will be put off by excessive displays. Marketers for status brands need to understand these distinctions because their customers may or may not value products with explicit logos and other highly visible cues that signal conspicuous consumption.[117] Figure 12.3 summarizes these four types and provides one set of contrasting products the researchers used in their study: quiet versus loud Gucci sunglasses.

Veblen's inspiration came from anthropological studies of the Kwakiutl Indians, who lived in the Pacific Northwest. At a *potlatch* ceremony, the host showed off his wealth and gave extravagant presents to the guests. The more he gave away, the greater his status. Sometimes, the host employed an even more radical strategy to flaunt his wealth. He would publicly *destroy* some of his property just to demonstrate how much he had.

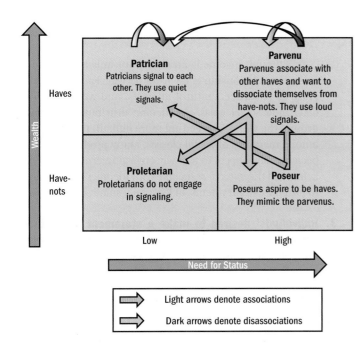

Figure 12.3 A TYPOLOGY OF STATUS SIGNALING

Note: "Quiet" sunglasses (L) do not include a prominent designer logo, while "Loud" (R) sunglasses do.

Source: Young Jee Han, Joseph C. Nunes, and Xavier Drèze (2010), "Signaling Status with Luxury Goods: The Role of Brand Prominence," *Journal of Marketing* 74 (July), 15–30, from Figures 2 and 3.

And the plot thickens: Because guests had to reciprocate by giving a gift of equal value, the host could humiliate a poorer rival with an invitation to a lavish *potlatch*. The hapless guest would eventually be forced into bankruptcy because he needed to give away as much as the host, even though he could not afford to do so. If this practice sounds "primitive," think for a moment about many modern weddings. Parents commonly invest huge sums of money to throw a lavish party and compete with others for the distinction of giving their daughter the "best" or most extravagant wedding, even if they have to dip into their retirement savings to do it.

Like the *potlatch* ritual, in modern times our desire to convince others we have a surplus of resources creates the need for us to exhibit the evidence that we do. Accordingly, we may prioritize consumption activities that use up as many resources as possible in nonconstructive pursuits. This *conspicuous waste*, in turn, shows others that we have assets to spare. Veblen wrote, "We are told of certain Polynesian chiefs, who, under the stress of good form, preferred to starve rather than carry their food to their mouths with their own hands."[118]

As the competition to accumulate status symbols escalates, sometimes the best tactic is to switch gears and go in reverse. One way to do this is to deliberately *avoid* status symbols—that is, to seek status by mocking it. Social scientists call this sophisticated form of conspicuous consumption **parody display**.[119] Hence, the popularity of old, ripped blue jeans (or more likely, the ones companies stonewash and treat so that they *look* old and ripped), "utility" vehicles such as Jeeps among the upper classes (like the Caldwells in the chapter opener), and brands with a strong blue-collar heritage like Von Dutch truckers' hats and Red Wing boots.

MyLab Marketing

To complete the problems with the ✪, go to EOC Discussion Questions in the MyLab as well as additional Marketing Metrics questions only available in MyLab Marketing.

CHAPTER SUMMARY

Now that you have finished reading this chapter, you should understand why:

1. **Our confidence in our future, as well as in the overall economy, determines how freely we spend and the types of products we buy.**

   The field of behavioral economics studies how consumers decide what to do with their money. Consumer confidence—the state of mind consumers have about their own personal situation, as well as their feelings about their overall economic prospects—helps to determine whether they will purchase goods and services, take on debt, or save their money.

2. **We group consumers into social classes that say a lot about where they stand in society.**

   A consumer's *social class* refers to his or her standing in society. Factors including education, occupation, and income determine the class to which we belong. Virtually all groups make distinctions among members in terms of relative superiority, power, and access to valued resources. This social stratification creates a status hierarchy in which consumers prefer some goods to others.

   Although income is an important indicator of social class, the relationship is far from perfect. Factors such as place of residence, cultural interests, and worldview also determine social class. As income distributions change around the world, it is getting more difficult to distinguish among members of social classes; many products succeed because they appeal to a newly emerging group that marketers call the *mass class* (people with incomes high enough to purchase luxury items, at least on a small scale).

3. **Individuals' desires to make a statement about their social class, or the class to which they hope to belong, influence the products they like and dislike.**

   Conspicuous consumption, when a person flaunts his status by deliberately using up valuable resources, is one way to "buy up" to a higher social class. *Nouveau riches,* whose relatively recent acquisition of income rather than ancestry or breeding accounts for their enhanced social mobility, are the most likely to do this. We use status symbols (usually scarce goods or services) to communicate our standing to others. Parody display occurs when we seek status by deliberately avoiding fashionable products.

KEY TERMS

Affluenza, 457
Bottom of the pyramid, 453
Brand prominence, 470
BRIC nations, 462
CEO pay ratio, 448
Chavs, 461
Codes, 463
College wage premium, 452
Conspicuous consumption, 469
Consumer confidence, 448
Cosmopolitanism, 457
Cougars, 470
Credit score, 449
Cultural capital, 466
Digital Divide, 454
Discretionary income, 447
Dominance–submission hierarchy, 455

Elaborated codes, 464
Female-to-male earnings ratio, 452
Frugalistas, 451
Glamping, 465
Habitus, 464
Hedonic adaptation, 451
Homogamy, 455
Income inequality, 448
Invidious distinction, 469
Leisure class, 469
Mass class, 462
Nouveau riches, 453
Occupational prestige, 456
One Percenter, 448
Online gated communities, 466
Parody display, 471

Plutonomy, 448
Reputation economy, 466
Restricted codes, 464
Savings rate, 448
Social capital, 448
Social class, 455
Social mobility, 449
Social stratification, 456
Status anxiety, 453
Status crystallization, 459
Status hierarchy, 456
Status signaling, 470
Status symbols, 468
Taste culture, 462
Trophy wives, 469
Worldview, 469

REVIEW

12-1   How have women contributed to the overall rise in income in our society?

12-2   Define *discretionary income.*

12-3   How does consumer confidence influence consumer behavior?

12-4   What is a *pecking order*?

⭐ 12-5   Explain what is meant by achieved versus ascribed status.

12-6   What is the significance of lower fertility rates in higher- and middle-class families?

12-7   Is income alone a good determinant of social class?

12-8   What is *income inequality*, and why is it a problem?

12-9   How are attitudes toward luxury categorized according to SRI Consulting Business Intelligence?

12-10   In some countries it is difficult to measure and quantify social class. Why might this be the case?

12-11   What are the main motivators in purchasing a status symbol?

12-12   What is the term used to describe an individual's aesthetic and intellectual preferences?

12-13   Describe the difference between a restricted and an elaborated code. Give an example of each.

12-14   How do the elites restrict access to their group?

12-15   What are the three identified strategies used by consumers if counterfeiting is common in their preferred brands?

12-16   What roles do status symbols play in purchase decisions?

12-17   What is meant by the term "calculated consumption"?

12-18   What is a current example of parody display?

12-19   Describe what we mean by the term *mass class* and summarize what causes this phenomenon.

CONSUMER BEHAVIOR CHALLENGE

■ DISCUSS

12-20   Consumer confidence is an indicator of the level of optimism that consumers have about the performance of their country's economy. How might consumer confidence affect the decisions of marketers and brand owners?

12-21   What are some of the obstacles to measuring social class in today's society? Discuss some ways to get around these obstacles.

12-22   Some countries have similar stratified social classes to the United States and Western Europe, but many do not. Is it possible to apply social stratification to all societies?

12-23   Read the brief review of the social classes in China, Japan, Middle East, the United Kingdom, or India provided in the chapter. Suggest a new product or service suitable for the market.

12-24   In today's economy, it's become somewhat vulgar to flaunt your money—if you have any left. Do you think this means that status symbols like luxury products are passé? Why or why not?

12-25   Basil Bernstein (1924–2000) was the first to contrast restricted and elaborated codes. How would you apply this to a key target market in your country?

12-26   Research suggests that social class influences how much compassion people show to others who need help. For example, one study reported that luxury car drivers were more likely to cut off other motorists instead of waiting for their turn at the intersection. Another showed that less-affluent people are more likely to agree with such statements as, "I often notice people who need help," and "It's important to take care of people who are vulnerable." Other studies have demonstrated that upper-class people are not as good at recognizing others' emotions. One explanation is that more resources provide a sense of independence; the less we have to rely on others, the less we care about their feelings.[120] Do you agree that wealthy people are less caring? Why or why not?

12-27   This chapter observes that some marketers find "greener pastures" when they target low-income people. How ethical is it to single out consumers who cannot afford to waste their precious resources on discretionary items? Under what circumstances should we encourage or discourage this segmentation strategy?

■ APPLY

12-28   Compile a list of occupations and ask a sample of students in a variety of majors (both business and nonbusiness) to rank the prestige of these jobs. Can you detect any differences in these rankings as a function of students' majors?

12-29   Conspicuous consumption is a sign of class and position in some societies. Is this important in your own country? Which brands are particularly prized, and why is this the case?

Case Study

SUCCESS AT THE BOTTOM OF THE PYRAMID? P&G'S GILLETTE GUARD SHOWS IT'S POSSIBLE

Consumer behavior is influenced by internal and external factors. One of the external factors that sets real boundaries for consumers is their level of income. Some marketers refer to strategies directed at different income tiers as targeting certain levels of a pyramid. Marketing to the "bottom of the pyramid," focusing on consumers with very limited financial means, became well-known in 2004 when C. K. Prahalad wrote *The Fortune at the Bottom of the Pyramid*. He envisioned companies marketing affordable products to the millions of consumers around the world with limited income and unmet needs. He believed that companies could help consumers and be profitable at the same time.

A number of companies have attempted to make this model work. Puriet, an in-home water purification system manufactured by Hindustan Unilever Limited, was developed for low-income consumers and has found success by offering a 6-month installment plan to make the $25 price more manageable. The Nokia 105, introduced by Microsoft, is a $25 basic cell phone with an alarm clock, flashlight, and FM radio. It was priced specifically for low-income consumers and has sold millions of phones since its introduction in 2013.

However bottom of the pyramid strategies are not always as workable as companies would have imagined. The Nokia 5 has struggled to be financially sustainable and has faced challenges as low-income consumers gravitate toward smart phones that are decreasing in cost. Other companies missed the mark because of a lack of research, discovering in the end that consumers could not afford their product or could opt for a cheaper, more local offering. Some companies have been pushed by investors to show profitability in the short-term with their low-income market initiatives, which has been difficult to accomplish. In some instances the only way to make their business model work over the long term is to partner with a nongovernmental organization (NGO) which could help them to gain access to consumers through their established connections within countries.

Let's consider the possibilities in India, a country with considerable bottom of the pyramid potential. World Bank 2013 data show India's population at 1.24 billion people and per capita income at $125 a month. The McKinsey Global Institute estimates that 78 percent of the that population fall into the bottom of the pyramid category, with the majority living in rural India. They predict that this market may be worth $1.5 trillion by 2020. The sheer numbers of consumers and the overall potential make this market appealing to marketers, but still the low level of income poses considerable challenges.

For years Procter & Gamble (P&G) has worked to find ways to capture market share of the men's razor market in India. They felt that there was a significant opportunity to meet the shaving needs of Indian men at the bottom of the pyramid. Unfortunately, early efforts, like their Vector razor, were undermined by a misunderstanding of the shaving process for men in India, many of whom did not have access to running water. More recently, P&G introduced the Gillette Guard. This razor was developed based on 3,000 hours of research over 18 months, some of it conducted in the homes of low-income Indian men. They asked the men about their shaving rituals and observed them in the process of shaving. What P&G found is that they typically shave on the floors of their huts with no

electricity, using a bowl of water and no mirror. Their primary objective is to avoid cutting themselves. This research proved to be invaluable in the development of the new razor.

The Gillette Guard was the result of what Alberto Carvalho, vice president, global Gillette, described as a focus on not only producing a razor that would meet the needs of these consumers, but doing it at "ruthless cost." This meant paying attention to the smallest details, designing a stripped down single blade razor with only four components versus the 25 found in more sophisticated razors. Jim Keighley, associate director for product engineering, says "I can remember talking about changes to this product that were worth a thousandth, or two thousandths of a cent." In the end they were able to produce a razor that cost one third of the previously introduced Vector. Selling price for the Gillette Guard ended up at 15 rupees (34 cents) and razor blades at 5 rupees (12 cents).

As a result of their painstaking research and attention to the needs of this unique target audience, P&G's market share for razors and blades has grown significantly in India and at a faster rate than any other P&G brand in India. Despite the challenges they encountered it appears that the Gillette Guard can be considered a bottom of the pyramid success story.

DISCUSSION QUESTIONS

CS 12-1 Using the "4A's" framework in Figure 12.1, analyze the considerations that went into the development of the Gillette Guard razor for the Indian market.

CS 12-2 Are companies targeting the bottom of the pyramid taking advantage of vulnerable consumers with limited resources?

CS 12-3 More than half of U.S. workers earn less than $30,000 a year, barely above the poverty line for a family of five. What would you recommend to a company looking to target the bottom of the pyramid consumers in the United States?

Sources: Marc Gunther, "The Base of the Pyramid: Will Selling to the Poor Pay Off?" May 22, 2014, http://www.theguardian.com/sustainable-business/prahalad-base-bottom-pyramid-profit-poor, accessed June 28, 2015; Mae Anderson, "How India Helped Gillette Rethink the Razor," https://www.bostonglobe.com/business/2013/10/03/cheap-razor-made-after-watches-indians-shave/NSQpOGAotpEfarkNmxIfcK/story.html, accessed June 24, 2015; Procter & Gamble-India website, http://www.pg.com/en_IN/, accessed June 28, 2015; Ryan Britton, "Value for the Money: Four Ways to Advertise to the Low-Income Shopper," http://maxpoint.com/us/digital-advertising-company/onpoint-blog/2014/10/21/4-ways-to-advertise-to-the-low-income-shopper, accessed June 29, 2015; Sophie Wilson, "Companies Target Billion-Dollar Potential By Marketing to the Poor," http://www.globalenvision.org/2014/10/02/companies-target-billion-dollar-potential-marketing-poor, accessed June 28, 2015; Glyn Atwal, Douglas Bryson, and Ambi Parameswaran, "Decrypting the Aspiring Indian Low-Income Consumer," March 26, 2015, http://www.worldfinancialreview.com/?p=3648, accessed June 25, 2015.

MyLab Marketing

Go to the Assignments section of your MyLab to complete these writing exercises.

12-30 Status symbols are products, such as Rolex watches or expensive sports cars, that we value because they show others how much money or prestige we have. Do you believe that your peer group values status symbols? Why or why not? If yes, what are the products that you think are status symbols for consumers your age? Do you agree with the assertion that a cell phone is a status symbol for many young people?

12-31 As we continue to emerge from The Great Recession, many people live frugally; they cut back on visits to restaurants, buy fewer high-end clothes and other luxury goods, and hold onto their cars much longer. Are we witnessing a long-term shift in consumer behavior, or do you believe this is just a temporary situation?

NOTES

1. Christopher D. Carroll, "How Does Future Income Affect Current Consumption?" *Quarterly Journal of Economics* 109 (February 1994): 111–147.
2. "Costco Net Falls on Weak Discretionary Spending," *Reuters* (May 28, 2009), www.reuters.com/article/newsOne/idUSTRE54R1GJ20090528, accessed June 17, 2009.
3. Daniel Kahneman and Angus Deaton, "High Income Improves Evaluation of Life But Not Emotional Well-Being," *Proceedings of the National Academy of Sciences* 107, no. 38 (2010): 16489–16493, http://www.pnas.org/content/107/38/16489.abstract, accessed April 14, 2015.
4. Quoted in Philip Jackman, "What Makes a Tightwad? Study Finds That People Who Are Stingy Report Feeling Emotional Pain When Spending Money," *Toronto Globe & Mail* (March 19, 2008), www.theglobeandmail.com, accessed March 22, 2008; http://webuser.bus.umich.edu/srick/Globe%20and%20Mail%203-19-08.pdf, accessed September 24, 2011.
5. José F. Medina, Joel Saegert, and Alicia Gresham, "Comparison of Mexican-American and Anglo-American Attitudes Toward Money," *Journal of Consumer Affairs* 30, no. 1 (1996): 124–145.
6. Kirk Johnson, "Sit Down. Breathe Deeply. This Is Really Scary Stuff," *New York Times* (April 16, 1995): F5; cf. also Matthew J. Bernthal, David Crockett, and Randall L. Rose, "Credit Cards as Lifestyle Facilitators," *Journal of Consumer Research* 32 (June 2005): 130–145.
7. Xinyue Zhou, Kathleen D. Vohs, and Roy F. Baumeister, "The Symbolic Power of Money: Reminders of Money Alter Social Distress and Physical Pain," *Psychological Science* 20, no. 6 (2009): 700–706.
8. Fred van Raaij, "Economic Psychology," *Journal of Economic Psychology* 1 (1981): 1–24.
9. Richard T. Curtin, "Indicators of Consumer Behavior: The University of Michigan Surveys of Consumers," *Public Opinion Quarterly* (1982): 340–352.
10. Patricia Cohen, "Oxfam Study Finds Richest 1% is Likely to Control Half of Global Wealth by 2016," *New York Times* (January 19, 2015), http://www.nytimes.com/2015/01/19/business/richest-1-percent-likely-to-control-half-of-global-wealth-by-2016-study-finds.html?smid=nytcore-iphone-share&smprod=nytcore-iphone&_r=1, accessed February 26, 2015.
11. Chris Matthews, "Wealth Inequality in America: It's Worse Than You Think," *Fortune* (October 31, 2014), http://fortune.com/2014/10/31/inequality-wealth-income-us/, accessed April 15, 2015.
12. Bige Saatcioglu and Julie L. Ozanne, "Moral Habitus and Status Negotiation in a Marginalized Working-class Neighborhood," *Journal of Consumer Research* 40, no. 4 (2013): 692–710. cf. also N. Ordabayeva and P. Chandon, "Getting Ahead of the Joneses: When Equality Increases Conspicuous Consumption Among Bottom-Tier Consumers," *Journal of Consumer Research* 38, no. 10 (2011): 27–41.
13. Elizabeth Holmes, "Luxury Goods Sparkle," *Wall Street Journal* (May 4, 2011), http://professional.wsj.com/article/SB1000142405274870334804576300941315031916.html?mg=reno-secaucus-wsj, accessed June 16, 2011.
14. Dionne Searcey and Robert Gebeloff, "Middle Class Shrinks Further as More Fall Out Instead of Climbing Up," *New York Times* (January 25, 2015), http://www.nytimes.com/2015/01/26/business/economy/middle-class-shrinks-further-as-more-fall-out-instead-of-climbing-up.html?smid=nytcore-iphone-share&smprod=nytcore-iphone&_r=0, accessed February 25, 2015.
15. Gretchen Morgenson, "Despite Federal Regulation, C.E.O.-Worker Pay Gap Data Remains Hidden," *New York Times* (April 10, 2015), http://www.nytimes.com/2015/04/12/business/despite-federal-regulation-ceo-worker-pay-gap-data-remains-hidden.html?ref=business&_r=0, accessed April 14, 2015; Patricia Cohen, "One Company's New Minimum Wage: $70,000 a Year," *New York Times* (April 13, 2015), http://www.nytimes.com/2015/04/14/business/owner-of-gravity-payments-a-credit-card-processor-is-setting-a-new-minimum-wage-70000-a-year.html?ref=business&_r=0, accessed April 14, 2015.
16. Mark Gongloff, "The U.S. Has the Worst Income Inequality in the Developed World, Thanks to Wall Street: Study," *The Huffington Post* (August 15, 2013), http://www.huffingtonpost.com/2013/08/15/income-inequality-wall-street_n_3762422.html, accessed April 14, 2015.
17. Jonathan H. Turner, *Sociology: Studying the Human System*, (Santa Monica, CA: Goodyear, 1981), 260.
18. See Ronald Paul Hill and Mark Stamey, "The Homeless in America: An Examination of Possessions and Consumption Behaviors," *Journal of Consumer Research* 17 (December 1990): 303–321; "The Homeless Facts and Figures," NOW (May 2, 2007), www.ask.com/bar?q=What+Percentage+of+Americans+Are+Homeless&page=1&qsrc=6&ab=0&u=http://www.pbs.org/now/shows/305/homeless-facts.html, accessed June 17, 2009.
19. Joseph Kahl, *The American Class Structure* (New York: Holt, Rinehart & Winston, 1961).
20. "A Family Affair: Intergenerational Social Mobility Across OECD Countries," Organization for Economic Co-Operation and Development (2010), http://www.oecd.org/tax/public-finance/chapter%205%20gfg%202010.pdf, accessed March 17, 2013; Dan Froomkin, "Social Immobility: Climbing the Economic Ladder Is Harder in the U.S. Than in Most European Countries," *The Huffington Post* (September 21, 2010), http://www.huffingtonpost.com/2010/03/17/social-immobility-climbin_n_501788.html, accessed September 25, 2013.
21. Steve Hargreaves, "The Myth of the American Dream," *CNN Money* (December 9, 2013), http://money.cnn.com/2013/12/09/news/economy/america-economic-mobility/index.html, accessed April 14, 2015.
22. David Leonhardt, "In Climbing Income Ladder, Location Matters," *New York Times* (July 22, 2013), http://www.nytimes.com/2013/07/22/business/in-climbing-income-ladder-location-matters.html?_r=0, accessed February 26, 2015.
23. Quoted in Jessica Silver-Greenberg, "*Perfect 10? Never Mind That. Ask Her for Her Credit Score*," *New York Times* (December 25, 2012), http://www.nytimes.com/2012/12/26/business/even-cupid-wants-to-know-your-credit-score.html, accessed April 15, 2015.
24. "The Great Recession," Economic Policy Institute, http://stateofworkingamerica.org/great-recession/, accessed April 14, 2015.
25. Matt Richtel, "Austere Times? Perfect," *New York Times* (April 10, 2009), www.nytimes.com/2009/04/11/business/economy/11cheap.html?_r=1, accessed April 13, 2015; www.stretcher.com, accessed April 13, 2015; www.allthingsfrugal.com, accessed April 13, 2015;; www.frugalmom.net, accessed April 13, 2015.
26. Tami Luhby, "Income is on the Rise ... Finally!," *CNN Money* (August 20, 2014) http://money.cnn.com/2014/08/20/news/economy/median-income/, accessed April 13, 2015.
27. Wendy Koch, "Mini-apartments are the Next Big Thing In U.S. Cities," *USA Today* (August 1, 2013), http://www.usatoday.com/story/news/nation/2013/07/30/tiny-apartments-apodments-catch-on-us-cities/2580179/, accessed February 18, 2015.

28. Stephanie Rosenbloom, "But Will It Make You Happy?," *New York Times* (August 7, 2010), http://www.nytimes.com/2010/08/08/business/08consume.html?pagewanted=1&_r=2&ref=business, accessed April 10, 2011.

29. Carmen DeNavas-Walt and Bernadette D. Proctor, Income and Poverty in the United States: 2013, Report Number P60-249, *United States Census Bureau* (September 16, 2014), http://www.census.gov/library/publications/2014/demo/p60-249.html, accessed April 14, 2015; *Occupational Employment and Wage Estimates*, Bureau of Labor Statistics, www.bls.gov/oes/oes_data.htm, accessed April 16, 2015.

30. Annie Lowrey, "The Premium From a College Degree," *New York Times* (June 7, 2013), http://economix.blogs.nytimes.com/2013/06/07/the-premium-from-a-college-degree/, accessed April 14, 2015; Troy Onink, "Federal Reserve: College Education Worth $830,000 More Than High School Diploma," *Forbes* (May 5, 2014), http://www.forbes.com/sites/troyonink/2014/05/05/federal-reserve-college-education-worth-830000-more-than-high-school-diploma/, accessed April 14, 2015.

31. "Reading the Buyer's Mind," *U.S. News & World Report* (March 16, 1987): 59.

32. Shelly Reese, "The Many Faces of Affluence," *Marketing Tools* (November–December 1997): 44–48.

33. Rebecca Gardyn, "Oh, the Good Life," *American Demographics* (November 2002): 34.

34. Paul Fussell, *Class: A Guide Through the American Status System* (New York: Summit Books, 1983): 29.

35. Elizabeth C. Hirschman, "Secular Immortality and the American Ideology of Affluence," *Journal of Consumer Research* 17 (June 1990): 31–42.

36. Richard C. Coleman and Lee Rainwater, *Social Standing in America: New Dimensions of Class* (New York: Basic Books, 1978), 150.

37. Kerry A. Dolan, "The World's Working Rich," *Forbes* (July 3, 2000): 162.

38. Jason DeParle, "Spy Anxiety: The Smart Magazine That Makes Smart People Nervous About Their Standing," *Washingtonian Monthly* (February 1989): 10.

39. For an examination of retailing issues related to the need for status, cf. Jacqueline Kilsheimer Eastman, Leisa Reinecke Flynn, and Ronald E. Goldsmith, "Shopping for Status: The Retail Managerial Implications," *Association of Marketing Theory & Practice* (Spring 1994): 125–130; also cf. Wilfred Amaldoss and Sanjay Jain, "Pricing of Conspicuous Goods: A Competitive Analysis of Social Effects," *Journal of Marketing Research* 42 (February 2005): 30–42.

40. Martin Fackler, "Pajamas: Not Just for Sleep Anymore," *Opelika-Auburn News* (September 13, 2002): 7A.

41. Paula Mergenhagen, "What Can Minimum Wage Buy?," *American Demographics* (January 1996): 32–36.

42. A. T. Kearney, *Serving the Low-Income Consumer: How to Tackle This Mostly Ignored Market* (2011), http://www.atkearney.com/index.php/Publications/serving-the-low-income-consumer.html, accessed March 17, 2013; cf. also Kelly D. Martin and Ronald Paul Hill, "Life Satisfaction, Self-Determination, and Consumption Adequacy at the Bottom of the Pyramid," *Journal of Consumer Research* 38, no. 6 (April 2012): 1155–1168.

43. Stephanie Strom, "Multinational Companies Court Lower-Income Consumers," *New York Times* (September 17, 2014), http://www.nytimes.com/2014/09/18/business/international/multinational-companies-court-lower-income-consumers.html?smid=nytcore-iphone-share&smprod=nytcore-iphone&_r=0, accessed February 26, 2015; http://www.dlight.com/, accessed April 15, 2015.

44. Teddy Wayne, "Digital Divide Is a Matter of Income," *New York Times* (December 12, 2010), http://www.nytimes.com/2010/12/13/business/media/13drill.html?adxnnl=1&src=busln&adxnnlx=1304179556-CFuBrgamrMhyRJjRfjj9Zg, accessed April 30, 2011.

45. Matt Richtel, "Wasting Time is New Divide in Digital Era," *New York Times* (May 29, 2012), http://www.nytimes.com/2012/05/30/us/new-digital-divide-seen-in-wasting-time-online.html, accessed April 16, 2015.

46. Richard P. Coleman, "The Continuing Significance of Social Class to Marketing"; W. Lloyd Warner and Paul S. Lunt, eds., *The Social Life of a Modern Community* (New Haven, CT: Yale University Press, 1941).

47. Floyd L. Ruch and Philip G. Zimbardo, *Psychology and Life*, 8th ed. (Glenview, IL: Scott Foresman, 1971).

48. Jonathan H. Turner, *Sociology: Studying the Human System*, 2nd ed. (Santa Monica, CA: Goodyear, 1981).

49. Richard P. Coleman, "The Continuing Significance of Social Class to Marketing," *Journal of Consumer Research* 10 (December 1983): 265–280; Turner, *Sociology: Studying the Human System*.

50. Rebecca Gardyn, "The Mating Game," *American Demographics* (July–August 2002): 33–34.

51. Richard C. Coleman and Lee Rainwater, *Social Standing in America: New Dimensions of Class* (New York: Basic Books, 1978): 89.

52. Coleman and Rainwater, *Social Standing in America*.

53. Turner, *Sociology: Studying the Human System*.

54. Coleman and Rainwater, *Social Standing in America*.

55. Coleman and Rainwater, *Social Standing in America*.

56. Jeffrey F. Durgee, "How Consumer Sub-Cultures Code Reality: A Look at Some Code Types," in Richard J. Lutz, ed., *Advances in Consumer Research* 13 (Provo, UT: Association for Consumer Research, 1986): 332–337.

57. Paul C. Henry, "Social Class, Market Situation, and Consumers' Metaphors of (Dis)Empowerment," *Journal of Consumer Research* 31 (March 2005): 766–778.

58. David Halle, *America's Working Man: Work, Home, and Politics Among Blue-Collar Owners* (Chicago: University of Chicago Press, 1984); David Montgomery, "America's Working Man," *Monthly Review* (1985): 1.

59. Coleman and Rainwater, *Social Standing in America*, 139.

60. Roger Brown, *Social Psychology* (New York: Free Press, 1965).

61. Kit R. Roane, "Affluenza Strikes Kids," *U.S. News & World Report* (March 20, 2000): 55.

62. Mark Cleveland, Michel Laroche, and Nicolas Papadopoulos, "Cosmopolitanism, Consumer Ethnocentrism, and Materialism: An Eight-Country Study of Antecedents and Outcomes," *Journal of International Marketing* 17, no. 1 (2009): 116–146; cf. also Dana Alden, James Kelley, Petra Reifler, Julie Lee, and Geoff Soutar, "The Negative Impact of Global Companies: A Three Country Study on Global Company Animosity," *Journal of International Marketing*, June 2013, Vol. 21, No. 2, pp. 17-38.

63. See Coleman, "The Continuing Significance of Social Class to Marketing"; Charles M. Schaninger, "Social Class Versus Income Revisited: An Empirical Investigation," *Journal of Marketing Research* 18 (May 1981): 192–208.

64. Coleman, "The Continuing Significance of Social Class to Marketing."

65. August B. Hollingshead and Fredrick C. Redlich, *Social Class and Mental Illness: A Community Study* (New York: Wiley, 1958).

66. John Mager and Lynn R. Kahle, "Is the Whole More Than the Sum of the Parts? Re-evaluating Social Status in Marketing," *Journal of Business Psychology* 10 (Fall 1995): 3–18.

67. Beeghley, *Social Stratification in America: A Critical Analysis of Theory and Research*.

68. R. Vanneman and F. C. Pampel, "The American Perception of Class and Status," *American Sociological Review* 42 (June 1977): 422–437.

69. Coleman, "The Continuing Significance of Social Class to Marketing"; Donald W. Hendon, Emelda L. Williams, and Douglas E. Huffman, "Social Class System Revisited," *Journal of Business Research* 17 (November 1988): 259.

70. Gerhard E. Lenski, "Status Crystallization: A Non-Vertical Dimension of Social Status," *American Sociological Review* 19 (August 1954): 405–412.

71. Richard P. Coleman, "The Significance of Social Stratification in Selling," in Martin L. Bell, ed., *Marketing: A Maturing Discipline: Proceedings of the American Marketing Association 43rd National Conference* (Chicago: American Marketing Association, 1960): 171–184.

72. Erin Carlyle, "2014 Foreclosure Filings Hit Lowest Level Since 2006, Realty Trac Says," *Forbes* (January 15, 2015), http://www.forbes.com/sites/erincarlyle/2015/01/15/foreclosure-filings-drop-by-18-in-2014-hit-lowest-level-since-2006-realtytrac-says/, accessed April 15, 2015.

73. E. Barth and W. Watson, "Questionable Assumptions in the Theory of Social Stratification," *Pacific Sociological Review* 7 (Spring 1964): 10–16.

74. Zick Rubin, "Do American Women Marry Up?" *American Sociological Review* 33 (1968): 750–760.

75. K. U. Ritter and L. L. Hargens, "Occupational Positions and Class Identifications of Married Working Women: A Test of the Asymmetry Hypothesis," *American Journal of Sociology* 80 (January 1975): 934–948.

76. Howard W. French, "Chinese Children Learn Class, Minus the Struggle," *New York Times* (September 22, 2006), www.nytimes.com, accessed September 22, 2006; Bay Fang, "The Shanghai High Life," *U.S. News & World Report* (June 20, 2005), www.usnews.com/usnews/biztech/articles/050620/20china.b2.htm, accessed June 20, 2005; Janine Gibson, "Den of Equity," *The Guardian* (May 12, 2001), http://travel.guardian.co.uk/cities/story/0,7450,489488,00.html, accessed June 20, 2005; Russell Flannery, "Long Live the $25 Cigar," *Forbes* (December 27, 2004): 51; Clay Chandler, "China Deluxe," *Fortune* (July 26, 2004): 149–156; Matthew Forney, "How Nike Figured Out China," *Time* (November 2004): A10–A14; J. David Lynch, "Emerging Middle Class Reshaping China," *USA Today* (November 12, 2002): 13A.

77. Brook Larmermach, "The Price of Marriage in China," *New York Times* (March 9, 2013), http://www.nytimes.com/2013/03/10/business/in-a-changing-china-new-matchmaking-markets.html?pagewanted=2&_r=0&ref=global-home, accessed February 25, 2015.

78. Sebastian Moffett, "The Japanese Paradox: Pinched by Economic Slump, Women Buy More Handbags from Vuitton, Prada, Hermes," *Wall Street Journal* (September 23, 2003), www.wsj.com, accessed September 23, 2003.

79. Vijay Mahajan, "Understanding the Arab Consumer," *Harvard Business Review* (May 2013), https://hbr.org/2013/05/understanding-the-arab-consumer, accessed April 15, 2015.

80. Frank Skinner, "Take Not the Moat Out of the Tory's Eye," *Times of London* (May 15, 2009), www.timesonline.co.uk/tol/comment/columnists/frank_skinner/article6289313.ece, accessed June 17, 2009.

81. Quoted in Sarah Lyall, "Multiplying the Old Divisions of Class in Britain," *New York Times* (April 3, 2013), http://www.nytimes.com/2013/04/04/world/europe/multiplying-the-old-divisions-of-class-in-britain.html?_r=0,accessed April 11, 2013; "Huge Survey Reveals Seven Social Classes in UK," *BBC News UK* (April 3, 2013), http://www.bbc.co.uk/news/uk-22007058, accessed April 11, 2013.

82. Quoted in Catherine Ostler, "As Romeo Beckham stars in their new ad, how Burberry went from chic to chav to chic again," *Daily Mail* (November 5, 2014), http://www.dailymail.co.uk/femail/article-2822546/As-Romeo-Beckham-stars-new-ad-Burberry-went-chic-chav-chic-again.html#ixzz3XPfKw2yb, accessed April 15, 2015; Robert Guy Matthews, "Bawdy British Ads Target Hot Youth," *Wall Street Journal* (April 20, 2005): B9.

83. Heather Timmons, "Vogue's Fashion Photos Spark Debate in India,"*New York Times* (August 31, 2008), www.nytimes.com/2008/09/01/business/worldbusiness/01vogue.html?_r=1&ref=busi; accessed September 1, 2008.

84. Quoted in Timmons, "Vogue's Fashion Photos Spark Debate in India."

85. Sara C. Nelson, "Vagina 'Brightener': Indian Feminine Hygiene Product Promises to Make Genitals 'Many Shades Fairer'," *Huffington Post UK*, http://www.huffingtonpost.co.uk/2012/04/12/vagina-brightener-indian-feminine-hygiene-product-promises-to-make-genitals-many-shades-fairer_n_1420052.html?just_reloaded=1, accessed January 11, 2013.

86. "India's Middle Class Population to Touch 267 Million in 5 Yrs," *Hindustan Times*, http://www.hindustantimes.com/India-news/NewDelhi/India-s-middle-class-population-to-touch-267-million-in-5-yrs/Article1-659159.aspx, accessed March 17, 2013.

87. "Indian Consumer Market: A Change from Pyramid to Sparkling Diamond," KS Oils, http://www.ksoils.com/whitepapers/KS_WHITEPAPER_INDIAN_CONSUMER_MARKET.Pdf, accessed March 17, 2013.

88. Jennifer Steinhauer, "When the Joneses Wear Jeans," *New York Times* (May 29, 2005), www.nytimes.com, accessed May 29, 2005.

89. "Welcome to the post-BRIC world," *The Economist* (May 6th 2013,) http://www.economist.com/blogs/freeexchange/2013/05/global-economy, accessed April 16, 2015; Mike Bird, "China Just Overtook The US As The World's Largest Economy," *Business Insider* (October 8, 2014), http://www.businessinsider.com/china-overtakes-us-as-worlds-largest-economy-2014-10#ixzz3XU8vMG9d, accessed April 16, 2015.

90. Paul F. Nunes, Brian A. Johnson, and R. Timothy S. Breene, "Moneyed Masses," *Harvard Business Review* (July–August 2004): 94–104; *Trend Update: Massclusivity*, report from Reinier Evers and Trendwatching.com, Zyman Institute of Brand Science, Emory University, www.zibs.com, accessed February 25, 2005.

91. Philip J. Mazzocco, Derek D. Rucker, Adam D. Galinsky, and Eric T. Anderson, "Direct and Vicarious Conspicuous Consumption: Identification with Low-Status Groups Increases the Desire for High-Status Goods," *Journal of Consumer Psychology* 22, no. 4 (2012): 520–528.

92. David Dubois, Derek D. Rucker, and Adam D. Galinsky, "Super Size Me: Product Size as a Signal of Status," *Journal of Consumer Research* 38, no. 6 (2012): 1047–1062.

93. Herbert J. Gans, "Popular Culture in America: Social Problem in a Mass Society or Social Asset in a Pluralist Society?" in Howard S. Becker, ed., *Social Problems: A Modern Approach* (New York: Wiley, 1966).

94. Eugene Sivadas, George Mathew, and David J. Curry, "A Preliminary Examination of the Continuing Significance of Social Class to Marketing: A Geodemographic Replication," *Journal of Consumer Marketing* 41, no. 6 (1997): 463–479.

95. Edward O. Laumann and James S. House, "Living Room Styles and Social Attributes: The Patterning of Material Artifacts in a Modern Urban Community," *Sociology & Social Research* 54 (April 1970): 321–342; see also Stephen S. Bell, Morris B. Holbrook, and Michael R. Solomon, "Combining Esthetic and Social Value to Explain Preferences for Product Styles with the Incorporation of Personality and Ensemble Effects," *Journal of Social Behavior & Personality* 6 (1991): 243–274.

96. Morris B. Holbrook, Michael J. Weiss, and John Habich, "Class-Related Distinctions in American Cultural Tastes," *Empirical Studies of the Arts* 22, no. 1 (2004): 91–115.

97. Nick Bilton, "A Line Is Drawn in the Desert: At Burning Man, the Tech Elite One-Up One Another," *New York Times* (August 20, 2014), http://www.nytimes.com/2014/08/21/fashion/at-burning-man-the-tech-elite-one-up-one-another.html?smid=nytcore-iphone-share&smprod=nytcore-iphone, accessed April 16, 2015.

98. Pierre Bourdieu, *Distinction: A Social Critique of the Judgment of Taste* (Cambridge, UK: Cambridge University Press, 1984); cf. also Douglas B. Holt, "Does Cultural Capital Structure American Consumption?," *Journal of Consumer Research* 1 (June 1998): 1–25; Tuba Ustuner and Douglas B. Holt, "Toward a Theory of Status Consumption in Less Industrialized Countries," *Journal of Consumer Research* 37, no. 1 (2010): 37–56; James S. Coleman, "Social Capital in the Creation of Human Capital," *American Journal of Sociology* 94 (1988): 95–120.

99. Nicole Ellison, Charles Steinfield, and Cliff Lampe, "The Benefits of Facebook 'Friends': Social Capital and College Students' Use of Online Social Network Sites," *Journal of Computer-Mediated Communication* 12 (2007): 1143–1168.

100. Anya Kamenetz, "The Perils and Promise of the Reputation Economy," *Fast Company* (November 25, 2008), www.fastcompany.com/magazine/131/on-the-internet-everyone-knows-youre-a-dog.html, accessed June 17, 2009.

101. Quoted from www.hotenough.org, accessed April 16, 2015.

102. Charla Mathwick, Caroline Wiertz, and Ko de Ruyter, "Social Capital Production in a Virtual P3 Community," *Journal of Consumer Research* 34 (April 2008): 832–849; cf. also Jonah Berger and Morgan Ward, "Subtle Signals of Inconspicuous Consumption," *Journal of Consumer Research* 37, no. 4 (2010): 555–569.

103. Molly Oswaks, "'This.' Has People Clamoring for an Invite," *New York Times* (January 28, 2015), http://www.nytimes.com/2015/01/29/fashion/this-has-people-clamoring-for-an-invite.html?smid=nytcore-ipad-share&smprod=nytcore-ipad, accessed February 25, 2015.

104. Ruth LaFerla, "A Facebook for the Few," *New York Times* (September 6, 2007), www.nytimes.com, accessed September 6, 2007; www.asmallworld.com, accessed April 16, 2015.

105. Xavier Drèze and Joseph C. Nunes, "Feeling Superior: The Impact of Loyalty Program Structure on Consumers' Perceptions of Status," *Journal of Consumer Research* (April 2009): 890–905; cf. also Eesha Sharma and Adam L. Alter, "Financial Deprivation Prompts Consumers to Seek Scarce Goods," *Journal of Consumer Research* 39, no. 3 (October 2012): 545–560.

106. Derek Rucker and Adam D. Galinsky, "Desire to Acquire: Powerlessness and Compensatory Consumption," *Journal of Consumer Research* 35 (August 2008): 257–267.

107. "China: The Land Where Fake Brands Reign Supreme," *WeirdAsia News* (October 22, 2010), http://www.weirdasianews.com/2010/10/22/china-the-land-fake-brands-reign-supreme/, accessed June 16, 2011.

108. Suraj Commuri, "The Impact of Counterfeiting on Genuine-Item Consumers' Brand Relationships," *Journal of Marketing* 73 (May 2009): 86–98.

109. Quoted in Jennifer Steinhauer, "When the Joneses Wear Jeans," *New York Times* (May 29, 2005), http://www.nytimes.com/2005/05/29/national/class/CONSUMPTION-FINAL.html?pagewanted=all, accessed April 16, 2015.

110. Rod Nordland, "Iraqis Snap Up Hummers as Icons of Power," *New York Times* (March 29, 2009), http://www.nytimes.com/2009/03/30/world/middleeast/30hummer.html?scp=1&sq=Iraqis%20Snap%20Up%20Hummers%20as%20Icons%20of%20Power&st=cse, accessed March 29, 2009.

111. Melissa Healy, "China's 'Little Emperor' Generation Fits Stereotypes, Study Finds," (January 11, 2013), *Los Angeles Times*, http://articles.latimes.com/2013/jan/11/science/la-sci-china-little-emperors-20130111, accessed April 16, 2015.

112. Robert Frank, "Biggest Billionaire Losers in 2014? The Russians," *CNBC* (March 2, 2015), http://www.cnbc.com/id/102468463, accessed April 16, 2015. Andrew E. Kramer, "New Czars of Conspicuous Consumption," *New York Times* (November 1, 2006), www.nytimes.com, accessed November 1, 2006.

113. Tom Wright, "Ringing Up Sales in Indonesia: Nokia's Bulky Smart Phones Find Niche Following There as Business Status Symbol," *Wall Street Journal* (May 22, 2007): B1.

114. John Brooks, *Showing Off in America* (Boston, MA: Little, Brown, 1981), 13.

115. Naughton Keith, "The Perk Wars," *Newsweek* (September 30, 2002): 42–46.

116. http://www.wikihow.com/Know-if-a-Woman-is-a-Cougar, accessed July 29, 2013; Alexia Elejalde-Ruiz, "Age Gap: She's Old Enough to Be his ... Wife," *Chicago Tribune* (September 19, 2012), http://articles.chicagotribune.com/2012-09-19/features/sc-fam-0918-age-gap-romance-20120919_1_age-gap-age-difference-age-matters, accessed March 17, 2013; Jessica Leshnoff, "Cougars and Their Cubs," *AARP* (February 2008), www.aarp.org/family/love/articles/cougars_and_their.html, accessed June 17, 2009; Robert Campbell, "For the Mature Woman Who Has Everything: A Boy Toy," Reuters (January 30, 2008), http://www.reuters.com/article/2008/01/30/us-speeddating-odd-idUSN3061371020080130, accessed July 29, 2013.

117. Young Jee Han, Joseph C. Nunes, and Xavier Drèze, "Signaling Status with Luxury Goods: The Role of Brand Prominence," *Journal of Marketing* 74 (July 2010): 15–30.

118. Thorstein Veblen, *The Theory of the Leisure Class* (1899; reprint, New York: New American Library, 1953): 45.

119. John Brooks, *Showing Off in America: From Conspicuous Consumption to Parody Display*, 1984.

120. Daisy Grewal, "How Wealth Reduces Compassion," *Scientific American* (April 10, 2012), http://www.scientificamerican.com/article/how-wealth-reduces-compassion/, accessed February 26, 2015.

Chapter 13 • Subcultures

aria wakes up early on Saturday morning and braces herself for a long day of errands and chores. As usual, her mother is at work and expects Maria to do the shopping and help prepare dinner for the big family gathering tonight. Of course, her older brother Orlando would never be asked to do the grocery shopping or help out in the kitchen; these are women's jobs.

Family gatherings make a lot of work. Maria wishes that her mother would use prepared foods once in a while, especially on a Saturday when Maria has an errand or two of her own to do. But no, her mother insists on preparing most of her food from scratch. She rarely uses any convenience products, to ensure that the meals she serves are of the highest quality.

Resigned, Maria watches a *telenovela* (soap opera) on Univision while she dresses and then she heads down to the *carnicería* (small grocery store) to buy a newspaper—almost 40 different Spanish newspapers are published in her area, and she likes to pick up new ones occasionally. Then Maria buys the grocery items her mother wants. The list is full of well-known brand names that she gets all the time, such as Casera and Goya, so she's able to finish quickly. With any luck, she'll have a few minutes to go to the *mercado* (shopping center) to pick up that new Reggaeton CD by Daddy Yankee. She'll listen to it in the kitchen while she chops, peels, and stirs.

Maria smiles to herself: Los Angeles is a great place to live, and what could be better than spending a lively, fun evening with *la familia*?

Source: Evok20/Shutterstock.

OBJECTIVE 13-1
Consumer identity
derives from "we" as
well as "I."

Ethnic and Racial Subcultures

Sí, Maria lives in Los Angeles, not Mexico City. More than one in four Californians are Hispanic, and overall the state has more non-white than white residents. In fact, more people watch Spanish-language Univision in Los Angeles than any other network; it's the fifth-largest network in the United States.[1]

Maria and other Hispanic Americans have much in common with members of other racial and ethnic groups who live in the United States. They observe the same national holidays, the country's economic health affects what they spend, and they may root for Team USA in the Olympics. Nonetheless, although U.S. citizenship provides the raw material for some consumption decisions, enormous variations in the social fabric of the country profoundly affect many others. The United States truly is a "melting pot" of hundreds of diverse groups, from Italian and Irish Americans to Mormons and Seventh-Day Adventists.

As we saw in Chapter 11, groups exert a lot of influence on our individual consumer decisions. Still, some of our affiliations are more central to our essence than are others.[2] In this chapter we'll look at some of the external linkages that play a big role in defining who we are and what we value: gender, race/ethnicity, religion, age, and where we live. Each of these is a **subculture**, which is a group whose members share significant beliefs and common preferences.

The rapidly growing diversity of U.S. culture is one of the most important drivers of change in this century. The U.S. Census Bureau projects that by 2018, it won't be possible to place a majority of children younger than the age of 18 into a single racial or ethnic group. Over the next 45 years, the Bureau expects the Hispanic population to more than double; by 2060 almost one in three Americans will identify as Hispanic. The Asian population will double during the same time period. Furthermore, traditional subcultural categories are breaking down. The Census Bureau also predicts that by 2050, people who identify themselves as multiracial will make up almost 4 percent of the U.S. population. Among U.S. children, the multiracial population has increased almost 50 percent, to 4.2 million, since 2000, making it the fastest-growing youth group in the country. The number of people of all ages who identified themselves as both white and black soared by 134 percent since 2000 to 1.8 million people.[3] Our country truly is a "melting pot" of people who belong to many different racial and ethnic subcultures.

Many major marketers are keenly aware of this change. McDonald's U.S. chief marketing officer (CMO) observes, "The ethnic consumer tends to set trends. So they help set the tone for how we enter the marketplace." He notes that feedback from minority consumers shape McDonald's menu and ad choices, which it then markets to all of its customers. In fact, the chain's U.S. strategy is called "Leading with Ethnic Insights." The company includes a disproportionate number of blacks, Hispanics, and Asians in focus groups. It asks its marketers to imagine how they would sell a product if the U.S. population were *only* African American, Hispanic, or Asian. For example, the fruit combinations in McDonald's latest smoothies reflect taste preferences in minority communities. And when the company started heavily advertising coffee drinks last year, the ads emphasized the indulgent aspects of sweeter drinks like mochas, a message that resonated with African Americans. Ethnic practices also get picked up in mainstream advertising: In one commercial called "Big Day," a young boy at a wedding looks bored while watching the bride and groom kiss and jump over a broom—an African American wedding tradition. His eyes light up when he gets to his seat and finds a Happy Meal.[4]

One important subcultural difference is how abstract or literal the group is. Sociologists make a basic distinction: In a **high-context culture**, group members tend to be tightly knit, and they infer meanings that go beyond the spoken word. Symbols and gestures, rather than words, carry much of the weight of the message. In contrast, people who belong to a **low-context culture** are more literal. Compared to Anglos (who tend to be low-context), many minority cultures are high context and have strong oral traditions, so consumers are more sensitive to nuances in advertisements that go beyond the message copy.

OBJECTIVE 13-2
Our memberships in
ethnic, racial, and
religious subcultures
often guide our
consumption choices.

Subcultural Stereotypes

Adidas provoked outrage when in 2014 the company posted a photo of a new design, the JS Roundhouse Mids, on its Facebook page. The shoes come with bright orange shackles and the tagline, "Got a sneaker game so hot you lock your kicks to your ankles?" Many users complained that this image is highly offensive to African Americans because it evokes imagery of slavery and chain gangs. The company claimed the design had nothing to do with these issues, but the damage was done.[5]

In the past, it was fairly common for marketers to use racial or ethnic symbolism as shorthand to convey certain product attributes. Before these actions became taboo, they often employed crude and unflattering images when they depicted African Americans as subservient or Mexicans as bandits.[6] Aunt Jemima sold pancake mix and Rastus was a grinning black chef who pitched Cream of Wheat hot cereal. The Gold Dust Twins were black urchins who peddled a soap powder for Lever Brothers, and Pillsbury hawked powdered drink mixes via characters such as Injun Orange and Chinese Cherry—who had buck teeth.[7] As the civil rights movement gave more power to minority groups and their rising economic status began to command marketers' respect, these negative stereotypes began to disappear. Frito-Lay responded to protests by the Hispanic community and stopped using the Frito Bandito character in 1971, and Quaker Foods gave Aunt Jemima a makeover in 1989.

Many subcultures have powerful stereotypes the general public associates with them. In these cases, outsiders assume that group members possess certain traits. Unfortunately, a communicator can cast the same trait as either positive or negative, depending on his or her biases or intentions. For example, the Scottish stereotype in the United States is largely positive, so we tend to look favorably on their (supposed) frugality. The 3M company uses Scottish imagery to denote value (e.g., Scotch tape), as does Scotch Inns, a motel chain that offers inexpensive lodging. However, the Scottish "personality" might carry quite different connotations to the British or Irish. One person's "thrifty" is another's "stingy."

Ethnicity and Acculturation

Although some people feel uncomfortable with the notion that marketers should explicitly take into account people's racial and ethnic differences when they formulate their strategies, the reality is that these subcultural memberships do shape many needs and wants. Research indicates, for example, that members of minority groups find an advertising spokesperson from their own group more trustworthy, and this enhanced credibility in turn translates into more positive brand attitudes.[8] However, marketers need to avoid the temptation to paint all members of an ethnic or racial group with the same brush; not only are these generalizations inaccurate, but they also are likely to turn off the very people a company wants to reach.[9]

Acculturation is the process of movement and adaptation to one country's cultural environment by a person from another country.[10] This is an important issue for marketers due to our increasingly global society. As people move from place to place, they may quickly assimilate to their new homes, or they may resist this blending process and choose to insulate themselves from the mainstream culture. It's typical for a new arrival in the United States, for example, to feel ambivalence or conflict about relinquishing old ways (and consumer behaviors) for new ones. Home Depot segments its campaigns when the retailer speaks to the Hispanic market; it creates different ads for "acculturated Hispanics" (second- or third-generation Americans) than it shows to consumers who almost always speak Spanish.[11]

A study of Mexican immigrants that used the research technique of *ethnography* probed their acculturation as they adapted to life in the United States.[12] Indeed, after the researchers interviewed these people in their natural settings, they reported a lot of ambivalence. On the one hand, they are happy about the improvements in the quality of their lives because of greater job availability and educational opportunities for their children. On the other hand, they report bittersweet feelings about leaving Mexico. They miss their friends, their holidays, their food, and the comfort that comes from living in familiar surroundings.

Many factors affect the nature of the transition process. Individual differences, such as whether the person speaks English, influence how rocky the adjustment will be. The person's contact with **acculturation agents**—people and institutions that teach the ways of a culture—are also crucial. Some of these agents come from the *culture of origin* (in this case, Mexico), including family, friends, the church, local businesses, and Spanish-language media that keep the consumer in touch with his or her country of origin. Other agents come from the *culture of immigration* (in this case, the United States) and help the consumer to learn how to navigate in the new environment. These include public schools, English-language media, and government agencies.

Several processes come into play as immigrants adapt to their new surroundings. *Movement* refers to the factors that motivate people to physically uproot themselves from one location and go to another. In this case, people leave Mexico because of the scarcity of jobs and the desire to provide a good education for their children. On arrival, immigrants encounter a need for *translation*. This means they try to master a set of rules for operating in the new environment, whether it's learning how to decipher a different currency or figuring out the social meanings of unfamiliar clothing styles. This cultural learning leads to a process of *adaptation*, by which people form new consumption patterns. For example, some of the Mexican women in the study started to wear shorts and pants once they settled in the United States, although people in Mexico frown on this practice.

During the acculturation process, many immigrants undergo *assimilation*, during which they adopt products, habits, and values they identify with the mainstream culture. At the same time, there is an attempt at *maintenance* of practices they associate with the culture of origin. Immigrants stay in touch with people in their country, and like Maria, many continue to eat Hispanic foods and read Spanish-language newspapers. Their continued identification with Mexican culture may cause *resistance* because they resent the pressure to submerge their Mexican identities and take on new roles. Finally, immigrants (voluntarily or not) tend to exhibit *segregation*; they are likely to live and shop in places physically separated from mainstream Anglo consumers. These processes illustrate that ethnicity is a fluid concept and that members of a subculture constantly recreate its boundaries.

The **progressive learning model** helps us to understand the acculturation process. This perspective assumes that people gradually learn a new culture as they increasingly come in contact with it. Thus, we expect that when people acculturate, they will mix the practices of their original culture with those of their new or **host culture**.[13] Research that examines such factors as shopping orientation, the importance people place on various product attributes, media preference, and brand loyalty generally supports this pattern.[14] When researchers take into account the intensity of ethnic identification, they find that consumers who retain a strong ethnic identification differ from their more assimilated counterparts in these ways:[15]

- They have a more negative attitude toward business in general (probably caused by frustration because of relatively low income levels).
- They access more media that's in their native language.
- They are more brand loyal.
- They are more likely to prefer brands with prestige labels.
- They are more likely to buy brands that specifically advertise to their ethnic group.

The acculturation process occurs even when we relocate from one place to another within the same country. If you have ever moved (and it's likely you have), you no doubt remember how difficult it was to give up old habits and friends and adapt to what people in your new location do.

A study of Turkish people who moved from the countryside to an urban environment illustrates how people cope with change and unfamiliar circumstances. The authors describe a process of **warming**, which they describe as transforming objects and places into those that feel cozy, hospitable, and authentic. The study's informants described what happened as they tried to turn a cold and unfamiliar house into a home that is *güzel* ("beautiful and good," "modern and warm"). In this context, that means they integrated

Green bagels to celebrate St. Patrick's Day illustrate the concept of deethnicization.
Source: J.R. Bale/123RF.

symbols of their former village life into their new homes: They blanketed them with the embroidered, crocheted, and lace textiles that people traditionally make by hand for brides' dowries in the villages. The researchers reported that migrants' homes contained far more of these pieces than they would have in their village homes because they used them to adorn their new modern appliances. The dowry textiles symbolize traditional norms and social networks of friends and family in the villages, so they link the "cold" modern objects with the owner's past. Thus, the unfamiliar becomes familiar.[16]

Of course, it's not unusual for consumers who don't belong to a subculture to use products they associate with that group. **Deethnicization** occurs when a product we link to a specific ethnic group detaches itself from its roots and appeals to other groups as well. Think about the popularity of bagels, a staple of Jewish cuisine that's mass-marketed today. Recent variations include jalapeño bagels, blueberry bagels, and even a green bagel for St. Patrick's Day.[17] Bagels now account for 3 to 6 percent of all U.S. breakfasts, and bagel franchisers such as Bruegger's Corporation and the Einstein/Noah Bagel Corporation operate hundreds of stores in cities that had never heard of a bagel just a few years ago.[18]

The dominant U.S. culture historically exerted pressure on immigrants to divest themselves of their origins and integrate with mainstream society. As President Theodore Roosevelt put it in the early part of the 20th century, "We welcome the German or the Irishman who becomes an American. We have no use for the German or the Irishman who remains such."[19]

Indeed, there is a tendency for ethnic groups with a relatively longer history in the United States to view themselves as more mainstream as they relax their identification with their country of origin. When the U.S. Census asked respondents to write up to two ancestries that defined their background, the results showed a clear decline in the number of people who identified themselves as of Irish, German, or other European origin. Compared to other subcultures, more people from these countries simply choose to call themselves "American."[20]

The "Big Three" American Ethnic Subcultures

African Americans, Hispanic Americans, and Asian Americans account for much of the current growth of the United States. The Hispanic population is now the largest ethnic subculture.[21] Asian Americans, though much smaller in absolute numbers, are the fastest-growing racial group.[22]

I am

LaTina.

MY Style:

I am trendy, fashionable and unapologetically feminine. I know that beauty comes in all shapes and sizes – and I love my body. I love to shop for clothes that reflect my personality and show off my curves. I crave excitement and variety. Other people describe me as confident, smart and independent – they're right!

MY
Language:

I am bilingual. I speak English with my friends and Spanish with *mi familia.* I'm a modern woman yet I'm firmly rooted in my traditions and culture.

Latina

120 REASONS TO LOVE BEING LATINA STARRING ...E SALDANA

Latina

SESSILEE LOPEZ
Fashion's Next It Girl

MY Magazine:

LATINA validates and enriches every aspect of my life. It entertains and inspires me and makes me proud to be a Latina.

MY World:

Hispanics represent 15% of the total U.S. population. We are the largest and fastest growing ethnic group in the U.S. – over 45 million strong. Our spending power is predicted to explode to $1.2 trillion within the next 5 years.

Me:

I'm about 33 years old. I was born in the U.S. but I was raised 100% Latina. I went to college and I have a career that I love. My income allows me to live comfortably and independently. I am part of the fastest growing, most affluent and influential segment of the Hispanic market — the bicultural Latina.

Sources: Latina Subscriber Study 2008; U.S. Census B2007

African Americans

African Americans make up more than 13 percent of the U.S. population.[23] As we saw in the case of McDonald's, many marketers recognize the huge impact of this racial subculture and work hard to identify products and services that will appeal to these consumers. The toy market is no exception; children tend to gravitate toward toys and characters that look like them. The Disney TV show Doc McStuffins that stars an African American character who fixes toys in her backyard clinic illustrates this appeal. The blockbuster show sold about $500 million in merchandise last year. Its success reflects demographic changes in the United States that create opportunities for a diversity of ethnic characters.[24]

Procter & Gamble launched a "My Black Is Beautiful" program for African American women after the company's research showed that these women think mainstream media does not represent them very well; three-quarters of the women the company surveyed said programs and ads portray them more negatively than other racial groups and that they worry about the negative impact these messages will have on teens.[25]

The Tangled Web

The popularity of some graphic video games underscores the concern of critics who argue that these games play on racial stereotypes, including images of African American youths who commit violent street crimes. For example, *Grand Theft Auto—San Andreas* is set in a city that resembles gang-ridden stretches of Los Angeles of the 1990s. It features a digital cast of African American and Hispanic men, some of whom wear braided hair and scarves over their faces and aim Uzis from low-riding cars.[27] A recent study found that when white men and women played the game *Saints Row 2* (which is similar to *Grand Theft Auto*) and were assigned a black avatar, they expressed more negative views of black people.[28]

The Mexican pop star Thalía Sodi has a new line of clothing and accessories at Macy's in the Unites States.
Source: Splash News/Newscom.

Research by Unilever illustrates how the body image dynamics we discussed in Chapter 6 vary across subcultures; the personal care products company found that skin takes on a deeper meaning for African Americans. In a poll it ran in *Essence* magazine, the company asked more than 1,400 African American women aged 18 to 64 to describe their skin, and the most common response was "beautiful" (59 percent). Another 30 percent described their skin as "strong." The survey also found that African American women rank skin as "most important to them" (49 percent); more so than their hair, figure, makeup, and clothes. About one-third say their skin is a source of their heritage, one-fourth say it's a source of pride, and "almost half of African American women say their skin tells a story of who they are and identifies them." This deep attachment is clear in posted comments such as "My skin is my life's historian," and "My skin represents the blending of my parents, an outward expression of their love."[26]

Hispanic Americans

Macy's recently launched a colorful new line of clothing and accessories with the hot Mexican pop star Thalía Sodi. Kmart sells a celebrity line for Hispanic women called Sofia by Sofia Vergara, named for the star of the popular television show *Modern Family*. Kohl's offers a clothing line with Jennifer Lopez.[29] As the attention these major retailers are showering on this subculture shows, today many major corporations avidly

court Hispanic consumers. No surprise: The 2010 Census reported a record 50 million Hispanics, or one in every six U.S. residents; this was a 42 percent increase from the 2000 Census. Hispanics are now the nation's second-largest consumer market after white non-Hispanics. They also are geographically concentrated, which makes it easier for marketers to reach them. About half of Hispanic consumers live in California and Texas. The other six states having more than 1 million Hispanics are Florida, New York, Illinois, Arizona, New Jersey, and Colorado.[30] Note: The umbrella term **Hispanic** describes people of many different backgrounds. Nearly 60 percent of Hispanic Americans are of Mexican descent. The next largest group, Puerto Ricans, make up just fewer than 10 percent of Hispanics. Other groups the Census includes in this category are Central Americans, Dominicans, South Americans, and Cubans.

In some ways, this growing segment also resembles our idealized concept of 1950s America. On average Hispanic consumers are young (their median age is about where the whole nation was in 1955) and they more often live in large, traditional, married-with-children families where grandparents log a lot of time. They're increasingly moving to the suburbs, they tend to be community oriented, and they have high aspirations for their children. The Hispanic birth rate went down dramatically in the years since The Great Recession, but this subculture continues to exert a major influence on U.S. culture and consumer activity.[31]

Many initial efforts to market to Hispanic Americans were, to say the least, counterproductive. Companies bumbled in their efforts to translate advertising adequately or to compose copy that captured the nuances advertisers intended. These mistakes do not occur so much anymore because marketers are more sophisticated when they talk to this segment and they tend to involve Hispanics in advertising production to ensure that they get it right. These translation mishaps slipped through before Anglos got their acts together:[32]

- Budweiser was the "queen of beers."
- Braniff (now defunct) promoted the comfortable leather seats on its airplanes with the headline, *Sentado en cuero*, which translates as "Sit naked."
- Coors beer's slogan to "get loose with Coors" appeared in Spanish as "get the runs with Coors."

More than one in three Hispanics in the United States are younger than 18 years old. This means they will acculturate much faster than their parents did. Already, almost half report that they are at ease when they speak English. Indeed, recent research shows that many Hispanics don't think of themselves as distinctly Latino or American, but rather somewhere in the middle or **ambicultural**.[33]

Asian Americans

The problems U.S. marketers encountered when they first tried to reach the Hispanic market popped up again when they began to target Asian Americans:[35]

- When Proctor & Gamble started selling its Pampers diapers in Japan, it used the image of a stork delivering a baby on the packaging. However, the folk myth was unfamiliar to Japanese customers and only confused them.
- Another ad by Proctor & Gamble in Japan showed a man entering a bathroom while his wife is bathing and touching her. The Japanese considered the act an invasion of privacy and the ad in very poor taste.
- A footwear ad depicted Japanese women performing foot binding, which only the Chinese did.

Few companies would make those mistakes today. Asian Americans have surpassed Hispanics as the fastest-growing racial group in the nation and have become the largest group of new immigrants to the United States. They boast $718 billion in buying power

Net Profit

Hispanic Americans spend triple the amount of time browsing online that non-Hispanics do, and nearly twice as much time (on average 5 hours per week) on social networks. One factor that accounts for this difference is the relative youth of this segment; Hispanics ages 13 to 34 use social networking sites about three times more than do those older than the age of 35. About 30 million Hispanics—or 60 percent of the U.S. Hispanic population—are online. A study from comScore, commissioned by Terra (a Spanish-language media network), suggests that Hispanics are more active online and more receptive to new technology than non-Hispanics. The research also says the Internet is the main media source of information for Hispanics in terms of services and products. The survey of several thousand respondents reported that 37 percent of Hispanics versus 30 percent of non-Hispanics said they would respond to online pitches, and 35 percent of Hispanics versus 27 percent of non-Hispanics said they are more open to advertising on sites where they read or contribute user-generated comments. Thirty-six percent of Hispanics, compared to 24 percent of non-Hispanics, said that Internet advertising has motivated them to visit a retail establishment; 35 percent of Hispanics versus 25 percent of non-Hispanics are likely to attend movies based on their online campaigns. Sixty percent of Hispanics polled, versus 42 percent of non-Hispanics, said they like things like iPad demonstrations, virtual shoppers, mobile coupons, and live streaming. The study also noted that Hispanics are more receptive to updates for offline activities via mobile text alerts, Twitter feeds, and Facebook. They are also more likely to visit a brand's fan page and to follow Twitter updates from artists.[34]

Family is a very high priority for many Asian Americans.
Source: Monkey Business/Fotolia.

that is expected to reach $1 trillion in just 5 years, equal to the 18th-largest economy in the world.

Asian Americans not only make up the fastest-growing population group, they also are the most affluent, best educated, and most likely to hold technology jobs of any ethnic subculture. Their median income is 28 percent higher than the U.S. average and they are almost twice as likely to have graduated from college. In addition they are geographically concentrated; almost 40 percent live in Los Angeles, New York, and San Francisco. A growing number belong in a segment Nielsen calls the "swayable shopaholics," who are the most active and impulsive buyers in the country. These consumers prefer well-known brands and lead the nation in their rate of online shopping.

The Asian American subculture can be hard to reach because it's composed of numerous culturally diverse subgroups that use different languages and dialects.[36] The term *Asian* refers to 20 ethnic groups, with Chinese being the largest and Filipino and Japanese second and third, respectively. Filipinos are the only Asians who speak English predominantly among themselves; like Hispanics, most Asians prefer media in their own languages. The languages Asian Americans speak most frequently are Mandarin Chinese, Korean, Japanese, and Vietnamese.

Despite this diversity, one unifying factor that helps to describe the Asian American subculture is an emphasis on family. A recent survey reported that 54 percent of Asian Americans feel that a successful marriage is one of the most important things in life compared to 34 percent of all Americans. However, "family" also includes grandparents, aunts and uncles, and so on; these consumers are twice as likely to live with other family members as is the average American.[37]

OBJECTIVE 13-3
Marketers increasingly use religious and spiritual themes to talk to consumers.

Religious Subcultures

In recent years we've seen an explosion of religion and spirituality in popular culture, including the box office success of Mel Gibson's movie *The Passion of the Christ*, the book *The Da Vinci Code*, and even the Broadway hit *The Book of Mormon*.[38] Mainstream marketers that used to avoid religion like the plague (pardon the pun) now actively court church members.

CB AS I SEE IT
Jerome D. Williams, *Rutgers University*

Multicultural consumer segments are of increasing importance to marketers. Current projections indicate that the combined buying power of African Americans, Hispanics, Asians, and American Indians exceeds $2 trillion. Despite this growth in multicultural purchasing power, there is continuing evidence of inequality in the U.S. marketplace in terms of how these groups are treated. My research collaborators and I have been conducting studies for many years on discrimination in the marketplace, and we've concluded that despite progress in race relations over the past several decades, and in the areas of housing, employment, and education, the harsh reality is that there still are remnants of discrimination in the marketplace.

Consider the results of just a few of our studies.

1. We examined 81 federal court decisions over a 12-year period and found evidence of customers' allegations of race and/or ethnic discrimination. This involved subtle and overt discriminatory treatment, degradation and denial of services, and criminal suspicion. We acknowledge that filing a lawsuit alone is not sufficient evidence of guilt by the marketer/retailer.

2. We analyzed negative publicity resulting from consumer racial profiling and its effect on brand image. We found it had a negative effect on consumers' image of the retail brand, but the effect was temporary. However, the rate of image recovery varied with exposure to marketing communication and the personal moral philosophy of the consumer.

3. We examined how consumers perceive consumer discrimination and what actions they felt the victim should take. We found that participants' own racial/ethnic backgrounds influenced their perceptions and their reactions to it. Consumers of color more strongly agreed that victims should engage in system-challenging behaviors when confronted with discrimination.

4. We compared the experience of Hispanic, African American, and White mystery shoppers when they visited banks. The results showed even when the shoppers were identical "on paper," minorities were treated more poorly by bank officers than their White counterparts.

5. We conducted a mail survey of 1,000 households and found that 86 percent of African Americans felt that they were treated differently in retail stores based on their race, compared to 34 percent of Whites. When comparing our results with those of other surveys, we found there always was a disparity in attitudes. For example, according to the reality show *What Would You Do?*, 54 percent of African Americans reported that they were not treated equally in retail stores, whereas only 15 percent of White respondents said they felt that way.

Based on our research, it is appropriate to continue asking the question "Is the glass half empty, or is the glass half-full?" in terms of progress being made in eradicating discrimination in the marketplace. If marketers continue to remain insensitive to multicultural consumers, they run the risk of alienating these segments and, as a result, suffering severe economic consequences with the loss of dollars as these consumers shift their purchasing power to more "diversity-friendly" shopping environments. So rather than thinking of this as solely a "black versus white" issue, the smart marketers will focus on the color that matters most in meeting the needs of multicultural consumers, namely, "green."

You don't have to be active in an organized religion to "worship" products. A study of a brand community centered on the Apple Newton illustrates how religious themes spill over into everyday consumption, particularly in the case of "cult products." Apple abandoned the Newton PDA years ago, but many avid users still keep the faith. The researchers examined postings in chat rooms devoted to the product. They found that many of

Movies and plays like *The Book of Mormon* accelerate the intersection between religion and popular culture.

Source: Randy Duchaine/Alamy.

the messages have supernatural, religious, and magical themes, including the miraculous performance and survival of the brand, as well as the return of the brand creator. The most common postings concerned instances in which dead Newton batteries magically come back to life. Here is an excerpt from one story, posted on a listserv under the heading "Another Battery Miracle":

> The battery that came with the 2100 that I just received seemed dead.... I figured that the battery was fried and I have nothing to lose. While "charging," I unplugged the adapter until the indicator said it was running on batteries again, and then plugged it back in until it said "charging" ... after a few times, the battery charge indicator started moving from the left to right and was full within 10 minutes! ... I've been using the Newt for about 4 hours straight without any problems. Strange. It looks like there has been yet another Newton battery miracle! Keep the faith.[39]

In addition to organized religion, numerous other types of groups serve similar functions for consumers—and indeed, they may be loosely based on religious principles (like the highly successful 12-step program that guides Alcoholics Anonymous and other addiction support groups). Weight Watchers, the world's largest support group for weight loss, similarly follows a **spiritual-therapeutic model** even though it is a profitable business.[40]

Organized Religion and Consumption

Marketers have not studied organized religion extensively, possibly because many view it as a taboo subject.[41] As one research director noted, "Religion, along with sex and politics, is one of the three taboo topics that we're never supposed to talk about."[42] Religious sensibilities vary around the world, and big trouble can result if marketers violate taboo subjects in other cultures. Here are some examples:[43]

- Winning entries in the Doritos/Pepsi MAX "Crash the Super Bowl" challenge get broadcast as ads during the Super Bowl. One entry caused a lot of controversy: "Feed the Flock" showed a "pastor" succeeding in bringing in new church parishioners by serving Doritos and Pepsi MAX from the altar—a scenario that some Catholics interpreted as mocking the religion's sacrament of Holy Eucharist (formerly Holy Communion). A petition appeal went out to Catholic organizations urging PepsiCo not to approve the entry, which was described as a "horrific blasphemy." The entry wasn't chosen as a finalist and PepsiCo removed it from the gallery of thousands of entries that were posted on the contest's Web site. However, the creators of the video posted it on YouTube, where it generated well more than 100,000 views.
- A Lipton ad won the prestigious Gold Lion award in Cannes, but the company had to decline the honor in the face of objections. The ad mocked the Catholic Church as it showed a man standing in the communion line with a bowl of onion dip in his hand.
- In Salt Lake City, a proposed billboard for Polygamy Porter beer aroused the ire of Mormons worldwide. The billboard company under contract with the brewery refused to erect the ad. The board, which was going to show a picture of a scantily clad man, cherubs, and a six-pack of spouses, advises drinkers to "take some home for the wives."
- An ad for Levi's jeans produced in London shows a young man who buys condoms from a pharmacist and then hides them in the small side pocket of his jeans. When he goes to pick up his date, he discovers that her father is the same pharmacist. The commercial was a hit in the United Kingdom, but people in strongly Catholic Italy and Spain didn't appreciate it at all.
- The Urban Outfitters chain was called out recently for selling a shirt that features a pink triangle against gray and white stripes. The design is similar to the uniforms that gay male prisoners were forced to wear in Nazi concentration camps. A few years previously the stores caught flack when they sold a shirt by the same designer that sported what resembled a Star of David emblem on the pocket like the ones Jews were forced to wear in Nazi Europe to identify themselves.[44]

Despite the occasional blunder, it's clear that religious dietary or dress requirements do create demand for certain products. For example, less than a third of the 6 million consumers who buy the 86,000 kosher products now on the market are Jewish. Seventh-Day Adventists and Muslims have similar dietary requirements, and other people simply believe that kosher food is of higher quality. Indeed only 15 percent of people who buy kosher do it for religious reasons. That's why some of the nation's largest manufacturers, like Pepperidge Farm, offer a wide range of kosher options.[45]

Born Again Consumers

Mainstream churches are marketing themselves aggressively these days. In the United States, there are approximately 1600 **megachurches** and each serves 2,000 or more congregants per week (some actually attract more than 20,000 to Sunday services!).[46] As a church marketing consultant observes, "Baby boomers think of churches like they think of supermarkets. They want options, choices, and convenience. Imagine if Safeway was open only one hour a week, had only one product, and didn't explain it in English."[47] Clearly, religion is big business.

**Megachurches are spiritual homes to
thousands of members.**
Source: Frank E. Lockwood/MCT/Newscom.

In the United States, we trace most religious marketing activity to "born again" Christians, who follow literal interpretations of the Bible and acknowledge being born again through belief in Jesus. Theirs is among the fastest-growing religious affiliations in the United States. One research company reported that about 72 million of the 235 million Christians in the United States say they are born again.[48]

The strength of the evangelical movement has caught the attention of many marketers who want to reach these consumers; marketers involved in faith-based marketing strategies include Pfizer, Merck, Tyson, Smucker's, several major automakers, and even the Curves fitness chain. Suzuki sponsored the Christian rock band Kutless on its national tour to promote its motorcycle and SUV lines.[49]

Islamic Marketing

Muslims will be more than one-quarter of the Earth's population by 2030, and during that same time period analysts expect the number of U.S. Muslims to more than double. If immigration patterns and Muslims' comparatively higher birth rates continue, experts predict that their numbers in the United States will climb from 2.6 million people to 6.2 million. In several European countries, it's predicted that Muslim populations will exceed 10 percent of the country's total population.[50] That's a consumer market to take seriously. The Whole Foods grocery store chain recently became the first major supermarket to run a Ramadan

Not of This World specializes in Christian-themed apparel and accessories.
Source: Courtesy of NOTW.

marketing campaign that caters to Muslims who eat lavish meals during the month when they fast each day.[51]

Nike committed a legendary error when it released a pair of athletic shoes in 1996 with a logo on the sole that some Muslims believed resembled the Arabic lettering for Allah. Muslims consider the feet unclean, and the company had to recall 800,000 pairs of the shoes globally. Today, some companies listen more closely to the needs of this religious subculture. For example, a Malaysian commercial for Sunsilk's Lively Clean & Fresh shampoo depicts a young, smiling woman, but there is not a strand of hair in sight. Her head is completely covered by a *tudung*, the head scarf worn by many Muslim women in that country. Sunsilk's pitch is that it helps remove excess oil from the scalp and hair, a common problem among wearers of *tudungs*.

Mindful of the success of kosher certification, some Muslims recognize that **halal** foods (permissible under the laws of Islam) also may appeal to mainstream consumers. The Islamic Food and Nutrition Council of America certifies halal products with a "crescent M," much like the circled "O" of the Orthodox Union, the largest kosher certifier. Both kosher and halal followers forbid pork, and both require similar rituals for butchering meat. Religious Jews don't mix milk and meat, nor do they eat shellfish, whereas religious Muslims don't drink alcohol. Neither group eats birds of prey or blood.[52]

Halal as a descriptor is being used for more and more commodities, services, and activities, including milk, water, nonprescription medicine, holidays, washing powder, tissues, cosmetics, Web sites, and music. Many major companies are taking steps to reassure consumers that all of their products—not just food—are halal by having them officially certified.

- Colgate-Palmolive claims to be the first international company to have obtained halal certification in Malaysia for toothpaste and mouthwash products. Some mouthwashes may contain alcohol, which would be forbidden under halal guidelines. Colgate's products now bear the halal logo, which also is featured in the company's television commercials.

The Muslim subculture represents an attractive market for many retailers.
Source: Iain Masterton/Alamy.

- Nokia introduced a phone for the Middle East and North Africa markets that came loaded with an Islamic Organizer including alarms for the five daily prayers, two Islamic e-books, and an e-card application that lets people send SMS greeting cards for Ramadan.
- Ogilvy & Mather established a new arm, Ogilvy Noor (Noor means "light" in Arabic), which the ad agency describes as "the world's first bespoke Islamic branding practice." Ogilvy also introduced the Noor index, which rates the appeal of brands to Muslim consumers. The index was formulated on the basis of how consumers ranked more than 30 well-known brands for compliance with *Shariah*, or Islamic law. Lipton tea, owned by Unilever, topped the list, followed by Nestlé. Ogilvy's research shows that young Muslim consumers are different from their Western counterparts; they believe that by staying true to the core values of their religion, they are more likely to achieve success in the modern world.[53]

OBJECTIVE 13-4
Our traditional notions about families are outdated.

The Family Unit and Age Subcultures

We've seen that subcultural identities revolve around shared experiences and perspectives. That's why it's so important for marketers to think about both when consumers are born and the family structure into which they're born. Age groups and the family unit helps to shape people's experiences, needs, and preferences. In this section we'll take a quick look at the family unit and then dive into age subcultures to understand how these identities influence consumer behavior.

Family Structure

Family size depends on such factors as educational level, the availability of birth control, and religion. Demographers define the **fertility rate** as the number of births per year per 1,000 women of childbearing age. Marketers keep a close eye on the population's birth rate to gauge how the pattern of births will affect demand for products in the future.

Worldwide, surveys show that many women want smaller families today. Ironically, while populations boom in some underdeveloped parts of the world, industrialized countries face future crises because there will be relatively fewer young people to support their elders. For population levels to remain constant, the fertility rate has to be 2.0 so that the two children can replace their parents. That's not happening in places such as Spain, Sweden, Germany, and Greece, where the fertility rate is 1.4 or lower. As a benchmark, the U.S. rate is 2.1. More babies were born in the United States in 2007 than in any other year in U.S. history—but this figure mostly reflects a greater number of women of childbearing age.[54]

The **extended family** used to be the most common family unit. It consists of three generations who live together, and it often includes grandparents, aunts, uncles, and cousins. Like the Cleavers of *Leave It to Beaver* and other TV families of the 1950s, the **nuclear family**—a mother, a father, and one or more children (perhaps with a sheepdog thrown in for good measure)—largely replaced the extended family, at least in U.S. society.

However, we've witnessed many changes since the days of Beaver Cleaver. Although many people continue to base their image of the typical family on old TV shows, demographic data tell us that this "ideal" image of the family is no longer realistic. The U.S. Census Bureau regards any occupied housing unit as a **household** regardless of the relationships among the people who live there. Thus, one person living alone, three roommates, or two lovers (whether straight or gay) constitute a household.

The family unit continues to evolve and marketers need to challenge their cherished assumptions:[55]

- The birth rate in the United States today is half what it was in 1960; less than one-fourth of the people are younger than the age of 18. The fertility rate has dropped from about 3 in the 1970s to 2.1 now.
- Nearly half of all women between the ages of 25 and 29 have never been married, up from about a quarter of that age group in 1986. In 1950, the median age of first marriages was 23 for men and 20 for women. One reason for this drop is that it's really expensive to raise a kid today (as if you didn't know that): The government estimates that it will cost the average middle-class couple $241,080 to raise a child to age 18. Of course, that doesn't even count college costs. The percentage of women of childbearing age who define themselves as **voluntarily childless** is on the rise. Twenty percent of women ages 40 to 44 have no children, double the level of 30 years ago. Childless couples are an attractive market segment for some companies (but obviously not for others, such as Gerber Baby Food). So-called **DINKS** (double income, no kids) couples are better educated on average than are two-income couples with children. According to the U.S. Census Bureau, 30 percent of childless couples consist of two college graduates, compared with 17 percent of those with kids. Many childless couples feel snubbed by a child-oriented society. In recent years they formed networking organizations such as Childfree by Choice to support this lifestyle decision.
- The likelihood of a woman following the traditional path of marriage and then a baby carriage is strongly influenced by social class. Whereas 90 percent of U.S. women who have a college degree or higher get married first, 57 percent of women with high school diplomas or less are unmarried when they give birth to their first child. More than one-quarter of these unwed mothers live with a partner who is not necessarily their child's biological father. The number of couples who **cohabitate** (live together without being married) jumped from 2.9 million in 1996 to 7.8 million in 2012.
- Circumstances such as divorce, the need for a breadwinner to live in a different place, and military service make it more common for family networks to be scattered geographically so parents, children, and extended family members need to work harder (and rely more on digital platforms like Skype) to maintain their connections with one another.
- Children are more likely to live at home after graduating from college rather than taking their own places. Demographers call these returnees **boomerang kids** (you

throw them out ... they keep coming back). In today's shrinking job market, many young people are forced to redefine the assumption that college graduation automatically means living on their own. About 40 percent of adults between 25 and 29 are now living, or have lived recently, with their parents.

- Many adults care for their own parents as well as for their children. In fact, Americans on average spend 17 years caring for children, but 18 years assisting aged parents.[56] Some label middle-aged people the **Sandwich Generation** because they must support both the generation above them and the one below them. As family living arrangements change, home builders need to come up with new footprints that can accommodate boomerang children, aging parents, and single people. Lennar, one of the largest homebuilders in the country, offers a 3000 square foot house that also includes a separate one-bedroom apartment with its own entrance and garage.[57]

Because they recognize that family needs and expenditures change over time, marketers apply the **family life cycle (FLC)** concept to segment households. The FLC combines trends in income and family composition with the changes these demands place on this income. As we age, our preferences and needs for products and activities tend to change. Twenty-somethings spend less than average on most products and services because their households are small and their incomes are low. Income levels tend to rise (at least until retirement), so that people can afford more over time. Older consumers spend more per capita on luxury items such as gourmet foods and upscale home furnishings. In addition, we don't need to repeat many purchases we make when we start out. For example, we tend to accumulate durable goods such as large appliances and replace them only as necessary.

A life-cycle approach to the study of the family assumes that pivotal events alter role relationships and trigger new stages of life that alter our priorities and brand loyalties.[58] In addition to the birth of a first child, other pivotal events include the departure of the last child from the house, the death of a spouse, retirement of the principal wage earner, and divorce. At Web sites like The Bump, women find tools such as an Ovulation Calculator and lists of baby names; The Knot offers a range of wedding-related services when those babies grow up and get hitched.

As people move through these life stages, we observe significant changes in expenditures in leisure, food, durables, and services, even after we adjust the figures to reflect changes in income.[59] We simply attribute some of these changes to variations in functional needs, whereas others reflect deeper motivations as we transition from one role to another. For example, researchers find that new mothers undergo profound changes in self-concept during pregnancy and after delivery; these changes influence the types of products they consume to reflect their new identities.[60]

Over the years, researchers have proposed several models to describe family life-cycle stages, but with limited effect because most failed to take into account such important social trends as the changing role of women, the acceleration of alternative lifestyles, childless and delayed-child marriages, and single-parent households. We need to focus on four variables to adequately describe these changes:

1 Age
2 Marital status
3 The presence or absence of children in the home, and
4 The ages of children, if present.

Today, we have to relax our definition of marital status to include *any* couple living together in a long-term relationship. Thus, although we might not consider roommates "married," for marketing purposes a man and woman who have established a household would be, as would two homosexual men or lesbian women who have a similar understanding. When we update our outlook, we identify a set of categories that includes many more types of family situations.[61] Consumers we classify into these categories show marked differences in consumption patterns:

- Young bachelors and newlyweds are the most likely to exercise; to go out to bars, concerts, movies, and restaurants; and to drink alcohol. Although people in their twenties account for less than 4 percent of all household spending in the United States, their expenditures are well above average in such categories as apparel, electronics, and gasoline.[62]

- Families with young children are more likely to consume health foods such as fruit, juice, and yogurt; those made up of single parents and older children buy more junk foods. The dollar value of homes, cars, and other durables is lowest for bachelors and single parents but increases as people go through the full-nest and childless-couple stages.

- Partly because they score wedding gifts, newlyweds are the most likely to own appliances such as toaster ovens and electric coffee grinders. Babysitter and day-care usage is, of course, highest among single-parent and full-nest households, whereas older couples and bachelors are most likely to employ home maintenance services (e.g., lawn mowing).

OBJECTIVE 13-5
We have many things in common with others because they are about the same age.

Age Cohorts

The era in which you grow up bonds you with the millions of others who come of age during the same time period. Obviously, your needs and preferences change as you grow older—often in concert with others of your own age (even though some of us don't really believe we'll ever get older). For this reason, our age is a big part of our identity. All things equal, we are more likely to have things in common with others of our own age than with those younger or older. These similarities can create opportunities for marketers (just ask any social media executive) or they can raise red flags: younger consumers, for example, don't drink nearly as much coffee on a daily basis as do older people.[66]

An **age cohort** consists of people of similar ages who have similar experiences. They share many common memories about cultural icons (e.g., John Wayne versus Brad Pitt), important historical events (e.g., the Great Depression versus the Great Recession), and so on. Although there is no universally accepted way to sort people into age cohorts, each of us seems to have a pretty good idea what we mean when we refer to "my generation." Marketers often target products and services to a specific age cohort; our possessions help us identify with others of a certain age and express the priorities and needs we encounter at each life stage.[67]

Although there is general consensus when analysts describe age cohorts, the labels and cutoff dates they use to put consumers into generational categories are subjective. One rough approximation looks like this:[68]

- **The Interbellum Generation**—People born at the beginning of the 20th century.
- **The Silent Generation**—People born between the two World Wars.
- **The War Baby Generation**—People born during World War II.
- **The Baby Boom Generation**—People born between 1946 and 1964.
- **Generation X**—People born between 1965 and 1985.
- **Generation Y**—People born between 1986 and 2002.
- **Generation Z**—People born 2003 and later.

Children: Consumers-in-Training

Disney estimates the North American baby market, including staples like formula, to be worth $36.3 billion annually. A representative of the Disney Baby program that operates in 580 maternity hospitals in the United States visits a new mother and offers a free Disney Cuddly Bodysuit, a variation of the classic Onesie. The rep provides bedside demonstrations and asks mothers to sign up for email alerts from DisneyBaby.com. As one company executive observes, "To get that mom thinking about her family's first park experience before her baby is even born is a home run."[69]

Marketing Opportunity

Almost one-third of all U.S. households have at least one pet, and 92 percent of pet owners consider their furry friends members of the family—83 percent call themselves "Mommy" or "Daddy" when they talk to their pets.[63] Many of us assume that pets share our emotions; perhaps that helps to explain why more than three-quarters of domestic cats and dogs receive presents on holidays and birthdays.[64] The pet industry pulls in more revenue (almost $40 billion annually) than either the toy or candy industries. Here are a few examples of pet-smart marketing:[65]

- Kennels look a lot more like spas for the furry. At some of them, dogs can hike, swim, listen to music, watch TV, and even get a pedicure—complete with nail polish. Heated tile floors and high-tech ventilation systems are common. When a dog stays in the "ambassador suite" at Club Bow-Wow, a staff member sleeps overnight in the room. PetSmart, the largest U.S. pet-store chain, opened a chain of PetsHotels, where furry guests lounge on hypoallergenic lambskin blankets and snack on lactose-free, fat-free ice cream. The suites feature raised dog beds and a television that plays videos, such as *Lady and the Tramp* and *101 Dalmatians*.

- Companies that make human products, such as Gucci, Juicy Couture, Harley-Davidson, IKEA, Lands' End, Paul Mitchell, and Ralph Lauren, also sell products for pets, ranging from shampoos to nail polish to gold-plated bowls. Harley-Davidson started its pet collection after it noticed that customers at rallies and other events bring along their dogs; some ride shotgun in the motorcycles' saddle bags or side cars. Customers can buy denim and leather jackets for their pets, as well as riding goggles, bandanas, spiked leather collars, and even squeaky toys shaped like oil cans.

- Designer water for dogs? A California company started things off when it introduced a vitamin-enriched water product for dogs. A Florida company sells "DogWater" in containers that double as throwing toys. Then there's K9 Water Inc., a company whose catalog lists products such as "Gutter Water" and chicken-flavored "Toilet Water." Make that a double.

(Continued)

● What happens when our four-legged companion goes to the great kennel in the sky? One trend is to freeze-dry the departed pet rather than bury it or cremate it. The bereaved say that turning furry friends into perma-pets helps them deal with loss and maintains a connection to their former companions. Once dried, the animal's body doesn't decay, so it can continue to occupy that special place on the couch.

The author's pug, Kelbie Rae.
Source: Photo courtesy of Michael Solomon.

In Chapter 4 we discussed how people learn to be consumers. As you well know, this process starts when we are young. Parents often reward their kids with products and punish them by taking things away. This form of **material parenting** shapes children's behavior. A recent study found that kids whose parents use products to shape behavior are more likely to be materialistic as adults.[70]

It's a no-brainer that kids represent a huge market for toys, apparel, and even electronics; already more than half of kids aged 8 to 12 have their own cellphone and there are numerous tablets designed for them as well.[71] However, kids also play a big role in many other household purchases. **Parental yielding** occurs when a parental decision maker "surrenders" to a child's request.[72] Yielding drives many product selections because about 90 percent of these requests are for a specific brand. Researchers estimate that children directly influence about $453 billion worth of family purchases in a year. They report that on average children weigh in with a purchase request every 2 minutes when they shop with parents.[73] In recognition of this influence, Mrs. Butterworth's Syrup created a $6 million campaign to target kids directly with humorous ads that show the lengths to which adults will go to get the syrup bottle to talk to them. An executive who worked on the campaign explained, "We needed to create the *nag factor* [where kids demand that their parents buy the product]."[74]

OBJECTIVE 13-6
Teens are an important age segment for marketers.

Gen Y and Gen Z

In 1956, the label *teenager* entered the general U.S. vocabulary when Frankie Lymon and the Teenagers became the first pop group to identify themselves with this new subculture. Believe it or not, the concept of a teenager is a fairly new idea. Throughout most of history a person simply made the transition from child to adult. It was common for kids in their late teens to be married and start their own families (of course, life expectancies were much shorter as well).

The magazine *Seventeen* was first published in 1944; its founders realized that modern young women didn't want to be little clones of Mom. Following World War II, the teenage conflict between rebellion and conformity began to unfold as teen culture pitted Elvis Presley, with his slicked hair and suggestive pelvis swivels, against the wholesome Pat Boone, with his white bucks and whiter teeth. Today, this rebellion continues to play out

ABOUT   PRIVATE TREND SCHOOLS

A DAY OF DISCOVERY

TREND SCHOOL IS IMMERSIVE, INTIMATE, AND INTERACTIVE...AND IT WILL TRANSFORM YOU.

Thousands of executives have gained the awareness and vision necessary to connect with young consumers by attending Trend School. Part grad class, part mini-conference, part networking event, Trend School takes you beyond what's happening with young consumers by delving into why they do what they do. Comprehensive Cassandra Report presentations. Pervasive macro trends. Amazing guest speakers. Product samples. Taste tests. Tech demos. Ideation exercises. Cool music. Hot videos. Gen Y consumer panels. It's all there, in one intense day.

as pubescent consumers forsake their Barbies for the likes of Paris Hilton, Lindsay Lohan (when they're not in jail or rehab), Justin Bieber, or the teen heartthrob *du jour.*[75]

The global youth market is massive. It represents about $100 billion in spending power! Much of this money goes toward "feel-good" products: cosmetics, posters, and fast food—with the occasional nose ring thrown in. Because teens are interested in so many different products and have the resources to obtain them, many marketers avidly court them.

As anyone who has been there knows, puberty and adolescence are both the best of times and the worst of times. Many exciting changes happen as we leave the role of child and prepare to assume the role of adult. These transitions create a lot of uncertainty about the self, and the need to belong and to find one's unique identity as a person becomes pressing. At this age, our choices of activities, friends, and clothes are crucial. Teens constantly search for cues for the "right" way to look and behave from their peers and from advertising. Advertising to teens is typically action-oriented and depicts a group of "in" teens who use the product.

Consumers in this age subculture have a number of needs (including some that conflict with one another) such as experimentation, belonging, independence, responsibility, and approval from others. Product usage is a significant medium that lets them satisfy these needs. For example, many kids view smoking cigarettes as a status activity because of the numerous movies they've seen that glorify this practice. In one study, ninth graders watched original movie footage with either smoking scenes or control footage with the smoking edited out. Sure enough, when the young viewers saw the actors smoking, this enhanced their perceptions of smokers' social stature and increased their own intent to smoke. (The good news: When kids see an antismoking advertisement before the film, these effects cancel out.)[76]

Teenagers in every culture grapple with fundamental developmental issues when they transition from childhood to adult. Throughout history young people have coped with insecurity, parental authority, and peer pressure (although each generation has trouble believing it's not the first!). According to Teenage Research Unlimited, the five most important social issues for teens are AIDS, race relations, child abuse, abortion, and the environment. Today's teens often have to cope with additional family responsibilities as well, especially if they live in nontraditional families where they have significant responsibility for shopping, cooking, and housework. It's hard work being a teen in the modern world. The Saatchi & Saatchi advertising agency identified four basic conflicts common to all teens:

● **Autonomy versus belonging**—Teens need to acquire independence, so they try to break away from their families. However, they need to attach themselves to a support structure, such as peers, to avoid being alone.

Marketing Pitfall

Marketers refer to kids aged 8 to 14 as **tweens** because they are "between" childhood and adolescence, and they exhibit characteristics of both age groups. Many marketers want to appeal to these consumers; they spend about $43 billion annually! Tweens are keen to experiment with products that make them appear older, even though they may not be psychologically or physically ready. Abercrombie & Fitch crossed the line way back in 2002, when the clothing chain had to pull a line of thong underwear for young girls after many adults protested. Since that time, however, the line between childhood and adolescence continues to blur. In 2005 the NPD Group reported that the average age at which women began to use beauty products was 17. By 2009, that average had dropped to 13. Another study by Experian found that 43 percent of 6- to 9-year olds use lipstick or lip gloss, and 38 percent use hairstyling products. In addition to adult shows like *Extreme Makeover*, tweens watch TV shows like MTV's *16 and Pregnant* and movies like *Little Miss Perfect*, which tells the story of a high school freshman who encounters an online pro-eating disorder subculture (the movie's tagline: "Thinner is the winner").[79]

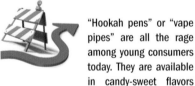

Marketing Pitfall

"Hookah pens" or "vape pipes" are all the rage among young consumers today. They are available in candy-sweet flavors like Bubblicious, Candyfloss, and Caribbean Twist. The real twist, however, is that chemically they are virtually identical to the e-cigarettes older people puff, including the addictive nicotine and various other chemical additives. Analysts project that in the next decade sales of these products will pass those of conventional cigarettes.[81]

- **Rebellion versus conformity**—Teens need to rebel against social standards of appearance and behavior, yet they still need to fit in and be accepted by others. They prize "in-your-face" products that cultivate a rebellious image.
- **Idealism versus pragmatism**—Teens tend to view adults as hypocrites, whereas they see themselves as being sincere. They have to struggle to reconcile their view of how the world should be with the realities they perceive around them.
- **Narcissism versus intimacy**—Teens tend to obsess about their appearance and needs. However, they also feel the desire to connect with others on a meaningful level.[77]

These needs often collide, sometimes in unpleasant ways (there's nothing more venomous than a teenager who's having a bad hair day!). One researcher explored the role of *ridicule* as a mechanism through which adolescents exchange information about consumption norms and values. He found that—often beginning in middle school—adolescents use ridicule to ostracize, haze, or admonish peers who violate consumption norms. One result of this painful process is that kids internalize their peers' stereotypes about aspirational and avoidance groups (remember Chapter 11) and often significantly alter their consumption patterns to try to align themselves with the former and distance themselves from the latter. For example, one of the kids in the study quickly exchanged a pair of white sneakers for more stylish black ones after his peers ridiculed him.[78]

Gen Z

Gen Z describes kids who were born in the late 1990s to early 2000s, so they will start entering college in just a few years. This is the first generation of the 21st century and it's the most diverse we've ever experienced: 55 percent are Caucasian, 24 percent are Hispanic, 14 percent are African American and 4 percent are Asian. Many have friends from other racial and ethnic subcultures and they assume this to be the norm. They are accustomed to blurred gender roles, where household responsibilities don't split along traditional lines. And, of course they are "Digital Natives" who spend a big chunk of their time online, so they expect brands to engage them in two-way digital conversations.

Marketers are just starting to figure out what this new group of young consumers will look like. Having grown up during the Great Recession, they are not as likely to believe in an idealized, carefree world. They tend to be independent and gravitate to stores like Free People rather than Abercrombie & Fitch.[80] They learn about new styles from around the globe via social media, so they are equally at home watching *The Hunger Games* or listening to Korean K-pop. Their idols are "self-made" Internet stars like the Swedish video producer PewDiePie, who has the world's most subscribed YouTube channel, and the teenage video sensation Evan who has 25 million followers.

Gen Y

A brand overhaul by Pepsi that included its new smiley-face logo had the so-called **Gen Y** age segment squarely in its sights. Young people have always been Pepsi's lifeblood, but that blood has drained or thinned a bit over the past few years, as young people gravitate toward energy drinks and fortified waters. The company's research showed that this age group—which also goes by the labels **Millennials** and **Echo Boomers**—is hopeful about the future; almost all of them agree that it's important to maintain a positive outlook on life. Pepsi also found that 95 percent of Millennials have positive associations with the word *change* and that they link the word to others like *new, progress, hope,* and *excitement*.[82]

Gen Yers were born between 1986 and 2002. They already make up nearly one-third of the U.S. population, and they spend $170 billion a year of their own and their parents' money. They are "jugglers" who value being both footloose and connected to their "peeps" 24/7. The advertising agency Saatchi & Saatchi labels this new kind of lifestyle **connexity**. To help Millennials feel connected with one another, companies including Apple and Philips developed miniature devices such as the iPod and MP3 key ring that store music and images for kids on the run—and they plug directly into a USB port for up- and downloading. When Toyota developed its youth-oriented Scion model, researchers learned that Echo Boomers practically live in their cars; for example, one-quarter of Gen Yers keep a full change of clothes in their vehicles. So Toyota's designers made the Scion resemble a home on wheels, with fully reclining front seats so drivers can nap between classes and a 15-volt outlet so they can plug in their computers.[83]

Gen Yers love brands like Sony, Patagonia, Gap, Aveda, and Apple. However, a lot of marketers have run into trouble as they try to keep up with changes in their tastes. This can be difficult because these consumers like to "trade up and down," that is, they fluctuate between upscale brands and less expensive ones. That helps to explain why both Louis Vuitton and Target both make the list of their most favorite brands.[84] Another issue is that apparel no longer is as important to this age group; youth-oriented chains like Wet Seal and Hot Topic have gone bankrupt because tech has replaced clothing as the hot status item. As a magazine editor observed, "You try to get them talking about what's the next look, what they're excited about purchasing in apparel, and the conversation always circles back to the iPhone 6. Having a cool phone to show you're plugged in is a huge part of people's style, a huge part of life these days."[85]

A research firm analyzed data from several million Millennials and concluded that three major forces have shaped their experience:

1   **Economy:** The company identified a subgroup of ambitious go-getters. Women in particular seem very aware of their "self-brand" and work hard to project a professional image via clothing and home décor. Men tend to identify with a "frat boy" culture and spend a lot of time and money on technology, gaming and sports. However, these Millennials are a minority. Many are stuck in "economic purgatory"; they are overeducated but underemployed and focus on economizing by living with roommates and clipping coupons. Even this more frugal group, however, considers technology like smartphones a must-have.

2   **Globalization:** Millennials are eager to experience other cultures, but they do this in different ways. Ironically, those who are underemployed and thus less invested in their current jobs are more likely to travel to foreign countries. Many of those who are actually on a desired career path settle for being "foodies" who like to patronize restaurants that serve exotic cuisine so they can vicariously collect these experiences.

3   **Social media:** Gen Y is constantly open to public observation because every new post or status update reveals something about themselves. Some are what the report terms "Exuberants" who are avid posters and constantly blog about their experiences. However, most are "Collectors" who passively absorb others' experiences. A smaller number, such as YouTube star Bethany Mota, are digital gatekeepers who curate or edit style options from the huge number of options and then advise their followers what to buy.[86]

Unlike their parents or older siblings, Gen Yers tend to hold relatively traditional values and they prefer to fit in rather than rebel. Their acculturation agents (like those we discussed previously in this chapter) stress teamwork—team teaching, team grading, collaborative sports, community service, service learning, and student juries. Violent crime among teenagers is down 60 to 70 percent. The use of tobacco and alcohol is at an all-time low, as is teen pregnancy. Five out of 10 Echo Boomers say they trust the government, and virtually all of them trust Mom and Dad.[87]

We've already discussed the overwhelming importance of the online world in the lives of consumers, especially young ones. Millennials are the first generation to grow up with computers at home in a 500-channel TV universe. They are *multitaskers* who easily engage their cell phones, music downloads, and IMs at the same time. They are totally at home in a *thumb culture* that communicates online and by cell phone (more likely via text and IM than by voice).

Within the Gen Y subculture, college students are a special segment. There are more than 21 million students in the United States today, and they spend $163 billion per year on discretionary purchases. Of this amount, about $50 billion goes to food purchases, $31 billion to automotive expenses, and greater than $18 billion to clothing and shoes. No surprise: college students love gadgets. They own an average of 6.8 devices, including laptops, smartphones, and video game consoles. Although they spend much of their time on social media, about one third say they avoid advertising on these sites. They would rather connect with brands by receiving product samples and attending sponsored events. [88]

Gen X

The **Gen X** age subculture consists of 46 million Americans who were born between 1965 and 1985. This group got the label following publication of the best-selling novel *Generation X: Tales for an Accelerated Culture* by Douglas Coupland. Some called them "slackers" or "baby busters" because of their supposed alienation and laziness, and these stereotypes live on in movies such as *Clueless* and in music groups such as Marilyn Manson.[89]

Advertisers fell all over themselves to create messages that would not turn off the worldly Generation X cohort. Many of them referenced old TV shows such as *Gilligan's Island* or showed commercials that featured disheveled actors in turned-around baseball caps who tried their best to appear blasé. This approach actually turned off a lot of Busters because it implied that they had nothing else to do but sit around and watch old television reruns. Subaru sponsored one of the first commercials of this genre. It showed a sloppily dressed young man who described the Impreza model as "like punk rock" as he denounced the competition as "boring and corporate." The commercial did not play well with its intended audience, and Subaru eventually switched advertising agencies.

Today, Gen Xers have grown up, and in fact members of this generation are responsible for many culture-changing products and companies such as Google, YouTube, and Amazon. A book that laments the bad rap Gen X has gotten sums it up: *X Saves the World: How Generation X Got the Shaft But Can Still Keep Everything from Sucking.*[90]

The Mature Market

Restylane is the top-selling dermal injection to reduce the appearance of wrinkles. The company decided to pitch it directly to consumers for the first time, so in keeping with new media trends it launched a multipronged campaign that recognizes the technical prowess of many middle-aged people. A conventional TV spot features before-and-after results along with women who talk about how frequently men check them out after the treatment. But a second component is a video skit on YouTube that supposedly takes place during a woman's 50th birthday party. While her son works on a video birthday card, Mom gets caught smooching with a younger man on a couch. Viewers don't know the skit is an ad until the last 15 seconds. A third prong is a contest to name the "Hottest Mom in America": Contestants submit videos to a Web site and the winner gets cash, free treatments for a year, and an interview with a modeling agency.[91] Today's Mom isn't exactly June Cleaver, the ideal mother depicted in the old TV show *Leave it to Beaver*. Let's take a closer look at the changing face of mature consumers—some of them aren't as mature as they used to be.

OBJECTIVE 13-7
Baby Boomers are the most economically powerful age segment.

Baby Boomers

The **Baby Boomer** age subculture consists of people whose parents established families following the end of World War II and during the 1950s when the peacetime economy was strong and stable. As a general rule, when people feel confident about how things are going in the world, they are more likely to decide to have children, so this was a "boom" time for delivery rooms. As teenagers in the 1960s and 1970s, the "Woodstock generation" created a revolution in style, politics, and consumer attitudes. As they aged, they fueled cultural events as diverse as the Free Speech movement and hippies in the 1960s to Reaganomics and yuppies in the 1980s. Now that they are older, they continue to influence popular culture.

As the Restylane campaign demonstrates, this generation is much more active and physically fit than its predecessors; Baby Boomers are 6 percent more likely than the national average to engage in some kind of sports activity.[92] In addition. Baby Boomers

now it's Pepsi-for those who **think** young
Thinking young is a wholesome attitude, an enthusiastic outlook. It means getting the most out of life, and everyone can join in. This is the life for Pepsi —light, bracing, clean-tasting Pepsi. Think young. Say "Pepsi, please!"

ENJOY THE STEVE ALLEN SHOW PRESENTED BY PEPSI WEEKLY ON ABC-TV

This 1962 Pepsi ad highlights the emphasis on youth power that began to shape our culture as Baby Boomers came of age in the 1960s.
Source: Pepsi is a registered trademark of PepsiCo, Inc. Used with permission.

are now in their peak earning years. As one commercial for VH1, the music video network that caters to those who are a bit too old for MTV, pointed out, "The generation that dropped acid to escape reality ... is the generation that drops antacid to cope with it." A study found that the majority of Boomers want to be "surprised and delighted" by brands. Offerings that especially appeal to them include Swiffer for the home; Keurig for the palate; Amy's Kitchen for organic foods, Dove, and Trader Joe's.[93]

Demographers distinguish between two subgroups of Baby Boomers: "Leading-edge" boomers, born between 1946 and 1955, grew up during the Vietnam War and Civil Rights eras. "Trailing-edge" boomers, who were born between 1956 and 1964, came of age after Vietnam and the Watergate scandal. The Great Recession had a greater impact on trailing-edge boomers than leading-edge boomers. The relatively older group is less burdened by expenses like college tuitions and mortgage payments, so they are able to buy more discretionary products and experiences despite the bad economic conditions of the last 5 years or so.[94]

To appreciate the impact middle-aged consumers have and will have on our economy, consider this: At current spending levels, a 1 percent increase in the population of

This British AIDS awareness message targets men over the age of 50.

Source: www.fpa.org.uk Created by theethicalagency.co.uk.

householders aged 35 to 54 results in an additional $8.9 billion in consumer spending. Ironically, however, most marketers neglect this incredibly important group: For example, although Boomers spend 38.5 percent of consumer packaged goods (CPG) dollars, Nielsen estimates that only 5 percent of advertising dollars are currently targeted toward adults 35 to 64 years old. Nielsen's research says that Boomers dominate 1,023 out of 1,083 CPG categories, and watch 9.34 hours of video per day—more than any other segment. They also constitute a third of all TV viewers, online users, social media users, and Twitter users and are significantly more likely to have broadband Internet. As a Nielsen executive observed, "Marketers have this tendency to think the Baby Boomers—getting closer to retirement—will just be calm and peaceful as they move ahead, and that's not true. Everything we see with our behavioral data says these people are going to be active consumers for much longer. They are going to be in better health, and despite the ugliness around the retirement stuff now, they are still going to be more affluent. They are going to be an important segment for a long time."[95]

OBJECTIVE 13-8

Seniors are a more important market segment than many marketers realize.

Seniors

The old woman sits alone in her dark apartment while the television blares out a soap opera. Once every couple of days, her arthritic hands slowly and painfully open her triple-locked door as she ventures out to the corner store to buy essentials such as tea, milk, and cereal—of course she always picks the least expensive items. Most of the time she sits in her rocking chair and thinks sadly about her dead husband and the good times they used to have together.

Is this the image you have of a typical elderly consumer? Until recently, many marketers did. They neglected the elderly in their feverish pursuit of the youth market. But as our population ages and we live longer and healthier lives, the game is rapidly changing. A lot of businesses are updating their old stereotype of the poor recluse. The newer, more accurate image is of an active person who is interested in what life has to offer, who is an enthusiastic consumer with the means and willingness to buy many goods and services, and who maintains strong loyalty to favorite brands over the years.

Think about this: The United Nations says that people older than 60 are the fastest-growing age group on Earth. There are 700 million of them now, and there will be 2 billion by midcentury. In the United States, by 2030, 20 percent of the population will be over the age of 65.[96] By 2100, there will be 5 million of us who are at least 100 years old.[97] Few of us may be around then, but we can already see the effects of the **senior market** today. Older adults control more than 50 percent of discretionary income, and worldwide consumers older than the age of 50 spend nearly $400 billion a year.[98] We're living longer and healthier because of more wholesome lifestyles (at least some of us), improved medical diagnoses and treatment, and changing cultural expectations about appropriate behaviors for the elderly.

Larger numbers of older people lead more active, multidimensional lives than we assume. Nearly 60 percent engage in volunteer activities, one in four seniors aged 65 to 72 still works, and more than 14 million provide care for their grandchildren.[99] It is also crucial to remember that income alone does not express seniors' spending power. Older consumers are finished with many of the financial obligations that siphon off the income of younger consumers. Eighty percent of consumers older than age 65 own their own homes. In addition, child-rearing costs are over. As the popular bumper sticker proudly proclaims, "We're Spending Our Children's Inheritance!" Some of the important areas that stand to benefit from the surging gray market include exercise facilities, cruises and tourism, cosmetic surgery and skin treatments, and "how-to" books and university courses that offer enhanced learning opportunities.

Research confirms the popular wisdom that age is more a state of mind than of body. A person's mental outlook and activity level have a lot more to do with longevity and quality of life than does *chronological age*, the actual number of years the person has actually been alive. That's why **perceived age**, or how old a person *feels*, is a better yardstick to use. Researchers measure perceived age on several dimensions, including "feel-age" (i.e., how old a person feels) and "look-age" (i.e., how old a person looks).[100] The older consumers get, the younger they feel relative to their actual age.

A study investigated what the authors call **consumer identity renaissance**; this refers to the redefinition process people undergo when they retire. The research identified two different types of identity renaissance: revived (revitalization of previous identities) or emergent (pursuit of entirely new life projects). Even though many retirees cope with losses (of professional identity, spouses, and so on), many of them focus on moving forward. They engage in a host of strategies to do this, including affiliation, where they reconnect with family members and friends (in many cases online), and *self-expression*. This latter strategy may involve revisiting an activity they never had time to adequately pursue when they were younger, learning new skills, or perhaps moving into an urban area to reengage with cultural activities.[101]

OBJECTIVE 13-9

Birds of a feather flock together in place-based subcultures.

Place-Based Subcultures

Geodemography refers to analytical techniques that combine data on consumer expenditures and other socioeconomic factors with geographic information about the areas in which people live to identify consumers who share common consumption patterns. Researchers base this approach on the common assumption that "birds of a feather flock together"—people who have similar needs and tastes also tend to live near one another, so it should be possible to locate "pockets" of like-minded people whom marketers can reach more economically by direct mail and other methods. For example, a marketer who wants to reach white, single consumers who are college educated and tend to be fiscally conservative may find that it is more efficient to mail catalogs to zip codes 20770 (Greenbelt, MD) and 90277 (Redondo Beach, CA) than to adjoining areas in either Maryland or California, where there are fewer consumers who exhibit these characteristics.

One popular clustering technique is Nielsen's **PRIZM** system. This system classifies every U.S. Zip Code into 1 of 66 categories, ranging from the most affluent "Blue-Blood Estates" to the least well-off "Public Assistance." It terms a resident of southern California "Money & Brains" if she lives in Encino (Zip Code 91316), whereas someone living in Sherman Oaks (Zip Code 91423) is a "Young Influential."

Residents of different clusters display marked differences in their consumption of products, from annuities to Ziploc bags. The system also ranks these groupings by income, home value, and occupation (i.e., a rough index of social class) on a ZQ (Zip Quality) scale. Table 13.1 provides an idea of how dramatically different the consumption patterns of two clusters can be. It compares consumption data for two different clusters primarily composed of young people without kids. You can check out your own Zip Code at MyBestSegments.com. [102]

Although consumers in two different clusters may purchase a product at an equivalent rate, these similarities end when we take their other purchases into account. These differences highlight the importance of going beyond simple product-category purchase data and demographics to really understand a market (remember the discussion of product complementarity). For example, people in "Urban Gold Coast," "Money & Brains," and "Blue-Blood Estates" communities buy a lot of high-quality binoculars, but so do those in the "Grain Belt," "New Homesteaders," and "Agri-Business" clusters. The difference is that the former groups use the binoculars to watch birds and other wildlife, whereas the latter use them to help line up the animals in their gun sights. Furthermore, whereas the bird watchers do a lot of foreign travel, listen to classical music, and host cocktail parties, the bird hunters travel by bus, like country music, and belong to veterans' clubs.

TABLE 13.1   A Comparison of Two Different Youth-Oriented PRIZM Clusters

Segment #4: Young Digerati	Segment #24: Up-and-Comers
Tech-savvy consumers who live in trendy urban neighborhoods filled with fitness clubs, boutiques, and microbreweries.	A transition segment for young, middle-class singles before they marry and establish families. Primarily live in mid-size cities and includes many recent college graduates who are into athletic activities, technology, and nightlife.
Much more likely than the average consumer to:	Much more likely than the average consumer to:
Shop at Bloomingdale's	Order from Priceline.com
Travel to Asia	Travel to South America
Read *Dwell*	Read *Cigar Aficionado*
Watch Independent Film Channel	Watch *South Park*
Drive an Audi A3	Drive a Nissan Altima Hybrid

Adapted from "My Best Segments," Nielsen, http://www.claritas.com/MyBestSegments/Default.jsp?ID=30&pageName=Segment%2Bexplorer, accessed April 21, 2015.

CHAPTER SUMMARY

Now that you have finished reading this chapter, you should understand why:

1. Consumer identity derives from "we" as well as "I."

Consumers identify with many groups that share common characteristics and identities, but some of these affiliations are more central to how we define ourselves. Subcultures are large groups that exist within a society, and membership in them often gives marketers a valuable clue about individuals' consumption decisions. Important sources of consumer identity include gender, race/ethnicity, religion, age, and place of residence.

2. Our memberships in ethnic, racial, and religious subcultures often guide our consumption choices.

A person's ethnic origins, racial identity, and religious background often are major components of his or her identity. African Americans, Hispanic Americans, and Asian Americans are the three most important ethnic/racial subcultures in the United States. Key issues to reach members of racial/ethnic subcultures are consumers' degree of acculturation into mainstream U.S. society and the recognition of important cultural differences among subgroups (e.g., Puerto Ricans, Cubans, and Mexicans).

3. Marketers increasingly use religious and spiritual themes to talk to consumers.

The quest for spirituality influences demand in product categories including books, music, and cinema. Although the impact of religious identification on consumer behavior is not clear, some differences among religious subcultures do emerge. Marketers need to consider the sensibilities of believers carefully when they use religious symbolism to appeal to members of different denominations.

4. Our traditional notions about families are outdated.

We've seen that subcultural identities revolve around shared experiences and perspectives. That's why it's so important for marketers to think about both when consumers are born and the family structure into which they're born. Age groups and the family unit help to shape people's experiences, needs, and preferences.

5. We have many things in common with others because they are about the same age.

Consumers who grew up at the same time share many cultural memories because they belong to a common age cohort, so they respond well to marketers' nostalgia appeals that remind them of these experiences.

6. Teens are an important age segment for marketers.

Teenagers are in the middle of a transition from childhood to adulthood, and their self-concepts tend to be unstable. They are receptive to products that help them to be accepted and enable them to assert their independence. Because many teens earn money but have few financial obligations, they are a particularly important segment for many nonessential or expressive products, ranging from chewing gum to clothing fashions and music. Because of changes in family structure, many teens also are taking more responsibility for their families' day-to-day shopping.

7. Baby Boomers are the most economically powerful age segment.

Baby Boomers are the most powerful age segment because of their size and economic clout. Boomers continue to affect demands for housing, child care, automobiles, clothing, and many other products.

8. Seniors are a more important market segment than many marketers realize.

As the population ages, the needs of older consumers will become increasingly important. Many marketers ignore seniors because of the stereotype that they are too inactive and spend too little. This stereotype is no longer accurate. Many older adults are healthy, vigorous, and interested in new products and experiences—and they have the income to purchase them. Marketing appeals to this age subculture should focus on consumers' perceived ages, which tend to be more youthful than their chronological ages.

9. "Birds of a feather flock together."

Geodemography refers to analytical techniques that combine data on consumer expenditures and other socioeconomic factors with geographic information about the areas in which people live to identify consumers who share common consumption patterns. Researchers base this approach on the common assumption that "birds of a feather flock together." Marketers can increase the efficiency of their messages when they focus on the similarities among consumers who choose to live in the same place.

KEY TERMS

REVIEW

⭐ **13-1** What is a subculture?

13-2 One important subcultural difference is how abstract or literal the group is. What are the distinctions between the two?

13-3 How do marketers promote products and services to ethnic subcultures?

13-4 What is deethnicization? Give an example.

13-5 Why are Hispanic American consumers attractive to marketers?

⭐ **13-6** What is *acculturation*? How does it differ from *enculturation*?

13-7 Who are acculturation agents? Give two examples.

13-8 Describe the processes involved when a person assimilates into a new host culture.

13-9 Why might a marketer be interested in the second largest ethnic group in a market? Is this group difficult for marketers to reach?

13-10 Is it true that religious, cultural, or traditional events impact consumption?

13-11 What is a *nuclear family*, and how is it different from an *extended family*?

13-12 What are *boomerang kids*?

13-13 What is the *FLC*, and why is it important to marketers?

⭐ **13-14** Can children be considered "consumers-in-waiting"?

13-15 How important is the global youth market? Suggest products and services they would want to use.

13-16 What are the rules of engagement for young consumers?

13-17 What is geodemography? Is it straightforward to apply it to any market or country?

CONSUMER BEHAVIOR CHALLENGE

■ DISCUSS

13-18 Geodemographic techniques assume that people who live in the same neighborhood have other things in common as well. Why do they make this assumption, and how accurate is it?

13-19 Should members of a religious group adapt marketing techniques that manufacturers customarily use to increase market share for their secular products? Why or why not?

13-20 The United Kingdom is one of the many countries that do not overtly ban advertising that is likely to cause offense to certain religious groups. Extreme cases would not be authorized for broadcast or print and could well be subject to criminal proceedings. Instead, the United Kingdom's Advertising Standards Authority (ASA), a non-governmental organization, provides advice and guidance for advertisers. However, in an increasingly diverse and complex United Kingdom, advertisers can inadvertently make mistakes. The ASA advises avoiding anything linked to a central tenet or sacred symbol, texts, or spiritual figures. It also makes the point that as Christianity is the predominant faith, the public are more accommodating providing the advertising is not disrespectful. Is it necessary to legislate to protect religious beliefs?

13-21 Describe the progressive learning model and discuss why this perspective is important when we market to subcultures.

13-22 Discuss the pros and cons of the voluntarily childless movement.

13-23 When they identify and target newly divorced couples, do you think marketers exploit these couples' situations? Are there instances in which you think marketers may actually be helpful to them? Support your answers with examples.

13-24 The Cornetto ice cream brand in Malaysia was losing market share to local brands. The traditional Cornetto image was seen as too old-fashioned and not edgy enough. Internationally, Cornetto's advertising message revolved around love, but in Malaysia they merged love with a four-part story centering on the ghost characters Po and Lang to attract the high-consumption teen market (ghost stories are very popular with teens in Malaysia). Cornetto's new campaign successfully managed to make a connection with the target market. Four webisodes featuring the ghosts were released on YouTube, Facebook, and Twitter.[103] Cornetto also used vloggers and bloggers to spread the buzz about the story. When users clicked banner ads, they received a call on their mobile phone from one of the characters in the story. Cornetto sales rose by 21 percent over the course of the campaign.[104]

This campaign is an exemplary instance of advertising adaptation. Identify an advertising adaption of a global brand in your own country.

13-25 Religious symbolism appears in advertising, even though some people object to this practice. For example, a French Volkswagen ad for the relaunch of the Golf showed a modern version of *The Last Supper* with the tagline, "Let us rejoice, my friends, for a new Golf has been born."[105] A group of clergy in France sued the company and the ad was removed from 10,000 billboards. One of the bishops involved in the suit said, "Advertising experts have told us that ads aim for the sacred in order to shock, because using sex does not work anymore." Do you agree? Should religion be used to market products? Do you find this strategy effective or offensive? When and where is this appropriate, if at all?

13-26 The human race has been on the move for countless generations. The process of acculturalization describes the process of adapting to or adopting traits from another culture. Populations can even shift from one continent to a new one. Is the process more difficult for these people compared to a less radical migration?

13-27 The chapter discussed the dramatic changes in family structure today. The reality is that many other *types* of families continue to grow rapidly as well. Indeed, some experts argue that as traditional family living arrangements wane, we place even greater emphasis on siblings, close friends, and other relatives who provide companionship and social support.[106] Some people join *intentional families*, groups of unrelated people who meet regularly for meals and who spend holidays together.[107] Indeed, for some the act of meeting together to consume homemade food plays a central role in defining family: It is a symbolic way to separate a family unit from other social groups by allowing the cook(s) to personalize the meal and express affection via the effort that went into preparing the feast.[108] What evidence do you find of the impact of nontraditional family structures? How will these alternative lifestyles change the way we think about consumer behavior?

13-28 This chapter describes members of Gen Y as much more traditional and team oriented than their older brothers and sisters. Do you agree?

13-29 Many parents worry about the time their kids spend online, but this activity may actually be good for them. A study by the MacArthur Foundation claims that surfers gain valuable skills to prepare them for the future. The study also finds that concerns about online predators are overblown; most kids socialize with friends they know from other situations like school or camp.[109] What's your take on this? Are concerns about excessive Web surfing unjustified?

13-30 What are some of the positives and negatives of targeting college students? Identify some specific marketing strategies you feel have either been successful or unsuccessful. What characteristics distinguish the successes from the failures?

13-31 Is it practical to assume that people age 55 and older constitute one large consumer market? How can marketers segment this age subculture? What are some important variables to keep in mind when we tailor marketing messages to this age group?

■ APPLY

13-32 Locate current examples of marketing stimuli that depend on an ethnic or religious stereotype to communicate a message. How effective are these appeals?

13-33 To understand the power of ethnic stereotypes, conduct your own poll. For a set of ethnic groups, ask people to anonymously provide attributes (including personality traits and products) most likely to characterize each group, using the technique of free association where they simply say what comes to mind when you mention each group. How much agreement do you obtain across respondents? To what extent do the characteristics derive from or reflect negative stereotypes? Compare the associations for an ethnic group between actual members of that group and nonmembers.

13-34 Observe the interactions between parents and children in the cereal section of a local grocery store (remember to take earplugs with you). Prepare a report on the number of children who expressed preferences, how they expressed their preferences, and how parents responded, including the number who purchased the child's choice.

13-35 Select a product category and, using the life-cycle stages this chapter describes, list the variables likely to affect a purchase decision for the product by consumers in each stage of the cycle.

13-36 Consider three important changes in the modern family structure. For each, find an example of a marketer who seems to be conscious of this change in its product communications, retailing innovations, or other aspects of the marketing mix. If possible, also try to find examples of marketers who have failed to keep up with these developments.

13-37 One study asked young people in the United States and the Netherlands to write essays about what is "cool" and "uncool" and to create visual collages that represent what it means to be cool.[110] The researchers found that cool has multiple meanings to kids in these two cultures. Some of the common dimensions include having charisma, being in control, and being a bit aloof. Many of the respondents also agreed that being cool is a moving target: The harder you try to be cool, the more uncool you are! Here are some of their actual responses:

- "Cool means being relaxed, to nonchalantly be the boss of every situation, and to radiate that" (Dutch female)
- "Cool is the perception from others that you've got 'something' which is macho, trendy, hip, etc." (Dutch male)
- "Cool has something standoffish, and at the same time, attractive" (Dutch male)

- "Being different, but not too different. Doing your own thing, and standing out, without looking desperate while you're doing it" (American male)
- "When you are sitting on a terrace in summer, you see those machos walk by, you know, with their mobile [phones] and their sunglasses. I always think, 'Oh please, come back to earth!' These guys only want to impress. That is just so uncool" (Dutch female)
- "When a person thinks he is cool, he is absolutely uncool" (Dutch female)
- "To be cool we have to make sure we measure up to it. We have to create an identity for ourselves that mirrors what we see in magazines, on TV, and with what we hear on our stereos" (American male)

Replicate this study in your area. Recruit a group of teenagers to construct individual collages that represent what they feel is "cool." Analyze their choices—what patterns do you see?

13-38 Authenticity and evolution are the two key words when a brand is tackling the notoriously fickle teen market.[111] A teen chooses to eat, sleep, and breathe a particular lifestyle for a brief time, and the brand needs to connect with this in an authentic way. A teen can always spot a fake brand that is based on teen stereotypes. The brand has to do is to recognize that teens evolve quickly. Their likes and dislikes can change overnight. The brand needs to grow and adapt with them to keep them committed. If you were launching a new brand for teens, where would you start?

13-39 Locate one or more consumers (perhaps family members) who have emigrated from another country. Interview them about how they adapted to their host culture. In particular, what changes did they make in their consumption practices over time?

13-40 Find good and bad examples of advertising that targets older consumers. To what degree does advertising stereotype the elderly? What elements of ads or other promotions appear to determine their effectiveness in reaching and persuading this group?

13-41 Interview some retired people. How are they reconstructing their identities? What opportunities do their desires present for marketers?

Case Study

WELLS FARGO BANKS ON EMBRACING SAME-SEX MARRIAGE

With the U.S. Supreme Court decision that upheld the constitutional right to same-sex marriage in June 2015, the cultural landscape changed dramatically. Although only 13 states had continued to oppose same-sex marriage, the decision was a significant moment for the LGBT community and for many other citizens who saw the issue as national confirmation of a fundamental civil right for a sizable portion of the population. Regardless of where individuals stand on this issue, many companies and brands are realizing that they must pay attention and respond strategically to this increasingly visible subcultural group.

The Supreme Court ruling comes at a time when public opinion on the issue is evolving as well. Polls indicate that most Americans now approve of same-sex unions and a recent Google study shows that almost 50 percent of Millennials would be more likely to support a brand after seeing an ad with a theme of equality.

Additional evidence of the changing marketplace includes a study by PR firm Edelman that identifies gay, lesbian, and single parents as the new traditional family. Less than half of today's families fall into the 2010 U.S. Census definition of "traditional," and 2 million children are being raised by lesbian, gay, bisexual, and transgender (LGBT) parents. The study points out that companies need to make sure that all aspects of their marketing, from imagery to language, lend themselves to a variety of audiences, including this new family demographic. In a more specific finding, the study reported that 66 percent of gay dads are more likely to buy products that run ads reflecting their sexual orientation.

Some companies have already reached out to the LGBT market. Initial strategies focused on being involved in gay-related events or placing ads in LGBT-specific media. In "Advertisers Come Out of the Closet, Openly Courting Gay Consumers," Rich Ferraro, VP of communications at GLAAD, reminds us that the history of gay people in advertising is relatively short. Brands like Bud Light and Absolut Vodka made early moves to market directly to gay men in gay magazines or at gay events.

Robert Klara from *Adweek* goes on to identify the "coded ads" that would be understood by the gay market, but missed by straight consumers. He points to the Volkswagen Golf ad, "Sunday Afternoon—DaDaDa," an ad with two guys driving around. The two guys could be interpreted to be friends or boyfriends, depending on the viewer's sexual orientation. Coding ads was seen as a step forward, while allowing brands to remain somewhat ambiguous and face less potential backlash.

Most recently companies with even more traditional products have incorporated overtly LGBT themes into mainstream campaigns, Honey Maid, Kindle, Marriott, Target, Burger King, and Chevrolet, to name a few. Do these moves represent real social progress? As Klara points out, the reality is probably more a reflection of how competitive the marketplace is today. As he says, "If you're not appealing to every minority community, be that racial or in terms of sexual orientation, you're missing out on market share."

In the banking world, a notoriously conservative industry, Wells Fargo appears to be ahead of the curve, as demonstrated by their willingness to associate their company name with same-sex marriage. When they launched their 2015 ad, "Learning Sign Language," they became the first U.S. bank to feature an LGBT relationship in a national ad campaign. The ad features a lesbian couple learning sign language in preparation to adopt a deaf child.

Wells Fargo Chief Marketing Officer Jamie Moldafsky points out several noteworthy aspects of the campaign:

The campaign's goal was to reflect the diversity of customers and to tell emotional stories that illustrate universal truths.

The bank felt that it was a great way to both represent the notion of family and adoption—both an important part of their communities and many of their customers' lives—and to do it in a way that felt very true to their perspectives about diversity and inclusion.

Wells Fargo knew that there would be potential backlash to the campaign. Several religious groups have publicly boycotted the bank, including Franklin Graham of the Billy Graham Evangelical Association. Graham pulled all of his organization's accounts and then publicized the decision on social media. Wells Fargo's reply was that they would not be swayed by boycotts and would continue with the ad. Moldafsky commented that this ad is not their first marketing effort targeted at the LGBT market. The bank has supported the LGBT community over the long term in a variety of ways and even has a business unit that specializes in financial advice for same-sex couples.

DISCUSSION QUESTIONS

CS 13-1 Some criticize the actions of companies that try to align themselves with the values and views of subcultures as simply moves to make more money rather than attempting to make a social statement. What is your evaluation of this criticism?

CS 13-2 Is there a point at which a subculture becomes so "mainstream" that unique marketing approaches are no longer appropriate or necessary? Discuss.

Sources: Adam Liptak, "Supreme Court Ruling Makes Same-Sex Marriage a Right Nationwide," http://www.nytimes.com/2015/06/27/us/supreme-court-same-sex-marriage.html?_r=0,accessedJune27,2015;SonariGlinton,"Advertisers Come Out of the Closet Openly Courting Gay Consumers," http://www.npr.org/2014/06/29/326524942/advertisers-come-out-of-the-closet-openly-courting-gay-consumers, accessed June 24, 2015. Andrew McMains, "Wells Fargo Features a Lesbian Couple in Its First Big Campaign From BBDO," April 23, 2015, http://www.adweek.com/news/advertising-branding/wells-fargo-features-lesbian-couple-its-first-big-campaign-bbdo-164245,accessedJune 3, 2015; Caroline Bologna, "Sweet Wells Fargo Ad Features Lesbian Couple Learning Sign Language for Their Daughter, http://www.huffingtonpost.com/2015/04/28/wells-fargo-lesbian-couple-asl_n_7163254.html,accessedJune25, 2015; Dawn Ennis, "Wells Fargo Won't Pull Ad Featuring Lesbians," http://www.advocate.com/politics/marriage-equality/2015/06/15/wells-fargo-won-t-pull-ad-featuring-lesbians, accessed June 23, 2015; P. J. Bednarski, "Do Millennials Respond to "Equality-Themed Ads? Google Says Yes," http://www.mediapost.com/publications/article/248335/do-millennials-respond-to-equality-themed-ads-g.html, accessed June 25, 2015; Jill Finney, "Traditionall: Marketing to the Nontraditional Family," http://socialmediacertificate.net/2015/03/marketing-tradition-family/,accessedJune27,2015;"TheModern Family: A Study in Marketing," http://www.edelman.com/insights/intellectual-property/edelman-marketing-to-the-modern-family-study/

MyLab Marketing

Go to the Assignments section of your MyLab to complete these writing exercises.

13-42 Some industry experts feel that it's acceptable to appropriate symbols from another culture even if the buyer does not know their original meaning. They argue that even in the host society there is often disagreement about these meanings. What do you think?

13-43 What advice would you give to a marketer who wants to appeal to Gen Y? What are major do's and don'ts? Can you provide some examples of specific marketing attempts that work or don't work?

NOTES

1. Alex Cohen, "How Univision is adapting to a new generation of Latino viewers in the US," *KPCC Public Radio* (May 8, 2012), accessed April 17, 2015; Jaime Mejia and Gabriel Sama, "Media Players Say 'Si' to Latino Magazines," *Wall Street Journal* (May 15, 2002), www.wsj.com, accessed May 15, 2002.
2. Kay Deaux, "Social Identity," http://www.utexas.edu/courses/stross/ant 393b_files/ARTICLES/identity.pdf, accessed March 13, 2013.
3. Michael Cooper, "Census Officials, Citing Increasing Diversity, Say U.S. Will Be a 'Plurality Nation'," *New York Times* (December 12, 2012), http://www.nytimes.com/2012/12/13/us/us-will-have-no-ethnic-majority-census-finds.html, accessed February 18, 2015; Susan Saulny, "Census Data Presents Rise in Multiracial Population of Youths," *New York Times* (March 24, 2011), http://www.nytimes.com/2011/03/25/us/25race.html?_r=2&ref=census, accessed April 24, 2011.
4. Burt Helm, "Ethnic Marketing: McDonald's Is Lovin' It," *Bloomberg Businessweek* (July 8, 2010), http://www.businessweek.com/magazine/-content/10_29/b4187022876832.htm, accessed April 24, 2011.
5. Shirley Brady, "Adidas Sparks Uproar with Shackled 'Slavery Shoe'," *Brandchannel* (June 18, 2012), http://www.brandchannel.com/home/post/2012/06/18/Adidas-Originals-Jeremy-Scott-Slavery-061812.aspx accessed January 29, 2015.
6. Marty Westerman, "Death of the Frito Bandito," *American Demographics* (March 1989): 28.
7. Stuart Elliott, "Uncle Ben, Board Chairman," *New York Times* (March 30, 2007), www.nytimes.com, accessed March 30, 2007.
8. Rohit Deshpandé and Douglas M. Stayman, "A Tale of Two Cities: Distinctiveness Theory and Advertising Effectiveness," *Journal of Marketing Research* 31 (February 1994): 57–64.
9. Warren Brown, "The Potholes of Multicultural Marketing," *Washington Post* (June 10, 2007): G2.
10. See Lisa Peñaloza, "*Atravesando Fronteras*/Border Crossings: A Critical Ethnographic Exploration of the Consumer Acculturation of Mexican Immigrants," *Journal of Consumer Research* 21 (June 1994): 32–54; Lisa Peñaloza and Mary C. Gilly, "Marketer Acculturation: The Changer and the Changed," *Journal of Marketing* 63 (July 1999): 84–104; Carol Kaufman-Scarborough, "Eat Bitter Food and Give Birth to a Girl; Eat Sweet Things and Give Birth to a Cavalryman: Multicultural Health Care Issues for Consumer Behavior," *Advances in Consumer Research* 32, no.1 (2005): 226–269; Søren Askegaard, Eric J. Arnould, and Dannie Kjeldgaard, "Postassimilationist Ethnic Consumer Research: Qualifications and Extensions," *Journal of Consumer Research* 32, no. 1 (2005): 160.
11. Stuart Elliott, "1,200 Marketers Can't Be Wrong: The Future Is in Consumer Behavior," *New York Times* (October 15, 2007), www.nytimes.com, accessed October 15, 2007.
12. Peñaloza, "*Atravesando Fronteras*/Border Crossings."
13. Melanie Wallendorf and Michael D. Reilly, "Ethnic Migration, Assimilation, and Consumption," *Journal of Consumer Research* 10, no. 3 (December 1983): 292–302.
14. Ronald J. Faber, Thomas C. O'Guinn, and John A. McCarty, "Ethnicity, Accessed Ulturation and the Importance of Product Attributes," *Psychology & Marketing* 4 (Summer 1987): 121–134; Humberto Valencia, "Developing an Index to Measure Hispanicness," in Elizabeth C. Hirschman and Morris B. Holbrook, eds., *Advances in Consumer Research* 12 (Provo, Utah: Association for Consumer Research, 1985): 118–121.
15. Rohit Deshpandé, Wayne D. Hoyer, and Naveen Donthu, "The Intensity of Ethnic Affiliation: A Study of the Sociology of Hispanic Consumption," *Journal of Consumer Research* 13 (September 1986): 214–220.
16. Güliz Ger, "Warming: Making the New Familiar and Moral," *Journal of European Ethnology* (special issue of the journal *Ethnologia Europea*), Richard Wilk and Orvar Lofgren, eds. (forthcoming) 35, no. 1–2: 19–21.
17. Eils Lotozo, "The Jalapeño Bagel and Other Artifacts," *New York Times* (June 26, 1990): C1.
18. Dana Canedy, "The Shmeering of America," *New York Times* (December 26, 1996): D1.
19. Peter Schrag, *The Decline of the WASP* (New York: Simon & Schuster, 1971): 20.
20. "Nation's European Identity Falls by the Wayside," *Montgomery Advertiser* (June 8, 2002): A5.
21. U.S. Census Bureau, *Census 2000 Brief: Overview of Race and Hispanic Origin* (U.S. Department of Commerce, Economics and Statistics Administration, March 2001).
22. Padmananda Rama, "U.S. Census Show Asians Are Fastest Growing Racial Group," NPR (March 23, 2012), http://www.npr.org/blogs/thetwo-way/2012/03/23/149244806/u-s-census-show-asians-are-fastest-growing-racial-group, accessed March 16, 2013.
23. U.S. Census Bureau, http://quickfacts.census.gov/qfd/states/00000.html, accessed March 16, 2013.
24. Elizabeth A. Harris and Tanzina Vega," Race in Toyland: A Nonwhite Doll Crosses Over," *New York Times* (July 26, 2014), http://www.nytimes.com/2014/07/27/business/a-disney-doctor-speaks-of-identity-to-little-girls.html?_r=0, accessed February 23, 2015.
25. www.myblackisbeautiful.com, accessed June 18, 2009; Karl Greenberg, "P&G Borrows 'Black Power' Phrase for Campaign," *Marketing Daily*, (August 10, 2007), www.mediapost.com, accessed August 10, 2007.
26. www.skinvoice.com, accessed June 18, 2009; Sarah Mahoney, "Unilever Finds Skin Takes on Deep Meaning Among Black Women," *Marketing Daily* (May 23, 2007), www.mediapost.com, accessed May 23, 2007.
27. http://www.rockstargames.com/sanandreas/, accessed April 17, 2015.
28. Alan Neuhauser, "Study: Video Games May Reinforce Racist Stereotypes," *U.S. News & World Report* (March 21, 2014), http://www.usnews.com/news/articles/2014/03/20/video-games-may-reinforce-racist-stereotypes-study-finds, accessed April 17, 2015.
29. Elizabeth A. Harris, "To Expand Reach, Retailers Take Aim at Hispanic Shoppers," *New York Times* (December 5, 2013), http://www.nytimes.com/2013/12/05/business/to-expand-reach-retailers-take-aim-at-hispanic-shoppers.html?hpw&rref=business, accessed February 22, 2015.
30. Peter Francese, "Hispanic Market Hits Tipping Point," *Advertising Age* (July 26, 2010), http://adage.com/article/hispanic-marketing/hispanic-market-hits-tipping-point/145095/, accessed April 24, 2011.
31. Haya El Nasser, "Poor Economy Slows Hispanic Birthrate," *USA Today* (November 28, 2011), http://usatoday30.usatoday.com/news/nation/story/2011-11-27/economy-causes-drop-in-hispanic-births/51425394/1?loc=interstitialskip, accessed February 18, 2015.
32. Schwartz, "Hispanic Opportunities," *American Demographics* (May 1987): 56–59.
33. Karl Greenberg, "More Latinos See Themselves As Bicultural," *Marketing Daily* (February 20, 2013), http://www.mediapost.com/publications/article/193900/more-latinos-see-themselves-as-bicultural.html?edition=56909#axzz2LyoalJqc, accessed February 22, 2015.
34. Karl Greenberg, "Study: Hispanics Are Ideal Online Consumers," *Marketing Daily* (January 3, 2011), http://www.mediapost.com/publications/?fa=Articles.showArticle&art_aid=142204&nid=122251, accessed April 24, 2011; Karl Greenberg, "Hispanics' Web Savvy Surpassing Others," *Marketing Daily* (March 25, 2009), www.mediapost.com, accessed March 25, 2009.

35. Marty Westerman, "Fare East: Targeting the Asian-American Market," *Prepared Foods* (January 1989): 48–51; Eleanor Yu, "Asian-American Market Often Misunderstood," *Marketing News* (December 4, 1989): 11.

36. For a discussion of Asian identity, cf. Julien Cayla and Giana M. Eckhardt, "Asian Brands and the Shaping of a Transnational Imagined Community," *Journal of Consumer Research* 35 (August 2008): 216–230.

37. *State of the Asian American Consumer*, Nielsen, (Quarter 3 2012), http://www .nielsen.com/content/dam/corporate/us/en/microsites/publicaffairs/ StateoftheAsianAmericanConsumerReport.pdf, accessed April 17, 2015; Anh Do, "Asian Americans' Shopping Habits Make Retailers' Eyes Light Up," *Los Angeles Times* (December 5, 2013), http://articles.latimes.com/ 2013/dec/05/local/la-me-ff-1206-asian-spending-20131206, accessed April 17, 2015.

38. Dan Brown, *The Da Vinci Code* (New York: Doubleday, 2003).

39. Albert M. Muñiz, Jr., and Hope Jensen Schau, "Religiosity in the Abandoned Apple Newton Brand Community," *Journal of Consumer Research* 31 (March 2005): 737–747.

40. Risto Moisio and Mariam Beruchashvili, "Questing for Well-Being at Weight Watchers: The Role of the Spiritual-Therapeutic Model in a Support Group," *Journal of Consumer Research* 36, no. 5 (2010): 857–875.

41. For a couple of exceptions, see Michael J. Dotson and Eva M. Hyatt, "Religious Symbols as Peripheral Cues in Advertising: A Replication of the Elaboration Likelihood Model," *Journal of Business Research* 48 (2000): 63–68; Elizabeth C. Hirschman, "Religious Affiliation and Consumption Processes: An Initial Paradigm," *Research in Marketing* (Greenwich, CT: JAI Press, 1983): 131–170.

42. Quoted in Joe Mandese, "MindShare Turns SoulShare, Puts Faith in Evangelicals," *Media Daily News* (May 15, 2008), http://www.mediapost .com/publications/index.cfm?fa=Articles.showArticle&art_aid=82586 &passFuseAction=PublicationsSearch.showSearchReslts&art_sear ched=&page_number=0, accessed May 15, 2008.

43. Karlene Lukovitz, "PepsiCo Pulls Controversial Video Entry from Site," *Marketing Daily* (January 5, 2011), http://www.mediapost.com/publi cations/?fa=Articles.showArticle&art_aid=142406&nid=122346, accessed April 25, 2011; Jack Neff, "Dip Ad Stirs Church Ire," *Advertising Age* (July 2, 2001): 8; G. Burton, "Oh, My Heck! Beer Billboard Gets the Boot," *Salt Lake Tribune* (November 6, 2001); "Religion Reshapes Realities for U.S. Restaurants in Middle East," *Nation's Restaurant News* 32 (February 16, 1998); Sarah Ellison, "Sexy-Ad Reel Shows What Tickles in Tokyo Can Fade Fast in France," *Wall Street Journal* (March 31, 2000), www.wsj.com, accessed March 31, 2000; Claudia Penteado, "Brazilian Ad Irks Church," *Advertising Age* (March 23, 2000): 11; "Burger King Will Alter Ad That Has Offended Muslims," *Wall Street Journal* (March 15, 2000), www.wsj.com, accessed March 15, 2000.

44. Abe Sauer, "Why Wood Wood Urban Outfitters Continue to Carry Offensive Label?" *Brandchannel* (February 10, 2015), http://www.brand channel.com/home/post/2015/02/10/150210-Urban-Outfitters-Of fensive-Design.aspx?utm_campaign=150210-Urban-Outfitters&utm_ source=newsletter&utm_medium=email, accessed February 23, 2015.

45. Kim Severson, "For Some, 'Kosher' Equals Pure," *New York Times* (January 12, 2010), http://www.nytimes.com/2010/01/13/dining/13kosh.html? pagewanted=all&_r=0, accessed March 15, 2010.

46. Ed Stetzer, "The Explosive Growth of U.S. Megachurches, Even While Many Say Their Day is Done," *Christianity Today* (February 19, 2013), http://www .christianitytoday.com/edstetzer/2013/february/explosive-growth-of-us- megachurches-even-while-many-say.html?paging=off, accessed April 17, 2015; Patricia Leigh Brown, "Megachurches as Minitowns: Full-Service Havens from Family Stress Compete with Communities," *New York Times* (May 9, 2002): D1; Edward Gilbreath, "The New Capital of Evangelicalism: Move Over, Wheaton and Colorado Springs—Dallas, Texas, Has More Megachurches, Megaseminaries, and Mega-Christian Activity Than Any Other American City," *Christianity Today* (May 21, 2002): 38; Tim W. Ferguson, "Spiritual Reality: Mainstream Media Are Awakening to the Avid and Expanding Interest in Religion in the U.S.," *Forbes* (January 27, 1997): 70.

47. Richard Cimino and Don Lattin, *Shopping for Faith: American Religion in the New Millennium* (New York: Jossey-Bass, 2002).

48. Michael Fielding, "The Halo," *Marketing News* (February 1, 2005): 18–20.

49. Mandese, "MindShare Turns SoulShare, Puts Faith in Evangelicals"; Karlene Lukovitz, "Evangelicals More Diverse Than Might Be Assumed," *Marketing Daily* (November 7, 2007), http://www.mediapost.com/publi cations/?fa=Articles.showArticle&art_aid=70553, accessed November 7, 2007.

50. Cathy Lynn Grossman, "Number of U.S. Muslims to Double," *USA Today* (January 27, 2011), http://www.usatoday.com/news/religion/2011-01- 27-1Amuslim27_ST_N.htm, accessed June 22, 2011. For a theoretical account, cf. E. Izberk-Bilgin, "Infidel Brands: Unveiling Alternative Meanings of Global Brands at the Nexus of Globalization, Consumer Culture, and Islamism," *Journal of Consumer Research* 39, no. 4 (2012): 663–687.

51. Neal Ungerleider, "Whole Foods Celebrates, Monetizes Ramadan," *Fast Company* (July 28, 2011), http://www.fastcompany.com/1769739/whole- foods-celebrates-monetizes-ramadan, accessed February 22, 2015.

52. Barry Newman, "Halal Meets Kosher in Health-Food Aisle," *Wall Street Journal* (May 5, 2006): B1; Louise Story, "Rewriting the Ad for Muslim- Americans," *New York Times Online* (April 28, 2007), www.nytimes.com, accessed April 28, 2007.

53. Liz Gooch, "Advertisers Seek to Speak to Muslim Consumers," *New York Times* (August 11, 2010), http://www.nytimes.com/2010/08/12/business/ media/12branding.html?pagewanted=1&_r=1&ref=media, accessed April 25, 2011.

54. Natalie Angier, "The Changing American Family," *New York Times*, November 25, 2013, http://www.nytimes.com/2013/11/26/health/families. html?_r=0, accessed February 20, 2015; Erik Eckholm, "'07 U.S. Births Break Baby Boom Record," *New York Times* (March 18, 2009), www.ny times.com/2009/03/19/health/19birth.html?_r=1, accessed March 18, 2009.

55. Sabrina Tavernise, "Study Finds Women Slower to Wed, and Divorce Easing," *New York Times* (May 18, 2011), http://www.nytimes.com/ 2011/05/19/us/19marriage.html?_r=1&scp=1&sq=age%20of%20 marriage&st=cse, accessed June 4, 2011; Katie Zezima, "More Women Than Ever Are Childless, Census Finds," *New York Times* (August 18, 2008), www.nytimes.com, accessed August 19, 2008; Amber M. Epp, Hope Jensen Schau, and Linda L. Price, "The Role of Brands and Mediating Technologies in Assembling Long-Distance Family Practices," *Journal of Marketing* 78, no. 3 (2014): 81–101; Penelope Green, "Under One Roof, Building for Extended Families," *New York Times* (November 29, 2012), http://www.nytimes.com/2012/11/30/us/building-homes-for-modern- multigenerational-families.html, accessed February 20, 2015.

56. "Mothers Bearing a Second Burden," *New York Times* (May 14, 1989): 26.

57. Penelope Green, "Under One Roof, Building for Extended Families," *New York Times* (November 29, 2012), http://www.nytimes.com/2012/11/30/ us/building-homes-for-modern-multigenerational-families.html, accessed February 20, 2015.

58. Giang Trinh, Malcolm Wright, and Philip Stern, "The Relationship Between Household Life Cycle and Brand Loyalty," Paper presented at the annual meeting for the Association for Consumer Research, (2014), Baltimore, MD.

59. http://www.thebump.com/, accessed April 20, 2015; https://www.thek not.com/, accessed April 20, 2015; Edmondson, "Do the Math."

60. The VOICE Group, "Buying into Motherhood? Problematic Consumption and Ambivalence in Transitional Phases," *Consumption Markets & Culture* 13, no. 4 (2010): 373–397.

61. These categories are an adapted version of an FLC model proposed by Gilly and Enis (1982). Based on an empirical comparison of several competing models, Charles M. Schaninger and William D. Danko found that this framework outperformed others, especially in terms of its treatment of nonconventional households, though they recommend several improvements to this model as well. See Mary C. Gilly and Ben M. Enis, "Recycling the Family Life Cycle: A Proposal for Redefinition," in Andrew Mitchell, ed., *Advances in Consumer Research* 9 (Ann Arbor: Association for Consumer Research, 1982): 271–276; Schaninger and Danko, "A Conceptual and Empirical Comparison of Alternative Household Life Cycle Models," *Journal of Consumer Research* 19, no. 4 (March 1993): 580–594; Scott D. Roberts, Patricia K. Voli, and Kerenami Johnson, "Beyond the Family Life Cycle: An Inventory of Variables for Defining the Family as a Consumption Unit," in Victoria L. Crittenden, ed., *Developments in Marketing Science* 15 (Coral Gables, FL: Academy of Marketing Science, 1992): 71–75; George P. Moschis, "Life Course Perspectives on Consumer Behaviour," *Journal of the Academy of Marketing Science* 35 (2007): 295–307.

62. Edmondson, "Do the Math."

63. Rebecca Gardyn, "Animal Magnetism," *American Demographics* (May 2002): 31–37.

64. For a review, cf. Russell W. Belk, "Metaphoric Relationships with Pets," *Society & Animals* 4, no. 2 (1996): 121–46.

65. "Pets Win Prizes on Recession Bites," *Virgin Money* (April 23, 2009), http:// uk.virginmoney.com/virgin/news-centre/press-releases/2009/Pets_win_ prizes_as_recession_bites.jsp, accessed June 16, 2009; Carla Baranauckas, "A Dog's Life, Upgraded," *New York Times* (September 24, 2006), www.nytimes .com, accessed September 24, 2006; Thom Forbes, "PetSmart's Hotels Offer Doggies the Lap of Luxury," *Marketing Daily* (December 28, 2006), http://www.mediapost.com/publications/?fa=Articles.printFriendly&art_ aid$$$=53099, accessed December 28, 2006; Stephanie Thompson, "What's Next, Pup Tents in Bryant Park?" *Advertising Age* (January 29, 2007): 4; Maryann Mott, "Catering to the Consumers with Animal Appetites," *New York Times on the Web* (November 14, 2004), http://www .nytimes.com/2004/11/14/business/yourmoney/14pet.html, accessed September 9, 2011; http://www.k9waterco.com/, accessed June 14, 2011;

Jim Carlton, "For Finicky Drinkers, Water from the Tap Isn't Tasty Enough," *Wall Street Journal* (March 11, 2005), www.wsj.com, accessed March 11, 2005.

66. Karlene Lukovitz, "Coffee Marketers Need to Woo Young Adults," *Marketing Daily* (October 8, 2010), http://www.mediapost.com/publications/?fa=Articles.showArticle&art_aid=137318, accessed April 29, 2011.

67. Anil Mathur, George P. Moschis, and Euehun Lee, "Life Events and Brand Preference Changes," *Journal of Consumer Behavior* 3, no. 2 (December 2003): 129–141; James W. Gentry, Stacey Menzel Baker, and Frederic B. Kraft, "The Role of Possessions in Creating, Maintaining, and Preserving Identity: Variations Over the Life Course," in Frank Kardes and Mita Sujan, eds., *Advances in Consumer Research* 22 (Provo, Utah: Association for Consumer Research, 1995): 413–418.

68. Cf. Neil Howe and William Strauss, *Generations: The History of America's Future, 1584 to 2069* (New York: Harper Perennial, 1992). The yearly ranges in this list are the author's synthesis of a variety of generational schemes and as such are approximations.

69. www.disneybaby.com, accessed March 16, 2013; Quoted in Brooks Barnes, "Disney Looking into Cradle for Customers," *New York Times* (February 6, 2011), http://www.nytimes.com/2011/02/07/business/media/07disney.html?_r=1&ref=business#, accessed April 19, 2011.

70. Marsha L. Richins and Lan Nguyen, "Material Parenting: How the Use of Goods in Parenting Fosters Materialism in the Next Generation. *Journal of Consumer Research* 2015, Volume 41, Issue 6 Pp. 1333 - 1357

71. Paulina Smith, "Is Your Child Ready for a Cell Phone?" Verizon, http://www.verizonwireless.com/mobile-living/home-and-family/cell-phones-for-kids/, accessed April 20, 2015; "Best Tablets for Kids," *Consumer Reports*, http://www.consumerreports.org/cro/news/2014/11/best-tablets-for-kids-android/index.htm, accessed April 20, 2015.

72. Kay L. Palan and Robert E. Wilkes, "Adolescent-Parent Interaction in Family Decision-Making," *Journal of Consumer Research* 24 (September 1997): 159–69; cf. also Tiffany Meyers, "Kids Gaining Voice in How Home Looks," *Advertising Age* (March 29, 2004): S4.

73. Russell N. Laczniak and Kay M. Palan, "Under the Influence," *Marketing Research* (Spring 2004): 34–39.

74. Stephanie Thompson, "Mrs. Butterworth's Changes Her Target," *Advertising Age* (December 20, 1999): 44.

75. Stephen Holden, "After the War the Time of the Teen-Ager," *New York Times* (May 7, 1995): E4.

76. Cornelia Pechmann and Chuan-Fong Shih, "Smoking Scenes in Movies and Antismoking Advertisements Before Movies: Effects on Youth," *Journal of Marketing* 63 (July 1999): 1–13.

77. Junu Bryan Kim, "For Savvy Teens: Real Life, Real Solutions," *New York Times* (August 23, 1993): S1.

78. Excerpted from David B. Wooten, "From Labeling Possessions to Possessing Labels: Ridicule and Socialization Among Adolescents," *Journal of Consumer Research* 33 (September 2006): 188–198.

79. Ilya Marritz, "Brands Target Tween Girls in Bid to Keep them as Long-time Customers," NPR, (April 9, 2015), http://www.npr.org/2015/04/09/395091935/to-get-em-while-they-re-young-brands-target-tween-girls, accessed April 21, 2015; Tweens 'R Shoppers: A Look at the Tween Market & Shopping Behavior, POPAI (March 2013), http://www.popai.com/uploads/downloads/POPAIWhitePaper-Tweens-R-Shoppers-2013.pdf, accessed April 21, 2015; "Little Miss Perfect," IMDB, http://www.imdb.com/media/rm3226402560/tt3276618?ref_=tt_ov_i, accessed April 21, 2015; "16 and Pregnant," MTV, http://www.mtv.com/shows/16_and_pregnant/, accessed April 21, 2015; Leslie Earnest, "Store's Thongs for Kids Stir Outrage," *Los Angeles Times* (May 23, 2002), http://articles.latimes.com/2002/may/23/nation/na-thong23, accessed April 21, 2015.

80. Ruth Bernstein, "Move Over Millennials—Here Comes Gen Z," *Advertising Age* (January 21, 2015), http://adage.com/article/cmo-strategy/move-millennials-gen-z/296577/, accessed April 20, 2015; Laurence Benhamou, "Everything You Need to Know About Generation Z," *Business Insider* (February 12, 2015), http://www.businessinsider.com/afp-generation-z-born-in-the-digital-age-2015-2#ixzz3XsRYBXX6, accessed April 20, 2015; https://www.youtube.com/user/evantherock, accessed April 20, 2015.

81. Matt Richtel, "E-Cigarettes, by Other Names, Lure Young and Worry Experts." *New York Times* (March 4, 2014), http://www.nytimes.com/2014/03/05/business/e-cigarettes-under-aliases-elude-the-authorities.html?action=click&module=Search&region=searchResults%230&version=&url=http%3A%2F%2Fquery.nytimes.com%2Fsearch%2Fsitesearch%2F%3Faction%3Dclick%26region%3D3DMasthead%26pgtype%3DHomepage%26module%3DSearchSubmit%26contentCollection%3DHomepage%26t%3Dqry940%23%2Fe-cigarettes%2F24hours%2F&_r=0, accessed January 29, 2015.

82. Natalie Zmuda, "Pepsi Embraces 'Optimistic' Millennials in New TBWA Work," *Advertising Age* (December 11, 2008), http://adage.com/article/news/pepsi-embraces-optimistic-millennials-tbwa-work/133211/, accessed January 12, 2008; James Ledbetter, "Obama, the Pepsi Candidate," *Slate* (August 21, 2008), www.slate.com/id/2198198, accessed June 19, 2009.

83. Michael J. Weiss, "To Be about to Be," *American Demographics* (September 2003): 29–48.

84. Dionne Searcey, "Marketers Are Sizing Up the Millennials," *New York Times* (August 21, 2014), http://www.nytimes.com/2014/08/22/business/marketers-are-sizing-up-the-millennials-as-the-new-consumer-model.html?smid=nytcore-iphone-share&smprod=nytcore-iphone&_r=0, accessed February 22, 2015.

85. Quoted in Elizabeth A. Harris and Rachel Abrams, "Plugged-In Over Preppy: Teenagers Favor Tech Over Clothes," *New York Times* (August 27, 2014), http://www.nytimes.com/2014/08/28/business/less-prep-more-plugs-teenagers-favor-tech-over-clothes.html?smid=nytcore-iphone-share&smprod=nytcore-iphone&_r=0, accessed January 29, 2015; Hiroko Tabuchi, "Chapter 11 for Wet Seal as Tastes Change," *New York Times* (January 16, 2015), http://www.nytimes.com/2015/01/17/business/wet-seal-files-for-chapter-11-bankruptcy.html?_r=0, accessed February 22, 2015; Sheila Shayon, "McDonald's Struggles to Woo Millennials," *Brandchannel* (March 25, 2013), http://www.brandchannel.com/home/post/2013/03/25/McDonalds-McWrap-Millennials-032513.aspx, accessed February 22, 2015.

86. "The Millennial That Marketers Are Targeting Does Not Exist," *Mashable* (October 3, 2014), http://mashable.com/2014/10/03/millennial-marketing/, accessed February 22, 2015.

87. Steve Kroft, "The Echo Boomers," *CBS News* (October 3, 2004), www.cbsnews.com, accessed October 3, 2004.

88. "Tech-Savvy College Students Maintain Healthy Spending, Continue to Gather Gadgets and Prefer Campus Marketing Tactics," *Reuters* (June 25, 2014), http://www.reuters.com/article/2014/06/25/idUSnGNX8YFczg+1d8+GNW20140625, accessed April 21, 2015; The Purchasing Power of College Students, Retail Connection (October 2, 2013), http://retailconnection.dstewart.com/2013/10/02/the-purchasing-power-of-college-students/, accessed April 21, 2015.

89. Paul Taylor and George Gao, "Generation X: America's Neglected 'Middle Child'," Pew Research Center (June 5, 2014), http://www.pewresearch.org/fact-tank/2014/06/05/generation-x-americas-neglected-middle-child/, accessed April 21, 2015.

90. Jeff Gordinier, *X Saves the World: How Generation X Got the Shaft But Can Still Keep Everything from Sucking* (New York: Viking Adult, 2008); M. J. Stephey, "Gen-X: The Ignored Generation?" *Time* (April 16, 2008), www.time.com/time/arts/article/0,8599,1731528,00.html, accessed June 19, 2009.

91. http://www.restylaneusa.com/, accessed March 16, 2013; Angel Jennings, "Contests, YouTube and Commercials Converge for Skin Product," *New York Times Online* (July 26, 2007), http://www.nytimes.com/2007/07/26/business/media/26adco.html?_r=0, accessed September 25, 2013; cf. also Isabelle Szmigin and Marylyn Carrigan, "Consumption and Community: Choices for Women over Forty," *Journal of Consumer Behaviour* 5, no. 4 (2006): 292.

92. Jennings, "Contests, YouTube and Commercials Converge for Skin Product"; cf. also Szmigin and Carrigan, "Consumption and Community."

93. Gavin O'Malley, "Boomers Value Brands That Champion 'Youthful' Style," *Marketing Daily* (April 13, 2011), http://www.mediapost.com/publications/?fa=Articles.showArticle&art_aid=148507&nid=125673, accessed April 24, 2011.

94. John H. Fleming, "Baby Boomers Are Opening Their Wallets," *Gallup Business Journal* (January 30, 2015), http://www.gallup.com/businessjournal/181367/baby-boomers-opening-wallets.aspx, accessed April 21, 2015.

95. Quoted in Sarah Mahoney, "Nielsen: Time to Recommit to Boomers," *Marketing Daily* (July 21, 2010), http://www.mediapost.com/publications/article/132364/nielsen-time-to-recommit-to-boomers.html?edition=, accessed April 21, 2015.

96. Hiawatha Bray, "At MIT's AgeLab Growing Old Is the New Frontier," *Boston Globe* (March 23, 2009), www.boston.com/business/technology/articles/2009/03/23/at_mits_agelab_growing_old_is_the_new_frontier/?s_campaign=8315, accessed March 23, 2009.

97. D'Vera Cohn, "2100 Census Forecast: Minorities Expected to Account for 60% of U.S. Population," *Washington Post* (January 13, 2000): A5.

98. Catherine A. Cole and Nadine N. Castellano, "Consumer Behavior," in James E. Binnen, ed., *Encyclopedia of Gerontology*, vol. 1 (San Diego, CA: Academic Press, 1996), 329–339.

99. Rick Adler, "Stereotypes Won't Work with Seniors Anymore," *Advertising Age* (November 11, 1996): 32.

100. Benny Barak and Leon G. Schiffman, "Cognitive Age: A Nonchronological Age Variable," in Kent B. Monroe, ed., *Advances in Consumer Research* 8 (Provo, UT: Association for Consumer Research, 1981): 602–606.

101. Hope Jensen Schau, Mary C. Gilly, and Mary Wolfinbarger, "Consumer Identity Renaissance: The Resurgence of Identity-Inspired Consumption

in Retirement," *Journal of Consumer Research* 36 (August 2009): 255–276; cf. also Michelle Barnhart and Lisa Peñaloza, "Who Are You Calling Old? Negotiating Old Age Identity in the Elderly Consumption Ensemble," *Journal of Consumer Research* 39, no. 6 (2013): 1133–1153.

102. http://www.claritas.com/MyBestSegments/Default.jsp, accessed April 21, 2015.

103. Spikes Asia 2016, "Ice Scream, You Scream: Ghostly Campaign 'Haunts' Consumers," https://www.spikes.asia/winners/2015/media/entry.cfm?entryid=2113&award=101&order=4&direction=1

104. Mobile Marketing Association, "Cornetto: The Ghost Is Calling," http://www.mmaglobal.com/case-study-hub/case_studies/view/36693.

105. Penteado, "Brazilian Ad Irks Church."

106. Robert Boutilier, "Targeting Families: Marketing to and Through the New Family," in *American Demographics Marketing Tools* (Ithaca, NY: American Demographics Books, 1993): 4–6; W. Bradford Fay, "Families in the 1990s: Universal Values, Uncommon Experiences," *Marketing Research: A Magazine of Management & Applications* 5 (Winter 1993): 47.

107. Ellen Graham, "Craving Closer Ties, Strangers Come Together as Family," *Wall Street Journal* (March 4, 1996): B1.

108. Risto Moisio, Eric J. Arnould, and Linda L. Price, "Between Mothers and Markets: Constructing Family Identity Through Homemade Food," *Journal of Consumer Culture* 4, no. 3 (2004): 361–384.

109. Quoted in Tamar Lewin, "Teenagers' Internet Socializing Not a Bad Thing," *New York Times* (November 19, 2008), www.nytimes.com/2008/11/20/us/20internet.html?ex=1384923600&en=c3467e945b431625&ei=5124, accessed November 24, 2008.

110. Gary J. Bamossy, Michael R. Solomon, Basil G. Englis, and Trinske Antonidies, "You're Not Cool If You Have to Ask: Gender in the Social Construction of Coolness," paper presented at the Association for Consumer Research Gender Conference, Chicago, June 2000; see also Clive Nancarrow, Pamela Nancarrow, and Julie Page, "An Analysis of the Concept of Cool and Its Marketing Implications," *Journal of Consumer Behavior* 1 (June 2002): 311–322.

111. LeeAnna Buis, "Two Must-Haves for Effective Teen Marketing," *MediaPost*, http://www.mediapost.com/publications/article/257640/two-must-haves-for-effective-teen-marketing.html.

Chapter 14 • **Culture**

When you finish reading this chapter you will understand why:

14-1 A culture is a society's personality.

14-2 We distinguish between high culture and low culture.

14-3 Myths are stories that express a culture's values, and in modern times marketing messages convey these values to members of the culture.

14-4 Many of our consumption activities—including holiday observances, grooming, and gift-giving—relate to rituals.

14-5 We describe products as either sacred or profane, and it's not unusual for some products to move back and forth between the two categories.

14-6 New products, services, and ideas spread through a population over time. Different types of people are more or less likely to adopt them during this diffusion process.

14-7 Many people and organizations play a role in the fashion system that creates and communicates symbolic meanings to consumers.

14-8 Fashions follow cycles and reflect cultural dynamics.

14-9 Western (and particularly U.S.) culture has a huge impact around the world, although people in other countries don't necessarily ascribe the same meanings to products as we do.

14-10 Products that succeed in one culture may fail in another if marketers fail to understand the differences among consumers in each place.

Source: Rob Marmion/Shutterstock

Stephanie is at her wits' end. It's bad enough that she has a deadline looming on that new Christmas promotion for her gift shop. Now, there's trouble on the home front as well: Her son Mark had to go and flunk his driver's license road exam, and he's just about suicidal because he feels he can't be a "real man" if he doesn't have a license. To top things off, now she'll have to postpone her much-anticipated vacation to Disney World with her stepdaughter Arya because she just can't find the time to get away.

When Stephanie meets up with her buddy Lenny at their local Starbucks for their daily "retreat," her mood starts to brighten. Somehow the calm of the café rubs off as she savors her grande cappuccino. Lenny consoles her with the ultimate remedy to beat the blues: Go home, take a nice long bath, and then consume a quart of Starbucks Espresso Swirl ice cream. Yes, that's the ticket. It's amazing how the little things in life can make such a big difference. As she strolls out the door, Stephanie makes a mental note to get Lenny a really nice Christmas gift this year. She's earned it.

OBJECTIVE 14-1
A culture is a society's personality.

Cultural Systems

Stephanie's experiences illustrate how everyday events reflect deeper meanings; overcoming challenges like a driver's test, planning "pilgrimmages" to destinations like Disney World, choosing gifts to thank others, even calming ourselves with that daily latte or bowl of favorite ice cream. Marketers can only appreciate the importance of these activities when they understand what they signify and that's why this final chapter will explore some of the underlying elements. **Culture** is a society's personality. It includes both abstract ideas, such as values and ethics, and material objects and services, such as the automobiles, clothing, food, art, and sports a society produces. Put another way, it's the accumulation of shared meanings, rituals, norms, and traditions among the members of an organization or society.

We simply can't understand consumption unless we consider its cultural context: Culture is the "lens" through which people view products. Ironically, the effects of culture on consumer behavior are so powerful and far-reaching that it's sometimes difficult to grasp their importance. We don't always appreciate this power until we encounter a different culture. Suddenly, many of the assumptions we take for granted about the clothes we wear, the food we eat, or the way we address others no longer seem to apply. The effect when we encounter such differences can be so great that the term *culture shock* is not an exaggeration.

Our culture determines the overall priorities we attach to different activities and products, and it also helps us decide whether specific products will satisfy these priorities. A product that provides benefits to members of a culture at any point in time has a much better chance to achieve marketplace acceptance. For example, U.S. culture began to emphasize the concept of a fit, trim body as an ideal of appearance in the mid-1970s. The premium consumers put on thinness, which stemmed from underlying values such as mobility, wealth, and a focus on the self, greatly contributed to Miller's success when the brewer launched its Lite beer. However, a decade earlier when Gablinger's introduced a similar low-cal beer in the 1960s, the product failed. This beverage was "ahead of its time" because U.S. beer drinkers during that era (who were almost all men) weren't worried about cutting down on calories.

The relationship between consumer behavior and culture is a two-way street. On the one hand, consumers are more likely to embrace products and services that resonate with a culture's priorities at any given time. On the other hand, it's worthwhile for us to understand which products do get accepted, because this knowledge provides a window into the dominant cultural ideals of that period. Consider, for example, some U.S. products that successfully reflected dominant values during their time:

- The TV dinner reflected changes in family structure and the onset of a new informality in U.S. home life.
- Cosmetics made from natural materials without animal testing reflected consumers' apprehensions about pollution, waste, and animal rights.
- Condoms packaged in pastel carrying cases for female buyers signaled changes in attitudes toward sexual responsibility and openness.

Cultural Systems

Culture is not static. It evolves continually as it synthesizes old ideas with new ones. A *cultural system* consists of these functional areas:[1]

- **Ecology**—The way a system adapts to its habitat. The technology a culture uses to obtain and distribute resources shapes its ecology. The Japanese, for example, greatly value products that make efficient use of space because of the cramped conditions in their urban centers.[2]

- **Social structure**—The way people maintain an orderly social life. This includes the domestic and political groups that dominate the culture (e.g., the nuclear family versus the extended family; representative government versus dictatorship).
- **Ideology**—The mental characteristics of a people and the way they relate to their environment and social groups. As we saw in Chapter 12, they share a common *worldview* that includes ideas about principles of order and fairness. They also share an *ethos*, or a set of moral and aesthetic principles. A theme park in Bombay called *Water Kingdom* that caters to India's emerging middle class illustrates how distinctive a culture's worldview can be. Many consumers there are unfamiliar with mixed-sex swimming in public, so the park rents swimsuits to women who have never worn them before. No thongs here, though: The suits cover the women from wrists to ankles.[3]

The Yin and Yang of Marketing and Culture

Even though inner-city teens represent only 8 percent of all people in that age group and have incomes significantly lower than their white suburban counterparts, their influence on young people's musical and fashion tastes is much greater than these numbers suggest. "Urban" fashion now is a mainstay in the heartland, as major retail chains pick up on the craze and try to lure legions of young middle-class shoppers. Macy's and JC Penney carry Sean John and FUBU ("for us by us"); labels like Versace, Tommy Hilfiger, Enyce, Ecko, Nautica, and Affliction are standard issue for junior high kids. Web sites like Krunkgrillz.com and Hiphopbling.com sell other emblems of hip-hop such as "pimp cups," gold plated "grillz," and Bellagio spoke rims.[4] Why does this subculture influence the mass market so strongly?

Outsider heroes—whether John Dillinger, James Dean, or Dr. Dre—who achieve money and fame without being hemmed in by societal constraints have always fascinated Americans. That helps to explain the devotion of many white suburban teens to the urban music scene. As one executive of a firm that researches urban youth noted, "People resonate with the strong anti-oppression messages of rap, and the alienation of blacks."[5] It's common for mainstream culture to modify symbols from "cutting-edge" subcultures for a larger audience to consume. As this occurs, these cultural products undergo a process of **cooptation** in which outsiders transform their original meanings.[6] The spread of hip-hop fashions and music is only one example of what happens when the marketing system takes a set of subcultural meanings, reinterprets them, and reproduces them for mass consumption.

Of course, the countercultures that originate these movements don't just sit still for this. They develop strategies to reclaim their symbols and practices. For example, large food manufacturers and retailers today recognize shifting consumer tastes as they co-opt vegan or organic food cultures and repackage food products for mainstream grocery shoppers. Walmart sells organic food, and the huge conglomerate ConAgra purchased Ben & Jerry's ice cream. In response, adherents of a **locavore** lifestyle that emphasizes the purchase of locally produced meat and vegetables may find alternative channels of distribution, such as farmers' markets, to sell their "authentic" versions to true believers.[7]

In this section we'll look at how our culture creates these meanings—which often reside in everyday products—and how these meanings move through a society. As Figure 14.1 shows, the advertising and fashion industries play a key role in this process; they link functional products with symbolic qualities such as sexiness, sophistication, or just plain "cool." These goods, in turn, impart their meanings to us as we use these products to create and express our identities.[8]

Cultural Movement

Fairy tats. Tory Burch flats. Cage-free eggs. Ke$ha. High-tech furniture. Postmodern architecture. *Candy Crush.* Vine videos. Tablets. Emojis. *Real Housewives.* Selfies. Electric cars. Costa Rican ecotours. We inhabit a world that brims with different styles and possibilities. The food we eat, the cars we drive, the clothes we wear, the places we live and work, the music we listen to—the ebb and flow of popular culture and fashion influences all of them.

Figure 14.1 THE MOVEMENT OF MEANING

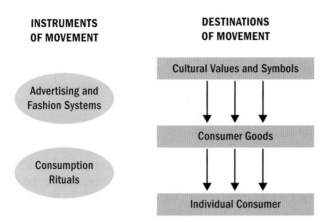

At times we may feel overwhelmed by the sheer number of choices available to us in the marketplace. A person who wants to choose something as routine as a necktie or a lipstick shade may look at hundreds of alternatives! Despite this seeming abundance, however, the options available to us at any point in time actually represent only a small fraction of the *total* set of possibilities. Figure 14.2 shows that when we select certain alternatives over others—whether automobiles, dresses, computers, recording artists, political candidates, religions, or even scientific methodologies—our choice actually is

Figure 14.2 THE CULTURE PRODUCTION PROCESS

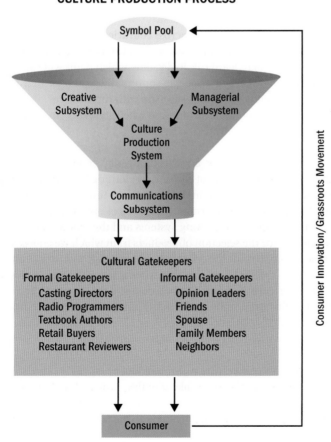

only the culmination of a complex filtration process that resembles a funnel. Many possibilities initially compete for adoption; most of them drop out of the mix as they make their way down the path from conception to consumption. We call this winnowing-out process **cultural selection.**

We don't form our tastes and product preferences in a vacuum. The many images mass media present to us drive our choices, as well as our observations of those around us, and even our desires to live in the fantasy worlds marketers create in the ads we see all around us. These options constantly evolve and change. A clothing style or type of cuisine that is "hot" one year may be "out" the next.

Hip-hop was born way back in 1968 by a DJ in the Bronx, New York. The music and fashions that grew up around it grew over the years and began to garner mainstream status when Columbia Records bought the Def Jam record label in 1985. By the mid-2000s, entrepreneurs branched out into other categories including sports (Jay Z became part owner of what is now the Brooklyn Nets), beverages (Nelly launched Pimp Juice, an energy drink) and fragrances (Queen by Queen Latifah, Pink Friday by Nicki Minaj, Girl by Pharrell Williams). Ghostface Killah sold a $500 action figure of himself; it came with a mixtape, a real 14k gold chain, and a chalice lined with Swarovski crystals. Eventually hip-hop grew beyond its U.S. roots as artists in other countries (even an aborigine in Australia) developed their own interpretations. The widespread adoption of hip-hop style illustrates some of the characteristics of fashion and popular culture:

- Styles reflect more fundamental societal trends (e.g., politics and social conditions).
- A style begins as a risky or unique statement by a relatively small group of people and then spreads as others become aware of it.
- Styles usually originate as an interplay between the deliberate inventions of designers and businesspeople and spontaneous actions by ordinary consumers who modify these creations to suit their own needs. Designers, manufacturers, and merchandisers who anticipate what consumers want will succeed in the marketplace. In the process, they help to fuel the fire when they encourage distribution of the item—especially if they persuade opinion leaders to use it first.
- Cultural products travel widely, often across countries and even continents.
- Influential people in the media and increasingly everyday "influencers" who are active in social media play a significant role in deciding which items will succeed.
- Most styles eventually wear out as people continually search for new ways to express themselves and marketers scramble to keep up with these desires.
- The cultural selection process never stops, so when styles become obsolete others wait to replace them in popular culture.

No single designer, company, or advertising agency creates popular culture. Many parties contribute to every hit song, hot car, or new clothing style. A **culture production system (CPS)** is the set of individuals and organizations that create and market a cultural product.[9] The structure of a CPS determines the types of products it creates. Factors such as the number and diversity of competing systems and the amount of innovation versus conformity each influence the selection of products from which we choose at any point in time. For example, an analysis of the country/western music industry showed that the hit records it produces are similar to one another when a few large companies dominate the industry, but when a greater number of labels compete we see more diversity in musical styles.[10] Table 14.1 illustrates some of the many cultural specialists that jointly create a hit CD like singer Beyoncé's platinum album 4.

A culture production system has three major subsystems:

1 A *creative subsystem* to generate new symbols and products
2 A *managerial subsystem* to select, make tangible, produce, and manage the distribution of new symbols and products
3 A *communications subsystem* to give meaning to the new product and provide it with a symbolic set of attributes

TABLE 14.1 Cultural Specialists in the Music Industry

Specialist	Functions
Songwriter(s)	Compose music and lyrics; must reconcile artistic preferences with estimates of what will succeed in the marketplace
Performer(s)	Interpret music and lyrics; may be formed spontaneously, or may be packaged by an agent to appeal to a predetermined market (e.g., The Monkees, Menudo, and New Kids on the Block)
Teachers and coaches	Develop and refine performers' talents
Agents	Represent performers to record companies
A&R (artist & repertoire) executives	Acquire artists for the record label
Publicists, image consultants, designers, stylists	Create an image for the artists that is transmitted to the buying public
Recording technicians, producers	Create a recording to be sold
Marketing executives	Make strategic decisions regarding performer's appearances, ticket pricing, promotional strategies, and so on
Video directors	Interpret the song visually to create a music video that will help to promote the record
Music reviewers	Evaluate the merits of a recording for listeners
Disc jockeys, radio program directors	Decide which records will be given airplay and/or placed in the radio stations' regular rotations
Record store owners	Decide which of the many records produced will be stocked and/or promoted heavily in the retail environment

An example of the three components of a culture production system for a music release is (1) a singer (e.g., singer Beyoncé, a creative subsystem); (2) a company (e.g., Columbia Records distributes Beyoncé's CDs, a managerial subsystem); and (3) the advertising agencies and corporations such as PepsiCo that work with the singer's company Parkwood Entertainment to promote her music and arrange for her appearances in venues including the Super Bowl and even on a limited edition set of Pepsi soda cans.[11]

Many judges or "tastemakers" have a say in the products we consider. These **cultural gatekeepers** filter the overflow of information as it travels down the "funnel." Gatekeepers include movie, restaurant, and car reviewers; interior designers; disc jockeys; retail buyers; magazine editors; and increasingly a fan base that obsessively follows and shares the latest gossip, styles, TV and film plots, and other pieces of popular culture. Collectively, social scientists call this set of agents the *throughput sector*.[12]

High and Low Culture

OBJECTIVE 14-2
We distinguish between high culture and low culture.

Question: What do Beethoven and Kanye West have in common? Although we associate both the famous composer and the rap singer with music, many would argue that the similarity stops there. Culture production systems create many kinds of products, but we make some basic distinctions.

An **art product** is an object we admire strictly for its beauty or because it inspires an emotional reaction in us (perhaps bliss, or perhaps disgust). In contrast, we admire a **craft product** because of the beauty with which it performs some function (e.g., a ceramic ashtray or hand-carved fishing lures).[13] A craft tends to follow a formula that permits rapid production.[14]

Characters from popular culture often serve as a form of "shorthand" for companies the world over to communicate with their customers. This ad is from Nigeria but the figures in it are familiar to people in many countries.
Source: Courtesy of Noah's Ark Communications Ltd.

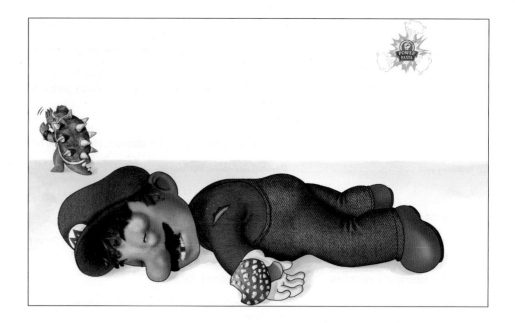

To appreciate this distinction, consider the phenomenal success of the late artist Thomas Kinkade. This painter sold 10 million digital reproductions of his work. Even after his death in 2012, his studio continues to mass-produce pictures at a factory in California, where workers reproduce a digital photograph of each original thousands of times onto thin plastic film they glue to canvasses. Then "high-lighters" sit along an assembly line where they dab oil paint onto set spots. The company also licenses images that appear on coffee mugs, La-Z-Boy recliners, and even a romance novel cover.[15]

As Kinkade's "formula for success" demonstrates, the distinction between high and low culture is not as clear as it used to be. In addition to the possible class bias that drives such a distinction (i.e., we assume that the rich have culture but the poor do not), today high and low culture blend together in interesting ways. In addition to the appliances, tires, and cereals it sells by the case, the warehouse club Costco stocks fine art, including limited-edition lithographs by Pablo Picasso, Marc Chagall, and Joan Miró.

A multinational team of consumer researchers extended the study of high and low art to the realm of **street art** where artists create paintings, murals, and other pieces in public places. They identified numerous sites where the art became an instrument that was used for "transactions" between the artists and the people who lived in the area. Although not all reactions were positive, it was common to observe that people's experiences of public spaces were enhanced because the street art created a feeling of empowerment and ownership in formerly barren places.[16]

Marketers often invoke high-art imagery to promote products. They may feature works of art on shopping bags or sponsor artistic events to build public goodwill.[17] When observers from Toyota watched customers in luxury car showrooms, the company found that these consumers view a car as an art object. The company then used this theme in an ad for the Lexus with the caption, "Until now, the only fine arts we supported were sculpture, painting, and music."[18]

Cultural Formulae

Moviegoers won't be surprised to learn that there's not that much new in theaters today. The majority of blockbuster movies are sequels, prequels, or adaptations of successful franchises that include *Lego*, *Harry Potter*, *Star Wars*, Marvel Comics, even *Fast and Furious*. This is a steadily increasing trend: One analysis found that whereas in 1984 about 59 percent of movies from major studios were based on original stories, today this proportion is less than 25 percent.[19]

The reliance on established plots and characters illustrates how mass culture churns out products that aim to please the average taste of a mass audience. Rather than being unique, they are predictable because they follow a well-defined pattern. Many popular art forms, such as detective stories or science fiction, follow a **cultural formula** in which familiar roles and props occur consistently.[20] For example, we expect characters in a classic western to ride horses to get around, while in a science fiction movie they use spaceships; hard-boiled detectives drive a beat-up car and characters in a family sitcom ride in a minivan. Similarly, a six-gun or rifle is the weapon in a classic western, ray guns appear in science fiction movies, a hard-boiled detective uses a pistol or his fists, and the actors in a family sitcom fight one another with verbal insults. Romance novels are an extreme case of a cultural formula. Computer programs even allow users to "write" their own romances by systematically varying certain set elements of the story.[21]

As members of the creative subsystem rely on these formulae, they tend to *recycle* images as they reach back through time for inspiration. Thus, young people watch retro shows like *Full House* as well as remakes such as *Fuller House*; designers modify beaded dresses inspired by the hit British show *Downton Abbey* that is set in the early 1920s; hip-hop deejays sample sound bites from old songs and combine them in new ways; and Gap ran ads that featured celebrities in khaki pants, including Humphrey Bogart, Gene Kelly, and Pablo Picasso. With easy access to CD burners, digital cameras, and imaging software, virtually anyone can "remix" the past.[22]

OBJECTIVE 14-3

Myths are stories that express a culture's values, and in modern times marketing messages convey these values to members of the culture.

Cultural Stories and Ceremonies

Every culture develops *stories* and *ceremonies* that help its members to make sense of the world. When we hear about some strange practice that goes on in another place, it may be hard to figure out just what these people think they're doing. Yet, our own cultural practices seem quite normal—even though a visitor may find them equally bizarre! Just take a European to a NASCAR race, and you'll understand that culture is relative.

To appreciate how "primitive" belief systems influence our supposedly "modern" rational society, consider the avid interest many of us have in magic. Marketers of health foods, anti-aging cosmetics, exercise programs, and gambling casinos often imply that their offerings have "magical" properties that prevent sickness, old age, poverty, or just plain bad luck. People by the millions play their "lucky numbers" in the lottery, carry rabbits' feet and other amulets to ward off "the evil eye," and own "lucky" clothing.[23] In a set of studies, researchers examined how people come to regard products as lucky: They looked at **conditioned superstition**; consumers who don't feel they have control over their outcomes come to associate a product that is paired with a reward with the outcome itself (see Chapter 4). You may have observed this process; for example, a friend wears a certain T-shirt to a big game and the team wins. This person may choose to wear the same shirt to future games to "help" the team.[24] A recent advertising campaign for Budweiser featured fans with bizarre superstitions and the tagline, "It's only weird if it doesn't work."

Interest in the occult tends to spike when members of a society feel overwhelmed or powerless; magical remedies simplify our lives when they give us "easy" answers. Many consumers regard the computer with awe as a sort of "electronic magician" with the ability to solve our problems (or, in other cases, to cause data to magically disappear!).[25] Software developers even supply "wizards" that guide the uninitiated through their programs! Or, we may even think a person's soul inhabits an object: Kids (and maybe some adults as well) believe that when they put on their Air Nikes they magically absorb some of the athletic ability of Michael Jordan or Dwyane Wade. Sound preposterous? The movie *Like Mike* had this exact storyline. In this section, we'll discuss myths and rituals, two aspects of culture common to all societies from the ancients to the modern world.

Myths

A **myth** is a story with symbolic elements that represents a culture's ideals. The story often focuses on some kind of conflict between two opposing forces, and its outcome serves as a moral guide for listeners. In this way, a myth reduces anxiety because it provides consumers with guidelines about their world. Most members of a culture learn these stories, but usually we don't really think about their origins.

The familiar *Little Red Riding Hood* myth started as a peasant's tale in 16th-century France, where a girl meets a werewolf on her way to Granny's house (there is historical evidence for a plague of wolf attacks during this time, including several incidents where men were put on trial because they allegedly turned themselves into the deadly animals). The werewolf has already killed Granny, stored her flesh in the pantry, and poured her blood in a bottle. Contrary to the version we know, however, when the girl arrives at the house she snacks on Granny, strips naked, and climbs into bed with the wolf! To make the story even more scandalous, some versions refer to the wolf as a "gaffer" (a contraction of "grandfather"), implying incest as well. This story first appeared in print in 1697; it was a warning to the loose ladies of Louis XIV's court (the author puts her in red in this version because this color symbolizes harlots). Eventually, the Brothers Grimm wrote their own version in 1812, but they substituted violence for sex to scare kids into behaving. And to reinforce the sex-role standards of that time, in the Grimm version, a man rescues the girl from the wolf.[26] So, this myth sends vivid messages about such cultural no-no's as cannibalism, incest, and promiscuity.

In some cases marketers adapt these stories and (perhaps unconsciously) pattern their messages along a mythic structure. Consider, for example, the way that McDonald's takes on "mythical" qualities.[27] The "golden arches" are virtually synonymous with U.S. culture. They offer sanctuary to Americans around the world, who know exactly what to expect once they enter. Basic struggles involving good versus evil play out in the fantasy world McDonald's advertising creates; for example, when Ronald McDonald confounds the Hamburglar. McDonald's even has a "seminary" (Hamburger University) where inductees go to learn the ways of the Golden Arches.

Corporations often have myths and legends in their history. Nike designates senior executives as "corporate storytellers" who explain the company's heritage to the hourly workers at Nike stores. They recount tales about the coach of the Oregon track team who poured rubber into his family waffle iron to make better shoes for his team—the origin of the Nike waffle sole. The stories emphasize the dedication of runners and coaches to reinforce the importance of teamwork. Rookie hires visit the track where the coach worked to help them appreciate the importance of the Nike legends. And rumor has it that senior Nike executives (including the CEO) have a "swoosh" tattoo on their backsides.[28]

Myths serve four interrelated functions in a culture:[29]

1 **Metaphysical**—They help to explain the origins of existence.
2 **Cosmological**—They emphasize that all components of the universe are part of a single picture.
3 **Sociological**—They maintain social order because they authorize a social code for members of a culture to follow.
4 **Psychological**—They provide models for personal conduct.

When we analyze myths, we examine their underlying structures, a technique the French anthropologist Claude Lévi-Strauss (no relation to the blue jeans company) pioneered. Lévi-Strauss noted that many stories involve **binary opposition** which represents two opposing ends of some dimension (e.g., good versus evil, nature versus technology).[30] Often a *mediating figure* resolves the conflict between mythical opposing forces; this links the opposites as it shares characteristics of each. For example, many myths are about animals that have human abilities (e.g., a talking snake) to bridge the gap between humanity and nature, just as marketers often give cars (technology) animal names (nature) such as Cougar, Cobra, or Mustang.

We associate myths with the ancient Greeks and Romans, but in reality comic books, movies, holidays, and yes, even commercials embody our own cultural myths. Furthermore, researchers report that some people create their own **consumer fairy tales**. They tell stories that include magical agents, donors, and helpers to overcome villains and obstacles as they seek out goods and services in their quest for happy endings.[31]

Smart marketers are more than happy to help us live out these fairy tales. Consider the popularity of the elaborate weddings Disney stages for couples who want to reenact their own version of a popular myth: At Disney World, the princess bride wears a tiara and rides to the park's lakeside wedding pavilion in a horse-drawn coach, complete with two footmen in gray wigs and gold lamé pants. At the exchange of vows, trumpets blare as Major Domo (he helped the Duke in his quest for Cinderella) walks up the aisle with two wedding bands he gently places in a glass slipper on a velvet pillow. Disney stages about 2,000 of these extravaganzas each year. The company continues to expand the appeal of this myth as it moves into the bridal gown business. It sells a line of billowing princess gowns complete with crystal tiaras. Fairy tale brides can walk down the aisle costumed as Elsa, Cinderella, Snow White, Belle, Sleeping Beauty, Jasmine, or Ariel.[32]

Many "blockbuster" movies and hit TV shows draw directly on mythic themes. Although dramatic special effects and attractive stars certainly don't hurt, a number of these movies also owe their huge appeal to their presentation of characters and plot structures that follow mythic patterns. Here are three examples of mythic blockbusters:[33]

- *Gone with the Wind*—Myths often take place in times of upheaval such as wars. In this story, the North (which represents technology and democracy) battles the South (which represents nature and aristocracy). The movie depicts a romantic era (the antebellum South) when love and honor were virtues. Following the war, newer values of materialism and industrialization (i.e., modern consumer culture) replace these priorities. The movie paints a picture of a lost era where man and nature existed in harmony.
- *E.T.: The Extra-Terrestrial*—*E.T.* represents a familiar myth involving messianic visitation. The gentle creature from another world visits Earth and performs miracles (e.g., he revives a dying flower). His "disciples" are neighborhood children; they help him combat the forces of modern technology and an unbelieving secular society. The myth teaches that the humans God chooses are pure and unselfish.
- *Star Trek*—The multiple television series and movies, prequels, and sequels that document the adventures of the starship *Enterprise* also link to myths, such as the story of the New England Puritans who explore and conquer a new continent ("the final frontier"). Encounters with the Klingons mirror skirmishes with American Indians. In addition, at least 13 out of the original 79 episodes employed the theme of a quest for paradise.[34]

Advertisements sometimes represent mythic themes. Commercials for Pepperidge Farm ask consumers to "remember" the good old days (lost paradise) when products were wholesome and natural. Avis famously used the theme of the underdog prevailing over the stronger foe (i.e., David and Goliath).[35] A commercial that encouraged Hispanic consumers to buy more milk featured a female phantom who wails as she walks through a home. She is *La Llorona* (the crying one), a character in a Hispanic myth who murders her children, commits suicide, and roams for all eternity as she seeks her lost family. In this version, however, the moaning phantom makes her way to the refrigerator, only to find an empty milk carton.[36]

Rituals

OBJECTIVE 14-4

Many of our consumption activities—including holiday observances, grooming, and gift-giving—relate to rituals.

A **ritual** is a set of multiple, symbolic behaviors that occurs in a fixed sequence and is repeated periodically.[37] Bizarre tribal ceremonies, perhaps involving animal or human sacrifice, may come to mind when you think of rituals. In reality many contemporary consumer activities are ritualistic. Researchers find that when people consume products like chocolate as part of a ritual, they report they enjoy them more than if there is no context.[38]

Consider a ritual that many beer drinkers in the United Kingdom and Ireland hold near and dear to their hearts: the spectacle of a pub bartender "pulling" the perfect pint of Guinness. According to tradition, the slow pour takes exactly 119.5 seconds as the bartender holds the glass at a 45-degree angle, fills it three-quarters full, lets it settle, and tops it off with its signature creamy head. Guinness wanted to make the pull faster so the bar could serve more drinks on a busy night, so it introduced FastPour, an ultrasound technology that dispenses the dark brew in only 25 seconds. You probably guessed the outcome: The brewer had to scrap the system when drinkers resisted the innovation. Note: Diageo (which owns Guinness) hasn't given up, and it continues to experiment with more efficient techniques in markets where this ritual isn't so inbred. A system it calls Guinness Surger shows up in Tokyo bars, many of which are too small to accommodate kegs: The bartender pours a pint from a bottle, places the glass on a special plate, and zaps it with ultrasound waves that generate the characteristic head.[39]

Source: Oli Scarff/Getty Images

Many businesses benefit because they supply **ritual artifacts** to consumers. These are items we need to perform rituals, such as wedding rice, birthday candles, diplomas, specialized foods and beverages (e.g., wedding cakes, ceremonial wine, or even hot dogs at the ball park), trophies and plaques, band uniforms, greeting cards, and retirement watches.[40] In addition, we often follow a **ritual script** to identify the artifacts we need, the sequence in which we should use them, and who uses them. Examples include graduation programs, fraternity manuals and etiquette books.

A wedding ceremony is one of our most familiar rituals. If you've ever planned or participated in a wedding, you know the many scripted activities are serious stuff. They're expensive, too: Americans spend $70 billion a year on weddings, more than we spend on pets, coffee, toothpaste and toilet paper combined.[41] The massive wedding industry continues to find new ways for consumers to compete in their own *potlach* ceremonies (see Chapter 12) as they vie to offer the most lavish or novel attractions. Destination weddings, online gift

Retirement is a milestone that includes ritual artifacts.
Source: bst2012/Fotolia

Robots are popping up as guests at weddings.
Source: Kaku Kurita/Newscom

registries, save-the-date cards, chocolate fountains; you name it and someone will have it. A company called Anybots even rents robots to guests who can't attend; the mechanical wedding crashers boogie with the crowd and allow the absent revelers to videoconference during the event.[42]

As we'll see shortly, some rituals symbolize a transition from one status to another. Certainly weddings do that, as two single people now become a unit. Many parts of the ritual script hold great meaning, even if most of us today don't remember the original symbolism:[43]

- **Giving away the bride:** Years ago it was common for fathers to use daughters as currency to pay off a debt or to appease a member of a more powerful tribe. The bride wore a veil so that the payee would not refuse her as payment in case she turned out to be less attractive than he desired.
- **The best man:** His original job was to stand next to the couple to be sure the bride wasn't kidnapped during the ceremony. He was chosen because he was "best" with his sword. Similarly, bridesmaids were instructed to dress similarly to the bride to confuse potential kidnappers and evil spirits; somehow this custom evolved to the design of hideous gowns that make the bride look better by comparison!
- **The tossing of the garter:** At one time the bride and groom were expected to conclude the marriage ceremony and retire immediately to a nearby room to "close the deal." To make the consummation official, witnesses would crowd around the nuptial bed and hope to grab a lucky piece of the bride's gown as it was ripped from her body. Over time, modesty prevailed and the guests had to settle for a symbolic piece of her undergarments.
- **Throwing rice:** Rice is a symbol of fertility; this action is supposed to encourage the newlyweds to get busy and start producing offspring. More recently many couples have replaced rice with butterflies or other items because of the false rumor that birds who eat the rice will die when it expands in their stomachs.

Many colleges boast unique rituals in which students engage in some scripted group activity, though in recent years some institutions have abolished these because of safety concerns or because they encourage underage drinking. Casualties include spring couch burning at the University of Vermont and Texas A&M's bonfire on the eve of the annual football game against the University of Texas (the bonfire ritual has since been revived off campus).[44] However, UC–Santa Barbara still offers an Undie Run. Naked Harvard

Marketing Opportunity

Tailgating at college and pro ballgames is one of the most visible group rituals around today. According to legend, this practice started in the 19th century when fans had to cook meals in their carriages after they journeyed to the site of a football game. Today tailgating is also big business. A survey Coca-Cola sponsored reported that 41 percent of tailgaters spend more than $500 a season on food and supplies. Now, everyone from food conglomerates to camping suppliers tries to get a piece of these boisterous pregame rituals:[44] The NFL sells $100 million a year of tailgating merchandise, including keg-shaped grills. The Buffalo Bills provide showers and changing rooms in the parking lot, and the Denver Broncos pick a "most valuable tailgater" at each home game. The Houston Texans sponsor "Tailgating 101" classes at a local sporting goods store. For the truly hard-core, California customizer Galpin Motors sells a tailgaters' pickup truck complete with a huge grill, taps for two beer kegs, a blender, and a flip-down TV screen for "only" $70,000.

A modern take on a wedding ritual.
Source: Courtesy of Prolam Y&R

students let off steam just before finals in The Primal Scream, and Yale seniors run naked through campus libraries at the end of each semester to toss candy at underclass students as they cram for finals. Denison University celebrates Naked Week and Tufts has a Naked Quad Run. Are you starting to see a pattern here?

A study the BBDO Worldwide advertising agency conducted illustrates the close relationship between brands and rituals.[46] It labels items that we use to perform our rituals **fortress brands** because once they become embedded in our ceremonies—whether we use them to brush our teeth, drink a beer, or shave—we're unlikely to replace them. The study ran in 26 countries, and the researchers found that, overall, people worldwide practice roughly the same consumer rituals. The agency claims that 89 percent of people always use the same brands in their sequenced rituals; three out of four are disappointed or irritated when something disrupts their ritual or their brand of choice isn't available. For example, the report identifies one common ritual category it calls *preparing for battle*. For most of us this means getting ready for work. Relevant rituals include brushing the teeth, taking a shower or bath, having something to eat or drink, talking to a family member or partner, checking email, shaving, putting on makeup, watching TV or listening to the radio, and reading a newspaper.

Rituals occur at several levels. Some reinforce broad cultural or religious values. Public rituals such as the Super Bowl, presidential inaugurations, and graduation ceremonies are communal activities that affirm our membership in the larger group and reassure us that we are reading from the same script as everyone else.[47] In one study, researchers documented the collective ritual of *head banging* at heavy metal music concerts. They showed how participants, who tend to come from lower economic classes and feel disempowered in other settings, participate collectively in a performance that is a cathartic experience where they are rejuvenated and validated (perhaps this presents an opportunity for companies that sell headache remedies?).[48]

Tailgating is a hugely popular group ritual.
Source: Mike Stobe/NHLI/ Getty Images

CB AS I SEE IT
Cele C. Otnes, *University of Illinois at Urbana–Champaign*

In 2015, Virgin Atlantic chose to celebrate its new nonstop route between Manchester, United Kingdom, and Atlanta, Georgia, by offering the first planeload of U.S.-bound customers a special send-off. The plan was to "christen" the plane with spray from a high-pressure water cannon. Unfortunately, the employee in charge pressed the button marked "foam" instead of "water," shooting gallons of goopy muck into the plane's delicate engines. What could have been an enjoyable event cascaded into hours of

delays and ultimately, a canceled flight. With passengers forced to spend the night in hotels and fly the next morning, Virgin Atlantic's hoped-for fanfare transitioned quickly into fiasco.

Practitioners and scholars would describe this (chaotic) episode as an example of a "marketplace ritual," a concept based on the consumption ritual, introduced by marketing scholar Dennis Rook more than 30 years ago.[48] Rook argues that often, seemingly ordinary consumption-laden activities help structure people's lives and contribute to their individual and social identities. Meaningful, repeated activities also can serve as sources of reassurance and relaxation (think stress-reducing bubble baths or Thursday night pizza parties). Rook identifies four key aspects of these rituals: (1) artifacts (symbolic items); (2) scripts (rules that specify how the ritual unfolds); (3) performance roles (who does what), and (4) the ritual audience (non-participants who observe how others engage in the event).

Expanding on Rook, we recently define marketplace rituals as activities in commercial spaces (e.g., stores or service sites) that are often repeated, involve a performance of some kind, and symbolically mark an occurrence significant to a firm or its stakeholders (e.g., customers, stockholders, or employees).[50] Marketers' goals for

offering such rituals can include enhancing the customer's marketplace experience, fostering long-term brand loyalty, spurring word-of-mouth (WOM), or deepening consumers' emotional connections to brands. Some marketplace rituals specifically involve consumer co-creation. For example, a bakery could set up a space where its employees help customers decorate baked goods being purchased, to enhance the personal and creative dimensions of the purchase experience.

Our study also found that when marketers design rituals for their customers, they rely on all four of Rook's ritual dimensions. But they also stressed the need to include two other elements: (1) the aesthetics of the ritual, or the way it is designed to appeal to have sensory appeal and (2) the language providers employ when engaging in the ritual. Consider how the Ritz-Carlton hotel chain trains its staff to greet customers with their correctly pronounced name. Furthermore, employees at every level, from housekeepers to managers, adhere to this ritual form of greeting. In fact, we found a wide range of marketplace rituals in use, from simple greetings/partings to incredibly elaborate experiences. Just ask the Hollywood stars attending the Oscars who receive gift bags with contents worth thousands of dollars!

Grooming Rituals

Whether you brush your hair 100 strokes a day or give yourself a pep talk in the mirror before a big date, virtually all of us practice private **grooming rituals**. These ceremonies help us to transition from our private self to our public self. Grooming rituals help to inspire confidence before we face the world, and they "cleanse" us of impurities. When consumers talk about their grooming rituals, some of the dominant themes that emerge from these stories reflect the almost mystical qualities we attribute to grooming products and behaviors. Many people emphasize a before-and-after phenomenon, whereby the person feels magically transformed after she uses certain products (similar to the Cinderella myth).[51]

Some companies that make personal care products understand the power of these rituals and supply the artifacts we need to make them happen. Nair, the depilatory maker, expanded its customer base when it targeted younger girls with its Nair Pretty product—a market the industry calls "first-time hair removers." Researchers conducted focus groups with mothers and their daughters, where they learned that "[w]hen a girl removes hair for the first time, it's a life-changing moment." Some of the respondents actually held hair removal slumber parties, where the moms bought products for the teens to remove their hair. So, instead of a focus on boys or romance, ads for Nair Pretty suggest that the depilatory is a stubble-free path to empowerment. "I am a citizen of the world," reads the ad copy. "I am a dreamer. I am fresh. I am so not going to have stubs sticking out of my legs."[52]

Grooming rituals express two kinds of binary opposition: *private/public* and *work/leisure*. Many beauty rituals reflect a transformation from a natural state to the social world (as when a woman "puts on her face") or vice versa. To her, a bath may be a cleansing time, a way to wash away the "sins" of the profane world.[53] In these daily rituals, women reaffirm the value their culture places on personal beauty and the quest for eternal youth. This cleansing ritual is clear in ads for Oil of Olay Beauty Cleanser that proclaim, "And so your day begins. The Ritual of Oil of Olay."

Gift-Giving Rituals

In a **gift-giving ritual**, we procure the perfect object, meticulously remove the price tag, carefully wrap the object (where we symbolically change the item from a commodity to a unique good), and deliver it to the recipient.[54] Gifts can be store-bought objects, homemade items, or services. Some recent research even argues that music file-sharing systems such as Megaupload (which the government shut down), KaZaa, or Morpheus are really all about gifting. This work finds, for example, clear evidence of the gift-giving norm of *reciprocity*; people who download files but who don't leave their own files available to others are "leeches."[55]

Researchers view gift-giving as a form of *economic exchange* in which the giver transfers an item of value to a recipient, who in turn must reciprocate. However, gift-giving also involves *symbolic exchange*. In fact, researchers who analyzed the personal memoirs of World War II concentration camp inmates found that even in such a brutal environment, where people had to focus primarily on survival, a need to express humanity through generosity prevailed. The authors found that gift-giving, which symbolized recognition of others' plight as well as one's own, was an act of defiance against the dehumanizing existence the camps forced on their prisoners.[56]

Some research indicates that gift-giving evolves as a form of social expression. It is more exchange oriented (instrumental) in the early stages of a relationship (where we keep track of exactly what we give and receive to be sure we're not getting ripped off), but it becomes more altruistic as the relationship develops.[57]

Every culture dictates certain occasions and ceremonies to give gifts, whether for personal or professional reasons. The birthday gift ritual alone is a significant contributor to our economy. Each American on average buys six birthday gifts a year—about 1 billion gifts in total.[58] Business gifts are an important way to define and maintain professional relationships. Expenditures on business gifts exceed $1.5 billion per year, and givers take great care to ensure that they purchase the appropriate gifts (sometimes with the aid of professional

You don't want it. He can't have it back.

gift consultants). Most executives believe that corporate gift-giving provides both tangible and intangible results, including improved employee morale and higher sales.[59]

The gift-giving ritual proceeds in three distinct stages:[60]

1 During **gestation** the giver procures an item to mark some event. This event may be either *structural* (i.e., prescribed by the culture, as when people buy Christmas presents) or *emergent* (i.e., the decision is more personal and idiosyncratic).
2 The second stage is **presentation** or the process of gift exchange. The recipient responds to the gift (either appropriately or not), and the donor evaluates this response.
3 In the **reformulation** stage, the giver and receiver redefine the bond between them (either looser or tighter) to reflect their new relationship after the exchange. Negativity can arise if the recipient feels the gift is inappropriate or of inferior quality. For example, the hapless husband who gives his wife a vacuum cleaner as an anniversary present is just asking to sleep on the couch, and the new suitor who gives his girlfriend intimate apparel probably won't score many points. The donor may feel that the response to the gift was inadequate or insincere or a violation of the **reciprocity norm**, which obliges people to return the gesture of a gift with one of equal value.[61]

Japanese gift-giving rituals show how tremendously important these acts are in that culture, where the wrapping is as important (if not more so) than the gift itself. The Japanese view gifts as an important aspect of one's duty to others in one's social group. Giving is a moral imperative (*giri*). Highly ritualized acts occur when a person gives both household/personal gifts and company/professional gifts. Each individual has a well-defined set of relatives and friends with which he shares reciprocal gift-giving obligations (*kosai*). People give personal gifts on social occasions, such as at funerals, for a hospitalization, to mark movements from one life stage to another (e.g., weddings, birthdays), and as greetings (e.g., when one meets a visitor). They give company gifts to commemorate the anniversary of a corporation's founding, the opening of a new building, or the announcement of new products. In keeping with the Japanese emphasis on saving face, the recipient doesn't open the present in front of the giver so that he won't have to hide any disappointment with what he gets.[62]

Holiday Rituals

On holidays, we step back from our everyday lives and perform ritualistic behaviors unique to those occasions.[63] Each cultural celebration typically relates to the adventures of one or more special characters, such as St. Patrick in Ireland or Yue Lao in China. These special events require tons of ritual artifacts and scripts. The Thanksgiving holiday script includes serving (in gluttonous portions) foods such as turkey and cranberry sauce that many of us consume only on that day, complaining about how much we've eaten (yet rising to the occasion to find room for dessert), and (for many) a postmeal trip to the couch for the obligatory football game.

Net Profit

The Chinese e-commerce giant Alibaba single-handedly turned a minor holiday into a blockbuster sales event. Traditionally, unmarried Chinese men gathered together each year on November 11 to lament their single status on what was called Bachelors' Day. They chose this date because the calendar shows it as 11.11 (four singles). The company decided to turn this day into an excuse for shopping and in 2009 it began to promote Singles' Day. By 2014, this "anti-Valentine's Day" surpassed Black Friday as the most lucrative online shopping day. The company racked up $9 billion in sales in a 24-hour period. That's a lot of lonely bachelors.[64]

Most holidays commemorate a cultural myth, often with a historical (e.g., Miles Standish on Thanksgiving) or imaginary (e.g., Cupid on Valentine's Day) character as the story's hero. These holidays persist because their basic elements appeal to our deep-seated needs.[65]

- **Christmas**—Myths and rituals fill the Christmas holiday, from Santa's adventures at the North Pole to others' adventures under the mistletoe. The meaning of Christmas evolved quite dramatically during the past few hundred years. In colonial times, Christmas celebrations resembled carnivals and public rowdiness was the norm. Most notable was the tradition of "wassailing," in which roving packs of rowdy young men laid siege to the rich and demanded food and drink. By the end of the 1800s, the mobs were so unruly that city fathers in Protestant America invented a tradition whereby families conducted Christmas gatherings around a tree, a practice they "borrowed" from early pagan rites. In an 1822 poem Clement Clarke Moore, the wealthy son of a New York Episcopal bishop, invented the modern-day myth of Santa Claus. The Christmas ritual slowly changed to a focus on children and gift-giving.[66] One of the most important holiday rituals, of course, stars Santa, a mythical figure for whose arrival children eagerly await (even if their house doesn't have a fireplace). Indeed, an Australian study that analyzed the letters children write to Santa found they specify their brand preferences quite carefully and often employ sophisticated request strategies to be sure they get what they want from the Big Guy.[67] In opposition to Christ, Santa is a champion of materialism. Perhaps it is no coincidence, then, that he appears in stores and shopping malls—secular temples of consumption. Whatever his origins, the Santa Claus myth socializes children because it teaches them to expect a reward when they are good and that people get what they deserve (which may be a lump of coal).

- **Halloween**—Halloween began as a pagan religious ceremony, but it's clearly a secular event today. However, in contrast to Christmas, the rituals of Halloween (e.g., trick-or-treating and costume parties) primarily involve nonfamily members. Halloween is an unusual holiday because its rituals are the opposite of many other cultural occasions. In contrast to Christmas, it celebrates evil instead of good and death rather than birth. It encourages revelers to extort treats with veiled threats of "tricks" rather than rewards for the good. Because of these oppositions, Halloween is an **antifestival**—an event that distorts the symbols we associate with other holidays. For example, the Halloween witch is an inverted mother figure. The holiday also parodies the meaning of Easter because it stresses the resurrection of ghosts, and it mocks Thanksgiving because it transforms the wholesome symbolism of the pumpkin pie into the evil jack-o-lantern.[68] Furthermore, Halloween provides a ritualized, and therefore socially sanctioned, context that allows people to try on new roles: Children can go outside after dark, stay up late, and eat all the candy they like for a night. The otherwise geeky guy who always sits in the back of class dresses as Jason from *Friday the 13th* and turns out to be the life of the party. Halloween of course is big business as well: Americans spend $350 million in costumes, and that's just what they're shelling out for their pets' getups.[69]

- **Valentine's Day**—On Valentine's Day, we relax our standards about sex and love and we express feelings we may hide during the rest of the year (in Japan, it's the women who send gifts to the men). A study that investigated Valentine's Day rituals explored how marketing communications help to shape the holiday. The authors identify five familiar classes of rituals:

  1 Exchanging gifts and cards
  2 Showing affection
  3 Going out
  4 Preparing and consuming food and drink
  5 Special attention to grooming and clothing

Costumes are big business during Halloween, and many of those are for our pets.
Source: Courtesy of Beneva Flowers

Many of their informants (primarily men) understood the holiday as an obligatory occasion for them to buy their partners expensive, "romantic" gifts. One guy posted this warning: "If you want her happy always remember: the gift has to shine or smell [good] or she should be able to wear it! Otherwise, you're doomed." Some informants expressed negative associations with the holiday, including painful emotions because of broken relationships (or a lack of relationships altogether) and aversion to the "forced" consumption and artificial displays of affection the day requires.[70] But, as much as some of us may grumble about it, this holiday ritual is too powerful to ignore (unless you like sleeping on the couch).

Rites of Passage

What does a dance for recently divorced people have in common with a fraternity Hell Week? Both are modern **rites of passage**, rituals we perform to mark a change in social status. Every society, both primitive and modern, sets aside times for these changes. Some may occur as a natural part of our life cycles (e.g., puberty or death), whereas others are more individual (e.g., getting divorced and reentering the dating market).

Much like the metamorphosis of a caterpillar into a butterfly, a rite of passage consists of three phases. Let's see how this works for a young person who changes his social status to become a college student:[71]

1 In the first stage, *separation*, he detaches from his original group or status as a high school kid and leaves home for campus.

2 *Liminality* is the middle stage, where he is in limbo between statuses. Think of those bewildered new first-year students who try to find their way around campus during orientation.

3 In the *aggregation* stage, he returns to society with his new status. Our hero returns home for Thanksgiving break as a cocky college "veteran."

Many types of people undergo rites of passage, including fraternity pledges, recruits at boot camp, or novitiates at a convent. We observe a similar transitional state when people prepare for occupational roles. For example, athletes and fashion models typically undergo a "seasoning" process. They leave their normal surroundings (athletes go to training camps, young models move to Paris or New York), they get indoctrinated into a new subculture, and then they return to the real world in their new roles (if they successfully pass the trials of their initiation and don't "get cut").

Death also involves rites of passage. Funeral ceremonies help the living organize their relationships with the deceased. Action is tightly scripted, down to the costumes (e.g., the ritual black attire, black ribbons for mourners, the body laid out in its best clothes) and specific behaviors (e.g., sending condolence cards or holding a wake). Passing motorists award special status to the *cortege* (the funeral motorcade) when they obey the strong social norm that prohibits cutting in as the line of cars proceeds to the cemetery.[72]

Funeral practices vary across cultures, but they're always rich in symbolism. For example, a study of funeral rituals in Ghana found that the community there determines a person's social value *after* he dies; this status depends on the type of funeral his family gives him. One of the main purposes of death rituals is to negotiate the social identities of deceased persons. This occurs as mourners treat the corpse with a level of respect that indicates what they think of him. The Asante people who were the subjects of the study don't view death as something to fear; it's just part of a broader, ongoing process of identity negotiation.[73] People in parts of Madagascar go a step further: They regularly remove the bodies of their ancestors from their tombs so that family members can caress the skeletal outlines that protrude through their burial shrouds. This ritual is called a *famadihana*, and many believe this is a time to convey the latest family news to the deceased and ask them for blessings and guidance.[74]

Net Profit

As we've seen, the marriage ritual represents a rite of passage. Social scientists have long studied how people prepare themselves for these transitions or what we referred to as liminality. Now a group of researchers has looked at the way people represent these changes in their online behavior. They identified more than 900 Twitter accounts that belonged to people who posted publicly that they had become engaged and then analyzed their posts both before and after these announcements. The study found that not too surprisingly the people they studied were less likely to use the terms *boyfriend* or *girlfriend* after the engagement and more likely to talk instead about a fiancé or fiancée. They included the word *we* in their posts to a greater extent, and they shared more comments about things they did as a couple such as cooking and traveling together. And, some of the engaged people they studied used social media to vent about the stress of preparing for the wedding. One posted this complaint: "Two of my bridesmaids are coworkers. They have not ONCE asked me if they could help with anything. They don't ask how anything is going."[75]

Funeral ceremonies are a rite of passage that include scripted symbolism including a *cortege*.

Source: mario beauregardFotolia

Sacred and Profane Consumption

Nike recently had to pull a new line of Pro Tattoo Tech Gear clothing line for women after the news came out that the graphics it used came from a sacred Samoan tattoo that only men wear. Consumers started a Change.org petition online and bombarded the brand's Facebook page with negative comments.[76]

As we saw when we discussed the structure of myths, many types of consumer activities involve the demarcation, or binary opposition, of categories, such as good versus bad, male versus female—or even regular cola versus diet. One of the most important distinctions we find is between the sacred and the profane. **Sacred consumption** occurs when we "set apart" objects and events from normal activities and treat them with respect or awe. Note that in this context the term *sacred* does not necessarily carry a religious meaning, although we do tend to think of religious artifacts and ceremonies as "sacred." **Profane consumption** in contrast, describes objects and events that are ordinary or everyday; they don't share the "specialness" of sacred ones. Again, note that in this context we don't equate the word *profane* with obscenity, although the two meanings do share some similarities.

Often we're unaware of the distinction between these two domains—until they conflict with one another. Then, the sparks fly—sort of like the collision between matter and antimatter on *Star Trek*. A conflict in Thailand illustrates this process. It seems that several Bangkok nightclubs, inspired by the film *Coyote Ugly* about women who dance seductively on a New York bar, began to feature their own "Coyote Girls" dancers. The trend caught on and soon the dancers showed up at auto shows, in shopping malls, and at outdoor festivals. That's when the trouble started: Thailand's queen learned of one performance the girls put on near a Buddhist temple on a holy day that marks the end of a 3-month period where Buddhists refrain from impure thoughts and deeds (sort of like the Christian season of Lent). When the queen saw TV news reports about a motorcycle shop that hired Coyote Girls to promote its wares, she was outraged by the intrusion of profane activity into a sacred domain. Coyote Girls are now banned from dancing in public places.[77]

Sacralization

Sacralization occurs when ordinary objects, events, and even people take on sacred meaning. Many consumers regard events such as the Super Bowl and people such as Elvis Presley as sacred. Indeed, virtually anything can become sacred. Skeptical? Consider the Web site that sells *unlaundered* athletic wear that members of the Dallas Cowboys football team have worn. Former quarterback Troy Aikman's shoes sold for $1,999, and an unwashed practice jersey that retains the sweat of an unknown player goes for $99. Used socks fly out the door at $19.99 a pair. Says the owner, "Fans who have never been able to touch the Cowboys before now have an opportunity."[78]

Objectification occurs when we attribute sacred qualities to mundane items (such as smelly socks). One way that this process occurs is via **contamination** whereby objects we associate with sacred events or people become sacred in their own right. This explains many fans' desire for items that belonged to (or were even touched by) famous people. Even the Smithsonian Institution in Washington, DC, maintains a display that features such "sacred items" as the ruby slippers from *The Wizard of Oz*, a phaser from *Star Trek*, and Archie Bunker's chair from the television show *All in the Family*—all reverently protected behind sturdy display glass.[79]

In addition to museum exhibits that display rare objects, we often set apart mundane, inexpensive things in collections; when we do so we transform them from profane items to sacred ones. An item is sacralized as soon as it enters a collection, and it takes on special significance to the collector that outsiders may find hard to comprehend. For example, you may know someone who collects matchbooks that mark visits to out-of-town restaurants: Just try to use one of these books if you actually need to light a match.

Collecting refers to the systematic acquisition of a particular object or set of objects. We distinguish this from **hoarding**, which reflects a reluctance to discard used objects.[80] Hoarding is a problem in some cities where residents' refusal to properly dispose of old newspapers, food, or even deceased pets results in fires, eviction, and even the removal of children from the home. A dozen cities run hoarding task forces to combat this problem.[81]

Collecting typically involves both rational and emotional components. On the one hand, avid collectors carefully organize and exhibit their treasures.[82] On the other hand, they are ferociously attached to their collections. A teddy bear collector summed up this fixation: "If my house ever burns down, I won't cry over my furniture, I'll cry over the bears."[83]

Some consumer researchers feel that collectors acquire their "prizes" to gratify their materialism in a socially acceptable manner. When he systematically amasses a collection, the collector "worships" material objects but he doesn't have to feel guilty or petty. Another perspective argues that collecting is actually an aesthetic experience; for many collectors, the pleasure comes from creating the collection. Whatever the motivation, hard-core collectors often devote a great deal of time and energy to maintaining and expanding their collections, so for many this activity becomes a central component of their extended selves (see Chapter 6).[84]

OBJECTIVE 14-5
We describe products as either sacred or profane, and it's not unusual for some products to move back and forth between the two categories.

Domains of Sacred Consumption

Sacred consumption events permeate many aspects of our lives. We find ways to "set apart" all sorts of places, people, and events. In this section, we'll look at ways that "ordinary" consumption is sometimes *not* so ordinary after all.

Sacred Places

A society "sets apart" sacred places because they have religious or mystical significance (e.g., Bethlehem, Mecca, Stonehenge) or because they commemorate some aspect of a country's heritage (e.g., the Kremlin, the Emperor's Palace in Tokyo, the Statue of Liberty, or Ground Zero in Manhattan). *Contamination* makes these places sacred: Something sacred happened on that spot, so the place itself takes on sacred qualities. Hard-core fans buy Yankees Sod, the first officially licensed grass. Although it costs a few thousand dollars to fill out a good-sized lawn, proud fans can boast of turf that grows from the same seeds the groundskeepers use at the stadium, and the sod comes with a certificate of authenticity from Major League Baseball and a counterfeit-proof hologram that declares it the official grass of the New York Yankees.[85]

Still other places start out as profane, but we endow them with sacred qualities. Grauman's Chinese Theater in Hollywood, where movie stars leave their footprints in concrete for posterity, is one such place. Theme parks are a form of mass-produced fantasy that take on aspects of sacredness. In particular, Disney World and Disneyland (and their outposts in Europe, Japan, and China) are destinations for "pilgrimages" by consumers around the globe. Disney World displays many characteristics of more traditional sacred places. Some even believe it has healing powers, which helps to explain why a trip to the park is the most common "last wish" for terminally ill children.[86]

As the saying goes, "Home is where the heart is."[87] In many cultures, the home is a particularly sacred place. It's a barrier between the harsh, external world and consumers' "inner space." Americans spend more than $50 billion a year on interior decorators and home furnishings, and our home is a central part of our identity. People all over the world go to great lengths to create a feeling of "homeyness." They personalize their dwellings with door wreaths, mantel arrangements, and a "memory wall" for family photos.[88] Even public places such as Starbucks cafés strive for a homelike atmosphere to shelter customers from the harshness of the outside world.

Sacred People

Two friends in San Francisco maintain Tumblr and Instagram sites, *#WWYW or What Would Yeezus Wear*, devoted to their idols, the glam couple Kim Kardashian and Kanye

West. They post paparazzi photos of the celebs' outfits, then add photos of themselves wearing the same things. Hundreds of fan clubs like Always Elvis memorialize the King. Katy Perry has more than 40 million "Katy Cat" followers on Twitter.[89]

We idolize sacred people as we set them apart from the masses, and sometimes people come to believe that these individuals have "superhuman" abilities. Souvenirs, memorabilia, and even mundane items these celebrities have touched acquire special meanings (the celebrities "contaminate" the items). Newspapers pay *paparazzi* hundreds of thousands of dollars for candid shots of stars or royalty. Indeed, many businesses thrive on our desire for products we associate with the famous. There is a flourishing market for celebrity autographs, and objects that celebrities owned, such as Princess Diana's gowns or John Lennon's guitars, sell on eBay for astronomical prices.

Sacred Events

Sometimes public events resemble sacred, religious ceremonies. Think about fans who hold their hands over their hearts and solemnly recite the "Pledge of Allegiance" before a ball game, or how others reverently light matches (or hold up illuminated cell phones) during a rock concert.[90]

The world of sports is sacred to many of us (recent doping and gambling scandals aside). We find the roots of modern sports events in ancient religious rites, such as fertility festivals (e.g., the original Olympics).[91] And it's not uncommon for teams to join in prayer prior to a game. The sports pages are like the scriptures (and we all know ardent fans who read them "religiously"), the stadium is a house of worship, and the fans are members of the congregation. Devotees engage in group activities, such as tailgate parties and the "Wave," where sections of the stadium take turns standing up. The athletes and coaches that fans come to see are godlike; devotees believe they have almost superhuman powers. One study documented more than 600 children whose parents named them after the legendary University of Alabama coach Paul "Bear" Bryant![92]

Athletes are central figures in a common cultural myth known as the *hero tale*. In these stories, the player must prove himself under strenuous circumstances, and he achieves victory only through sheer force of will. On a more mundane level, devotees consume certain ritual artifacts during these ceremonies (such as hot dogs at the ballpark). Sales of snack foods and beverages spike around the time of the Super Bowl; people spend $10 million more on tortilla chips than during a normal 2-week period and more than $15 million extra on beer in the weeks surrounding the big game.[93]

Tourism is another category of sacred experience. People occupy sacred time and space when they travel on vacation (though you may not think so if you get stuck sleeping on an airport floor because of a plane delay). The tourist searches for "authentic" experiences that differ from his normal world (think of Club Med's motto, "The antidote to civilization").[94] This traveling experience involves binary oppositions between work and leisure and being "at home" versus "away." Often, we relax everyday (profane) norms regarding appropriate behavior as tourists, and participate in illicit or adventurous experiences we would never engage in at home ("What happens in Vegas, stays in Vegas").

The desire of travelers to capture these sacred experiences in objects forms the bedrock of the souvenir industry, which really sells sacred memories. Whether it's a personalized matchbook from a wedding or New York City salt-and-pepper shakers, a souvenir represents a tangible piece of the consumer's sacred experience.[95] In addition to personal mementos, such as ticket stubs you save from a favorite concert, these are some other sacred souvenir icons:[96]

- Local products (e.g., wine from California)
- Pictorial images (e.g., postcards)
- "Piece of the rock" (e.g., seashells, pine cones)
- Symbolic shorthand in the form of literal representations of the site (e.g., a miniature Statue of Liberty)
- Markers (e.g., Hard Rock Cafe T-shirts)

A souvenir commemorates a consumer's
sacred experience.
Source: glowonconcept/Fotolia

From Sacred to Profane, and Back Again

Just to make life interesting, some consumer activities move back and forth between the sacred and profane spheres over time.[97] A study of tea preparation in Turkey illustrates this movement. Although we are more likely to think of thick Turkish coffee, in reality Turks consume more tea *per capita* than any other country. In Turkish culture people drink tea continuously, like (or instead of) water. Tea is an integral part of daily life; many households and offices boil water for tea in the traditional *çaydanlik* (double teapot) first thing in the morning, and keep it steaming all day so that the beverage is ready at any time. The tea drinking process links to many symbolic meanings—including the traditional glasses, clear to appreciate the tea's color, and hourglass-shaped like a woman's body—and rituals, such as blending one's own tea, knowing how finely to grind the tea leaves, and how long to steep the tea for optimal flavor. When Lipton introduced the modern tea bag in 1984, Turkey was intent on modernization and soon consumers snapped up electric *çaydanliks* and mugs instead of small, shapely tea glasses. Tea became a symbol of the quick and convenient, and the drinking act became more of a fashion statement. Now, many Turkish consumers opt to return to the sacred, traditional rituals as a way to preserve authenticity in the face of rapid societal changes.[98]

The transition of Turkish tea to a mass-market product illustrates the process of **desacralization**. This occurs when we remove a sacred item or symbol from its special place or duplicate it in mass quantities so that it loses its "specialness" and becomes profane. Souvenir reproductions of sacred monuments such as the Washington Monument or the Eiffel Tower, artworks such as the *Mona Lisa* or Michelangelo's *David*, or reproductions of sacred symbols such as the U.S. flag on T-shirts eliminate their special aspects. They become inauthentic commodities with relatively little value.

Religion itself has to some extent become desacralized. Religious symbols like stylized crosses or New Age crystals often pop up on fashion jewelry.[99] Critics often charge that Christmas has turned into a secular, materialistic occasion devoid of its original sacred significance. A similar process occurs in relatively Westernized parts of the Islamic Middle East, where the holy month of Ramadan (that people traditionally observe by fasting and praying) is starting to look like Christmas: People buy lights in the shape of an Islamic crescent moon, send Ramadan cards to one another, and attend lavish fast-breaking feasts at hotels.[100]

The Diffusion of Innovations

OBJECTIVE 14-6
New products, services, and ideas spread through a population over time. Different types of people are more or less likely to adopt them during this diffusion process.

The originators of skateboarding in 1970s southern California (who were portrayed in the popular documentary *Dogtown and Z-Boys*) wouldn't recognize the sport today. At that time, boarders were outlaws; as one of the main characters in the film says, "We get the beat-down from all over. Everywhere we go, man, people hate us."

Now skateboarding is about as countercultural as *The Simpsons*. More kids ride skateboards than play basketball, and many of them snap up pricey T-shirts, skate shoes, helmets, and other accessories. In fact, boarders spend almost six times as much on "soft goods," such as T-shirts, shorts, and sunglasses (about $4.4 billion in a year), than on hard-core equipment, including the boards themselves. To real afficionados, skateboarding has simply become a way for big companies like Nike to sell its SB Dunks and Janoski shoes.[101]

The progression of skateboarding from a cult-like activity with rebellious undertones to a mainstream sport mirrors the journey many products and services take through popular culture. **Diffusion of innovations** refers to the process whereby a new product, service, or idea spreads through a population. An **innovation** is any product or service that consumers perceive to be new. It may take the form of an activity (skateboarding), a clothing style (Thom Browne T-shirts), a new manufacturing technique (the ability to design your own running shoe at nike.com), a new variation on an existing product (Parkay Fun Squeeze Colored Margarine in electric blue and shocking pink), a new way to deliver a product (Uber), or a new way to package a current product (Campbell's Soup at Hand Microwaveable Soup that comes in a travel mug).[102]

The social media explosion takes the diffusion process to a whole different level. As we've seen, the media democratization we witness today means that there are fundamental disruptions in the way consumers become aware of new products and the rate at which these innovations reach their markets. In this section, we'll step back and examine the basic process of diffusion.

If an innovation is successful (most are not!), it spreads through the population. First only a trickle of people decides to try it. Then, more and more consumers decide to adopt it, until sometimes it seems that almost everyone is buying it—if it's a "hit." The rate at which a product diffuses varies. For example, within 10 years after introduction, 40 percent of U.S. households watched cable TV, 35 percent listened to compact discs, 25 percent used answering machines, and 20 percent bought color TVs. It took radio 30 years to reach 60 million users and TV 15 years to reach this number. In contrast, within 3 years 90 million of us surfed the Web.[103]

How Do We Decide to Adopt an Innovation?

Our adoption of an innovation resembles the decision-making sequence we discussed in Chapter 9. We move through the stages of awareness, information search, evaluation, trial, and adoption. The relative importance of each stage differs, however, depending on how much we already know about an innovation as well as on cultural factors that affect our willingness to try new things.[104]

As Figure 14.3 shows, roughly one-sixth of the population (innovators and early adopters) are quick to adopt new products, and one-sixth (**laggards**) are slow. The other two-thirds, so-called **late adopters** are somewhere in the middle. These consumers are the mainstream public. They are interested in new things, but they do not want them to be *too* new. In some cases, people deliberately wait to adopt an innovation because they assume that the company will improve its technology or that its price will fall after it has been on the market awhile (have you been holding off on that iPhone purchase to see what Apple will come up with next?).[105] Keep in mind that the proportion of consumers who fall into each category is an estimate; the actual size of each depends on such factors as the complexity of the product, its cost, and how much risk people associate with it.

Even though **innovators** represent only about 2.5 percent of the population, marketers are eager to identify them. These are the brave souls who are always on the lookout for novel products or services and who are first to try something new. An innovator tends to be a risk-taker. He or she also is likely to have a relatively high educational and income level and to be socially active. In some cases an innovator is an admired celebrity to whom others look for leadership. Luxury brands understand this, and they often work hard to "seed adoptions" by providing their exclusive items to high-profile people. This is the strategy Apple followed when the company launched its Apple Watch. Rather than making the new item widely available as it does with iPhones, Apple at first restricted access to celebrities including Pharrell Williams, Katy Perry, Drake, and Beyoncé. As Apple hoped, the celebs in turn posted Instagram photos of themselves sporting their new toys that stoked the fires of desire for the rest of us.[106]

Early adopters share many of the same characteristics as innovators. An important difference is their high degree of concern for social acceptance, especially with regard to expressive products such as clothing and cosmetics. Generally speaking, an early adopter is receptive to new styles because he or she is involved in the product category and he or she values being in fashion.

What appears on the surface to be a fairly high-risk adoption (e.g., wearing a skirt three inches above the knee when most people wear them below the knee) is actually not *that* risky. Innovators who truly took the fashion risk have already "field-tested" the style change. We're likely to find early adopters in "fashion-forward" stores that feature the latest "hot" designer brands. In contrast, we're more likely to find true innovators in small boutiques that carry merchandise from as-yet-unknown designers.

Figure 14.3 TYPES OF ADOPTERS

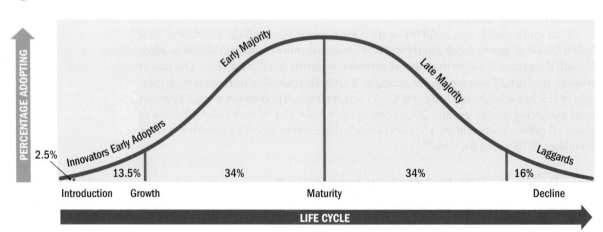

Behavioral Demands of Innovations

We categorize innovations by the degree to which they demand adopters to change their behavior. One widely used approach to predicting whether people will adopt a new form of technology or information system is the **Technology Acceptance Model (TAM)**. The TAM suggests that the likelihood of change is based on two factors: The perceived usefulness of the new option and its perceived ease of use. This model is based the theory of reasoned action we discussed in Chapter 8; it stresses that because there may be other constraints at work such as access to resources or the expectations of our peers, we can't necessarily predict if an innovation will be successful just because consumers have a positive or negative attitude toward it. We also have to consider whether they believe it will provide *utility* for them (e.g., if they believe that by using the new item this will enhance their performance in some way). The TAM model has been used to understand, for example, whether consumers will use e-commerce platforms depending on how useful they perceive them to be relative to traditional purchase strategies.[107]

Researchers identify three major types of innovations, though these three categories are not absolutes. They refer, in a relative sense, to the amount of disruption or change they bring to people's lives.

1. A **continuous innovation** is a modification of an existing product, such as when General Mills introduces a Honey Nut version of Cheerios or Levi's promotes shrink-to-fit jeans. The company makes small changes to position the product, add line extensions, or merely alleviate consumer boredom. Most product innovations are of this type; they are *evolutionary* rather than *revolutionary*. When a consumer adopts this kind of new product, she only has to make minor changes in her habits. A type-writer company, for example, many years ago modified its product to make it more "user friendly" to secretaries. Its engineers made the tops of the keys concave because women told them it was hard to type with long fingernails on a flat surface. This change endures today on our computer keyboards.

2. Some innovations present us with a new way to use an existing product. This may be more effective, but we still have to alter our habits to use it. A Japanese clothing company introduced a line of Shower Clean business suits that allow traveling executives to bypass the dry cleaner; they wash their suits in a warm shower and need not press or iron them.[108] A **dynamically continuous innovation** is a significant change to an existing product. When IBM introduced its Selectric typewriter that used a typing ball rather than individual keys, the new design permitted secretaries to instantly change the typeface of manuscripts as they replaced one Selectric ball with another.

3. A **discontinuous innovation** creates really *big* changes in the way we live. Major inventions, such as the airplane, the car, the computer, and the television, radically changed modern lifestyles. The personal computer replaced the typewriter; it also allows some of us to "telecommute" from our homes. Of course, the cycle continues, as new continuous innovations such as mobile apps and cloud software transform how we access data and connect to others online.

What Determines If an Innovation Will Diffuse?

Regardless of how much we have to change what we do, a successful innovation should possess these attributes:[109]

- **Compatibility**—The innovation should be compatible with consumers' lifestyles. A manufacturer of personal care products tried unsuccessfully several years ago to introduce a cream hair remover for men as a substitute for razors and shaving cream. This formulation was similar to what many women use to remove hair from their legs.

Net Profit

M-Pesa (M for mobile, *pesa* is Swahili for money) is a mobile-phone-based money transfer service that is popular in parts of Africa, where most consumers do not have access to bank branches. As many other people around the world start to transact more of their banking business online, M-PESA provides valuable lessons on how to design an app that transforms how we relate to our financial institutions. This service is an example of **reverse innovation** (or trickle-up innovation). This term refers to the process whereby a product is initially to meet the needs of developing nations and then is adapted elsewhere. Battery-operated medical instruments first designed for use in countries with limited infrastructure are another example.

Although the product was simple and convenient to use, it failed because men were not interested in a product they perceived to be too feminine and thus a threat to their masculine self-concepts.

- **Trialability**—Because we think an unknown product is risky, we're more likely to adopt an innovation if we can experiment with it before making a commitment. To reduce this risk, companies may spend a lot of money to distribute free "trial-size" samples of new products.

- **Complexity**—The product should be low in complexity. All things being equal, we will choose a product that's easier to understand and use rather than a more complex one. This strategy requires less effort from us and it also lowers our perceived risk. Manufacturers of DVD recorders, for example, put a lot of effort into simplifying usage (e.g., on-screen programming) to encourage nontechies to adopt them.

- **Observability**—Innovations that are readily apparent are more likely to spread because we can learn about them more easily. The rapid proliferation of fanny packs (pouches people wear around the waist in lieu of wallets or purses) was a result of their high visibility. It was easy for others to see the convenience this alternative offered (even if they were a bit nerdy).

- **Relative advantage**—Most importantly, the product should offer relative advantage over other alternatives. The consumer must believe that it will provide a benefit other products cannot offer. For example, the Bugchaser is a wristband that contains insect repellent. Mothers with young children like it because it's nontoxic and nonstaining—these are clear advantages over alternatives. In contrast, the Crazy Blue Air Freshener, which emits a fragrance when you turn on your car wipers, fizzled: People didn't see the need for the product and felt there were simpler ways to freshen their cars.

The Fashion System

OBJECTIVE 14-7

Many people and organizations play a role in the fashion system that creates and communicates symbolic meanings to consumers.

Style is important to many of us, even when the style is to *not* be in style. That was the case in recent years as a fashion movement known as **Normcore** started to take off. This term describes a trend among young urbanites to foresake hipster styles like skinny jeans, wallet chains, and flannel shirts, for bland, suburban attire like Gap cargo shorts, a Coors Light T-shirt, a Nike golf hat, white sneakers, and "dad jeans." More broadly, some analysts stated that normcore reflected an effort by young bohemain types to "get over themselves." They devoted tremendous effort to set themselves apart from others with quirky style flourishes like handlebar moustaches and drinking obscure microbrews, and so they felt a need to throw themselves back into mainstream culture. The normcore buzz grew quickly, to the point where a Google search of the term yields almost 1 million hits. Fashion insiders couldn't take it anymore; one person created the Google Chrome extension No More #NORMCORE, which blocks references to the term.[110] Time to move on to the next trend.

The **fashion system** includes all the people and organizations that create symbolic meanings and transfer those meanings to cultural goods. Although we often equate fashion with clothing, it's important to keep in mind that fashion processes affect *all* types of cultural phenomena, including music, art, architecture, and even science (i.e., certain research topics and individual scientists are "hot" at any point in time). Even business practices are subject to the fashion process; they evolve and change depending on which management techniques are in vogue, such as total quality management (TQM), just-in-time inventory control (JIT), or managing by walking around (MBWA). All of these domains are affected by the "movement of meaning" in a culture that we discussed previously in this chapter.

At the outset, let's distinguish among some confusing terms. **Fashion** is the process of social diffusion by which some group(s) of consumers adopts a new style. In contrast, *a fashion* (or style) is a particular combination of attributes (say, stovepipe jeans that women wear with a tunic top). To be *in fashion* means that some reference group positively

The recent Normcore style reflects the fashion of not being in fashion.
Source: Eugenio Marongiu/Shutterstock

evaluates this combination (i.e., *Vogue* endorses this look as "in" for this season). Thus, the term *Danish Modern* refers to particular characteristics of furniture design (i.e., a fashion in interior design); it does not necessarily imply that Danish Modern is a fashion that consumers currently desire.[111]

Behavioral Science Perspectives on Fashion

Fashion is a complex process that operates on many levels. At one extreme, it's a societal phenomenon that affects many of us simultaneously. At the other, it exerts a personal effect on individual behavior. Many of us desire to be in fashion, and this motivates us as to what we buy. Fashion products also are aesthetic objects that reflect a culture's artistic traditions and history. For this reason, there are many perspectives on the origin and diffusion of fashion. Let's summarize some major approaches.[112]

Psychological Models of Fashion

Many psychological factors help explain what motivates us to be fashionable. These include conformity, desires for variety seeking, the need to express personal creativity, and sexual attraction. For example, many consumers seem to have a "need for uniqueness": They want to be different (though not necessarily *too* different!).[113] As a result, people may conform to the basic outlines of a fashion, but still improvise to make a personal statement within these general guidelines.

One of the earliest theories of fashion argued that "shifting **erogenous zones** (sexually arousing areas of the body) accounted for fashion changes and that different zones become the object of interest because they reflect societal trends. J. C. Flugel, a disciple of Freud, proposed in the 1920s that sexually charged areas wax and wane as we grow bored with them; clothing styles change to highlight or hide the parts that currently are the focus of attention. For example, it was common for Renaissance-era women to drape their abdomens in fabrics to give a swollen appearance; successful childbearing was a priority in the disease-ridden 14th and 15th centuries. Now, some suggest that the current prevalence of the exposed midriff in women's fashion reflects the premium our society places on fitness.[114]

Economic Models of Fashion

Economists approach fashion in terms of the model of supply and demand. Items in limited supply have high value, whereas our desire decreases for readily available products.

This ad for Maidenform illustrates that fashions have accentuated different parts of the female anatomy throughout history.

Source: Courtesy of Hanesbrands Inc.

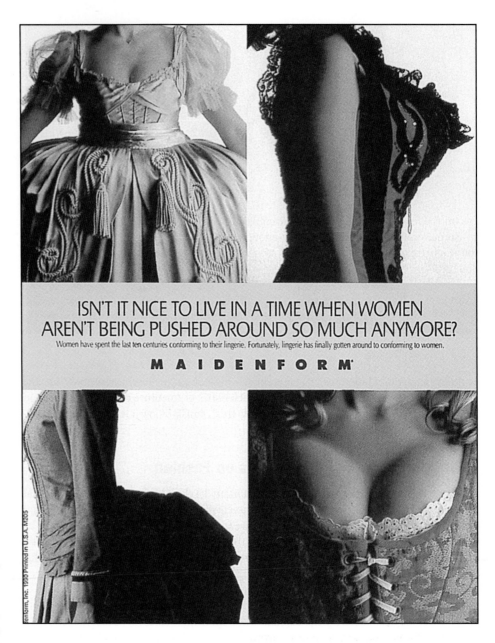

ISN'T IT NICE TO LIVE IN A TIME WHEN WOMEN AREN'T BEING PUSHED AROUND SO MUCH ANYMORE?

Women have spent the last ten centuries conforming to their lingerie. Fortunately, lingerie has finally gotten around to conforming to women.

M A I D E N F O R M®

Marketing Pitfall

The sociological perspective that emphasizes the tension between dominant and subordinate groups highlights a basic **paradox of fashion**. A brand often has cachet *because* only a select group of people own it; either because it is expensive or perhaps because only people "in the know" select it. As more consumers outside of this inner circle start to adopt it, it is no longer exclusive and its original meaning is lost. Therefore, *the item is a victim of its own success.* Popular brands including Levi Strauss and Harley-Davidson continue to struggle with this problem as their core users abandon them precisely because they gain wider market acceptance. Some companies such as the luxury car brand Aston Martin even limit access to some of their models only to current customers.

Rare items command respect and prestige. As we discussed in Chapter 12, the writer Thorstein Veblen argued that the wealthy practice *conspicuous consumption* to display their prosperity. As we also noted, this approach is somewhat outdated; upscale consumers today engage in *parody display* where they deliberately buy inexpensive products (especially during a recession). Other factors also influence the demand curve for fashion-related products. These include a **prestige–exclusivity effect** where high prices still create high demand, and a **snob effect** whereby lower prices actually reduce demand ("If it's that cheap, it can't be any good").[115]

Sociological Models of Fashion

This perspective focuses on a subculture's adoption of a fashion (idea, style, etc.) and its subsequent diffusion into society as a whole. To understand this process, think about the integration of Goth culture into the mainstream. This fashion started as an expression of rebellion by young outcasts who admired 19th-century romantics. Goths defied conventional styles with their black clothing (often including over-the-top fashion statements such as Count Dracula capes, fishnet stockings, studded collars, and black lipstick) and punk music from bands such as Siouxsie & the Banshees and Bauhaus. Today, music stores sell vampire-girl lunchboxes, and mall outlets sell tons of clunky cross jewelry and black lace. You can find a T-shirt that looks like a corset at Kmart. At the Hot Topic Web site, teen surfers can buy a "multi-ring choker." Hard-core Goths are not amused, but hey, that's fashion for you.[116]

Trickle-down theory which the sociologist Georg Simmel first proposed in 1904, is one of the most influential sociological perspectives on fashion. It states that two conflicting forces drive fashion change. First, subordinate groups adopt the status symbols of the groups above them as they attempt to climb up the ladder of social mobility. Dominant styles thus originate with the upper classes and *trickle down* to those below.

Now the second force kicks in: Those people in the superordinate groups keep a wary eye on the ladder below them to be sure followers don't imitate them. When lower-class consumers mimic their actions, they adopt new fashions to distance themselves from the mainstream. These two processes create a self-perpetuating cycle of change—the machine that drives fashion.[117]

The integration of hip-hop phrases into our vocabulary illustrates how people who set fashions resist mainstream adoption by the broader society. The street elite shunned some slang terms, such as *bad, fresh,* and *jiggy,* once they became too mainstream. The rap community even held a funeral (with a eulogy by Reverend Al Sharpton) for the word *def* once the *Oxford English Dictionary* included it in its new edition.[118]

Trickle-down theory applies to a society with a stable class structure that allows us to easily identify lower- versus upper-class consumers. This task is no longer so easy. In contemporary Western society, we have to modify this theory to account for new developments in mass culture:[120]

- A perspective we base on class structure can't account for the wide range of styles now available. We have many more choices today because of technological advances that let manufacturers drastically speed up production times and real-time media that keep us informed of style changes in minutes. Stores such as Zara and H&M can replenish their inventories in weeks rather than months. Suburban tweens watch MTV, chat on Facebook, or browse the virtual world Stardoll.com to stay on top of the latest trends; *mass fashion* thus replaces elite fashion because our media allow many market segments to learn about a style simultaneously.
- Consumers today are more influenced by opinion leaders who are similar to them, even if these innovators don't live in the same town or even country. As a result, each social group has its own fashion innovators who determine fashion trends. It's more accurate to speak of a **trickle-across effect** where fashions diffuse horizontally among members of the same social group.[121]
- Finally, current fashions often originate with the lower classes and we observe a **trickle-up effect**. Grassroots innovators typically are people who lack prestige in the dominant culture (e.g., urban youth). Because they are less concerned with maintaining the status quo, they are free to innovate and take risks.[122]

A Medical Model of Fashion

For many years, the lowly Hush Puppy was a shoe for nerds. Suddenly—almost overnight—the shoe became a chic fashion statement even though its manufacturer did nothing to promote this image. Why did this style diffuse through the population so quickly? **Meme theory** explains this process with a medical metaphor. A *meme* is an idea or product that enters the consciousness of people over time—examples include tunes, styles like the Hush Puppy, or even catch-phrases: The singer Taylor Swift trademarked several phrases from her album *1989,* including "Party like it's 1989," "this sick beat," and "nice to meet you, where you been."[124]

In this view, memes spread among consumers in a geometric progression just as a virus starts off small and steadily infects increasing numbers of people until it becomes an epidemic. Memes "leap" from brain to brain via a process of imitation. The memes

One pair of researchers distinguishes between two types of non-core users, however: They describe **brand immigrants** who try to claim membership within the community of users, and **brand tourists** who buy the brand but who do not claim membership. They found that brand immigrants do potentially dilute the value of the brand for core users, but brand tourists do not. Instead they can actually enhance the value of the brand because their experimentation with it demonstrates that the brand has value, but this usage does not threaten the identities of the core users. So, can a prestige brand have its cake and eat it too? These findings suggest one strategy: Create a museum dedicated to the myth of the brand (as Louis Vuitton, Valentino, Gucci, and Nike have done) and allow tourists to look but not touch.[119]

Net Profit

Big rewards await those who can identify memes or create new ones. Case in point: Ben Huh, a young entrepreneur, dipped into his own savings and bought a quirky site from two Hawaiian bloggers—the hugely successful *I Can Has Cheezburger* that pairs photos of cats with quirky captions. He realized that there's a huge demand for content that satisfies people's quirky cravings and now he's expanded his empire—The Cheezburger Network—to include numerous sites that serve up all kinds of offbeat humor. These include *Fail Blog* for photos and videos of disastrous mishaps and *There I Fixed It* where people post photos of bad repair jobs. There are also user-created meme animals such as Philosoraptor, Anti-Joke Chicken, Art Student Owl, and Pickup Line Panda. The network employs more than 40 people who scour the Web for new ideas to post. They are essentially meme miners who monitor cyberspace for themes that emerge on forums, blogs, and video sites. As the creator of a video series called "Know Your Meme" explained, "Cheezburger figures out what's starting to get popular and then harvests the humor from the chaff. Things like Lolcats and Fail are easy to make, easy to spread and hit on an emotional level that crosses a lot of traditional boundaries."[123]

The Tangled Web

Two 12 year-old Wisconsin girls stabbed a classmate 19 times, and later explained they did this at the urging of someone called "Slenderman." It turns out that he is not a real person; he's an Internet meme. The thin, faceless character in a dark suit appears in numerous YouTube videos, in PhotoShopped pictures and on blogs that described "sightings" around the country. The girls read about Slenderman on the Web site Creepypasta, where fans submit small fictional accounts of scary characters including zombies, vampires, and aliens. His creator, whose Web handle is "Victor Surge," says he invented Slenderman in 2009 as an "attempt to cooperatively create new folklore" by mixing a stock horror theme with the ability of the Internet to spread the message.[127] His formula seems to be working; in 2015 people in the United Kingdom started to post video sightings of Slenderman as well.

that survive tend to be distinctive and memorable, and the hardiest ones often combine aspects of prior memes. For example, the *Star Wars* movies evoke prior memes that relate to the legend of King Arthur, religion, heroic youth, and 1930s adventure serials. Indeed, George Lucas studied comparative religion and mythology as he prepared his first draft of the *Star Wars* saga, *The Story of Mace Windu*.[125]

The diffusion of many products in addition to Hush Puppies seems to follow the same basic path. A few people initially use the product, but change happens in a hurry when the process reaches the moment of critical mass—what one author calls the **tipping point**[126] For example, Sharp introduced the first low-priced fax machine in 1984 and sold about 80,000 in that year. There was a slow climb in the number of users for the next 3 years. Then, suddenly, in 1987 enough people had fax machines that it made sense for everyone to have one, and Sharp sold a million units. Cell phones followed a similar trajectory. Do you remember when you first heard about Instagram or Vine?

OBJECTIVE 14-8
Fashions follow cycles and reflect cultural dynamics.

Cycles of Fashion Adoption

In the early 1980s, Cabbage Patch dolls were all the rage among U.S. children. Faced with a limited supply of the product, some retailers reported near-riots among adults as they tried desperately to buy the dolls for their children. A Milwaukee deejay jokingly announced that people should bring catcher's mitts to a local stadium because an airplane was going to fly overhead and drop 2,000 dolls. He told his listeners to hold up their American Express cards so their numbers could be photographed from the plane. More than two dozen anxious parents apparently didn't get the joke: They showed up in subzero weather, mitts in hand.[128]

The Cabbage Patch craze lasted for a couple of seasons before it eventually died out, and consumers moved on to other things, such as Teenage Mutant Ninja Turtles, which grossed more than $600 million in 1989. The Mighty Morphin Power Rangers eventually replaced the Turtles, and Beanie Babies and Giga Pets in turn deposed them before the invasion of Pokémon, followed by Yu-Gi-Oh! cards, Webkinz, Transformers, Squinkies and Zoobles, Furbys, and on and on.[129]

Figure 14.4 illustrates that fashions begin slowly, but if they "make it," they diffuse rapidly through a market, peak, and then retreat into obscurity. We identify different classes of fashion when we look at the relative length of their **acceptance cycles**. Many fashions have a moderate cycle, taking several months or even years to work their way through the stages of acceptance and decline; others are extremely long lived or short-lived.

A **classic** is a fashion with an extremely long acceptance cycle. It is in a sense "anti-fashion" because it guarantees stability and low risk to the purchaser for a long period of time. Keds sneakers, introduced in 1917, appeal to those who are turned off by the high-fashion, trendy appeal of Nike or Reebok. When researchers asked consumers in focus groups to imagine what kind of building Keds would be, a common response was a country house with a white picket fence. In other words, consumers see the shoes as a stable, classic product. In contrast, participants described Nikes as steel-and-glass skyscrapers to reflect that brand's more modern image.[130]

A theme park in Japan offers "amusement baths" to visitors, including a wine bath, a green-tea bath, a coffee bath, a sake bath, and even a ramen-noodle bath. When they don their bathing suits and jump into the ramen bath (which looks like a soup bowl), they frolic in pepper-flavored water that contains collagen and garlic extracts the Japanese believe will improve the skin. A man dressed as a chef dispenses noodle-shaped bath additives and soy sauce to everyone in the tub.[131] A **fad** is a short-lived fashion. Relatively few people adopt a fad product, but it can spread quickly. Adopters may all belong to a common subculture, and the fad "trickles across" members but rarely breaks out of that specific group.

The *streaking* fad hit college campuses in the mid-1970s because it was briefly popular for students to run nude through classrooms, cafeterias, dorms, and sports venues.

Figure 14.4 COMPARISON OF THE ACCEPTANCE CYCLES OF FADS, FASHIONS, AND CLASSICS

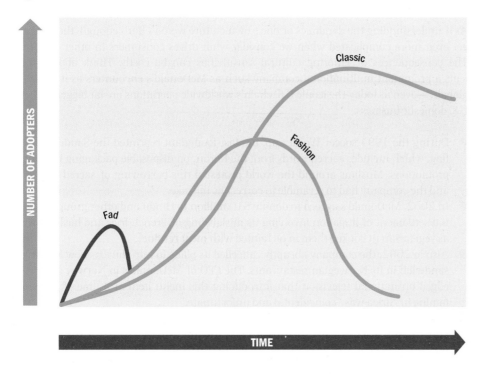

Although the practice quickly spread across many campuses, it was primarily restricted to college settings. Streaking highlights several of a fad's "naked truths:"[132]

● The fad is nonutilitarian; it does not perform any meaningful function.
● The fad often spreads impulsively; people do not undergo stages of rational decision making before they join in.
● The fad diffuses rapidly, gains quick acceptance, and dies just as quickly.

Music, furniture, and other cultural products undergo cycles of fashion adoption.
Source: Creative Director: João Santos, Art Director: Mariana Moreira, Copy: Daniel Pereira

Global Consumer Culture

As if understanding the dynamics of one's own culture weren't hard enough, these issues get even more complicated when we consider what drives consumers in other cultures. The consequences of ignoring cultural sensitivities can be costly. Think about problems a prominent multinational company such as McDonald's encounters as it expands globally—even as today the iconic U.S. chain's worldwide operations are far bigger than its U.S. domestic business: [133]

- During the 1994 soccer World Cup, the fast-food giant reprinted the Saudi Arabian flag, which includes sacred words from the Koran, on disposable packaging it used in promotions. Muslims around the world protested this borrowing of sacred imagery, and the company had to scramble to correct its mistake.
- In 2002, McDonald's agreed to donate $10 million to Hindu and other groups as partial settlement of litigation involving its mislabeling of French fries and hash browns as vegetarian (it cooked them in oil tainted with meat residue).
- Also in 2002, the company abruptly cancelled its plans to introduce its new McAfrika sandwich in its Norwegian restaurants. The CEO of McDonald's in Norway acknowledged on national television that introducing this menu item at a time of growing famine in Africa was "coincidental and unfortunate."
- In India, the company doesn't sell any of its famous beef hamburgers. Instead, it offers customized entrées such as a Pizza McPuff, McAloo Tikki (a spiced-potato burger), Paneer Salsa McWrap, and even a Crispy Chinese burger, to capitalize on the great popularity of Chinese food in India. It makes its mayonnaise without eggs, and all stores maintain separate kitchen sections for vegetarian and nonvegetarian dishes. Workers from the nonvegetarian section must shower before they cross over to the other area.
- In 2005, McDonald's introduced the spicy Prosperity Burger in nine countries, from South Korea to Indonesia, in recognition of the Lunar New Year.
- Although the Japanese are well-known for their healthy diets, McDonald's numerous customers there are clamoring for high-calorie sandwiches—even as the company's U.S. consumers welcome new diet-friendly entrées like the Premium Southwest salad. As part of its new Big America 2 campaign, McD's in Japan offer the 713-calorie Idaho burger (topped with melted cheese, a deep-fried hash brown, strips of bacon, onions, and pepper-and-mustard sauce) and several other U.S.-themed items. [134] It seems there's more than one way to translate "Big America."
- McDonald's introduced a new entrée to the German market: The McCurrywurst is a mix of pork bratwurst chunks in a spicy tomato sauce accompanied by shaker packs of either mild or sharp curry powder. This follows on the mini Nürnburger brat sandwich the chain introduced a few years ago. Germans love their bratwurst, so now they can eat it Golden Arches style. [135]
- Asian consumers regard McDonald's as less of an inexpensive meal on the run and more of a middle-class experience. People regard Western fast food chains as safe options: Food safety is a major concern, particularly in China because of a series of scandals involving contaminated products that resulted in deaths. McDonald's emphasized the quality of its ingredients with its Chickileaks campaign (the actual translation from the Chinese is "unveil the secret of chicken grown"), that focused on the integrity of the company's chicken supply chain. [136] Unfortunately, recent events show that these companies can't rest on their laurels: Sales at McDonald's as well as KFC slumped when in 2014 Chinese television uncovered yet another food safety problem; this time with a local supplier who was selling meat to both companies past its expiration date. [137]

More than 60 countries have a gross national product of less than $10 billion. There are at least 135 transnational companies that post more revenue than that figure. Many multinational firms are household names, widely recognized by literally billions of people.

CB AS I SEE IT

Julien Cayla, *Nanyang Business School, Singapore*

The more research I do in the Asia-Pacific region, the more I am amazed at the sheer diversity of consumer cultures, and the interconnections between cultures. With my French colleague Jean Baptiste Welté, I am currently involved in doing research on luxury boutiques in Asia, and we find that luxury consumers from Tokyo, Shanghai, and New Delhi are extremely different. While many Chinese consumers are interested in the way luxury items signal status and allow them to build relationships or *guanxi*, the Japanese were often more interested in limited editions of luxury brands. These differences can be partly explained by the fact that the penetration of luxury brands in Japan is much higher than in China. The Japanese market hence requires a completely different approach, emphasizing exclusivity.

In India, many luxury brands have struggled to generate sales given the high taxes and duties imposed on luxury products. But some brands have successfully adapted to the idiosyncrasies of the Indian luxury market. A case in point is Louis Vuitton. After building an understanding of the local culture, Louis Vuitton's management decided to focus more specifically on weddings. Building from the ancient custom in which the Indian bride takes a trunk of belongings with her when she joins her husband's household, Louis Vuitton uses its expertise in customizing luggage to deliver unique luggage pieces for lavish weddings, an occasion when even otherwise frugal Indian families are willing to splurge. Overall, what our research and other evidence suggest is that treating Asia or Asian consumers as homogenous, or summarizing their behavior as "collectivist" is misleading given the huge diversity and the complexity hiding behind those labels.

Second, I remain fascinated by the various types of exchanges and connections that exist between Asian nations. For instance, the Korean wave of pop culture or *hallyu* has generated a huge following and promoted the sense of an ideal Korean beauty, with features such as big eyes, tiny button noses, v-line shaped jaws and wide cheeks, in many parts of East Asia. An after-effect of this success has been the rise of Seoul as a cosmetic surgery center, with large numbers of Chinese tourists flocking to South Korea every year to resemble Korean television and pop music stars. In our research with Giana Eckhardt, we looked at some of these connections between Asian nations, and at the type of modernity promoted in Asia. We found that brands often invoked a very urban modernity, and the idea that Asians are experiencing the same dynamic wave of economic development. This dynamism, the connections existing between Asian cities, and the fascinating history of the region, is what appeals to me as I continue to do more work on consumer behavior in Asia.

The dominance of these marketing powerhouses creates a **global consumer culture** that unites people around the world by their common devotion to brand-name consumer goods, movie stars, celebrities, and leisure activities.[138] As developing countries generate millions of new middle-class consumers, people the world over value well-known brands that symbolize prosperity. Shopping evolves from a wearying, task-oriented struggle to locate even basic necessities to a leisure activity.

OBJECTIVE 14-9

Western (and particularly U.S.) culture has a huge impact around the world, although people in other countries don't necessarily ascribe the same meanings to products as we do.

It's a BRAND-New World

Although Chinese consumers enjoy exotic beverages such as snake bile wine and fresh-squeezed cucumber juice, they still buy more than one billion bottles of good old U.S. Coca-Cola per year. The National Basketball Association sells $500 million of licensed merchandise every year *outside* of the United States; China is its largest foreign market.[139] Patrons of the Starlite

Urban Drive-In in London sit in rows of cars as they watch U.S. "classics" like *Grease* and *Dirty Dancing* while they chow down on burgers, meatloaf, and sweet potato pie, followed by ice cream sundaes or chocolate brownies and cream. Starstruck fans of the reality show *Keeping up with the Kardashians* lined up 30 hours in advance for a chance to see Kim at a shopping mall in Sydney, Australia.

Walk the streets of Lisbon or Buenos Aires, and the sight of Nike hats, Gap T-shirts, and Levi's jeans will accost you at every turn. The allure of U.S. consumer culture spreads throughout the world, but with a lot of pushback in many places. Critics in other countries deplore the creeping Americanization of their cultures because of what they view as excessive materialism. One French critic summarized this resistance to the diffusion of U.S. culture: He described the Euro Disney theme park as "a horror made of cardboard, plastic, and appalling colors—a construction of hardened chewing gum and idiotic folklore taken straight out of a comic book written for obese Americans."[140]

A survey in Beijing found that nearly half of all children younger than age 12 think McDonald's is a domestic Chinese brand![141] The West (and especially the United States) is a net exporter of popular culture. Many consumers equate Western lifestyles in general and the English language in particular with modernization and sophistication, and numerous U.S. brands slowly but surely insinuate themselves into local cultures. Indeed, some global brands are so widespread that many are only vaguely aware of their countries of origin. In surveys, consumers routinely guess that Heineken is German (it's really Dutch) and that Nokia is Japanese (it's Finnish).[142]

One study looked at how Chinese consumers think about Western brands. The researchers found that their interpretations depended on their unique perspective about the history of relations between China and the West. The researchers in fact identified four different *narratives* (themes) in their sample: West as liberator, as oppressor, as subjugated, and as partner. Depending on which view they endorsed, respondents viewed Western brands as instruments of democratization, domination, a symbol of Asian ascendancy as Chinese domestic brands start to gain traction, or as instruments of economic progress that will help China to grow its economy in partnership with the United States and Western Europe.[143]

As the global consumption ethic spreads, rituals and product preferences in different cultures become homogenized. For example, some urbanites in Muslim Turkey now celebrate Christmas even though gift-giving is not customary in many parts of the country—even on birthdays. In China, Christmas fever grips China's newly rising urban middle class as an excuse to shop, eat, and party. People there snap up Christmas trees, ornaments, and Christian religious objects (even though the street vendors who peddle images of Jesus and Mary can't always identify who they are). Chinese consumers embrace Christmas because to them the holiday is international and modern, not because it's a traditional Christian celebration. The government encourages this practice because it stimulates consumer spending. To make the holiday even merrier, China exports about $1 billion worth of Christmas products every year, and its factories churn out $7.5 billion of the toys people worldwide put under their trees.[144]

Does this homogenization mean that in time consumers who live in Nairobi, New Guinea, or the Netherlands will all be indistinguishable from those in New York or Nashville? Probably not, because the meaning of consumer goods mutates to blend with local customs and values. For example, in Turkey some urban women use their ovens to dry clothes and their dishwashers to wash muddy spinach. A person in Papua New Guinea may combine a traditional clothing style such as a *bilum* with Western items such as Mickey Mouse shirts or baseball caps.[145]

These processes make it unlikely that global homogenization will overwhelm local cultures, but it is likely that there will be multiple consumer cultures, each of which blends global icons such as Nike's pervasive "swoosh" with indigenous products and meanings. In Vietnam, for example, local fast-food chains dominate the market as they duplicate a McDonald's approach but add a local flavor. The country's hugely successful Kinh Do red and yellow outlets sell specialties like dried squid buns. In the Philippines, the Jollibee Foods Corp. burger chain also copies the McDonald's look—and it outsells McDonald's there.[146]

Creolization occurs when foreign influences integrate with local meanings. In India, beggars sell bottles of Coke from tricycles, and Indipop, a popular music hybrid, mixes traditional styles with rock, rap, and reggae.[147] Young Hispanic Americans bounce between hip-hop and *Rock en Español*, blend Mexican rice with spaghetti sauce, and spread peanut butter and jelly on tortillas.[148] In Argentina, Coca-Cola launched Nativa, a soft drink flavored with the country's traditional *yerba mate* herbal tea, as part of a strategy to broaden its portfolio with products it makes from indigenous ingredients.[149]

Rather than ignore the global characteristics of their brands, firms have to manage them strategically. That's critical, because future growth for most companies will come from foreign markets. In 2002, developed countries in North America, Europe, and East Asia accounted for 15 percent of the world's population of 6.3 billion. By 2030, according to the World Bank, the planet's population will rise to 9 billion—and 90 percent of these people will live in developing countries.

As corporations compete in many markets around the world, the debate intensifies: Should an organization develop separate marketing plans for each culture, or should it craft a single plan to implement everywhere? Let's briefly consider each viewpoint.

Adopt a Standardized Strategy

As Procter & Gamble strategizes about the best way to speak to consumers around the world, the company finds large segments in many countries that share the same outlooks, style preferences, and aspirations. These include teenagers, working women who try to juggle careers and families, and baby boomers. As the head of P&G's Global Health and Feminine Care division explained, "We're seeing global tribes forming around the world that are more and more interconnected through technology. If you focus on the similarities instead of the differences [in these tribes], key business opportunities emerge." For example, brand managers find that teenage girls everywhere have the same concerns and questions about puberty, so the company makes the same content available in 40 countries.[150]

Proponents of a standardized marketing strategy argue that many cultures, especially those of industrialized countries, are now so homogenized that the same approach will work throughout the world. If it develops one approach for multiple markets, a company can benefit from economies of scale, because it does not have to incur the substantial time and expense to develop a separate strategy for each culture.[151] This viewpoint represents an **etic perspective**, which focuses on commonalities across cultures. An etic approach to a culture is objective and analytical; it reflects impressions of a culture as outsiders view it.

OBJECTIVE 14-10
Products that succeed in one culture may fail in another if marketers fail to understand the differences among consumers in each place.

Adopt a Localized Strategy

Unlike Disney World in Orlando, visitors to the Walt Disney Studios theme park at Disneyland Paris don't hear the voices of U.S. movie stars narrating their guided tours. Instead, European actors such as Jeremy Irons, Isabella Rossellini, and Nastassja Kinski provide commentary in their native tongues.

Disney learned the hard way about the importance of being sensitive to local cultures after it opened its Euro Disney Park in 1992. The company got slammed because its new location didn't cater to local customs (such as serving wine with meals). Visitors to Euro Disney from many countries took offense, even at what seem to be small slights. For example, initially the park only sold a French sausage, which drew complaints from Germans, Italians, and others who believed their own local versions to be superior. Euro Disney's CEO explained, "When we first launched there was the belief that it was enough to be Disney. Now we realize that our guests need to be welcomed on the basis of their own culture and travel habits."[152]

Disney applied the lessons it learned in cultural sensitivity to its newer Hong Kong Disneyland. Executives shifted the angle of the front gate by 12 degrees after they

Marketing Pitfall

The language barrier is one obvious problem that marketers who wish to break into foreign markets must navigate. Travelers abroad commonly encounter signs in tortured English, such as a note to guests at a Tokyo hotel that proclaims, "You are invited to take advantage of the chambermaid," a notice at a hotel in Acapulco reassuring people that "The manager has personally passed all the water served here," or a dry cleaner in Majorca who urges passing customers to "drop your pants here for best results." Local product names often raise eyebrows on visiting Americans who might stumble on a Japanese coffee creamer called Creap, a Mexican bread named Bimbo, or even a Scandinavian product to unfreeze car locks named Super Piss.

One technique marketers use to avoid this problem is **back-translation** in which a different interpreter retranslates a translated ad back into its original language to catch errors. Here are some errors that could have used a bit of back-translation:[157]

- Audi calls its sporty electric car the e-tron. Unfortunately, to a French speaker the word *étron* hardly connotes motoring sophistication. Instead, it translates as "excrement."[158]
- Kraft Foods reorganized recently and renamed itself Mondelēz International. Monde is French for *world* in French, and *delez*, with a long E in the final syllable, is a play on *delish*. However, to Russians the word sounds like a term for oral sex.[159]
- The Scandinavian company that makes Electrolux vacuum cleaners sold them in the United States with this slogan: "Nothing sucks like an Electrolux."
- Fresca (a soft drink) is Mexican slang for lesbian.
- Ford discovered that a truck model it called *Fiera* means "ugly old woman" in Spanish. Its Caliente model is slang for a streetwalker. In Brazil, Pinto is a slang term for "small male appendage."
- When Rolls-Royce introduced its Silver Mist model in Germany, it found that the word *mist* translates as excrement. Similarly, Sunbeam's hair-curling iron, called the Mist-Stick, translates as manure wand. To add insult to injury, *Vicks* is German slang for sexual intercourse, so the company had to change its name to Wicks in that country.
- IKEA had to explain that the Gutvik children's bunk bed is named "for a tiny town in Sweden" after German shoppers noted that the name sounded a lot like a phrase that means "good f***." IKEA has yet to issue an explanation for its Fartfull workbench or its Jerker computer table.[160]

consulted a *feng shui* specialist, who said the change would ensure prosperity for the park. Disney also put a bend in the walkway from the train station to the gate to make sure the flow of positive energy, or *chi*, did not slip past the entrance and out to the China Sea. Cash registers are close to corners or along walls to increase prosperity. The company burned incense as it finished each building, and it picked a lucky day (September 12) for the opening. One of the park's main ballrooms measures 888 square meters, because eight is a lucky number in Chinese culture. And because the Chinese consider the number four bad luck, you won't find any fourth-floor buttons in hotel elevators.

Disney's experience supports the view of marketers who endorse an **emic perspective** that stresses variations across cultures. They feel that each culture is unique, with its own value system, conventions, and regulations. This perspective argues that each country has a **national character**, a distinctive set of behavior and personality characteristics.[153] A marketer must therefore tailor its strategy to the sensibilities of each specific culture. An emic approach to a culture is subjective and experiential: It attempts to explain a culture as insiders experience it.

Sometimes this strategy means that a manufacturer has to modify what it makes or a retailer has to change the way it displays the product so that it's acceptable to local tastes. When Walmart started to open stores abroad in the early 1990s, it offered a little piece of America to foreign consumers—and that was the problem. It promoted golf clubs in soccer-mad Brazil and pushed ice skates in Mexico. It trained its German clerks to smile at customers—who thought they were flirting. Now Walmart tries to adapt to local preferences. Its Chinese stores sell live turtles and snakes and lure shoppers who come on foot or bicycle with free shuttle buses and home delivery for refrigerators and other large items.[154]

In some cases, consumers in one place simply do not like some products that are popular elsewhere, or their different lifestyles require companies to rethink their designs. IKEA finally realized that Americans use a lot of ice in their drinks and so they didn't buy the smaller European glasses the stores stocked. The Swedish furniture chain also figured out that compared to Europeans, Americans sleep in bigger beds, need bigger bookshelves, and like to curl up on sofas rather than sit on them.[155] Listerine sells an alcohol-free version in Muslim countries where spirits are forbidden and a Green Tea–flavored mouthwash in Asia. Cheetos come in many flavors around the world that have little to do with cheese, including Seaweed (Taiwan), Avocado Salad (Japan), Ketchup (Canada), Masala Balls (India), and Strawberry Yogurt (Vietnam).[156]

So, which perspective is correct, the emic or the etic? As you might guess, the best bet probably is a combination of both.[161] Some researchers argue that the relevant dimension to consider is **consumer style**: A pattern of behaviors, attitudes, and opinions that influences all of a person's consumption activities—including attitudes toward advertising, preferred channels of information and purchase, brand loyalty, and price consciousness. These researchers identified four major clusters of consumer styles when they looked at data from the United States, the United Kingdom, France, and Germany:[162]

- Price-sensitive consumers
- Variety seekers
- Brand-loyal consumers
- Information seekers

Given the sizable variations in tastes within the United States alone, it is hardly surprising that people around the world develop their own unique preferences. Panasonic touted the fact that its rice cooker kept food from getting too crisp—until the company learned that consumers in the Middle East *like* to eat their rice this way. Unlike Americans, Europeans favor dark chocolate over milk chocolate, which they think of as a children's food. Sara Lee sells its pound cake with chocolate chips in the United States, raisins in Australia, and coconut in Hong Kong. Crocodile handbags are popular in Asia and Europe but not in the United States.[163]

One of the most widely used measures of cross-cultural values is an instrument a Dutch researcher developed called **Hofstede Dimensions of National Culture**.[164]

This measure scores a country in terms of its standing on six dimensions so that users can compare and contrast values:[165]

- **Power Distance**—The extent to which the less powerful members of organizations and institutions (like the family) accept and expect that power is distributed unequally.
- **Individualism**—The degree to which individuals are integrated into groups.
- **Masculinity**—The distribution of roles between the genders.
- **Uncertainty Avoidance**—A society's tolerance for uncertainty and ambiguity.
- **Long-Term Orientation**—Values associated with long-term orientation are thrift and perseverance; values associated with short-term orientation are respect for tradition, fulfilling social obligations, and protecting one's "face."
- **Indulgence versus Restraint**—The extent to which a society allows relatively free gratification of basic and natural human drives related to enjoying life and having fun. A culture high on restraint suppresses gratification of needs and regulates it by means of strict social norms.

These dimensions are useful to marketers that want to understand how members of specific cultures may respond quite differently even though they encounter the same situations or marketing messages. For example, researchers found that there is a lower level of prosocial behavior, such as donating to charities, in countries characterized by lower Power Distance. They argue that because people expect and accept greater levels of inequality among citizens, they don't feel as much responsibility to help others.[166]

An entirely different analysis argued that Spanish consumers score high on the Uncertainty Avoidance dimension, which motivates them to avoid new products compared to other Europeans. It underscores the importance of providing "uncertain" customers like these with a relatively familiar experience and then gently innovating on that, rather than trying to introduce entirely new products. In Spain it is now popular to drink what the locals call a "gintonic." Specialty bars serve imaginative variations of the traditional "gin and tonic" that use tonic flavors like kaffir lime and pink peppercorn and gin infused with fresh fruits and spices. Apparently Spaniards consider these new offerings "easy to taste" because they are used to bitter-tasting brands of sparkling water. As a successful restaurateur explains it, "It's almost like we're seeing baby steps. Like we're not ready to take everything at once, but, for now, we'll try a cupcake. And then we'll try a burger. And then we will try a grapefruit slice in a gin and tonic. You take these little bits that, for whatever reason, you are comfortable with, and they are your first steps towards becoming multicultural." Spanish consumers suddenly became the second-highest *per capita* consumers of gin worldwide (the British still hold the title).[167]

Does Global Marketing Work?

So, what's the verdict? Does global marketing work or not? Perhaps the more appropriate question is, "*When* does it work?" Although the argument for a homogenous world culture is appealing in principle, in practice it hasn't worked out too well. One reason is that consumers in different countries have varying conventions and customs, so they simply do not use products the same way. Kellogg, for example, discovered that in Brazil people don't typically eat a big breakfast; they're more likely to eat cereal as a dry snack.

Some large corporations, such as Coca-Cola, have successfully crafted a single, international image. Still, even the soft-drink giant must make minor modifications to the way it presents itself in each culture. Although Coke commercials are largely standardized, the company permits local agencies to edit them so they highlight close-ups of local faces.[168] Coke's successful Share a Coke campaign started in Australia, then expanded to more than 50 countries where cans and bottles are imprinted with the most popular names in each place.

To maximize the chances of success for these multicultural efforts, marketers must locate consumers in different countries who nonetheless share a common *worldview*. This is more likely to be the case among people whose frame of reference is relatively more international or cosmopolitan, or who receive much of their information about the world from sources that incorporate a worldwide perspective. Who is likely to fall into this category? Two consumer segments are particularly good candidates: (1) affluent people who are "global citizens" and who come into contact with ideas from around the world through their travels, business contacts, and media experiences; and (2) young people whose tastes in music and fashion are strongly influenced by MTV and other media that broadcast many of the same images to multiple countries. For example, viewers of MTV Europe in Rome or Zurich can check out the same "buzz clips" as their counterparts in London or Luxembourg.[169]

A large-scale study of consumers in 41 countries identified the characteristics that people associate with global brands, and it also measured the relative importance of those dimensions when consumers buy products.[170] The researchers grouped consumers who evaluate global brands in the same way. They identified four major segments:

- **Global citizens**—The largest segment (55 percent of consumers) uses the global success of a company as a signal of quality and innovation. At the same time, they are concerned about whether companies behave responsibly on issues such as consumer health, the environment, and worker rights.
- **Global dreamers**—The second-largest segment, at 23 percent, consists of consumers who see global brands as quality products and readily buy into the myths they author. They aren't nearly as concerned with social responsibility as are the global citizens.
- **Antiglobals**—Thirteen percent of consumers are skeptical that transnational companies deliver higher-quality goods. They dislike brands that preach U.S. values, and they don't trust global companies to behave responsibly. They try to avoid doing business with transnational firms.
- **Global agnostics**—The remaining 9 percent of consumers don't base purchase decisions on a brand's global attributes. Instead, they evaluate a global product by the same criteria they use to judge local brands and don't regard its global nature as meriting special consideration.

MyLab Marketing

To complete the problems with the ⭐, go to EOC Discussion Questions in the MyLab as well as additional Marketing Metrics questions only available in MyLab Marketing.

CHAPTER SUMMARY

Now that you have finished reading this chapter, you should understand why:

1. A culture is a society's personality.

A society's culture includes its values, ethics, and the material objects its members produce. It is the accumulation of shared meanings and traditions among members of a society. We describe a culture in terms of ecology (the way people adapt to their habitat), its social structure, and its ideology (including moral and aesthetic principles).

2. We distinguish between high culture and low culture.

Social scientists distinguish between high (or elite) forms and low (or popular) forms of culture. Products

of popular culture tend to follow a cultural formula and contain predictable components. However, these distinctions blur in modern society as marketers increasingly incorporate imagery from "high art" to sell everyday products.

3. Myths are stories that express a culture's values, and in modern times marketing messages convey these values to members of the culture.

Myths are stories with symbolic elements that express the shared ideals of a culture. Many myths involve a binary opposition, defining values in terms of what they are and what they are not (e.g., nature versus technology). Advertising, movies, and other media transmit modern myths.

4. **Many of our consumption activities—including holiday observances, grooming, and gift-giving—are rituals.**

A ritual is a set of multiple, symbolic behaviors that occur in a fixed sequence and that we repeat periodically. Ritual is related to many consumption activities that occur in popular culture. These include holiday observances, gift-giving, and grooming.

A rite of passage is a special kind of ritual that marks the transition from one role to another. These passages typically entail the need to acquire ritual artifacts to facilitate the transition. Modern rites of passage include graduations, fraternity initiations, weddings, debutante balls, and funerals.

5. **We describe products as either sacred or profane, and it's not unusual for some products to move back and forth between the two categories.**

We divide consumer activities into *sacred* and *profane* domains. Sacred phenomena are "set apart" from everyday activities or products. *Sacralization* occurs when we set apart everyday people, events, or objects from the ordinary. *Objectification* occurs when we ascribe sacred qualities to products or items that sacred people once owned. *Desacralization* occurs when formerly sacred objects or activities become part of the everyday, as when companies reproduce "one-of-a-kind" works of art in large quantities.

6. **New products, services, and ideas spread through a population over time. Different types of people are more or less likely to adopt them during this diffusion process.**

Diffusion of innovation refers to the process whereby a new product, service, or idea spreads through a population. Innovators and early adopters are quick to adopt new products, and laggards are slow. A consumer's decision to adopt a new product depends on his or her personal characteristics as well as on characteristics of the innovation itself. We are more likely to adopt a new product if it demands relatively little behavioral change, is easy to understand, and provides a relative advantage compared to existing products.

7. **Many people and organizations play a role in the fashion system that creates and communicates symbolic meanings to consumers.**

The fashion system includes everyone involved in creating and transferring symbolic meanings. Many different products express common cultural categories (e.g., gender distinctions). Many people tend to adopt a new style simultaneously in a process of collective selection. According to meme theory, ideas spread through

a population in a geometric progression much as a virus infects many people until it reaches epidemic proportions. Other perspectives on motivations for adopting new styles include psychological, economic, and sociological models of fashion.

8. **Fashions follow cycles and reflect cultural dynamics.**

The styles prevalent in a culture at any point in time reflect underlying political and social conditions. We term the set of agents responsible for creating stylistic alternatives a culture production system. Factors such as the types of people involved in this system and the amount of competition by alternative product forms influence the choices that eventually make their way to the marketplace for consideration by end consumers.

Fashions follow cycles that resemble the product life cycle. We distinguish between two extremes of fashion adoption, classics and fads, in terms of the length of this cycle.

9. **Western (and particularly U.S.) culture has a huge impact around the world, although people in other countries don't necessarily ascribe the same meanings to products as we do.**

The United States is a net exporter of popular culture. Consumers around the world eagerly adopt U.S. products, especially entertainment vehicles and items they link to a U.S. lifestyle (e.g., Marlboro cigarettes, Levi's jeans). Despite the continuing "Americanization" of world culture, some people resist globalization because they fear it will dilute their own local cultures. In other cases, they exhibit creolization as they integrate these products with existing cultural practices.

10. **Products that succeed in one culture may fail in another if marketers fail to understand the differences among consumers in each place.**

Because a consumer's culture exerts such a big influence on his or her lifestyle choices, marketers must learn as much as possible about differences in cultural norms and preferences when they do business in more than one country. One important issue is the extent to which we need to tailor our marketing strategies to each culture. Followers of an etic perspective believe that people in many cultures appreciate the same universal messages. Believers in an emic perspective argue that individual cultures are too unique to permit such standardization; marketers must instead adapt their approaches to local values and practices. Attempts at global marketing have met with mixed success. In many cases this approach is more likely to work if the messages appeal to basic values or if the target markets consist of consumers who are internationally rather than locally oriented.

KEY TERMS

REVIEW

⭐ **14-1** What is *culture*? List three dimensions that social scientists use to describe a culture and give an example of each.

14-2 A myth is a special kind of story. What makes it special? What is an example of a modern myth?

14-3 How might a consumer behave if they exhibited signs of conditioned superstition?

⭐ **14-4** What is a *ritual*? Describe three kinds of rituals and provide an example of each.

14-5 List the three stages of a rite of passage ritual.

14-6 What is the difference between sacred and profane consumption? Provide one example of each.

14-7 How is a collection sacred? What is the difference between collecting and hoarding?

14-8 What is *collective selection*? Give an example.

14-9 Describe a culture production system and list its three components.

14-10 Define a *cultural gatekeeper*, and give three examples.

14-11 Describe the difference between arts and crafts.

14-12 What is a *cultural formula*? Give an example.

14-13 What are the two factors that underpin the technology acceptance model?

14-14 What are the differences among *fashion, a fashion,* and *in fashion*?

⭐ **14-15** Summarize some of the major approaches we can use to understand fashion from the perspectives of psychologists, economists, and sociologists.

14-16 What is an example of a *meme*?

14-17 What is the trickle-down effect? List some reasons why this theory is no longer as valid as it used to be.

14-18 What is the difference between a *fad*, a *fashion*, and a *classic fashion* life cycle?

CONSUMER BEHAVIOR CHALLENGE

■ DISCUSS

14-19 Is it possible for a commercial building or attraction to attain a status that borders on the sacred? Give an example from your own country or region.

14-20 Illustrate the concepts of separation, liminality, and aggregation in relation to your own specific culture. Are the concepts readily applicable?

14-21 Some products can be classified as being either sacred or profane. It is not usual for some products to move back and forth between the two categories. Why?

14-22 How could packaging design be used to suggest the binary opposition of natural and processed foods?

14-23 There is a tradition, particularly in subcultures, of having to go through some kind of entry rite at some point of time. Identify an example from your own country to illustrate this process.

14-24 Religious festivals and ceremonies are not immune to marketing. Many have become another opportunity for businesses to make sales. To what extent is this true? Give reasons for your answer.

14-25 Bridal registries specify clearly the gifts that the couple wants. How do you feel about this practice? Should people actually specify what you should buy for them, or should a gift be a more personal expression from you?

14-26 When a couple marry, the choice of gift is commonly either chosen from a wedding list or is a sum of money, often determined by culture. How does this work in your country?

14-27 Movie companies often conduct market research when they produce big-budget films. If necessary, they will reshoot part of a movie when viewers say they don't like it. Some people oppose this practice: They claim that movies, like books, songs, plays, and other artistic endeavors, should not conform to what the market wants, lest they sacrifice their integrity. What do you think?

14-28 Boots with 6-inch heels were a fashion rage among young Japanese women a few years ago. Several teens died after they tripped over their shoes and fractured their skulls. However, followers of the style claimed they were willing to risk twisted ankles, broken bones, bruised faces, and other dangers the platform shoes caused. One teenager said, "I've fallen and twisted my ankle many times, but they are so cute that I won't give them up until they go out of fashion."[171] Many consumers around the world seem willing to suffer for the sake of fashion. Others argue that we are merely pawns in the hands of designers, who conspire to force unwieldy fashions down our throats. What do you think? What is and what should be the role of fashion in our society? How important is it for people to be in style? What are the pros and cons of keeping up with the latest fashions? Do you believe that we are at the mercy of designers?

■ APPLY

14-29 Cristiano Ronaldo is one of the world's greatest footballers, but he may also be one of the most superstitious.[172] The Real Madrid star has built up a series of rituals that he insists on following while playing a game. He always steps on the pitch leading with his right foot. He always insists on wearing long-sleeve shirts regardless of the weather conditions. He always makes sure that he is the last member of his team to step onto the pitch, unless he is captaining the side (in which case he must be first). When traveling to and from a game, he demands to be seated at the front of an aircraft, but at the back of a coach or bus.

Many of us adopt strange superstitious rituals. Ask some people you know about their rituals. How did they develop? What do they fear might happen if they are not followed?

14-30 Interview people you know who collect some kind of object. How do they organize and describe their collections? Do you see any evidence of sacred versus profane distinctions?

14-31 Ask friends to describe an incident in which they received a gift they thought was inappropriate. Why did they feel this way, and how did this event influence the relationship between them and the gift giver?

14-32 How might the rise of peer-to-peer music sharing influence the structure of the music CPS? One guess is that this method erodes the dominance of the big labels because listeners are more likely to access music from lesser-known groups. Survey your friends to determine whether this in fact is happening. Do they listen to a wider variety of artists, or simply download more from the big-time groups?

14-33 Identify examples of high or low culture from your country or region in terms of music, art, literature, and TV entertainment. Which cultural formulae can be used to distinguish them?

14-34 U.S. television inspires knockoffs around the world. But to be fair, many U.S. viewers don't realize that U.S. reality show hits such as *Big Brother* and *American Idol* started out as European concepts that U.S. producers imported. In fact, the U.K. version of *Big Brother* briefly went off the air after a fight broke out and housemates threatened to kill each other.[173] In contrast, a Malaysian show that borrows the *American Idol* format is called *Imam Muda* (Young Leader). Contestants debate religious topics and recite passages from the Koran. The winner doesn't get a recording contract. Instead, he receives a job as an imam, or religious leader; a scholarship to study in Saudi Arabia; and an all-expenses-paid pilgrimage to Mecca, Islam's holiest city.[174] See if you can identify foreign versions of familiar reality shows. You should be able to find them online. How have the creators of these programs adapted them to appeal to local customs?

Case Study

MARKETING THE IKEA FANTASY AROUND THE WORLD

Companies who market internationally often have to work hard to find an effective and profitable balance between standardizing their marketing strategies while still reflecting an understanding of the unique characteristics and consumer behavior present in those markets.

IKEA, the Swedish furniture and furnishings company, is a good example of a retailer trying to find that sweet spot between standardization and adaptation. Its unique mission is to "create a better everyday life for the many people," in particular, helping consumers with "thin wallets," to be able to afford stylish furniture and home furnishings, as the store describes its niche. The company has 370 stores in 47 countries worldwide and a goal of 500 stores by 2020. To put its international footprint into perspective, IKEA has stores in more countries than Walmart and these are more profitable than Target and Lowe's. In Beth Kowitt's *Fortune* article "How IKEA Took Over the World," the company is recognized as having mastered one of the hardest retail challenges: selling high volumes of inventory at a consistently low price in vastly different marketplaces, languages, and cultures. How have they achieved a successful balance between standardization and adaptation in their international markets?

First of all, the company credits marketing research for much of its success. Mikael Ydholm, head of research, says "The more far away we go from our culture, the more we need to understand, learn, and adapt." At the same time it must look for points where cultures intersect. With a focus on volume production, IKEA does not want to have to adapt its products for each country market. But it has figured out how to show the same product working into the lifestyles of different locations around the world. By visiting the homes of consumers in different countries it has uncovered the similarities and differences in how consumers around the world use and interact with IKEA products.

Through its research, IKEA pays special attention to the subtle differences that are so important in international marketing. It also takes its time to develop strategy. For instance, it's taken the company 6 years to move into South Korea, but even with that kind of lead time mistakes were still made; for instance a map mislabeled what South Koreans call the East Sea as the Sea of Japan.

Much of IKEA's recent international growth has been built on the growing middle-class markets in emerging markets, which was a logical step for IKEA. It has always excelled at creating a sense of fantasy for customers who visit its stores. Tom Novak describes it as a creation of "domestic tableaux and scenes from a home life we imagine living." In his *Trend and Tonic* post he describes how "these fantasies of new living are crucial for emerging global powers like China, India, and Brazil who all have rising middle classes." IKEA is carefully tracking the growth of the middle class in these markets and has opened stores in countries like Croatia, Indonesia, Thailand, and China. In fact China is the market where it is experiencing the fastest growth and which has eight of the largest stores.

Novak argues that IKEA's minimalism translates well across cultures because its simple furniture is chic yet practical. He also suggests that Sweden as the "country of origin" for the IKEA concept may enjoy the unique ability to appeal politically or ideologically to other cultures. It may be seen as able to fill a void for international consumers who are drawn to the Western fantasy but who want to avoid Western controversy. In fact, products retain their Swedish names in markets around the world as a way to build on the positives of IKEA's brand identity.

Although IKEA may work hard to keep a more universal product approach, when it comes to its catalogs it defers to adaptation of language and culture. The company prints 212 million catalogs a year. Kowitt reports that catalogs come in 32 languages and 67 versions, which enables the company to do a better job of reflecting local customers and customs. Photo shoots for the catalogs are all done in a studio in Sweden where an employee is responsible for making sure that shots taken of each room set-up are appropriate and culturally sensitive for each of the different catalog versions being produced. For instance, they want to ensure that the Taiwanese catalog doesn't feature glass products from mainland China and that Israel's catalogs don't picture Persian rugs.

The company admits that it has made cultural *faux pas* in the past with its catalog, like photoshopping women out of catalogs for Saudi Arabia and removing a lesbian couple from a version for Russia. IKEA Communications officer Kajsa Orvarson says, "We have done mistakes, but we are becoming more and more aware of how to improve and to share our values."

IKEA has reexamined other aspects of its interational marketing strategy as well. For instance, the Chinese market required some interesting adaptations. IKEA redesigned in-store vignettes to more closely resemble Chinese rooms and kitchens, reconfigured the length of sofas to better fit the dimensions of Chinese apartments, located stores closer to city centers and public transportation, and lowered prices through local product sourcing. In addition, Chinese consumers are not used to assembling things themselves, so they typically hire cheap local labor to do it for them. IKEA has had to educate customers about assembling the furniture and persuade them that it is worth it in a market with low-cost competitors who typically include assembly in their price.

DISCUSSION QUESTIONS

CS 14-1 Discuss how IKEA's approach has helped you to better understand the debate that exists between standardization compared with adaptation for international markets.

CS 14-2 Compare and contrast two countries according to the Hofstede cultural model using the online tool at http://geert-hofstede.com/countries.html. How might this tool help a company like IKEA do a better job of marketing in each country?

CS 14-3 The text talks about the difference between low and high culture. Is IKEA trying to position its brand to be one or the other? Would this be different depending on the country location?

Sources: Tom Novak, "IKEA: Brand of Fantasies," June 23, 2015, http://trendantonic.thefuturescompany.com/ikea-brand-of-fantasies/, accessed June 26, 2015; Beth Kowitt, "How IKEA Took Over the World," March 15, 2015, http://fortune.com/ikea-world-domination/, accessed June 28, 2015; Steve Burt, Asa Thelander, and Ulf Johansson, "Standardized Marketing Strategies in Retailing? IKEA's Marketing Strategies in Sweden, the UK, and China," *Journal of Retailing and Consumer Services* (May 2011), http://www.research gate.net/profile/Steve_Burt/publication/223947182_Standardized_marketing_strategies_in_retailing_IKEAs_marketing_strategies_in_Sweden_the_UK_and_China/links/09e41511d21b1ca3e8000000.pdf, accessed June 25, 2015; http://franchisor.ikea.com/wp-content/uploads/2015/04/IKEA-2014_IKEA-retailing-facts-and-figures.pdf, accessed June 20, 2015.

MyLab Marketing

Go to the Assignments section of your MyLab to complete these writing exercises.

14-35 Identify the ritual elements of a football game.

14-36 The chapter states that a culture is a society's personality. If your culture were a person, how would you describe its personality traits?

NOTES

1. Clifford Geertz, *The Interpretation of Cultures* (New York: Basic Books, 1973); Marvin Harris, *Culture, People and Nature* (New York: Crowell, 1971); John F. Sherry, Jr., "The Cultural Perspective in Consumer Research," in Richard J. Lutz, ed., *Advances in Consumer Research* 13 (Provo, UT: Association for Consumer Research, 1985): 573–575.
2. William Lazer, Shoji Murata, and Hiroshi Kosaka, "Japanese Marketing: Towards a Better Understanding," *Journal of Marketing* 49 (Spring 1985): 69–81.
3. Celia W. Dugger, "Modestly, India Goes for a Public Swim," *New York Times* (March 5, 2000), www.nytimes.com, accessed March 5, 2000; cf. also Marius K. Luedicke, Craig J. Thompson, and Markus Giesler, "Consumer Identity Work as Moral Protagonism: How Myth and Ideology Animate a Brand-Mediated Moral Conflict," *Journal of Consumer Research* 36, no. 6 (2010): 1016–1032.
4. http://www.krunkgrillz.com/CategoryItems.aspx?CategoryIDX=1, accessed April 22, 2015; http://www.hiphopbling.com/, accessed April 22, 2015.
5. Marc Spiegler, "Marketing Street Culture: Bringing Hip-Hop Style to the Mainstream," *American Demographics* (November 1996): 29–34.
6. Damon Sajnani. "HipHop's Origins as Organic Decolonization," Decolonization .org (April 2, 2015), https://decolonization.wordpress.com/2015/04/02/hi phops-origins-as-organic-decolonization/, accessed April 22, 2015; Elizabeth M. Blair, "Commercialization of the Rap Music Youth Subculture," *Journal of Popular Culture* 27 (Winter 1993): 21–34; Basil G. Englis, Michael R. Solomon, and Anna Olofsson, "Consumption Imagery in Music Television: A Bi-Cultural Perspective," *Journal of Advertising* 22 (December 1993): 21–34.
7. Craig Thompson and Gokcen Coskuner-Balli, "Countervailing Market Responses to Corporate Co-optation and the Ideological Recruitment of Consumption Communities," *Journal of Consumer Research* 34 (August 2007): 135–152.
8. Grant McCracken, "Culture and Consumption: A Theoretical Account of the Structure and Movement of the Cultural Meaning of Consumer Goods," *Journal of Consumer Research* 13 (June 1986): 71–84.
9. Richard A. Peterson, "The Production of Culture: A Prolegomenon," in Richard A. Peterson, ed., *The Production of Culture, Sage Contemporary Social Science Issues* 33 (Beverly Hills, CA: Sage, 1976); Elizabeth C. Hirschman, "Resource Exchange in the Production and Distribution of a Motion Picture," *Empirical Studies of the Arts* 8, no. 1 (1990): 31–51; Michael R. Solomon, "Building Up and Breaking Down: The Impact of Cultural Sorting on Symbolic Consumption," in J. Sheth and E. C. Hirschman, eds., *Research in Consumer Behavior* (Greenwich, CT: JAI Press, 1988): 325–351. For a study that looked at ways consumers interact with marketers to create cultural meanings, cf. Lisa Peñaloza, "Consuming the American West: Animating Cultural Meaning and Memory at a Stock Show and Rodeo," *Journal of Consumer Research* 28 (December 2001): 369–398. Cf. also Markus Giesler, "Conflict and Compromise: Drama in Marketplace Evolution," *Journal of Consumer Research* 34 (April 2007): 739–753.
10. Richard A. Peterson and D. G. Berger, "Entrepreneurship in Organizations: Evidence from the Popular Music Industry," *Administrative Science Quarterly* 16 (1971): 97–107.
11. Ben Sisario, "In Beyoncé Deal, Pepsi Focuses on Collaboration," *New York Times* (December 9, 2012), http://www.nytimes.com/2012/12/10/

business/media/in-beyonce-deal-pepsi-focuses-on-collaboration.html?
smid=tw-nytimesmusic&seid=auto&_r=1&, accessed February 16, 2013.

12. Paul M. Hirsch, "Processing Fads and Fashions: An Organizational Set
Analysis of Cultural Industry Systems," *American Journal of Sociology* 77,
no. 4 (1972): 639–659; Russell Lynes, *The Tastemakers* (New York: Harper
& Brothers, 1954); Michael R. Solomon, "The Missing Link: Surrogate
Consumers in the Marketing Chain," *Journal of Marketing* 50 (October
1986): 208–219.

13. Howard S. Becker, "Arts and Crafts," *American Journal of Sociology* 83
(January 1987): 862–889.

14. Herbert J. Gans, "Popular Culture in America: Social Problem in a Mass
Society or Social Asset in a Pluralist Society?" in Howard S. Becker, ed.,
Social Problems: A Modern Approach (New York: Wiley, 1966).

15. http://thomaskinkade.com/, accessed April 24, 2015; Karen Breslau,
"Paint by Numbers," *Newsweek* (May 13, 2002): 48.

16. Luca M. Visconti, John F. Sherry Jr., Stefania Borghini, and Laurel
Anderson, "Street Art, Sweet Art? Reclaiming the 'Public' in Public Place,"
Journal of Consumer Research 37, no. 3 (2010): 511–529.

17. Annetta Miller, "Shopping Bags Imitate Art: Seen the Sacks? Now Visit the
Museum Exhibit," *Newsweek* (January 23, 1989): 44.

18. Kim Foltz, "New Species for Study: Consumers in Action," *New York Times*
(December 18, 1989): A1.

19. Adam K. Raymond, "How Unoriginal Is Hollywood? Very—and We've
Got the Stats to Prove It," *Yahoo!* (November 4, 2014), Yahoo!, https://
www.yahoo.com/movies/how-unoriginal-is-hollywood-very-and-weve-
got-the-101773800642.html, accessed February 16, 2015.

20. Arthur A. Berger, *Signs in Contemporary Culture: An Introduction to Semiotics*
(New York: Longman, 1984).

21. Adam Popescu, "Why Write Your Own Book When An Algorithm Can Do
It For You?," *Readwrite* (January 15, 2013), http://readwrite.com/2013/
01/15/why-write-your-own-book-when-an-algorithm-can-do-it-for-you,
accessed April 23, 2015.

22. http://www.vintagedancer.com/1920s/1920-downton-abbey-inspired-
clothing/, accessed April 22, 2015; Michiko Kakutani, "Art Is Easier the
2d Time Around," *New York Times* (October 30, 1994): E4.

23. Cf. Karen V. Fernandez and John L. Lastovicka, "Making Magic: Fetishes in
Contemporary Consumption," *Journal of Consumer Research* 38, no. 2 (2011):
278–299.

24. E. J. Hamerman and G. V. Johar, "Conditioned Superstition: Desire for Control
and Consumer Brand Preferences," *Journal of Consumer Research* 40, no. 3
(2013), 428–443.

25. Molly O'Neill, "As Life Gets More Complex, Magic Casts a Wider Spell," *New
York Times* (June 13, 1994): A1.

26. Susannah Meadows, "Who's Afraid of the Big Bad Werewolf?," *Newsweek*
(August 26, 2002): 57.

27. Conrad Phillip Kottak, "Anthropological Analysis of Mass Enculturation,"
in Conrad P. Kottak, ed., *Researching American Culture* (Ann Arbor:
University of Michigan Press, 1982), 40–74; cf. also Teresa Davis and Olga
Kravets, "Bridges to Displaced Meaning: The Reinforcing Roles of Myth
and Marketing in Russian Vodka Labels," *Advances in Consumer Research*
32, no. 1 (2005): 480.

28. Eric Ransdell, "The Nike Story? Just Tell It!" *Fast Company* (January–
February 2000): 44.

29. Joseph Campbell, *Myths, Dreams, and Religion* (New York: E. P. Dutton, 1970).

30. Claude Lévi-Strauss, *Structural Anthropology* (Harmondsworth, England:
Peregrine, 1977).

31. Tina Lowrey and Cele C. Otnes, "Consumer Fairy Tales and the Perfect
Christmas," in Cele C. Otnes and Tina M. Lowrey, eds., *Contemporary
Consumption Rituals: A Research Anthology* (Mahwah, NJ: Lawrence
Erlbaum, 2003).

32. "Wedding Dresses Fit for a (Disney) Princess," *CBS News*, http://www
.cbsnews.com/pictures/disney-princess-wedding-gowns, accessed April 22,
2015; Merissa Marr, "Fairy-Tale Wedding? Disney can Supply the Gown,"
Wall Street Journal (February 22, 2007): B1.

33. Elizabeth C. Hirschman, "Movies as Myths: An Interpretation of Motion
Picture Mythology," in Jean Umiker-Sebeok, ed., *Marketing and Semiotics:
New Directions in the Study of Signs for Sale* (Berlin: Mouton de Gruyter,
1987), 335–374.

34. See William Blake Tyrrell, "Star Trek as Myth and Television as
Mythmaker," in Jack Nachbar, Deborah Weiser, and John L. Wright, eds.,
The Popular Culture Reader (Bowling Green, OH: Bowling Green University
Press, 1978): 79–88.

35. Bernie Whalen, "Semiotics: An Art or Powerful Marketing Research Tool?"
Marketing News (May 13, 1983): 8.

36. Eduardo Porter, "New 'Got Milk?' TV Commercials Try to Entice Hispanic
Teenagers," *Wall Street Journal* (December 28, 2001), www.wsj.com, accessed December 28, 2001.

37. See Dennis W. Rook, "The Ritual Dimension of Consumer Behavior,"
Journal of Consumer Research 12 (December 1985): 251–264; Mary A.

Stansfield Tetreault and Robert E. Kleine, III, "Ritual, Ritualized Behavior,
and Habit: Refinements and Extensions of the Consumption Ritual
Construct," in Marvin Goldberg, Gerald Gorn, and Richard W. Pollay, eds.,
Advances in Consumer Research 17 (Provo, UT: Association for Consumer
Research, 1990): 31–38.

38. Kathleen D. Vohs, Yajin Wang, Francesca Gino, and Michael I. Norton,
"Rituals Enhance Consumption," *Psychological Science* 24, no. 9 (2013):
1714–1721.

39. Deborah Ball, "British Drinkers of Guinness Say They'd Rather Take It
Slow," *Wall Street Journal* (May 22, 2003), www.wsj.com, accessed May
22, 2003.

40. For a study that looked specifically at rituals pertaining to birthday par-
ties, see Cele Otnes and Mary Ann McGrath, "Ritual Socialization and the
Children's Birthday Party: The Early Emergence of Gender Differences,"
Journal of Ritual Studies 8 (Winter 1994): 73–93.

41. Natalie Angier, "The Changing American Family," *New York Times*,
November 25, 2013, http://www.nytimes.com/2013/11/26/health/fami-
lies.html?_r=0, accessed February 20, 2015.

42. Ashley Hoffman, "I Now Present Mr. and Mrs. Jetson," *New York Times* (January
23, 2014), http://www.nytimes.com/2014/01/26/fashion/weddings/i-now-
present-mr-and-mrs-jetson.html, accessed February 23, 2015.

43. Jenn Grabenstetter, "The Bizarre Origins of 8 Wedding Traditions," *Mental
Floss* (June 23, 2008), http://mentalfloss.com/article/18915/bizarre-origins
-8-wedding-traditions, accessed April 23, 2015; "Against the Grain," Snopes
.com, http://www.snopes.com/critters/crusader/birdrice.asp, accessed
April 23, 2015.

44. Emily Shire, "5 Weirdest Naked College Traditions," *The Week* (September 27,
2013), http://theweek.com/articles/459469/5-weirdest-naked-college-
traditions, accessed April 22, 2015; Stan Beck and Jack Wilkinson, *College
Sports Traditions: Picking Up Butch, Silent Night, and Hundreds of Others*
(Lanham, MD: Scarecrow Press, 2013).

45. Nancy Keates and Charles Passy, "Tailgating, Inc.," *Wall Street Journal*
(August 29, 2003), www.wsj.com, accessed August 29, 2003; www.tail
gating.com, accessed April 24, 2015.

46. Karl Greenberg, "BBDO: Successful Brands Become Hard Habit for Consumers to Break," *Marketing Daily* (May 14, 2007), www.mediapost.com,
accessed May 14, 2007.

47. Virginia Postrel, "From Weddings to Football, the Value of Communal
Activities," *New York Times* (April 25, 2002), www.nytimes.com, accessed
April 25, 2002.

48. Paul Henry and Marylouise Caldwell, "Headbanging as Resistance or
Refuge: A Cathartic Account," *Consumption, Markets, and Culture*, 10 (June
2007): 159–174.

49. Dennis Rook, "The Ritual Dimension of Consumer Behavior," *Journal of
Consumer Research* 12 (1985): 251–264.

50. Cele C. Otnes, Behice Ece Ilhan, and Atul Anil Kulkarni, "The Language of
Marketplace Rituals: Implications for Customer Experience Management,"
Journal of Retailing 88 (2012): 367–383.

51. Dennis W. Rook and Sidney J. Levy, "Psychosocial Themes in Consumer
Grooming Rituals," in Richard P. Bagozzi and Alice M. Tybout, eds.,
Advances in Consumer Research 10 (Provo, UT: Association for Consumer
Research, 1983): 329–333.

52. Quoted in Andrew Adam Newman, "Depilatory Market Moves Far Beyond
the Short-Shorts Wearers," *New York Times* (September 14, 2007), www
.nytimes.com, accessed September 14, 2007.

53. Diane Barthel, *Putting on Appearances: Gender and Advertising* (Philadelphia:
Temple University Press, 1988).

54. Russell W. Belk, Melanie Wallendorf, and John F. Sherry, Jr., "The Sacred and
the Profane in Consumer Behavior: Theodicy on the Odyssey," *Journal of
Consumer Research* 16 (June 1989): 1–38; Jean-Sebastien Marcoux, "Escap-
ing the Gift Economy," *Journal of Consumer Research* 36, no. 4 (December
2009): 671–685.

55. Markus Giesler and Mali Pohlmann, "The Anthropology of File Sharing:
Consuming Napster as a Gift," in Punam Anand Keller and Dennis W.
Rook, eds., *Advances in Consumer Research* 30 (Provo, UT: Association for
Consumer Research 2003); Markus Giesler, "Consumer Gift Systems,"
Journal of Consumer Research 33, no. 2 (2006): 283.

56. Jill G. Klein and Tina M. Lowrey, "Giving and Receiving Humanity: Gifts
among Prisoners in Nazi Concentration Camps," *Advances in Consumer
Research* 33, no. 1 (2006): 659.

57. Suri Weisfeld-Spolter, Cindy B. Rippé, and Stephen Gould, "Impact of Giving on
Self and Impact of Self on Giving," *Psychology & Marketing* 32, no. 1 (2015):
1–14; Tina M. Lowrey, Cele C. Otnes, and Julie A. Ruth, "Social Influences on
Dyadic Giving over Time: A Taxonomy from the Giver's Perspective," *Journal of
Consumer Research* 30 (March 2004): 547–558; Russell W. Belk and Gregory
S. Coon, "Gift Giving as Agapic Love: An Alternative to the Exchange Paradigm
Based on Dating Experiences," *Journal of Consumer Research* 20 (December
1993): 393–417. See also Cele Otnes, Tina M. Lowrey, and Young Chan Kim,
"Gift Selection for Easy and Difficult Recipients: A Social Roles Interpretation,"

Journal of Consumer Research 20 (September 1993): 229–244; Burcak Ertimur and Ozlem Sandikci, "Giving Gold Jewelry and Coins as Gifts: The Interplay of Utilitarianism and Symbolism," *Advances in Consumer Research* 32, no. 1 (2005):322–327.

58. Monica Gonzales, "Before Mourning," *American Demographics* (April 1988): 19.

59. Alf Nucifora, "Tis the Season to Gift One's Best Clients," *Triangle Business Journal* (December 3, 1999): 14.

60. John F. Sherry, Jr., "Gift Giving in Anthropological Perspective," *Journal of Consumer Research* 10 (September 1983): 157–168.

61. Daniel Goleman, "What's Under the Tree? Clues to a Relationship," *New York Times* (December 19, 1989): C1; John F. Sherry, Jr., Mary Ann McGrath, and Sidney J. Levy, "The Dark Side of the Gift," *Journal of Business Research* (1993): 225–244.

62. Colin Camerer, "Gifts as Economics Signals and Social Symbols," *American Journal of Sociology* 94 (Supplement 1988): 5, 180–214; Robert T. Green and Dana L. Alden, "Functional Equivalence in Cross-Cultural Consumer Behavior: Gift Giving in Japan and the United States," *Psychology & Marketing* 5 (Summer 1988): 155–168; Hiroshi Tanaka and Miki Iwamura, "Gift Selection Strategy of Japanese Seasonal Gift Purchasers: An Explorative Study," paper presented at the Association for Consumer Research, Boston, October 1994; cf. also Tonya Williams Bradford, "Intergenerationally Gifted Asset Dispositions," *Journal of Consumer Research* 36 (June 2009): 93–111.

63. See, for example, Russell W. Belk, "Halloween: An Evolving American Consumption Ritual," in Richard Pollay, Gerald Gorn, and Marvin Goldberg, eds., *Advances in Consumer Research* 17 (Provo, UT: Association for Consumer Research, 1990): 508–517; Melanie Wallendorf and Eric J. Arnould, "We Gather Together: The Consumption Rituals of Thanksgiving Day," *Journal of Consumer Research* 18 (June 1991): 13–31.

64. Jennifer Booton, "Alibaba's 'Singles' Day' Sales Top $9 Billion, Bigger Than Black Friday," *Market Watch* (November 11, 2014), http://www.marketwatch.com/story/alibabas-singles-day-bigger-than-black-friday-2014-11-10, accessed April 24, 2015.

65. Bruno Bettelheim, *The Uses of Enchantment: The Meaning and Importance of Fairy Tales* (New York: Alfred A. Knopf, 1976).

66. Kenneth L. Woodward, "Christmas Wasn't Born Here, Just Invented," *Newsweek* (December 16, 1996): 71.

67. Aron O'Cass and Peter Clarke, "Dear Santa, Do You Have My Brand? A Study of the Brand Requests, Awareness and Request Styles at Christmas Time," *Journal of Consumer Behavior* 2 (September 2002): 37–53.

68. Theodore Caplow, Howard M. Bahr, Bruce A. Chadwick, Reuben Hill, and Margaret M. Williams, *Middletown Families: Fifty Years of Change and Continuity* (Minneapolis: University of Minnesota Press, 1982).

69. Sarah Halzack, "Shoppers to Spend $350 Million On Halloween Costumes This Year—For Their Pets," *The Washington Post* (October 29, 2014), http://www.washingtonpost.com/news/business/wp/2014/10/29/shoppers-to-spend-350-million-on-halloween-costumes-this-year-for-their-pets/, accessed April 24, 2015.

70. Angeline Close and George M. Zinkhan, "A Holiday Loved and Loathed: A Consumer Perspective of Valentine's Day," *Advances in Consumer Research* 33, no. 1 (2006): 356–365.

71. Arnold Van Gennep, *The Rites of Passage*, trans. Maika B. Vizedom and Shannon L. Caffee (London: Routledge & Kegan Paul, 1960; orig. published 1908); Michael R. Solomon and Punam Anand, "Ritual Costumes and Status Transition: The Female Business Suit as Totemic Emblem," in Elizabeth C. Hirschman and Morris Holbrook, eds., *Advances in Consumer Research* 12 (Washington, DC: Association for Consumer Research, 1995): 315–318.

72. Walter W. Whitaker, III, "The Contemporary American Funeral Ritual," in Ray B. Browne, ed., *Rites and Ceremonies in Popular Culture* (Bowling Green, OH: Bowling Green University Popular Press, 1980): 316–325. For an examination of funeral rituals, see Larry D. Compeau and Carolyn Nicholson, "Funerals: Emotional Rituals or Ritualistic Emotions," paper presented at the Association of Consumer Research, Boston, October 1994.

73. Samuel K. Bonsu and Russell W. Belk, "Do Not Go Cheaply into That Good Night: Death-Ritual Consumption in Asante, Ghana," *Journal of Consumer Research* 30 (June 2003): 41–55; cf. also Stephanie O'Donohoe and Darach Turley, "Till Death Do Us Part? Consumption and the Negotiation of Relationships Following a Bereavement," *Advances in Consumer Research* 32, no. 1 (2005): 625–626.

74. Barry Bearak, "Dead Join the Living in a Family Celebration," *New York Times* (September 5, 2010), http://nytimes.com/2010/09/06/world/africa/06madagascar.html?scp=2&sq=madagascar&st=cse, accessed April 28, 2011.

75. Natasha Singer, "Love in the Time of Twitter," *New York Times* (February 13, 2015), http://bits.blogs.nytimes.com/2015/02/13/love-in-the-times-of-twitter/?smid=nytcore-iphone-share&smprod=nytcore-iphone, accessed February 23, 2015.

76. Mark J. Miller, "Nike Pulls Tattoo-Inspired Line After Outcry from Samoan Community," *Brandchannel* (August 15, 2013), http://www.brandchannel.com/home/post/2013/08/15/Nike-Pulls-Tattoo-Line-081514.aspx, accessed February 16, 2015.

77. "Queen Prompts Thailand to Restrict 'Coyote Ugly' Dance Troupes," *New York Times* (December 28, 2006), www.nytimes.com, accessed December 28, 2006.

78. http://www.sportsmemorabilia.com/sports-memorabilia/football-game-used/, accessed April 23, 2015; J. C. Conklin, "Web Site Caters to Cowboy Fans by Selling Sweaty, Used Socks," *Wall Street Journal* (April 21, 2000), www.wsj.com, accessed April 21, 2000.

79. http://americanhistory.si.edu/press/fact-sheets/ruby-slippers, accessed April 23, 2015; George E. Newman, Gil Diesendruck, and Paul Bloom, "Celebrity Contagion and the Value of Objects," *Journal of Consumer Research* 38, no. 2 (August 2011): 215–228.

80. Dan L. Sherrell, Alvin C. Burns, and Melodie R. Phillips, "Fixed Consumption Behavior: The Case of Enduring Acquisition in a Product Category," in Robert L. King, ed., *Developments in Marketing Science* 14 (1991): 36–40.

81. Anne Underwood, "Hoarders Pack It In," *Newsweek* (July 26, 2004): 12.

82. Russell W. Belk, "Acquiring, Possessing, and Collecting: Fundamental Processes in Consumer Behavior," in Ronald F. Bush and Shelby D. Hunt, eds., *Marketing Theory: Philosophy of Science Perspectives* (Chicago: American Marketing Association, 1982): 85–90.

83. Ruth Ann Smith, *Collecting as Consumption: A Grounded Theory of Collecting Behavior* (unpublished manuscript, Virginia Polytechnic Institute and State University, 1994): 14.

84. For a discussion of these perspectives, see Smith, *Collecting as Consumption*.

85. John Branch, "Yankees Grass Is Now a Brand," *New York Times* (March 21, 2009), www.nytimes.com/2009/03/22/sports/baseball/22grass.html?scp=1&sq=Yankees%20Grass%20Is%20Now%20a%20Brand&st=cse, accessed March 21, 2009.

86. Kottak, "Anthropological Analysis of Mass Enculturation."

87. Joan Kron, *Home-Psych: The Social Psychology of Home and Decoration* (New York: Clarkson N. Potter, 1983); Gerry Pratt, "The House as an Expression of Social Worlds," in James S. Duncan, ed., *Housing and Identity: Cross-Cultural Perspectives* (London: Croom Helm, 1981): 135–179; Michael R. Solomon, "The Role of the Surrogate Consumer in Service Delivery," *Service Industries Journal* 7 (July 1987): 292–307.

88. Grant McCracken, "'Homeyness': A Cultural Account of One Constellation of Goods and Meanings," in Elizabeth C. Hirschman, ed., *Interpretive Consumer Research* (Provo, UT: Association for Consumer Research, 1989): 168–184.

89. Karen Mizoguchi, "Keeping Up with Kimye! Two Fans of Kim Kardashian and Kanye West Imitate the Fashion Icons by Posting Identical Outfit Pictures on Their Blog," *Daily Mail* (October 29, 2014), http://www.dailymail.co.uk/tvshowbiz/article-2813529/Kim-Kardashian-Kanye-West-fans-imitate-fashion-icons-posting-nearly-identical-outfit-pictures-blog.html#ixzz3Y9ppUNMY, accessed April 23, 2015; Always Elvis Fan Club, http://www.alwayselvisfanclub.com/about-alwayselvi.html, accessed April 23, 2015; Gregory E. Miller and Carrie Seim, "The 10 Most Rabid Celebrity Fan Groups Online," *New York Post* (March 4, 2014), http://nypost.com/2014/03/04/which-celebrity-has-the-craziest-fans-on-twitter/, accessed April 23, 2015.

90. Émile Durkheim, *The Elementary Forms of the Religious Life* (New York: Free Press, 1915).

91. Susan Birrell, "Sports as Ritual: Interpretations from Durkheim to Goffman," *Social Forces* 60, no. 2 (1981): 354–376; Daniel Q. Voigt, "American Sporting Rituals," in Browne, ed., *Rites and Ceremonies in Popular Culture*.

92. Ronald W. Pimentel and Kristy E. Reynolds, "A Model for Consumer Devotion: Affective Commitment with Proactive Sustaining Behaviors," *Academy of Marketing Science Review* 5 (2004): 1.

93. Mark A. Stein, "Block That Snack," *New York Times* (February 4, 2007): 2.

94. Dean MacCannell, *The Tourist: A New Theory of the Leisure Class* (New York: Shocken Books, 1976).

95. Belk et al., "The Sacred and the Profane in Consumer Behavior."

96. Beverly Gordon, "The Souvenir: Messenger of the Extraordinary," *Journal of Popular Culture* 20, no. 3 (1986): 135–146.

97. Belk et al., "The Sacred and the Profane in Consumer Behavior"; Amber M. Epp and Linda L. Price, "The Storied Life of Singularized Objects: Forces of Agency and Network Transformation," *Journal of Consumer Research* 36, no. 5 (2010): 820–837.

98. Güliz Ger and Olga Kravets, "Rediscovering Sacred Times in the Mundane: Tea Drinking in Turkey," *Consuming Routines: Rhythms, Ruptures, and the Temporalities of Consumption*, International Workshop, European University Institute, Florence, Italy, May 3–5, 2007; cf. also Güliz Ger, "Religion and Consumption: The Profane Sacred," *Advances in Consumer Research* 32, no. 1 (2005): 79–81.

99. Deborah Hofmann, "In Jewelry, Choices Sacred and Profane, Ancient and New," *New York Times* (May 7, 1989), www.nytimes.com, accessed October 11, 2007.

100. Lee Gomes, "Ramadan, a Month of Prayer, Takes on a Whole New Look," *Wall Street Journal* (December 4, 2002), www.wsj.com, accessed December 4, 2002.

101. http://store.nike.com/us/en_us/pw/mens-skateboarding-shoes/7puZbrkZ9yq, accessed April 23, 2015; Anthony Pappalarado, "Is This the End of the Skateshop?" *Ride* (November 13, 2014), http://theridechannel.com/features/2014/11/end-of-skateboard-shops, accessed April 23, 2015; Damien Cave, "Dogtown, U.S.A.," *New York Times* (June 12, 2005), www.nytimes.com, accessed June 12, 2005.

102. Emily Nelson, "Moistened Toilet Paper Wipes Out After Launch for Kimberly-Clark," *Wall Street Journal* (April 15, 2002), www.wsj.com, accessed April 15, 2002.

103. Robert Hof, "The Click Here Economy," *BusinessWeek* (June 22, 1998): 122–128.

104. Eric J. Arnould, "Toward a Broadened Theory of Preference Formation and the Diffusion of Innovations: Cases from Zinder Province, Niger Republic," *Journal of Consumer Research* 16 (September 1989): 239–267; Susan B. Kaiser, *The Social Psychology of Clothing* (New York: Macmillan, 1985); Thomas S. Robertson, *Innovative Behavior and Communication* (New York: Holt, Rinehart & Winston, 1971).

105. Susan L. Holak, Donald R. Lehmann, and Fareena Sultan, "The Role of Expectations in the Adoption of Innovative Consumer Durables: Some Preliminary Evidence," *Journal of Retailing* 63 (Fall 1987): 243–259.

106. Nick Bilton, "What's That on Beyoncé's Wrist? Let Me Guess ... an Apple Watch," *New York Times* (April 22, 2015), http://www.nytimes.com/2015/04/23/style/whats-that-on-beyonces-wrist-let-me-guess-an-apple-watch.html, accessed April 23, 2015.

107. Fred D. Davis, Richard P. Bagozzi, and Paul R. Warshaw, "User Acceptance of Computer Technology: A Comparison of Two Theoretical Models," *Management Science* 35 (1989): 982–1003; Viswanath Venkatesh and Hillol Bala, "Technology Acceptance Model 3 and a Research Agenda on Interventions," *Decision Sciences* 39, no. 2 (2008): 273–315.

108. "Trends in Japan," http://web-japan.org/trends/08_lifestyle/lif080707.html, accessed March 19, 2013.

109. Everett M. Rogers, *Diffusion of Innovations*, 3rd ed. (New York: Free Press, 1983).

110. Alex Williams, "The New Normal," *New York Times* (April 2, 2014), http://www.nytimes.com/2014/04/03/fashion/normcore-fashion-movement-or-massive-in-joke.html?src=dayp, accessed April 18, 2015.

111. Melanie Wallendorf, "The Formation of Aesthetic Criteria Through Social Structures and Social Institutions," in Jerry C. Olson, ed., *Advances in Consumer Research* 7 (Ann Arbor, MI: Association for Consumer Research, 1980): 3–6.

112. For more details, see Kaiser, *The Social Psychology of Clothing*; George B. Sproles, "Behavioral Science Theories of Fashion," in Michael R. Solomon, ed., *The Psychology of Fashion* (Lexington, MA: Lexington Books, 1985): 55–70.

113. C. R. Snyder and Howard L. Fromkin, *Uniqueness: The Human Pursuit of Difference* (New York: Plenum Press, 1980).

114. Linda Dyett, "Desperately Seeking Skin," *Psychology Today* (May–June 1996): 14; Alison Lurie, *The Language of Clothes* (New York: Random House, 1981). Note: Until recently, the study of fashion focused almost exclusively on women. Some researchers today also probe the meanings of the fashion system for men, but not nearly to the same extent. Cf., for example, Susan Kaiser, Michael Solomon, Janet Hethorn, Basil Englis, Van Dyk Lewis, and Wi-Suk Kwon, "Menswear, Fashion, and Subjectivity," paper presented in Special Session: Susan Kaiser, Michael Solomon, Janet Hethorn, and Basil Englis (Chairs), "What Do Men Want? Media Representations, Subjectivity, and Consumption," at the ACR Gender Conference, Edinburgh, Scotland, June 2006.

115. Harvey Leibenstein, *Beyond Economic Man: A New Foundation for Microeconomics* (Cambridge, MA: Harvard University Press, 1976).

116 Nara Schoenberg, "Goth Culture Moves into Mainstream," *Montgomery Advertiser* (January 19, 2003): 1G.

117. Georg Simmel, "Fashion," *International Quarterly* 10 (1904): 130–155.

118. Maureen Tkacik, "'Z' Zips into the Zeitgeist, Subbing for 'S' in Hot Slang," *Wall Street Journal* (January 4, 2003), www.wsj.com, accessed January 4, 2003; Tkacik, "Slang from the 'Hood Now Sells Toyz in Target," *Wall Street Journal* (December 30, 2002), http://www.ytlcommunity.com/-commnews/shownews.asp?newsid=5112, accessed September 13, 2011.

119. Silvia Bellezza and Anat Keinan, "Brand Tourists: How Non-Core Users Enhance the Brand Image by Eliciting Pride," *Journal of Consumer Research* 41, no. 2 (2014): 397–417.

120. Grant D. McCracken, "The Trickle-Down Theory Rehabilitated," in Michael R. Solomon, ed., *The Psychology of Fashion* (Lexington, MA: Lexington Books, 1985): 39–54.

121. Charles W. King, "Fashion Adoption: A Rebuttal to the 'Trickle-Down' Theory," in Stephen A. Greyser, ed., *Toward Scientific Marketing* (Chicago: American Marketing Association, 1963): 108–125.

122. Alf H. Walle, "Grassroots Innovation," *Marketing Insights* (Summer 1990): 44–51.

123. http://icanhas.cheezburger.com/tag/Memes, accessed April 23, 2015; Tracy Tuten and Michael R. Solomon, *Social Media Marketing* 2nd ed. (London: SAGE, 2015).

124. Ken Paulson, "Cost of Cashing in on Catchphrases," *USA Today* (February 2, 2015), http://www.usatoday.com/story/opinion/2015/02/02/taylor-swift-copyright-ken-paulson/22702801/, accessed April 23, 2015.

125. Robert V. Kozinets, "Fandoms' Menace/Pop Flows: Exploring the Metaphor of Entertainment as Recombinant/Memetic Engineering," *Association for Consumer Research* (October 1999). The new science of memetics, which tries to explain how beliefs gain acceptance and predict their progress, was spurred by Richard Dawkins who in the 1970s proposed culture as a Darwinian struggle among "memes" or mind viruses. See Geoffrey Cowley, "Viruses of the Mind: How Odd Ideas Survive," *Newsweek* (April 14, 1997): 14.

126. Malcolm Gladwell, *The Tipping Point* (New York: Little, Brown, 2000).

127. Timothy H. Evans, "The Ghosts in the Machine," *New York Times* (June 7, 2014), http://www.nytimes.com/2014/06/08/opinion/sunday/the-ghosts-in-the-machine.html?partner=rss&emc=rss, accessed February 22, 2015; Ollie McAteer, "Ghostly Sightings of Slender Man Reported in UK Town, *Metro* (January 25, 2015), http://metro.co.uk/2015/01/25/ghostly-sightings-of-slender-man-reported-in-uk-town-5035922/, accessed April 23, 2015.

128. "Cabbage-Hatched Plot Sucks in 24 Doll Fans," *New York Daily News* (December 1, 1983).

129. www.Zoobles.com, accessed June 23, 2011; Ann Zimmerman, "How Toy Crazes Are Born: Collectibles Are Designed to Be Cute, Numerous, Affordable and Just Rare Enough," *Wall Street Journal* (December 16, 2010), http://online.wsj.com/article/SB1000142405274870482810457602143043493792.html, accessed April 28, 2011; John Lippman, "Creating the Craze for Pokémon: Licensing Agent Bet on U.S. Kids," *Wall Street Journal* (August 16, 1999), www.wsj.com, accessed August 16, 1999; "Turtlemania," *The Economist* (April 21, 1990): 32.

130. Anthony Ramirez, "The Pedestrian Sneaker Makes a Comeback," *New York Times* (October 14, 1990): F17.

131. Madden, "Japan's Latest Fads—Marketable in U.S.?"

132. B. E. Aguirre, E. L. Quarantelli, and Jorge L. Mendoza, "The Collective Behavior of Fads: The Characteristics, Effects, and Career of Streaking," *American Sociological Review* (August 1989): 569.

133. Peter Gumbel, "Big Mac's Local Flavor," CNNmoney.com (May 2, 2008), http://money.cnn.com/2008/04/29/news/companies/big_macs_local.fortune/index.htm, accessed May 2, 2008; Geoffrey A. Fowler, "For Prosperity Burger, McDonald's Tailors Ads to Asian Tastes," *Wall Street Journal* (January 24, 2005), www.wsj.com, accessed January 24, 2005; Saritha Rai, "Tastes of India in U.S. Wrappers," *New York Times* (April 29, 2003), www.nytimes.com, accessed April 29, 2003; Gerard O'Dwyer, "McD's Cancels McAfrika Rollout," *Advertising Age* (September 9, 2002): 14; "McDonald's to Give $10 Million to Settle Vegetarian Lawsuit," *Wall Street Journal* (June 4, 2002), www.wsj.com, accessed June 4, 2002; "Packaging Draws Protest," *Marketing News* (July 4, 1994): 1.

134. Mariko Sanchanta and Yoree Koh, "Beefing Up McDonald's," *Wall Street Journal* (January 12, 2011), http://online.wsj.com/article/SB10001424052748703791904576075450692538030.html, accessed April 10, 2011.

135. "McCurrywurst Time in Germany," *Burger Business* (February 18, 2013), http://www.burgerbusiness.com/?p=13289, accessed February 20, 2013.

136. Mike Ives, "McDonald's Opens in Vietnam, Bringing Big Mac to Fans of Banh Mi," *New York Times* (February 7, 2014), http://www.nytimes.com/2014/02/08/business/international/mcdonalds-chooses-its-moment-in-vietnam.html, accessed February 21, 2015; Ariel Schwartz, "Chickileaks: McDonald's and a Strange Farm-Fresh Chicken Campaign in China," *Fast Company* (April 8, 2011), http://www.fastcompany.com/1745477/chickileaks-mcdonalds-and-strange-farm-fresh-chicken-campaign-china, accessed February 21, 2015.

137. Lian Zi, "Despite Sales Slump, Fast Food Moves Ahead in China," *ChinaDaily USA* (December 12, 2014), http://usa.chinadaily.com.cn/us/2014-12/12/content_19069145.htm, accessed April 24, 2015.

138. Russell W. Belk, "Hyperreality and Globalization: Culture in the Age of Ronald McDonald," *Journal of International Consumer Marketing* 8 (1995): 23–38.

139. "Coffee and Soft Drinks in China," *Facts and Details* (January 2014), http://factsanddetails.com/china/cat11/sub73/item1875.html, accessed April 24, 2015; Terry Lefton, "NBA Merchandise Sales Could Set Another Record," *Sports Business Journal* (October 20, 2014), http://www.sportsbusinessdaily.com/Journal/Issues/2014/10/20/In-Depth/Merchandise.aspx, accessed April 24, 2015; "British Drive In Movies," NBC.co.uk, http://www.vidsnet.com/nbc/watch.php?vid=10df4d623, accessed April 24, 2015; Monica Tan, "Kim Kardashian and Her Fans Defy Polite Society and the Sneers of the Elite," *The Guardian* (September 14, 2014), http://www.theguardian.com/lifeandstyle/australia-culture-blog/2014/sep/14/sass-meets-ass-kim-kardashian-goes-west-and-fans-turn-out-in-force, accessed April 24, 2015.

140. Alan Riding, "Only the French Elite Scorn Mickey's Debut," *New York Times* (April 13, 1992): A1.

141. Elisabeth Rosenthal, "Buicks, Starbucks and Fried Chicken. Still China?" *New York Times* (February 25, 2002), www.nytimes.com, accessed February 25, 2002.

142. Special Report, "Brands in an Age of Anti-Americanism," *BusinessWeek* (August 4, 2003): 69–76.

143. Lily Dong and Kelly Tian, "The Use of Western Brands in Asserting Chinese National Identity," *Journal of Consumer Research* 36 (October 2009): 504-523.

144. David Murphy, "Christmas's Commercial Side Makes Yuletide a Hit in China," *Wall Street Journal* (December 24, 2002), www.wsj.com, accessed December 24, 2002.

145. This example courtesy of Professor Russell Belk, University of Utah, personal communication, July 25, 1997.

146. James Hookway, "In Vietnam, Fast Food Acts Global, Tastes Local," *Wall Street Journal* (March 12, 2008), http://online.wsj.com/article/Sb12052 8509133029135.html?mod=mm_hs_marketing_strat,accessedMarch12, 2008.

147. Miriam Jordan, "India Decides to Put Its Own Spin on Popular Rock, Rap and Reggae," *Wall Street Journal* (January 5, 2000), www.wsj.com, accessed January 5, 2000; Rasul Bailay, "Coca-Cola Recruits Paraplegics for 'Cola War' in India," *Wall Street Journal* (June 10, 1997).

148. Rick Wartzman, "When You Translate 'Got Milk' for Latinos, What Do You Get?" *Wall Street Journal* (June 3, 1999).

149. Charles Newbery, "Coke Goes Native with New Soft Drink," *Advertising Age* (December 1, 2003): 34.

150. www.beinggirl.com/en_US/home.jsp, accessed June 25, 2009; Carol Hymowitz, "Marketers Focus More on Global 'Tribes' than on Nationalities," *Wall Street Journal* (December 10, 2007): B1.

151. Theodore Levitt, *The Marketing Imagination* (New York: Free Press, 1983).

152. Geoffrey A. Fowler, "Main Street, H.K.: Disney Localizes Mickey to Boost Its Hong Kong Theme Park," *Wall Street Journal* (January 23, 2008): B1; Merissa Marr, "Small World: Disney Rewrites Script to Win Fans in India; China, Latin America Are Also in Turnaround," *Wall Street Journal* (June 11, 2007): A1; Laura M. Holson, "The Feng Shui Kingdom," *New York Times* (April 25, 2005), www.nytimes.com, accessed April 25, 2005; Keith Bradsher, "Disneyland for Chinese Offers a Soup and Lands in a Stew," *New York Times* (June 17, 2005): A1; Paulo Prada and Bruce Orwall, "Disney's New French Theme Park Serves Wine—and Better Sausage," *Wall Street Journal* (March 12, 2002), www.wsj.com, accessed March 12, 2002.

153. Terry Clark, "International Marketing and National Character: A Review and Proposal for an Integrative Theory," *Journal of Marketing* 54 (October 1990): 66–79.

154. Geraldo Samor, Cecilie Rohwedder, and Ann Zimmerman, "Innocents Abroad? Walmart's Global Sales Rise as It Learns from Mistakes; No More Ice Skates in Mexico," *Wall Street Journal* (May 16, 2006): B1.

155. Marc Gobé, *Emotional Branding: The New Paradigm for Connecting Brands to People* (New York: Allworth Press, 2001).

156. Rachel Abrams, "Adapting Listerine to a Global Market," *New York Times* (September 12, 2014), http://www.nytimes.com/2014/09/13/business/adap ting-listerine-to-a-global-market.html?ref=international&_r=0, accessed February 21, 2015; Jeffrey Lin, "Cheetos Flavors from Around the World That Makes You Want to Give Up Your American Citizenship," *Foodamentals* (June 30, 2014), http://www.foodamentals.com/cheetos-flavors-from-around-the-world-that-makes-you-want-to-give-up-your-american-citizenship/, accessed April 24, 2015.

157. Shelly Reese, "Culture Shock," *Marketing Tools* (May 1998): 44–49; Steve Rivkin, "The Name Game Heats Up," *Marketing News* (April 22, 1996):

8; David A. Ricks, "Products That Crashed into the Language Barrier," *Business & Society Review* (Spring 1983): 46–50.

158. "Oh, Crap: Audi Mucks Up E-Tron Name in French, *AutoBlog* (September 13, 2010), http://www.autoblog.com/2010/09/13/oh-crap-audi-mucks-up-e-tron-name-in-french/, accessed February 21, 2015.

159. Kate MacArthur, "Kraft's Name Brings New Meaning to Snacking in Russia: Mondelēz International Comes Close to Local Translation for Oral Sex," *Advertising Age* (March 22, 2012), http://adage.com/article/global-news/kraft-s-close-russian-translation-oral-sex/233459/?utm_source=global_news&utm_medium=newsletter&utm_campaign=adage, accessed February 16, 2015.

160. Mark Lasswell, "Lost in Translation," *Business* (August 2004): 68–70.

161. For a case study that explores how the Guinness brand does this, cf. John Amis and Michael L. Silk, "Transnational Organization and Symbolic Production: Creating and Managing a Global Brand," *Consumption Markets & Culture* 13, no. 2 (2010): 159–179.

162. Martin McCarty, Martin I. Horn, Mary Kate Szenasy, and Jocelyn Feintuch, "An Exploratory Study of Consumer Style: Country Differences and International Segments," *Journal of Consumer Behaviour* 6, no. 1 (2007): 48.

163. Julie Skur Hill and Joseph M. Winski, "Goodbye Global Ads: Global Village Is Fantasy Land for Marketers," *Advertising Age* (November 16, 1987): 22.

164. Geert Hofstede, *Culture's Consequences: Comparing Values, Behaviors, Institutions, and Organizations across Nations* (Thousand Oaks, CA: Sage, 2001).

165. Geert Hofstede, Gert Jan Hofstede, Michael Minkov, "Cultures and Organizations, Software of the Mind", Third Revised Edition, McGrawHill 2010, ISBN 0-07-166418-1.Geert Hofstede B.V. quoted with permission.

166. Karen Page Winterich and Yinlong Zhang, "Accepting Inequality Deters Responsibility: How Power Distance Decreases Charitable Behavior," *Journal of Consumer Research* 41, no. 2 (2014): 274–293.

167. Quoted in Libby Garrett, "G&T Moments: Influencing Conservative Cultures," *Canvas 8*, August 2, 2012, http://www.canvas8.com/content/2012/08/02/safe-space-creativity-in-conservative-markets.html,accessed February 18, 2015.

168. Shahrzad Warkentin, "What Can We Learn from Coca-Cola's International Marketing Success? *Smartling* (December 18, 2014), https://www.smartling.com/2014/12/18/what-can-we-learn-from-coca-colas-global-marketing-success/, accessed April 24, 2015.

169. MTV Europe, personal communication, 1994; cf. also Dannie Kjeldgaard and Søren Askegaard, "Consuming Modernities: The Global Youth Segment as a Site of Consumption, *Advances in Consumer Research* 31 (2004): 104–105; Teresa J. Domzal and Jerome B. Kernan, "Mirror, Mirror: Some Postmodern Reflections on Global Advertising," *Journal of Advertising* 22 (December 1993): 1–20.

170. Douglas B. Holt, John A. Quelch, and Earl L. Taylor, "How Global Brands Compete," *Harvard Business Review* (September 2004): 68–75.

171. Calvin Sims, "For Chic's Sake, Japanese Women Parade to the Orthopedist," *New York Times* (November 26, 1999), www.nytimes.com, accessed November 26, 1999.

172. Luis Miguel Pereira and Juan Ignacio Gallard, *The Secrets of the Machine* (Prime Books 2014).

173. Suzanne Kapner, "U.S. TV Shows Losing Potency around World," *New York Times* (January 2, 2003), www.nytimes.com, accessed January 2, 2003; "Big Brother Nipple Sparks Outrage," *BBCNews* (September 10, 2004), www.bbcnews.com, accessed September 10, 2004.

174. Liz Gooch, "A Reality Show Where Islam Is the Biggest Star," *New York Times* (July 28, 2010), http://www.nytimes.com/2010/07/29/world/asia/29imam.html?scp=1&sq=islamic%20reality%20show&st=cse, accessed April 10, 2011.

SECTION 4   GOING GLOBAL WITH CAPABLE JUICE

BACKGROUND

You are the CMO (Chief Marketing Officer) for CAPABLE JUICE. CAPABLE JUICE is a company that sells a line of premium, all-natural juices. CAPABLE JUICE is marketed as a tasty beverage particularly well-suited for people who emphasize health and wellness in their lives. To date, your company has only sold in the United States, but you are now preparing to make your first expansion into a foreign market.

Previous research has narrowed the candidate countries down to three. Regardless of which country is selected, it has already been determined that CAPABLE JUICE will be sold to local distributors who will then be responsible for selling to local retailers and, ultimately, consumers. Your Chief Financial Officer (CFO) has provided you some preliminary financial information, and you have also been handed a report created from the 2014 GfK Consumer Trends Global Consumer Survey. This survey reports information about each country. Importantly, it dives deeper and also segments consumers by their relative income and occupational status. In the United States, income and occupation have been important characteristics to identify CAPABLE JUICE consumers.

YOUR GOAL

Review the data from the CFO and from the GfK consumer report. Then, make some preliminary financial estimates about the likely financial performance of CAPABLE JUICE. Based on your estimates, make some preliminary recommendations for CAPABLE JUICE's future international expansion.

THE DATA

- **About the data from the CFO:**
  - **PRICE:** The CFO has provided you with the assumed sale price per bottle of CAPABLE JUICE. The price has been adjusted into US dollars and is assumed to be constant for each of the three countries and for any quantity of CAPABLE JUICE that is sold.
  - **MARKET SIZE:** The CFO has asked you to assume that CAPABLE JUICE will account for a specific percentage of the foreign market after a single year. The market for a country is defined as the quantity of total fruit juices or fruit drinks sold in a given year.
- **About the GfK data:** The GfK Consumer Trends Global Survey is a large survey of many countries. Results for

each country are adjusted to be representative of the country's population that is 15 years or older. Each country has results for four different consumer segments from the combination of income (high/low) and occupation (white collar/other occupation).

- **Size (000s) of Group:** The estimated number of people (in thousands) who are in each segment of a country. This estimate uses the CIA Factbook's 2014 estimate of the number of 15+ year olds in each country as the base to determine the total estimated size of a group.

- **% Country:** The estimated % of the entire country that is comprised of people within a particular segment

- **% Group:** The "% Group" means the percentage of people within a segment who meet the criteria for a specific survey question

- **Personal Values, Health and Fitness:** The percentage of segment members who scored the 2 highest possible values on how important "health and fitness" were as part of their personal values.

- **Satisfaction with Primary Shopping Location: Availability of healthy foods and beverages:** The percentage of segment members who scored the 2 highest possible values on how satisfied they were with the availability of healthy foods/beverages.

- **Drink fruit juice daily:** The percentage of segment members who said they drink fruit juice "daily"

- **Drink Fruit juice weekly:** The percentage of segment members who said they drink fruit juice "weekly"

- **Drink fruit drinks daily:** The percentage of segment members who said they drink fruit drinks "daily"

- **Drink fruit drinks weekly:** The percentage of segment members who said they drink fruit drinks "weekly"

- **Regularly eat healthy, nutritious foods for: physical health:** The percentage of segment members who said this is a motivation to eat healthy foods.

- **Regularly eat healthy, nutritious foods for: mental/emotional health:** The percentage of segment members who said this is a motivation to eat healthy foods.

- **Regularly eat healthy, nutritious foods for: appearance:** The percentage of segment members who said this is a motivation to eat healthy foods.

	Country	GERMANY				UK				USA			
	Income Group	High		Medium		High		Medium		High		Medium	
	Occup. Group	White Collar	Blue Collar	White Collar	Blue Collar	White Collar	Blue Collar	White Collar	Blue Collar	White Collar	Blue Collar	White Collar	Blue Collar
Est. Population of Country 15+ years old (CIA Factbook, 2014)	(millions)	70.4				52.6				257.02			
Country Segment, % of Country	% of Group	3.9	2.1	16.2	11.7	9.7	4.0	9.3	9.3	7.5	3.7	9.2	7.2
Size of Group	(000s)	2,745.6	1,478.4	11,404.8	8,236.8	5,102.2	2,104.0	4,891.8	4,891.8	19,276.5	9,509.7	23,645.8	18,505.4
Personal Values: Health and Fitness	% of Group	59.7	60.3	54.0	52.4	47.0	55.5	36.1	44.8	60.0	49.0	44.4	54.7
Satisfaction with Primary Shopping Location: Availability of healthy foods and beverages	% of Group	87.7	66.0	75.3	77.5	75.1	71.5	66.6	75.2	77.2	75.4	72.6	68.6
Drink fruit juice daily	% of Group	17.3	20.4	17.0	11.6	32.1	35.2	22.2	24.2	36.1	18.5	20.5	26.8
Drink Fruit juice weekly	% of Group	38.9	43.3	39.3	31.8	35.3	39.9	33.9	43.1	29.0	32.3	39.8	38.9
Drink fruit drinks daily	% of Group	6.9	3.5	5.3	3.3	13.8	12.0	12.5	15.1	21.3	5.6	8.6	14.0
Drink fruit drinks weekly	% of Group	31.8	25.5	25.8	23.3	31.7	48.2	29.6	32.9	38.7	15.8	33.0	34.9
Regularly eat healthy, nutritious foods for: physical health	% of Group	55.8	62.8	51.5	49.2	61.0	75.3	49.7	54.3	70.0	66.0	60.8	49.0
Regularly eat healthy, nutritious foods for: mental/emotional health	% of Group	32.7	39.3	29.9	24.1	30.2	47.7	30.5	33.9	38.5	32.7	33.2	30.7
Regularly eat healthy, nutritious foods for: appearance	% of Group	46.4	33.5	37.2	35.8	29.3	45.7	40.7	37.0	50.8	31.7	39.4	34.7
CFO Data: Price per bottle to local distirbutors (US $)		$ 0.75	$ 0.75	$ 0.75	$ 0.75	$ 0.75	$ 0.75	$ 0.75	$ 0.75	$ 0.75	$ 0.75	$ 0.75	$ 0.75
Number of Daily Drinks in Segment (000s)		659.2											
Beverages sold per year to segment (000s)		240,614.8											
Estimated number of annual fruit juice/drink beverages consumed per year by segment member		87.64											
CFO Data: Estimated Market Share within Segment		10%											
Estimated Annual Sales (000s)		$18,046											
Estimates Sales per Consumer		$6.57											

Task 1: Understanding the Data

Before providing recommendations to the CFO, make sure you understand how to interpret the information presented in the table.

1 Which country has the segment with the fewest consumers in it?

2 Which country has the largest total number of potential consumers in it?

3 Find the country that has the consumer segment that makes up the largest percentage of its total amount of consumers. What is that percentage?

4 Which segment prioritizes physical appearance as a motivation for eating/drinking healthy?

5 Which segment prioritizes mental/emotional health as a motivation for eating/drinking healthy?

Task 2: Estimating Sales

Using some assumptions provided by the CFO, you are tasked with estimating the annual sales (in $) for each segment in each country. To do so, you will need to make the following assumptions:

- **Actual consumption:**

  - When someone says they drink juice or drinks fruit drinks "daily," we assume they actually have 0.7 of that drink on a typical day.

  - When someone says they drink juice of drinks fruit drinks "weekly," we assume they actually have 0.1 of that drink on a typical day.

  - For all other answers, we assume that they don't drink the beverage at all.

  - There are 365 days in a year.

- Using the data provided by GfK and the assumptions above, what are total estimated number of fruit drinks & juices (combined) that are estimated to be sold to consumers of each segment in a typical year (365 days)? The answers have been provided to you for the first column.

- **CALCULATION:**

- Estimated Units Sold Per Segment per Year =

  [(Segment Total Size) × (% daily drink) × (assumed daily consumption) + (Segment Total Size) × (% weekly drink) × (assumed daily consumption) + (Segment Total Size) × (% daily drink)*(assumed daily consumption) + (Segment Total Size) × (% weekly drink)*(assumed daily consumption)] × 365

- According to these estimates, how many beverages would we assume a typical person in each segment consumes per year?

- **CALCULATION:**

  - Average yearly consumption per consumer =

    [For each segment, take the answers immediately above]/[total size of segment]

Task 3: Estimating Sales

The CFO is impressed with your initial estimates. She would like you to go even further and estimate the total sales expected within each segment after one year. Again, the CFO has provided you with some important estimates to help you make your calculations.

- **Financial Assumptions:**

  - (1) The per unit price sold to distributors will be $0.75, regardless of country or quantity sold.

  - (2) The estimated market share for sales depends on how much a segment sees health and wellness as being essential to their lives. If healthy and wellness is a priority for a segment, the CFO assumes a 10% market share in that segment during the first year is reasonable. If health and wellness is not a major priority, the market share is assumed to only be 5%. Health and wellness is considered to not be a priority for a segment if less than 50% of the members of that segment identify it as a priority.

- **Question 1:** Using the GfK data and the information provided by the CFO, what is the estimated annual sales for each segment?

  - **CALCULATION:**

    - **Annual Sales $ estimated per segment =**

      [(Original Estimated Units Sold Per Segment per Year) × (Assumed Market Share, per CFO's rules) × (Price per unit to distributors)]

- **Question 2:** Which country, overall, has the highest estimated annual sales? Which country has the lowest estimated annual sales?

- **Question 3:** Based on these estimates, how much money per consumer would we expect for each segment?

DISCUSSION AND DEBATE:

1. Based solely on the information that was analyzed, which country do you think CAPABLE JUICE should expand to? Why?

2. While making its financial estimates, CAPABLE JUICE did not consider the impact of every GfK survey question reported in the table above. For example, CAPABLE JUICE did not consider if each segments' satisfaction with the availability of healthy foods and beverages at grocery stores might impact their market share within a given segment. From your perspective, how might CAPABLE JUICE incorporate the rest of the GfK information into their estimates? Which questions do you think may lead to you increasing or decreasing different estimates?

3. Think about other important consumer behavior factors that might impact the success of CAPABLE JUICE in a foreign market. What other important information do you think is pertinent for CAPABLE JUICE to know but was not present in the table above? Why?

 GfK Consumer Life (Roper Reports © Worldwide).

Sources of Secondary Data

Many organizations in the government and private sector collect information on consumer buying patterns. One good place to start is GfK, the international marketing research company that supplied data for the exercises in this book: www.gfk.com.

A selected list of other secondary data sources and indices that are particularly useful to consumer researchers follows. Many of these sources are available in the reference section of your library.

Commercial Sources

- *ABI/Inform Ondisc.* Ann Arbor, MI: University Microfilms International. These are abstracts (on compact disc) of articles from business journals.
- *Aging America: Trends and Projections.* Washington, DC, Government Printing Office: U.S. Senate Special Committee on Aging and the American Association of Retired Persons. This gives data on demographic characteristics and growth projections on the elderly over the next 30 years.
- *American Marketing Association International Directory & Marketing Services Guide.* Chicago: American Marketing Association. This complete directory of AMA members includes both individual and corporate listings and a guide to marketing research firms, by area of specialization (published annually).
- *Ipsos Reid Group Inc.* Many syndicated studies are available for purchase. The cost of the surveys depends on their age.
- *BAR/LNA Multi-Media Service.* New York: Leading National Advertisers. This is a listing of advertising expenditures for media and specific brands (updated quarterly).
- *Business Information Sources.* Berkeley: University of California Press. Listed are sources of information about market research and statistical data.
- *Business Periodicals Index.* New York: H.W. Wilson Company. This is an index of business periodicals (updated monthly).
- *Communication Abstracts.* Beverly Hills, CA: Sage Publications, Inc. This is an index of articles and books on topics related to advertising and marketing (published quarterly).
- *Directory of Online Databases.* Santa Monica, CA: Cuadra Associates, Inc. The directory lists databases that are accessible by computer.
- *Dissertation Abstracts International.* Ann Arbor, MI: University of Microfilms International. This is an index of doctoral dissertations, including relevant studies in the humanities and social sciences section, from major universities (updated monthly).
- *Encyclopedia of Information Systems and Services.* Detroit: Gale Research Company. The encyclopedia is a source of information about producers of various databases.
- *Financial Post Canadian Markets.* Toronto: Maclean-Hunter. Contains forecasts for consumer spending along with economic and demographic information.
- *FINDEX: The Directory of Market Research Reports, Studies, and Surveys.* Bethesda, MD: Cambridge Information Group. This international guide to reports is produced by research companies.
- *Guide to Consumer Markets.* New York: The Conference Board. Data on consumer spending and income is published (annually) in this guide.
- *Print Measurement Bureau Production Profile Guide.* This is product data in a two-year database from a sample of more than 20,000 respondents (1-800-PMB-0899).
- *Social Sciences Citation Index.* Philadelphia: Institute for Scientific Information. This is an index of articles in social science periodicals (updated three times a year).
- *Standard Directory of Advertisers.* Wilmette, IL: National Register Publishing Company. This directory is a guide ompanies whose advertising spending exceeds $75,000 and includes information such as their agencies, types of media used, and specific products advertised.

Academic, Industry, and Nonprofit Sources

Center for Mature Consumer Studies
College of Business Administration
Georgia State University
University Plaza
Atlanta, GA 30303
(404) 651-4177

The Conference Board
Consumer Research Center
845 Third Avenue
New York, NY 10022
(212) 759-0900

Marketing Science Institute
1000 Massachusetts Avenue
Cambridge, MA 02138–5396
(617) 491-2060

International Sources

Statistics Canada
R.H. Coats Building
Tunney's Pasture
Ottawa, ON K1A OT6
(613) 951-7277

The Roper Center for Public Opinion Research
P.O. Box 440
Storrs, CT 06268
(203) 486-4440

Center for International Research
U.S. Bureau of the Census
Washington, DC 20233
(301) 763-4014

Population Institute
East-West Center
1777 East-West Road
Honolulu, HI 96848
(808) 944-7450

European Society for Opinion and Marketing
Research (ESOMAR)
Central Secretariat
J.J. Viottastraat 29
1071 JP Amsterdam
Netherlands
31-20-664-21-41

Euromonitor
87–88 Turnmill Street
London ECIM 5QU
England
0171-251-8024

The European Community
2100 M Street, NW
Suite 707
Washington, DC 20037
(202) 862-9500

Latin American Demographic Centre (CELADE)
Casilla 91
Santiago, Chile
011-56-2-485051

The Organisation for Economic Co-operation and
Development
2001 L Street, NW
Suite 700
Washington, DC
20036-4905

Population Reference Bureau, Inc.
1875 Connecticut Avenue, NW
Suite 520
Washington, DC 20009
(212) 483-1100

United Nations
Public Inquiries Unit
Public Services Section
Department of Public Information
Room GA–057
New York, NY 10017

The World Bank
1818 H Street, NW
Washington, DC 20433
(202) 473-2943

Major Websites

- *www.orcinternational.com:* A commercial service that performs regular industry analyses and provides one-page industry profile summaries online
- *www.fuld.com:* A competitive intelligence service with corporate information online
- *www.marketingpower.com:* American Marketing Association
- *www.amic.com:* Advertising Media Internet Center; information about Internet commerce, a link to the Advertising

Research Foundation, a link to Georgia Tech Web-user survey, plus many more links

- *www.nielsen.com*
- *www.kpmg.com*
- *www.ipsos.com*

- *www.comscore.com:* The websites for research firms that sell summaries of reports on various topics
- *www.pantone.com*
- *www.strategicbusinessinsights.com*
- *www.visioncritical.com*

APPENDIX II

Careers in Consumer Research

An understanding of consumers is, of course, essential in virtually every aspect of marketing. To prepare for a career in a consumer-related field, consider getting involved in relevant research that one of your professors may be doing. In addition to your Consumer Behavior course, be sure to take as many courses as possible in other aspects of marketing. Also, try to achieve proficiency in statistics and computer skills. Courses in the social sciences, particularly psychology and sociology, are also helpful.

Career Paths

The following list identifies aspects of marketing where knowledge of consumer behavior is particularly valuable:

- *Marketing research:* Researchers define problems and collect information needed to resolve them. They typically design projects, analyze data, present findings, and make recommendations to management. Researchers may be employed by corporations that maintain their own market research staffs, or they may work for independent market research firms, trade organizations, advertising agencies, the government, or nonprofit organizations.
- *Brand management:* Managers oversee and direct marketing efforts for a specific product or line of products. They oversee all aspects of product strategy, including research, packaging, sales, promotion, and forecasting.
- *Customer affairs:* A customer affairs representative acts as a liaison between the firm and its customers. He or she handles complaints and may act as an advocate for the customer within the company.
- *Global marketing:* As firms globalize their operations they need managers who understand the importance of cultural differences and who can adapt strategies to foreign markets.
- *Advertising copywriters:* Copywriters translate a brand's positioning strategy into concrete form by creating words and visual images that convey this imagery. They need to understand the target market to employ imagery that will create the desired response.

- *Advertising account executives:* An account executive supervises the development of a marketing plan and makes sure that the agency's clients understand and are happy with the plan. This job requires knowledge about all aspects of marketing, including an understanding of target markets.
- *Retail managers and merchandisers:* A department or store manager must make decisions about such factors as the store's sales force and how merchandise is displayed in the store. He or she must understand the factors that add to or subtract from the quality of the customer's experience while in the store.
- *Retail buyers:* A buyer purchases merchandise for a store. A good buyer is always "tuned in" to upcoming trends and fashions and is sensitive to the wants and needs of the store's clientele.
- *Public relations:* A public relations specialist is responsible for maintaining positive public awareness of the firm and minimizing negative reactions to company activities. Knowledge of how people's perceptions are influenced by the media is integral to this job.

The Industry Route

Many entry-level jobs are available to a competent person with a bachelor's degree (though in some fields it is increasingly difficult to get hired without at least a master's degree). A typical starting position for a university graduate in a marketing research firm, for example, would be as an assistant project manager. This person assists in the design and administration of studies and ensures that they are enacted within the prescribed budget. The beginner may also be assigned to supervise field operations, overseeing the actual collection of data and perhaps coding and analyzing it.

Over time the person would move up to a supervisory position with increasing responsibility. Eventually the person might attain the position of vice-president of marketing research, where he or she would be responsible for the entire company's marketing research efforts and be part of senior management. Chances of moving up tend to improve greatly if the individual received advanced training in statistics, experimental design, and other aspects of consumer psychology.

The Academic Route

Another alternative is to consider training to become a scholar in the field of consumer behavior. Many major business schools offer doctoral programs in marketing in which it is possible to specialize in consumer behavior research. In addition, some psychology departments offer doctoral programs in consumer psychology. The typical doctoral program involves from four to seven years of intensive study, during which the student is trained in both theoretical and technical aspects of consumer research. Many doctoral students in business have already earned an M.B.A., though this is not always the case.

Most consumer behavior Ph.D.s who did not obtain their degrees in marketing were trained in psychology. Other possible fields of study—as the discipline's perspective continues to widen—are sociology, anthropology, economics, history, English, human ecology, and others.

These individuals may take faculty positions in a business school, where they conduct research that is published in such academic journals as the *Journal of Consumer Research*. They may also work as consultants to corporations, advertising agencies, and the government. Also, those with Ph.D.s are in demand for full-time non-academic positions, such as in consulting firms and "think tanks," or in advertising agencies, manufacturing companies, trade groups (e.g., the Wool Bureau or the Conference Board), or government agencies.

For further insight on these possibilities, consider asking your professor about his or her educational background and research activities.

GLOSSARY

ABC model of attitudes a multidimensional perspective stating that attitudes are jointly defined by affect, behavior, and cognition

Absolute threshold the minimum amount of stimulation that can be detected on a given sensory channel

Acceptance cycles a way to differentiate among fashions in terms of their longevity

Accommodative purchase decision the process of using bargaining, coercion, compromise, and the wielding of power to achieve agreement among group members who have different preferences or priorities

Acculturation the process of learning the beliefs and behaviors endorsed by another culture

Acculturation agents friends, family, local businesses, and other reference groups that facilitate the learning of cultural norms

Activation models of memory approaches to memory stressing different levels of processing that occur and activate some aspects of memory rather than others, depending on the nature of the processing task

Activity stores a retailing concept that lets consumers participate in the production of the products or services being sold in the store

Actual self a person's realistic appraisal of his or her qualities

Adaptation the process that occurs when a sensation becomes so familiar that it no longer commands attention

Advergaming online games merged with interactive advertisements that let companies target specific types of consumers

Advertising wear-out the condition that occurs when consumers become so used to hearing or seeing a marketing stimulus that they no longer pay attention to it

Affect the way a consumer feels about an attitude object

Affluenza well-off consumers who are stressed or unhappy despite of, or even because of, their wealth

Age cohort a group of consumers of approximately the same age who have undergone similar experiences

Agentic goals an emphasis on self-assertion and mastery, often associated with traditional male gender roles

AIOs (activities, interests, and opinions) the psychographic variables researchers use to group consumers

Allegory a story told about an abstract trait or concept that has been personified as a person, animal, or vegetable

Alternate-reality game (ARG) an application that blends online and offline clues and encourages players to collaborate to solve a puzzle

Ambicultural an identity that is a mixture of two subcultures

Androgyny the possession of both masculine and feminine traits

Anthropomorphism the tendency to attribute human characteristics to objects or animals

Antibrand communities groups of consumers who share a common disdain for a celebrity, store, or brand

Anticonsumption the actions taken by consumers involving the deliberate defacement or mutilation of products

Antifestival an event that distorts the symbols associated with other holidays

Approach–approach conflict a person must choose between two desirable alternatives

Approach–avoidance conflict a person desires a goal but wishes to avoid it at the same time

Archetypes a universally shared idea or behavior pattern, central to Carl Jung's conception of personality; archetypes involve themes—such as birth, death, or the devil—that appear frequently in myths, stories, and dreams

Art product a creation viewed primarily as an object of aesthetic contemplation without any functional value

Aspirational reference group high-profile athletes and celebrities used in marketing efforts to promote a product

Associative network a memory system that organizes individual units of information according to some set of relationships; may include such concepts as brands, manufacturers, and stores

Asynchronous interactions message posts that don't require all participants to respond immediately

Atmospherics the use of space and physical features in store design to evoke certain effects in buyers

Attention the assignment of processing activity to selected stimuli

Attitude a lasting, general evaluation of people (including oneself), objects, or issues

Attitude accessibility perspective an attitude will guide the evaluation of the object but *only* if a person's memory activates it when she encounters the object

Attitude models frameworks that identify specific components and combine them to predict a consumer's overall attitude toward a product or brand

Attitude object (A_o) anything toward which one has an attitude

Attitude toward the act of buying (A_{act}) the perceived consequences of a purchase

Audio watermarking a technique where composers and producers weave a distinctive sound/motif into a piece of music that sticks in people's minds over time

Augmented reality technology applications that layer digital information over a physical space to add additional information for users

Automated attention analysis (AAA) the automated recording of how long people look at images, words, people, places, and products, if their pupils dilate, how their heads and postures change, how fast they blink, and what emotions they show

Autonomic decision when one family member chooses a product for the whole family

Avoidance-avoidance conflict a choice situation where both alternatives are undesirable

Avoidance groups reference groups that exert a negative influence on individuals because they are motivated to distance themselves from group members

B2C e-commerce businesses selling to consumers through electronic marketing

Baby Boomer a large cohort of people born between the years of 1946 and 1964 who are the source of many important cultural and economic changes

Back-translation A technique in which a different interpreter retranslates a translated ad back into its original language to catch errors

Badges evidence of some achievement consumers display either in the physical world or on social platforms

Balance theory a theory that considers relations among elements a person might perceive as belonging together, and people's tendency to change relations among elements to make them consistent or "balanced"

Basking in reflected glory the practice of publicizing connections with successful people or organizations to enhance one's own standing

Beacons devices in a retail environment that communicate with shoppers' phones as they walk through the aisles

Behavior a consumer's actions with regard to an attitude object

Behavioral economics the study of the behavioral determinants of economic decisions

Behavioral learning theories the perspectives on learning that assume that learning takes place as the result of responses to external events

Being space a retail environment that resembles a residential living room where customers are encouraged to congregate

Belief systems a person's underlying beliefs; the extent to which people share a belief system is a function of individual, social, and cultural forces. Believers tend to be exposed to information that supports their beliefs.

Big Data the collection and analysis of extremely large datasets to identify patterns of behavior in a group of consumers

Big Five a set of five dimensions that form the basis of personality: openness to experience, conscientiousness, extroversion, agreeableness, and neuroticism

Binary opposition a defining structural characteristic of many myths in which two opposing ends of some dimension are represented (e.g., good versus evil, nature versus technology)

Bioterrorism a strategy to disrupt the nation's food supply with the aim of creating economic havoc

Bitcoin an online currency system that uses peer-to-peer technology and does not coordinate with any central authority or banks

Body image a consumer's subjective evaluation of his or her physical self

Body image distortions psychological disorders that cause the patient to believe that

his or her body is bigger or smaller than others see it

Boomerang kids grown children who return to their parents' home to live

Botnets a set of computers that are penetrated by malicious software known as *malware* that allows an external agent to control their actions

Bounded rationality a concept in behavioral economics that states because we rarely have the resources (especially the time) to weigh every possible factor into a decision, we settle for a solution that is just good enough

Bottom of the pyramid the huge number of consumers around the world who have low incomes

Brand arrogance a type of brand personality that conveys a sense of smugness or superiority

Brand community a set of consumers who share a set of social relationships based on usage or interest in a product

Brand equity a brand that has strong positive associations in a consumer's memory and commands a lot of loyalty as a result

Brand immigrants noncore users who try to claim membership within a community of users

Brand loyalty repeat purchasing behavior that reflects a conscious decision to continue buying the same brand

Brand personality a set of traits people attribute to a product as if it were a person

Brand prominence the display of blatant status symbols to ensure that others recognize one's luxury brands

Brand storytelling a marketing communications approach that emphasizes the importance of giving a product a rich background to involve customers in its history or experience.

Brand tourists noncore users who buy the brand but who do not seek admittance into a community of users

Brandfests a corporate-sponsored event intended to promote strong brand loyalty among customers

BRIC nation the bloc of nations with rapid economic development: Brazil, Russia, India, and China

Bromance a relationship characterized by strong affection between two straight males

Business ethics rules of conduct that guide actions in the marketplace

Business-to-business (B2B) e-commerce Internet interactions between two or more businesses or organizations

Business-to-business (B2B) marketers specialists in meeting the needs of organizations such as corporations, government agencies, hospitals, and retailers

Buyclass theory of purchasing a framework that characterizes organizational buying decisions in terms of how much cognitive effort is involved in making a decision

Buying center the part of an organization charged with making purchasing decisions

Buzz marketing messages that consumers perceive to be authentic and consumer generated

C2C e-commerce consumer-to-consumer activity through the Internet

Category exemplars brands that are particularly relevant examples of a broader classification

Cause marketing a strategy that aligns a company or brand with a cause to generate business and societal benefits

Celebrity endorsements a communications tactic whereby an organization retains a well-known person to tout a product or cause on its behalf

CEO pay ratio a ratio that compares the salary of a company's chief executive to the earnings of a typical employee

Chavs British term that refers to young, lower-class men and women who mix flashy brands and accessories from big names such as Burberry with track suits

Chunking a process in which information is stored by combining small pieces of information into larger ones

Classic a fashion with an extremely long acceptance cycle

Classical conditioning the learning that occurs when a stimulus eliciting a response is paired with another stimulus that initially does not elicit a response on its own but will cause a similar response over time because of its association with the first stimulus

Closure principle the *Gestalt* principle that describes a person's tendency to supply missing information to perceive a holistic image

Co-branding strategies linking products together to create a more desirable connotation in consumer minds

Co-consumers other patrons in a consumer setting

Co-creation involving consumers in the process of developing advertising and other marketing actions

Codes the ways members of a shared culture express and interpret meanings

Coercive power influence over another person because of social or physical intimidation cohesiveness

Cognition the beliefs a consumer has about an attitude object

Cognitive-affective model proposes that an emotional reaction is just the last step in a series of cognitive processes that follows sensory recognition of a stimulus and retrieval of information from memory that helps to categorize it.

Cognitive learning theory approaches that stress the importance of internal mental processes; this perspective views people as problem solvers who actively use information from the world around them to master their environment

Cohabitate people who live together without being married

Collaborative consumption a term to describe the new sharing economy, where people rent or barter what they need rather than buying it

Collecting the systematic acquisition of a particular object or set of objects

Collective decision making situations in which more than one person chooses the products or services that multiple consumers use

Collective self a process of self-definition whereby an individual's identity is largely derived from his or her group memberships

Collective value creation the process whereby brand community members work together to develop better ways to use and customize products

College wage premium the gap between what workers with a college degree earn compared with those without one

Color forecasts predictions that manufacturers and retailers buy so they can be sure they stock up on the next hot hue

Communal goals an emphasis on affiliation and the fostering of harmonious relations, often associated with traditional female gender roles

Communications model a framework specifying that a number of elements are necessary for communication to be achieved, including a source, message, medium, receivers, and feedback

Comparative advertising a strategy in which a message compares two or more specifically named or recognizably presented brands and makes a comparison of them in terms of one or more specific attributes

Compatibility in the context of diffusion of innovations, the extent to which a new product fits with a consumer's preexisting lifestyle

Compensatory consumption product choice driven by a threat to the self-concept

Compensatory rules a set of rules that allows information about attributes of competing products to be averaged in some way; poor standing on one attribute can potentially be offset by good standing on another

Complexity in the context of diffusion of innovation, the extent to which a new product is difficult to use or to integrate into a person's daily life

Compliance belief that we form an attitude because it helps us to gain rewards or avoid punishment

Compulsive consumption the process of repetitive, often excessive, shopping used to relieve tension, anxiety, depression, or boredom

Conditioned response (CR) a response to a conditioned stimulus caused by the learning of an association between a conditioned stimulus (CS) and an unconditioned stimulus (UCS)

Conditioned stimulus (CS) a stimulus that produces a learned reaction through association over time

Conditioned superstition consumers who don't feel they have control over their outcomes come to associate a product that is paired with a reward with the outcome itself

Conformity a change in beliefs or actions as a reaction to real or imagined group pressure

Conjunctive rule the decision maker establishes cut-offs for each attribute and chooses a brand if it meets all the cutoffs, but rejects a brand that fails to meet any one cut-off

Connexity a lifestyle term coined by the advertising agency Saatchi & Saatchi to describe young consumers who place high value on being both footloose and connected

Conscientious consumerism a new value that combines a focus on personal health with a concern for global health

Consensual purchase decision a decision in which the group agrees on the desired purchase and differs only in terms of how it will be achieved

Consideration set the products a consumer actually deliberates about choosing

Conspicuous consumption the purchase and prominent display of luxury goods to provide evidence of a consumer's ability to afford them

Constructive processing a thought process in which a person evaluates the effort he or she will need to make a particular choice, and then tailors the amount of cognitive "effort" expended to make this decision

Consumed consumers those people who are used or exploited, whether willingly or not, for commercial gain in the marketplace

Consumer a person who identifies a need or desire, makes a purchase, or disposes of the product

Consumer addiction a physiological or psychological dependency on products or services

Consumer behavior the processes involved when individuals or groups select, purchase, use, or dispose of products, services, ideas, or experiences to satisfy needs and desires

Consumer confidence the extent to which people are optimistic or pessimistic about the future health of the economy

Consumer confusion in legal contexts, the likelihood that one company's logo, product design, or package is so similar to another that the typical shopper would mistake one for the other

Consumer culture theory (CCT) the study of consumption from a cultural perspective rather than a psychological or economic focus

Consumer fairy tales stories that consumers create involving products that help them to overcome villains and obstacles

Consumer hyperchoice the profusion of options in the modern marketplace that forces us to make repeated decisions that may drain psychological energy while decreasing our abilities to make smart choices

Consumer identity renaissance the redefinition process people undergo when they retire

Consumer satisfaction/dissatisfaction (CS/D) the overall attitude a person has about a product after it has been purchased

Consumer socialization the process by which people acquire skills that enable them to function in the marketplace

Consumerspace marketing environment where customers act as partners with companies to decide what the marketplace will offer

Consumer style a pattern of behaviors, attitudes, and opinions that influences all of a person's consumption activities—including attitudes toward advertising, preferred channels of information and purchase, brand loyalty, and price consciousness

Consumption communities Web groups where members share views and product recommendations online

Consumption constellation a set of products and activities used by consumers to define, communicate, and perform social roles

Consumption situation includes a buyer, a seller, and a product or service—but also many other factors, such as the reason we want to make a purchase and how the physical environment makes us feel

Contamination when a place or object takes on sacred qualities because of its association with another sacred person or event

Contemporary Young Mainstream Female Achievers (CYMFA) modern women who assume multiple roles

Context effects subtle cues in the environment that influence a person's decisions

Continuous innovation a modification of an existing product

Contrast stimuli that differ from others around them

Conventions norms that regulate how we conduct our everyday lives

Cooptation a cultural process by which the original meanings of a product or other symbol associated with a subculture are modified by members of mainstream culture

Core values common general values held by a culture

Corporate social responsibility (CSR) processes that encourage the organization to make a positive impact on the various stakeholders in its community including consumers, employees, and the environment

Corrective advertising messages an organization releases (voluntarily or not) that inform consumers of previous messages that were inaccurate or misleading

Cosmopolitanism a cultural value that emphasizes being open to the world and striving for diverse experiences

Cosplay a form of performance art in which participants wear elaborate costumes that represent a virtual world avatar or other fictional character

Cougars older women who date younger men

Counteractive construal exaggerating the negative aspects of behaviors that will impede the attainment of a goal as a strategy to avoid them and reach the goal

Counterarguing the tendency for consumers to think of reasons why they should not believe a message

Counterfeiting companies or individuals sell fake versions of real products

Country of origin (COO) original country from which a product is produced; it can be an important piece of information in the decision-making process

Covariation assumed associations among events that may or may not actually influence one another

Craft product a creation valued because of the beauty with which it performs some function; this type of product tends to follow a formula that permits rapid production, and it is easier to understand than an art product

Credit score a measure of financial well being based upon a consumer's debt and payment histories

Creolization foreign influences are absorbed and integrated with local meanings

Crescive norms unspoken rules that govern social behavior

Crowdsourcing the growing practice of soliciting ideas for new products and even advertising campaigns from a user community

Cryptocurrency a system that relies upon encryption techniques rather than banks to regulate the generation of units of currency and verify the transfer of funds.

Cult products items that command fierce consumer loyalty and devotion

Cultural capital a set of distinctive and socially rare tastes and practices that admits a person into the realm of the upper class

Cultural formula a sequence of media events in which certain roles and props tend to occur consistently

Cultural gatekeepers individuals who are responsible for determining the types of messages and symbolism to which members of mass culture are exposed

Cultural selection the process by which some alternatives are selected over others by cultural gatekeepers

Culture the values, ethics, rituals, traditions, material objects, and services produced or valued by the members of a society

Culture jamming strategies that attempt to disrupt or satirize messages from corporations

Culture of participation the driving philosophy behind social media that includes a belief in democracy; the ability to freely interact with other people, companies, and organizations; open access to venues that allow users to share content from simple comments to reviews, ratings, photos, stories, and more; and the power to build on the content of others from your own unique point of view

Culture production system (CPS) the set of individuals and organizations responsible for creating and marketing a cultural product

Curation a source such as a store or a celebrity selects a set of products to simplify shoppers' decisions

Custom a norm that controls basic behaviors, such as division of labor in a household

Cyberbullying when one or more people post malicious comments online about someone else in a coordinated effort to harass him or her

Cybermediary intermediary that helps to filter and organize online market information so that consumers can identify and evaluate alternatives more efficiently

Dadvertising a new trend that depicts fathers as wise and benevolent in advertising

Database marketing tracking consumers' buying habits very closely, and then crafting products and messages tailored precisely to people's wants and needs based on this information

Decay structural changes in the brain produced by learning decrease over time

Deethnicization process whereby a product formerly associated with a specific ethnic group is detached from its roots and marketed to other subcultures

Default bias a tendency in decision making that makes it more likely for people to comply with a requirement than to make the effort not to comply

Deindividuation the process whereby individual identities get submerged within a group, reducing inhibitions against socially inappropriate behavior

Demographics the observable measurements of a population's characteristics, such as birthrate, age distribution, and income

Desacralization the process that occurs when a sacred item or symbol is removed from its special place, or is duplicated in mass quantities, and becomes profane as a result

Determinant attributes the attributes actually used to differentiate among choices

Differential threshold the ability of a sensory system to detect changes or differences among stimuli

Diffusion of innovations the process whereby a new product, service, or idea spreads through a population

Digital Divide the gulf between wealthy and poor people in terms of online access

Digital Native young people who have grown up with computers and mobile technology; multitaskers with cell phones, music downloads, and instant messaging on the Internet; people who are comfortable communicating online and by text and IM rather than by voice

Digital self elements of self-expression that relate to a person's online identity

Digital virtual consumption (DVC) purchases of virtual goods for use in online games and social communities

Digital wallets electronic devices that allow an individual to make e-commerce transactions

DINKS acronym for double income, no kids; a consumer segment with a lot of disposable income

Disclaimers content at the end of a commercial message that supplies additional information the advertiser is required to provide

Discontinuous innovation a new product or service that radically changes the way we live

Discretionary income the money available to a household over and above that required for necessities

Dispreferred marker effect the tendency to couch negative product reviews in softer terms to avoid looking harsh and judgmental

Dominance-submission hierarchy a "pecking order" within a culture that dictates which members are relatively higher in status than other members

Doppelgänger brand image a parody of a brand posted on a Web site that looks like the original but is in fact a critique of it

Dramaturgical perspective a view of consumer behavior that views people as actors who play different roles

Drive the desire to satisfy a biological need to reduce physiological arousal

Drive theory concept that focuses on biological needs that produce unpleasant states of arousal

Dyadic encounters relationships in which both parties must reach some agreement about the roles of each participant during a process of identity negotiation

Dynamically continuous innovation a significant change to an existing product

E-sports a growing activity that involves spectators who watch videogamers compete with one another

Early adopters people who are receptive to new products and adopt them relatively soon, though they are motivated more by social acceptance and being in style than by the desire to try risky new things

Echo Boomers people born between 1986 and 2002, also known as *Gen Y* and *Millennials*

Ecology the way members of a culture adapt to their physical habitat

Ego the system that mediates between the id and the superego

Ego-defensive function attitudes we form to protect ourselves either from external threats or internal feelings

80/20 rule a rule-of-thumb in volume segmentation, which says that about 20 percent of consumers in a product category (the heavy users) account for about 80 percent of sales

Elaborated codes the ways of expressing and interpreting meanings that are more complex and depend on a more sophisticated worldview, which tend to be used by the middle and upper classes

Elaboration likelihood model (ELM) the approach that one of two routes to persuasion (central versus peripheral) will be followed, depending on the personal relevance of a message; the route taken determines the relative importance of the message contents versus other characteristics, such as source attractiveness

Elaborative rehearsal a cognitive process that allows information to move from short-term memory into long-term memory by thinking about the meaning of a stimulus and relating it to other information already in memory

Elimination-by-aspects rule a rule that selects the brand that is the best on the most important attribute, but that imposes specific cut-offs or "must haves"

Embarrassment an emotion driven by a concern for what others think about us

Embeds tiny figures inserted into magazine advertising by using high-speed photography or airbrushing; these hidden figures, usually of a sexual nature, supposedly exert strong but unconscious influences on innocent readers

Embodied cognition the perspective that our behaviors and observations of what we do and buy shape our thoughts rather than vice versa

Emic perspective an approach to studying (or marketing to) cultures that stresses the unique aspects of each culture

Emotions intense affective reactions, such as happiness, anger, and fear

Emotional oracle effect a finding reported by researchers that people who trust their feelings are able to predict future events better than those who do not

Empty self a shift toward a greater focus on the self as traditional points of reference such as family and cultural traditions recede in importance

Enclothed cognition as a demonstration of the more general phenomenon of embodied cognition, the symbolic meaning of clothing changes how people behave

Encoding the process in which information from short-term memory enters into long-term memory in a recognizable form

Enculturation the process of learning the beliefs and behaviors endorsed by one's own culture

Endowment effect encouraging shoppers to touch a product encourages them to imagine they own it, and researchers know that people value things more highly if they own them

Endowed progress effect people are more motivated to attain a goal when they are provided with the illusion of a "head start" even though the actual effort required to reach the goal does not change

Envy a negative emotion associated with the desire to reduce the gap between oneself and someone who is superior on some dimension

Episodic memories memories that relate to personally relevant events; this tends to increase a person's motivation to retain these memories

Erogenous zones sexually arousing areas of the body

Etic perspective an approach to studying (or marketing to) cultures that stresses commonalities across cultures

Evaluations positive or negative reactions to events and objects that are not accompanied by high levels of physiological arousal

Evaluative criteria the dimensions used by consumers to compare competing product alternatives

Evoked set those products already in memory plus those prominent in the retail environment that are actively considered during a consumer's choice process

Exchange a transaction in which two or more organizations or people give and receive something of value

Executive control center the part of the brain that we use to make important decisions

Expectancy disconfirmation model states that we form beliefs about product performance based on prior experience with the product or communications about the product that imply a certain level of quality: (1) if something performs the way we thought it would, we may not think much about it; (2) if it fails to live up to expectations, this may create negative feelings; (3) if performance exceeds our initial expectations, we are satisfied

Expectancy theory the perspective that behavior is largely "pulled" by expectations of achieving desirable outcomes, or positive incentives, rather than "pushed" from within

Experiential hierarchy of effects an attitude is initially formed on the basis of a raw emotional reaction

Expert power influence over others as a result of specialized knowledge about a subject

Exposure an initial stage of perception during which some sensations come within range of consumers' sensory receptors

Extended family traditional family structure in which several generations live together

Extended self the external objects we consider a part of our self-identity

Extinction the process whereby a learned connection between a stimulus and response is eroded so that the response is no longer reinforced

Eyeball economy the argument that in today's media environment marketers compete for consumers' attention rather than their money

Fad a short-lived fashion

Family branding an application of stimulus generalization when a product capitalizes on the reputation of its manufacturer's name

Family financial officer (FFO) the individual in the family who is in charge of making financial decisions

Family identity the definition of a household by family members that it presents to members and to those outside the family unit

Family life cycle (FLC) a classification scheme that segments consumers in terms of changes in income and family composition and the changes in demands placed on this income

Fantasy a self-induced shift in consciousness, often focusing on some unattainable or improbable goal; sometimes fantasy is a way of compensating for a lack of external stimulation or for dissatisfaction with the actual self

Fashion the process of social diffusion by which a new style is adopted by some group(s) of consumers

Fashion system those people and organizations involved in creating symbolic meanings and transferring these meanings to cultural goods

Fatshionistas plus-sized consumers who are avidly interested in fashion and want more options from mainstream fashion marketers

Fattism a preference for thin people and/or discrimination against overweight people

Fear appeals an attempt to change attitudes or behavior through the use of threats or by highlighting negative consequences of noncompliance with the request

Fear of Missing Out (FOMO) a popular explanation for the addictive nature of social networks

Feature creep the tendency of manufacturers to add layers of complexity to products that make them harder to understand and use

Feedback loop a strategy to help a person regulate his or her behavior by providing information about his or her actions in real time, and then offering a chance to change those actions

Female-to-male earnings ratio is 0.78, which means that on average a woman earns 78 cents for every dollar a man brings home

Fertility rate a rate determined by the number of births per year per 1,000 women of childbearing age

Figure-ground principle the *Gestalt* principle whereby one part of a stimulus configuration dominates a situation whereas other aspects recede into the background

Fishbein Model a widely-used perspective that measures several attributes to determine a person's overall attitude

Fixed-interval reinforcement after a specified time period has passed, the first response an organism makes elicits a reward

Fixed-ratio reinforcement reinforcement occurs only after a fixed number of responses

Flaming a violation of digital etiquette when a post is written in all capital letters

Flow exchanges of resources, information, or influence among members of an online social network

Focus groups small set of consumers tries out a new product while being observed by company personnel

Follower brands brands that enter a market after another brand has already tested the waters

Food desert a geographic area where residents are unable to obtain adequate food and other products to maintain a healthy existence

Foot-in-the-door technique approach based on the observation that a consumer is more likely to comply with a request if he or she has first agreed to comply with a smaller request

Fortress brands brands that consumers closely link to rituals; this makes it unlikely they will be replaced

Framing a concept in behavioral economics that the way a problem is posed to consumers (especially in terms of gains or losses) influences the decision they make

Frequency marketing a marketing technique that reinforces regular purchasers by giving them prizes with values that increase along with the amount purchased

Frugalistas fashion-conscious consumers who pride themselves on achieving style on a limited budget

Frugality a personality trait that describes people who prioritize ways to save money

Functional theory of attitudes states that attitudes exist *because* they serve some function for the person; consumers who expect that they will need to deal with similar situations at a future time will be more likely to start to form an attitude in anticipation

Functionally illiterate a person whose reading skills are not adequate to carry out everyday tasks

Game platform an online interface that allows users to engage in games and other social activities with members of a community

Gamification the process of injecting gaming elements into tasks that might otherwise be boring or routine

Gemba Japanese term for the one true source of information

Gen X people born between 1965 and 1985

Gen Y people born between 1986 and 2002; also known as *Echo Boomers* and *Millennials*

Gen Z the age cohort born in the late 1990s to early 2000s

Gender-bending product a traditionally sex-typed item adapted to the opposite gender

Gender identity the elements of self-concept that reflect sex roles

Gender socialization elements of culture, including advertising, that provide guidelines regarding "appropriate" sex role behavior for members

Genre in the context of social gaming, the method of play such as simulation, action, and role-playing

Geodemography techniques that combine consumer demographic information with geographic consumption patterns to permit precise targeting of consumers with specific characteristics

Geospatial platforms online applications that use smartphones to identify consumers' physical locations

Gestalt meaning derived from the totality of a set of stimuli, rather than from any individual stimulus

Gestation the first stage of the gift-giving ritual where the giver procures an item to mark the event

Gift-giving ritual the events involved in the selection, presentation, acceptance, and interpretation of a gift

Glamping a new trend that combines camping with luxury travel

Global consumer culture a culture in which people around the world are united through their common devotion to brand name consumer goods, movie stars, celebrities, and leisure activities

Goal a consumer's desired end state

Golden triangle the portion of a Web site that a person's eyes naturally gravitate to first, which makes it more likely that search results located in that area will be seen

Green marketing a marketing strategy involving an emphasis on protecting the natural environment

Greenwashing inflated claims about a product's environmental benefits

Gripe sites Web sites that consumers create to share frustrations about bad experiences with companies

Grooming rituals sequences of behaviors that aid in the transition from the private self to the public self or back again

Group dieting online forums devoted to encouraging people to go on crash diets

Guerrilla marketing unconventional marketing campaigns that place unusual messages in places where consumers don't expect to encounter advertising.

Guilt an individual's unpleasant emotional state associated with possible objections to his or her actions, inaction, circumstances, or intentions

Gyges effect the anonymity of the Internet can cause otherwise moral people to experience a loss of inhibition and post things they would never say to a person in the real world

Habitual decision making choices made with little or no conscious effort

Habitus ways in which we classify experiences as a result of our socialization processes

Halal food and other products whose usage is permissible according to the laws of Islam

Halo effect a phenomenon that occurs when people react to other, similar stimuli in much the same way they respond to the original stimulus

Happiness a mental state of well-being characterized by positive emotions

Happiness economy an economy based upon well-being rather than material wealth

Haptic touch-related sensations

Haul videos a genre of YouTube video that consists of a shopper who describes in detail apparel he or she has just purchased

Heavy users a name companies use to identify their customers who consume their products in large volumes

Hedonic adaptation belief that to maintain a fairly stable level of happiness we tend to become used to positive and negative events in our lives

Hedonic consumption the multisensory, fantasy, and emotional aspects of consumers' interactions with products

Heuristics the mental rules of thumb that lead to a speedy decision

Hierarchy of effects a fixed sequence of steps that occurs during attitude formation; this sequence varies depending on such factors as the consumer's level of involvement with the attitude object

Hierarchy of Needs (Maslow's) a framework that specifies different levels of motives that depends on the consumer's personal situation

Hierogamy when physically attractive women "marry up"

High-context culture group members tend to be close-knit and are likely to infer meanings that go beyond the spoken word

High-involvement hierarchy the sequence of attitude formation when a person approaches a product decision as a problem-solving process.

Highlighting effect the order in which consumers learn about brands determines the strength of association between these brands and their attributes

Hispanic people whose geographic and/or cultural origins are in Latin American countries

Hoarding unsystematic acquisition of objects (in contrast to collecting)

Hofstede Dimensions of National Culture a measurement system that scores a country in terms of its standing on six dimensions so that users can compare and contrast values

Homeostasis a stable state of physiological arousal

Home shopping party a selling format where a company representative makes a sales presentation to a group of people who gather at the home of a friend or acquaintance

Homogamy the tendency for individuals to marry others similar to themselves

Homophily the degree to which a pair of individuals is similar in terms of education, social status, and beliefs

Hook an element in a title that increases the likelihood people will click on it

Horizontal revolution a fundamental change in how consumers communicate via social media, whereby information doesn't just flow from big companies and governments; information flows *across* people as well

Host culture a new culture to which a person must acculturate

Household according to the U.S. Census Bureau, an occupied housing unit

Humor appeals a marketing message that relies upon humor to sell a product

Hybrid ad a marketing communication that explicitly references the context (e.g., TV show) in which it appears

Hybrid products items that feature characteristics from two different product domains

Hype marketing messages that consumers perceive to be inauthentic and company generated

Hyperreality the becoming real of what is initially simulation or "hype"

Icon a sign that resembles the product in some way

Id the Freudian system oriented toward immediate gratification

Ideal of beauty a model, or exemplar, of appearance valued by a culture

Ideal self a person's conception of how he or she would like to be

Identification the process of forming an attitude to conform to another person's or group's expectations

Identity a component of self-concept

Identity marketing a practice whereby consumers are paid to alter some aspects of their selves to advertise for a branded product

Identity negotiation the process that occurs when both participants in an encounter reach agreement about the role of each person

Identity theft the unauthorized use of personal information

Ideology the mental characteristics of a people and the way they relate to their environment and social groups

IKEA effect the tendency for consumers to like products more when they are involved in building or assembling them

Imbibing idiot bias the assumption that people who drink alcohol are less intelligent

Implementation intentions "if-then" plans that may dictate how much weight we give to different kinds of information (emotional or cognitive), a timetable to carry out a decision, or even how we will deal with disruptive influences that might interfere with our plans

Impression management our efforts to "manage" what others think of us by strategically choosing clothing and other cues that will put us in a good light

Impulse buying a process that occurs when the consumer experiences a sudden urge to purchase an item that he or she cannot resist

Incidental brand exposure motives that can lurk beneath the surface and cues in the environment that can activate a goal even when we don't know it

Incidental learning unintentional acquisition of knowledge

Income inequality the extent to which resources are distributed unevenly within a population

Independence hypothesis argues that affect and cognition are separate systems so that it's not always necessary to have a cognition to elicit an emotional response.

Index a sign that is connected to a product because they share some property

Inertia the process whereby purchase decisions are made out of habit because the consumer lacks the motivation to consider alternatives

Influence impressions brand-specific mentions on social media posts

Influence network a two-way dialogue between participants in a social network and opinion leaders

Information cascades an online communication process where one piece of information triggers a sequence of interactions

Information power influence over others because of the possession of inside knowledge

Information search the process by which the consumer surveys his or her environment for appropriate data to make a reasonable decision

Innovation a product or style that is perceived as new by consumers

Innovators people who are always on the lookout for novel developments and will be the first to try a new offering

Instrumental conditioning also known as *operant conditioning*, occurs as the individual learns to perform behaviors that produce positive outcomes and avoid those that yield negative outcomes

Instrumental values goals endorsed because they are needed to achieve desired end states or terminal values

Intelligent agents software programs that learn from past user behavior to recommend new purchases

Interference one way that forgetting occurs; as additional information is learned, it displaces the previous information

Internalization deep-seated attitudes become part of our value system

Internet trolls people who experience a loss of inhibition and post things they would never say to a person in the real world

Interpretant the meaning derived from a sign or symbol

Interpretation the process whereby meanings are assigned to stimuli

Interpretivism as opposed to the dominant positivist perspective on consumer behavior, instead stresses the importance of symbolic, subjective experience and the idea that meaning is in the mind of the person rather than existing "out there" in the objective world

Intersex children children born with both genitals or ambiguous sex characteristics

Invidious distinction the use of status symbols to inspire envy in others through display of wealth or power

Involvement the motivation to process product-related information

Juggling lifestyle working mothers' attempts to compromise between conflicting cultural ideals of motherhood and professionalism

Just noticeable difference (JND) the minimum difference between two stimuli that can be detected by a perceiver

Kansei engineering a Japanese philosophy that translates customers' feelings into design elements

Kin-network system the rituals intended to maintain ties among family members, both immediate and extended

Knowledge bias the effectiveness of a source decreases because we question his or her knowledge about the topic

Knowledge function the process of forming an attitude to provide order, structure, or meaning

Knowledge structure organized system of concepts relating to brands, stores, and other concepts

Laddering a technique for uncovering consumers' associations between specific attributes and general values

Laggards consumers who are exceptionally slow to adopt innovations

Late adopters the majority of consumers who are moderately receptive to adopting innovations

Lateral cycling a process in which already-purchased objects are sold to others or exchanged for other items

Latitudes of acceptance and rejection in the social judgment theory of attitudes, the notion that people differ in terms of the information they will find acceptable or unacceptable; they form latitudes of acceptance and rejection around an attitude standard—ideas that fall within a latitude will be favorably received, but those falling outside of this zone will not

Leaderboards an element of game design that provides information about all participants' progress in the game

Learning a relatively permanent change in a behavior caused by experience

Legitimate power influence over others due to a position conferred by a society or organization

Leisure class wealthy people for whom work is a taboo

Lexicographic rule a simple rule that selects the brand that is the best on the most important attribute

Licensing popular marketing strategy that pays for the right to link a product or service to the name of a well-known brand or designer

Lifestyle a pattern of consumption that reflects a person's choices of how to spend his or her time and money

Lifestyle marketing perspective strategy based on the recognition that people sort themselves into groups on the basis of the things they like to do, how they like to spend their leisure time, and how they choose to spend their disposable income

Lifestyle segmentation typologies Research projects that cluster a large group of consumers into a set of distinct lifestyle groups

Linkbaiting in website design, the careful crafting of a title that markets the content

List of Values (LOV) scale identifies consumer segments based on the values members endorse and relates each value to differences in consumption behaviors

Locational privacy the extent to which a person's activities and movements in the physical world are tracked by his or her devices such as smartphones

Locavore a lifestyle that emphasizes the purchase of locally produced meat and vegetables

LOHAS an acronym for "lifestyles of health and sustainability"; a consumer segment that worries about the environment, wants products to be produced in a sustainable way, and spends money to advance what they see as their personal development and potential

Long tail states that we no longer need to rely solely on big hits (such as blockbuster movies or best-selling books) to find profits; instead, companies can also make money if they sell small amounts of items that only a few people want—if they sell enough different items

Long-term memory (LTM) the system that allows us to retain information for a long period of time

Look-alike packaging package designs that mimic the shapes and colors of well-known brands

Looking-glass self the process of imagining the reaction of others toward oneself

Loss aversion the tendency for people to hate losing things more than they like getting things

Lovemark a passionate commitment to a brand

Low-context culture in contrast to high-context cultures that have strong oral traditions and that are more sensitive to nuance, low-context cultures are more literal

Low-involvement hierarchy of effects the process of attitude formation for products or services that carry little risk or self-identity

Lurkers passive members of an online community who do not contribute to interactions

M-commerce the practice of promoting and selling goods and services via wireless devices including cell phones, PDAs, and iPods

M-PESA a mobile-phone-based money transfer service that is popular in parts of Africa

Market access the extent to which a consumer has the ability to find and purchase goods and services

Market beliefs common assumptions about relationships between product quality and other factors such as price

Market maven a person who often serves as a source of information about marketplace activities

Market segmentation strategies targeting a brand only to specific groups of consumers who share well-defined and relevant characteristics

Marketplace sentiments consumers' feelings about companies or market practices.

Martyrdom effect the tendency for people to donate more to a cause if they also have to sacrifice something or experience discomfort

Masculinism study devoted to the male image and the cultural meanings of masculinity

Mass class a term analysts use to describe the millions of global consumers who now enjoy a level of purchasing power that's sufficient to let them afford many high-quality products

Mass connectors highly influential members of social media networks

Mass customization the personalization of products and services for individual customers at a mass-production price

Materialism the importance consumers attach to worldly possessions

Material accumulation the instinct to earn more than we can possibly consume

Material parenting a style of raising children that involves giving and taking away of possessions to shape behavior

Maximizing solution the extensive cognitive decision strategies we use when we want to identify the best possible choice

Means–end chain model assumes that people link specific product attributes (indirectly) to terminal values such as freedom or safety

Media literacy a consumer's ability to access, analyze, evaluate, and communicate information

Media multiplexity in a social media context, when flows of communication go in many directions at any point in time and often on multiple platforms

Media snacker consumers who visit media venues about 27 times per nonworking hour—the equivalent of more than 13 times during a standard half-hour TV show

Medical tourism a rapidly growing sector of the global economy that encourages consumers to travel to other countries for surgical procedures that might be unavailable, more dangerous, or more expensive where they live

Medication adherence the extent to which people fill and actually take prescribed medicines

Meerkating the act of shooting a live video stream

Megachurches very large churches that serve between 2,000 and 20,000 congregants

Megacity a metropolitan area with a total population of more than 10 million people

Megaphone effect the ability of individual bloggers to share their opinions about products with large numbers of online followers

Membership reference group ordinary people whose consumption activities provide informational social influence

Meme theory a perspective that uses a medical metaphor to explain how an idea or product enters the consciousness of people over time, much like a virus

Memory a process of acquiring information and storing it over time so that it will be available when needed

Mental accounting principle that states that decisions are influenced by the way a problem is posed

Mental budgets consumers' preset expectations of how much they intend to spend on a shopping trip

Mere exposure phenomenon the tendency to like persons or things if we see them more often

Message involvement properties of the medium and message content that influence a person's degree of engagement with the message

Metaphor the use of an explicit comparison ("A" is "B") between a product and some other person, place, or thing

Microframe a period of notoriety due to a surge of interest on the Internet

Milieu in the context of social gaming, the visual nature of the game such as science fiction, fantasy, horror, and retro

Millennials people born between 1986 and 2002; also known as *Echo Boomers* and *Gen Y*

Minimal group paradigm the common finding that even when people are arbitrarily assigned to a group they tend to favor those who are placed in the same group

Minipreneurs one-person businesses

Minnesota Multiphasic Personality Inventory (MMPI) a widely used instrument to identify personality traits

Mixed emotions affect with positive and negative components

MMORPGs (massive multiplayer online role-playing games) online role-playing games that typically involve thousands of players

Mobile shopping apps smartphone applications that retailers provide to guide shoppers in stores and malls

Mode in the context of social gaming, the way players experience the game world

Modeling imitating the behavior of others

Modified rebuy in the context of the buyclass framework, a task that requires a modest amount of information search and evaluation, often focused on identifying the appropriate vendor

Moods temporary positive or negative affective states accompanied by moderate levels of arousal

Mood congruency the idea that our judgments tend to be shaped by our moods

More a custom with a strong moral overtone

Morning morality effect people are more likely to cheat, lie, or even commit fraud in the afternoon than in the morning.

Motivational research a qualitative research approach, based on psychoanalytic (Freudian) interpretations, with a heavy emphasis on unconscious motives for consumption

Multiattribute attitude models those models that assume a consumer's attitude (evaluation) of an attitude object depends on the beliefs he or she has about several or many attributes of the object; the use of a multiattribute model implies that an attitude toward a product or brand can be predicted by identifying these specific beliefs and combining them to derive a measure of the consumer's overall attitude

Multiple-intelligence theory a perspective that argues for other types of intelligence, such as athletic prowess or musical ability, beyond the traditional math and verbal skills psychologists use to measure IQ

Multitasking processing information from more than one medium at a time

Myers-Briggs Type Indicator a widely-used personality test based upon the work of Carl Jung

Myth a story containing symbolic elements that expresses the shared emotions and ideals of a culture

Nanoframe a very brief period of "buzz" about someone who posts online or who appears in an online video

Narrative product information in the form of a story

Narrative transportation the result of a highly involving message where people become immersed in the storyline

National character the belief that a country has a distinctive set of behavior and personality characteristics

Native advertising a new advertising strategy that focuses on digital messages designed to blend into the editorial content of the publications in which they appear

Natural user interface a philosophy of computer design that incorporates habitual human movements

Near field communication (NFC) technology that allows devices near to one another (like a smartphone and an NFC terminal in a store) to establish radio communication

Need a basic biological motive

Negative reinforcement the process whereby the environment weakens responses to stimuli so that inappropriate behavior is avoided

Negative state relief the view that helping others is a way to resolve one's own negative moods

Negative word-of-mouth consumers passing on negative experiences relating to products or services to other potential customers to influence others' choices

Net neutrality ensures that everyone—individual users and behemoth companies—is guaranteed equal access to the "pipes" we rely on to access cyberspace

Network effect each person who uses a product or service benefits as more people participate

Neuroendocrinological science the study of the potential role of hormonal influences on preferences for different kinds of products or people

Neuromarketing a new technique that uses a brain scanning device called *functional magnetic resonance imaging* (fMRI) that tracks blood flow as people perform mental tasks; scientists know that specific regions of the brain light up in these scans to show increased blood flow when a person recognizes a face, hears a song, makes a decision, senses deception, and so on; therefore, they are now trying to harness this technology to measure consumers' reactions to movie trailers, choices about automobiles, the appeal of a pretty face, and loyalty to specific brands

New task in the context of the buyclass framework, a task that requires a great degree of effort and information search

Nodes members of a social network connected to others via one or more shared relationships

Noncompensatory rules decision shortcuts a consumer makes when a product with a low standing on one attribute cannot make up for this position by being better on another attribute

Normative influence the process in which a reference group helps to set and enforce fundamental standards of conduct

Normcore a trend among young urbanites to forsake hipster styles like skinny jeans, wallet chains, and flannel shirts for bland, suburban attire

Norms the informal rules that govern what is right or wrong

Nostalgia a bittersweet emotion; the past is viewed with sadness and longing; many "classic" products appeal to consumers' memories of their younger days

Nouveau riches affluent consumers whose relatively recent acquisition of income rather than ancestry or breeding accounts for their enhanced social mobility

Nuclear family a contemporary living arrangement composed of a married couple and their children

Nudge a subtle change in a person's environment that results in a change in behavior

Object in semiotic terms, the product that is the focus of a message

Objectification when we attribute sacred qualities to mundane items

Observability in the context of diffusion of innovations, the extent to which a new product is something that is easy for consumers to see in use to motivate others to try it

Observational learning the process in which people learn by watching the actions of others and noting the reinforcements they receive for their behaviors

Occupational prestige a system in which we define people to a great extent by what they do for a living

One Percenter a label applied by the Occupy Wall Street Movement to people who earn the top 1 percent of income

Online community the collective participation of members who together build and maintain a digital social network

Online gated communities digital social networks that selectively allow access to people who possess criteria such as wealth or physical attractiveness

Open rates the percentage of people who open an email message from a marketer

Opinion leader person who is knowledgeable about products and who frequently is able to influence others' attitudes or behaviors with regard to a product category

Organizational buyers people who purchase goods and services on behalf of companies for use in the process of manufacturing, distribution, or resale

P2P commerce the notion of doing business with other consumers rather than with companies

Paradigm a widely accepted view or model of phenomena being studied; the perspective that regards people as rational information processors is currently the dominant paradigm, although this approach is now being challenged by a new wave of research that emphasizes the frequently subjective nature of consumer decision-making

Paradox of fashion a brand has cachet *because* only a select group of people own it. As more consumers outside of this inner circle start to adopt it, it is no longer exclusive and its original meaning is lost. Therefore, the item is a victim of its own success.

Paradox of low involvement when we *don't* care as much about a product, the way it's presented (e.g., who endorses it or the visuals that go with it) increases in importance

Parental yielding the process that occurs when a parental decision-maker is influenced by a child's product request

Parody display deliberately avoiding status symbols; to seek status by mocking it

Pastiche mixture of images

Perceived age how old a person feels as compared to his or her true chronological age

Perceived risk belief that a product has potentially negative consequences

Perception the process by which stimuli are selected, organized, and interpreted

Perceptual defense the tendency for consumers to avoid processing stimuli that are threatening to them

Perceptual selection process by which people attend to only a small portion of the stimuli to which they are exposed

Perceptual vigilance the tendency for consumers to be more aware of stimuli that relate to their current needs

Permission marketing popular strategy based on the idea that a marketer will be much more successful in persuading consumers who have agreed to let them try

The Personal Data Notification & Protection Act pending legislation that would require consumers to be notified when their personal information has been compromised

Personality a person's unique psychological makeup, which consistently influences the way the person responds to his or her environment

Personality traits identifiable characteristics that define a person

Persuasion an active attempt to change attitudes

Phablets a combination of the features of a cellphone and a tablet

Phantom Vibration Syndrome the tendency to habitually reach for your cell phone because you feel it vibrating, even if it is off or you are not even wearing it at the time

Phishing Internet scams where people receive fraudulent emails that ask them to supply account information

Pioneering brand the first brand to enter a market

Pleasure principle the belief that behavior is guided by the desire to maximize pleasure and avoid pain

Plinking™ act of embedding a product or service link in a video

Plutonomy an economy that a small number of rich people control

Point-of-purchase (POP) stimuli the promotional materials that are deployed in stores or other outlets to influence consumers' decisions at the time products are purchased

Popular culture the music, movies, sports, books, celebrities, and other forms of entertainment consumed by the mass market

Pop-up stores temporary locations that allow a company to test new brands without a huge financial commitment

Positioning strategy an organization's use of elements in the marketing mix to influence the consumer's interpretation of a product's meaning vis-à-vis competitors

Positive reinforcement the process whereby rewards provided by the environment strengthen responses to stimuli and appropriate behavior is learned

Positivism a research perspective that relies on principles of the "scientific method" and assumes that a single reality exists; events in the world can be objectively measured; and the causes of behavior can be identified, manipulated, and predicted

Postpurchase evaluation the final stage of consumer decision making when we experience the product or service we selected

Power posing standing in a confident way in order to increase self-confidence

Power users opinion leaders in online networks

Prediction market an approach based on the idea that groups of people with knowledge about an industry are jointly better predictors of the future than are any individuals

Presentation the second stage of the gift-giving ritual when the gift is presented to the recipient

Prestige–exclusivity effect high prices create high demand

Pretailer an e-commerce site that provides exclusive styles by prodding manufacturers to produce runway pieces they wouldn't otherwise make to sell in stores

Priming properties of a stimulus that evoke a schema that leads us to compare the stimulus to other similar ones we encountered in the past

Principle of cognitive consistency the belief that consumers value harmony among their thoughts, feelings, and behaviors and that they are motivated to maintain uniformity among these elements

Principle of least interest the person who is least committed to staying in a relationship has the most power

PRIZM (Potential Rating Index by Zip Market) clustering technique that classifies every zip code in the United States into one of 66 categories, ranging from the most affluent "Blue-Blood Estates" to the least well off "Public Assistance."

Problem recognition the process that occurs whenever the consumer sees a significant difference between his or her current state of affairs and some desired or ideal state; this recognition initiates the decision-making process

Product authenticity information about an item's origins and history

Product complementarity the view that products in different functional categories have symbolic meanings that are related to one another

Product disposal choices people make regarding how to get rid of items once they no longer are of value to them

Product involvement a consumer's level of interest in a particular item

Product line extension new products based upon an established brand

Product personalization a manufacturing process that allows each user to customize their own design

Product placement the process of obtaining exposure for a product by arranging for it to be inserted into a movie, television show, or some other medium

Productivity orientation a continual striving to use time constructively

Profane consumption the process of consuming objects and events that are ordinary or of the everyday world

Progressive learning model the perspective that people gradually learn a new culture as they increasingly come in contact with it; consumers assimilate into a new culture, mixing practices from their old and new environments to create a hybrid culture

Prospect theory a descriptive model of how people make choices

Provenance the origin of a product and a preference for "authentic" items

Psychographics the use of psychological, sociological, and anthropological factors to construct market segments

Psychological time a person's subjective evaluation of the passage of time, which may not correspond closely to the actual time elapsed

Psychophysics the science that focuses on how the physical environment is integrated into the consumer's subjective experience

Public self-consciousness a personality trait that makes a person very aware of how he or she appears to others

Punishment the learning that occurs when a response is followed by unpleasant events

Purchase momentum initial impulses to buy to satisfy our needs increase the likelihood that we will buy even more

Queuing theory the mathematical study of waiting lines

Rational perspective the assumption that people calmly and carefully integrate as much information as possible with what they already know about a product, painstakingly weigh the pluses and minuses of each alternative, and arrive at a satisfactory decision

Reader-response theory an approach to understanding literature that focuses on the role of the reader in interpreting a story rather than just relying upon the author's version

Reality engineering the process whereby elements of popular culture are appropriated by marketers and become integrated into marketing strategies

Reality principle principle that the ego seeks ways that will be acceptable to society to gratify the id

Real-time bidding an electronic trading system that sells ad space on the Web pages people click on at the moment they visit them

Recall the process of retrieving information from memory; in advertising research, the extent to which consumers can remember a marketing message without being exposed to it during the study

Reciprocity norm a culturally learned obligation to return the gesture of a gift with one of equal value

Recognition in advertising research, the extent to which consumers say they are familiar with an ad the researcher shows them

Recommerce the practice of trading or reselling used possessions in the underground economy rather than purchasing new items from retailers

Red market the global market for body parts

Red sneakers effect we assume someone who makes unconventional choices is more powerful or competent

Reference group an actual or imaginary individual or group that has a significant effect on an individual's evaluations, aspirations, or behavior

Referent power influence over others because they are motivated to imitate or affiliate with a person or group

Reformulation the third stage of the gift-giving ritual when the relationship between the two parties is redefined following the exchange

Refutational arguments calling attention to a product's negative attributes as a persuasive strategy where a negative issue is raised and then dismissed; this approach can increase source credibility

Relationship marketing the strategic perspective that stresses the long-term, human side of buyer–seller interactions

Relative advantage in the context of diffusion of innovations, the extent to which a new product or service is an improvement over alternatives that are already available in the market

Repetition multiple exposures to a stimulus

Reporting bias the effectiveness of a source decreases because he or she has the required knowledge but we question his or her willingness to convey it accurately

Reputation economy a reward system based on recognition of one's expertise by others who read online product reviews

Resonance a literary device, frequently used in advertising, that uses a play on words (a double meaning) to communicate a product benefit

Response bias a form of contamination in survey research in which some factor, such as the desire to make a good impression on the experimenter, leads respondents to modify their true answers

Restricted codes the ways of expressing and interpreting meanings that focus on the content of objects, which tend to be used by the working class

Retail theming strategy where stores create imaginative environments that transport shoppers to fantasy worlds or provide other kinds of stimulation

Retail therapy the act of shopping in order to improve mood or mental state

Retrieval the process whereby desired information is recovered from long-term memory

Retro brand an updated version of a brand from a prior historical period

Reverse innovation the process whereby a product is created initially to meet the needs of developing nations and then is adapted elsewhere

Reward power a person or group with the means to provide positive reinforcement

Rich media elements of an online ad that employ movement to gain attention

Rites of passage sacred times marked by a change in social status

Ritual a set of multiple, symbolic behaviors that occur in a fixed sequence and that tend to be repeated periodically

Ritual artifacts items (consumer goods) used in the performance of rituals

Ritual script a predetermined sequence of effects that identifies how people should interact with products and services

Role theory the perspective that much of consumer behavior resembles actions in a play

Sacralization a process that occurs when ordinary objects, events, or people take on sacred meaning to a culture or to specific groups within a culture

Sacred consumption the process of consuming objects and events that are set apart from normal life and treated with some degree of respect or awe

Sadvertising advertising that uses inspirational stories to generate an emotional response

Salience the prominence of a brand in memory

Sandwich Generation a description of middle-aged people who must care for both children and parents simultaneously

Satisficing solution a decision strategy that aims to yield an adequate solution (rather than the best solution) to reduce the costs of the decision-making process

Savings rate the proportion of income consumers put aside for future expenses

Schema an organized collection of beliefs and feelings represented in a cognitive category

Script a learned schema containing a sequence of events an individual expects to occur

Search engines software that examines the Web for matches to terms the user provides

Search engine optimization (SEO) the procedures companies use to design the content of Web sites and posts to maximize the likelihood that their content will show up when someone searches for a relevant term.

Selfie a picture a smartphone user takes of himself or herself

Self-concept the beliefs a person holds about his or her own attributes and how he or she evaluates these qualities

Self-esteem the positivity of a person's self-concept

Self-fulfilling prophecy a person acts according to the way he or she believes others expect, thus confirming this assumption

Self-image congruence models research that suggests we choose products when their attributes match some aspect of the self

Self-monitors individuals who are very conscious of their behavior in social situations

Self-perception theory an alternative (to cognitive dissonance) explanation of dissonance effects; it assumes that people use observations of their own behavior to infer their attitudes toward some object

Self-regulation a person's deliberate efforts to change or maintain his actions over time

Semiotics a field of study that examines the correspondence between signs and symbols and the meaning or meanings they convey

Senior market consumers over the age of 50 who control a large amount of discretionary income

Sensation the immediate response of sensory receptors (eyes, ears, nose, mouth, fingers) to such basic stimuli as light, color, sound, odors, and textures

Sensory marketing marketing strategies that focus on the impact of sensations on our product experiences

Sensory memory the temporary storage of information received from the senses

Sensory overload a condition where consumers are exposed to far more information than they can process

Sensory threshold the point at which a stimulus is strong enough to make a conscious impact on a person's awareness

Sentiment analysis a process (sometimes also called *opinion mining*) that scours the social media universe to collect and analyze the words people use when they describe a specific product or company

Serial reproduction a technique to study how information changes as people transmit it to another where each person has to repeat the stimulus for the next person

Serial wardrobers shoppers who buy an outfit, wear it once, and return it

Service scripts the sequence of events a consumer expects to experience in a service situation

Sex appeals marketing communications for products that feature heavy doses of erotic suggestions that range from subtle hints to blatant displays of skin

Sex roles a culture's expectations about how members of the male or female gender should act, dress, or speak

Sexting the growing trend of young people posting sexually suggestive photos of themselves online

Sex-typed products products that reflect stereotypical masculine or feminine attributes

Sex-typed traits characteristics that are stereotypically associated with one gender or the other

Shaping the learning of a desired behavior over time by rewarding intermediate actions until the final result is obtained

Shared endorsements users who follow or rate a product or service may find that their endorsements show up on the advertiser's page

Sharing economy a business model where people rent or barter what they need rather than buying it

Shopping orientation a consumer's general attitudes and motivations regarding the act of shopping

Short-term memory (STM) the mental system that allows us to retain information for a short period of time

Showrooming the process lamented by traditional retailers whereby consumers shop their stores to obtain product information and then purchase the chosen product online at a lower price

Shrinkage the loss of money or inventory from shoplifting or employee theft

Sign the sensory imagery that represents the intended meanings of the object

Similarity principle a view that consumers tend to group together objects that share similar physical characteristics

Simile comparing two objects that share a similar property

Simple additive rule select the option that has the largest number of positive attributes

Situational involvement the extent to which a shopper is engaged with a store, Web site, or a location where people consume a product or service

Situational self-image the role a person plays in a specific social context that helps to determine how he or she feels

Six Degrees of Kevin Bacon a popular game that illustrates how closely linked people are in our online culture

Slacktivism token expressions of support for a cause that ironically may substitute for more concrete actions.

Sleeper effect the process whereby differences in attitude change between positive and negative sources seem to diminish over time

Snob effect lower prices reduce demand

Social capital organizational affiliations and experiences that provide access to desirable social networks

Social class the overall rank of people in a society; people who are grouped within the same social class are approximately equal in terms of their income, occupations, and lifestyles

Social comparison the basic human tendency to compare ourselves to others

Social default a shortcut to learning that involves the mimicry of others' behaviors

Social game a multi-player, competitive, goal-oriented activity with defined rules of engagement and online connectivity among a community of players

Social graphs social networks; relationships among members of online communities

Social identity theory a perspective that argues each of us has several "selves" that relate to groups. These linkages are so important that we think of ourselves not just as "I," but also as "we"

Social judgment theory the perspective that people assimilate new information about attitude objects in light of what they already know or feel; the initial attitude acts as a frame of reference, and new information is categorized in terms of this standard

Social loafing the tendency for people not to devote as much to a task when their contribution is part of a larger group effort

Social marketing the promotion of causes and ideas (social products), such as energy conservation, charities, and population control

Social media the set of technologies that enable users to create content and share it with a large number of others

Social media addiction dependency on interaction with social networking platforms to the extent that signs of withdrawal appear if the person is unable to connect

Social mobility the movement of individuals from one social class to another

Social network a group of people who connect with one another online due to some shared interest or affiliation

Social power the capacity of one person to alter the actions or outcome of another

Social shopping an emerging form of e-commerce that allows an online shopper to simulate the experience of shopping in a brick-and-mortar store with other shoppers

Social stratification the process in a social system by which scarce and valuable resources are distributed unequally to status positions that become more or less permanently ranked in terms of the share of valuable resources each receives

Social structure the way members of a culture maintain an orderly social life

Sociometric methods the techniques for measuring group dynamics that involve tracing communication patterns in and among groups

Sock puppeting a company executive or other biased source poses as someone else to tout his organization in social media

Sound symbolism the process by which the way a word sounds influences our assumptions about what it describes and attributes such as size

Source attractiveness the dimensions of a communicator that increase his or her persuasiveness; these include expertise and attractiveness

Source credibility a communication source's perceived expertise, objectivity, or trustworthiness

Source derogation a possible downside to comparative advertising because the consumer may doubt the credibility of a biased presentation

Spacing effect the tendency to recall printed material to a greater extent when the advertiser repeats the target item periodically rather than presenting it over and over at the same time

Spectacles a marketing message that takes the form of a public performance

Spiritual-therapeutic model organizations that encourage behavioral changes such as weight loss that are loosely based on religious principles

Spokescharacters the use of animated characters or fictional mascots as product representatives

Spontaneous recovery ability of a stimulus to evoke a weakened response even years after the person initially perceived it

Spreading activation meanings in memory are activated indirectly; as a node is activated, other nodes linked to it are also activated so that meanings spread across the network

Stage of cognitive development the ability to comprehend concepts of increasing complexity as a person matures

State-dependent retrieval people are better able to access information if their internal state is the same at the time of recall as when they learned the information

Status anxiety the apprehension newly wealthy consumers experience as they try to act and consume in a way that is appropriate for affluent people

Status crystallization the extent to which different indicators of a person's status (income, ethnicity, occupation) are consistent with one another

Status hierarchy a ranking of social desirability in terms of consumers' access to resources such as money, education, and luxury goods

Status signaling the extent to which a brand employs prominent signs of status such as a well-known logo on merchandise

Status symbols products whose primary function is to communicate one's social standing to others

Stimulus discrimination the process that occurs when behaviors caused by two stimuli are different, as when consumers learn to differentiate a brand from its competitors

Stimulus generalization the process that happens when the behavior caused by a reaction to one stimulus occurs in the presence of other, similar stimuli

Store image a store's "personality," composed of such attributes as location, merchandise suitability, and the knowledge and congeniality of the sales staff

Storage stage the stage of memory processing when we integrate incoming information with existing data and store it until needed

Straight rebuy in the context of the buyclass framework, the type of buying decision that is virtually automatic and requires little deliberation

Street art paintings, murals, and other pieces in public places

Strength of weak ties the referral process that provides access to members of new groups due to a slight connection to someone in that group

The Student Digital Privacy Act a law that would prevent companies from selling student data to third parties

Subculture a group whose members share beliefs and common experiences that set them apart from other members of a culture

Subjective norm (SN) an additional component to the multiattribute attitude model that accounts for the effects of what we believe other people think we should do

Subliminal perception the processing of stimuli presented below the level of the consumer's awareness

Sunk-cost fallacy the belief that if we pay more for something we should not waste it

Superego the system that internalizes society's rules and that works to prevent the id from seeking selfish gratification

Surrogate consumer a professional who is retained to evaluate or make purchases on behalf of a consumer

Sustainability An emphasis on creating and maintaining the conditions under which humans and nature can exist in productive harmony, that permit fulfilling the social, economic and other requirements of present and future generations

Swatting a prank where someone falsely reports criminal activity in order to initiate a police SWAT team investigation

Swishing people organize parties to exchange clothing or other personal possessions with others

Symbol a sign that is related to a product through either conventional or agreed-on associations

Symbolic interactionism a sociological approach stressing that relationships with other people play a large part in forming the self; people live in a symbolic environment, and the meaning attached to any situation or object is determined by a person's interpretation of these symbols

Symbolic self-completion theory the perspective that people who have an incomplete self-definition in some context will compensate by acquiring symbols associated with a desired social identity

Synchronous interactions a conversation that requires participants to respond in real-time

Syncretic decision purchase decision that is made jointly by both spouses

Synoptic ideal a model of spousal decision-making in which the husband and wife take a common view and act as joint decision-makers, assigning each other well-defined roles and making mutually beneficial decisions to maximize the couple's joint utility

Taste culture a group of consumers who share aesthetic and intellectual preferences

Technology acceptance model (TAM) a widely used approach to predicting whether people will adopt a new form of technology or information system

Terminal values end states desired by members of a culture

Theory of cognitive dissonance theory based on the premise that a state of tension is created when beliefs or behaviors conflict with one another; people are motivated to reduce this inconsistency (or dissonance) and thus eliminate unpleasant tension

Theory of reasoned action an updated version of the Fishbein multiattribute attitude theory that considers factors such as social pressure and A_{act} (the attitude toward the act of buying a product), rather than simply attitudes toward the product itself

Theory of trying states that the criterion of behavior in the reasoned action model of attitude measurement should be replaced with *trying* to reach a goal

Third-gender movement the push to expand the definition of gender beyond the traditional categories of male and female

Tie strength the nature and potency of the bond between members of a social network

Time poverty a feeling of having less time available than is required to meet the demands of everyday living

Timestyle an individual's priorities regarding how he or she spends time as influenced by personal and cultural factors

Tipping point moment of critical mass

Torn self a condition where immigrants struggle to reconcile their native identities with their new cultures

Total quality management (TQM) management and engineering procedures aimed at reducing errors and increasing quality; based on Japanese practices

Trade dress color combinations that become strongly associated with a corporation

transformative consumer research (TCR) promotes research projects that include the goal of helping people or bringing about social change

Transitional economies a country that is adapting from a controlled, centralized economy to a free-market system

Transmedia storytelling the use of a mix of social media platforms to create a plot that involves consumers who try to solve puzzles or mysteries in the narrative

Trialability in the context of diffusion of innovations, the extent to which a new product or service can be sampled prior to adoption

Trickle-across effect fashions diffuse horizontally among members of the same social group

Trickle-down theory the perspective that fashions spread as the result of status symbols associated with the upper classes "trickling down" to other social classes as these consumers try to emulate those with greater status

Trickle-up effect fashion originate in a lower-class group and diffuse into the mass market

Triple bottom-line orientation business strategies that strive to maximize financial, social, and environmental return

Trophy wives attractive spouses that rich men deploy as status symbols

Tweens a marketing term used to describe children aged 8 to 14

Two-factor theory the perspective that two separate psychological processes are operating when a person is repeatedly exposed to an ad: repetition increases familiarity and thus reduces uncertainty about the product, but over time boredom increases with each exposure, and at some point the amount of boredom incurred begins to exceed the amount of uncertainty reduced, resulting in wear-out

Two-step flow model of influence proposes that a small group of *influencers* disseminate information because they can modify the opinions of a large number of other people

Unboxing videos a genre of YouTube video that features consumers who show how to unpack a new gadget it, assemble it or use it

Unconditioned stimulus (UCS) a stimulus that is naturally capable of causing a response

Underdog brand biography a communications approach that includes details about a brand's humble origins and how it defied the odds to succeed

Underground economy secondary markets (such as flea markets) where transactions are not officially recorded

Unipolar emotions emotional reactions that are either wholly positive or wholly negative

Unplanned buying when a shopper buys merchandise she did not intend to purchase, often because she recognizes a new need while in the store

User-generated content consumers voice their opinions about products, brands, and companies on blogs, podcasts, and social networking sites such as Facebook and Twitter, and film their own commercials that they post on sites such as YouTube

Utilitarian function states that we develop some attitudes toward products simply because they provide pleasure or pain

Value a belief that some condition is preferable to its opposite

Value-expressive function states each individual develops attitudes toward products because of what they say about him or her as a person

Value system a culture's ranking of the relative importance of values

Values and Lifestyles System (VALS2™) a psychographic segmentation system

Vanity sizing deliberately assigning smaller sizes to garments

Variable-interval reinforcement the time that must pass before an organism's response is reinforced varies based on some average

Variable-ratio reinforcement method in which you get reinforced after a certain number of responses, but you don't know how many responses are required

Variety seeking the desire to choose new alternatives over more familiar ones

Viral marketing the strategy of getting customers to sell a product on behalf of the company that creates it

Virtual goods digital items that people buy and sell online

Virtual makeover software that allows consumers to manipulate aspects of their appearance in a photograph they post online

Virtual reality (VR) provides a totally immersive experience that transports the user into an entirely separate three-dimensional environment

Virtual worlds immersive three-dimensional virtual environments such as Second Life

Voluntarily childless women of childbearing age who consciously decide not to have children

Von Restorff effect techniques like distinctive packaging that increase the novelty of a stimulus and also improve recall

Want the particular form of consumption chosen to satisfy a need

Warming process of transforming new objects and places into those that feel cozy, hospitable, and authentic

Wearable computing devices that integrate digital interactions with the physical body

Web 2.0 the current version of the Internet as a social, interactive medium from its original roots as a form of one-way transmission from producers to consumers

Weber's Law the principle that the stronger the initial stimulus, the greater its change must be for it to be noticed

Weighted additive rule select the option that has the largest number of positive attributes, but taking into account the relative importance of the attributes by weighting each one in terms of its relative importance to the decision maker

Wisdom of crowds a perspective that argues that, under the right circumstances, groups are smarter than the smartest people in them; implies that large numbers of consumers can predict successful products

Word-of-mouth (WOM) product information transmitted by individual consumers on an informal basis

Word–phrase dictionary in sentiment analysis, a library that codes data so that the program can scan the text to identify whether the words in the dictionary appear

Worldview a perspective on social norms and behaviors that tends to differ among social classes

INDEXES

Page numbers with *f* represent figures, n represent notes, *p* represent photos, and *t* represent tables.

Name

Aaker, David A., 408n79
Aaker, Jennifer L., 55n20, 55n27, 55n46, 170n114, 198n24, 198n33, 237n42, 277n23, 277n89, 278n29, 278n39, 329n9, 330n53
Aarabi, Parham, 236n21
Abelson, R. P., 330n34
Abraham, Chris, 333n147
Abrams, Rachel, 512n85, 561n156
Achenreiner, Gwen Bachmannn, 169n60
Adamy, Janet, 90n129
Adaval, Rashmi, 169n74
Addis, Michela, 444n54
Adkins, Natalie Ross, 89n73, 89n74
Adler, Alfred, 246
Adler, G., 277n12
Adler, Keith, 128n40
Adler, Rick, 512n99
Aerosmith, 231
Aggarwal, Pankaj, 129n86
Agrawal, Jagdish, 331n59
Aguirre, B. E., 560n132
Ahrensa, Anthony H., 240n153
Ahuvia, Aaron, 236n5
Aikman, Troy, 533
Aishwarya Rai, 235
Ajzen, Icek, 330n32
Aknin, Lara B., 198n33
Aksoy, Lerzan, 88n36
Alba, Joseph W., 168n25, 169n68, 170n103, 170n108, 170n111, 199n59
Albanese, Paul J., 240n168, 277n25
Albanesius, Chloe, 88n56
Alden, Dana L., 476n62, 559n62
Alexander, J., 423
"Alex from Target," 201
Alger, Horatio, 453
Al-Greene, Bob, 90n95
Allan, David, 331n56
Allen, Chris T., 167n10, 168n36
Allen, Michael W., 128n51
Allen, Woody, 48
Alleyne, Richard, 378n106
Allsopp, J. F., 277n25
Allvine, Fred C., 444n67
Alpert, Frank, 128n28, 377n67
Alpert, Lewis, 279n66
Alpert, Mark I., 332n98, 332n102
Alsop, Ronald, 376n47
Alt, Matt, 239n117
Alter, Adam L., 477n105
Alter, Charlotte, 240n156
Altman, Irwin, 237n60
Alwitt, Linda F., 330n34
Amaldoss, Wilfred, 476n39
Ames, B. Charles, 377n77
Amis, John, 561n161
Anand, Punam, 330n10, 559n71

Anderson, B. B., 332n109
Anderson, Chris, 376n36
Anderson, Eric T., 477n91
Anderson, Erin, 377n81
Anderson, Hans Christian, 209
Anderson, Helen H., 332n107
Anderson, Laurel, 513n111, 558n16
Anderson, Mae, 474
Anderson, Paul, 199n56, 279n94
Anderson, Ronald D., 90n122
Andreasen, Alan R., 88n34, 88n54
Andrews, Edmund L., 378n109
Andrews, J. Craig, 331n65
Andrus, Bruce W., 236n30
Andruss, Paula Lyon, 169n61
Angier, Natalie, 378n98, 378n107, 511n54, 558n41
Aniston, Jennifer, 309
Ante, Spencer E., 90n109
Antonides, Trinske, 513n110
Apperley, Thomas, 444n83, 444n85
Appleton-Knapp, S. L., 169n94
Aradhna, Krishna, 128n33
Areni, Charles S., 407n52
Argo, J. J., 408n86
Ariely, Dan, 199n61, 377n59
Armstrong, Gary, 169n62
Arndt, Johan, 279n66, 443n42, 443n46
Arnold, Stephen J., 238n96
Arnould, Eric J., 55n42, 55n44, 87n14, 443n38, 510n10, 513n108, 559n63, 560n104
Aronoff, J., 277n4
Arora, Neeraj, 199n60
Arsel, Zeynep, 278n36
Arsena, Ashley Rae, 238n98
Arthur, Lisa, 55n16
Ashford, Susan J., 236n30
Ashman, Rachel, 368t, 378n115
Ashmore, Richard D., 239n144
Askegaard, Søren, 128n27, 197n7, 279n94, 510n10, 561n169
Aspara, Jaakko, 377n78
Assael, Henry, 278n62
Assmus, Gert, 330n44
Atalay, A. Selin, 129n67, 129n75
Atkinson, Claire, 333n128
Atkinson, R. C., 169n67
Attaway, Jill S., 444n50
Atwal, Glyn, 474
Austin, W. G., 443n5
Avery, Jill, 278n32
Aydinoğlu, Nilüfer Z., 240n157
Aylesworth, Andrew B., 128n59, 329n9
Azalea, Iggy, 144, 226
Azhari, A. C., 331n62

Baar, Aaron, 170n98, 240n188, 329n5
Babin, Barry J., 406n25, 406n27, 408n71, 444n50
Baca-Motes, K., 89n79
Bacon, Kevin, 430
Bagozzi, Richard P., 170n126, 277n10, 330n42, 407n69, 558n51, 560n107
Bahn, Kenneth D., 169n56
Bahr, Howard M., 559n68

Bailay, Rasul, 561n147
Bailenson, Jeremy N., 238n81
Baird, Julia, 239n127
Bajarin, Tim, 196
Bakalar, Nicholas, 129n82
Baker, Courtney Nations, 88n47, 88n49
Baker, Julie, 391, 406n14
Baker, Stacy Menzel, 69, 87n16, 88nn47–50, 171n146, 512n67
Baker, Stephen, 330n44, 332n111
Bala, Hillol, 560n107
Bales, Robert F., 378n96
Ball, A. Dwayne, 237n59
Ball, Deborah, 279n84, 558n39
Ball, Jeffrey, 87n6
Bamossy, Gary J., 128n27, 442n3, 513n110
Bandura, Albert, 168nn40–41
Banfield, Jillian C., 330n16
Banjo, Shelly, 407n65
Banks, Tyra, 423
Banner, Lois W., 239n145
Bannon, Lisa, 240nn148–149
Barak, Benny, 512n100
Baranauckas, Carla, 511n65
Barbaro, Michael, 168n26
Barbosa, David, 55n28
Bardhi, Fleura, 270
Bardzell, Jeffrey, 333n133
Bardzell, Shaowen, 333n133
Barger, Victor A., 128n44
Bargh, John A., 377n64
Barker, Nigel, 423
Barnes, Brooks, 127n2, 332n111, 512n69
Barnes, Susan B., 443n19
Barnhart, Michelle, 513n101
Baron, Alma S., 378n97
Baron, Robert A., 167n2, 329n1, 377n66
Barone, Michael J., 329n9
Barro, Josh, 197n6
Barron, Kelly, 442n3
Barrow, Karen, 89n69
Barth, E., 476n73
Barthel, Diane, 558n53
Bartlett, Frederic, 425
Barton, Roger, 129n70
Basil, Debra Z., 198n39, 330n26
Basil, Michael D., 198n39
Basu, Kunal, 406n21, 406n23
Batra, Rajeev, 129n69, 406n24
Baumeister, Roy F., 55n27, 55n46, 169n74, 198n38, 236n6, 475n7
Baumgardner, Michael H., 170n102, 331n63
Baumgarten, Steven A., 444n65
Baumgarten, Hans, 278n25, 375n13
Baumgatner, Felix, 276
Baumrucker, Craig, 127n1
Beaglehole, Ernest, 237n68
Beales, Howard, 377n69
Bearak, Barry, 559n74
Bearden, William O., 376n52, 377n56, 408n80, 443n29, 443n32
Beasley, Deena, 90n108
Beatty, Sharon E., 279n93, 330n11, 376n52, 376n54, 378n94
Bechara, Antonie, 237n44
Beck, Stan, 558n44

587

Company/Brand Name

Subject Index